● Rethinking Political Thinkers

Rethinking Political Thinkers

Edited by
Manjeet Ramgotra
Simon Choat

OXFORD
UNIVERSITY PRESS

OXFORD
UNIVERSITY PRESS

Great Clarendon Street, Oxford, OX2 6DP,
United Kingdom

Oxford University Press is a department of the University of Oxford.
It furthers the University's objective of excellence in research, scholarship,
and education by publishing worldwide. Oxford is a registered trade mark of
Oxford University Press in the UK and in certain other countries

© Oxford University Press 2023

The moral rights of the authors have been asserted

All rights reserved. No part of this publication may be reproduced, stored in
a retrieval system, or transmitted, in any form or by any means, without the
prior permission in writing of Oxford University Press, or as expressly permitted
by law, by licence or under terms agreed with the appropriate reprographics
rights organization. Enquiries concerning reproduction outside the scope of the
above should be sent to the Rights Department, Oxford University Press, at the
address above

You must not circulate this work in any other form
and you must impose this same condition on any acquirer

Published in the United States of America by Oxford University Press
198 Madison Avenue, New York, NY 10016, United States of America

British Library Cataloguing in Publication Data
Data available

Library of Congress Control Number: 2022947800

ISBN 978-0-19-884739-7

Printed in the UK by
Bell & Bain Ltd., Glasgow

Links to third party websites are provided by Oxford in good faith and
for information only. Oxford disclaims any responsibility for the materials
contained in any third party website referenced in this work.

Praise for Rethinking Political Thinkers

'This well-conceived and well-executed book offers accessible and thoughtful chapters on theorists (including Gandhi, C.L.R. James, Du Bois and Fanon) and themes (including Black consciousness and colonial domination) that do not usually find a place in political theory textbooks, and yet have been central to political thinking in modern times. It will be welcomed by teachers and students who want to avoid the seemingly incorrigible Eurocentrism of their discipline.'

—**Professor Sanjay Seth, Professor of Politics and Director of the Centre for Postcolonial Studies, Goldsmiths, University of London, UK**

'The book provides a refreshing overview of key political thinkers, bringing to the fore ideas and authors which have long been unjustly neglected in the discipline and thus offering a richer and more inclusive introduction to the defining questions and debates in political theory.'

—**Dr Davide Schmid, Senior Lecturer in International Relations, Manchester Metropolitan University, UK**

'*Rethinking Political Thinkers* answers a long-felt need of students and faculty alike. Through obviously careful planning, Ramgotra and Choat have pulled together a superb resource to restructure political theory curricula so as to bring critical engagement with questions of race, gender, sexuality, and colonialism into university courses, positioning such questions as integral rather than supplemental to understanding the history, present, and future of political theory. *Rethinking Political Thinkers* will very quickly become an essential text for undergraduate courses.'

—**Professor Samantha Frost, Professor in the Department of Political Science, the Department of Gender and Women's Studies, and the Unit for Criticism and Interpretive Theory at the University of Illinois, Urbana-Champaign, USA**

'This is the dream textbook we have been looking for. It offers a way to rethink the teaching of political theory that does not abandon the canon, but instead expands and interrogates it, situating the thinkers within contemporary concerns.'

—**Dr David Moon, Senior Lecturer in Politics, University of Bath, UK**

'An excellent volume which can be used to widen the curriculum of political theory to include more diverse authors and cover important subjects such as colonialism, imperialism, slavery, non-Western philosophy, feminism, and poststructuralist critiques. Accessible for students, and a clear resource for lecturers keen to vary their teaching, it is a welcome addition to the field.'

—**Dr Charles Devellennes, Senior Lecturer in Political and Social Thought, University of Kent, UK**

'This is a ground-breaking introduction to political thought. It offers an indispensable tool for students and teachers and shows how political theory can be taught in a way that respects diversity and shows the radical potential of political thought.'

—**Dr Alasia Nuti, Senior Lecturer in Political Theory, University of York, UK**

'This timely volume highlights positive possibilities for the future of political theory and philosophy. By refocusing our attention on many of those intellectual voices who have usually held them the least, the volume's chapters refuse—in theme and method—to narrowly conform to the accepted modes of the discipline. Indeed, the volume excels in making clear that, should it wish to, political theory and philosophy are eminently capable of allowing for innovations in thought and method drawn from as full an epistemic range as the historical and contemporary world offers. As the editors emphasize, the benefit will be to the discipline and, also, to the intellectual understandings of our societies. Certainly, this volume will inspire new and diverse entrants into political thought—who will, as a result, be unafraid to break and cultivate ever more original ground.'

—Dr Eniola Anuoluwapo Soyemi, Lecturer in Political Philosophy and Public Policy, Blavatnik School of Government, University of Oxford, UK

Acknowledgements

The editors would like to thank those who have helped and supported them in the book's production, in particular Sarah Iles and Katie Staal at Oxford University Press and each of the contributing authors. Manjeet thanks Elizabeth Bowker and Catherine Temma Davidson for reading drafts of her chapters and making useful suggestions. She thanks her son Neel for reading sections of chapters and mostly for his patience and constant encouragement and her mother Pushpinder K. Ramgotra for her love and support. She is indebted to Simon for his patience and excellent suggestions in the process of writing and editing all parts of this textbook. Simon would like to thank Mark Cowling, Terrell Carver, Thomas Nail, Andy Higginbottom, and John Grant for reading the first draft of Chapter 13. He would also like to thank Elizabeth Evans and William and Josephine Choat, and finally Manjeet for initiating the volume and her friendship. We would both like to thank Kevin Ochieng Okoth. As this book was inspired by our teaching practices, we would like to thank our colleagues and students with whom we have taught and learnt political theory over the years.

We would like to dedicate this book to the memory of Charles Mills (1951–2021), who offered us invaluable support and encouragement for the book from its inception but who sadly died before it could be published. This book would not have been possible without his foundational work.

About the editors

Simon Choat is Associate Professor and Head of the Department of Economics at Kingston University London. He is the author of *Marx Through Post-Structuralism: Lyotard, Derrida, Foucault, Deleuze* (Continuum, 2010) and *Marx's 'Grundrisse': A Reader's Guide* (Bloomsbury, 2016). He has published articles on, among other topics, neoliberalism, contemporary anarchism, the philosophers Ernesto Laclau and Michael Sandel, and the theories of the 'new materialists', such as Bruno Latour. He has been teaching political theory for nearly 20 years. He has published research on decolonizing the political theory curriculum and is currently collaborating on a comparative study of Politics and Economics curricula at UK universities. He is a member of the Political Economy Research Group at Kingston University and is co-convener of the Political Studies Association specialist group on Political Thought.

Manjeet Ramgotra is a Senior Lecturer in Political Thought in the Department of Politics and International Studies at SOAS University of London. She is a Fellow of the Independent Social Research Foundation and was a visiting researcher at the School of Politics and IR at QMUL. Her research examines the history of republican ideas extending from classical European to twentieth-century, anti-colonial political thought. She is the author of several articles on republicanism and is co-editor of *Decolonising Curricula and Pedagogy in Higher Education* (Routledge, 2021). Currently, she is working on a project on postcolonial republicanism in India. She is a Trustee on the Political Studies Association executive committee and a member of the Centre for Comparative Political Thought at SOAS.

List of contributors

Signy Gutnick Allen is a historian of political thought and political theorist who has worked at Queen Mary University of London, the University of York, and the London School of Economics, UK. She has particular interests in Hobbes's theory of crime and punishment, as well as in the political implications of his model of authorization. She is currently undertaking a Postdoctoral Fellowship as part of the Just City research project at the University of Zurich, Switzerland, where she is investigating debates over the nature and extent of justice in seventeenth- and eighteenth-century political writing. Her chapter has received funding from the European Research Council (ERC) under the European Union's Horizon 2020 research and innovation program (grant agreement No. 864309).

Elvira Basevich is an Assistant Professor of Philosophy at University of California, Davis, USA, and a Laurance S. Rockefeller Visiting Faculty Fellow at Princeton University, USA. Her first monograph *W.E.B. Du Bois: The Lost and the Found* was published in 2020 with Polity Press. Her next monograph, titled *A DuBoisian Theory of Justice: On Political Constructivism, Democratic Development, and Revolution*, is forthcoming.

Terrell Carver is Professor of Political Theory at the University of Bristol, UK. He is the author of *Masculinities, Gender and International Relations*, *Marx* in the 'Classic Thinkers' series, *Men in Political Theory*, *The Postmodern Marx*, and numerous articles and chapters. He is co-editor-in-chief of *Contemporary Political Theory* and co-general editor of three book series: Globalization; Marx, Engels and Marxisms; and Routledge Innovators in Political Theory. He has served on the executive committees of the Political Studies Association of the UK and the International Political Science Association.

Alan Coffee teaches Global Ethics and Human Values at King's College London, UK. He is the co-editor of *The Social and Moral Philosophy of Mary Wollstonecraft* (OUP, 2016) and *The Wollstonecraftian Mind* (Routledge, 2019) and the author of a forthcoming book on *Mary Wollstonecraft* (Polity). His research focuses on republicanism and the recovery of historically marginalized or forgotten voices in this tradition. Alan has written several articles on Catharine Macaulay and African-American political thought.

Claire Colebrook is Edwin Erle Sparks Professor of English, Philosophy and Women's and Gender Studies at Penn State University, USA. She has written books and articles on contemporary European philosophy, literary history, gender studies, queer theory, visual culture, and feminist philosophy. Her most recent book is *What Would You Do and Who Would You Kill to Save the World?* (2022).

Nikita Dhawan holds the Chair in Political Theory and History of Ideas at the Technical University Dresden, Germany. Her research and teaching focus on global justice, human rights, democracy, and decolonization. She received the Käthe Leichter Award in 2017 for outstanding achievements in women's and gender studies. Selected publications include *Impossible Speech: On the Politics of Silence and Violence* (2007); *Reimagining the State: Theoretical Challenges and Transformative Possibilities* (as co-editor, 2019); *Rescuing the Enlightenment from the Europeans: Critical Theories of Decolonization* (forthcoming).

LIST OF CONTRIBUTORS

Ashley Dodsworth is a Senior Lecturer in Politics at the University of Bristol, UK. Her research and teaching focus on environmental politics, human rights, and the history of Western political thought. She is the co-editor of *Environmental Human Rights: A Political Theory Perspective* and *Green Politics and Civic Republicanism* (Routledge, 2018).

Allauren Forbes is an Assistant Professor in the Department of Philosophy and Gender and Social Justice at McMaster University, Canada. Her primary research and teaching focus is the history of feminist philosophy, especially with respect to socio-epistemic relations in early modern European thinking. Another strand of her research and teaching extends into contemporary theorizing about love, sex, and race. She has published on several early modern women philosophers, though Astell is probably her favourite.

Kiara Gilbert is a graduate student at the intersection of ethics, political theory, and African American Studies. Her research is rooted in the lived experiences and philosophies of Afro-diasporic communities. She graduated with a BA in African American Studies from Princeton University, USA, and an interdisciplinary MPhil in Criticism and Culture from the University of Cambridge, UK. She is currently pursuing an MSc in Philosophy and Public Policy at the London School of Economics, UK, as a two-year Marshall Scholar.

Peter Hallward teaches at the Centre for Research in Modern European Philosophy at Kingston University London, UK. He has written books on the French philosophers Alain Badiou and Gilles Deleuze, on postcolonial literature, and on contemporary Haitian politics. He is currently finishing a book on mass sovereignty entitled *The Will of the People* (forthcoming from Verso), and is working his way through a related series of shorter studies on figures like Blanqui, Marx, Che Guevara, and Fanon.

Kei Hiruta is a Lecturer in Philosophy at the Tokyo University of Foreign Studies, Japan. He is the author of *Hannah Arendt and Isaiah Berlin: Freedom, Politics and Humanity* (Princeton University Press, 2021) and editor of *Arendt on Freedom, Liberation, and Revolution* (Palgrave Macmillan, 2019). He is a former fellow of the Aarhus Institute of Advanced Studies, Aarhus University, Denmark, and his chapter draws on a project that has received funding from the European Union's Horizon 2020 research and innovation programme under the Marie Skłodowska-Curie grant agreement No 754513 and The Aarhus University Research Foundation.

Ruth Kinna is a political theorist and historian of ideas at Loughborough University, UK, specializing in late-nineteenth- and early-twentieth-century socialism. She is the author of *The Government of No One* (Pelican, 2019), *Kropotkin: Reviewing the Classical Anarchist Tradition* (University of Edinburgh, 2016), and *William Morris: The Art of Socialism* (University of Wales, 2000). She has published studies of several important yet marginalized figures, including Guy Aldred, Ernest Belfort Bax, Varlam Cherkezishvili, Ananda Coomaraswamy, and Dora Marsden and ten pamphlets (*Great Anarchists*, Dog Section Press) on leading anarchist movement activists.

Jimmy Casas Klausen is an Associate Professor at the Institute of International Relations of the Pontifical Catholic University of Rio de Janeiro, Brazil, where he teaches on global inequality; identity, alterity, and resistance; and indigeneity and race. Author of *Fugitive Rousseau: Slavery, Primitivism, and Political Freedom* (Fordham, 2014), he has published widely on empire in European political theory and anticolonial theory in South Asia. He currently researches population politics and Indigenous genocide after political decolonization.

Hagar Kotef is a Professor in Political Theory and Comparative Political Thought at SOAS, University of London, UK. She is the Chair of the Centre for Comparative Political Thought at SOAS and the author of *Movement and the Ordering of Freedom: On Liberal Governances of Mobility* (Duke University Press, 2015) and *The Colonizing Self: Home and Homelessness in Israel/Palestine* (Duke University Press, 2020).

Patrizia Longo is Professor of Politics at Saint Mary's College of California, USA. Her teaching and research focus on political theory, particularly on gender, racial and food justice, and on decolonizing the curriculum. Her publications include two books: *The Statue of Glaucus: Rousseau's Modern Quest for Authenticity* (Peter Lang, 1991) and *Justice Unbound: Voices of Justice for the 21st Century* (Rowman & Littlefield, 2019) as well as several journal articles.

Victoria Margree is a Principal Lecturer at the University of Brighton, UK, who works across politics, philosophy, and literature. She is the author of several articles on Shulamith Firestone and contemporary feminism as well as the book *Neglected or Misunderstood: The Radical Feminism of Shulamith Firestone* (Zero Books, 2018). Her monograph on *British Women's Short Supernatural Fiction, 1860–1930* (Palgrave Macmillan) was published in 2019. Her two current projects concern the politics of reproduction, and neo-Victorian literature and culture.

Inder S. Marwah is Associate Professor in the Department of Political Science at McMaster University, Canada, and the author of *Liberalism, Diversity and Domination: Kant, Mill and the Government of Difference* (Cambridge University Press, 2019). His research focuses on the intersections of race, empire, and political theory, and his current project examines the influence of Darwinism and evolutionary theory on anti-colonialism at the turn of the twentieth century.

Keally McBride is a Professor of Politics at the University of San Francisco, USA. She teaches on colonialism, decolonization, Marxism, environmentalism, and California politics. Her current research examines the colonial histories and capitalist economic formation of California. Her publications include *Mr. Mothercountry: The Man Who Made the Rule of Law* (Oxford University Press, 2016), *Political Theories of Decolonization: Postcolonialism and the Problem of Foundations* (co-authored with Margaret Kohn, Oxford University Press, 2011) and *Punishment and Political Order* (University of Michigan Press, 2007).

Maeve McKeown is an Assistant Professor in Political Theory at Campus Fryslân, University of Groningen. She has two forthcoming books: a monograph *With Power Comes Responsibility: The Politics of Structural Injustice* (Bloomsbury Academic) and an edited volume with Jude Browne *What is Structural Injustice?* (Oxford University Press). She works on structural injustice, Iris Marion Young, reparations, and feminism, and has a background in theatre.

Esme G. Murdock is an Assistant Professor of American Indian Studies and Associate Director of the Institute for Ethics and Public Affairs at San Diego State University, USA. Her research interests include environmental justice, Indigenous and Afro-descended environmental ethics, settler colonial theory, and decolonization as land/resource rematriation. Her work centres conceptions of land found within both Indigenous and African-American/Afro-descended environmental philosophies. She comes to this work as a descendant of enslaved Africans and European settlers in North America.

Viren Murthy teaches at the University of Wisconsin-Madison, USA. He is the author of *The Political Philosophy of Zhang Taiyan: The Resistance of Consciousness* (Brill, 2011) and *The Politics of Time in China and Japan* (Routledge, 2022). He is co-editor of *A Companion to Global Historical Thought* (with Prasenjit Duara and Andrew Sartori, Blackwell, 2014), co-editor of *East Asian Marxisms and Their Trajectories* (with Joyce Liu, Routledge, 2017), and co-editor of *Confronting Capital and Empire: Rethinking Kyoto School Philosophy* (with Max Ward and Fabian Schäfer, Brill, 2017).

LIST OF CONTRIBUTORS

Eva-Maria Nag is a political theorist and the Senior Executive Editor of *Global Policy* at the School of Government and International Affairs, Durham University, UK. Her research interests include theories of democracy and violence in South Asia, global governance architecture, and climate governance in the developing world. She teaches on modules in democratic theory and the history of Western political thought.

Ayesha Omar is a Senior Lecturer in Political Theory in the Department of Political Studies at the University of the Witwatersrand (Wits), South Africa, a Mellon Early Career Scholars Fellow, and Research Associate at SOAS, University of London, UK. She works in the area of comparative political theory, with a focus on Islamic and African political thought and South African Black intellectual history. She has published various articles and book chapters on these topics. She is currently working on her monograph, which deals with political authority in Islam.

Paul Patton is Hongyi Chair Professor of Philosophy at Wuhan University, China, editor of the *Journal of Social and Political Philosophy*, and Emeritus Professor of the University of New South Wales, Australia. He has published widely on French poststructuralist philosophy and contemporary political philosophy, including the rights of colonized Indigenous peoples. He is the author of *Deleuze and the Political* (Routledge, 2000) and *Deleuzian Concepts: Philosophy, Colonization, Politics* (Stanford, 2010).

Rahul Rao is Lecturer in International Political Thought at the University of St. Andrews, UK. He is the author of *Out of Time: The Queer Politics of Postcoloniality* (2020) and *Third World Protest: Between Home and the World* (2010), both published by Oxford University Press. He is a member of the *Radical Philosophy* collective.

Karen Salt is an interdisciplinary scholar who specializes in systems of governance, historical shocks, and transformative decision-making. She has led large collaborative research teams and has run a policy and evidence centre focused on rights and justice. Now a senior policymaker, she remains committed to developing policies and processes that learn from the past in order to shape more just political futures.

Stella Sandford is Professor in the Centre for Research in Modern European Philosophy at Kingston University, London, UK. Her research and writing focus critically on the concept of 'sex' in the history of philosophy and psychoanalysis; recent work also includes essays on Kant's philosophy and his concept of race. Her book *Vegetal Sex: Philosophy of Plants* was published by Bloomsbury in 2022.

Deepshikha Shahi is Associate Professor of International Relations at the O. P. Jindal Global University, India. Her current research interests revolve around the theoretical frameworks of Global IR, non-Western intellectual resources, pedagogical practices, politics of knowledge-production, Indian politics, Afghan politics, and global politics. She performs symptomatological readings of the classical texts to theorize IR and to boost the transdisciplinary synergies between Humanities and Social Sciences.

Robbie Shilliam is Professor of International Relations at Johns Hopkins University, USA. His most recent book is *Decolonizing Politics* (Polity, 2021).

Neus Torbisco-Casals is Senior Research Fellow at the Albert Hirschman Centre on Democracy and a Faculty member at the Geneva Academy of International Humanitarian Law and Human Rights, Geneva Graduate Institute, Switzerland, where she teaches courses relating to international human rights law and transitional justice. She is the author of *Group Rights as Human*

Rights: A Liberal Approach to Multiculturalism (Springer, 2006). She would like to thank Juliana Santos de Carvalho for her assistance in preparing her contribution to this book.

Varun Uberoi is a Reader in Political Theory and Public Policy at Brunel University London, UK. His research focuses on the nature and origins of multicultural political thought and he has published *Multiculturalism Rethought* (Edinburgh University Press, 2015) and numerous peer-reviewed journal articles on this subject in *History of Political Thought*, *Political Studies*, *Critical Review of International Social and Political Philosophy*, *Ethnicities*, and many other journals.

Willow Verkerk is a Lecturer in Continental Philosophy and Social Philosophy at the University of British Columbia, Canada, and a Postdoctoral Researcher with the Gendered Mimesis Project at KU Leuven, Belgium. She is the author of *Nietzsche and Friendship* (Bloomsbury, 2019) and other academic texts on continental and feminist philosophy. Willow supports the decolonization of the curriculum and regularly lectures on changing the tradition of philosophical thought.

Caroline Williams is Visiting Senior Research Follow at Queen Mary University of London, UK. Caroline's research interests cut across political theory, philosophy, the history of ideas, and critical theory. She is the author of *Contemporary French Philosophy: Modernity and the Persistence of the Subject* (Continuum, 2001) and has published extensively on Spinoza within political theory and Continental philosophy.

Yves Winter is Associate Professor of Political Science at McGill University, Canada, where he teaches the history of political thought and contemporary social and political theory. He is the author of *Machiavelli and the Orders of Violence* (Cambridge University Press, 2018).

Clare Woodford is Principal Lecturer in Political Philosophy and Director of the Centre for Applied Philosophy, Politics and Ethics (CAPPE) Critical Theory research group strand at the University of Brighton, UK. She specializes in political theory and contemporary French and Italian philosophy and has published widely on topics ranging from democratic activism and performance, feminism and gender politics, populism, post-truth, and UK politics and policy.

Guide to the Book

Comparing and contrasting dominant and marginal voices, *Rethinking Political Thinkers* is the only textbook to explore key political concepts through a truly diverse range of political thinkers. This textbook is enriched with a range of learning features to help you navigate the text and reinforce your knowledge and understanding of political theory. This guide shows you how to get the most out of your book.

The online resources which accompany this book are available at: www.oup.com/he/ramgotra-choat1e

Chapter guides

Identify the scope of the material to be covered and which themes and issues you can expect to learn about with Chapter Guides at the beginning of each chapter.

Key concepts

Develop your understanding of core principles in political theory with Key Concept boxes throughout the text.

Key thinkers

Contextualize your learning with information about key figures in political theory with Key Thinker boxes.

Key thinker biographies

Contextualize your understanding of the key thinkers explored in this volume with detailed thinker biographies, available on the online resources: www.oup.com/he/ramgotra-choat1e.

Study questions

Assess your understanding of core themes and reflect critically on key ideas with carefully devised end-of-chapter questions.

Further reading

Broaden your learning with guided primary and secondary further reading recommendations, where the authors highlight additional resources you may wish to read, with explanations of why these readings are helpful.

Web links

Access the online resources at www.oup.com/he/ramgotra-choat1e for an annotated list of important websites, blogs, journal articles, videos, and more for each chapter, which will help you take your learning further and conduct further research.

Outline contents

Acknowledgements — vii
About the editors — ix
List of contributors — xi

1 Introduction — 1
Simon Choat and Manjeet Ramgotra

PART I Boundaries of the political

2 Socrates, Plato, and Sojourner Truth — 21
Patrizia Longo

3 Aristotle and bell hooks — 39
Manjeet Ramgotra

4 Kautilya — 57
Deepshikha Shahi

PART II Social contract theory and its critics

5 Thomas Hobbes — 79
Signy Gutnick Allen

6 Baruch Spinoza — 97
Caroline Williams

7 John Locke — 115
Hagar Kotef

8 Mary Astell — 131
Allauren Forbes

9 Jean-Jacques Rousseau — 147
Peter Hallward

10 Carole Pateman and Charles Mills — 163
Terrell Carver

PART III Liberal modernity and colonial domination

11 Charles-Louis de Secondat, Baron de la Brede et de Montesquieu — 185
Manjeet Ramgotra

OUTLINE CONTENTS

12	**John Stuart Mill**	203
	Inder S. Marwah	
13	**Karl Marx**	221
	Simon Choat	
14	**Friedrich Nietzsche**	239
	Willow Verkerk	
15	**Sayyid Qutb**	257
	Ayesha Omar	
16	**Edward W. Said**	273
	Rahul Rao	

PART IV **Freedom and revolution**

17	**Catharine Macaulay and Edmund Burke**	295
	Alan Coffee	
18	**C.L.R. James**	313
	Robbie Shilliam	
19	**Hannah Arendt**	331
	Kei Hiruta	
20	**Zhang Taiyan**	349
	Viren Murthy	

PART V **Inclusion and equality**

21	**Mary Wollstonecraft**	371
	Ashley Dodsworth	
22	**Iris Marion Young**	389
	Neus Torbisco-Casals	
23	**Bhikhu Parekh**	407
	Varun Uberoi	
24	**Gayatri Chakravorty Spivak**	427
	Nikita Dhawan	

PART VI **Violence, power, and resistance**

25	**Niccolò Machiavelli**	447
	Yves Winter	
26	**Emma Goldman**	465
	Ruth Kinna	

27	**Mohandas (Mahatma) Gandhi**	485
	Jimmy Casas Klausen	
28	**Frantz Fanon**	505
	Keally McBride	

PART VII The liberal self and black consciousness

29	**Immanuel Kant**	527
	Stella Sandford	
30	**Frederick Douglass**	545
	Kiara Gilbert and Karen Salt	
31	**W.E.B. Du Bois**	565
	Elvira Basevich	
32	**John Rawls**	581
	Maeve McKeown	

PART VIII Sex and sexuality

33	**Michel Foucault**	603
	Paul Patton	
34	**Shulamith Firestone**	621
	Victoria Margree	
35	**Angela Y. Davis**	639
	Manjeet Ramgotra	
36	**Judith Butler**	657
	Clare Woodford	

PART IX The environment, human, and non-human

37	**Dipesh Chakrabarty**	679
	Eva-Maria Nag	
38	**Donna Haraway**	697
	Claire Colebrook	
39	**Indigenous ecologies**	713
	Esme G. Murdock	

Index   731

Detailed contents

Acknowledgements vii
About the editors ix
List of contributors xi

1 Introduction 1
Simon Choat and Manjeet Ramgotra

1.1 Rethinking political thinkers 1
1.2 Political thought 2
1.3 The history of political thought 5
1.4 The canon of political thought 8
1.5 Overview of the book 12

PART I Boundaries of the political

2 Socrates, Plato, and Sojourner Truth 21
Patrizia Longo

2.1 Introduction 21
2.2 Three political thinkers 22
    2.2.1 Socrates 22
    2.2.2 Plato 23
    2.2.3 Sojourner Truth 23
2.3 Plato: knowledge, education, and politics 25
    2.3.1 The ideal state 26
    2.3.2 The allegory of the cave: knowledge and politics 27
    2.3.3 Women Guardians in the ideal state 28
2.4 Socrates and Sojourner Truth: knowledge and education 29
2.5 Sojourner Truth's speeches 31
    2.5.1 The representation of Black women 31
    2.5.2 Narrative and humour 33
2.6 Conclusion 34

3 Aristotle and bell hooks 39
Manjeet Ramgotra

3.1 Introduction 39
3.2 Two political thinkers 40
    3.2.1 Aristotle 40
    3.2.2 bell hooks 40

		3.3	Locations of politics	40
		3.4	Theories of knowing and being	43
			3.4.1 Aristotle on knowing and being	43
			3.4.2 hooks on knowing and being	44
		3.5	Human nature and subjectivity	46
			3.5.1 Aristotle on human nature	46
			3.5.2 bell hooks on subjectivity	48
		3.6	The domestic sphere	49
			3.6.1 Aristotle on the household	49
			3.6.2 hooks on homeplace	52
		3.7	Conclusion	54

4 Kautilya — 57
Deepshikha Shahi

	4.1	Introduction	57
	4.2	Unfolding the philosophical foundation	58
	4.3	Circles of states and foreign policy	60
		4.3.1 The ends of political rule	62
		4.3.2 Political reality and morality	64
	4.4	Untangling the knots of 'gender' and 'caste'	67
		4.4.1 The many faces of womanhood	67
		4.4.2 The groundwork of a social order	68
	4.5	Conclusion	70

PART II Social contract theory and its critics

5 Thomas Hobbes — 79
Signy Gutnick Allen

5.1	Introduction	79
5.2	The state of nature and the laws of nature	80
	5.2.1 A modern theorist?	80
	5.2.2 The origins of *warre*: Hobbes on the state of nature	81
	5.2.3 The natural law	82
	5.2.4 Gender and the natural law	84
	5.2.5 Locating the state of nature	85
5.3	The social contract	87
	5.3.1 Authorization and representation	87
	5.3.2 Absolute sovereignty	89
	5.3.3 The duties of sovereignty	90
	5.3.4 The limits of covenanting	90

	5.4	Rebellion and state breakdown	91
		5.4.1 Protection and obligation	91
		5.4.2 A right to rebel?	91
		5.4.3 Hobbes's legacy	92
	5.5	Conclusion	92

6 Baruch Spinoza — 97
Caroline Williams

	6.1	Introduction	97
	6.2	From *Ethics* to politics	98
		6.2.1 The critique of religion	99
		6.2.2 Bodies and minds	100
	6.3	Politics and power	103
		6.3.1 From right to power	103
		6.3.2 The political shadow of the multitude	105
	6.4	Democracy: politics beyond the state	106
		6.4.1 The unity of the multitude	108
	6.5	Conclusion	110

7 John Locke — 115
Hagar Kotef

	7.1	Introduction	115
	7.2	Locke, sovereignty, and the state of nature	116
	7.3	Social and sexual identities and hierarchies	119
		7.3.1 Class: labour, accumulation, and Locke's 'individual'	119
		7.3.2 Gender: the questions of limited rule and forced subjection	121
	7.4	Global considerations	123
		7.4.1 Place: colonization and the establishment of European access to the world's resources	123
		7.4.2 Race: slavery and the question of freedom	126
	7.5	Conclusion	128

8 Mary Astell — 131
Allauren Forbes

	8.1	Introduction	131
	8.2	Astell's philosophical projects	132
		8.2.1 An interpretive puzzle	132
		8.2.2 Social contract theory and liberalism	133
	8.3	Problematizing social contract theory	134
		8.3.1 Human nature	135
		8.3.2 Sovereignty	136
		8.3.3 Consent	138
		8.3.4 Freedom and slavery	140

		8.4	Marriage as a social contract?	142
		8.5	Conclusion	144

9 Jean-Jacques Rousseau — 147
Peter Hallward

	9.1	Introduction	147
	9.2	A revolutionary agenda	148
		9.2.1 Mass sovereignty	149
		9.2.2 Solitary by nature	150
		9.2.3 Free will	153
	9.3	Sovereign by choice	154
		9.3.1 Sustained by virtue	155
		9.3.2 Commanders-in-chief	159
	9.4	Conclusion	159

10 Carole Pateman and Charles Mills — 163
Terrell Carver

	10.1	Introduction	163
	10.2	The social contract	163
		10.2.1 Peaceful agreements and equal individuals	164
		10.2.2 The people and the state	166
		10.2.3 Some are more equal than others	167
		10.2.4 Some are more violent than others	168
	10.3	The sexual contract	169
		10.3.1 Women and marriage	170
		10.3.2 Women and prostitution	171
	10.4	The racial contract	172
		10.4.1 Universalism and hypocrisy	173
		10.4.2 Whiteness and ignorance	174
	10.5	The settler contract	175
	10.6	Conclusion	177

PART III Liberal modernity and colonial domination

11 Charles-Louis de Secondat, Baron de la Brede et de Montesquieu — 185
Manjeet Ramgotra

	11.1	Introduction	185
	11.2	Context and scope	187
		11.2.1 Transatlantic commerce, economic and political change	187
		11.2.2 Climatology	188
	11.3	Theory of the separation and balance of powers and individual freedom	189
		11.3.1 Divided sovereignty	189

		11.3.2	The separation of powers: checks and balances	191
		11.3.3	Types of government	192
	11.4	Time, progress, and conquest		194
		11.4.1	Time and progress	194
		11.4.2	Conquest	196
	11.5	Commerce and slavery		197
		11.5.1	Commerce	197
		11.5.2	Slavery	198
	11.6	Conclusion		200
12	**John Stuart Mill**			**203**
	Inder S. Marwah			
	12.1	Introduction		203
	12.2	Liberalism and utilitarianism		204
		12.2.1	Liberty	204
		12.2.2	Liberty of thought and discussion	206
		12.2.3	Liberty of action	206
		12.2.4	Individuality	207
		12.2.5	Utilitarianism	208
	12.3	Government and democracy		210
		12.3.1	Government	210
		12.3.2	Democracy	211
	12.4	Race, gender, empire		213
		12.4.1	Race	213
		12.4.2	Gender	214
		12.4.3	Empire	216
	12.5	Conclusion		218
13	**Karl Marx**			**221**
	Simon Choat			
	13.1	Introduction		221
	13.2	The materialist conception of history		223
		13.2.1	Modes of production	223
		13.2.2	Base and superstructure	224
		13.2.3	Ideology	226
	13.3	The origins and nature of capitalism		227
		13.3.1	Commodification	227
		13.3.2	Exploitation	228
		13.3.3	Primitive accumulation	230
	13.4	The state and political transformation		231
		13.4.1	The state and the ruling class	231

		13.4.2	Marx and the anarchists	232
		13.4.3	The end of capitalism	234
	13.5	Conclusion		234

14 Friedrich Nietzsche — 239
Willow Verkerk

	14.1	Introduction		239
	14.2	Physician of culture		240
		14.2.1	Perspectivism	241
		14.2.2	'Woman' and 'truth'	242
		14.2.3	Contesting the truth of opposite values	243
	14.3	Will to power		244
		14.3.1	*Agon* and the state	245
		14.3.2	Slave and master moralities	246
		14.3.3	Morality has no rational foundation	247
	14.4	Democracy and the problem of equality		248
		14.4.1	Sexism, racism, and colonialism	249
	14.5	Conclusion		252

15 Sayyid Qutb — 257
Ayesha Omar

	15.1	Introduction		257
	15.2	Colonialism and *jahilliyyah*		259
		15.2.1	Intellectual context and reception	259
		15.2.2	States of ignorance: *jahilliyyah*	261
	15.3	Sovereignty as *Hakimiyyah*		263
	15.4	*Jihad* (holy war)		267
	15.5	Conclusion		270

16 Edward W. Said — 273
Rahul Rao

	16.1	Introduction		273
	16.2	Orientalism and the politics of knowledge		274
		16.2.1	'"We" are this, "they" are that'	274
		16.2.2	Critiques of *Orientalism*	276
	16.3	Empire and hybridity		278
		16.3.1	'Overlapping territories, intertwined histories'	278
		16.3.2	Resistance to empire	280
	16.4	Partisan for Palestine		281
		16.4.1	Narrating Palestine	281
		16.4.2	For, against, and beyond nationalism	284
	16.5	The intellectual vocation		285
	16.6	Conclusion		287

PART IV Freedom and revolution

17 Catharine Macaulay and Edmund Burke — 295
Alan Coffee

- 17.1 Introduction — 295
- 17.2 Catharine Macaulay — 297
  - 17.2.1 Accountable government — 298
  - 17.2.2 Three connected values: independence, virtue, equality — 299
  - 17.2.3 Government and education — 301
- 17.3 Edmund Burke — 301
  - 17.3.1 Conservation and correction — 302
  - 17.3.2 Rights as convention — 303
  - 17.3.3 The spirit of a gentleman and the spirit of religion — 304
- 17.4 Criticisms and relevance — 305
  - 17.4.1 Can Macaulay reconcile universal principles with social context? — 305
  - 17.4.2 Does Burke have sufficient safeguards against the abuse of power? — 307
- 17.5 Conclusion — 309

18 C.L.R. James — 313
Robbie Shilliam

- 18.1 Introduction — 313
- 18.2 James's Marxism — 314
  - 18.2.1 The dialectic of freedom — 314
  - 18.2.2 The radical intelligentsia and the masses — 315
  - 18.2.3 The dialectic of freedom in world history — 316
- 18.3 The native intelligentsia — 318
  - 18.3.1 Colonial education and European civilization — 318
  - 18.3.2 The Haitian Revolution versus European civilization — 319
- 18.4 Black freedom/European civilization — 321
  - 18.4.1 Trinidad and the racial sources of self-determination — 321
  - 18.4.2 The challenge of Garveyism to James — 322
  - 18.4.3 The challenge of Rastafari to James — 324
  - 18.4.4 Black women and the dialectic of freedom — 325
- 18.5 Conclusion — 326

19 Hannah Arendt — 331
Kei Hiruta

- 19.1 Introduction — 331
- 19.2 The burden of our time — 333
  - 19.2.1 A new form of government — 333
  - 19.2.2 Crystallization — 335

		19.3	The meaning of politics	336
			19.3.1 The specificity of the political	336
			19.3.2 Philosophy and politics	337
		19.4	'The end of revolution is the foundation of freedom'	339
			19.4.1 France and America (and Haiti)	339
		19.5	Between feminism and anti-feminism	340
			19.5.1 Arendt as an anti-feminist	341
			19.5.2 Arendt as a (proto-)feminist	342
		19.6	Arendt's 'Negro question'	342
			19.6.1 Arendt's 'horrific racial stereotypes'	343
			19.6.2 The world and its other	344
		19.7	Conclusion	345
20	**Zhang Taiyan**			**349**
	Viren Murthy			
		20.1	Introduction	349
		20.2	Zhang Taiyan as anti-Manchu revolutionary	350
			20.2.1 Zhang's classical learning amidst political events	350
			20.2.2 Zhang's nationalism in relation to reformers	351
			20.2.3 The revolutionary Zhang Taiyan	353
		20.3	Pan-Asianism and different types of transnationalism	355
			20.3.1 In defence of anti-colonial nationalism	355
			20.3.2 The roots of socialism in Chinese culture	356
			20.3.3 India and China at the centre of Asian unity	357
		20.4	Buddhism vs Hegel: towards a new universality	359
			20.4.1 Zhang's confrontation with Hegel	359
			20.4.2 Zhang's alternative to Hegel: a philosophy of difference	360
		20.5	Conclusion	362

PART V Inclusion and equality

21	**Mary Wollstonecraft**			**371**
	Ashley Dodsworth			
		21.1	Introduction	371
		21.2	Women's emancipation	372
			21.2.1 Form	372
			21.2.2 *A Vindication of the Rights of Woman*	373
		21.3	Reason and republicanism	376
			21.3.1 Reason	376
			21.3.2 Liberalism or republicanism	377

		21.4 Slavery and the global context	378
		21.4.1 Global context	379
		21.5 Tensions	381
		21.5.1 Class	381
		21.5.2 Motherhood	382
		21.6 Conclusion	384
22	**Iris Marion Young**		**389**
	Neus Torbisco-Casals		
		22.1 Introduction	389
		22.2 Oppression and structural inequality	390
		22.2.1 Social groups and structural inequalities	392
		22.3 Equality, justice, and inclusion	394
		22.4 Citizenship, democracy, and representation	397
		22.4.1 Citizenship and the 'politics of difference'	397
		22.4.2 Representation, deliberation, and inclusion	398
		22.4.3 Relations between representative and represented person	402
		22.5 Conclusion	403
23	**Bhikhu Parekh**		**407**
	Varun Uberoi		
		23.1 Introduction	407
		23.2 Culture and cultural diversity	409
		23.3 Intercultural dialogue	410
		23.4 Legitimizing cultural differences in a polity	413
		23.5 Encouraging unity among culturally diverse citizens	415
		23.6 *The Parekh Report*: political philosophy and practice	417
		23.7 Reception and interpretations of Parekh's work	419
		23.8 Conclusion	421
24	**Gayatri Chakravorty Spivak**		**427**
	Nikita Dhawan		
		24.1 Introduction	427
		24.2 Subalternity	429
		24.2.1 Representation	429
		24.2.2 Subaltern Studies	430
		24.2.3 Imperialist feminism	432
		24.3 Alter-globalization and subalternity	434
		24.3.1 Transnational solidarity	435
		24.3.2 Desubalternization	436
		24.4 The European Enlightenment and empire	437
		24.4.1 Decolonizing the Enlightenment	439
		24.5 Conclusion	441

DETAILED CONTENTS

PART VI Violence, power, and resistance

25 Niccolò Machiavelli — 447
Yves Winter

- 25.1 Introduction — 447
- 25.2 Power and the state — 448
  - 25.2.1 Machiavelli's life and times — 448
  - 25.2.2 Principalities and republics — 448
  - 25.2.3 Power — 449
- 25.3 Virtue and fortune — 452
  - 25.3.1 Virtù — 452
  - 25.3.2 Fortuna — 453
- 25.4 Freedom and conflict — 454
  - 25.4.1 The Roman republic — 454
  - 25.4.2 Freedom — 455
  - 25.4.3 Conflict — 457
- 25.5 Violence, conquest, and empire — 458
  - 25.5.1 Violence as spectacle — 458
  - 25.5.2 The paradox of conquest — 459
  - 25.5.3 Republics and empire — 460
- 25.6 Conclusion — 461

26 Emma Goldman — 465
Ruth Kinna

- 26.1 Introduction — 465
- 26.2 Goldman's anarchism — 467
  - 26.2.1 Radicalization: Haymarket — 468
  - 26.2.2 Love with open eyes — 469
  - 26.2.3 The spirit of revolt — 469
  - 26.2.4 Goldman's anarchist imaginary — 470
- 26.3 Theory and practice — 472
  - 26.3.1 Theory and experience — 472
  - 26.3.2 Power — 474
  - 26.3.3 Class, sex, 'race', and representation — 476
- 26.4 Slavishness and rights — 478
  - 26.4.1 Slavery and slavishness — 478
  - 26.4.2 Rights and resistance — 479
- 26.5 Conclusion — 480

27 Mohandas (Mahatma) Gandhi   485
Jimmy Casas Klausen

- 27.1 Introduction   485
- 27.2 Gandhi as global icon   486
- 27.3 *Hind Swaraj*: anti-colonial resistance   488
- 27.4 *An Autobiography*: struggle towards nonviolence   491
  - 27.4.1 Gandhi's hidden biases   491
  - 27.4.2 Self-purification and *satyagraha*   493
  - 27.4.3 Miscalculation: moral politics and the masses   494
- 27.5 Campaigns of nonviolent resistance: theory and practice   496
- 27.6 Conclusion   499

28 Frantz Fanon   505
Keally McBride

- 28.1 Introduction   505
- 28.2 Fanon's life   505
- 28.3 Race, gender, and psychology   508
- 28.4 The violence of colonization and decolonization   511
- 28.5 Achieving lasting decolonization   515
- 28.6 Conclusion   519

PART VII The liberal self and black consciousness

29 Immanuel Kant   527
Stella Sandford

- 29.1 Introduction   527
- 29.2 Fundamentals of Kant's philosophy   528
- 29.3 Kant's political philosophy   530
  - 29.3.1 Universal history and teleology   531
  - 29.3.2 *A priori* foundations for political theory   532
- 29.4 'Ideal' and 'non-ideal' political theory   535
  - 29.4.1 Problems in the *a priori* foundations   536
  - 29.4.2 Problems in relation to universal history and teleology: the theory of race and the colonial context   538
- 29.5 Conclusion   540

30 Frederick Douglass   545
Kiara Gilbert and Karen Salt

- 30.1 Introduction   545
- 30.2 Slavery and freedom   545
  - 30.2.1 The fugitive's philosophy   546

		30.2.2	Activating freedom	548
		30.2.3	Silences within slavery	550
	30.3	The freedman's philosophy		550
		30.3.1	Heroic violence	552
		30.3.2	The promise of the US Constitution	553
		30.3.3	Suffragists, Natives, and the Constitution	555
	30.4	The statesman's philosophy		558
		30.4.1	(Re)colonizing the Caribbean	558
	30.5	Conclusion		559

31 W.E.B. Du Bois — 565
Elvira Basevich

	31.1	Introduction		565
	31.2	The problem of exclusion		567
		31.2.1	Du Bois's philosophy of resistance and race	569
	31.3	Du Bois on gender and the Black family		571
		31.3.1	Slavery and the Black family	571
		31.3.2	Motherhood and the freedom to love	573
	31.4	Du Bois's socialist politics		574
		31.4.1	Du Bois among liberals and labour organizers	574
	31.5	Conclusion		577

32 John Rawls — 581
Maeve McKeown

	32.1	Introduction		581
	32.2	*A Theory of Justice*: The basics		582
		32.2.1	The basic structure	582
		32.2.2	Ideal theory	583
		32.2.3	The original position	583
		32.2.4	The principles of justice	585
	32.3	The original position and the Rawlsian self		586
		32.3.1	The feminist critique	587
		32.3.2	The critical race critique	588
		32.3.3	The disability critique	589
	32.4	The basic structure and the Rawlsian society		591
		32.4.1	What is the basic structure?	591
		32.4.2	Critique of the 'distributive paradigm'	592
		32.4.3	The scope of justice	593
	32.5	Conclusion		595

PART VIII Sex and sexuality

33 Michel Foucault — 603
Paul Patton

- 33.1 Introduction — 603
- 33.2 Sexuality — 604
- 33.3 Discourse, truth, and power — 607
  - 33.3.1 Discourse and truth — 607
  - 33.3.2 Disciplinary power — 608
- 33.4 Race, government, and power — 611
  - 33.4.1 Biopower and state racism — 611
  - 33.4.2 Liberal and neoliberal government — 613
  - 33.4.3 Power and the government of conduct — 614
- 33.5 Conclusion — 616

34 Shulamith Firestone — 621
Victoria Margree

- 34.1 Introduction — 621
- 34.2 The Women's Liberation Movement — 622
  - 34.2.1 The personal is political — 622
  - 34.2.2 Liberal, socialist, and radical feminisms — 623
  - 34.2.3 Reproductive rights — 624
- 34.3 Reproductive biology and women's oppression — 625
  - 34.3.1 A historical materialism rooted in sex — 625
  - 34.3.2 Natural oppression — 626
  - 34.3.3 Pregnancy and childbirth — 627
- 34.4 Reproductive technology and feminist revolution — 629
  - 34.4.1 Abolishing the family — 630
  - 34.4.2 The 'racial family' — 631
  - 34.4.3 The household — 632
  - 34.4.4 Children's oppression — 632
- 34.5 Sexual and reproductive politics in the twenty-first century — 633
  - 34.5.1 Queering sex and gender — 633
  - 34.5.2 Reproductive politics — 635
- 34.6 Conclusion — 636

35 Angela Y. Davis — 639
Manjeet Ramgotra

- 35.1 Introduction — 639
- 35.2 Davis's radical political theory — 641
  - 35.2.1 Marxism and Communism — 641
  - 35.2.2 Consciousness — 642
- 35.3 Abolition of prisons — 644
  - 35.3.1 Prisons, racism, and slavery — 644
  - 35.3.2 Prisons and policing — 645
  - 35.3.3 Delinking crime from punishment — 646
  - 35.3.4 Reparative justice — 647
- 35.4 Women, race, and class — 648
  - 35.4.1 Black women's struggles and resistance — 648
  - 35.4.2 The category of woman — 651
- 35.5 Conclusion — 653

36 Judith Butler — 657
Clare Woodford

- 36.1 Introduction — 657
- 36.2 Gender, feminism, and identity — 658
- 36.3 Parody and performativity — 660
- 36.4 Subjectivity, resistance, and the psyche — 663
- 36.5 Morality and ethics — 666
- 36.6 Politics — 668
- 36.7 Conclusion — 670

PART IX The environment, human, and non-human

37 Dipesh Chakrabarty — 679
Eva-Maria Nag

- 37.1 Introduction — 679
- 37.2 What is the Anthropocene? — 680
  - 37.2.1 Historical time and geological time — 683
- 37.3 A story of globalization and capitalism: freedom and fossil fuels — 684
  - 37.3.1 Freedom — 684
  - 37.3.2 Global capitalism — 685
  - 37.3.3 The global and the planetary — 685
  - 37.3.4 Critical debates and defence — 686

		37.4	Old and new images of the human: free agent and geological force	687
			37.4.1 Different, equal, and conjoined	688
			37.4.2 Species thinking	689
		37.5	Justice-sensitivity and justice-blindness	690
			37.5.1 Intra-human justice	690
			37.5.2 Inter-species justice	690
			37.5.3 Justice-blindness	691
		37.6	Conclusion	692
38	**Donna Haraway**			**697**
	Claire Colebrook			
		38.1	Introduction	697
		38.2	Cyborg	699
			38.2.1 'A Cyborg Manifesto'	699
			38.2.2 Cyborgs, humans, and non-humans	700
			38.2.3 Production and reproduction	702
		38.3	Organisms, mechanisms, vitalism	703
		38.4	The reinvention of nature	705
		38.5	Anthropocene, Capitalocene, Plantationocene, Chthulucene	707
		38.6	Conclusion	709
39	**Indigenous ecologies**			**713**
	Esme G. Murdock			
		39.1	Introduction	713
		39.2	Indigenous thinking vs. industrial thinking	714
		39.3	Indigenous governance	717
			39.3.1 Indigenous governance in action: the Haudenosaunee Confederacy	718
			39.3.2 Gender systems and land	719
		39.4	Interruptions and disruptions of Indigenous ecologies and sovereignties	721
		39.5	Difference, incommensurability, and solidarity	723
		39.6	Extractivism, fossil fuels, and Indigenous lands	725
		39.7	Conclusion	728

Index	731

1 Introduction

SIMON CHOAT AND MANJEET RAMGOTRA

1.1 Rethinking political thinkers

Textbooks of political thought have until now tended to present a 'canon' of great thinkers whom, it is claimed, one must read and understand in order to develop an adequate knowledge of the discipline of Politics. This canon, however, is typically constituted almost exclusively of white European men. Yet while the voices of women and People of Colour—including, of course, women of colour—have hitherto been excluded from the canon, and hence also from books such as this, thinking and writing about politics have never been activities limited only to white men. *Rethinking Political Thinkers* invites you to reconsider and rethink politics by listening to and engaging with voices that have not usually been heard.

While our textbook will introduce you to a wide range of political thinkers, it differs from other books in three important ways. First, alongside the predominantly white male thinkers of the traditional canon, we also include women and non-white thinkers whose work has often been ignored, excluded, or devalued. In this way, we bring previously marginalized voices into debates about some core political issues. Second, we believe that all political thinkers must be read with an acknowledgement and appreciation that they lived and wrote in a world characterized by certain power relations, specifically those of patriarchy, imperialism, and, in the modern world, capitalism and white supremacy. This means that special attention must be given to the relations and structures of race, gender, and class which different theories have reflected, defended, or challenged. Finally, we contend that the best way to understand and study political ideas, concepts, and debates is to compare them across time and space rather than viewing them as moments in a linear and progressive trajectory. The typical historical approach, which narrates a progression of ideas from the Greek city-state to present-day liberal democracy, is problematic. By viewing the history of political thought as a conversation over time in which participants build on the work of earlier theorists, it has tended to exclude alternative and critical voices from this conversation. As such, our book is organized not purely chronologically but thematically. The next two chapters (Chapters 2 and 3), for example, juxtapose classical thinkers of ancient Greece with nineteenth- and twentieth-century Black feminist theorists, and the nine Parts of the book are organized around themes rather than periods of time. We do this not because we believe all thinkers are addressing the same questions and can therefore be read and understood in isolation from the contexts in which they wrote. To the contrary, we believe that juxtaposing thinkers from different eras will encourage you to consider how the position, identity, and context of each thinker affect their understanding of politics, while simultaneously recognizing that ideas and themes can persist, recur over time, and be subjected to reuse and reinterpretation (Ramgotra, 2015).

The aim of this initial chapter is to introduce you to the study of political thought and to explain and justify the contents, approach, and organization of this book. Section 1.2 examines political thought as a specific way of understanding and analysing politics, highlighting some recent debates and developments, including the development of comparative political thought. In doing so, it also reflects on the meaning of 'politics' itself. Section 1.3 looks at why and how we might study the *history* of political thought. We will explore different approaches to the study of the history of political thought and reflect on a range of methodological and interpretative issues. Section 1.4 considers *who* we should be studying and, in particular, explores calls to decolonize political thought. This chapter aims to demonstrate that political thought can be understood and studied in a variety of ways and to show why it is important to include voices that have been excluded or silenced. It concludes, in Section 1.5, by providing a brief overview of the book and explaining its pedagogical features.

1.2 Political thought

Not all of the thinkers included in this book called themselves political theorists or political philosophers. They include sociologists, economists, historians, literary theorists, activists, and politicians. Many of them worked across academic disciplines, or lived in a time when the current disciplinary boundaries had not been shaped and solidified, and many did not work in universities at all. Indeed, one of the claims of this book is that it is anachronistic to think that political thought must always be written in a certain way or even that it must meet certain thresholds or adhere to particular standards. Political thought is developed in a variety of locations and is written in very many styles. Even classic works by well-established thinkers, such as Niccolò Machiavelli, Jean-Jacques Rousseau, and Karl Marx, come in a wide range of forms: letters, manifestos, newspaper articles, novels, plays, fragmentary drafts, and notebooks. Many significant works, from *The Federalist* (Hamilton et al., 2003) to the Combahee River Collective's (1977) 'Statement', were not originally attributed to specific authors at all.

All of the thinkers in this book can nonetheless be said to have contributed to the discipline of political theory in the sense that they all reflect theoretically on politics. Of course, at some level, all political analysis is 'theoretical': rather than simply reporting what happens, the study of politics must use concepts and models to develop theories that explain events and processes. But what further distinguishes political theory from other types of political analysis is that political theory is *normative*: it seeks to establish, clarify, question, and challenge norms or standards. As Jonathan Floyd (2019) argues, the distinguishing question of political philosophy is: 'How should we live?'. This question is normative—it asks how we *should* live rather than how we *do* live—and it is collective, asking how *we* should live rather than simply how each of us should act as individuals.

Although the question 'How should we live?' may seem abstract and unwieldy, it is of vital importance to all of us: it asks what it is that we value and how we think society should be organized. Moreover, it can and must be broken down into innumerable further questions that address more obviously concrete issues: Should the rich pay more tax? What limits, if any, should be put on freedom of speech? Should animal rights be recognized in law? What role, if any, should the state play in governing our sexual activity? Should reparations be paid to the victims of slavery or colonialism and their descendants? How should we address climate change? These are all normative questions that political theory can help us answer. Many political theorists contend that normative theory is intricately bound to the real world: part of what Marc Stears (2005: 347) calls the 'drama' of politics, 'a drama that [theorists] can understand, shape, and perhaps even rewrite'.

In this book, we do not restrict 'political' thought to analysis of the state or relations between states. We contend that 'the political' is not simply the arena in which those who rule gather to deliberate on public business. If we confine our definition of politics to the formal politics of government, then those groups who have historically been denied the right to participate in government, including women, People of Colour, and Indigenous peoples, will face a double exclusion: excluded from the activity of politics and simultaneously excluded from our understanding and discussions of politics. In order, therefore, to include formerly (or currently) excluded groups and individuals in our analyses of politics—as this book tries to do—then we cannot simply add their voices and experiences to our existing conception of politics: inclusion must mean rethinking our political concepts and theories, including the concept of politics itself (Hanchard, 2010). One of the central contributions of women and People of Colour to political thought has precisely been to challenge and expand our understanding of 'politics'. Think, for example, of the slogan 'The personal is political', with which second-wave feminists not only demanded the inclusion of women in formal politics but also sought to undermine the traditional divide between the 'private' and the 'public' spheres, widening the scope of the political (see Section 34.2.1 of Chapter 34 for further discussion). If, as the radical feminist Kate Millett (2016) claims, 'the essence of politics is power', then arguably every area of human (and even non-human) life is amenable to political analysis.

What distinguishes the thinkers in this book, therefore, is not their varied approaches to analysing a common object named 'politics'—because what they understand by 'politics' varies. We can say that politics is about disagreement, in at least two senses. First, if there were no disagreement—in particular about how to order and organize our societies—then there would be no politics. But, second, this disagreement extends to the very definition of politics: the concept of 'politics' is itself political, in that there is no agreement about how to define it.

The Belgian political theorist Chantal Mouffe (1943–) uses the term 'the political' to refer to the dimension of our world that is necessarily characterized by forms of conflict and antagonism that can never be eliminated. She defines 'politics', meanwhile, as 'the set of practices and institutions through which an order is created, organizing human coexistence in the context of conflictuality provided by the political' (Mouffe, 2005: 9). In making this argument, Mouffe is drawing in part on the work of the German legal and political theorist Carl Schmitt (1888-1985). For Schmitt (2007: 36), what distinguishes the political is the friend/enemy distinction: 'Every religious, moral, economic, ethical, or other antithesis transforms into a political one if it is sufficiently strong to group human beings effectively according to friend and enemy.' For Schmitt, all political communities are determined by their choice of who is the friend and who is the enemy—or, as Mouffe puts it, all political identities consist of a 'we' which is defined against a 'they'. Unlike Schmitt, however, Mouffe is fully committed to democratic pluralism: the we/they distinction is necessary, but to act democratically is to view our opponents ('they') not as enemies to be eradicated but as adversaries with whom we share some common ground.

Political thought is also characterized by disagreement at the methodological level: just as there is no agreement about the meaning of 'politics', there is no consensus about *how* it should be studied. Indeed, not everyone agrees that political theory must be normative (see, e.g., Kelly, 2018). In the English-speaking world, however, an explicit commitment to normative theorizing has certainly been the dominant form of political philosophy over the past half-century. This in part reflects the influence of John Rawls' 1971 book, *A Theory of Justice*, which is commonly credited with reviving normative political philosophy (e.g., Kymlicka, 2002: 10) (see Chapter 32 on Rawls). This is perhaps a somewhat narrow claim: even in the English-speaking world, important normative theorizing was taking place between the end of the Second World War and the publication of *A Theory of Justice*, and, across the world, normative theories continued to be propounded, not least as part of anti-colonial movements and demands for civil rights. Yet, for a long time, many Anglophone political philosophers viewed their discipline through an exclusively Rawlsian or post-Rawlsian lens, to the extent that, in some university departments, studying political philosophy meant studying Rawls and his critics and their varying answers to the question 'What is justice?'

Even in Anglophone analytic philosophy, however, the dominance of Rawlsian approaches has recently been challenged. For Rawls and many of his critics, political philosophy essentially involves the identification and application of moral ideals concerning justice, rights, freedom, and so forth.

This approach is rejected by so-called political realists, who argue that we have politics at least in part because there exists moral disagreement over our collective aims and values (Williams, 2005; Geuss, 2008). Realists agree that politics requires normative standards—to judge whether a particular political regime is legitimate, for example—but argue that these standards arise from within politics itself and are not found in a pre-political moral realm. In this sense, the political is autonomous of morality—or, at least, political judgements cannot be reduced to or straightforwardly derived from moral norms (Rossi and Sleat, 2014). Political realism encompasses a variety of types, but all agree that political theorists must take facts about the political world more seriously, paying more attention to real-world politics and its history (Galston, 2010).

This emphasis on the facts of concrete politics has led to accusations that political realism is conservative, especially when such facts are invoked to place limits on what is possible. Which facts we identify as salient and how we interpret them are surely just as disputable as our moral values. What counts as 'realistic', in other words, is a *political* question: it cannot be established outside of or beyond the space of political disagreements (Finlayson, 2017). It can be argued, therefore, that there is in the work of (some) recent political realists a 'displacement of politics' (Honig, 1993) similar to what we find in the work of the Rawlsians: an attempt to fix in place the social order by the introduction of constraints—whether moral (as with the Rawlsians) or 'factual' (as in realism)—that are supposedly beyond the antagonisms and conflicts of politics (see also Mouffe, 1993).

The dominance of Rawls-inspired theory in the final third of the twentieth century may also have contributed to a narrowing of the range of political thought as researched and taught in English-speaking universities, crowding out alternative traditions from the non-Western world in particular (von Vacano, 2015: 477). The twenty-first century has seen the welcome development of *comparative* political thought, which seeks to engage with varieties of political thought that exist outside of Europe and North America. This growth of comparative political thought responds to the unjust exclusion of non-Western voices and reflects the emergence and need for cultural interaction and dialogue in an increasingly globalized world (Jenco, 2007; Dallmayr, 2010; Godrej, 2011; Tully, 2016). Certain forms of comparative political thought have been criticized for demarcating too strongly between 'Western' thought and 'non-Western' thought (El Amine, 2016; Idris, 2016). Yet rather than simply studying non-Western traditions, comparative political theorists have sought equally to de-centre the West and disrupt the distinction between 'Western' and 'non-Western'. An understanding of different cultures can be seen as fundamental and necessary to political thought. As Roxanne Euben (2004) shows, the ancient Greek *'theôria'*—from which we take our word 'theory'—drew connections between travel and wisdom: travel distances a person from their homeland and a particular way of seeing things, introducing other ways of being and understanding the world.

This is not a book of comparative political thought. Many, though by no means all, of its thinkers are European and American. That is partly because the book is produced in Europe (though not all of our chapter authors are European or American). It is also because Europe and the United States have dominated global affairs for the past half-millennium: the ideas produced by European and American thinkers have played a significant role in justifying and maintaining that dominance, and so are worth interrogating. Moreover, rather than *comparing* 'Western' and 'non-Western' thought by placing them side by side, we seek to demonstrate their mutual imbrication—to show how the very idea of 'the West' and 'Western' political thought was formed through the (often violent and oppressive) encounter with the 'non-West'. Yet we nevertheless endorse the claims of comparative political theorists that there is a plurality of approaches, traditions, norms, and methods, with no single 'correct' way of doing political thought.

This does not, however, mean that we cannot judge political theories or that one thinker or theory is as good as every other. The normativity of political thought can make judgement difficult. A thinker may make erroneous or mistaken factual claims in support of their arguments, for which they can be justly criticized but, ultimately, normative claims can never be true or false. There are nonetheless a number of different criteria by which we can judge political theories. We can question their coherence and consistency: does a theory hold together or does it contradict itself? We can ask whether a theory fits with our values and judgements: does a theory have contemporary relevance and application? We can challenge the feasibility and desirability of a theory: would it be possible to implement what it proposes, and would doing so produce the kind of society we want? Finally, we can interrogate the assumptions made by a thinker: does a theory assume certain ideals of political agency or action that exclude others?

The answers to these questions will not automatically produce reasons for rejecting a thinker. A thinker might contradict themselves in interesting and even productive ways. Their values might be very different to our own—but that might cause us to rethink our own principles. Feasibility is as contestable as desirability: many things which were once deemed 'impossible' have since come to pass. A thinker may be sexist, racist, or ableist—as indeed are many of the thinkers in this book—and yet still have important and useful things to say. We believe that political thinkers must be read *critically*—but that means evaluating their arguments rather than setting out to denounce or reject them.

1.2 Political thought: Key Points

- Definitions of politics and approaches to studying politics are themselves political in the sense that they are subject to disagreement and contestation.
- Political thought is typically normative, asking how we *should* live—in particular, how we should order our societies—but it can and does take a variety of forms and come from a variety of sources.
- Comparative political thought has sought to draw attention to 'non-Western' thinkers and theories but also to disrupt the distinction between 'Western' and 'non-Western'.

1.3 The history of political thought

We have so far tried to show why political thought as normative analysis is of vital importance. But what is the point of studying political thinkers from the past? One answer might be that past thinkers can help solve our present problems, because those thinkers faced the same problems that we face. From this perspective, the questions asked by the great thinkers of the past—concerning the purpose of the state, the meaning of justice, or the origins of rights—are also our questions. Different thinkers across the ages have, of course, given very different answers to those questions—but that, it can be argued, is why we need to study the history of political thought, in order to survey and assess their different answers: how, for example, did Aristotle, Hobbes, and Kant answer the question 'What is justice?', and who was right?

This kind of approach, in which we study past thinkers in order to benefit from their timeless wisdom, was criticized by the English philosopher R.G. Collingwood (1889-1943). For Collingwood (2013), the study of philosophy must be properly historical. To understand the statements that a thinker made, Collingwood argued, we need to understand the questions to which those statements were answers, and we should not assume that all thinkers through history have been asking the same questions. For Collingwood (ibid.: 58), we must therefore reconstruct the questions asked by a thinker, which involves 'getting inside other people's heads, looking at their situation through their eyes'. This historical approach does not mean that for Collingwood the ideas of the past are of no use to us today or that we should study them only for their intrinsic historical interest. While thinkers ought to be studied in their contexts, and the past is quite different from the present, the present has emerged from the past. As Collingwood says, '[T]he past which an historian studies is not a dead past, but a past which in some sense is still living in the present' (ibid.: 97). So although the study of history cannot provide us with any ready-made rules for how to act in the present, it can offer us insight, and it can do this because the past is not dead but alive and active in the present.

Others have argued that the past persists in the present not just in ideas but in the material world around us—in objects, architecture, nature, and the design and structure of institutions and systems. As the Haitian anthropologist Michel-Rolph Trouillot (1995) explains, material objects embody ideas and collective memories, constituting an archive of their own that persists in the present; sometimes they convey silences or stories that have been erased in what historians choose to convey. As such, the study of the past should not be limited to the written record. For instance, the practices and ideologies that justified colonial empires—and the material symbols, such as statues, that celebrate those empires—continue to shape the present and are important for understanding contemporary patterns of racial injustice.

Collingwood was an important influence on the work of the English intellectual historian Quentin Skinner (1940-) (Skinner, 1988: 103). Skinner's work, which has over the past half-century been enormously influential on readings in political thought, has an affinity with the work of other historians, including John Dunn (1968), J.G.A. Pocock (2009), and James Tully (1988). These authors, who all emphasize the importance of intellectual contexts to understanding past ideas, have often been grouped under the name of the 'Cambridge School of historians'. Like Collingwood, Skinner rejects the idea that the thinkers of the past have all addressed the same questions. The uses and meanings of concepts change over time: failure to recognize this, Skinner argues, will lead us to anachronistic readings—blaming a thinker for failing to meet standards that we have imposed on them or, conversely, crediting a thinker for saying something that they could never have intended to say. Instead of imposing our preconceptions on the past, we must try to recover thinkers' points of view. Skinner argues that we cannot understand a thinker simply by reading what they have written. This is not only because meanings change—and so we need to understand what a concept meant for the author who used it—but also because to understand *any* text we need 'to grasp not merely what people are saying but also what they are *doing in* saying it' (Skinner, 2002: 82). To say something is at the same time to do something (to warn, to promise, to inform, to condemn, etc.) and we need to know what an author was doing in saying something: for example, did they intend their arguments to be taken literally or did they mean them ironically?

Whereas Collingwood wanted to get into other people's heads, Skinner (ibid.: vii, 120) argues that this is neither possible nor necessary: to recover the intentions of a thinker—'to see things their way'—we do not need to think their private thoughts, because intentions are public and social. We should view political texts as interventions into pre-existing debates, and in order to understand what an author intended to do in a text, we need to explore the intellectual context within which the author wrote—specifically, the 'wider linguistic context' which both constrains what an author can say but also allows them to say something new (ibid.: 87).

Yet if political problems are always historically specific, as Skinner argues, then what is the point of studying past thinkers? Why study Machiavelli, for example, when the context in which he wrote, and hence the questions that he asked and problems he addressed, are so different from our own twenty-first-century context and concerns? Skinner's answer is that past texts do not provide us with 'directly applicable "lessons"' but rather help reveal a more general lesson that all problems and their solutions—including our own—are historically specific (ibid.: 88). Studying past thinkers allows and encourages us to 'stand back from our own assumptions and systems of belief', demonstrating their contingency and enlarging our horizons (ibid.: 125). In this sense, the merit of the history of political thought is similar to that of comparative political thought: they both help to deflate our parochialism, showing us that our ways of seeing and understanding are not unique (Euben, 2004; Blau, 2021). But this analogy between historical and comparative thought, if anything, calls into question the value of the former: if we can learn the same lesson from studying geographically distant authors, why study temporally distant authors? More broadly, Skinner's justification of his method does not seem to give us a very strong reason for reading specific authors or for reading widely: if both Machiavelli and Aristotle reveal the same general truth—that no social arrangements or beliefs are timeless—then why read them both? Indeed, notwithstanding the fact that we might simply derive some pleasure from doing so, why read *any* past thinker, given that Skinner's moral can be understood and accepted without a detour through the past?

Perhaps Skinner (2002: 88) is simply wrong to assert that 'there are no perennial problems in philosophy'. In making this point, Skinner claims to be drawing on Collingwood—but Collingwood (2013: 67-68) actually states that there are no *eternal* problems in philosophy, which is quite different (Lamb, 2009). A problem might be 'perennial'—that is, lasting for a long time—without being eternal and hence somehow timeless; or, as Collingwood argued, problems, questions, and concepts can change over time while nonetheless being linked by a historical process, such that there is both continuity and discontinuity. Even if we were to acknowledge that there are perennial problems or questions, however, this raises the question of *what* those problems are. Until very recently, imperial conquest, slavery, genocide, and the settler state have not figured among the perennial problems worthy of study within the discipline of political theory, despite being defining features of the modern world. The Jamaican anthropologist David Scott (2004: 4) has framed the recurrence of particular issues over time in terms of what he calls 'problem-spaces': 'an ensemble of questions and answers around which a horizon of identifiable stakes (conceptual as well as ideological-political stakes) hangs'. The questions that inhabit Scott's problem-spaces are not those that are typically associated with the conversation had over time by the 'great men' of the canon. Using this framework, Scott examines frequently silenced or neglected problems of race, colonialism, and slavery.

Scott's work engages appreciatively though critically with that of Skinner, but also with Marxism (especially via the writings of C.L.R. James and Stuart Hall). Like Skinner, the Marxist tradition also places great emphasis on the contexts in which texts were written—but it does so in a very different way. Understanding ideas for Marxists means relating them not so much to the discursive contexts in which authors wrote (the debates in which they intervened) but rather to the social, economic, and political contexts within which those ideas were produced, reflecting on the class interests that they might serve. 'The ruling ideas of each age have ever been the ideas of its ruling class' (Marx and Engels, 1976: 503). To what extent and in what ways, for example, does the celebration by liberal thinkers of the ideals of freedom and equality further the interests of the capitalist class? (See Chapter 13 on Marx.)

The risk for Skinner and others of the Marxist approach is that it seems to eliminate the role of intentionality: if texts are reflective of or even wholly determined by their economic context, then the author's specific intentions become irrelevant. Whether or not this is a legitimate criticism of the Marxist approach to the history of ideas, there are other approaches that more explicitly dismiss the significance of intentions. The French historian and philosopher Michel Foucault (1926-1984), for example, shifts the focus of attention away from the author altogether. Rather than trying to establish what people intended to say, Foucault (1970; 1977a) analysed the underlying systems of rules—or discourses—that made it possible for some things to be said rather than others. In his later works, Foucault (1977b; 1980) became interested in how discourses are connected to power relations. But, unlike Marxists, Foucault did not understand this in relation to the power of the ruling class: power for Foucault does not come from a single, central source, like the state or the bourgeoisie; power is everywhere and there are multiple power relations. (See Chapter 33 on Foucault.)

In developing his own approach to reading texts, Foucault drew upon the ideas of Friedrich Nietzsche (1844-1900) and Martin Heidegger (1889-1976). Nietzsche emphasized the perspectival nature of all knowledge—we always see and understand from a certain point of view—or what Heidegger referred to as our 'thrownness': we are always-already in the world, such that our understanding of ourselves and the world is always historical and situated. The French philosopher Jacques Derrida (1930-2004) also drew upon Nietzsche and Heidegger. In doing so, he developed an approach very different from that of Foucault, though one that similarly downplayed the significance of authorial intentionality. Derrida (1976; 1988) rejected the idea that the meaning of a text can be reduced to either its context or its author's intentions. Advocating a strategy he named 'deconstruction'—which sought to reveal the inconsistencies, paradoxes, and tensions in a text—Derrida argued that texts do not have a single, fixed meaning: they are open to multiple competing interpretations and can contain meanings not intended by their authors.

The kind of poststructuralist approach undertaken by Foucault and Derrida does not mean that we can take whatever we like from a text: both Derrida and Foucault demonstrated enormous care and rigour in their readings of texts. But it might mean that there are multiple legitimate interpretations of any thinker. This entails that a selective reading—in which we take certain insights from a thinker but not others—would not only be legitimate but necessary. It might even be that *mis*interpretations can be productive: misreading a text might make a reader a bad historian but it might simultaneously (though, of course, not necessarily) make that reader an interesting theorist.

This book does not advocate any specific method for reading political thinkers, whether idealist, contextualist, postcolonialist, Marxist, or poststructuralist. Each chapter attempts to analyse critically the ideas of a thinker by presenting them in their historical and intellectual contexts. The authors of our chapters have different approaches to political thought and come from various disciplines. We also believe that it can be fruitful to compare thinkers across time, including by placing side by side thinkers separated by centuries. This is not because we view the history of political thought as following a linear trajectory of progress; to the contrary, it is because we recognize that the history of ideas is punctuated by moments of change, repetition, crisis, and rupture, with thinkers both reviving older ideas and concepts and introducing innovations. This is why we present thinkers thematically rather than chronologically, presenting political ideas, concepts, and debates as recurrent and comparing thinkers across time and space.

> ### 1.3 The history of political thought: Key Points
>
> - The ideas and texts of past thinkers can be studied using a variety of methods.
> - Historians of political thought have provided competing justifications for studying past thinkers: some have argued that ideas are timeless, others that the past is living in the present, and still others that the differences of the past help demonstrate the contingency and historical specificity of all beliefs.
> - There are debates over whether ideas must be related to the contexts of their production in order to be understood and whether we need to understand the original intentions of authors.

1.4 The canon of political thought

If you agree that studying the history of political thought is important, there still remains the question of *who* we should study. There is a well-established canon of political thought: a list of thinkers typically included in books like this and on the modules and courses that such books serve. Students often begin with Machiavelli or Hobbes, sometimes starting earlier with Plato and Aristotle, and then go on to study Locke, Rousseau, Kant, Mill, and Marx, perhaps bringing things up to date with Rawls and his critics. The status and nature of this canon have been challenged in recent years, but it is not uncommon for textbooks on political thinkers to feature no female thinkers, and it is the norm for them to feature only white (and usually European) thinkers (Choat, 2021; Ramgotra, 2022).

The white male canon has endured for a number of reasons. Political theory can be a slow-moving discipline, and inertia means that political theorists and philosophers, who themselves are often white men, teach the next generation what they themselves were taught, thus perpetuating a static canon. Women have only relatively recently gained access to higher education, and barriers to academic study and advancement persist, in particular for women of colour (Begum and Saini, 2019). Many women and People of Colour found outlets to make their voices heard elsewhere, in non-governmental organizations, the media, social movements, and other fora (Owens et al., 2022). Yet these voices were frequently marginalized and in effect silenced, often by claims that they do not meet standards of knowledge worthy of study and inclusion on university curricula. Such standards, however, are set by those in power or in high-ranking university positions, with existing structures operating to maintain power and knowledge as the privileged domain of a white male minority (McClain, 2021). Fundamentally, the exclusion of women, Indigenous people, and People of Colour from the canon of political thought reflects their exclusion more generally—from the institutions in which political thought has been written and from participation in formal politics. If the canon of political thought is white and male, this reflects a world which is, in bell hooks' (2004) felicitous phrase, an 'imperialist white-supremacist capitalist patriarchy' (see Chapter 3 for more on bell hooks).

One way to address the problems with the existing canon might be simply to abandon the canon altogether. In line with the Cambridge School insistence that all texts are interventions into specific debates (see Section 1.3), we could undertake a history of political thought that focuses much less on great thinkers and their theories and much more on arguments, debates, and discourses—on 'a plurality of competing, overlapping and interacting political languages' (Stuurman, 2000: 161). Yet this would be no guarantee that the voices of women and thinkers of colour would be heard. To the contrary, organizing the study of ideas around thinkers can be a useful way of including hitherto marginalized voices. While we acknowledge the importance of historical and discursive contexts, we think that there are pedagogical benefits to studying individual thinkers: foregrounding thinkers can be a useful way of making vivid what are often complex and abstract ideas. It also recognizes the importance of the figures in this book not only as thinkers but also as politicians and activists. Moreover, it allows us to acknowledge the *positionality* of thinkers. By 'positionality' we refer not only to the position in which a thinker stands in relation to their ideas, but also to their situation within society: a thinker's gender, race, class, sexuality, languages, and so on—their position in the world—can affect how they read and think about the world (Spivak, 1988; Collins, 1989). So, as Hutchings and Owens (2021) argue in relation to the canon of international relations, rather than simply *rejecting* the canon, we can try to *reconstitute* it and in so doing *recover* forgotten or suppressed contributions (which have often criticized and challenged the authority of the canon itself).

As women and non-white people have begun to win political power and influence, so has the white, male, European canon been contested. The challenge to the maleness of the canon was inspired in large part by second-wave feminism. Since the 1970s in particular, feminist political theorists and intellectual historians have sought to criticize the sexism of canonical thinkers, recover the work of women thinkers which has been neglected or marginalized, and create new concepts—such as patriarchy and intersectionality—to serve feminist ends (e.g., Okin, 1979; Pateman, 1988; Shanley and Pateman, 1991; Coole, 1993). This book tries to build on the work of pioneering feminist theorists and historians. As well as including chapters on well-known women thinkers, such as Mary Wollstonecraft (Chapter 21), we have included more neglected figures, such as Mary Astell

(Chapter 8) and Catharine Macaulay (Chapter 17). While some of the women thinkers in this book, such as Shulamith Firestone (Chapter 34), Iris Marion Young (Chapter 22), and Carole Pateman (Chapter 10), are straightforwardly feminist, others are not. Hannah Arendt (Chapter 19) was one of the most important thinkers of the twentieth century but she showed little interest in feminism or gender. Others, such as Emma Goldman (Chapter 26) and Judith Butler (Chapter 36), have an ambivalent or complicated relationship to feminism. Some, such as Gayatri Chakravorty Spivak (Chapter 24) and Donna Haraway (Chapter 38), are committed feminists, but are as well known for their work in other fields as for their contributions to feminism.

Opposition to the whiteness of the canon has perhaps taken longer to gain ground than the challenge to its maleness, and has taken a variety of forms. As we saw in Section 1.2, comparative political thought has drawn the attention of European and North American scholars to non-European traditions of political thought. Demands to decolonize the university have also called into question Eurocentric canons (Mbembe, 2016; Bhambra et al., 2018). Calls to decolonize our ways of thinking are not new. The great anti-colonial theorist and activist Frantz Fanon (2004) believed that decolonization must involve the complete overthrow of colonial power structures *and* the forms of knowledge that held them in place (see Chapter 28 on Fanon). Decolonial critics such as Anibal Quijano (2000) and Walter Mignolo (2007) have argued that colonialism produced power relations that have endured into the postcolonial period, including relations of knowledge production. Of all academic disciplines, political thought is as good a place to start decolonizing as any because, as we have seen, its canon is dominated by white men (Omar, 2016).

While decolonization is a contested concept and it can take many forms, its applicability to political thought begins from the recognition that forms of knowledge, epistemologies, and pedagogies exist that were dismissed and suppressed by colonial domination: 'legitimate' knowledge was claimed to be that produced by white, European men. Decolonization, therefore, must involve bringing in non-white, non-European, and women authors, figures, and thinkers. It does *not* mean jettisoning the work of white men. Thinkers like Locke, Kant, and Mill are highly significant and influential figures, so should continue to be taught. But one of the ways in which they have been influential is by developing and propagating concepts and arguments that have been used to justify and promote colonialism. As such, we should continue to read these thinkers but do so *critically*, highlighting the colonial contexts within which their concepts, arguments, and theories were developed and advanced. The aim should not be to scapegoat, dismiss, or diminish the so-called 'dead white men' who have traditionally constituted the canon: to the contrary, it is only by placing these thinkers in their contexts and interrogating *all* aspects of their thought—including their often-neglected views on race and gender—that we can do justice to the sophistication and nuances of their arguments.

The feminist strategies identified above for theorizing gender in the works of political thinkers (criticizing sexism, recovering forgotten women thinkers, and creating new concepts) have their parallel when theorizing race: uncovering the racism of white thinkers; rediscovering neglected works of anti-racism; and reconceptualizing politics using new or repurposed terms, such as white supremacy (Mills, 1998: 120–126). As with women thinkers, the works of non-white thinkers included in this book are highly varied, from more scholarly works by postcolonial thinkers like Edward Said (Chapter 16) and Spivak to the slave narratives and speeches of Frederick Douglass (Chapter 30). Some of the thinkers we have included would not necessarily meet commonly held standards about what political theory should look like: the women's rights and abolitionist activist Sojourner Truth (Chapter 2), for example, is not a political theorist in the sense that she does not provide a systematic, conceptually sophisticated, comprehensive, and rigorous theory. But her words are powerful, influential, and ultimately theoretically significant.

While 'decolonizing' involves both diversifying the canon by adding non-white authors and directly addressing the racist defences of colonialism found in the writings of canonical thinkers, it also entails reconsidering what knowledge is, who produces it, and how it is produced. This does not mean endorsing an 'anything goes' relativism but rather creating a space for different voices to speak and be heard. The aim is not to effect a crude levelling, wherein all voices are equally significant, but to deflate the 'pretended universalism of modern Western philosophy' (Maldonado-Torres et al., 2018: 76). Robbie Shilliam (2021) has helpfully characterized the work of decolonizing the study of politics in terms of three 'manoeuvres'. First, we *recontextualize*, placing thinkers in their imperial and colonial contexts. Second, in the light of those newly emphasized contexts, we reconsider thinkers' concepts and categories—we *reconceptualize* their ideas. Third, we *reimagine* the discipline, challenging the existing canon and bringing in voices from the margins. This is what we attempt to do in this textbook: to recontextualize, reconceptualize, and reimagine the contours of political thought.

Some may acknowledge that the thinkers of the past were often racist and sexist but argue that it is nonetheless anachronistic to judge those thinkers by the standards of our age. It might be claimed that the sexism and racism of Kant, for example, simply reflect the times in which he lived and wrote. But the ideas in any historical period are always varied and contested. While many thinkers of the eighteenth and nineteenth centuries, for example, ignored or justified slavery and imperialism, many others strongly and explicitly opposed those institutions (Losurdo, 2014). Kant did not hold racist and sexist views because those views were universally held during his lifetime: he held them in opposition to those of his contemporaries who resisted and contested such views. It is true, of course, that the legitimacy and conventionality of ideas change over time. Almost no one today would explicitly defend or endorse slavery, and yet that is exactly what some of the canonical thinkers in this book did. Yet if all a thinker did was to reflect or repeat the common beliefs and opinions of their time, then they would not be worth reading. We read the likes of Kant, Locke, and Mill precisely because they challenged and upset the conventions and prejudices of their day and offered novel and even revolutionary arguments that transcend their context. If, therefore, we find sexist or racist assumptions or claims in their work, then it is legitimate to ask, given they were so adept at rising above and challenging the views held by their contemporaries, why could they not also challenge the racial and sexual prejudices of their time? It is because the thinkers in this book managed in some ways to transcend the historical contexts in which they wrote—creating something *new*—that their ideas remain influential today. That continuing influence is another reason why we should seek to expose and challenge their racism and sexism. As the American political philosopher Susan Moller Okin (1979: 3) puts it: 'the analysis and criticism of the thoughts of political theorists of the past [are] not an arcane academic pursuit, but an important means of comprehending and laying bare the assumptions behind deeply rooted modes of thought that continue to affect people's lives in major ways'.

That many great political thinkers held prejudicial and even contemptuous views towards those who were not able-bodied, property-owning, white males is an undeniable fact and we should not hide this fact behind spurious appeals to historical context. But nor should we stop reading a thinker on discovery of such views. An extreme example can be found in two thinkers who do not have chapters in this book but whom we have already encountered (in Section 1.3): Carl Schmitt and Martin Heidegger. Both Schmitt and Heidegger joined the Nazi Party in 1933. Although Schmitt was the more active and enthusiastic member, until their deaths, in 1985 and 1976 respectively, neither Schmitt nor Heidegger expressed any regret or remorse for their affiliation with the Nazis. Both are thus arguably complicit in the systematic murder of approximately six million Jews that was perpetrated by the Nazi regime.

Yet our view is that Schmitt and Heidegger should still be read today. To read a thinker is not to support their arguments, still less to endorse every single thing they ever wrote, said, or did. The works of any serious thinker are varied and open to competing interpretations. That Schmitt and Heidegger might have had interesting and significant things to say, despite their membership of the

Nazi Party, is demonstrated by the fact that they have been read and used by very many subsequent thinkers from across the political spectrum, from conservatives to feminists, liberals to Marxists, and including Jewish thinkers, such as Arendt and Derrida. This does not mean that we should ignore their connection to Nazism. To the contrary, one reason to continue to read them is to see where they went wrong and consider how we can avoid the same fate. How could men so erudite, thoughtful, and cultured have supported such a despicable ideology? What traces—subtle or overt— of anti-Semitism or fascism can we find in their writings? If we can continue to read literal Nazis, and do so profitably, then, in our view, there is no thinker whose writings should be censored. We can legitimately avoid reading a thinker because they are uninteresting or unoriginal, but should not do so because they express hateful sentiments.

> ### 1.4 The canon of political thought: Key Points
>
> - The traditional canon of political thought is dominated by white, European men.
> - Feminist theorists have sought to expose and challenge the maleness of the canon by criticizing the sexism of canonical thinkers, recovering forgotten women thinkers, and creating new concepts, such as patriarchy and intersectionality.
> - Projects to decolonize political thought have focused on placing canonical thinkers in their colonial contexts, highlighting the contributions of non-white and non-European thinkers, and reflecting on the processes of knowledge production.

1.5 Overview of the book

This book is divided into nine themed Parts. Part I explores the 'Boundaries of the Political', reflecting on who and what is included or excluded in the political and why. Our first two chapters read ancient political thinkers—Plato and Socrates (Chapter 2) and Aristotle (Chapter 3)—alongside nineteenth- and twentieth-century Black feminist thinkers—Sojourner Truth (Chapter 2) and bell hooks (Chapter 3)—whose experience of oppression leads them to contest boundaries that limit, exclude, and hierarchize. We then examine the ancient Indian thinker Kautilya (Chapter 4), whose work provides points of comparison and contrast with thinkers from the Western canon. Part II, 'Social Contract Theory and Its Critics', looks at the work of classical social contract thinkers, interrogating the often patriarchal, racist, and colonialist underpinnings of their work and examining critics of the social contract—both contemporaries of the classical contract thinkers and present-day critics. Part III, 'Liberal Modernity and Colonial Domination', explores the responses of different thinkers to the development of modernity, including liberal and anti-liberal thinkers, revolutionaries and reactionaries. We pay special attention to the ways in which modernity is entwined with colonialism. In Part IV, 'Freedom and Revolution', we consider how freedom has been understood in both European and anti-colonial contexts, reflecting on both opponents and defenders of revolution. Part V, 'Inclusion and Equality', considers feminist, multiculturalist, and postcolonial thinkers and their analyses of equality and calls for inclusion. All of the thinkers in this book are to some extent theorists of power; in Part VI, 'Violence, Power, and Resistance', we look at thinkers who have explicitly reflected on the nature of power and in so doing have defended or condemned the use of violence. In Part VII, 'The Liberal Self and Black Consciousness', we problematize the abstract liberal self in the light of Black consciousness, placing two of the most influential white liberals, Immanuel Kant (Chapter 29) and John Rawls (Chapter 32), side by side with two of the most important African-American theorists of racial oppression, Frederick Douglass (Chapter 30) and W.E.B. Du Bois (Chapter 31). In this book we endorse a broad understanding of politics, and this is reflected in Part VIII,

'Sex and Sexuality', which examines thinkers who have explored the political dimensions of sex. We end, in Part IX, 'The Environment, Human, and Non-Human', by moving beyond the human world to consider the politics of nature and our interactions with non-human life.

Some chapters cover a single thinker while others look at two or more thinkers, allowing us to draw out pertinent comparisons and contrasts. Chapter 39, on 'Indigenous ecologies', is not organized around thinkers at all, showing that not all traditions of thought foreground the contributions of individual authors. Every chapter of this book will introduce a thinker or thinkers, providing an overview of their main writings, concepts, and arguments and placing them in their historical and intellectual contexts (with special attention given to the contexts and legacies of male domination and European expansion); will explore any tensions, contradictions, exclusions, or unspoken assumptions in the thinker's work; and consider the reception and influence of the works of the thinker or thinkers and the different interpretations to which they have been subject. As noted in Section 1.3, we do not endorse any particular methodology for reading texts, and our chapter contributors work in a variety of academic disciplines. Yet, while we have chosen thinkers whom we think can help us explain and understand politics today, we recognize that appreciation of the contexts within which thinkers wrote is important for understanding their arguments. As such, chapters try both to place thinkers in their relevant contexts, and also to explain how thinkers have transcended those contexts, producing novel ideas that remain of interest to us today.

To help you get to grips with some often complex ideas, each of the following chapters includes a number of pedagogical features, including a chapter guide that outlines the aims and contents of the chapter; 'Key Thinker' boxes that provide short summaries of significant thinkers who are not the subjects of chapters in the book; 'Key Concept' boxes covering both novel concepts introduced by specific thinkers and common concepts that are used by thinkers in particular ways; annotated Further Reading lists, covering primary writings by each thinker and secondary writings that act as commentaries on or critiques of the thinkers; and a list of study questions that encourage you to reflect on and evaluate what you have learned.

While we hope that you find this book useful, our intention is that it should complement and enhance—rather than replace—reading the works of the thinkers themselves. We have provided comprehensive overviews of each thinker, but all interpretations are necessarily partial and a strong understanding of any thinker requires reading their primary writings. Above all, we hope that you come away from this book with an appreciation of the many ways in which political ideas reflect, inform, and change our world. The relationship between political theory and 'real-world' politics can be complex and at times even appear tenuous. Debates in political theory can seem arcane or self-referential. This may be because, since the twentieth century, most political theory has been produced within universities, with academics writing for other academics and acting as the gatekeepers of what counts as 'proper' theory. As bell hooks (1994: 64) has argued, work which is not written in an 'academic' style can find itself delegitimized and designated as inferior in a way that establishes and reinforces hierarchies. But as hooks (ibid.: 69) goes on to argue, simply rejecting theory and dismissing theorists only compounds this problem: anti-intellectualism is merely the flipside of elitism, with both promoting the erroneous idea that 'there is a split between theory and practice'. For hooks, theory—and its production, circulation, and consumption—is not divorced from practice but is itself a type of practice. hooks wishes to emphasize the necessity of theory to liberation struggles, but we could say the same of conservative or reactionary struggles: *all* political movements depend on theory in some way. The formulation and articulation of political demands necessarily rely on a conceptual vocabulary—of justice, rights, freedom, equality, etc.—that is fundamentally theoretical. All attempts to change the world *and* attempts to resist such change are ultimately normative: they rely on claims about what the world *should* look like. This book provides you with a wide range of theoretical analyses of our world and may even give you some ideas for how you can change it.

Take your learning further by accessing the online resources for a library of web links for each chapter, and detailed biographies for every thinker covered in this book: **www.oup.com/he/Ramgotra-Choat1e**.

Further reading

Arneil, B. and Hirschmann, N.J. (eds) (2016) *Disability and Political Theory*. Cambridge: Cambridge University Press.
Valuable collection on an important topic of growing interest to political theorists.

Browning, G. (2016) *A History of Modern Political Thought: The Question of Interpretation*. Oxford: Oxford University Press.
Useful volume which in its first part explains some approaches to studying the history of political thought, including those of Collingwood, Skinner, Derrida, and Foucault, and in its second part applies those approaches to some canonical thinkers.

Buxton, R. and Whiting, L. (eds) (2020) *The Philosopher Queens: The Lives and Legacies of Philosophy's Unsung Women*. London: Unbound.
Readable introductory collection of essays on women philosophers.

Dallmayr, F. (ed.) (2010) *Comparative Political Theory: An Introduction*. New York: Palgrave Macmillan.
Set of essays on Islamic, Indian, and East Asian thought, with a useful introductory chapter by the editor.

Dryzek, J.S., Honig, B., and Philips, A. (eds) (2008) *The Oxford Handbook of Political Theory*. Oxford: Oxford University Press.
Comprehensive set of introductory essays on a variety of themes, issues, and concepts by some of the world's leading political theorists.

Edwards, A. and Townshend, J. (eds) (2002) *Interpreting Modern Political Philosophy: From Machiavelli to Marx*. London: Bloomsbury.
Essays focusing on the interpretative debates surrounding thinkers from the white, male canon.

Gabrielson, T., Hall, C., Meyer, J.M., and Schlosberg, D. (eds) (2016) *The Oxford Handbook of Environmental Political Theory*. Oxford: Oxford University Press.
Wide-ranging collection covering a diversity of concepts, approaches, debates, and thinkers.

Klosko, G. (ed.) (2011) *The Oxford Handbook of the History of Political Philosophy*. Oxford: Oxford University Press.
Contains entries on methodological approaches as well as traditions, themes, and concepts.

Park, P.K.J. (2013) *Africa, Asia, and the History of Philosophy: Racism in the Formation of the Philosophical Canon, 1780–1830*. Albany, NY: State University of New York Press.
Explores the ways in which Africa and Asia contributed to the development of philosophy and the ways in which they were excluded from the canon of philosophy.

Pinder, S.O. (ed.) (2020) *Black Political Thought: From David Walker to the Present*. Cambridge: Cambridge University Press.
Compilation of writings mainly by African-American thinkers and activists.

Sandel, M.J. (2010) *Justice: What's the Right Thing to Do?* London: Penguin.
Highly accessible introduction to some key debates in Anglo-American political philosophy, focused on the concept of distributive justice.

Shanley, M.L. and Pateman, C. (eds) (1991) *Feminist Interpretations and Political Theory*. Cambridge: Polity Press.
Collection of feminist interpretations of (mainly male) canonical thinkers from Plato to Habermas.

Shilliam, R. (2021) *Decolonizing Politics: An Introduction*. Cambridge: Polity.
Functions as both an illuminating discussion of decolonizing the discipline of politics—including the sub-discipline of political theory—and a fine example of how it can be done.

Skinner, Q. (2002) *Visions of Politics*, vol. I: *Regarding Method*. Cambridge: Cambridge University Press.
Collection of methodological essays of outstanding quality and significance by arguably the most influential historian of ideas of the last century.

References

Begum, N. and Saini, R. (2019) 'Decolonising the Curriculum'. *Political Studies Review*, 17(2): 196–201.

Bhambra, G.K., Gebrial, D., and Nişancıoğlu, K. (eds) (2018) *Decolonising the University*. London: Pluto Press.

Blau, A. (2021) 'How (Not) to Use the History of Political Thought for Contemporary Purposes'. *American Journal of Political Science*, 65(2): 359–372.

Choat, S. (2021) 'Decolonising the Political Theory Curriculum'. *Politics*, 41(3): 404–420.

Combahee River Collective (1977) 'Statement'. Available at https://combaheerivercollective.weebly.com/the-combahee-river-collective-statement.html# (accessed 17 January 2022).

Collingwood, R.G. (2013) *An Autobiography and Other Writings*. Oxford: Oxford University Press.

Collins, P.H. (1989) 'The Social Construction of Black Feminist Thought'. *Signs*, 14(4): 745–773.

Coole, D. (1993) *Women in Political Theory: From Ancient Misogyny to Contemporary Feminism*. Hemel Hempstead: Harvester Wheatsheaf.

Dallmayr, F. (ed.) (2010) *Comparative Political Theory: An Introduction*. New York: Palgrave Macmillan.

Derrida, J. (1976) *Of Grammatology*. Trans. G.C. Spivak. Baltimore, MD: Johns Hopkins University Press.

Derrida, J. (1988) *Limited Inc*. Ed. G. Graff. Evanston, IL: Northwestern University Press.

Dunn, J. (1968) 'The Identity of the History of Ideas'. *Philosophy*, 43(164): 85–104.

El Amine, L. (2016) 'Beyond East and West: Reorienting Political Theory through the Prism of Modernity'. *Perspectives on Politics* 14(1): 102–120.

Euben, R.L. (2004) 'Travelling Theorists and Translating Practices'. In S.K. White and J.D. Moon (eds), *What Is Political Theory?* London: Sage Publications.

Fanon, F. (2004) *The Wretched of the Earth*. Trans. R. Philcox. New York: Grove Press.

Finlayson, L. (2017) 'With Radicals Like These, Who Needs Conservatives? Doom, Gloom, and Realism in Political Theory'. *European Journal of Political Theory*, 16(3): 264–282.

Floyd, J. (2019) *What's the Point of Political Philosophy?* Cambridge: Polity.

Foucault, M. (1970) *The Order of Things: An Archaeology of the Human Sciences*. London: Tavistock.

Foucault, M. (1977a) *The Archaeology of Knowledge*. Trans. A. Sheridan. London: Tavistock.

Foucault, M. (1977b) *Discipline and Punish: The Birth of the Prison*. Trans. A. Sheridan. London: Allen Lane.

Foucault, M. (1980) *Power/Knowledge: Selected Interviews and Other Writings, 1972–1977*. Ed. C. Gordon, trans. C. Gordon et al. New York: Pantheon Books.

Galston, W. (2010) 'Realism in Political Theory'. *European Journal of Political Theory*, 9(4): 385–411.

Geuss, R. (2008) *Philosophy and Real Politics*. Princeton, NJ: Princeton University Press.

Godrej, F. (2011) *Cosmopolitan Political Thought: Method, Practice, Discipline*. New York: Oxford University Press.

Hamilton, A., Madison, J., and Jay, J. (2003) *The Federalist with Letters of 'Brutus'*. Cambridge: Cambridge University of Press.

Hanchard, M. (2010) 'Contours of Black Political Thought: An Introduction and Perspective'. *Political Theory*, 38(4): 510–536.

Honig, B. (1993) *Political Theory and the Displacement of Politics*. Ithaca, NY: Cornell University Press.

hooks, b. (1994) *Teaching to Transgress: Education as the Practice of Freedom*. New York: Routledge.

hooks, b. (2004) *The Will to Change: Men, Masculinity, and Love*. New York: Atria Books.

Hutchings, K. and Owens, P. (2021) 'Women Thinkers and the Canon of International Thought: Recovery, Rejection, and Reconstitution'. *American Political Science Review*, 115(2): 347–359.

Idris, M. (2016) 'Political Theory and the Politics of Comparison'. *Political Theory*, July, 1–20. https://doi.org/10.1177/0090591716659812 (accessed 20 January 2022).

Jenco, L.K. (2007) '"What Does Heaven Ever Say?" A Methods-Centered Approach to Cross-Cultural Engagement'. *American Political Science Review*, 101(4): 741–755.

Kelly, M.G.E. (2018) *For Foucault: Against Normative Political Theory*. Albany, NY: SUNY Press.

Kymlicka, W. (2002) *Contemporary Political Philosophy: An Introduction*. Oxford: Oxford University Press.

Lamb, R. (2009) 'Quentin Skinner's Revised Historical Contextualism: A Critique'. *History of the Human Sciences*, 22(3): 51–73.

Losurdo, D. (2014) *Liberalism: A Counter-History*. Trans. G. Elliott. London: Verso.

Maldonado-Torres, N., Vizcaíno, R., Wallace, J., and We, J.E.A. (2018) 'Decolonising Philosophy'. In G.K. Bhambra, D. Gebrial, and K. Nişancıoğlu (eds), *Decolonising the University*. London: Pluto Press.

Marx, K. and Engels, F. (1976) 'Manifesto of the Communist Party'. In K. Marx and F. Engels, *Collected Works*, vol. 6. London: Lawrence and Wishart.

Mbembe, A.J. (2016) 'Decolonizing the University: New Directions'. *Arts & Humanities in Higher Education*, 15(1): 29–45.

McClain, P.D. (2021) 'Crises, Race, Acknowledgement: The Centrality of Race, Ethnicity, and Politics to the Future of Political Science'. *Perspectives on Politics*, 19(1): 7–18.

Mignolo, W.D. (2007) 'Delinking: The Rhetoric of Modernity, the Logic of Coloniality and the Grammar of De-Coloniality'. *Cultural Studies*, 21(2–3): 449–514.

Millet, K. (2016) *Sexual Politics*. New York: Columbia University Press.

Mills, C.W. (1998) *Blackness Visible: Essays on Philosophy and Race*. Ithaca, NY: Cornell University Press.

Mouffe, C. (1993) *The Return of the Political*. London: Verso.

Mouffe, C. (2005) *On the Political*. London: Routledge.

Okin, S.M. (1979) *Women in Western Political Thought*. Princeton, NJ: Princeton University Press.

Omar, A. (2016) 'Moving Beyond the Canon: Reflections of a Young African Scholar of Political Theory'. *Arts & Humanities in Higher Education*, 15(1): 153–159.

Owens, P., Rietzler, K., Hutchings, K., and Dunstan, S. (eds) (2022) *Women's International Thought: Towards a New Canon*. Cambridge: Cambridge University Press.

Pateman, C. (1988) *The Sexual Contract*. Cambridge: Polity Press.

Pocock, J.G.A. (2009) *Political Thought and History: Essays on Theory and Method*. Cambridge: Cambridge University Press.

Quijano, A. (2000) 'Coloniality of Power, Eurocentrism, and Latin America'. *Nepantla: Views from South*, 1(3): 533–580.

Ramgotra, M. (2015) 'On Teaching Political Theory to Undergraduates'. https://psawomenpolitics.wordpress.com/2015/12/21/on-teaching-political-theory-to-undergraduates/ (accessed 11 January 2022).

Ramgotra, M. (2022) 'Power from the Margins: Uncovering the Silences and Decolonising the Canon'. In K. Hutchings, S. Dunstan, P. Owens, et al., 'On Canons and Question Marks: The Work of Women's International Thought'. *Contemporary Political Theory*, 21: 114–141.

Rossi, E. and Sleat, M. (2014) 'Realism in Normative Political Theory'. *Philosophy Compass*, 9(10): 689–701.

Schmitt, C. (2007 [1932]) *The Concept of the Political*. Trans. G. Schwab. Chicago: University of Chicago Press.

Scott, D. (2004) *Conscripts of Modernity: The Tragedy of Colonial Enlightenment*. Durham, NC: Duke University Press.

Shanley, M.L. and Pateman, C. (eds) (1991) *Feminist Interpretations and Political Theory*. Cambridge: Polity Press.

Shilliam, R. (2021) *Decolonizing Politics: An Introduction*. Cambridge: Polity.

Skinner, Q. (1988) 'Analysis of Political Thought and Action'. In J. Tully (ed.) *Meaning and Context: Quentin Skinner and His Critics*. Princeton, NJ: Princeton University Press.

Skinner, Q. (2002) *Visions of Politics*, vol. I: *Regarding Method*. Cambridge: Cambridge University Press.

Spivak, G.C. (1988) 'Can the Subaltern Speak?' In C. Nelson and L. Grossberg (eds), *Marxism and the Interpretation of Culture*. Urbana, IL: University of Illinois Press.

Stears, M. (2005) 'The Vocation of Political Theory: Principles, Empirical Inquiry and the Politics of Opportunity'. *European Journal of Political Theory*, 4(4): 325–350.

Stuurman, S. (2000) 'The Canon of the History of Political Thought: Its Critique and a Proposed Alternative'. *History and Theory*, 39(2): 147–166.

Trouillot, M-R. (1995) *Silencing the Past: Power and the Production of History*. Boston, MA: Beacon Press.

Tully, J. (ed.) (1988) *Meaning and Context: Quentin Skinner and His Critics*. Princeton, NJ: Princeton University Press.

Tully, J. (2016) 'Deparochializing Political Theory and Beyond: A Dialogue Approach to Comparative Political Thought'. *Journal of World Philosophies*, 1(1): 1–18.

von Vacano, D. (2015) 'The Scope of Comparative Political Theory'. *Annual Review of Political Science*, 18: 465–480.

Williams, B. (2005) *In the Beginning Was the Deed: Realism and Moralism in Political Argument*. Ed. G. Hawthorn. Princeton, NJ: Princeton University Press.

Part I

Boundaries of the Political

2	Socrates, Plato, and Sojourner Truth	Patrizia Longo	21
3	Aristotle and bell hooks	Manjeet Ramgotra	39
4	Kautilya	Deepshikha Shahi	57

Both boundaries and the political are contested concepts. The concept of the political has a long history and is a present in the very first human associations, when human beings began to organize their collective lives according to rules, norms, and structures. The political is typically understood as the space in which members of the community (usually a set of people who share in a common way of life and agree to coexist) gather to make collective decisions on rules regarding how people should live together and how they should behave—i.e., what is good and bad conduct or what is right and wrong—and how these rules should be enforced. The political is a space of moral and ethical deliberation where people determine these questions. In this space, people decide who should have power and authority, who should be included or not in the association or community and who should be listened to or not. It is also an imagined space that encompasses the idea of the association as well as notions of how it operates. The political space sets boundaries that operate to include and exclude those deemed fit to make the rules that would govern over society. Gender, race, class, age, disability, and knowledge are often used as criteria to determine inclusion and exclusion. As such, only part of society represents and speaks for society.

The political also holds jurisdiction over the physical territory that society occupies. It sets physical borders that determine entry to its space. Who belongs or not to the community, the nation, the state is often based on ethnicity, nationality, religion, or ideology. State borders operate to establish conceptions of nation or community and determine who is entitled to rights and privileges. Many people who come from beyond the boundary, such as immigrants, asylum-seekers, or refugees are excluded from either the state itself or political processes. Even if admitted, they are often denied political and social rights. For instance, Aristotle was a foreigner in Athens. He did not enjoy citizenship or political rights, and when his protectors died, he had to flee the city. Carl Schmitt theorizes the political in terms of the friend/enemy distinction which includes those who support the ruling ideology and excludes those who don't. The move to democratize and calls for greater participation in the political aim at pushing and expanding the boundaries so that not only a particular segment of society governs. Most societies ask questions regarding the nature of the political, about power, authority, *who* should rule, governance—ruling and being ruled—and inclusion or exclusion. These are contested, and hence appeals to nature, the natural order of the universe, God and religion, brute force, convention or agreed procedures—such as elections—operate to legitimate political authority and power.

The European term political derives from the ancient Greek *polis*, which was one of the earliest formations of a political community. *Polis* refers to the ancient Greek city-state, which was a union of tribes that came together to provide for their mutual needs and mutual protection. Classical Greek thinkers, such as Plato and Aristotle, considered this union of tribes into *poleis* (city-states) as permanent and described the life within the state as *polis*-life or political life. Although these tribes often disagreed, Plato believed they had to learn to resolve differences and to take account of one another. In the Greek city-state, the public space (*agora*) operated as a marketplace, a place of worship, of social interaction, public meetings, and decision-making. With the *polis* came the distinction between the private and the public, between the household (the primary political unit) and the political space. This distinction between the public and private sets boundaries of inclusion/exclusion, notably in Western political thinking and practice, and it is widely contested by Marxists and feminists, who argue that power is everywhere and the personal is political.

To Aristotle, politics was an ethical idea, according to which the natural ends of man—he excluded women, children, and slaves—were to be a citizen engaged with other citizens, equal in status, in the deliberation of what is best for the whole of the *polis*. On entering the public arena, one would put their personal and private concerns aside and take on the public persona of the citizen in order to deliberate in terms of the public good. Thus, men would realize their highest ends as political animals. Aristotle's conception that the political is composed of equal citizens who reason in terms of the public good underpins the ethics of democracy, whereby either the people as a body or their elected representatives rule according to this principle. Nevertheless, the public good is often read through and shaped by people's positionalities, especially if the deliberative body is comprised of a single gender, class, or race, such as white male heads of households.

Knowledge is not only critical in determining who should rule, but it is also deeply intertwined with power. Plato conceptualized a dividing line to distinguish the world of ideas, timelessness, and truth from the real world of belief and changing circumstance. This line also operated to separate out those who can access the world of ideas from those who cannot. He considered that only those with intellectual propensity ought to be educated and to rule as Philosopher Kings, for they would know what is good for all. Yet Plato followed Socrates, a humble man who lacked formal education and who holds a place in our imagination as one of the first philosophers, for he claimed that he knew he did not know.

Access to education has historically played a decisive role in determining inclusion/exclusion in the political. Education has often separated the propertied classes from the working classes, for the former enjoy the freedom from work to pursue learning and the latter must work to survive and therefore do not have the time for learning. Today we consider that education is a universal good and that all should have the opportunity to develop their intellectual capacities. Sadly, in some places, this continues to be limited by race, gender, class, and disability. Moreover, those who are more privileged have access to better schools and higher education, and are not hindered by the lack of wealth, or the need to work to live and provide for their families. These boundaries operate to maintain hierarchies in society and to exclude many from sharing in ruling even in democratic societies that promote liberty, equality, and human rights.

The four chapters of this Part of the book introduce readers to the study of political theory through both classical and contemporary thinkers. Chapters 2-4 pair unlikely sets of thinkers on their conceptions of knowledge, the political, and its boundaries by juxtaposing classical and modern political thinkers. These chapters contend that while we have much to learn from classical political theory on the fundamentals of politics, we do not always need to start there. Contemporary contestations of the political and its boundaries are just as important.

Chapter 2 reads Plato/Socrates alongside Sojourner Truth. Although Socrates never recorded his ideas, Plato did. As such, Socrates appears in many of Plato's writings. Therefore, it is difficult to distinguish their ideas. Similarly, other people recorded Sojourner Truth's ideas as she was illiterate. Both Socrates and Truth occupy a place in the political imaginary as two important figures who spoke truth to power. They educated people on uncovering and understanding truth in the light of very inegalitarian and oppressive politics of the democratic regimes of their day. Although Plato reconstructed Socrates' ideas in his philosophical works, his views differed.

To Plato, philosophy was directed to the pursuit of knowledge and the understanding of the essence of things in their unchangeable forms; whereas, in the real world, politics is characterized by speech, communication, difference, negotiation, and deliberation.

Socrates and Truth engaged in the pursuit of justice. Socrates aimed to discover justice in the city and the individual soul. In *The Republic*, Plato depicts Socrates as advancing a hierarchical conception whereby each person would know their place and due in society. By contrast, Truth laid bare the violence and terror of slavery, called for its abolition, and sought to change society and social relations so that Black people would be recognized as equal human beings and Black women as women. These are very different thinkers, yet their conceptions of knowledge, truth, and justice are fundamental to the study of politics. They demonstrate that although we can imagine ideal and moral values, in the real world, truth and justice are often violated and manipulated to serve the interests of those in power. Socrates was executed for corrupting the youth and Truth represented the injustice of racism, sexism, and slavery.

Chapter 3 puts Aristotle in conversation with the African-American feminist bell hooks. It examines Aristotle's conception of the political and how it establishes the power and authority of male heads of households in the political since they have experience of ruling over their wives, children, and slaves. In his ideal *polis*, that aims at achieving the good of all, Aristotle limits the political to include only property-owning men. By contrast, bell hooks contests the boundaries of the political. She criticizes the patriarchal household and disrupts conceptions of power relations within the family and household to create a more liberatory politics that does not rely on knowledge and power produced by privileged, educated white men. She contends that knowledge is based on the experience and standpoint of the oppressed, notably of groups that experience multiple oppressions and exclusions, based on race, gender, and class. She argues for a liberatory politics and theory that not only provide educational opportunities but which cultivate critical thinking and the questioning of structures that exclude. In turn, this supports a more participatory and democratized basis of politics.

Finally, Chapter 4 presents the thought of an ancient Indian thinker known as Kautilya, who produced a work on the science of politics and notably on power politics, called *Arthaśāstra*, which means the science of material gain. Written in the fourth century BCE, this work advises kings on how best to maintain their power, especially in light of other neighbouring and potentially aggrandizing powers. It sees political regimes as organic entities composed of the material elements of power, yet aimed at the moral good of the whole body. Nevertheless, the work focuses on maintaining power and forging alliances that will either preserve or extend the territorial boundaries of the king's power. Kautilya conceptualizes the relations with other regimes in terms of friends and enemies and analyses the intellectual, psychological, and material aspects of power. Produced around the same time as Plato and Aristotle were writing, the *Arthaśāstra* was rediscovered in the late nineteenth century. It extends our understanding of the machinations of politics and power in the classical world.

By combining ancient and modern thinkers in single chapters, we disrupt the canonical and chronological study of political theory that begins with the exploration of basic questions in the classics and works its way through time to the present. By reading thinkers in conversation with each other, we can compare their ideas on a conceptual and analytical basis, notably in relation to questions about how people know (epistemology), how they exist (ontology) in the world, and how these contribute to different visions and constructions of politics and the political. How we know and exist in the world influences how we structure our political institutions and, conversely, how these political and social structures constitute subjectivities, subjects, ways of being and knowing. The chapters in this Part pay attention to historical and intellectual contexts, but also they bring the classics into the present and emphasize that although their times and ideas are very different from contemporary ones, they are worth reading since their ideas continue to influence our conceptions of politics.

2 Socrates, Plato, and Sojourner Truth

PATRIZIA LONGO

Chapter guide

Philosophy is often introduced through its history, beginning with Socrates, who banished the weeping women, as a prelude to the real business of philosophizing. Today, despite the spread of feminism and multiculturalism, and their impact on fields ranging from literature to anthropology, it is possible to study philosophy without hearing anything about the historical contributions of women and People of Colour to the field. The canon remains dominated by white males. This chapter examines the concepts of knowledge, education, and politics in the teachings of Socrates, Plato, and Sojourner Truth through a gender and racial lens and aims to show that the categories of gender and race, although foundational to philosophy from its inception, are often ignored, naturalized, and divided. While recognizing the importance of studying ancient Greek philosophers, such as Socrates and Plato, the inclusion of thinkers who have been excluded from the political philosophy canon expands not only the number of participants, but also the number of vantage points and thus provides a broader range of perspectives, visions, and concerns.

2.1 Introduction

Race, gender, and class are often factors of exclusion in philosophy, and they are interrelated: philosophical justifications for the superiority of one group over another have been influenced by and have in turn reinforced racist, sexist, and classist biases. Hence our analysis of these exclusions in the history of political philosophy has to focus on their intersectionality (see Key Concept: Intersectionality for a definition of this). If we approach Plato's texts through a gender and racial lens, we discover the way in which philosophers' culturally inherited beliefs about women and 'barbarians' affect their theories, and expose the fact that their theories are neither gender-neutral nor race-neutral. It exposes the fact that philosophers in general, and Plato (c. 428–348/7 BCE) in our analysis, have inscribed gender, race, and class biases in the central categories of their theories—what it means to be human, rational, knowledgeable, moral, and a political agent. We then discover that we can no longer read the philosophical narrative as offering a universal perspective, since philosophers are influenced by the cultural values they have inherited and, like all of us, privilege some experiences and ways of seeing over others. In other words, to understand a philosophical text we must read it within the framework of this larger context. As Charles Mills (1997: 123) writes, 'we need to see differently, ridding ourselves of class and gender bias, coming to recognize as political what we had previously thought of as apolitical or personal, doing conceptual innovation, reconceiving the familiar, looking with new eyes at the old world around us.'

> **Key Concept: Intersectionality**
>
> Intersectionality is a theoretical framework for understanding how social categorizations such as race, class, gender, and sexuality may combine to create multiple forms of discrimination and oppression experienced by an individual. The term was coined in the 1980s by the African-American legal scholar Kimberlé Crenshaw (1959–) but the idea can arguably be traced back to at least the 1970s—the Combahee River Collective (1977) discuss 'interlocking' systems of oppression—and perhaps even earlier to figures such as Sojourner Truth, whom we explore in this chapter. While the concept originally emerged out of Black feminism to analyse forms of discrimination unique to Black women, today it is used to challenge other potential axes of oppression, such as sexuality, disability, education, language, and nationality.

In that spirit, rather than taking the traditional historical and chronological approach to political theory, this chapter will pair Greek philosophers Socrates (c. 470–400 BCE) and Plato with the African-American former slave and preacher Sojourner Truth (c. 1797–1883) and compare their epistemological and political questions across time and space.

2.2 Three political thinkers

2.2.1 Socrates

Socrates is regarded as the first political philosopher. We come to know him primarily through one of his students, Plato, as he did not leave behind any writings. Socrates was born in Athens, Greece, and grew up during the years when Athens was a flourishing democracy under the statesman Pericles and had hegemony over the rest of Greece and its colonies. The second part of Socrates' life, however, was overshadowed by the defeat of Athens by Sparta during the Peloponnesian War (431–404 BCE) and the loss of Athenian leadership.

Socrates went around Athens engaging in conversation with both friends and hostile interlocutors, such as the Sophists (see Key Thinker: The Sophists), asking questions about the meaning of concepts, such as virtue, piety, justice, employing the 'Socratic method', which consisted of leading his audience to think through a problem to a logical conclusion.

Socrates' open criticism of prominent Athenian politicians had made him many enemies. Seen as a threat to the political status quo, he was accused of religious impiety and corruption of the Athenian youth by the democratic faction in power, tried, convicted, and condemned to death by poison.

*Read more about **Socrates'** life and work by accessing the thinker biography on the online resources: www.oup.com/he/Ramgotra-Choat1e.*

> **Key Thinker: The Sophists**
>
> The Sophists were itinerant teachers who went from city to city in ancient Greece offering expert instruction in various subjects for a fee. They studied forensic debate and oratorical persuasion and were best known for teaching rhetoric. Their teachings had a considerable influence on thought in the fifth century BCE. The most famous representatives of the sophistic movement are Protagoras, Gorgias, Antiphon, Hippias, and Thrasymachus.

2.2.2 Plato

Born circa 428 BCE, Plato was a student of Socrates and a teacher of Aristotle. Both of his parents came from the Greek aristocracy. As a young man, Plato experienced two major events that influenced his course in life. One was meeting the great Greek philosopher Socrates (see Section 2.2.1). Socrates' methods of dialogue and debate impressed Plato so much that he became one of his followers and dedicated his life to the pursuit of questions of virtue and justice. In *The Republic* (375 BCE) and other works, Plato presents Socrates' philosophical dialogues with various people.

The other significant event was the Peloponnesian War between Athens and Sparta, in which Plato served for a brief time. The defeat of Athens ended its democracy, which the Spartans replaced with an oligarchy. After the oligarchy was overthrown and democracy restored, Plato briefly considered a career in politics, but he abandoned the idea; the politically motivated sentence of his mentor in 399 BCE prompted him to reflect on politics, corruption, power, truth, and justice, and contributed to his call to bear witness to posterity of 'the best, . . . the wisest and most just' person that he knew (*Phaedo*: 118).

After Socrates' death, Plato travelled for twelve years throughout the Mediterranean region, studying mathematics, geometry, geology, astronomy, and religion. Upon his return to Athens, at around 40 years of age, Plato founded the first known institution of higher learning in the West, the Academy, named for its location in the Grove of Academus. Among its alumni was Aristotle, who would take his mentor's teachings in new directions.

Read more about **Plato's** life and work by accessing the thinker biography on the online resources: www.oup.com/he/Ramgotra-Choat1e.

2.2.3 Sojourner Truth

As with Socrates, we come to know about Sojourner Truth primarily through the writings of others—in this case, the autobiography she dictated to a white abolitionist, Olive Gilbert, since she could neither read nor write. Sojourner Truth was born in upstate New York around 1797, where the Dutch had settled in the seventeenth century. She was given the name Isabella by her Dutch owner, and she grew up speaking Dutch. She was the youngest of several (ten or twelve) children. Her parents were slaves and all their children, except for Isabella and her brother Peter, were sold away. In her *Narrative*, she describes the grief of her parents over the loss of their children and her own fear of separation. She also recalls her mother teaching her children that 'there is a God, who hears and sees you and when you are beaten, or cruelly treated, or fall into any trouble, you must ask help of him and he will always hear and help you' (Gilbert, 1998: 12).

At around the age of 9, Isabella and her brother were sold at the slave auction, and she dated her 'trials in life' from that time when she started working as a slave. She worked under harsh conditions, often beaten and whipped for not understanding and speaking English (ibid.: 17–18). After about a year she was sold to another family, and at around the age of 12, in 1810, sold again to John Dumont where she lived for about sixteen years (ibid.: 20). As was the case for most slaves in rural areas in the North, Truth lived isolated from other African-Americans and suffered from abuse at the hands of her owners. She married an older slave and between 1815 and 1826, bore five children (ibid.: 24–25).

In 1799, the state of New York began the process of gradual emancipation, and slavery ended on 4 July 1827. Dumont promised Isabella that he would free her one year early if she continued to work hard. She did but hurt her right hand. On 4 July 1826, when her master refused to free her, claiming she had not worked hard enough because of her injury, Isabella fled his household with her infant daughter Sophia and was taken in by an abolitionist family, the Van Wagenens, whom she had known for years (ibid.: 26–28). Isabella took their last name and lived with them for about a year, until emancipated. This time with the Van Wagenens, devout Methodists, was an important period in her spiritual life and delineated her path to activism. She was introduced to Perfectionism, a branch of Methodism, whose followers believed they were guided by an inner light that endowed them with spiritual authority, and that certain people achieved holiness through traumatic experiences and encounters with the Holy Ghost. This certainly applied to Isabella who had endured slavery, beatings, whippings, and sexual abuse, and who had employed her mother's teachings to always turn to God in her trials.

In 1828, Isabella moved to New York and secured domestic employment. Here she was put in touch with many activists who would have a profound influence on her political views and commitment to social change. During this period, she preached at the religious camp meetings that convened around New York City and became very popular.

On 1 June 1843, the day of Pentecost, Isabella was 'called in spirit' to flee a 'wicked city' and move east. Significantly, on that date she embraced a new identity as Sojourner Truth and embarked on a new life, participating in the growing Northern reform movements. She joined the Northampton Association of Education and Industry in Massachusetts, a commune that supported abolition, women's rights, pacifism, and religious tolerance. There she met Frederick Douglass (see Chapter 30) and William Lloyd Garrison; in 1850, Garrison published her life story, *Narrative of Sojourner Truth: A Northern Slave*, that she had dictated to Olive Gilbert, a white woman who was also a member of the Northampton Association. The *Narrative* marks a turning point in the biography of Sojourner Truth, her first step into a deliberate representation of herself. The proceeds from her autobiography allowed her to support herself and buy a home.

Key Thinker: Elizabeth Cady Stanton

Elizabeth Cady Stanton (1815–1902) was probably the best-known advocate of women's rights and suffrage in the nineteenth century. She was the first president of the National Woman Suffrage Association in 1869, and with Susan B. Anthony, another famous activist, she compiled a six-volume *History of Woman Suffrage*. Sojourner Truth worked with Stanton in the fight to attain women's right to vote.

Read more about **Truth's** life and work by accessing the thinker biography on the online resources: www.oup.com/he/Ramgotra-Choat1e.

In 1853, Truth met Harriet Beecher Stowe, a year after Stowe's publication of *Uncle Tom's Cabin*, which fuelled opposition to slavery. During the Civil War, Sojourner Truth met President Lincoln (Gilbert, 1998: 120–121), recruited Black soldiers to the Union Army, and began the process of integrating the streetcars of Washington, DC, by sitting in their white-only sections almost ninety years before Rosa Park did so in 1955 (ibid.: 124–125). After the Civil War, she unsuccessfully urged Congress to make Western land grants to freed slaves who were suffering from poverty and violence in the South (ibid.: 133–134). In addition to equal rights for women and Black people, Truth also spoke on behalf of prison reform and against capital punishment.

Truth died in 1883, at about 86. The first obituaries came from the great abolitionists Frederick Douglass and Wendell Phillips. The *Christian Recorder* called her 'one of the most remarkable characters of the day' and the *New York Globe* wrote of her remarkable intelligence despite her lack of education (Painter, 1996: 255). Both branches of women's suffrage saluted her memory, calling her 'the most wonderful woman the colored race has ever produced' (Stanton et al., 1887: 531–532).

Over one hundred years after her death, Sojourner Truth remains one of the most powerful symbols and examples of American Black feminism. She took pride in being a *Black woman* and fought to remind both male abolitionists that female slaves needed freedom as much as male slaves did, and white women's rights activists, such as Elizabeth Cady Stanton (see Key Thinker: Elizabeth Cady Stanton) and Susan B. Anthony, that women of colour should be included in their cause as well. She ultimately split with Douglass, who believed suffrage for formerly enslaved men should come before women's suffrage; she thought both should occur simultaneously. At Truth's famous address at the First Annual Meeting of the American Equal Rights Association in New York in 1867, she stated: 'There is a great stir about colored men getting their rights but not about the colored women; and if colored men get their rights, and not colored women theirs, you see the colored men will be masters over the women, and it will be just as bad as it was before', points to the intersectionality of sexist and racist oppression for Black women. (Stanton et al., 1887: 72–73). At a time when women were seen as white and slaves as males, Truth embodied the fact that among Blacks are women and among women are Blacks (Painter, 1996: 4).

In 2009, Sojourner Truth became the first African American woman to be memorialized with a bust in the US Capitol.

2.2 Three political thinkers: Key Points

- Race, gender, and class are interrelated factors of exclusion in political philosophy; philosophical justifications for the superiority of one group over another have often been shaped by culturally inherited beliefs, racial, sexist, and classist biases.
- In general, philosophers have inscribed gender, race, and class biases in the central categories of their theories, notably in what it means to be human, rational, knowledgeable, moral, and a political agent; as such, we cannot read philosophical narratives as offering a universal perspective.
- Philosophers are influenced by the cultural values they have inherited and they privilege some experiences and ways of seeing over others: to understand a philosophical text, we must read it within the framework of this larger context that considers exclusions, cultural values, and experiences.

2.3 Plato: knowledge, education, and politics

For Plato (as well as Sojourner Truth), the aim of politics was the creation of a just society, and philosophy to Plato was 'the knowledge by which we are to make other men good' (*Laws*: 771). The reform of society and the moral improvement of its members had to go hand-in-hand since, in a corrupt society, citizens would be corrupted. For Plato, the state is first and foremost an educational institution: if virtue is knowledge, then it can be taught, and the educational system to teach it becomes an indispensable part of a good state and cannot be left to private demand. A plan for a compulsory, state-controlled system of education was perhaps Plato's most important innovation; he placed the utmost importance on education as the means by which the ruler could shape human nature to produce a harmonious state.

Governing is an art depending on exact knowledge: the philosopher had to rule because he alone possessed the knowledge of the Good and the true ends of the community; at the same time, the character of the ruler had to be shaped by education and the removal of possible causes of self-interest and temptations of power, such as the institution of the family and private property. Without the philosopher's vision of the Good, the members of the community were condemned to live in a cave of illusions, with distorted images of reality and irrational desires. Those who could ascertain the Good would be philosopher-kings who would rule in Plato's ideal state.

2.3.1 The ideal state

For Plato, since every state is made up of individuals, it follows that once the pattern of justice in a man can be duplicated in several other men, the state would turn out to be a just one; in Plato's words, 'the state is the soul writ large' (*The Republic*: 368d7).

Plato conceives of the human soul as containing three elements: (1) the philosophic; (2) the spirited; and (3) the appetitive (ibid.: 37b–441c). The philosophical disposition is the desire for knowledge, as shown by Socrates' continuous questioning and search for knowledge. The spirited element is the passion for combat and honour and characterizes the warriors. The appetitive element likes material possessions, is interested in economics, and characterizes the farmers and artisans. Although each element is present in everyone, different dispositions are dominant in different people, thus rendering them unequal. Those who are interested in philosophy and the search for truth have the philosophical element as dominant. Accordingly, citizens should be divided into three social groups or classes: the Philosophers as the rulers, the Warriors as the defenders of the city, and the Producers as the suppliers of material goods (ibid.: 374d–376e). The philosophers rule because they alone know the virtues of each class and can give them the appropriate education to perform their function, with each contributing to sustaining the whole society and the common good. It follows that justice reflects the natural inequality of individuals and is rooted in the division of labour where each citizen and class do that for which they are most suited, leading to harmony between the classes (ibid.: 427d–434c).

Socrates suggests that the citizens should be told a 'noble lie' (ibid.: 414b–c) so that they agree to the three-class social order. According to the 'myth of the metals', every citizen is born out of the earth; but the Gods have framed them differently, mixing different metals into their soul: gold for the rulers, silver for the auxiliaries, and brass or iron for the producers and craftsmen. If the people believed 'this myth . . . [it] would have a good effect, making them more inclined to care for the state and one another' and thus promote the stability of the state (ibid.: 415c–415d).

Membership in a class is determined by moral and intellectual qualities rather than birth or sex. Although Plato believed that children for the most part reflected the qualities of their biological parents ('nature'), it would not always be the case, and Plato's programme of intensive training and testing represented his attempt to identify those who possessed the qualities appropriate to ruling.

There is a hereditary component to virtue—it is 'according to nature' for good men to have good sons (*Cratylus*: 393c–394a), which is presumably why the ideal city seeks to improve its citizens by strictly regulating procreation (ibid.: 459a–461b). However, even with the controlled breeding in the ideal city, parents of a certain type sometimes give birth to children of another type (ibid.: 415bc, 460c, 546bd). Heredity is not a sufficient condition of virtue for, in the absence of a good education, good men will have bad sons as they do in Athens (*Meno*: 93c–94e), and even philosophic natures are perverted (*The Republic*: 497b). Thus, for Plato, a just order must be brought about by rational planning and education, not just by natural and social selection.

According to Plato, boys and girls should receive the same kind of education and both men and women should have access to all positions, thus making available to the state a large supply of natural talent. Education ('nurture') is a social process and its goal becomes the careful cultivation of each member in their specialized skill, and the restriction of each person to one function alone. The Guardians or Rulers live apart from others, and are to receive a specific education in literature, music, and gymnastics. Women as well as men are to be Guardians, but there are clear restraints: Guardians cannot own property or money; they are provided with their necessities and will live together (ibid.: 451d–471c); they are not allowed to marry; wives are held in common; and children are not to have contact with their biological parents and are raised in public crèches.

After describing the ideal state, Plato explains that it could come into existence only if the rulers were philosophers (ibid.: 473c–473d). Here Socrates presents one of the most popular images in ancient philosophy, the allegory of the cave, to show why the philosopher should rule the city and why such a proposal may seem absurd to those who live in non-ideal societies. We explore this in Section 2.3.2.

2.3.2 The allegory of the cave: knowledge and politics

Socrates starts with a distinction between knowledge and belief: knowledge concerns what is, while belief concerns both what is and what is not. Ignorance concerns itself only with what is not. In Plato's terminology, the objects of knowledge are the Forms, the true essence of things. The physical objects surrounding us are those things that are and are not since they are constantly changing and are the object of belief. Where people concern themselves with beautiful things, only the philosophers concern themselves with beauty itself. For instance, there are many dogs, and all differ from each other, but we are still able to recognize them all as dogs, and the same dog will be different at one and at ten years. What they have in common is the Form of 'dogness', the immutable essence of being a dog. The Forms are unchangeable, eternal, perfect concepts or ideals that transcend time and space. The physical realm is only a shadow or image of the true reality of the realm of the Forms. For Plato, understanding the Forms is the goal of philosophy, and the knowledge of the Form of the Good is essential to establish a city governed by perfect justice, because without knowing the nature of goodness, the philosopher cannot understand what is good about the other Forms (ibid.: 505a–505b).

Plato uses metaphors and analogies to help us understand his theory. In the metaphor of the Divided Line, the world is divided into the realm of the 'sensible'—detectable through our senses—and the realm of the 'intelligible'—discoverable using the intellect. Opinion relates to the former, knowledge to the latter. In the allegory of the Sun, Socrates compares the Form of the Good to the sun (ibid.: 508a–509b): like the sun illuminates the objects around us and makes them visible, the Form of the Good renders all the other Forms intelligible. Finally, Socrates provides a story, the Allegory of the Cave, to explain that knowledge gained through the senses is mere opinion, while real knowledge can be achieved only through philosophical reasoning. The allegory shows the philosopher leaving behind the impermanent, material world of darkness and ignorance for the permanent, intelligible world of light and knowledge.

We are to imagine a cave where prisoners are chained since birth to some rocks in such a way that they cannot look at anything but the wall in front of them. Behind them there is a fire and behind the wall there are people walking and carrying statues (ibid.: 514b). Because of the firelight, the prisoners can see the shadows of the statues on the wall and, having never seen the real objects, believe that the shadows are the real objects. They engage in pointless games of guessing which shadow would appear next. We, according to Plato, are like the prisoners and the political debates in our societies are like the meaningless games played by the prisoners. Political societies dwell in a shadowy realm 'where men live fighting one another about shadows and quarrelling for power, as if that were a great prize' (ibid.: 520).

If a prisoner escaped and left the cave, they would be shocked by the sunlight and would not believe that it was real. However, as they become accustomed to the light and their surroundings, they would realize that their former view of reality was wrong (ibid.: 516a). The freed prisoner is the philosopher who understands the Forms, using the Form of the Good as the prisoner uses the light of the sun to see the real things outside of the cave. When he returns to the cave to inform the other prisoners of his findings, they do not believe him and threaten to kill him if he sets them free. The other prisoners are those who believe in empirical knowledge and are thus trapped in a cave of false perceptions.

The chances of achieving justice in the real world are slim, and Socrates admits that the only way a philosopher could get to rule a city would be by the lucky chance that a philosophically inclined person was born to a king and inherited their throne. The other difficulty would be in convincing the philosophers to abandon their life of contemplation in the sunlight and descend into the dark cave of politics. Socrates says that the reluctance of the philosopher would prove his selflessness and his commitment to justice would make him take command of the city (ibid.: 520c). The best way to avoid conflict within a city is to give power to those who are reluctant to wield it (ibid.: 520d). Women could also be philosophers, according to Socrates, as we shall see in Section 2.3.3.

2.3.3 Women Guardians in the ideal state

In *The Republic*, Plato argued for allowing women to engage in traditionally 'male' tasks, even if he realized that the idea that women could be Guardians would provoke laughter (ibid.: 452a). Plato points out that not all differences between people are relevant (ibid.: 454c) and that the simple fact of reproductive differences between women and men is insufficient reason to conclude that the roles of women and men must differ: the only relevant differences are those which are 'pertinent to the pursuits themselves', the differences in the souls of individuals; some women, like some men, are better than others at learning or at philosophy, the love of wisdom (ibid.: 456a). Without discounting gender differences, Plato saw class differences as more important. Although Plato admits that men with an aptitude for philosophy will be superior to women with the same aptitude (ibid.: 455d), it would be a waste of resources for the city not to make some women Guardians.

Plato may seem unique among ancient philosophers, who typically regarded women as inferior and different from men. However, he still sees women as worse versions of men (in the creation myth in the *Timaeus*, he argued that cowardly men are punished by being born as women in their next life), and their inclusion as Guardians is framed by specific parameters. In fact, women are shared by men in common; although the raising of children will be delegated to women who are not Guardians, the Guardian women must bear children, and the best of them will bear the most children (*The Republic*: 459d–460b); these women, 'beginning at the age of twenty, shall bear for the state to the age of forty' (ibid.: 460e). There is to be no private home or family among the Guardians because this could create tension between their personal needs and desires and the needs of the state, thus removing the distinction between the private and the public. There is also no recognition of motherhood or women's needs and desires as different from men, and women's difference is negated for the good of the city, not for their benefit, liberation, or advancement.

It is important to recognize that Plato did not subscribe to a rights-based view of justice. Justice involved maximizing the well-being and goodness of the state, and 'all social and political arrangements within the state should be for the good of the community' (Buchan, 1999: 135–136). In the *Laws*, Plato's concern in regulating the private realm and women comes from the possible risks to the good of the state caused by the lack of such regulation: 'Woman—left without chastening restraint—is not . . . merely half the problem; nay, she is a two-fold and more than a two-fold problem, in proportion as her native disposition is inferior to man's' (ibid.: 781b). We can then conclude that Plato's assertion of equal laws and equal roles for women and men is consistent with his view of women as inferior to men. Women can serve as Guardians only insofar as they are capable of being like men. Plato's gender bias is an integral part of his philosophy: women's rational faculties are inferior to men's, and they are more likely to act driven by their passions. This belief in the relative weakness of women's rational faculties became an accepted tenet in Western philosophy.

> **2.3 Plato: knowledge, education, and politics: Key Points**
>
> - For Plato, the human soul contains three elements: the appetitive, the spirited, and the philosophical; each is dominant in different people, thus rendering them unequal.
> - Justice is the proper ordering of the different elements in different social groups, reflecting the natural inequality of individuals.
> - The philosopher should rule because only he knows the Good and such knowledge is essential to establish a just city; women as well as men can be Guardians if they manifest the right disposition.
> - We are like the prisoners in the cave who are trapped by false beliefs; knowledge through the senses is mere opinion, while real knowledge can be achieved only through philosophical reasoning.

2.4 Socrates and Sojourner Truth: knowledge and education

As we saw in the analysis of Plato's *The Republic*, the task of the philosopher is to pursue truth and knowledge, and to imagine and put in place a just society. Socrates was put on trial in 399 BCE for impiety and corruption of the youth of the city-state. At this trial, he explained that his method of questioning others in the search for truth started when his friend Chaerephon told him that the Oracle at Delphi had proclaimed that Socrates was the wisest man in Greece. Puzzled, Socrates set out to disprove the Oracle by finding a man in Athens wiser than himself.

> I gave a thorough examination to . . . one of our politicians . . . and in conversation I formed the impression that although in many people's opinion, and especially in his own, he appeared to be wise, in fact he was not. Then when I began to try to show him that he only thought he was wise and was not really so, my efforts were resented both by him and by many of the other people present. However, I reflected as I walked away: 'Well, I am certainly wiser than this man.' . . . it seems that I am wiser than he is to this small extent, that I do not think that I know what I do not know.
>
> (*Apology*: 21c)

Thus, Socrates defined wisdom as the recognition of one's ignorance and the lifelong search for truth. In matters of morality, it was most important to pursue genuine knowledge and to expose false pretentions, for, according to Socrates, virtue and moral knowledge were the same thing: no one who knew what was the right thing to do could do otherwise, and all wrongdoing was the product of ignorance (*Gorgias*: 475e, *Protagoras*: 458d).

Both Socrates and Truth saw the emancipatory role of philosophy in a social context. Both considered their roles to be a 'gadfly' whose mission it was to sting Socrates' sluggish fellow citizens and Truth's white audiences out of complacency by raising questions about their most basic beliefs.

Socrates saw as his role to help people to give birth to what they already knew as it was something they already possessed. Contrary to Plato's view of education in *The Republic*, Socrates neither wanted to nor could educate his followers as he knew that he did not know. Rather he wanted simply to help them be more truthful by improving their opinions through dialogue.

Socrates did not claim he himself possessed the wisdom sufficient to keep a man from wrongdoing, but he claimed that he relied on an inner divine voice that would intervene if he went in the wrong direction (*Apology*: 41d). Sojourner Truth, like Socrates, claimed to be guided by divine inspiration, the voice of the Holy Spirit, a route to knowledge through faith. In her *Narrative*, Sojourner Truth reported that the voice of God had instructed her to leave on her own and become a free woman. She described her spiritual conversion when God revealed Himself to her as a flash of lightning (Gilbert, 1998: 45). According to her autobiography, she prayed for instruction and the Lord gave her the name Sojourner because she 'was to travel up an' down the land, showin' the people their sins, an' bein' a sign unto them', and Truth because she 'was to declare the truth to the people' (ibid.: 111). She began to claim a special authority to teach others of a God who bore the message of salvation and equal rights for Black people and white women.

Socrates believed that virtue is knowledge and, as such, can be learned and taught. Virtue is knowledge of the good. What separates the virtuous from the unvirtuous person is not the desire for what is good, since everyone desires what they think to be good, but rather the knowledge of what the good really is.

For Socrates, knowledge must be continuously pursued with humility as wisdom consists in knowing that we do not know. He approached the problems of philosophy in ethical terms, by eliciting answers from his interlocutors about man and society and engaging them in the task of finding out for themselves what they knew and what they did not know. To discover the limits of one's knowledge, it is necessary first to find out what one really believes. The opinion will need to be tested, but to have it formulated and thought through its implications and connections with other beliefs is already a step towards self-knowledge. Self-knowledge is an indispensable motivating condition, because the greatest obstacle to intellectual and moral progress is people's unwillingness to confront their own ignorance.

Self-knowledge, then, is not only the goal of Socratic education; it is also, right from the beginning, a vital force in the process itself, which involves and is sustained by the pupil's growing awareness of their own cognitive resources, their strengths, and their limitations.

In Plato's *Theaetetus* (148e–151d), Socrates compares himself to a midwife and his method of dialectical questioning to the midwife's art of delivery. The metaphor here is 'intellectual midwifery', the mind giving birth to ideas it has conceived. The youth has the pregnancy; Socrates merely helps to bring forth his conception.

Here, then, are two contrasting notions of education. The sophist treats his pupil as an empty receptacle to be filled from the outside with the teacher's ideas. Socrates respects the pupil's own creativity, holding that, with the right kind of assistance, they will produce ideas from their own mind and will be enabled to work out for themselves whether they are true or false. Like childbirth, the process may be painful, for it hurts to be made to formulate one's own ideas and, having done so, to find out for oneself what they are worth (ibid.: 151a, c). This leads to the growth in self-knowledge, the awareness of what one knows and does not know (ibid.: 210bc). Self-knowledge is the benefit peculiarly associated with the Socratic method, while orthodox teaching does not have the same effect. This contrast, between putting ideas into the pupil's mind and drawing them out from within, is also the key contrast in *Meno*'s exposition of the theory that learning is recollection (81e–82a): in the dialogue, Socrates' questions lead an uneducated slave to the solution of a mathematical problem. Therefore, Socratic inquiry, if pursued with sincerity and determination, can lead to knowledge.

In her speeches, Sojourner Truth also raised questions about knowledge and communication. She had no education beyond her thirty-year experience of slavery. Her first teacher was her mother who taught her the Lord's Prayer and the efficacy of prayer, offering her a mental escape from her abusive masters. From her parents Isabella also learned her family's history of grief and loss through the slave trade. Sojourner Truth's rhetoric, in her speeches and in her *Narrative*, served to validate her as a Black woman and a former slave, and her particular embodied ways of knowing through her experiences as a slave, a labourer, and a mother.

Sojourner Truth's method of communicating, to relate to her audience, and preaching was different from the Socratic method as she employed a relational type of rhetoric that made her audience recognize her life's physical journeys, beginning with her status as a slave, and culminating in her position as an influential civil rights activist. She saw herself as educating people through the use of moral and legal arguments and presented herself as an example when discussing the condition of slaves, women, and former slaves. Like Socrates, who believed that philosophy should work for the ethical well-being of society, Truth did not see herself as simply a preacher and evangelist, but rather as helping to bring about social and political change for slaves, women, and former slaves. Her decision to change her name also reflected her role as an itinerant preacher (as Socrates was an itinerant philosopher) who discussed the truth of human experience as she travelled from community to community.

Patricia Hill Collins (2008: 22) writes that, because Black women's lives differ from the lives of white women, they have 'a specialized knowledge', through which they interpret their own reality as it is lived by them. At the core of this experience there is struggle against oppression and for the right of self-definition. Their specific rhetoric intervenes in the presupposed 'truth' of the dominant discourse. That is how Sojourner Truth employed rhetoric to validate the knowledge derived from her experiences as a slave, a labourer, a breeder, and later as a channel of the Holy Spirit and a moral reform agent.

2.4 Socrates and Sojourner Truth: knowledge and education: Key Points

- Wisdom to Socrates was the recognition of one's ignorance—to know that we do not know—and education was a continuous process of questioning our opinions and beliefs in search of the truth.
- Sojourner Truth's method of educating her audience was through presenting herself and her life as validation of her knowledge.
- Both Truth and Socrates saw the task of education as one of bringing forth the truth and thus improving society.
- Truth's and Socrates' speeches and questions served to unmask the alleged validity of the dominant discourse of those in power.

2.5 Sojourner Truth's speeches

Like Socrates, Truth may have preferred the dialogic rather than written form as more engaging and able to provide an adequate account of the truth. While Sojourner Truth had no formal rhetorical or oratorical training, she would have been familiar with the common oratorical styles of the day and with the importance of oratory in general. She would also have become familiar with common oratorical styles and conventions through her attendance at political and religious meetings and revivals. These were similar to Socrates' dialectical style, since the reaction of the interlocutor checks the truth-value of the preacher's claims.

Truth learned the skills she used as a speaker through both practice and rehearsal. In the late 1820s and early 1830s, she preached regularly at camp meetings around New York City, so by the time she joined the abolitionist movement and feminist lecture circuit in the late 1840s, she was a practised public speaker.

2.5.1 The representation of Black women

Truth faced a host of troubling representations of African-American female bodies, and she had to navigate her way through these models as she presented her own bodily identity. In pro-slavery literature as well as in some abolitionist discourse, Black women were depicted as overly sexual and animalistic, and their bodies as particularly suited for hard labour, clearly deviating from the true womanly ideal.

In one of her best-known speeches, commonly called 'Ain't I a Woman?' (Gilbert, 1998: 92), Truth declared her physical equality with men, by talking about her experience as a worker on the farm and her muscular strength in ploughing, reaping, husking, weeding, and mowing: 'I am as strong as any man that is now.' With the line 'ain't I a woman?', Truth positioned herself as one who had been cast out of the cult of true womanhood. Her claims are supported by her past as a slave, when she was required to do physical labour that the average middle-class white woman would have found impossible; she presents her real body which contradicts the ideal body of 'true womanhood' and shows this ideal to be lacking: '"Look at me. Look at my arm," and she bared her right arm to the shoulder, showing its tremendous muscular power.' Truth undercuts dominant nineteenth-century assumptions about women's embodiment, and her self-definition in terms of strength and labour implies a new vision of women's roles and the questioning of the male/female binary (Piepmeier, 2004: 108–109). She challenged the rhetoric of woman's submissive place and limited abilities. In fact, she claimed equality of intellect as well, asserting women's ability to handle the responsibility that rights entail and suggesting that men might benefit from women's enfranchisement, and their rights 'won't be so much trouble'. Truth used the category 'woman' both to demonstrate that women are like men, strong and capable of physical work, and, unlike men, able 'to turn the world upside down' and transform it, thus both acknowledging and subverting the constraints of 'true womanhood'.

> **Key Concept: The cult of true womanhood**
>
> The cult of true womanhood, or cult of domesticity, was a (white) conservative response to the suffragist movement that developed in particular in the United States in the nineteenth century. It defined womanhood as relegated to the domestic sphere, a morally superior position that was not to be sullied by politics: women were seen as pure, submissive, and pious, out of the public eye and, of course, white.

The question, 'ain't I a woman?' addressed both white women's suffrage activism and race inequities regarding women of colour. African-American women were seen as sexually promiscuous and thus not pure and modest as 'true womanhood' dictated.

With the sentence 'I am a woman's rights', Truth stresses how the battle for women's rights is particularly pertinent to her life experiences. Her physical strength refutes the notion expressed in the cult of true womanhood that women are weaker than men (Fitch and Mandziuk, 1997: 73). By telling the audience, 'look at me!', and mentioning 'the lash' and her mother's grief, she asks those present to consider her life as a Black woman, a slave, and a mother whose children were taken away and sold into slavery (Gilbert, 1998: 92). When Truth talks of being helped over mud puddles, something reserved for women of high rank, she points to class distinctions. Using her personal history to connect her physical strength, the inhumanity of slavery, and issues of class, Truth attempts to raise the consciousness of her white audience to the inhumanity and horrors of slavery as well as to the endurance of women in the face of sexism.

Finally, in her speech, Truth presents herself as a messenger of God and refers to the weeping women who demonstrated their faith in Jesus. Then she asks: 'And how came Jesus into the world? Through God who created him and woman who bore him. Man, where is your part?' (ibid.). The use of biblical references was employed also to counter the view of Black women's questionable morality implicit in the notion of 'true womanhood'. Truth's mentions of Eve and Mary also show women's important role in Christianity as well as their strength and resilience and suggest that only women can 'fix' the wrongs of the world (Fitch and Mandziuk, 1997: 77).

During a speech in Indiana in 1858, a group of pro-slavery sympathizers accused her of being a man disguised in women's clothing. Truth responded by baring her breast that had 'suckled many a white babe' and asked the men in the audience whether 'they too wished to suck' (Gilbert, 1998: 95). Truth not only called into question the assumption that Black women were not truly women in any embodied sense, but she also shamed the white men who taunted her by belittling them, and resisting the racist characterization of 'true' nineteenth-century women. Without shame, she claimed her authority and knowledge not simply as a woman but as a Black woman who bore the scars of slavery on her body, and once more challenged the 'naturalness' of the male/female dichotomy. As Painter (1996: 140) notes: 'Truth has turned the challenge upside down. Her skilful re-making employed the all-too-common exhibition of an undressed black body, with its resonance of the slave auction that undressed women for sale. What had been intended as degradation became a triumph of embodied rhetoric.' Finally, Truth proclaimed her truthfulness but not in the terms of her accusers. She rather employed the 'mammy' stereotype to call attention to the public nature of Black women's breasts. Truth's words, therefore, drew attention to the public availability of Black women as mammies, while Truth's body called attention to the public availability of Black women on the auction block. Truth again used her body to challenge cultural discourses on race and gender that stigmatized the body.

2.5.2 Narrative and humour

Like Plato, Sojourner Truth used narrative and stories, and, like Socrates, she often used irony and humour to disarm her opponents and convey her message. During a lecture in her Midwest tour, Truth was heckled by a man in the audience who accused her of not supporting the United States' Constitution. To set the man straight, Truth narrated a story that revolved around a kind of beetle, called a weevil, that had damaged the wheat crop in Ohio that year.

> 'Children,' she said, 'I talk to God and God talks to me. I go out and talk to God in the fields and the woods. This morning I was walking out, and I got over the fence. I saw the wheat holding up its head, looking very big. I go up and take hold of it. You believe it, there was no wheat there?' I say, 'God, what is the matter with this wheat?' And he says to me, 'Sojourner, there is little weevil in it.' Now I hear talking about this Constitution and the rights of man. I come up and take hold of this Constitution. It looks mighty big, and I feel for my rights, but there ain't any there. Then I say, 'God, what ails this Constitution?' He says to me, 'Sojourner, there is a little weevil in it.'
>
> (Gilbert, 1998: 100–101)

Through humour, Truth pointed out a fault in the Constitution, namely, that it did not provide for the rights of all people.

During her famous 'ain't I a woman?' speech, to men's claims of superior rights due to their superior intellect, Truth replied: 'What's that got to do with woman's rights or Negroes' rights? If my cup won't hold but a pint and yours holds a quart, wouldn't it be mean not to let me have my little half measure-full?' (ibid.: 92). The implication is that since men claimed superior rights based on their superior intellect, then women with some intellect, even if just a 'pint', should have some rights. Instead of denying the offending claim, Truth subverted it and reassured her audience that, since women lack intellectual capacity, men had no need to fear them. A discussion of intellect is beside the point; women and Black people deserve the same kinds of rights as white men; white men need to give a portion of their rights to the rest of the population towards the goal of equality for all. Like Socrates, who saw those who lacked virtue as merely ignorant of the good, she portrayed opponents of equality as merely confused: 'The poor men seem to be all in confusion, and don't know what to do. Why, children, if you have woman's rights, give it to her and you will feel better. You will have your rights, and they won't be so much trouble.' According to one observer, the audience responded with long and loud cheering (Stanton et al., 1887: 116).

Finally, arguing against the idea that women did not deserve equal rights because Jesus was a man, Truth claimed that Jesus came to the world through God and a woman, with man playing no part (Gilbert, 1998: 92). Again, she used humour in emphasizing the role of a woman in the story of Jesus.

Truth's humour also worked to soften her audience's hostility towards her as an African-American ex-slave ('A buzz of disapprobation was heard all over the house'). By the end of the speech Truth had won most people over (Painter, 1996: 166).

As these examples illustrate, Sojourner Truth was very brave, had a strong sense of self, and always spoke in the first person, never afraid to call attention to herself when advancing an argument. Her use of wit and her own life experiences seemed to be consistently effective in disarming hostile crowds.

2.5 Sojourner Truth's speeches: Key Points

- While female Black bodies were represented as deviating from the ideal of true womanhood, Truth attacked the stereotype in the cult of true womanhood in her speeches and used her life and experiences to validate her rhetoric.
- Fighting against the racism and sexism of which she was the victim, Truth employed storytelling as a powerful way to connect with her audience as well as the subversive use of humour to disarm her opponents.
- She presented herself as a vessel of God's message, using biblical references to validate her spiritual authority.

2.6 Conclusion

In the *Thaetetus*, Socrates tells the story of Thales who, while looking at the sky and the stars, fell into a well. A maidservant laughed at him and told him that while he might want to know all things in the universe, he missed the things in front of his nose (174A–174B). The hearty laughter of the young slave woman at Thales' exclusive concern with the life of the mind has often been interpreted as the simple-mindedness of ignorant people mocking theory and the contemplative life of the philosopher. 'Truth' is a higher reality that supposedly distracts the thinker from the ordinary affairs of the world where he is out of place. A sense of a world that is elsewhere, that is not of this world, thus emerges with Thales, the first philosopher. The only hint of resistance and derision in the face of philosophy's negation of reality is found in the maidservant's laughter. She belongs to this world, exists in the female world of bodily needs and provision of nourishment (Cavarero, 1995).

Plato's theory of the Forms means that acquiring knowledge involves turning away from the world of the senses, which can only ever produce opinion, towards the Forms and the world of the intellect. Sojourner Truth, however, like the maidservant, could not turn away from her daily life of struggle against racism, misogyny, and classism. She transmitted knowledge to others through the story of her life experiences, as embedded knowledge rather than theoretical knowledge.

For Plato, the task of philosophy is the pursuit and love of knowledge of what is eternal, immutable, and unchanging. The Forms—the essence of things—constitute the proper object of philosophical contemplation. Such knowledge, moreover, is incommunicable. The essence of politics, however, is communication: public speech, made possible by a shared language. Without it, there could be no politics but only, as Hannah Arendt (1998: 25–26) said, 'mute violence'.

Socrates, Plato, and Sojourner Truth were critical of the politics of their times and spent their lives speaking truth to power. Both Socrates and Truth were itinerant speakers, neither was formally educated, and neither left anything written behind, so their lives and ideas were recorded in the writings of their contemporaries. They employed oratory and often humour while engaging with their audiences to expose hypocrisy and the arrogance of the powerful.

Both Socrates and Truth explored the meaning of justice and claimed they were guided by an inner divine voice in their pursuit of truth. Both were subjected to oppressive and brutal political power under democratic regimes. Both defended their positions and refused to give up their quest. Socrates confronted a bellicose Thrasymachus, and in the end, after his trial, chose to die rather than stopping his questioning; Truth experienced a normalized and everyday violence under slavery, and then faced hostile and angry mobs as a preacher, but continued speaking up for abolitionism and women's rights. Socrates and Truth differed, however, in their views of justice.

In *The Republic*, Socrates starts looking for justice in its greater extent, in a city, and later in an individual (ibid.: 369a). The state is merely the individual 'writ large' and justice concerns the proper ordering of elements within each. Justice requires the recognition of these different elements and the acceptance of inequality among individuals and classes in society. Justice, therefore, is 'giving each his due'. The just individual knows and performs his or her task responsibly and respects others for their function and contribution to the good of the whole society. Only the philosopher knows the particular virtues of each class and gives them their 'due', or what is necessary to perform their functions, and establish justice. It follows that it is necessary for him to rule, and the good state will emerge only when political power is merged with a philosophical intellect: 'Unless the philosophers rule as kings or those now called kings . . . philosophize . . . there is no rest from ills for the cities' (ibid.: 473d–473e).

Contrary to Socrates and Plato, Truth maintained that equality is foundational to justice. In her speeches she addressed the need for racial and sexual equality, for the franchise for Black people and women. She also stressed economic equality and the need for reparations for former slaves:

> We have been a source of wealth to this republic. Our labor supplied the country with cotton . . . Beneath a burning southern sun have we toiled, in the canebrake and the rice swamp, urged on by the merciless driver's lash, earning millions of money; and so highly were we valued there, that should one poor wretch venture to escape from this hell of slavery, no exertion of man or trained bloodhound was spared to seize and return him to his field of unrequited labor . . . Our unpaid labor has been a stepping stone to its financial success. Some of its dividends must surely be ours.
> (Gilbert, 1998: 132)

Truth's critique of racism, sexism, and classism reverberates today in societies that may have eliminated legal discrimination against women and minorities but still maintain it de facto.

Finally, Socrates' and Truth's courage in pursuing the truth is a valuable lesson for all. They show us the relevance of political theory and the importance of engaging in the quest for knowledge, truth, and justice, since, as Socrates said, 'the unexamined life is not worth living'. And let us not forget, as Sojourner Truth reminds us, that 'Life is a hard battle anyway. If we laugh and sing a little as we fight the good fight of freedom, it makes it all go easier' (Notecard, *The New York World*, 13 May 1867).

Take your learning further by accessing the online resources for a library of web links to relevant videos, articles, blogs, and useful websites for this chapter: **www.oup.com/he/Ramgotra-Choat1e**.

Study questions

1. How are virtue and knowledge related, according to Socrates and Sojourner Truth?
2. How is the concept of intersectionality woven into Truth's famous speech 'Ain't I a woman?'
3. According to Plato, the philosophers should rule. What might Sojourner Truth reply to Plato?
4. In which social group would Sojourner Truth be placed by Plato in *The Republic*?
5. What does Plato's ideal state tell us about his views of woman's nature and abilities and how do Sojourner Truth's life experiences refute them?
6. What is the value of storytelling in both Plato's work and Truth's speeches?
7. What is the relation between justice and equality for Plato and for Sojourner Truth?
8. Socrates, Plato, and Sojourner Truth claim that they are pursuing the 'truth'—but what does 'truth' mean and why is it a contested concept?

Further reading

Primary sources

Gilbert, O. (1998) *Narrative of Sojourner Truth*. Ed. N.I. Painter. New York: Penguin Books.
Chronicles Truth's experiences as a slave and her transformation into an abolitionist and preacher.

Plato (2005) *The Collected Dialogues of Plato: Including the Letters*. Princeton, NJ: Princeton University Press.
Wide range of Platonic dialogues and letters.

Secondary sources

Kraut, R. (ed.) (1992) *The Cambridge Companion to Plato*. Cambridge: Cambridge University Press.
Essays discussing Plato's philosophy.

Morrison, D. (ed.) (2010) *The Cambridge Companion to Socrates*. Cambridge: Cambridge University Press.
A range of perspectives on the controversial figure of Socrates.

Painter, N.I. (1996) *Sojourner Truth: A Life, a Symbol*. New York: W.W. Norton.
Ground-breaking biography of the life of Sojourner Truth.

Rudebusch, G. (2009) *Socrates*. New York: Wiley-Blackwell.
Accessible study of Socrates' life and work with lessons applicable to our lives.

Stanton, E.C. et al. (eds) (1887) *History of Woman Suffrage*. Rochester, NY: Charles Mann.
Primary documentation about the women's suffrage movement.

Washington, M. (2009) *Sojourner Truth's America*. Urbana, IL: University of Illinois Press.
Describes the political landscape of nineteenth-century America through the life of Sojourner Truth and her journey from slavery to self-emancipation.

References

Arendt, H. (1998) *The Human Condition*. Chicago: The University of Chicago Press.

Buchan, M. (1999) *Women in Plato's Political Theory*. London: Palgrave Macmillan.

Cavarero, A. (1995) *In Spite of Plato: A Feminist Rewriting of Ancient Philosophy*. Trans. S. Anderlini-D'Onofrio and A. O'Healy. New York: Routledge.

Collins, P.H. (2008) *Black Thought: Knowledge Feminist, Consciousness and the Politics of Empowerment*. New York: Routledge.

Combahee River Collective (1977) 'Statement'. Available at https://combaheerivercollective.weebly.com/the-combahee-river-collective-statement.html# (accessed 28 March 2022).

Fitch, S.P. and Mandziuk, R.M. (1997) *Sojourner Truth as Orator: Wit, Story, and Song*. Westport, CT: Greenwood Press.

Gilbert, O. (1998) *Narrative of Sojourner Truth*. Ed. N,I. Painter. New York: Penguin Books.

Mills, C. (1997) *The Racial Contract*. Ithaca, NY: Cornell University Press.

Painter, N.I. (1996) *Sojourner Truth: A Life, a Symbol*. New York: W.W. Norton.

Piepmeier, A. (2004) *Out in Public*. Chapel Hill, NC: University of North Carolina Press.

Stanton, E.C., Anthony, S.B., Gage, M.J., and Harper, I.H. (eds) (1887) *History of Woman Suffrage*. Rochester, NY: Charles Mann.

3 Aristotle and bell hooks

MANJEET RAMGOTRA

Chapter guide

This chapter compares Aristotle's and bell hooks' rich but radically distinct conceptions of politics composed for two different communities located in different spaces and times. It demonstrates that how we understand the world, the individual subject, and the household shapes human relations and political institutions. Section 3.3 looks at the spaces in which politics is located and considers boundaries that separate and exclude. Section 3.4 examines Aristotle's theory of teleology in relation to knowing and being, which it then contrasts with hooks' conception of knowledge as constructed through experience and positionality in relation to marginalized groups. Section 3.5 compares Aristotle's understanding of human nature comprised of reason, appetite, and spirit to hooks' view that human beings are political subjects constituted by systems of power that situate them in hierarchical categories, but who can reclaim agency and create their own subjectivities. Section 3.6, the final section, focuses on the home as the first social institution in which individuals learn about authority, gender, and social relations. It contrasts Aristotle's defence of patriarchy with hooks' conception of homeplace as a site of resistance that Black women created to nurture and restore human dignity.

3.1 Introduction

Both Aristotle (384–322 BCE) and bell hooks (1952–2021) address the questions: what is the political? what are its boundaries? Both consider who should participate in the activity of politics and why. Even though he was a foreigner in Athens and therefore not a citizen, Aristotle writes from the position of the ruling classes; whereas bell hooks writes from the position of a Black American woman. Aristotle explains how various constitutions work and determines which one is the best; he promotes a political order in which the freemen rule. By contrast, hooks challenges the political institutions and movements that exclude. In her words, she criticizes 'imperialist white supremacist capitalist patriarchy' systems that intersect and 'work together to uphold and maintain cultures of domination' (hooks, 2012: 4). She aims to break boundaries that separate and create hierarchies on the basis of race and gender. Such exclusions are not simply the result of force, but also depend on the sort of power associated with knowledge and being: how we know the world and how we are in it. Social hierarchies are justified by theories that evaluate the worth of categories of people. By accepting such justifications, we allow them to have power over us and to regulate our behaviour. Such power pervades customs, ways of being, norms, and practices, all of which underpin social and political institutions. Theory is central in creating, criticizing, and challenging political structures and norms.

> **Key Concept: Race in antiquity**
>
> In the ancient world, there were no conceptions of race and colour in the way we understand these today. Racism is an ideology that emerged in the modern world and justified imperial domination and slavery. It is structural. In antiquity, distinctions were made between ethnicities, languages, and place of birth. Foreigners, *metics*, were excluded from political processes and did not enjoy full citizenship. Nevertheless, there is debate on whether race existed in the ancient world (Bernal, 1991; Benjamin, 2006; Rodriguez, 2016; Frank, 2019; Hanchard, 2019).

By putting Aristotle in conversation with bell hooks, we reframe the lens through which to read Aristotle. By shifting the frame, we do not simply read him as one of the first Western political thinkers whose legacy permeates the history of political ideas, but rather we view him in a contemporary light, and acknowledge that we can reconstruct his ancient world only to a limited extent. To do so disrupts the conventional way of reading political theory through the canon of great and mostly white male thinkers who are thought to be in conversation across time. Although Aristotle and hooks write in very different times and places, we can still compare their ideas in relation to the common questions they address and examine their divergent languages and perspectives on political activity, political activism, identity, social roles, patriarchy, and feminism.

3.2 Two political thinkers

3.2.1 Aristotle

Read more about **Aristotle's** life and work by accessing the thinker biography on the online resources: www.oup.com/he/Ramgotra-Choat1e.

Aristotle lived in ancient Greece and was a protégé of Plato's (see Chapter 2 for coverage of Plato) and tutor to Alexander the Great, whereas bell hooks (1952–2021) lived as an independent woman in a modern twentieth-century liberal democracy. Yet both thinkers shared the experience of social and political exclusion from two great powers of the classical and modern worlds. Aristotle was a *metic*, a foreigner in Athens. He was excluded from political life and when he did not enjoy Plato's or Alexander's protection, he had to flee the city.

3.2.2 bell hooks

Read more about **hooks'** life and work by accessing the thinker biography on the online resources: www.oup.com/he/Ramgotra-Choat1e.

bell hooks grew up in a racially segregated town in Kentucky, USA. She attended a segregated school and transitioned to an integrated school when the laws changed. hooks was from a working-class family. Aristotle was from a well-off educated one. His work with eminent rulers and philosophers shaped his outlook. hooks obtained a PhD and worked her way up a system that did not readily promote Black women. She did not reproduce the norms of the academy but bucked the trend. Her name was Gloria Watkins, but she took a pseudonym, spelt it in lower case, thus making a stand against social conventions.

3.3 Locations of politics

In *The Politics* (350 BCE), Aristotle presents a compelling conception of the political that continues to shape how we think of politics today. He considers that politics is a uniquely human activity through which human beings can realize their capacities and aptitudes, such as speech and reason.

The political represents the physical space in which equal citizens gather to make collective decisions through reasoned debate, negotiation, and deliberation in relation to the common good. It is also an imagined ethical space in which citizens leave behind their private concerns and think themselves part of a greater collective whole. They cultivate virtue, they reason in terms of the common good, and aim at realizing this noble end. In Aristotle's conception of the political, men share in ruling and being ruled.

Many theorists do not consider that politics is restricted to the public sphere. According to many feminists and critical theorists 'politics is everywhere' (Squires, 2004: 119), including the private space of the home. The slogan, 'the personal is political' (Hanisch, 1970) stresses that the home is very 'political', for power and authority play a major role in family relations. To feminists and Marxists (see Chapter 13 on Marx), politics exists in the relations we forge with each other, in our behaviour, customs, and norms that structure collective living and reinforce the apparatus of power. We begin to learn about behaviour, norms, social roles, and hierarchies in the home.

To Aristotle, the home was the basic unit of the *polis*. It was distinct from the public space; and, generally, it was owned and managed by the male head of the household. Ruling over the household provided men with the experience to rule in the public domain. This distinction of the private from public realms supported paternalistic and patriarchal rule in the domestic sphere and the rule of the citizen or freeman in the public domain.

Key Concept: The *polis*

The ancient Greek term *polis* translates as city-state. It refers to the political community that arose from the conglomeration of several tribes into a single unity. *Polis* emerged for the mutual defence of these tribes against common enemies and for the satisfaction of mutual needs, both material and intellectual. Speech, language, and communication made such association possible. The *polis* further refers to political life in the public space constituted by men of equal standing, who, as part of the greater whole, reasoned and ruled for the collective good. The *polis* was central to human flourishing and the good life, which amounted to the realization of all human potential and the common good both through the fulfilment of needs and good governance. The *polis* allowed men to reach their highest moral ends and virtue as political animals through participation in ruling for the common good.

Feminists contest the exclusion of the household from the political realm especially since it creates the structures through which men are liberated from everyday responsibilities to take part in public affairs (Anderson, 1999). The household is the space in which we first experience the exercise of power and authority and gendered, social, and racial divisions of labour. To exclude the domestic sphere from the political is to disregard a major element of society and of politics.

hooks (1984: 21, 35–39) characterizes the American patriarchal household as imperialist, as structured according to the norms of white supremacist colonizers. In the USA, when slavery was legal, the household was the place of the brutal abuse of power, perpetuating sexism, racism, and the commodification of human beings and relations. The hierarchies established in the home between men and women and white and Black people pervaded public spaces and regulated all aspects of life.

Boundaries created in the home continued to operate in the public space, in the architecture of space. hooks contests the regulation of populations based on race and gender. Her observation that exclusion operates not only in segregated schools, but also in the organization of space poignantly demonstrates that racial inequality is deeply embedded in the layout of American towns. For instance, railway tracks constitute a line that divides neighbourhoods and living spaces in terms of colour and class, Black from white, rich from poor.

> As black Americans living in a small Kentucky town, the railroad tracks were a daily reminder of our marginality. Across those tracks were paved streets, stores we could not enter, restaurants we could not eat in, and people we could not look directly in the face. Across those tracks was a world we could work in as maids, as janitors, as prostitutes, as long as it was in a service capacity. We could enter that world but we could not live there. We had always to return to the margin, to cross the tracks, to shacks and abandoned houses on the edge of town.
>
> (hooks, 1982: Preface, i)

The organization of space in which people can move freely or not or from which they are prohibited sets boundaries. As a foreigner, Aristotle's life in Athens was also restricted (Frank, 2004; Dietz, 2012).

Public spaces reflect how a society conceptualizes power and authority. Symbols, artwork, billboards, and statues represent and commemorate power and authority while other artistic articulations contest power. In turn, these shape perceptions and conceptions about politics, where power is situated, and how individuals fit into or are positioned within the wider architecture of society. Space was central to ancient Greek life, notably the *agora*, the open space that was used for public assemblies and the market. Boundaries also exist between groups of people. Aristotle justifies these, whereas hooks teaches people to transgress borders that hierarchize, divide, and exclude.

Access to education is another boundary that hooks highlights. Women and People of Colour have not always enjoyed equal access to education and public life. There is weight in her observation that in the United States:

> there are so many settings . . . where the written word has only slight visual meaning, where individuals who cannot read or write can find no use for a published theory however lucid or opaque. Hence, any theory that cannot be shared in everyday conversation cannot be used to educate the public.
>
> (hooks, 1994: 64)

The same could be said of ancient Greece. Due to high levels of illiteracy, there were probably many settings where the written word held little meaning, but the architecture of space, buildings, statues, and artwork reflected and enforced the structures of power and society. To the ancients, speech, dialogue, and reason, even among the illiterate were important to understand and shape the world.

Those who have access to knowledge, the educated, have a voice. In turn, this justifies their access to power. The denial of education operates to silence; the denial of a voice demands obedience. This counters contemporary democratic principles that conceptualize the public space as belonging to everyone. As politics affects everyone, thus, everyone—regardless of gender, race, class, or level of education—ought to have a say in how they are ruled. You do not have to be educated to take part in public life. All people constitute the political. Nevertheless, many are excluded. Aristotle considers that the rational and educated have greater authority to rule; whereas those who are deemed incapable of reasoning have no authority (Aristotle, 1996: 1254b–1255a, 1276b–1281a). His distinction between political and domestic spaces was reiterated in the separation of the public from the private and propped up by male governance in the state and patriarchal rule in the home. bell hooks opposes these binaries that run deep in the canon of Western political thought and are reflected in the physical edifices of public spaces.

> **3.3 Locations of politics: Key Points**
>
> - Politics is not located only in public spaces; power and authority are everywhere and are often manifest in art and the architecture of space, as well as in human relations.
> - Boundaries operate to exclude, differentiate, segregate, and maintain inequalities.
> - Boundaries are present in physical space, education; they exist between individuals, between groups of people; and divide public from private spaces.

3.4 Theories of knowing and being

Both Aristotle and hooks were teachers, and considered knowing and experiencing the world as central to how human beings exist in the world and how they structure their collective lives.

3.4.1 Aristotle on knowing and being

To Aristotle, we learn about and know the world through our senses; we see, feel, touch, taste, smell, and hear the material, living, and inanimate world around us. Aristotle observed nature, plants, animals, inanimate objects, and forms of social organization, such as political constitutions. He organized and classified what he saw according to common characteristics and purposes into species, categories, and groups. In his view, the cosmos formed a holistic whole in which all living things are connected (Oakeshott, 2006: 60–63). Each living thing has a nature or essence of its own that is discernible through its behaviour and movement. This essence is apparent in the cycle of birth, growth, becoming, and decline. This cycle allows us to observe and understand change. Objects have both an essence and a permanence as well as physical features subject to change cycles of growth and decay.

According to Aristotle, each object has a *telos* or a purposive end towards which it moves to both perfect itself and achieve its final state (see also Key Concept: *Telos*). All things in the universe have purposive ends that are contained within their essences. Even relations and connections between living things have specific ends and functions defined by the structure and order of the universe. In this conception of the universe, teleological movement or change reflects living beings pursuing their ends and displaying their nature.

> **Key Concept: *Telos***
>
> The *telos* or final state of an object is also its nature or essence. The *telos* is inherent in an object and defines it. For instance, a seed has the potential to become a flower. The final object is both prior to and contained within the seed. The *telos* of the seed is becoming a flower. Logically the concept of the fully developed product—the flower—exists prior to the seed, even though it is contained in the seed. Its essence exists prior to the planting, development, and growth of the seed. We must understand the *telos* or end-state of an object before we can understand its existence, but in order to understand its nature and essence, we have to comprehend its existence. The argument and logic are circular, similar to the chicken and egg scenario. At the same time, movement towards final ends can be truncated, and the object put to new use. For example, trees are cut down and the timber can be used to build a new object.

Living things flourish and fulfil their ends under the right conditions. Seeds need fertile soil, water, air, and sunlight to become flowers. Human beings also thrive under certain conditions. At a minimum, they need food, clothing, and shelter to develop their potential and move towards their purposive ends. Aristotle assigns a hierarchy of ends to human beings where the lowest is that of the slave who is considered a tool for work and the highest is that of the rational man engaged in political activity, who satisfies the highest human ends as a political animal. This stratification of the different types of ends includes, for example, the role of women to bear and raise children, of various craftsmen to produce the material goods necessary for life. Each is assigned a role according to their 'nature' or 'essence'. Aristotle developed this theory of purposive ends, or teleology, through observation of ancient societies. His categorization into species and groups of animate objects bears a certain rationale that underpins the logic of his argumentation.

Aristotle's teleological understanding of the cosmos is contested, notably for its essentialism (Arneil, 1999: 14–15). Effectively, essentialism implies that individuals are assigned certain roles according to gender, intellectual ability, and class. It categorizes individuals according to 'nature' and determines their role, place, and ends in society, leaving little room for the freedom to choose one's own path or way of life. Present-day responses to Aristotelian essentialism demonstrate that it is unrealistic to think that an individual has a single path and end in life. People's lives are rarely straightforward trajectories defined by a single end. Moreover, such essences are artificially constructed and created. Conceptions of ideal types are based on human ideas and social norms which, in turn, construct notions about who we are and how we should be (Hacking, 1999). Social roles and identities are neither natural nor a matter of biology, these are constructed in society and according to individual self-understandings.

3.4.2 hooks on knowing and being

bell hooks does not offer a prescriptive theory about the universe and knowledge as Aristotle does. Rather, she focuses on pedagogy (the method and practice of teaching), learning, and how individual experience and standpoints shape understandings and contribute to the wider body of knowing and being in the world. Her political theory centres on the oppressed, notably Black women and their perspectives on politics and power. These experiences form a body of knowledge and being. Such knowledge is different from epistemologies (the nature of knowledge) and ontologies (the nature of being) derived from first principles which prescribe how things in the universe are and ought to be. Rather, hooks approaches political theory from the standpoint of those who experience the effects of power, of oppression, whose perspective is to resist and oppose structures of power rather than justify these. She sees knowledge production as constructed, and tends to deconstruct systems of knowledge that function to maintain power structures that dominate. She considers theory as a liberatory site where critical thinking can take place. She challenges processes of teaching and learning that discipline students to co-opt them into the socio-political structures that govern society.

Unlike Aristotle, hooks works from the 'bottom up', examining how the oppressed experience education rather than educating the privileged. She focuses on lived experience, considers how it shapes knowing, and queries why it is frequently silenced and invalidated. To hooks, education and how we know are political. To Black folks who had been denied education, it was political. She recalls her experience in her all-Black grade school where teachers situated education in 'antiracist struggle' and she 'experienced learning as revolution' since learning and 'a life of the mind, was a counter-hegemonic act, a fundamental way to resist every strategy of white racist colonization' (hooks, 1994: 2). By contrast, when she entered university, the classroom became oppressive, as learning became an exercise in memorizing and repeating rather than thinking critically. Learning was about acquiring knowledge to be reproduced as needed, rather than engaging creatively in thinking and learning.

hooks recalls her experience at university when members of marginalized groups were not readily admitted. Her aspirations to be a critical thinker threatened authority. Marginalized students were expected to conform, whereas white male students were free to 'chart their intellectual journeys'. Difference was 'viewed with suspicion' and seen to mask 'inferiority or work'. hooks (1994: 4–5) recounts:

> In those days, those of us from marginal groups who were allowed to enter prestigious, predominantly white colleges were made to feel that we were there not to learn but to prove that we were the equal of whites. We were there to prove this by showing how well we could become clones of our peers.

In *Teaching to Transgress*, hooks argues that theory should liberate (hooks, 1994). Learning should be about the practice of freedom, questioning, challenging norms, and being able to express oneself from one's own positionality and perspective without having to conform to standards and roles that society imposes and expects.

In the classroom, hooks does not see students and teachers as separate where one disseminates knowledge that others consume. Rather, she considers that teaching and learning should engage students to actively participate in their learning. Teachers ought to value the presence of all members of a class and recognize that in the classroom, everyone influences and contributes to the dynamic (ibid.: 7–12). As all are located or positioned in society differently, recognizing diverse standpoints is important to creating an open space in which all learn from each other. By breaking the boundaries between students and teacher and opening the learning space to diverse perspectives, hooks begins to dissolve social, racial, and gender hierarchies between students and members of society. hooks (ibid.: 10) advances a radical approach to education through combining 'anticolonial, critical, and feminist pedagogies'. This opens the possibility of moving beyond boundaries to interrogate 'biases in curricula that re-inscribe systems of domination' and to innovate teaching methods for diverse sets of students. hooks decolonizes education. She challenges top-down models of teaching and questions bodies of knowledge that reinforce oppressive systems of power. Her work on Black women thinkers brings marginal voices to the classroom and opens new pedagogical avenues (hooks, 1982; 1984; 1994).

When individuals speak from the standpoint of identity, experience, and positionality, they do so from their own particular perspective. Although this perspective is forged out of shared experience among people of that particular identity group, it is not essentialist since it does not claim to be a universalist perspective that determines how members of a particular group ought to be. For example, when talking of a Black woman's experience, hooks refers to the position of Black women in society and their particular experiences. For instance, she cites Anna Julia Cooper who wrote: 'The colored woman of today occupies . . . a unique position in this country . . . She is confronted by a woman question and a race problem, and is as yet an unknown or unacknowledged factor in both' (hooks, 1984: 166). She further cites Mary Church Terrell, a 'black female activist' who appealed to white women to join with Black women 'in the anti-lynching crusade' (ibid.: 169–170). Her understanding of different groups and their relations is textured. She considers various perspectives. She does not make blanket statements about being, rather, she shows how groups of people experience such statements and become categorized, stereotyped by false perceptions and myths. Like Aristotle, hooks observes what happens in the real world, however, she does not draw conclusions regarding rigid essences and the nature of things. Instead, she develops an understanding of the present through examination of ways of being, of social, gender, and racial relations, of the ideas and structures that keep these in place; in turn, she deconstructs these to show that they are fluid and could be otherwise.

> ### 🛈 3.4 Theories of knowing and being: Key Points
>
> - To Aristotle, all life is connected and living things have purposive ends and essences.
> - Aristotle argues that all movement in the universe is of animate objects fulfilling their potentials and ends. It reflects the cycle of birth, growth, and decay.
> - Aristotle observes that we know the physical world through our senses and experience; from this experience we can formulate conceptual knowledge. To Aristotle, this is essentialist, whereas, to hooks, it is constructed from the perspective of the knowing (individual) subject.
> - To hooks, knowledge is constructed and all innovative thinking comes from those on the margins who contest set bodies of knowledge.
> - hooks sees theory as critical thinking and a site of liberation.

3.5 Human nature and subjectivity

Most political theorists examine human nature in terms of the category of man and construct understandings of social organization for men. The focus on man excludes women as political agents. Other theorists, namely feminists and poststructuralists, consider that human beings are socialized beings who are constructed by society through processes of socialization. These two approaches are central to political theory.

3.5.1 Aristotle on human nature

Like other gregarious animals, human beings are social, they live together. But they are unique because they have the capacity for language and speech. Human beings can communicate with each other, organize their collective lives, and choose their political structures (Aristotle, 1996: 1252b–1253a). Aristotle asserts that man's highest end is to be active in politics and to advance the good of all. 'Hence it is evident that the state is a creation of nature, and that man is by nature a political animal. And he who by nature and not by mere accident is without a state, is either a bad man or above humanity' (ibid.: 1253a). Man's essence and meaning can be realized only through living in a political community. The *polis* is not defined by the individuals that comprise it; rather, the city-state is natural and antecedent to the individual which is a part of the whole. Moreover, when well constituted, the *polis* is the 'highest of all' political communities and 'it aims . . . at the highest good' (ibid.: 1252a). The end (*telos*) of the *polis* is the good life.

In his understanding of human beings, Aristotle distinguishes between the soul and the body. The soul (or psyche) is associated with reason, language, and culture. It represents the rational part of a person and corresponds to the mind (Arneil, 1999: 5, 17). The body is associated with nature and instinct; it is not rational. Aristotle further distinguishes between two parts of the body: the spirit which motivates individuals to act (ambition or passion) and appetite (desire and need). 'A living creature', he observes, 'consists in the first place of soul and body, and of these two the one is by nature the ruler and the other the subject' (Aristotle, 1996: 1254a). The rational part of the soul is subdivided into practical and theoretical reason. Individuals use practical reason to calculate, deliberate, and make decisions in their daily lives about variable things in the present moment. In the real world, things are subject to change and the decisions made in the everyday world are not permanent. Individuals use theoretical reason to contemplate unchanging and timeless first principles. This type of reasoning requires knowledge and a capacity to use logic and mathematical analysis to develop understandings of truth, final ends, and essences (Aristotle, 1980: 1141a–1142b).

The irrational part is also subdivided into two parts: the nutritive and appetitive. The nutritive is instinctive and distinct from reason. Human beings act according to instinct when they need to eat or sleep. The appetitive is based on desire and want, not instinctive need and must be controlled by reason such that it is satisfied but not over-indulged (Roberts and Sutch, 2004: 50–51; Oakeshott, 2006: 122–123).

To Aristotle, reason ought to dominate instinct and appetite, as opposed to the inverse. Individuals use reason to deliberate and make choices between many impulses, such as the expedient and inexpedient, good and evil, just and unjust. Individuals use reason to choose the best course of action to achieve their ends to the best of their ability and to realize the excellence inherent in human nature by fulfilling their potential. Individuals can achieve happiness (*eudaimonia*) when acting in moderation and making choices that align with the moral excellence of character. To Aristotle, happiness is the goal of human life, and it obtains when individuals achieve their *telos*. When individuals act in moderation, they neither deny irrational instinct or impulse nor over-indulge these. Rather, they satisfy their bodily needs without excess. In this manner, they achieve a balance or a mean. This balance of the soul and the capacity to make reasoned choices to fulfil one's ends produces happiness (Coleman, 2000: 158; Oakeshott, 2006: 123). However, this applies mainly to men since they have the full capacity to reason and deliberate (Aristotle, 1980: 1141a).

As Aristotle looks for 'the intentions of nature', he does not examine corrupt or imperfect objects, rather, he studies 'the man who is in the most perfect state both of body and soul for in him we shall see the true relation of the two' (Aristotle, 1996: 1254b). He sets a normative and ideal standard against which others are measured. In the perfect man, the soul rules over the body and the rational over the passionate. This is a natural and expedient relationship that reflects the order of the universe. Any equality between the superior (rational) and inferior parts (the instinctive and appetitive) of a person or a reversal of these roles is harmful. In like manner, in the perfect city-state, the rational part of the community should rule over the less rational parts that are associated with work and producing the material objects necessary for life.

According to Aristotle, women and children do not have the full capacity to reason and deliberate; slaves lack reason altogether. Although boys will grow to acquire reason, women and slaves are seen to be dominated by passion and are associated with the body. Women produce children and slaves use their body for work. Aristotle's assertion that women have only partial capacity to reason bars them from taking part in public debate and in ruling. Without access to education, women were denied the opportunity to develop their rational capacities and theoretical reason.

The division between the soul and the body corresponded to a division between the public and private spaces. Aristotle considered male heads of households best suited to rule since they enjoyed the full capacity to reason, were educated, and were experienced in ruling over the home. When these men leave the private sphere and enter the public sphere, they are transformed as they come together with other like men out of choice as equals to rule for the whole of the city. They become citizens. Life in the *polis* creates a new type of relationship: friendship.

For men to reach their ends as rational and moral beings, certain social and economic conditions must be met. These conditions can be fulfilled in a political community: a *polis*. The various parts of the community contribute to creating a self-sufficient *polis* that would satisfy the mutual needs of all and provide the conditions for all to fulfil their roles in life, notably for men to obtain the highest human potential as political animals by sharing in ruling and being ruled. This is the good life, by which Aristotle does not mean bare life consisting in the simple provision of minimal needs and security. Rather, the good life obtains when all parts fulfil their ends and satisfy mutual needs, including intellectual, artistic, and material needs. The division of roles and labour allows the city-state to function well and flourish (Aristotle, 1980: 1162a).

3.5.2 bell hooks on subjectivity

bell hooks does not present a fixed sense of human nature or any idea of what human beings should be. Instead, she talks about subjectivity. She understands human beings as subjects who are constructed through the social and political fabric within which they exist. They are not objects constructed through the eyes of those in power, rather, they are agents who can resist and forge their own selves and identities (hooks, 2015: 15). The freedom to resist society's conceptualization of individuals and their specific roles is central to her understanding of human agency.

To fully understand one's subjectivity from a critical standpoint, a person should acknowledge where they are coming from, along with the bias attached to that perspective. In addition, one must recognize the broader societal structures that constitute identities. Once individuals understand their subjectivity in this complex manner, then they are able to liberate themselves from personal bias and oppose the social constraints that define, categorize, and label. hooks (ibid.: 15), explains that the process of becoming subjects emerges as one understands how systems of 'domination work in one's own life, as one develops critical thinking and critical consciousness, as one invents new, alternative habits of being, and resists from that marginal space of difference inwardly defined'. This is a process of resistance and one can never completely free oneself of the environmental factors that produce the person. But one can produce one's subjectivity in one's own way.

As an African-American woman, hooks is particularly concerned with the struggle for radical Black subjectivity. She argues that the quest to make the self and identity involves opposing normative power structures and liberating the subject from these. From the vantage point of the margins, she observes that the dominant class believes it constitutes the norm and the ideal human being; moreover, it essentializes marginalized groups in disparaging ways. Although it is liberating to refute the idea that there is a Black 'essence', this is not the same process as constituting Black identity. hooks (1990) argues that Black subjectivity emerges from the 'experiences of exile and struggle'.

As individuals acknowledge their subjectivity with respect to their own self-conceptions, positionalities as well as how others view them and how they see others (see also the work of W.E.B. Du Bois, explored in Chapter 31), then they can begin to break down barriers and relate to themselves and others on a new 'deconstructed' terrain.

> **Key Concept: Positionality and standpoint**
>
> Positionality refers how one's standing, outlook, and prospects in society are formed by gender, race, class, sexuality, disability, and age. The intersection of these also affects privilege and oppression. So, a white heteronormative, middle-class man occupies a position of authority and privilege by virtue of his masculinity, whiteness, and economic security; whereas a working-class, Black woman occupies a position of oppression, given her femininity, Blackness, and economic precarity. Positionality situates subjects within the world, shapes how they experience, know and interpret it, and read others. Acknowledgement of one's positionality allows one to recognize their standpoint and bias.

hooks considers how identity operates in persistent gender, racial, and social hierarchies that stratify present-day society. On the one hand, identity is essentialized as it functions to categorize and organize groups of people into a hierarchy of privileged to underprivileged. On the other hand, although one may be part of a particular group, this does not mean that they are necessarily defined essentially by that group. One's personal experience will not necessarily conform to the essentialist definition and might operate to repudiate it. hooks (1990) rejects essentialism and outdated understandings of identity that impose 'a narrow constricting notion of blackness' on Black folk.

She concurs with postmodernist 'critiques of essentialism which challenge notions of universality and static over-determined identity within mass culture and mass consciousness', for this sort of critical thinking opens 'new possibilities for the construction of the self and the assertion of agency'.

hooks (2003: 18) speaks from the position of a Black woman who grew up in the segregated American South; even though she now occupies a position of privilege as an academic, she still defends and articulates the position of the oppressed. In her view, the most 'fascinating construction of Black subjectivity emerges' from these margins (hooks, 2015: 19).

> ### 3.5 Human nature and subjectivity: Key Points
>
> - Aristotle understands human beings to be constituted by rational and irrational parts: the mind, which operates according to reason, and the body, driven by desire and instinct.
> - According to Aristotle, reason must dominate over desire and instinct; individuals use theoretical reason to contemplate abstract ideas and practical reason which draws on concrete knowledge to deliberate and function in the everyday world.
> - Subjectivity, to hooks, refers to how individual subjects are constituted by external powers, their capacity to negate these and to assert their own personhood.
> - In hooks' view, subjectivity is a repudiation of not being an object (defined by others and objectified) and being a subject (constituting oneself).

3.6 The domestic sphere

3.6.1 Aristotle on the household

To understand the political community, Aristotle breaks the whole into its component parts until he gets to the smallest unit. He examines the ends of each part, the relations between the parts as well as the ends of these relations.

Aristotle considered the union between man and woman to be the oldest type of community and the basic unit of the family. Human beings are born into and live in families. Family was the main centre of life, and extended family provided a broader social network and support system (Springborg, 1992: 12–15). The family reproduced life, provided basic needs, and nurtured both emotionally and physically (Aristotle, 1996: 1252a; Arneil, 1999: 14). Household and family arrangements teach children about authority and obedience. These structures underpin political order and determine who has the authority to rule (Brunt, 1993: 356–359). Aristotle observed that the household is constituted by freemen, women, children, and slaves, and is ruled by men: 'the rule of a household is a monarchy, for every house is under one head; whereas constitutional rule which is a government of freemen and equals' (Aristotle, 1996: 1255b). Within the household, there were several types of rule that the head exercised over each of the parts. Patriarchal rule (*oikonomikon*) characterized the authority of husband over wife, paternalistic rule (*basilikon*) of father over child, and despotic rule (patrimonial) of master over slave (Springborg, 1992: 10).

Each type of rule reflects the degree of control over the parts. Patriarchal rule of men over women gives men access to women's bodies for reproduction (Pateman, 1988: 2). Paternalistic rule teaches children about male power, notably that fatherly authority focuses on caring for children for their own good in the same way that a king rules over his subjects for their own good. Despotic rule over slaves is the absolute command over human beings who are considered to be the material property and patrimony of the master (Springborg, 1992: 10). Each type of power is justified on the basis of nature and the natural order of things: that the rational part (men) dominate over the less rational parts (women, children, slaves).

The household is a reproductive structure and each relationship has a *telos*. The relationship between man and woman is reproduction and that between the master and slave produces work to support the household structure as well as basic needs. The structure of the household stratifies the various roles of individuals that contribute to the overall well-being of society. However, as these are essentialized—defined by purposive ends—they become rigid and there is little room for mobility and change. In addition, socio-economic relations between property owners and non-property owners, between wealthy and popular social classes—the *demos*—were unequal. Poor people, 'slaves, peasant farmers, craftsmen or day labourers' were not included in Aristotle's political society (Brunt, 1993: 358). Propertied classes enjoyed the leisure time to be educated and to rule. They possessed the authority of knowing and this underscored their political authority.

Together households form tribes that associate with others to create a community. The political association arises for the exchange of goods without which there would be no association (Aristotle, 1980: 1133b). The *polis* furnishes the mutual needs of society and creates the setting in which men can reach their highest human potential as political animals. Each part has a function and an end. Together they work in harmony for the common good and the good life.

3.6.1.1 Slaves

Aristotle contends that there are slaves by nature. He develops his argument for natural slavery in the first book of *The Politics*. It is important to consider his arguments, for they were revisited in the Renaissance (from the fourteenth to the seventeenth centuries) and used to justify the enslavement of Indigenous peoples and Africans in the new World (Brunt, 1993: 343–346; Blackburn, 1998: 35). Aristotle categorizes slaves as tools, as bodies that are owned and absolutely subordinate to the household head.

> The master is only the master of the slave; he does not belong to him, whereas the slave is not only the slave of his master, but wholly belongs to him. Hence we see what is the nature and office of a slave; he who is by nature not his own but another's man, is by nature a slave; and he may be said to be another's man who, being a slave, is also a possession. And a possession may be defined as an instrument of action, separable from the possessor.
>
> (Aristotle, 1996: 1254a)

Again, the principle that the rational soul ought to rule over the irrational physical body applies. To Aristotle, the master controls the slave's body as if it were an extension of his own body. The slave is 'part of the master, a living but separated part of his bodily frame' (ibid.: 1255b; 1980: 1134a; Brunt, 1993: 358–359). Slaves are denied their existence as human beings. They are considered to be objects, tools used for work in the household and are entirely dependent on the command of the master. Aristotle (1996: 1253b) states: 'in the arrangement of the family, a slave is a living possession, and property [is] a number of such instruments'.

Aristotle's view of slaves is dehumanizing. He compares slaves to domesticated animals since both use their bodies to provide the things for life. Aristotle draws on 'reason and fact' to defend such claims. He asks if nature *intended* some to be slaves. He determines that it is necessary and expedient 'that some should rule and others be ruled' and that 'from the hour of their birth, some are marked out for subjection, others for rule' (ibid.: 1254a). His justification of slavery is instrumental because it is expedient for slaves to do work, and moral since nature intends some people for slavery (ibid.: 1255b). Any abuse of the authority that the master exercises over the slave would cause injury to both, since the interests of the whole and part, soul and body are the same.

Aristotle also recognizes slavery by convention, where it is justified to enslave peoples conquered in a just war (ibid.: 1255a; Brunt, 1993: 354).

Aristotle's defence of slavery is tenuous and constructed. Slavery is a relationship of power. Absolute domination requires not only the power of a master, but also the complicity of local social, economic, and political structures to maintain it. Some people may be dependent on others since they do not have the capacity to live independently. Yet this neither means that there is a complete lack of rationality and deliberation, nor does it follow that they should be enslaved, exploited, or tied to domestic labour with neither voice nor freedom.

Aristotle's view that slavery is natural because slaves lack rational and deliberative capacities is morally and ethically questionable. Despotic rule over slaves prevented rational and deliberative development. It entailed the systematic denial of education, enforced labour, physical, emotional, and psychological brutalization. His perspective is not simply a consequence of his time and place. In his day, slavery was controversial. Not all Greeks thought that slavery was natural. Some considered all men free and none a slave. For example, Alcidamas and Antiphon, fourth- and fifth-century BCE thinkers, respectively, made statements against slavery (Brunt, 1993: 351–359).

Aristotle's views on slavery were authoritative and travelled across space and time. Thomas Aquinas and John Locke (see Chapter 7 on Locke) rearticulated Aristotelian justifications for slavery (ibid.: 345–355) and his justification of slavery was debated in the Spanish Valladolid Debates of 1550 on the enslavement of Africans in the Americas (Blackburn, 1997). In the modern world, as in ancient Greece, slaves were treated as commodities to 'be bought, sold, hired, pledged, bequeathed like any other asset' (Brunt, 1993: 347). In the USA, Black Africans were enslaved and forced to work in the plantation household. In the context of European colonial empire, the argument that some are naturally superior and others inferior was reformulated in terms of race. Whiteness was seen to be superior to Blackness (Mills, 2007).

3.6.1.2 Women

Aristotle draws on a similar rationale to justify the subordination of women in the home. Unlike slaves, Aristotle concedes that women have partial rational and deliberative capacities since they raise children. Yet their capacities lack authority (Aristotle, 1996: 1260a; 1980: 1161a–1162b). On the one hand, he recognizes that women, like men, are capable of reason and deliberation. On the other, he argues that men and women do not have the same temperament, courage, and justice. At bottom, he subordinates women to men: 'the male is by nature superior, and the female inferior; and the one rules, and the other is ruled; this principle, of necessity, extends to all mankind' (Aristotle, 1996: 1254b). This claim is universal and categorical. In addition, he assigns roles to each sex which if fulfilled would advance excellence of character. Men command and women obey (ibid.: 1260a).

In *The Politics*, Aristotle cites and endorses the poet Sophocles' claim that 'Silence is a woman's glory'. Immediately after, he distinguishes that this is not a man's glory (ibid.: 1260a). This speech act dismisses women's voices as insignificant and excludes women from public life as well as education. At the same time, the attempt to silence women displays a fear of women's voices and demonstrates that women are not inferior.

Aristotle's position on gender inequality is constructed through the hierarchies of the household and in the power relations between men and women (Samaras, 2016). At the time, this was not a universal perspective. Socrates held that women and men were equally apt. Some women, such as the poet Sappho, had a voice, and in Greek mythology women held powerful roles and some ruled, such as Helen of Troy (Aristotle, 1980: 1160; Dubois, 1988).

> ### Key Thinker: Sappho
>
> Plato (see Chapter 2) called Sappho (c. 610–570 BCE) the tenth muse for she comprised nine volumes of poetry that explored eroticism, beauty, goodness, and community. She is best-known for her love poems addressed to women. Her work also touched on pre-Socratic philosophical themes such as the notions of permanence and change. Unfortunately, much of her work is lost as it was stored in the Library of Alexandria, which burnt down. Some complete poems and fragments exist and continue to be found (Lardinois, 2014).

Aristotle conceptualized the household as the cornerstone of society; it provided the necessaries for life and included both material and living parts. The household head had slaves and women to produce what he needed to live and reproduce. In this conception, the household was the property and extension of the life of man (Arneil, 1999: 17).

3.6.2 hooks on homeplace

hooks' conception of 'homeplace' subverts the patriarchal household that Aristotle imagines. She considers home foundational to political society since the values and types of authority learned in the home are reproduced in society. Therefore, she argues that home ought to be a place of nurturing that supports and affirms human dignity.

hooks (2015) presents an understanding of the African-American homeplace as a humanizing space in which Black people escaped the dehumanizing violence of slavery and racism. Homeplace subverted debasing master-slave relations. In the white supremacist patriarchal plantation household, slaves were denied the possibility of building lasting relationships. They could be sold at the master's whim. Marriage was illegal; partners, mothers and children were torn apart. Black women were raped by white men and forced to breed with other slaves (hooks, 1982: 35–45). The culture of slavery continues to pervade American society in the form of white supremacy and racism. It seeks to eradicate the space and conditions under which Black people could develop self-esteem and self-love.

hooks (2015: 43) avers: 'For those who dominate and oppress us benefit most when we have nothing to give our own, when they have so taken from us our dignity, our humanness that we have nothing left, no "homeplace" where we can recover ourselves.' One could retreat to homeplace both physically and emotionally. This was a safe space where Black people could validate each other, share their humanity, and heal the injuries of white aggression. Here, African Americans affirmed their dignity, Blackness, and integrity of being (ibid.: 46). Homeplace could be found in the slave hut, the wooden shack during reconstruction and, eventually, after emancipation, the family home on the other side of the tracks.

Homeplace was a creation of Black women and represented their conscious resistance to white supremacist oppression and degradation. They did not do this because it was their 'natural' role. Black women worked long hours, yet they were determined to create transformative nurturing spaces in which their families were valued, could develop critical consciousness and learn 'to be revolutionaries able to struggle for freedom', such as Frederick Douglass (see Chapter 30) (hooks, 2015: 44). Black women gave positive values to their families and community. Homeplace became the site for political organization in the struggle for liberation. It was the backbone for Black solidarity, political consciousness, and community values.

After emancipation from slavery, family was important for Black people as it provided 'the only sustained support system for exploited and oppressed peoples' (hooks, 1984: 37). As African

Americans built family life, racist myths made it difficult to maintain supportive relations. Black men were seen to be emasculated, and Black women were portrayed as strong 'masculinized sub-human creatures' (hooks, 1982: 71) who could withstand any abuse. To provide for the family, women had to work, usually in debasing domestic service jobs. Often, Black men were unemployed either due to racism or because they rejected menial jobs that de-masculinized and un-manned them. As such, the Black family was portrayed as matriarchal. To hooks (1982: 71–91), this was a false assumption since Black men neither relinquished their role as household head nor their masculinity. 'Many black men who did not feel at all personally de-masculinized absorbed sexist ideology' (ibid.: 79) Yet, hooks discerns, 'White sociologists presented the matriarchy myth in such a way that it implied black women had "power" in the family and black men had none . . . and these [false] conclusions fostered divisiveness between black men and women' (ibid.: 80). Nevertheless, these myths made Black men reassert their manliness by subjugating Black women. These myths devalued Black women, reinforced patriarchy, and sexism and undid their work in creating homeplace and resisting racism. Sexism prevented Black women and men from uniting against racism.

3.6.2.1 Struggles for freedom and the alienation of Black women

Two decades after the American Civil Rights movement, hooks wondered why systemic inequality persisted when women and Black people had acquired civil and political rights. In *Ain't I a Woman: Black Women and Feminism*, a title that takes its name from Sojourner Truth's famous speech (see Chapter 2 on Truth), hooks (1982: 1) detects 'a profound silence engendered by resignation and acceptance of one's lot' among Black women. She contends Black women felt powerless because they were subject to racism from white men and women and sexism from white and Black men.

Black male leaders of both the nineteenth-century struggle for the vote and the 1960s Black Power movement alienated Black women. Black men expected Black women to support them, but they did not advocate that Black women get the vote or acquire equal rights (by contrast, see Angela Davis, 1983: 43–53, and Chapter 35 on Davis). Even in the 1960s, Black men expected Black women to submit to their authority (hooks, 1982: 91–95). Black women found themselves in an awkward position: to support the movement would promote patriarchy; to withdraw support amounted to going against anti-racist struggles and their own people. This overt sexism prevented Black men and women from uniting to resist racism (ibid.: 115). Although hooks (ibid.: 5) recognizes the radical gains Black Americans achieved through these movements, she criticizes Black Power for changing its goal to 'free all black people from racist oppression' to establishing Black male patriarchy.

Similarly, the nineteenth-century suffragist movement for the vote and the 1960s Women's Liberation struggle for equality excluded Black women and were racist against them. In the nineteenth century, Black women did not fit the idea of woman as white (see also the ideas of Sojourner Truth, explored in Chapter 2). In the twentieth century, white women claimed to speak for all women and equated their oppression with that of Black people, effectively silencing the voice of Black women. Each time white women compared their position with that of Black people, Black women were diminished (ibid.: 135–142). hooks points out that this erasure reflected a subtle form of racism whereby 'the dominant race . . . reserves for itself the luxury of dismissing racial identity while the oppressed race is made daily aware of their racial identity' (ibid.: 138). The dominant race makes their experience seem representative. In her view, white women were not genuinely concerned about the plight of Black people. They aligned themselves with Black Power to advance their own interests against white men, to depict themselves as non-racist and non-classist. Moreover, their sisterhood with Black women was rhetorical. Inequality between white and Black women in the workforce persisted. Often, Black women worked for white women in domestic service. Relations between Black and white women were complex and steeped in racism and classism.

hooks (1984: 37) acknowledges the radical potential of feminism to repudiate gender inequality in the home, especially since sexist oppression is the most common and accepted practice of domination, and children are exposed to it early on.

hooks stresses that both Black men and white women aspired to be part of the white capitalist patriarchal system. Black men wanted to maintain patriarchy and be equal to white men. White women wanted to equally share in the capitalist society. Moreover, since both groups desired equality within white male power structures, they would effectively give white men the privilege and power to determine the grounds of equality. She laments that racism in the women's liberation movement undermined its radical potential and that sexism in the Black Power movement prevented it from overthrowing patriarchy (hooks, 1982: 156–158).

hooks advocates a radical Black feminist movement that 'has as its fundamental goal the liberation of all people' (ibid.: 15). This would require the eradication of both racism and sexism. In her understanding of the home and liberation, there is an intersection of homeplace and feminism. Both subvert the white patriarchal household that serves the interests of the state and upholds coercive authority. Homeplace acts as a site of resistance to racism and supports humanizing relations in families and community. Feminism insists 'the purpose of family structure is not to reinforce patterns of domination in the interests of the state' (hooks, 1984: 37–38). Both struggles contain the radical potential to reinvent family life and to create a 'positive social equality that grants all humans the opportunity to shape their destinies in the most healthy and communally productive way' (hooks, 1982: 117).

> **3.6 The domestic sphere: Key Points**
>
> - Structures of the home and family relations reflect and support political structures.
> - Aristotle promotes the superiority of the rational (men) over the inferior less rational parts of the household (women, slaves, and children) as the best sort of rule.
> - hooks develops an innovative understanding of Black women's resistance to imperialist patriarchal domination in homeplace through the creation of a nurturing safe space.
> - Black women suffer sexist and racist oppression from white men, Black men and white women, and exclusion from Black male and white feminist political struggles for freedom.

3.7 Conclusion

We do not associate 'identity politics' with Aristotle, yet it is clear that one's gender, social class, race, and the location or city-state in which one was born affect the role one has in life as well as the political, social, and economic privileges that one may enjoy. The legacy of hooks is to show that race and sex shape who we are and that their intersection can both oppress and privilege. She does not advance a system of equality in which all would be the same. Rather, she seeks to eliminate the structures and systems that underpin inequality in the relations between genders and races. These radically different conceptions of politics determine boundaries in different manners. To Aristotle, there is a natural order to the universe that structures the place and role of all individuals; whereas, to hooks, both the political subject and political society are constructed and mutually constitutive. As such, there is room for change.

Take your learning further by accessing the online resources for a library of web links to relevant videos, articles, blogs, and useful websites for this chapter: **www.oup.com/he/Ramgotra-Choat1e**.

Study questions

1. How does positionality affect Aristotle's and hooks' political thinking?
2. According to Aristotle, what is teleology?
3. How does teleology influence contemporary understandings of human development and struggle?
4. To what extent do Aristotle's and bell hooks' languages of 'political activity' and 'political activism' construct contrasting perspectives and understandings of politics?
5. How does Aristotle's understanding of human nature differ from bell hooks' notion of subjectivity?
6. Are there similarities between Aristotle's conception of social roles and identity?
7. Is home a place of hierarchy or resistance?
8. How does hooks' view of knowledge and being undermine arguments for hierarchy as natural?

Further reading

Primary sources

Aristotle (1984) *The Complete Works of Aristotle: The Revised Oxford Translation*. Princeton, NJ: Princeton University Press.
This volume brings together all of Aristotle's surviving works.

Aristotle (1996) *The Politics and the Constitution of Athens*. Trans. B. Jowett, ed. S. Everson. Cambridge: Cambridge University Press.
This standard translation of Aristotle's *Politics* is useful. It contains parts of other works and a glossary of terms.

Aristotle (2011) *Aristotle's Nicomachean Ethics*. Trans. R.C. Bartlett and S.D. Collins. Chicago: Chicago University Press.
This recent translation tries to be literal and consistent in rendering ancient Greek words into English.

hooks, b. (1982) *Ain't I a Woman: Black Women and Feminism*. London: Pluto Press.
Without doubt, hooks' best-known work that examines the double oppression of Black women.

hooks, b. (1984) *Feminist Theory from Margin to Center*. Boston: South End Press.
This follow-up to *Ain't I a Woman* develops hooks' theory and refines her thinking.

hooks, b. (1994) *Teaching to Transgress: Education as the Practice of Freedom*. London: Routledge.
An excellent collection of essays that challenges educators to change traditional practices and pushes theorists to reconsider how theory and practice can liberate.

hooks, b. (2015) *Yearning: Race, Gender, and Cultural Politics*. Abingdon: Routledge.
A recent volume of essays that explores homeplace and subjectivity.

Secondary sources

Florence, N. (1998) *bell hooks' Engaged Pedagogy: A Transgressive Education for Critical Consciousness*. Westport, CT: Bergin & Garvey.
Explores the main themes of hooks' critical, social, and educational theories, notably in relation to intersectional oppressions.

Frank, J. (2005) *A Democracy of Distinction: Aristotle and the Work of Politics*. Chicago: Chicago University Press.
Provides a comprehensive understanding of Aristotle's politics in light of contemporary debates on democracy.

Freeland, C.A. (1998) *Feminist Interpretations of Aristotle*. University Park, PA: Pennsylvania State University Press.
A broad collection of essays that looks at gender in various aspects of Aristotle's thinking.

References

Anderson, E.A. (1999) 'What Is the Point of Equality?' *Ethics*, 109(2): 287-337.

Aristotle (1980) *The Nicomachean Ethics*. Trans. D. Ross, revised by J.L. Ackrill and J.O. Urmson. Oxford: Oxford University Press.

Aristotle (1996) *The Politics and the Constitution of Athens*. Trans. B. Jowett, ed. S. Everson. Cambridge: Cambridge University Press.

Arneil, B. (1999) *Politics & Feminism*. Oxford: Blackwell Publishers Ltd.

Benjamin, I. (2006) *The Invention of Racism in Classical Antiquity*. Princeton, NJ: Princeton University Press.

Bernal, M. (1991) *Black Athena: The Afroasiatic Roots of Classical Civilization*, vol. I: *The Fabrication of Ancient Greece*. London: Vintage.

Blackburn, R. (1998) *The Making of New World Slavery: From the Baroque to the Modern, 1492-1800*. London: Verso.

Brunt, P.A. (1993) 'Aristotle and Slavery'. In *Studies in Greek History and Thought*. Oxford: Oxford University Press, pp. 343-388.

Coleman, J. (2000) *A History of Political Thought from Ancient to Early Christianity*. Vol. I. Oxford: Blackwell.

Davis, A. (1983) *Women, Race and Class*. New York: Vintage Books.

Dietz, M.G. (2012) 'Between Polis and Empire: Aristotle's Politics'. *American Political Science Review*, 106(2): 275-293.

Dubois, P. (1988) *Sowing the Body: Psychoanalysis and Ancient Representations of Women*. Chicago: University of Chicago Press.

Frank, J. (2004) 'Citizens, Slaves, and Foreigners: Aristotle on Human Nature'. *American Political Science Review*, 98(1): 91-104.

Frank, J. (2019) 'Athenian Democracy and Its Critics'. *Ethnic and Racial Studies*, 42(8): 1306-1312.

Hacking, I. (1999) *The Social Construction of What?* London: Harvard University Press.

Hanchard, M. (2019) 'Response to Ethnic and Racial Studies Interlocutors'. *Ethnic and Racial Studies*, 42(8): 1333-1340.

Hanisch, C. (1970) 'The Personal Is Political'. In S. Firestone and A. Koedt (eds), *Notes from the Second Year: Women's Liberation Major Writings of the Radical Feminists*. New York: Radical Feminism.

hooks, b. (1982) *Ain't I a Woman: Black Women and Feminism*. London: Pluto Press.

hooks, b. (1984) *Feminist Theory from Margin to Center*. Boston: South End Press.

hooks, b. (1990) 'Postmodern Blackness'. *Postmodern Culture: Journal of Interdisciplinary Thought of Contemporary Cultures*, 1(1). doi: 10.1353/pmc.1990.0004 (accessed 10 April 2020).

hooks, b. (1994) *Teaching to Transgress: Education as the Practice of Freedom*. London: Routledge.

hooks, b. (2003) *Teaching Community: A Pedagogy of Hope*. Abingdon: Routledge.

hooks, b. (2012) *Writing Beyond Race: Living Theory and Practice*. Abingdon: Routledge.

hooks, b. (2015) *Yearning: Race, Gender, and Cultural Politics*. Abingdon: Routledge.

Lardinois, A. (2014) 'Introduction'. In *Sappho: A New Translation of the Complete Works*. Ed. and trans. D. Rayor. Cambridge: Cambridge University Press.

Mills, C.W. (2007) 'White Ignorance'. In S. Sullivan and N. Tuana (eds), *Race and Epistemologies of Ignorance*. Albany, NY: State University of New York Press.

Oakeshott, M. (2006) *Lectures in the History of Political Thought*. Ed. T. Nardin and L. O'Sullivan. Exeter: Imprint Academic.

Pateman, C. (1988) *The Sexual Contract*. Stanford, CA: Stanford University Press.

Roberts, P. and Sutch, P. (2004) *An Introduction to Political Thought: A Conceptual Toolkit*. Edinburgh: Edinburgh University Press.

Rodriguez, P-A. (2016) 'L'impérialisme institutionnel et la question de la race chez Aristote'. *European Review of History/Revue Européenne d'Histoire*, 23(4): 751-767.

Samaras, T. (2016) 'Aristotle on Gender in *Politics* I'. *History of Political Thought*, 37(4): 595-605.

Springborg, P. (1992) *Western Republicanism and the Oriental Prince*. Austin, TX: University of Texas Press.

Squires, J. (2004) 'Politics Beyond Boundaries: A Feminist Perspective'. In A. Leftwich (ed.), *What Is Politics? The Activity and Its Study*. Cambridge: Polity Press, pp. 119-134.

4 Kautilya

DEEPSHIKHA SHAHI

Chapter guide

This chapter presents the seminal work of Kautilya—*Arthaśāstra*. The *Arthaśāstra* (literally meaning 'the science of material gain') has been unanimously accepted not only as one of the most precious works of Sanskrit literature, but also as an ancient Indian compendium of principles and policies related to political science. The historiography of Kautilya's *Arthaśāstra* has provoked a fierce debate. In addition to the unsolved controversies around its chronological origins and authorship, various scholars have differently interpreted Kautilya's writings on the role of political morality. Kautilya's *Arthaśāstra* is increasingly recognized as a valuable textual resource in today's globalized world. This chapter draws insights from the English translations of Kautilya's *Arthaśāstra* to foreground its political theory. The chapter develops in three sections. Section 4.2 unfolds the 'philosophical foundation' of Kautilya's *Arthaśāstra*. A systematic study of this foundation clarifies the moral footing of Kautilya's political theory. Section 4.3 unpacks the structural and functional outlook of Kautilya's *Arthaśāstra*. A meticulous analysis of this outlook makes obvious how Kautilya's political theory is eclectic, as it fuses the allegedly conflicting rational/prudential and abstract/ideal concerns in politics, thereby outdoing the prescriptions of Eurocentric realpolitik. Finally, Section 4.4 inspects the position of gender and caste in Kautilya's political theory. In so doing, it probes the gaps between Kautilya's theoretical plan and its practical performance.

4.1 Introduction

Kautilya was the chief counsellor to Chandragupta Maurya (fourth century BCE), the first ruler of India's Maurya Dynasty. Kautilya is well known for his incredibly vast treatise—*Arthaśāstra*. Kautilya wrote *Arthaśāstra* to assist Chandragupta Maurya in his political venture to unify the Indian subcontinent as an empire. The Kautilya-inspired Maurya Dynasty, under the reign of its third ruler Aśoka (third century BCE), formed the largest historically known Indian subcontinental empire. Not surprisingly, Kautilya's *Arthaśāstra* acquired widespread recognition as an immensely important work in the entire collection of Sanskrit texts. The intellectual tradition of *Arthaśāstra* remained known through numerous citations of it in the extant Sanskrit texts, e.g., Viśākhadatta's *Mudrārākṣasa* and Kamandaka's *Nītisāra*. During his time as an Indologist at the Oriental Research Institute of Mysore in South India, R. Shamasastry received the palm-leaf manuscripts of *Arthaśāstra* from an unnamed person. When it was received in 1905, it was inscribed in the *grantha* script popularly employed by Tamil linguists. Shamasastry instantly identified the received palm-leaf manuscripts as 'Kautilya's *Arthaśāstra*', and published their Sanskrit and English translations in 1909 and 1915 respectively.

Read more about **Kautilya's** life and work by accessing the thinker biography on the online resources: www.oup.com/he/Ramgotra-Choat1e.

Over the years, a number of fresh English translations (which draw information from the discovery of additional manuscripts) have emerged—the major ones are composed by Kangle (1963) (see Key Thinker: R.P. Kangle), Rangarajan (1992), and Olivelle (2013). Due to the all-encompassing composition of this classical Indian treatise, its re-readings have influenced a variety of academic disciplines, including political science, administrative studies, jurisprudence, economics, history, and anthropology. The myriad Western and non-Western re-readings have narrowly construed this treatise as an early compendium of 'political realism'—a theory that primarily perceives political reality as a rational and prudential struggle for power (see Key Concept: Realism in Section 25.2.3 of Chapter 25). Some re-readings have criticized this treatise for its sexist and racist (casteist) standpoint. In the light of these re-readings, this chapter aims to elucidate the theoretical postures of Kautilya's *Arthaśāstra*. To do so, it is necessary to reveal its philosophical foundation. Sections 4.2 and 4.3 offer a brief discussion of the origins and authorship of Kautilya's *Arthaśāstra* before examining its philosophical foundation.

> ### Key Thinker: R.P. Kangle
>
> R.P. Kangle (1899-1999) was born into a low-ranked social group known as the Arya Kshatriya community. Despite the discrimination faced by this group, due to his extraordinary scholarly achievements, Kangle served as a professor of Sanskrit for over thirty years in several government colleges located in Gujarat, Maharashtra, and Bombay. After his retirement in 1954, between 1965 and 1972, Kangle published his research findings on Kautilya's *Arthaśāstra* in the form of a three-volume historical-critical edition: Volume I, the original Sanskrit text; Volume II, the English translation; and Volume III, a critical commentary in English, in which he explained the origin of the literary tradition of *Arthaśāstra* as a science, the issues related to its date and authorship, and its strategic relevance for contemporary statecraft, law, economics, administration, and foreign policy. He also published several other texts that revolve around the themes of ancient Indian poetics, plays, and politics.

4.2 Unfolding the philosophical foundation

Different scholars locate the origins of Kautilya's *Arthaśāstra* around the second to the fourth centuries BCE (Olivelle, 2013; Liebig and Mishra, 2017). Despite its vague chronological origins, it is commonly accepted that Kautilya's *Arthaśāstra*—stretched across 15 books, 150 chapters, 180 topics, and 6000 verses—enabled Chandragupta Maurya to fortify the Indian subcontinent as an empire. R. Boesche (2002: 8) comments:

> Kautilya was ... the genius of the strategy undertaken by the king – Chandragupta Maurya (317–293 B.C.E.), who defeated the Nanda kings, stopped the advance of Alexander the Great's successors, and first united the Indian subcontinent in empire ... [Kautilya states:] 'This science [i.e., *Arthaśāstra*] has been composed by him, who in resentment, quickly regenerated the science and the weapon and [conquered] the earth that was under control of the Nanda kings' ... Claiming only that he 'regenerated' the *Arthashastra*, Kautilya [admits that he] borrowed from previous works.

Expanding upon the regenerated character of Kautilya's *Arthaśāstra*, Olivelle (2013: 6) remarks that it is important to know whether

> [Kautilya] created a fresh text ex novo, or made use of existing material in his composition ... [*Arthaśāstra*] states at the very beginning: 'This singular Treatise on Success (*Arthaśāstra*) has been composed for the most part by drawing together the Treatises on Success (*Arthaśāstras*) composed by former teachers for gaining and administering the earth.'

The treatise of *Arthaśāstra* includes Kautilya's individual writings (Kautilya's Recession) and later textual interpolations by other scholars (Śāstric Redaction)—that is, a few books written by scholars other than Kautilya were inserted into *Arthaśāstra* (Trautmann, 1971). This *Arthaśāstra* (including the elements of Recession and Redaction) allowed Chandragupta Maurya to justify crushing the widely detested wicked regime of the Nanda kings (Bhargava, 1996).

Intriguingly, Kautilya's *Arthaśāstra* is itself not free from moral criticism. It is argued that Kautilya depicts the 'reality as it is', not as 'it ought to be' (Boesche, 2003) and, in this manner, he 'openly discards ideals' (Smith, 1957), delivers a 'document of immoral practices of kings and ministers' (Sarkar, 1919), thereby showing 'no special preference for peace in politics' (Winternitz, 1923). It was Max Weber who first noted that in comparison to the furious realpolitik (i.e., politics that prefers rational/prudential use of power) of Kautilya's *Arthaśāstra*, Machiavelli's writings were not as ruthless as they seemed to some analysts. In his famous lecture, 'Politics as a Vocation', Weber (1978: 220) notes: 'Truly radical "Machiavellianism", in the popular sense of that word, is classically expressed in . . . the Arthashâstra of Kautilya (written long before the birth of Christ, ostensibly in the time of Chandragupta [Maurya]): compared to it, Machiavelli's "Prince" is harmless.' Although this moral criticism persists, Kautilya's *Arthaśāstra* delineates the following philosophical principles:

> *Sāṃkhya, Yoga* and [*Lokāyata*] are [the] three schools of philosophy [that form the bedrock of *Arthaśāstra*] . . . One should study philosophy because it helps one to distinguish between *dharma* [moral] and *adharma* [immoral] in the study of the *Vedas* [or religious scriptures], between material gain and loss in [the study of] economics, and between good and bad policies in the study of politics . . . it teaches one the distinction between good and bad use of force [i.e., legitimacy] . . . philosophy [i.e., *anvikshaki*] is the lamp that illuminates all 'sciences'.
>
> (Rangarajan, 1992: 106)

Key Concept: *Anvikshaki* (philosophy of science)

Anvikshaki is the 'philosophy of science' that drives Kautilya's *Arthaśāstra*. It contains three philosophical constructs: *Sāṃkhya*/'numbers', *Yoga*/'aggregate', and *Lokāyata*/'worldly ones'. *Sāṃkhya* and *Yoga* accept the infallibility of God, whereas *Lokāyata* reject the infallibility of God. Kautilya reconciles these metaphysical divides to support pragmatic or practical politics. In practical politics, *Sāṃkhya*, *Yoga*, and *Lokāyata* support the following presuppositions. First, the device to explore and cope with the worldly reality is 'perception'. Second, the 'self' (as it uses perception) is interested in defending the 'identity of body and soul': the body-interest (i.e., material gratification and corporeal pleasure) and the soul-interest (i.e., moral integrity and self-liberation) are 'co-dependent'. Third, in practical politics, the 'identity of body and soul' can be defended through the conditional implementation of some moral-ethical doctrines, e.g., material enjoyment, non-injury, truthfulness, not stealing, and altruism.

A careful reading of these philosophical principles makes clear that Kautilya essentially calls for a moral judgement that separates good from bad actions as undertaken in the realms of religion, economics, and politics. This moral judgement is politically decisive as it helps to determine what is legitimate and what is illegitimate (Kangle, 1997; Olivelle, 2013). Furthermore, the strategic significance of this moral judgement indicates that Kautilya is not insensitive to the comparable consequences of 'realpolitik' (defined earlier as politics that prefers rational/prudential use of power) and 'moralpolitik' (i.e., politics that encourages abstract/ideal use of power). The Eurocentric realpolitik in the writings of Thucydides, Machiavelli, Hans Morgenthau, and Kenneth Waltz aims to realize the moral goal of self-survival through rational/prudential use of power by the 'self', which in turn, hampers the power of the 'other/s' (Forde, 1992; Rösch, 2015; Lundborg, 2018). By contrast, Kautilya attempts to merge realpolitik and moralpolitik. He exceeds the moral goal of 'survival' (*yogakshema*) and strives to achieve 'collective benefit and happiness' (*lokasamgraha*)—a vision that simultaneously promotes rational/prudential and abstract/ideal use of power so as to expand the concerted power of 'self' as well as 'other/s'.

When Kautilya strives to achieve collective benefit and happiness (*lokasamgraha*), he depends upon the concept of a 'state' made up of seven primary elements: (1) king; (2) council of ministers; (3) countryside; (4) fort; (5) treasury; (6) army; and (7) ally. These elements act like the 'seven limbs' of the allegorical organism called the state. According to this organic theory, the dynamic operation of the state needs proper synchronization between its seven elements. All these seven elements are important. Nonetheless, Kautilya proclaims that 'a king endowed with the ideal personal qualities enriches the other elements when they are less than perfect', thereby arguing that 'whatever character the king has, the other elements also come to have the same' (Sihag, 2004: 146). Kautilya divides the treatise of *Arthaśāstra* into two interrelated halves: domestic administration and foreign affairs. The first five elements (i.e., king, ministers, countryside, fort, and treasury) constitute the first half of *Arthaśāstra*, in which Kautilya discusses the matters related to domestic administration of the state. And the last two elements (i.e., army and ally) shape the second half of *Arthaśāstra*: here, Kautilya outlines the issues of diplomacy, warfare, and foreign affairs.

In the arena of foreign affairs, the conception of *mandala* (circles of states) designates the 'structural layout' of the states-system. And the principles of *sadgunya* (six-fold foreign policy) decides the 'functional orientation' of different states vis-à-vis each other. The debates on *mandala* and *sadgunya* have attracted the most attention from those scholars who intend to express the philosophical aptitude of the Asian world (Mahbubani, 2009), or display the rising power reputation of India in the contemporary world (Mitra and Liebig, 2016), as Kautilya's *Arthaśāstra* presents an established, classical, non-Western textual tradition. Moreover, recent renewed interest in this work overcomes the problem of 'Eurocentrism' which promotes the primacy of European/Western politico-experiential realities in knowledge production.

Section 4.3 explains how the structural and functional aspects of *mandala* (circles of states) and *sadgunya* (sixfold foreign policy) come together to formulate Kautilya's political theory. Here, it is important to remember that Kautilya's political theory assumes a compulsory correlation between domestic and international politics.

> ### 4.2 Unfolding the philosophical foundation: Key Points
>
> - Kautilya's *Arthaśāstra* is based on the philosophies of *Sāṃkhya*, *Yoga*, and *Lokāyata*.
> - These philosophies promote some moral-ethical doctrines in national and international politics, i.e., material enjoyment, non-injury, truthfulness, non-stealing, and altruism.
> - For Kautilya, the state is an organism with seven basic limbs: (1) king; (2) council of ministers; (3) countryside; (4) fort; (5) treasury; (6) army; and (7) ally.
> - Proper coordination among these limbs helps the state to skilfully handle domestic administration and foreign affairs.
> - The ultimate end that the state aims to achieve in domestic and international politics is twofold: (1) *yogakshema* (survival); and (2) *lokasamgraha* (benefit and happiness of all).

4.3 Circles of states and foreign policy

The notion of *mandala* (circles of states) signifies the 'structural layout' of the states-system: this layout resembles a set of abstract concentric circles which mark the strategic positioning of individual states in the states-system. Since a possible conqueror state always positions itself at the centre of *mandala*, it frequently evokes *sadgunya* (sixfold foreign policy) to decide its 'functional orientation' vis-à-vis other states. Kangle (1997: 248) clarifies:

> Foreign policy is summed up in the formula of *sadgunya* or the six measures. This formula is associated with ... the theory of *rajamandala* or circles of kings. This *mandala* is said to consist of twelve kings or states: (1) *vijigishu*, the would-be conqueror; (2) *ari*, the enemy, whose territory is contiguous to that of the *vijigishu*; (3) *mitra*, the *vijigishu*'s ally, with territory beyond that of the *ari*; (4) *arimitra*, the enemy's ally, with territory beyond that of the *mitra*; (5) *mitramitra*, the ally of the *vijigishu*'s ally, with territory beyond that of the *arimitra*; (6) *arimitramitra*, the ally of the enemy's ally, beyond *mitramitra*; (7) *pārsnigraha*, the enemy in the rear of the *vijigishu*; (8) *ākranda*, the *vijigishu*'s ally in the rear; (9) *pārsnigrahasara*, the ally of the *pārsnigraha*, behind the *ākranda*; (10) *ākrandasāra*, the ally of the *ākranda*, behind the *pārsnigrahasara*; (11) *madhyama*, the middle king with territory adjoining those of the *vijigishu* and the *ari* and stronger than either of these; and (12) *udāsina*, the king 'lying outside' or the indifferent or neutral king, more powerful than the *vijigishu*, the *ari*, and the *madhyama*.

Kautilya states: 'Any king, whose kingdom shares a common border with that of the conqueror is an antagonist, and a king whose territory has a common boundary with that of an antagonist ... is an ally' (Rangarajan, 1992: 520). These statements have created a fallacy that Kautilya sees a neighbour-state as an enemy, and the neighbour-state's enemy as a friend (Michael, 2013). However, this rigid principle of 'geographical determinism' conforms to a naive and rudimentary conclusion that Kautilya perceives the issues of political enmities/friendships as an offshoot of the geographical location (Karsh, 1986). This, in turn, fuels another implausible implication whereby the hope of peace with a bordering state remains dim—since two kings are enemies when they share a common border, peace remains only a transitory phase where the conqueror amplifies his relative power so as to initiate a military strike against the enemy, if necessary (Rangarajan, 1992). Though Kautilya reinforces the tenets of political realism when he approves an incessant preparedness for war (Weber, 1978; Bandyopadhyaya, 1993; Singh, 2011), he also instructs the states (including neighbour-states) to bear the strategic responsibility to prefer peace to war in selected situations. Kautilya recommends that: 'When the advantages derivable from peace and war are of equal character, one should prefer peace; for disadvantages, such as the loss of power and wealth, sojourning, and sin are ever-attending upon war' (Shamasastry, 1915: 374).

Noticeably, Kautilya is fully cognizant of the everlasting flaws of war. He, thus, advises that a mindful priority should be assigned to the goal of securing self-benefits before deciding to go to war or choose peace with any states (including neighbour-states). Kautilya breaks that image of *mandala* wherein a neighbour is compulsorily considered an enemy and the hostility with that 'neighbour-enemy' is anticipated as an inescapable incidence. G. Modelski (1964: 554) discerns that we might call the *mandala* 'a checkerboard model, because the basis of it is the proposition that one's neighbour's enemy is therefore one's obvious friend. This regular alteration between friends and enemies produces, for the system, a checkerboard effect.' He notes, however, that 'the "locational determinism" implied in Kautilya's circle needs to be qualified and was, in fact qualified, in the Arthaśāstra'.

Kautilya does mention some qualifications for allocating the identities of different states. For example, Kautilya distinguishes between a 'natural enemy', who has a similar 'high birth' and inhabits a kingdom in the vicinity of the potential conqueror state, and 'factitious enemy', who is openly hostile and forms enemies to the potential conqueror state. Kautilya also distinguishes between a 'natural friend', whose alliance is inherited from ancestors and who lives close to the kingdom of a direct enemy, and an 'acquired friend', whose alliance is invited for self-preservation (Shamasastry, 1915: 368). In addition, Kautilya distinguishes between an 'ally of diverse utility', who provides support with the supplies of his villages, seaports, mines, jungles, and elephants, and an 'ally of great utility', who offers military and financial services (Poddar, 2016). Put simply, Kautilya stresses the need to distinguish between various types of enemies as per their relative strengths and weaknesses, and friends according to the quality of one's relationships (McClish and Olivelle, 2012).

After distinguishing between different types of enemies and friends, the potential conqueror state must fix their momentary strategic positioning in the aforesaid twelve categories of *mandala*. Depending on this momentary strategic positioning of different types of enemies and friends, the potential conqueror state has to cautiously implement a sixfold foreign policy towards them: (1) *samdhi*, making a peace treaty with clear terms and conditions; (2) *vigraha*, the policy of antagonism; (3) *asana*, not marching on an expedition; (4) *yana*, marching on an expedition; (5) *samsraya*, looking for shelter with another king; and (6) *dvaidhibhava*, the policy of peace with one king and antagonism with another at the same juncture. Kautilya offers a detailed illustration of how the sixfold foreign policy may be implemented in diverse circumstances (Kangle, 1997). Presumably, adherence to the sixfold foreign policy can continually maximize the power of the potential conqueror state as it forges ahead on the path of the conquest of the world.

> **Key Concept: Power**
>
> Kautilya mentions three types of power: (1) 'intellectual' (wisdom to provide good counsel); (2) 'physical' (economic reserves and armed forces); and (3) 'psychological' (moral-energetic acts). However, Kautilya does not consider power as the most treasured political asset. He prefers 'skill for intrigue' (i.e., the use of one's knowledge of the science of polity) to power or enthusiasm. Kautilya states:
>
> > [H]e who . . . is acquainted with the science of polity can with little effort make use of his skill for intrigue and succeed by means of conciliation and other strategic means [e.g., donating gifts, sowing dissent, etc.] . . . in over-reaching even those kings who are possessed of enthusiasm and power . . . [O]f the three acquirements . . . enthusiasm, power and skill for intrigue, he who possesses more of the quality mentioned later than the one mentioned first in the order of enumeration will be successful in over-reaching others.
> >
> > (Shamasastry, 1915: 491)

4.3.1 The ends of political rule

For Kautilya, the ruler's self-interest is fulfilled only if they achieve *yogakshema* (survival) and *lokasamgraha* (benefit and happiness) of the subjects (or citizens) through a 'just' use of power. Here *yogakshema* means protection from internal and external threats to life, and *lokasamgraha* implies the capability to realize the world's potential for virtue and to obtain happiness therefrom for 'self' and 'other/s' (Iyer, 2000: xii). Kangle (1997: 120) elaborates:

> An unjust or improper use of . . . power by the ruler might lead to serious consequences, the most serious being a revolt of the subjects against the ruler . . . [A] large number of acts on the part of the ruler . . . are likely to make the subjects disaffected with his rule . . . if the subjects become disaffected [at the domestic level], they may join hands with the ruler's enemies [at the international level] . . . [This] threat . . . is expected to serve as a check on the wanton use of coercive power by the ruler. This shows at the same time how the ruler's authority is, in the last analysis, dependent on the contentment of the subjects.

Although the ruler's self-interest is defined in terms of power, Kautilya requests the ruler should be self-critical as they set out to maximize power. As the ruler's self-interest/power is dependent on the contentment of the subjects, the ruler's power is diminished if they declare a war against a just state where the subjects, loyal to their virtuous ruler, might put up a resilient counter-attack (Olivelle, 2013). This means that the ruler must preferably enter a war with an unjust state where the disaffected subjects, tired of injustice, might join the war against their own unjust ruler (Rangarajan, 1992). Certainly, the ruler's power is enhanced if they avoid 'hurting the leaders of the people and despising the worthy' or 'insulting the good and commending the wicked' (Shamasastry, 1915: 386–387). In all circumstances, a blind imposition of the ruler's self-interest over other-interest is unscientific and evil. Kautilya proclaims:

> [W]hoever, as a king, is destitute of good temper and amiable character cannot, by reason of his habitual hatred of the science of polity and an inborn proclivity to evil ways, maintain his sovereignty... [A king] shall... keep away from hurting the women and property of others; avoid... falsehood... Not violating righteousness and economy, he shall enjoy his desires... the three pursuits of life, charity, wealth, and desire... are inter-dependent... Any one of these three, when enjoyed to an excess, hurts not only the other two, but also itself.
>
> (ibid.: 17, 352–353)

For an aggrandizing state interested in *lokasamgraha* (the benefit and happiness of all), the war with a 'neighbour-enemy' is worthy only if the 'neighbour-enemy' is comparatively weaker and unjust. This is because the thrust for *lokasamgraha* sets the moral responsibility for an aggrandizing state in such a manner that it has to locate itself in a place where it can guarantee the benefit and happiness of all the subjects afflicted by war. Tactically, the aggrandizing state can locate itself in that place if it declares war only against a comparatively weaker and unjust state (and strikes a peace deal with an equally strong or a reasonably stronger state). Once the aggrandizing state succeeds in defeating the unjust state, Kautilya advises that the conqueror must not threaten or abuse the subjects of that unjust state, but rule in a manner that is beneficial and agreeable to them, and be tolerant towards their culture, fairs, festivals, religion, etc., thereby acting as if the conqueror state belonged to them (Chande, 1998)—which dilutes the 'self-other distinction' in politics. As the goal of *lokasamgraha* entails the benefit and happiness of people who live not only in one's own state (inside) but also in other states (outside), one may posit that Kautilya does not endorse a strict demarcation between domestic and international politics (Acharya and Buzan, 2009).

Practically, the likelihood of war is nil if the 'neighbour-enemy' is comparatively stronger than the 'potential conqueror state'. But if the war is imposed upon the potential conqueror state by an equally strong or a reasonably stronger 'neighbour-enemy', then the potential conqueror state must select a suitable form of war on the basis of the norms of righteousness (i.e., *dharma*). According to Morkevičius (2018: 180–181), 'Kautilya envisions three types of battles': open battles (*prakashayuddha*), concealed battles (*kutayuddha*), and silent battles (*tsuniyuddha*), such as guerrilla warfare. Of the three, *prakashayuddha* is the most honourable. It is a sort of 'just war' which ought to be 'fought between evenly matched militaries' and according to agreed and stipulated rules. Moreover, 'only kings whose power is superior to their opponents should fight using such tactics. Kings who are weaker than their opponents, or who are not sure about their relative power, should use *kutayuddha* or *tsuniyuddha*. Which tactics are considered legitimate are contingent on the state's relative power.'

It is evident that the estimated relative strength and weakness, not geographical location, determine the 'likelihood' and 'form' of war between different states. Of course, not all the Kautilyan military tactics are unequivocally moral. Mishra (2017: 215–216) affirms that although 'Kautilya suggests resort to violence, deception and secretive punishments to the enemies',

> [he] 'never suggests violence as the immediate resort'. The violent use of coercion, sanction, assassination, and so on—*danda*—is the last tool... out of the four [tools], the other three being

sama (conciliation), *dana* (gift) and *bheda* (sowing dissent) ... *Arthaśāstra* holds that the means of diplomacy ... are superior ... than violent means ... [T]he morality of Kautilya is purely guided by the changing nature and dynamics of the political agents in which the 'good' is dynamic in the functional sense.

4.3.2 Political reality and morality

In theory, Kautilya's description of political reality is 'dualistic'—that is, the 'self' (one's own state) always remains separated from the 'other/s' (other states). Yet, when different states interact, they seek to attain the ultimate end of survival along with the benefit and happiness of the people living in one's own state (inside) as well as other states (outside). One of the mechanisms to attain this ultimate end is power. But not all states possess equal intellectual, physical, and psychological power. After undertaking a rational assessment of their power in relation to others, different states find themselves in a relative position of decline, stability, or growth. Regardless of the position, every state must operationalize the sixfold foreign policy to maximize power, so as to preserve growth, or to progress from decline to stability and, subsequently, from stability to growth. When states strive to maximize power, they must not always show an aggressive spirit: at various moments in interaction with other states, the increase in power of one's own state requires not only a relative reduction in power of other states (zero-sum view) but also coordinated expansion in power of other states (variable-sum view).

> **Key Concept: Zero-sum power vs. variable-sum power**
>
> If a state acts according to the view of zero-sum power, it assumes that an increase of power in one place causes equal loss of power in other places. If a state acts on the basis of the view of variable-sum power, it guesses that there can be a mutual increase of power not compensated by equal loss in other places (positive-sum), and mutual loss of power not compensated by equal gain in other places (negative-sum). As Kautilya offers the option of coordinated expansion in the power of one's own state and other states, he seems to advocate a variable-sum approach to power.

To calculate when it is appropriate to act in accordance with either the zero-sum or variable-sum views of power, different states must assess the 'identities' and 'interests' of each other. Keeping a variety of material and ideational factors in mind (for instance, relative strength/weakness, past proof of friendship/enmity, observable signs of good/bad intentions, etc.), a state can allocate three types of identities to other states: enemy/*ari*, friend/*mitra*, and rival/*samantas* (Shahi, 2014). But different states hold their identities only 'on a momentary basis' and 'with varying intensity': different states can be allocated the identities of various categories of enemy, friend, or rival at different junctures. These identities (enemy, friend, or rival) allow states to discern at different junctions the interests of other states. When a state interacts with those states whose identities and/or interests are those of an enemy or a rival, then it must act according to the view of zero-sum power. By contrast, when a state interacts with those states that share the identities and/or interests of a friend, then it must act according to the view of variable-sum power. Over time, the assessment of identities or interests of different states undergoes a change. Accordingly, the dynamics of power relations among different states also undergoes a change.

Kautilya believes that a ruler can promote justice in politics only if they make minimal use of organized violence. Kautilya reminds a potential conqueror state that it should not let the causes of decline, greed, and disaffection among the subjects to appear, or, should they appear, they should be instantly defused (Deb, 1938), thereby preventing violent repercussions that might arise from retaliatory responses of the disaffected subjects. Kautilya also suggests that those who 'cause violent death to men or women, hijack travellers, commit house-breaking, and enforce unjust penalty upon others' should be executed (Shamasastry, 1915: 324), so as to deter violence in political life. He further warns: 'the vehemence of someone who reenters a battle without regard for his life becomes irrepressible', therefore, it is wise not to 'harass a man who has [already] been crushed' (Olivelle, 2013: 380). A just use of power seeks to harmonize the four goals of human life: (1) material well-being/*artha*; (2) physical pleasure/*kama*; (3) righteousness/*dharma*; and (4) self-liberation/*moksha*. Thus, when a ruler makes a just use of power to attain material well-being, they must not block the prospects of spiritual well-being.

For Kautilya, the supply of righteousness/*dharma* is not a ruler's exclusive duty, but a combined discursive endeavour on the part of the ruler, ministers, and other experts of sacred laws (Shamasastry, 1915: 213). Nonetheless, the ruler plays a special role. Kautilya pronounces:

> The king who administers justice in accordance with sacred law, evidence, history, and edicts of kings ... will be able to conquer the whole world bounded by the four quarters. Whenever there is disagreement between history and sacred law or between evidence and sacred law, then the matter shall be settled in accordance with sacred law. But whenever sacred law is in conflict with rational law, then reason shall be held authoritative.
>
> (ibid.: 218)

To assure a just use of power, the ruler must discharge two kinds of duty: (1) specific duty (*viśesa dharma*), i.e., the ruler's exclusive duty; and (2) general duty (*sāmānya dharma*), i.e., the inclusive duty common to all. Distinguishing between these two kinds of duty, Chemburkar (1999: 65) observes that, for Kautilya, '*sāmānya dharma* includes duties ... which are common to all irrespective of any distinction such as class, caste, creed, sex, time-space', for example, forgiveness (Shamasastry, 1915: 11). However, *viśesa dharma* 'differ from individual to individual' and are determined through individual relations with others (Chemburkar, 1999: 65). For instance, the ruler has the specific duty to obtain material well-being for the subjects (Kangle, 1997: 131). Because the ruler remains related to the whole social fabric (including 'self' and 'other/s') in a specific way, they carry the specific duty to secure material well-being for all subjects. But the ruler who is guided by righteousness/*dharma* must strive to harmonize material well-being with altruistic spiritual well-being.

In real-life situations, the rulers are likely to face tensions when they reasonably aspire to secure the two allegedly conflicting ends of material and spiritual well-being. As Shah (1982: 61; 70–71) explains, Kautilya does not deny that '*artha* [material well-being] has to be pursued in accordance with *dharma* [spiritual well-being]'. The institutions and structures to achieve such fulfilment are state, government, and administration. However, unlike modern academic disciplines in which these institutions and structures are treated separately, and distinctions are made between different subdisciplines of politics, the *Arthaśāstra* makes 'no clear-cut distinction between political science, political philosophy and political policy'. This, Shah maintains, has its merits and 'prevents the theory from being empty and the facts from being simple facts without a focus'.

To be sure, these disciplines and their boundaries did not exist in Kautilya's day as they do presently. As such, Kautilya's theoretical scheme can be seen as interdisciplinary in today's terms. On the basis of this scheme, the politico-administrative interest in securing material well-being is conceptualized in terms of an interest in securing spiritual well-being, or general earthly well-being. Kangle (1997: 2) illustrates:

> With *artha* understood, by implication, in the sense of the earth where men live and seek their material well-being, it ceases to be a goal pursued by individuals and appears as the means of ensuring

the well-being of men in general. And since state activity alone can make such general well-being possible, the protection of earth [becomes] an essential part of state activity. [*Arthaśāstra*] . . . shows how this activity of the . . . protection of the earth should be carried out.

For Kautilya, the protection of the Earth is the 'superseding principle' to settle the allegedly conflicting goals of material well-being/*artha* and spiritual well-being/*dharma*. In a way, Kautilya favours the ruler's 'non-selfishness' as the supreme behavioural approach for resolving the tussles between material and spiritual duties in political life (Chemburkar, 1999). On the whole, Kautilya furnishes an eclectic political theory which makes reflective-moralpolitik (or abstract universal ideals aiming to protect the Earth) as a 'necessary condition' for the pursuit of rationalist-realpolitik (or a rational/prudential hunt for material well-being on Earth). Interestingly, Kautilya's eclectic political theory resonates with the latest 'post-human turn' (Zolkos, 2018), i.e., a theoretical turn that offers an inclusive account of the human as well as non-human actors in politics, such as nature, plant, and animal systems, Earth's processes, the technosphere, and viruses (see also Part IX of this book, which explores the environment, human, and non-human). While Kautilya specifies multiple methods of wildlife conservation and orders severe punishment for those found guilty of cruelty to animals, he tends to replace the Kantian 'human/non-human dualism' with 'human/non-human hybridity'. The Kantian human/non-human dualism assumes that the humans, despite their self-incurred immaturity, are rational agents but the non-humans (e.g., animals) are not and, thus, they merely possess an instrumental value. But Kautilya's human/non-human hybridity appreciates the agency of both human and non-human actors. Despite sharing a dualistic approach that typifies Eurocentric political realism, Kautilya's eclectic political theory innovatively presents itself as an advocate of 'political realism between realpolitik and moralpolitik' (Shahi, 2018).

In negotiating between realpolitik and moralpolitik, Kautilya's theory is quite inventive in three specific senses. First, it is atypical in the way it defends the rational and prudential self-interests of the states defined in terms of power, and still accepts the abstract universal ideals of the protection of the Earth as a necessary condition for realization of those rational and prudential self-interests. In so doing, it challenges the customary conflict between rational/prudential and abstract/ideal concerns that cause an uneasiness in scores of Eurocentric political theories. Second, its dynamic rendering of the states-system (which notices continually changing identities/interests of various states) pertains to three kinds of power, i.e., 'intellectual' (good counsel), 'physical' (economic reserves and armed forces), and 'psychological' (moral-energetic acts). Since Kautilya's political theory acknowledges the moral-energetic action as a form of power (i.e., psychological power), it provokes a curious reconsideration of the 'power vs. morality' debates that preoccupy many Western political theories. Third, contrary to the ongoing debates on the relative impact of state and non-state actors in politics, Kautilya's political theory transfers the focus to the 'personal (re)actions of the rulers' (not considering their political status as state/non-state actors). As such, it plainly asserts that the legitimate exercise of power requires a detached or non-selfish personal (re)action of the rulers, whereby they stay 'actively engaged with' yet 'consciously distanced from' the immediate instances of success and failure in politics (ibid.).

4.3 Circles of states and foreign policy: Key Points

- The structural and functional dimensions of *mandala* (circles of states) and *sadgunya* (sixfold foreign policy) unite to formulate Kautilya's political theory.
- In this conception, different states occupy different momentary strategic positioning in the states-system (*mandala*); regardless of their positioning, the states must use the sixfold foreign policy (*sadgunya*) to boost their power.

- Because he prescribes the use of power to attain survival and benefit/happiness of the people living in one's own state and other states, Kautilya does not erect a strict partition between domestic and international politics.
- To promote justice in politics, Kautilya advises that the rulers of different states must support the legitimate exercise of power, make minimal use of organized violence, and strike a balance between rational/prudential goals of material-well-being and abstract/ideal goals of spiritual-well-being; in order to strike this kind of a balance, one needs a 'post-human' attitude that values the agency of both human and non-human actors.

4.4 Untangling the knots of 'gender' and 'caste'

Though Kautilya's political theory aims to maintain a balance between the material and spiritual aspects of life, it sporadically appears to be torn between the imperatives of concrete political action and abstract political philosophy (Banerjee, 2012). Sil (1985: 125–126) laments:

> One major problem in determining the extent of Kautilya's moral susceptibility is that he is seldom consistent in his contentions . . . He might occasionally appear secular and amoral, though, on closer scrutiny, his fundamental moralism becomes obvious . . . [For example,] he observes that . . . 'material well-being alone is supreme, for, spiritual . . . and sensual pleasures depend on material well-being' . . . Yet, on another occasion, Kautilya comments that a king must preserve his body, not wealth; for, what regret can there be for wealth that is impermanent?

The fragmented re-readings of Kautilya's inconsistent remarks on the political issues related to 'gender' and 'caste' have become a source of criticism. A few critics claim that Kautilya professes a strong belief in gender inequalities and hierarchies—that is, the comparative superiority or inferiority of men or women, depending on varying socio-political circumstances, defined in terms of the caste system (Chandrasekaran, 2006). In what follows, an attempt has been made to examine the extent to which Kautilya's views can be branded as sexist or casteist.

4.4.1 The many faces of womanhood

There is a lack of synthesized study of the position of women in Kautilya's *Arthaśāstra* (Bhattacharjee, 2018). Almost no attempt has been made to analyse how the position of women, as portrayed in Kautilya's *Arthaśāstra*, speaks to traditional Eurocentric feminist theories. But a careful look at the many faces of womanhood in *Arthaśāstra*—for example, wife, widow, spinster, prostitute, and slave—makes it obvious that Kautilya considers both men and women as political agents. Kautilya neither builds a wall of separation between the personal and political spheres of a woman's life nor belittles a woman's rational capacities. Kautilya announces:

> A poor widow . . . very clever, and desirous to earn her livelihood is a woman ascetic . . . [Also, a] woman-spy under the guise of an ascetic . . . may allure each prime minister one after another, saying 'the queen is enamoured of thee and has made arrangements for thy entrance into her chamber; besides this, there is also the certainty of large acquisitions of wealth'. If they [prime ministers] discard the proposal, they are pure. This is what is styled love-allurement.
>
> (Shamasastry, 1915: 23)

In addition to women spies and women assassins, Kautilya also discusses women archers and, during war, asks women (with prepared food and beverage) to stand behind the fighting lines and utter encouraging words to the men in the front (Sen, 2013). Kautilya not only promotes women's visibility in public spaces, but also legalizes women's claim to marriage and property. For instance, if a woman enters into a marriage and receives wealth (*stridhana*) in the form of a gift, Kautilya asserts that she must have full ownership of that property. Even when she becomes a widow, if she decides to remarry, she retains full ownership of that property and could transfer that property to her daughter or daughter-in-law. Under specific conditions, a daughter could even inherit property from her father. Kautilya permits the ownership of property by skilled women who could financially support themselves by the spinning of yarn. The spinning of yarn could offer a living not only to free women, but also to female slaves, spinsters, widows, women with physical impairments, and women who had left home to live separately. Even women who had committed some offence and were fined could pay it off in the form of personal labour by spinning of yarn. Kautilya may be the only author who mentions women tenants tilling for half produce (Jaiswal, 2001). At times, Kautilya permits a woman's claim to equal pay for equal work. He sanctions the same salary to women spies as given to men who worked as engineers, miners, doctors, and village overseers (Singh, 2012).

Yet Kautilya's conservatism is exposed when he stipulates the main role of wives as reproduction, preferably of sons (Rangarajan, 1992). In *Arthaśāstra*, while prostitutes are made dependent on their clients for money, wives are made dependent on their husbands and sons (Boesche, 2003). Although female slaves and prostitutes are given legal protection against violence, the violent treatment of wives is permitted in certain cases. Of course, wives are allowed to divorce on the basis of mutual consent, but only if their marriage was not pious. The *Arthaśāstra* classifies eight types of marriages: *brahma*, *daiva*, *arsha*, and *prajapatya* are pious marriages as they respect the authority of a bride's father, whereas *asura*, *gandharva*, *rakshasa*, and *paisacha* are not pious marriages as they weaken the authority of a bride's father. A daughter could inherit property from her father only if she was born of a pious marriage and there were no sons (Shirin, 2009). The instances of biased treatment of men and women surely convey a constricted 'male gaze' (Mukherjee, 1994). However, Kautilya is attentive not only to 'sexual differences' (arising from the biological make-up of men/women) but also to 'gender differences' (resulting from social constructs of masculinity/femininity). Kautilya problematizes the essentialist representations of 'masculine' and 'feminine' nature and advocates punishments for the wrongdoings of both men and women. Kautilya commands:

> Any woman who murders her husband . . . shall be torn off by bulls . . . No man shall have sexual intercourse with any woman against her will . . . When a person commits rape with a captive . . . he shall be punished with the first amercement [fine]; when he commits rape with the wife of a thief . . . he shall be punished with the middlemost amercement; and when he commits rape with an *Arya* [upper caste] woman . . . he shall be punished with the highest amercement. When a man performs witchcraft to win . . . his own daughter-in-law, daughter, or sister, he shall have his limb cut off and also put to death, while any woman who yields herself to such an offender shall also receive similar punishment.
>
> (Shamasastry, 1915: 319–327, 334)

Overall, Kautilya's *Arthaśāstra* endorses a complex stratification not only of men and women, but also of men and men, and women and women. Furthermore, on many occasions, the complex stratification of men and men, and women and women, is situated upon the conception of '*varna-ashrama-dharma*', which, in due course, unleashed the degenerated form of caste system that still underpins India's hierarchical social structure.

4.4.2 The groundwork of a social order

Kautilya upholds the notion of *varna-ashrama-dharma* which institutionalizes a social order based upon a neat division of labour among people. People are grouped according to four functional categories or *varna*: *brahmin* (learners and teachers), *kshatriya* (army personnel), *vaishya* (farmers, cattle-rearers, and traders), and *sūdra* (artisans and actors). Furthermore, people's lives are divided into four stages or *ashrama*: namely, *brahmacharya* (learning stage), *grihastha* (household stage), *banprastha* (retirement stage), and *sanyas* (renunciation stage) (Prasad, 1978). For Kautilya, governance is about making people discharge their specific duty (*viśesa dharma*) as per their functional categories (i.e., *varna*) and life-stages (i.e., *ashrama*). Kautilya, therefore, asks the ruler that they should not allow the specific duty of people to be transgressed. Kautilya argues that the observance of one's specific duty leads to endless bliss. In the case of its transgression, in contrast, the ruler must punish the transgressors. Kautilya writes:

> A son begotten by a *Brahman* [or *brahmin*] on a woman of next lower caste [*varna*], shall, if endowed with manly or superior qualities, take an equal share (with other sons of inferior qualities); similarly, *Anantara* sons of *Kshatriya* or *Vaisya* fathers shall, if endowed with manly or superior qualities, take half or equal shares (with others). An only son to two mothers of different castes shall take possession of the whole property and maintain the relatives of his father.
>
> (Shamasastry, 1915: 235)

According to Drekmeier (1962), the *varna-ashrama-dharma* could be compared with the Platonic theory of justice or Aristotle's definition of nature, i.e., 'what each thing is when at its best, that we call its nature'. However, it cannot be denied that the practice of the *varna* system gradually degenerated into the caste system. The original idea of *varna* as 'non-hierarchical functional categories' (decided by one's labour) was replaced with the idea of caste or *jati* as 'hierarchical social groups' (decided by one's birth). In addition, the depiction of '*dharma* as righteousness' was later perverted to '*dharma* as religion'.

As expected, these degenerations affected the translations of *Arthaśāstra*. In Shamasastry's English translation, one finds repeated references to the criteria of 'high birth' and 'low birth'. Shamasastry implies that Kautilya used the criteria of high birth and low birth to perform a range of administrative activities, such as the management of armies, military alliances, trade deals, penalties, marriages, etc. But the references to birth indicate the ascribed status of caste/*jati*, not *varna*. While caste/*jati* claims a superior or purer position for the social group of *brahmin* in India's hierarchical socio-cultural settings, the non-hierarchical functional categories of *varna* seek to infuse a cooperative dependence among social groups in the form of a division of labour, wherein no social group claims hierarchical superiority and purity or inferiority and impurity. With a view to avoiding semantic confusions arising from the usage of the term birth/caste/*jati*, Rangarajan and Kangle's English translations prefer to use the term *varna*. However, Kangle (1997: 144) confesses that the 'preeminent position of the *brahmin* [*varna* is] self-evident. Nevertheless, the text does not . . . explicitly declare the *brahmin* to be above the law or independent of the state and its authority. [For sure,] special privileges are intended for . . . a *brahmin* learned in the Vedas.' Kautilya not only differentiates between learned and ignorant *brahmins* but also rejects all kinds of *brahmins* as poor soldiers, thereby preferring *kshatriyas*, *vaishyas*, and *sūdras* as superior candidates for a standing army (Gautam, 2013). While the *brahmins* are exempted from forced labour, torture, and capital punishment, they are intermittently expected to pay higher fines than other social classes for committing specific crimes. Kautilya is aware of the overwhelming power of vice in life, so he recommends punishment even for the reprobate ascetics—'for righteousness, overpowered by evil, destroys the ruler, if neglected' (Sil, 1985: 125). But, then again, one may spot how Kautilya authorizes special disadvantages for the people of allegedly lower *varna* (*sūdra*) and outside *varna* (or outcasts/*antávasáyins*).

Olivelle (2013: 23–24) suspects that the *varna*-based special (dis)advantages—usually aroused to disclose the so-called chauvinistic stance of Kautilya—were 'possibly added later' to the treatise of

Arthaśāstra. Because the interpolations of *varna* in the treatise of *Arthaśāstra* are repeatedly 'given at the end of a sentence containing a prescription', Olivelle surmises that this is due to Śāstric Redaction (i.e., alterations by authors other than Kautilya) and not Kautilya's Recession (i.e., Kautilya's personal contributions). Like Olivelle, some other Indologists also suggest that the *varna*-based discriminations were later inserted by authors other than Kautilya. But ahistorical re-readings of *Arthaśāstra* refer to these discriminations to label Kautilya as sexist/casteist and *Arthaśāstra* as non-secular or non-empirical. For all those who adopt an ahistorical route to indiscreetly tag Kautilya's *Arthaśāstra* as a 'brahminical text' (and, thus, a non-secular text), McClish (2019: 223) throws open a number of unanswered questions:

> Who brought this new [brahminical] orthodoxy into the halls of counsel? Was it a new class ... or a transformation within the old ministerial lineages? What role did foreign invasion play? How does this map onto the [brahminical] appropriation of state law? Did states actually begin at this point to enact policies reflecting [brahminical] priorities?

A methodical study of these unanswered questions could develop a better understanding of the multifarious and, sometimes, incongruous text of Kautilya's *Arthaśāstra*.

> **4.4 Untangling the knots of 'gender' and 'caste': Key Points**
>
> - Kautilya envisaged a socio-political order based on a complex stratification of men and women, men and men, and women and women: here, men and women with different personal/social/professional statuses were subjected to varying proscriptions and obligations.
> - This complex stratification of men and women was situated within the imagination of *varna-ashrama-dharma*: governance involved making people discharge their duty/*dharma* according to their functional categories/*varna* and life-stage/*ashramas*.
> - People were grouped into four functional categories/*varna*: learners, army personnel, farmers-traders-cattle-rearers, and artisans-actors.
> - The life span of people was divided into four stages/*ashrama*: learning, household, retirement, and renunciation.
> - Because the non-hierarchical functional categories/*varna* (decided by one's labour) degraded into the hierarchical social groups of caste/*jati* (decided by one's birth), and the notion of '*dharma* as righteousness' perverted to '*dharma* as religion', Kautilya's writings are often (mis)interpreted as sexist/casteist.

4.5 Conclusion

At the core of Kautilya's political thinking lies the 'philosophy of science' called *anvikshaki*. *Anvikshaki*, as inspired by the ancient Indian philosophical discourses of *Sāṃkhya*, *Yoga*, and *Lokāyata*, calls not only for the use of 'perception' to know reality but also for the application of moral-ethical principles to secure survival/*yogakshema* and benefit and happiness/*lokasamgraha*. For Kautilya, the goal of securing survival and benefit and happiness extends to the people who live both in one's own state (inside) and in other states (outside). Thus, Kautilya's political thinking goes beyond the limits of nationalism/internationalism and orientalism/occidentalism, embodying a spirit of 'globalism'. As today's global politics continues to grapple with the problems of 'inside-outside difference', especially in the context of the execution of moral-ethical norms related to climate change, pandemics, economic recession, humanitarian intervention, and so on, Kautilya's *Arthaśāstra* emerges as a relevant textual tradition. In contrast to several Eurocentric political theories that revolve around the debates of 'rational vs. abstract', 'power vs. morality', and 'state vs. non-state', a comprehensive re-reading of the non-Western intellectual tradition of Kautilya's *Arthaśāstra* conveys an eclectic political theory that transcends these debates and tries to reconcile the apparently contradictory ends of material well-being and spiritual well-being of all people belonging to all social groups in domestic and international politics.

Take your learning further by accessing the online resources for a library of web links to relevant videos, articles, blogs, and useful websites for this chapter: **www.oup.com/he/Ramgotra-Choat1e**.

Study questions

1. What is the 'philosophy of science' underlying Kautilya's famous treatise *Arthaśāstra* and what does this philosophy promote?
2. In what ways does Kautilya provide an organic theory of the state?
3. How do the notions of 'interests' and 'identities' in *mandala* (circles of states) and *sadgunya* (sixfold foreign policy) come together to shape Kautilya's political theory?
4. In what ways, if any, is the concept of 'power' central to Kautilya's understanding of politics?
5. How does Kautilya reconcile the apparently divergent ends of material well-being (*artha*) and spiritual well-being (*dharma*)?
6. How did Kautilya define *yogakshema*/survival and *lokasamgraha*/benefit and happiness?
7. What are the unconventional traits of Kautilya's eclectic political theory?
8. In what ways, if any, might Kautilya's writings be considered sexist and casteist?

Further reading

Primary sources

Kangle, R.P. (1963) *Arthaśāstra*. Bombay: University of Bombay.
   The first English translation enriched with modern critical and explanatory commentaries.

Olivelle, P. (2013) *King, Governance, and Law in Ancient India: Kautilya's Arthasastra*. New York: Oxford University Press.
   The latest English translation, incorporating a number of important advances in the knowledge of the texts, inscriptions, and archaeological remains from the period in Indian history to which the *Arthaśāstra* belongs.

Rangarajan, L.N. (1992) *The Arthashastra*. New Delhi: Penguin Books.
   Useful rearrangement of several chapters, topics, and verses of Kautilya's *Arthaśāstra* along some key concepts.

Shamasastry, R. (1915) *Kautilya's Arthashastra*. Bangalore: Government Press.
   The earliest English translation of the originally received palm-leaf manuscripts.

Secondary sources

Bandyopadhyaya, N. C. (1927) *Kautilya or An Exposition of His Social Ideal & Political Theory*. Calcutta: Chuckervertty, Chatterjee & Co.
Discusses the historical evolution of the text of *Arthaśāstra* and simplifies Kautilya's ethical, social, and political thought.

Bisht, M. (2019) *Kautilya's Arthashastra: Philosophy of Strategy*. New York: Routledge.
Comprehensive study of Kautilya's statecraft as it rests at the intersection of political theory and International Relations.

Gautam, P.K. (2015) *Kautilya's Arthashastra: Contemporary Issues and Comparison*. IDSA Monograph Series No. 47. New Delhi: Institute for Defence Studies and Analyses.
Rationalizes the policy relevance of Kautilya's *Arthaśāstra* in contemporary times.

Jog, K.P. (ed.) (1999) *Perceptions on Kauṭilīya Arthaśāstra: In Commemoration of Prof. R.P. Kangle's Birth Centenary*. Mumbai: Popular Prakashan.
Lucid discussion of the miscellaneous themes in Kautilya's writings that are present and missing in Kangle's translation.

Leibig, M. and Mishra, S. (eds) (2017) *The Arthaśāstra in a Transcultural Perspective: Comparing Kautilya with Sun-Zi, Nizam al-Mulk, Barani and Machiavelli*. New Delhi: Pentagon Press.
Comparative review of the overlapping Western and non-Western political thinking of Kautilya, Sun-Zi, Nizam al-Mulk, Barani, and Machiavelli.

McClish, M. (2019) *The History of the Arthaśāstra: Sovereignty and Sacred Law in Ancient India*. Cambridge: Cambridge University Press.
Extensive exploration of the *Arthaśāstra's* historiography and textual interpolations.

Mital, S.N. (2000) *Kauṭilīya Arthaśāstra Revisited*. PHISPC Monograph Series, Vol. 11. New Delhi: PHISPC.
Logical refutation of the scholarly claims that the *Arthaśāstra* was not authored by a single man and the date of its composition cannot be attributed to a single century.

Shahi, D. (2018) *Kautilya and Non-Western IR Theory*. Cham: Palgrave Macmillan.
Accessible restatement of Kautilya's world-view as a non-Western International Relations theory.

Sihag, B. (2016) *Kautilya: The True Founder of Economics*. New Delhi: Vitasta Publishing.
Bold exposition of the monumental contribution of Kautilya to economic thought.

Sil, N.P. (1989) *Kautilya's Arthasastra: A Comparative Study* (American University Studies). New York: Peter Lang Publishing.
Brilliant comparison of Kautilya's *Arthaśāstra* to the writings of Plato, Aristotle, and Machiavelli.

References

Acharya, A. and Buzan, B. (eds) (2009) *Non-Western International Relations Theory: Perspectives On and Beyond Asia*. London: Routledge.

Bandyopadhyaya, J. (1993) *A General Theory of International Relations*. New Delhi: Allied Publishers.

Banerjee, P. (2012) 'Chanakya/Kautilya: History, Philosophy, Theater and the Twentieth-Century Political'. *History of the Present*, 2(1): 24–51.

Bhargava, P.L. (1996) *Chandragupta Maurya: A Gem of Indian History*. New Delhi: D.K. Printworld Ltd.

Bhattacharjee, B. (2018) 'Position of Women in Kautilya's Arthashastra'. *International Journal of Humanities & Social Science Studies*, 4(4): 108–115.

Boesche, R. (2002) 'Moderate Machiavelli? Contrasting *The Prince* with the *Arthasastra* of Kautilya'. *Critical Horizons*, 3(2): 253–276.

Boesche, R. (2003) *The First Great Political Realist: Kautilya and His Arthashastra*. Lanham, MD: Lexington Books.

Chande, M.B. (1998) *Kautilyan Arthasastra*. New Delhi: Atlantic Publishers.

Chandrasekaran, P. (2006) *Kautilya: Politics, Ethics and Statecraft*. Munich Personal RePEc Archive, Available at: https://mpra.ub.uni-muenchen.de/9962/ (accessed 21 August 2021).

Chemburkar, J. (1999) 'Kautilya's *Arthaśāstra* and the Early Dharmasūtras: Some Observations on Rājadharmas'. In K.P. Jog (ed.), *Perceptions on Kauṭilīya Arthaśāstra: In Commemoration of Prof. R.P. Kangle's Birth Centenary*. Mumbai: Popular Prakashan.

Deb, H.K. (1938) 'The Kautilya Arthasastra on Forms of Government'. *Indian Historical Quarterly*, 14.

Drekmeier, C. (1962) *Kingship and Community in Early India*. Stanford, CA: Stanford University Press.

Forde, S. (1992) 'Varieties of Realism: Thucydides and Machiavelli'. *The Journal of Politics*, 54(2): 372–393.

Gautam, P.K. (2013) *One Hundred Years of Kautilya's Arthasastra*. IDSA Monograph Series, No. 20. Available at: https://idsa.in/system/files/monograph20.pdf (accessed 24 August 2021).

Iyer, S. (2000) 'Religion and Economics of Fertility in South India'. PhD thesis, University of Cambridge. https://doi.org/10.17863/CAM.16513 (accessed 1 September 2021).

Jaiswal, S. (2001) 'Female Images in the *Arthasastra* of Kautilya'. *Social Scientist*, 29(3/4): 51–59.

Kangle, R P. (1963) *Arthaśāstra*. Bombay: University of Bombay.

Kangle, R.P. (1997) *The Kauṭilīya Arthaśāstra: A Study*. Vol. 3. Delhi: Motilal Banarsidass Publishers.

Karsh, E. (1986) 'Geographical Determinism: Finnish Neutrality Revisited'. *Cooperation and Conflict*, 21(1): 43–57.

Liebig, M. and Mishra, S. (2017) *The Arthàstra in a Transcultural Perspective: Comparing Kauäilya with Sun-Zi, Nizam al-Mulk, Barani and Machiavelli*. New Delhi: Pentagon Press.

Lundborg, T. (2018) 'The Ethics of Neorealism: Waltz and the Time of International Life'. *European Journal of International Relations*, 25(1): 229–249.

Mahbubani, K. (2009) *Can Asians Think?* Singapore: Times Book International.

McClish, M. (2019) *The History of the Arthaśāstra: Sovereignty and Sacred Law in Ancient India*. Cambridge: Cambridge University Press.

McClish, M. and Olivelle, P. (eds) (2012) *The Arthasastra: Selections from the Classic Indian Work on Statecraft*. Indiana, IN: Hackett Publishing.

Michael, A. (2013) *India's Foreign Policy and Regional Multilateralism*. Basingstoke: Palgrave Macmillan.

Mishra, S. (2017) 'Rājadharma, Legitimacy and Sovereignty in the *Arthaśāstra*'. In M. Leibig and S. Mishra (eds), *The Arthaśāstra in a Transcultural Perspective: Comparing Kautilya with Sun-Zi, Nizam al-Mulk, Barani and Machiavelli*. New Delhi: Pentagon Press.

Mitra, S.K. and Liebig, M. (2016) *Kautilya's Arthashastra: An Intellectual Portrait: The Classical Roots of Modern Politics in India*. Baden-Baden, Germany: Nomos.

Modelski, G. (1964) 'Kautilya: Foreign Policy and International System in the Ancient Hindu World'. *The American Political Science Review*, 58(3): 549–560.

Morkevičius, V. (2018) *Realist Ethics: Just War Traditions as Power Politics*. Cambridge: Cambridge University Press.

Mukherjee, P. (1994) *Hindu Women: Normative Models*. Calcutta: Orient Blackswan.

Olivelle, P. (2013) *King, Governance, and Law in Ancient India: Kautilya's Arthasastra*. New York: Oxford University Press.

Poddar, P. (2016) 'The Differential Uses of Kautilya's *Arthaśāstra*'. *Akademisk Kvarter*, 14: 96–109.

Prasad, D.M. (1978) 'Politics and Ethics in Kautilya's *Arthashastra*'. *The Indian Journal of Political Science*, 39(2): 240–249.

Rangarajan, L.N. (1992) *The Arthashastra*. New Delhi: Penguin Books.

Rösch, F. (2015) *Power, Knowledge, and Dissent in Morgenthau's Worldview*. New York: Palgrave Macmillan.

Sarkar, B.K. (1919) 'The Hindu Theory of International Relations'. *The American Political Science Review*, 13(3): 400–414.

Sen, S. (2013) 'Benoy Kumar Sarkar and Japan'. *Economic and Political Weekly*, 48(45/46): 61–70.

Shah, K.J. (1982) 'Of Artha and the *Arthaśāstra*'. In T.N. Madan (ed.) *Way of Life: King, Householder, Renouncer: Essays in Honour of Louis Dumont*. Delhi: Motilal Banarsidass Publishers.

Shahi, D. (2014) 'Arthashastra Beyond Realpolitik: The "Eclectic" Face of Kautilya'. *Economic and Political Weekly*, 49(41): 68–74.

Shahi, D. (2018) *Kautilya and Non-Western IR Theory*. Cham: Palgrave Macmillan.

Shamasastry, R. (1915) *Kautilya's Arthashastra*. Bangalore: Government Press.

Shirin, P. (2009) 'The Position of Women in Kautilya's Arthashastra'. *Journal of the Asiatic Society of Bangladesh*, 54(1): 123–134.

Sihag, B.S. (2004) 'Kautilya on the Scope and Methodology of Accounting, Organizational Design and the Role of Ethics in Ancient India'. *Accounting Historians Journal*, 31(2): 125–148.

Sil, N.P. (1985) 'Political Morality vs. Political Necessity: Kautilya and Machiavelli Revisited'. *Journal of Asian History*, 19(2): 101–142.

Singh, M.P. (2011) *Indian Political Thought: Themes and Thinkers*. New Delhi: Pearson.

Singh, N.K. (2012) *Eastern and Cross-Cultural Management*. New Delhi: Springer.

Smith, V.A. (1957) *The Early History of India*. Oxford: Clarendon Press.

Trautmann, T.R. (1971) *Kauṭilya and the Arthaśāstra: A Statistical Investigation of the Authorship and Evolution of the Text*. Leiden: E.J. Brill.

Weber, M. (1978) 'Politics as a Vocation'. In W. Runciman (ed.) and E. Matthews (trans.), *Max Weber: Selections in Translation*. Cambridge: Cambridge University Press.

Winternitz, M. (1923) 'Kautilya and the Art of Politics in Ancient India'. *Vishva Bharati Quarterly*, 1(3).

Zolkos, M. (2018) 'Life as a Political Problem: The Post-Human Turn in Political Theory'. *Political Studies Review*, 16(3): 192–204.

Part II
Social Contract Theory and Its Critics

5	**Thomas Hobbes**	Signy Gutnick Allen	79
6	**Baruch Spinoza**	Caroline Williams	97
7	**John Locke**	Hagar Kotef	115
8	**Mary Astell**	Allauren Forbes	131
9	**Jean-Jacques Rousseau**	Peter Hallward	147
10	**Carole Pateman and Charles Mills**	Terrell Carver	163

Many—though by no means all—political thinkers place the state at the centre of their analyses: they set out to explain the origins, purpose, and nature of the state. One of the best-known and most influential methods for addressing these issues is social contract theory. All social contract theories aim to justify the state—to show why it is necessary to have a state—but also to justify a specific theory of the state: what powers the state should have, who should exercise those powers, what limits (if any) should be placed upon them, and so on. In order to establish why we need a state and what functions the state should perform, social contract thinkers ask us to imagine what life would be like without a state in a so-called 'state of nature'. Social contract theorists claim that the disadvantages of life in the state of nature would lead people to agree—to contract with each other—to leave the state of nature and establish a political order.

For social contract theorists, therefore, the state is an artificial construct, not a natural development. In the pre-political realm of the state of nature, people do possess natural rights—that is, rights that they have simply by virtue of being human, independently of government. How these rights are conceptualized and what role they play vary between different social contract thinkers: depending on the theory, the establishment of government can mean that we give up (most of) our rights or that our natural rights are better protected. Contract theorists disagree about the *purpose* of government: to secure peace, guarantee our rights, or restore our liberty. All contract theorists agree, however, that the basis of government is *consent*: we have government because we have consented to it—or, rather, because we *would have* consented to it had we found ourselves in the state of nature.

This emphasis on consent reflects the emergence of social contract theory in the early modern period, when the divine right of kings to rule was being challenged and an alternative source of legitimation was being sought. The first great contract theorist, Thomas Hobbes, wrote his *Leviathan* during the English Civil War (1642–1651), as debates between supporters of the King and supporters of Parliament erupted into violence. Another context for the development of social contract theory—not always emphasized or even mentioned in the literature—was European colonial expansion. It is no coincidence that the 'state of nature' was conceptualized at a time when white Europeans were encountering people who lived very differently—and, indeed, seemed to some European eyes to be living precisely in a pre-political state of nature. For most contract thinkers, the state of nature was primarily hypothetical rather than historical: rather than something which did exist in the past (or still exists today), the 'state of nature' was above all a device for representing the benefits of government. It asks what life *would* look like without government rather than what life *did* look like. Yet, Hobbes offered as an example of an actually existing state of nature 'the savage people in many places of America'. In the work of John Locke, the use of the idea of the state of nature to justify the colonization of the Americas is even more direct and explicit. As Charles Mills has argued, contract theorists took the 'state of nature' to be temporary or hypothetical for white people yet real and permanent for non-white people, who could therefore be portrayed as savages unsuited to political society and in need of being ruled by 'whites'.

When thinking about the social contact, therefore, we must simultaneously think about *who* makes the contract: who are the contracting parties—and, hence, who is it who consents to government? Just as non-whites, non-Europeans, and Indigenous peoples were excluded from different versions of the social contract, so were women and white European men who did not own property.

Each of the following chapters in this Part focuses on a central thinker in the social contract tradition or a major critic of that tradition, beginning with Chapter 5 on Hobbes. Thomas Hobbes was a complex thinker who began from premises which might today be called 'liberal' yet reached highly conservative conclusions that prioritized order and security over freedom. Hobbes's state of nature is one of conflict between self-interested, rational individuals who cannot agree on common moral values. His solution is to propose a highly authoritarian form of government both domestically as well as over acquired territories. As Chapter 5 shows, the complexity and ambiguity of Hobbes's work are also evident in his discussion of family relations: while he assumes and accepts the dominance of patriarchal family structures in most societies, he does not locate the origins of this dominance in any natural right of men over their wives and children.

While studies of modern social contract often begin with Hobbes, such studies do not always include the Dutch philosopher Baruch Spinoza. Yet, as Chapter 6 shows, Spinoza can also be considered a social contract theorist, albeit of an unorthodox kind. Where Hobbes saw relations between people in the state of nature as characterized by competition and conflict, Spinoza emphasized cooperation and reciprocity. And where Hobbes proposed a sovereign with absolute power, Spinoza extolled the advantages of democracy and paid special attention to 'the multitude'. Yet, as was common in the seventeenth century, Spinoza excluded women from political life. Despite the role of the Netherlands as a major colonial power, he also had little to say about colonialism.

Similar exclusions are evident in the work of John Locke, as discussed in detail in Chapter 7. If Hobbes's social contract theory was forged during the English Civil War, and so was preoccupied with the breakdown of sovereignty, Locke was contributing to post-Civil War debates concerning the limits of sovereignty, property rights, and the legitimacy of resisting the sovereign. Locke's state of nature is formulated in such a way that he reaches very different conclusions to those of Hobbes. Locke presents a relatively peaceful state of nature, the theory of which he uses to delineate the rights and duties given to us by God. He places limits on the power of the sovereign and argues that people have the right to resist a sovereign who oversteps those limits. In this way, Locke's work provided many of the foundations for later liberal arguments. Yet Locke's egalitarianism and universalism—and, indeed, that of liberalism more generally—go hand in hand with various forms of exclusion and domination. By focusing especially on Locke's exclusion of wage labourers, women, Indigenous Americans, and slaves, Chapter 7 illuminates the limits of social contract theory.

It is not anachronistic to criticize Locke for his views on class, gender, and race. Rather than simply neglecting particular groups of people, he went to great lengths to justify their exclusion from the social contract. Moreover, some of Locke's own contemporaries either offered more radical theories or were critical of his claims. A good example is discussed in Chapter 8: the English philosopher Mary Astell, born in the seventeenth century, a few years after Locke, offered an early feminist critique of contract theory. She explored the similarities and contradictions between the social contract and the marriage contract, contrasting the freedom and equality given to men in the political sphere with the subordination and domination of women in the domestic sphere. As Chapter 8 shows, Astell's use of irony, rhetoric, and equivocation raises interpretative issues about how her work should be read. Astell's own work can also be criticized: her characterization of wives as slaves is, at the very least, provocative at a time when thousands of African and Indigenous peoples were literally enslaved.

The Genevan philosopher Jean-Jacques Rousseau was also critical of existing social contract theories, while proposing his own version. Rousseau argued that a social contract could become a form of domination and that we need a new contract that will make the people sovereign. He was critical of earlier contract theorists, such as Hobbes, for projecting into the state of nature characteristics which man has actually only acquired in society. Rousseau wanted to show that inequality, dependence, and corruption were not 'natural'. Rather than seeking a return to the state of nature, however, Rousseau sought a form of association in which all will be free and the general will can be expressed. As Chapter 9 suggests, Rousseau's work has provoked hostility from liberal and reactionary critics and provided inspiration for radical and revolutionary thinkers.

Critics of social contract theories in effect have two options: (1) they can argue that contract theory should be abandoned altogether; or (2) they can propose different forms of social contract. These two options are taken by, respectively, Carole Pateman and Charles Mills, who together are the subjects of Chapter 10. Pateman's book *The Sexual Contract* is a landmark text which argued that a prior sexual contract excluded women from the social contract and reinforced the domination of women by men. It inspired Mills's *The Racial Contract*, which argues that there is a racial contract made between whites to exclude and subordinate non-whites. Though she disagrees with Mills on the question of whether contract theory is redeemable, Pateman has in turn drawn upon Mills's analysis of the racial contract to develop the idea of the settler contract, by which white settlers excluded Indigenous peoples.

5 Thomas Hobbes

SIGNY GUTNICK ALLEN

Chapter guide

This chapter examines the ideas of Thomas Hobbes, focusing on the account provided in *Leviathan* (1651). Following an introduction which sets out elements of his historical context, Section 5.2 outlines Hobbes's presentation of the state of nature, natural right, and the laws of nature, linking his analysis to his materialist science. Section 5.3 turns to Hobbes's explanation of the origins of the state and explores his argument that the political relationship is fundamentally representative. It then explains his understanding of sovereignty, as well as his theory of inalienable rights. Section 5.4 examines the possibility that this retained right is the seed of a right to rebel against the sovereign and ends with a brief consideration of Hobbes's legacy.

5.1 Introduction

Thomas Hobbes (1588–1679) occupies both a central and a controversial place in the history of political thought. Born in the year of the Spanish Armada, he developed his key political ideas in the context of the seventeenth-century Civil War between supporters of King Charles I and the English Parliament, which culminated in Charles's beheading in 1649. He thus began his life under the shadow of foreign invasion but published his masterpiece *Leviathan* (1651) to warn of the dangers of the state tearing itself asunder from within.

Hobbes's own political leanings in these struggles were often difficult to identify, even to his own contemporaries. He was an advocate of the absolute power of the sovereign and was part of the English Royalist community in exile in Paris throughout in the 1640s. However, his rejection of the divine right of kings in favour of government by consent and his emphasis on the relationship between subjects' security and their obligation to their rulers meant that he was frequently suspected of supporting and justifying the anti-monarchical Republican regimes which followed the king's execution. As we will see, Hobbes's ideas were often formed in response to specific political challenges, such as the Parliamentarian claim that a king could not represent the people. Nonetheless, he presented his theories as transcending specific contexts or ideologies, declaring his work *De Cive*, or *On the Citizen* (1642/7), to be the first to develop a true 'civil philosophy', or political science, which developed universal rules of government based on empirical observation (quoted in Skinner, 1990: 121).

By emphasizing the importance of centralized state power underpinned by individuals' consent the Hobbesian approach to politics highlights a set of key questions. What does it mean to be a citizen? What are the grounds, nature, and limits of political authority and obligation? The answers Hobbes gave were strikingly different from alternatives available at the time. The Hobbesian community is not a natural entity made up of active citizens whose flourishing depends on continuous participation in governance, as had been argued in earlier Aristotelian and Republican traditions. Instead, Hobbes tells us that it is in subjects' interest to devolve their rights of self-rule and judgement to an all-powerful figure who represents the commonwealth and acts on their behalf.

Read more about **Hobbes's** life and work by accessing the thinker biography on the online resources: www.oup.com/he/Ramgotra-Choat1e.

The key feature of the good citizen is obedience, and politics is a project of artifice and human creation. The only alternative is the pervasive risk of war and death found outside the protection of the state. This account, which is grounded in his theory of human psychology, has struck many as overly pessimistic. But while many readers of Hobbes have rejected his conclusions, it is undeniable that his work continues to play an influential role in both political theory and theories of international relations.

With this focus on the individual, on interests, and on consent as the basis of legitimacy, Hobbes is often included among the social contract thinkers. However, his theory is in many ways unique within, and even in tension with, this tradition, helping us to recognize challenges which would face later philosophers operating within it. The extent to which a single unifying will of the state could be identified, for instance, or what rights citizens hold against the state are problems to which Hobbes provided striking and, in many cases, provocative, answers.

5.2 The state of nature and the laws of nature

5.2.1 A modern theorist?

In presenting the state as a human creation Hobbes emphasized its role as a tool for meeting our interests. Accompanying this shift from nature to artifice was his transformation of natural law from a universal and external moral standard, such as that provided by God, to an account of what any given individual needs to do to guarantee their own self-preservation. This prudentialist account of the role of morality meant that he was often accused of atheism in his own life, and 'Hobbist' was a term of abuse in the early modern period.

Hobbes's strategy of starting with individuals as the 'units' of the state drew on his materialist account of the world in which the universe consists purely of matter in motion. Hobbes rejected key tenets of Christian orthodoxy, including the existence of an immaterial soul, and argued that all perceptions of the external world are caused by external physical stimuli. There is thus no way to access the 'true nature' of something which is outside us, nor is there a universal or objective experience of some external object or concept. Instead, all our responses to the outside world need to be understood as the result of our unique perception, a consequence of the world's material generating reactions within our bodies and of how these reactions make us feel. When we say 'this water is cold' not only do we really mean 'this water is cold *to me*', but we also connect the experience of cold water to wanting to pull away from it (if it is freezing) or of being drawn to it (if it is a hot day). This experience of desire or aversion is inseparable from our knowledge about the water itself, which has implications not only for perception, but also for our decision-making processes (Hobbes, 2010: 13–14, 37–39).

> **Key Concept: Deliberation and the will**
>
> Hobbes broke with earlier philosophical traditions in declaring that all human action was ultimately the result of our passions. When we consider a future course of action, or 'deliberate', these passions alternate in our minds. We might consider the positive outcomes of taking a risk, for instance, before turning away because of the fear of potential harm. In the end, one final passion proves stronger than the others and we either engage in the action or not. Hobbes labels this final passion the 'Will' and so it is a striking feature of his thought that in this sense we have willed, and therefore desired, any actions we undertake following deliberation (ibid.: 44).

It is this inevitable solipsism (the inability to understand the world outside of our own perception) which means both that human beings can be understood scientifically (because we can trace the sources of cause and effect which lead to our actions) and which makes us so prone to conflict. Crucially, this doesn't mean that Hobbes thought that humans are evil or even necessarily antagonistic towards each other (Hobbes, 2008: 11). But it does mean that if cooperation is going to happen between human beings, this must be because we perceive it to be in our own self-interest. It also means that we need to generate a mechanism, like the state, which can be the source of, and enforce, a common set of terms and definitions about the world, including for moral terms like 'good' or 'evil'.

5.2.2 The origins of *warre*: Hobbes on the state of nature

It was a crucial element of Hobbes's account of civil science that just as understanding how a watch works requires taking it apart to see the functioning of its wheels and cogs, understanding something as complex as a state requires studying its constituent elements: human beings (ibid.: 10). In seeking to explain the nature and benefits of life under government, Hobbes developed one of the most notorious elements of his theory: a state of nature in which there is no political power, and our actions are only limited by the brute strength of others. As a result, those living in such a state find themselves in a perpetual 'Warre, where every man is Enemy to every man' and in which life is, famously, 'nasty, brutish and short' (Hobbes, 2010: 89).

The Hobbesian state of nature is characterized, at both the theoretical and the physical levels, by equality. What is striking about his argument is that it is this equality which must be overcome, rather than generated, by politics. While individuals may differ in physical characteristics, such as age and strength, they nonetheless all pose a potential threat to each other. Even the strongest person is vulnerable when asleep (Hobbes, 2008: 26). This physical equality is compounded by a form of moral equality: in the absence of both shared definitions and standards of judgement, there is simply no way to generate an enforceable hierarchy between people, many of whom believe that they are superior to each other (Hobbes, 2010: 87). This moral and physical equality results in an equality of rights. Hobbes believed that we are all primarily driven by our desire to preserve ourselves. No moral system would be legitimate, let alone 'scientific', were it to deny this fact. As a result, we all have the natural right to whatever is needed to achieve this goal. We can connect this argument to Hobbes's materialism. Due to our solipsism, it is not only our perception of the material world which is filtered through our own experiences, but also the way that we understand concepts. Terms like 'bad' and 'good' must be understood as 'bad *for me*' or 'good *for me*' and so among humans of equal power, it is impossible to generate a universal moral standard of 'goodness' or 'badness' which can be used to judge actions. In the absence of any overarching political structures, individuals are the only arbiters of what they may need to feel secure, and so this right to self-preservation becomes, from the perspective of enforceability, a universal right to all things.

It is for this reason that our natural right does not result in any limitations on the behaviour of others. In contrast to other theories which also deploy a version of the state of nature, this right to self-preservation is not balanced by an obligation not to violate the same rights of others (as we see in Locke, see Chapter 7) and, as a claim about *rights* rather than about human nature, it is not placed alongside a tempering sympathy for others (as is found in Rousseau, see Chapter 9).

Even if we assume material abundance in the state of nature, these varying understandings of what is necessary and therefore legitimate for each person to claim for self-preservation would generate discord. The challenge, in other words, is not one of distribution, but of multiple manifestations of right. Hobbes is already hinting at what a state must provide: it must be empowered as a source of common definitions of concepts such as 'just' and 'unjust', so that humans' private definitions will not be a cause of war.

> **Key Concept: Claim rights and liberty rights**
>
> Hobbes's presentation of rights in the state of nature can seem counterintuitive: he argues that before the establishment of the state, we all have equal rights to everything, even after something has been initially taken by someone else. As a result, we might think that none of these claimants have any particular right at all. Many scholars have followed Wesley Hohfeld's (2001 [1919]) distinction between 'liberty rights' and 'claim rights' to explain the gap between Hobbes's account and our intuitions. 'Claim rights' involve duties on the parts of others. A right to private property, for instance, involves a claim on the rest of society not to use, appropriate, or destroy your property without permission. But a 'liberty right', which is the kind of right held by all individuals in the Hobbesian state of nature, simply means that you do not have a duty to do otherwise, and does not demand anything of anyone else.

The potential for legitimate conflict introduced by this universal right is compounded by the psychological portrait Hobbes presents of pre-political humanity. He is aware that the drive to self-preserve manifests itself differently in different individuals, but three core features of human nature stand out as sources of conflict: diffidence (fear), competition, and glory-seeking. Even if only a relatively small number of individuals behave in the latter two ways, this will cause genuine fear in others, who may engage in pre-emptive aggression in response. Here again we see the consequences of solipsism: actions which appear to be aggressive may, from the perpetuator's perspective, simply be natural defensiveness and so the cycle continues, leading to a generalized mistrust of others. This is the dynamic which we see in attempts to generate agreements in the state of nature. As we cannot guarantee that others will keep their promises, especially if their situation changes and the agreement is no longer beneficial, our own self-interest dictates that we anticipate the possibility of others reneging by being the first to break faith. The surprising conclusion is that it might be entirely rational and rightful to behave in ways which most moral systems condemn.

The result of these conditions is that, while the state of nature may not always involve active conflict, all those within it nonetheless experience constant insecurity. In this context, it is impossible to generate the kinds of long-term plans and cultural and scientific advances which Hobbes associates with civilization:

> there is no place for Industry; because the fruit thereof is uncertain: and consequently no Culture of the Earth; no Navigation, nor use of commodities that may be imported by Sea; no commodious Building . . . no Knowledge of the face of the Earth; no account of Time; no Arts; no Letters; no Society.

(Hobbes, 2010: 88–89)

5.2.3 The natural law

The combination of Hobbes's materialism and his belief in the rightful pursuit of self-preservation generates a coordination problem. Given the sources of conflict in the state of nature we might think that escape is impossible, with humans permanently trapped by their inability to settle on universal standards of behaviour. However, Hobbes also believed that the self-preservation drive, which was the source of the natural right to all things, could also lead to constraints on it. He called these constraints the Laws of Nature. In turning to natural law, Hobbes both availed himself of a long-standing tradition in political thought and fundamentally transformed it, rendering what had been understood as an external, and often religious, form of moral guidance into one which emerged from human interests.

Hobbes provides a list of twenty distinct laws of nature over the course of *Leviathan*, with each following on from what he calls the 'fundamentall law': that we have an obligation to seek peace whenever possible, but that if we are unable to do so, we may use any means necessary for our self-preservation. Our natural right and individual interests are thus fundamentally integrated into the system of natural law. Importantly, peace is not presented as a good in itself; we are obliged to create it because it is in our own self-interest to do so. As a result, the laws of nature cannot command that we sacrifice ourselves at their altar, something which is also emphasized in the second natural law which is the basis of the political community: that in the pursuit of peace we must lay down our right to all things to set up the state, but that we only need to do so if all others make the same agreement (ibid.: 92).

Due to their integral role in the structure of Hobbes's theory it is unsurprising that the nature of these laws has been a source of controversy in the scholarship of Hobbes, and that different interpretations have led to fundamentally different views on how we should approach Hobbes as a thinker. According to scholars such as Howard Warrender (1957), the laws must have divine origins: law must be the command of someone with authority, leaving God as the only possible candidate. Such a reading places Hobbes's account closer to traditional natural law theories, according to which they are universal and potentially enforceable on Earth. But other interpreters, including Quentin Skinner (1966), have stressed that Hobbes himself clearly defines these specific laws as not being 'law' properly speaking but as precepts of reason: they are non-enforceable guidelines for how to maximize one's own self-preservation (Hobbes, 2010: 111).

The argument that the Hobbesian laws of nature are not, strictly speaking, external laws but are instead the precepts of reason has led some readers to claim that they are best understood as amoral, and that Hobbesian man should be seen as not merely solipsistic but as fundamentally egotistical. On this reading, because we not only will, but are *permitted* to seek our own best interest in any situation, reason tells us that even once we have left the state of nature, unjust behaviour such as the breaking of contracts is allowed so long as we do not think we will be caught (ibid.: 101). Hobbes seems to have found himself in a bind: by attempting to generate a moral system from self-preservation, he appears to have reduced morality to self-interest, and thus merely reproduced the potential for mutual mistrust which characterizes the state of nature.

This suggestion, though powerful, ignores the distinction between our long-term interests (and especially, our interest in self-preservation) and our more fleeting desires. Someone who continually breaks agreements is unlikely to be accepted into civil society, and so it is in fact in our long-term interest to limit our actions to generate peace (ibid.: 101–102). We can see Hobbes's logic in the structure of his list of the laws of nature. While the first law is indeed a right to act as we need to, the logic of peace-seeking leads to requirements which might be at home within almost any moral framework: we are told to keep promises, to demonstrate gratitude and complaisance, and to avoid arrogance. The normative ground for these laws is still self-interest; these are ways of treating others which help us to avoid conflict. But they also place demands on us, asking us to behave in ways which force us to keep our desires in check for both the greater good and our own (ibid.: 106–107). Recognizing and following the laws of nature is thus shown to be a way to both create and maintain the state; the self-interest which is at the root of conflict can instead be a motivation to limit our own behaviour.

We seem, then, to have quite a traditional account of morality grounded in new ways. Indeed, Hobbes was keen to emphasize that his laws of nature were congruent with Christian teaching, spending chapters in *De Cive* outlining this consistency and, in *Leviathan*, summarizing them in a version of the golden rule: '*Do not that to another, which thou wouldest not have done to thy selfe*' (ibid.: 109).

The laws of nature can also be understood as producing a virtuous circle. Not only do they call for establishing the state because it is our best chance to avoid conflict, but conditions of peace are also the conditions in which the laws themselves are most easily followed. This is clear in Hobbes's claim about their applicability. As he argues, the laws always apply internally (*in foro interno*, or within our own conscience). We must always be aware of what they would demand under ideal circumstances where others are also compliant, even if the laws do not require us to act on them (*in foro externo*, or in our conduct) when obeying them would make us vulnerable to others (ibid.: 110). With the creation of the state and an external force which punishes transgressions, we see a context in which more of the laws of nature will bind in both ways. Hobbes has thus provided us with a type of universal standard, but it is one which is both minimalistic, in that it assumes only that humans share an interest in self-preservation, and contextual, in that the demands it places on individuals vary according to their specific circumstances. This also explains why, for Hobbes, the state is necessary. The challenge is not merely that humans may find following the demands of natural law difficult without an external enforcement mechanism, but also that in the absence of the state, these laws alone will not necessarily lead to less conflict even when people are aware of them and follow them as they should.

5.2.4 Gender and the natural law

These foundational commitments justify Hobbes's theory of natural law and explain why in some places his account differs from more traditional presentations. As Susanne Sreedhar (2020) has argued, unlike earlier thinkers, Hobbes does not include a discussion of sexuality or marriage under the framework of natural law. This seems to be a result of his view that specific family or relationship structures are not necessarily more or less conducive to peace. By removing these areas of life from the jurisdiction of reason or nature, Hobbes permits different societies to come to different conclusions about how to organize this element of life.

This feature of Hobbes's thought has been of particular interest to feminist scholars. As they have emphasized, in the state of nature, families are governed by the laws of nature but this does not automatically lead to a set of patriarchal norms, as might be expected from a seventeenth-century text. Instead, we see a striking account of natural parental authority which foregrounds the rights of the mother. Hobbes suggests that while paternal dominion is common in established states, children naturally owe allegiance to the person who has protected them in infancy, leading to a theory of natural maternal right. He thus challenges standard early modern views on the family in at least two ways. In grounding even family relationships in a form of contract, Hobbes emphasizes the extent to which all human cooperation is rooted in the protection of interests. Second, in denying that men have a natural right over their female partners and children, Hobbes suggests that social structures which many considered to be immutable were simply conventional (Hobbes, 2010: 139–140). At the same time, we should take care not to overplay Hobbes's radicalism. The conditions of the state of nature are intended to be overcome precisely through artificial convention. Maternal right is presented as an early pre-political form of power, and Hobbes does reference examples of matriarchal communities like the Amazons as forms of alternative domestic and political arrangements which can be developed through contracts. Nonetheless, it is also true that the creation of the state is shown as a means of reasserting and legitimizing patriarchal family structures in most societies. As Hobbes observes: 'for the most part Common-wealths have been erected by the Fathers, not by the Mothers of families' (ibid.: 139–140).

The question of why naturally free and equal women, who themselves have dominion over others (children), would enter into 'a pact that subordinated women to men in civil society' (Pateman, 1988: 49) has been debated by feminist readers of Hobbes. The theorist Carole Pateman (see Chapter 10) argued that among the classic social contract theorists the political contract generating the state is preceded by a sexual contract determining family structure and female subservience.

In the case of Hobbes, this occurs when individual women, weakened by the duties of childcare, are conquered by individual men and subsequently agree to a role which is akin to that of a servant whose master has spared her life. These men, who thus confirm their position as the heads of their households, covenant on these households' behalf with other men. The generation of the state goes hand in hand with the legal consolidation of women's inferior status. Women thus have no civil personality, merely a domestic one (ibid.: 44–50).

This reading has been challenged by Nancy Hirschmann, who argues that women's ability to extract loyalty from children should be seen as a source of strength rather than as a weakness. The choice by (most) Hobbesian sovereigns to mandate authoritarian patriarchal families is thus a means of generating social stability in the face of feminine power, and so this family structure follows rather than precedes the creation of the state (Hirschmann, 2008: 44–63). In this telling, women enter into the state-creating covenant on equal terms but are subordinated for the benefit of the commonwealth, rather than this subordination being its pre-condition. While we can draw a clear contrast between Pateman's and Hirschmann's interpretations, both connect Hobbes's assumption about the dominance of patriarchal structures with female biology. This may in turn complicate a reading of Hobbes which suggests that he fully departs from explanations for patriarchy grounded in nature even if in his account not all societies will follow this patriarchal model.

5.2.5 Locating the state of nature

While the Hobbesian state of nature could be understood as an early modern thought experiment, Hobbes was insistent that there existed real examples which his readers could observe to verify his claims: the international sphere; a state experiencing civil war; and, the Americas. In each case, he suggested, we see the same lack of a shared authority, and hence both universal right and universal enmity. While Hobbes did not flesh out these comparisons, considering how he frames them and what he is using them to illustrate sheds light on important aspects of his theory.

The argument that we can see a parallel between states in the international sphere and pre-political individuals, sometimes referred to as the 'domestic analogy', was a common one in the early modern period and Hobbes used it to illustrate how entities will behave when they are solely governed by the laws of nature (Grewal, 2016). Importantly, this set of laws was the same as the interpersonal one which is explored above: a model which prioritized self-preservation under conditions of inevitable natural insecurity. This contrasted with many of his predecessors and contemporaries who had argued for the existence of a separate *ius gentium*, or 'law of nations', which could be used to set standards for distinguishing between just and unjust war, and the treatment of foreign soldiers or traders (Tuck, 1999). Due to Hobbes's rejection of a model of binding international law he has been adopted as an inspiration in the field of international relations. According to some, Hobbes can be understood as one of the forefathers of international realism, in which conflict between states is assumed and sovereign nations will act in much the same way as individuals: they will seek power as a means of ensuring security; they will invade others when needed, including pre-emptively; and they will do so with moral impunity when they have a genuine belief in the necessity of their actions. The international sphere, on this reading, is international anarchy (Beitz, 1979).

More recently, scholars such as Noel Malcolm (2002) have argued that while individual states alone are the arbiters of what is necessary for their own security, as the international sphere becomes more and more stable, the range of permissible actions taken in good faith decreases. Because states differ from individuals in important ways (for instance, the differences in strength and power are more obvious), the international state of nature may be less unpredictable than the interpersonal one. As a result, there are fewer excuses for setting aside the more demanding natural laws. Because states will generally cater to the needs of their own populations even as they may put those of other states at risk, the fact of nations being in a 'posture of War' against each other does not lead to 'that misery, which accompanies the Liberty of particular men' (Hobbes, 2010: 90). There is thus no imperative for international sovereignty, as later thinkers, such as Kant, would claim (see more on Kant in Chapter 29).

> ### Key Thinker: Hugo Grotius
>
> Hugo Grotius (1583–1645) was an influential Dutch theorist and legal scholar. His major work *The Rights of War and Peace* (1625) argued that natural law regulates human interactions even among those who do not share a sovereign. As a result, we can differentiate between just and unjust wars, as well as between just and unjust conduct during war. This idea was predicated on a community of states, which he believed permitted a balance between our right to preserve ourselves and our possessions, on the one hand, and, on the other, our obligations towards other members of this international community. Grotius's work was important for the twentieth-century 'English School' of international relations, and, as a fellow rights and contract theorist, he provides an important contrast to Hobbes, particularly on the topic of the *ius gentium* ('law of nations', or international law).

Understanding Hobbes's positioning of all states as being at war with each other, even if they are not actually fighting, helps to shed light on the two further examples he provides of the state of nature. By stating that men in a condition of 'civill Warre' have returned to a state of nature in which they regain all natural rights, including the right to seek out protection wherever they can, Hobbes suggested that both sides in such a conflict are equally legitimate in defending themselves. This claim disturbed his Royalist contemporaries who argued that actions by their Parliamentarian opponents were necessarily illegitimate. Turning to the third example, Hobbes's framing of Indigenous Americans as living in a 'brutish manner' with 'no government at all' reminds us that his works were written at a time of increasing expansion into and colonization of the so-called 'New World' (Hobbes, 2010: 89–90). His account of the right of states to engage in whatever actions they perceive as necessary to their own survival has clear implications for the legitimacy of such expansion.

From 1622 Hobbes himself was a shareholder in the Virginia Company, and so would have been familiar with a range of justifications for colonialism (Malcolm, 2002: 54). While there are relatively few references to the Americas in Hobbes's texts, the illustrated frontispiece of his work *De Cive* contrasts the state of *Libertas* ('Liberty'), portrayed as a nearly naked, haggard figure representing an Indigenous American woman, with the healthy, robed, and European figure of *Imperium* ('Command'). Such imagery, alongside his use of terms such as 'savage people' (Hobbes, 2010: 89) to describe the original inhabitants of the Americas, has suggested to some readers that Hobbes is deploying a 'tacit racial logic', according to which 'the *literal* state of nature is reserved for nonwhites' while 'for whites the state of nature is *hypothetical*' (Mills, 1997: 66). The case of civil war suggests that Europeans not only can but do also experience a version of the state of nature, but as Charles Mills has pointed out, part of the shock of Hobbes's theory to his contemporaries may have been the suggestion that 'without a sovereign *even Europeans* could descend [to the level of Indigenous Americans], and that the absolutist government appropriate for nonwhites could also be appropriate for whites' (ibid.: 66) (see more on Mills in Chapter 10).

Hobbes's account of the international anarchy has clear implications for colonialism. While Hobbes writes that the 'insatiable appetite' of 'enlarging Dominion' is a danger to the stability of the colonizing state (Hobbes, 2010: 230), he nonetheless argues that when the population of a given nation has grown so large that domestic institutions are unable to provide for it, it is acceptable for the state to set up settler colonies elsewhere (ibid.: 175–176, 234). This appears to be justified through his account of the international sphere as a state of nature; the actions of the settlers are legitimized through their universal natural right, rather than through civilizational superiority over other populations. Hobbes's theory therefore might not actively encourage imperial expansion, but this reasoning doesn't place any meaningful barriers in its way. Moreover, as Pat Moloney (2011) has argued, the suggestion that non-Europeans had not formed properly constituted commonwealths was used by later thinkers who argued that international law and its protections applied specifically to states, and therefore not to peoples without sovereignty (as it had been defined in European political thought). Regardless of Hobbes's own project, his framing of the opposition between the 'Old' and 'New' Worlds as being about a difference in sovereignty thus introduced the possibility of a tiered international sphere and the relegation of Indigenous peoples to a position outside the community of states.

> **5.2 The state of nature and the laws of nature: Key Points**
>
> - Prior to the creation of government, humans possess a right to self-preservation which, because we are all entitled to judge what is needed for our own self-preservation, becomes a right to all things.
> - This right is a source of conflict in the pre-political state of nature, which Hobbes thought could be observed in the international sphere, during civil war, and among Indigenous communities.
> - The only escape from this state is to recognize and follow the laws of nature; these explain that it is in our own self-interest to impose mutual obligations on ourselves to obey a common sovereign and thus enter into the commonwealth.

5.3 The social contract

5.3.1 Authorization and representation

As we saw in the discussion of the second law of nature, it is central to Hobbes's project that to escape the state of nature, individuals must covenant with others to each lay down their right to all things. This right can also be understood as a right of judgement or self-governance, and the purpose of the state is therefore to overcome the dangers of the state of nature which emerge from these inevitably disparate, yet equally legitimate, judgements. As a result of this process, Hobbes argues, we can generate a single, unified standard of behaviour, and a mechanism to enforce it. The covenant which generates the state is therefore the means, required by reason, by which people best secure their own individual self-preservation.

To generate this unity, all future subjects transfer their right to all things to some individual (or group), thus designating the future sovereign. Rights are not like physical tokens, as Hobbes recognized, and they cannot be concretely traded or 'given up'. Instead, what this right-transfer requires is that future subjects pledge to not frustrate the sovereign's actions and to aid the sovereign in any way legally required (Hobbes, 2010: 92–93, 120–121). The sovereign, importantly, does not make any direct promises of its own, and can be understood as an indirect or third-party beneficiary of this agreement. This focus on the individual who covenants with others as an individual sets Hobbes apart from many other members of the social contract tradition. He did not suggest that those in the state of nature come together first as a 'people' who then subsequently engage in a contract with a specific government or ruler. This initial stage was often used to theorize conceptions of popular sovereignty, including the right of 'the people' to replace their sovereign by force if necessary.

Hobbes used the concepts of representation and authorization to characterize the political relationship between subjects and sovereign. His understanding of these terms is different from both contemporary and seventeenth-century views on political representation. It is a good example of his ability to co-opt and defang political conceptions used by his political adversaries to demonstrate that their ideas could be used to advocate for a very different kind of politics. When subjects engage in the initial rights-transfer, they agree, according to the most mature version of Hobbes's theory, to 'authorize' the sovereign to act on their behalf (ibid.: 111–121). Today, we often think of political representation as a form of delegation, in which representatives take direction from the individual or group which they represent. Misrepresentation might therefore occur when a representative, such as an elected politician, deviates from their instructions or mandate. This is not how Hobbes used the concept. While he does argue that the sovereign's actions should track the interests of those who have transferred their rights, this is only true in the broadest possible sense. The sovereign must act to secure *salus populi* ('the safety of the people') (ibid.: 9, 231). But it is ultimately up to them how to achieve this, and indeed evidence that the sovereign has failed in this task might only emerge in the context of state breakdown. According to Hobbes, representation simply means that an authorized representative is permitted to act on behalf of the represented entity. Once this relationship is established, the represented then takes responsibility for the actions of their representative. In the case of the covenant which establishes sovereignty, subjects all agree that in authorizing the sovereign, they will take the latter's will for their own. Importantly, the sovereign is here acting in a dual representative capacity. It represents the will of each subject, but in the process of the creation of this unified will, a new entity also comes into existence: the commonwealth, which Hobbes labels the 'Leviathan'. The sovereign thus not only speaks for—and defines the will of—each subject, but it also has the exclusive right to do the same for this new state.

> ### Key Concept: Religious imagery of the Leviathan
>
> Hobbes's discussion of political power is replete with religious symbolism. In *Leviathan*, he describes the commonwealth as a 'Mortall God'; in the same text he suggests that subjects be taught a list of duties towards the sovereign which is framed as a secular, political version of the Ten Commandments. The title of *Leviathan* is itself Biblical and is derived from the Book of Job. Not only is his commonwealth compared to the terrifying sea monster 'Leviathan', the latter is called the 'King of all the children of pride' (Job 41.34), an apt label, given the self-interested and competitive human beings Hobbes envisages as the building blocks of his theory (Hobbes, 2010: 221).

This model of representation thus gives the sovereign representative immense power. Not only is there no such thing as 'a people' capable of acting independently of the sovereign, but the sovereign is the only mechanism by which the will of both the commonwealth itself, and the political will of each member, can be known. To act against the will of the sovereign is thus not only to act against the will of the state but is also a form of impermissible self-contradiction on the part of the subject.

When Hobbes put forward his theory, it was commonly held that the representative and represented needed to share some key characteristics for this representation to be legitimate. A king, as an individual, would be incapable of representing a pluralistic nation. Hobbes's account of representation dismisses this Parliamentarian objection to monarchy. Representation, he argued, is a legal or juridical relationship, not an aesthetic one. Any entity can be given the right to speak for any other entity if they have been chosen and authorized by the represented figure.

Hobbes is clear that the central principles regarding the nature of the state and the relationship between subjects and sovereign apply to all properly constituted commonwealths. At the same time, he is aware that what he labels the 'commonwealth by institution', according to which individuals come together and covenant in the state of nature, is a highly idealized model. Instead, he argued that states would most likely come about, and expand, through conquest, or what he called the 'commonwealth by acquisition'. Both are generated by consent and are, from Hobbes's perspective, equally legitimate: in one case, one authorizes the sovereign out of fear of one's fellow humans in the state of nature, and in the other one does the same from fear of the invading foreign sovereign. This conqueror offers individuals the choice between joining their commonwealth on the same terms as all other citizens, or destruction (ibid.: 138–139, 486). This choice will strike many readers as one inevitably made under duress, and we can question whether future subjects are able to offer meaningful consent at all. However, for Hobbes, decisions made due to fear must be recognized as free and it is this account of freedom, alongside his understanding of human decision-making, which lead him to generate an internally coherent account of political consent, albeit one which is at odds with contemporary views.

> **Key Concept: Liberty**
>
> Hobbes famously defines liberty in *Leviathan* as the absence of external impediments (ibid.: 145). In other words, we are free to the extent that our actions are not constrained by outside physical forces, an extreme example of what Isaiah Berlin labelled 'negative liberty' (Berlin, 1969). This means that many actions which we might consider to be 'unfree', such as those performed under duress, are technically 'free' on Hobbes's account. However, there is a second concept of freedom which operates throughout Hobbes's theory: liberty as the absence of obligation, such as our obligations to the state. A question which emerges is whether these two accounts are compatible. While Hobbes does label the laws 'Artificiall Chains', these do not actually physically constrain (Hobbes, 2010: 147). At most, it might be the fear of the consequence of lawbreaking which pushes our deliberative process towards obedience. As fear is not an external impediment, it appears that we are equally free when we obey *or* break the law.

5.3.2 Absolute sovereignty

Hobbes's account of authorization and the role it plays in the creation of the state helped him to explain and justify, using the language of his political opponents, a concept of absolute sovereignty. The argument that political sovereignty requires the centralization of authority in a specific individual or group which cannot be overridden was not entirely new. The French theorist and jurist Jean Bodin (1530–1596) had previously argued that in all states there has been some power which has historically emerged as the final decision-maker. In Hobbes's case, absolute sovereignty is not merely a descriptive reality but a theoretical necessity. As a precondition of true unity and statehood, there must be a means of overcoming the problem of individual judgement, according to which there will be multiple different accounts of 'the good' or 'justice'. There must, in other words, be a single arbiter and final decision-maker; to have this authority is the essence of sovereignty. Hobbes is clear that whatever the constitutional form of a state, there will be some identifiable sovereign: the king or queen in a monarchy, a class in an aristocracy, and the people in a democracy. What is logically impossible is a mixed constitution, as this would simply replicate the dangers of the state of nature by perpetually threatening the possibility of civil war.

As a result of this view of sovereignty, Hobbes argued that several rights and powers must be attached to the sovereign, even when they appear to function as separate organs of the state. Sovereigns must have absolute rights over precisely the branches of government which Hobbes's

Parliamentarian opponents of the 1640s argued that they, rather than the king, should control, such as the militia and taxation. The sovereign must also have legislative capacity (ibid.: 121–129). This is not merely a claim about civil law, or the specific laws passed in each state (sometimes referred to as 'positive law'): sovereigns also have the right to interpret the laws of nature for their subjects. Thus, 'theft' might be universally held as a wrong under the natural law, but different sovereigns might come to different conclusions about what falls under the category of 'stealing' (Hobbes, 2008: 86). This is true even though the authority of these laws pre-dates and exists outside of the authorization of the sovereign. Finally, Hobbes's theory of sovereignty took direct aim at one of the institutions he saw as most responsible for the outbreak of civil war in his own times: the Church. As the frontispiece to the *Leviathan* illustrates, the commonwealth holds both the sword of war and a bishop's crozier, indicating that the sovereign controls both secular and religious government, a philosophical position known as 'Erastianism'. The state church is therefore not a separate entity with its own legitimacy and decision-making structures and the sovereign has the right both to determine religious doctrine and to appoint ministers.

5.3.3 The duties of sovereignty

While Hobbes's theory of sovereignty and account of the authorization process entailed that the sovereign had no direct obligations to subjects, he nonetheless argued that the sovereign had a duty to generate peace and stability. Hobbes is clear that performing this duty is in the interest of the sovereign as well, not least due to their personal interest in avoiding rebellion, which might arise if large numbers of subjects consistently feel insecure. While Hobbes allows a range of possible social arrangements across different commonwealths, he nonetheless outlines certain political and social institutions which sovereigns should create. These include systems of national education in which subjects are taught the principles behind the commonwealth, as well as national work and welfare programmes, so that the basic self-preservation of each subject is guaranteed (Hobbes, 2010: 234–239). Hobbes also goes into detail about the legal and criminal justice systems, outlining permissible and impermissible justifications of punishment and the legal rights which all subjects have under the law, including following criminal conviction.

5.3.4 The limits of covenanting

The authorization which individuals give to their future sovereign is uniquely wide-ranging and covers nearly all aspects of life in the commonwealth. However, the rights-transfer is not absolute and subjects retain a right of self-preservation. As a result, the authorizing covenant involves the unspoken caveat that no subject agrees to help the sovereign harm them, with Hobbes insisting that even if an individual seeks to transfer or contract away this fundamental right, we are not to take this transfer seriously (ibid.: 150–152). This retained right of self-preservation is explained in two ways: (1) that it would be illogical to expect people to enter a covenant in which the purpose of the agreement (self-preservation) is undermined, and (2) that it is psychologically impossible to expect individuals not to try rescue themselves when needed, and so a theory of political obligation which demands this is simply untenable. Importantly, the individual's retained right does not imply that the sovereign has an obligation to facilitate this self-preservation. The theory therefore outlines a seemingly paradoxical situation in which individuals who are legally condemned to death or imprisonment are permitted to resist a sovereign who is exercising their (legitimate) right to punish lawbreakers (ibid.: 214).

This account of inalienable rights complicates how we should think of Hobbes's theory. For some readers, the emphasis on the individual and their retained rights has indicated that Hobbes should be seen as a proto-liberal thinker, or at the very least as a 'liberal illiberal' (Ryan, 2012; Malcolm,

2016). Others have argued that these rights are not politically salient in the face of overwhelming sovereign power (Baumgold, 1988). Finally, we might question the extent to which they are compatible with Hobbes's theory more broadly. According to Jean Hampton (1986), the right to self-preservation must act in the commonwealth, as it did in the state of nature, as a right of judgement regarding what this right allows us to do. As a result, a model of state formation which involves giving up private judgement is impossible if subjects retain this right, and sovereign authority is fatally undermined.

> ### 5.3 The social contract: Key Points
>
> - All states must have an absolute sovereign, who has wide-ranging powers over war and peace, criminal justice, education, and taxation, as well as the right to determine doctrine.
> - The relationship between the sovereign and their subjects is a representative one: in transferring their rights, subjects agree that the sovereign may define their will and act on their behalf.
> - This rights transfer is not absolute; all subjects retain a right to self-preservation, though scholars disagree about how impactful this retained right really is.

5.4 Rebellion and state breakdown

5.4.1 Protection and obligation

Hobbes emphasizes in his account of the origin of the state that the political relationship is the result of subjects' consent to be represented. However, he also argued that the reason we have an obligation towards our sovereign is independent of any concrete agreement we have made; it is instead because sovereigns provide us with security. It is thus not our consent or the legitimacy that this confers on the state that are important but instead the question of who (we believe) is able and willing to protect us (Hobbes, 2010: 484–485). This has led some readers to argue that Hobbes is ultimately more concerned with pragmatic reality and power than with theoretical legitimacy (Hoekstra, 2004). This pragmatism can also be connected both to Hobbes's account of the duties of the sovereign and to his theory of state breakdown. Regardless of whether subjects have a right to rebel, he is very aware that if sovereigns fail to either assert their authority, such as by failing to properly regulate doctrine, or ignore the needs of their subjects, as when criminal justice is not delivered equitably, rebellion is a likely outcome.

5.4.2 A right to rebel?

This emphasis on the authority of the sovereign being derived from their power and practical abilities rather than from some other legitimating process led some of Hobbes's contemporaries to suggest that *Leviathan* was in fact, as the royalist Bishop John Bramhall put it, a 'rebel's catechism', according to which fighting against one's sovereign and winning effective control is an entirely legitimate and rightful means of gaining political authority (Bramhall, 1995: 145). More recently, Susanne Sreedhar (2010) has controversially argued that, despite Hobbes's emphasis on absolute and centralized state power, a genuine right to rebel can be constructed from the Hobbesian right to self-preservation because individuals can, in situations of extreme necessity, work together to protect each other against a common threat posed by the state itself (Hobbes, 2010: 152).

5.4.3 Hobbes's legacy

While early readers found Hobbes's focus on self-interest and the apparently secular nature of his moral system shocking, it was precisely these elements of his thought which appealed to a new wave of twentieth-century contractarian thinkers who sought to integrate insights from rational choice and game theory into political philosophy (Gauthier, 1979; Hampton, 1986; Kavka, 1986). His account of politics as shaped by conflict and competing interests has also appealed to political thinkers who adopt a 'realist' as opposed to a 'moralist' approach to politics, at both the domestic and international levels (Douglass, 2020). Among readers drawing on Marxist or Republican frameworks, however, some of the most pernicious features of modern politics can be traced back to his thought. C.B. Macpherson argued that Hobbesian psychology is really the application of 'the essential characteristics of the competitive market' to interpersonal relations; even if modern capitalism did not exist at the time of Hobbes's writing, he helped pave the way for modern bourgeois society (Macpherson, 2011: 39). Hannah Arendt (2017: 182–186) claimed that the reduction of all politics to interests meant that individuals would seek a constant accumulation of power, something which she argued spurred European imperialism (see more on Arendt in Chapter 19).

> **5.4 Rebellion and state breakdown: Key Points**
>
> - Hobbes's emphasis on the relationship between obligation and protection suggests he can be understood both as a pragmatic theorist of power and as a theorist of consent-based legitimacy.
> - This focus on protection and the retained right to self-preservation might, under certain conditions, constitute the grounds of a genuine right to rebel against the sovereign.
> - Hobbes's focus on rights and the individual has led to a complicated legacy in the history of political thought. His ideas have been adopted by some Liberal and Realist thinkers but, among theorists drawing on Republican and Marxist traditions, he has been held responsible for pernicious features of modern politics, including imperialism and an individualistic, interest-based model of society.

5.5 Conclusion

Hobbes's account of politics is an attempt to answer the question of how humans can overcome their mutual suspicion, pride, and competitive drives to live together in the absence of natural sociability. His solution, a sovereign who has the right to define the political wills of all their subjects as well as that of the commonwealth itself, has struck many readers as extreme or dangerous. However, it is also one which raises crucial questions about the scope and nature of the social contract, especially in the context of divided sovereignty resulting in political deadlock or conflict.

As this chapter has shown, Hobbes achieved this by transforming and deploying concepts which had long been part of the political discourse of his time. In presenting the laws of nature as the precepts of reason which support us in our quest for self-preservation rather than as external and universal constraints on our behaviour, he was able to provide an account of morality grounded in self-interest. While the consequence of these laws—the all-powerful Leviathan—has long been used as a byword for terrifyingly absolute rule, Hobbes sought to demonstrate that life under such a system was nonetheless infinitely preferable to its alternative and could even be a site of human flourishing. While sovereigns are not party to the covenants which empower them and do not have any direct duties towards their subjects, we saw that Hobbes was nonetheless concerned with outlining a model of good rule which would promote peace and security.

SOCIAL CONTRACT THEORY AND ITS CRITICS

This emphasis on the interests of the individual led to one of the most confounding elements of Hobbes's theory: the right to resist harm to one's person, even after we have entered a political community, and even in the context of the state's legitimate right to harm us. For some readers, this suggests that even Hobbes was unable to avoid including a version of a right to rebel against the state in his theory, raising the question of the nature and extent of the absolutism of any political model based on consent, rights, and human interests.

Take your learning further by accessing the online resources for a library of web links to relevant videos, articles, blogs, and useful websites for this chapter: www.oup.com/he/Ramgotra-Choat1e.

Study questions

1. What are the causes of 'warre' in the Hobbesian state of nature, and what does he mean by this term?
2. Once individuals have left the Hobbesian state of nature, do the laws of nature still have a role to play?
3. In what ways is the Hobbesian sovereign a representative?
4. Does Hobbes have a coherent account of freedom?
5. Is the Hobbesian international sphere best described as an 'anarchy'?
6. Why, according to Hobbes, does sovereignty need to be absolute?
7. Why does Hobbes argue for an original maternal, rather than paternal, right over children and what might be some implications of this argument?
8. To what extent is Hobbes a theorist of the social contract?

Further reading

Primary sources

Hobbes, T. (2008) *On the Citizen*. Eds R. Tuck and M. Silverthorne. Cambridge: Cambridge University Press.
   An English translation of Hobbes's Latin work *De Cive*, originally printed in 1642 and published in 1647 with additional material.

Hobbes, T. (2010) *Leviathan*. Ed. R. Tuck. Cambridge: Cambridge University Press.
   An accessible, one-volume edition of Hobbes's (1651) masterpiece, with a very helpful Introduction.

Secondary sources

Hampton, J. (1986) *Hobbes and the Social Contract Tradition*. Cambridge: Cambridge University Press.
   A classic text illustrating the use of game theory and rational choice models to analyse Hobbes's thought.

Hirschmann, N. and Wright, J. (eds) (2012) *Feminist Interpretations of Thomas Hobbes*. University Park, PA: Pennsylvania State University Press.
   This collection of essays examines the role of women in Hobbes's theory and considers what insights we might gain for current debates.

Lloyd, S.A. (ed.) (2012) *Hobbes Today*. New York: Cambridge University Press.
   An edited volume which explores Hobbesian responses to contemporary topics such as bipartisanship, conscription, and taxation.

Malcolm, N. (2002) *Aspects of Hobbes*. Oxford: Oxford University Press.
   This volume of essays showcases the contextualist method of reading past political texts and includes a helpful biography and discussion of Hobbes's involvement in the Virginia Company.

Skinner, Q. (2008) *Hobbes and Republican Liberty*. Cambridge: Cambridge University Press.
   An exploration of Hobbes's theory of liberty and its relationship to a Republican account of liberty as non-domination.

Sommerville, J.P. (1992) *Thomas Hobbes: Political Ideas in Historical Context*. Basingstoke: Macmillan.
   A thematically organized discussion of key Hobbesian concepts, engaging in both textual and contextual analysis.

Sreedhar, S. (2010) *Hobbes on Resistance: Defying the Leviathan*. Cambridge: Cambridge University Press.
   The best modern argument for the existence of a Hobbesian right to rebel.

Tuck, R. (1989) *Hobbes*. Oxford: Oxford University Press.
   A short, clear account of Hobbes's life, thought, and works, which highlights his engagement with continental thinkers, including Descartes.

References

Arendt, H. (2017) *The Origins of Totalitarianism*. London: Penguin.

Baumgold, D. (1988) *Hobbes's Political Theory*. Cambridge: Cambridge University Press.

Beitz, C. (1979) *Political Theory and International Relations*. Princeton, NJ: Princeton University Press.

Berlin, I. (1969) 'Two Concepts of Liberty'. In I. Berlin, *Four Essays on Liberty*. London: Oxford University Press, pp. 118-172.

Bramhall, J. (1995) 'The Catching of Leviathan, or the Great Whale'. In G.A.J. Rogers (ed.), *Contemporary Responses to the Political Theory of Thomas Hobbes*. Bristol: Thoemmes Press, pp. 115-179.

Douglass, R. (2020) 'Hobbes and Political Realism'. *European Journal of Political Theory*, 19(2): 250-269.

Gauthier, D.P. (1979) *The Logic of Leviathan: The Moral and Political Theory of Thomas Hobbes*. Oxford: Clarendon Press.

Grewal, D.S. (2016) 'The Domestic Analogy Revisited: Hobbes on International Order'. *Yale Law Journal*, 125(3): 618-680.

Hampton, J. (1986) *Hobbes and the Social Contract Tradition*. Cambridge: Cambridge University Press.

Hirschmann, N. (2008) *Gender, Class and Freedom in Modern Political Theory*. Princeton, NJ: Princeton University Press.

Hobbes, T. (2008) *On the Citizen*. Ed. R. Tuck and M. Silverthorne. Cambridge: Cambridge University Press.

Hobbes, T. (2010) *Leviathan*. Ed. R. Tuck. Cambridge: Cambridge University Press.

Hoekstra, K. (2004) 'The de facto Turn in Hobbes's Political Philosophy'. In T. Sorell and L. Foisneau (eds), *Leviathan after 350 Years*. Oxford: Oxford University Press, pp. 33-74.

Hohfeld, W.N. (2001 [1919]) *Fundamental Legal Conceptions as Applied in Judicial Reasoning*. Ed. D. Campbell and P. Thomas. Aldershot: Ashgate.

Kavka, G.S. (1986) *Hobbesian Moral and Political Theory*. Princeton, NJ: Princeton University Press.

Macpherson, C.B. (2011) *The Political Theory of Possessive Individualism: Hobbes to Locke*. Ed. F. Cunningham. Don Mills, ON: Oxford University Press.

Malcolm, N. (2002) *Aspects of Hobbes*. Oxford: Oxford University Press.

Malcolm, N. (2016) 'Thomas Hobbes: Liberal Illiberal'. *Journal of the British Academy*, 4: 113-136.

Mills, C.W. (1997) *The Racial Contract*. Ithaca, NY: Cornell University Press.

Moloney, P. (2011) 'Hobbes, Savagery, and International Anarchy'. *American Political Science Review*, 105(1): 189-204.

Pateman, C. (1988) *The Sexual Contract*. Redwood City, CA: Stanford University Press.

Ryan, A. (2012) *The Making of Modern Liberalism*. Princeton, NJ: Princeton University Press.

Skinner, Q. (1966) 'The Ideological Context of Hobbes's Political Thought'. *The Historical Journal*, 9(3): 286–317.

Skinner, Q. (1990) 'Thomas Hobbes on the Proper Signification of Liberty: The Prothero Lecture'. *Transactions of the Royal Historical Society*, 40: 121–151.

Sreedhar, S. (2010) *Hobbes on Resistance: Defying the Leviathan*. Cambridge: Cambridge University Press.

Sreedhar, S. (2020) 'Hobbes on Sexual Morality'. *Hobbes Studies*, 33(1): 54–83.

Tuck, R. (1999) *The Rights of War and Peace: Political Thought and the International Order from Grotius to Kant*. Oxford: Oxford University Press.

Warrender, J.H. (1957) *The Political Philosophy of Hobbes: His Theory of Obligation*. Oxford: Clarendon Press.

6 Baruch Spinoza

CAROLINE WILLIAMS

Chapter guide

This chapter will focus on the major works of Baruch Spinoza as they impact upon politics. Attention will be given primarily to the posthumously published *Ethics*. This broadly philosophical work, composed over fifteen years, opens up many important ideas that are further developed in Spinoza's two explicitly political works, the *Theologico-Political Treatise* and the unfinished *Political Treatise*. After an introduction, Section 6.2 explores some of the key ideas and concepts to be found in the *Ethics*, including the concepts of nature, individuality, mind and body, imagination, and freedom. Section 6.3 deepens the political ground of these concepts by addressing power and democracy. Section 6.4 advances Spinoza's idea of the multitude and considers some of the political exclusions present in his political philosophy. While there may be limits in the perception of political equality, gender, and race to be found in his works, Spinoza's analysis of the relationship between the human condition and the natural world remains deeply prescient for many radical political thinkers reflecting on such themes today. Overall, the aim will be to highlight the many ways in which Spinoza is truly our contemporary.

6.1 Introduction

The writings of Spinoza (1632–1677) have long occupied a marginal position within the canon of political thought. His name has often remained concealed between the twin figures of Hobbes and Machiavelli (see Chapters 5 and 25, respectively) within political thought, and overshadowed by the presence of Descartes (see Key Thinker: René Descartes box in Section 6.2.1) within philosophy. It is therefore to be celebrated that Spinoza's name is included in a volume drawing attention to hidden and absent elements of our political history. If, at times, his position appears ambivalent in relation to these elements, there are, nonetheless, many resources within his thought upon which feminists and radical thinkers continue to draw.

Spinoza was born in 1632 in Amsterdam, which was the central hub of Dutch mercantile capitalism. Both the Dutch East India Company (founded in 1603) and the Dutch West India Company (founded in 1612) were involved in the slave trade that would last well into the nineteenth century, and the period is marked by ongoing conflicts in the colonies (largely between Holland and Portugal) that reverberated on the domestic stage. It is noteworthy that we find only one significant reference to this dominant postcolonial imaginary made by Spinoza in the form of his experience of a dream that we will consider later in the chapter. Spinoza's family developed an import-export business trading in goods from Brazil. He showed little interest in the family business and chose instead to mix in the intellectually progressive circles that debated the relationship between science and theology. Could science be brought to bear upon theological explanations of the world? Might philosophy develop any autonomy from the theological claims of divine reason? Both of these themes are developed in Spinoza's major writings. At this time, universities were largely institutions for the teaching and advancement of theology, and to think outside of this framework was considered treasonable. We should remain unsurprised that Spinoza in 1673 refused the offer of a post at the University of Heidelberg, preferring to practise and maintain his own philosophical freedom and independence. It was in this shifting intellectual and historical context that Spinoza began to discuss and build the key arguments of the *Ethics*.

Despite his notable academic concealment, Spinoza was actually a key thinker of the Enlightenment whose writings scandalized his time with their radical rejection of any transcendent God inseparable from the world. In the *Ethics*, Spinoza writes of God as identical with nature itself, setting in motion competing cries of atheism and pantheism (where God and reality are interchangeable) that were to fuel philosophical disputes for many decades to come. His thought became associated with a movement rather than simply a philosophy, and to be labelled a Spinozist was therefore associated with all forms of atheism. His *Tractatus Theologico Politicus* (*TTP*), the only work to be published during his own lifetime (its first edition being clandestinely published in Latin in 1670 under a false title page and publisher), was considered by many of his contemporaries to be a subversive political tract. Its core argument was a secular attack upon belief in religious revelation, asserting the power of natural philosophical reason above superstitious belief, and highlighting individual freedom and power as key political goals. For many political philosophers it represents a preliminary statement of liberal democracy, and was studied carefully by Rousseau and the young Marx (see Israel, 2001). This so-called 'golden age' of European Enlightenment was inseparable from the growth of capitalism, itself stimulated by voyages of colonial exploration that increasingly gave these new ideas of freedom, contract, and individuality an unacknowledged ideological blindness as well as an important gender and racial subtext.

Spinoza paid for this deep commitment to freedom of thought when he was excommunicated from the Jewish community. His intellectual work could not be halted, however, and he continued to circulate and discuss drafts of the yet unpublished *Ethics*, as well as receive visits from some of the most significant figures of his time, the context of which are portrayed in the many letters he exchanged (see Spinoza, 1985a; 2016a).

While it is common to situate Spinoza in relation to an emerging liberalism, this is arguably a one-sided view and this chapter will show the many faces of Spinoza. Like Machiavelli, Spinoza is a realist who does not attempt to idealize either man or politics. He wishes to take the human being as immersed in a life of passion and action. Like Marx, he can also be described as a thinker of the masses since he understands the individual not as the pure, uncontaminated element of politics but as part of nature and a product of relationships, both human and non-human. He is also, like Nietzsche, an excavator of morality who recognizes that moral norms must be interrogated and are not a guide for either knowledge or politics. Placed alongside these three political figures, Spinoza appears as a critic of liberalism rather than one of its founders. He is also, however, one of its friends, pushing liberalism to reframe its conception of the individual, which can only truly blossom in community. Indeed, if we could agree that one of the perennial problems shaping political philosophy, and liberalism in particular, is the relationship between the individual and community, or the collective sphere of politics, then Spinoza offers us new conceptual tools to reimagine the shape of politics.

Read more about **Spinoza's** life and work by accessing the thinker biography on the online resources: www.oup.com/he/Ramgotra-Choat1e.

6.2 From *Ethics* to politics

Spinoza's *Ethics* was a controversial text with a complex history, punctuated by his deep reflections, in the *TTP*, upon politics and superstition. The *Ethics* is therefore far from being a self-contained text and we must be aware of the trails to and from his political works. The *Ethics* presents us with a theory of nature, a psychology of the passions and how they might limit our freedom and action, together with an important statement of Spinoza's political theory and its relation to his philosophy. Its five parts are written in a very distinctive geometric style, establishing key axioms, propositions, and proofs that sometimes appear overly abstract and detached, but are also balanced by more explanatory, critical reflections (called scholia), as well as short appendices that more directly draw the reader in. What, then, are the central tenets of Spinoza's thought that necessitated his excommunication?

By far the most shocking aspect of Spinoza's philosophy is his radical monism. Monism attributes oneness to the world. Spinoza refuses Descartes' idea of many different substances, where God is a divine substance beyond the world (see Key Thinker: René Descartes). He similarly rejects a dualism between the human and non-human, as well as between mind and body. His monist view identifies one substance, God, that is expressed in infinite ways, and where human thought and bodily extension are but two of many expressions. Since everything in reality expresses and is a part of this infinite substance known as God, Spinoza writes of God as identical with nature itself: *Deus, sive Natura* (God, that is Nature) where the Latin term *sive* is used to signify equivalence. This connection of God with Nature scandalized his time and helps us to account for claims regarding his atheism, as well as his pantheism, where God is found in every thing. Indeed, the rich diversity within interpretations of Spinoza is largely due to the metaphysical fascination with this knot between God and the world (see Moreau, 1996). It is also what makes his philosophy most relevant to contemporary environmental thought where the relationship between the human and non-human is so important.

6.2.1 The critique of religion

The kernel of Spinoza's argument here is presented most accessibly in the Appendix to Part 1 of the *Ethics*. Spinoza sweeps away the dominant ideas of a transcendent, other-worldly God who creates the world, and of a hierarchical chain of being from God to human existence. God is not a being who fashions the world according to certain ends, nor intervenes to radically change its course. All such final ends are nothing but human fictions, for Spinoza. Neither can a God be vengeful or benign, cruel or virtuous. These are anthropomorphic, human-centred, characteristics that are invested in the figure of God. In this way, superstition and religious belief come to take the place of a more rational understanding of nature.

Key Thinker: René Descartes

René Descartes (1596–1650) was an influential French philosopher who was closely read by Spinoza. His writings had a significant impact upon the modern age, specifically his *Meditations* (1642), where he constructs the self as a thinking thing, and develops his famous formulation *cogito ergo sum* (I think, therefore I am). Here he distinguishes between the mind and the body, as two separate substances with two quite different functions. He views the body as an unreliable source of desire, passion, and sensory experience, hence denigrating its role and value. In contrast, Descartes views the mind more positively. While we might be misled by confused thoughts and by imagination, it is via the vehicles of reason and rationality that the mind comes to understand clearly and distinctly God's existence and the principles of science and mathematics. Descartes constructs a self that is radically detached from the world, a pure thinking thing without a body. This dualist conception is challenged by Spinoza's monist perspective where all kinds of things, mind and body included, are each modes of a single substance. Thinkers of race and feminism, such as Charles Mills and Judith Butler (see Chapters 10 and 36, respectively), also critique and deconstruct such dualist conceptions of the self in order to radically undermine the atomistic, disengaged, and instrumental characteristics of such a position.

Much of this argument was initially received through the *Tractatus Theologico Politicus*, which directly challenged the legitimacy of the revelatory power of scripture. For Spinoza, the method for interpreting religion was no different to studying nature. In this he follows the ancient atomists, Democritus, Epicurus, and Lucretius (thinkers who were also read closely by Marx and Nietzsche) and finds in them the first elements of a materialist theory of the universe. It is alongside these ancient thinkers that Spinoza begins to reflect upon the power of the imagination and the ways in which it is used to harness particular passions and emotions, constructing forms of identification (in particular, relations of servitude and mystification) that are necessary for the maintenance and legitimation of religious power. The greatest power of religion, Spinoza writes, in a manner that influences Marx's own critique of ideology, 'is to keep man in a state of deception, and with the specious title of religion to cloak the fear by which they must be held in check, so that they will fight for their servitude as if for salvation' (Spinoza, 2002: 389–390).

The key message of the *TTP* asserts the power of reason over superstition. Religion generates irrational hopes and fears, and grounds these unstable emotions in rituals and religious beliefs that are dominated by superstition. Hence Spinoza argues in the Appendix of *Ethics*, Part 1, that we often confuse what is real with what is imaginary. In taking his critique of religion to the heart of biblical exegesis, this argument is perhaps more damaging than the demystifying strategies of either Marx's analysis of ideology or Nietzsche's destruction of morality. Religious prophecy occupied the horizon of imagination; prophets had no supernatural or otherworldly powers. But how might the passions tie individuals together as a collectivity? How might we come to understand this horizon of imagination? It was precisely these questions that Spinoza sought to investigate in the *Ethics* and the *TTP*.

While it is certainly the case that the main focus of the *Ethics* becomes a precise investigation of human bodies, minds, and passions, we have also drawn attention to the important argument whereby every element of nature, human and non-human, is causally connected by a kind of network or web, and each is a mode of substance, a part of a whole. This argument has presented many challenges to Spinoza's readers. How can Spinoza's objective be that of freedom when he appears to subordinate the individual to a schema of causal necessity where human agency is forever determined by some other cause and free will is contested? Spinoza writes, 'in the mind, there is no absolute or free will, but the mind is determined to will this or that by a cause which is also determined by another cause, and this again by another, and so to infinity' (*Ethics*, Part II, Proposition 48). Hegel found this position entirely uncompromising, arguing that Spinoza's substance is static and determines everything, depriving all things of their freedom and dialectical movement. But this view tells us only part of the story, and where Hegel finds Spinoza's philosophy overshadowed by necessity and determinism, others (for example, contemporary thinkers, such as Étienne Balibar and Antonio Negri) identify a novel account of collective freedom discussed in Section 6.3. Let us follow the steps that might give rise to such an account of freedom, and begin to clarify this age-old opposition between freedom and necessity.

6.2.2 Bodies and minds

Rather like Hobbes, Spinoza understands all bodies to be constituted by power. But significantly, this is not simply part of an account of human nature, as it is for Hobbes, since we have seen that Spinoza recognizes no clear distinction and necessary autonomy between human and non-human bodies. Each and all are characterized by this striving for power and perseverance, including the boundless forms of the natural world itself. Spinoza calls this primary power *conatus*, and it is an essential element of all living forms. Such a formulation requires that we revise carefully our assumptions about what constitutes an individual. Spinoza's concept of the individual, or *individuum*, therefore, has little to do with modern liberal conceptions of the individual that are found wanting by critical political theorists (see Key Concept: Individualism).

> ### Key Concept: Individualism
>
> We often mark the birth of the concept of the individual with the Enlightenment, and specifically liberal political philosophy, when many thinkers began to ground ideas of human subjectivity in rationality, free will, reason, and the inner sanctuary of thought. Early modern thinkers, such as Descartes, and later Kant (see Chapter 29), laid the foundations for this flourishing of the individual subject as a thinking being and as the epistemological centre for scientific knowledge, while Locke and Mill (see Chapters 7 and 12, respectively) gave it a liberal political grounding. Individualism is closely allied with humanism, which assigns a special value to human beings among other things in nature, attributing them natural rights and emphasizing the primacy of a distinctly human perspective that also seeks to justify its elevation above other life forms. This broad understanding of individualism has many critics who find an insidious connection between 'possessive individualism' and the rise of capitalism (Macpherson, 2010); locate an insurmountable tension between the universalist pretensions of liberal freedoms and the rise of colonialism (Said, 1994; Spivak, 1999); and identify myriad exclusions to be haunting liberalism's ideology of the solitary, self-contained individual. Spinoza's profoundly relational concept of individuality supports such critiques in emphasizing the way in which we live simultaneously as individuals and as a collective. Thus, he writes: 'Man is not a dominium within a dominium' (Spinoza, 1985b: Part III, Pref.). Together, these observations incite us to think very carefully about how many of our political concepts remain tied to the tradition of liberal individualism.

In contrast, Spinoza's interest lies in the production of an individual conceived as a composite of different bodies and relations, so that what we might think of as a distinctly human body always requires a wider body of organic and inorganic elements to maintain its existence. Such a perspective resonates strongly with the early Marx, for whom nature and the self are intimately connected and require each other in order to flourish. According to Spinoza, individuals can be more or less complex, from atoms and cells, multi-cell organisms to 'the whole of Nature ... whose parts i.e. all bodies, vary in infinite ways, without any change in the whole Individual' (ibid.: Part II, P13, L7S). For example, an individual might be a forest, a storm, an amoeba, an eco-system, as well as an animal, or a human being. The greater the complexity of the individual, we might say, the greater is the power to interact with the rest of nature (see Key Concept: Knowledge). Knowledge of this complexity might enable the human individual in particular to accommodate, include, and recognize politically many forms of diversity and difference. There is, then, an important reciprocity between what Spinoza calls substance (as the one-ness of the world) and the multiplicity of interacting individual bodies. It would be rather short-sighted to view this as a kind of determinism that overshadows freedom.

> **Key Concept: Knowledge**
>
> In the *Ethics*, Part II, P40, Spinoza (1985b) distinguishes three kinds of knowledge. The first kind of knowledge, wholly one-dimensional and inadequate, begins from immediate everyday experience: opinion, signs, distorted beliefs, the realm where Marx understood ideology to be made. The second kind of knowledge commences from a shared knowledge where understanding of the value of certain relations and the causes and properties of things is present. Here an understanding of the shared utility of such social knowledge produces common notions based on reason. The third kind of knowledge, discussed extensively in Part V of the *Ethics*, Spinoza calls intuitive knowledge, which is wholly adequate to itself and appears to be linked to a contemplation of eternity and the formal properties of God or Nature.

In Part II of the *Ethics*, Spinoza (1985b) continues his challenge to Cartesian philosophy and develops an argument that would later be of interest to many feminist thinkers. Mind and body are not separate substances with distinct realities; likewise, the body and the passions are not simply dominated by the mind. Rather, each must be portrayed as interconnected expressions of the *same* human form. If the mind has ideas, they are ideas of the body. Thus, Spinoza writes: 'the mind does not know itself except insofar as it perceives ideas and affections of the body' (ibid.: Part II, P23). In other words, mind is a 'thinking body' and cannot be separated from its relation to the body, as it can for Descartes. Each of its ideas has their source in images regarding the affective state of the body.

Part III of the *Ethics* is entitled '*De Affectibus*' or 'Concerning the Origin and Nature of the Affects'. It offers a psychology of the passions, how they are shaped, their various intensities, and how they are affected by different objects. In the Preface to this Part, Spinoza considers the passions as a physics or geometry 'just as if it were an investigation of lines, planes, or bodies'. What we understand by consciousness is not the act of thinking per se but a mind conscious of its *conatus*, that is, its striving or power (ibid.: Part III, Proposition 9, Scholium). The individual is mobilized to act according to three primary primitive affects: desire, joy, and sadness. But it is the way in which desire combines with joy and sadness that gives rise to the intensity and the shape of the resulting passion.

Ethics, Part III presents us with a wide range of passions deriving from the three primary affects, from hatred, anger, scorn, envy, pity, and despair, to love, hope, wonder, self-esteem, compassion, and gratitude (see ibid.: Part III, Definitions of the Emotions). These different emotional states either increase or decrease our power to act. Indeed, the power of a body is diminished by passions resulting from sadness, where envy, for example, leaves us consumed by objects over which we have no control. Its power is increased by those passions, such as compassion and gratitude resulting from joy. Spinoza recognizes that the passions are intensely transformative states and it therefore becomes important to understand the causes underlying our actions. Can we come to experience more joyful affects?

The implications of these questions are far-reaching and have deep political effects. Spinoza went to great lengths to expose the role that fear might play in the constitution and life of political society, striving to grasp and understand the passions that might develop reason and virtue, mutuality and friendship and thus permit a different vision of the political state (see Gatens and Lloyd, 1999). Despite offering us a very nuanced account of affective dynamics, Spinoza's underlying concept of the individual still remains socially abstracted from the concrete questions of race and gender. We will have to consider how and to what degree his politics might accommodate these omissions in Section 6.3.

> **6.2 From *Ethics* to politics: Key Points**
>
> - Spinoza refuses any dualism between human and non-human orders of being and adopts a monist position, where all things are modes of a single substance and are interconnected.
> - He contests the idea of free will, arguing instead that an understanding of the causal connections between things leads to true knowledge.
> - With Spinoza, the conception of the individual takes on a new shape: a composite of social relations, interactive and reciprocal.
> - The power to act depends upon the affective state of the body that can be increased by joy or diminished by sadness; an understanding of affect informs Spinoza's politics.

6.3 Politics and power

In this section, we will explore Spinoza's politics and consider whether he is best presented as a social contract theorist in the manner of Hobbes, Locke, and Rousseau. Our aim is to build upon some of the key arguments of the *Ethics* and explore Spinoza's close regard for the affects and their role in the constitution of political society, together with his understanding of the individual as a relational being. How might these ideas inform and enrich our understandings of freedom and equality, democracy, and political power?

The central concern of the *Tractatus Theologico Politicus* (*TTP*), as we saw in Section 6.1, was a secular attack upon religious despotism and this concern cannot be separated from the core arguments of the *Ethics*. Both were written out of a love for philosophy, the freedom to philosophize, for those who dared to think; in short, for the power of reason. In the *TTP*, this regard for freedom of expression is closely allied with an anti-ecclesiastical, anti-monarchical, anti-aristocratic politics. Spinoza will argue that the more a political state seeks to limit the freedom of thought and judgement of its members, the greater the distance from their most natural state becomes and consequently the more oppressive the state (Spinoza, 2002: 247). In the final chapter of this work, Spinoza will claim that the *raison d'être* of the state is freedom, and that democracy is the most natural and absolute form for the state to take, thus identifying himself as the first early modern thinker since the ancient Greeks to argue for the intrinsic value of democratic political institutions.

6.3.1 From right to power

Spinoza begins his theorization of politics in Chapter XVI of the *TTP* by considering the concept of natural right. Here his argument is not simply derived from a state of nature argument, as it is for Hobbes and Locke. Instead it arises from the primary principle of his whole philosophy: *Deus sive Natura*, which is, as the political philosopher C.E. Vaughan observes, 'a speculative principle which unravels the secret of the whole universe' (Vaughan, 1925: 68).

For Spinoza, the power of nature is identical with the power of God; everything in nature acts according to its natural determinations, whatever its individual disposition and moral implication (see Negri, 1991: 108–113; Spinoza, 2002: 526–535). It follows that an individual's natural right is also coextensive with its power. Thus, Spinoza writes:

> [I]t is certain that Nature, taken in the absolute sense, has the sovereign right to do all that she can do; that is, Nature's right is co-extensive with her power. For Nature's power is the very power of God, who has sovereign right over all things. But since the universal power of Nature as a whole is

> nothing but the power of all individual things taken together, it follows that each individual thing has the sovereign right to do all that it can do; i.e. the right of the individual is co-extensive with its determinate power.
>
> (ibid.: 527)

Spinoza's naturalism is deeply political, disrupting the classical opposition within social contract theory between nature and culture, or institution, requiring that politics be understood in terms of the dynamic field of forces that underscore and determine its power rather than in terms of the established rule of law. However, Spinoza does not suggest that this sovereign right be equated with the right of the strongest, or the most powerful, since *all* individuals, like all other singularities in nature, are able to exercise their natural right, according to their corresponding power. There is no privileged place for man and no natural hierarchy in nature; it follows that right is neither a property nor a possession restricted to man. The intrinsic power of each thing to exist and persevere will certainly still produce inequalities of power within and between individuals since there is no singular thing in nature that cannot be overpowered and destroyed by another (Spinoza, 1985b: Part IV, Axiom 1). Ultimately, any body or thing can be overpowered by something stronger, and a degree of antagonism is a natural reality. But will these inequalities naturally produce insurmountable hostilities and differences? Can this dual understanding of power and right be alienated from its natural foundation to become political or juridical right? Can natural right be *transferred* easily to a sovereign power? What is the role of the social contract or pact in Spinoza's argument, and where might we place him in the social contract tradition from Hobbes to Kant?

As if in response to these questions, Spinoza makes his own position quite explicit in Letter 50: 'As far as politics is concerned . . . the difference between Hobbes and myself is this: I always preserve natural Right unimpaired and I maintain that in each state the Supreme Magistrate has no more right over its subjects than it has greater power over them' (Spinoza, 2016a: 406). While for Hobbes, man's natural state is one marked by relentless competition, enmity, hostility, and fear of others, giving rise to a constant threat of war, resolved only through the medium of absolute authority, Spinoza's emphasis is upon the tendency towards mutuality and cooperation between individuals. The challenge posed by Spinoza's thought is to understand how a deeper knowledge of differential power relations can be pursued virtuously in order to generate an understanding of human and non-human relations, connections, and interactions (see Key Concept: Knowledge). This, in turn, implies a much richer conception of reason than the rational calculus preferred by Hobbes, where man seeks peace only to escape a fearful, warlike natural state. Spinoza's concept of reason, while being a deeply passionate state of being, is also closely tied to a capacity for virtue and understanding (see Key Concept: Knowledge). Recognizing that 'the life of men without mutual assistance must necessarily be most wretched and must lack the cultivation of reason', Spinoza argues that it is only by uniting as one body that the good of men can be achieved, since 'the good which everyone who seeks virtue wants for himself, he also desires for other men' (Spinoza, 1985b, Part IV, Proposition 37). In Proposition 35 of Part IV of the *Ethics*, Spinoza famously writes: 'there is no single thing in nature that is more useful to man than a man who lives under the guidance of reason'. These extracts from the *Ethics* identify the idea that reason brings with it a sense of virtue, mutuality, and social cooperation, as well as the shared utility to be gained by the formation of a civil body. They also reinforce Spinoza's philosophy of individual freedom and power, which is always enlarged and never reduced by the constitution of a state.

However, we have understood Spinoza also as a realist who recognizes that, in the absence of reason, individuals may be moved to obedience by the passions. Specifically by fear, but also by 'all the possible means by which [government] can induce men to obey its commands' (Spinoza, 2002: 536), to habituate beliefs so that obedience is no longer lived as bondage but as freedom itself. It is imagination which plays the role that reason cannot perform, and this imagination is all the more effective, the more individuals believe—or imagine—that they have instituted an agreement according to free will. The idea of a transfer of right by way of a contract is wholly *imaginary*; it is the fiction of the contract that itself sustains obedience. Politics always has this ineradicable imaginary component that draws on the passions as well as reason. It is this reality that furnishes Spinoza's deep regard for the relations of force and passion underscoring the political, and the means used by states to bind individuals to its laws, to nurture their obedience and consent. For him, it is the combining of forces that creates political power rather than simply the legal title to it.

Thus, Spinoza once again reveals himself to be rather Machiavellian. This bold refusal to contaminate natural right with juridical or moral questions has led several commentators to reject the terms of his political thought, concerned that its lack of a theory of obligation and duty may serve ultimately to legitimate rather than prevent forms of political tyranny (Rosen, 1987; Berlin, 2002). Like Machiavelli, Spinoza has little interest in the question of the legitimacy of the modern state. Rather, his concern is with what factors permit a state to endure or contribute to its destruction, specifically with how its power is produced and reproduced over time. His focus is, in other words, upon how individuality is itself produced and reproduced to become a nation or a community, a people, or a discrete series of individuals.

Indeed, Spinoza argues in the *TTP* that it is the political mass or the multitude who are most receptive to superstitious belief and less receptive to reasonable argument. Similarly, his discussion, in the *Ethics*, Part IV of the vacillation, or instability, of affects (between hope and fear, happiness and despair) can make the mass a sometimes unpredictable, inconstant political force, guided more by that which generates recognition of their immediate experience and world-view (i.e., the power of imagination) than by that which might increase reason and joyful affects. By the time Spinoza began to write the unfinished *Political Treatise* (TP) his growing political realism had led him to appreciate that the right of the state is determined by the power not of each individual but of the multitude itself (Spinoza, 2016b, III, 2). The state is continuously exposed to the often unstable political relations that constitute it, therefore a political system that excludes the mass, he concluded, is unlikely to remain peaceful and will tend to provoke their indignation and possible rebellion (ibid.: VI, 6).

6.3.2 The political shadow of the multitude

It is necessary to pause our discussion of Spinoza's political thought here and reflect upon the context shaping political events at this time. Spinoza's silence upon the broader political and economic conditions shaping colonial power and conflict follows the path of many political thinkers, ancient and modern. But it is unfortunate, particularly since, as Montag (1999: 85–89) argues, his work remains haunted by excluded figures. What might be the value of an argument for a democratic state when vast swathes of the political body—from women, understood as the weaker sex (see Section 6.4.1), to servants, and the common people—remain excluded and unrecognized by politics? How does Spinoza theorize this power of the multitude that determines the state and provokes in it fear and the risk of rebellion?

Before considering these questions in Section 6.4, we must note that there is some evidence of Spinoza's reflection upon the presence of colonialism, albeit symbolically and in the relating of a dream. Some scholars (for example, Rosenthal, 2005; Goetschel, 2016) have drawn attention to a letter from Spinoza (1985a: Letter 17) to Pieter Balling, a merchant engaged in trade with Spain and the Spanish holdings in the Americas, who had written to him about the worrying omen of his own son's death. In the course of responding to his friend, Spinoza relates his own dream where the image of a Black Brazilian man appears, lingers, and vividly imprints itself for some time afterward, before only gradually disappearing from sight. Some have seen the dream itself as a symbol of

Spinoza's hope, where the image points to the figure of Henrique Dias, a prominent Brazilian soldier and militia leader of enslaved and free Afro-Brazilians, who had liberated himself from oppression and sought the liberation of his troops. Others have seen in Dias the embodied threat of the defeat of Dutch colonial rule in Brazil, the challenge to liberal freedoms, and hence a symbol of Spinoza's fear. At the very least, we must identify in this dream fragment the profound role that colonial conflict has played within the formation of the modern subject and consider to what extent Spinoza's political thought can help the contemporary scholar accommodate and recognize the facts of this conflict.

It is certainly the case that we can identify a clear shift in Spinoza's writings, as the political mass becomes a pivotal focus. Having identified its power towards the end of the *TTP*, as well as entertained some of its characteristics in the *Ethics*, Spinoza begins to give the concept of the multitude much greater attention. This makes his construction of politics somewhat unique within modern political thought. In his final work, this dynamic relationship between multitude and state becomes the over-riding interest.

However, we clearly cannot equate the multitude simply with a ready-made mass or collective body. Every political body is built upon a fine balance between reason and imagination, influenced in turn by political hope or fear that will entail very different political forms. As Spinoza writes in the unfinished *Tractatus Politicus* (Spinoza, 2016b: Chapter V, para. 2): 'Citizens are not born but made'; there is no universal citizen, each is situated in changeable historical contexts, shaped by laws, customs, passions, and interests. As Hobbes also recognized, the multitude is the *body* of the state. But Spinoza appreciated that it was also continuously produced and reproduced by the relationship between them. Might the multitude govern itself by reason, or must it be manipulated and brought to a state of obedience? Does Spinoza share the Hobbesian solution where the sovereign appeals to fear in order to bring about obedience? These questions highlight Spinoza's deep regard for the physics of bodies and their political formation. What, then, is the optimum relationship between multitude and state?

> ### 6.3 Politics and power: Key Points
> - The central aim of Spinoza's political writings is to protect the freedom of thought of its members.
> - Spinoza's powerful form of naturalism, where there is no hierarchy and no privileged place for the human being, understands right as co-extensive with power (*potentia*).
> - Spinoza's conception of reason underscores the role of cooperation and virtue.
> - He also recognizes, like Hobbes, that individuals may be moved to obedience through sad passions like fear and enmity.
> - For Spinoza, a state that excludes the multitude will risk instability and rebellion.

6.4 Democracy: politics beyond the state

The focus of Spinoza's political theory changed between the *Tractatus Theologico-Politicus* and the *Tractatus Politicus* (TP). The later *Political Treatise* is often viewed as offering a scientific, classical view of politics that explores the three main types of government (monarchy, aristocracy, democracy), and it rarely touches on religious and political matters with the kind of depth and detail found in the earlier *TTP*. While the *TTP* devotes considerable space to democracy, the unfinished nature of the *TP*, which famously ends only four sections into Chapter XI, 'On Democracy', makes its own consideration of the topic somewhat lacking.

Nevertheless, Spinoza does not completely put aside an interest, developed in both the *TTP* and the *Ethics*, in the advantages of democracy as the form of government best approximating man's natural state where right and power coexist. The consistent emphasis throughout upon consultation and inclusion; his profound interest in the mass as a political subject *par excellence*, where the rule of the multitude is considered the most absolute rule; and the tendency to introduce democratically inclusive measures into every political structure of power each point to the importance of democracy. Thus in Chapter III of the *Political Treatise*, Spinoza writes: 'The Right of a state, or of the supreme powers is nothing more than the Right of nature, determined not by the power of each person, but by the power of a multitude, led as if by one mind' (Spinoza, 2016b: III, 2). Indeed, if a contrast with the *TTP* is to be noted, it is surely in the strategic concern with the most 'absolute' state, where absolute must be understood in terms of its activity rather than in the usual terms of the state's monolithic or despotic power.

Spinoza's approach once again follows Machiavelli's observations of the conflictive, discontinuous, and shifting scene of politics. Both thinkers are interested in the practical function of the state and its relation to the social forces that compose it (Del Lucchese, 2009). This focus upon a shifting changeable scene also echoes Spinoza's concept of substance (or nature) as an infinitely variable form, subject to continuous generation and destruction. The absolute character of a state is not simply a reflection of its stability but the extent to which a government may act effectively while allowing the state to maintain a condition of peace, where peace also signifies political agreement and common unity. In this regard, *any* state may be considered absolute—monarchy and democracy alike—although Spinoza continues to describe democracy as the most absolute of states. How is this the case?

In the *TP*, each typology of government analysed by Spinoza considers different combinations of the relationship between right and power, state and multitude (see Key Concept: Power). This relationship is inseparable from the passionate forces that are formed in the multitude, which are themselves a modality of the way the state functions (Spinoza, 2016b: IV, 2; III, 8). Spinoza's considerations of monarchy, aristocracy, and (albeit partially) of democracy each focus on the balance of forces between the masses and institution. He is at pains to show that the greatest threat is always an internal one, and argues that the state is increasingly stable the more it tends to bring itself into equilibrium with the political body. Both monarchy and aristocracy should therefore build into their political structures the political deliberation of citizens:

> It is sheer stupidity to want to do everything in secrecy, and then expect the citizens not to judge the government's actions wrongly, and not to interpret everything perversely. If the plebians could restrain themselves, and suspend judgement on matters they know little about, or judge correctly from scanty information, they would be more worthy to rule, than be ruled.
>
> (Spinoza, 2016b: VII, 27)

In his reading of the *Political Treatise*, Étienne Balibar (1994) suggests that democracy is a regulative mechanism that all kinds of state can strive to realize. Democracy functions as a measure of a state's consciousness of its own internal parts, and the degree of their democratic inclusion. Thus, when Spinoza considers the political abuse of power, and the problem of (dis)order in monarchy and aristocracy, it is by introducing more democratic practices (such as variations and extensions to the qualifying right for aristocracy, or establishing of a representative council in a monarchy) that stability is preserved and the state governs in closest proximity to the common good. If we follow this reading of the democratizing tendency of all political forms, we can make sense of Spinoza's description of democracy as the most absolute of states where finally, in the third type of state, the multitude becomes a placeholder for the state itself and the people ('led as if by one mind') hold public office, make collective decisions, vote and, most importantly, actively shape the final result on public matters. They are—to utilize Rousseau's (1973) later formulation, perhaps written in the spirit of Spinoza—both sovereign and subject.

> **Key Concept: Power**
>
> The concept of power plays a key role in most political theories as the relationship between the state or political power and individual power is negotiated. We can identify two quite distinctive conceptions of power in Spinoza's writings. *Potestas* can be defined as political rule, or command secured through law, while *potentia* is a capacity to act, a power of becoming, that is tied closely to the right of the individual/ multitude. *Potentia* can never be completely subordinated to *potestas*. But Spinoza does present *potentia* as hindered and restrained by sad passions (fear, anger, despair) and thus subject to manipulation by the state. Similarly, *potentia* is not unlimited because it must be understood vis-à-vis a dependence on the evolving *potentia* of others. Spinoza's concept of power shows his interest in the construction of individualities and politics (with their reciprocal actions and reactions), as dynamic and changeable processes, a view shared by, among others, Machiavelli, Foucault, and Butler.

6.4.1 The unity of the multitude

This connection between the sovereignty of the multitude and body politic begs the question of its unity, and whether—and how far—we might take it in the direction of Rousseau's general will. To what extent can we think of the state as embodying such an organic principle of unity, and corresponding to the mind of the multitude? Some older, but nonetheless very interesting readings draw attention to precisely this connection (Eckstein, 1944); others claim that Spinoza's multitude could only ever be a majority will—with all the exclusions this might entail (Geismann, 1991; Negri, 1991: 231). Given Spinoza's radical critique of free will as caught in a mesh of causes (see Section 6.2), it seems hard to entertain the pure agency of even a united will. Similarly, Spinoza refuses to sacrifice the individual to the collective in the manner of Rousseau. Instead he will describe various different kinds of state formation that might incorporate the multitude in different ways and to different degrees. We have already observed how democracy is conditional upon the development of social forces that constitute and reproduce the state. The democratic solution, while favoured by Spinoza as the optimum or most absolute state, is not put forth as a utopian ideal as it is in Rousseau.

There is some evidence that Rousseau was familiar with Spinoza's *Tractatus Theologico-Politicus* (Eckstein, 1944; Israel, 2001). The most striking and notable parallel is the use both thinkers make of a civic religion to engender a sense of virtue in citizens and hence help solder a social bond between them (Smith, 1997: 117). Rousseau similarly displays a strong regard for the passions and stands virtually alone within the Enlightenment in his view that reason alone is insufficient to secure man's obligations to his fellow men, as well as his civic duty, and consent to the state. Yet ultimately Spinoza's texts are political rather than moral, and while it is clear that both Spinoza and Rousseau may be viewed as exponents of positive liberty, the former does not seek to simply marry liberty with obedience to the moral law (Berlin, 1993; West, 1993). Spinoza brackets the problem of morality, and when he writes of natural right, it is in relation to the wider laws of nature that the problem is posed.

The question of the possible unity of the multitude raised at the start of this section thus persists: how might the multitude reach an agreement that might form the basis of its unity as 'one mind'? If we understand the multitude as a plural composition that is continually affected by its interactions (rather as Spinoza understood the individual in Section 6.1), how can its common outlook be nurtured? This question is particularly relevant when we bear in mind Spinoza's observation that participation in a democratic body will depend upon legal qualification of citizenship, which might be enjoyed by many or only a few. Spinoza recognizes that we can therefore conceive of many kinds of democracy but endeavours to discuss only one where 'absolutely everyone' bound to the laws of his native land and being their own masters have the right to vote and stand for public office (Spinoza, 2016b: XI, 3). Spinoza's own qualifications here are far from acceptable. Excluded are foreigners, who, he writes, 'are counted as under someone else's control', women, servants, and children, all of whom are under the power of someone else (ibid.: XI, 3). These exclusions are also bolstered by essentialist arguments regarding the natural subjection of women:

> If women were by nature equal to men, both in strength of character and in native intelligence ... surely among so many and such diverse nations we would find some where each sex ruled equally, and others where men were ruled by women, and so educated that they could do less with their native intelligence, But since this has not happened anywhere, we can say without reservation that women do not, by nature, have an equal right to men's, but that they necessarily submit to men. So it cannot happen that each sex rules equally, much less that men are ruled by women.
>
> (ibid.: XI, 4)

Readers of Spinoza have rightly been perplexed by the conservatism of these views expressed in the *Political Treatise*, especially since they appear entirely at odds with the philosophical positions developed in the *Ethics*, where Spinoza understands marriage, for example, as an expression of freedom for both, as well as in agreement with the life of reason (Spinoza, 1985b: Part IV, Appendix XX), and where many of the dualisms that have organized political thought are unravelled and questioned by him. Feminists have long argued that the tradition of political thought reinforces dualist ways of thinking between body and mind, passion and reason, nature and culture, private and public, the feminine and the masculine. These dualisms are then mirrored in the insidious political powers of the modern (masculine) political subject (see, for example, Lloyd, 1984). Spinoza's thought arguably frees itself from such dualisms by stressing the interconnections between reason, affect, or passion, and forms of social structure that enhance or diminish freedom (Lloyd, 2009). It has evidently continued to offer conceptual resources for feminists despite the anti-feminism of the *Political Treatise* (Sharp, 2021). In the *Ethics*, Spinoza argues that the human body requires many other bodies to live and regenerate itself (both human and non-human). The complex mesh of reciprocal relations that form the individual is always changing. Sexual difference and gendered minds and bodies are each produced through the shifting play of power relations that likewise underscore the formation of the multitude. Spinoza's arguments about gender in the *Political Treatise* are inherently weak because they contradict his philosophy. The Marxist critic might suggest that they also point to the absence in his writings of any analysis of civil society, the emerging division between private and public realm, as well as the transatlantic slave trade that continued to shape and influence European politics. This gives his thought a certain ideological blindness. Without an understanding of the fissures and conflicts that are built into the foundations of democracy, particularly in relation to the emergence of particular social groups as they capture resources and power (for example, merchants, property owners), Spinoza's politics, and the concept of the multitude, can look rather one-dimensional.

Given the unfinished nature of Spinoza's final work, perhaps it is left for the reader to explore both the theoretical and practical implications of democracy. Clearly, there are dangers here. We cannot simply rescue or reinvent Spinoza, attempt to fill the gaps and absences in his thought, or consider his oversights as historically determined omissions. It is perhaps instead a question of understanding how, even as Spinoza retreats from the page where he writes about democracy, his writings can still inform and permeate contemporary political problems. The figure of the multitude cannot simply be contained within whatever political form Spinoza (or any other political thinker) has described. The presence of the unrepresented, those without a voice, the excluded, remains and overflows its containment by any political form. Spinoza's multitude is at once the mob-like mass that must itself be dissolved to fragment the base of monarchical power in his native Holland, just as it is the free multitude that must be constituted to enlarge the democratic base of a republic (see Key Concept: Power). It is the incipient power of this mass that Spinoza's politics was most aware of, and he sought to place it at the epicentre of his political reflections. Spinoza's political philosophy also reminds us that democracy takes many different forms and shapes. It is for him a fragile achievement not simply because collective agreement will always be finely balanced and precarious (rather than uniform), but because wherever they are to be found, democratic structures risk being destroyed from within by the very forces that compose them.

> ### 6.4 Democracy: politics beyond the state: Key Points
>
> - Spinoza's attention to the multitude continues into his final work, where the changing relationship between the multitude and the state becomes a key focus.
> - It is important to consider the possible unity of the multitude since every mass reflects a diverse range of voices.
> - Spinoza's exclusion of women and his mostly absent attention to the impact of colonial politics upon the state arguably weaken his politics, but his philosophical naturalism contradicts these views.
> - Given Spinoza's final work is unfinished, the theoretical and practical implications of democracy are unclear, but his analysis of the role of democratic practices within all types of government is nonetheless important.

6.5 Conclusion

Is Spinoza's philosophy difficult to classify—a 'savage anomaly' as Antonio Negri (1991) argued? Is it, as Nietzsche claimed of his own thought, a philosophy for the future? Certainly at a time when Enlightenment philosophies—and sciences—of knowledge and freedom were just beginning to fight against religion for the primacy of the human subject, Spinoza began to question and radicalize the foundations of their political arguments. Rather than viewing the self as independent and self-contained, he understood human bodies and minds to rely upon an elemental relationality and reciprocity, thus transforming the way in which freedom and equality might be viewed (Armstrong et al., 2019; Vardoulakis, 2018), and identifying the future possibility for new compatibilities and combinations between a great many entities—human and non-human alike (Haraway, 2008). We are, as Spinoza (2016a: Letter 32) writes in one of his Letters, 'part of nature', and the more we understand the causal connections between things (nature, cultures, human and non-human lives), they will cease to be outside our understanding. While Spinoza's thought is marked by many political exclusions that throw his naturalist equation of political right and power into question, his thought continues to be an important resource for feminists, Marxists, radical ecologists, and environmentalists for whom we cannot separate nature from the life-building processes of the world and what (or who) we might become. Spinoza's political thought shares this deep regard for human freedom with liberal political philosophy, but he encourages liberalism to recognize the collective aspects of individuality. As a key thinker of the masses, Spinoza joins Marx in his appreciation of the importance of collective politics. It is perhaps here that his understanding of the multitude can support and invigorate contemporary discussions of democracy, equality, inclusion, and the shape of contemporary politics.

> *Take your learning further by accessing the online resources for a library of web links to relevant videos, articles, blogs, and useful websites for this chapter: www.oup.com/he/Ramgotra-Choat1e.*

Study questions

1. Would you describe Spinoza as a radical or a conservative?
2. On what grounds does Spinoza critique religion?
3. How might Spinoza's thought speak to the challenges of an environmental politics?
4. To what extent do you agree with the characterization of Spinoza as an individualist?
5. Is Spinoza best described as a social contract theorist?
6. In what ways might Spinoza's thought be utilized by feminist theory?
7. How does Spinoza describe and understand democracy?
8. What is the multitude, as defined by Spinoza?

Further reading

Primary sources

Spinoza, B. (1985a) *The Collected Works of Spinoza*, vol. I. Ed. and trans. E. Curley. Princeton, NJ: Princeton University Press.
   A readable translation of the *Ethics* along with his earliest works and letters. Full and very helpful glossary and Introduction.

Spinoza, B. (2007) *Theological-Political Treatise*. Ed. J. Israel. Cambridge: Cambridge University Press.
   Helpful Introduction and chronology by Israel.

Spinoza, B. (2016a) *The Collected Works of Spinoza*, vol. II. Ed. and trans. E. Curley. Princeton, NJ: Princeton University Press.
   This second volume adds the *Tractatus Theological Politicus* and the *Tractatus Politicus* and the remaining library of letters.

Secondary sources

Balibar, E. (1998) *Spinoza and Politics*. London: Verso Books.
   A thought-provoking engagement with Spinoza's political thought that encourages creative thinking about his influence on political theory today.

Deleuze, G. (1988) *Spinoza: Practical Philosophy*. New York: City Lights.
   Several engaging short essays and dictionary-type discussion of many concepts and ideas in Spinoza's thought.

Gatens, M. (ed.) (2009) *Feminist Interpretations of Benedict Spinoza*. University Park, PA: Pennsylvania University Press.
   A broad range of essays exploring Spinoza's legacy for feminism and how we might bring his thought into present discussions

Gatens, M. and Lloyd, G. (1999) *Collective Imaginings: Spinoza, Past and Present*. London: Routledge.
   Explores Spinoza's concept of imagination and discusses the ways in which his thought exceeds the liberal paradigm.

Lloyd, G. (1996) *Spinoza and the Ethics*. London: Routledge.
   A helpful and accessible introduction to the structure and main themes of the *Ethics*.

Lord, B. (2010) *Spinoza's Ethics: An Edinburgh Philosophical Guide*. Edinburgh: Edinburgh University Press.
Designed to be read alongside the *Ethics*, provides useful summary of the text, explains key terms, and unpacks arguments.

Montag, W. and Stolze, T. (eds) (1997) *The New Spinoza*. Minneapolis, MN: Minnesota University Press.
Collects together key essays by French and Italian scholars, showing the breadth and creativity present in contemporary Spinoza studies.

Nadler, S. (1999) *Spinoza: A Life*. Cambridge: Cambridge University Press.
Informative biographical study.

Negri, A. (1991) *The Savage Anomaly: The Power of Spinoza's Metaphysics and Politics*. Trans. M. Hardt. Minneapolis, MN: Minnesota University Press.
Situates Spinoza in Dutch politics, considers the genesis of Spinoza's thought, and assesses him critically against figures such as Hobbes, Rousseau, Kant, and Hegel.

Rosen, S. (1987) 'Benedict Spinoza'. In L. Strauss and R. Cropsey (eds), *History of Political Philosophy*, 3rd edn. Chicago: University of Chicago Press.
An accessible and general commentary on Spinoza's political philosophy.

Rosenthal, M. (2005) 'The Black, Scabby Brazilian: Some Thoughts on Race and Early Modern Philosophy'. *Philosophy and Social Criticism*, 31(2): 211–221.
A very helpful look at discussions of race in the history of political thought, and how we might recognize and use it today.

Sharp, H. (2011) *Spinoza and the Politics of Renaturalization*. Chicago: University of Chicago Press.
This book draws on Spinoza's naturalism to rethink human agency, ethics, and political practice.

References

Armstrong, A., Green, K., and Sangiacomo, A. (eds) (2019) *Spinoza and Relational Autonomy: Being with Others*. Edinburgh: Edinburgh University Press.

Balibar, E. (1994) 'Spinoza, The Anti-Orwell: The Fear of the Masses'. In *Masses, Classes, Ideas: Studies on Politics and Philosophy Before and After Marx*. London: Routledge.

Berlin, I. (1993) 'A Reply to David West'. *Political Studies*, 41: 297–298.

Berlin, I. (2002) 'Two Concepts of Liberty'. In H. Hardy (ed.), *Liberty*. Oxford: Oxford University Press.

Del Lucchese, F. (2009) *Conflict, Power, and Multitude in Machiavelli and Spinoza*. London: Continuum.

Eckstein, W. (1944) 'Rousseau and Spinoza'. *Journal of the History of Ideas*, 5: 259–291.

Gatens, M. and Lloyd, G. (1999) *Collective Imaginings: Spinoza, Past and Present*. London: Routledge.

Geismann, G. (1991) 'Spinoza: Beyond Hobbes and Rousseau'. *Journal of the History of Ideas*, 52(1): 35–53.

Goetschel, W. (2016) 'Spinoza's Dream'. *The Cambridge Journal of Postcolonial Literary Inquiry*, 3(1): 39–54.

Haraway, D.J. (2008) *Where Species Meet*. Minneapolis, MN: University of Minnesota Press.

Israel, J. (2001) *Radical Enlightenment: Philosophy and the Making of Modernity 1650–1750*. Oxford: Oxford University Press.

Lloyd, G. (1984) *The Man of Reason: 'Male' and 'Female' in Western Philosophy*. London: Routledge.

Lloyd, G. (2009) 'Dominance and Difference: A Spinozistic Alternative to the Distinction between "Sex" and "Gender"'. In M. Gatens (ed.), *Feminist Interpretations of Benedict Spinoza*. University Park, PA: University of Pennsylvania Press.

Macpherson, C.B. (2010) *The Political Theory of Possessive Individualism*. Oxford: Oxford University Press.

Montag, W. (1999) *Bodies, Masses, Power: Spinoza and His Contemporaries*. London: Verso Books.

Moreau, F. (1996) 'Spinoza's Reception and Influence'. In D. Garrett (ed.), *The Cambridge Companion to Spinoza*. Cambridge: Cambridge University Press.

Negri, A. (1991) *The Savage Anomaly: The Power of Spinoza's Metaphysics and Politics*. Trans. M. Hardt. Minneapolis, MN: Minnesota University Press.

Rosen, S. (1987) 'Benedict Spinoza'. In L. Strauss and R. Cropsey (eds), *History of Political Philosophy*, 3rd edn. Chicago: University of Chicago Press.

Rosenthal, M. (2005) 'The Black, Scabby Brazilian: Some Thoughts on Race and Early Modern Philosophy'. *Philosophy and Social Criticism*, 31(2): 211–221.

Rousseau, J.J. (1973) *The Social Contract and Discourses*. Trans. G.D.H. Cole. London: J.M. Dent and Sons.

Said, E. (1994) *Culture and Imperialism*. London: Vintage Books.

Sharp, H. (2021) 'Spinoza and Feminism'. In Y.Y. Melamed (ed.), *A Companion to Spinoza*. Hoboken, NJ: Wiley Blackwell.

Smith, S. (1997) *Spinoza, Liberalism and the Question of Jewish Identity*. New Haven, CT: Yale University Press.

Spinoza, B. (1985a) *The Collected Works of Spinoza*, vol. I. Ed. and trans. E. Curley. Princeton, NJ: Princeton University Press.

Spinoza, B. (1985b) 'Ethics'. In *The Collected Works of Spinoza*, vol. I. Ed. and trans. E. Curley. Princeton, NJ: Princeton University Press.

Spinoza, B. (2002) 'Tractatus Theologico-Politicus'. In *Spinoza: Complete Works*. Ed. S. Shirley. Indianapolis, IN: Hackett.

Spinoza, B. (2016a) *The Collected Works of Spinoza*, vol. II. Ed. and trans. E. Curley. Princeton, NJ: Princeton University Press.

Spinoza, B. (2016b) 'Tractatus Politicus'. In *The Collected Works of Spinoza*, vol. II. Ed. and trans. E. Curley. Princeton, NJ: Princeton University Press.

Spivak, G. (1999) *A Critique of Postcolonial Reason: Towards a History of the Vanishing Present*. Cambridge, MA: Harvard University Press.

Vardoulakis, D. (2018) 'Equality and Power: Spinoza's Reformulation of the Aristotelian Tradition of Egalitarianism'. In A.K. Kordela and D. Vardoulakis (eds), *Spinoza's Authority*, vol. 1: *Resistance and Power in the Ethics*. London: Bloomsbury.

Vaughan, C.E. (1925) *Studies in the History of Political Philosophy Before and After Rousseau*, vol. 1. Manchester: Manchester University Press.

West, D. (1993) 'Spinoza on Positive Freedom'. *Political Studies*, 41: 284–296.

7 John Locke

HAGAR KOTEF

Chapter guide

In the seventeenth and eighteenth centuries, the social contract became one of the primary frameworks of political thought. Locke is often considered one of the most important theorists of the social contract and, alongside Rawls' later adaptation, the paradigmatic representative of its liberal version. This chapter focuses on Locke's theory of the social contract, and hence primarily on one of his books: *The Second Treatise of Government*, first published in 1689. Section 7.1 offers a quick review of the social contract as a paradigm, while Section 7.2 provides an overview of a common reading of Locke's version of it. Sections 7.3 and 7.4 situate Locke's contract within a global historical context by focusing on the voices that have been excluded from or marginalized within this story. This will allow an understanding of the hidden politics at stake.

7.1 Introduction

The story of the social contract, in its many versions, begins with two main assumptions: first, that, by nature, man is not a political creature. He—and we will return to this gendered pronoun—lives in what is called 'the state of nature': a mode of living *before* or perhaps simply *outside of* a condition of common rule. Second, and relatedly, the assumption is that, by nature, man is free. Freedom in this context is conceived primarily as freedom *from* the coercion of the state, and the social contract should provide a bridge of sorts—between natural freedom, on the one hand, and subjection to often coercive state apparatuses, on the other. It allows us to imagine subjection that does not contradict freedom, since it is based on consent: under certain conditions and with particular limitations, all individuals agreed to 'leave' the state of nature, to 'enter' a political community, and to be ruled by someone else. Accordingly, the importance of the state of nature is often more theoretical than historical: the history of the consolidation of the political community is important only as far as it is a tool for *justifying* a particular form of political organization and/or to criticize it/others. In other words, it is an effort to understand the conditions that have or would have pushed men to abandon the freedom they enjoy in the state of nature and agree to being subjected to a sovereign, in order to understand the limits and remits of any legitimate form of government.

In all these stories, then, we begin with an assumption of how men live 'naturally'—a concept that plays a dual role: it describes the *essence* of man, but also a *moment* in time, a specific mode of being, that is about to change. The social contract is the act through which this transition from 'the state of nature' to a political state is made. Often, political theorists' analyses of social contract theories focus on two closely related questions:

1. the nature of the original conditions (what are the conditions that push people to come together as a political body and that the political formation thus needs to address?);

2. the scope of derivative limitations upon government (what would the original contractors have agreed upon in order to gain political protections?).

The harsher the original conditions, the fewer limitations will be set on the ruling powers, because the stakes of the failure of sovereignty will be too high (see more on Hobbes in Chapter 5). If, however, the state of nature is a fairly peaceful state of being, as John Locke (1632–1704) contends, then sovereignty must be limited. Since political theory tends to focus on questions concerning the nature of rule, the structure of governance, state institutions, and the justification of those, it tends to foreground this dual discussion when considering the social contract. But political life is composed of more than the institutions and the structure of rule; it is composed, above all, of the people who come to share life as a community. Therefore, as important as the above questions may be, it is just as important to ask: 'Who are the agents engaging in the agreement?' That is, how does political theory imagine those who consented? What are their needs or fears? What do they have to gain or lose? Which is also to ask: who are the people with whom we imagine sharing life and who are those whom we cannot even see as candidates for sharing the world? These questions reveal a great deal about how we imagine our political communities; they are also crucial in shaping political institutions and laws. This chapter will focus on them.

Charles Mills and Carole Pateman (see Chapter 10) have called our attention to the fact that the contracting individuals in the story of the social contract are very clearly positioned as men (Pateman, 1988), white (Mills, 1997), and are globally positioned as the dominating part of imperial and colonial powers (Pateman and Mills, 2007). Macpherson's (2011 [1962]) analysis further allows us to see how the working classes and the poor have been excluded from the imaginary process of contracting. The social contract takes place only after women, non-whites, the propertyless, and the colonized have been subjugated via other means. Their subjugation is justified from the outset, before politics even 'begins'. Therefore, this subjugation does not interrupt the assumptions of equality tethered into the contract, and allows it to coexist alongside a reality and ideology of gender, racial, class, and global inequality.

This chapter presents Locke's social contract theory from the perspective of those excluded voices. It begins by providing a schematic version of Locke's social contract theory, and moves to unpack it from the above perspectives: class, gender, global positionality, and race.

Read more about **Locke's** life and work by accessing the thinker biography on the online resources: www.oup.com/he/Ramgotra-Choat1e.

7.2 Locke, sovereignty, and the state of nature

Locke famously begins with a pleasant, pastoral state of nature. Unlike the Hobbesian state of nature, there is no mutual fear but mutual respect and tolerance (Locke, 2003: §4ff). Since Locke sees us as essentially rational beings, he believes that even without a 'power to keep them all in awe' (as Hobbes would have it), humans could live in relative peace with each other, form social bonds, and regulate themselves according to the Laws of Nature. For Locke, these Laws essentially forbid us to hurt others or their property (ibid.: §6). The source of these Laws is God, and their rationale is that we are not allowed to destroy God's creation (including other people and ourselves; ibid.). In this sense, there is a form of rule at play already in the state of nature, in which religion, rationality, and self-rule intersect. The state of nature is thus a state of freedom but not of 'licence'. It is 'a state of perfect freedom to order their actions and dispose of their possessions and persons, as they think fit, within the bounds of the law of nature' (ibid.: §4). Note that 'freedom' is immediately followed by 'order', and that it is confined by 'the bounds of the law of nature'. It is precisely the presence of this ordered freedom that will allow Locke to limit state power: it renders a strong, invasive state unnecessary and thus illegitimate. *Consent* is the source of legitimacy for Locke and people would not have consented to an invasive state. Also note how this freedom is tied to property from the outset. We shall return to all of these soon.

It is important to note here that we are not born such subjects but must *become* people who are able to identify the law of nature and self-regulate: 'we are born free, as we are born rational; not that we have actually the exercise of either: age, that brings one, brings with it the other too' (ibid.: §61). Locke accordingly emphasizes education as the means facilitating children's development into self-disciplined adults. Whereas the *Treatise* does not elaborate much on this issue, it is key to other writings of Locke, specifically *Thoughts Concerning Education* and, to a lesser degree, 'An Essay on the Poor Law'. This creates something of a tension: we need to *become* the autonomous individuals Locke *assumes* us to be. Locke indeed does not believe we can all become fully rational subjects, even if *potentially* we are all free and rational. Disabled people, the poor, and to some degree Indigenous Americans will never obtain this status of free and rational persons, according to him (Mehta, 1992; Hirschmann, 2007; Kotef, 2015).

The law of nature allows us to regulate our own action, but also allows each to regulate others: if some people violate this natural law, each and every one of us can put ourselves in the position of a judge and punish the offender (Locke, 2003: §§7–8). With the law of nature, then, arises an entire social network that is still part of what Locke defines as the state of nature: there are outlaws, who can be legitimately punished; there are families, aiding children to develop as rational creatures; there are even small societies that are the results of large family formations; and there is property, and even the use of money, on which most societies agree in their pre-contract formation (ibid.: §§37–38). This rich social texture exists *before* the social contract, and circumvents it. That is, by constructing the state of nature in this way, one of the *Treatises*' most important arguments can be justified: the limitation of state power. First, the original individual freedom must be secured under any state formation, and, second, the state emerges as the greatest potential risk to our freedom (as it is secured within the state of nature). This dual understanding—of a state that both protects and potentially threatens our liberty—would become one of the foundations of liberal theory.

Indeed, the *Second Treatise* is above all a text advocating freedom from excessive, tyrannical, or unjust rule. The book was published in 1689, one year after the 'Glorious Revolution' of 1688, in which King James II was ousted (read more in Chapter 17 on Macaulay and Burke). It was read as a justification of this revolution, although it was written earlier and, at least in part, its object of critique was another absolutist king, Charles II. The text is one of the most important treatises on the limits of monarchy and of state power more broadly. It asserts, beyond the idea that the monarch him/herself is subject to the law and thus limited, an initial idea of separation of powers (specifically the independence of the judging authority), innate human rights and an explicit right of rebellion. Thus, even if Locke was not himself a 'liberal' (a concept emerging only in the eighteenth century), this text provided some of the most important foundations for liberal thought, as did other texts of Locke's such as his 'Letter Concerning Toleration', also published in 1689.

> ### Key Concept: Toleration
>
> Toleration refers to the peaceful coexistence of conflicting beliefs and practices. Locke's 'Letter Concerning Toleration' (1689) was written during a time of religious conflict and persecution across Europe. Locke argued in favour of religious toleration, and in so doing he tried to establish the extent to which the state should be allowed to interfere in people's beliefs and practices. He set out various

> principles which would later be central to liberalism, including the separation of church and state, the necessity of government neutrality, freedom of belief, the division between public and private spheres, and an emphasis on individual conscience. The 'Letter' also arguably highlights the limits of liberalism: not only does Locke argue that we should not tolerate the intolerant, but also that we should not tolerate atheists (because promise and oaths means nothing to them) and apparently Catholics (because they owe their allegiance to a foreign ruler, namely the Pope).

Key to the arguments of the *Second Treatise* is Locke's understanding of self-ownership: the idea that the individual owns their own person and body, which is the basis for their freedom. In Section 7.3, we will see how this concept of freedom, that is so tightly linked to ownership and thus to property, ultimately serves to exclude propertyless people and slaves (who were the property of others and thus could not own themselves or other property). This notion ties freedom, as well as individuality itself, to possession. But for now we can emphasize how the idea of self-ownership served to entrench important ideas, such as bodily integrity and boundaries. Moreover, the idea that I own myself and my actions means that any change to my status requires my consent. From this emerges the scheme of the social contract. Accordingly, if, for Hobbes, sovereignty is based on a consent which can always be assumed (given the horrid life in his state of nature), in Locke, consent gains content and becomes a meaningful political apparatus. Let us return, then, to that moment of original consent: the social contract.

Despite the relative comfort of the state of nature, there are benefits to political organization which eventually push people to form a political body. Above all, the state allows us to better secure our property, and frees each and every man from the need to be his own judge. The latter further gives way to the separation between judgement (interpreting the law), legislation (the making of laws—even if only by the means of re-articulating natural ones), and government (the implementation of laws by executive power). It can thus give rise to a good state-formation in which sovereignty is divided (another important liberal idea promoted by Locke). Property and the law thus become the two main foundations of the state. Property is the state's *raison d'être*, and the law is in many ways its form: what we give to the sovereign in Locke's version of the social contract, thereby constituting it, is the right to *judge*. This means that the state is primarily a judicial function, or a legislative body (it is not, for example, primarily a military or security apparatus, as we find in Hobbes). Moreover, its legislative activities are limited by the form and content of the law itself, with principles such as visibility, non-arbitrariness, and egalitarianism that protect people against tyranny. This idea of the rule of law would be another one of the main foundations of the liberal state.

These ideas that emerge around Locke's theory of the social contract will continue to be developed by Locke and many of his followers. They allow Locke to do the following:

- criticize conquest as granting political rights;
- criticize various form of absolute power beyond the state: of husbands over wives, parents over children, and more, thereby expanding realms of individual freedom;
- advocate religious toleration.

All these and more have been crucial politically as well as philosophically in imagining and advocating spheres of freedom, some of which were previously almost inconceivable. Yet they have also been the subject of much critique. Sections 7.3 and 7.4 works through some critiques as they emerge from the question of positionality with which we began.

> ### 🛈 7.2 Locke, sovereignty, and the state of nature: Key Points
>
> - Locke presents a liberal version of social contract theory that advocates limits on sovereign power, mixed government (or divided sovereignty), the rule of law, self-ownership, and the equality of all before the law.
> - Because the Lockean state of nature is relatively peaceful, there is no *justification* for limitless sovereignty—we would not have agreed to it in that originary moment.
> - Because we have an ability to regulate ourselves, we do not *need* a sovereign who would rule us tyrannically in order to provide security.
> - Our freedom is regulated via the law of nature, which *limits* not only our behaviour but also what is permitted to the sovereign.

7.3 Social and sexual identities and hierarchies

I proposed that in trying to understand the social contract as both a political and theoretical project we need to understand how the contracting agents are imagined. The rest of this chapter will be organized around an analysis of the main social positions forming the identity of these agents. Section 7.3 will consider questions of class and gender, while Section 7.4 will consider global positioning and race. Together these sections seek to demonstrate how the egalitarian, universal project of liberalism can work in tandem with a reality of various forms of domination.

7.3.1 Class: labour, accumulation, and Locke's 'individual'

Locke says repeatedly that the main reason we enter a social contract is to protect property (e.g., Locke, 2003: §8). But the fifth chapter of the *Second Treatise*, 'On Property', opens not with the idea of private property but with the assumption that the world has been given to all men in common. In fact, one of the main challenges of the chapter is to explain how we move from a system of common use to a system of private property. In seventeenth-century England, with the gradual elimination of the commons through processes of enclosure, this was indeed an urgent question. Locke's answer has to do with labour: what I have laboured on is mine. This is because of the time invested in it, as well as due to a model of spatial annexation wherein property is extended from the body to anything the body is 'mixed with' through labour (Kotef, 2020). Both time and annexation add value to the natural object, Locke contends, thus producing property. Accordingly, while God gave us the land ('the world') in common, once I start cultivating it—once I add to it something that was not there by nature—I have a right to the product of my toil. This is both a material argument (I have rights in the outcomes of my investment, the added value I put into objects through labour) and a religious one (property emerges from creation: we are the property of God since he created us, and we can create property ourselves). Importantly, this notion of labour and creation is anchored in the individual body. First, it begins from the idea of self-ownership mentioned above: this idea is the conceptual foundation for property. Second, the body is what *makes* property: 'The labour of his body, and the work of his hands, we may say, are properly his' (Locke, 2003: §27).

Yet, quite quickly, we see that this is not the entire story: although Chapter 5 begins with a close link, if not complete equivalence, between body, labour, and property, somewhere along the way the product of labour is severed from the labouring 'hands' and 'body'. It is not just what my toil has produced that is mine; also 'the grass my horse has bit; the turfs my servant has cut; and the ore I have digged . . . become my property' (ibid.: §28). Putting the horse aside for now, if property is generated through labour, then the labour of the servant should generate property for *them*, rather than for 'me'. Yet Locke makes a different claim.

To understand how this hierarchical order of property emerges—why some people become property-owners while some people must work for others—we need to retell the story of the contract. Locke's narration progresses along a dual trajectory. In both, Locke begins with an assumption of equality in the state of nature. This equality is not just a formal one in which we are all equal before and under the law of nature. It is also a material one: we all have equal access to the goods of the world that is given to us in common. In the first trajectory, there is a series of limitations on material accumulation that restrain inequality to some degree. The natural equality is thus (more or less) maintained and is carried into the social contract. In the political community, equality is preserved and protected as formal equality. Note that equality in this version is not a matter of fact (as it is for Hobbes, for example) but a matter of *principle*, a normative demand: we *should* be treated equally, even though we are, in fact, different.

At the same time, we find an almost opposite trajectory, which begins with the same equal access of each and every man to natural resources, but ends in a radical inequality. We begin, then, with the world given to us in common, and with an original economy based on consumption. (Locke's examples of property in the state of nature often revolve around food.) We move to small units of property, that are limited both by primitive cultivation techniques and by the principle of no spoilage: the idea that natural spoilage limits what can technically and morally be accumulated (ibid.: §§36, 37). In other words: if I take from nature more than I can consume, this is a violation of natural law. Imagine a small farm, where people consume what they produce and thus cannot accumulate indefinitely; or a primitive economy based on exchange, which is itself limited. At this stage, the gaps between different units of cultivation are small enough, although gaps do begin to emerge. Rather than the primitive mode of accumulation with which Locke begins, wherein we consume that for which we labour (I pick an apple or an acorn, I hunt a deer; therefore these are mine) and wherein, accordingly, property is linked to the body both as that which produces it and as that which enjoys it, we move to small units of accumulations: households, farms, plantations. In those units, there are women and children, horses, sheep, and perhaps also servants.

If you recall our original question concerning the property of the servant (who labours and yet does not obtain the property rights for the fruits of his labour), we see that, at this point, property departs from the labouring body and starts being attached to another person: the property-owner. Although we must keep asking ourselves: if there is enough for everyone, why would one want to work for another rather than cultivating their own plot of land? Why would one freely choose to become a servant? Locke has an answer to this, that is hidden already in the first trajectory above: some of us are more talented, creative, and hard-working, and thus would be able to quickly establish successful units of accumulation; presumably the lazy and less talented would find themselves working for the former. But it is safe to say that beneath this answer we can find another one hiding: there is simply not enough land for everyone within the system Locke proposes. At any rate, with trade, these gaps are growing, especially with money they acquire (see Key Thinker: C.B. Macpherson).

Key Thinker: C.B. Macpherson

The Canadian political theorist C.B. Macpherson (1911–1987) offered a combination of Marxist principles with democratic values. Through his notion of 'possessive individualism', he showed how pre-capitalist thinkers, such as Hobbes and Locke, provided a theoretical foundation for the later development of capitalism. He further showed how accumulation is defended by Locke, facilitating radical inequality.

> While Locke introduced several limits on accumulation—leading to some interpretations of his theory of property as founded on a commitment to ethics—Macpherson (2011 [1962]) showed how the vast majority of Locke's theory of property is dedicated to *removing these limits*, setting the ground for what Macpherson termed 'unlimited accumulation'. Most importantly, money allows the removal of the limit set by natural spoilage: although Locke contended that I can rightly own only what I can use, as long as it does not spoil in my possession, money never spoils and property can therefore grow indefinitely once it is introduced.

Importantly, all this occurs *before the contract has taken place*. By the time we contract in, we are therefore not equal in terms of our access to material resources. Moreover, some of us are not at all included in the category to which Locke refers as the 'I', the contracting individual: if 'the turfs *my* servant has cut . . . become *my* property', then the servant is already not part of this story. The servant here is significantly part of the household, but he/she represents each and every wage labourer. This is because the servant's labour is hired by the landowner, who temporarily owns the servant's labour power, as well as the products of the servant's labour. The servant is thus a prototype of wage labourers: an entire class of propertyless people who are therefore not considered as agents in or of the social contract. If, then, we began with an origin story of rational, toiling protagonists, whose property is a function of their hard labour and who enter the social contract as equal individuals, in this second version, the individual quickly undergoes two related transformations. First, its universality emerges as fractured—or, in other words, only some appear to be represented by the Lockean concept of the 'individual'. Second, its very individuality is threatened, or perhaps expands: rather than an individual body that produces individual property, the political imagination of Locke seems to be shifting into a model of households as the basic contracting units, including wives, horses, servants, and, as we shall see, also slaves. It is through the second process that the first occurs: Locke's framework of property allows one representative of the unit of accumulation (the husband/father/landlord) to 'swallow' all the other members of the household, rendering them irrelevant or invisible once the game of contracting begins (Kotef, 2020).

Accordingly, while the property-holder contracts to protect his property, the servant does not participate in the decision-making process that shapes the political community and the forms of rule to which he/she is subjected. Indeed, as we have seen, Locke tells us that the main reason men enter into a social contract is to protect their property and, thus, the main *raison d'être* of the state is securing private property. We can presume that the interests and desires of servants, or other propertyless people, will not be represented by the set of rules the contract contrives. The formal story of equality, therefore, cannot be separated from the material story of inequality. The society that Locke imagines is a society of property-holders, and the law (upon which they agreed, which they have shaped, and which formally treats everyone the same) aims at protecting *them*; its content, limits, and scope would be those that *they* see as necessary or desirable.

7.3.2 Gender: the questions of limited rule and forced subjection

The above story tells the story not only of the servant, but also that of the wife: in the formation of the household as the primary property-making unit that then becomes the contracting unit, not only are the servant and the horse 'swallowed' by the landlord; the wife also somehow disappears and comes to be represented by the husband. Carole Pateman (1988) argues that the only consistent way to read Locke's account of women in the *Second Treaties* is to assume that the wife is but another servant. The wife, too, labours for another person, both in her domestic work and through reproductive labour. One could therefore tell a very similar story to the one above, focusing on gender, rather than class. As many feminists have taught us, these categories of gender and class, as well as race, must be understood together, through their intersections.

But, if in the story of property women somehow fade away and become hidden by the structure of the household, they take a more central stage in Locke's argument against absolute power. One of the main adversaries of Locke in this argument was Robert Filmer, who was Locke's explicit opponent in the *First Treatise*. Filmer argued that the power of the sovereign, as an absolute monarch, can be derived from the original right given by God to the original sovereign, Adam. The godly right/power of Adam over his sons provides both the origin and the principle of absolute sovereignty. Locke seeks to refute this theory in several ways. One of them is by proving that power over children is not *paternal* but rather *parental*: it belongs to the mother as well as the father. The fact that both parents have some power over the child means that no one enjoys absolute power over anyone, and both the historical story and the theoretical principle are void. Adam never had absolute power over his sons, as he shared this power with Eve. Arguing that the wife/mother shares power with the husband/father is therefore essential to one of Locke's main arguments in the *Treatises*. Accordingly, some saw him as an early feminist (see Hirschmann and McClure, 2007, especially the chapters by Shanley and Butler). He even grants women the right to divorce—which was very uncommon at the time—as part of the same argument: there is no natural absolute power, and the power of husband over wife, much like the power of the sovereign over his subjects, is dependent on her consent and is therefore limited and conditional (Locke, 2003: §82). Thus, the conditionality of the marriage contract is yet another path through which Locke justifies the right to rebellion.

Nevertheless, as important as her role may be for his argument against absolute power, the wife/mother/woman disappears when it comes to the contract itself. As we saw above, Locke's state of nature includes families, and it is families that enter into the contract, represented by the head of the household. For some reason, the head of the household is 'naturally' the man. Sharing responsibilities for children, therefore, does not amount to a full equality: in case of disagreements, 'the last determination, i.e., the rule, should be placed somewhere', and it 'naturally falls to the man's share' (ibid.: §82). Where did this 'natural' course of things come from? If mothers have a shared authority over their children—and if, moreover, only a few paragraphs earlier Locke points to matriarchal societies in America, wherein women have multiple husbands and have greater authority over their children than the men involved (ibid.: §65)—then why it is 'natural' for the father to become the ruler within the (European) household? Locke's words may insinuate the answer: the man is 'the abler and the stronger'. But how did physical superiority come to transform a consensual agreement between equals into a relation of subordination? Pateman (1988: 104–105) proposes that at the foundation of any social contract, there is rape. In other words: men's physical strength served to subjugate his partner, creating the 'natural' course of things. Either way, by the time politics 'begins', that is, by the time we 'contract in', this subjugation has already happened. We enter the contract after women (and children, and servants, and slaves) have become subordinated to 'man', represented by his figure thereby. Thus, even though Locke begins Chapter 6 ('On Paternal Power') with seeing Eve and Adam—or women and men—as having joint authority over their children, this equality is not carried into the political sphere.

> **Key Concept: The private sphere**
>
> The division between the private and the political spheres is an important principle of liberalism, that has its roots in early political thought. (For example, when Aristotle insisted that 'the roles of a statesman' are different *in kind* to those of the head of the household [Aristotle, 1981: 1252a1].) Within liberalism, this differentiation of spheres is often theorized in relation to the principle of limited state power: the private sphere is a domain of non-state-intervention, defending us from excessive state power. The state cannot intervene in questions of love, for example, or in how we educate our children. Yet as many feminists have argued, this structure allows an entire domain of hierarchies and domination to remain unregulated. The privatization of domestic issues—from sex to property—withholds protection from those whose primary injury takes place in the household. Their injury remains not only hidden; it becomes a private matter, unintelligible as a *political* injury.

This fact further means that the woman's power over her children becomes a *private* rather than a *political* power. Locke tells us in Section 2 of the *Second Treatise* that we must distinguish between 'political power' and the power of 'the father over his children, a master over his servants, a husband over his wife, and a lord over his slaves'. Indeed, he says, 'these two powers, political and paternal, are ... perfectly distinct and separate, are built on... different foundations, and are given to ... different ends' (Locke, 2003: §71). The rationale for this separation is to refute the argument for absolute *political* power, by separating from political power the presumably absolute control that the original man (Adam) held over his sons. At the same time, however, this distinction marks the very border of political power and creates a separation between two spheres or logics of governance: the political and the domestic. And it *is the very existence of the private sphere* that excludes women from the political sphere. Thus, after using the power of the mother over her children to refute one of the main doctrines of absolute power, Locke uses her to demarcate the borders of the political sphere and to create its paradigmatic 'outside': the private sphere.

> **7.3 Social and sexual identities and hierarchies: Key Points**
>
> - While seemingly presenting a universal individual, Locke's social contract theory in fact contrives only specific individuals as the contracting agents: propertied, European (if not English) men.
> - Wage labourers without property are excluded from the social contract through the figure of the 'servant', who is presumed to be a part of the household rather than an 'individual' who can freely enter the social contract (which becomes a tool to secure property).
> - Women are ultimately confined by Locke to the private, domestic sphere as a non-political sphere and thus excluded from the story of the social contract.

7.4 Global considerations

In this section we will continue to question the egalitarianism and universalism of Locke's project, this time by reflecting on global positioning and race.

7.4.1 Place: colonization and the establishment of European access to the world's resources

The context given above was an English one, focusing on the structure of English monarchy. Many have further noted that Locke's justification of private property comes to address the process of enclosure that took place in England at the time of his writing. In the last two decades, others have shown that just as important for Locke, in both his conceptualization of the state of nature and in his defence of enclosure, was the context of the colonization of America.

More than his writing—and probably tightly related to his theory—the colonies occupied Locke's personal and financial interests. Locke served in both private and public colonial administration roles, including serving as the secretary of the Lords Proprietors of Carolina (1671-1675) and drafting its constitution (Armitage, 2004). Crucially, the *Fundamental Constitutions of Carolina* anchored slavery in law and guaranteed 'Absolute dominion and power over slaves' (recall Locke's objection to absolute power as one of the main arguments of the *Second Treatise*). Locke was further involved in colonial enterprises and the trading of enslaved people via his patron, Anthony Ashley Cooper (later the first Earl of Shaftesbury), whose household Locke joined in 1667. Cooper was a Lord Proprietor of Carolina, a part-owner of a sugar plantation in Barbados—the most significant slave-holding British colony at the time—and a supporter of and investor in the trading of enslaved people. Finally, Locke was invested in the two companies trading enslaved people: the Bahamas Company and the Royal Africa Company.

Yet it is not enough to point to the colonial *practices* of Locke as something that is in conflict with his liberal *theory*. These are not, as Uday Mehta (1999: 46) aptly states, 'ships passing in the night, spurred on by unrelated imperatives and destinations'; it is not, in other words, a matter of a reality betraying 'the pristine motives of theory'. We need to understand *Locke's theory itself* as providing justifications for these practices. Indeed, America was central to Locke's writing, notably in the *Second Treatise* and particularly (though not exclusively) in Chapter 5, 'On Property'. In this chapter, America was the paradigm of the state of nature, a place wherein the lack of apparent sovereignty allowed free political agents to assemble and contract a new commonwealth; a place wherein people 'still live' without any government, demonstrating not just the coherency but the validity of the theory of the state of nature. It was also a site providing various examples of 'early' societies. Finally, this space of origin served to help Locke to justify his theory of property.

Locke begins his theory of labour with a commonsensical example: it is evident that when I eat something, it is mine: 'He that is nourished by the acorns he picked up under an oak, or the apples he gathered from the trees in the wood, has certainly appropriated them to himself. Nobody can deny but the nourishment is his' (Locke, 2003: §28).

But, Locke asks: 'When did they begin to be his? when he digested? or when he eat? or when he boiled? or when he brought them home? or when he picked them up? and it is plain, if the first gathering made them not his, nothing else could.' Labour, he explains, 'put[s] a distinction' between the objects that can be seen as private property and the commons (ibid.: §28). But this seemingly straightforward theory of labour—that begins with eating an apple and is carried through the time and effort invested in picking it if not growing it—was in fact based on a very specific model of European agriculture. Whereas everyone has the right to the apple they eat or the deer they kill, not everyone has a right to the land on which apples grow or deer run. To gain right to the land, Locke says, people need to invest labour in the land itself, and he defined this labour 'in terms of European agriculture and industry: cultivating, subduing, tilling, and improving' (Tully, 1994: 160). The first right, to things, did not 'interfere with England's plans for settlement in the same way that claim over land [would] do' (Arneil, 1996b: 62). The second right, to land, was solely permitted to those who practised European models of working the land, primarily enclosure.

Unlike the model described in the pages of Chapter 5, Indigenous agriculture was based on crop rotation and a degree of moving between plots to secure the fertility of the land. Locke was aware of these agricultural methods and their effectiveness, and even read documented cases in which such practices saved European settlers from starvation (Tully, 1993: 65-87, 118-132, 140-141; Arneil, 1996a: 23-41; Hsueh, 2006: 200-205). Nevertheless, he chose to portray Indigenous Americans as hunter-gatherers, and chose to identify only enclosed lands as producing value from the territory. The land in America could thus be classified as 'free'—that is, free for European (English) appropriation. This was part of a much wider system of justification for colonial expansion: 'From the 1620s to the 1680s in Britain, and then in North America, Australia, and Africa well into the nineteenth century, the argument from vacancy (*vacuum domicilum*) or absence of ownership (*terra nullius*) became a standard foundation for English, and later British dispossession of indigenous people', argues David Armitage (2000: 97). Locke, he continues, provided 'the most extensive presentation of this argument'. Locke's justification of enclosure was therefore not only a justification of land privatization in England. It was also a way of isolating a single model of agriculture, thereby dismissing Indigenous work on the land, denying their right to the land, making it available for European settlement.

This argument was key to Locke's justification of private property *and* to his justification of colonialism. One of the principles that limits property in Locke is an ethical principle, according to which private ownership is just only as long as it does not injure (take away from) everyone else. This can work only as long as there is no shortage in this world. Yet, Locke was fully aware that we no longer live in an age of abundance: there is not enough land for everyone. Indeed, the practice of enclosure, which created a whole new class of people without basic means of substance, demonstrated this vividly. America, as a space of presumably available land, solved this predicament. Those who have nothing left in England should simply go and 'plant in some inland, vacant places of America' (Locke, 2003: §36). Without this colonial possibility, Locke's moral argument concerning private property collapses. Of course, the reality was very different: it was one in which only few 'planted' freely. The rest—both those who were transported from the coasts of Africa and the vast majority of those who arrived from the coasts of England—were kidnapped and sold or (in the case of the latter) 'leased' into forced labour.

But Locke's defence of enclosure did more: it served to frame any territorial wars with Indigenous Americans as just wars. Locke claims that land is much more valuable when enclosed. He estimates that 'an acre of land' in America produces 'not one thousandth' of an acre of cultivated, enclosed land 'here' (ibid.: §43). (A few paragraphs beforehand he provides the more moderate ratio of one to ten, or perhaps to a hundred (ibid.: §37).) And since 'he who appropriates land to himself' by enclosing 10 acres produces 'a greater plenty of the conveniences of life . . . than he could have from an hundred left to nature', Locke can argue that this person does not *take* away from the 'common stock of human kind', but actually *gives* 'ninety acres to mankind' (ibid.: 37). In a move that completely overturns the working of private property, Locke thus proposes that enclosure does not reduce the commons but enlarges what everyone can enjoy. Moreover, he points to those who 'know no enclosure' (ibid.: §26)—specifically, Indigenous Americans—as *denying* goods to the rest of humanity. If you recall, the world was given to us in common, but not to lie waste. God gave it to us to cultivate and enjoy. Those who fail to act according to this 'common law of nature' (ibid.: §37) sin towards humanity and lose not just their own rights to the land, but also their status as free, rational, members of society.

Locke's most famous example of a violation of this law of nature commanding us to enjoy, use, and cultivate what God gave us is a man accumulating beyond what he can consume. This man over-accumulates goods; goods that therefore 'perished, in his possession, without their due use; . . . the fruits are rotted, or the venison putrefied' (ibid.: §37). Like this man, the failure to enclose can also be seen as an act against God's will and against the natural law. But whereas the man of greed is redeemed once money is introduced into the picture (as money cannot rot and so the greedy man can accumulate without any interruption), Indigenous Americans' 'failure' to enclose is portrayed by Locke as a failure to organize society according to and within the limit of laws of nature. Moreover, unlike that hypothetical man, Locke's 'Indians' represent not an isolated sin, but a systematic social order that cannot cross the threshold of natural law. Importantly, the law itself is often metaphorically referred to by Locke as a fence (Brown, 2010: 44) and, accordingly, the refusal of fences echoes a refusal to live within the bounds of the law. This, again, places Indigenous Americans as enemies of mankind; any war against them is therefore a just war. In such wars, territorial gains are fully justified, he claimed. To be sure, Locke emphasized that the only case in which an *unjust* conqueror can have the right to the land of the vanquished is when this land 'lies waste' (Locke, 2003: §184). From this perspective, too, colonization became justifiable.

Locke's theory of property was thus a theory of and for colonization. It both dismissed and erased Indigenous Americans' legitimate claims to the land and portrayed them as enemies of mankind. In making these arguments Locke clearly ignored not just Indigenous practices of land cultivation in order to portray land in America as vacant. He further ignored the political forms of sovereignty among Indigenous Americans, rendering them non-political subjects from this perspective as well. All the societies he sees in America are explicitly classified by him as pre-contract (non-political) societies. Ultimately, even if they occupy the state of nature as free, rational, individuals, they seem to fail to cross to its other side, to come together to form a contract. The story of the social contract is therefore not their story—much like women or the propertyless, who were excluded from it before it even began.

> **Key Concept: Rationality**
>
> Rationality is a key concept for various strands of liberal theory: from the autonomous man, whose freedom is a function of his ability to give himself and follow rules (Locke, Kant), to the *homo oeconomicus*, whose rationality allows him to identify and follow his best interest (Smith, neoliberalism). Many of the opponents of liberalism—from Nietzsche to Freud—argued, however, that human beings act according to their passions, desires, and aggression, rather than reason (see also Hobbes). But even though rationality is often seen by liberalism as part of human nature, it also serves to create hierarchies. Critics of Locke have shown how the poor (Hirschmann, 2009), non-Europeans (Mehta, 1999; Seth, 2010), or the physically and mentally disabled (Arneil, 2009; Clifford, 2014) lack the material conditions that allow rationality to develop. Since rationality for Locke is the foundation for political freedom as well as economic prosperity, only some end up enjoying both freedom and the plenty of the world.

7.4.2 Race: slavery and the question of freedom

Much like the 'Indian', who is ultimately not the protagonist of the transition from a state of nature to political society, the people kidnapped in Africa, transported across the Middle Passage, and enslaved, are not the protagonists of Locke's concept of freedom. Paradoxically, this means they are also not the subjects of his fierce critique of slavery. Locke's ardent objection to slavery is woven into most of the *Second Treatise*. It is part of his insistence on natural freedom; slavery is presented as the most illegitimate violation of the law of nature (see, e.g. Locke, 2003: §§17, 18, 23, 172). Since men are equal and God's creation, and thus have no absolute power even over their own lives, no one can have such power over anyone else. Yet, Locke was a supporter of slave labour and trade and was involved in forming the first American colony in which owning slaves was guaranteed by the Constitution. How can the two be reconciled?

Some have claimed that cannot be reconciled; others have pointed to a temporal schism, between a young Locke, supporter of kings and slavery, and an older one, who cherished freedom (although David Armitage's [2004] meticulous historical work refutes this claim). Many have suggested that the term 'slavery' to which Locke refers throughout most of the *Second Treatise* does not refer to real slaves, but is in fact a metaphor for people (Englishmen) living under tyrannical power. Indeed, Chapter 4, 'On Slavery', focuses on life under tyranny and not on concrete enslavement, and accordingly, targets the English monarchy. This last claim merits at least two reservations.

First, one may wonder about this metaphorical use, at a time when the slave trade was flourishing across the Empire, especially by someone who was actively involved in it. How can Locke refer to slavery as an analogy, knowing too well it is the living-condition of so many people (see also Buck-Morss, 2005)? Second, Locke *does* refer to real slaves, and not all mentions of the term in the *Treatise* are metaphorical. We saw some of them above, when discussing the question of class. In fact, when he refers to concrete slaves, whom he sees as part of the household, he seems to be quite at ease with their existence: the slave's presence in the household is repeatedly mentioned alongside the wife or servant, and Locke even grants absolute power to the master over them (Locke, 2003: §85).

This, indeed, is the only case of justified absolute power in the *Treatise*, as all other forms of power are limited either in time (as in the case of children or servants) or in scope and extent (as in the case of wives or the king's subjects).

This may not seem surprising, given the fact that in some of the English colonies (including Carolina and Barbados, to which Locke had significant links), slaves were probably the most important property and the main means of acquiring more property (both through their physical labour and through the reproductive labour of enslaved women). As a chief defender of property, Locke's freedom somehow found its limit when it came to the freedom of those who themselves became property and who as a result could own none. If individual freedom is defined as a state in which one is able 'to order their actions and dispose of their possessions and persons, as they think fit' (ibid.: §4), absolute dominion and power over the enslaved paradoxically appear as consistent with freedom. The slave, then, is neither the subject of freedom nor its negation to Locke. His/her story is not relevant to the story of 'the individual' and the political principles protecting him.

This eviction from any consideration is also manifested, quite surprisingly, in the moments Locke *defends* slavery. Despite his condemnation of slavery, Locke provided justification for it under some *very restricted* conditions. When I have a right to kill someone—in a just war—death can be suspended and replaced with slavery. This is a very limited justification: to be just, the war should be one of self-defence, and it is only then that it can grant the right to kill, or to suspend death and exert absolute arbitrary power instead (ibid.: §23). It is only if an 'aggressor' threatens to kill me or subjugate me to his own absolute power,

> he renders himself liable to be destroyed by the injured person, and the rest of mankind, that will join with him in the execution of justice, as any other wild beast, or noxious brute, with whom mankind can have neither society nor security. And thus captives, taken in a just and lawful war, and such only, are subject to a despotical power.
>
> (ibid.: §172)

Slavery, he says, is 'nothing else, but the state of war continued, between a lawful conqueror, and captive' (ibid.: §24).

On the one hand, this justification is given under such strict limitations that Farr (1986; 2008) argued that 'if Locke intended his just war theory to justify the execrable practices of new world slavery, about which he knew so much, then he did a spectacularly bad job of it'. It is quite difficult to explain commercial, New World slavery via this paradigm of just wars against an aggressor. Farr (2008: 500) thus concludes that, 'there are reasons to believe that he did not so intend the theory, in whatever contradictions this lands him'. If we take the context of those enslaving and trading companies in which Locke was invested, kidnapping people in Africa and transporting them into the colonies' plantations as slaves, it is difficult to see how slavery can be justified by claims such as this one: 'The aggressor' who 'unjustly invades another man's right' can 'never have the right over the conquered' (Locke, 2003: §176). Yet, these trading companies invaded Africa (even if by proxies), not the other way around. Moreover, Locke insists that the absolute right given over to the aggressor in a just war does not extend to the aggressor's offspring (ibid.: §182). This stood in contradiction not only to the common practices and laws governing New World slavery, but specifically to the *Fundamental Constitution of Carolina* that Locke partially drafted, both of which rendered servitude hereditary. A possible explanation is that these arguments should be understood vis-à-vis the English context, specifically the Norman Conquest, to which Locke refers explicitly soon thereafter (ibid.: §177): Locke wanted to refute the right of kings who were linked to a history of conquest, and assert, further, that if conquest did give an original right in the case of 1066, this right cannot be carried through generations. 'The aggressor' in this story is a monarch overstepping his authority, and the just war is the right of rebellion. Even in his defence of slavery as the outcome of a just war, Locke was unable to see enslaved people.

> ### 🔑 7.4 Global considerations: Key Points
>
> - Indigenous Americans are identified by Locke as pre-political agents, not as contracting individuals, in two main ways: through their relation to land and through their social structures.
> - Slaves, being property, are likewise not defined as political agents, and in their reality remain almost completely unseen by Locke.
> - Locke was not only *historically involved* in projects of colonization and slave trade, but his *theory* provided a systematic justification for the former and a less-systematic erasure of the latter.

7.5 Conclusion

Through these different figures—the servant (wage labourer), the wife, the Indigenous American, and the slave—we see a series of tensions between formal equality and material, racial, and gender inequalities. The universality of the theory emerges as fragile, if not fraudulent, and yet it is still held as the theory's main merit. Importantly, at stake are not abstract concepts and a theorization that remain limited to philosophy books. Locke was actively involved in the shaping of the world we still inhabit, and both his ideas and acts of governance were important in the entrenchment and justification of concrete histories and world orders.

Trying to understand the role of these marginalized figures in Locke's thinking is not always straightforward. Precisely because they interrupt the liberal pretence of universality, their positioning within the theory is not always stable. In this chapter, I have offered several possible interpretations, but at times these interpretations leave us with more questions than answers. I propose not to be frustrated by these instabilities and tensions, but rather to see them as productive: it is through these inconsistencies that those marginalized voices can enter the space from which they are systematically excluded. Their very insistence on being present in the story—our very insistence as readers to read them back into the story—is often the source of these tensions and so perhaps in our act of reading, we should not be trying to resolve them.

Take your learning further by accessing the online resources for a library of web links to relevant videos, articles, blogs, and useful websites for this chapter: www.oup.com/he/Ramgotra-Choat1e.

Study questions

1. What are Locke's main critiques of absolute power?
2. In what ways can we identify in Locke's theory the foundation for liberal thought and politics?
3. What are the different historical backdrops and political projects against which Locke's story of the social contract should be read?
4. Why can the servant be thought of as a prototype of the wage labourer and why does this status exclude them from the contract?
5. Why does Locke seek to replace 'paternal' power with 'parental' power and what are the different implications this has on political institutions and structures in his theory?

6. How is Locke's theory of property relevant to his justification of colonialism?
7. What are the links and tensions between Locke's critique of tyranny and his account of slavery?
8. What are the intersections and meeting points between the exclusion or marginalization of women, the poor, the colonized and the enslaved subjects in Locke's story?

Further reading

Primary sources

Locke, J. (1693) *Some Thoughts Concerning Education*. London: A. and J. Churchill.
An often-neglected writing of Locke's that helps reveal the hidden assumptions beyond his conceptualizations of subjectivity and rationality.

Locke, J. (1854) *An Essay Concerning Human Understanding*. Philadelphia: Hayes and Zell.
This is not a text in political theory, but Locke's epistemological theory can help understand his conception of the human.

Locke, J. (1997) *Political Essays*. Ed. M. Goldie. Cambridge: Cambridge University Press.
Includes several important essays by Locke, including 'On the Poor Law and Working Schools'.

Locke, J. (2003) *Two Treatises of Government and a Letter Concerning Toleration*. Ed. I. Shapiro. New Haven, CT: Yale University Press.
An edition containing the two most influential political writings of Locke, with an excellent introduction by Ian Shapiro.

Secondary sources

Armitage, D. (2000) *The Ideological Origins of the British Empire*. Cambridge: Cambridge University Press.
Among many other important contextualizations of Locke's thinking in relation to the imperial project, this book provides detailed accounts of Locke's personal involvement with colonialism in America.

Bell, D. (2014) 'What Is Liberalism?' *Political Theory*, 42(6): 682–715.
This brief article provides a nuanced and historically grounded understanding of liberalism and Locke's role in it.

Hirschmann, N. and McClure, K. (eds) (2007) *Feminist Interpretations of John Locke*. University Park, PA: Pennsylvania State University Press.
A great collection of feminist accounts of Locke.

Ince, O.U. (2018) *Colonial Capitalism and the Dilemmas of Liberalism*. Oxford: Oxford University Press.
A comprehensive work on the links between political theories and colonial capitalism.

Macpherson, C.B. (2011 [1962]) *The Political Theory of Possessive Individualism: Hobbes to Locke*. Oxford: Oxford University Press.
An important work linking Locke to early capitalism.

Mehta, U.S. (1999) *Liberalism and Empire: A Study in Nineteenth-Century British Liberal Thought*. Chicago: University of Chicago Press.
A revolutionary book explaining the philosophy of Locke (among others) and its deep links to imperial practices.

Tully, J. (1980) *A Discourse on Property: John Locke and His Adversaries*. Cambridge: Cambridge University Press.
An excellent book on Locke's theory of property and its context.

Williams, E. (1994) *Capitalism & Slavery*. Chapel Hill, NC: The University of North Carolina Press.
A ground-breaking work on the relation of capitalism and world slavery.

References

Aristotle (1981) *The Politics*. Trans. T.A. Sinclair and T.J. Saunders. Harmondsworth: Penguin.

Armitage, D. (2000) *The Ideological Origins of the British Empire*. Cambridge: Cambridge University Press.

Armitage, D. (2004) 'John Locke, Carolina, and the Two Treatises of Government'. *Political Theory*, 32(5): 602–627.

Arneil, B. (1996a) *John Locke and America: The Defence of English Colonialism*. Oxford: Clarendon Press.

Arneil, B. (1996b) 'The Wild Indian's Venison: Locke's Theory of Property and English Colonialism in America'. *Political Studies*, 44(1): 60–74.

Arneil, B. (2009) 'Disability, Self Image, and Modern Political Theory'. *Political Theory* 37(2): 218–242.

Brown, W. (2010) *Walled States, Waning Sovereignty*. New York: Zone Books.

Buck-Morss, S. (2005) *Hegel, Haiti, and Universal History*. Pittsburgh, PA: University of Pittsburgh Press.

Clifford, S. 'The Capacity Contract: Locke, Disability, and the Political Exclusion of "Idiots"'. *Politics, Groups, and Identities*, 2(1): 90–103.

Farr, J. (1986) '"So Vile and Miserable an Estate": The Problem of Slavery in Locke's Political Thought'. *Political Theory*, 14(2): 263–289.

Farr, J. (2008) 'Locke, Natural Law, and New World Slavery'. *Political Theory*, 36(4): 495–522.

Hirschmann, N.J. (2007) 'Intersectionality Before Intersectionality Was Cool: The Importance of Class to Feminist Interpretations of Locke'. In N.J. Hirschmann and K.M. McClure (eds), *Feminist Interpretations of John Locke*. University Park, PA: Pennsylvania State University Press, pp. 155–186.

Hirschmann, N.J. (2009) *Gender, Class, and Freedom in Modern Political Theory*. Princeton, NJ: Princeton University Press.

Hirschmann, N. and McClure, K. (eds) (2007) *Feminist Interpretations of John Locke*. University Park, PA: Pennsylvania State University Press.

Hsueh, V. (2006) 'Cultivating and Challenging the Common: Lockean Property, Indigenous Traditionalisms, and the Problem of Exclusion'. *Contemporary Political Theory*, 5(2): 193–214.

Kotef, H. (2015) *Movement and the Ordering of Freedom: On Liberal Governances of Mobility*. Durham, NC: Duke University Press.

Kotef, H. (2020) *The Colonizing Self : Home and Homelessness in Israel/Palestine*. Durham, NC: Duke University Press.

Locke, J. (2003) *Two Treatises of Government and a Letter Concerning Toleration*. Ed. I. Shapiro. New Haven, CT: Yale University Press.

References to this text give the section number of the *Second Treatise*.

Macpherson, C.B. (2011 [1962]) *The Political Theory of Possessive Individualism: Hobbes to Locke*. Oxford: Oxford University Press.

Mehta, U.S. (1992) *The Anxiety of Freedom: Imagination and Individuality in Locke's Political Thought*. Ithaca, NY: Cornell University Press.

Mehta, U.S. (1999) *Liberalism and Empire: A Study in Nineteenth-Century British Liberal Thought*. Chicago: University of Chicago Press.

Mills, C.W. (1997) *The Racial Contract*. Ithaca, NY: Cornell University Press.

Pateman, C. (1988) *The Sexual Contract*. Cambridge: Polity.

Pateman, C. and Mills, C. (2007) *Contract and Domination*. Cambridge: Polity.

Seth, V. (2010) *Europe's Indians*. Durham, NC: Duke University Press.

Tully, J. (1993) *An Approach to Political Philosophy: Locke in Contexts*. Cambridge: Cambridge University Press.

Tully, J. (1994) 'Aboriginal Property and Western Theory: Recovering a Middle Ground'. *Social Philosophy and Policy*, 11(2): 153–180.

8 Mary Astell
ALLAUREN FORBES

Chapter guide

This chapter explores the ways in which Mary Astell offered a thoroughgoing and sustained critique of social contract theory in *Some Reflections Upon Marriage* (first published in 1700; authoritative edition in 1706; reprinted 1996) and *A Serious Proposal to the Ladies* (first published in 1694, second part published in 1697; reprinted 2002). The chapter begins with a brief introduction to Astell's philosophical methods and an overview of the philosophical positions to which Astell was responding. The majority of the chapter addresses Astell's criticisms of central features of social contract theory, particularly in the context of marriage as an analogue for the social contract. Section 8.4 asks whether the analogue holds or whether it was simply a rhetorical device and what this means for how Astell understands marriage. The chapter closes with the suggestion that Astell's critique of social contract theory, and especially its application to marriage, was an attempt to reshape the socio-political terrain of her time.

8.1 Introduction

Mary Astell (1666–1731) was an English philosopher, feminist, and political theorist. She was born in Newcastle Upon Tyne, England, but moved to Chelsea in London in her early adulthood. She never married. Astell supported herself through her writing and through the patronage of her like-minded female friends. Although she wrote about a wide variety of philosophical and political issues that were hotly debated in her time, Astell has not traditionally been considered a canonical figure.

Astell, like many other philosophers and political theorists marginalized on the basis of their identities, was keenly attuned to the views, institutions, and systems of power that were used to perpetuate oppression. Astell uses one such socio-political institution—marriage—as a microcosm of a larger problem. In *Some Reflections Upon Marriage* (hereafter, *Reflections*), Astell draws a series of parallels between marriage and social contract theory which problematize the latter. There are good reasons to think that Astell is hinting at a much more radical project. Women ought to be free, and one way to obtain this, Astell seems to suggest, is a fundamental revision of the socio-political institution of marriage.

The central claim of this chapter is that Astell was not only critical of social contract theory for theoretical reasons, but also because those criticisms offered her a vehicle to argue for significant socio-political change, particularly in terms of improving the condition of women. This is complicated by Astell's occasional use of irony.

Read more about **Astell's** life and work by accessing the thinker biography on the online resources: www.oup.com/he/Ramgotra-Choat1e.

8.2 Astell's philosophical projects

8.2.1 An interpretive puzzle

Astell's main interest is improving the status of women. This is the central aim of *A Serious Proposal to the Ladies* (hereafter, *Proposal*)—that women should have access to formal education at her proposed educational retreat (in modern terms, something like a women's college) because, contrary to popular arguments about the nature of women, Astell argues that women are fundamentally equal to men. Women's apparent inferiority is the result of deficient social and political conditions: if women are educated, she argues, they will develop greater epistemic skills (i.e., they will become better thinkers and knowers), they will become virtuous and good Christians, and they will become meaningfully free (Astell, 2002; see also, Astell, 2013).

It is with this commitment to women's equality and the improvement of their social and political conditions in the background that Astell takes on some of the classical political topics and questions of her time. She entered the political debates between the Tories and the Whigs as a political pamphleteer, writing *Moderation Truly Stated*, *A Fair Way with the Dissenters and their Patrons*, and *An Impartial Enquiry into the Causes of Rebellion* (all published in 1704). Before getting into her philosophical differences with John Locke, it is important to note an interpretive complication with *Reflections*; that is, it should be read with an eye to irony and disingenuous, rhetorical speech. Writing political and philosophical treatises in this time was a dangerous prospect for women. Many, including Astell, sometimes published anonymously to avoid public backlash, or engaged in substantial philosophical and political projects through genres coded as appropriate for women, such as fiction or poetry. For unmarried women like Astell, public censure ran the risk of alienating patrons, publishers, or potential employers—her sources of financial stability. That she and other women in this time did write such works is a testament to their resilience and their commitment.

> **Key Thinker: Damaris Cudworth Masham**
>
> Damaris (1658-1708) was the daughter of Cambridge Platonist philosopher Ralph Cudworth and grew up with the works of several philosophers in this tradition. She had fruitful philosophical correspondences with famous philosophers John Locke and Gottfried Wilhelm Leibniz. Her friendship with Locke was so close that he eventually came to live with her and her husband Sir Francis Masham at their home in Essex. Though she published her philosophical writings anonymously, scholars have identified two of her works: *A Discourse Concerning the Love of God* (1696) and *Occasional Thoughts in Reference to a Virtuous or Christian Life* (1705). Her *Discourse* was written in response to Astell and John Norris's *Letters Concerning the Love of God* (Astell and Norris, 2005) and her *Occasional Thoughts* was written in response to Astell's *The Christian Religion* (1705), which was itself a response to Damaris's *Discourse*.

The problem, especially for a modern reader, is that it can be very difficult to determine just what Astell is claiming. Is she saying something that she thinks is patently absurd so that the reader will conclude the opposite, or is she speaking plainly? This chapter considers some cases where Astell's intent is not obvious, particularly in showing that the structure of social contract theory is rotten at its core. So, why did Astell write in ways that she must have known would make understanding her true meaning more difficult? Astell probably used irony because she was offering a radical view, and she knew that she had to be careful in how she articulated it. Using irony provides plausible deniability. Plain speech about contentious matters is safe only for privileged groups and, though Astell was not impoverished, she was in a precarious social and financial position. Astell opens the Preface of *Reflections* with the observation:

> 'Tis a very great Fault to regard who it is that Speaks, than what is Spoken, and either to submit to Authority, when we should only yield to Reason . . . Bold Truths may pass while the Speaker is *Incognito*, but are not endur'd when he is known; few Minds being strong enough to bear what Contradicts their Principles and Practices without Recriminating when they can.
>
> (Astell, 1996: 7)

Speaking truth to power has always been dangerous, and always even more dangerous for some than others. Nevertheless, the truth ought to win. If one must use rhetorical devices to achieve this, well, then the reader must strive to meet the challenge.

8.2.2 Social contract theory and liberalism

One of the central political questions of Astell's time pertains to political obligation and legitimate authority. Astell and her contemporaries were interested in determining who was a legitimate ruler and what subjects owed to them. This mattered a great deal, for if hereditary monarchs are made legitimate by divine right, then their authority echoes that of God. If, on the other hand, monarchs are made legitimate and granted authority by agreements among the citizens, then the balance of power looks very different. Social contract theory engages with the questions of political obligation and legitimacy largely from the latter perspective.

Thomas Hobbes (1588–1679)—see more in Chapter 5—and John Locke (1632–1704)—see more in Chapter 7—are two of the most famous social contract theorists, and Astell was familiar with and writing in the context of their views. Hobbes's (2017) social contract theory emerges out of concerns with stability and safety. He imagines a pre-political world, called a state of nature, in which there are no governments or socio-political institutions. He argues that a state of nature is a state of war, a conflict of all against all, in which people compete for scarce resources. This works against people's inherent self-interest. The only way to ensure safety and flourishing—the means for commodious living that all people desire—is for the people to consent to give up nearly all their rights and individual powers to the Sovereign, who becomes a near-absolute ruler. The real promise of the Sovereign, for Hobbes, is that the Sovereign solves the assurance problem: if it is known that there is a political body empowered to punish those who would break rules or contracts, individuals are less likely to do so. Thus, society is stabilized. The Sovereign is legitimate because it is authorized and empowered by the consent of the people, and people's obligations to the Sovereign are near-absolute.

Like Hobbes, consent plays a founding role in Locke's social contract theory. According to Locke (2003), a government is legitimate only if all rational members of society in a state of equal freedom and political right, as in a state of nature, could have consented to it. For Locke, consent is genuine only if it occurs without duress or coercion, and if it maintains the human duty to God—the fundamental law of nature—to preserve oneself and all mankind. So, the social contract is a test: if rational, free, and equal people could have voluntarily agreed to the present government—the people were not coerced or forced; it would be expressive of their wills—then the present government is legitimate, and one has political obligations to it. This view fits with the Whig aims of political reform and limited monarchies: such a view is incompatible with the absolute political power of hereditary monarchs, as rational, free, and equal people could not have chosen that system.

Locke (see more on Locke in Chapter 7) is sometimes called the first great liberal, and while there have been many debates on the history, nature, and iterations of liberalism, the organizing principle of liberalism is that certain individual liberties or rights are of fundamental political significance. Hobbes, while not a liberal, also focuses on the individual insofar as he is concerned primarily with the drive for self-preservation via safety and stability. Astell, on the other hand, focuses on communities—the community of women, of friends, of families. In adopting this more social perspective, she criticizes social contract theory through the microcosm of marriage. Many of her contemporaries, including Hobbes and Locke, drew a structural parallel between the social contract relation holding between subjects and ruler and the relation between wife and husband. Just as the ruler of the land is properly appointed (or could have been appointed) by the consent of the governed, so too do wives become subject to the authority of their husbands by consenting to the marriage contract (Locke, 2003; Hobbes, 2017). This is consonant with political thinking at the time—that the family is a miniature commonwealth, or that the monarch is 'wedded' to the commonwealth. Some theorists, most notably Patricia Springborg (1996; 2005), have argued that Astell condemns the connection drawn between social contract theory and marriage contracts because both require an incorrect model of contractarianism. Springborg argues that, for Astell, humans do not give consent and thus power to rulers or husbands; rather, God authorizes the Sovereign just as He authorizes marriage as a sacrament of Christianity. It is important to distinguish here between the sacrament of marriage and the socio-political institution of marriage. Astell is concerned with—though is not always clear about—both forms.

The view in this chapter is that Astell does not reject the parallel between the social contract and the marriage contract, but instead uses it to show that the structure of social contract theory is deeply flawed. She shows the reader that core structural elements of social contract theory present in both Hobbes's and Locke's theories go awry in the case of marriage. Such features include a particular conception of human nature, sovereignty, consent, and freedom in opposition to slavery. Astell shows that social contract theory and marriage are absurd for the same reasons: this reveals a more radical political aim than is usually attributed to her.

8.2 Astell's philosophical projects: Key Points

- Astell is committed to improving the social and political condition of women.
- Some of Astell's claims are ironic, rhetorical, and non-literal.
- Astell uses and critiques parallels between marriage and social contract theory.

8.3 Problematizing social contract theory

Like many other women philosophers of her time, Astell writes with the knowledge that she will endure more scrutiny than her male peers. This may be why she problematizes social contract theory so subtly—open criticisms might have caused her too much trouble. Even so, Astell clearly does not think highly of the social contract. Astell's criticisms lay bare problems not only with social contract theory but also with more fundamental philosophical and political commitments, including power, agency, and the nature of political subjecthood. One way to obtain women's freedom, Astell seems to suggest, is a fundamental revision of the socio-political institution of marriage into a relation between radical equals. She illustrates this by problematizing structural elements of social contract theory—human nature, sovereignty, consent, and freedom and slavery—as they appear in the context of marriage.

8.3.1 Human nature

Claims about human nature are often central to philosophical and political thought. If one can grasp the essential truth of what it is to be human, then the laws, institutions, and values one takes up should be informed by this truth: human nature is thought to dictate the limits of what is possible and desirable for human societies. The *querelle des femmes*, a contentious debate about the nature and worth of women, began in medieval literature and continued through the eighteenth century (see, for example, Kelly, 1984). Are men and women equals, or could they be made into equals through education or some other means? Astell's works are part of this debate, but there is also an important overlap with social contract theories. Like many other philosophers, Hobbes and Locke build their views about the correct organization of society on the notion of what humans are really like—their essence or nature—prior to governments or, rather, in a 'state of nature'. Astell has a view about human nature, too, but her view suggests a kind of rhetorical flaw in both the content and the approach of tying political organization to pre-social humans. Astell rejects the natural inferiority of women, and she suggests that the real challenge in forming socio-political institutions and practices lies in the way that people are now, not an imagined pre-social nature.

Astell rejects the widely held notion that women are naturally subordinate to men—a claim which was a key structural feature in explaining how marriage endowed a husband with the powers of a ruler. Astell notes that the proposed claim, *all men are superior to all women*, is inconsistent with lived experience; moreover, if this were true 'it wou'd be a Sin in *any* Woman to have Dominion over *any* Man, and the greatest Queen ought not to command but to obey her Footman, because no Municipal Laws can supersede or change the Law of Nature' (Astell, 1996: 9). If women were naturally inferior, men's oaths to queens such as Queen Anne (r. 1702–1714) would be incoherent. So, men must choose whether they want a ruler who is no ruler at all and the chaos that would bring about, or to admit their own inconsistency. And if the claim is meant to be that *some men are superior to some women*, then this is not especially surprising, but it will mean that at least some women are equal (or superior) to some men.

For Astell (2002), the natural state of men and women is one of radical equality. Humans are rational souls first and foremost; only bodies are sexed. And, by virtue of being created as rational souls by God, humans are equal. Astell (1996; 2002) assembles scriptural evidence to suggest that men and women are not only equal, but that they need one another to be as God wishes humans to be. Astell also points out that there is a structural inequality in access to the knowledge that would allow most women to make this argument for themselves. Women are made to rely on men to tell them the contents of scripture: 'Women without their own Fault, are kept in Ignorance of the Original, wanting Languages and other helps to Criticise on the Sacred Text, of which they know no more, than Men are pleas'd to impart in their Translations' (Astell, 1996: 14). Astell hints that this asymmetry in knowledge is deliberate: women are made dependent on the religious knowledge men design to impart to them.

Here, one might be tempted to think that this view of men and women as natural equals is consistent with Hobbes and Locke. After all, Hobbes says that people in the state of nature are equal enough, and the Lockean state of nature is one of perfect freedom and of equality of men (Locke, 2003; Hobbes, 2017). Astell clearly has natural equality in mind. However, there are two notable differences here. First, Astell is specifically and intentionally addressing the natural equality of *women*. This may sound trivial, but it is not. Locke (2003) suggests that men should rule their wives because they are naturally stronger and more able. In fact, the notion that men are naturally stronger and therefore the rightful rulers of women was thematic in the *querelle des femmes* (Kelly, 1984). By centring the more essential aspect of humans, souls rather than bodies, Astell is arguing for a foundational kind of equality such that, if human nature determines the correct political system, one must reconsider the political role of women and wives.

The second notable difference between Astell and her social contract predecessors is that, unlike Hobbes and Locke, Astell is arguing that whatever disparities exist between men and women are a result of human convention rather than nature. Where government is the solution to significant problems for both Hobbes and Locke—stability and protecting property rights—for Astell, these institutions have taken humans much further away from where they ought to be. In arguing that women are not naturally inferior (or at least not in the way that matters), Astell points to the complications presented by custom.

In *Proposal*, Astell argues that custom—the set of norms, values, and practices that shape how we think and behave—can cause serious problems if they are predicated on bad beliefs or practices inconsistent with what God wants humans to be (Astell, 1996; 2002). Custom stands in a mutually-reinforcing relation with socio-political institutions. If *x* is raised to value democracy, it is unlikely that *x* would support an absolute monarchy, and if *x* grows up in an absolute monarchy, it is unlikely that *x* would endorse democratic values. How someone sees and experiences the world depends on their social and political conditions; people are the products of their environments. If one's environment is epistemically, socially, or politically deficient, it is unsurprising that there is knowledge or understanding that is unavailable or at least obscured by those poor circumstances. Astell's point in bringing up custom in *Reflections* is to show how socio-political systems are vulnerable to unseen harms. In shaping how one sees, experiences, and understands the world, custom makes it *appear* that men are superior to women—it was customary that women did not have access to formal education, for example—but this does not reflect some essential truth so much as an accident of political values and institutional organizations (Astell, 1996; 2002). Hobbes's and Locke's shared commitment that government institutions are the answer is not obvious to Astell: for her, institutions are only as good as the values that structure them.

Astell's point about custom also suggests a sly problematization of the methodology of social contract theory. Astell (1996: 10) says: 'That the Custom of the World has put Women, generally speaking, into a State of Subjection, is not deny'd; but the Right can no more be prov'd from the Fact, than the Predominancy of Vice can Justifie it.' Here, Astell rejects the claim that one can derive an ought—what *should* be the case—from a descriptive claim about what *is* the case. Astell implicitly challenges social contract theory's methodology of moving from descriptive claims about humans to normative claims about what should be the case for humans. One might worry that her own claims about humans as rational souls would fall prey to similar concerns. Astell would likely say that this is not the case since she is appealing to God's notion of humans rather than a mere descriptor of humans but, even so, the bare fact that there is another descriptive story to tell suggests that there is a methodological flaw in appealing to claims about nature as the basis of normative views. Behind every interpretation is an interpreter.

8.3.2 Sovereignty

One of the more obvious parallels between Astell's discussion of marriage and social contract theory, and the site of some of her criticisms, is the connection Astell draws between sovereigns of nations—the Sovereign created by the social contract—and 'domestic sovereigns' or husbands. Like Hobbes and Locke, Astell (ibid.) discusses legitimacy and power in the course of considering domestic sovereigns. However, she also problematizes the notion of the sovereign in at least two ways: she exposes a crucial inconsistency in social contract theorists' attitudes towards women; and her proposed model of marriage and proper sovereignty challenges both constitutional and hereditary monarchies.

A husband, Astell notes, is granted the power of a sovereign. Once in this state, there is nothing women can do to remedy the situation. When a woman marries,

> [She] . . . Elects a Monarch for Life, who gives him an Authority she cannot recall however he misapply it, who puts her Fortune and Person entirely in his Powers; nay even the very desires of her Heart according to some learned Casuists, so as that it is not lawful to Will or Desire any thing but what he approves and allows . . .
>
> (ibid.: 48)

The power of the domestic sovereign is absolute. It is also a power borne of strength which demands complete obedience, even in the face of domestic violence. Astell (ibid.) is clear, however, that good government and legitimate power over others are grounded not in brute force, but in superior understanding—a greater degree of knowledge and intellectual skill. Great understanding fulfils humanity's God-given purpose of rational achievement, and, as such, it brings one closer to God. Brute power is granted by mere strength and belongs to the bodily rather than the divine realm.

One should submit only to the force of reason—God's will and that which is concordant with it—for humans are rational creatures. Even God does not require blind obedience, but rather offers principles that are intelligible, good, reasonable, and thus independently motivating (ibid.). The problem with domestic sovereigns is that their power is deficient. The origin of this power is in physical rather than intellectual superiority; not all domestic sovereigns are rational men of great understanding (ibid.). Thus, their absolute reign is unwarranted. To cast gender, without regard to reason, as the sole determinant of political hierarchies is not just bad for women, but an affront to God's design.

Sovereigns need not be absolute or brutish; they could hold their power in trust for those they rule. The obligation of the ruled, under these circumstances, is respect and cheerful compliance with their efforts rather than total obedience, but this is neither blind nor unearned (ibid.). Astell suggests that the right model of marriage is one where the parties stand in a kind of unfelt, albeit divinely instituted hierarchy, where the marital relation begins from a place of friendship and radical equality (ibid.). On this view, wives are subordinate only in a formal sense: marriage is not about wifely obedience but, rather, two agents acting from their duty as rational creatures to support one another (ibid.).

There is a strong similarity between Astell and her social contract predecessors on this point. Her notion of a domestic sovereign gone awry looks much like Hobbes's Sovereign, a ruler with absolute power that demands (and can expect) complete obedience (Hobbes, 2017). And, like Hobbes, this kind of ruler will procure a kind of stability even if that stability comes at great cost. Astell's preferred model of domestic sovereignty as a kind of power held in trust is both more in keeping with Locke's concern that the government is one to which people could have consented, and also consistent with his notion of political power as being for the public good. However, again, Astell seems to be taking elements of social contract theory and twisting them just enough to cast doubt. One such case is Astell's contention that women have been rightful sovereigns over men. Drawing on scripture, Astell (ibid.) again points to many cases of women possessing a greater understanding than men and using their power for the benefit of others below them, including their husbands. This implies that the unfelt hierarchy she proposes need not result in the husband being in charge.

Astell is quite clear throughout *Reflections* that there is a disconnect between social contract theory and the best interests of women. She says:

> Again, if Absolute Sovereignty be not necessary in a State, how comes it to be so in a Family? or if in a Family why not in a State; since no Reason can be alledg'd for the one that will not hold more strongly for the other? If the Authority of the Husband so far as it extends, is sacred and inalienable, why not of the Prince? The Domestic Sovereign is without Dispute Elected, and the Stipulations and Contract are mutual, is it not then partial in Men to the last degree, to contend for, and practice that Arbitrary Dominion in their Families, which they abhor and explain against in the State? For if Arbitrary Power is evil in itself, and an improper Method of Governing Rational and Free Agents it ought not to be Practis'd any where . . .
>
> (Astell, 1996: 17)

Astell is exposing men's hypocrisy. Some, like Robert Filmer (1991), argued that just as God gave Adam authority, so too do fathers rightly rule over families and kings rule over nations. On this kind of view, ruling is paternalistic and by divine right. Social contract theorists like Locke (2003) were explicitly criticizing this notion of hereditary monarchy as an absolute tyranny, as a kind of power over others that is inconsistent with the very nature of men. And yet, 'how much soever Arbitrary Power may be dislik'd on a Throne, not *Milton* himself wou'd cry up Liberty to poor *Female Slaves*, or plead for the Lawfulness of Resisting a Private Tyranny' (Astell, 1996: 46–47). If tyranny is bad, it is bad for women, too. The social contract does not permit women to be citizens or active participants, and yet they are to be ruled by it, and are expected to submit to it, even in the absence of their consent. A system that fails to recognize this fails to live up to its own ideals.

One might also think that Astell's discussion of marriage as being properly modelled on friendship challenges the notion of appointing a sovereign at all. Astell uses the language and structures of social contract theory in her discussions of marriage to criticize both marriage and social contract theory. However, she also offers a positive model of marriage, albeit briefly, as a kind of unfelt hierarchy—much like having a boss who never flexes their authority—between true friends (ibid.). What is the reader meant to make of this? Astell says that she is not making seditious claims or fomenting women's rebellion, and yet this small change to marriage is quietly revolutionary. For this to take place, women must be permitted the same means of growth allowed to men, such as formal education, and husbands must see their wives as persons, equals, and political subjects—a view of women which was extremely progressive for the time. Making her remarks against the backdrop of social contract theory allows Astell not only to challenge a major political system, but also to provide cover for a more radical view of her own.

8.3.3 Consent

Astell's discussion of consent and its importance for legitimizing government is a crucial piece of her critique of social contract theory. While she is focused more narrowly on the government of husbands over wives, her concerns point to a structural flaw in social contract theory. Over the course of *Reflections*, Astell addresses two questions about consent: first, *do wives consent to marriage and the rule of their husbands?*, and, second, *is consent sufficient to ground political obligation?* Recall that Astell writes using irony and layered meanings: this allow her to make bold claims, but this also presents a challenge. In addressing these two questions, Astell seemingly answers each question in *both* the affirmative and in the negative. This ambiguity and the plausibility of each answer suggest that Astell is rightly pressing on a structural weakness in social contract theory. To make sense of Astell's seeming self-contradiction, this sub-section will assess each question and its possible answers before turning to Astell's true position.

Astell seems to offer an affirmative answer to the first question. After all, 'The Domestic Sovereign is without Dispute Elected' (ibid.: 17). Astell points out that wives promise to obey, and she describes the beginning of a marriage as a kind of transfer of power from the woman to the man through which the woman grants the man a permanent authority over her (ibid.). Astell spends a great deal of time in *Reflections* and *Proposal* trying to persuade women that marrying is a significant and most likely irreversible decision, and one which they must approach carefully. Women should assess the merits of their suitors independently from what society says is valuable about men—e.g., wealth or gallantry—and instead ascertain whether they have the kind of good and virtuous character that will make marriage bearable (Astell, 1996; 2002). Collectively, these claims suggest that Astell thinks that women consent to marry and thus consent to the rule of their husbands. Moreover, marriage is permanent and binding, being formalized in oath, so women's consent is even more important.

> **Key Concept: The Mazarin case**
>
> Astell credits the high-profile divorce of the Duke and Duchess of Mazarin as the occasion for writing *Reflections*. Both sides alleged misconduct: the duke was accused of a host of strange and controlling behaviours, while the duchess, Hortense Mancini, was publicly excoriated when she escaped in disguise and proceeded to live in the public eye (Astell, 1996: 35; 34). Perhaps unsurprisingly, it was Mancini rather than her estranged husband who was disinherited and discredited by these events. Astell used this popular event to critique both marriage and the social conversation about women. She points out that Mancini and others were in a difficult position: if they sought refuge from a miserable marriage in pleasant diversions, they damaged their own reputations; if they fled altogether, they suffered the same (ibid.: 34–35). In marriage and in general, women's freedom and credibility were curtailed.

But Astell also observes the social conditions under which women make their choices are epistemically and politically deficient. She says, 'A Woman indeed can't properly be said to Choose, all that is allow'd her, is to Refuse or Accept what is offer'd' (ibid.: 43). Women cannot really consent because they are not provided with meaningful options. They are taught from birth that their sole aim ought to be to marry well. Women are deprived of formal education and are subjected to customs that demean them and cast them as being for the service of men rather than God, and so they lack the knowledge that should inform their choice (Astell, 2002). Custom also grants men a greater degree of credibility and political power, such that practices of courtship are stacked so as to deceive women about the character and capacities of the men they would marry (Astell, 1996). It might look like consent, insofar as women say 'I do', but there was no other kind of life on offer, and no means to support themselves should the marriage become untenable.

Astell provides similar ambiguity in answering the second question, whether consent can ground political obligation. Astell thinks that marriage is binding. A plausible way of construing this, particularly given her remarks about electing or choosing a domestic sovereign, is that by virtue of the woman's consent and the power that her consent transfers to her husband in beginning a marriage, she takes on political obligations of obedience and being a good and dutiful subject. The subordination of wives is, as Astell (ibid.) points out, supported by law. Moreover, marriage transferred all material assets to husbands, thereby making independence impossible. Social contract theorists like Hobbes and Locke argue that consent is the only thing that could justify political obligation, for all men are by nature equal and free. By appealing to law and practices of obedience, and Astell's constant refrain that women understand just what it is that they are signing up for, she seems to imply that consent to marriage and all it includes really does ground political obligation.

Then again, Astell may not even think that women are capable of giving consent, let alone allowing consent to be the explanation for their political obligations. At least one other candidate for women's required obedience is the fact that marriage is not only a socio-political institution, but a Christian sacrament. Men and women are equal in terms of their souls and have obligations to God in virtue of becoming husbands and wives, but God created marriage as a hierarchical relation in which husbands rule wives (ibid.). Importantly, a husband's rule should be unfelt, as marriage should be modelled on the respect attendant in a friendship. If there is rightful obedience of wives, it is to God first, and husbands second and *only* as God's proxies. Consent is irrelevant; rather, what matters are one's duties to fulfil God's wishes.

Moreover, Astell points to a worry with consent as the basis for political obligation in appealing to Locke's notion of express versus tacit consent. Express consent is explicit, like the process of becoming a citizen of a new country: *x* states that in joining this society, *x* is subject to its laws. Tacit consent is only implied. Famously, Locke notes that the use of a highway—participation in the infrastructure of another land—implies a temporary agreement to be subject to its laws and government (Locke, 2003). But as Astell points out, a highwayman could be using those same roads: 'And if mere Power gives a Right to Rule, there can be no such thing as Usurpation; but a Highway-Man so long as he has strength to force, has also a right to require our Obedience' (Astell, 1996: 16). Astell is suggesting that under conditions of inequality of social, political, and epistemic power, one cannot tell genuine and forced consent apart. This problematizes consent as a means of political obligation.

If it is impossible to determine whether consent is legitimate, then it seems unwise to make it the basis of political obligation: political obligation is necessary for a functioning government, and Hobbes, Locke, and Astell all want this. Astell's point is that consent is not necessarily the best means to get there, and so this reading offers undermines a central pillar of social contract theory. One might point out that while Hobbes was fine with consent under duress—for in the state of nature as the state of war, all parties fear for their lives and consent to the Sovereign because of that fear—Astell and Locke would agree: coerced consent cannot be the basis for political obligation. And yet, Locke overlooks the complicated conditions of consent—and its *merely apparent* unforced nature—for women in marriage. Astell's criticism suggests that, at best, Locke overlooked how things are meaningfully different for women and, at worst, women's genuine consent did not matter to his view of political obligation.

Which answers does Astell really endorse? It is likely that her true view was the negative in both cases, not only because Astell says more in support of this view, but also because it is more consistent with her overall project of improving women's social and political conditions. An important first step in this project is showing what has gone wrong, and this discussion of consent and its deficiencies makes that case. But, if so, one might wonder why she even suggests the contrary. Astell knows that her claims seem seditious, so she is careful about how she makes them. Moreover, she is not contradicting herself if the affirmative answers and the remarks that constitute them are read as ironic or dripping in sarcasm. This strategy allows her to escape censure while still offering a critical political perspective.

8.3.4 Freedom and slavery

Hobbes and Locke begin their social contract theories with the claim that men are by nature equal and free. It is not clear that these accounts include women. For Locke, women are properly subordinated to men not only because of men's natural superiority, but also because property—the primary value of his system, and that which makes someone free—is largely inaccessible to women. Common Law in England in the seventeenth and eighteenth centuries made wives subject to coverture: their legal personhood became subsumed under their husbands' (Stretto and Kesselring, 2013). As non-persons, they could not acquire property and their pre-marital property was transferred to their husbands. Wives were akin to slaves; they were property-less and subject to an arbitrary and absolute power of their masters.

Astell makes the point that women and especially wives are slaves explicitly:

> If *all Men are born free*, how is it that all Women are born slaves? as they must be if the being subjected to the *inconstant, uncertain, unknown, arbitrary Will* of Men, be the *perfect Condition of Slavery?* and if the Essence of Freedom consists, as our Masters say it does, in having a *standing Rule to live by?* And why is Slavery so much condemn'd and strove against in one Case, and so highly applauded and held so necessary and so sacred in another?
>
> (Astell, 1996: 19)

Astell seems to be targeting Locke here. The italicized sections correspond almost exactly to excerpts from his *Two Treatises of Government*, as Patricia Springborg (2005) and Jacqueline Broad

(2014) have both pointed out. However, these scholars disagree on how to interpret Astell here. Broad (2014) has argued that Astell is not being ironic but literal. Marriage really is a kind of Lockean slavery, and so it is a morally bad state. For Springborg (2005), Astell is trying to illustrate Locke and other Whigs' hypocrisy in expecting women to obey in the domestic realm but being unwilling to do so themselves in the political realm. It seems likely that Astell did regard marriage as a kind of slavery and so morally bad, and that she was also trying to get the Whigs to reckon with their own inconsistency. Broad's interpretation is consistent with Astell's overall project to advocate for women and their advancement, insofar as women were not taken to be political subjects or of political consequence, and Springborg's interpretation highlights a frequent strategy of Astell's: to expose a kind of internal contradiction to problematize a view. One concern one might have here is that since marriage is also a Christian sacrament, Astell cannot possibly think that it is God's will that women enter a subordinating relation that turns them into slaves, particularly if this is a morally bad result. Broad (2014) clarifies that while Astell does seem to endorse a kind of passive obedience, especially for wives, it is not a blind or unreflective one: women can resist those who would enslave them by force or ask them to sin. For Astell, one's primary responsibility is to God, not to one's ruler. One may also recall that marriage is both a socio-political relation and a Christian sacrament. While the socio-political dimension might result in women's enslavement given certain practical facts, the Christian sacrament can never be so since it is a divinely instituted hierarchy for human good.

Suggesting that wives are like slaves, even if it was meant ironically, is provocative. It is interesting to consider, as Broad (ibid.) points out, who is included when early modern figures think about slavery as an immoral state. Locke thinks that slavery is morally wrong, though he makes an exception for those captured in a just war. In practice, however, this means that Locke objects to the enslavement of white men to a tyrannical ruler, but not to the enslavement of the Africans and Indigenous peoples enslaved in colonial nations. Though there is some philosophical literature from philosophers who were enslaved in Africa and brought to new worlds—for example, Anton Wilhelm Amo (1703-1759) and Olaudah Equiano (1745-1797)—much of the discussion of slavery in this period focuses on the natural freedom of white men (see Equiano, 2001; Amo, 2020).

Astell and some other women philosophers of her time—Judith Drake, for example—drew a direct parallel between the conditions of women and slavery. But which sort of slavery was the target of their comparison, the potential enslavement of white men to a tyrannical king, or the generations of enslavement of African and Indigenous peoples? Broad makes a compelling case for the interpretation that Astell truly regarded women as enslaved through marriage, but the conditions of white women in marriage were unlikely to be as terrible as those of people stolen from their homelands; the slavery at issue simply is not comparable. It is an unfortunate failing of Astell's that she does not discuss slavery in more depth, and particularly the injustice inflicted upon generations of African and Indigenous peoples, perhaps especially so upon the women in these groups.

Key Thinker: Judith Drake

Very little is known of Judith Drake (active 1696-1723), a contemporary and friend of Astell's. Some of their views were so similar that Drake's *An Essay in Defence of the Female Sex* (published anonymously in 1696) was originally attributed to Astell. In this work, Drake challenges some of the claims of female intellectual inferiority, especially those which are said to be based on the science of male and female physical difference. Drake was, in some ways, more progressive than Astell: she draws on notions of class as well as nature to make the point of women's equality, and she is explicit in the connection between the enslavement of women by men and the enslavement of Africans by white folks.

This failure aside, Astell's point in addressing the issue of natural freedom, particularly of women, is part of her larger strategy to problematize the social contract. How Astell thinks of freedom, and therefore how governments ought to be organized, is somewhat unclear. In the passage above, Astell adopts the language of Locke and Republicanism—that unfreedom is being subject to arbitrary power—and also suggests, as she does in *Proposal*, that freedom is living by one's own, self-given rules (Astell, 2002). The former is a common conception of freedom in this period, and the latter is closer to what most people tend to think of when they think of autonomy—it is essentially individual in origin. However, in *Proposal*, Astell also seems to approximate a view called *relational autonomy*, which was formalized only in the twentieth century. On this view, what it is to be free is to stand in the right kind of relations with others—ones of respect, esteem, and equality (see Forbes, 2021). No matter which of these views in fact captures Astell's notion of freedom, each case offers the reader a reason to think that the Lockean notion of natural freedom and the purpose of the Lockean social contract have gone awry.

On Locke's view, the most important thing about humans is the right to hold property. It is true even prior to civil society in the state of nature, and it is property rights in one's self and one's labour that prevent humans from being permitted to harm one another. Per Locke, property rights make men free—a condition of freedom is at minimum owning oneself. Astell's point that women elect a domestic sovereign with absolute power over them should also be read as a concern with Locke's view: Locke believes that women belong to men through marriage, but also holds that individuals are free and self-owned, and that one cannot sell one's self into slavery. Yet this is what happens when women marry.

One of the main purposes of the social contract is to protect property rights and adjudicate any disputes that might arise. But Astell was writing at a time where women were made incapable of ownership, as Broad points out, and it is also significant that on each of the potential views of freedom that Astell may have endorsed, social conditions bear on how free an individual can be. Whatever Astell's view of freedom truly was, conceiving of freedom as being tied up in property rights is something that Astell rejects. If property is the source of freedom, and women are categorically denied property, then they are categorically denied freedom. Astell's critique of the social contract with respect to freedom and slavery is that it neither fully reckons with the sociality of freedom nor how this might be accounted for by a contract.

> ### 8.3 Problematizing social contract theory: Key Points
>
> - Astell argues that institutions have created what appears to be natural inequalities between men and women.
> - Astell's preferred form of marriage, an unfelt hierarchy, challenges the parallel between monarchy and marriage.
> - Astell asks two questions about how consent grounds marriage; her ambiguity in answering them is a strategy to escape censure.
> - Astell is critical of how social contract theory denies women access to freedom.

8.4 Marriage as a social contract?

Most of Astell's criticisms of social contract theory appear in the context of discussing marriage, and certainly other folks around her time treat marriage as an iteration of the social contract. In the *Second Treatise*, Locke (2003) says that marriage is a kind of conjugal society made by a voluntary compact, and while it is natural and just for the man to rule over the wife, for he is her natural superior, the terms of the compact have no natural determinant other than what is conventional in the society. One might think that this sounds quite progressive, which would be consistent with subsequent depictions of Locke's overall position: it is simply a matter of getting the terms of the contract right. But in the same breath Locke describes women as naturally inferior, and it is hard not to think that he was aware that women's assumed inferiority and actual lack of political power meant that the terms of the marriage contract would never be in their favour. This asymmetry in setting the terms of the social contract—called a threat advantage—is something that twentieth-century philosopher John Rawls (1971) points to as a failing in Locke's form of the social contract. Rawls (see more on Rawls in Chapter 32) criticizes this as an asymmetry in knowledge and therefore power: if *x* knows more than *y*, then *x* is in a better (and potentially unjustly so) position to negotiate favourable terms of the contract; this is why he implements the veil of ignorance as to personal details when determining the principles of justice. While Astell does not use the term 'threat advantage', she spills a great deal of ink in both *Reflections* and *Proposal* arguing that women ought to be educated and tries to help women to understand what marriage looks like and the burdens it entails in order to avoid the effects of such an asymmetry.

The question remains whether Astell thought of marriage as a kind of social contract or whether she uses that assumption as a kind of rhetorical device to undermine social contract theory. This seems particularly pressing because if it is a social contract, then it would be subject to all the same criticisms discussed in the previous section, in which case, Astell would no longer be simply criticizing the political view of Whigs who wanted to limit the monarchy, but criticizing a foundational socio-political institution. Though Astell never explicitly says that marriage is this kind of social contract, she implies that this view governs the practices of marriage and the election of a domestic sovereign—how else can an assent to a proposal transfer a woman's power and subjecthood to her husband? But then again, this does not fit with her religious commitments and claims that marriage is a Christian sacrament. Astell capitalizes on that ambiguity in order that her somewhat subversive and radical criticisms of marriage appear as legitimate conservative worries about Whig views.

When Astell discusses marriage, she does not distinguish between two parallel things: marriage *qua* Christian sacrament, and marriage *qua* socio-political institution. This ambiguity likely explains why Astell is sometimes interpreted as quite progressive and other times as deeply conservative. It is possible, of course, that Astell herself was conflicted and alternately pulled in each direction—sometimes endorsing women's subordination and hereditary monarchies as God's will, and sometimes arguing that women are men's equals and that tyranny is unacceptable in both the family and on the throne—but given the context and the enormous risks she knew herself to be taking, it seems far more likely that this ambiguity is a deliberate strategy just as is her use of irony. Astell's main concern is improving the conditions of women. Doing so in a way that does not undermine her standing and which will have the desired rhetorical effect without activating the defensive postures of conservative interlocutors is a tricky balance to strike.

Astell rejects the notion that marriage *qua* sacrament is a social contract because this is a divinely instituted hierarchy. However, marriage *qua* socio-political institution *is* a kind of social contract. In pre-marital society, men and women exist in a of state of nature. They are natural equals and free, but in consenting (or merely assenting, given impoverished socio-political and epistemic conditions) to a relation, a domestic sovereign is established and women are expected to obey. Women lose their freedom in a meaningful sense—whether this is understood as arbitrary domination, or not being self-governing, or whether it is standing in relations of inequality—and women are made into domestic slaves. Social contract theory and marriage as a socio-political institution are bad for the same reasons: they fail to reckon with the way that humans really are, what God really wants for humans, and the conditions under which humans flourish—that is, freedom and mutual support rather than arbitrary domination by an unjust ruler. *Reflections* is an attempt to persuade the reader that bringing the socio-political institution in line with the sacrament requires revision. Recall that Astell endorses a notion of marriage based on genuine friendship, equality, and respect. This is at odds with the practice of marriage in her time. The laws do not support this, nor do the practices of courtship or women's defective educational practices. Astell wants to problematize social contract theory and use this insight to revise marriage, for the same reasons, and for the same ends.

> **8.4 Marriage as a social contract?: Key points**
> - Marriage has two senses for Astell: socio-political institution and Christian sacrament.
> - Equivocating on the sense of marriage allows her to make radical political criticisms.

8.5 Conclusion

So, what was Astell *really* doing in *Reflections*? Astell was not only offering criticisms of the structures and claims underlying social contract theory, but also using the parallel between the social contract and the socio-political institution of marriage to show that they suffer from the same flaws. In doing so, Astell was laying the groundwork for a radical revision of marriage to be more in line with her philosophical views on human nature and capacities, and also offering a way to reshape the socio-political terrain of her time. Feminist philosophers have long argued that the public/private distinction, which mirrors the political/domestic division, is deeply problematic and disadvantageous to women, given the historical relegation of women to homes rather than the *polis*. A common refrain in this literature is that the personal *is* political: what happens in the private sphere is relevant to and shaped by public political practices and values. In linking marriage and social contract theory, especially in a way that shows they suffer from similar structural flaws, Astell is making just this point.

In clothing poor political structures in a veneer of legitimacy provided by consent, bad governments can appear as good ones. So too can bad marriages appear as legitimate and important socio-political institutions, given the precedence of the family in constructing and supporting a society. Astell's point is that if 'what one could consent to' is an appropriate means by which to measure the legitimacy of a government (the Lockean consent thesis at the core of the social contract), then we need to provide a socio-political background in which meaningful consent is possible. She shows us that marriage—and its seemingly acceptable forms—are a product of the political society and systems we endorse. By suggesting a way in which we might revise this framework, Astell is hinting at a revolutionary improvement in the lives of men and especially women. Marriage is a legitimate matter of political and social significance. In short, Astell's point is that women are political subjects and must be regarded as such. The first step in doing so will be reforming the socio-political relation that has historically affected their lives and continues to disproportionately do so.

> *Take your learning further by accessing the online resources for a library of web links to relevant videos, articles, blogs, and useful websites for this chapter:* **www.oup.com/he/Ramgotra-Choat1e**.

Study questions

1. What is a plausible reason for Astell's use of irony?
2. Why does Astell talk about marriage alongside concepts from social contract theory?
3. How does Astell's view of human nature differ from Hobbes and Locke's?
4. What does Astell think a marriage is and how does that compare to what she thinks a marriage should be?
5. What is the significance of Astell's claim that domestic sovereigns are elected?
6. Why does Astell critique consent as the basis of political obligation?
7. What does Astell mean by comparing marriage to slavery?
8. What are the two senses of marriage at work in Astell's thinking?

Further reading

Primary sources

Astell, M. (2002) *A Serious Proposal to the Ladies (Pts. I & II)*. Ed. P. Springborg. Toronto: Broadview Press Ltd.
  Astell's best-known work concerning women's education and the need for it across epistemic and moral dimensions.

Astell, M. (2013) *The Christian Religion, as Professed by a Daughter of the Church of England*. Ed. J. Broad. Toronto: Iter, Inc.
  Astell's most in-depth treatment of religion, epistemology, and metaphysics along with very useful context and explanation from Broad.

Springborg, P. (1996) *Astell: Political Writings*. Cambridge: Cambridge University Press.
  A collection of Astell's political texts, including *Reflections Upon Marriage* as well as some of her political pamphlets.

Secondary sources

Arndal, M.F.L. (2021) 'Mary Astell's Radical Criticism of Gender Inequality'. *Intellectual History Review*, 31: 91–110.
  Discusses Astell's rejection of patriarchy.

Bejan, T.M. (2019) '"Since All the World is mad, why should not I be so?" Mary Astell on Equality, Hierarchy, and Ambition'. *Political Theory*, 47: 781–808.
  Discussion of Astell's seemingly internally inconsistent moral and political commitments.

Broad, J. (2015) *The Philosophy of Mary Astell: An Early Modern Theory of Virtue*. Oxford: Oxford University Press.
  An insightful and comprehensive discussion of Astell's moral theorizing and conception/use of virtue as the crux of all her philosophical projects.

Forbes, A.S. (2019) 'Mary Astell on Bad Custom and Epistemic Injustice'. *Hypatia*, 34: 777–801.
  Interprets Astell as a theorist of epistemic injustice in the effects of bad social and political customs.

Kolbrener, W. and Michelson, M. (eds) (2007) *Mary Astell: Reason, Gender, Faith*. Aldershot: Ashgate.
  A collection of essays which span Astell's writings on religion, politics, and ethics.

Perry, R. (1986) *The Celebrated Mary Astell*. Chicago: University of Chicago Press.
  A comprehensive biography which highlights the seeming internal conflicts in Astell's thinking and publishing efforts.

Sowaal, A. (2007) 'Mary Astell's *Serious Proposal*: Mind, Method, and Custom'. *Philosophy Compass*, 2: 227–243.
: Offers a thorough analysis of Astell's understanding of custom and her theory of mind.

Sowaal, A. and Weiss, P. (2016) *Feminist Interpretations of Mary Astell*. University Park, PA: Pennsylvania State University Press.
: A collection of essays about Astell that spans her moral, political, metaphysical, and epistemic theorizing.

Springborg, P. (2005) *Mary Astell: Theorist of Freedom from Domination*. Cambridge: Cambridge University Press.
: A book which highlights Astell's political philosophy and which places her in context with some of her peers (e.g., Judith Drake).

References

Amo, A.W. (2020) *Anton Wilhelm Amo's Philosophical Dissertations on Mind and Body*. Ed. S. Menn and J.E.H. Smith. New York: Oxford University Press.

Astell, M. (1996) 'Some Reflections Upon Marriage'. In *Astell: Political Writings*. Ed. P. Springborg. Cambridge: Cambridge University Press.

Astell, M. (2002) *A Serious Proposal to the Ladies (Pts. I & II)*. Ed. P. Springborg. Toronto: Broadview Press Ltd.

Astell, M. (2013) *The Christian Religion, as Professed by a Daughter of the Church of England*. Ed. J. Broad. Toronto: Iter, Inc.

Astell, M. and Norris, J. (2005) *Letters Concerning the Love of God*. Ed. D. Taylor and M. New. London: Ashgate.

Broad, J. (2014) 'Mary Astell on Marriage and Lockean Slavery'. *History of Political Thought*, 35: 717–738.

Drake, J. (1696) *An Essay in Defence of the Female Sex*. London printed for A. Roper and E. Wilkinson at the Black Boy and R. Clavel at the Peacock, in Fleetstreet (Folger Library, A4058a).

Equiano, O. (2001) *The Interesting Narrative of the Life of Olaudah Equiano, or, Gustavus Vassa*. Ed. A. Costanzo. Peterborough, ON: Broadview Press.

Filmer, R. (1991) *Patriarcha and Other Writings*. Ed. J. Sommerville. New York: Cambridge University Press.

Forbes, A.S. (2021) 'Astell, Friendship, and Relational Autonomy'. *European Journal of Philosophy*, 29(2): 487–503.

Hobbes, T. (2017) 'Leviathan'. In *Thomas Hobbes' Political Theory*. Ed. D. Baumgold. New York: Cambridge University Press.

Kelly, J. (1984) *Women, History, and Theory*. Chicago: University of Chicago Press.

Locke, J. (2003) 'Second Treatise of Government'. In *Two Treatises of Government and A Letter Concerning Toleration*. Ed. I. Shapiro. New Haven, CT: Yale University Press.

Rawls, J. (1971) *A Theory of Justice*. Cambridge, MA: Harvard University Press.

Springborg, P. (1996) *Astell: Political Writings*. Cambridge: Cambridge University Press.

Springborg, P. (2005) *Mary Astell*. Cambridge: Cambridge University Press.

Stretto, T. and Kesselring, K. (eds) (2013) *Married Women and the Law: Coverture in England and the Common Law World*. Montréal: McGill-Queen's University Press.

9 Jean-Jacques Rousseau

PETER HALLWARD

Chapter guide

Jean-Jacques Rousseau was Europe's first great thinker of popular sovereignty, which he equated with the exercise of a collective or 'general' will. As he argued in his main political works, the *Discourse on Political Economy* (1755) and *The Social Contract* (1762), if it is sufficiently forceful, such a collective will can counteract the forms of inequality and servitude that have accompanied the historical rise of propertied and exploitative classes, a process he reconstructs in his 1755 *Discourse on the Origins of Inequality*. This chapter examines some of the central tensions that characterize Rousseau's egalitarian account of sovereignty. He formulates this account as the basis for a participatory 'social contract', meaning a voluntary form of association that aims to be both general enough to include the people as a whole, yet concentrated enough to command their government and to overpower the divisive influence of a wealthy elite. Rousseau's radical conception of mass power would soon inspire the most uncompromising sequences of the French Revolution, but its emancipatory promise was also limited by its author's sexism, his anachronism, and his failure to engage with some emerging forms of inequality and power, notably those associated with the rise of commerce, capitalism, and the transatlantic slave trade.

9.1 Introduction

Writing in absolutist France in the 1750s and 1760s, Rousseau (1712–1778) anticipated many of the questions that would shape Europe's political future. By equating sovereign power with the exercise or willing of a 'general will', he helped to foreground a distinctively modern tension between the involuntary and the voluntary dimensions of social life, between the things that we suffer because we must and the things we choose because we can. This allowed him to frame what remains the fundamental questions of any emancipatory practice: how might an oppressed and coerced group of people free themselves from this coercion and acquire the power they need to determine their own course of action, deliberately and 'willingly', in the face of the obstacles such action might confront? How can we assume and maintain a degree of collective control over the direction of our lives, in accordance with the old adage that 'united we stand, divided we fall'?

Asking this, Rousseau's approach immediately raises a series of related questions. In any given situation, who is this 'we', and how does it come to be constituted? What does this we really want, and why? What are we prepared to do, and at what cost, in order to achieve what we want?

Rousseau put these questions at the centre of the political agenda and perhaps did more than any of his contemporaries to hasten and clarify the 'inevitable revolutions' he saw looming on the historical horizon. These revolutions would surely challenge all existing social hierarchies, and strip inherited privileges of their legitimacy. They might allow 'nobles to become commoners, the rich to become poor, the monarch to become subject' (Rousseau, 2010 [1762]: 343). At a time when even the most 'enlightened' social thinkers took it for granted that 'the common people is the most insolent tyrant there can be' (Montesquieu, 1964: 327) and that a properly 'balanced' constitution should do everything necessary 'to protect the minority of the opulent against the [poor] majority' (Madison, speech of June 1787, cited in Yates, 1911: 431), Rousseau insisted instead that since 'man is the same in all stations', 'all civil distinctions' should simply 'disappear . . . It is the people who compose humankind', and 'what is not the people is so slight a thing as not to be worth counting' (Rousseau, 2010 [1762]: 377).

If Rousseau helped frame the political questions of the future, there is no denying that he tends to answer them in ways that draw on an idealized and limited conception of the past. But before we consider his limitations, we need to understand what made Rousseau such an incendiary and inspiring figure in his own day, and most especially for the generation that would seek, only a few years after his death in 1778, to put many of his ground-breaking ideas into practice.

9.2 A revolutionary agenda

Born into an artisan's family in Geneva in 1712, Rousseau's mother died soon after his birth. His youth was marked both by repeated experiences of dislocation and a strong emotional investment in republican ideals of patriotism and civic self-sacrifice. After working as a servant, a tutor, and a music copyist, Rousseau first found his public voice when in 1749 he won an essay competition on the development of the arts and sciences, in which he advanced the rather startling proposition that both scientific progress and artistic refinement—two central dimensions of the ongoing process of Enlightenment—were in fact socially divisive, elitist, and corrupting. He followed this *succès de scandale* with a second and even more provocative essay on *The Origins of Inequality* (written in 1754) and its corrosive effects on society. After sketching some aspects of a more egalitarian vision of society in a brief *Discourse on Political Economy* (1755), he spent the next years writing the works that would secure his fame: the best-selling novel *Julie, ou La Nouvelle Héloïse* (1761) and then his two principal philosophical works *Emile* (1762) and *The Social Contract* (1762). Both of these books were quickly condemned as subversive, forcing their harried author into exile first in Switzerland and then in England. Eventually allowed to return to a quiet life in France in 1767, he spent his last years as a botanist and a copyist, and composing more introspective texts, including his posthumously published and genre-stretching autobiography, the *Confessions* (1782).

Read more about **Rousseau's** life and work by accessing the thinker biography on the online resources: www.oup.com/he/Ramgotra-Choat1e.

The simplest way to position Rousseau's political thought is to locate it as a pivotal moment in a much longer historic shift in ways of thinking about legitimate power. Rousseau marks a turning point in Europe's slow, uneven, and partial transition from aristocratic to democratic conceptions of sovereignty. In broad terms, throughout most of Europe's ancient and medieval history, ruling elites could generally justify their dominance in terms of top-down authority and divine justification. This began to change in the sixteenth and seventeenth centuries, with the broad movement from a medieval-feudal to a modern-capitalist order of things. For political theory, the immediate consequence of this transition was a growing realization that power could no longer be secured and justified in the literally old-fashioned terms of necessity and obedience. Stable governments now needed to retain at least a degree of popular consent. By the time that the French Revolution held out the promise of an unprecedented opportunity to remake the social order, the most influential pamphleteer of the day (the Abbé Sieyès) could take it for granted, following Rousseau's logic, that 'every man has an inherent right to deliberate and will for himself', and 'either one wills freely or one is forced to will, there cannot be any middle position' (Sieyès, 2003: 10). Along with other more radical members of the Jacobin Club, Maximilien Robespierre soon came to emphasize the kinds of discipline, commitment, and equality involved in the collective exercise of such a free will.

> ### Key Thinker: Maximilien Robespierre
>
> Of all the major leaders to emerge during the French Revolution, Maximilien Robespierre (1758-1794) did perhaps the most to put Rousseau's 'utopian' theories into vigorous and contested practice. By June 1793, he recognized that if a revolutionary affirmation of civic equality was to prevail, in a divided society on the verge of civil war, it needed to concentrate 'ONE will [*une volonté UNE*]' (Robespierre, 1828: 15) in its defence, and to rally it around a 'single centre of forces and resources'—its literally 'capital' city, Paris (Robespierre, 1958: 553, 559). The forceful steps that Robespierre and other Jacobin members of the Committee of Public Safety took in 1792-1793, to win this war and to secure this rallying point, allowed him to celebrate, in a speech of 5 December 1793, the conversion of mere 'dreams' of justice into the sort of 'imposing realities' Rousseau had anticipated. 'Morality used to be in philosophers' books; we have put it in the government of nations' (Robespierre, 2007: 93-94).

Sovereign power could certainly still be understood in terms of will and command, but it was now the will of the people, and not the will of a king or a God, that claimed the authority to lay down the law. Where sovereign commands once ran from the top of the social pyramid down to its base, the people rule when it's *their* will that prevails over the wills of those who might seek to dominate or exploit them. A great many subsequent projects of mass empowerment—from the Bolsheviks' 'all power to the Soviets!' to the Black Panthers' 'all power to the people!'—can be understood as distinct variations on this same broad effort.

9.2.1 Mass sovereignty

As Rousseau conceives it, a just social order is one instituted by its members on the basis of their collective freedom and equality, through a process that is itself voluntary and egalitarian. Such a process begins when a certain number of people, frustrated by the inequities of their existing society, decide that to protect themselves from injustice and insecurity they should assemble in ways that might allow them to work out what their common interests are, and what must be done to achieve them. Where one exists, the collective or 'general will' to pursue these things constitutes itself, in the process, as the 'sovereign' or law-giving authority of a new social order. Rousseau calls the foundation of this order a 'social contract' because its constitution is grounded in the free decision of all its adherents to obey this authority, as the basis of a 'form of association that will defend and protect the person and goods of each associate with the full common force' (Rousseau, 1997c [1762]: 49 [1:6]).

> ### Key Concept: The general will
>
> Every individual has a natural desire to pursue what they see as essential to their well-being. In addition to their particular will to advance their personal interests, through participation in a group that has or acquires some common interests, they can also come to share in the elaboration and realization of collective purposes—for instance, they might seek to protect the group's security, or to ensure an equitable sharing of its resources and opportunities. A general will to pursue such things prevails or is 'sovereign' in situations where its participants' commitment to these common priorities is more powerful, in practice, than all the tendencies that might instead tempt them to favour their private advantage at the public's expense.

Any general will or popular sovereign will then face two pressing practical challenges. First, since steps taken to promote the general interest may often threaten the particular interests of a privileged minority, so the assembled people must consolidate whatever power they might need to over-power those that Rousseau typically condemns as *les riches*. The more resistance they encounter from wealthy or elite interests, the more power the people must concentrate in the executive agent or government they need to appoint to carry out the decisions they make. Hence the second challenge: in order to ensure that this agent doesn't itself eventually come to usurp their power and oppress them anew, the people will need to sustain practices and institutions that allow them to over-power both the rich and the government.

As it addresses these challenges, any popular sovereign simultaneously answers, one way or another, the two basic questions posed by its persistence over time and its coherence across space. Both questions follow from the deceptive simplicity of the new formula for democratic rule, 'the will of the people': who are the people, and what is their will? On the one hand, if the only legitimate sovereign is a popular sovereign, if the power to command or to prescribe laws rightly belongs to the people, then who now makes up 'the people', and by what criteria? In any given people, who is included as a citizen and who is excluded as an outsider or an enemy? Who has an active voice or vote, and who is silenced? On the other hand, how does any group of people actually arrive at some sort of common will? How do 'some' people become 'a' people? What do people really want, and what are they willing to do in order to realize it? What kinds of influence, power, and capacity are at play, in the determination of such a shared or general will? In the following reconstruction of Rousseau's account of politics we will explore these questions in turn.

9.2.2 Solitary by nature

Like many of his contemporaries and predecessors, Rousseau frames his account of society and politics with an account of nature, but unlike most of these contemporaries, he emphatically refuses to found the legitimacy of the former upon what supposedly prevails in the latter. Early modern writers like Hobbes (see Chapter 5), Locke (see Chapter 7), or Grotius (see Key Thinker: Hugo Grotius in Chapter 5, Section 5.2.5) observed how people behaved in their proto-capitalist societies, and inferred that it is simply human nature to be selfish, aggressive, deferential, and so on; a social order regulated by an absolute monarch, or one dominated by private property and the pursuit of profit, can then be justified by reference to the apparently natural and universal order of things. Societies structured by hierarchy and inequality, if not overt slavery and submission, thereby figure as consistent with the way people most fundamentally *are*, and consequently with what they should need and want.

Rousseau rejects this whole conception out of hand, in part by refusing to acknowledge any sort of 'natural' sociability at all. According to Rousseau, early human beings were by nature solitary and non-social. Affirming this allows him to posit socialization as a historical process that has *happened* to people, as something that they have suffered or instituted, rather than a dimension of what they are. What most fundamentally 'makes a people a people' is then always a deliberate 'act', rather than a natural orientation or way of being (Rousseau, 1997c [1762]: 49 [1:5]). Because social configurations are contingent and artificial constructs, established by specific groups of people for specific reasons in specific times and places, so then they can be changed, and changed radically, whenever enough people are sufficiently determined to change them. A just social configuration, 'rather than destroying natural equality, on the contrary substitutes a moral and legitimate equality for whatever physical inequality nature may have placed between people', such that 'while they may be unequal in force or in genius, they all become equal by convention and by right' (ibid.: 56 [1:9]).

Rousseau's brief speculative sketch of an originary human nature, outlined in the first part of his *Discourse on the Origins of Inequality* (1754) is less a documented reconstruction of humanity's actual early history than a space-clearing gesture designed to discredit any attempt to justify social hierarchies as somehow natural or necessary. According to Rousseau, human nature per se is not shaped by constituent forms of relations with others; human beings are better understood as made to *become* sociable, through the very processes of association they initiate. Rather than reconstruct human nature via the mediation of kinship, status, or communication, Rousseau's relatively minimalist account emphasizes only three equiprimordial attributes, three 'birthright' qualities common to every human being. These are:

1. the 'self-love' [*amour de soi*] we experience in common with all sentient beings, an irreducible 'natural sentiment' that motivates both our interest in our own welfare and the pity or compassionate interest we further take in beings we recognize as similar to ourselves (Rousseau, 1997a [1755]: 127; cf. Rousseau, 2010 [1762]: 363);
2. the 'freedom' or free will that distances our capacity to act from merely 'instinctual' forms of behaviour or compulsion, that delegitimizes any form of servitude, and that entitles us to independence and autonomy;
3. the 'perfectibility' of our distinctively human faculties, i.e. our ability over time to bring to full fruition those capacities (notably freedom, reason, morality, and conscience) that, in the early stages of both socio-historical and personal-psychological development, remain largely potential or virtual.

Taken together, these qualities serve both to condemn any social order that perverts or violates them (for instance, any social order that converts healthy self-love into vain and pernicious self-regard [what Rousseau terms '*amour propre*'], or that tolerates slavery, or that inhibits the popular exercise of reason or conscience), and to ground a legitimate social order in an ongoing exercise of public will. Rousseau's reconstruction of social development is designed to legitimate a genuinely voluntary social contract or order, not to evoke an Edenic utopia. Contrary to a widespread misconception, Rousseau does not think of the slow transition from nature to society solely in terms of corruption and loss. His priority is rather to establish that there is no natural and thus trans-historical basis for corruption. There is no natural equivalent of 'original sin', and so no natural need for the equivalent of a church, or a prison.

Rather than pursue any sort of 'return to nature', rather than yearn for our lost solitude, Rousseau insists, on the contrary, that there can be no turning the clock back.

> Good social institutions are those that best know how to denature man, to take his absolute existence from him in order to give him a relative one and transport the I into the common unity, with the result that each individual believes himself no longer one but a part of the unity and no longer feels except within the whole.
>
> (Rousseau, 2010 [1762]: 164)

What Rousseau idealizes is less the state of nature than virtuous states that appear to favour an unconditional commitment to the common good, for instance the sort of self-sacrificing patriotism he associates with ancient Sparta or republican Rome.

What's at stake in the daunting 'institution' of a people, in other words, involves nothing less than a qualitative shift in what it means to be human. The transition from 'natural' to 'social' requires the transformation of 'each individual who by himself is a perfect and solitary whole into part of a larger whole from which that individual would as it were receive his life and his being', thereby 'substituting a partial and moral existence for the independent and physical existence we have all received from nature.' The more perfect and far-reaching this substitution, the more equitable and durable is the social order that results. The ideal outcome would be a state in which 'each Citizen is nothing and can do nothing except with all the others' (Rousseau, 1997c [1762]: 69 [2:7]). A suitably socialized person loses a limited independence in exchange for a share in incomparably greater collective capacities. Such a person, Rousseau explains in the *Social Contract*, is deprived of the scant benefits of solitude but:

> gains such great advantages in return, his faculties are exercised and developed, his ideas enlarged, his sentiments ennobled, his entire soul is elevated to such an extent, that if the abuses of this new condition did not often degrade him to beneath the condition he has left, he should ceaselessly bless the happy moment which wrested him from it forever, and out of a stupid and bounded animal made an intelligent being and a man.

(ibid.: 53 [1:8])

Our historical problem is simply that the degrading 'abuses of our new condition' have indeed tended, so far, to eclipse its advantages. Actually-existing societies arose by establishing and reinforcing inequalities of wealth, property, distinction, and rank. They exist to serve the interests of the rich at the expense of the poor. Rousseau pushes this point about as far, and eventually further, than was legally possible in mid-eighteenth-century France. As Rousseau describes it, 'the demon of property infects everything it touches. A rich man wants to be the master everywhere', and *les riches* have successfully rigged the whole social order in their favour (Rousseau, 2010 [1762]: 527–528; cf. Rousseau, 1997b: 32). In all its forms, Rousseau 'hate[s] servitude as the source of all the ills of human kind' (Rousseau, 2001b [1755]: 92), and 'in the relations between man and man the worst that can happen to one is to find himself at the other's discretion' (Rousseau, 1997a [1755]: 176).

> **Key Concept: Inequality**
>
> Rousseau emphasized the social rather than natural origins of inequality, and traced its development to the seizure and transmission of private property, reinforced by the emergence of class distinctions and accompanying differences in status and occupation. Modern societies are dominated by the wealthy few, who use their economic power and cultural 'refinement' to preserve a hypocritical social order structured by fear, envy, and deference.

The first priority of a 'popular government', then, should be to block the accumulation of wealth and power in the hands of a few. Although it's essential to 'protect the poor against the tyranny of the rich', 'the greatest evil has already been done where there are poor people to defend and rich people to restrain' (Rousseau, 1997b [1755]: 19). As if in anticipation of the way Marx (see Chapter 13) will understand the exploitation that sustains capitalist production, the goal of political economy should be to ensure that 'no citizen be so rich that he can buy another, and none so poor that he is compelled to sell himself' (Rousseau, 1997c [1762]: 78 [2:11]).

In principle, the transition from nature to society should have liberated and empowered human beings but it has instead, so far, mostly oppressed and limited us. Since there can be no going back to nature, Rousseau's solution to the problems created by the way we've been 'de-natured' is to propose an egalitarian re-naturing. We have been mis-educated; let us then be re-educated. Our history is the story of how we have 'become wicked and unhappy in becoming sociable'; the task of an emancipatory politics, therefore, is to interrupt this history, and by inventing new forms of socialization, to 'attempt to draw from the ill itself the remedy that should cure it' (Rousseau, 1994b, 20 [2:12]).

9.2.3 Free will

Such a re-naturing begins with our natural capacities, but seeks to re-orient and transform their exercise. Rousseau takes both self-love and a free will to be properly basic components of human nature, and draws on them as principles of explanation, rather than as things that themselves need to be explained. Whereas other animals appear to be guided by instinct and impulses, humans as a species are to some extent free to set their own course: 'Nature alone does everything in the operations of the Beast, whereas man contributes to his operations in his capacity as a free agent. The one chooses or rejects by instinct, the other by an act of freedom' (Rousseau, 1997a [1755]: 140; cf. 2010 [1762]: 437–438; 2001b [1763]: 43). Freedom thus figures here as 'a consequence of man's nature' pure and simple (Rousseau, 1997c [1762]: 42 [1:2]), so 'it always appears peculiar to me', Rousseau admits,

> to ask a free people why it is free. It is as if one asked a man who has his two arms why he is not one-armed. The right to liberty is born from itself, it is the natural state of man. This is not the case for domination, whose right needs to be proved when it exists.
>
> (Rousseau, 2001c [c. 1764]: 120)

To suggest then, as defenders of domination like Grotius or Hobbes tried to do, that people might 'freely give away their freedom' is literally to say something 'absurd', indeed deranged, and the political equivalent of 'madness' cannot serve as a principle of right (Rousseau, 1997c [1762]: 45 [1:4]).

Rousseau is quite happy to accept, for the same sort of reasons Kant (see Chapter 29) will accept after him, that we don't seem capable of understanding the apparently 'spiritual' foundation of our freedom, at least not with minds better equipped to discern mechanical laws—but this theoretical limitation on our understanding puts no restriction on what we can do in practice. 'The will is known to me by its acts, not by its nature' (Rousseau, 2010 [1762]: 434), and where the will is concerned, intentional and consequential acts are all that we need to know.

We know, in practice and through practice, that willing and doing are bound up with each other. Before Rousseau, a rationalist philosopher like Descartes (see Key Thinker: René Descartes in Section 6.2.1 of Chapter 6) could affirm the boundless or indeterminate freedom of human *volonté* (will) as our most 'god-like' faculty, but only by severing its relation with action—rather than an account of free will, he offered what might be better described as an embrace of boundless 'free wish' (Descartes, 1985b: 40; cf. 1985a: 343 [article 41]). Rousseau, by contrast, links willing and doing in a way that resonates with standard English usage. We may be free to wish for whatever we want, but we can only properly *will* those ends that we might in principle achieve. Rousseau knows as well as the Russian revolutionary Leon Trotsky or the Marxist philosopher Antonio Gramsci (see Key Thinker: Antonio Gramsci) that 'whoever wills the end cannot refuse the means' (Rousseau, 1997b [1755]: 23; cf. Gramsci, 1994: 99; Trotsky, 2017 [1920]: 25), and he condenses the relation between *vouloir* and *pouvoir*, between will and capacity, in a rhyming formula he calls his 'fundamental maxim': 'the truly free man wills [or wants] only what he can do, and he does what he pleases [*l'homme vraiment libre ne veut que ce qu'il peut, et fait ce qu'il lui plaît*]' (Rousseau, 2010 [1762]: 215). This is the basic psycho-political foundation of Rousseau's whole theory. His mouthpiece in *Emile* posits as a matter of 'dogma', or as an 'article of faith', that 'the principle of every action is in the will of a free being. One cannot go back beyond that. It is not the word freedom which means nothing; it is the word necessity' (ibid.: 422).

Affirmation of freedom over necessity is for Rousseau an assumed point of departure, which allows him to treat broadly psychological, moral, and political problems as part of a single broad continuum. What cannot be assumed as given, however, is the scope and power of this freedom. The more general and more expansive a will, the more power it has; the more people who will a common purpose, the more they can do to bring it about. How far, then, might we expand our circles of association? How far might we generalize our interest, purposes, or priorities? These remain matters of political effort or exercise precisely because our mere nature puts no limits on our historical achievements. 'We do not know what our nature permits us to be' (ibid.: 190), 'it is only our lukewarm will which causes all of our weakness', and the power of a will can grow or diminish. '*Volenti nihil difficile* [nothing is difficult for those who will]' (ibid.: 494), so the limits of political possibility depend directly on the relative strength or weakness of our common will. Here Rousseau follows the logic of Roman philosopher Seneca's maxim: 'It is not because things are difficult that we do not dare; it is because we do not dare that they are difficult' (Seneca, 1969: 192).

> ### 9.2 A revolutionary agenda: Key Points
>
> - People were originally or 'naturally' solitary, and the way they subsequently combined to form societies introduced artificial (and thus mutable) forms of inequality and corruption.
> - Every individual has a natural 'love of self' or concern for their own well-being, and an equitable society is one that allows this concern to expand to embrace the well-being of all its members.
> - The faculty that allows people to prioritize social or general priorities over private ones is the will (*la volonté*), whose own capacities vary with its scope and intensity.

9.3 Sovereign by choice

To foreground the will as the practical element of political life, as Rousseau conceives it, is immediately to focus attention on its *capacity*, i.e., on its extent, lucidity, cohesion, discipline, determination, power, force, and so on. A general will is itself a will in the same basic sense as the will of an isolated individual, and Rousseau regularly refers to communities as 'moral beings' that have the political equivalent of bodies, minds, and desires (Rousseau, 1997b [1755]: 6; Rousseau, 1997c [1762]: 50 [1:6]). By expanding its exercise and scope, however, a political will is qualitatively stronger and clearer than any merely individual will. It's this generalization and intensification of the will that Rousseau identifies as the central concern of politics. The most basic features of his account of an egalitarian society follow as so many corollaries of this guiding concern.

First and foremost, a group of individuals becomes 'a people' through the inaugural act of free association, which Rousseau posits as 'the most voluntary act' in the world (ibid.: 123 [4:2]). By combining together in pursuit of their common interests or projects, the members of an emergent society share in the elaboration of a common will, and, like any will, this shared or general will is free to determine its own course of action, limited only by its natural and thus invariable obligation to pursue what it sees as its best interest. Rousseau's own main examples are adapted from his idealized, Plutarch-inspired conceptions of ancient Sparta and republican Rome, but in principle his logic applies to any sort of group that coalesces around a common project—contemporary readers might find his logic applies better to groups like a social movement, trade union, political party, or other kind of voluntary organization than it does to a modern nation-state. In every such process of association what is transformative is the substitution of the general or common cause for partial or particular interests, rather than the geographic scope or social configuration of the group that results. Alongside ancient city-states, Rousseau considers modern would-be nations like Corsica and Poland, and ponders on the Jewish diaspora as an especially remarkable and durable case in point:

> It is an amazing and truly unique spectacle to see an expatriate people, without either location or land for nearly two thousand years; a people that has been modified, oppressed, and mingled with foreigners for even longer . . . a scattered people, dispersed over the earth, subjected, persecuted, scorned by all nations, and yet preserving its customs, its laws, its morals, its patriotic love, and its initial social union when all its links appear broken. The Jews give us this amazing spectacle.
>
> (Rousseau, 1994b: 34 [4:24]; cf. Rousseau, 2005 [1772]: 171–172)

Second, whether it be bounded by geography or held together by shared priorities, what holds a community or people together is ultimately nothing other than their common *will* to hold themselves together. Although he pays some secondary attention to the 'sub-voluntary' factors like climate, history, and geography that might facilitate or discourage the development of such a common will, for Rousseau (unlike his contemporary Montesquieu [see Chapter 11]), it's always the active willing itself that sustains a people (or a movement, a union, or a party). Do people actually want to prioritize their common interests over their particular ones? This is a thoroughly practical question, one decided by active participation and direct exercise, for 'it is as true of freedom as it is of innocence and virtue that one appreciates their worth only as long as one enjoys them oneself' (Rousseau, 1997a [1755]: 176). The decisive question to be addressed in any political sequence, regardless of scale or configuration, thus always comes down to this: do the people involved participate, yes or no, in a common will? Do they assume that it's everyone for themselves, or are they willing to act on the principle of 'all for one and one for all'? Rousseau sees this as a stark binary choice. Either a 'will is general or it is not; it is either the will of the body of the people, or that of only a part' (Rousseau, 1997c [1762]: 58 [2:2]).

Third, where a general will prevails, the very fact of its prevailing invests it with sovereign or commanding power—or in Rousseau's compressed formulation, 'the Sovereign, by the mere fact that it is, is always everything it ought to be' (ibid.: 52 [1:7]). A general will is thus sovereign in a broadly post-Hobbesian sense: it prevails 'simply' as a matter of volition (rather than of custom, or counsel), i.e., as a command issued by an authority whose mere 'instruction is the reason for obedience' (Hobbes, 1998: 154 [Chapter XIV]). Precisely because it's a matter of will, so then sovereign power, if or where it exists, is radically free and independent, as well as indivisible, inalienable, and unrepresentable. Any will evaporates if it loses or abandons its capacity to determine its own ends, so as soon as a 'people promises simply to obey, it dissolves itself by this very act, it loses its quality of being a people; as soon as there is a master, there is no more sovereign, and the body politic is destroyed forthwith' (Rousseau, 1997c [1762]: 57 [2:1]). For the same reason, if it is to endure, a sovereign or general will cannot over-rule itself, so to speak. The sovereign should not try to 'impose on itself a law that it cannot break' (ibid.: 52 [1:7]), since 'sovereignty, which is only the exercise of the general will is, like it, free, and is not subject to any kind of engagement . . . The sovereign never acts because it willed, [in the past,] but because it wills', in the present (Rousseau, 1994b [1755]: 24 [3:11]). Where no such willing prevails, as is usually the case, then there is no free association either, but only the dreary continuation of what has normally prevailed across human history: dominance and oppression.

9.3.1 **Sustained by virtue**

The perseverance of a popular sovereign or general will depends on its capacity to manage two over-arching tensions, one internal to it, the other external.

The first tension applies to the 'generality' or extension of a general will. On the one hand, the more a will expands and widens, the more 'enlarging' and 'elevating' are its psycho-political effects on its participants, the more numerous are its adherents, and the more powerful they become.

'The more the State expands, the more its real force increases' (Rousseau, 1997c [1762]: 88 [3:2]), and 'the most general will is also the most just', such that 'the voice of the people is indeed the voice of God' (Rousseau, 1997b [1755]: 8). In principle, the most just and equitable will would be one affirmed by humanity as a whole.

On the other hand, however, the more a will expands, the more its own active mobilizing force is stretched and consequently weakened. 'Interest and commiseration must in some way be constricted and compressed in order to be activated', Rousseau concedes, and 'it would seem that the sentiment of humanity dissipates and weakens as it spreads to the whole earth' (ibid.: 15). Rousseau trusts the sincerity and intensity of focused patriotic dedication more than abstract declarations of cosmopolitan sympathy (Rousseau, 1994a [c. 1761]: 81; Rousseau, 2010 [1762]: 163–164). This is partly because, as he conceives it, a commitment to the common good is initially rooted in our natural and irreducible love of self, one's own self, which can then progressively expand to include a love of others whom we see as in some ways linked or similar to ourselves—but which can only extend so far, before it begins to fade in intensity. It's also a function of the way Rousseau understands the exercise of force itself. If the extent of a force varies with its scope or generality, its intensity or energy varies with its level of concentration. The least forceful actors are the most scattered or fragmented. Rousseau admits that a dictator is better placed to act decisively than a committee or assembly, and the principle applies as much to popular actors as it does to organizations or governments. As a rule, 'the people's force acts only when concentrated, it evaporates and is lost as it spreads, like the effect of gunpowder scattered on the ground and which ignites only grain by grain. The least populous countries are thus the most suited to Tyranny: wild beasts reign only in wildernesses' (Rousseau, 1997c [1762]: 104 [3:8]).

Any steps taken to generalize a will and to broaden its extension, therefore, must be compensated by measures designed to heighten its intensity and increase its density. Rousseau's Jacobin admirers would face the practical consequences of this principle soon enough, when in the early 1790s they developed a network of thousands of revolutionary clubs across France. It's also a principle that Jean-Paul Sartre and Frantz Fanon (see Chapter 28) would subsequently affirm, in recognizably Rousseauist terms, in the context of anti-colonial and national-liberation struggles of the 1950s, and it's one that's been corroborated by the experience of a good many organizing efforts and social movements ever since. The 'Black Power' campaigns for civil rights in the US are a suggestive case in point (Singh, 2004; Gordon, 2014). Black nationalism, rather like French or Haitian 'Jacobinism', was primarily conceived as a step towards a more inclusive internationalism and a less compromised humanism. As the Black Panthers' Fred Hampton put it, 'there's power anywhere where there's people' (Hampton, 1969); 'we don't see ourselves as a national unit for racist reasons', his comrade Bobby Seale added, 'but as a necessity for us to progress as human beings', and as a means of building a collective unity based on 'people's right to self-determination', whoever and wherever they might be (cited in Singh, 2004: 197). Under heavy pressure from an oppressive state, civil rights groups like the Panthers, or the pioneering Student Non-Violent Coordinating Committee (SNCC), were also confronted by versions of Rousseau's warning, that rushed expansion of a common project makes it easier to divide or corrupt it.

The generic name that Rousseau gives to the various kinds of discipline and training that might ward off division is 'virtue'. Virtue is a matter of literal 'will-power' in the sense that virtuous practices and institutions lend the will the power it needs to overcome the obstacles posed by both social corruption and 'natural' temptation. Since 'virtue is only the collection of the most general wills' (Rousseau, 1994b: 22 [3:6]) and since every person is 'virtuous when their particular will conforms in all things to the general will', then if you want to ensure that a general will prevails, your task is simply 'to make virtue reign' (Rousseau, 1997b [1755]: 15, 13).

Rousseau's account of virtue as the practice of political will has at least four distinguishable but overlapping and mutually reinforcing aspects, most of which return, in one guise or another, in later contributions to neo-Jacobin politics like those championed by Gramsci, Sartre, or Fanon.

First, as its etymology suggests, virtue is a matter of effort and struggle, of 'fortitude' and strength (*force*), with further connotations of 'manliness' and virility (Rousseau, 2010 [1762]: 633–634). Since the tempting 'vices' of division and corruption are irreducible, if it is to endure, a 'virtuous' group must remain as forceful as the needs of unity and discipline require. Recognition of this point is what leads Rousseau to formulate perhaps his most notorious principle, one that his liberal critics never fail to attack. Since 'each individual may, as a man, have a particular will contrary to or different from the general will he has as a Citizen', so then in order that it 'not to be an empty formula, the social compact tacitly includes the following engagement which alone can give force to the rest, that whoever refuses to obey the general will shall be constrained to do so by the entire body: which means nothing other than that he shall be forced to be free' (Rousseau, 1997c [1762]: 53 [1:7]). Rather than a recipe for totalitarian oppression, Rousseau affirms this logic as a simple consequence of the rule of law, itself no more controversial than an insistence that all residents must pay their taxes or that all drivers must stop at red lights. Given Rousseau's further insistence that legitimate laws must be passed by the people themselves, so long as they remain an actively willing participant in law-making any 'citizen consents to all the laws, even to those passed in spite of him, and even to those that punish him when he dares to violate any one of them' (ibid.: 124 [4:2]). The alternative is exile (from a people) or resignation (from a union or party), and with it a return to the relative unfreedom and political incapacity of an isolated individual.

Concretely, this means that 'when a law is proposed in the People's assembly, what they are being asked is not exactly whether they approve the proposal or reject it [as isolated individuals], but whether it does or does not conform to the general will' that they share as members of the group, and which they must determine together. A proposal is discussed, alternatives are considered, competing priorities are weighed up, and then votes are cast; in the absence of unanimity, 'the tally of the votes yields the declaration of the general will. Therefore when the opinion contrary to my own prevails, it proves nothing more than that I made a mistake, and that what I took to be the general will was not' (ibid.: 124 [4:2]). When members of a trade union deliberate about whether they should go on strike, for instance, this is the kind of decision they will need to make. So long as the will and practices that sustain commitment to the group (or the trade union, or political party, or social movement) are sufficiently strong, Rousseau is confident that 'a good plan once adopted will change the mind' even of those members who initially opposed it, and who personally stood to gain from a different configuration of things (Rousseau, 2005 [1772]: 239).

Second, since it involves the actual exercise of will and force, it follows that virtuous practice cannot be delegated to others, or undertaken by proxy. Citizens either will and do what their collective obligations prescribe, or they don't. This is why delegates can be chosen to execute collective decisions, but not to make or influence them. Where it exists, a sovereign or general will is unalienable and unrepresentable by definition: the sovereign 'can only be represented by itself; power can well be transferred, but not will' (Rousseau, 1997c [1762]: 57 [2:1]). Again, 'sovereignty consists essentially in the general will, and the will does not admit of being represented' (ibid.: 114 [3:15]), so anyone who purports to 'represent' the will of the people—for instance, members of the UK Parliament, or of the US Congress—are in fact guilty of usurping it. Rousseau recognizes that even the smallest and most concentrated peoples will need to delegate the actual execution of their decisions to particular agents, but when it comes to its sovereign or law-making power, 'the instant a People gives itself Representatives, it ceases to be free; it ceases to be' (ibid.: 115 [3:15]).

Third, virtuous commitment must be 'voluntary' in the sense of deliberate and sincere—a matter of genuine *engagement*, in something like the sense that Sartre, de Beauvoir, and Fanon will later invest in that term. 'As soon as someone says about affairs of State What do I care? the State has to be considered lost' (ibid.: 114 [3:15]). Although any 'politics of sincerity' or enthusiasm risks pitfalls, Rousseau's stark insistence on this point has the advantage of foregrounding rather than evading some of the difficulties that so often shadow activist political projects. Since 'it is useless to preach to anyone who has no desire to act rightly' (Rousseau, 1994b: 29 [4:7]), Rousseau argues, then 'as long as Laws only concern actions and say nothing to the will, they will always be badly observed' (ibid.: 31 [4:11], 495). As revolutionaries from Mexico to Cuba and Vietnam have well understood, *morale* is a decisive strategic value in any insurgent struggle, and the ultimate dimension of any 'battle of wills' is moral rather than economic or institutional, since 'morals alone penetrate internally and direct wills' (ibid.: 71 [16:6]).

Hence the explicitly pedagogical or educational dimension of virtuous practice. This is a fourth characteristic.

> While it is good to know how to use men as they are, it is much better still to make them what one needs them to be; the most absolute authority is that which penetrates to man's inmost being, and affects his will no less than it does his actions . . . The mainspring of public authority is in the hearts of the citizens, and nothing can replace morals in sustaining government.
>
> (Rousseau, 1997b [1755]: 13)

Virtuous self-mastery can only be acquired through a process of collective self-education, rather than in isolation, or via the 'involuntary' coordination of an invisible hand. If the initial steps of such a process need to be guided temporarily by the equivalent of a political 'educator' or avant-garde—in *The Social Contract*, the role is played by Rousseau's controversial 'legislator' or constitution-maker (Rousseau, 1997c [1762]: 67–72 [2:7])—a virtuous society is sustained by egalitarian practices of self-education. Once a collective will has been established, in order to sustain its orientation to the common good, each participant 'necessarily submits to the conditions which he imposes on others', such that 'every genuine act of the general will either obligates or favours all Citizens equally' (ibid.: 63 [2:4]). A common will can only extend as far as this equality applies, i.e., as far as it can invent the means for overcoming, step by step, the distinctions (between classes, occupations, ethnicities) that might serve to divide it. Virtue unites, vice dissolves, and any embattled group of people is 'ruined without resource if you remain divided' (Rousseau, 2001a [1765]: 306).

Key Thinker: Antonio Gramsci

Arguably no recent political thinker has done more than the great Italian Marxist Antonio Gramsci (1891–1937) 'to put the "will", which in the last analysis equals practical or political activity, at the base of philosophy' (Gramsci, 1971: 345). Inspired by Lenin as much as by Marx, in the early 1920s Gramsci was a leading figure in the most revolutionary wing of the Italian Communist Party. Arrested by Mussolini's police in 1926, the 'prison notebooks' he composed over the remainder of his life are remarkable, among other things, for the way he shows how class domination or 'hegemony' involves not merely a monopoly on coercive force but also the manipulation and preservation of more consensual forms of submission among subaltern groups. In opposition to the determinist priorities that dominate some understandings of historical materialism, Gramsci conceives of reality as 'a product of the application of human will to the society of things', so 'if one excludes all voluntarist elements . . . one mutilates reality itself'. Just as 'only the man who wills something strongly can identify the elements which are necessary to the realisation of his will' (Gramsci, 1971: 345), so too 'no mass action is possible unless the mass itself is convinced of the ends it wishes to achieve and the methods to apply' (Gramsci, 1994: 321; cf. 40).

9.3.2 Commanders-in-chief

The second broad tension or challenge confronting any general will is easier to summarize, and concerns the way it relates to the agent it must institute to execute its commands or apply its laws. Rousseau limits the scope of 'government' to such executive power, and thereby preserves an important distinction between government and sovereign (Tuck, 2015: 124–130). The sovereign wills and commands; government's role is simply to do what the sovereign people tells it do. The people should formulate laws, their government should apply them, simple as that.

In practice, of course, the relationship is never so simple, since we know that Rousseau also accepts an 'intensive' understanding of political force—and any government is necessarily a more concentrated agent than its people. Here again, Rousseau's approach has the virtue of directly addressing rather than evading the problem at hand. As a corporate entity with a particular will of its own, a government will tend over time to become more powerful than the people it is supposed to serve, and as its capacities grow, its own corporate ambitions will tend to grow along with them. The stronger its government becomes, the harder a people must work in order to control it, through its own forms of assembly, organization, and assertion. Rousseau concedes that contemporary social conditions may make mass assembly difficult, but as a matter of both principle and practice, 'where right and freedom are everything, inconveniences are nothing'. In a virtuous state 'everyone flies to the assemblies' as a matter of course (Rousseau, 1997c [1762]: 114 [3:15]). The fact that Rousseau draws most of his own exemplars from ancient history did not prevent his admirers from addressing this problem in distinctly modern forms, from the Jacobins' Clubs and the first industrial combinations or trade unions through to international associations of the working class.

9.3 Sovereign by choice: Key Points

- A social group retains a 'general will' if its members are more committed to promoting the interests they all have in common than to pursuing advantages that might divide or corrupt them.
- A general will operates by means of association and concentration, and 'virtuous' social practices are those that promote common interests over divisive ones.
- Where one exists, a general will exercises sovereign or commanding power, and it cannot be represented, divided, or alienated without undermining it.
- The simplest way to disempower a general will is prevent its participants from assembling, or to divide them by promoting class differences and social particularisms at the expense of political unity.

9.4 Conclusion

The limits to Rousseau's own broad understanding of assembly offer a helpful way of framing the limits to his project as a whole. In the first and most obvious place, like some other defenders of popular sovereignty before and after him, he restricts participation in the sovereign to adult men. Although he doesn't insist on the ownership of property as a criterion for citizenship, he pointedly confines women to the domestic sphere, and the portrait of gentle, maternal, self-sacrificing paragons of femininity that he paints in *Emile* was clichéd and stifling even by the standards of his day. If Rousseau seeks to purge his social contract of relations of dependence and subordination, the same certainly cannot be said of the way he conceives of the 'sexual contract' (Pateman, 1988: 75–76, 96–102; Wollstonecraft, 2014: 43–44, 118–119, 130–131).

Although racialized concepts were not central to Rousseau's thought in the same way that they were for figures like Locke (see Chapter 7), Kant (see Chapter 29), or Hegel, for all his emphasis on freedom and equality, Rousseau also had very little to say about the contemporary slave trade and its consequences. While he condemned the rapacity and corruption of European colonizers in the New World, and had some respect for the vigorous efforts of 'savage' peoples to keep them at bay—'nothing can overcome their invincible repugnance against adopting our morals and living in our way' (Rousseau, 1997a [1755]: 219 [note XVI])—his apparent indifference to the broader implications of racialized slavery has been the object of a good deal of critical discussion in recent decades (e.g., Mills, 1997: 68-9; Estève, 2002: 163-202; Sala-Molins, 2006: 73-74, 80-81; Gordon and Roberts, 2009: 3-16; Klausen, 2014). In the *Social Contract* he briefly considers 'unfortunate circumstances', like those that prevailed in ancient slave-owning Sparta, in which 'one can preserve one's own freedom only at the expense of someone else's, and the Citizen can be perfectly free only if the slave is utterly enslaved'. But when he then pivots to address his European contemporaries, he not only ignores but effectively denies their ownership of slaves, in order to condemn instead their reliance on parliamentary representatives: 'As for you, modern peoples, you have no slaves, but are yourselves slaves; you pay for their freedom with your own', an exchange that smacks 'more of cowardice than humanity' (Rousseau, 1997c [1762]: 115 [3:15]). The fact that many of these modern people own slaves overseas doesn't detain him.

Marxist critics, meanwhile, have regularly drawn attention to Rousseau's 'petty bourgeois' defence of peasant farmers and their private property, and his failure to anticipate the looming effects of industrialization and proletarianization, to say nothing of the consolidation of associated forms of class and state power.

To defend Rousseau's legacy certainly isn't to downplay his blind spots, or to suggest that 'he got everything right' (Gordon, 2014: 16-17). But however limited his ability to answer them, Rousseau marks a turning point in the history of European philosophy for framing questions that anticipated the concerns of a whole range of emancipatory movements, including many anti-racist and anti-patriarchal ones. Rousseau asked about the ways an oppressed group might try to free itself from domination. How inclusive and expansive can such groups become? How might they acquire the political force required to overcome the obstacles confronting them, without thereby creating new mechanisms of oppression? These are the questions that Rousseau asked, and that his liberal or reactionary critics have consistently tried to evade or foreclose. They are also questions that later revolutionary movements would repeatedly address, in terms that soon exceeded the limits of Rousseau's own historical imagination.

Take your learning further by accessing the online resources for a library of web links to relevant videos, articles, blogs, and useful websites for this chapter: **www.oup.com/he/Ramgotra-Choat1e**.

Study questions

1. Does Rousseau's account of human nature provide a convincing basis for social analysis?
2. According to Rousseau, what enables a group of individuals to become 'a people'?
3. Does Rousseau's conception of politics deny the rights and freedoms of individuals?
4. How does Rousseau understand the relation between sovereignty, on the one hand, and government, on the other?
5. Why does Rousseau condemn recourse to means of political representation?
6. To what extent is Rousseau's conception of civic equality compromised by his exclusion of women and his indifference to racism?

7. Why does Rousseau put so much emphasis on processes of civic or political education?
8. Does Rousseau's readiness to 'force people to be free' mean that he is best understood as an authoritarian thinker?

Further reading

Primary sources

Rousseau, J.-J. (1990–2009) *The Collected Writings of Rousseau*, 13 vols. Hanover, NH: Dartmouth College Press.
This is the most complete English-language edition of Rousseau's work.

Secondary sources

Bertram, C. (2003) *Rousseau and The Social Contract*. London: Routledge.
A helpful student guide to Rousseau's main political text.

Cohen, J. (2011) *Rousseau: A Free Community of Equals*. Oxford: Oxford University Press.
A sympathetic overview of Rousseau's political philosophy.

Gordon, J.A. (2014) *Creolizing Political Theory: Reading Rousseau through Fanon*. New York: Fordham University Press.
A fruitful recent reading of Rousseau's legacy.

Shklar, J. (1969) *Men and Citizens: A Study of Rousseau's Social Theory*. Cambridge: Cambridge University Press.
An influential, pessimistic reading of Rousseau as a utopian thinker who emphasized the 'awful' and unbridgeable gap between the way contemporary societies are and the way they should be.

Spector, C. (2019) *Rousseau*. Cambridge: Polity Press.
A useful recent overview.

Starobinski, J. (1988) *Transparency and Obstruction*. Trans. A. Goldhammer. Chicago: University of Chicago Press.
Still the best and most insightful 'deconstructive' reading of the tensions and frustrations that inflect Rousseau's literary and confessional writings in particular.

Wood, E.M. (2012) 'Jean-Jacques Rousseau'. In *Liberty and Property: A Social History of Western Political Thought from the Renaissance to Enlightenment*. London: Verso, pp. 189–209.
A brief overview by an important Marxist historian of ideas.

References

Descartes, R. (1985a) 'The Passions of the Soul'. In *The Philosophical Writings of Descartes*, vol. 1. Cambridge: Cambridge University Press.

Descartes, R. (1985b) 'Meditations on First Philosophy'. In *The Philosophical Writings of Descartes*, vol. 2. Cambridge: Cambridge University Press.

Estève, L. (2002) *Montesquieu, Rousseau, Diderot: du genre humain au bois d'ébène*. Paris: UNESCO.

Gordon, J. (2014) *Creolizing Political Theory: Reading Rousseau through Fanon*. New York: Fordham University Press.

Gordon, J. and Roberts, N. (2009) 'Introduction: The Project of Creolizing Rousseau'. *The C.L.R. James Journal*, 15(1): 3–16.

Gramsci, A. (1971) *Selections from the Prison Notebooks of Antonio Gramsci*. London: Lawrence & Wishart.

Gramsci, A. (1994) *Pre-Prison Writings*. Cambridge: Cambridge University Press.

Hallward, P. (2023) *Rousseau and Political Will*. London: Verso, forthcoming.

Hampton, F. (1969) *Power Anywhere Where There's People!* Chicago: Black Panther Party. Available at: https://www.marxists.org/archive/hampton/1969/misc/power-anywhere-where-theres-people.htm.

Hobbes, T. (1998) *On the Citizen*. Ed. R. Tuck. Cambridge: Cambridge University Press.

Klausen, J.C. (2014) *Fugitive Rousseau: Slavery, Primitivism, and Political Freedom*. New York: Fordham University Press.

Mills, C.W. (1997) *The Racial Contract*. Ithaca, NY: Cornell University Press.

Montesquieu, C. de (1964) 'Voyages'. In *Œuvres complètes*. Paris: Le Seuil.

Pateman, C. (1988) *The Sexual Contract*. Cambridge: Polity.

Robespierre, M. (1828) *Papiers inédits trouvés chez Robespierre Saint-Just, Payan, etc. supprimés ou omis par Courtois*. vol. 2. Paris: Baudouin Frères.

Robespierre, M. (1958) *Œuvres complètes*, vol. 9. Paris: PUF.

Robespierre, M. (2007) *Virtue and Terror*. Ed. S. Žižek, London: Routledge.

Rousseau, J-J. (1994a [c. 1761]) 'The Geneva Manuscript'. In *Collected Writings of Rousseau*, vol. 4: *The Social Contract*. Ed. R.D. Masters and C. Kelly. Hanover, NH: Dartmouth College Press.

Rousseau, J-J. (1994b) 'Political Fragments'. In *Collected Writings of Rousseau*, vol. 4. Hanover, NH: Dartmouth College Press.

Page references to this text are followed by the editors' section and article numbers, inside square brackets.

Rousseau, J-J. (1997a [1755]) 'Discourse on the Origins and Foundation of Inequality Among Men'. In J-J. Rousseau, *The Discourses and Other Early Political Writings*. Ed. V. Gourevitch. Cambridge: Cambridge University Press.

Rousseau, J-J. (1997b [1755]) 'Discourse on Political Economy'. In J-J. Rousseau, *The Social Contract and Other Later Political Writings*. Ed. V. Gourevitch. Cambridge: Cambridge University Press.

Rousseau, J-J. (1997c [1762]) 'On the Social Contract'. In J-J. Rousseau, *The Social Contract and Other Later Political Writings*. Ed. V. Gourevitch. Cambridge: Cambridge University Press.

Page references to this text are followed by Rousseau's book and chapter numbers, inside square brackets.

Rousseau, J-J. (2001a [1765]) 'Letters from the Mountain'. In *Collected Writings of Rousseau*, vol. 9: *Letter to Beaumont and Related Writings*. Ed. C. Kelly and E. Grace. Hanover, NH: Dartmouth College Press.

Rousseau, J-J. (2001b [1763]) 'Letter to Beaumont'. In *Collected Writings of Rousseau*, vol. 9. Hanover, NH: Dartmouth College Press.

Rousseau, J-J. (2001c [c. 1764]) 'History of the Government of Geneva'. In *Collected Writings of Rousseau*, vol. 9. Hanover, NH: Dartmouth College Press.

Rousseau, J-J. (2005 [1772]) 'Considerations on the Government of Poland'. In *Collected Writings of Rousseau*, vol. 11: *The Plan for Perpetual Peace and Other Writings on History and Politics*. Ed. C. Kelly. Hanover, NH: Dartmouth College Press.

Rousseau, J-J. (2010 [1762]) 'Emile, or, On Education'. In *Collected Writings of Rousseau*, vol. 13. Ed. and trans. C. Kelly and A. Bloom. Hanover, NH: Dartmouth College Press.

Sala-Molins, L. (2006) *Dark Side of the Light : Slavery and the French Enlightenment*. Minneapolis, MN: University of Minnesota Press.

Seneca, L. (1969) *Letters from a Stoic: Epistulae morales ad Lucilium*. Ed. and trans. R. Campbell. Harmondsworth: Penguin.

Sieyès, E.J. (2003) 'Views of the Executive Means Available to the Representatives of France in 1789'. In E.J. Sieyès, *Political Writings*. Ed. and trans. M. Sonenscher, Indianapolis, IN: Hackett.

Singh, N.P. (2004) *Black Is a Country: Race and the Unfinished Struggle for Democracy*. Cambridge, MA: Harvard University Press.

Trotsky, L. (2017 [1920]) *Terrorism and Communism: A Reply to Karl Kautsky*. London: Verso.

Tuck, R. (2015) *The Sleeping Sovereign: The Invention of Modern Democracy*. Cambridge: Cambridge University Press.

Wollstonecraft, M. (2014) *A Vindication of the Rights of Woman*. Ed. E. Botting. New Haven, CT: Yale University Press.

Yates, R. (1911) 'Notes of the Secret Debates of the Federal Convention of 1787'. In M. Farrand (ed.), *The Records of the Federal Convention of 1787*, vol. 1. New Haven, CT: Yale University Press.

10 Carole Pateman and Charles Mills

TERRELL CARVER

Chapter guide

This chapter explains how social contract theories emerged in early modern north-west Europe as a critique of monarchical absolutisms. Those absolutisms assumed inequalities that were fixed by inheritance of social rank and privilege. Contractual theory, by contrast, presumes an equality of individuals. From that basis, social contract theories then explained hypothetically how society itself, and an obligation to obey government, *could* arise by contractual agreement. Contract theorists thus argued that absolutist monarchical governments were illegitimate. In recent years, political theorists Carole Pateman and Charles Mills have signally exposed the exclusionary violence (Section 10.2.4) and inclusionary discriminations related to gender (Section 10.3), race (Section 10.4), and class (Section 10.2.3) that lay within this apparently universal egalitarianism. To do this, they have theorized three *prior* contracts of domination. Each prior contract explains hypothetically how self-selected individuals have agreed, one with another, that they can subordinate those whom they have already excluded. Thus the subsequent social contract legitimates, not the human equality implied in its stated premises, but the inequalities that it fails to disclose. This chapter also registers the development of a further 'capacity' or 'ableist' contract modelled on the prior contracts of gender, race, and class. It also examines the principles of contractual egalitarianism in relation to the subordinating dynamics of capitalist inequality.

10.1 Introduction

Carole Pateman (1940–) and Charles W. Mills (1951–2021), writing both separately and together, have constructed major critiques of one of the most important and politically effective concepts in modern political theory: the social contract. Their theorizations originated in political movements related to the identity politics of gender and race, understood by them within postcolonial and decolonizing perspectives.

This chapter will start from the beginning by explaining the bare-bones terms of contractualism. It will briefly review the classical political theorists who have contributed in different, broadly overlapping ways, to what the concept has become at present. And it will show how the work of Pateman and Mills has held liberal egalitarianism to account against its own ideals.

10.2 The social contract

Social contract theory, as a significant political force, emerged in revolutionary circumstances during the seventeenth and eighteenth centuries in north-west Europe. In that context, those theorizations were not merely controversial but rather treasonous, and thus punishable with penalties up to

Read more about **Pateman's** life and work by accessing the thinker biography on the online resources: www.oup.com/he/Ramgotra-Choat1e.

Read more about **Mills's** life and work by accessing the thinker biography on the online resources: www.oup.com/he/Ramgotra-Choat1e.

and including death. Most contractarian authors, now famous as political theorists, endured some periods of personal repression and involuntary exile. The major theorists were Thomas Hobbes (see more in Chapter 5), John Locke (see more in Chapter 7), and Jean-Jacques Rousseau (see more in Chapter 9).

> **Key Concept: Contract**
>
> A contract is a mutual and binding agreement between two or more parties that something will be done, or not done. It may be explicit or implicit, but either way mutual obligations are incurred. In a more specific sense, it also refers to a commercial agreement for supply of goods or performance of services, such as employees render to employers, or sellers render to buyers, in exchange for money or articles of value. In both cases non-fulfilment of an obligation will have consequences, usually legal enforcement. Where there is no legal enforcement, the social contract explains how individuals may legitimately generate sovereignty and thus legality. In this contractual way, legality and sovereignty arise to enable and protect commercial relations of ownership and exchange.

For classical theorists, the English Civil War (1642–1649), the Glorious Revolution (1688–1689), and the American Revolution (1776–1783) were foundational events. These liberalizing processes continued through further revolutionary wars in Europe, the Middle East, and the Caribbean, including widespread anti-colonial struggles throughout the Americas (Hampsher-Monk, 2006). Continuing into the nineteenth and twentieth centuries, there were wars of national liberation from colonial powers, civil wars of nation-building in Africa and Asia, and the establishment of post-Soviet successor states (James, 2001). Overwhelmingly these political processes are not peaceful, and anti-authoritarian liberalization comes with considerable violence.

10.2.1 Peaceful agreements and equal individuals

The social contract presumes human individuals are capable of making a formal agreement or promise, and of understanding the obligations into which they have therefore entered. Agreeing in that way is a social activity that exists only as and when individuals make the requisite declarations autonomously and then perform in full what the obligations require. There is thus a transfer of a right, and consequent imposition of a duty.

Of course, any individual may fail to fulfil an obligation. Without giving an excuse that convinces others of continued good intentions, that person will then rightfully suffer punitive consequences. But if such non-compliance becomes widespread, and thus general, the institution of agreement-making itself will collapse. Once a tipping point is reached, the words 'I agree' and 'I promise' will become meaningless (Taylor, 1976). Contracts are thus fragile, because individuals who are damaged by non-fulfilment must resort to their own powers of coercion to secure the expected benefit. Or they may resort to others whom they authorize to act on their behalf. That latter circumstance can arise only if others promise to help. These encounters—agreeing, contracting, promising—constitute contractualism.

Contractualism admits, whether overtly or covertly, the existence of considerable power differentials between individuals (Nozick, 2013). Those power differentials may be physical, intellectual, or psychological. They may also be the result of prior social and economic advantage or disadvantage, or luck or misfortune. Or individuals may gain power as they fulfil the contracts which they make, or indeed lose such advantages when others do better elsewhere at their expense. If all this is so, then in what sense are the contracting parties equal?

The answer is that the scenario is circular. The equality in question is the very abstract one that—by definition—each individual already possesses by being capable of entering into a contractual agreement.

That abstraction arises from quite concrete practices and circumstances. The practice of making and performing contracts goes back to the beginning of written records, approximately the third millennium BCE. The formalization of this practice emerged gradually in post-Roman times as commercial trading developed in western and southern Europe. Monetary validity in and through these practices is itself an artefact of social processes of promising and agreeing, contracting, and performing (Hont, 2015).

However, not all individuals will in fact see their essential, or even circumstantial, identity and values wholly or even partly aligned with commercialism (Scanlon, 2000). Many important human relationships, based on trust, honour, loyalty, love, and kinship, including practices of charitable giving, even doing 'good turns' for others, are typically defined in opposition to it.

Key Concept: Commercialism

Commercialism is the spirit, or attitude of mind, that values and validates trading activities. These are buying and selling merchandise through contractual transactions, typically involving monetary exchange, and to mutual advantage. As a predominating value it excludes or even devalues other ways of behaving and living, because it links utility to objects, objects to wealth, and wealth to security. Philosophically, it references a materialism of desires fulfilled by objects, and an avoidance of pain by securing future supply. That view of human activity invokes a utilitarian psychology and moral framework mirroring a mechanical model of transactional accumulation. In that way, it reinforces a bodily individualism, which abstracts from societal relationships. It also presumes a competitive urge to economic advantage, and a fearful view of others as potential competitors.

The abstract theorizations of contractualism mirror a world of idealized commercial stability (Macpherson, 2010). Remember, however, that this ideal of peaceful market-trading was accompanied by, and arose within, widespread political processes of intimidation and violence.

As opposed to commercial contracts for an exchange of goods or services, with respective obligations to fulfil the stated terms, a *social contract* institutes a governing body. That body is thus legitimately empowered to maintain internal order and external defence with force of arms. This is possible precisely because all contractors are obliged, by virtue of the contract, to aid enforcers designated by the governing body, or to be enforcers themselves, if required and capable. Political obligation is thus a consequence of the social contract. Acts of the sovereign law-maker, created through that device, must be obeyed. Disobedience will result in forceful punishment or other punitive sanction.

Citizen-contractors are therefore obliged to obey governments whose legitimacy arises from their own action in making and fulfilling the social contract. Those who might choose non-fulfilment are at risk from their fellows, acting as enforcers. If that were not the case, then government and society itself would unravel and collapse.

Here we have reached a paradox. Most human societies have, or have had, some authoritative promulgation of rules, or at least some respected adjudication on custom and practice. Repetitive obedience under those terms constitutes rule-governed behaviour and therefore some degree of stability. What need, then, is there to fulfil social contract theory? And why was it politically revolutionary?

10.2.2 The people and the state

In early modern north-west Europe, monarchical absolutisms, based on the doctrine of the divine right of kings, were overthrown, and new institutions were set up after violent revolutions and ensuing civil wars. Or absolutisms were sometimes made to concede to some devolutions of power in more gradual and less violent ways. Those liberalizing processes have generated constitutional landscapes that can be rationalized as consistent with the social contract. In that way their institutions and procedures are rendered legitimate. The social contract, in its various forms, did important service in this revolutionary and/or evolutionary politics, because it was developed in the first place to be a potent assemblage of theory and practice (Pettit, 2012).

> **Key Concept: Sovereignty**
>
> Sovereignty refers to the possession or exercise of supreme power, such as that of a ruler or monarch. Sovereignty and the sovereign are thus identified in a physical individual. In republican or other constitutional arrangements, through which monarchy has been constrained, sovereignty refers to the power of the state. In this way, state sovereignty is heir to monarchical sovereignty. The state thus claims and exercises supreme authority, usually within a bounded territory. Sovereign power may be legitimated, according to various criteria, such as popular ratification or continuing consent. Or it may be branded illegitimate, because of usurpation, when a legitimate sovereign power is overthrown, or because it has become indubitably tyrannical, that is, exercising absolute power detrimental to the public good.

As a device, the social contract solved two problems. One problem was that of legitimating *non*-absolutist government, which rejects monarchy or limits it constitutionally, and thus shares out power more liberally. The other problem was that of civil war and anarchy, which only sovereign authority could solve through institutionalized law-making and enforcement. It would do this by having an obligated citizenry ready to defend the government that they themselves as individuals had authorized. Thus by exercising the social contract, the people would preserve the peace and promote the public good.

However, if, in terms of sovereignty, the people are sole legitimators, as a matter of theoretical reasoning, then two practical questions arise. Who exactly are the people? What exactly do they need to agree to?

Both questions raise problems of definition, because inclusion will have bounded limits, and therefore exclusions. Which individuals or groups are to be excluded altogether, or not included as fully entitled members? And what matters are excluded from the terms of the agreement and are therefore not subject to governmental control?

> **Key Concept: The people**
>
> The people is a collective of individuals, whether subjects of a singular ruler, or citizens of a republic. Subjects may have no relationship to rulers other than obedience, or rulers may construct a relationship with their subjects that allows or requires some elements of consultation and participation. In republics, forms of popular assembly were instituted in place of monarchical authority. The people, in some larger or smaller bodies, were then invested with sovereign authority. As a collective, 'the people' was typically defined through exclusions so that only some of the populace could be full and equal citizens. Governing activities were then undertaken by very small groups and/or a single individual, said in some sense to be representative, and chosen through a variety of formal procedures.

Social contract theorists have been quite precise about the contractual terms of agreement. But from the beginning, and over time, those theorists have been notably obscure and indeed hypocritical concerning the definition of the people, in theory and in practice. This hypocrisy arises through discriminatory exclusions and subordinating inclusions (Canovan, 2005). That is where more recent theorists—in particular, Pateman and Mills—come in.

10.2.3 Some are more equal than others

In their texts, the classical writers listed some exclusions in explicit terms. The first was the servant-class, that is, persons in domestic and other forms of servitude, and therefore of inferior legal and social status. Hence their economic agency as contract-makers was highly restricted or non-existent. It followed that their agency in relation to participating in the social contract was insufficient. This was because contract-making presupposed individuals with access to private property as owners of exchangeable objects, including money. From the logic of the social contract, it did *not* follow that servants were also excluded from an obligation to obey the sovereign institutions that the social contract-makers had legitimated.

Hobbes derives the need for a social contract from an individualism of fearfulness that someone's life, liberty, and possessions are at risk from any other person. He understands persons, however, not as autonomous individuals, but as already within a family structure of fatherly rule. A father rules over his children and servants, thus comprising an ordered household or 'family'. In Chapter XX of his masterwork, *Leviathan*, published in 1651, he writes that a family 'consists of a man, and his children, and his servants together; wherein the father or master is the sovereign' (Hobbes, 2019: [143]). Pateman (1988: 48) concludes that for Hobbes, '[a]ll servants are subject to the political right of the master'. Thus, it is only household rulers who are free as autonomous persons to consider agreeing to the social contract.

Locke is even clearer on the subject. In the second of his two *Treatises of Government*, published in 1689, he states in Chapter 5 that 'the grass my horse has bit, the turfs my servant has cut . . . become my property' (Locke, 2012: §28). For Locke, the social contract secures the natural right to life, liberty, and property against physical threat from robbers, and political threat from tyrants. It follows that only those in a position to have property will be contractors, since others are not fully at liberty in their lives to gain it.

The second exclusion was often put less overtly, though it was clearly analogous. By status, women were unmarried daughters, wives, and widows and thus economic dependants, almost always within a household or only barely tolerated outside one. That was a realm of private, patriarchal householders, quite separate from the public realm of contract-making. Individuals undertaking the social contract were therefore conceptualized as males, even though the language defining the individual autonomous contractor, which invoked a generic abstract humanity, suggested otherwise.

Hobbes's 'family' apparently subsumes wives within the category of servants, who were excluded from obligating themselves freely into political society (Pateman, 1988: 50). Locke, however, is much clearer, not just about households and marriage, but about male superiority in general. In Section 82 of the second *Treatise of Government*, he writes:

> But the husband and wife, though they have but one common concern, yet having different understandings, will unavoidably sometimes have different wills too; it therefore being necessary that the last determination, i.e. the rule, should be placed somewhere; it naturally falls to the man's share, as the abler and the stronger.

Perceived similarities in language, religion, culture, race, capacity, or ableism and such like categorial markers were also at work in the classical texts, just as they were in the contemporary politics of the writers. In their political theories, hierarchies of power produced relations of domination and categories of discrimination which they did not contest. The egalitarian logic of contractualism then legitimated those already established exclusions and subordinations.

10.2.4 Some are more violent than others

Monetized commodification, which presumes a commercial contract, has more often been imposed throughout the world than voluntarily accepted. Contract-making, because it is understood abstractly to arise in peaceable circumstances, is therefore ideal for legitimating economic systems established or re-made through aggressive commercialisms. Those processes of violence and intimidation included internal repression, external colonization, imperial conquest, systematic dispossession, and similar forms of money-driven exploitation of resources and peoples. Through an abstract scenario, the actual circumstances of invasion, colonialism, displacement, forced labour, genocide, and the like are set aside (Ince, 2018).

> **Key Concept: Settler societies**
>
> The term 'settler societies' refers to colonies and enclaves formed by governmental power and commercial enterprise in order to transfer some people, either forcibly or voluntarily, to sites where they were expected or required to make permanent settlement. Governments explicitly or implicitly authorized settlers to dispossess such inhabitants as were already there, so as to give settlers unimpeded access to land and further resources. Existing inhabitants were thus variously subjected to genocide, slavery, marginalization, and discrimination, as well as to forcible erasure of culture and tradition. They were also stigmatized in historical writing and in day-to-day practice, as well as excluded from full and equal citizenship, or sometimes even human status. Successor states to those colonies and enclaves have so far offered only minimal acknowledgement and insignificant reparations.

The moral mythology of commercial contractualism then functioned as an exemplar for, and paradigm of, rectitude, freedom, progress, and modernity (Armitage, 2013). That convergence of power with knowledge-making has made it difficult for dominant nations and persons even to see the exclusionary practices and inclusionary violence described above. Hence they have resisted, most often with considerable violence, many of the struggles against their domination. Those repressions and suppressions were and are commonplace, even though the oppressed and subordinated peoples often invoke the inclusivity and peacefulness through which the social contract was defined (Césaire, 2000).

> **10.2 The social contract: Key Points**
>
> - The social contract invokes the individualistic, egalitarian logic of autonomous individuals empowered to make agreements and thus incur obligations.
> - The liberalizing politics of anti-absolutism, based on contractualism, aligns exactly with the violent politics of aggressive commercialisms.
> - The social contract is a moralizing mythology of equality and self-interest that presumes and legitimates prior exclusions from 'the people'.
> - Those prior exclusions represent hierarchies of domination and subordination.

10.3 The sexual contract

As we have seen, liberalizing struggles to establish constitutional governments have been grounded in the egalitarian individualism of the social contract. That politics of securing and extending rights and liberties was therefore aligned with the presumptions of commercial contract-making (Whyte, 2019: 10–14). In both cases, the inclusion of female individuals as human beings equal to male ones in political and commercial life should not have been problematic. And their exclusion from competitive male hierarchies of power and wealth would clearly be illegitimate.

Feminists have, however, presented detailed historical and contemporary research demonstrating that, as matters of fact, women were systematically excluded and disadvantaged. Male-dominated structures of political and economic power discriminated against them in public and subordinated them in private. Women do not own and control economic and political resources in any respect equal to what, through male-dominated structures of power, men afford to themselves. To explain how this could be, and to understand why it has such widespread legitimacy, Pateman turned to political theory.

In *The Sexual Contract*, Pateman (1988) deduced that the narratives through which contractualism was explained actually negated the human equalities that they expressed. That is, contrary to textual appearances, the human universal was construed by classical theorists in male-centric terms. In that way, women were conceived as unequal to men or, rather, the human universal was clearly not conceived as female.

Rousseau's *Social Contract*, published in 1762, removes commercialism from contractualism by placing his equal individuals in an idealized bucolic setting of household and collective sufficiency, rather than locked into competitive hierarchies of economic domination and subordination. But his view of sexual difference was extreme, arguing explicitly in various writings that women were unsuited to citizenship and civic life, and required—by their nature—subjection to men in patriarchal households (Pateman, 1988: 96–102).

The possible inclusion of at least some women in male hierarchies of power and wealth became acutely visible as an issue in the 1790s. The *Declaration of the Rights of Women and the Female Citizen* (De Gouges, 2018), and *A Vindication of the Rights of Woman with Strictures on Political and Moral Subjects* (Wollstonecraft, 2004), occasioned much debate and violent struggle. De Gouges herself was executed on the guillotine (read more about Wollstonecraft in Chapter 21). Subsequently—nearly two hundred years later—those works entered the otherwise all-male history of political thought.

In the nineteenth and twentieth centuries, there have been some inclusionary successes for women in certain respects, notably in equality before the law, and access to the franchise. But in more recent eras of increasing egalitarianism, albeit within racialized and other structures of domination, why have exclusionary discrimination, and persistent economic disadvantage, so affected so many women so persistently? Why did female citizens have to fight so hard to get the vote? Why did so many men resist this, and other equalizations, so determinedly, even violently? Why do so many male-centric and female-unfriendly spaces and practices still exist? What are the moral and political economies of female prostitution or sex-work? Why is so much sexual violence against women understood as unimportantly domestic? Why is there a gender pay gap in wages and a glass ceiling in promotions?

Pateman's sexual contract is a parodic theorization that upends the male-centric abstractions through which the social contract is understood as egalitarian. It is therefore a powerful analytical and explanatory tool for understanding feminist politics and assessing what it is up against.

The human-centric universalisms of the classical social contract, according to Pateman, are already construed within a hierarchical politics of power and authority. That politics is in fact a self-legitimated practice of sexual control by men over women. Insubordinate and rebellious women are therefore considered a threat to the legitimacy of the entire social order. Sexual difference is thus a *political* hierarchy of men over women. It follows that any grant to women of higher social status, or conditional inclusion into hierarchies of power, is men's alone to grant.

10.3.1 Women and marriage

As a feminist, Pateman's first target, in bringing down illegitimate structures of men's control over women, was marriage. To do this, she distinguished it sharply from other concepts, such as the family, parenthood, childcare, and the like (Pateman and Mills, 2007: 222–224).

Marriage, as a customary and religious institution, has been very largely construed in terms of male superiority and dominance. Moreover, women as marriage partners were not understood as fully human, but rather as sexual servants and status-markers for men. As property ownership became ever more crucial to aggressive commercialisms, contractualism in relation to marriage—whether as an implied transactional agreement or an explicit contract of property exchange—became the norm. Women were thus subordinated under men's control.

Why, Pateman (1988: 5–8) asked, would any woman freely sign a contract of marriage, or otherwise agree to be bound by such obviously disadvantageous terms? Or, to put it another way, how can the liberalizing politics, for which the social contract set such crucially egalitarian terms, so consistently support the patriarchal oppression and political subordination of women?

Pateman's answer was that the institutions of female subordination—marriage, maternity, family, domesticity, sexual objectification, prostitution, sex-work, and suchlike—had *already* been legitimated by men before the liberalizing politics of the social contract could be applied. Following the logic of the social contract—that legitimating authority arises only through contractualism—she concluded that there must have been a *prior* contract of domination. That prior contract would be an agreement among men, founded on the exclusion of women from their egalitarian contract-making. The subsequent *social* contract thus legitimates not only the sovereign authority of men but also their political and sexual subordination of women.

Pateman writes: 'The original pact is a sexual as well as a social contract: it is sexual in the sense of patriarchal – that is, the contract establishes men's political right over women – and also sexual in the sense of establishing orderly access by men to women's bodies' (ibid.: 2). As with the social contract itself, this prior contract need never have occurred. Rather, both contracts together are a way of understanding how legitimacy can be ascribed to social structures of exclusion, domination, and subordination, notwithstanding premises of inclusivity, equality, and autonomy.

Moreover, both contracts rest on consent, rather than on overt agreement. Overt agreement is an explicit action, whereas consent can be a kind of inaction, merely acting *as if* one had agreed. In that way, the social contract is unlike commercial contracts, which typically require explicit agreement signified with seals or signatures. Even implicit contracts are based on parties taking actions consistent with terms, evidently agreed without formalities.

Consent, though, can be merely ascribed to individuals, and the validity of the contract will still arise. Critics of the social contract have protested that ascribed consent to a hypothetical contract is an extraordinary device from which to derive a comprehensive obligation to obey (Wolff, 1998). But in Pateman's analysis, through the social contract, and the prior sexual contract, women are deemed by men to have consented to their bodily subordination, foremost in sexual terms, but also to their political subordination, again at men's disposal.

> ### Key Thinker: Susan Moller Okin
>
> Susan Moller Okin (1946–2004) published *Justice, Gender, and the Family* in 1989, a highly influential feminist critique of liberal presumptions. Okin (1991) argued that liberalism actively promoted injustice in relation to women. Liberal conceptions of justice, whether individualist or communitarian, did not consider relations of power within families, because liberals did not take family life seriously in political terms. Family relationships were structured within patriarchal presumptions through which women were disadvantaged as wives and mothers. Okin's argument thus aligns with Pateman's in *The Sexual Contract* (Pateman, 1988), because it shows how masculinist knowledge-production marginalizes women and legitimates their exclusion from positions of power. While Pateman focused on marriage and prostitution, and thus on women as individuals, Okin focused on the family-group, and similar domesticating relationships, within which women were treated by men as inferiors.

10.3.2 Women and prostitution

Pateman also used her analytical framework to examine another problematic institution through which men exert power over women. That institution was prostitution, a transactional practice that is typically denigrated and stigmatized. She argued that both marriage and prostitution were instances of, and supports for, the domination of men over women. Both, therefore, were effects of the sexual contract, undertaken by men, such that their exclusive participation in the social contract legitimated their sovereign authority over the other sex. 'Prostitution is part of the exercise of the law of male-sex right', Pateman (1988: 194) says, 'one of the ways in which men are ensured access to women's bodies'.

From that analysis it followed, for Pateman, that marriage and prostitution were more similar than different. In that way, they are mirror images of male hypocrisy, because egalitarian contractualism espouses autonomous individualism. Thus, in Pateman's analysis, the moral mythology of the social contract occludes the subordination of, and control over, women by men that actually take place. It has this effect precisely because it articulates abstractly an egalitarian politics that resists authoritarian domination.

Pateman's analysis of marriage and prostitution follows logically from the analytical framework that she establishes. In both cases, however, her specific points of criticism have in turn attracted feminist controversy (O'Neill, Shanley, and Young, 2008) (read more about Young in Chapter 22). In the case of prostitution, this has been particularly intense. It must be said that prostitution is a hugely controversial subject, so any opinion will generate a passionate reaction. Marriage, though, is rather different, being generally less controversial, even celebrated, and also well provided with defences and defenders. Yet, citing Wollstonecraft's famous remark, Pateman (1988: 190) notes that marriage can be described as legal prostitution, though unlike prostitutes, wives are not paid for their sexual services.

Other feminists have commented that, through contractual negotiations, prostitutes, in some circumstances, are striking agreements with men more freely than is usually the case in marriage. As one would expect, Pateman's critical riposte focuses on such contractarian narratives of individual freedom understood in terms of commercial exchange.

For Pateman, that freedom is based on a supposed separation between a woman's selfhood and her body, on the one hand, and the marketable commodity termed sexual services, on the other. Men, by contrast, are not subject to a self/body separation that commodifies the latter. The moral mythology of equal exchangers thus enables orderly access by men to women's bodies, not just within marriage, but also outside it (ibid.: 191). Moreover, men's economic empowerment over women as sexual objects also extends to liaisons, affairs, mistress-keeping, secondary households, and other arrangements. Those relations are transactional within a zone somewhat between prostitution and marriage (ibid.: 191–192). Freedom of contract is the cornerstone of what Pateman calls patriarchal capitalism, which privileges men as controllers of wealth and power.

Pateman's analysis moved heterosexual relations controversially into a zone of specifically political contestation. By contrast, the parameters through which those relations had been traditionally understood were typically set by religious teachings on family life or biological understandings of species-reproduction.

Rather than contesting religion or science, Pateman contests the legitimating narratives of political theory. Those egalitarian narratives of contract-making, based on commercial exchange, are the modes through which modern politics is understood. By using the prior contract as a device, Pateman is able to highlight the way that the female sex is construed as already subordinated to the male sex. Thus her theorizing denies legitimacy to the sovereignty that the social contract purports to justify.

> **10.3 The sexual contract: Key Points**
>
> - The sexual contract explains how the egalitarianism of the social contract is made consistent with the subordinated and disadvantaged position of women.
> - This is because a prior contract of exclusion has already been agreed among men which authorizes their orderly access to women's bodies.
> - In that way, marriage and prostitution are revealed to be effects of male sovereignty.
> - Contract-making, whether prior, social, or commercial, is thus a device integral to patriarchal capitalism.

10.4 The racial contract

Mills's (1997) book, *The Racial Contract*, references and mirrors Pateman's analysis in *The Sexual Contract* (Pateman, 1988). Just as Pateman detailed the legitimating logic through which women were disadvantaged and subordinated, so Mills similarly theorizes an exclusionary contract of domination prior to social-contract making. Pateman and Mills both use this device to argue that some persons are already excluded from the contract-makers who constitute 'the people' and are therefore sovereign. Thus, the apparently inclusive and egalitarian scenario of social contract-making among autonomous individuals disguises a prior agreement among some to exclude others whom they judge to be inferior. Yet those inferiorized individuals will be obligated to accept the resultant governing authority as legitimate. In that way Pateman accounts for systematic discrimination against women, by men, and Mills accounts for systematic discrimination against Black people, and People of Colour generally, by White people.

Mills's book also shows us that the production and reproduction of political theory by white people have excluded or marginalized, and thus inferiorized, other ways of making sense of politics and society. So the political theory canon of classic writers is very white in exactly the way that it is very male. The exclusionary and subordinating processes of discrimination and disadvantage are thus disguised by a moralizing mythology that takes whiteness as the human ideal and the exemplar of human achievement.

The same mythological moralizing also licenses the aggressive commercialisms through which human progress to modernity has been theorized and pursued by white people. Mills's racial contract, undertaken by white people among themselves, reveals not just the domination and subordination that belies the apparent egalitarianism of the social contract, but also a moral mission for white people to enforce their version of modernity on non-white peoples and their cultures. This combination of aggressive commercialisms and convictions of white superiority has justified and condoned slavery, massacres, brutality, conquest, invasion, colonialism, imperialism, pacification, nation-building, land-grabs, population removal, incarceration, seizure of children, cultural destruction, and similar phenomena.

As Mills (1997: 1–2) says, 'White supremacy is the unnamed political system that has made the modern world what it is today.' That status of being unnamed is not an accident, but a way of making sure that white domination 'is not seen as a political system at all'. Yet, Mills continues, 'the most important political system of recent global history' is the one 'by which white people have historically ruled over and, in certain important ways, continue to rule over non-white people'. Mills's conclusions (ibid.: 33) come with due acknowledgement of the work of Frantz Fanon (see Chapter 28), C.L.R. James (see Chapter 18), W.E.B. Du Bois (see Chapter 31), and many other writers of colour.

10.4.1 Universalism and hypocrisy

Mills's argument, however, is not about the desirability of including non-white persons in the privileged position of the sovereign people as set out in the classical social contract. He is well aware that those texts, as we have seen, explicitly excluded servants and implicitly, or sometimes even explicitly, excluded women. Those hierarchies, then, by virtue of the moral mythology of the social contract, are hypocritically understood to be consistent with the universal equality of all humans as autonomous individuals. Mills is thus drilling deeper by factoring white modernity and racial oppression into Pateman's critique.

Mills argues that white modes of knowledge-production, termed mainstream and authoritative in an apparently unraced way, have generated closed communities in philosophy, ethics, political theory, and the like. To maintain the fiction that the knowledge that these communities generate is unraced, those communities, he says, are preoccupied with very abstract, universalizing discussions of justice, equality, rights, authority, and legitimacy. The educational curricula, which license those abstractions and associated analytical methods, then obscure other ideas and knowledges, since abstractions have already claimed centre-stage.

Moreover, in that way, white knowledge-production occludes the actual historical struggles of non-white peoples against white domination. Thus the moralizing mythologies of contract-making push real struggles, actually made by real people, into the background. This take-over of knowledge-production has been termed epistemicide (De Sousa Santos, 2014).

Mills (1997: 4) references a number of alternative intellectual traditions, including 'Native American, African American, and Third and Fourth World political thought'. Those intellectual traditions have focused on the struggles through which the majority of the world's populations have resisted white domination. Thus, they offer explicitly raced, non-mainstream accounts of 'conquest, imperialism, colonialism, white settlement, land rights, race and racism, slavery, Jim Crow, reparations, apartheid, cultural authenticity, national identity, *indigenismo*, Afrocentrism' and the like.

Those histories have been misconstrued, obscured, and suppressed in white histories and are thus unknown to, or only superficially noticed by, students and intellectuals familiar solely with white knowledge-production. Indeed, whiteness itself functions as a criterion of significance and an index of truth. The racial contract, Mills says, thus bears witness to the political and economic imperialisms and colonialisms through which white knowledge-production proceeds.

Feminists had already experienced male domination personally and protested it publicly, such that Pateman could make it visible academically. By contrast, Mills notes that white domination, as a persistent and pervasive hierarchy, can scarcely be mentioned within white education and public life. White people do not have the experiences that come with racialized oppression, because they are the oppressors. In any case, they have little reason to enquire into their own complicity. For those reasons they have almost no sense that they are even a race.

10.4.2 Whiteness and ignorance

Mills (2017: 49–53) targets what he calls white ignorance. He develops this idea by linking the philosophies of the Enlightenment period, arising in north-west Europe, with the aggressive commercialisms fostered there. Put very simply, Mills is arguing that what academic establishments have taught as validated knowledge, and ways of acquiring it, have proceeded from the standpoint of elite, economically privileged, white males.

The contrasting non-white knowledges to which Mills appeals are ones proceeding from a view of the individual rooted in the histories and cultures of social groups, rather than in abstractions from human experience that are supposedly universal. Those supposed universalisms, Mills says, are suited to presumptions and erasures that enable one group to empower itself over others.

White knowledge-making proceeds not only by supporting the aggressive commercialisms that fund academic institutions, but also by eliminating rival intellectual systems that proceed from different, less abstract presuppositions. In Mills's view (2017: 51), 'the Marxist [class] critique is seemingly discredited, the feminist critique is marginalized, and the racial critique does not even exist' (read more about Marx in Chapter 13).

Thus, Mills is mapping a kind of knowledge-bubble of white privilege through which the world—as it is envisaged in and through the minds of white, propertied males—protects itself. That protection is accomplished not so much with falsehoods as with disdain for other points of view. In particular, the moralizing mythologies and rarefied abstractions of social contract-making are a key device for maintaining this studied incuriosity.

From that basis, Mills tackles the trade in Black humans, forced to labour as slaves, which propelled the aggressive commercialisms of the early modern period. From the late fifteenth to the late nineteenth century, this traumatizing set of practices flourished in a specifically racialized way. The global trade, notably around the Caribbean and also much further afield, even to Pacific Oceania, generated huge profits for western European elites and commercial middle classes (Williams, 1994).

In the first decades of the nineteenth century various European countries and the United States abolished the slave trade as a feature of their moralizing self-empowerment, though with convenient gaps in enforcement. The lucrative practice, deriving commercial profit from forced labour, continued for decades. Complete abolition of slavery itself, at least in principle, occurred in various colonies and countries, with Brazil the last in 1888. Compensation went exclusively to slave-holders and their heirs who had personal ownership of human beings, and to holders of investment shares in slave-owning enterprises. Nothing went to former slaves; indeed some were bound to further labour to repay the former owners' investments (Manjapra, 2020).

The moral mythology of contractualism has survived quite well as the foundational argument for inclusionary political practices, such as promises of non-discrimination and policies of affirmative action. Those inclusionary practices beg the question as to what kind of society formerly excluded and subordinated persons were being included in, as well as exactly what inclusion in white-dominated economic and political systems would entail. As a mode of theorizing, contractualism itself is history-less, so it erases, rather than acknowledges, the violent histories and institutional persistence of white racism.

> ### 🔑 10.4 The racial contract: Key Points
>
> - The racial contract is a prior contract of exclusion through which some agree among themselves to dominate and subordinate others along lines they determine as race.
> - The apparent egalitarianism of the subsequent social contract then legitimates a racialized hierarchy of white persons over Persons of Colour.
> - Through white ignorance, knowledge-making from subordinated points of view is marginalized or erased.
> - In that way, whiteness itself goes unacknowledged as a racialized category and racializing practice.

10.5 The settler contract

Mills pays tribute to Pateman's work on the contract of sexual domination prior to, but suppressed by, the classical terms of the social contract itself. In turn, Pateman takes up Mills's racial contract in relation to the actual practices of nation-states, expanding on what he had briefly termed the settler contract.

Pateman points out that sending white settlers out globally for permanent and dominant occupation elsewhere required particular attention to the establishment of continuing sovereignty. Settlers' sovereignty needed legitimation, because otherwise they would appear as conquerors of territory that belonged to others and as usurpers over their sovereignty.

Pateman tackles the settler contract by considering how the USA, Canada, and Australia were colonized by white people. In that way, she reinterprets the theory and practice of the classical contractarians themselves, not just textually in their theoretical writings, but personally in archival material, notably with Hobbes and Locke.

While the concept of race is not posed explicitly by Hobbes and Locke, both theorists included colonization within their theorizations of the social contract. Those theorizations explained what sorts of peoples, namely North American Indigenous, were excluded from, or not yet suitable for, inclusion in the peaceable agreements of social contractualism. However, those excluded persons were nonetheless obliged to obey the governing body that the social contract-makers had legitimated.

Both Hobbes and Locke, Pateman points out, were involved in the commercial and governmental colonial schemes through which settlements were organized. Hobbes was associated with the Virginia Company, and Locke was affiliated to the Lords Proprietors of the Carolinas. Both enterprises were encouraged, protected, and defended by British governments, which both Hobbes and Locke, in somewhat different ways and at somewhat different times, were involved in legitimating (Pateman and Mills, 2007: 35–41).

Pateman traces the narrative arguments through which Indigenous people were excluded from being sovereign peoples in their own right, and thus from having their own governing structures, which colonists might have been obliged to respect. Those structures typically included occupying and using lands and waterways, engaging in systems of production and exchange that were already in place, and continuing the activities of knowledge-production and cultural meaning-making through which they understood themselves and others. As contractarian narratives of sovereignty were developed further, from a basis in texts by Hobbes and Locke, the doctrine of *terra nullius* or 'empty land' emerged in political parlance.

Pateman shows how the colonizing powers used this device to declare their settlements to be legitimate outposts of home-country sovereignties. That device inferiorized Indigenous peoples by characterizing them as uncivilized, dangerous, and subhuman, thus legitimizing expropriation and extirpation. Those narratives also provided exoneration for the civilized white man, and subordinately, white woman, who would otherwise be adjudged perpetrators of injustice.

With that prior agreement among white people, understood by Pateman as the settler contract, the aggressive commercialisms, licensed at home by contractual individualism, were also licensed in colonial spaces, yet without the moral opprobrium of conquest and usurpation. As a corollary, the moral justification of self-defence was often invoked *against* Indigenous resistance. For Indigenous peoples, any right to such action had been negated already by the settler contract. That agreement among the white settlers, one with another, dehumanized Indigenous peoples to a status below that of slaves. Slaves, after all, had a market-value, whereas Indigenous people were worthless.

Pateman summarizes this succinctly: 'In a *terra nullius* the original contract takes the form of a *settler contract*.' It follows from this logic that 'settlers alone [can be said to] conclude the original pact'. 'Native peoples', she says, 'are not part of the settler contract', because in the required sense of civilized white humanness, they are 'not really present or even existent'. However, they are 'henceforth subject to it', and 'their lives, lands and nations are reordered by it' (Pateman and Mills, 2007: 56; emphasis in original).

Pateman identifies two variants in British colonial practice: one in North America, beginning in 1607, and the other in Australia, beginning in 1788. In the USA, as the successor state from the Treaty of Paris in 1783, some remnants of territorial integrity and subordinated legalities were imposed by government on Indigenous peoples. In Canada, though, as successor state from the British North America Act of 1867, some elements of devolved sovereignty and property ownership have been negotiated by Indigenous peoples with the government. In both cases, those arrangements were pragmatically undertaken as a result of persistent resistance by Indigenous peoples by whatever means they could muster.

By contrast, in Australia, the logic of *terra nullius* was 'elevated to the law of the land' and 'an entire continent was deemed uninhabited'. With the Indigenous communities there were no official negotiations or treaties signed, since Indigenous individuals did not exist other than in forms of total exclusion and physical marginalization. They were said to be dying races and cultures, and, as some have commented, treated as enemies of the state (ibid.: 61, 70–71).

Pateman then circles back from histories to theories, commenting that the classical social contract proceeds in a way that abstracts from embarrassing origins, and erases current inequalities. The egalitarian narrative of autonomous individual contract-making thus removes from view the continuing effects of violent occupation and genocidal colonization. Contractualism has worked so well reciprocally with the moralizing politics of nation-building, because it mirrors the practical goals of the white commercial order.

Like the racial contract, the settler contract proceeds on racialized presumptions of whiteness, but subsumes this into an apparently race-less 'everyman' individual. Like the racial contract, it legitimates the involuntary inclusion of some subordinated, even enslaved, persons into a system of commercial sovereignty. But unlike the racial contract, it also legitimates the involuntary exclusion of subordinated persons, sometimes through genocidal murder, from *their own lands*.

10.5 The settler contract: Key Points

- White settlers empower themselves to exclude Indigenous peoples from their lands and other physical and cultural resources.
- Those acts of usurpation, annexation, marginalization, and murder then require legitimation within white systems of morality.
- The settler contract, undertaken prior to the social contract, excludes Indigenous persons from 'the people' and sometimes even from human status.
- Nonetheless, in colonized spaces and successor states, Indigenous peoples are made subject to the sovereignty that white contractualism legitimates.

10.6 Conclusion

Where does this leave the social contract? Does it follow from Pateman's and Mills's critiques that the social contract is inherently and necessarily hypocritical? And, if so, what way of theorizing sovereignty, and of distinguishing legitimate forms of rule from illegitimate ones, could replace it?

On this point, Pateman and Mills disagree somewhat. Mills identifies and defines the domination contract as an 'exclusionary, manipulative contract deployed by the powerful to subordinate others in society under the pretext of including them as equals' (Pateman and Mills, 2007: 82). But, for him, the fault is not with the idea of equals making a contract in order to make governmental sovereignty legitimate. The fault lies in the *kind of contract-making*, that is, a prior one and a subsequent social one, which together perform the subterfuge.

Against that kind of dual-contract, and to address the injustices that it legitimates, Mills proposes a revisionist contract. In that format the reasoning will not be nearly so abstract, because it will take the facts of historic injustice into account. Moreover, individuals will be understood as having agency in and through group memberships and identities, specifically those of sex, race, and class. By taking the historical and current realities of domination and subordination on board, contract-making would be more usefully inclusive. It would depart from universalizing presumptions of an ideal equality, and from timeless presumptions of history-less autonomy. It would therefore leave behind the hypocrisies that Pateman and Mills (ibid.: 94–101) have identified.

Mills's revisionist position is invoked in the 'capacity contract', which also uses Pateman's device of the prior contract (Simplican, 2015). The projection of the general category of mental incapacity by self-defined and self-empowered 'fully capable' persons on to other persons so as to dominate them follows the model that Pateman and Mills have powerfully argued. Rather similarly Simplican shows that major theorists and philosophers in the liberal tradition have graded the social acceptability and even human status of individuals in relation to ideals originating with privileged white males. Those ideals of mental capacity represent standards of minimal, functional, and exemplary humanness through which gradations of subordination and degrees of control can be exercised. The subsequent, hypocritical social contract thus legitimates those hierarchical and exclusionary presumptions and practices.

The 'ableist' contract follows similar lines of critique but also includes physical disability. Pinheiro (2016: 45–46) argues that in contract theory, as is very generally the case in politics, the able mind and the able body cannot be strictly separated. Moreover, bodily development is commonly understood as necessary for mental development, and indeed classical contract theorists wrote extensively to make that point. Hence, in contractualism, an abstract presumption of 'able' personhood is deployed to exclude and subordinate those whose 'singularities' threaten this idealized self-image.

In contrast to Mills's position and to other revisionist contractualisms, Pateman argues that contractual processes among dispassionate individuals, even if everyone is historically informed and determined on justice, could not possibly work to overcome the violent histories by which today's individuals already form their identities and views. While contending that her position is not one of hopelessness, she looks to political processes of practical negotiations, compromises, and trade-offs, rather than to a reversion to the abstractions of the social contract. That kind of unrealism, she argues, allows hypocrisies to creep back in (Pateman and Mills, 2007: 164).

Pateman also finds contractual theorizing suspect, because it presupposes commercialism. Identifying freedom with a system that necessarily fosters inequality, since that is what monetary exchange ensures, merely creates new forms of domination and subordination (ibid.: 208–209). Alternatively, Pateman conceptualizes freedom as autonomy, that is, thinking and acting within a robust and inclusive set of political institutions. Concepts of equality and justice would thus emerge in relation to, rather than be derived from, the principles and practices of commercialism.

That realistic process, she argues, would be truer to the promise of liberalizing anti-absolutism than circular reasoning from abstract premises (ibid.: 228–229).

Many people today hold the view that governmental legitimacy derives from claims to authority understood as traditional. These include monarchical succession, religious revelation, and constitutional conventions and institutions. There are few, if any cases, of actual government-making by contract, hence the social contract is much more a heuristic device than a real-world instruction kit. Allegations of illegitimacy, though, have a real-world role in liberalizing authoritarian regimes so that governmental powers are exercised within bounds and would-be tyrants called to account. The true test of legitimacy, then, is whether the government acquiesces to the officers of the legal system—supreme courts, constitutional councils, guardian authorities or special prosecutors, and the like—and thus maintains the rule of law.

The concepts through which to understand legitimacy, and to grasp how important it is, are all quite abstract. Hence they require an articulation in theory that lays out first principles, whether of absolute or limited power, authoritarian or participatory decision-making, divine sanction, or human effort. Those theorizations tell us how we have agreed already—that is, consented—to our obligation to obey. But they also tell us how we can 'unconsent', though with downsides and difficulties. While consent binds us as individuals, theorizations of unconsent always require a collective.

The social contract has functioned both ways in getting people on board for political action, get-out-the-vote as an individual affirmation of consent, and throw-the-rascals-out as a collective act of rebellion. In the political philosophy of modern times, though, as Pateman contends, the abstract scenario of individual agreement and collective obligation often disguises exclusions and hierarchies that need to be worked through, not forgotten, marginalized, or erased. However, as Mills contends, some degree of abstraction is required in order to theorize the legitimacy or otherwise of governmental power, so the pairwise egalitarianism of contract-making is often a good place to start.

It is unlikely that anyone's version of the social contract will tell us exactly what we need to know and do in order to generate individual consent, and to empower collective unconsent, so as to realize the elusive public good. It seems equally unlikely that resolving all such questions into groupwise ongoing political negotiations represents an attractive option, given powerful interests and human gullibility. The alignment of the social contract with the procedures and values of aggressive commercialism suggests that the device is only helping us to beg questions about power, hierarchy, and legitimacy, rather than to pose them. However, the apparatus of rights, duties, and obligations, arising from autonomous choices made by equal individuals, has been politically potent for over three hundred years. This is not at all a purely philosophical debate. It dominates the news every day.

Take your learning further by accessing the online resources for a library of web links to relevant videos, articles, blogs, and useful websites for this chapter: **www.oup.com/he/Ramgotra-Choat1e**.

Study questions

1. What do you think politicians mean when they invoke a social contract?
2. Citizens are obliged to obey legitimate governments. If this is not the result of the social contract, how else could it come about?
3. Consider the apparently raceless principles of human rights. Can liberal individualism ever be raceless?

4. In what ways is there a politics of whiteness? Consider both white supremacism and settler-society apologies.
5. Consider what the sexual contract says about men. Are there ways of disempowering them?
6. Consider the man/woman binary in relation to domination and subordination. Is heterosexuality the basis for female oppression?
7. What is the relationship between political and commercial individualisms?
8. Consider the consequences of injustices done to individuals now deceased. Can living individuals acquire or exercise any rights as a consequence?

Further reading

Primary sources

Mills, C.W. (1997) *The Racial Contract*. Ithaca, NY: Cornell University Press.
Classic statement of this original conception that racializes global history.

Mills, C.W. (2017) *Black Rights/White Wrongs: The Critique of Racial Liberalism*. Oxford: Oxford University Press.
Critical essays on race in theory and politics, revising analytical perspectives.

Pateman, C. (1988) *The Sexual Contract*. Cambridge: Polity.
Classic and still controversial statement of this original conception.

Pateman, C. (2017) *Democracy, Feminism, Welfare*. Ed. T. Carver. Abingdon: Routledge.
Collection of shorter writings on major themes in political theory.

Pateman, C. and Mills, C. (2007) *Contract and Domination*. Cambridge: Polity.
Jointly conceived argumentative work with separately signed chapters.

Secondary sources

Bell, D. (2019) *Reordering the World*. Princeton, NJ: Princeton University Press.
Comprehensive review of the relationship between Anglophone liberalism, aggressive commercialisms, and imperial-colonial rule.

Claeys, G. (2012) *Imperial Sceptics: British Critics of Empire 1850–1920*. Cambridge: Cambridge University Press.
Historical analysis of important contemporary critiques of imperialism and colonialism.

De Sousa Santos, B. (2014) *Epistemologies of the South: Justice Against Epistemicide*. Abingdon: Routledge.
Argumentative development of cognitive justice as alternative to liberal universalism.

Ivison, D. (2020) *Can Liberal States Accommodate Indigenous Peoples?* Cambridge: Polity.
Reviews histories of white settler societies, arguing transformation of popular sovereignty.

Kukathas, C. (2003) *The Liberal Archipelago: A Theory of Diversity and Freedom*. Oxford: Oxford University Press.
Argumentative work exploring liberal individualism.

Losurdo, D. (2011) *Liberalism: A Counter-History*. Trans. G. Elliott. London: Verso.
Thorough historical investigation of the relationship between liberalism and exclusion, subordination, and violence.

Okin, S.M. (ed.) (1999) *Is Multiculturalism Bad for Women?* Princeton, NJ: Princeton University Press.
Feminist critique from individualist principles with outstanding critical engagements from an array of leading scholars.

Pinder, S.O. (ed.) (2019) *Black Political Thought: From David Walker to the Present*. Cambridge: Cambridge University Press.
  Major collection altering the political theory canon.

Smith, L.T. (2012) *Decolonising Methodologies: Research and Indigenous Peoples*. 2nd edn. London: Zed Books.
  Rethinking political theory and practice from Indigenous and feminist perspectives.

References

Armitage, D. (2013) *Foundations of Modern International Thought*. Cambridge: Cambridge University Press.

Canovan, M. (2005) *The People*. Cambridge: Polity.

Césaire, A. (2000) *Discourse on Colonialism*. Trans. J. Pinkham. New edn. New York: Monthly Review.

De Gouges, O. (2018) *The Declaration of the Rights of Women: The Original Manifesto for Justice, Equality and Freedom*. London: Ilex Press.

De Sousa Santos, B. (2014) *Epistemologies of the South: Justice Against Epistemicide*. Abingdon: Routledge.

Hampsher-Monk, I. (2006) *A History of Modern Political Thought: Major Thinkers from Hobbes to Marx*. 2nd edn. Oxford: Wiley-Blackwell.

Hobbes, T. (2019) *Leviathan*, rev. student edn. Ed. R. Tuck. Cambridge: Cambridge University Press, ebook.

Hont, I. (2015) *Politics in Commercial Society: Jean-Jacques Rousseau and Adam Smith*. Cambridge, MA: Harvard University Press.

Ince, O.U. (2018) *Colonial Capitalism and the Dilemmas of Liberalism*. Oxford: Oxford University Press.

James, C.L.R. (2001) *The Black Jacobins*. Harmondsworth: Penguin.

Locke, J. (2012) *Two Treatises of Government*. Ed. P. Laslett. Cambridge: Cambridge University Press, ebook.

Macpherson, C.B. (2010) *The Political Theory of Possessive Individualism: Hobbes to Locke*. Reprint edn. Toronto: Oxford University Press.

Manjapra, K. (2020) *Colonialism in Global Perspective*. Cambridge: Cambridge University Press.

Mills, C.W. (1997) *The Racial Contract*. Ithaca, NY: Cornell University Press.

Mills, C.W. (2017) *Black Rights/White Wrongs: The Critique of Racial Liberalism*. Oxford: Oxford University Press.

Nozick, R. (2013) *Anarchy, State, and Utopia*. 2nd edn. New York: Basic Books.

Okin, S.M. (1991) *Justice, Gender and the Family*. New York: Basic Books.

O'Neill, D.J., Shanley, M.L., and Young, I.M. (eds) (2008) *Illusion of Consent: Engaging with Carole Pateman*. University Park, PA: Pennsylvania State University Press.

Pateman, C. (1988) *The Sexual Contract*. Cambridge: Polity.

Pateman, C. and Mills, C. (2007) *Contract and Domination*. Cambridge: Polity.

Pettit, P. (2012) *On the People's Terms: A Republican Theory and Model of Democracy*. Cambridge: Cambridge University Press.

Pinheiro, L.G. (2016) 'The Ableist Contract: Intellectual Disability and the Limits of Justice in Kant's Political Thought'. In B. Arneil and N.J. Hirschmann (eds), *Disability and Political Theory*. Cambridge: Cambridge University Press, pp. 43–78.

Scanlon, T.M. (2000) *What We Owe to Each Other*. New edn. Cambridge MA: Harvard University Press.

Simplican, S.C. (2015) *The Capacity Contract: Intellectual Disability and the Question of Citizenship*. Minneapolis, MN: University of Minnesota Press.

Taylor, M. (1976) *Anarchy and Cooperation*. Oxford: Blackwell.

Whyte, J. (2019) *The Morals of the Market: Human Rights and the Rise of Neoliberalism*. London: Verso.

Williams, E.E. (1994) *Capitalism and Slavery*. Durham, NC: University of North Carolina Press.

Wolff, R.P. (1998) *In Defence of Anarchism*. Reprint edn. Berkeley, CA: University of California Press.

Wollstonecraft, M. (2004) *A Vindication of the Rights of Woman*. Rev. edn. Ed. M. Brody. Harmondsworth: Penguin.

Part III

Liberal Modernity and Colonial Domination

11	Charles-Louis de Secondat, Baron de la Brede et de Montesquieu	Manjeet Ramgotra	185
12	John Stuart Mill	Inder S. Marwah	203
13	Karl Marx	Simon Choat	221
14	Friedrich Nietzsche	Willow Verkerk	239
15	Sayyid Qutb	Ayesha Omar	257
16	Edward W. Said	Rahul Rao	273

This Part of the book includes thinkers who have sought to diagnose modernity and its dominant ideology of liberalism—either by embracing liberal modernity, rejecting it, or taking up a more ambivalent position which recognizes its contradictory features.

Exactly what characterizes 'modernity' is a matter of debate. Historians typically view the modern age as beginning around 1500 and identify it with a series of economic, social, political, and intellectual developments in Europe in particular that marked a break with the medieval period. Economically, modernity is characterized by the decline of a primarily agrarian, feudal economy and the emergence of capitalism and, eventually, industrialization. These economic changes led to various sociological upheavals, with increasing urbanization and the development of new class relations, as the power of the aristocracy waned and that of the bourgeoisie grew. The new working classes also made increasing demands, and more democratic forms of governance slowly developed. Political power was consolidated in the nation state, at least in part at the expense of the Catholic Church, with power shifting from the Pope and monarchs to elected representatives of the people.

Intellectual developments functioned as both causes and consequences of these transformations. The transition from the Middle Ages to modernity coincided with the Renaissance, a flourishing of intellectual and artistic innovation inspired in part by the revival of classical Greek and Roman learning. Political thought during the Renaissance began to shift from justifications of the monarch's power to discussions of the rights of citizens to participate in political life. Later, the Scientific Revolution and the Age of Enlightenment both reflected and helped to accelerate the decline of religious authority and the growth of secular faith in reason and progress. In the nineteenth century in particular, modern political ideologies coalesced to offer competing visions of society, reflecting increasingly pluralist societies and the new need to legitimize expanding state power without reference to religious authority.

The primary ideology was liberalism—both in the sense that it was the first modern ideology to develop and that it was and arguably remains the dominant ideology. Central to liberalism is individualism. This is posited as both a methodological principle—with a claim that knowledge of society should begin with the individual, understood as rational, self-interested, and competitive—and an ethical goal: the aim of politics, liberals argue, should be to protect the individual and their liberties and rights (especially to property). Individualism ties together a number of liberalism's central tenets: the reliance on individual reason rather than on religious or traditional authorities; the ascription of inalienable rights to free and equal individuals; the call to limit the power of the state, which simultaneously protects and threatens those rights; and the emphasis on the toleration of differences.

The high point of modernity and its governing liberal ideology was the 'long nineteenth century' that stretched between the revolutions in France in 1789 and Russia in 1917. Many argue that since the mid-/late-twentieth century we have moved into a new era of postmodernity, in which nation states have become less important and new forms of capitalism have altered the class structure, with new social movements developing. Concomitantly, postmodern theories have challenged and questioned modern ideologies' emphasis on reason, progress, and universality.

The brief summary of liberal modernity offered thus far resembles standard accounts found elsewhere, but such accounts are typically highly Eurocentric in at least two ways. First, they do not acknowledge that temporal categories applied to Europe may be ill-suited to other regions of the globe. To claim that there was a rebirth of learning in the late medieval and early modern period, for example, may be applicable to Europe, but makes less sense for the Islamic world, which from the eighth to the fourteenth centuries saw huge advances in knowledge and learning. Second, such accounts ignore what is arguably the central and constitutive feature of modernity: European colonial expansion and domination. Decolonial scholars have used the term 'modernity/coloniality' to emphasize the centrality of colonialism to every aspect of modernity. We will not have understood the development of the modern capitalist economy if we conceptualize it only in terms of the growth of markets within Europe while ignoring its dependence on colonial exploitation. The expansion of the franchise and other political rights in Europe went hand in hand with the brutal denial and suppression of the same rights in European colonies; many European states secured legitimacy by redistributing to their citizens wealth that had been plundered from elsewhere.

The 'universal' rights celebrated by early theorists of liberalism were in practice restricted to white, European, male property-owners. Pressure for the extension of democratic rights came from below and was not always welcomed by liberals, who were often wary of the majoritarian impulses of democracy. In some cases, liberal thinkers simply omitted women, the working classes, and non-European and Indigenous peoples from their reflections on politics, while others explicitly justified their exclusion.

The tensions in liberalism are in evidence in the works of the French Enlightenment thinker Montesquieu, who is often cited as one of the earliest liberal thinkers for his opposition to despotism, endorsement of the separation of powers, and belief that commerce promoted peace. Montesquieu was also one of the first thinkers consciously to reflect on the meaning and significance of modernity, contrasting modern and ancient types of rule and forms of liberty. Yet, as Chapter 11 shows, Montesquieu's 'modernity' was distinguished not only from European antiquity but also from supposedly 'pre-modern' non-European societies. His political sociology, which connected governmental systems to different climates and terrains, postulated that peoples of the South, in hot climates outside of Europe, were lazy and servile. It was partly on this basis that he defended slavery and the slave trade (even while continuing to insist on the pacific nature of commerce).

Perhaps the greatest theorist of liberalism was the English philosopher and political economist John Stuart Mill, whose work is discussed in Chapter 12. Mill's liberty principle, which states that we are free to act as long as we do not harm others, has become a cornerstone of modern liberalism. Yet Mill was also a leading proponent of utilitarianism, which holds that actions and policies are right insofar as they promote the greatest happiness of the greatest number of people. This commitment to the general welfare, even potentially at the expense of minorities or individuals, is in tension with Mill's defence of individual liberty. While Mill supported representative government, including working-class and women's suffrage, he viewed many non-Europeans as incapable of self-government and believed that the liberty principle should not be applied to 'backward' societies. Portraying non-European societies as less advanced than European nations, Mill explicitly justified colonial rule (while nonetheless endorsing the abolition of slavery). In Mill's work, therefore, we find illuminated the contradictions and limits of liberal modernity: dedicated to social progress and the extension of liberty, and supportive of women's rights, Mill nonetheless believed that European imperialism was just and rational; relatively progressive in what he advocated for Europeans, Mill was reactionary and even racist in what he denied to non-Europeans.

Other thinkers of the nineteenth century more directly confronted the contradictions of liberal modernity. Perhaps the two greatest critics of modernity were the German philosophers Karl Marx and Friedrich Nietzsche, discussed in Chapters 13 and 14, respectively. Marx was, in one sense, a typical heir to the Enlightenment, committed to using reason to achieve human emancipation. Yet while Marx celebrated aspects of the modern world, he also revealed the darker side of social progress. For Marx, analysis of modernity meant analysis of capitalism. He argued that increased productivity and wealth had come at the expense of intensified exploitation; expanded commerce had not brought peace but was rather reliant on violence and colonial domination. Liberalism was for Marx the ideology of capitalism: its view of the state as a protector of free and equal individuals concealed class oppression.

Whereas Marx criticized modern capitalism, Nietzsche undertook a critique of modern culture and morality that characterized modernity as an age of nihilism: the decline of Christianity—the 'death of God'—had produced a crisis of values and meaning. Yet this disturbing condition was for Nietzsche also a moment of opportunity—an opportunity to destroy our old values in the name of new values. Nietzsche's efforts to link morality, reason, and truth to forms of power have been highly influential on postmodern thinkers. Challenging our faith in objective knowledge, his work has been interpreted in a variety of conflicting ways. Like Marx, his work has been taken up by feminist and postcolonial scholars even while racist and sexist elements can be found in both their works.

In their different ways, both Marx and Nietzsche viewed liberal modernity not as the culmination of human history but as a step towards an alternative future. Chapter 15 considers a more conservative critic of modernity: the twentieth-century Egyptian thinker Sayyid Qutb sought not to accelerate modernity but in effect to reverse it. Writing from and about the Arab world, Qutb saw clearly that the transition to modernity had resulted from colonial dispossession and occupation. Many Muslim thinkers and activists borrowed Western ideas and arguments to oppose Western imperialism, and later adapted socialist and Marxist critiques of liberalism to promote postcolonial reform and modernization. In contrast, Qutb sought Islamic alternatives to the Westernization and secularization that he rejected. Citing the Qur'an as the ultimate source of ethics, he conceptualized freedom as the submission to divine sovereignty and Islamic law. Qutb's anti-colonialism was socially conservative, especially with respect to gender roles, and since his death it has been associated with violent *Jihad*. But, as with other thinkers, his inclusion in this book does not imply endorsement of his ideas, and his work articulates an influential rejection of and alternative to Western political values.

A very different critique of Western imperialism was offered by the final thinker in this Part. The Palestinian American critic Edward Said is best known for his analysis of Orientalism, through which he explored the portrayal and constitution of the 'Orient' as backward, despotic, and superstitious, in contrast to the West's self-understanding as modern, enlightened, and rational. Unlike Qutb, however, Said's aim was not to reinforce the distinctions between the 'West' and the 'East'. Said instead emphasized the intertwined, hybrid histories and cultures produced by imperialism and of which his own life and work were examples. This emphasis on hybridity does not dilute opposition to imperialism—to the contrary, resistance to imperialism itself draws on these hybrid cultures, as when thinkers and activists use the language and ideas of the colonizer to oppose colonialism. Again, Said's own work is a good example here, and he continued to criticize and oppose both historical and contemporary forms of colonialism, including Israel's dispossession and occupation of Palestinian lives and lands (while simultaneously denouncing authoritarian Arab regimes).

In Said's work, we find analysis of the complex dynamics of liberal modernity/coloniality that are examined in all of the chapters in this Part: the simultaneous and interdependent growth of liberty and oppression, equality and exploitation, democracy and domination, with liberal modernity providing the resources to challenge and dismantle the ills to which it itself gave rise.

11 Charles-Louis de Secondat, Baron de la Brede et de Montesquieu

MANJEET RAMGOTRA

Chapter guide

This chapter briefly introduces the political theory and writings of French Enlightenment thinker, Montesquieu. It contends that Montesquieu's constitutional theory of the separation of powers promoted a strong government which advanced individual freedom, maintained internal stability against absolutism and populism and allowed the state to expand its boundaries at a moment in history when European powers were fighting each other to establish colonial empires across the world. Sections 11.1 and 11.2 present Montesquieu and the contexts in which he composed *The Spirit of the Laws*. Section 11.3 examines his constitutional theory and typology of governments. Section 11.4 analyses the various notions of time and progress that undergird Montesquieu's view of how the various constitutions in the world are ordered. Finally, Section 11.5, on commerce, peace, colonialism, and slavery, brings to light the tensions in Montesquieu's thought, notably in relation to freedom.

11.1 Introduction

Montesquieu (1689–1755) published *The Spirit of the Laws*, his key theoretical work, in 1748. Within two years, it had been translated into English, followed by the publication of multiple English editions within its first few decades. The work, circulated widely, was highly acclaimed, immensely influential, and impacted on many Enlightenment thinkers, including David Hume, Jean-Jacques Rousseau, and Edmund Burke (read more about Burke in Chapter 17). Montesquieu is best known for his constitutional theory of the separation and balance of powers and his view that commerce brings peace, both of which came to be considered as pillars of liberalism. Therefore, Montesquieu is regarded as an early liberal thinker (Pangle, 1973). Montesquieu's constitutional theory influenced the founding of the American and French Republics. It was discussed in the *Federalist Papers* and in the French constitutional deliberations (Appleby, 1992). In addition, his constitutional theory impacted on early twentieth-century post-colonial republican founding, including Turkey (Turnaoğlu, 2017) and India (Austin, 1966).

Key Thinker: David Hume

The Scottish Enlightenment philosopher David Hume (1711–1776) corresponded with Montesquieu and admired his thought. He agreed with Montesquieu that the hereditary nobility provided a barrier to despotism and acted to protect liberty (Moore, 2008). Hume treated the developing political economy

> of his day in the light of commerce, empire, and slavery. Like Montesquieu, Hume considered that commerce was a civil activity opposed to the plunder and destruction of conquest. Nevertheless, he glossed over the brutality of slavery and colonial empire in this understanding of commerce. Hume's main works include *A Treatise of Human Nature* (1740), *Enquiries Concerning Human Understanding* (1748), *Enquiries Concerning the Principles of Morals* (1751), and *History of England in eight volumes* (1754–1761).

Montesquieu's novel, *The Persian Letters* (Montesquieu (1973 [1721]) was also massively successful and widely read. It tells the story of two Persian aristocrats, Usbek and Rica, who travel from Isfahan (present-day Iran) to Paris. Montesquieu writes the novel in the form of letters written between the two Persian travellers, their friends, and wives, who live in seraglios (harems) back home. In these letters, the travellers recount their impressions and experiences of Western European culture in comparison to their own. In this way, Montesquieu imagines how his society appears through the eyes of the 'Eastern' Other. Throughout the novel, Montesquieu shifts between his own standpoint as a Frenchman and that of the Persian Other; as such, he reiterates an orientalist perspective of political and domestic rule in the East (Bourdieu, 1980). The novel also compares the position of women in the West to that of women in the East who live in harems and are subject to the sexual domination of men. This portrayal of domination in the domestic sphere symbolizes the despotic rule of the so-called Oriental Prince who governs according to whimsical desire. The *Persian Letters* are considered a work of satire that criticizes Parisian society and its decadence; yet, at the same time, the novel praises Western notions of reason and modernity. These themes are picked up in *The Spirit of the Laws*.

Montesquieu composed *The Spirit of the Laws* over a period of 20 years. In the book's Preface, he implored his readers not to judge this work on a hasty reading or on 'some few sentences', but 'to seek the design of the author . . . in the design of the work' (Montesquieu, 1989 [1748]: xliii). The work is encyclopaedic and counts over 30 books with numerous chapters. Inspired by his travels across Europe and the travel writings of merchants and explorers in the Americas, Africa, the Middle East, and Asia, it examines ideas and ways of life from across the world (Althusser, 1959: 11–27). The subtitle of this work reflects the book's vast scope that treats 'the relation the laws must have with the constitution of each government, mores, climate, religion, commerce, etc.' (Montesquieu, 1951: 227). Montesquieu draws on philosophical reflection, sociology and the historical experience of various types of political rule, including monarchic, republican, and despotic to develop a comprehensive understanding of the laws and ways of the world.

The Spirit of the Laws opens with a broad definition of the laws which 'are the necessary relations deriving from the nature of things' (Montesquieu, 1989 [1748]: 3 [I:1]). In addition, divinity, superior intelligences, beasts, men, and the material world have their own laws. To Montesquieu, laws are the relations between a primary reason (natural reason/law) and different beings, as well as 'the relations of these various beings to each other' (ibid.: 3 [I:1]). Human beings, as well as animate and inanimate objects are subject to the invariable laws of the universe, physics, and biology. Yet they are also subject to laws that govern relations between them. Hence there is a certain determinism and relativism about these laws and relations. Human beings are free:

> man constantly violates the laws god has established and changes those he himself establishes; he must guide himself, and yet he is a limited being; he is subject to ignorance and error, as are all finite intelligences; he loses even the imperfect knowledge he has. As a feeling creature, he falls subject to a thousand passions.
>
> (ibid.: 5 [I:1])

Montesquieu examines how things relate to each other through reason (intelligence), feelings (passion), and invariable laws (necessity). The laws that arise from these relations comprise the spirit of the laws. This approach underpins much of his analysis and conclusions, and also explains the complexity as well as contradictions of his massive work.

11.2 Context and scope

11.2.1 Transatlantic commerce, economic and political change

Montesquieu lived and wrote during a period of great change as European nations extended colonial empire across the world. This entailed the decline of feudalism and the early development of industrial capitalism. This was also the period of Enlightenment when the arts, sciences, and mechanics flourished. Liberty, equality, and one's place in the world were debated. Yet, this moment was also characterized by conflict between European nations over their colonies.

At the beginning of the eighteenth century, the slave trade was at its most lucrative. From 1701 to 1800, European, mainly English, Portuguese, and French, slave traders kidnapped and sold approximately 6,132,900 Africans into slavery in the New World (Blackburn, 1997: 383). In this context, Montesquieu (1989 [1748]: 338–339 [XX: 1–2]) portrayed commerce as a peaceful activity. In a chapter on Europe and 'the discovery of two new worlds', he describes the trade that connected America, 'Asia and Africa to Europe'. This included the triangular slave trade between Europe, Africa, and the West Indian colonies. To Montesquieu, the French colonies in the Antilles were 'admirable' and trade with them was equitable, based on mutual need and exchange: 'they have objects of commerce that we do not and cannot have; [and] they lack that which is the object of our commerce'. He further underlines claims that human trafficking was necessary: 'voyages to Africa became necessary; they furnished men to work the mines and lands of America' (ibid.: 392 [XXI: 21]). In concluding this chapter, he observes that Europe was at the height of its power, given its military engagements and commercial presence across the world (ibid.: 392–393 [XXI: 21]).

Montesquieu justified the slave trade on the basis of necessity. This allowed him to override the question regarding the morality of this trade and to assert that there was no other choice. International trade and commerce generated a great deal of wealth and supported the rise of a newly rich merchant class of people. These changing socio-economic circumstances led to social instability as the feudal system began to give way to a market economy. At the same time, the French monarchy had become increasingly absolute, which provoked a series of aristocratic and popular uprisings in the seventeenth century known as *La Fronde*. The nobility protested against the usurpation of its political authority in the *parlements* (twelve regional courts that originated in the thirteenth century and ensured that the crown ruled according to the laws), through which they could challenge and halt the king's legislative decisions (De Dijn, 2013). Poor people, peasants, and artisans were increasingly impoverished. Their lives were subject to great insecurity due to war, oppression, and taxation which they also rebelled against (Keohane, 1980: 9). In response, the monarchy became increasingly absolute. Therefore, Montesquieu theorized a 'fundamental constitution' (1989 [1748]: 164 [XI: 6]) that would allow the state to pursue colonial empire without collapsing into disarray or absolutism. At the same time, this constitution would have to be robust enough to confront change and to harness a new political economy based on trade and the market. The political structures he proposed would limit the scope and power of a centralized monarchical power, locate political authority in the body of the landed nobility, and broaden the political base to give greater political voice to those who contributed to the public wealth through their commercial endeavours abroad and at home (Larrère, 2001: 346–353; Ramgotra, 2014).

Read more about **Montesquieu's** life and work by accessing the thinker biography on the online resources: www.oup.com/he/Ramgotra-Choat1e

11.2.2 Climatology

The colonialist and global contexts led Montesquieu to consider how the material world shapes people, their ways of life, culture, mores, and habits, all of which are related to laws. He developed a theory of climatology which asserted that human beings are influenced by the climate in and terrain on which they live. These affect the production of the material necessities of life and influence human behaviour. Montesquieu (1989 [1748]) conducted experiments on a sheep's tongue to analyse the reactions of the fibres and muscles of the body to hot and cold temperatures. He also considered how the fertility or barrenness of the land impacted work ethics, property, and governmental types. He then made assumptions about how cold and hot climates affect human character (ibid.: 231–234 [XIV: 2]).

To Montesquieu, people of the North, mainly Europeans, are subject to cold climates and live on barren lands. He describes Northerners as vigorous, 'courageous' and 'confident'. Their muscles are taut and springy which makes them stronger as more blood goes to the heart. Yet their land is barren, so they have to cultivate and work it to make it bear fruit. Consequently, they are industrious, sober, and free. Moreover, he notes, Northerners recognize their superiority and are less vengeful because they think themselves secure (ibid.: 232 [XIV: 2]). By contrast, people of the South are subject to heat. Montesquieu contends that their muscles are lax, weak, less springy, which makes them slack since less blood circulates to the heart. Their land is fertile, which contributes to their sloth as they do not have to cultivate it to yield fruit. They can subsist simply by gathering the fruit (ibid.: 231–234 [XIV: 2]). Montesquieu concludes that Southerners are 'weak', fearful, 'timid', lazy, impassioned, and servile. His observation that many fertile parts of the world are uninhabited and that infertile places are populated by great peoples supports arguments for colonization. In the North, 'the terrain seems to refuse everything' and populations lack necessary goods to subsist, therefore Northerners have to look for more fertile countries to preserve their life and satisfy their needs. This, Montesquieu notes, leads to 'invasion and devastation' (ibid.: 286–287 [XVIII: 2–4]). By contrast, inhabitants of fertile lands have no need to look elsewhere for subsistence.

In part, his argument is supported by the view that the cultivation of land also cultivates human beings. Those who do not work the land not only lack cultivation, but they do not have any real notion about property ownership and the freedom this procures. By contrast, those who own property enjoy independence and autonomy since they are not dependent on others for their subsistence. In Western understandings of property ownership, the ownership of land and management of an estate contribute to one's independence and freedom; whereas lack of ownership leads to dependence (ibid.: 285–291, 238 [XVIII: 1–12]; Aristotle, 1996; Locke, 2003).

To Montesquieu, the effect of the climate on human character is deterministic. Yet, these biases that promoted the superiority of the West through the association of freedom, strength, and virtue with peoples from cold northern climates and inferiority, servility, weakness and vice with peoples of hot southern climates were discriminatory (Bourdieu, 1980; Montesquieu, 1989 [1748]: 234–235). Montesquieu's writings convey a Eurocentric perspective that considers the North as superior to the South and in which Africans are seen to be barbaric, Indigenous peoples in the Americas as savage, Asians as servile, and Europeans as free, cultivated, and civilized (ibid.: 283, 284, 290–291, 355 [XVII: 6–7; XVIII: 10–12; XXI: 2–3]). These myths that derive from a tenuous sociological understanding of the material existence of different people in different geographies supported the colonial domination of superior and reasoned peoples over inferior and sub-rational peoples. They also informed his understanding of political constitutions.

11.2 Context and scope: Key Points

- Montesquieu composed his main political writings in contexts of: social and political unrest; the decline of feudalism and the early development of industrial capitalism; the Enlightenment; conflict between European nations over their colonies, and increasingly absolutist monarchy.
- Montesquieu lauds Europe's power in the world, considers their colonies admirable and sees the slave trade as necessary.
- Montesquieu's theory of climate asserts that cold and hot temperatures affect bodily fibres and muscles, making people of the North strong, courageous, industrious, and free and peoples of the South weak, timid, lazy, and servile.
- Montesquieu's claims that divided sovereignty guarantees freedom and commerce produces peace are considered cornerstones of liberalism.

11.3 Theory of the separation and balance of powers and individual freedom

Although Montesquieu was not the first to argue that power ought to be separated into its different functions and distributed to different institutional bodies, his examination of the English constitution as a moderate type of government that had political liberty as its object has been highly influential and is seen to be an early articulation of a key principle of liberal democracy. He refers to it as the 'fundamental constitution'. It provides the basis of his ideal conception that builds upon the English and to a certain extent Roman constitutions.

11.3.1 Divided sovereignty

According to Montesquieu (1989 [1748]), in every state, there are three kinds of powers: legislative and two types of executive power. Legislative power entails the authority to make laws either for a fixed time or in perpetuity and to correct, change or repeal existing laws. The first type of executive power regards the right of nations. It includes the political power to make peace and war, send or receive embassies, establish security and prevent invasions. This power has at its disposal the use of force to maintain external and internal security and to enforce the laws. Montesquieu calls this power 'the executive power of the state' (ibid.: 156–157 [XI: 6]).

The second type of executive power deals with civil right. By this power, the executive 'punishes crimes or judges disputes between individuals'. Montesquieu calls this the 'power of judging'. He situates it in an independent judiciary and stipulates that it should be absolutely independent from the legislative and executive powers. If the power to judge was not distinct from legislative authority, 'the power over the life and liberty of the citizens would be arbitrary'. Were it 'joined to the executive power, the judge could have the force of an oppressor' (ibid.: 156–157 [XI: 6]).

The role of the judiciary is to provide fair judgement and to ensure that the state is ruled by laws. To Montesquieu, the roles and functions of the executive and legislative powers are distinct and ought to be attached to different institutions so that power does not become despotic. For if the legislative and executive powers were united in a single person or in a single institution, 'there is no liberty, because one can fear that the same monarch or senate that makes tyrannical laws will execute them tyrannically' (ibid.: 156–157 [XI: 6]).

To Montesquieu, the separation of these powers guarantees individual liberty. Only when these powers are distinct and exercised by different institutions can individuals be free since they would not be subject to arbitrary, absolute or oppressive power. This constitutional structure divides sovereignty and creates the background conditions that would promote the rule of law and limit power. Its conceptual opposite is the undivided, absolute, and arbitrary sovereignty that unites all powers in the body of one man or an assembly of men.

Montesquieu challenges Bodin's and Hobbes's prevailing theory of absolute sovereign power as the final authority of the state (Hobbes, 1996: 121–142 [XVIII–XX]) (read more about Hobbes in Chapter 5). An absolute sovereign created unity, maintained peace domestically, and allowed the state to expand without collapsing. By contrast, republics based on the mixed constitution incorporated the nobility and people in governing institutions, but lacked the central unity to expand externally without collapsing internally. Montesquieu's theory of divided sovereignty resolved this weakness since it established a centralized executive power that could facilitate colonial expansion and mediate social conflict between the nobles and people.

> ### Key Thinker: Jean Bodin
>
> French Renaissance thinker, Jean Bodin (1529/30–1596) was a lawyer, philosopher, and historian. He is best known for his conception of undivided, absolute, and perpetual sovereignty as the supreme power to make laws—the highest and final power of the state. This conception of sovereignty was distinguished from government. Bodin developed this conception in his major work *The Six Books of the Commonwealth* (1576). Although this work explored various types of constitutions and mixed forms of government, he articulated a preference for monarchy.

Montesquieu (1989 [1748]: 63 [V: 14]) observes that most peoples are subject to despotic government and even though people try to resist it, it is very difficult to establish a moderate government that divides sovereign power. For 'one must combine powers, regulate them, temper them, make them act; one must give one power a ballast . . . to put it in a position to resist another; this is a masterpiece of legislation that chance rarely produces and prudence is rarely allowed to produce'. On the other hand, despotic government 'is uniform throughout' for 'only passions are needed to establish it, everyone is good enough for that'.

Montesquieu's constitutional theory is based on a mechanistic and scientific analysis of power that would hold for all places and times. Unless power is stopped by another countervailing power, it will become absolute, and liberty will be lost.

> Political liberty is found only in moderate governments. But it is not always in moderates states. It is present only when power is not abused, but it has eternally been observed that any man who has power is led to abuse it; . . .
> So that one cannot abuse power, power must check power by the arrangement of things.
>
> (ibid.: 155 [XI: 4])

At the same time, he draws on the sociological understanding of the state to distribute the various powers and functions of government to the social classes. In doing so, he broadens the political base by incorporating the newly rich bourgeoisie and the landed nobility in a new constitutional form based on the separation and balance of powers.

> **Key Concept: Liberty**
>
> Liberty is a multi-layered concept. On the one hand, individual liberty is the freedom to live in security without fear of domination from either the state or other members of society. Therefore, political power must be limited and exercised according to laws and citizens must abide by these. To Montesquieu (1989 [1748]: 155 [XI: 3]), liberty is the freedom to act within the constraints of the law and not beyond. On the other hand, liberty is the power to make laws, to rule, and be ruled according to these. Yet not all people can rule. However, by electing representatives, the people govern indirectly and must be contented with the freedom to live in security. In his ideal constitution, the landed nobility enjoy the privilege and political authority to make laws and the people gain the political freedom to contest these laws in order to ensure their government does not become oppressive.

11.3.2 The separation of powers: checks and balances

Montesquieu allocates executive power to the rule of one person, either a monarch or president, and shares the legislative power between the hereditary nobility and the wealthy portion of the people. The legislature, or legislative assembly, is divided into upper and lower chambers. The nobility sit in the upper chamber and enjoy the authority to propose laws. As they have a fixed stake in the state, it is important that they initiate laws that would have jurisdiction over their property. The elected representatives of the people comprise the lower chamber. They are not allowed to propose laws but are granted the liberty to discuss the proposed legislation of the upper chamber and to reject these. The absence of contestation would signal their acceptance of the laws. In this manner, the people make and consent to the laws. Effectively, each social class has its own proceedings and contributes to the legislative aspect of sovereign power (Montesquieu, 1989 [1748]: 160–163 [XI: 6]).

Both chambers can veto each other. The lower chamber can veto or annul a proposal made by the upper chamber and the upper chamber can stop the lower chamber's proceedings. The executive power can veto either of the two legislative chambers and thus mediate any conflict between the social classes. However, neither legislative chamber can veto the executive. The legislature can check to see that the executive power carries out its duties well, but it cannot stop it from acting. As 'the legislative body is composed of two parts', Montesquieu writes, 'the one will be chained to the other by their reciprocal faculty of vetoing. The two will be bound by the executive power, which will itself be bound by the legislative power' (ibid.: 164 [XI: 6]). As they are bound by each other, they can only move forward when they act in concert.

Executive power is situated in the body of one person who is sacred (ibid.: 162 [XI: 6]). The executive is limited to executing the laws. Montesquieu promotes a strong central power that would direct the state, command the army and police, maintain internal stability by mediating social conflict between the nobles and people, defend the state from external threats and facilitate colonial expansion abroad. Equally, Montesquieu advocates individual freedom and considers individuals as political units who can vote, if they meet property requirements. This constitution could withstand both the internal threats of absolutism from above and rebellion from below. It limits executive power to the execution of the laws and protection of the state, and incorporates the voice of the newly rich people who heralded social and economic change. This extends the political base and allows the state to reap the benefits of empire and create a new market economy that would allow this wealth to circulate. Finally, it creates stability by maintaining the privilege and authority of the nobility as a moderating power.

Montesquieu limits inclusion in the political process. Although he claims that, 'in a free state, every man considered to have a free soul, should be governed by himself' (ibid.: 159 [XI: 6]), he does not consider all men to be free. Moreover, those who are free would be too numerous to assemble in order to participate directly in government. Therefore, he recommends that the people enter government only to elect representatives.

Montesquieu does not extend suffrage to all members of the population; he excludes women, children, and those men whose 'estate is so humble that they are deemed to have no will of their own' (ibid.: 160 [XI: 6]). These people, in Montesquieu's opinion, do not have free souls since they are governed by and are dependent on others. Only the higher and more wealthy ranks of the popular social classes who owned adequate property were included.

It is widely debated as to whether this constitution is a constitutional monarchy or a republic since it includes both a monarch and the elements of aristocratic and democratic republics. To Montesquieu, it is a free state, a fundamental constitution that sets political liberty as its goal and divides sovereignty to create the conditions under which citizens could enjoy 'that tranquillity of spirit which comes from the opinion each one has of his security, and in order for him to have this liberty the government must be such that one citizen cannot fear another citizen' (ibid.: 157 [XI: 6]).

11.3.3 Types of government

In his study of the various governments that exist and have existed in history, Montesquieu advances a new typology of constitutions. He rejects the classical Aristotelian typology of simple constitutions that classifies government in terms of the one, the few, and the many, which translates into monarchy, aristocracy, and democracy when political rule aims at the common good, or tyranny, oligarchy, and anarchy when power is corrupt. These simple types are prone to corruption since they combine both executive and legislative power in a single body of rulers. Again, without any countervailing powers to stop the abuse of power, rulers will inevitably govern in their own interests. To Montesquieu, the exercise of power for the good of all is insufficient, the institutional structure must keep power in check. Therefore, he devises a typology of mixed constitutions which divide power among the constituent groups of the state. These include monarchies and republics as moderate types and despotism as the opposing, corrupt type.

11.3.3.1 Monarchy

Montesquieu underlines that the ancients lacked a proper understanding of monarchy since they did not conceptualize the subordinate and intermediate powers with which the monarch rules (ibid.: 167 [XI: 8]). Monarchy is a moderate form of government in which power is channelled through the body of the nobility (ibid.: 17–18 [II: 4]). In feudal monarchies and those of Montesquieu's time, the nobility of robe and sword protected the laws and the realm (ibid.: 351 [XX: 22]). Through the institution of the *parlements* (see Section 11.2.1), the nobility maintained a depository of laws and ensured that the monarch ruled according to laws. Without the nobility, there would be no monarchy. If the monarch ruled alone, the state would be despotic and power, arbitrary and absolute (ibid.: 18 [II: 4]).

Each constitution in Montesquieu's typology is characterized by the spring that puts it into motion which is distinct from the structure of each government. Honour, the spring of monarchy, reflects merit, distinction, pre-eminence, rank and 'hereditary nobility'. As individuals strive to distinguish themselves in the pursuit of honour, they bind the social whole and make it move forward: 'each person works for the common good, believing he works for his individual interests' (ibid.: 27 [III: 7]). This way of thinking about politics differs from the classical perspective where the pursuit of self-interest leads to corruption. Here, the individual pursuit of private interest advances the public good and contributes to the public wealth.

11.3.3.2 Republics

In his classification of republics, Montesquieu rejects the pure democracy of ancient times when the people as a body ruled, since they were unstable and prone to corruption. Rather, he defends a mixed type of democratic republic in which the people participated in government alongside the landed nobility. To Montesquieu, the Roman republic presented a powerful historical example of a mixed constitution in which the people selected their magistrates to do their business and were 'guided by a council or senate' (ibid.: 11 [II: 2]). He considered these republics as moderate since the people and nobles checked each other's power.

He does not reject pure aristocratic republics and defends the privilege and position of the landed nobility, whose power, he argues, ought to be hereditary. They do not require as much virtue as the people since they are 'equal among themselves', few in number, leisured, educated, and bring 'reason' to the state. They can more readily see the public interest beyond their private interests (ibid.: 24 [III: 4], Carrithers, 2001: 138–147; Rahe, 2001: 70). To Montesquieu, their virtue is the 'spirit of moderation', which is the 'soul' of aristocracy since it tempers the excesses of the power of one and the many (Montesquieu, 1989 [1748]: 25, 51 [III: 5, V: 8]). Moderate political rule divides sovereignty and advances the rule of law and reason.

> **Key Concept: Political virtue**
>
> Political virtue, the spring of republics, entails 'love of the homeland and of equality' (ibid.: xli [Author's Foreword]). In ancient thought, political virtue obliged people to prioritize public over private interests. This required a measure of self-denial, a 'renunciation of oneself', which Montesquieu describes as 'painful' and impracticable (ibid.: 35 [IV: 5]). Therefore, he transforms the meaning of virtue to 'love of the republic' (ibid.: 22–23 [III: 3]). As love 'is a feeling' and not a consequence of knowledge, both the lowest and highest men of the republic could share in it (ibid.: 42 [V: 2]). Here political virtue is not an objective end obtained through the reasoned deliberation of equals on what is best for all. It is a feeling, a passion that does not require reason. Virtue becomes 'love of the laws and homeland' (ibid.: 36 [IV: 5]). Effectively, Montesquieu reconceptualizes political virtue to promote obedience to the rule of law and the public good.

In addition, Montesquieu envisions a commercial republic. He emphasizes that commerce is related to the constitution. It neither suits monarchy nor despotism. Rather, it suits the government of the many since it integrated the people who had acquired wealth through commerce (ibid.: 340 [XX: 4]; Douglass, 2012). They desired political voice and could be incorporated as citizens who would cultivate a love for the republic and its laws, exercise minimal positive rights and contribute their newfound wealth. He remarks that 'the spirit of commerce brings with it the spirit of frugality, economy, moderation, work, wisdom, tranquillity, order, and rule. Thus, as long as this spirit continues to exist the wealth it produces has no bad effect' (Montesquieu, 1989 [1748]: 48 [V: 6]). Merchants provide a steady flow of goods that they trade across the world and increase their business and profits incrementally. Montesquieu refers to this as 'economic commerce' (ibid.: 340–345 [XX: 4–11]). Based on free market exchange, this commerce was presented as peaceful, even though it used slave labour to extract natural resources from European colonies, this was depicted as different from plunder and the pursuit of luxury.

11.3.3.3 Despotism

To Montesquieu, people obey a despotic ruler out of fear. Fear, the spring of despotism, suppresses courage and ambition. Individuals are reduced to an extreme equality as they are all equally subject to despotic oppression (ibid.: 28 [III: 9]). Despotism unites legislative, executive and judicial power in a single person who 'governs according to his will and caprices' (ibid.: 21 [III: 2]). As one person makes the laws and enforces them, there is no independent body or depository of laws 'which announce[s] the laws when they are made and recall[s] them when they are forgotten'. Such 'fundamental laws' do not exist in despotic states (ibid.: 19 [II: 4]).

It is frequently argued that Montesquieu uses the Oriental Prince as a foil to criticize the absolutist French monarchy of his day; however, he invariably associates despotism with the Oriental Prince who owns all property, controls absolutely everything in his state and subjects his people to political servitude. As the people do not own private property, they lack the independence to oppose the despot and lack the autonomy to cultivate virtue and experience in ruling (ibid.: 61 [V: 14]). Montesquieu portrays the subjects of oriental despots as lazy, lascivious, and servile (ibid.: 20 [II: 5], 62–63 [V: 14]). Despotism is an extreme, oppressive, and immoderate form of rule. It is the opposite of all moderate government including monarchy, republics, and Montesquieu's fundamental constitution. Montesquieu locates despotism in three places: (1) conceptually in Bodin's and Hobbes's theories of indivisible and absolute sovereignty; (2) in the Eurocentric and orientalist construction of the Oriental Prince; and, (3) historically, in the Spanish threat of universal monarchy (Ramgotra, 2014).

> ### 11.3 Theory of the separation and balance of powers and individual freedom: Key Points
>
> - Montesquieu devises a fundamental constitution that divides sovereign power into its executive and legislative functions and establishes an independent judiciary. This constitution moderates political power and guarantees individual liberty, namely the freedom to live in security.
> - Montesquieu's constitution incorporates those who own landed property and those who own mobile property (acquired through commerce) on a hierarchical basis within the legislature and establishes a strong centralized executive power.
> - To Montesquieu, monarchy is a moderate and mixed type of government that depends on the nobility to channel power and maintain the laws.
> - Montesquieu analyses a variety of republics and advances those that include both the noble and popular social classes in a mixed form of government.
> - Montesquieu reconceptualizes political virtue to mean the love of the laws and homeland.

11.4 Time, progress, and conquest

11.4.1 Time and progress

There are three temporalities in Montesquieu's theory: (1) cyclical, in which the simple constitutions are subject to the cycle of growth, decay, decline, and death; (2) linear, in which human beings progress from existing as solitary creatures to living in society; and (3) rupture, where cyclical time is disrupted with the creation of stable constitutions that stand outside of recurring revolutions and where change is so great that the past is no longer relevant to the present and imagined futures. Montesquieu draws a boundary between the ancient and modern worlds. Although much could be learned from antiquity, it was no longer appropriate for imitation in the modern world, given the shift in ways of being, new geographies, and scientific progress. In antiquity, states followed the cyclical pattern and found stability in mixed (monarchical and republican) forms of government. Many states, in Montesquieu's day, were either monarchical or despotic. They were legitimated by divine right or created through social contract. Yet, to Montesquieu, neither ancient types of rule nor absolute sovereignty were suitable for a new mode of existence in which international trade produced great sources of wealth that was distributed more broadly. Therefore, he presents an evolutionary story of man's progress from his solitary existence in the state of nature to the creation of society, war, and the founding of states according to law and right. This story underpins his constitutional theory and serves to categorize various states according to levels of development and decay.

Montesquieu (1989 [1748] : 6–7 [I: 2]) concurs with natural law theorists that natural laws existed prior to those made by men in society (Courtney, 2001: 51–56; Macdonald, 2003: 121–123). He delineates four stages in the state of nature. Initially, men lived as solitary, sentient, timid and fearful creatures. As they encountered other human beings, they felt themselves as inferior, not equals. They did not attack each other since they felt their weakness rather than strength. The realization that their fear was mutual allowed them to overcome it, to approach one another, to feel attracted to the opposite sex and enjoy being together. From these first encounters, they began to communicate with each other and developed reason and speech. They formed a primitive type of society in which they lived together as equals. To Montesquieu, the laws of nature reflect the conditions necessary to sustain life and arise from the sentient nature of human beings. The first law is peace, the second is 'to seek nourishment'. The natural attraction and inclination human beings have for each other form the third law; and the fourth is 'living in society' not as brute animals but as communicative and rational beings (Montesquieu (1989 [1748]: 6–7 [I: 2]).

Montesquieu's depiction of this peaceful state of nature challenges Hobbes's negative conception of this state as one of competition, mistrust, violent conflict, and war. Montesquieu contends that war, domination, and empire are complex ideas that would not exist in the state of nature where man's rational and intellectual faculties lay dormant (ibid.: 6–7 [I: 2]). These would only occur in society, where individuals compete and conflict. Contrastingly, in the state of nature, men had the capacity to know, but not knowledge. They were guided by their feelings which led to their mutual attraction, procreation, and development of society. However, once men lost their timidity and weakness, they began to feel their strength, to distinguish themselves, which gave rise to inequality and eventually war (ibid.: 7 [I: 3]).

In the aftermath of war, men create positive laws. These include: the right of nations which regulates relations between states; political right that concerns 'the relation between those who govern and those who are ruled'; and civil right that regulates relations between citizens (ibid.: 7 [I: 3]). Montesquieu does not present a social contract theory through which all relinquish their right of nature to an indivisible sovereign power and state. Rather, he claims that the 'union of all individual strengths' forms the political state, and the union of individual wills forms the civil state (ibid.: 8 [I: 3]). The principle of divided sovereignty underscores this conception. The union of strengths constitutes executive power, and the union of wills constitutes the legislative will. The former has the power to enforce the authority of the latter.

These registers of time are at play in Montesquieu's work: the cyclical conception maps onto states that existed historically and shows their fragility and sensitivity to the cycles of creation, growth, and decline (Krause, 2002: 714–720). The linear understanding of time demonstrates development from the state of nature to civil society and decline. It also allows for states to exist outside the unstable and recurring cycle of revolutions, brought about through change and corruption. These temporalities map onto his classification of contemporaneous peoples and places. For instance, tribal societies in Africa and America were depicted as being in the state of nature, most European states were portrayed as moderate political societies (monarchies or republics), and Oriental and Asian civilizations were seen to be in decline, subject to despotism. Even though Montesquieu advances a hierarchical view of the world as comprised of barbaric, tribal, civilized, and corrupt states in constant flux and evolution, he nevertheless asserts the universality of the modern civilized state, which was strong, stable, and could dominate over underdeveloped or decaying states.

From this tableau of ancient and modern constitutions, stages of civilizations and types of states, Montesquieu devised a fundamental constitution based on his theory of divided sovereignty that would guarantee individual freedom from absolute and arbitrary political rule. In addition, it had the capacity to withstand cyclical change and rupture as encountered through complete and unanticipated shifts in knowledge or ways of being. Such ruptures in time represent decisive breaks with the past, as in Montesquieu's preference for the modern over the ancient. This figured into an understanding of modernity and the modern world characterized by science, better knowledge of the world acquired through increased communications, exchange of ideas and goods from across the globe, empirical method, individual liberty, and free political rule in developed states. This concept of modernity was not only constituted through its opposition to antiquity as a period in time, but also it was constructed through its opposition to states and societies considered premodern (underdeveloped, savage, or barbaric) or in decline and subject to despotic rule (Estève, 2002; Ramgotra, 2022). Although Montesquieu is disparaging of the ways of life and knowledge of European 'others', these knowledges did inform European science and progress (Chakrabarty, 2000: 10–13; Koselleck, 2002).

11.4.2 Conquest

In books IX and X, Montesquieu (1989 [1748]) examines the laws in relation to defensive and offensive force. These books defend the expansive state and justify conquest and colonialism. In book IX, he proposes a combination of monarchy and republics to create a strong constitution that defends against external aggression, for small republics are subject to the pitfalls of invasion and large ones to internal vice. Most governments, he observes, would be ruled by one person alone had men not 'devised a constitution that has all the internal advantages of republican government and the external force of monarchy' (ibid.: 131 [IX: 1]). This is the 'federal republic'. It assembles several small states into a large one. The strength of this constitution lies in its combination of the spirit of republics which is 'peace and moderation' with the spirit of monarchy which is 'war and expansion' (ibid.: 132 [IX: 1]). Montesquieu's fundamental constitution outlined in book XI, Chapter 6 does precisely this: it combines the advantages of republics and monarchies to create stability (peace and moderation) at home and empire (war and expansion) abroad.

In Book X, Montesquieu defends the use of pre-emptive force as the right of natural defence (ibid.: 138 [X: 1]) and defines conquest as an 'acquisition that carries with it the spirit of preservation and use, and not that of destruction' (ibid.: 139 [X: 3]). This refers to European colonies abroad which were exploited for their natural resources. He characterizes this approach to conquest as modern and contrasts it with ancient Roman ways of plunder and destruction of conquests. Modern Europeans had advanced in their reason, religion, philosophy, and customs. Even though the Spanish reproduced the extreme violence of the ancients in their conquest of the New World, the Dutch, French, and British sought to protect their conquests and were less brutal. With regard to the plight of the conquered and whether they can be enslaved, Montesquieu discerns that 'servitude is never the purpose of conquest, but it is sometimes a necessary means for achieving preservation' (ibid.: 140 [X: 3]). From a moral point of view, Montesquieu considers slavery to be wrong as an end in and of itself; nevertheless, he admits it on a temporary basis and justifies it as a means to preserve conquered territories. Preservation and use are tied to commerce and the continual exploitation of West Indian colonies for their raw materials, such as sugar, cotton, indigo, and tobacco that were cheaply and expediently obtained through slave labour.

These two books precede the famous Book XI on 'Political Liberty and the Constitution'. They support Montesquieu's construction of the fundamental constitution that combines the power of the monarchy in the executive and the moderation of republics in the legislature. The strength of this constitution lies in its ability to guarantee individual freedom and security, to confront external aggression, to expand and integrate the mobile wealth acquired through the commercial exploitation of its colonies and finally to adapt to new economic structures.

11.4 Time, progress, and conquest: Key Points

- Three temporalities run throughout Montesquieu's work: cyclical, linear, and rupture.
- Montesquieu depicts the state of nature as solitary and peaceful from which are derived fundamental laws of nature: peace, nourishment, reproduction, and living in society.
- Montesquieu presents an understanding of political societies in the world as hierarchical.
- Montesquieu's fundamental constitution combines a republican spirit of peace and moderation and a monarchical spirit of war and expansion to create a strong state.
- Conquest is an acquisition that must be preserved.

11.5 Commerce and slavery

11.5.1 Commerce

Montesquieu is widely acclaimed for his notion that '*le doux commerce*'—soft or sweet commerce—is a gentle activity which 'cures destructive prejudices' and promotes peace since it is better to trade than to engage in violent conflict to acquire goods. Commerce also refers to the exchange of ideas; as Montesquieu remarks, it spreads 'knowledge of the mores of all nations everywhere' which has good consequences. It produces an exact sense of justice between trading partners and places nations in a mutual dependency to fulfil their needs and interests in buying and selling (Montesquieu (1989 [1748]: 338–339 [XX: 1–2]). Peaceful trading relations occurred between equals, among European nations with each other; whereas trade relations between Europe and the rest of the world were colonial. Moreover, the main commerce of his day was the slave trade. Colonialism and the slave trade were brutal and dehumanizing activities that entailed the domination of others, not the peaceful commerce Montesquieu describes.

Montesquieu discusses colonialism in the chapters on conquest and commerce. He contrasts the Spanish who treated 'newly discovered lands' as 'objects of conquest' with the refined nations of Europe who saw these lands as 'objects of commerce'. These refined nations allowed trading companies to establish empire for trade and to act as auxiliary powers to govern 'these distant states' without 'encumbering the principal state'. Overseas colonies were placed in a 'kind of dependence' on the European metropole, and their 'purpose', Montesquieu remarks, was 'to engage in commerce under better conditions than one has with neighbouring peoples with whom all advantages are reciprocal'. The mother country maintained a monopoly of trade with the colony because 'the goal of the establishment was to extend commerce, not to found a town or a new empire' (ibid.: 391 [XXI: 21]). Although Montesquieu presents the creation of colonies for trade as refined and civilized, he acknowledges that trading companies maintained the empire for the metropole which ultimately backed them by military force.

Montesquieu outlines some 'fundamental laws' of Europe. First, commerce between the metropole and the foreign colony is 'a pure monopoly' enforceable by law; trade within the colonies is prohibited. Second, the loss of the colonies' freedom to trade is compensated by the military and legal 'protection of the mother country'. Third, given the prohibition of foreign commerce with a colony, navigation of its seas is illegal unless provided for by treaty (ibid.: 391–392 [XXI: 21]). To Montesquieu, it is contrary neither to natural right nor positive law for a people to cede their lands and/or seas to another power: 'Nations, which are to the entire universe what individuals are to a state, govern themselves as do the latter by natural right and by laws they have made for themselves. A people can give up the sea to another as it can give up land' (ibid.: 392 [XXI: 21]).

In Montesquieu's view, conquest is an acquisition to be preserved. The metropole protects its colonies whose purpose is trade which entails the exploitation of the lands and peoples. This is 'economic commerce' where resources are extracted and traded on a regular basis, according to the principles of frugality, need and use rather than luxury and ostentation (ibid.: 340–341 [XX: 4–5]). Yet, the extraction of these resources depended on slave labour; and, as noted above, Montesquieu considered voyages to Africa to supply the labour to work the mines and lands as necessary.

11.5.2 Slavery

Part three of *The Spirit of the Laws* treats laws and slavery in relation to the nature of climate and terrain. Three of its six books are on slavery: civil, domestic, and political (XV–XVII). Montesquieu (1989 [1748]) defines civil slavery as the right of one man to absolutely possess and control another as in the master/slave relation, and domestic slavery as the subjugation of women to men in the home. Montesquieu does not discuss gender inequality in Europe but focuses on polygamy and the subjugation of women in Asia and the Middle East (ibid.: 264–271 [XVI: 2–15]). He understands political servitude as the complete subjection of a people to the despotic rule of one man alone. Montesquieu's approach is comparative and relativist. He examines slavery in countries of the Global South and not in the North, where slavery had been abolished, which is regarded as a consequence of climate. Throughout his work, Montesquieu makes categorical statements that things cannot be other than they are, such as: 'the cowardice of the peoples of hot climates has almost always made them slaves and that the courage of the peoples of cold climates has kept them free' (ibid.: 278 [XVII: 2]). Montesquieu's logic is deterministic and supports a Eurocentric ideology of race that operates to justify slavery and colonization of the Global South.

In Book XV on civil slavery, Montesquieu attempts to find the 'origin of the right of slavery' (ibid.: 247–251 [XV: 2–7]). He refutes Aristotle arguing that slavery does not exist by nature since 'all men are born equal'. However, Montesquieu's argument slips into relativism since he considers geographical location and contradicts this universal precept of equality. In certain countries, he contends, slavery 'may be founded on a natural reason'. He distinguishes these countries 'from the countries of Europe, where 'natural reasons reject it' and 'it has . . . been abolished' (ibid.: 252 [XV: 7]). Montesquieu gives three reasons to found slavery by right. First, the right of nations, allows conquering states to enslave the vanquished temporarily to preserve an acquired territory. Second, 'the gentle right of slavery is founded on the free choice of the master . . . and forms a reciprocal agreement between two parties' (ibid.: 251 [XV: 6]). This contradictory, hypocritical, and dubious claim seems to refer to a contract between two parties selling and buying slaves treated as chattel rather than the deliberate selling of one's own person into slavery (ibid.: 247–248 [XV: 2]). Third, he acknowledges that European powers had created legal codes to permit and regulate the enslavement and trading of Africans, such as the French '*Le Code Noir*'. Montesquieu remarks that although it pained Louis XIII to ratify this code, he consented since 'this was the surest way to convert' Africans to Christianity (ibid.: 249 [XV: 4]; Sala-Molins, 1987).

The most controversial chapter of *The Spirit of the Laws* is entitled 'Of the Slavery of Negroes', which is a term that Montesquieu uses, but that today is considered offensive (Montesquieu (1989 [1748]: 250 [XV: 5]). Montesquieu rehearses the arguments for the enslavement of Africans in the New World. It opens in the conditional voice: 'If I had to defend the right we had of making Negroes slaves, here is what I would say.' This conditional voice has led many scholars to contend that Montesquieu does not defend but mocks the views of society and by doing so he tempers and refutes these (Volpilhac-Auger, 2003; Samuel, 2009). Yet, Montesquieu nowhere explicitly refutes these views. Rather, as noted above, he sees this slavery as necessary. Europeans exterminated the peoples of the Americas, therefore they 'had to make slaves of Africans' to clear the land. Moreover, the cost of sugar would be too high without slavery (Montesquieu (1989 [1748]: 250 [XV: 5]). He goes as far to state that, given their colour, it is 'impossible to feel sorry for them' and difficult to believe that God would have 'put a soul . . . in a body that was entirely black'. He observes that it is 'natural to think that colour constitutes humanity'. Finally, he questions their humanity: 'if we assumed they were men, one would begin to believe that we ourselves were not Christians'. He concludes that small minds 'exaggerate too much the injustice done the Africans. For, if it were as they say, would it not have occurred to the princes of Europe, who make so many useless agreements with one another, to make a general one in favour of mercy and pity?' (ibid.: 250 [XV: 5]; Sala-Molins, 1987; 1992). Yet he acknowledged that princes had ratified codes, such as *Le Code Noir*, to regulate the trade. Montesquieu implies that if things were as bad as they are made out to be, surely there would be laws to stop this. The chapter as a whole is almost too blatant to be the stance of an Enlightenment political philosopher renowned for his view that slavery 'is not good by nature' and is opposed to civil and natural right (Montesquieu (1989 [1748]: 246, 248 [XV: 1-2]). Montesquieu declares slavery wrong from a moral point of view, yet he admits its practice and recognizes it as a right. The tensions and contradictions in this book are open to interpretation. Nevertheless, Montesquieu does not explicitly oppose any of the reasons that justify the slavery of Africans in the West Indies.

In the book on domestic slavery, Montesquieu contends that women of the Global North have greater freedom and are treated with greater respect by men than women of the Global South whose dependence reflects the brutality of power. He criticizes marital and sexual practices of hot southern countries, including polygamy, and characterizes women as excessively lustful and focused on youthful beauty rather than reason (ibid.: 264, 271 [XVI: 2, 10]). By contrast, women of the cold European North are chaste, not as lustful, and marriage is monogamous (ibid.: 264–265 [XVI: 2]). The domestic and political spheres are related. In republics, where there is 'public liberty' and citizens are 'equal, gentle and moderate', women cannot be dominated. In hot countries, however, women endure absolute subjection to the desires and whims of husbands in the harem from which they are unfree to leave. This domestic slavery corrupts society and goes 'hand in hand' with despotic government (ibid.: 270 [XVI: 9]). This contrast between women of the North and South is caricatural and orientalist. It plays a major role in the portrayal of non-European societies as decadent, declining, and subject to despotism. Moreover, it ignores the fact that European women were not equal to men and were subject to absolute tyrants in the home (Astell, 1996: 17, read more about Astell in Chapter 8).

In Book XVII on political servitude, Montesquieu relates the laws to the climate and geography. He asserts that peoples of the North are courageous and conquer as freemen: 'valiant nations . . . go out of their own countries to destroy tyrants and slaves'. By contrast, peoples of the South, notably Asians, conquer as slaves for a despot (Montesquieu (1989 [1748] : 282–283 [XVII: 5-6]). We often read Montesquieu's concept of liberty in terms of individual freedom of security or from domination. Yet in these chapters on slavery, freedom's opposite, Montesquieu develops another facet of freedom as characteristic of peoples of the North who are brave and hardy since they are subject to cold climates and harsh terrains. This freedom is valiant and glorious. It allows men to break the shackles of despotic domination and servitude yet at the same time it permits them to dominate others. For a 'conquest can destroy harmful prejudices, and, if I dare speak in this way, can put a nation under a better presiding genius' (ibid.: 142 [X: 4]).

Montesquieu's contrast of moderate (monarchical or republican) government with oriental despotism parallels his opposition between the free North to the servile South. In the Global North, slavery is abolished, political rule is moderate, and women are relatively free; whereas, in the Global South, slavery persists, political rule is despotic, and women are tied to domestic servitude in the seraglio. This contrast operates to vilify the Global South and to demonstrate European superiority. It underpins the orientalist and racist ideology that legitimized modern European colonial domination over peoples and places in Africa, Asia, and the Americas.

> **11.5 Commerce and slavery: Key Points**
>
> - Montesquieu's claim that commerce brings peace sits in tension with his understanding of colonial trade and the necessity of slavery.
> - Montesquieu's categorization of peoples of the North as free and those of the South as servile creates a legitimating narrative for the subjection of countries of the Global South.
> - Fundamental laws of Europe legitimize a trading monopoly of the metropole over the colony which becomes economically dependant and loses its right to trade. This is supported by the military protection and administration offered by the metropole.
> - Slavery is practised in countries other than European ones and can be understood in terms of gender (domestic slavery), master/servant relations (civil slavery), and despotism (political servitude).

11.6 Conclusion

This chapter has developed a critical reading of Montesquieu's core ideas within the historical contexts of political instability, growing absolutism in France and the development of and competition for European colonial empire. Through examination of his views on commerce, colonialism, slavery, and climate, combined with his historical understanding of political constitutions, moderate and immoderate governments, this chapter contends that Montesquieu advanced a conception of a 'fundamental' political constitution that not only aimed at the guarantee and protection of individual freedom, but also designed political institutions and powers that would maintain stability at home and support empire abroad. It argues that this formed part of the political ideology to support colonial empire along with the political sociology that Montesquieu drew from history, travel writings, and the comparisons of different peoples across time and space. Finally, through his comparisons of the Global North and South, Montesquieu extends the concept of freedom beyond the individual freedom to security against arbitrary domination within the state and the independence of the self-governing state to the domination of others across the globe.

Take your learning further by accessing the online resources for a library of web links to relevant videos, articles, blogs, and useful websites for this chapter: www.oup.com/he/Ramgotra-Choat1e.

Study questions

1. Why does Montesquieu argue that commerce brings peace?
2. How does the theory of the separation of powers guarantee freedom?
3. Does Montesquieu's theory of climate and progress support a hierarchical understanding of peoples and countries in the global order?
4. Why does Montesquieu associate despotism with the Oriental Prince?
5. To what extent, if any, does Montesquieu justify slavery?
6. Is Montesquieu's fundamental constitution a constitutional monarchy or a republic?

7. To what extent is Montesquieu's fundamental constitution able to deal with both internal and external change?
8. How should we read an Enlightenment thinker who is hailed for his anti-imperialism and anti-slavery views in the light of what he says about climate, commerce, and slavery?

Further reading

Primary sources

Montesquieu (1949 [1748]). *The Spirit of the Laws*. Trans. T. Nugent. Ed. F. Neumann. London: Collier Macmillan.
This edition, based on an early translation of 1750, captures the language, expression and tone of the time.

Montesquieu (1989 [1748]) *The Spirit of the Laws*. Trans. and ed. A.M. Cohler, B.C. Miller, and H. Stone. Cambridge: Cambridge University Press.
The latest English translation with updated language and style.

Montesquieu (1999 [1734]). *Considerations on the Causes of the Greatness of the Romans and Their Decline*. Trans. D. Lowenthal. Indianapolis, IN: Hackett Publishing.
Montesquieu's early work on Rome that influenced *The Spirit of the Laws*.

Montesquieu (2018 [1721]). *The Persian Letters*. Trans. M. Mauldon. Ed. A. Kahn. Oxford: Oxford World Classics.
An accessible and recent translation.

Secondary sources

Carrithers, D.W., Mosher, M.A., and Rahe, P.A. (eds.) (2001) *Montesquieu's Science of Politics: Essays on The Spirit of Laws*. Oxford: Oxford University Press.
An excellent collection of articles and recent interpretations of Montesquieu's thought.

De Dijn, A. (2008) *French Political Thought from Montesquieu to Tocqueville: Liberty in a Levelled Society?* Cambridge: Cambridge University Press.
A careful study of aristocratic power in Montesquieu's constitutional theory and his influence on Tocqueville.

Kingston, R. (ed.) (2008) *Montesquieu and His Legacy*. Ithaca, NY: State University of New York Press.
This comprehensive collection of articles by leading scholars presents new readings of Montesquieu's ideas and his legacy beyond his impact on political constitutions.

Pangle, T. (1973) *Montesquieu's Philosophy of Liberalism: A Commentary on 'The Spirit of the Laws'*. Chicago: University of Chicago Press.
A thorough study of Montesquieu's political philosophy that portrays him as a liberal.

Ramgotra, M. (2022) 'Time, Modernity and Space: Montesquieu's and Constant's Ancient/Modern Binaries'. *History of European Ideas*, 48(3): 263–279.
Explores the relevance of Montesquieu's use of ancient versus modern binary in conceptions of modernity and freedom.

Shackleton, R. (1961) *Montesquieu: A Critical Biography*. Oxford: Oxford University Press.
One of the few authoritative and comprehensive biographies of Montesquieu.

Sullivan, V. (2017) *Montesquieu and the Despotic Ideas of Europe: An Interpretation of 'The Spirit of the Laws'*. Chicago: University of Chicago Press.
Analyses Montesquieu's concept of despotism and his responses to Machiavelli and Hobbes.

References

Althusser, L. (1959) *Montesquieu: La politique et l'histoire*. Paris: Presses Universitaires de France.

Appleby, J. (1992) *Liberalism and Republicanism in the Historical Imagination*. Cambridge, MA: Harvard University Press.

Aristotle (1996) 'The Politics'. In S. Everson (ed.), B. Jowett (trans.), *The Politics and The Constitution of Athens*. Cambridge: Cambridge University Press.

Astell, M. (1996 [1700]) 'Some Reflections upon Marriage, Occasioned by the Duke and Duchess of Mazarine's Case'. In P. Springborg (ed.), *Astell: Political Writings*. Cambridge: Cambridge University Press.

Austin, G. (1966) *The Indian Constitution: Cornerstone of a Nation*. Oxford: Clarendon Press.

Blackburn, R. (1997) *The Making of New World Slavery: From the Baroque to the Modern, 1492–1800*. London: Verso.

Bourdieu, P. (1980) 'Le Nord et le Midi : Contribution à une analyse de l'effet Montesquieu'. *Actes de la Recherche en Sciences Sociales*, 35: 21–25.

Carrithers, D.W. (2001) 'Democratic and Aristocratic Republics: Ancient and Modern'. In D.W. Carrithers, M.A. Mosher, and P.A. Rahe (eds), *Montesquieu's Science of Politics*. Oxford: Oxford University Press, pp. 109–158.

Chakrabarty, D. (2000) *Provincializing Europe: Postcolonial Thought and Historical Difference*. Princeton, NJ: Princeton University Press.

Courtney C.P. (2001) 'Montesquieu and Natural Law'. In D.W. Carrithers, M.A. Mosher, and P.A. Rahe (eds), *Montesquieu's Science of Politics*. Oxford: Oxford University Press, pp., 41–67.

De Dijn, A. (2013) 'Montesquieu's Controversial Context: The Spirit of the Laws as a Monarchist Tract'. *History of Political Thought*, 34(1): 66–88.

Douglass, R. (2012) 'Montesquieu and Modern Republicanism'. *Political Studies*, 60: 703–719.

Estève, L. (2002) *Montesquieu, Rousseau, Diderot: Du genre humain au bois d'ébène: Les silences du droit naturel*. Paris: UNESCO.

Hobbes, T. (1996) *Leviathan*. Ed. R. Tuck. Cambridge: Cambridge University Press.

Keohane, N. (1980) *Philosophy and the State in France: The Renaissance to the Enlightenment*. Princeton, NJ: Princeton University Press.

Koselleck, R. (2002) 'The Eighteenth Century as the Beginning of Modernity'. In *The Practice of Conceptual History: Timing, History, Spacing Concepts*. Trans. T.S. Presner et al., Stanford, CA: Stanford University Press, pp. 154–169.

Krause, S. (2002) 'The Uncertain Inevitability of Decline in Montesquieu'. *Political Theory*, 30(5): 702–727.

Larrère, C. (2001) 'Montesquieu on Economics and Commerce'. In D.W. Carrithers, M.A. Mosher, and P.A. Rahe (eds), *Montesquieu's Science of Politics: Essays on The Spirit of Laws*. Oxford: Oxford University Press, pp. 335–373.

Locke, J. (2003) 'Two Treatises of Government'. In J. Dunn et al. (eds), *Two Treatises of Government and A Letter Concerning Toleration*. London: Yale University Press.

MacDonald, S. (2003) 'Problems with Principles: Montesquieu's Theory of Natural Justice'. *History of Political Thought*, 34(1): 109–130.

Montesquieu (1951) *De l'Esprit des Lois*. Ed. R. Callois. Paris: Editions Gallimard.

Montesquieu (1973 [1721]) *Les Lettres Persanes*. Paris: Editions Gallimard.

Montesquieu (1989 [1748]) *The Spirit of the Laws*. Trans. and ed. A.M. Cohler, B.C. Miller, and H. Stone. Cambridge: Cambridge University Press.

Moore, J. (2008) 'Montesquieu and the Scottish Enlightenment'. In R. Kingston (ed.), *Montesquieu and His Legacy*. Ithaca, NY: State University of New York Press.

Pangle, T. (1973) *Montesquieu's Philosophy of Liberalism: A Commentary on 'The Spirit of the Laws'*. Chicago: University of Chicago Press.

Rahe, P.A. (2001) 'Forms of Government: Structure, Principle, Object, and Aim'. In D.W. Carrithers, M.A. Mosher, and P.A. Rahe (eds), *Montesquieu's Science of Politics: Essays on The Spirit of Laws*. Oxford: Oxford University Press, pp. 69–108.

Ramgotra, M. (2014) 'Republic and Empire in Montesquieu's *Spirit of the Laws*'. *Millennium*, 42(3): 790–816.

Ramgotra, M. (2022) 'Time, Modernity and Space: Montesquieu's and Constant's Ancient/Modern Binaries'. *History of European Ideas*, 48(3): 263–279.

Sala-Molins, L. (1987) *Le Code Noir ou le Calvaire de Canaan*. Paris: Presses Universitaires Françaises.

Sala-Molins, L. (1992) *Misères des Lumières: Sous la raison, l'outrage*. Paris: Presses Universitaire Françaises.

Samuel, A.J. (2009) 'The Design of Montesquieu's "The Spirit of the Laws": The Triumph of Freedom over Determinism'. *American Political Science Review*, 103(2): 305–321.

Turnaoğlu, B. (2017) *The Formation of Turkish Republicanism*. Princeton, NJ: Princeton University Press.

Volpilhac-Auger, C. (2003) 'Pitié pour les nègres'. *L'Information Littéraire*, 55(1): 11–16.

12 John Stuart Mill

INDER S. MARWAH

Chapter guide

This chapter introduces John Stuart Mill's political philosophy, focusing on two particular features of his thought. First is Mill's relation to the liberal political tradition. Second are his writings on race, gender, and empire, which have in recent years come into greater prominence. Following a brief introduction, Section 12.2 highlights Mill's contributions to liberal political theory and utilitarian ethics, the two traditions of thought with which he's most commonly associated. Section 12.3 elaborates his views on government (widely) and democracy (more narrowly). Section 12.4 considers Mill's views on human diversity and difference, showing how his treatments of race, empire, and gender intersect with his liberalism. The chapter concludes with a brief reflection on how one might think about his political philosophy in light of his imperialist entanglements.

12.1 Introduction

Few philosophers have lived as many lives as John Stuart Mill (1806–1873), both in their own time and since. Mill was Victorian England's most influential philosopher—by some accounts, the most influential English-language philosopher of the nineteenth century. He was a pre-eminent public figure, a high-ranking administrator in the East India Company, a member of the Philosophical Radicals surrounding Jeremy Bentham, an outspoken feminist, a Member of Parliament (briefly), and an accomplished botanist. He wrote on every conceivable subject that might interest the era's foremost public intellectual, from better-known excurses on liberty, economics, government, utilitarian ethics, and the history of philosophy, to lesser-known tracts on international law, psychology, socialism, women's and working-class suffrage, character formation, race, gender, and more. Since his death in 1873, he has gained and lost reputations for being a leader of the utilitarian movement (or a lapsed utilitarian), a champion of free speech, an unrepentant imperialist, and, most often, the forefather of modern liberalism.

Key Thinker: Jeremy Bentham

Jeremy Bentham (1748–1832) was a jurist, philosopher, and political reformer widely credited as the originator of classical utilitarianism. While his philosophical writings touched on ethics, law, logic, political economy, and more, he is best known as a leader of an early nineteenth-century reformist movement seeking to develop legal, civil, penal, and political institutions grounded in utilitarian principles. Bentham believed that human experience could be reduced to a balance of pleasures and pains, whose proportions would yield a more or less happy life. Social institutions should, then, aim to maximize the overall happiness by increasing overall pleasure and decreasing overall pain. His utilitarianism is hedonistic: it aims to maximize the quantity of pleasures experienced by human beings, gauged by a 'felicific calculus' measuring the intensity, duration, certainty, and proximity of experiences of pleasure or pain.

Read more about **Mill's** life and work by accessing the thinker biography on the online resources: www.oup.com/he/Ramgotra-Choat1e.

There are, then, different Mills that we might discuss depending on where our interests lie, and where we choose to focus in the thousands of pages he penned over a long and turbulent life. This chapter examines Mill's political philosophy and his place in the liberal tradition, highlighting his major contributions to social ethics and political theory. It also widens beyond these better-known topics by exploring Mill's views on human difference—racial, gender-based, and class-based—and his work as a high-ranking bureaucrat in the East India Company from 1823 until 1858. The idea isn't just to sit these topics side by side, but to consider how they influenced one another. Mill's celebrated writings on liberty, for instance, excluded the very populations over which he presided as a colonial administrator, and his concerns for women's autonomy shaped the extent and form of the liberties he defended. The chapter will thus outline the liberal commitments for which Mill is renowned and show how his thoughts on race, gender, empire, and civilization intersect with them.

12.2 Liberalism and utilitarianism

Mill is best known for two principles that pull in opposing directions. These are the liberty principle, often taken as the touchstone of modern liberalism, and the principle of utility, the ethical core of his moral and political thought. This section begins by sketching out the liberty principle and the arguments following from it in *On Liberty*; it then looks at the ideal of individuality, central to Mill's liberalism and utilitarianism alike; it concludes by sketching out Mill's utilitarianism, pointing to its stress points in relation to the liberty principle.

12.2.1 Liberty

In his *Autobiography*, Mill (1981: 259) speculated that as 'a kind of philosophical text-book of a single truth', '[t]he *Liberty* is likely to survive longer than anything else that I have written'. He was right. *On Liberty* is Mill's best-known and most enduring contribution to the canon of political philosophy, widely considered a foundational expression of classical liberalism (despite its affinities with modern liberalisms as concerned with social welfare as with individual freedom).

On Liberty's purpose is to ascertain 'the nature and limits of the power which can be legitimately exercised by society over the individual' (Mill, 1977a: 217). While questions surrounding the extent of political authority stretch back to antiquity, Mill's inquiry is set within the conditions of his era, in the context of ascendant popular governments. He lived in a period in which increasingly representative forms of government were beginning to replace the largely monarchical institutions that had ruled Europe for centuries, and was attuned to democracy's promise and anxieties. *On Liberty* thus aims to determine the scope of social and political power over individuals in a democratic context.

Popular governments present two dangers to individuals, one political and the other social. The first, the 'tyranny of the majority', is that:

> [t]he 'people' who exercise the power are not always the same people with those over whom it is exercised; and the 'self-government' spoken of is not the government of each by himself, but of each by all the rest. The will of the people, moreover, practically means the will of the most numerous or the most active part of the people; the majority.

(ibid.: 219)

From an institutional standpoint, democracy enables majorities to dominate minorities. The second problem lies in the power of majorities to exert, through customs and moral codes, 'a social tyranny more formidable than many kinds of political oppression, since, though not usually upheld by such extreme penalties, it leaves fewer means of escape, penetrating much more deeply into the details of life, and enslaving the soul itself' (ibid.: 219). Mill concludes that individuals need protection not only from overweening political authorities, but from prevailing opinions proscribing a person's choices, preferences, and behaviours.

The question is where to draw the line between those areas where society might interfere with an individual's actions, and those where they should enjoy complete liberty. Mill's answer lies in 'one very simple principle', which is that:

> the sole end for which mankind are warranted, individually or collectively, in interfering with the liberty of action of any of their number, is self-protection. That the only purpose for which power can be rightfully exercised over any member of a civilized community, against his will, is to prevent harm to others. His own good, either physical or moral, is not a sufficient warrant . . . The only part of the conduct of any one, for which he is amenable to society, is that which concerns others. In the part which merely concerns himself, his independence is, of right, absolute.
>
> (ibid.: 223)

This is the liberty principle or, as it's also called, the harm principle. The liberty/harm principle is seemingly transcendent because it appears so simple, clear, and intuitive: we should be free to do what we choose so long as it doesn't harm others. This moral obviousness, to late-liberal societies, has undoubtedly contributed to its longevity.

Without denying its appeal, Mill's account of liberty has faced challenges since he first enunciated it. First, the idea of harm is overly fluid and under-specified. Can one consent to be harmed? Is injurious language harmful, or are harms strictly material/physical? If it's the former, what kinds of language cross the threshold from protected to injurious speech? Second, how exactly are we to distinguish 'self-regarding' from 'other-regarding' actions, since nearly everything we do affects those in proximity to us? Finally, Mill's conceptualization of liberty is itself ambiguous. Is liberty intrinsically valuable (good in itself) or instrumentally valuable (good as a conduit to other goods)? Should we understand it in negative terms, as a sphere of non-interference, or does it require social or institutional supports? Is liberty a qualified good that holds only under certain conditions, or an unqualified good, regardless of time or place? This last question is sharpened by Mill's infamous declaration, in *On Liberty*, that the liberty principle did not extend to 'backward states of society' (ibid.: 224). He considered insufficiently 'advanced' societies, such as the one over which he governed in India, as benefiting from the despotic government of European colonists. This was because the liberty principle did not apply 'anterior to the time when mankind have become capable of being improved by free and equal discussion' (ibid.: 224). Such societies, he believed, could only progress through the forceful direction of 'civilized' Europeans. His account of liberty, then, is connected to his defence of imperialism and to his prejudiced assessment of non-Europeans.

Without resolving all these tensions, I take Mill to express the conviction that one's liberty is inviolable except in those cases where its exercise encroaches upon certain *rights* of others (and not their preferences, sensibilities, or interests). These would be entitlements in which we have a primary, justice-based interest lexically superior to other kinds of interests and to which we have a fundamental political claim—a core human interest (Donner, 2017: 436). Despite Mill's appeal to harm, he appears to defend the view that the right to liberty is sacrosanct unless other basic rights are threatened by it. This would rule out limiting a person's liberty to prevent them from, for instance, offending public sentiments, or acting against the majority's will, or injuring their own interests, or joining a dissident organization.

Understood this way, Mill defends (1) liberty of thought and discussion; (2) liberty of choice and action; and (3) freedom of assembly. 'No society in which these liberties are not, on the whole, respected,' he maintains, 'is free' (Mill, 1977a: 226).

12.2.2 Liberty of thought and discussion

Mill's account of the right of free speech is deceptively complex, combining several distinctive but related arguments to defend a broad-ranging liberty to hold and disseminate one's views. He addresses three possible scenarios: (1) cases where we do not know whether our ideas are true or false; (2) cases in which they are correct; and (3) cases in which they are 'in error'.

Starting with the first, Mill holds, most simply, that freedom of speech is necessary because the suppressed opinion may be true. Beyond its surface truth, Mill makes a historical argument, an epistemic one, and a sociological one.

The historical argument is that silencing certain opinions assumes the infallibility of our own judgements, and that the most self-evident truths of a given people are almost always the object of bewilderment, consternation, or ridicule of future generations. The belief that we are warranted in censoring unpleasant, immoral, or socially dangerous views is not only baseless, but pernicious: it prevents present and future generations from questioning ideas and making social progress.

This leads to the epistemic argument. Given the fallibility of our judgements, our best chance of approaching the truth on any given matter is to expose it to as many counter-opinions as possible. '[A]ny person whose judgement is really deserving of confidence', Mill (ibid.: 232) maintains, earns it by 'his practice to listen to all that could be said against him'. To shield them from argument because we are certain that they're correct is the best way of limiting our capacity to assess the truth of our convictions.

Finally, the sociological argument: democratic conditions increase social pressures towards conformity, custom, and convention, against which liberty of thought and discussion, and the critical spirit they engender, serve as a bulwark. In the modern world, we don't need to burn heretics at the stake; they simply censor themselves in societies that don't actively encourage and defend liberty of thought. The harm isn't just to contrarians and originals, but to society itself, as the best and brightest minds are quietly dwarfed and pacified.

These all fall under Mill's first scenario: that suppressed opinions may be true or false. He goes on to defend liberty of thought and discussion when we know our ideas to be correct and the truth is not in question.

Even here, Mill argues, liberty of discussion remains invaluable as a means of learning the grounds of our own convictions. Most of us settle into our beliefs without subjecting them to careful examination; defending them renews their truth and recalls their foundations, without which they devolve into dead dogma, articles of faith whose vitality is sapped by time and habit. Free speech invigorates conviction, forcing us to confront *why* we believe our beliefs at all.

Finally, Mill addresses the more common case than either of the above: when truth is shared between conflicting doctrines. Historical reflection and a consciousness of our own fallibilism are, again, key to recognizing that no person, civilization, or doctrine contains the entire truth on any given matter. Much more frequently, given systems of thought hold *some* portion of it, which can only be supplemented through freewheeling discussion airing out dissenting views. Even 'incorrect' doctrines, then, reveal some measure of truth. As obvious as this may seem, few philosophical, religious, or moral systems acknowledge their own incompleteness. Free speech, then, remains an important reminder of it.

12.2.3 Liberty of action

Mill's arguments concerning liberty of action borrow from Wilhelm von Humboldt's dictum that humanity's efflorescence depends on 'freedom, and variety of situations' (ibid.: 261). Just as human beings should be able to hold a wide range of opinions, 'so is it that there should be different experiments of living' (ibid.: 260–261). Mill's view is, again, restricted by his prejudices, as he fails to see the worth of such differences in many non-European societies. These 'inferior and more backward portion[s] of the human race' should instead be absorbed by 'highly civilized and cultivated people' (Mill, 1977b: 449).

Despite these limitations, Mill provides both individual and social justifications for 'experiments of living'. From the individual standpoint, different human beings have different ways of being in the world which may be ill-fitted to the customary way, particularly in the case of dissentient minorities. This is an argument about autonomy, development, and flourishing: forcing individuals to live as most people do cramps the human spirit to the detriment of eccentrics, mavericks, and geniuses. 'Human nature', Mill (1977a: 263) famously holds, 'is not a machine to be built after a model, and set to do exactly the work prescribed for it, but a tree, which requires to grow and develop itself on all sides, according to the tendency of the inward forces which make it a living thing.'

From the collective standpoint, reducing the breadth of ways that we might think and live inhibits social progress. True originals by definition act outside and often against social conventions. Only by allowing them to do so are the bounds of social existence widened. As Mill (ibid.: 267) observes, 'these few are the salt of the earth; without them, human life would become a stagnant pool', as '[g]enius can only breathe in an *atmosphere* of freedom'. Here, Mill reflects the anxieties of his early democratic era, in which popular opinion was becoming increasingly powerful, constraining through both law and custom all but the most ordinary ways of life. '[T]he despotism of custom,' he reminds, 'is everywhere the standing hindrance to human advancement' (ibid.: 272).

While carving out a fairly expansive sphere for individual autonomy, Mill's defence of liberty is, by design, limited. Liberty is not a licence to incite violence or harm. My freedom to argue that property is theft does not extend to inciting others to destroy my neighbour's property. Liberty also does not shield abuses of power in the private sphere, particularly those that men inflict on women. Mill's argument here tallies with feminist scholarship: the state's obligation to respect individual liberty must be balanced against the 'almost despotic power of husbands over wives' (ibid.: 301). Liberty's good is thus neither unconstrained nor intrinsic.

It is equally restricted in the economic sphere, where Mill steadfastly resists the free-market economics often attributed to liberalism. His mature economic and political thought is in fact inflected by socialism, recognizing the necessity of curbing capitalism's excesses. Without embracing stronger forms of state socialism, Mill endorsed workers' collectives, for instance, to improve the material and educational prospects of the working classes. He also argued against unlimited economic growth in advanced societies in favour of a redistributive system elevating the entire population's standard of life. His liberalism, then, remains more nuanced and heterodox than is often credited.

12.2.4 Individuality

Individuality is a central concern of Mill's and of liberal political thought more generally. Liberalism's focus on the individual has long been an object of non-liberal criticism, from communitarians taking aim at its atomism to postcolonial scholars pointing to its Eurocentrism. While such criticisms are in many cases warranted, Mill prizes individuality not as against community, but as a part of it.

For Mill, individuality has an intrinsic and extrinsic worth. From the intrinsic standpoint, individuality is valuable in relation to the human capacity for self-development, our unique ability to improve ourselves by fostering an active and self-directing character (Donner, 1991). This is against the 'ape-like imitation' to which we consign ourselves by thinking and acting in conformity with dominant opinions—the despotism of custom that withers the human spirit (Mill criticizes this very deformation in *The Subjection of Women*: women's individuality is sacrificed by the passive character forced upon them). Autonomy and dependency, however, need not conflict. Mill recognizes that our capabilities for individual self-development do not exist independently of social intercourse but are rather anchored in a social existence whose tendencies to overreach are checked by basic liberties. Human autonomy depends on a properly limited social and political life; Mill's valuation of individuality is not libertarian.

From the extrinsic—or social—standpoint, individuality is an engine of progress, the more of which exists, the better. As Mill (1977a: 272) puts it, 'the only unfailing and permanent source of improvement is liberty, since by it there are as many possible independent centres of improvement as there are individuals'. A nation that fails to preserve individuality, in this view, faces the eventuality of sliding into social stagnancy. Critics such as Uday Singh Mehta (1999) and Bhikhu Parekh (1994) have criticized Mill on this front, given his characterization of 'the whole East' as nations in which 'the despotism of Custom is complete' (Mill, 1977a: 272). Given his conviction that India could only be jolted out of its stationary state through British rule, Mill's focus on individuality has come under fire for its Eurocentrist presumptions and for rationalizing imperialism.

12.2.5 Utilitarianism

As with many of Mill's intellectual commitments, his relationship to utilitarianism is anything but straightforward. That relationship is partly biographical. Mill was raised in an intellectual milieu dominated by his father and Jeremy Bentham, leading proponents of classical utilitarianism, which aimed to reform nineteenth-century social, political, and legal institutions. J.S. Mill shared in those ambitions and developed his own utilitarianism but retained a certain ambiguity in his commitments as he drifted from his father's influence. There are also deep tensions between the principles of liberty and utility. As a result, commentators vary widely in interpreting Mill's utilitarianism and reconciling it with his liberalism.

> **Key Concept: Utilitarianism**
>
> Utilitarianism is a normative theory of ethics that holds that the morally correct action is the one that maximizes good outcomes. It is consequentialist, taking the *results* of actions as the object of our moral concern. This is in contrast with deontological ethics—where what's morally correct is given by a rule or maxim, for example, 'thou shalt not kill'—or virtue ethics, which take a person's character as the object of moral concern. Generally speaking, utilitarian theories aim to maximize the overall good, which includes both one's own good and that of others. Though variants have existed throughout the history of ethics, classical utilitarianism came into prominence in the nineteenth century, primarily through the legal, political, and moral philosophies of Jeremy Bentham, James Mill, John Stuart Mill, and Henry Sidgwick.

Mill most clearly spells out his convictions in his 1859 essay, 'Utilitarianism'. 'Utility, or the Greatest Happiness Principle', he asserts,

> holds that actions are right in proportion as they tend to promote happiness, wrong as they tend to produce the reverse of happiness. By happiness is intended pleasure, and the absence of pain; by unhappiness, pain, and the privation of pleasure . . . pleasure, and freedom from pain, are the only things desirable as ends.
>
> (Mill, 1969: 209–210)

The utilitarian measure of happiness, Mill (ibid.: 218) specifies, is not the individual's, but 'that of all concerned'. Utility is, then, the basic ethical principle guiding Mill's practical philosophy, governing both how we ought to act in various spheres of action and the organization of our social and political institutions. It shapes our collective commitments, such that educational institutions, 'laws and social arrangements should place the happiness, or (as speaking practically it may be called) the interest, of every individual, as nearly as possible in harmony with the interest of the whole' (ibid.: 218).

Here, Mill steps into uncomfortable territory for liberals, for a few reasons. First, the argument flirts with perfectionism, the notion that there's a particular 'good life' that public institutions should push citizens to adopt. This runs afoul of the liberal commitment to a neutral public sphere. This is exacerbated by a second feature of Mill's view: his distinction between higher pleasures (which employ the 'higher faculties', such as the intellect) and lower pleasures (associated with base desire-satisfaction). Mill's utilitarianism prioritizes the former over the latter, suggesting that we should cultivate the higher pleasures as '[i]t is better to be a human being dissatisfied than a pig satisfied; better to be Socrates dissatisfied than a fool satisfied' (ibid.: 212).

These points of friction illuminate the tension between Mill's liberalism and his utilitarianism. At best, they pull in conflicting directions; at worst, they are irreconcilable. The utility principle enjoins us to maximize human happiness, even if it means that some person or minority could be made to bear the brunt of a social policy that increases the overall happiness (such as, for instance, banning minority religious practices disliked by a majority). The liberty principle, conversely, is strictly egalitarian: no one should be denied basic liberties, even if their preservation lessens the overall happiness. The principle of utility prioritizes the general welfare, which liberty may undermine, and the principle of liberty prioritizes individual freedom, which may not maximize the general welfare.

There are a few responses to such inconsistencies. The first is that Mill simply *is* inconsistent—that he failed to square his commitments to utility and liberty. Isaiah Berlin (2015) most famously advances this view, suggesting that as Mill's liberalism developed, he drifted away from the utilitarian fold. A second tack is to argue that Mill sees individuality and autonomy as constitutive of human happiness; by preserving them, the liberty principle maximizes pleasure. A variant of this argument is that if we recognize human happiness as implicitly variable, then liberty is required to carve out the space for us to determine and seek our happiness. Finally, we might emphasize the temporal dimension of Mill's view when he describes utility, in *On Liberty*, 'as the ultimate appeal on all ethical questions: but it must be utility in the largest sense, grounded on the permanent interests of man as a progressive being' (Mill, 1977a: 225). The measure of happiness here is our long-term interests as beings that will always develop and progress, which only liberty—rather than any fixed principle of government—can enable us to do over time. Liberty ensures that we can deliberate and improve ourselves on an ongoing basis, taking as its object not our immediate happiness as individuals, but our enduring and collective happiness as continuously evolving creatures. None of these resolutions is entirely satisfying and objections can be raised against them all. Nevertheless, they point to some tensions in Mill's thought and to a few ways that he might have worked through them.

Another serious concern with Mill's utilitarianism is that it directly shapes his justification of imperialism. As he saw it, by pulling non-Europeans up the civilizational ladder, from the depths of barbarism into the light of modernity, the British Empire furthered overall human happiness. By raising ostensibly retrograde populations out of their social, intellectual, and political torpor, 'pedagogical' imperialism—understood as a 'civilizing mission'—performed a service to the species by increasing its sum pleasure. That the measures of happiness, civilization, progress, and pleasure were strictly European; that the empire's pedagogical mandate served its economic interests; that this service to humanity had to be performed by the force of arms; none of this appears to have sowed much doubt in Mill's mind concerning the empire's beneficence.

> ### 🔑 12.2 Liberalism and utilitarianism: Key Points
>
> - Mill's liberty principle, or harm principle, which states that we are free to act as long as we do not harm others, has been criticized for its ambiguous conceptualizations of 'harm' and 'liberty' and for failing clearly to distinguish 'self-regarding' from 'other-regarding' actions.
> - Mill offers historical, epistemic, and sociological arguments in defence of liberty of thought and discussion, and individual and social justifications for liberty of choice and action.
> - Mill values individuality both for enabling individual self-development and as an engine of social progress.
> - Mill's defence of utilitarianism—which holds that actions are right insofar as they maximize overall happiness—is in tension with his liberalism.
> - Mill's valuations of liberty, individuality, and utility are qualified by, or contribute to, his justifications of British imperialism.

12.3 Government and democracy

12.3.1 Government

Mill measures government, like liberty, against the standard of utility, arguing that 'the influence of government on the well-being of society can be considered or estimated in reference to nothing less than the whole of the interests of humanity' (Mill, 1977b: 384). As above, this sits awkwardly with his liberalism by supporting more activist forms of government than are typically countenanced by classical liberal views.

This activist bent is apparent in Mill's two criteria for good government. The first is 'the degree in which it tends to increase the sum of good qualities in the governed, collectively and individually' (ibid.: 390). The second relates to 'the quality of the machinery itself; that is, the degree in which it is adapted to take advantage of the amount of good qualities which may at any time exist, and make them instrumental to the right purposes' (ibid.: 390–391). Taken together, these criteria balance principles of order (government should employ the population's existing resources and capacities) and progress (government should increase the population's resources and capacities). As Mill understands them, these principles are complementary: governments should maintain a stable foundation for their populations while also seeking to improve them, cultivating the 'active character' and self-developing individuality lauded in *On Liberty*.

How a government goes about this, however, depends on a society's 'state of civilization' (ibid.: 393). Mill does not espouse any fixed, singular form of government, resisting the notion that political institutions can be set out from a speculative void. Governments should be fitted to a people's social, cultural, and historical circumstances and must satisfy three basic conditions:

> [t]he people for whom the form of government is intended must be willing to accept it . . . They must be willing and able to do what is necessary to keep it standing. And they must be willing and able to do what it requires of them to enable it to fulfil its purposes.
>
> (ibid.: 376)

These conditions are a double-edged sword. On one hand, Mill's view of government is attractive in registering the nature of its population and adapting to it. There is no universally best form of government, which varies according to its population's needs. On the other hand, Mill's attention to a people's state of civilization sustains the argument for colonial domination over 'unfit' or 'barbaric' non-Europeans. While 'the ideally best form of government is that in which the sovereignty, or supreme controlling power in the last resort, is vested in the entire aggregate of the community' (ibid.: 403), this is only the case for 'advanced' peoples—Europeans. By contrast, 'a people in a state of savage independence . . . is practically incapable of making any progress in civilization until it has learnt to obey . . . To enable it to do this, the constitution of the government must be nearly, or quite, despotic' (ibid.: 394). For such people, Mill argues, 'a government under their own control would be entirely unmanageable by them. Their improvement cannot come from themselves, but must be superinduced from without' (ibid.: 395).

Mill's sensitivity to the conditions of government, then, yields very different forms of rule for different societies. For 'civilized' Europeans, the best governments are popular, free, and democratic, while 'uncivilized' non-Europeans benefit from 'benevolent' European despotism. He reconciles the contradiction by appealing to an ideal of progress: Europeans' advancement enables them to benefit from liberty and self-rule, while non-Europeans' underdevelopment leads them to require external direction.

12.3.2 Democracy

Mill's democratic theory is most clearly enunciated in *Considerations on Representative Government*. While certain commentators have found it more elitist than democratic, some such charges are mitigated by a close reckoning of his aims and concerns.

Mill's milieu, in which popular sovereignty and representative governments were ascendant but by no means the norm that they are today, shapes his democratic theory. Like Alexis de Tocqueville—with whom Mill corresponded, and whose landmark *Democracy in America* he reviewed—Mill endeavours to strike a balance between giving voice to the masses and mitigating its possible excesses. In his Victorian context, that meant balancing between Britain's working class, who were gradually gaining voting rights, and elites, who largely controlled Parliament. Ultimately, his democratic theory aims to weigh principles of equality and inclusiveness (by increasing working-class participation in government) against those of competence and education (by preserving some of the upper-class's political power and raising the educational level of the working class). Mill was a lifelong advocate for women's and working-class suffrage, both in his theoretical work and in his brief parliamentary career. His conviction that the working class should be educated before being enfranchised, however, also betrays his democratic hesitations.

> #### Key Thinker: Alexis de Tocqueville
>
> Alexis de Tocqueville (1805–1859) was a French aristocrat, historian, and politician, whose *Democracy in America* (Tocqueville, 2003 [1835, 1840]) is among the nineteenth century's most wide-ranging and enduring analyses of democracy. It was one of the earliest examinations of modern, mass democracies, capturing both their promise and the anxieties they provoked, especially, the worry about the tyranny of the masses that in turn shaped Mill's political thought. Like Mill, with whom he corresponded, Tocqueville led an active political life domestically and abroad as a colonial official. While he criticized slavery and the treatment of Black Americans in the United States, he advocated French domination of North Africans in Algeria.

For Mill (1977b: 404), popular government 'is both more favourable to present good government, and promotes a better and higher form of national character, than any other polity whatsoever'. Democracies preserve citizens' rights and flourishing while also ensuring that 'the general prosperity attains a greater height, and is more widely diffused' (ibid.: 404). Democratic governments carry particular advantages in relation to individuals' interests and development.

As regards the first, Mill (ibid.: 404) sees that 'the rights and interests of every or any person are only secure from being disregarded, when the person interested is himself able, and habitually disposed, to stand up for them'. This concerns the working class, traditionally excluded from political leadership. For Mill, working-class interests can only be defended through democratic inclusion in decision-making processes, by incorporating its members into political institutions rather than depending on representation by other classes. 'Every class knows some things not so well known to other people', Mill (1988: 65) proclaims in an 1866 speech before Parliament, 'and every class has interests more or less special to itself, and for which no protection is so effectual as its own'.

Democracy's second advantage is pedagogical. Drawing citizens into the machinery of government develops their civic capacities, teaching them to become self-governing. Local democracy and small-scale politics cultivate citizens' habits of collective action. Mill is again thinking of the working class, whose disconnect from civic life is redressed by incorporating them into democratic political institutions that foster public habits. By contributing to democratic processes,

> [the citizen] is called upon, while so engaged, to weigh interests not his own; to be guided, in case of conflicting claims, by another rule than his private partialities; to apply at every turn, principles and maxims which have for their reason of existence the common good . . . He is made to feel himself one of the public.
>
> (Mill, 1977b: 412)

Democratic participation thus develops our abilities for self-government and self-development, individually and collectively.

However, Mill hardly endorses unchecked universal suffrage, given his trepidations regarding democracy's potential pathologies such as social domination, class-specific interests, waning public spirit, failures of representation, political pandering, and more. The greatest of these is the tyranny of the majority, democracy's ability to empower majorities to run roughshod over the rights of minorities. Despite his support of working-class suffrage, Mill worried about the dangers presented by unrestricted enfranchisement, given its numerical preponderance. Without regulation, democracy made it all too easy for the working class's interests to surpass the common interest. A second and related concern, outlined above, concerns competence: the working class's lack of education (generally) and experience in government (more narrowly). Democracy's inclusiveness runs the risk of drawing into government citizens unaccustomed to considering the public good. As a result, Mill (ibid.: 287) frets, 'the benefits of completely universal suffrage cannot be obtained without bringing with them, as it appears to me, a chance of more than equivalent evils'. He thus turned from championing 'pure democracy' early in his career 'to the modified form of it, which is set forth in my *Considerations on Representative Government*' (Mill, 1981: 199).

The middle chapters of *Considerations* address these problems, and Mill's solutions contribute to his reputation as an elitist. These include a weighted voting scheme endowing the better educated with greater civic power; Thomas Hare's single-transferable voting system, which limited the numerical power of the majority and enabled an 'instructed minority' (Mill, 1977b: 457) to air its views in Parliament; and imposing conditional voting restrictions on citizens dependent on, or abusive of, the public weal (tax defrauders, welfare recipients, etc.). While such inequalities are deeply problematic, Mill's context is crucial in understanding his apprehensions. Enfranchising a large mass of uneducated voters in a class-divided society carried a risk of class-driven legislative action and of quashing minority views. What Mill fails to state more directly, however, is the threat that working-class enfranchisement presented to governing elites' power and interests.

Mill's claims about competence and the shortcomings they reveal in this democratic theory are also connected to his defence of colonialism. As he sees it, both the working class and colonized peoples are incapable of self-government due to their supposed incapacities and are thus relegated to political subjection until deemed to have acquired sufficient 'maturity'. While domestically, Mill championed working-class education, internationally, the argument about competence rationalized colonial powers' indefinite deferral of Indian self-determination.

Mill's democratic theory does not, then, advocate the absolute sovereignty of the masses but rather aims to strike a balance between competing social blocs, forces, and principles—the working and employing classes, participation and competence, equality and experience. It aims to maximize the benefits of popular sovereignty while limiting its possible excesses. More generally, it operationalizes Mill's belief that progress depends on the antagonism between divergent social powers and that societies lacking such a tension sink into immobility. This notion of progress also underlies his conviction that such 'stagnant' societies—invariably non-European, such as China and India—require the strong arm of European imperialism to get back on the civilizational track. We now turn to just this topic.

> ### 12.3 Government and democracy: Key Points
>
> - Rather than advocating a single form of government, Mill argues that governments should be fitted to a people's social, cultural, and historical circumstances.
> - For 'civilized' Europeans, Mill supports representative government and working-class enfranchisement, emphasizing the advantages of democracy in defending working-class interests and promoting capacities for self-government and self-development.
> - Like Alexis de Tocqueville, Mill worries about what he views as the dangers of democracy, including the 'tyranny of the majority'.
> - While supporting the education of the working class, Mill also proposes a weighted voted system giving greater power to the better educated.
> - Mill sees many non-Europeans as incapable of self-government and as best governed through European despotism.

12.4 Race, gender, empire

12.4.1 Race

In an era when biological racism was commonplace, Mill swam against the tide. To be sure, he employs racist stereotypes in the frequent and troubling aspersions he casts upon variously 'uncivilized', 'barbaric', and 'savage' peoples. However, Mill emphatically opposes biological racism, actively—and publicly—declaiming against it.

He also draws clear links between the oppression of non-white races and women: both take as natural an inequality grounded in social conventions. In criticizing the presumption of women's inferiority, Mill asks:

> Was there ever any domination which did not appear natural to those who possessed it? . . . Did [Southern slaveholders] not call heaven and earth to witness that the dominion of the white man over the black is natural, that the black race is by nature incapable of freedom, and marked out for slavery?

(Mill, 1984a: 269)

Slavery and women's subordination, Mill argues, trade in the same fallacy and are both as unjust as they are regressive. He registers their parallels, recognizing that '[w]hat, in unenlightened societies, colour, race, religion . . . are to some men, sex is to all women; a peremptory exclusion from almost all honourable occupations' (ibid.: 340).

Mill most famously opposes racial essentialism in 'The Negro Question' (1850), an essay that strenuously contests Thomas Carlyle's endorsement of biological racism and slavery in 'Occasional Discourse on the Negro Question' (1849). Against Carlyle's claim that West Indians should be 'emancipated' from their own indolence through white domination, Mill (1984a: 93) charges Carlyle with 'the vulgar error of imputing every difference which he finds among human beings to an original difference of nature'. Mill (1974: 859) cuts to the root of the problem: beyond their evident prejudices, biological racists fail to attribute 'mental differences to the outward causes by which they are for the most part produced, and on the removal of which they would cease to exist'. Cognitive capacities are shaped by environment and education, and Mill (ibid.: 859) lambasts dogmatists treating such differences as 'ultimate facts, incapable of being explained or altered' rather than as remediable by more just institutions.

These convictions shape Mill's politics. He was a committed abolitionist, supporting the Union in the American Civil War, which he saw as 'a war of principle for the complete extirpation of that curse [slavery]' (Mill, 1986: 1204–1205). As a Member of Parliament, he also chaired a committee seeking to bring Edward John Eyre, governor of Jamaica, to trial for using brutal and excessive force to put down a native rebellion. The attempt was ultimately unsuccessful but Mill was, here, prescient. Eyre's British supporters were 'the same kind of people who had so long upheld negro slavery' (Mill, 1981: 282) and their views, he correctly saw, would sink into obsolescence.

12.4.2 Gender

Mill's views on gender are justly recognized as ahead of their time. His firm belief in women's equal rights, his advocacy for women's suffrage, his consciousness of the multiple levels of women's subordination, and his fierce criticisms of patriarchal rights and institutions contribute to his deserved reputation as an early feminist.

Mill's feminism shaped his thought as much as his personal life. From a biographical standpoint, he regarded Harriet Taylor Mill, with whom he shared a decades-long intellectual partnership and, ultimately, a marriage, as an intellectual equal. He publicly recognized her part in developing his most celebrated ideas—*On Liberty*'s dedication is '[t]o the beloved and deplored memory of her who was the inspirer, and in part the author, of all that is best in my writings'. 'Like all that I have written for many years,' Mill (1977a: 217) acknowledges, 'it belongs as much to her as to me.' While Mill himself ascribed to Taylor Mill an equal share in his intellectual endeavours, her subsequent reception has been decidedly more ambivalent. Early commentators treated Mill's effusive praise of Taylor Mill as an embarrassing flattery. Some took his assessment of Taylor Mill's capacities as embellished, others depicted her as having had little sway over his thought, and others still regarded her as corrupting his liberalism and dragging him towards socialism.

Key Thinker: Harriet Taylor Mill

Harriet Taylor (1807–1858)—Harriet Taylor Mill as of 1851—was a British philosopher and an interlocutor of Mill's for nearly 30 years. Following her first husband's death, she and Mill married and remained so until her passing in 1858. Mill saw Taylor Mill as an intellectual equal and partner, crediting her in his autobiography with playing a major role in developing the ideas of *On Liberty*, *Principles of Political Economy*, and *On the Subjection of Women*, and in newspaper articles published throughout the 1840s

> and 1850s (he did not, however, list her as co-author on any of them). Taylor Mill's interests were chiefly in social and political philosophy, where she addressed socialism, women's rights, legal reform, individual liberty, and more. The precise extent of her influence over Mill has long been a matter of controversy.

More recent scholarship has sought to understand better their entanglements, raising important questions about how we measure contributions to the intellectual labour of canonical thinkers (McCabe, 2017; Philips, 2018). Though Mill 'held the pen' (Mill, 1981: 252), there is no doubt that Taylor Mill was the interlocutor with whom his thoughts developed. They held similar views on marriage, the family, women's education, and a wide range of subjects touching on gender and justice, all of which they discussed closely. Their shared affinities stretched well beyond women's rights. A note of Taylor Mill's from 1831–1832 reads '[e]very human being has a right to all *personal* freedom which does not interfere with the happiness of some other' (cited in McCabe, 2017: 117), prefiguring *On Liberty*'s central argument by nearly 30 years. They converged on such topics as resisting custom and public opinion, education's centrality to democratic citizenship, and the need to improve working-class conditions.

Mill's feminist commitments are spelled out in *On the Subjection of Women*, which holds that 'the legal subordination of one sex to the other . . . is wrong in itself, and now one of the chief hindrances to human improvement . . . it ought to be replaced by a principle of perfect equality' (Mill, 1984c: 261). Reflecting the utilitarian standard against which he gauges all social policies, Mill makes the case for the individual and societal advantages of women's accession to complete civil and legal equality. The essay confronts two stances defending women's inequality: that their 'natural' subordination to men is beneficial to women themselves (an individual good); and that society benefits from confining women to those occupations for which they're best fitted (a social good). Mill raises moral, practical, and historical objections against both propositions.

Chief among them is that we don't actually know what women's nature is. 'What is now called the nature of women,' he maintains, 'is an eminently artificial thing—the result of forced repression in some directions, unnatural stimulation in others' (ibid.: 276). Women's purportedly inborn qualities are instilled by social institutions that have from time immemorial cemented their subjection and then rationalized it by appealing to those very qualities. Their near-universal subordination is a form of social inertia, little more than 'the primitive state of slavery lasting on' (ibid.: 264). Given men's unbridled power over women in the private sphere, this domination is also totalizing, in contradiction of all considerations of right and justice. Against this, Mill applies *On Liberty*'s argument to women's circumstances. If we accept that individuals are best judges of their own good, then we must reject a social condition in which 'to be born a girl instead of a boy, any more than to be born black instead of white, or a commoner instead of a nobleman, shall decide the person's position through all life' (ibid.: 274).

While Mill criticizes many social and political institutions sustaining women's inequality, two are especially pernicious. The first is marriage, through which 'the wife is the actual bondservant of her husband: no less so, as far as legal obligation goes, than slaves' (ibid.: 284). He points to the deep asymmetry of the marriage relation: women have no rights or control over property, finances, or children; they are subject to domestic violence against which they have no recourse; they have no legal advantages over their husbands, to whose absolute and arbitrary authority they are subject and from which, barring exceptional circumstances, they are powerless to free themselves. Under such conditions, Mill maintains, marriage is akin to a contract of slavery, one-sided to the point of invalidity by any passable moral measure. The solution lies in '[t]he equality of married persons before the law', 'the sole mode in which that particular relation can be made consistent with justice' (ibid.: 293). As elsewhere, Mill here conjoins principled argument and sociological observation.

Where inequality renders marriage and family despotic, based on relations of command and obedience unacceptable in other spheres of social life, marital equality would be aligned with modern moral sentiments and make it a 'school of moral cultivation' (ibid.: 293).

The second social institution that Mill criticizes is property. Rejecting the automatic legal transfer of women's property to their husbands through marriage, he proposes that 'whatever would be the husband's or wife's if they were not married, should not be under their exclusive control during marriage' (ibid.: 297). Control over one's material existence, he sees, is a pre-condition for autonomy. Few social institutions maintain women's subordination more firmly than a marital contract ensuring women's economic dependency on their husbands.

Mill then addresses the social question: whether society benefits from

> excluding half the human race from the greater number of lucrative occupations and from almost all high social functions; ordaining from their birth either that they are not, and cannot by any possibility become, fit for employments which are legally open to the stupidest and basest of the other sex.
>
> (ibid.: 299)

The social benefits argument, he observes, works on the presumption that no women are suited to certain employments, such that the most capable women would do a worse job than the dullest of men. The contention is plainly ludicrous. Despite systemic disadvantages, women persistently demonstrated their excellence in the highest posts of the highest offices, Queen Victoria—Britain's ruling monarch for most of Mill's life—being only the most obvious example.

Women's peremptory exclusion from a wide range of social and political positions creates at least two problems. First is the straightforward injustice of banning half the species from even competing for certain positions. Second is the loss to humanity of an inestimably deep well of resources. Women's accession to all occupations would double the pool of doctors, engineers, scientists, professors, advocates, politicians, and so on, benefiting the overall social good. Women should, then, have the right to compete for the opportunities presented to men. Mill argues that this should begin with suffrage, the starting point of widespread social reform aiming at women's total equality.

12.4.3 Empire

Recent years have witnessed an important development in the scholarship on Mill, part of a wider 'turn to empire' in political theory excavating the imperial and colonial foundations of modern Western political thought. This has not only altered our view of certain canonical figures, but of modern political theory's conceptual landscape, showing how the categories constructing our political world are enmeshed with imperialism. Ideas such as right, liberty, the social contract, and property are neither natural, neutral, nor universal, but rather reflect the preoccupations of Euro-Americans engaged in projects of empire. Against the fiction that our political ideas emerged from discussions between and about Europeans, the turn to empire has illuminated the outward-looking face of modern political thought.

With the possible exception of John Locke (see more on Locke in Chapter 7), no figure better exemplifies those embroilments than Mill. He has come to be regarded as a paradigmatic liberal imperialist, synthesizing a defence of liberty domestically with commitments to empire abroad. Mill is related to empire in three ways in particular.

The first is biographical. Mill was drafted into the East India Company (which ruled colonial India) by his father at the age of 17, in 1823, and occupied a high-ranking post until its dissolution in 1858.

His father was a chief administrator of the Company from 1819 until his death in 1836. This was the only real employment of J.S. Mill's life and while he dismissed it as little more than a day job, his views on the benefits of civilizing imperialism pervade his philosophical writings. His conviction that non-Europeans should be elevated by despotic rule was undoubtedly shaped by his decades in an administration enacting it over hundreds of millions. Just as he was a pivotal figure in nineteenth-century liberal reformism, so too was he a pivotal figure in the East India Company during the same period.

Second, from a conceptual standpoint, Mill treats Euro-Americans as at the apex of human civilization and non-Europeans as further down the developmental ladder. This civilizational scale structures his view of historical advancement, rationalizing British imperialism as the only way to pull retrograde societies forward, for their own good. This is no appendage to Mill's political philosophy but rather goes to its core. He stipulates that the liberty principle 'is meant to apply only to human beings in the maturity of their faculties', such that 'we may leave out of consideration those backward states of society in which the race itself may be considered as in its nonage'. 'Despotism,' he concludes, 'is a legitimate mode of government in dealing with barbarians, provided the end be their improvement' (Mill, 1977a: 224). The linchpin of Mill's liberalism is qualified by a developmentalism that excludes the majority of the world's populations. His democratic theory is also touched by this understanding of social progress. In *Considerations*, he suggests that 'it is possible for one nationality to merge and be absorbed in another: and when it was originally an inferior and more backward portion of the human race, the absorption is greatly to its advantage' (Mill, 1977b: 549). Mill's commitments to liberty and democracy, both pivotal to his liberalism, are thus inflected by his imperialism: their goods are limited to those civilizations he deemed sufficiently advanced. Both also contribute directly to his defence of colonialism.

Finally, there is the problem of Eurocentrism, Mill's unquestioning faith in Euro-American civilization's superiority over 'backward' peoples. That he was culturally myopic is unsurprising, but no less problematic is his readiness to depict non-European societies as frozen in time, relics of Europe's own past. Mill (1977c: 120) describes 'the uncivilized' as 'wandering or thinly scattered over a vast tract of country', having 'no commerce, no manufactures, no agriculture', 'little or no law, or administration of justice', and as incapable of 'systematic employment of the collective strength of society'. 'The savage,' he argues, 'cannot bear to sacrifice, for any purpose, the satisfaction of his individual will. His social cannot even temporarily prevail over his selfish feelings, nor his impulses bend to his calculations' (ibid.: 122). Given that '[t]heir minds are not capable of so great an effort, nor their will sufficiently under the influence of distant motives', Mill (1984b: 118) excludes such peoples from the rules of international exchange governing free states. His Eurocentrism thus shapes his assessment of non-Europeans' incapacities, justifying their political domination. 'To suppose that the same international customs, and the same rules of international morality, can obtain between one civilized nation and another, and between civilized nations and barbarians,' Mill reflects, 'is a grave error' (ibid.: 119).

These problems have led to an important revision of Mill's ethical and political thought. While his defences of liberty and self-government undoubtedly remain compelling, they also served to deny those goods to 'unfit' populations. Mill can no longer simply be regarded as the fountainhead of liberalism, or as advancing politically neutral notions of liberty and democracy. He is also a theorist of empire, and these facets of his thought are imbricated. The scholarship is divided in its response to this revised Mill. Some commentators take Mill's views of the uncivilized as regrettable but philosophically inconsequential, the marks of his era's prejudices; others take the civilizational hierarchies qualifying his liberalism as impugning it entirely.

> ### 12.4 Race, gender, empire: Key Points
>
> - Mill was an early feminist who supported women's rights, including suffrage, and denounced gender-based inequalities in marriage and property rights.
> - While Mill opposes biological racism and endorses the abolition of slavery, he simultaneously portrays many non-Europeans as 'backward', 'barbaric', or otherwise 'uncivilized'.
> - Mill's belief in the superiority of Euro-American civilization shapes his defence of imperialism, which he also helped carry out as an employee of the East India Company.

12.5 Conclusion

Mill was a great champion of liberty, self-government, working-class suffrage, and women's equality, and his political philosophy remains a bedrock of liberal political thought. His imperialism, however, cannot be extricated from his political philosophy. What this means for his liberalism, or for liberalism more generally, remains an open question. But to read Mill's defences of liberty, democracy, freedom, progress, and self-government in isolation from the imperialist context within which he conceptualized them is to read them incompletely. This does not mean that we should throw them out, whatever that might entail. But it does mean that any full understanding of Mill's moral and political philosophy cannot afford to disregard its imperialist features. This is all the more so in a world increasingly coming to terms with empire's long shadow and catastrophic global impacts, past and present. Mill's legacy is, in this sense, the legacy of liberalism itself, caught in the tension between universalist aspirations to equality, freedom, and self-determination and the persistent limitation of those goods to Euro-American populations alone.

Take your learning further by accessing the online resources for a library of web links to relevant videos, articles, blogs, and useful websites for this chapter: www.oup.com/he/Ramgotra-Choat1e.

Study questions

1. How does the utilitarian ethical standpoint differ from deontology and virtue ethics?
2. What, according to Mill, is the liberty principle?
3. Should harmful speech be limited by the state, or should all forms of speech/expression be permitted?
4. How do Mill's commitments to liberty and utility relate to his defence of colonialism?
5. Are Mill's political ideas undermined or contradicted by his work as an imperialist?
6. Do Mill's feminist arguments still hold today, in contexts where women have formally equal marriage and voting rights?
7. What are some of the limitations of Mill's democratic theory?
8. Do contemporary democracies remain subject to the 'tyranny of the majority'?

Further reading

Primary sources

Mill, J.S. (2015) *On Liberty, Utilitarianism and Other Essays*. Ed. M. Philp and F. Rosen. Oxford: Oxford University Press.
This collection draws together Mill's four best-known political essays.

Secondary sources

Capaldi, N. (2012) *John Stuart Mill: A Biography*. Cambridge: Cambridge University Press.
A lucid intellectual biography that traces shifts in Mill's views across distinctive periods of his life.

Donner, W. (1991) *The Liberal Self: John Stuart Mill's Moral and Political Philosophy*. Ithaca, NY: Cornell University Press.
Argues that Mill's liberalism revolves around the formation and development of moral character.

Kinzer, B., Robson, A., and Robson, J. (1992) *A Moralist in and out of Parliament: John Stuart Mill at Westminster, 1865–1868*. Toronto: University of Toronto Press.
Examines Mill's political career as a Member of the British Parliament.

Mehta, U.S. (1999) *Liberalism and Empire: A Study in Nineteenth-Century British Liberal Thought*. Chicago: University of Chicago Press.
Analyzes Mill's 'liberal imperialism', arguing that the impulse to dominate non-Europeans is embedded in his liberalism.

Miller, D. (2010) *J. S. Mill*. Cambridge: Polity Press.
An excellent introduction to Mill's social and moral thought.

Pitts, J. (2005) *A Turn to Empire: The Rise of Imperial Liberalism in Britain and France*. Princeton, NJ: Princeton University Press.
Argues that nineteenth-century British liberalism—including Mill's—became increasingly imperialistic, in contrast to eighteenth-century liberalisms generally opposed to European colonialism.

Thompson, D.E. (1979) *John Stuart Mill and Representative Government*. Princeton, NJ: Princeton University Press.
Argues that Mill's notion of representative government balances principles of political participation and civic competence.

Urbinati, N. (2002) *Mill on Democracy: From the Athenian Polis to Representative Government*. Chicago: University of Chicago Press.
Demonstrates that Mill's democratic theory incorporates features of ancient Athenian political life.

Zastoupil, L. (1994) *John Stuart Mill and India*. Stanford, CA: Stanford University Press.
Treats the interrelation of Mill's professional work at the East India Company and his political philosophy.

References

Berlin, I. (2015) 'John Stuart Mill and the Ends of Life'. In J. Gray and G.W. Smith (eds), *Mill's On Liberty in Focus*. London: Routledge.

Donner, W. (1991) *The Liberal Self: John Stuart Mill's Moral and Political Philosophy*. Ithaca, NY: Cornell University Press.

Donner, W. (2017) 'Mill on Individuality'. In C. Macleod and D.E. Miller (eds), *A Companion to Mill*. Malden, MA: Wiley-Blackwell.

McCabe, H. (2017) 'Harriet Taylor Mill'. In C. Macleod and D.E. Miller (eds), *A Companion to Mill*. Malden, MA: Wiley-Blackwell.

Mehta, U.S. (1999) *Liberalism and Empire: A Study in Nineteenth-Century British Liberal Thought*. Chicago: University of Chicago Press.

Mill, J.S. (1969) 'Utilitarianism'. In *The Collected Works of John Stuart Mill*, vol. X: *Essays on Ethics, Religion and Society (Utilitarianism)*. Ed. J.M. Robson. Toronto: University of Toronto Press/London: Routledge & Kegan Paul.

Mill, J.S. (1974) 'A System of Logic Ratiocinative and Inductive: Being a Connected View of the Principles of Evidence and the Methods of Scientific Investigation'. In *The Collected Works of John Stuart Mill*, vol. VIII: *A System of Logic Part II*. Ed. J.M. Robson. Toronto: University of Toronto Press/London: Routledge & Kegan Paul.

Mill, J.S. (1977a) 'On Liberty'. In *The Collected Works of John Stuart Mill*, vol. XVIII: *Essays on Politics and Society Part 1 (On Liberty)*. Ed. J.M. Robson. Toronto: University of Toronto Press/London: Routledge & Kegan Paul.

Mill, J.S. (1977b) 'Considerations on Representative Government'. In *The Collected Works of John Stuart Mill*, vol. XIX: *Essays on Politics and Society Part II*. Ed. J.M. Robson. Toronto: University of Toronto Press/London: Routledge & Kegan Paul.

Mill, J.S. (1977c) 'Civilization'. In *The Collected Works of John Stuart Mill*, vol. XVIII: *Essays on Politics and Society Part I (On Liberty)*. Ed. J.M. Robson. Toronto: University of Toronto Press/London: Routledge & Kegan Paul.

Mill, J.S. (1981) 'Autobiography'. In *The Collected Works of John Stuart Mill*, vol. I: *Autobiography and Literary Essays*. Ed. J.M. Robson and J. Stillinger. Toronto: University of Toronto Press/London: Routledge & Kegan Paul.

Mill, J.S. (1984a) 'The Negro Question'. In *The Collected Works of John Stuart Mill*, vol. XXI: *Essays on Equality, Law, and Education (Subjection of Women)*. Ed. J.M. Robson. Toronto: University of Toronto Press/London: Routledge & Kegan Paul.

Mill, J.S. (1984b) 'A Few Words on Non-Intervention'. In *The Collected Works of John Stuart Mill*, vol. XXI: *Essays on Equality, Law, and Education (Subjection of Women)*. Ed. J.M. Robson. Toronto: University of Toronto Press/London: Routledge & Kegan Paul.

Mill, J.S. (1984c) 'On the Subjection of Women'. In *The Collected Works of John Stuart Mill*, vol. XXI: *Essays on Equality, Law, and Education (Subjection of Women)*. Ed. J.M. Robson. Toronto: University of Toronto Press/London: Routledge & Kegan Paul.

Mill, J.S. (1986) '"The Civil War in the United States", *Our Daily Fare*, 21 June, 1864'. In *The Collected Works of John Stuart Mill*, vol. XXV: *Newspaper Writings Part IV*. Ed. A.P. Robson and J.M. Robson. Toronto: University of Toronto Press/London: Routledge & Kegan Paul.

Mill, J.S. (1988) 'Representation of the People, 13 April 1866'. In *The Collected Works of John Stuart Mill*, vol. XXVIII: *Public and Parliamentary Speeches Part I*. Ed. B.L. Kinzer and J.M. Robson. Toronto: University of Toronto Press/London: Routledge & Kegan Paul.

Parekh, B. (1994) 'Decolonizing Liberalism: A Critique of Locke and Mill'. In A. Shtromas (ed.), *The End of 'Isms'? Reflections on the Fate of Ideological Politics after Communism's Collapse*. Oxford: Blackwell, pp. 85–103.

Philips, M. (2018) 'The "Beloved and Deplored" Memory of Harriet Taylor Mill: Rethinking Gender and Intellectual Labor in the Canon'. *Hypatia*, 33(4): 626–642.

Tocqueville, A. de (2003 [1835, 1840]) 'Democracy in America', 2 vols. In G.E. Bevan (trans.), *Democracy in America and Two Essays on America*. New York: Penguin Classics, pp. 1–863.

13 Karl Marx

SIMON CHOAT

> **Chapter guide**
>
> This chapter will focus on the works written by Karl Marx from 1845 onwards, because it was then that the theories and concepts for which he is best known were developed. His earlier writings will be discussed briefly in Section 13.1. Section 13.2 explains Marx's materialist conception of history, mainly through the manuscripts published posthumously as *The German Ideology* (originally co-authored 1845–1846 with Friedrich Engels) and the 1859 'Preface'. It explores some of Marx's main concepts, including mode of production, class struggle, and ideology. Section 13.3 turns to Marx's critical analysis of the capitalist mode of production, especially as found in the *Communist Manifesto* (1848, with Engels) and *Capital*, Volume 1 (1867). Section 13.4 examines Marx's views on the state and contrasts them with those of his anarchist contemporaries. While acknowledging Marx's weaknesses, especially with respect to the analysis of race and gender, the chapter defends his continuing relevance.

13.1 Introduction

Karl Marx (1818–1883) is not a typical political thinker. Modern political thinkers since Machiavelli have tended to take the state as the focus of their investigations. In contrast, Marx (1974: 329; 1987b: 263) viewed the state as an 'excrescence', arguing that what he called the 'legal and political superstructure' is derivative of the 'real foundation' of society, which is its 'economic structure'. For Marx, therefore, neither social analysis nor revolutionary activity should focus primarily on the state, whose role fundamentally is to defend the interests of the ruling class. Marx's critics claim that his preoccupation with economics and class meant that he not only underestimated the importance of the state but also that he failed adequately to grasp other forms of political agency and struggle, such as those of gender, race, nationality, and sexuality. Others claim that political thought is about defining and exploring concepts, such as justice, equality, and freedom—but Marx showed little interest in that kind of analysis either.

This chapter will maintain that Marx was nonetheless a deeply political thinker. If it can be difficult to appreciate Marx's *political* significance, this is primarily because Marx was one of many thinkers who have expanded our understanding of what 'politics' can mean. Rather than reducing everything to economics, as his critics claim, Marx shows how our economic relations are also political. 'Economic' should not here be understood narrowly but rather as referring to the production and reproduction of our conditions of life. As such, from Marx's perspective, politics is not something that takes place simply in parliaments or at the ballot box: the class struggle affects all aspects of our lives.

There are other difficulties in interpreting Marx's work, not least of which is that he wrote an incredible amount, most of which was not published during his lifetime: the complete works of Marx and Engels are expected to contain 114 volumes. Like any thinker, Marx's ideas changed over time, meaning that any interpretation of his work must necessarily be selective and contestable.

Marx himself is reputed by Engels (2001: 7) to have said: 'All I know is that I'm not a Marxist.' This chapter will focus on the works that Marx wrote from 1845 onwards, because it is in those works that he develops the distinctive approach and set of concepts for which he is today celebrated as a novel and influential thinker. As such, the rest of this section will outline very briefly Marx's early (pre-1845) works before turning to his mature theories.

> ### Key Thinker: Friedrich Engels
>
> Friedrich Engels (1820–1895) was born in Barmen, Prussia. The son of an industrialist, as a young man he was sent to work for the family firm in Manchester, England. There he wrote *The Condition of the Working Class in England* (1845). Engels and Marx first met in 1842 in Cologne but did not become friends until meeting again in Paris in 1844. In the 1840s in particular, they collaborated on a number of works and throughout Marx's life Engels provided financial and emotional support. After Marx's death, Engels played a central (though sometimes controversial) role in editing and publishing Marx's unfinished writings. Engels was the author of many books, perhaps the most important of which is *The Origin of the Family, Private Property and the State* (1884), in which he argued that the patriarchal family and the oppression of women originated with the development of private property.

As a student in Berlin in the 1830s, Marx began to associate with a group named the Young Hegelians, who sought to redeploy the philosophy of Hegel for radical ends (see Key Thinker: Georg Wilhelm Friedrich Hegel in Section 36.4 of Chapter 36). The influence of Hegel on the later Marx is a matter of fierce debate, but he was undoubtedly a central reference point for the young Marx. In the 1844 Introduction to his critique of Hegel's *Philosophy of Right*, we can see early versions of some of the claims and concepts that will be central to Marx's mature work. He calls for revolution and identifies the agent of revolution as the proletariat: 'a class with *radical chains*, a class of civil society which is not a class of civil society' (Marx, 1975a: 186). The proletariat are the working class—those who own nothing but their capacity to work and so must work for others in order to live—but it was only when Marx began to engage with political economy that he could explicate and defend this identification of the proletariat as the revolutionary class.

In 1843, Marx moved to Paris and undertook an intensive study of the classical political economy of Adam Smith, David Ricardo, and others. A central concept of his *Economic and Philosophic Manuscripts* (written in Paris in 1844 but not published until 1932) is that of alienation, which Marx derives ultimately from Hegel. The basic meaning of alienation is that two things that belong together become separated: something which belongs to you or that you have created becomes an alien force. In earlier works Marx, like other Young Hegelians, had criticized religion as a form of alienation: our desires, aspirations, and powers are projected onto God as an alien force outside of ourselves. In the 1844 *Manuscripts*, Marx turns to economic alienation. He argues that in 'bourgeois society' (capitalism) the worker is alienated from:

1. the product of his labour;
2. the activity of labour ('The worker . . . feels at home when he is not working, and when he is working he does not feel at home' [Marx, 1975b: 274]);
3. his fellow workers;
4. his 'species-being', or his uniquely human ability to engage in creative labour free from need and instinct.

Throughout this analysis, Marx uses 'man' to refer to humankind, yet he also uses gender relations as a measure of alienation and argues that only when men and women are equal can they lead fully developed, non-alienated lives (Brown, 2012: 28–31). While some (for example, McLellan, 1973) have argued that the concept of alienation remains central to Marx's theory throughout his life, the concept has a rather different meaning in later texts (see Cowling, 2006). For example, when used in the *Grundrisse* (a set of notebooks written in 1857–1858 but published posthumously), 'alienation' refers not to the alienation of the worker from his human nature but to the alienation of workers from their own collective powers: what is social (the collective powers of labour) appears as what is private (as a product of privately owned capital).

Read more about **Marx's** life and work by accessing the thinker biography on the online resources: www.oup.com/he/Ramgotra-Choat1e.

13.2 The materialist conception of history

Marx's youthful writings can be described as 'humanist' because they criticize capitalism on the basis that it denies or represses our human essence or 'species-being'. The ultimate aim of critique for the young Marx is human emancipation: by overcoming our alienation, we will regain control of our essential powers and abilities and hence realize our true human nature. For some readers of Marx, this humanism is a strength: in the mid-twentieth century, many Western European Marxists drew upon the 1844 *Manuscripts* in order to develop a humanist Marxism that could counter the economistic and deterministic Marxism of Stalinism. Others—perhaps most famously the French philosopher Louis Althusser (1969)—have sought to show that the mature Marx abandoned his earlier humanism. Either way, it is certainly the case that Marx's political thought develops over time and that 1845 is an important moment in that development.

13.2.1 Modes of production

In a series of manuscripts written in 1845–1846 and first published in 1932 under the title *The German Ideology*, Marx and Engels develop what has been called 'the materialist conception of history' or historical materialism. They are materialists because the premises they start from are 'real individuals, their activity and the material conditions under which they live, both those which they find already existing and those produced by their activity' (Marx and Engels, 1976a: 31). Marx no longer writes of 'species-being' or attempts to establish the essence of human nature. As he writes in the so-called 'Theses on Feuerbach', written in 1845 but only published by Engels in 1888: 'the essence of man is no abstraction inherent in each single individual. In its reality it is the ensemble of the social relations.' If one starts with 'an abstract—*isolated*—human individual', one will never be able to grasp human individuals as they exist in the real world (Marx, 1976c: 4).

Hence, instead of beginning from some idea of human nature—from 'Man' in the abstract—we must instead begin from concrete social relations. While they do not begin from some notion of the human essence, Marx and Engels (1976a: 31) do distinguish humans from animals: the former '*produce* their means of subsistence'. To understand human life, then, we must examine how humans satisfy their needs by producing and reproducing their conditions of life. This necessarily means analysing humans within society. This is not a moral point that we are necessarily sociable or altruistic rather than individualistic or egotistical; Marx's point is that humans cannot produce and satisfy their needs in isolation, outside of society.

> **Key Concept: Dialectics**
>
> Marx adapted Hegel's dialectical method. Simplifying somewhat, 'dialectics' for Hegel meant viewing history as a series of stages, each of which is in tension with itself. The limits and contradictions of each stage lead to its dissolution, leading to a new stage which transcends the old stage while preserving some of its features. Marx adopts this emphasis on historical change, but whereas Hegel understood history as the movement of ideas or forms of consciousness, Marx sees it as the movement of the material conditions from which ideas emerge. This is why Marx (1976a: 103) claimed that with Hegel the dialectic 'is standing on its head. It must be inverted, in order to discover the rational kernel within the mystical shell.' A dialectical approach to capitalism entails recognition that capitalism is not 'natural' or eternal: there were pre-capitalist societies and there will be post-capitalist societies—and it is capitalism's own contradictions which are pushing it towards its dissolution.

Marx is a materialist, then, because he believes that the analysis of any society must begin with the *material* conditions of production, or what he calls its 'mode of production'. This is a *historical* materialism because he further argues—in dialectical fashion (see Key Concept: Dialectics)—that the mode of production changes through history. In the 1859 'Preface' to *A Contribution to the Critique of Political Economy*—the most condensed and concise summary of his method available to us—Marx (1987b: 263) distinguishes 'the Asiatic, ancient, feudal and modern bourgeois modes of production'. Each of these modes of production is characterized by specific forces of production—the activity of production and its tools and technology—and relations of production. Except in the very early societies that Marx calls 'primitive communism', relations of production have always been *class* relations: a ruling class owns and controls the means of production, while most people belong to an oppressed class whose emancipation can only be achieved with the creation of a new society. As Marx and Engels (1976b: 482) state at the start of the *Communist Manifesto*: 'The history of all hitherto existing society is the history of class struggles.' In the capitalist mode of production—which is what Marx spends most of his time criticizing—the ruling class are the bourgeoisie and the oppressed class are the proletariat, who will only be free with the overthrow of capitalism and the advent of communism: a classless society in which the means of production are owned in common.

13.2.2 Base and superstructure

Marx's methodological approach has often been understood in terms of a distinction between the 'base' and the 'superstructure'. As he puts it in the 1859 'Preface':

> The totality of these relations of production constitutes the economic structure of society, the real foundation, on which arises a legal and political superstructure and to which correspond definite forms of social consciousness . . . The changes in the economic foundation lead sooner or later to the transformation of the whole immense superstructure.
>
> (Marx, 1987b: 263)

Yet this model raises some problems and questions, not all of which are satisfactorily answered elsewhere in Marx's work. First, there is the question of human agency. Marx has been accused of economic determinism—of claiming that history is driven by economic structures and relations that determine our lives, leaving no room for the agency of individuals or groups. While such an interpretation would not be wholly illegitimate, it would be unfair on Marx, whose position is better summarized in his 1852 essay, *The Eighteenth Brumaire of Louis Bonaparte*: 'Men make their own history, but they do not make it just as they please; they do not make it under circumstances chosen by themselves, but under circumstances directly encountered, given and transmitted from the past' (Marx, 1979b: 103). In *The German Ideology*, Marx and Engels do tend to suggest that the forces of production determine the relations of production: as the forces develop, they outgrow their relations, and a social revolution ushers in new relations that better correspond to the newly developed productive forces. Such a formulation, however, risks presenting the progress of modes of production as inevitable—merely a question of waiting for productive forces to ripen—and hence minimizes the role of class struggle in social revolutions and the active participation of the exploited classes as agents of their own emancipation. In later works, Marx will place greater emphasis on the dialectical nature of the relationship between forces and relations of production, presenting them as reciprocally determined.

The charge of economic determinism has also been used to claim that Marx obliterates the efficacy or autonomy of non-economic, 'superstructural' forces. It is certainly true that in the 1859 'Preface'—whose concision has meant that it has been taken as a distillation of Marx's essential methodological principles—the superstructure is presented as merely reflecting or expressing the base that determines it. In other writings, however, Marx awards the superstructure greater autonomy, in the sense that legal, political, and cultural developments can affect the base. In the 'Introduction' to the *Grundrisse*, Marx (1986b: 46) refers to the 'unequal [or uneven] development of material production' relative to legal, intellectual, and cultural forms, such as art, implying that the latter are not strictly determined by the economic base. In *Capital*, Volume 1, Marx acknowledges that in some societies non-economic forces may play a dominant role, for example, the Catholic religion in the Middle Ages, or politics in Ancient Athens and Rome. But he insists that even in these societies the *determining* role is still played by economic production, because the satisfaction of our needs (for food, shelter, etc.) through economic production is necessarily at the foundation of any society: 'the Middle Ages could not live on Catholicism, nor could the ancient world on politics. On the contrary, it is the manner in which they gained their livelihood that explains why in one case politics, in the other case Catholicism, played the chief part' (Marx, 1976a: 176).

But why must production be understood in terms of *class*? Even many sympathetic critics of Marx have argued that he is economically deterministic in the sense that his privileging of economic class as both a lens of analysis and an agent of change relegates other forms of struggle and oppression—such as those of gender and race—as superstructural and thus secondary to class. This criticism certainly has some validity. Marx did not develop any systematic theory of gender, despite paying attention to the position of women and the role of the family in capitalism. His theory is gender-blind in that he takes the *male* worker as his model, with women labourers tending to feature alongside children as cheap competition (they could work for less money than men and so lowered wages as they entered the labour force). That Marx himself may have subsumed the oppression of women to the class struggle, however, does not mean that feminists cannot make use of Marxism (Hartmann, 1979). The concept of social reproduction, for example, builds on Marx to explore the domestic labour that is essential for capitalism but which is unwaged and often unrecognized and is usually performed by women (Bhattacharya, 2017).

Marx and Engels both used racial slurs in their private correspondence (Mills, 2003: 152) and in his early 'On the Jewish Question', Marx (1975c) plays ironically but unwisely with anti-Semitic tropes even as he defends Jewish emancipation. At best, his work is at best often highly Eurocentric. For example, the 'Asiatic mode of production', which Marx conceptualized as a pre-capitalist social form typified by despotism, has been criticized for its apparent dismissal of the non-European world as autocratic, stationary, and backward and for its implication that non-European societies are significant only insofar as they can help us understand the development of European capitalism. On the other hand, the concept of the Asiatic mode of production can be read as a challenge to Eurocentric models of history, demonstrating that there is more than one path to capitalism and communism. In later life, Marx (1989b: 200-201) himself cautioned against using his work as a universal, all-purpose 'historico-philosophical theory of general development, imposed by fate on all peoples, whatever the historical circumstances in which they are placed'.

13.2.3 Ideology

For Marx, then, to understand a society we should examine not its main ideas—its religious values, moral principles, legal codes, or philosophical theories—but rather the material production which gives rise to those ideas. As Marx and Engels (1976a: 37) write: 'It is not consciousness that determines life, but life that determines consciousness.' The idealist belief that *ideas* are the ruling force in society—and hence that we need only combat bad ideas in order to transform society—is attributed by Marx and Engels to the Young Hegelianism that they now reject and which they contrast to their own materialism. This is what they mean by 'ideology': an ideologist is someone who has inverted the relation between ideas and practice, believing that consciousness determines life. But simply to denounce the ideology of the Young Hegelians would itself be ideological: it would be to remain at the level of ideas, stuck within philosophical debate, in place of the empirical investigation of material conditions that Marx and Engels are advocating. What they set out to demonstrate, therefore, is how the ideological inversion of ideas and practice developed historically. They show that the belief that ideas are autonomous in relation to material practice is not wholly illusory, because the production of ideas *has* become separated from material production: there is a division of mental and manual labour. Just as material production is dominated by the ruling class, so is the production of ideas. As Marx and Engels (ibid.: 59) put it: 'The ideas of the ruling class are in every epoch the ruling ideas.' The ruling class 'regulate[s] the production and distribution of the ideas of their age'. This is the meaning of 'ideology' most associated with Marx, referring not simply to the mistaken belief that ideas are the ruling force in any society, but to those specific ideas that defend and perpetuate the interests of the ruling class.

Against the German ideologists, therefore, Marx and Engels argued that we must relate ideas to the material conditions of their production—but because production is always dominated by a ruling class, this means that we must also consider the class interests which are served by particular ideas. What defines history for Marx, however, is not simply class rule but class *struggle*. If class rule was unchallenged, then the ruling class would not need ideology to advance its interests. So ideology is not something that is simply imposed upon us: it is contested and can become a battleground in the class war (Marx, 1987b: 263).

With the concept of ideology, Marx provides a way of critically reading other political theories. Marx was in particular a critic of liberalism, which for Marxists is the ideology of capitalism. The liberal focus on the individual both misleadingly suggests that we can understand societies as collections of individuals—rather than in terms of conflictual classes—and legitimizes and encourages the kind of individualism which capitalism perpetuates and on which it depends. For Marx, the *formal* freedoms and rights awarded to individuals by the liberal revolutions of the late-eighteenth and nineteenth centuries were empty, concealing the reality of economic oppression and exploitation. As Charles Mills (2003) (see Chapter 10) and others have claimed, however, this critique of liberalism arguably underplays and obscures the fact that even the formal freedoms and rights of liberalism were reserved for white European men. It could be said, therefore, that Marx's own theory was sometimes 'ideological' in the broad sense that it obscured the reality of certain power relations, especially those of white supremacy and patriarchy.

> ### 🔑 13.2 The materialist conception of history: Key Points
>
> - Marx and Engels' materialist conception of history posits that we should understand societies as modes of production which can be analysed in terms of their forces and (class) relations of production.
> - The forces and relations of production constitute the economic structure or base which determines or conditions the political, legal, and ideological superstructure, but the superstructure can itself affect and influence the base, such that the two are not necessarily strictly distinguished.
> - Marx and Engels' claim that the history of society hitherto is the history of class struggle can be criticized for obscuring other forms of oppression and conflict, such as those of gender and race.

13.3 The origins and nature of capitalism

In 1847, Marx and Engels joined the newly formed Communist League, for whom they wrote the *Communist Manifesto*. Because of his radical activities, Marx was expelled from a number of European countries and in 1849 he and his family settled in London, where he began work on *Capital*, a planned multi-volume work of which only the first volume was published in Marx's lifetime.

13.3.1 Commodification

Marx opens *Capital*, Volume 1 (first published in 1867) with an analysis of the commodity. A commodity is a product that has been produced in order to be exchanged. It is only under capitalism that 'the commodity becomes *the general form of the product*, that every product must take on the commodity form' (Marx, 1976a: 950). This is in contrast to previous modes of production, in which goods were produced in order to be consumed, and only that which was surplus to requirements was exchanged. It is not just things that become commodities under capitalism, but services, knowledge, emotions. Or, as Marx (1976b: 113) puts it in *The Poverty of Philosophy*, 'virtue, love, conviction, knowledge, conscience, etc.' have all 'passed into commerce'.

Marx does not simply denounce this commodification. Capitalism is for Marx revolutionary, and some passages from certain texts of his work read almost as celebrations of capitalism—though Marx at the same time condemns capitalism in the strongest terms and both hopes and expects that it will be superseded by communism. As the Marxist cultural theorist Fredric Jameson (1993: 47) puts it, Marx asks us 'to understand that capitalism is at one and the same time the best thing that has ever happened to the human race, and the worst'. Capitalism for Marx is revolutionary in part because it unleashes enormous productive energy. In the *Manifesto*, Marx and Engels (1976b: 489, 487) claim that the 'bourgeoisie, during its rule of scarce one hundred years, has created more massive and more colossal productive forces than have all preceding generations together', accomplishing 'wonders far surpassing Egyptian pyramids, Roman aqueducts, and Gothic cathedrals'.

In revolutionizing productive forces, capitalism simultaneously and necessarily revolutionizes our social relations. All of our traditional values and modes of living are undermined by capitalism. As one of the most memorable passages of the *Manifesto* declares: 'All fixed, fast-frozen relations, with their train of ancient and venerable prejudices and opinions, are swept away, all new-formed ones become antiquated before they can ossify. All that is solid melts into air, all that is holy is profaned' (ibid.: 487). Traditional beliefs, practices, and sources of authority—religious, moral, political—are swept away as every aspect of our lives becomes commodified and thus governed by capital. As well as extending down deeper into our lives, capitalism also spreads it way across the globe in its search for new markets and for new sources of raw material and labour power. In the *Manifesto*, this point is made in rather Orientalist and even racist terms, as Marx and Engels (ibid.: 488) argue that capitalism 'draws all, even the most barbarian, nations into civilisation. The cheap prices of commodities are the heavy artillery with which [the bourgeoisie] batters down all Chinese walls, with which it forces the barbarians' intensely obstinate hatred of foreigners to capitulate.' This 'civilizing' influence of capital is a major theme of Marx's *Grundrisse*. The line of argument is perhaps at its most troubling in Marx's journalistic writings on India of the 1850s, criticized by Edward Said (1995: 154) for their 'Romantic Orientalist vision' (see Chapter 16 on Said). In articles for the *New York Tribune*, Marx (1979a; 1979c) suggested that British colonialism, although brutally violent and not immediately benefitting the Indian people, could nonetheless be viewed as a progressive force, because by facilitating economic and social development it helped to lay down the conditions for a possible future communist society. This claim is at the very least highly Eurocentric—apparently suggesting that India must follow the same path of development as Britain—and at worst relies on racist tropes of Britain's civilizing mission in India (though we should note that Marx's later writings on non-European societies are far more sophisticated: see Anderson, 2016).

This near-celebratory depiction of a triumphant capitalism spreading civilization is echoed in the attitude towards nature that Marx sometimes displays. Indeed, there is some overlap with his often patronizing dismissal of other cultures: in his articles on India he mocks their 'worship of nature' and failure to recognize man as the 'sovereign of nature' (Marx, 1979a: 132). Yet, in general, Marx's understanding of the relationship between human and non-human nature is much more subtle and even prescient. Humans, he argues, are themselves part of nature and their labour in and on non-human nature transforms both them and nature. Hence 'the history of nature and the history of men' are 'inseparable' (Marx and Engels, 1976a: 28). Although, of course, we could not expect Marx to have anticipated climate change, he does warn of the destruction of the Earth by capital. A strand of eco-Marxism has developed in the twenty-first century that places much emphasis on Marx's (1976a: 637–638; 1981: 949–950) references in *Capital* to a 'metabolic rift', or the way in which capitalist production disturbs the metabolism between humans and the Earth (for example, by exhausting the fertility of the soil) (Foster, 2000; Burkett, 2014; Saito, 2017). It is, however, the exploitation of workers rather than of nature which lies at the heart of Marx's critique of capitalism.

13.3.2 Exploitation

Borrowing from Adam Smith, Marx claims that each commodity has two aspects: it is a *use value*, because it can be used to satisfy some need or desire, and it is an *exchange value*, because it can be exchanged for any other commodity. If commodities can be exchanged with each other in different proportions, it is because they all share something in common: they are all products of human labour. The value of a commodity thus depends on the amount of labour required to produce it. More specifically, the value of a commodity is determined by the 'labour-time socially necessary to produce it' (Marx, 1976a: 293).

> **Key Concept: Value**
>
> The classical political economist David Ricardo supported the labour theory of value: the value of commodities is determined by labour time. It is often claimed that Marx adopted the labour theory of value and used it to argue that workers should be given the full value of their labour. But that method better describes a group of early nineteenth-century radical economists called the Ricardian socialists. Ricardo had asked what determines the value of commodities; his answer was labour time. But Marx asks a different question: why are products produced as commodities at all? It is only under capitalism that

> most products are produced as commodities—or, to put it another way, it is only under capitalism that 'labour is expressed in value' (Marx, 1976a: 174). So 'value' is not a category applicable to all societies: it is the form that wealth takes in capitalist society. Exchange value is the form that value takes when commodities are exchanged; money represents values abstractly and capital is defined as 'self-expanding value'.

In pre-capitalist societies, the aim of production was to produce use values to be consumed; in capitalist societies, the aim is to produce values for exchange. This is expressed in what Marx (1976a: 257) calls the 'general formula of capital' or 'M - C - M': capitalists use money (M) to buy commodities (C) which are used to make more money (M'). This is 'valorization': value has been created. But the puzzle here is how valorization has taken place: how can the capitalist create value and therefore make a profit simply by buying and selling commodities? One answer might be that he buys cheaper than he sells: he buys commodities that have a value of £1000 but he sells them for £1100, for example, making a profit of £100. But while this might explain how one individual capitalist had made a profit at the expense of the others, it does not explain how all capitalists can make a profit—how value can be created. The capitalist production process creates more value than that with which it begins: a *surplus value* is created.

The answer to the puzzle is that the capitalist buys, along with raw materials and machinery, a special commodity which is 'a source not only of value, but of more value than it has itself' (ibid.: 301). That commodity is labour power: the capacity of the labourer to perform labour. The value of labour power is calculated in the same way as all other commodities—by the amount of labour required to produce it. Let us say, for example, that a worker needs £20 to meet her needs for a day and so to keep her in a condition in which she can continue to labour: the value of her labour power is therefore £20. So the worker is paid £20 per day—but in one day's labour she can produce commodities that have a value of £30. The worker has produced a *surplus value* of £10, which is appropriated by the capitalist and is the source of the capitalist's profit. It is, therefore, the unique property of labour power to create more value than it is itself worth which allows the capitalist to extract surplus value.

Key Concept: Exploitation

Marx defines exploitation as the production of a surplus that is appropriated by the ruling class. Exploitation is present in all class societies, but it is more obvious in pre-capitalist societies: the performance of surplus labour by slaves or serfs is clear. In capitalist societies, exploitation is less obvious: workers are (at least in some senses) free to choose their employer and they receive a day's wage for a day's work. But the wage-labourer under capitalism is still exploited, albeit in a different way: of her day's labour, some is necessary labour—reproducing value equivalent to that needed to meet the worker's needs, which is returned to the worker as wages—and some will be surplus labour: unpaid, because it produces value beyond that which is paid to the worker as wages. The surplus value produced is appropriated by the capitalist.

The exchange between the worker and capitalist is 'fair' and 'equal' in the sense that the capitalist pays the correct value of the labour power. The root of capitalist exploitation lies not in an unequal exchange but in the relations of production which underlie exchange relations: capitalists own the means of production, while workers own nothing but their labour power, which they are therefore forced to sell to a capitalist (even if they can in many cases choose which particular capitalist to work for). Both the problem and its solution therefore lie in the relations of production and not in the sphere of distribution. The objection to capitalism posed by Marx is not that workers are treated 'unfairly' or that they deserve higher wages or a greater slice of the pie. The exploitation of the proletariat will only be ended with the overthrow of capitalism.

There are two ways that the capitalist can increase surplus value. The first produces what Marx calls *absolute surplus value* and involves extending the working day, thereby increasing the total amount of labour performed. There is thus a struggle over the working day: workers can resist its extension and legal limits can be placed on its length. The second method is to reduce necessary labour: this produces *relative surplus value* (so-called because it increases the amount of surplus labour relative to necessary labour). This is achieved through the introduction of machinery (which increases productivity, thereby cheapening commodities and decreasing the value of labour power).

Far from making labour easier, machinery increases the intensity and danger of labour for workers. It also has an effect on gender relations. With the physical strength of the worker transferred to machinery, women (and children) could now be employed in factories, often in the worst and most dangerous jobs and for lower wages (ibid.: 517). As well as undermining traditional family relationships—a development which Marx (ibid.: 621) views ambivalently (or dialectically), on the basis that it creates 'a new economic foundation for a higher form of the family and of relations between the sexes'—this employment of low-paid women and children increased competition between workers and potentially divided the workforce. The unity of the proletariat was undermined by national and ethnic as well as gender divisions. Immigration from Ireland provided the English bourgeoisie with a reserve of labour, thus forcing down the wages of English workers who, whipped up by the ruling class, resented the Irish as competitors. In the Reconstruction-era USA, a similar hostility of white towards Black workers hindered proletarian unity (Marx, 1988). Marx (1989c: 340) urged working-class cooperation, declaring that 'the emancipation of the producing class is that of all human beings without distinction of sex or race'.

13.3.3 Primitive accumulation

The capitalist mode of production has two fundamental conditions: workers who sell their labour power and capitalists who employ that labour power to create surplus value. But how did these conditions come into being? How was it that one class was separated from the means of production and therefore forced to work for another class who owned the means of production? Marx (1976a: 873) answers this question in an exploration of 'primitive accumulation', so called because it was 'an accumulation which is not the result of the capitalist mode of production but its point of departure'. According to Marx (ibid.: 874), this was not a peaceful process: 'In actual history, it is a notorious fact that conquest, enslavement, robbery, murder, in short, force, play the greatest part.' Beginning in the sixteenth century, labourers were forcibly expropriated from the land that they worked by a variety of methods, including the enclosure of common land. This expropriation was initiated for a number of reasons, but the common result was the conversion of a largely independent peasantry into a proletariat separated from the means of production. Ruthless laws against vagrancy and begging compelled this newly created proletariat to move to towns and cities to look for work.

While some peasants were pushed down into the newly emergent proletariat, other independent farmers, already employing some wage labour, rose up into the new class of capitalists. Feudal restrictions on money were dissolved and new and larger markets developed, allowing this new class to accumulate wealth. Crucially, Marx (ibid.: 915) insists that European colonization of non-European lands and enslavement of their peoples were central to primitive accumulation.

'The treasures captured outside Europe by undisguised looting, enslavement and murder flowed back to the mother-country and were turned into capital there' (ibid.: 918). Later scholars investigated the place of colonialism in the development of capitalism in more detail. The historian (and later Prime Minister of Trinidad and Tobago) Eric Williams (1994), for example, argued that colonialism and the slave trade had helped to stimulate the Industrial Revolution in Britain: slaves were purchased using British goods and transported by British companies; the processing of raw materials from the colonies, such as cotton and sugar, created new industries and employment in Britain; and the colonies provided new markets to which the processed goods could be sold. Profits from the slave trade were invested in industries whose production and markets the trade itself had stimulated: many slave traders became bankers or supplied capital to heavy industry. Others, such as Cedric Robinson (1983), have argued that colonialism and slavery must be seen as central not only to capitalism's pre-history of primitive accumulation but also to modern capitalism itself. As such, we should recognize that opposition to what Robinson called 'racial capitalism' came not only from the European proletariat but also from Black rebellions and uprisings outside Europe.

Marx's discussion of primitive accumulation is significant for a number of reasons. To uncover the origins of capitalism is to contest the liberal view of capitalism as 'natural' and eternal. Against the view of liberal thinkers from Adam Smith onwards that commerce generates peace, Marx reveals capitalism's violent beginnings and its reliance on colonialism. And whereas Smith and others distinguished the state and the market—politics and economics—Marx demonstrates the often brutal role of the state in establishing and maintaining the capitalist 'free' market.

13.3 The origins and nature of capitalism: Key Points

- Marx argued that capitalism revolutionized both the forces and relations of production and in some texts even presented capitalism as a progressive or 'civilizing' force.
- Marx condemns capitalism on the grounds that it exploits workers, where 'exploitation' refers to the appropriation by capital of a surplus value produced by labour.
- In his analysis of 'primitive accumulation'—the pre-history of capitalism—Marx assigns a central role to colonialism.

13.4 The state and political transformation

Marx's view of the state is quite different from the standard liberal view of the state as a neutral referee that defends the rights and freedoms of individuals. From Locke (see Chapter 7) to Rawls (see Chapter 32) and beyond, liberals have used the idea of a social contract to illuminate their claim that the authority of the state rests on the consent of the governed. For Marx, in contrast, the role of the state is to defend the interests of one group, namely the ruling class. The state is based not on consent but on oppression and ultimately it uses violence to maintain the dominance of the ruling class.

13.4.1 The state and the ruling class

Whereas liberals tend to place the state—and its origins, purpose, powers, and limits—at the centre of their theories, we have seen that, for Marx, the state is part of the superstructure and hence secondary to the economic base. But this does not mean that the state is irrelevant to political analysis or action, for the state must play its part in protecting and maintaining the economic structure of society, by securing the conditions of reproduction of capitalist relations of production. This might include: regulation of competition (stepping in where necessary to reduce instability and resolve crises); enforcement of the legal system (which is itself not neutral but favours the bourgeoisie); regulation of class struggle (in favour of capital—but this might involve providing concessions to the working class such as the provision of welfare); and the promotion of bourgeois values. The state is itself dependent on capitalism: its funding through taxation depends on a growing capitalist economy.

At times, Marx implies that the state is something like a tool of the ruling class. In perhaps their most famous pronouncement on the state, in the *Manifesto*, Marx and Engels (1976b: 486) write: 'The executive of the modern State is but a committee for managing the common affairs of the whole bourgeoisie.' This formulation—which implies that the ruling class directly controls the state—is problematic for at least two reasons. First, it underplays the extent to which the state is itself a site of conflict and struggle. The working class respond to the state not merely with obedience but by making demands upon it, for example, for a shorter working day. Second, viewing the state as a tool of the ruling class tends to obscure the extent to which there are divisions *within* the ruling class. Not only are there different types of capital—for example, the industrial capital that produces commodities and the commercial capital that sells those commodities—but each individual capitalist firm is in competition with every other. The role of the state, therefore, is not merely to express and realize the interests of the bourgeoisie but also to negotiate, aggregate, and reconcile those interests. In *The Eighteenth Brumaire of Louis Bonaparte*, Marx argued that the state could rule *on behalf of* the bourgeoisie, who need not directly possess political power themselves. In this sense, the state can have what Althusser (1969) calls 'relative autonomy'.

The question of how the ruling class rule and the role that the state plays in their rule is significant not only for the analysis of capitalism but also for thinking about the transition to a post-capitalist society. Given that the central purpose of the state is to defend the interests of the ruling class, there will be no need for a state in communist society, in which the means of production will be owned in common and classes will not exist. But could the proletariat *use* the state to end capitalism and usher in communism? And how, if at all, should Marxists engage with the state in capitalist societies? It is, fundamentally, in the answers to these questions that the dispute between Marxists and anarchists arises.

Key Thinker: Pierre-Joseph Proudhon

It is believed that the first person to call themselves an 'anarchist' was the French theorist and activist Pierre-Joseph Proudhon (1809-1865), who was one of the best-known radical thinkers in Europe in the mid-nineteenth century. His first book, *What Is Property?* (1840), answered 'property is theft!' Marx initially admired and supported Proudhon but soon broke with him: the title of Marx's *The Poverty of Philosophy* (1847) is a play on Proudhon's *The Philosophy of Poverty* (1846). Marx argued that Proudhon had identified only the superficial problems of capitalism, such as the existence of money and exchange, and had failed adequately to address what for Marx was the fundamental question of the ownership of the means of production.

13.4.2 Marx and the anarchists

One of the most influential anarchists of the mid- to late-nineteenth century was the Russian Mikhail Bakunin. Bakunin admired Marx and largely accepted his analysis of capitalism. Both men desired a classless and stateless future—but they disagreed about the correct path to reach that future. Bakunin and his anarchist followers rejected all forms of political authority and organization: they would not form political parties, stand or vote in elections, or lobby the state for improved conditions. The state must be smashed. For Marx and Engels, the anarchist position was both naïve and untenable. The refusal of political action, they argued, denied the working class the most effective means of challenging the status quo. Moreover, even if abstention from politics was a good idea, it would not be possible: workers are always already involved in political struggles because they are subjected to the political oppression of the bourgeoisie.

So although he was a revolutionary who wanted to overthrow the capitalist mode of production and the capitalist state, Marx differed from the anarchists in his belief that engagement in party and electoral politics could benefit the proletariat. In many of his writings Marx also claimed that the state could be a tool of revolution: the proletariat could seize the state and use it to transform capitalism into communism. 'Between capitalist and communist society,' wrote Marx (1989a: 95) in the *Critique of the Gotha Programme*, 'there lies the period of the revolutionary transformation of the one into the other. Corresponding to this is also a political transition period in which the state can be nothing but *the revolutionary dictatorship of the proletariat*.' This notion of the 'dictatorship of the proletariat' was taken up by later Marxists such as Lenin (1992). The idea was that the proletariat must take over and make use of the state before abolishing it.

Bakunin (1990: 179) thought this was dangerously misguided: 'no dictatorship can have any other objective than to perpetuate itself, and . . . it can engender and nurture only slavery in the people who endure it'. From the anarchist's perspective, Marx and his followers did not understand that *all* states—including so-called workers' states—are pernicious. Bakunin contended that Marx's authoritarian tendencies were rooted in part in his reductionist theory. Because Marx reduced all forms of power and conflict to the class struggle, he did not understand that the state is itself an autonomous source of oppression (and not simply secondary to the economic base): he was therefore too complacent, Bakunin argued, in his view that the state could be used as a tool of revolution. Marx, Bakunin argued, also interpreted the class struggle too narrowly, privileging the proletariat as the agent of change and dismissing the revolutionary potential of other classes such as the peasantry. This single-minded focus on one struggle, anarchists have argued, lends itself to an authoritarian politics: it leads Marxists to argue that if there is only one struggle—proletariat against capital—then it makes sense for that struggle to be led by a centralized, disciplined party (such as that advocated by Lenin).

The dispute between Marx and Bakunin is illuminated by their divergent responses to the Paris Commune. This was the name given to a revolutionary government established in Paris in March 1871 by workers and soldiers. At the end of May 1871, the Commune was savagely repressed, with thousands of Communards executed. Bakunin (1973: 199, 206) celebrated the Commune as 'a bold and outspoken negation of the State' whose initial triumph and eventual failure vindicated his anarchist belief in popular organization from below: 'The future social organization must be made solely from the bottom upwards, by the free association or federation of workers.' While Marx (1986a) also welcomed the Commune as an expression of working-class agency, he argued that its failure showed that the workers were engaged in a long struggle against capitalism and that neither the state nor capitalism could be overthrown immediately. Marx mocked the anarchists for thinking that a revolution could be started through sheer force of will and insisted that the success of any revolution depended on the right economic conditions being in place: the contradictions of capitalism must develop and sharpen before it can be overthrown.

These disagreements came to a head in the International Workingmen's Association, which had been established in London in 1864 to unite workers across the world. At the 1872 Congress, the International split into two factions: the 'communist anarchists' behind Bakunin and the 'state communists' behind Marx. Bakunin was expelled and Marx stepped down from the General Council, marking the effective end of the International as a unifying force on the left.

13.4.3 The end of capitalism

Marx did not view himself as a prophet and so did not say much about the nature of future communist society, beyond indicating that it will be a stateless, classless society in which the means of production are owned in common. Similarly, Marx does not try to establish the exact mechanism by which capitalism will be transformed into communism. He always retained his faith in revolution but, especially after the 1848 revolutions and the subsequent counter-revolutions that had swept across Europe, he began to insist that a *'new revolution is possible only in consequence of a new crisis'* (Marx, 1978: 135). Yet he also thought that crisis is inevitable: capitalism is inherently contradictory and unstable. In *Capital*, Volume 3, Marx (1981) identifies a 'law of the tendential fall in the rate of profit'. Without here going into technical details, Marx claims that this tendency of the rate of profit to fall is rooted ultimately in the increased use of machinery by capitalists. If expected profits are low, then capitalists will not invest and demand falls, leading to crises of overproduction. In texts such as the *Grundrisse*—which Marx began writing in the midst of a major global economic crisis—these crises are presented as increasingly cataclysmic events that will inevitably lead to capitalism's 'violent overthrow' (Marx, 1987a: 134). In later works, such as *Capital*, Volume 3, Marx instead emphasizes factors that counteract the tendency of the rate of profit to fall and claims that capitalism's economic crises do not necessarily produce *political* crises that will lead to its overthrow.

In the final fifteen years of his life, Marx became increasingly interested in pre-capitalist and non-European social forms, seeing in them possible alternative paths to communism. With their sensitivity to historical and cultural difference, his ethnological notebooks can be contrasted with his earlier enthusiasm for the modernizing and 'civilizing' role of capitalism. In place of the Asiatic mode of production, Marx recognizes a range of forms of production and paths of development. He suggests that some communal forms of ownership could form the basis of a transition to communism without first having to pass through capitalism. In the 1880s, Marx and Engels (1989) speculated, for example, that the Russian peasant commune might be a starting point for the development of communism—if, that is, a Russian revolution can spark and connect with a proletarian revolution in the West.

> **13.4 The state and political transformation: Key Points**
>
> - Marx claimed that the role of the state was to defend the interests of the ruling class, while also recognizing that the state is a site of class struggle.
> - Marx and anarchists like Bakunin both looked forward to a stateless future but they disagreed over the need to engage in bourgeois politics and the possibility of a workers' state that could transform capitalism into communism.
> - Marx did not offer a blueprint for a communist society or for the end of capitalism, but in his later writings suggested that there might be more than one path of development towards communism.

13.5 Conclusion

At the heart of Marx's political thought is the concept of class struggle. This is both his strength and his weakness. Marx shows that politics is not about consensus or compromise but conflict. This conflict occurs because one class owns and controls the means of production, and it is therefore not restricted to a single arena but rather lies at the foundation of our lives as human beings. Within the capitalist mode of production, the conflict can be ameliorated but not ended: it will only be overcome with the overthrow of capitalism. In one sense, this is a widening of the scope of 'politics' beyond the common-sense liberal focus on formal political institutions, such as parliaments. The concept of class struggle can be and has been used to analyse almost every aspect of our lives. Yet Marx's focus on class is also restrictive. 'Political power, properly so called,' Marx and Engels (1976b: 505) state in the *Manifesto*, 'is merely the organized power of one class for oppressing another.' This suggests that politics will cease to exist in the classless society that will be communism. There is a tendency in the works of Marx and subsequent Marxists to subordinate other forms of political oppression, such as sexism and racism, to the class struggle (or even to ignore them altogether), with the assumption that those forms of oppression will automatically disappear with the advent of communism.

Yet Marx never claimed to have founded a universal theory that could explain everything. He developed a critique of capitalism that remains the most sophisticated we possess and has lost none of its relevance. Our lives are still structured by class relations and capitalism remains prone to crisis. Marx may have underestimated the resilience of capitalism but, as we experience the deepening of an ecological crisis that Marx himself anticipated, it is increasingly clear that capitalism is unsustainable and perhaps unreformable. This crisis will not necessarily be resolved: revolution is not inevitable and class struggles can end in 'the common ruin of the contending classes' (ibid.: 482).

As has been argued by generations of thinkers and activists—from anti-colonialists, such as Frantz Fanon (see Chapter 28) and Amical Cabral, to Black Marxist feminists, such as Claudia Jones and the Combahee River Collective—to say that Marx's theory requires supplementation is not to say that it should be abandoned. Oppression has many forms and takes place along many axes but they all necessarily intersect with class—because class in the Marxian sense concerns the production and reproduction of the conditions of our life. Indeed, given ever-increasing commodification and the extension of market relations into more and more spheres of life, Marx's focus on economics can be seen as a strength rather than a weakness.

Take your learning further by accessing the online resources for a library of web links to relevant videos, articles, blogs, and useful websites for this chapter: **www.oup.com/he/Ramgotra-Choat1e**.

Study questions

1. What are the main claims of Marx's materialist conception of history?
2. What is the distinction between base and superstructure and how might it be criticized?
3. How did Marx define 'ideology'?
4. What did Marx have to say about women, gender, and the family?
5. What role has colonialism played in the development of capitalism, according to Marx?
6. What did Marx think was the role of the state and how did this view differ from anarchist views?
7. How did Marx think capitalism would end?
8. In what ways, if any, might Marx's work be considered Orientalist or racist?

Further reading

Primary sources

Marx, K. (2000) *Selected Writings.* Ed. D. McLellan. Oxford: Oxford University Press.
　Probably the best single-volume collection of Marx's writings, including among other things the entire texts of key writings, such as the *Communist Manifesto*, the 1859 'Preface', *The Eighteenth Brumaire*, and the 'Introduction' to the *Grundrisse*.

Marx, K. (2007) *Dispatches for the New York Tribune: Selected Journalism of Karl Marx*. Ed. J. Ledbetter. London: Penguin.
　Useful collection of Marx's enlightening journalism on contemporary events, including British parliamentary politics, the Opium Wars in China, the British Raj, and the American Civil War.

Marx, K. (2019) *The Political Writings*. Ed. D. Fernbach. London: Verso.
　Wide-ranging selection of texts from 1848 onwards, including essays, articles, speeches, letters, and documents from the First International.

Secondary sources

Anderson, K. (2016) *Marx at the Margins: On Nationalism, Ethnicity, and Non-Western Societies*. Chicago: University of Chicago Press.
　Explores Marx's lesser-known writings on colonialism, race, slavery, and nationalism.

Brown, H. (2012) *Marx on Gender and the Family: A Critical Study*. Leiden: Brill.
　Comprehensive study of the place of gender throughout Marx's work.

Carver, T. (2018) *Marx*. Cambridge: Polity Press.
　Introduction by a leading scholar of Marx that emphasizes Marx's political activism.

Choat, S. (2016) *Marx's Grundrisse: A Reader's Guide*. London: Bloomsbury.
　Accessible introduction to one of Marx's central writings.

Foster, J.B. and Burkett, P. (2016) *Marx and the Earth: An Anti-Critique*. Leiden: Brill.
　Explication and defence of the ecological reading of Marx by two of its founding advocates.

Harvey, D. (2018) *A Companion to Marx's Capital: The Complete Edition*. London: Verso.
　Introduction to the first two volumes of *Capital* by one of today's most influential Marxist theorists.

Heinrich, M. (2012) *An Introduction to the Three Volumes of Karl Marx's Capital*. Trans. A. Locascio. New York: Monthly Review Press.
　Brilliant summary of Marx's most important work.

McLellan, D. (1973) *Karl Marx: His Life and Thought*. London: Macmillan.
　The best biography of Marx is also a very clear overview of his political thought.

Robinson, C. (1983) *Black Marxism: The Making of the Black Radical Tradition*. London: Zed Books.
　Analyses the roles of racism, colonialism, and slavery in capitalism, the limits of Marx's thought, and the place of Marxism in Black radicalism.

Vogel, L. (2013) *Marxism and the Oppression of Women: Toward a Unitary Theory*. Leiden: Brill.
　Key text in Marxist feminism that includes analysis of Marx and Engels' views on women and gender.

Wolff, J. (2003) *Why Read Marx Today?* Oxford: Oxford University Press.
　Highly accessible summary of Marx's main ideas.

References

Althusser, L. (1969) *For Marx*. Trans. B. Brewster. London: NLB.

Anderson, K. (2016) *Marx at the Margins: On Nationalism, Ethnicity, and Non-Western Societies*. Chicago: University of Chicago Press.

Bakunin, M. (1973) 'The Paris Commune and the Idea of the State'. In A. Lehning (ed.), *Selected Writings*. London: Jonathan Cape.

Bakunin, M. (1990) *Statism and Anarchy*. Ed. M.S. Shatz. Cambridge: Cambridge University Press.

Bhattacharya, T. (ed.) (2017) *Social Reproduction Theory: Remapping Class, Recentering Oppression*. London: Pluto Press.

Brown, H. (2012) *Marx on Gender and the Family: A Critical Study*. Leiden: Brill.

Burkett, P. (2014) *Marx and Nature: A Red and Green Perspective*. Chicago: Haymarket Books.

Cowling, M. (2006) 'Alienation in the Older Marx'. *Contemporary Political Theory*, 5: 319–339.

Engels, F. (2001) 'Letter to Conrad Schmidt. 5 August 1890'. In K. Marx and F. Engels, *Collected Works*, vol. 49. London: Lawrence and Wishart.

Foster, J.B. (2000) *Marx's Ecology: Materialism and Nature*. New York: Monthly Review Press.

Hartmann, H.I. (1979) 'The Unhappy Marriage of Marxism and Feminism: Towards a More Progressive Union'. *Capital & Class*, 3(2): 1–33.

Jameson, F. (1993) *Postmodernism, or, The Cultural Logic of Late Capitalism*. London: Verso.

Lenin, V.I. (1992) *The State and Revolution*. Trans. R. Service. London: Penguin.

Marx, K. (1974) *Ethnological Notebooks*. Ed. L. Krader. Assen: Van Gorcum.

Marx, K. (1975a) 'Contribution to the Critique of Hegel's Philosophy of Law: Introduction'. In K. Marx and F. Engels, *Collected Works*, vol. 3. London: Lawrence and Wishart.

Marx, K. (1975b) 'Economic and Philosophic Manuscripts of 1844'. In K. Marx and F. Engels, *Collected Works*, vol. 3. London: Lawrence and Wishart.

Marx, K. (1975c) 'On the Jewish Question'. In K. Marx and F. Engels, *Collected Works*, vol. 3. London: Lawrence and Wishart.

Marx, K. (1976a) *Capital: A Critique of Political Economy*, vol. 1. Trans. B. Fowkes. Harmondsworth: Penguin.

Marx, K. (1976b) 'The Poverty of Philosophy: Answer to the Philosophy of Poverty by M. Proudhon'. In K. Marx and F. Engels, *Collected Works*, vol. 6. London: Lawrence and Wishart.

Marx, K. (1976c) 'Theses on Feuerbach'. In K. Marx and F. Engels, *Collected Works*, vol. 5. London: Lawrence and Wishart.

Marx, K. (1978) 'The Class Struggles in France, 1848 to 1850'. In K. Marx and F. Engels, *Collected Works*, vol. 10. London: Lawrence and Wishart.

Marx, K. (1979a) 'The British Rule in India'. In K. Marx and F. Engels, *Collected Works*, vol. 12. London: Lawrence and Wishart.

Marx, K. (1979b) 'The Eighteenth Brumaire of Louis Bonaparte'. In K. Marx and F. Engels, *Collected Works*, vol. 11. London: Lawrence and Wishart.

Marx, K. (1979c) 'The Future Results of British Rule in India'. In K. Marx and F. Engels, *Collected Works*, vol. 12. London: Lawrence and Wishart.

Marx, K. (1981) *Capital: A Critique of Political Economy*, vol. 3. Trans. B. Fowkes. Harmondsworth: Penguin Books.

Marx, K. (1986a) 'The Civil War in France'. In K. Marx and F. Engels, *Collected Works*, vol. 22. London: Lawrence and Wishart.

Marx, K. (1986b) 'Economic Manuscripts of 1857–58'. In K. Marx and F. Engels, *Collected Works*, vol. 28. London: Lawrence and Wishart.

Marx, K. (1987a) 'Economic Manuscripts of 1857–58'. In K. Marx and F. Engels, *Collected Works*, Vol. 29. London: Lawrence and Wishart.

Marx, K. (1987b) 'A Contribution to the Critique of Political Economy'. In K. Marx and F. Engels, *Collected Works*, vol. 29. London: Lawrence and Wishart.

Marx, K. (1988) 'Letter to Sigfrid Meyer and August Vogt, 9 April 1870'. In K. Marx and F. Engels, *Collected Works*, vol. 43. London: Lawrence and Wishart.

Marx, K. (1989a) 'Critique of the Gotha Programme'. In K. Marx and F. Engels, *Collected Works*, vol. 24. London: Lawrence and Wishart.

Marx, K. (1989b) 'Letter to *Otechestvenniye Zapiski*, November 1877'. In K. Marx and F. Engels, *Collected Works*, vol. 24. London: Lawrence and Wishart.

Marx, K. (1989c) 'Preamble to the Programme of the French Workers' Party'. In K. Marx and F. Engels, *Collected Works*, vol. 24. London: Lawrence and Wishart.

Marx, K. and Engels, F. (1976a) 'The German Ideology'. In K. Marx and F. Engels, *Collected Works*, vol. 5. London: Lawrence and Wishart.

Marx, K. and Engels, F. (1976b) 'Manifesto of the Communist Party'. In K. Marx and F. Engels, *Collected Works*, vol. 6. London: Lawrence and Wishart.

Marx, K. and Engels, F. (1989) 'Preface to the Second Russian Edition of the *Manifesto of the Communist Party*'. In K. Marx and F. Engels, *Collected Works*, vol. 24. London: Lawrence and Wishart.

McLellan, D. (1973) *Karl Marx. His Life and Thought*. London: Macmillan.

Mills, C.W. (2003) *From Class to Race: Essays in White Marxism and Black Radicalism*. Lanham, MD: Rowman & Littlefield.

Robinson, C. (1983) *Black Marxism: The Making of the Black Radical Tradition*. London: Zed Books.

Said, E. (1995) *Orientalism*. London: Penguin.

Saito, K. (2017) *Karl Marx's Ecosocialism: Capitalism, Nature, and the Unfinished Critique of Political Economy*. New York: Monthly Review Press.

Williams, E. (1994) *Capitalism & Slavery*. Chapel Hill, NC: The University of North Carolina Press.

14 Friedrich Nietzsche

WILLOW VERKERK

Chapter guide

This chapter takes into consideration many of Nietzsche's major works, with a concentration on his middle and later texts, to reflect on the problem of 'the political' in his oeuvre. After the Introduction, Section 14.2 identifies Nietzsche as a philosopher of culture whose perspectivist theory of knowledge challenges dualistic systems of truth. In Section 14.3, Nietzsche's concept of the will to power is explained, with reference to how it functions at the level of the state and the individual. Nietzsche's critique of morality is presented. Section 14.4 examines Nietzsche's difficult writings on equality and democracy and interrogates his positions on sex, race, and colonization. This chapter neither seeks to dismiss nor defend Nietzsche. It aims to provide a foundation for understanding Nietzsche's philosophical concepts and methodologies, so that each reader can use the tools of critical thinking to assess the relevance of his philosophy for themselves.

14.1 Introduction

There is no consensus on the status of Friedrich Nietzsche (1844–1900) as a political thinker. He has been called apolitical and anti-political, anti-feminist, and racist. At the same time, he has been read and quoted by decolonial thinkers for his inspirational force and studied and used by feminist theorists to deconstruct the gender binary. His writings influenced a generation of post-war leftist French philosophers, yet, not long before this, his work was misappropriated by the Nazis. More recently, it has been contended that his notion of *agon*, meaning struggle or contest in ancient Greek, gives evidence for his support of democracy. Nietzsche has been used and abused theoretically and practically by thinkers on all sides of the political spectrum. This makes his position as a political theorist a complicated one. What is most often agreed upon is that Nietzsche is a violent thinker who is concerned, above all, with power and how it operates.

According to Nietzsche, all life is will to power at its foundations. At the instinctual level, human beings are a combination of struggling forces that seek to express themselves. Human nature is wilful; culture allows the inclination to cruelty that is part of this disposition to be sublimated into sport, work, and art, among other things. Nietzsche believes that human beings are trained through moral and societal disciplinary practices, which he calls 'the morality of custom' and the 'social straitjacket', to be 'good' moral subjects and citizens (Nietzsche, 2014: 248). These disciplinary practices change the *form* that the will to power takes. This is what is meant by sublimation when applied to the will to power: how the will to power is expressed changes from being in its raw and instinctual form into something that is more culturally acceptable.

The scholarly assertion that Nietzsche is a violent thinker does not refer to his notion of human nature. It refers to his no-saying style, in which he questions, critiques, and denies traditional presumptions in the history of philosophy. Nietzsche attacks the ideas and characters of philosophers without refrain. Nothing is sacred. He calls for the destruction of old beliefs and values, declaring that, 'to what is falling one should give it a further push!' (Nietzsche, 2005b: 182). Nietzsche's proclamation that God is dead (and we have killed him) and that 'good' and 'evil' are human constructions, were provocative statements in the nineteenth century, and arguably are still so today. Without God, people lack values, according to Nietzsche, and this leads to widespread nihilism—the notion that life is without meaning. These statements, and especially *how* Nietzsche writes them, exemplify why he is considered a violent thinker.

Nietzsche calls the state 'the coldest of all cold monsters' (ibid.: 43). Yet, he is more concerned with culture and concepts and how societal values and practices shape and control people psychologically through morality, religion, and belief. Nietzsche employs what he terms a genealogical method to study the generation and development of concepts, as well as their progressions and modifications over time. In doing so, he challenges the premise that concepts have a fixed and objective meaning. He claims, instead, that they are dynamic and perspectival. The upshot of this is that people and institutions can mould and modify concepts for their own use. Nietzsche's self-defined role, said by him to be the most creative role of a philosopher, is to change concepts.

Nietzsche is considered a great stylist. He writes in unconventional forms for a philosopher, employing aphorism and narrative, poetry, and jokes, as well as the essay. In addition to the interpretive challenges of understanding Nietzsche's literary tropes, there is further debate about which of Nietzsche's texts are most important. His published works or his notes? His late period or some other? The three periods of his writings are generally understood to be the following: early 1872–1876; middle 1878–1882; late 1883–1888.

Read more about **Nietzsche's** life and work by accessing the thinker biography on the online resources: **www.oup.com/he/Ramgotra-Choat1e**.

The notion that Nietzsche's texts have periods is used to understand the focus of his different writings, as well as the biographical and historical contexts during which they were written. Good practice is to concentrate on his published works and consider his unpublished works when unresolved questions emerge, and further information is required. This chapter focuses on the middle and late periods of Nietzsche's published works: *Human, All Too Human, Daybreak, The Gay Science, Thus Spoke Zarathustra, Beyond Good and Evil*, and *On the Genealogy of Morality*. These include Nietzsche's most widely read texts, with the late period often assumed to include Nietzsche's mature thoughts.

14.2 Physician of culture

Throughout his oeuvre, Nietzsche is preoccupied with the themes of sickness and health and applies these notions to the body, as well as to the spirit and the intellect, to society and to culture. Nietzsche argues that with the death of God and an increasingly secular world, value systems are eroding, and many people struggle to find meaning, becoming hopeless without the comfort of faith. Instead of attempting to create new values, people focus on their productivity as good workers and citizens. According to Nietzsche, the rise of industrialization meant that there was less time for learning, reflection, and friendship. Nietzsche writes that the shifts from a religious world-view to a scientific one, from feudalism to capitalism and to the politics of the petty bourgeoisie, have harmed the individual through perpetuating mediocrity. These harms are broadly described by him as involving a sickness that infiltrates life. For this reason, he contends that a physician of culture is required to make diagnoses and put forward remedies. The physician of culture must be adept in human psychology, which Nietzsche contends is 'ruler of the sciences' and the path to the fundamental problems (Nietzsche, 2014: 26).

Nietzsche views his books as means to interject into the minds and beliefs of his readers, to affect them as individuals and, through this, have an impact on society. He writes that he is 'a psychologist without equal' (Nietzsche, 2007: 105). Nietzsche diagnoses modern European culture with nihilism, so that its subjects can seek out a cure or, at minimum, become aware of it. Nietzsche writes about two types of nihilists: the passive nihilist and the active nihilist. Most people are passive nihilists. They seek out escapism to forget the disorientation and despair caused by the loss of meaning. The kind of nihilist that Nietzsche admires, and recognizes as dangerous, is the active nihilist who aims to destroy values. The active nihilist is aware that for new values to emerge, those in decay must first be destroyed. The way in which Nietzsche writes, specifically his confrontational style, is used to enlighten readers to the collective need for the re-evaluation of values.

> **Key Concept: Nihilism**
>
> Modern European culture was, according to Nietzsche, nihilistic. He claimed that the move away from Christianity left Europeans without a justification for existence. Formerly, the higher values of Europe, such as justice, virtue, beauty, and truth, found their authority in a metaphysical world-view associated with God and the rewards of the afterlife. Nietzsche explains that the loss of this authority impacts all Europeans, not only religious folk, because it reveals the absence of a higher order. According to Nietzsche (2014: 2), Christianity is 'Platonism for the people' and the loss of belief in God also affects belief in the higher ideals that regulate society. As a result, people come to doubt whether there are objective moral or religious foundations for human life. The consequence of this is that life seems senseless, even absurd, and people become hopeless and suffer from despair.

Nietzsche employs stylistic devices to select his readers. He writes esoterically and exoterically: there is a hidden meaning (esoteric) and a literal meaning (exoteric). He argues that comprehension requires work and time and he wants readers willing to put in the effort required to access the complexity of his thought. Nietzsche states: 'My writings have been called a schooling in suspicion, even more in contempt, but fortunately also in courage, indeed in audacity' (Nietzsche, 2005a: 5). The French philosopher Paul Ricoeur (2008: 32) categorizes Nietzsche, along with Marx (see more on Marx in Chapter 13) and Freud, as a master of suspicion who unmasks the real from the apparent and provides a critique of false consciousness.

Nietzsche proposes that beliefs are creative productions, not objective facts. He aims to train the reader to think more carefully about those facts that they take to be true, and the interests that are at work in determining which beliefs rule over society. Nietzsche was one of the first philosophers to illuminate the relationship between power and truth and show that reason can be instrumentalized. Contra Kant, Nietzsche argues that reason is not pure; it can be employed for variant ends which need not be good or just.

14.2.1 Perspectivism

Nietzsche's theory of perspectivism argues that objective truth does not exist as a God eye's view or neutral location. Knowledge is of a situated kind: it is dependent upon the perspectives and experiences of the individual. However, this does not mean that Nietzsche is a relativist; he does not propose that all beliefs are of equal value or are equally 'true'. Instead, to discover the relevance of a supposition, it is important to examine it from more than one position so that one's prejudicial thinking can be countered by other points of view. For Nietzsche, disinterested knowledge does not exist. However, it is possible to come to a more accurate view of a belief through approaching the problem from a plurality of perspectives (Nietzsche, 2014: 308). Nietzsche admits that his own propositions too reflect a point of view and require further questioning and interrogation from perspectives different from his own.

Nietzsche disputes the epistemological claim that knowledge is justified true belief by questioning the proposal that what is 'true' can be defined as that which is reasonable. He points out that the logic of discovery, or how a belief becomes justified, is infiltrated by networks of power at both individual and societal levels. The thinking subject is affected by culture, by their social categories, by their life experiences, and the presuppositions they bring to any new or old belief. Nietzsche's critique of objective knowledge has been important for postmodern and feminist thinkers who question the cogency of the unbiased rational subject and the presumption that belief can be freed of perspective.

14.2.2 'Woman' and 'truth'

Nietzsche explores the problem of perspective when he writes about the 'prejudices of philosophers' in *Beyond Good and Evil* (Nietzsche, 2014). He creates an analogy between 'woman' and 'truth' to show how the idealism of philosophers is a kind of dogmatism that limits their knowledge (ibid.: 1). According to Nietzsche, philosophers project an image of 'woman' onto women which prevents them from seeing and understanding real living women. They do so similarly with truth: they have a notion of 'the truth' inherited from the Christian-Platonic tradition which shapes their pursuit of knowledge and narrows their point of view.

Nietzsche rejects the Platonic system of ideal forms which supposes the existence of concepts of 'the good', 'the true', and 'the beautiful'. Just as there is no perfect woman, or 'eternal feminine' waiting to be discovered, there is no perfect truth to be uncovered through education or enlightenment. Instead of serving to enlighten, Nietzsche claims that the idealisms of Plato (see more on Plato in Chapter 2) and Kant (see more on Kant in Chapter 29) perpetuate a naïve dogmatism, inhibiting the pursuit of knowledge which necessarily requires a plurality of perspectives.

This line of critique has been pursued from a feminist perspective in the work of Luce Irigaray, who agrees with Nietzsche that we lack perspective, but claims that the problem has specifically to do with an absence of the feminine perspective. Although she acknowledges Nietzsche's challenge to dualistic systems of meaning, she argues that Nietzsche too remains locked in a logic of the same, in which the masculinist perspective creates a specular image of woman that perpetuates a false representation of 'woman' (Irigaray, 1991). Further, she argues that Nietzsche not only creates his own image of woman, he wants to become her, and in doing so, leaves no space for women to be themselves.

Nietzsche was aware of certain pitfalls in his thinking that Irigaray brings to light. He admits that his beliefs about 'woman' and 'man' are a result of a situated perspective, of his own inherited values. He writes that one's convictions about such concepts as man and woman are 'the footsteps of our self-knowledge, signposts to the problem that we are—more correctly to the great stupidity that we are' (Nietzsche, 2014: 136). This admission shows that Nietzsche understood the limitations of his own belief system and was seeking to move beyond them. While it is the case that Nietzsche does make misogynistic remarks in his writings, it is important to consider the textual context. Paying close attention to Nietzsche's styles is key, as he uses metaphor and hyperbole to attain a greater response from his readers. As can be seen in the work of Irigaray, Nietzsche's writings on women are productive for feminist critique, even if they are disturbing.

> #### Key Thinker: Luce Irigaray
>
> Luce Irigaray, born in Blaton, Belgium, in the 1930s, is a philosopher, feminist, linguist, and psychoanalyst with two doctorates, one in philosophy and the other in linguistics. She is Director of Research in Philosophy at the Centre National de la Recherche Scientifique in Paris. Her work, which examines the problem of sexual difference in the history of Western philosophy and psychoanalysis, has been highly influential. So much so that the publication of her second dissertation, *Speculum of the Other Woman*

in 1974, made her lose her place at the Freudian School and in the Lacanian community, as well as her position as an instructor at the University of Vincennes. Since this time, Irigaray has continued to challenge major figures and concepts in philosophy and psychoanalysis through her own style of feminist critique, writing over thirty books, including *This Sex Which Is Not One* (1977), *Marine Lover of Friedrich Nietzsche* (1980), and *An Ethics of Sexual Difference* (1984).

One of Nietzsche's goals as a philosopher of culture is to expose the beliefs, including his own, that create stagnancy in society. His diagnosis of the prejudices of philosophers aims to help philosophers reinvent themselves so that they can pursue knowledge more effectively. According to Nietzsche, most people inherit their belief systems without taking the time to consider them. Rather than studying their opinions and habits to determine their worth, people refer to their inherited beliefs when it comes to making judgements. Nietzsche introduces the notion of the intellectual conscience as a second-order self-awareness to measure and reflect upon the origins of beliefs. He describes the intellectual conscience as a 'conscience behind your "conscience"' which impels you to inquire into the origins and developments of your judgements (Nietzsche, 1974: 263). The intellectual conscience brings probity to presuppositions so that beliefs can be examined more carefully, and individuals can develop greater self-honesty.

14.2.3 Contesting the truth of opposite values

Just as good religious folk follow a faith, Nietzsche argues that good moral subjects follow a faith which is based upon the convictions of the metaphysicians, namely a belief in the opposition of values (Nietzsche, 2014: 6). Nietzsche's critique of dualistic systems of truth such as good and evil, man and woman, truth and falsity, poison and cure, demonstrates that binaries are more related to one another than is supposed. Nietzsche argues that binary concepts originate in their opposites and, in some instances, formerly shared the same attributes as their opposites. For example, he argues that what is taken to be true and just in society can become so through deception and injustice.

Nietzsche explains that beliefs that are in fact errors can be supported beliefs because over time, due to their usefulness, they have gained authority (Verkerk, 2019: 54). He argues that even if a counter-example has more evidence, it can be rejected in the interest of the useful belief (Nietzsche, 1974: 169). In many instances, that which is useful to the authority governing the truth becomes part of the accepted knowledge. For example, the notion that women are weaker and more emotional may be false, but this belief can be used to maintain gender inequality in a patriarchal society. One of Nietzsche's central aims as a physician of culture is to reveal these deceptions so that individuals can think more critically about what they take to be true, and question whether they want to support the authority which governs that belief.

14.2 Physician of culture: Key Points

- Nietzsche writes as a physician of culture to diagnose the cultural condition of nihilism in modern European society; he also aims to challenge collectively held belief systems and provoke questioning of said beliefs in the reader.
- Nietzsche's theory of perspectivism disputes the theory of objective truth and the postulation of a neutral subject of knowledge by claiming that knowledge is situated, shaped by one's perspectives and experiences.
- Nietzsche rejects idealistic theories of knowledge by claiming that there is no perfect concept of 'woman' or 'the truth'.

14.3 Will to power

The will to power is the foundational concept in Nietzsche's thinking. It provides a description of existence in both macro and micro terms: it is the stuff that makes up all of life. According to Nietzsche, human nature is governed by the will to power and so are culture and society. What does this mean? Instead of pleasure, happiness, or self-preservation being the impulse of life, we are motivated by a drive to possess and experience greater power. Nietzsche writes that the will to power is a '*primordial fact* of all history' (Nietzsche, 2014: 170). Although conventions and institutions change the forms of representation that the will to power takes through sublimation, it remains there as the instinct that drives things on.

Nietzsche claims that the 'fundamental instinct of life' aims at '*the expansion of power*' (Nietzsche, 1974: 291). Life as will to power is constituted by a combination of forces, each of which seeks to assimilate and incorporate the other forces into itself so that it can increase its power. The will to power is agonistic, which means that it is engaged in and determined by contest. An individual is an organization of struggling drives held together as the will to power and should be viewed as a verb, not a noun, because it is in continual movement, 'always reorganizing' (Aydin, 2007: 30). The human is composed of many different drives, each seeking mastery.

> **Key Concept: *Agon***
>
> *Agon*, translated as competition, struggle, or contest, is a governing concept for Nietzsche's thinking. He drew on the writings of Homer to develop his notion of *agon*, as well as on the lectures of his friend Jacob Burckhardt, who was a historian of European art and culture. At the level of being, Nietzsche views human nature to be agonistic and contends that *agon* must be maintained for a healthy political community to exist. As a philosopher, Nietzsche writes agonistically and attempts to encourage the spirit of *agon* in his readers, urging them to struggle against him. *Agon* is proposed as a remedy for passive nihilism. While passive nihilism leads to apathy and escapism, the competitive energy of *agon* forces the individual to find value in activity and pursue goals in the interest of both individual and collective growth.

It is incorrect to view Nietzsche's notion of the will to power in simple terms of dominance and submission. Existence is always in a process of becoming, in a movement of struggle, which requires that forces intermingle. Forces of variant degrees permeate and modify each other. Furthermore, the attainment of greater power need not be achieved through a direct route. Although the energy of the will to power seeks to be expressed overtly, often it cannot and finds other ways to express itself. We will see later how Nietzsche examines this in greater detail through his account of the slave and master.

Nietzsche often brings up his concept of the will to power to analyse the meaning and the purpose of a human work. He argues that behind what we see, whether it be a penal system, a story of history, or a work of art, is a psychic life that seeks a fuller expression of their power. He then asks, how is this thing a manifestation of the will to power? Philosophical theories too are viewed to be a result of the philosopher's will to power. Nietzsche argues that a theory is a way to imprint oneself on the world and the specific way in which the theory is articulated can reveal much about the thinker's inner life. For this reason, Nietzsche views biography as important to consider in the interpretation of a thinker's overall project.

Regarding Nietzsche's biography, he planned for but later abandoned a manuscript called *The Will to Power*. In his *Genealogy of Morality*, he writes that he is preparing a work called *The Will to Power: Attempt at a Revaluation of All Values* (Nietzsche, 2014: 346). However, this title was only one stage of his planned magnum opus (Brobjer, 2006) and the book which exists with this title today is not actually a book written by Nietzsche, but a selection of writings from his notebooks modified and rearranged by several editors under the direction of his sister Elisabeth Förster-Nietzsche. Elisabeth outlived her brother (until 1935) and after he died she used the book to misrepresent Nietzsche's views and align him with National Socialism and Hitler in Germany.

The postulation that all life is will to power has been and continues to be a tempting formulation for those looking for a justification for violence. The faulty reasoning goes something like this: if we are by nature creatures who seek greater power, then any mechanisms are appropriate to achieve this (might makes right). Key to note is that this line of justification requires that one ignore that the will to power is agonistic and its health depends on it being in ongoing conflict, with a plurality of drives and *not* in a state of resolution where one force dominates. It also overlooks that Nietzsche discusses the benefits that culture and society bring to the raw drives of the will to power, allowing for it to develop through structure and discipline, beyond its vulgar instincts. While his monistic theory of life is surely incomplete, the will to power is not the call to brutality that some have supposed it to be.

14.3.1 *Agon* and the state

Is the will to power compatible with democracy? When questioning how Nietzsche's notion of the will to power as an agonistic plurality can be used to understand society, scholars turn to an early essay of Nietzsche's called 'Homer's Contest' of 1872 (Nietzsche, 2008), where he discusses the relationship between nature and culture through the Greek concept of *agon*. This essay provides insight into Nietzsche's thinking about the existence of the state which is further explored in his *Genealogy*. At the start of 'Homer's Contest', Nietzsche writes that there is no separation between humanity and nature. He argues that the state is a continuation of nature, and much of what is most admirable in society has come into existence through impulses that may be considered animalistic or inhumane. These impulses, however, drive competition and are the source of much of human greatness, according to Nietzsche. The desire for cruelty, which Nietzsche later argues is a shared human trait and a compulsion of the will to power, is sublimated through the practice of agonistics in society.

Nietzsche claims that sport, education, art, politics, and friendship involve a spiritualized cruelty that motivates people to achieve greatness through competition. This not only allows for the individuals involved to develop and improve their skills, but it also serves the health of the state by increasing its reputation and genius. In 'Homer's Contest', Nietzsche explains that the struggle that inspires excellence is not one orientated towards destruction of the other but is one in which contestants rely upon the skill of the opponent and offer each other mutual respect to lift each other up in the interest of shared advancement.

At the level of the state, Nietzsche writes that 'the contest is vital, if the well-being of the state is to continue' (ibid.: 178). Although there is evidence to suppose that Nietzsche favoured an aristocratic political system over a democracy, the principle of *agon* requires, like democracy, that a plurality of voices be maintained, and open dialogue and public debates be supported. The role of contest in politics calls for ongoing discussion and dissensus to allow for the social community to develop together. Political dispute between different perspectives is considered essential to the democratic process (Hatab, 2008: 185).

For Nietzsche, a harmonious political community in which all agree is a stagnant one. There, the forces of life are supressed. He claims that we should be wary of living in a place without visible competition, disagreement, and envy. The appearance of conflict shows an active political community whereas its absence suggests a tyranny which suppresses the diversity of life. Nietzsche states that the forces of the will to power do not abate when they are repressed. Instead, they wait under the surface for the right time to strike, taking on new forms of development so that they can exert their powers most effectively when the time is right.

14.3.2 Slave and master moralities

In *Beyond Good and Evil* and *Genealogy of Morality*, Nietzsche writes about two kinds of moralities: those of the master and the slave. Rather than stating one type is superior, Nietzsche is engaging in a cultural analysis, providing a genealogy of the two types he considers are predominant in the history of morality. The account is a descriptive one; it becomes polemical because it aims to make readers aware of the dogmatic attachments they have to moral paradigms. Nietzsche argues, through his description of the slave revolt in morality, that many of the values that we consider admirable originated from their opposite and are not as praiseworthy as they appear.

Nietzsche associates the master morality with nobility and often connects its characteristics to ancient Greece and the writings of Homer. The master type forms the notions of 'good' and 'bad' in relation to their capacities as a straightforward expression of their nature. Nietzsche explains that it is 'a morality of self-glorification' which involves an overt expression of power (Nietzsche, 2014: 171). What is 'good' is like them: it is proud, affirmative, strong, truthful, and courageous. The master rejects the pity of others and accepts friendship only with their peers, enjoying relationships that are agonistic. They believe in a hierarchical system of value, in the importance of honour, in backgrounds, and bloodlines. Nietzsche states that this type of morality is generally unpalatable to modern people, representative of an older more 'barbaric' time in which the will to power was less restrained. He highlights the attributes of the master morality as one way to critique nineteenth-century values, which he argues are generally governed by slave moralities.

Nietzsche claims that slave morality began with the Jewish tradition, has further developed through Christianity, 'and has shifted from our view because it has been—victorious' (ibid.: 226). He explains it as a revolt against the masters which occurred because an oppressed people needed to find new routes to gain power. Slave morality inverts the values of the masters and defines those things as 'good' that can alleviate suffering and bring the oppressed greater advantage. These traits include charity, compassion, patience, industriousness, humility, and kindness. Slave morality transforms the notions of 'good' and 'bad' into 'good' and 'evil', making evil that which harms them. As such, power and danger are said to be evil and pride a sin: this allows the slaves to vilify characteristics of the masters. While the goals of the slave morality are freedom and happiness, the masters do not care for either; they are concerned with honour and reverence.

According to Nietzsche, the slave revolt occurs because a community of people are not able to directly express their nature. They are oppressed and look for a way to assert themselves in reaction to those who are their oppressors. Nietzsche explains that when a people's will to power is not able to affirm and express itself, it is forced to turn inward and look for alternative routes from which to act. The oppression that the slaves experience from the masters makes them want to take revenge upon them, but since they are not strong enough to do so, they become frustrated. However, this frustration becomes creative and 'gives birth to values: the *ressentiment* of those beings who are denied genuine reaction, that of the deed, who make up for it only through imaginary revenge' (ibid.: 228). Nietzsche claims that slave morality becomes a weapon against the masters from which the slaves can find routes to exercise their repressed will to power.

> **Key Concept: *Ressentiment***
>
> Nietzsche uses the French word *ressentiment* to explain the psychological desire for revenge that forms within a person or group of people when they are unable to express their will to power. His meaning is different from the English 'resentment' which is defined as a moral emotion, a response to an injustice from a specific harm. By *ressentiment*, Nietzsche is describing the instinctual and reactive mood experienced by people who feel oppressed. *Ressentiment*, according to Nietzsche, is the affective force behind the slave revolt in morality: motivated by hatred, envy, and vengeance, the slaves transform the meaning of concepts and create new values that will serve them. While Nietzsche admires the generative strength of *ressentiment*, he is critical of the values that have originated from it, such as 'good' and 'evil', 'equality' and 'justice'. He asks: If the modern notions of justice and equality were formulated by a group of people who were seeking revenge, how epistemically sound can they be?

14.3.3 Morality has no rational foundation

Nietzsche believes that society and individuals are made up of a combination of slave and master moralities that struggle with one another. He provides an account of master and slave moralities as an alternative to the hypothesis that morality is an extension of the human capacity for reason. Nietzsche disputes the claim that moral principles are connected to some innate qualities within us that strive for fairness. Instead, they are in an ongoing state of contestation.

The problem with presuming that there is a definite foundation to morality for Nietzsche is that it obscures the fact that there are many kinds of moralities and, in doing so, overlooks that morality itself needs to be questioned. Nietzsche argues that those who think that they are practising a science of morality are bound by beliefs related to their own class, environment, faith, culture, and region (ibid.: 81). Nietzsche thinks that the attempt to create a system in a disinterested framework or set up some kind of universalism such as Kant's categorical imperative, is a kind of armchair philosophy that tells us more about the psyche of its creator, and the community that has adopted it, than about what we should or should not do.

When we follow a system of morals without questioning it, we are being commanded by an authority that acts to serve their own interests, according to Nietzsche. We act in service to a community, as a member within it, rather than from a position of reflective self-interest. Nietzsche writes that morality shows the needs of a community or a 'herd'. 'Morality trains the individual to be a function of the herd and to ascribe value to himself only as a function' (Nietzsche, 1974: 174).

Yet Nietzsche does think that morality as a series of commands is necessary because it acts as a disciplinary apparatus for human development. Nietzsche believes that it is through obedience, through the compulsion to follow a specific system of belief that something new can be created. Morality is a tool that can train human nature to express itself through specific channels. For example, Nietzsche states that it was through the pressures of Christian morality that 'the sex drive sublimated itself into love' (Nietzsche, 2014: 85) and new cultural practices and works of art associated with romantic love emerged. Although morality can be used to stifle life, it can also be used to develop a specific mode of life which gives rise to new creations.

Nietzsche's aim is to transform morality so that it no longer serves what he argues is the lowest common denominator of 'the herd', but instead serves the development of human excellence. Nietzsche's concept of virtue involves a return to the Aristotelian notion of human flourishing. However, Nietzsche's notion of flourishing is not connected to happiness but instead to the activation of the will to power. Nietzsche believes that the state should use systems of values, such as morality, to serve cultural development. A morality that can sublimate the will to power into new channels of human genius is of great worth to Nietzsche.

> **14.3 Will to power: Key Points**
>
> - In Nietzsche's view, human nature, society, and culture are all governed by the will to power: the will to power is the impulse of life, in a state of ongoing struggle, it seeks to experience and have greater power.
> - A healthy political community for Nietzsche is one which supports a plurality of agonistic perspectives.
> - Nietzsche argues that morality is not innate or rational. It is a disciplinary apparatus for human development.

14.4 Democracy and the problem of equality

How do Nietzsche's scathing remarks about equality impact his analysis of democracy? Do his remarks on these topics show him to be an elitist? Certainly, there are statements made by Nietzsche that appear to support prejudicial thinking. There is a reason that radical and fascist figures have used Nietzsche's incendiary words as inspiration—however, this does not mean that they understood him well. The challenge is to decipher him accurately, which is no small feat, considering how varied are scholarly interpretations of Nietzsche on all topics, but most especially on these ones.

Nietzsche's writings on democracy appear to suffer from contradictions; however, there are important distinctions to note which help us to understand their meaning better. Nietzsche often writes about a democratic sentiment or taste, which does not refer to democracy as a political system but instead to a characteristic or set of values. In addition, while his earlier texts show a genuine support for democracy as an agonistic and pluralistic system that bolsters the community, protecting it from tyranny, his later texts (from 1880 onwards) critique democracy for promoting uniformity and mediocrity and becoming the 'tyranny of the people' (Siemens, 2009: 20). Nietzsche's focus and style change in his later texts: he becomes more critical and provocative, increasingly concerned with his project of re-evaluation. One benefit to Nietzsche's contesting analyses of democracy is that they encourage independent thinking and debate, with other members of the political community, which are themselves principles of democracy.

Nietzsche's critique of equality is primarily concerned with the notion of moral equality. He argues that while scientific atheism has prevailed over Christian faith, the tenets of Christian morality remain entrenched in the modern European subject. He is referring specifically to the Christian notion that all are equal under God and are thus of equal worth. Christian beliefs are translated into democratic values, according to Nietzsche: the claims for equal rights and equal opportunities, the call for fairness, as well as the demands for compassion for those who suffer. Nietzsche's proposal is the following: if God is dead, why should we hold on to these beliefs and especially if they inhibit the development of individual excellence? One may argue that Nietzsche is writing as an active nihilist, to topple what he believes to be the remaining idols of the Christian-Platonic value system. Alternatively, it is also possible to claim that he is challenging the reader to find arguments for moral equality which do not circle back to Christianity.

Nietzsche writes about equality in positive terms when he states that the rule of law comes into effect through an agreement between equals (Nietzsche, 2005a: 314) and explains that a 'balance' is required for all contracts and consequently for all law (Nietzsche, 2014: 210–211). What is key to note here is that his positive notions of equality and being 'equals' refer to individuals who have 'no superiority of force' (Nietzsche, 2005a: 49). For Nietzsche, being among equals amounts to having roughly similar degrees of power. As is the case for opponents in a competition, there is a shared respect for one another and the assumption that the other competitor is one's peer. This does not refer to brute physical force, but rather to skill and character which can be composed of a variety of attributes.

In *Human, All Too Human*, Nietzsche writes about two types of the 'will to equality' (ibid.: 136). One kind involves the desire to bring others down to one's own level through doing them harm. This is the will to equality that Nietzsche argues is most active in a society that involves a 'tyranny of the people'. The other kind aims to raise others and oneself up and is viewed by Nietzsche as being active in agonistic relationships and communities founded on competition and excellence. The kind that Nietzsche attacks is of the first kind: this will to equality is viewed by him as a mechanism which subdues growth and differentiation and acts to bring down others to a lower level of being, promoting conformity. An example of this kind of levelling could be found in a populist movement which argues against intellectualism and higher education, promoting the nuclear family, cultural assimilation, and 'an honest day's work' for everyone. Nietzsche is concerned that this will to equality will detract from one's individuality and personal autonomy, encroaching on one's duties to oneself (Owen, 2002: 119). He is genuinely worried about the emergence of a conformist society and argues that the will to equality has a key role to play in its coming.

Nietzsche takes issue with what we know today as the principle of formal equality: that for fairness to ensue, people should be treated roughly in the same way. Broadly speaking, he associates equality with the move to treat everyone in similar ways and make people alike. For example, he defines equality as 'a certain factual increase in similarity that the theory of "equal rights" only gives expression to' (Nietzsche, 2007: 212). Nietzsche argues that the discourse of equality, which claims that everyone is equal under God and, as such, should have the same rights and protections, is a strategy of slave morality. As an ideology, it denigrates hierarchical systems of values and allows those who are or were once oppressed to take part in self-affirmation and minimize power disparities between themselves and the masters. While the discourse of equality helps to raise up the oppressed, Nietzsche argues that it also acts as an authoritarian levelling device by demanding the same kind of treatment for everyone.

Nietzsche claims that the call for equality ignores that power disparities are an inevitable part of life and are a requirement for human development. He argues that human beings are plastic and have, through their own efforts, the ability to overcome their circumstances. The move to treat everyone in the interest of fairness, in which all have security and comfort, freedom from danger and suffering does not respect human nature and its potential for growth, according to Nietzsche (2014: 45). He views it as repressive, an expression of a will against life. Nietzsche claims that resilience in the face of hardship builds one's character and is necessary for the development of self-knowledge. The popular saying 'what doesn't kill me makes me stronger' is a quotation from Nietzsche's *Twilight of the Idols* (Nietzsche, 2007: 157).

Considering Nietzsche's critique of equality, it is important to reassess whether Nietzsche can be considered a democratic thinker. For, if communal participation is considered important for a healthy society to protect it from tyranny, as he claims in his pre-1880 texts, then some foundational moral principles are required to allow for real participation. Otherwise, so-called 'democratic' *agon* is only expressed by a select few who have the power to do so, and Nietzsche can be viewed as a proponent of aristocratic radicalism. What should not be overlooked is that Nietzsche's analysis of equality is polemically charged: infused with the spirit of *agon*, he writes in search for respondents who are willing to answer to his cultural diagnoses and, in doing so, act as philosophers of culture themselves.

14.4.1 Sexism, racism, and colonialism

Nietzsche's self-defined role as a physician of culture has him diagnosing the circumstances of race, class, and gender and indicating what he considers to be the strengths and limitations of these categories. Nietzsche works with stereotypes to illuminate and deconstruct them, sometimes showing (and admitting to) his own prejudices about these topics. He should be held to account for the serious limitations of what he himself calls his own 'stupidity' (Nietzsche, 2014: 136). For there are sexist and racist statements in Nietzsche's books. However, Nietzsche also aims to make his readers uncomfortable, to force them to question their beliefs, and to reflect upon the limitations of prevalent belief systems by drawing out their contradictory attributes.

Nietzsche addresses problems of sexism and class when he discusses the construction of the concept of 'woman'. He argues that the notion of 'woman' has a genealogy as complex and dynamic behind it as the notions of 'truth' and 'evil' and is one which is overdetermined by the interest of men. In *The Gay Science* he writes, 'For it is man who creates for himself the image of woman, and woman forms herself according to this image' (Nietzsche, 1974: 126). Nietzsche notes that women face a 'psychic knot' when it comes to their relationship with men and with themselves, one which is reified through their domestic relationships with their husbands (ibid.: 128). Readers presume that Nietzsche is a misogynist because they overlook his writings on women in *The Gay Science* which contrast considerably with those in *Beyond Good and Evil*. To address these differences sufficiently a comparative reading of the two texts is necessary with attention given to Nietzsche's styles, his genealogical method, and his periods, as well as to biographical and historical context.

> **Key Concept: Genealogy**
>
> Genealogy is a methodology of critical analysis which examines the historical narrative of a concept or cultural practice to show how it came to have its current meaning and position. This process involves a study of the development of that thing which serves to denaturalize the meaning of it through providing alternative accounts of its generation. In this way, Nietzsche casts doubt on the integrity of moral concepts and entrenched cultural practices. He shows that important components of human life have not been established through historical progress. Instead, they are contingent and contestable, based on complex struggles for power. Those who follow the practice of Nietzschean genealogy reject the principle of epistemic certainty and attempt to track the development and effects of belief systems so that they can be better understood.

Nietzsche suggests that the notion of 'race' also requires a genealogical investigation, namely one which deconstructs the power networks at stake in the formulation of the concept (ibid.: 35). Yet, he does not take it up. However, other philosophers, such as Michel Foucault (2003) in *Society Must be Defended* and Cornel West (1982) in *Prophesy Deliverance*, have used the Nietzschean investigative tool of genealogy to analyse race and racism (see more on Foucault in Chapter 33).

It is now generally agreed that Nietzsche is not an anti-Semite. Scholars have pointed to his critique of nationalism as evidence that he was not an anti-Semite and to his emphasis on being a 'good European' over a German citizen. For example, the post-war French philosopher Georges Bataille (2015: 165–168) wrote that Nietzsche's values are 'in opposition to racist values', not compatible with fascism. More recently, contemporary scholar, Maudemarie Clark has argued that Nietzsche's notion of 'breeding' has to do with culture and not genes (Clark, 2013: 287).

Nietzsche makes stereotypical statement about races and national identities, sometimes using the notions of 'nation' and 'a people' as interchangeable with 'race'. He denigrates and celebrates various attributes of 'the Germans', 'the French', 'the English', 'the Chinese', and 'the Jews', among others. He comments on their morality, religion, values, arts, and cultures, as well as their problems related to sickness. Nietzsche does this not to create firmer boundaries between different national or cultural identities, but to demarcate what he contends to be the strengths and weaknesses of different cultures, emphasizing the importance of creating a stronger Europe through the amalgamation of different values and peoples. He calls himself a 'good European' and implores his readers to join him to bring Europeans together to build a stronger Europe (Nietzsche, 2005a: 174–175).

Nietzsche connects being a good European with being a free spirit (Nietzsche, 2014: 3) and states that one of his aims is to bring free spirits into existence (Nietzsche, 2005a: 6). He describes the free spirit as a critical thinker who questions the prevalent values of their age and what is expected of them, who has a lifestyle and system of beliefs that differ from the majority and more specifically from their origins and environment (ibid.: 108). The free spirit pursues philosophical honesty through examining their beliefs, rejecting epistemic certainty, and looking to understand concepts from a plurality of perspectives. Nietzsche explains that the free spirit differs from the fettered spirit whose beliefs are based on unquestioned habit. Nietzsche is also quite specific that the free spirit is a relative concept because the ways in which one develops radical honesty has to do with one's unique position and how one takes up critical self-analysis. Following Nietzsche's own account, then, we can ask: how free is he from the conventional beliefs of his time about European colonization? Does his enthusiasm for the 'good European' make him a 'good' colonialist too?

Like Hegel and Kant, Nietzsche encourages European expansion and global rule. While he is critical of Germany, its anti-Semitism and racism, as well as nationalism more broadly, when it comes to writing about world leadership, he is *for* Europe. He writes that those who are good Europeans must learn to write well so that their ideas can be shared with others. This appears as an admirable point, but the making of the ideas of the 'good European' available is, he writes, for the 'great task: the direction and supervision of the total culture of the earth' (ibid.: 332).

Nietzsche explains the good European as a person without a home who is of mixed racial descent. He uses the word 'we', speaking about himself and a community of admirable others who are his prospective friends, as if these are the kinds of people who can build a new European world. It is also the case that when he writes about the free spirit, as a higher type of human being, he is adamant that free spirits can come from any background. But what of Nietzsche's racial stereotypes? For example, in his *Genealogy*, Nietzsche claims that Black people have a greater capacity to endure pain and links the ability to withstand pain with being less cultured and more primitive (Nietzsche, 2014: 256). His use of a set of characteristics to fallaciously distinguish a group of people indicates both scientific ignorance and racist belief (Bernasconi, 2017). Nietzsche also makes erroneous generalizations about Chinese people, claiming, for example, that they have greater perseverance and diligence and, for this reason, can be a good resource for Europe (Nietzsche, 2003: 127). There are racist and colonial elements in Nietzsche's thinking. At the same time, there is a long tradition of decolonial and feminist thinkers turning to Nietzsche's critical philosophy: to his deconstruction of dualistic norms, to his analysis of the will to power, and to his notion of overcoming, among other topics.

This is because a good portion of Nietzsche's writing is concerned with the problem of liberation, in helping the 'fettered spirit' become free (Nietzsche, 2005a: 108). The feminist anarchist Emma Goldman (see more on Goldman in Chapter 26) recognized this, arguing that Nietzsche's critiques of morality and his stress on the importance of self-creation are crucial to a project aimed towards emancipation. She was an avid proponent of Nietzsche's philosophy, even designating him as an honorary anarchist. In his *Black Skin, White Masks*, Frantz Fanon (see more on Fanon in Chapter 28) references Nietzsche's notion of the will to power, turning to it to discuss actional power and the overcoming of racialized colonial indoctrination (Fanon, 2008: 197). Huey P. Newton also discusses Nietzsche's notion of the will to power. He writes about how power operates behind concepts that are taken to be 'true' and how the transformation of words can work to move power around. For example, the statement 'All Power to the People' shows that the 'Black community has its own will to power' (Hilliard and Weise, 2002: 227). For progressive and radical thinkers, Nietzsche can provide both deconstructive and constructive tools to analyse current paradigms so that they can be re-evaluated and, it is hoped, transformed.

> ### Key Thinker: Huey P. Newton
>
> Huey P. Newton was born in Monroe, Louisiana, USA, in 1942, the youngest of seven children. He was an activist, revolutionary thinker and writer, and, with Bobby Seale, co-founder of the Black Panther Party (1966–1982). Newton and Seale wrote the Ten-Point Program for the Black Panther Party which stipulated the party's principles and goals, including the right to self-defence for Black people in America, the right to full employment, decent housing, and anti-racist education. The Black Panther Party created over sixty community support programmes in the 1960s under Newton's leadership. They also created the Black Panther newspaper and the Free Breakfast for Children programme. Although Newton was convicted in 1968 for killing John Frey, an Oakland police officer, he was later released under public pressure, the Free Huey! Campaign, and a legal appeal. Newton published his book, *Revolutionary Suicide*, in 1973.

> ### 14.4 Democracy and the problem of equality: Key Points
>
> - Nietzsche supports and critiques democracy: he believes that democracy should support pluralism and avoid tyranny, whether it be of the one or the many.
> - Nietzsche argues that the principle of moral equality is a threat to individuality and autonomy, and that it creates a political climate in which difference and genius are discouraged.
> - There are racist and anti-racist, misogynist, and proto-feminist elements in Nietzsche's thinking.
> - The broad adoption of Nietzsche's concepts and methods by thinkers and activists shows that his thinking is political and can be put to different kinds of practical use.

14.5 Conclusion

Nietzsche performs an agonistic operation when he writes about politically contentious subjects. By appearing to write both for and against a claim, he expresses contradictory positions to bring attention and inquiry to these topics. In the spirit of critical engagement and agonistic friendship, he invites the reader into analysis and argument with him.

Nietzsche is above all a philosopher of modern European culture, focused on how values and beliefs are formed in the history of European society over time. He employs a genealogical method to unmask the development of tradition, holding no institution or system of knowledge to be free from critique. Nietzsche has injected philosophy with a heavy dose of doubt about objective truth and the universal subject. These doubts have been pursued further especially by French, feminist, and decolonial thinkers in the twentieth century. They have proven useful to those looking to deconstruct and transform concepts. There are, admittedly, troubling aspects to his thought which illuminate his own prejudices. However, Nietzsche's perspectivism holds that these are not fixed positions, they are agonistic claims made as provocations to his readers that are to be questioned and challenged.

Nietzsche's monistic theory of life, the will to power, claims that we are regulated by a drive that seeks power. This claim surely overlooks other key attributes of human nature, found in feminist, Indigenous, and Africana philosophies, as well as in science and psychoanalysis. Yet, Nietzsche's ruminations on power and morality often seem apt for diagnosing world conditions driven by white supremacy, colonialism, sexism, heteronormativity, and ableism. In addition, his articulation of the activation of the will to power, which involves the overcoming of restraint and the transformation of *ressentiment*, to bring about change, is important for an emancipatory politics.

For readers who read Nietzsche well, it is vital to cultivate our own perspective on his writings, to measure out which aspects of his thinking are to be kept, and which others must be rejected or transformed. Nietzsche is looking for readers who will think more carefully about the systems of truth and power that govern their lives. He is also looking for intellectual comrades who will challenge him with their own arguments. In Nietzsche's words, 'One repays a teacher poorly if one always remains only a student. And why would you not pluck at my wreath?' (Nietzsche, 2005b: 68).

Take your learning further by accessing the online resources for a library of web links to relevant videos, articles, blogs, and useful websites for this chapter: www.oup.com/he/Ramgotra-Choat1e.

Study questions

1. How does Nietzsche use his stylistic devices to affect his readers?
2. Critically evaluate Nietzsche's theory of perspectivism.
3. Critically examine Nietzsche's notion of the will to power.
4. Explain Nietzsche's claim that *agon* is an important principle for a healthy political community.
5. How does Nietzsche define the slave and master moralities?
6. Provide an argument against Nietzsche's critique of equality.
7. What are some of the racist and colonialist elements in Nietzsche's thinking?
8. Discuss which parts of Nietzsche's philosophy are helpful for a politics of liberation.

Further reading

Primary sources

Nietzsche, F. (2006) *The Nietzsche Reader*. Ed. K.A. Pearson and D. Large. Malden, MA: Blackwell.
This reader provides a comprehensive introduction to Nietzsche with substantial selections from his works and insightful commentary from the editors.

Nietzsche, F. (forthcoming) *The Complete Works of Friedrich Nietzsche*. Ed. A.D. Schrift, D. Large, and A. Del Caro. Stanford, CA: Stanford University Press.
This series of Nietzsche's published works will be the definitive edition, and will include of all his writings, both published and unpublished, once it is complete. For missing Stanford editions, see the Cambridge Nietzsche editions from *Cambridge Texts in the History of Philosophy*.

Secondary sources

Acampora, C.D. and Pearson, K.A. (2011) *Nietzsche's 'Beyond Good and Evil': A Reader's Guide*. London: Bloomsbury.
Guide to reading *Beyond Good and Evil*.

Burnham, D. (2015) *The Nietzsche Dictionary*. London: Bloomsbury.
A dictionary of Nietzsche's terminology.

Kaufmann, W. (1974) *Nietzsche: Philosopher, Psychologist, Antichrist*. Princeton, NJ: Princeton University Press.
This early biography of Nietzsche's life remains important today.

Knoll, M. and Stocker, B. (2014) *Nietzsche as Political Philosopher*. Berlin: De Gruyter.
A collection of essays on Nietzsche and political theory.

Lampert, L. (1986) *Nietzsche's Teaching: An Interpretation of Thus Spoke Zarathustra*. New Haven, CT: Yale University Press.
An analysis of *Thus Spoke Zarathustra* which allows for a greater understanding of Nietzsche's philosophy overall.

Oliver, K. and Pearsall, M. (eds) (1998) *Feminist Interpretations of Friedrich Nietzsche*. University Park, PA: Pennsylvania State University Press.
Collection of essays on Nietzsche and feminist theory.

Oppel, F.N. (2005) *Nietzsche on Gender*. Charlottesville, VA: University of Virginia Press.
A study of the topics of gender, sex, and sexuality in Nietzsche.

Owen, D. (2014) *Nietzsche's Genealogy of Morals*. London: Routledge.
An analysis of and guide to reading Nietzsche's *Genealogy*.

Patton, P. (ed.) (1993) *Nietzsche, Feminism and Political Theory*. London: Routledge.
Collection of essays on the intersections between political theory and feminism in Nietzsche's thought.

Richardson, J. (1996) *Nietzsche's System*. New York: Oxford University Press.
Nietzsche is approached as a systematic thinker.

Safranski, R. (2003) *Nietzsche: A Philosophical Biography*. Trans. S. Frisch. New York: W.W. Norton and Co.
An introduction to Nietzsche's life and ideas.

Scott, J. and Franklin, A.T. (eds) (2006) *Critical Affinities: Nietzsche and African American Thought*. Albany, NY: State University of New York Press.
An exploration between the thinking of Nietzsche and themes in African-American philosophy.

Siemens, H.W. and Roodt, V. (eds) (2008) *Nietzsche, Power and Politics: Rethinking Nietzsche's Legacy for Political Thought*. Berlin: De Gruyter.
This collection discusses the topic of Nietzsche's political thinking from a variety of perspectives.

References

Aydin, C. (2007) 'Nietzsche on Reality as Will to Power: Towards an "Organization-Struggle" Model'. *Journal of Nietzsche Studies*, 33: 25-48.

Bataille, G. (2015) *On Nietzsche*. Trans. S. Kendall. New York: SUNY Press.

Bernasconi, R. (2017) 'Nietzsche as a Philosopher of Racialized Breeding'. In N. Zack (ed.), *The Oxford Handbook of Philosophy and Race*. Oxford: Oxford University Press.

Brobjer, T.H. (2006) 'Nietzsche's Magnum Opus'. *History of European Ideas*, 32(3): 278-294.

Clark, M. (2013) 'Nietzsche Was No Lamarckian'. *Journal of Nietzsche Studies*, 44(2): 282-296.

Fanon, F. (2008) *Black Skin, White Masks*. Trans. R. Philcox. New York: Grove Press.

Foucault, M. (2003) *Society Must Be Defended: Lectures at the Collège de France, 1975-76*. Trans. D. Macey. New York: Picador.

Hatab, L. (2008) 'Breaking the Contract Theory: The Individual and the Law in Nietzsche's Genealogy'. In H.W. Siemens and V. Roodt (eds), *Nietzsche, Power and Politics: Rethinking Nietzsche's Legacy for Political Thought*. Berlin: De Gruyter.

Hilliard, D. and Weise, D. (eds) (2002) *The Huey P. Newton Reader*. New York: Seven Stories Press.

Irigaray, L. (1991) *Marine Lover of Friedrich Nietzsche*. Trans. G.C. Gill. New York: Columbia University Press.

Nietzsche, F. (1974) *The Gay Science*. Trans. W. Kaufmann. New York: Vintage.

Nietzsche, F. (2003) *Daybreak*. Trans. R.J. Hollingdale. Cambridge: Cambridge University Press.

Nietzsche, F. (2005a) *Human, All Too Human*. Trans. R.J. Hollingdale. Cambridge: Cambridge University Press.

Nietzsche, F. (2005b) *Thus Spoke Zarathustra,*. Trans. G. Parkes. Oxford: Oxford University Press.

Nietzsche, F. (2007) *The Anti-Christ, Ecce Homo, Twilight of the Idols*. Trans. J. Norman. Cambridge: Cambridge University Press.

Nietzsche, F. (2008) 'Homer's Contest'. In *On the Genealogy of Morality*. Trans. C. Diethe. Cambridge: Cambridge University Press.

Nietzsche, F. (2014) *Beyond Good and Evil/On the Genealogy of Morality*. Trans. A. Del Caro. Stanford, CA: Stanford University Press.

Owen, D. (2002) 'Equality, Democracy, and Self-Respect: Reflections on Nietzsche's Agonal Perfectionism'. *Journal of Nietzsche Studies*, 24: 113–131.

Ricoeur, P. (2008) *Freud and Philosophy: An Essay on Interpretation*. Trans. D. Savage. New Haven, CT: Yale University Press.

Siemens, H.W. (2009) 'Nietzsche's Critique of Democracy (1870–1886)'. *Journal of Nietzsche Studies*, 38: 20–37.

Verkerk, W. (2019) *Nietzsche and Friendship*. London: Bloomsbury.

West, C. (1982) *Prophesy Deliverance*. Philadelphia, PA: Westminster.

15 Sayyid Qutb

AYESHA OMAR

> **Chapter guide**
>
> This chapter explores some of the key ideas of Sayyid Qutb, a prominent Egyptian, Muslim political theorist and anti-colonial thinker. After an Introduction, Section 15.2 sets Qutb's ideas in their intellectual contexts and discusses his theory of *jahilliyyah* (condition of ignorance), exploring how and why Qutb prescribes measures to counter the effects of *jahilliyyah*. Section 15.3 then unpacks Qutb's conception of *hakimiyyah* (divine sovereignty), which is central to his project for Islamic renewal. Finally, Section 15.4 considers Qutb's contribution to revolutionary resurgence and in particular his theory of offensive *jihad*. Overall, the chapter highlights and problematizes Qutb's enduring legacy as both a militant and decolonial political thinker and underscores the manner in which his ideas continue to garner interest in the contemporary world.

15.1 Introduction

Sayyid Qutb (1849–1905) exerts an enormous influence on Islam in the modern period and is frequently described as one of the most important intellectuals and radical ideologues of the twentieth century. Qutb's name rose to global prominence after the attacks on the United States on 9/11 in 2001, when political commentators traced the intellectual origins and source material of Al-Qaeda directly to his political ideology. His copious writings routinely circulating in the Muslim world have been translated into an extraordinary number of languages and he is read from Indonesia to Sudan. Some have argued that Qutb's untimely execution and inability to clarify controversial terms have led to the radical interpretation of his writings (Musallam, 2005: ix).

This chapter will show how and why Qutb's writings are useful for understanding Islam's relationship to liberal modernity and secularism, the politics of the Islamic world, and the concept of freedom. It argues that while Qutb's ideas are susceptible to a militant Islamic reading which has pernicious consequences, his ideas are also significant for the manner in which he responds to the dominant, Western philosophical and epistemological paradigm that proclaims the superiority of rationalist and Enlightenment values. This approach, which moves beyond the narrow binaries of Samuel Huntington's 'clash of civilizations' thesis, recognizes the immanent limitations of key aspects of Qutb's work, especially on gender and violent resistance, but simultaneously seeks to understand why Qutb thought that rehabilitating Islamic teachings through reform and revival were critical in confronting the challenges of liberal modernity. Rather than engaging in an orientalist exercise which merely reduces Qutb's ideas to the antithesis of liberal modernity, the chapter articulates how and why Qutb contested and undermined liberal modernity and which decolonial approach he sought as an alternative. Hence, the chapter claims that Qutb's arguments for moral and spiritual renewal as an antidote to imperial encroachment must be read alongside a broader awareness of his writings' entanglement with violent ideology and social conservatism. Like other

Western thinkers presented in this volume, it is important that Qutb's writings are interrogated and subjected to a critical gaze.

Qutb categorically repudiates the claim that a rationalist, secular, Western framework is the source of human freedom and progress. Interestingly, he does not question the genealogy of the Western 'secular' tradition of political thought or that its major exponents (such as Locke—see more on Locke in Chapter 7) were Christian thinkers and their thought was deeply marked by Christianity. Instead, through his rejection of liberal modernity, partly informed by his experience of colonial occupation, Qutb articulates an alternative possibility for how we think about freedom and revolution, grounded in a moralizing ethic. Qutb's impact on transnational politics and his ability to craft an Islamic response to Western colonialism need to be appreciated in the context of European expansion and imperial control. His ideas, concerned with reinstating religious purpose and ethical meaning, are a reaction to exploitation and dispossession which the colonial experience had delivered in Egypt and elsewhere in the Muslim world. The method and literary style which Qutb utilizes in his political thought are shaped by his pedagogical training. His writings, although multi-layered, contain a 'strong strain of didacticism' and are instructive in tone (Akhavi, 2013: 161). But his writings are also, as Tripp (1994: 154–155) correctly points out, 'confessional' in nature, and experiences such as his personal disillusionment with a morally corrupt Egyptian society or his decade-long imprisonment ought to be understood as events which directed how he thought about politics and society and the place of Islam in the world.

Qutb's impact on political movements and actors in the Muslim world has meant that key concepts and ideas contained in his ideology have attained notoriety far beyond the academic study of political Islam (March, 2019: 114). As such, Qutb's writings are often associated with the idea of *Islamism*, defined as the practical realization of the formation of a state and society according to a set of Islamic principles derived fundamentally from Quranic scripture. It is Qutb's contribution in constructing the theoretical basis of Islamism in the postcolonial Sunni Muslim world that draws attention to the remarkably complex nature of his intellectual project and the convictions which underscored his ideological certainty.

The early twentieth-century Muslim tradition, typified in the work of thinkers such as Muhammad Abduh, supported borrowing some aspects of Western thought in order to modernize and reform. In contrast, Qutb wrote from a 'self-consciously Islamic standpoint' and wholly rejected the West, calling for widespread Islamic renewal rooted in Islamic ideas and principles (Tripp, 1994: 155). Qutb's quarrel with the Western-inspired philosophical method of inquiry was that it was an aberration of the Islamic way. As Akhavi (2013: 162) points out, this does not mean he opposed rational discourse, but rather 'that the discursive logic that he upheld was one that was at the outset premised upon divine axioms that restricted the scope of inquiry within the bounds of transcendental faith'. Fundamental to Qutb's vision was the conviction that Islam encompassed a total and complete way of life and that the crisis in the Muslim world represented a deviation from the recognition of this totalizing mission. To this end, for Qutb, it was critical for Muslims to once again recognize Islam as 'religion and the world' (*din wa-dunya*).

Qutb's ideas must be analysed with particular reference to the socio-political contexts which inspired their development. This contextual feature of Qutb's work is particularly salient for understanding his critique of liberal modernity and the religio-centric framework he proposed as the method for urgent redress in Egypt and elsewhere in the Muslim world. Qutb's political thought, as Euben (1999: 53) suggests, is not just 'a matter of intellectual interest or enrichment' but contends with the very urgencies that animate political realities in the Muslim world. Moreover, as Calvert (2013: ix) argues, Qutb is 'a man who drew upon the hallowed corpus of the Islamic heritage in order to craft a vision of life and governance that is ostensibly different'. What this means is that Qutb sought to restore the Islamic tradition to its imagined true form as a way of providing the Muslim world with an alternative to liberal modernity and colonial domination.

> **Key Thinker: Muhammad Abduh**
>
> Muhammad Abduh (1906–1966) was a nineteenth-century Egyptian, Muslim jurist, intellectual, and reformer. His early training was influenced by the reformist teachings of the theologian Jamal al-Din al-Afghani at the prominent institution for religious learning, Al-Azhar University. Abduh's major intellectual contribution was in legal and political reform, as he argued for the revival of rational inquiry and the harmony of religion and reason. He supported selective borrowing from the West, especially in the development of science and modern technology, where he argued that the West itself built upon the Islamic classical heritage. Abduh is thus viewed as a thinker of the tradition of Islamic modernism, which can be described as a tradition which advocates for the reform of the Qur'an and Islamic normative teachings to address the challenges of living in modern societies.

Read more about **Qutb's** life and work by accessing the thinker biography on the online resources: **www.oup.com/he/Ramgotra-Choat1e**.

15.2 Colonialism and *jahilliyyah*

15.2.1 Intellectual context and reception

Sayyid Qutb was born in the rural village of Musha in the province of Asyut, Upper Egypt. His early life coincided with the British occupation in Egypt, which involved colonial interference in the affairs of the Egyptian government and the effective control over the strategic Suez Canal region. The formative years of his life thus coincided with a shift in Egyptian society from tradition to modernity, exemplified by the westernization and secularization of social, educational, economic, and political affairs. Colonial occupation also produced localized public dissent and opposition to government policy. Qutb's father, a religious and educated landowner, was involved in the Nationalist Party, inspired by its resistance to Western encroachment. Qutb received his early elementary education at a local state school and at the age of 13 he was sent to Cairo to seek a secondary education that paved the way to his admittance at a tertiary college institution (*daru'l uloom*), where he trained as a teacher. As a newly trained teacher, Qutb joined the Egyptian Ministry of Education, engaging in civil service and socializing in Cairo's literary circles. His writings during this period reflect his interest in emerging literary debates and the work of secular intellectuals such as Taha Husayn and Abbas Mahmud al-Aqqad, and these early writings arguably contain a more secular orientation than his later works. Qutb's concern with questions of identity and representation allowed him to interrogate Egyptian and Arab nationalism as a response to the colonial condition. He regularly contributed to intellectual and literary journals and his wide-ranging publications feature poetry and literary critique, while he later developed an account of the aesthetic dimensions of the Qur'an.

But for Qutb, the post-Second World War context brought into sharp focus the consequences of imperial occupation, rising inequality and poverty, government corruption, and economic and social injustice. Despair with established political institutions intensified, creating a polarizing environment in which Egyptians were increasingly attracted to two main ideological groups: Marxism and the Muslim Brotherhood (Musallam, 2005: 2). It is in this context that Qutb's ideas can be rightfully assessed. Qutb's first major theoretical work, *Social Justice in Islam* (Qutb, 1996 [1949]), had a greater Islamic orientation than his earlier writings. Qutb's intellectual transition to an Islamic outlook was in part related to his growing affinity for the Muslim Brotherhood. *Social Justice in Islam*, however, is important for heralding the start of an unrelenting intellectual project to search for Islamic alternatives to Western ideologies including liberalism and socialism.

> **Key Concept: The Muslim Brotherhood (*al-Ikhwan al-Muslimeen*)**
>
> The Muslim Brotherhood is a religio-political and social movement founded in Egypt in 1928 by elementary school teacher Hasan al-Banna. The movement was conceptualized as a militant, Islamic revivalist organization in response to British colonialism and the perceived Western impingement on religious tradition. The movement concerned itself with advocating for social, political, and economic reform along religious lines and soon established a large following, with Qutb as one of its prominent members. Since then the movement has transformed into a major transnational organization, with members and branches spanning from Sudan to Indonesia. The movement was persecuted and banned in Egypt by President Nasser and subsequent authoritarian governments, therefore functioning primarily as an underground organization. The Muslim Brotherhood emerged as a major player during Egypt's first democratic election in 2012 but was soon deposed in a violent coup by the military.

Qutb's observations on the inadequacy of secular, rationalist epistemologies and Western political and social frameworks were concretized a year later when, on the invitation of the Ministry of Education, he travelled to the United States of America to study Western educational models. For Qutb, this trip served to illustrate the deviancy of Western culture, as he confronted for the first time what he observed to be the moral degeneration of Western society, its customs, dress, and sexual promiscuity championed in the name of freedom. Moreover, Qutb decries the fundamental essence of Western societies, underpinned by capitalist progress and development but driven by what he perceived as a reprehensible God-less, materialist disposition. The stark contrast between Western and Islamic values, for Qutb, served as a basis from which to carve a revolutionary path to freedom derived from Islamic ethics. Emboldened by this perspective, when Qutb returned from the United States, he actively sought membership of the Muslim Brotherhood, officially joining its ranks in 1952, soon becoming one of its most prominent and outspoken figures.

Qutb envisaged that the Muslim Brotherhood, with its strong focus on Islamic social justice and outreach, could engender a transformation of Egyptian politics. The growing discontent with imperial occupation and the corruption of the Egyptian government of King Farouk led to the formation of the Free Officers Movement, composed of a group of nationalist army officers ardently advocating change. The Free Officers incited the Egyptian Revolution of 1952 and soon established a new political regime. Qutb involved himself in the structures of the Free Officers Revolution, offering the movement political and religious guidance. By some accounts, Qutb became disenchanted with General Gamal-Abdal Nasser, who was unsympathetic to the Muslim Brotherhood and its programme for Islamic reform. Nasser's increasing petulance with the Muslim Brotherhood resulted in the banning of the organization and its subversive members and in 1954 Qutb served the first of his prison sentences. Despite his ill-health and horrific conditions of maltreatment and severe torture, Qutb used this opportunity to develop his intellectual ideas, producing two of his most important texts: *In the Shade of the Qu'ran* [*Fil Zilal al-Quran*] and *Signposts on the Road* [*Ma'alim fil al-Tariq*]. Qutb was briefly released from prison in 1964, but re-arrested on charges of sedition, treason, and conspiracy to overthrow the government and sentenced to death. Along with other Muslim Brotherhood activists, he was executed in 1966. Qutb's summary execution earned sympathy from many in the Muslim world and he is still deferentially referred to as a martyr (*Shaheed*).

Qutb's texts have been translated into a number of different languages, including Urdu, Malay, and Turkish, gaining a popular readership far beyond the borders of Egypt. The circulation of Qutb's texts, with their polemical tone and derision of the prevailing order, not only inspired the activities of the underground movement of the Muslim Brotherhood in Egypt, but transcended far beyond the political landscape of Egyptian politics. Qutb's intellectual proclivity led to the publication of a number of other important texts, such as *The Future Belongs to This Religion* [*Al-Mustaqbal li-hâdhà al-Din*] and *Components of the Islamic Conception* [*Muqaw- wimât al-Tasawwur al-Islàmï*]. Qutb's writings also drew extensively on the writings of South-Asian jurist and ideologue Abu A'la Maududi. Many of the important terms Qutb invokes in his writings are a replication of some of the distinctive conceptual vocabulary that Maududi had developed earlier.

> ### Key Thinker: Abu A'la Maududi
>
> Mawlana Sayyid Abu A'la Maududi was born in Hyderabad, India, in 1903. During his early life, he pursued a career in journalism. In the years preceding the 1947 partition of India and Pakistan, Maududi protested against British colonialism and criticized the politics of the day, culminating in the establishment of his political movement in 1941, the Jamaat-e-Islami Party, which operated for three decades. While Maududi remained firmly opposed to the initial formation of Pakistan, he thereafter participated actively in intellectual and political discussions on the nature and character of the state, arguing for a strongly Islamist state with a constitution embedded in Islamic principles. Maududi's politico-religious conceptualization of the Islamic state and his notion of sovereignty were read widely in the broader Islamic world, most notably by Qutb, and significantly informed the politics of his immediate context. The appeal of Maududi's writings to Qutb were ostensibly two-fold: (1) its strong juridical component, as Maududi's developed one of the best-known translations and commentaries of the Qur'an at the time; and (2) as a political theorist, Maududi emphasized the primacy of Islamic law in his political framework and actively sought to provide a model for Islamic constitutionalism and statehood firmly ensconced in Qura'nic principles.

15.2.2 States of ignorance: *jahilliyyah*

> Mankind today is on the brink of a destruction, not because of the danger of complete annihilation, which is hanging over its head—this being just a symptom and not the real disease—but because humanity is devoid of those vital values which are necessary not only for its healthy development but also for its real progress. Even the Western world realizes that the Western civilization is unable to present any healthy values for the guidance of mankind. It knows that it does not possess anything which will satisfy its own conscience and justify its existence.
>
> (Qutb 1990 [1954]: 23)

In this opening statement of Qutb's major polemical treatise, *Signposts Along the Road* [*Ma'alim fi al-Tariq*], Qutb sets a tone of despair for the trajectory of civilizational progress and development. This excoriating analysis of the ills of modern political societies is, for Qutb, a reminder to his readers that Western society, with its outward manifestations of political order and scientific progress, was in a self-inflicted moral and existential crisis. Qutb's charge is categorical: Enlightenment values had precipitated fundamental change in the Western world but this change was devoid of ethical meaning. This moral crisis, Qutb argued, was most vividly on display in American society, where he believed he encountered first-hand the immorality of Western culture: 'Look . . . at this individual freedom . . . this materialistic attitude which deadens the spirit; at this behaviour, like animals, which you call "Free mixing of the sexes" at this vulgarity . . .' (ibid.: 115).

This sort of sentiment captures Qutb's views on gender relations more generally. For Qutb, a wholesome family structure represents the Islamic ideal. He thus argues that the role of the family is to nurture morality and virtue in society, and male-female relations are realized in the institution of marriage. The stability and permanency of marriage will ensure that functions such as the man's financial obligation in maintaining the family and the women's role in child-rearing endure (Shehadeh, 2000: 50). While Qutb acknowledges that Islam permits women to participate in education and work, he argues that Western women are forced into the workplace environment as a result of the erosion of the family structure and this phenomenon has led to women being demeaned and exploited. While in certain religious, spiritual, and financial matters Qutb pronounced an equality between the two genders, he emphasized the distinctive natures of males and females. He argued for gendered roles premised on a selective interpretation of Quran'ic verses (ibid.: 49–53). For Qutb, Islam exemplified logic, beauty, humanity, and happiness, representing a simple and 'practical way of life' with solutions 'based on the foundation of the wholesome nature of man' (Qutb, 1990 [1954]: 155). This includes how women and men are to understand their roles and functions in the ideal Islamic society. Qutb's account of freedom and agency was therefore highly limited, as he declared women subservient to their husbands, limiting their agency and relegating them to a subjugated role.

Qutb surmised that Muslim societies were in a deep moral crisis, a condition of wilful ignorance (*jahilliyyah*). This state of ignorance was like an ocean that 'had encompassed the entire world', which was immersed in a form of modern-day paganism (ibid.: 27). Qutb uses the term *jahilliyyah* for its powerful invocation to pre-Islamic Arabia. Muslims had been taught that pre-Islamic Arabian society was steeped in immoral and depraved practices. This is, for example, a recurring motif of the Qur'an and Qutb presumably realized the powerful symbolism of *jahilliyyah* for his intellectual project of social and political reform. In its modern iteration, Qutb uses the term *Jahilliyyah* to describe the maleficent and wilful disobedience of Muslims with respect to God's divine injunctions. To this end, *jahilliyyah* is cast as a spiritual and social condition of backwardness in society which could occur in any place or at any time, but which has become a dominant condition in Qutb's own reading of his context. It is interesting that Qutb's portrayal of the *jahilliyyah* of the Western world is illustrated as backwardness, as this very skilfully 'inverts' this recurring Western judgement on the Islamic world (Shepard, 2003: 526). This present-day form of *jahilliyyah*, Qutb asserts, is far more sophisticated and insidious, able to use science in a perverted way and to masquerade as authentic Islam (ibid.: 526–527).

But, according to Qutb, the most pernicious aspect of *jahilliyyah* in its contemporary form was the replacement of God's sovereignty with human sovereignty, a condition which he depicts as a form of earthly rebellion:

> *Jahilliyyah* is based on rebellion against God's sovereignty on earth. It transfers to man one of the greatest attributes of God, namely sovereignty, and makes some men lord over others. It is now not in that simple and primitive form of the ancient *Jahilliyyah*, but takes the form of claiming that the right to create values, to legislate rules of collective behaviour, and to choose any way of life rests with men, without regard to what God Almighty has prescribed. The result of this rebellion against the authority of God is the oppression of His creatures.
>
> (Qutb, 1990 [1954]: 27)

Qutb considered *jahilliyyah* as an ill of modernity, a symptom of a greater societal malaise that has befallen all contemporary societies, including Muslim ones. He recommended ways to treat this problem in line with his reading of the practicality of Islamic tenets and the immutability of divine law. These recommendations are also important for the way in which we understand Qutb's conception of freedom, which is essentially moral in nature.

For Qutb, transcending *jahilliyyah* and ultimately creating a civilized community are a moral mission: 'real freedom is moral freedom, and true justice is Islamic justice' (Euben, 1999: 58). Qutb's first recommendation is the creation of an Islamic vanguard that would navigate the treacherous terrain of Western culture by keeping itself 'aloof' but maintaining 'some ties', so that it is able to detect the 'landmarks and the signposts of the road' (Qutb, 1990 [1954]: 28). Qutb's recommendations are for a Muslim audience; he views the Western world as beyond redemption.

Qutb thus states that the *Signposts* is written for the vanguard of Islam, a group that he considers to be a potential reality about to be materialized (ibid.: 28). The vanguard, according to Qutb, would be skilled in addressing the people of *jahilliyyah* in the language of Islamic discourse, and would have insight into the 'topics and problems [that] ought to be discussed; and where and how to obtain guidance in all these matters' (ibid.: 28). Moreover, they are enlightened individuals who derive their identity and legitimacy from the authority of God. The source of their guidance are the principles of the Qur'an and its fundamental tenets. For Qutb, the Qur'an represents the ultimate source of normative ethics, providing the signposts which guide the activities of the vanguard.

> **15.2 Colonialism and *jahilliyyah*: Key Points**
>
> - Qutb's writings must be understood in the context of colonialism and Western secularization in Egypt and elsewhere in the Muslim world.
> - Qutb envisaged specific gender roles for men and women in accordance with his view of the institution of marriage and family in the ideal Islamic society.
> - Qutb argued that the contemporary world is afflicted by *jahilliyyah*, a condition of extreme and widespread moral deterioration fundamentally produced by the human usurpation of God's divine sovereignty.

15.3 Sovereignty as *Hakimiyyah*

Qutb argued that the most important role of the vanguard would be to restore *Hakimiyyah*—divine sovereignty—or God's law on Earth. Liberal modernity, according to Qutb, can be charged with foreclosing the possibility for divine guidance and the contemporary world is thus steeped in ignorance. For Qutb (1990 [1954]: 38), *Hakimiyyah* should never be ascribed to any human entity, including priests, leaders of tribes, the wealthy, or rulers. In God alone should any legitimate legislative prerogative rest, and God's authority should prevail in 'the heart and conscience, in matters pertaining to religious observances and in the affairs of life such as business, the distribution of wealth and the dispensation of justice' (ibid.: 38). Qutb proposes that *Hakimiyyah* must be instituted throughout the Earth and can be enabled by the vanguard's commitment to upholding Islamic law as the source of legislative authority. In his theory of the state, Qutb (1996 [1949]: 111–112) once again emphasizes the importance of divine sovereignty as the basis on which political authority is derived:

> God exercises sovereignty in human life on one hand by directly controlling human affairs by His will and determination (*qadar*) and on the other hand by establishing the basic order of human life and human rights and duties and relationships and mutual obligations by His *Shari'ah* and His programme (*manhaj*).

> **Key Concept: *Shari'ah* (Islamic law)**
>
> *Shari'ah* can be translated into English as Islamic law. It has developed as a normative set of values and teachings drawing from four main sources. Islam's major scriptural text the *Qur'an* and the *Sunnah*, a tradition comprising of the life, sayings, and conduct of the Prophet Muhammad, constitute the two

> primary sources of law. The other two sources are *Qiyas*—analogical and deductive reasoning—and *Ijtihaad*: the consensus among Muslim jurists on various laws throughout history. The *Shari'ah* is constructed on these sources and forms a basis of legal legitimacy on foundational values and ethics. In Islam the *Shari'ah* is expected to permeate the private sphere by appealing to the private consciences of individuals and the public sphere through voluntary compulsion.

Fundamentally, then, for Qutb, all man-made systems of government with regulations and laws crafted on human authority or positive law are a rejection of the divinity of God and true sovereignty. These systems of government 'claim the characteristics of divinity for themselves', something which Qutb (ibid.: 112) regards as a clear act of 'disbelief'. In contrast, Qutb (ibid.: 112) makes a case for an Islamic state wherein the system of government differs profoundly from existing systems of government. An ideal Islamic polity is based on the acceptance and recognition on 'the sole divinity and sovereignty of God', 'on justice on part of the rulers, obedience on the part of the ruled, and consultation between rulers and ruled'.

Qutb contends that another of the fundamental characteristics of *jahilliyyah* is its renunciation of morality and a normative code of ethics as recommended by scripture. This has resulted in a social order of deviancy akin to that animalism. Thus Qutb (1990 [1954]: 111) portrays modern *jahili* societies as morally repugnant to such an extent that man and animal are indistinguishable. For Qutb, the prevailing condition of all contemporary societies, including Muslim societies, is *jahilliyyah*, because these states do not submit to divine sovereignty. This included Egypt, where after decades of colonialism a *jahili* order prevailed. Although he is not explicit in mentioning Nasser's Egypt, Qutb (ibid.: 91) indirectly refers to Egypt as a system where political authority is exercised in the 'name of the nation or a party or on some other basis'. Western societies, too, through their implementation of a range of political systems which venerate human sovereignty, are in direct violation of the principle of divine sovereignty and can therefore be regarded as illegitimate. These systems, in Qutb's view, ought to be dispensed with, as they have resulted in despondency and a state of moral retrogression.

Communism, for example, was guided by a deeply held impulse of envy and hatred by one class against another: 'such a selfish and vengeful society cannot but excite base emotions in its individuals' (ibid.: 61). He believed that the problem with communist societies is that they suppress individuality, which Qutb (ibid.: 91) perceives as a unique human characteristic: 'the individuality of a person is expressed in various ways, such as private property, the choice of work and the attainment of specialization in work, and expression in various art forms; and it distinguishes him from animals or from machines'. Communism, he argued, reduces human beings to the 'level of an animal' or 'a machine'.

Qutb (1990 [1954]: 27; 1996 [1949]: 345) charged capitalist societies with similar offences, arguing that their greed for accumulation of wealth through imperialism, usury, and monopoly control is a 'source of injustice to labour'. Idolatrous societies, as found in many places in the world, are also among the *jahili* societies, as they construct an elaborate system of devotional acts to propitiate false deities (Qutb, 1990 [1954]: 61–62).

In this way, Qutb did not contain his disdain to just one system, such as communism, but rather extended this judgement to all prevailing forms of society and contemporary governance, including capitalism, nationalism, democracy, and liberalism. He noted that all nationalistic and chauvinistic ideologies that have appeared in modern times, and all the movements and theories which followed from them have descended into a state of decay and decline. In sum, these are all systems that constitute 'individual or collective theories' that Qutb contends are failures and are therefore profoundly unsustainable (ibid.: 24).

> **Key Concept: *Hakimiyyah* (divine sovereignty)**
>
> According to Qutb, in order to establish God's rule on Earth there should be no individual that should raise his position above God, either through the creation of man-made law (positive law) or by assuming authority independent of God's sovereignty. Authority from God is not merely philosophical and passive. Rather it is a positive, practical, and dynamic idea that will establish a way of life where Muslims submit to divine sovereignty (*Hakimiyyah*) and the *Shari'ah* and are thus freed from the servitude of man. Man has tried to ignore this principle and has therefore fallen into the trap of *jahilliyyah*. By reforming political societies and states, through the establishment of *Hakimiyyah*, Qutb argued that Islamic renewal will proliferate.

Islam as a culturally authentic, programmatic ideology was for Qutb at odds with the various political orders dominating the Muslim world. Islam serves as a total way of life which brings about the development of noble human character benefiting all of human society. Qutb (ibid.: 61) argues that those who deviate from this perfect system and long for another system, 'whether it be based on nationalism, colour and race, class struggle, or similar corrupt theories, are truly enemies of mankind'. Islam, for Qutb, was conceived as a cosmic and human mission transcending time and place, thus Islamic history is imbricated in the story of human history. Qutb expands on these ideas in *Social Justice in Islam* (1996 [1949]), in which he concludes that while the tension between a communist Eastern bloc and a capitalist Western bloc seeks to divide the world on ideological grounds, there is greater congruency between these two systems than people are led to believe. The division, for Qutb (1996 [1949]: 349), is one 'based on interests and not on principles, a struggle for goods and markets and not for ideas and convictions'. This is evinced by the shared ideological commitment to materialism which, in the case of the West, promotes a utilitarian ethics fuelled by exploitative market-centred policies which embellish profiteering (ibid.: 349). Marxist materialism operates in a similarly vacuous way, and both these systems for Qutb are bereft of spirituality and cannot deliver true freedom.

For Qutb, it is Islam that threatens the existence of these ideological systems, offering an escape from the superficiality of materialism, as it contains a 'universal, complete and harmonious conception concerning existence and life that replaces struggle and conflict with social solidarity in the human sphere, and that gives life a spiritual basis that links it to its Creator' (ibid.: 350). This is how human freedom is attained—through morality and not through materialism. Moral freedom catalysed through the restoration of divine sovereignty and the enactment of Islamic law by the vanguard movement was a real form of freedom that would ensure the happiness and well-being of humankind. Accordingly, for Qutb, it is this kind of submission to a moral (divine) law that would ensure the creation of a virtuous society where citizens experience genuine freedom. Islam therefore means freedom from the wretchedness of *jahilliyyah* and this freedom from human sovereignty ensures lasting freedom which arises from submission to God's sovereignty and the divine law. Such freedom, for Qutb, must be secured at all costs.

Something can be said about the distinction of these two epistemological states, that of ignorance and that of the acceptance of divine sovereignty, or what Qutb deems as 'true knowledge' in opposition to modernity. For Qutb, modernity represents the negation of God's sovereignty insofar as it transformed the category of religion both institutionally and conceptually, circumscribing religion to the private sphere through the notion of secularism. Qutb responds to secularism as a term of opposition, thereby understanding 'the concept not only as a postcolonial plague of foreign design' but also in terms of 'what he saw as the history of secularism' which he recast into his own project (Salama and Friedman, 2012: 126). For example, Asad (2003; 207) highlights that the translation of the term 'secular' into Arabic appeared in the late nineteenth century as *alamiyyah* and therefore any intellectual attempts to advance the concept of secularism or to attack it 'was mediated by this work of translation'. But, as Salama and Friedman (2012: 110) note, '[i]n Qutb's writings, the idea of the secular gained ideological weight and became reified. In post-Qutb Egyptian popular discourse, the secular came to have a derogatory connotation akin to *kufr* or "atheism," referring to that which denigrates and even cancels divine power.' Qutb's ideas could in this way be read as decolonial, in that he reacts to secularism as a feature of modernity which essentialized and privatized the notion of religion (Asad, 2003) and which denies divine sovereignty in favour of secularism. Recent works by Quijano (2007), Maldonado-Torres (2014), and Mignolo (2000), for example, highlight the entanglement of modernity and coloniality in relation to the category of religion, arguing that secularism embodies the 'coloniality of power' insofar as secular rationality came to be universalized and hegemonic, with other forms of religious knowledge designated as inferior. The secular, both as an epistemic category and a political doctrine, is therefore connected to the project of coloniality, and Qutb may be offering a decolonial response which resists inferiorization and elevates the supremacy of the Islamic epistemological tradition in opposition to modernity. Qutb's decolonial lens, following Mignolo (ibid.: 4–5), is therefore valuable for constructing a 'locus of enunciation' where knowledge and understanding are complemented by thinking that emerges from those who experience colonial and postcolonial legacies and where hegemonic perspectives of modernity are confronted in order to undo the 'Eurocentric power projection inherent to them'.

Qutb's conception of freedom therefore differs significantly from a liberal account of freedom inherent in Western political thought. The important distinction here, as Euben (1999: 63) suggests, is that for Qutb freedom and equality cannot be realized unless divine sovereignty exists, where all members are equal by virtue of their mutual submission to God: 'This is not the Lockean idea of equality whereby all persons are free and equal in that each has a natural right to life, liberty, and property. Rather, it is the case that since all are equally subject to God's call, they are therefore equal.' Qutb's ideas in this way allow us to reconsider the limitations of accounts of freedom premised on Western epistemology. Moreover, they provide us with an interesting basis for comparative political inquiry and for situating Qutb's ideas in a decolonial tradition of political thinking as mentioned above. This approach forecloses the tendency of thinking about politics and political morality as rationalized in 'the West' as universalizing. However, one of the obvious tensions that arises when thinking of Qutb's opposition to liberal modernity in this way is whether in his thought abstract universalism is being replaced with a totalizing religious universalism. In other words, are the constraints Qutb places on the individual by renewing commitments to Islam entirely consistent with individual freedom and freedoms of conscience and association?

The task in Section 15.4 is to examine Qutb's invocation to revolution through his notion of *jihad* (striving in God's path), an idea which is commonly and reductively misunderstood to mean violent holy war and which erroneously implicates Qutb's political thought as a blanket sanctioning of the use of militant force in order to spread Islamic revivalism.

15.3 Sovereignty as *Hakimiyyah*: Key Points

- Qutb maintained that all forms of contemporary governance, including systems of liberalism, communism, and capitalism, placed man's sovereignty above God's divine sovereignty (*Hakimiyyah*) and were therefore morally reprehensible.
- Qutb believed that the Qur'an is the ultimate source of ethics and from which Islamic principles must be derived.

- Qutb argued that Islam is a way of life and offers a practical path to achieving happiness and freedom through the submission to the Islamic law (*Shari'ah*).
- Qutb's conception of freedom can be contrasted with a liberal account of freedom inherent in Western political thought.

15.4 *Jihad* (holy war)

Qutb devised a 'revolutionary Islamist political doctrine' underpinned by a modern theology of revivalist themes that speak to the 'renewal and authenticity' of Islam (March, 2019: 120). In short, this is his theory of *Jihad*, which can be understood as a form of offensive war and a legitimation of political violence against tyrannical governments. While Qutb's refusal of 'non-violent' *Jihad* can in part be explained as a response to the colonial call for pacification which leaves the violence of colonial powers undisturbed (Idris, 2016: 8), it is certainly plausible to question why Qutb's conception of *Jihad* finds so much appeal with militant and terrorist organizations. In other words, why has Qutb's theory of *Jihad* concomitantly elicited widespread disapproval and significant endorsement? How do we understand his theory of *Jihad* in the context of those who claim him as an influence, and those who accuse him of being an influence on global terrorism? What, then, are the mechanics of Qutb's argument of *Jihad*?

In his writings, Qutb frequently describes Islam as inseparable from the worldly purpose of its adherents, an idea termed as *din wa-dunya* (religion and the world). This idea is intimately tied with his conception of freedom and revolution. Freedom is the submission to divine sovereignty and to God's commands, but for Qutb this freedom is largely unattainable in the context of living in a *jahili* non-Muslim political order. According to Qutb, secular states inflict a war against Islam, a form of violence which quashes the freedom of Muslims by rejecting divine sovereignty and the *Shari'ah*. The suppression of Muslims and the associated erosion of spiritual values culminate in a loss of moral freedom which Qutb vehemently condemns. But, he retorts, a state in which Islamic law is upheld is one in which human beings are dignified and safeguarded from the enslavement of fellow man, as equality prevails by virtue of a shared submission to God:

> When, in a society, the sovereignty belongs to God alone, expressed in its obedience to the Shari'ah—the Divine Law—only then is every person in that society free from servitude to others, and only then does he taste true freedom. This alone is 'human civilization', as the basis of a human civilization is the complete and true freedom of every person and the full dignity of every individual of the society. On the other hand, in a society in which some people are lords who legislate and some others are slaves who obey them, then there is no freedom in the real sense, nor dignity for each and every individual.
>
> (Qutb, 1990 [1954]: 108)

In citing the famous Qur'anic verse (2:256) which declares that 'there is no compulsion in religion', Qutb concedes that religion is first of all a matter of choice and is voluntary. But there are circumstances in which an illegitimate internal enemy, such as the state, erodes the moral freedom of Muslims. Qutb considered *Jihad* as a revolutionary ideal. When Muslim societies have been provoked by an illegitimate government, *Jihad* will move beyond a defensive rationale and become an actively offensive pursuit. Propagating the religion is not confined to preaching and persuasion and, since Islam seeks to establish itself in opposition to *jahilliyyah*, it is sometimes necessary to use force. The result of these actions should be that man is free from human enslavement. *Jihad* enables the attainment of moral freedom.

Qutb's description above prompts him to seek a revolutionary response. He appeals to the existing tradition of *Jihad* in Islam which, he argues, has been misrepresented by defeatist and apologetic writers and interpreters. Here, the word *Jihad* typically bears two meanings. When derived from the Arabic root, it can be translated as 'to struggle, to strive, to endeavour, or to exert', generally against one's own self. In another meaning, *Jihad*, employed as a verb, also means to struggle for a cause, or to wage holy war in God's path. Typically, Qutb does not openly endorse the use of violence in order to respond to the ills of *jahilliyyah*. But he certainly makes reference to *Jihad*, which he envisages as a legitimate form of political action under specific circumstances. The first kind of *Jihad* to which he makes reference is the former—that of self-purification, a conscious assertion of the self against its base desires. Before one is to establish the Islamic social system and organize an Islamic polity, Qutb is attentive to the need for the vanguard to engage in *Jihad* of the inner dimension in order to achieve self-purification, since only those whose hearts are so purified 'are completely free of servitude to anyone other than God' and can build a political community (ibid.: 89–90). But in response to the condition of *jahili* states imposing their will on Muslim societies, Qutb prescribes the latter form of *Jihad*—that of a more explicit form, a revolutionary taking up of arms and the employment of violence where necessary. Qutb argues that many thinkers fundamentally misunderstood the role of *Jihad* in the Islamic revolutionary sense. While Islam, on the one hand, forbade the imposition of its belief by force, it attempted, on the other hand, 'to annihilate all those political and material powers which stand between people and Islam, which compel a people to bow before another and prevent them from accepting the sovereignty of God' (ibid.: 66). In other words, to Qutb, under certain conditions, it would appear appropriate for the vanguard to respond in a revolutionary manner, principally through the notion of *Jihad*.

One of Qutb's novel contributions was his conceptualization of *Jihad*, beyond the traditionally defined parameters. While *Jihad* constituted a war of defence against non-believers, Qutb is wary of those who confine the meaning of *Jihad* simply to the idea of 'defensive war'. *Jihad*, he argues, is an authentically Islamic idea, distinct from any modern notion of warfare, either by nature of its cause or in the way it is conducted, and contains an offensive component (ibid.: 66). Beyond this offensive aspect of *Jihad*, Qutb unconventionally argued that certain contexts permit a *Jihad* against internal enemies, including the state, especially if it has lost its moral legitimacy: 'If we insist on calling Islamic *Jihad* a defensive movement, then we must change the meaning of the word defence and mean by it the defence of man against all those elements which limit his freedom' (ibid.: 71).

Qutb maintains that the reasons for supporting *Jihad* should be guided by Islamic ideals and principles. Most important of these is the acceptance of the dominion of God on Earth, the abolition of the dominion of man and positive law, the restoration of divine sovereignty from those who have usurped it, and the enforcement of the Divine Law (ibid.: 68). These ends, Qutb notes, cannot be achieved only through a theoretical, philosophical, and passive proclamation. *Jihad* therefore becomes necessary in these circumstances, as 'those who have usurped the authority of God Almighty and are oppressing God's creatures are not going to give up their power merely through preaching' (ibid.: 68).

Qutb argues that the first characteristic of *Jihad* is that it is a practical and necessary system and as such it needs to be supported by Muslims. Propagating the religion is not confined to preaching and persuasion and sometimes it is necessary to use force, the ultimate outcome of which is man's freedom from human enslavement. This ties to the second and third characteristics of *Jihad*, which emphasize the practicality of the religion and the necessity for physical resources to achieve the mission of Islam. Islam does not posit abstract theories for freedom, but enables people to be free from the compulsion of servitude to man, which is the greatest freedom. The objective of *Jihad* is to provide people with the choice of freedom and servitude to God alone or to their worldly desires (ibid.; 69).

In other words, Islamic renewal involves the two-fold existence of preaching and *Jihad*. Knowledge is for action and, for Qutb, one way in which the divine will is realized on Earth is through 'the movement' of *Jihad*, which is an appropriate means of achieving Islamic renewal. First, through preaching it in the realm of 'beliefs and ideas' which are confronted, and, second, through 'the movement', material impediments are confronted (ibid.: 68). Hence, Qutb argues, these two aspects, preaching and *Jihad* united, realize true freedom: for the 'achievement of the freedom of man on earth—of all mankind throughout the earth—it is necessary that these two methods should work side by side' (ibid.: 69).

Put differently, *Jihad* becomes a necessary resort, according to Qutb, if moral freedom cannot be attained because of an internal or external enemy. The revolutionary zeal that Qutb prescribes is as follows: 'to strike hard at all those political powers which force people to bow before them and which rule over them, unmindful of the commandments of God, and which prevent people from listening to the preaching and accepting the belief if they wish to do so' (ibid.: 70). After extinguishing this authoritarian form of government, whether it be in a 'political or a racial form', or in the form of 'class distinctions', the revolutionary has achieved its purpose of engendering moral and political reform. Islam must then come to establish a new kind of order, a 'social, economic and political system, in which the concept of the freedom of man is applied in practice' (ibid.: 70). For Qutb, this is paramount, as it supplies the basis from which a regeneration occurs, ostensibly for the freedom of humans from servitude to other humans. The new political order is now established in the authority of God, through divine sovereignty, and the enactment of Divine law.

From the perspective of Western political theory, *Jihad* appears 'particularistic, irrational, and archaic' and is therefore pathologized as a form of onslaught against liberal modernity (Euben, 1999: 7). But this reading of *Jihad* ignores the analytical deployment of the term itself, which can be considered as a 'layered artefact of discourse' (Idris, 2016: 8) rather than just the violent ideology of the 'Other'. This entails an attempt to understand Qutb's arguments 'on as close to its own terms and categories as humanly possible' so as to preserve the common humanity of the subject (Euben, 1999: 90). Perhaps this is one way of mitigating against the tendency to think of Qutb's account of *Jihad* in purely adversarial terms which simply reproduces Eurocentric biases. For example, it is possible to compare Qutb's arguments to those of John Locke, who supported a right to rebellion against tyrannical governments. Central to Locke's arguments too are deeply held theological principles and Christian ideals. This is not in any way to suggest that Qutb's theory of *Jihad* cannot be criticized or should not be subject to scrutiny, but it might allow us to read Qutb's writings on their own terms.

15.4 *Jihad* (holy war): Key Points

- Qutb devises a revolutionary Islamic doctrine in line with his conception of *Hakimiyyah*.
- True freedom, or moral freedom, for Qutb, represented a submission to divine sovereignty and to God's commands.
- Qutb argued that moral freedom cannot be realized under a *jahili* non-Muslim political order and both preaching and *Jihad* would be necessary.
- Qutb claimed that Islam offers an all-encompassing clear set of guidelines on how to live a morally fulfilled life.
- *Jihad* is for Qutb not inherently violent but seeks to release mankind from its enslavement to human sovereignty.
- *Jihad* is a revolutionary ideal and is part of Qutb's project of Islamic renewal.

15.5 Conclusion

Sayyid Qutb is central to our contemporary understanding of politics. Reading and understanding Qutb allow us to interrogate the Western canon and consider perspectives which lie outside its approach. Rather than providing a dismissive treatment which casts Qutb's work as simply irrational and regressive, this chapter has sought to resituate his rejection of liberal modernity as an 'ethico-political vision' that is part of a broader critique of colonial domination and modernity (Euben, 1997: 28). It is, however, evident that there are various aspects of Qutb's ideas, including on gender and *Jihad*, that contain deeply problematic assumptions.

Yet what Qutb offers is a view of moral freedom and progress that fundamentally challenges the categories of our established conceptual vocabulary, providing critical purchase and a decolonial lens on ideas of freedom, legitimacy, equality, and sovereignty. His writings reveal the inherent power of a moralizing ideal which, despite all its weaknesses, could in part explain its global resonance. Qutb's critique of liberal modernity and indeed Western epistemology is underpinned by his rejection of secularism and its claims of the supremacy of the sovereignty of man over God. Divine sovereignty for Qutb entails submission to God's laws and authority, and secularism is viewed as a pernicious outcome of *jahilliyyah*. For Qutb, Islamic tradition has been problematically substituted with a range of ideologies and forms of governance: communism, capitalism, liberalism, materialism, and polytheism. Qutb responds to these so-called aberrations of human society by offering a perspective of moral freedom. His work can be considered to be decolonial in at least two respects. First, his critique of secularism as an epistemic category highlights the link of the former with coloniality through its essentialized view of religion as a private affair. Second, Qutb's own response to modernity venerates the supremacy of Islam, and thereby displaces the abstract universalism of Western epistemology as a hegemonic tool that shapes the conception of religion as a representational concept of knowledge and cognition (Mignolo, 2000: 22). Qutb's decolonial lens constructs a 'locus of enunciation' that seeks to challenge and undo the Eurocentric epistemic framework and its self-descriptive imaginary (ibid.: 4–5).

Qutb presents Islam as an all-encompassing creed with a clear set of guidelines that are essential to living a morally fulfilled life and attaining true freedom. Qutb's work is often accused of being imbued with a militant flavour and a palpable intolerance of political systems that do not operate according to an Islamic framework. This charge, however accurate, does not fully capture the extent of his political project, which must be reconsidered in the context of the history of colonialism and the relationship between tradition and modernity. As we have examined in this chapter, Qutb's conceptions of freedom and revolution are in stark contrast to the established liberal vocabulary on these ideas and offer us something substantively different. In this sense, Qutb's political thought enriches the purview of our political thinking to traditions and ideas beyond Western epistemology, ones which reveal that despite the anti-foundationalist, post-Enlightenment world we seek to reify, we assume that the 'exclusion of religious authority from the political realm' is a shared universal value (Euben, 1997: 31). Hence, as Euben (ibid.: 31) argues: 'In the contemporary Middle Eastern context, Islamic ideas such as Qutb's are compelling at least in part because they are a powerful challenge to both the legitimacy of secular, modernizing Middle Eastern regimes and to the Western rationalist and imperialist ways of understanding and thus organizing political life.'

Take your learning further by accessing the online resources for a library of web links to relevant videos, articles, blogs, and useful websites for this chapter: www.oup.com/he/Ramgotra-Choat1e.

Study questions

1. What is the distinction between human sovereignty and divine sovereignty in the context of Qutb's ideas?
2. How did Qutb describe *jahilliyyah*?
3. What, for Qutb, was the role of the vanguard in Islamic political renewal?
4. What was the influence of Maududi's ideas on the development of Qutb's political thought?
5. How does Qutb conceptualize the notion of freedom and how does it differ from a liberal account of freedom?
6. In what way does *Jihad* feature in Qutb's revolutionary Islamist doctrine?
7. In what ways, if any, can Qutb's ideas help us better understand political Islam and its influence in places like the Middle East?
8. Can Qutb be described as a decolonial thinker?

Further reading

Primary sources

Euben, R. and Zaman, Q. (eds) (2009) *Princeton Readings in Islamist Thought: Texts and Contexts from al-Banna to Bin Laden*. Princeton, NJ: Princeton University Press.
Includes useful primary text excerpts from Qutb's *Signposts* (or *Milestones*) and *Social Justice in Islam*.

Qutb, S. (2005) *A Child from the Village*. Trans., ed., and introduced by J. Calvert and W. Shepard. Cairo: American University in Cairo Press.
An interesting memoir of Qutb's early life, focusing on the years 1912–1918 when he observed the invention of modern Egypt.

Shepard, W.E. (1996) *Sayyid Qutb and Islamic Activism: A Translation and Critical Analysis of Social Justice in Islam*. Leiden: Brill.
An excellent and accessible translation with notes on commentary of Qutb's text, *Social Justice in Islam*.

Secondary sources

Bergese, A.J. (2017) *The Sayyid Qutb Reader: Selected Writings on Politics, Religion, and Society*. New York: Routledge.
A set of selected works on Qutb that serves as a valuable introduction to his key intellectual ideas.

Khatab, S. (1990) *The Political Theory of Sayyid Qutb: Theory of Jahiliyyah*. London: Routledge.
An important text centring Qutb's conception of *jahilliyyah* in his political thought.

Musallam, A.A. (2005) *From Secularism to Jihad: Sayyid Qutb and the Foundations of Radical Islamism*. Westport, CT: Praeger.
This is a useful biographical account of Qutb's life and scholarship with interesting information on his early life.

Shehadeh, L.R. (2000) 'Women in the Discourse of Sayyid Qutb'. *Arab Studies Quarterly*, 22(3): 45–55.
For a gender analysis of Qutb's work, this article provides an interesting overview on the question of women.

Shepard, W.E. (2003)' Sayyid Qutb's Doctrine of "Jāhiliyya"'. *International Journal of Middle East Studies*, 35(4): 521–545.
    A valuable analysis dedicated to Qutb's conception of *jahilliyyah*.

Toth, J. (2013) *Sayyid Qutb: The Life and Legacy of a Radical Islamic Intellectual*. Oxford: Oxford University Press.
    An interesting and valuable intellectual history account of Qutb's ideas.

References

Akhavi, S. (2013) 'Sayyid Qutb'. In J. Esposito and Shahin, E. el-din (eds), *The Oxford Handbook of Islam and Politics*. Oxford: Oxford University Press.

Asad, T. (2003) *Formations of the Secular*. Stanford, CA: Stanford University Press.

Calvert, J. (2013) *Sayyid Qutb and the Origins of Radical Islamism*. New York: Columbia University Press.

Euben, R.L. (1997) 'Comparative Political Theory: An Islamic Fundamentalist Critique of Rationalism'. *The Journal of Politics*, 59(1): 28–55.

Euben, R.L. (1999) *Enemy in the Mirror: Islamic Fundamentalism and the Limits of Modern Rationalism*. Princeton, NJ: Princeton University Press.

Idris, M. (2016) 'Political Theory and the Politics of Comparison'. *Political Theory*. Available at: https://doi.org.10.1177/0090591716659812 (accessed 9 January 2023).

Maldonado-Torres, N. (2014) 'Race, Religion and Ethics in the Modern Colonial World'. *The Journal of Religious Ethics*, 42(4): 691–711.

March, A. (2019) *The Caliphate of Man: Popular Sovereignty in Modern Islamic Thought*. Cambridge, MA: Harvard University Press.

Mignolo, W. (2000) *Local Histories/Global Designs: Coloniality, Subaltern Knowledges and Border Thinking*. Princeton, NJ: Princeton University Press.

Musallam, A.A. (2005) *From Secularism to Jihad: Sayyid Qutb and the Foundations of Radical Islamism*. Westport, CT: Praeger.

Quijano, A. (2007) 'Coloniality and Modernity/Rationality'. *Cultural Studies*, 21(2): 168–178.

Qutb, S. (1990) *Milestones*. Trans. A. Zakī Manṣūr Ḥammād. Indianapolis, IN: American Trust Publications.

Qutb, S. (1996 [1949]) *Social Justice in Islam*. Trans. W. Shepard. Leiden: Brill.

Salama, M. and Friedman, R. (2012) 'Locating the Secular in Sayyid Qutb'. *The Arab Studies Journal*, 20(1): 104–131.

Shehadeh, L.R. (2000) 'Women in the Discourse of Sayyid Qutb'. *Arab Studies Quarterly*, 22(3): 45–55.

Shepard, W.E. (2003) 'Sayyid Qutb's Doctrine of "Jāhiliyya"'. *International Journal of Middle East Studies*, 35(4): 521–545.

Tripp, C. (1994) 'Sayyid Qutb: The Political Vision'. In A. Rahmena (ed.), *Pioneers of Islamic Revival* London: Zed Books, pp. 154–183.

16 Edward W. Said

RAHUL RAO

> **Chapter guide**
>
> This chapter focuses on the major intellectual contributions of Edward Said, many of which laid the foundations for what would become the field of postcolonial studies. Sections 16.2 and 16.3 explore Said's views on how knowledge and power structure relations between Western imperial powers and non-Western states and societies, through critical readings of *Orientalism* and *Culture and Imperialism*, respectively. Section 16.4 explores Said's writings and activism as a spokesperson for Palestinian self-determination. Finally, Section 16.5 examines Said's views on what it means to be a public intellectual. While Said's ideas have become so influential as to be almost ubiquitous in cultural and postcolonial studies, the apparent familiarity of his ideas has allowed a forgetting of the nuance and complexity with which they were originally articulated. By offering a close re-reading of Said's best-known texts, the chapter aims to encourage a more careful appreciation of the ideas that were central to his political thinking.

16.1 Introduction

Edward Said is typically regarded as a founding figure of postcolonial studies. There is some irony to this claim, partly because influential currents of postcolonial theory would develop as critical responses to his work, and partly because Said would distance himself from some of these currents. Yet the claim is sound enough insofar as it honours the ground-breaking impact of his best-known work, *Orientalism* (Said, 1995 [1978]). In this book as well as in subsequent works, Said explores the dialectical relationship between knowledge and power in structuring imperial relations between the geopolitical abstraction that we have long referred to as the 'West' and its Other—once named the 'Orient' and more recently the Third World, the developing world, the Global South, and sometimes rather more negatively the 'non-West'. Drawing on Michel Foucault's notion of discourse, Said's major innovation in the study of imperialism was to supplement Marxist conceptualizations of imperialism in terms of the global extraction of resources and exploitation of labour by drawing attention to the constitutive force of culture. The argument was controversial from the very outset. Critics on the right bristled at Said's exposition of the racism and supremacism that lurked at the heart of metropolitan Western culture. Critics on the Marxist left took Said to task for supplanting Marxism's materialist focus on questions of political economy with the analysis of discourse. Voices across the ideological spectrum wondered whether a scholar of modern Western literature had the requisite disciplinary competence with which to make sweeping statements about the historical relationship between the West and the non-West over several centuries.

But there is another reason why Said has always been as controversial in some quarters as he has been celebrated in others. Born in Jerusalem in 1935 in the tiny Anglican Christian community in what was then the British mandate of Palestine, Said was a US citizen from birth by virtue of his father's service in the US Army. These multiple affiliations fuelled in him a sense of being 'out of place', a self-avowed condition that would supply the title of his evocative memoir of his early years growing up in Palestine, Lebanon, and Egypt (Said, 2000). As a Palestinian, Said evinced a passionate and lifelong commitment to the struggle for Palestinian self-determination, serving on the Palestinian National Council and writing extensively about the quest for liberation. As a US citizen educated at elite schools in Jerusalem, Cairo, and Massachusetts and, later, at Princeton and Harvard, steeped in the literary and musical high cultures of the West, he was well positioned to make an articulate and sophisticated case for Palestine to Western audiences at a time when Israel commanded their unthinking allegiance. His deep familiarity with Western political and cultural institutions enabled him to educate his Arab audiences about the ways in which they might challenge the baleful effects of Western power on their societies. Not fully at home anywhere, Said spared no opportunity to excoriate Arab regimes for their authoritarianism, corruption, and incompetence. His fusillades against state power everywhere won him few friends in high places, but earned him the respect, admiration, and love of countless people in a global anti-imperialist left.

Said was Professor of Literature at Columbia University in New York for most of his career. Yet his interests were expansive, ranging across the fields of literature, philology, philosophy, politics, history, anthropology, religion, media studies, and music. He was an accomplished pianist and music critic and briefly contemplated a career as a musician before turning to literature. This makes a survey of Said's works extremely challenging. One is immediately faced with the task of delineating the scope of the survey and justifying the exclusions. One approach that might seem appropriate for a volume on political thinkers is to focus on the more explicitly 'political' writings. Yet this is not a particularly useful criterion of exclusion in Said's case as politics suffuses his entire oeuvre. He was just as likely to reach political insights through a study of musical form as through an investigation of state discourse. And his political views on coexistence in the Middle East could be expressed as much through his political writings as through musical ventures, such as the West-Eastern Divan Orchestra that he co-founded with conductor Daniel Barenboim to demonstrate that Israelis and Palestinians could make music together despite disagreement. Yet because some criterion is necessary, this chapter will focus on those of Said's writings that deal with questions and concepts at the heart of political theory and international relations—the constitution and contestation of global imperial order, the relationship between states and citizens, and the role of the intellectual in interpreting and transforming these relations.

Read more about **Said's** life and work by accessing the thinker biography on the online resources: www.oup.com/he/Ramgotra-Choat1e.

16.2 Orientalism and the politics of knowledge

16.2.1 '"We" are this, "they" are that'

Said is best known for his landmark work, *Orientalism*, the 1978 publication of which is considered by some to have inaugurated the field of postcolonial studies. As its subtitle makes clear, the book surveys Western conceptions of that part of the world that was once described as the 'Orient'. Said names this Western gaze 'Orientalism', defining the term in three ways (Said, 1995 [1978]: 2–3). First, Orientalism describes an academic field encompassing 'anyone who teaches, writes about or researches the Orient'. Second, Orientalism is a 'style of thought' that produces distinctions between the 'Orient' and the 'Occident' (or, as they are more colloquially rendered, 'East' and 'West'). As Said explains, writers across an array of fields, genres, and ideological tendencies have tended to accept and reiterate distinctions between East and West as the starting point for explanatory and imaginative accounts of the world. Running through these accounts is a tendency to view the world through a series of dichotomies that juxtapose a rational, enlightened, developed, modern Occident against an Orient mired in superstition, barbarism, despotism, sensuality, and whatever other undesired characteristics Western writers anxiously project onto their civilizational Other. Third, from the late eighteenth century, as West European empires begin to take possession of vast expanses of territory and rule over their inhabitants, Orientalism becomes a 'corporate institution for dealing with the Orient . . . by making statements about it, authorizing views of it, describing it, by teaching it, settling it, ruling over it'; in short, Orientalism is 'a Western style for dominating, restructuring, and having authority over the Orient' (ibid.: 3).

At the heart of Orientalism is a complex dialectical relationship between knowledge and power. On the one hand, the vast material power differential in terms of technology, weapons, etc. between Western imperial states and their non-Western subjects enables the acquisition and production of certain kinds of knowledge. As Said observes, 'The scientist, the scholar, the missionary, the trader, or the soldier was in, or thought about, the Orient because he *could be there*, or could think about it, with very little resistance on the Orient's part' (ibid.: 7). On the other hand, 'knowledge of subject races or Orientals is what makes their management easy and profitable; knowledge gives power, more power requires more knowledge, and so on in an increasingly profitable dialectic of information and control' (ibid.: 36). Said illustrates this with reference to Napoleon's 1798 invasion of Egypt. Informed and facilitated by classical Orientalist knowledge, the invasion also enabled the further accumulation of such knowledge in the form of the monumental *Description de l'Egypte*, the 24-volume account of the expedition produced by the scores of scientists, scholars, and artists who accompanied Napoleon's army. Orientalist knowledge, for Said, does not simply describe a reality 'out there', but in fact constitutes it by providing the perceptual grid through which observation and description of the 'Orient' are filtered (ibid.: 6, 94). It also lays the foundation for interventions that reconstitute that reality. Thus, the construction of the Suez Canal, which we might view as yet another element in the European Orientalist knowledge-power project in Egypt, quite literally refashions the relationship between East and West including in material and geographical respects.

Part of what made *Orientalism* such an influential statement about the imbrication of power and knowledge in imperialist projects were the sweeping contours of its argument. As a 'style of thought', Said finds Orientalist tropes in the work of figures as diverse as Homer, Aeschylus, Euripides, Dante, and Marx, although the book mainly focuses on eighteenth- and nineteenth-century British and French Orientalists and their twentieth-century US successors. It ranges across an array of modes of writing, including literature, poetry, drama, travel writing, anthropology, economics, and public administration. And, as the book's pointed references to Marx make clear, far from being restricted to imperial apologists, Orientalism also infected their most implacable opponents.

While sketching its wide historical sweep, Said is attentive to elements of continuity and change in the discourse of Orientalism. *Orientalism* is organized roughly chronologically and structured around a series of inflection points, at each of which the discourse that it describes undergoes significant shifts in character, method, and form. Said (ibid.: 56–57) sees the distinction between the Orient and the West as already having been in place by the time of the *Iliad* in the eighth century BCE. He finds significant features of what will become Orientalism in the earliest Greek tragedies: in Aeschylus's *The Persians* and Euripides's *The Bacchae*, 'Europe is powerful and articulate; Asia is defeated and distant' (ibid.: 57). In the medieval and early modern period, Orientalism is expressed through an obsession with Islam, which is seen as a perverted version of Christianity. Said (ibid.: 116–123) then notes a series of important shifts in the eighteenth century—an increasing awareness of the Orient beyond the Biblical lands as transport and communication improve, the development of a sense of historicity, a tendency on the part of some authors to identify selectively and sympathetically with regions and cultures other than their own, and a strong impulse to classify nature and man into types. Under the combined influence of these trends, older religious tropes of Orientalism come to be 'reconstituted, redeployed, redistributed' in the emerging secular discipline of philology. This is also the juncture at which an essentially 'bookish' Orientalism pursued through textual study by scholars, many of whom have never visited the Orient, comes to be overtaken by a newer kind of Orientalist whose authority derives from residence and immersion—what we might call 'fieldwork'—in the geographical Orient (figures such as Edward Lane, Chateaubriand, and Richard Burton are representatives here). The nineteenth century sees Orientalist knowledge pressed more directly into the service of formal colonialism, while also being yoked to biological theses about racial inequality that impute a certain immutability and permanence to civilizational essences (ibid.: 206). Finally, Said brings the account of Orientalism into his present which is dominated by US empire, for whose benefit the 'area studies' specialist makes regional expertise available. Despite being couched in the technocratic and apparently neutral language of social science, this knowledge remains saturated with Orientalist dogmas about the unremitting difference and cultural hostility between West and East (ibid.: 300–301).

Alongside this careful charting of distinct phases in the life of Orientalism, Said is also nuanced about how individual writers relate to it. Central to his argument is the methodological depiction of Orientalism as a 'discourse' in Foucault's (2002 [1969]: 131) sense of the term: a pattern of statements and practices to which specialized knowledge must conform if it is to be regarded as true. As Said (1995: 3) puts it, 'so authoritative a position did Orientalism have that I believe no one writing, thinking, or acting on the Orient could do so without taking account of the limitations on thought and action imposed by Orientalism'. He explains how fields of learning are constrained 'by society, by cultural traditions, by worldly circumstance, and by stabilizing influences like schools, libraries, and governments' as a result of which 'learned and imaginative writing are never free, but are limited in their imagery, assumptions, and intentions' (ibid.: 201–202). Sometimes he appears to take this argument to an extreme, as when he claims, somewhat polemically, that 'every European, in what he could say about the Orient, was consequently a racist, an imperialist, and almost totally ethnocentric' (ibid.: 203). Yet in a crucial departure from Foucault, Said also insists on the 'determining imprint of individual writers upon the otherwise anonymous collective body of texts constituting a discursive formation like Orientalism' (ibid.: 23). There are several moments when he depicts scholars like Marx (ibid.: 155), Burton (ibid.: 196), and Massignon (ibid.: 270–271) as straining productively, but ultimately unsuccessfully, against the discursive limits within which they operate. Going further, he singles out contemporaries such as Jacques Berque and Maxime Rodinson as 'freeing themselves from the old ideological straitjacket' thanks to their exemplary methodological self-reflexivity (ibid.: 326). In a wonderful image that perhaps best captures Said's dialectical vision of the relationship between discursive structures and individual scholarly agency, he suggests that 'each individual contribution first causes changes within the field and then promotes a new stability, in the way that on a surface covered with twenty compasses the introduction of a twenty-first will cause all the others to quiver, then to settle into a new accommodating configuration' (ibid.: 273).

16.2.2 **Critiques of *Orientalism***

Orientalism itself caused more than a quiver, disrupting disciplinary boundaries, importing French theory into the US academy, inaugurating new fields such as colonial discourse analysis and postcolonial studies, and giving voice to the grievances of minoritized scholars in the academy. While criticism from the right on account of Said's putative 'anti-Westernism' was predictable, it would be critiques from Marxist and poststructuralist scholars that provoked further developments in postcolonial theory and indeed in the trajectory of Said's own oeuvre.

Among the most influential Marxist critiques are those advanced by Sadiq Jalal al-'Azm (1981) and Aijaz Ahmad (1992). Both take Said to task for his periodization of Orientalism as a discourse stretching from classical Greek antiquity to the present. For al-'Azm, this obscures the ideological processes by which nineteenth-century Orientalists sought to 'eternalize' the great divergence that capitalism had opened up between Europe and its colonial possessions. Both accuse Said of 'Orientalism in reverse' in what they saw as his essentialist treatment of the 'West', which ultimately reified the very categories that he otherwise seemed to want to deconstruct. And both disagree sharply with Said's (1995 [1978]: 153–156) characterization of Marx as an Orientalist on account of his view of British colonialism in India as playing a progressive role in sweeping away the remnants of 'Oriental despotism'. In their reading, far from singling out Asia or the Orient as backward and in need of regeneration by colonial modernity, Marx saw colonialism in the Orient in exactly the same terms as he saw capitalism in the West: as a necessary stage, but one that had to be transcended, in the journey to communism. In addition, Ahmad argues that *Orientalism*'s jettisoning of Marxist categories of analysis in 1978 was very congenial to the anti-communist and post-Marxist turn evident in global politics as well as in the Western academy at the time. He suggests that the book owed its success to its embrace by bourgeois Third World migrants to the Western metropolis for whom its antagonism towards Western colonial discourse in terms that avoided engagement with class provided them with an alternative way of claiming the moral high ground by presenting themselves as marginal and 'subaltern'.

For poststructuralists, such as Homi Bhabha, Said's notion of colonial discourse is too totalizing in its insinuation that power is possessed mainly by the colonizer. Bhabha (1994: 118) sees colonial discourse as ambivalent and less sure of itself than Said proposes. This can be seen in the stereotypes of 'natives' that abound in colonial discourse, which seem to oscillate between images of them as static and irredeemably inferior and also as unstable, threatening, but amenable to moral improvement and civilization. Ambivalence also marks strategies of colonial rule. Here the colonizer's cultivation of a class of what V.S. Naipaul called 'mimic men' among the native elite—who are intended to function as loyal agents of colonial authority—sometimes backfires by producing the first generations of anti-colonial nationalists. In these and other ways, Bhabha represents the colonial encounter as one of not straightforward negation (as suggested by the stark binaries of orientalist discourse) but 'negotiation', which results in 'the production of hybridization rather than the noisy command of colonialist authority or the silent repression of native traditions' (ibid.: 112).

Key Thinker: Homi Bhabha

Homi Bhabha has been extremely influential in generating a distinct strand of postcolonial studies. Many of his key ideas are articulated in *The Location of Culture* (1994). Bhabha offers less a fully-worked-out theory of colonialism than an analysis of some of the key features and tropes of colonial discourse. Among these are the stereotype, which Bhabha views as a dominant mode in which colonialism represents natives. Bhabha turns to psychoanalysis to understand the encounter between colonizer and colonized, which he argues is characterized not only by rejection but also by mimicry. While the colonized seek to mimic the colonizer in order to wrest power from them, the colonizer actively encourages the process of mimicry in order to create a class of native elites—who resemble their masters in all respects except race—through whom colonial rule can be enforced. Yet these processes of mimicry are fraught with menace, as the native agents of colonial rule sometimes become its leading opponents.

Gender has been a key terrain for the reproduction of orientalist difference. Said (1995 [1978]: 188) acknowledges that orientalist discourse constructs the Orient as a space of 'sexual promise (and threat), untiring sensuality, unlimited desire'. Yet as feminist scholars have pointed out, he does not pursue the implications of this important observation. Meyda Yeğenoğlu (1998: 11) has argued that gendered images and tropes in the colonial archive such as the veiled woman are not simply depictions of Oriental women as mysterious and exotic but also signify the Orient itself as feminine, veiled, seductive, and dangerous. She calls for a sexualized reading of Orientalism on the grounds that 'the discursive constitution of Otherness is achieved simultaneously through sexual as well as cultural modes of differentiation' (ibid.: 2). Such claims have also been foundational for queer postcolonial studies (Puar, 2007). From a more historical vantage point but one that shares a queer sensibility, Joseph Boone (2014: xxi) has argued that Said's occasionally gendered references to Orientalism as a process in which a masculine Occident penetrates a feminized Orient tend to be heteroerotic, obscuring the rich history of 'homoerotic fascination and homophobic aspersion' that participated in the construction of this mythic divide. Thus while Said himself is allusive and elusive on the question of gender in *Orientalism*, his work has been deeply generative for feminist and queer scholars who have sought to fill this gap in his work.

> ### 16.2 Orientalism and the politics of knowledge: Key Points
>
> - Said defines Orientalism as (1) an academic field comprising those who study the 'Orient'; (2) a style of thought positing essential distinctions between 'East' and 'West'; and (3) the set of institutions through which Western imperial powers dominated the colonized world.
> - Orientalism reveals the dialectical relationship between knowledge and power: knowledge is instrumentally useful in the exercise of power, but can also construct new power relations between those with and without authoritative knowledge.
> - Said regards Orientalism as a discourse that constrains, but does not fully determine, what can be said about the 'Orient'.
> - *Orientalism* provoked defensive reactions from the right against its claims about the racism of Western metropolitan culture.
> - It was criticized from the left by Marxists for its displacement of class analysis and by poststructuralists for being insufficiently attuned to the ambivalence of colonial discourse and its production of hybridity.

16.3 Empire and hybridity

16.3.1 'Overlapping territories, intertwined histories'

In response partly to poststructuralist critiques and partly to the ways in which he believed that *Orientalism* had been misread as reinforcing rather than deconstructing categorical designations such as Orient and Occident, hybridity is a key theme in Said's *Culture and Imperialism* (Said, 1994a [1993]) (even if his theorization of it bears little resemblance to Bhabha's essentially psychic account). The book was published in 1993, the same year in which Paul Gilroy's (1993) *The Black Atlantic*—with which it has considerable resonance—also appeared. Depicting the hierarchical interconnectedness of a world forged by empire, such works stood in stark contrast to both the one-world triumphalism of liberal commentators such as Francis Fukuyama (1992) and the conflictual civilizationist ontologies of conservatives such as Samuel Huntington (1993). The concurrence of these contradictory interventions recalls the uncertainty in public discourse about the shape of the world that was coming into being in the immediate aftermath of the Cold War.

Said's (1994a [1993]: xii–xiii) starting point in this text is that 'culture'—understood as practices of description, communication, and representation that often exist in aesthetic forms, one of whose principal aims is pleasure—plays a distinct and underappreciated role in the sustenance and contestation of imperialism. Narratives and stories, he tells us, are central to how colonial authorities construct, claim, and govern distant parts of the world but also to how colonized peoples assert their identities and existence. As he explains,

> the main battle in imperialism is over land . . . but when it came to who owned the land, who had the right to settle and work on it, who kept it going, who won it back, and who now plans its future—these issues were reflected, contested, and even for a time decided in narrative.
>
> (ibid.: xiii)

Said has a particular interest in how the European realistic novel secured and sustained metropolitan societies' consent to overseas conquest (ibid.: 12, 84). Drawing on Raymond Williams's notion of 'structures of feeling', Said suggests that by making constant reference to participation in empire, literary works create 'structures of attitude and reference' that support empire.

> In British culture, for instance, one may discover a consistency of concern in Spenser, Shakespeare, Defoe, and Austen that fixes socially desirable, empowered space in metropolitan England or Europe and connects it by design, motive, and development to distant or peripheral worlds (Ireland, Venice, Africa, Jamaica), conceived of as desirable but subordinate. And with these meticulously maintained references come attitudes—about rule, control, profit, and enhancement and suitability—that grow with astonishing power from the seventeenth to the end of the nineteenth century.
>
> (ibid.: 61)

The clearest exposition of the argument is in Said's reading of Jane Austen's *Mansfield Park*, in which he notes 'a mere half-dozen passing references to Antigua' (ibid.: 70). In contrast to the much more explicit incorporation of empire in the texts of later writers, such as Joseph Conrad and Rudyard Kipling working in the high noon of the imperial age, subtle references to empire are fairly typical of early eighteenth-century novels where—rather like the servants in grand households—the empire is 'taken for granted but scarcely ever more than named' (ibid.: 75). Nonetheless, these references are sufficient in Said's view to establish Austen's awareness of the relationship between the protagonist Sir Thomas Bertram's Northamptonshire country estate Mansfield Park and his slave plantations in Antigua: 'to hold and rule Mansfield Park is to hold and rule an imperial estate in close, not to say inevitable association with it. What assures the domestic tranquillity and attractive harmony of one is the productivity and regulated discipline of the other' (ibid.: 104).

In deciding what to make of these references to empire, Said argues that the task of the critic is 'to draw out, extend, give emphasis and voice to what is silent or marginally present or ideologically represented . . . in such works' (ibid.: 78). *Culture and Imperialism* is rich in illustrations of what is at stake in this method. We are presented with readings of Verdi's opera *Aida*, commissioned by Khedive Ismail to mark the opening of Cairo's new Opera House, as embodying both a European Orientalist conception of Egypt as well as the Khedive's vertiginous modernization ambitions. We learn that in Kipling's novel *Kim*, set amidst the so-called 'Great Game' in Afghanistan, Kim's liminal identity as Irish is deployed to portray an empire in which imperial rule is apparently beseeched by the colonized themselves. For Said, Camus's works are not only universal existentialist parables of the human condition but also participate in the justification of French rule in Algeria.

Two central themes emerge in these readings. First, Said refuses the separation between 'culture' and the political, insisting on 'the connection between the prolonged and sordid cruelty of such practices as slavery, colonialist and racist oppression, and imperial subjection, on the one hand,

and the poetry, fiction, and philosophy of the society that engages in these practices on the other' (ibid.: xiv, see also 66–67). Yet far from arguing that their implication in the dirty business of empire offers a reason to disavow these works, Said suggests that 'because of their *worldliness*, because of their complex affiliations with their real setting, they are *more* interesting and *more* valuable as works of art' (ibid.: 13, emphasis in original). It is almost as if their acknowledgement of the fact of empire elevates their status as art in Said's eyes. Second, by re-reading what are usually thought of as metropolitan European texts in ways that reveal their deep implication in and dependence on the periphery, Said represents the imperial encounter not as a clash between fully constituted essences but as producing 'overlapping territories, intertwined histories'. Later postcolonial work would draw on these insights to suggest a mutually constitutive relationship between the core and periphery of the world system (see, for example, Barkawi and Laffey, 2006).

Key Concept: Contrapuntal reading

Said describes the reading method that he develops in a number of works, but especially *Culture and Imperialism*, as 'contrapuntal'. To think contrapuntally is to be simultaneously aware of the dominant discourse as narrated in the metropolis as well as the other histories against which and together with which the dominating discourse acts. Said's inspiration for this method is the form of counterpoint in Western classical music, where 'various themes play off one another, with only a provisional privilege being given to any particular one; yet in the resulting polyphony there is concert and order, an organized interplay that derives from the themes, not from a rigorous melodic or formal principle outside the work' (Said 1994a [1993]: 59–60). If his reading of *Mansfield Park* offers one illustration of this method, elsewhere he reads C.L.R. James's *The Black Jacobins* as placing the Haitian and French Revolutions within the same history, so that 'events in France and in Haiti criss-cross and refer to one another like voices in a fugue' (ibid.: 332).

16.3.2 Resistance to empire

This methodological sensibility also marks Said's treatment of resistance to imperialism, which forms the other major preoccupation of *Culture and Imperialism*. Regretting that he had said little about anti-imperial resistance in *Orientalism*, he devotes a substantial section of the later text to this subject. The culture of resistance, as he sees it, is itself an instance of 'overlapping territories' because 'it must to a certain degree work to recover [or, one might add, recover from] forms already established or at least influenced or infiltrated by the culture of empire' (ibid.: 253). By way of example, Said reminds us that the struggle over Africa in the twentieth century is over territories and boundaries drawn by European colonists. Similarly, the African novel in the hands of writers such as Chinua Achebe, Ngũgĩwa Thiong'o, and Tayeb Salih is partly a response to the racism of Conrad's images of Africa especially as articulated in his *Heart of Darkness* (Achebe, 1990 [1988]). For Said,

> [these post-imperial writers] bear the past within them—as scars of humiliating wounds, as instigation for different practices, as potentially revised visions of the past tending towards a post-colonial future, as urgently reinterpretable and redeployable experiences, in which the formerly silent native speaks and acts on territory reclaimed as part of a general movement of resistance, from the colonist.
>
> (Said, 1994a [1993]: 256)

The terrain of resistance is vast and variegated and not all parts of it command Said's uncritical allegiance. He has harsh words for forms of resistance that reinforce identitarian divides between the rulers and the ruled while simply inverting their order of primacy, criticizing these as 'nativist', separatist, chauvinist, and authoritarian (I shall have more to say about this critique in Section 16.4). Conversely, perhaps on account of his own biography, he has a strong affinity for scholars, writers, artists, and intellectuals who, hailing from colonial or peripheral regions, make what he describes as 'the voyage in' to the metropolis. Organically connected to mass resistance movements in their countries of origin and functioning as conduits for those movements into the metropolis, these figures nonetheless write in 'imperial' languages and 'set themselves the revisionist, critical task of dealing frontally with the metropolitan culture, using the techniques, discourses, and weapons of scholarship and criticism once reserved exclusively for the European' (ibid,: 293). They produce hybrid cultural works that draw on mainstream Western discourses but also create new disciplinary and political approaches. Exemplary of this kind of figure, in Said's view, are C.L.R. James (see more on James in Chapter 18), George Antonius, Ranajit Guha, and S.H. Alatas, to whose work he devotes considerable attention.

In sum, if *Orientalism* described a world of warring essences discursively constructed by Western imperialism and ironically reinforced by its antagonists, *Culture and Imperialism* was Said's analytical riposte to this construction, demonstrating the inescapable entanglements of a world constituted by imperialism: 'Partly because of empire, all cultures are involved in one another; none is single and pure, all are hybrid, heterogeneous, extraordinarily differentiated, and un-monolithic' (ibid.: xxix).

> ### 16.3 Empire and hybridity: Key Points
>
> - Hybridity is a central theme of Said's *Culture and Imperialism*, which explores how culture both sustains and contests imperialism.
> - Said demonstrates how, in making constant reference to empire, metropolitan literary and musical cultures create 'structures of attitude and reference' that support empire.
> - He also demonstrates how cultural resistance to empire in turn finds itself working through and against structures, forms, and languages imposed by empire.
> - In this way, contrary to the view of imperialism as a clash of distinct cultural formations, Said regards it as having forged a world of 'overlapping territories, intertwined histories'.

16.4 Partisan for Palestine

16.4.1 Narrating Palestine

In describing the critical work of those who had undertaken 'the voyage in', Said might have been describing himself, particularly in his avatar as an advocate for Palestinian self-determination. Even when not explicitly invoked, a concern for his native Palestine infused everything Said wrote. We might read *Orientalism* as a deep genealogical investigation of the stereotypes through which Arabs and Palestinians were viewed in much of the Western media at the time, as terrorists, fanatics, corrupt oil-rich sheikhs, camel jockeys, and so forth. Conversely, when discussing cultures of resistance, arguments about the most effective and emancipatory strategies for the liberation of Palestine were never far from his mind.

Said's writing about Palestine is concerned, above all else, with making the case for Palestinian self-determination to Western and especially US audiences. In a time when social media offers the possibility of conveying Palestinian voices to the world even in the midst of the most brutal violence inflicted by the Israeli state, it is easy to underestimate just how difficult this was when Said was beginning to articulate the Palestinian viewpoint. Israeli Prime Minister Golda Meir's reported remark in 1969 that 'there is no Palestinian people' is a stark indication of the difficulties. In a context where the very peoplehood of Palestinians was denied by Israel and its powerful patrons and allies, 'the first task'—as Said (1994b: xvi) puts it—'was to get a place—literally anywhere—to say that we did exist'. This he does in clear and uncompromising terms with a steadfastness mirroring that of the people in the service of whose liberation he was writing:

> . . . on the land called Palestine there existed as a huge majority for hundreds of years a largely pastoral, a nevertheless socially, culturally, politically, economically identifiable people whose language and religion were (for a huge majority) Arabic and Islam, respectively. This people—or, if one wishes to deny them any modern conception of themselves as a people, this *group* of people—identified itself with the land it tilled and lived on (poorly or not is irrelevant), the more so after an almost wholly European decision was made to resettle, reconstitute, recapture the land for Jews who were to be brought there from elsewhere . . . Such as it is, the Palestinian actuality is today, was yesterday, and most likely tomorrow will be built upon an act of resistance to this new foreign colonialism.
>
> (Said, 1980 [1979]: 7–8)

Said's account of Palestinian peoplehood is articulated most clearly in *The Question of Palestine* (Said, 1980 [1979]). Partly a work of history, a critique of ideology, and a commentary on political events unfolding at the time of writing, the text begins by unpacking the discourse of Zionism from the perspective of its Palestinian victims. For European Jews, Zionism's offer of a homeland in the Holy Land promised refuge from the centuries of anti-Semitic persecution that they had suffered. Yet as Said (ibid.: 15–16) explains, the Arab inhabitants of that land experienced the 1917 Balfour Declaration—whereby a European power (Britain) offered a non-European territory (Palestine) to another foreign group (European Jews) in flagrant disregard of the presence and wishes of the existing residents of that territory—as an act of rank colonialism. Drawing attention to the convergence of British imperialism and Zionism in their common view of the Arabs in Palestine as 'natives' who merited no consideration, he demonstrates how Zionism drew its geopolitical strength from its resonance with its 'Western ideological parents', colonialism and orientalism (ibid.: 26). As he explains,

> what in Zionism served the no doubt justified ends of Jewish tradition, saving the Jews as a people from homelessness and anti-Semitism and restoring them to nationhood, also collaborated with those aspects of the dominant Western culture (in which Zionism institutionally lived) making it possible for Europeans to view non-Europeans as inferior, marginal, and irrelevant.
>
> (ibid.: 71)

Precisely because Palestinians have experienced Zionism as colonialism, he argues, they have been unable to see it as a legitimate response to European anti-Semitism (ibid.: 69). Even as he unpacks here why Palestinians have been unable and unwilling to see Zionism as anything other than colonialism, as Rashid Khalidi (2008: 48) reminds us, Said was also one of the first Palestinians to argue before Arab audiences for a recognition of the humanity of the Israeli people and for the necessity of understanding the trajectory of Jewish history that culminated in the horrors of the Holocaust.

Said then analyses the challenges of Palestinian resistance in the first three decades since the establishment of Israel. Central here is the ideological difficulty of organizing against 'the most morally complex of all opponents, Jews, with a long history of victimization and terror behind them', as a result of which, 'the absolute wrong of settler-colonialism is very much diluted and perhaps even dissipated when it is a fervently believed-in Jewish survival that uses settler colonialism to straighten out its own destiny' (Said (1980 [1979]: 119). As Said frequently points out, by drawing on these moral complexities and by representing itself as a geopolitical asset of the West capable of holding the line against Islam, the Soviet Union, and communism, Israel won the uncritical moral, political, and especially financial support of the US, becoming the largest recipient of US foreign aid since the Second World War. It is worth underscoring here the settler colonial status of the USA (along with other states 'founded' through acts of white European settlement that simultaneously dispossessed and exterminated Indigenous peoples), which in part accounts for its endorsement of Israeli settler colonialism.

In the face of these challenges, Palestinians have had the difficult task of organizing resistance across a fragmented and widely dispersed population comprising (1) exiles scattered in neighbouring Arab states, as well as Europe, North America, and further afield; (2) Palestinian citizens of Israel facing unrelenting racial and religious discrimination from the very inception of the state in 1948; and (3) Palestinians living under occupation in the West Bank and Gaza after 1967. Published in 1979, *The Question of Palestine* speaks admiringly of the Palestine Liberation Organization (PLO), which Said commends for its progressive vision of a secular and democratic state for all people in Palestine, culture of open debate, relative independence from unreliable Arab state allies, broad-based popular support, long history of struggle and success in forging a representative Palestinian position (ibid.: 160). While acknowledging legitimate criticisms of the PLO by other groups in the crowded landscape of Palestinian politics, Said is nonetheless admiring of the leadership of Yasser Arafat at this time (ibid.: 166).

This relatively warm assessment was offered at a time when Said was himself a member of the Palestinian National Council, the legislative organ of the PLO, and a close advisor to Arafat. From the signing of the Oslo I Accord in 1993, we see a significant shift in his attitude. Said (1993) was a harsh critic of the agreement, which he saw as a Palestinian capitulation and surrender to Israel. In exchange for Israel's recognition of the PLO as the representative of the Palestinian people and its concession of little more than municipal powers over an archipelago of disconnected territories that could never constitute a viable state, the Palestinian leadership renounced their most far-reaching demands while deferring the thorniest questions (the status of Jerusalem, dismantling of settlements in the Occupied Territories, as well as the network of roads and infrastructure connecting them, the right of return of Palestinian refugees, control of aquifers) to 'final status negotiations'. Said surmised, prophetically, that in transforming the Palestinian leadership into collaborators with Israel, and particularly by outsourcing the policing of Gaza to the PLO, the agreement would sow the seeds of division between the latter and rival groups such as Hamas, undermining Palestinian unity and ensuring that 'the interim stage may be the final one' (ibid.). In scores of essays that followed, many of which were written for the Cairo-based *Al-Ahram Weekly* and subsequently anthologized, he excoriated the Palestinian Authority (PA) created by the Accords for its authoritarianism and corruption. He lamented the inability of its Legislative Council to exercise any constitutional checks over Arafat – 'a despot who controls the budget' – or over 'his twenty security services who torture, kill, imprison critics and ban their books at the whim of Palestine's overweening tyrant' (Said, 2003 [2000]: 163). He described the PA as a 'dictatorship' and 'at bottom a kind of mafia' (ibid.: 22) operating in its own self-interest. At times he even posited a moral equivalence between Israel and the PA, writing that the latter's 'clamp-down on expression and democratic practices is as severe as under direct Israeli rule' and speaking of 'the double occupation of the Israelis and the Palestinian Authority' (ibid.: 67). These critiques paralleled his untiring fusillades against continuing Israeli expulsion, occupation, dispossession, and destruction of Palestinian lives, livelihoods, and land; the opportunism of despotic Arab states that paid lip-service to the Palestinian cause to shore up their legitimacy; and a US foreign policy that sustained these oppressive structures.

Israel's tightening grip on Palestine transformed Said's vision of what a just resolution of the conflict might look like. From being an early advocate of the 'two-state solution' that recognized Israel's right to exist in exchange for independent Palestinian statehood—a position for which he was criticized at the time—he came to espouse what has come to be called the 'one-state solution' (Said, 1999). This was prompted partly by the recognition that Jewish settlement building in the Occupied Territories was too extensive and irreversible, short of morally heinous measures such as mass population transfer, to permit separate and ethnically homogeneous entities: 'so tiny is the land area of historical Palestine, so closely intertwined are Israelis and Palestinians, despite their inequality and antipathy, that clean separation simply won't, can't really, occur or work' (ibid.). But it was also prompted by a moral opposition to the ideology of 'clean separation'. As Said (2003 [2000]: 264) remarks, 'What is it . . . that we have against Israel if we say that we want a "pure" Palestine, free of Jews, free of everything that isn't pure Arab and Muslim and Palestinian? Nothing at all: we would be mimicking exactly what it is that we attack.' The one-state solution, in his view, required both sides 'to soften, lessen and finally give up special status for one people at the expense of the other' (Said, 1999). In practical terms, this meant a 'trimming' of both the Law of Return for Jews and the right of return for Palestinian refugees and the establishment of a binational state on the basis of equal citizenship for all—a set of recommendations that has been difficult for both parties to contemplate, let alone accept.

16.4.2 For, against, and beyond nationalism

The trajectory of Said's thought on Palestine reflects his complex view of nationalism itself. Said recognizes nationalism as the vehicle that delivers marginalized and persecuted peoples from slavery, colonialism, and spiritual dispossession but also as bringing with it the temptation to launder the cultural past in the process of nationalist myth-making as well as a politics of supremacism and indoctrination (Said, 2001: 377, 421–425). These criticisms of nationalism's authoritarian tendencies did not amount to a simple anti-nationalist position. Indeed, Said rejects Western critiques of Third World nationalisms that seem to imply that formerly colonized peoples are less deserving of nationalism than, say, Germans or Italians (Said, 1994a [1993]: 261). Instead, he works through the necessity, but also the pitfalls, of nationalism in a number of ways.

In his most pessimistic moments, Said views nationalism as an inescapable tragic imperative imposed on colonized peoples. As he puts it:

> It's the tragedy, the irony, the paradox of all anti-imperial or decolonizing struggles that independence is the stage through which you must try to pass: for us independence is the only alternative to the continued horrors of the Israeli occupation, whose goal is the extermination of a Palestinian national identity.

(Wicke and Sprinker, 1992: 236–237)

In more optimistic moments, Said appears to suggest that the excesses of nationalism might be mitigated through a methodological transparency and self-awareness. A brief illustration of what this might entail can be found in his reflection on the status in Palestinian national consciousness of the battle of Karameh, fought in 1968 between the Israeli army on the one hand and the PLO and Jordanian army on the other and enshrined in Palestinian memory as the first significant military encounter between Israeli and *Palestinian* forces. Referring to this episode in Palestinian history, Said (1994b: 9) writes: 'All occurrences become events after they occur. In part events are mythic, but like all effective myths they record an important aspect of a real experience.' He goes on to explore why Karameh has come to occupy such a significant place in Palestinian nationalist mythology, out of all proportion to the strictly military significance of the encounter. There is a sympathetic appreciation of the myth and of why it has been nurtured, but we are nonetheless reminded of the disjunction between occurrence and event, between what happened and the layers of meaning with which it became encrusted. In moments such as these, we see Said as both a participant *in* nationalist discourse and a theorist and critic *of* nationalism, hopeful that the tension between these enterprises might be mitigated by the intellectual whose task is 'to show how the group is not a natural or god-given entity but is a constructed, manufactured, even in some cases invented object, with a history of struggle and conquest behind it, that it is sometimes important to represent' (Said, 1996 [1994]: 33).

Said is at his clearest on the process by which this tension might be mitigated when he reads Frantz Fanon (see more on Fanon in Chapter 28) as arguing in *The Wretched of the Earth* that 'unless national consciousness at its moment of success was somehow changed into a social consciousness, the future would hold not liberation but an extension of imperialism' (Said, 1994a [1993]: 323). For Fanon (2001: 115), failure to pass 'from total, undiscriminating nationalism to social and economic awareness' risks entrenching nationalist bourgeois parties and elites in positions of power and, moreover, thwarts the development of a universalist consciousness among the people with which they might challenge and overthrow these elites. In a provocation to think beyond the immediate imperatives of nationalist independence, Said (1996: 41) asks, 'Are we fighting just to rid ourselves of colonialism, a necessary goal, or are we thinking about what we will do when the last white policeman leaves?' Invoking Fanon and his fellow Martinican thinker Aimé Césaire, Said responds that 'the goal of the native intellectual cannot simply be to replace the white policeman with his native counterpart, but rather... the invention of new souls'. While Fanon can appear to suggest, in a somewhat Leninist vein, that the nationalist struggle against the white colonizer and the universalist struggle against the bourgeoisie are sequential stages, Said felt he had no choice but to initiate his critique of the native policeman well before the departure of his 'white' overlord has even become contemplatable.

16.4 Partisan for Palestine: Key Points

- Said was one of the most articulate and effective spokespersons for Palestinian self-determination in the West.
- In this capacity, he offered incisive critiques of Israel, Zionism, and Western support for both, and chronicled the struggle for Palestinian liberation.
- From the signing of the Oslo I Accord in 1993, he became a harsh critic of Palestinian leader Yasser Arafat and the PA, on account of their capitulation to Israeli demands and increasingly authoritarian rule.
- He was also a critic of undemocratic and authoritarian Arab states and insisted that the Palestinian liberation struggle had the potential to shine as a beacon for democracy in the region.
- Said's simultaneous participation in the Palestinian national struggle and critique of the nationalist leadership reflect his complex view of nationalism itself, which he sees as a necessary vehicle for liberation but also as harbouring tendencies of myth-making, authoritarianism, and supremacism.

16.5 The intellectual vocation

How did a professor of comparative literature in the upper echelons of the US academy with relatively esoteric interests in literary criticism, philology, and opera come to become one of the English-speaking world's most embattled and celebrated intellectuals? The answer to this question can be found in Said's views on what it means to be an intellectual, the clearest statement of which is found in his 1993 Reith Lectures. In these lectures, Said (1996: xvi) describes the intellectual as an 'exile and marginal, as amateur, and as the author of a language that tries to speak the truth to power'.

The figure of the exile recurs frequently in Said's work, prompted most obviously by the facts of Palestinian expulsion and dispossession. Reflecting on the habits of mind formed by the condition of exile, Said is quick to acknowledge its least attractive aspects—an exaggerated sense of group solidarity, hostility to outsiders, a narcissistic masochism that is the result of isolation and displacement, the pressure to join parties and movements and the consequent loss of critical perspective that this can engender (Said, 2001: 178, 183). But beyond these understandable and even justifiable expressions of self-assertion and survival, exile in Said's view can also bring a new self-awareness. Whereas most people are principally aware of one culture and one home, the exile is aware of at least two. This plurality of vision, which Said calls contrapuntal, allows for a critical perspective on both the place that has been left behind and the one to which the exile has arrived. Said hopes that the enlarged awareness that results from multiple location might 'diminish orthodox judgment and elevate appreciative sympathy' (ibid.: 186). Besides being an actual condition, Said (1996 [1994]: 52) also speaks of exile in a metaphorical register when he describes the vocation of the intellectual. The intellectual as exile is at odds with their society, an outsider to the privileges, power, and honours that are to be had as rewards for conformity. Less vulnerable to the seductions of power and more able to identify with the weak and marginalized, the alienated intellectual is also less likely to take social structures for granted and more attuned to the ways in which they are contingent, historically constituted and potentially revisable (ibid.: 52, 59). The very marginality of this position brings with it a kind of intellectual liberation. Not having acquired the trappings of power and success, the intellectual as exile is more willing to risk upsetting received wisdoms.

Closely related to the figure of the exile is that of the amateur who refuses to remain confined within the boundaries of disciplinary competence and expertise but ranges freely across them. Perhaps counterintuitively, Said identifies the greatest threat to intellectual life as emanating not directly from the state or the market but from what he calls the attitude of professionalism. By this, he means the preoccupation with 'what is considered to be proper, professional behavior—not rocking the boat, not straying outside the accepted paradigms or limits, making yourself marketable and above all presentable, hence uncontroversial and unpolitical and "objective"' (ibid.: 73). Professionalism brings with it the dangers of specialization—which confines thinkers within ever narrower remits of inquiry—an increasing emphasis on technical 'expertise' and a propensity to respond to agendas set by those in power. Said counterposes this attitude of professionalism with that of amateurism. Wresting the term away from its connotations of incompetence, amateurism for Said (ibid.: 76) is 'the desire to be moved not by profit or reward but by love for an unquenchable interest in the larger picture, in making connections across lines and barriers, in refusing to be tied down to a speciality, in caring for ideas and values despite the restrictions of a profession'. The amateur believes that as a thinking and concerned member of society, 'one is entitled to raise moral issues at the heart of even the most technical and professionalized activity' insofar as these affect matters of public import concerning the relationship between the state and its citizens as well as other states (ibid.: 82–83). Finally, amateurism entails choosing the risks and uncertainties of intervening in the public sphere over the relative safety and insularity of professional academic exchange.

Said's valorization of the figure of the amateur was in large part a response to his reading of the intellectual landscape of the US at the close of the twentieth century. As he saw it, the sense of an intellectual vocation had been swallowed up by a public culture polarized between policy-oriented intellectuals who had internalized the norms of the state and a left that had retreated into superspecialist and hermetic enclaves and been defanged by the academy. Predictably critical of intellectuals whispering into the ears of the powerful, he also had harsh words for the academic left:

> Cults like post-modernism, discourse analysis, New Historicism, deconstruction, neo-pragmatism transport them into the country of the blue; an astonishing sense of weightlessness with regard to the gravity of history and individual responsibility fritters away attention to public matters, and to public discourse. The result is a kind of floundering about that is most dispiriting to witness, even as the society as a whole drifts without direction or coherence.
>
> (Said 1994a [1993]: 366)

It is his commitment to a revival of the intellectual as amateur that draws Said out of his disciplinary specialization in modern European and American literature into broader conversations about the relationship between imperialism and culture including in its contemporary manifestations. It spurs him to comment regularly and incisively on the shifting configurations of this relationship in popular culture and public policy, particularly as it relates to the question of Palestine and other anti-imperialist struggles, thrusting him into battle in the mainstream print and electronic media in the West as much as in the Arab world. Along with contemporaries such as Stuart Hall, Said anticipates the social media age in which the admittedly compromised platforms of surveillance capitalism nonetheless offer something of a stage on which the rank amateur might sometimes speak truth to power.

> **16.5 The intellectual vocation: Key Points**
>
> - Said describes the intellectual as an exile, an amateur, and as someone who speaks truth to power.
> - As a metaphorical exile, the intellectual is at odds with their society and, in keeping their distance from the privileges and honours that it confers, better able to identify with and speak for the marginalized.
> - As an amateur, the intellectual refuses to be confined within narrow boundaries of disciplinary expertise, but makes connections between issues and asks the larger questions that are necessary to sustain democratic public spheres.

16.6 Conclusion

The relevance of Said's political thought to our contemporary world can hardly be overstated. His theorization of the relationship between power and knowledge continues to shape discussion of the problem of representation in an unequal world. While acutely attentive to its hierarchies, Said is also attuned to its interconnectedness. This is both an analytical insight and a normative commitment. Despite borrowing extensively from poststructuralist theory, he shares none of its anti-universalism and anti-humanism. At the same time, his debts to poststructuralism have incurred the criticism of Marxists, who regard his replacement of Marx with Foucault as inaugurating a turn away from materialist analysis and downplaying the structuring force of capitalism in producing the cultural forms that he is investigating.

And, yet, Said is not vulnerable—as other postcolonial and poststructuralist theorists are—to the accusation that he has turned away from the business of anti-imperialist struggle. Marxists have been particularly severe on Homi Bhabha's theorization of the colonial relationship as one of negotiation rather than negation, arguing that it represents the colonial encounter as a competition between peers rather than the brutally unequal, often existential, struggle that it is (Parry, 2004: 62–63). Said's conceptualization of hybridity has not suffered the same fate. This is not only because his arguments are rooted in the concrete realities of liberation struggles, but also because of his own lifelong and costly commitment to a particular liberation struggle—that of Palestine. Here too, Said never suspends his critical sensibilities, living by the mantra 'never solidarity before criticism' (Said, 1996: 32). His fierce criticisms of the Palestinian leadership and its collaboration with Israeli occupation proved to be prophetic. As an early advocate of the two-state solution and later, as this prospect was made implausible by the entrenchment of Israeli occupation, the one-state solution, he has always seemed ahead of his time.

Beyond the particular issues and causes to which Said lent his voice, it is his embodiment of the role of the public intellectual that may be his most lasting legacy. While he could sometimes idealize the university as the last redoubt of critical thinking and may not have reflected sufficiently on the unique possibilities afforded by the elite universities that he inhabited, Said always used his privileged position in the academy to battle on behalf of the marginalized and the unrepresented. In this regard, he remains a shining example of the dissident potentials of a thinking life.

Take your learning further by accessing the online resources for a library of web links to relevant videos, articles, blogs, and useful websites for this chapter: www.oup.com/he/Ramgotra-Choat1e.

Study questions

1. How does Said understand the relationship between knowledge and power in the discourse of Orientalism?
2. Does Said's analysis of Orientalism reify or deconstruct categories such as 'Orient' and 'Occident'?
3. How does Said understand the relationship between discursive structures and individual scholarly agency?
4. Should Orientalism be understood as a discourse originating in classical antiquity or as a more recent phenomenon sustaining European colonialisms in the modern age?
5. What is the value of contrapuntal reading?
6. How does Said link Zionism to colonialism and Orientalism?
7. Is Said a nationalist?
8. Is Said's vision of the public intellectual elitist?

Further reading

Primary sources

Said, E.W. (1980 [1979]) *The Question of Palestine*. New York: Vintage Books.
   A historical and political account of the emergence of Palestinian national identity and struggle that also offers critiques of Zionism and US foreign policy.

Said, E.W. (1994a [1993]) *Culture and Imperialism*. London: Vintage.
   A wide-ranging survey of literary, musical, and cultural texts that sustain and contest empire, revealing the entanglements of colony and metropole.

Said, E.W. (1995 [1978]) *Orientalism: Western Conceptions of the Orient*. London: Penguin.
   A ground-breaking study of British, French, and US conceptions of the 'Orient' between the eighteenth and twentieth centuries.

Said, E.W. (1996 [1994]) *Representations of the Intellectual: The 1993 Reith Lectures*. London: Vintage.
   A powerful essay on the vocation of the public intellectual.

Secondary sources

Brennan, T. (2021) *Places of Mind: A Life of Edward Said*. London: Bloomsbury.
   The first comprehensive biography of Said.

Ertur, B. and Sökmen, M.G. (eds) (2008) *Waiting for the Barbarians: A Tribute to Edward W. Said*. London: Verso.
   A collection of essays exploring the political and intellectual legacy of Said written by figures closely associated with him and published after his death.

Morefield, J. (2022) *Unsettling the World: Edward Said and Political Theory*. London: Rowman & Littlefield.
   A book-length treatment of Said's cultural criticism from the perspective of political theory.

Sprinker, M. (ed.) (1992) *Edward Said: A Critical Reader*. Oxford: Blackwell.
   The first book-length examination of Said's career, surveying his cultural and political writings.

References

Achebe, C. (1990 [1988]) *Hopes and Impediments: Selected Essays*. New York: Anchor Books.

Ahmad, A. (1992) *In Theory: Classes, Nations, Literatures*. London: Verso.

Al-'Azm, S.J. (1981) 'Orientalism and Orientalism in Reverse'. *Khamsin*, 8: 5–26.

Barkawi, T. and Laffey, M. (2006) 'The Postcolonial Moment in Security Studies'. *Review of International Studies*, 32(2): 329–352.

Bhabha, H.K. (1994) *The Location of Culture*. London: Routledge.

Boone, J. (2014) *The Homoerotics of Orientalism*. New York: Columbia University Press.

Fanon, F. (2001 [1961]) *The Wretched of the Earth*. Trans. C. Farrington. London: Penguin.

Foucault, M. (2002 [1969]) *The Archaeology of Knowledge*. London: Routledge.

Fukuyama, F. (1992) *The End of History and the Last Man*. New York: Free Press.

Gilroy, P. (1993) *The Black Atlantic: Modernity and Double Consciousness*. London: Verso.

Huntington, S. (1993) 'The Clash of Civilizations?' *Foreign Affairs*, 72(3): 22–49.

Khalidi, R. (2008) 'Edward Said and Palestine: Balancing the Academic and the Political, the Public and the Private'. In B. Ertur and M.G. Sökmen (eds), *Waiting for the Barbarians: A Tribute to Edward W. Said*. London: Verso.

Parry, B. (2004) *Postcolonial Studies: A Materialist Critique*. London: Routledge.

Puar, J.K. (2007) *Terrorist Assemblages: Homonationalism in Queer Times*. Durham, NC: Duke University Press.

Said, E.W. (1980 [1979]) *The Question of Palestine*. New York: Vintage Books.

Said, E.W. (1993) 'The Morning After'. *London Review of Books*, 15(20). https://www.lrb.co.uk/the-paper/v15/n20/edward-said/the-morning-after.

Said, E.W. (1994a [1993]) *Culture and Imperialism*. London: Vintage.

Said, E.W. (1994b) *The Politics of Dispossession: The Struggle for Palestinian Self-Determination 1969–1994*. London: Vintage.

Said, E.W. (1995 [1978]) *Orientalism: Western Conceptions of the Orient*. London: Penguin.

Said, E.W. (1996 [1994]) *Representations of the Intellectual: The 1993 Reith Lectures*. London: Vintage.

Said, E.W. (1999) The One-State Solution. *The New York Times Magazine*, January 10, https://www.nytimes.com/1999/01/10/magazine/the-one-state-solution.html.

Said, E.W. (2000) *Out of Place: A Memoir*. New York: Vintage.

Said, E.W. (2001) *Reflections on Exile and Other Literary and Cultural Essays*. London: Granta Books.

Said, E.W. (2003 [2000]) *The End of the Peace Process: Oslo and After*. New Delhi: Penguin.

Wicke, J. and Sprinker, M. (1992) 'Interview with Edward Said'. In M. Sprinker (ed.), *Edward Said: A Critical Reader*. Oxford: Blackwell Publishers.

Yeğenoğlu, M. (1998) *Colonial Fantasies: Towards a Feminist Reading of Orientalism*. Cambridge: Cambridge University Press.

Part IV

Freedom and Revolution

17	Catharine Macaulay and Edmund Burke	Alan Coffee	295
18	C.L.R. James	Robbie Shilliam	313
19	Hannah Arendt	Kei Hiruta	331
20	Zhang Taiyan	Viren Murthy	349

Freedom is a core political concept. Almost everyone agrees that freedom is both a condition and an important goal of a flourishing human life. Disagreement, therefore, concerns the definition of freedom and its relation to other political values and concepts (for example, advancing equality might mean restricting liberty). Both of these issues require us to think about the constraints on freedom; almost no one advocates unconstrained, absolute freedom, which is better termed 'licence'. Guaranteeing my freedom means placing some limits on your freedom (and vice versa). The question is, therefore, what counts as a legitimate constraint—but also, what counts as a constraint at all?

Many liberals in particular define freedom as the absence of constraints: a person is free when they can pursue their desires without deliberate obstruction by others. Governments must enforce some constraints (in order to protect the freedom of all), but government itself can also threaten our freedom—which is why liberals support limits on state power. This conception of freedom as the enjoyment of an individual right is self-consciously modern, in contrast to an ancient conception of freedom as the sharing of social power or the collective exercise of sovereignty.

The characterization of freedom as the absence of deliberate interference has been criticized. Even if no one is interfering with or coercing a person, their 'freedom' will be meaningless if they do not have the resources to realize it: a lack of money, time, or knowledge, for example, can be an obstacle to realizing my freedom. Constraints on freedom may not necessarily be the result of deliberate human action: many argue that there are *structural* constraints on freedom—such as capitalism, patriarchy, and white supremacy—which may not be intended by anyone but which nonetheless severely restrict the capacity of certain people to act.

It has also been argued that there are internal as well as external constraints on our freedom. According to this argument—which is associated in particular with the communitarian critique of liberalism—freedom cannot simply mean being able to pursue our desires without interference from others, because sometimes our desires themselves may obstruct our true purposes. Sometimes, for example, a person may be motivated by fear, anger, laziness, or greed in such a way as to prevent them from realizing their goals; or they may deceive themselves as to what those goals really are. Therefore, the argument goes, freedom depends not simply on being left alone, but on being able to discriminate between one's aims in life, which, communitarians would argue, is only possible within the context of a particular community from which one draws one's understanding of what is significant and valuable in life.

However it is defined, the desire to defend and expand our freedoms can be a strong motivating force in politics. The imposition of external constraints that are viewed as illegitimate can provoke resistance and opposition. Such opposition may pursue legal routes, but ultimately it can take the form of a revolution. While there are long-standing and wide-ranging debates concerning what counts as a revolution and what motivates them, revolutions play a central role in the modern political imaginary. Three revolutions in particular excite the Western imaginary: the American and French Revolutions of the late-eighteenth century that overthrew the *ancien régime* and advanced liberal rights and freedoms—for white men, at least—and the Russian Revolution of 1917 that remains the most comprehensive challenge to the dominance of liberal capitalism that the world has seen. The French and Russian Revolutions are sometimes seen as bookending the 'long nineteenth century' that is often taken as the high point of liberal modernity (see Part III). Of equal significance—though not always given equal attention by Western scholars—are the anti-colonial revolutions in Latin America in the nineteenth century and across Africa and Asia after the Second World War. The first great anti-colonial revolution was the Haitian Revolution of 1791–1804, a slave revolt against French colonial rule that established the world's first Black state. Individual revolutions can become totems within rival visions of politics, used to celebrate or discredit mass uprisings for enlarging or endangering freedom respectively.

Differing attitudes towards revolution are well captured in Chapter 17, which compares two important political thinkers of the late-eighteenth century: the Anglo-Irish philosopher and politician Edmund Burke and the English historian Catharine Macaulay, who was in her day a celebrated public intellectual. A supporter of the American and French Revolutions, Macaulay promoted a republican ideal of freedom as independence from arbitrary control. The freedom of the individual and society, she argued, required equality and virtue: inequality would create dependence, and virtue was needed to guide individual action and develop rational and effective laws. Although widely cited today as the father of conservatism, Burke's political position is in some ways harder to classify. He supported the American Revolution but is best known for his polemical opposition to the French Revolution. Burke believed that the principles and processes governing society were complex and that social change should be cautious and incremental. He was certainly not opposed to freedom, but believed that freedoms and rights were contextual and particularistic—a product of social convention and custom, passed down through generations, rather than abstract, rational ideals discovered by speculation.

An alternative reading of the French Revolution was offered by the twentieth-century Trinidadian Marxist, C.L.R. James. As Chapter 18 explains, James proposed a 'dialectic of freedom' whereby the pursuit of collective self-determination expanded freedoms but could also introduce new unfreedoms, depending on the interplay between the masses, the bourgeoisie, and the radical intelligentsia. James applied this novel interpretation of Marxism to the French and Russian Revolutions, though he is perhaps best known for his analysis of the Haitian Revolution. James insisted that struggles for freedom must ultimately draw on the ideals of European civilization, even when, as in Haiti, those struggles were fought against European empires.

The American and French Revolutions—although notably not the Haitian Revolution—were also important references for the twentieth-century philosopher Hannah Arendt, discussed in Chapter 19. She argued that, in 1789, France saw a rebellion rather than a fully-fledged revolution: the overthrow of an oppressive regime, but not the founding of a new order of freedom, as happened in America. She further argued that whereas the French rebellion had been motivated by poverty and hunger, the American Revolution had been driven by a specifically political motivation to establish a free republic. This contrast is based on Arendt's distinctive and highly influential understanding of politics. The political sphere for Arendt does not concern the satisfaction of our biological needs, but is rather the uniquely human sphere of freedom. This sphere of freedom is itself understood by Arendt not as liberty from constraints, but as acting and speaking in the public realm as a member of a community. Among other things, Arendt was concerned that the displacement of this model of politics and its concept of freedom would leave us less able to resist the threat of totalitarianism. This was a threat that had personal significance for Arendt, a German Jew who fled from the Nazis and eventually settled in the USA. Arendt emphasized the connection between twentieth-century totalitarianism and nineteenth-century European imperialism—although her analysis of the European colonization of Africa expresses racially biased sentiments, as did her later discussion of the US Civil Rights Movement.

The final chapter in this Part focuses on a thinker who supported a revolution which is probably not as well known to English-speaking readers as the French, American, Russian, or even Haitian revolutions; namely, the 1911 revolution that overthrew the Qing dynasty, the last Chinese dynasty. Zhang Taiyan, who is the subject of Chapter 20, was initially critical of reformers who drew upon the works of the Chinese philosopher Confucius, and instead aimed to create a Western-style republic. After a brief period of imprisonment for plotting to overthrow the government, however, Zhang turned to Buddhism and the classical Chinese philosophy of Daoism to develop a form of pan-Asian socialism that attacked Western imperialism and capitalism.

We include a chapter on Zhang, rather than a better-known Chinese philosopher such as Confucius, in part because doing so reflects the book's commitment to amplifying hitherto marginal voices. Yet decentring—or decolonizing—political thought does not simply entail moving away from the centre to the margins, but rather involves revealing the co-constitution and mutual dependence of the centre and the margins. Zhang's work is an excellent example of these logics: his arguments were developed in a creative tension with Western ideas (particularly, as Chapter 20 shows, the work of the German philosopher G.W.F. Hegel), reading Chinese and other Asian sources alongside and sometimes against European theories.

17 Catharine Macaulay and Edmund Burke

ALAN COFFEE

Chapter guide

This chapter examines the rival and contrasting political philosophies of Catharine Macaulay and Edmund Burke. The two were almost exact contemporaries in the eighteenth century and clashed on their understandings of the fundamental nature of political society and the correct approach to take on reform. Macaulay and Burke were opposites in many ways. As a woman, Macaulay was a political outsider while Burke was a successful politician. Macaulay was a radical and revolutionary republican who based her ideas on a few clear, immutable philosophical truths, while Burke was a cautious and conservative thinker who valued stability and continuity, appealing to tradition rather than speculative principle. Section 17.2 introduces Macaulay's philosophy, based on the core ideal of freedom as independence from arbitrary control. Section 17.3 presents Burke's contrasting organic, contextual, and pragmatic approach. Finally, Section 17.4 considers some of the weaknesses in each philosopher's work, particularly from the perspective of securing the equal citizenship rights of women and members of minority social groups.

17.1 Introduction

Catharine Macaulay and Edmund Burke were two of the most prominent political thinkers of the eighteenth century. It may seem surprising to many readers to see Macaulay and Burke mentioned in the same bracket like this. While Burke remains one of the best-known figures in the history of political ideas, Macaulay is largely unknown today, outside of a small cluster of scholars. Nevertheless, in her lifetime, Macaulay was one of the most celebrated public intellectuals in England, and someone Burke himself regarded as a formidable political opponent. That her thought has been neglected over the last two centuries and more is a reflection of the contingencies of the history of ideas rather than of the quality of Macaulay's thought. As a reflection of this, in our own time, her philosophy is undergoing a sustained scholarly revival. Burke, by contrast, has long been one of the most recognizable, influential, and quotable figures in the history of political thought.

I shall place Macaulay and Burke in dialogue on the questions of freedom, social stability and tradition, and revolution, as indeed they were during their careers. The two represented opposing positions on the political spectrum, with Macaulay offering a radical republican challenge to Burke's monarchist politics. Macaulay answered Burke twice in writing, in her *Observations on a Pamphlet entitled 'Thoughts on the Cause of the Present Discontents'* (Macaulay, 1770) and her *Observations on the Reflections of the Right Hon. Edmund Burke* (Macaulay, 1790b), which proved to be her final work. Nevertheless, we should be cautious in how we translate their eighteenth-century

Read more about **Macaulay's** life and work by accessing the thinker biography on the online resources: www.oup.com/he/Ramgotra-Choat1e.

differences into today's political distinctions. Burke is probably best known today as a foundational figure in conservative thought. However, while his influence on modern conservativism is indisputable, whether this best characterizes his political philosophy is not so clear. Certainly, Burke has not always been thought of as a conservative. He was, for example, routinely regarded as a liberal during the nineteenth century. Burke's influence has been such that he has continued to fascinate thinkers on the left, while being regularly appropriated by those on the right (Kramnik, 1983). The labels 'conservative' and 'liberal', however, are slippery designations, with roots in nineteenth-century political discourse which have taken on a variety of forms through to our present time (Bourke, 2018). Indeed, whether it makes sense to speak of a timeless core of liberal or conservative positions and ideals is itself highly questionable. More often than not, the decision to apply these terms reflects either current concerns or particular contexts.

Macaulay and Burke are not only opposites in their substantive views, but also in their style of philosophical thinking. Macaulay's position is straightforward, if often subtle. It was worked out systematically and consistently over almost thirty years, most famously in her eight-volume *History of England* (1763-1783) which presents a unified republican interpretation of English history from the accession of the Stuarts to the so-called Glorious Revolution (1688). Macaulay builds her analysis around the core republican principle of freedom as independence from arbitrary control (or non-domination as it is often known today) (Coffee, 2017; 2019). Although described as a conception of freedom, independence represents a composite ideal that brings together the notions of equality, virtue, community, and the rule of law, held together within a tight framework that republicans use to diagnose cases of political legitimacy or failings. Macaulay places this republican ideal at the centre of her political analysis, applying it with unflinching consistency across both history and political context, so much so that even friendly critics in her own time noted that she was apt to reduce all social and political matters to the single question of freedom.

> **Key Concept: The Glorious Revolution (1688)**
>
> The peaceful process by which England's King James II was replaced by his daughter, Mary II, and William of Orange (William III) has long been described as 'glorious', though both Macaulay and Burke simply refer to it as 'the Revolution'. Burke viewed the Revolution very positively, regarding it as preserving the nation's ancient 'indisputable laws and liberties' (Burke, 2009 [1790]: 31). Macaulay, more critically, considered the Revolution to have been an unstable compromise that ceded too much power to the monarch to bypass Parliament.

Burke, by contrast with Macaulay, is an elusive thinker whose work is notoriously difficult to distil and codify. This has given rise to 'the Burke Problem', whereby scholars have attempted to reconcile his 'liberal' ideas on natural rights, individual liberty, and commercial society with his 'conservative' stance on tradition, social stability, and political authority (Winch, 1985; and O'Neill [2016]: 10), who casts this question in terms of Burke's support for or opposition to empire). Scholars often identify an early Burke who, among other things, supported the cause of the American Revolution, and a later Burke whose opposition to the French Revolution serves as a canonical text for many modern conservatives. This disjunction was not lost on Burke's contemporaries, such as Macaulay, Mary Wollstonecraft (see more on Wollstonecraft in Chapter 21), Thomas Paine, and Joseph Priestley (e.g. Priestley, 1791: iv–xii). There is considerable critical debate over the extent to which Burke should be considered a consistent or systematic thinker, and how far his position may have shifted over his life. Richard Bourke describes Burke as 'not a systematic thinker but an engaged polemicist' who had 'no occasion to reveal the "foundations" of his thought' (Bourke, 2015: 18), while Daniel O'Neill argues for understanding Burke as 'a consistently conservative political thinker' (O'Neill, 2016: 1). To some extent, this issue of interpretation is not just about Burke, but arises for many writers whose output straddles the latter half of the eighteenth century with its dramatic social, economic, intellectual, and political changes. David Miller (1981: 200) sees the French Revolution as a particular watershed event in which the 'incompatibility between liberal demands for personal freedom, the rule of law, careers open to talents etc., and conservative commitments to institutional continuity, authority, social hierarchy, and so forth' were crystallized.

I shall concentrate on the 'conservative' interpretation of Burke as most fully articulated in his *Reflections on the Revolution in France* (Burke, 2009 [1790]). I do this for several reasons. In part, given the considerable range of interpretations of his work, a selective reading will allow greater depth and coherence. The conservative reading is also the most influential and widely known outside of specialists on Burke. While it may not represent the biographically definitive portrayal of his complex thinking, it does represent a recognizable and important position in the history of political thought. Finally, the conservative reading captures the Burke that Macaulay and other republicans and radicals saw themselves as debating, and so it will give context to our comparison in this chapter.

Read more about **Burke's** life and work by accessing the thinker biography on the online resources: www.oup.com/he/Ramgotra-Choat1e.

17.2 Catharine Macaulay

Catharine Macaulay (1731–1791) was one of the most prominent public British intellectuals of the late eighteenth century, best known in her own time for her monumental *History of England*. This book rivalled David Hume's six volumes written a decade earlier (1754–1763) on the same subject (see Key Thinker: David Hume in Section 11.1 of Chapter 11). Macaulay's history provided a radical and republican counterpoint to the Tory, pro-monarchical perspective of Hume's work. Today, however, Macaulay is better known for her *Letters on Education*, written shortly before her death, which had a profound influence on Wollstonecraft. Macaulay was active in radical and revolutionary politics, not only a supporter of the American and French Revolutions but a sought-after correspondent by many of the intellectual and political leaders of those movements, including Benjamin Franklin, George Washington, John Adams, and Jacques-Pierre Brissot. She carried out an intellectual correspondence for two decades with Mercy Otis Warren, discussing subjects such as the build-up to American independence, the early difficulties encountered by the fledgling republic, international politics, and the French Revolution. In France, Madame Roland expressed her desire to become the 'Macaulay of my country' (Bergès, 2016: 108), while the Marquis de Condorcet compared her favourably with Prime Minister William Pitt, asking 'will it be maintained that Mistress Macaulay would not have expressed her opinions in the House of Commons better than many representatives of the British nation' (Condorcet, 1912: 7)?

Macaulay mixed in the same circles of dissenters and republicans as activists such as Richard Price, Joseph Priestley, and Thomas Paine. From the end of the eighteenth century, and well into the nineteenth, republican political ideals fell almost completely out of favour in Britain which contributed to the scholarly neglect of not only Macaulay but of Price and Priestley as well. Because of the gendered way that philosophical canons are created, however, Macaulay's work was neglected: republican political ideals came instead to be associated with and appreciated through her male contemporaries. This was unfortunate not only for her legacy but for the discipline, too, as Macaulay developed a body of theoretical republican thought that matches, and possibly exceeds, any of her rivals (Coffee, 2017, 2023). Though Macaulay was an outstanding example, she was by no means the only woman writing prominently in the republican tradition during this period. Others included Anna Laetitia Barbauld (1743-1825), Mary Wollstonecraft (1759-1797), Mary Hays (1759-1843) and Mary Shelley (1797-1851) in Britain, Olympe de Gouges (1748-1793) and Sophie de Grouchy (1764-1822) in France, and Frances Wright (1795-1852) and Margaret Fuller (1810-1850) in the United States.

> ### Key Concept: The Whigs
>
> In spite of their intellectual and political differences, both Macaulay and Burke are identified with the Whig tradition. Historically, the Whigs were the successors to the English Civil War faction of the seventeenth century that had opposed both the monarchy and Catholic rule. By the late eighteenth century, the tradition had broadened and diversified, with several distinct groups claiming the Whig mantle. Macaulay was an ideological purist who drew on the values and arguments of the seventeenth-century republicans or Commonwealthmen, such as James Harrington, John Milton, Algernon Sidney, and John Locke, while Burke represented a more pragmatic and politically active wing, forming part of the Rockingham group led by the Marquess of Rockingham both as Prime Minister and in opposition. Whigs of whatever brand are united by their support for freedom and constitutional protections against the power of Parliament over the monarch.

17.2.1 Accountable government

Government, according to Macaulay, is something that human beings have created for their own collective benefit, namely their security and the protection of their natural rights (Macaulay, 1763–1783, vol. 4: 415–416). The form a government takes is not set in stone but can, and should, be changed as reason and experience dictate that the current form either no longer fulfils its objectives or could be improved. Certainly, government must not serve the interests of a faction or subsection of the population but must deliver its benefits—to 'secure the virtue, liberty, and happiness of society'—to the whole population in equal measure. The government's three goals of securing liberty, happiness, and virtue are all connected, with liberty as the primary vale, virtue as a constitutive element necessary for liberty, and happiness as the consequence of the other two values being fulfilled. These values can only be delivered where the state is organized in the right way. Accordingly, Macaulay argues for what she calls a 'democratical system, rightly balanced' (not a full democracy with universal enfranchisement, but nevertheless a representative government with frequent elections) (Macaulay, 1769: 29).

Macaulay's model for government is built on, and echoes, her conception of the human being. Just as liberty and virtue are necessary for the happiness of society, so are they for the individual, too. Macaulay makes this clear in the opening paragraph of the very first volume of her enormous *History*. Liberty, she says, 'lies latent in the breast of every rational being, till it is nipped by the frost of prejudice or blasted by the influence of vice' (Macaulay, 1763–1783, vol. 1: vii). Human beings are rational and moral agents. Freedom, then, is conditioned. We are not to follow our impulses or whims; rather, we must govern our conduct according to both reason (rather than 'prejudice') and the moral law (rather than 'vice'). This is what Macaulay means by 'virtue'. Since it is in our best interests to follow reason, then we can be sure that this will lead to our eventual happiness. This is why the model for government so closely reflects Macaulay's understanding of the person. If human beings are to live freely and virtuously, following the requirements of reason, then it follows that the laws under which they live must also be virtuous, embodying reason and the moral law.

> ### Key Thinker: Thomas Paine
>
> Political theorist and activist Thomas Paine (1737–1809) was an influential supporter of the revolutions in America and in France who promoted republican principles and natural rights. His pamphlet *Common Sense* (1776) was the most-read tract of the American war. The *Rights of Man* (1791) had a major impact in France, where he was elected to the National Convention. It was written in response to Burke's *Reflections*, following shortly after Macaulay's *Observations* and eclipsing it in popularity. Paine, like Macaulay, was a critic of the 1688 revolution in England and, in his later years, he went further than her in rejecting monarchical rule altogether. Paine was more explicit than Macaulay in his writing about the need for social welfare provision (*Agrarian Justice*, 1797) and in his opposition to slavery (*Old Truths and Established Facts*, anonymously written but attributed to Paine and Priestley, 1792).

17.2.2 Three connected values: independence, virtue, equality

Freedom, or liberty, for Macaulay is understood as independence. Free persons should be able to both decide on what to do for themselves, and they must be able to act upon those decisions. Independence, then, is both a property of the mind and of civil society. This entails both adequate education to equip people with the substantial mental skills that they will need to think and decide for themselves, and suitable social and political conditions. Freedom, then, contains both positive and negative elements. Alongside independence, freedom entails two other values, each of which is necessary for a free person and for a free society: virtue and equality.

Virtue is necessary for individual independence because free agents should neither be led by the ideas of others nor guided by the opinions and prejudices that they have imbibed from their social surroundings. Instead they should be in a position to stand back and critically reflect on their beliefs and actions rationally. Independence is not only a protection against external forces. The virtuous agent should also be able to use rational conviction to overcome the internal distortions that come from our passions and emotions, which were considered alien to the 'true' self and contrary to our genuine interests and happiness. Collectively, a virtuous population is necessary for a free society. If we are to have rational and effective laws and public policies, then we must have the requisite moral and empirical knowledge. This requires a population with both the intellectual qualities and the willingness to engage in the collaborative pursuit of truth and scientific enquiry. It further requires that the population has sufficient independence not to be biased by either prejudice or the need to serve the interests of the socially powerful rather than to follow the evidence. Macaulay makes clear that there is a pressing need for society to develop a reliable and improved science of politics, morals, and rational interests along the lines of the natural sciences, deeply regretting that while the physical sciences had made great progress of late, the same could not be said of politics and morals (Macaulay, 1790a: 169–170).

The third constitutive value of freedom is equality. In part, the necessity for equality follows from the remit of government, which is that it should be 'a fair and equal representation of the whole people', accountable to them and managing the state in their collective interests (Macaulay, 1790b: 48). Macaulay refers to the 'natural equality of men' and 'equal rights in men', giving a moral underpinning to the equality of the citizens (Macaulay, 1790a: 160; 1763–1783, vol. 4: 409). (Karen Green identifies Macaulay as the earliest known source of the phrase, the 'equal rights of men' in English, ahead of the more celebrated use by men such as Paine [Macaulay, 1763–1783, vol. 3: 78; Green, 2016].) Macaulay also has a pragmatic reason for including equality as a part of the broader ideal of freedom, which is that inequality has the effect of undermining the civic virtue that is necessary for a free society (Coffee, 2019). By 'equality', Macaulay means the equal standing of each individual as a citizen. However, since the role of government is to ensure the equal independence of all citizens ('governments are formed on principles which promise the equal distribution of power and liberty', Macaulay, 1763–1783, vol. 5: 19), this standing must translate into an equal opportunity and empowerment to act independently, including protection by law, representation in politics, and social legitimation. Macaulay anticipates substantial economic equality, believing that disparities in income and wealth are 'incompatible with a wise and just government' (Macaulay, 1790a: 190).

Independence, virtue, and equality are entwined not just conceptually but also causally. Where any one component is missing, this has the effect of undermining the other two. This process can take place at an individual level. Poor people, for example, are often dependent on others for their material survival. This makes it difficult for them to practise virtue by acting on conscience or for the common good. Instead, they are rationally compelled to put their own needs first, for example, by placating their patrons or engaging in deceit or flattery. Dependence typically breeds unvirtuous dispositions and character:

> as envy and covetousness are two passions which act powerfully on the peace and harmony of the mind, the virtue of citizens will be in a greater security where the wholesome restraint of sumptuary laws, or taxes properly imposed banish those objects from society, which are adapted to inflame cupidity, and excite a vicious emulation.
>
> (ibid.: 190–191)

The rich are similarly compromised. Not only are they able to circumvent many of the checks and balances in society through their wealth, but in having so much to lose, they are characteristically motivated to protect their advantage rather than advance the common good. Moreover, given people's human tendency to judge things from their own perspectives, the rich are likely to believe that their dominance is deserved, thereby undermining their ability to reason impartially (virtuously). While these effects take place within individuals, their effects spread. As in the case of rich and poor, there is a reciprocal effect whereby both dominator and dominated are implicated in the loss of virtue. However, since the moral character of the parties is affected, these come to infect their other relationships. In this connection, Mary Wollstonecraft, for example, describes how dominated wives often come to dominate their children and servants (Wollstonecraft, 1787: 63). Where patterns of inequality and dependence are systemic and substantial, they have the potential to undermine the virtue—and therefore the freedom—of the entire population.

Key Concept: Republicanism

Philosophically, Macaulay wrote in the neo-Roman strand of republican philosophy that has been articulated most clearly by Quentin Skinner (1998) and Philip Pettit (1997) (see also Coffee, 2017). The central concept ties the freedom of the individual with the freedom of the state as a whole. Freedom itself is understood as 'independence' or 'non-domination' and represents a complex idea that embodies several components, including equality, the rule of law, the common good, social standing, civic virtue, and public reason, held together in a delicate balance. Freedom is a socially and politically demanding condition in that it must be guaranteed by an effective law. A free republic is governed in the interests of the citizens, who have a voice in determining their own laws. Unfree, or arbitrary, rule is illegitimate and constitutes grounds for rebellion by those subject to it.

17.2.3 Government and education

To mitigate against this process of undermining (or 'corrupting') virtue, Macaulay offers two main kinds of protection. First, there is the institutional design of the state which should have frequent elections, strict term limits, the rotation of offices, and a separation of powers. She favours a bi-cameral system of government divided between an advisory senate comprised of experts and an elected executive chamber of representatives (Macaulay, 1769: 34). Macaulay has both a negative and a positive purpose in this design. She aims, first, to limit the potential for abuse by the leaders of the nation. However, in so doing she believes this will enable the population to harness the restless energies, as well as the talents, of the ambitious and so focus these towards serving the common, rather than their private or factional, interests. The second protection comes through education. Education, here, is a broad term that includes both formal teaching and the effects of an improved environment. Macaulay is optimistic about the human potential for virtue. The decadence, tyranny, and vices that she records in her history have come about through our inattention to the importance of safeguarding our political and social environment. The ruthlessly ambitious were able to usurp power though weak institutional protections. However, just as our environment not only has the potential to corrupt our virtue, so it can improve it.

Macaulay is, nevertheless, under no illusions about the scale of the undertaking involved in educating the population: 'every error thrown out in conversation, every sentiment which does not correspond with the true principles of virtue, is received by the mind, and like a drop of venomous poison' (Macaulay, 1790a: 103). The foundation of her recommendation is to educate people rationally, according to what she describes as 'immutable moral truths' (Macaulay, 1783; 1790a). However, while formal education is necessary, it is not enough since we learn far more from the example of others around us than we do from books and schoolteachers, particularly with regard to developing in people the necessary moral feelings and sympathies that will guide their abstract thinking (Macaulay, 1790a: 72; Coffee, 2017: 851–852). So Macaulay places a great deal of emphasis on public example, setting high standards from above by our leaders as well as in the sorts of activities that are encouraged or sponsored by the government. Gardening and cooking, for example, are to be encouraged, while an interest in women's fashion is not.

17.2 Catharine Macaulay: Key Points

- The purpose of government, according to Macaulay, is to serve the virtue, liberty, and happiness of society.
- For Macaulay, independence entails equality and civic virtue, while dependence and inequality undermine or 'corrupt' the virtue necessary for a free republic.
- Macaulay believes that corruption negates people's support for the common good and undermines the quality of public deliberation.
- Macaulay advocates rational education based on principles of 'immutable truths'.

17.3 Edmund Burke

Edmund Burke (1729–1797) was a prominent politician, renowned for his skills as an orator and as a writer. So celebrated was his speechmaking that admiration for it permeated society. C.L.R. James quotes a passage from an early book on cricket in which it is said of a famous batter of the nineteenth-century, 'he took the ball, as Burke did the House of Commons, between wind and water; not a moment too soon or late' (James, 1963: 6) (read more about James in Chapter 18). Burke has had a profound influence in the history of political thought and the history of ideas, as well as in fields such as international relations where he is often regarded as source of inspiration for what became the English School (Bourke, 2009). For all this, it is significant that he has not had anything like the same influence among political philosophers. Sustained analytical treatments of his positions are comparatively few, especially when compared to other political writers of his stature, such as Thomas Hobbes (see Chapter 5), John Locke (see Chapter 7), or Jean-Jacques Rousseau (see Chapter 9) (Harris, 2020 provides an excellent philosophical introduction). A key reason for this is, as we noted in the Introduction, Section 17.1, that Burke does not write in a systematic way by setting out foundational principles and building upon these in a consistent and coherent manner. Burke was first and foremost a statesman, a politician, and party loyalist. It is in the nature of political action that one works with the world as it is, reacting to the problems that present themselves, and marshals the arguments that will be most effective, adapting principle to reality where necessary. This is not to say his work is devoid of principle or that systematic positions cannot be identified, though it does perhaps help explain why Burke's work has been understood, or at least appropriated, in contradictory ways over the last two centuries. Neither is it to say that Burke is philosophically naïve or unaware. His *Philosophical Enquiry into the Origin of Our Ideas of the Sublime and Beautiful* (Burke, 1757) is a classic text on aesthetics that engages with the philosophy of mind, language, and morals. It might, therefore, be said that a lack of overt system was itself part of Burke's political philosophy.

As a politician, Burke owed his position and influence to his relationship to the Marquis of Rockingham, for whom he served as private secretary from 1765. Rockingham was an important Whig leader who became Prime Minister briefly from 1765–1776, and again for a few months in 1782 until his untimely death from influenza. Having earlier failed to break through into politics, Burke gained a safe parliamentary seat in a rotten borough through Rockingham, launching a career that would last almost three decades until his retirement. Burke's relationship with Rockingham's group was significant. After their brief spell in power, Burke had other offers to serve with other factions but elected to remain under the patronage of Rockingham. While later commentators would elevate Burke's standing within the Rockinghams, the reality was that in spite of his reputation as an orator, there was never any question of his becoming party leader. Rather, Burke was a 'follower not a leader' who understood and accepted the nature of his personal dependence on Rockingham (O'Gorman, 2004: 22). Seen through Macaulay's lens of independence, Burke's reliance on maintaining his standing with his sponsors is instructive: while Macaulay was fortunate enough to be financially independent whereas Burke was required to tailor his arguments to suit party and patron.

Though I present Burke and Macaulay in opposing terms, it is important to reiterate that they were both Whigs and so, superficially at least, they share a commitment to a range of political values, such as liberty, an idea of natural rights, and the sovereignty of Parliament and its ultimate accountability to the people it governs. It is, after all, on account of these values that the 'liberal' Burke of the nineteenth century, and its resurgence in the twenty-first, are able to be sustained. However, how these ideas are conceived and the framework in which they are housed differs radically between Burke and Macaulay.

17.3.1 Conservation and correction

The destructive violence and excesses that unfolded in the months and years following the French Revolution horrified observers from Britain across the political spectrum. Much of this was anticipated by Burke in his *Reflections*. Nevertheless, Burke's criticism of this rebellion in contrast with his earlier support for that of the Americans baffled and angered many British radicals. Though

Macaulay herself does not frame her reply to Burke in these terms, Priestley opens his response expressing regret 'that an avowed friend of the American revolution should be an enemy to that of the French, which arose from the same general principles, and in a great measure sprung from it, is to me unaccountable' (Priestley, 1791: iii). Burke's answer was straightforward enough: the two revolutions did not spring from the same principles (Burke, 1791). The earlier revolution, he maintained, represented an internal correction within a civilization and political tradition that rebalanced the necessary compromise between liberty and stability, whereas the later destroyed its civilization and tradition, not only obliterating its people's own prospects for freedom or peace but threatening the foundations of the civilizations around it.

At the heart of the difference between the radicals and Burke is a difference in philosophical approach. Whereas Macaulay, like Priestley, begins with abstract principles, or immutable truths, such as the natural right to liberty, and reasons towards a conclusion about how to govern society, Burke regards this as a very foolish—and dangerous—endeavour. Human society is far too complicated a matter to reduce to a simple, or even a complex, system based on a few bare axioms. 'The nature of man is intricate', Burke reasons, 'the objects of society are of the greatest possible complexity; and, therefore, no simple disposition or direction of power can be suitable either to man's nature or to the quality of his affairs', adding pointedly that 'when I hear the simplicity of contrivance aimed at and boasted of in any new political constitutions, I am at no loss to decide that the artificers are grossly ignorant of their trade or totally negligent of their duty' (Burke, 2009 [1790]: 62). Rather, society has emerged from a centuries-long process of accumulating experience which has become distilled in its particular traditions and institutions. We tamper with this inherited wisdom at our peril. It has come to serve us well by balancing the competing values and interests with the tendencies of human nature as these have come to us through our history. The result is a fine and intricate balance. This is not to say that change or reform is not possible. 'A state without the means of some change', Burke accepts, 'is without the means of its conservation' (ibid.: 21). The vicissitudes of history that have bequeathed our traditions and institutions are part of an ongoing process without any ideal end-state. The Restoration and subsequent Glorious Revolution, he argues, show the 'two principles of conservation and correction' in operation whereby what was deficient in the old constitution was regenerated 'through the parts which were not impaired'. There had been no wholesale revolution in these cases, as there was in France. Instead, a process of slow, cautious reform was adopted within the current arrangements. Within this tradition, Burke regarded himself, rightly, as a reformer.

In condemning the French Revolution, Burke did not mean to suggest that all was right with the way that the country was run. The failure of its leaders was undeniable. Burke's view, however, was that its institutions, perhaps with suitable reforms, were capable of correcting its errors. This would have allowed a gradual, sustainable change as the country adapted while maintaining the overarching framework of civilization that had long sustained it. This contrasts with Burke's view of the American situation. The American colonies had developed into a distinct society, albeit one within the same overarching civilization. The British government's policy to 'tax [the colonists] without their consent' amounted to a violation of its mandate as it had been embodied in England's long tradition of freedom (Burke, 1791: 26). Great Britain's freedom was, in effect, bought at the price of America's servitude, and so their revolution was made on a 'defensive footing', and, crucially, left its basic civilization and institutional structure in place.

17.3.2 Rights as convention

Burke accepts Macaulay's starting point that 'government is a contrivance of human wisdom to provide for human wants' and that ultimately it must be constituted for the benefit of all (Burke, 2009 [1790]: 60, compared with Macaulay, 1769: 29). Within this basic proviso, Burke also has room for the core Whig values of freedom, equality, rights, and representation, with those of virtue and stability, just as Macaulay does. The key difference between them is that, for Burke, these values are not abstract, foundational principles—they are not the products of speculative reasoning to be universalized and applied indiscriminately. Rather, they are practical solutions developed over time that are passed on 'as an entailed inheritance derived to us from our forefathers, and to be transmitted to posterity—as an estate specially belonging to the people of this kingdom, without any reference whatever to any other more general or prior right' (Burke, 2009 [1790]: 33). This history gives rights and freedoms a particular character that is limited by competing considerations within society as a whole. It is not that Burke sets limits on our basic rights that distinguishes him from Macaulay, but the tone in which he expresses those limits, and the basis upon which he does so.

So, regarding freedom, Burke accepts the premise that 'everything ought to be open', but adds the rider 'but not indifferently, to every man' (ibid.: 50). Likewise, with equality, Burke acknowledges that 'all men have equal rights' but qualifies this, adding 'but not to equal things' (ibid.: 59). However, when Burke goes on in this passage to discuss the rights to share in government, his conclusion is instructive:

> and as to the share of power, authority, and direction which each individual ought to have in the management of the state, that I must deny to be amongst the direct original rights of man in civil society; for I have in my contemplation the civil social man, and no other. It is a thing to be settled by convention.
>
> (ibid.: 59)

Rights are not prior to, but the outcome of, a social convention. 'Government', Burke insists in contrast to Macaulay, 'is not made in virtue of natural rights, which may and do exist in total independence of it' (ibid.: 60). It is convention that dictates the use and scope of our civil and political rights, rather than the other way around. We do not alter convention in light of our fundamental freedoms, we understand the freedoms we have through the lens of convention: 'if civil society be the offspring of convention, that convention must be its law. That convention must limit and modify all the descriptions of constitution which are formed under it' (ibid.: 59).

17.3.3 The spirit of a gentleman and the spirit of religion

The convention that the British had received, via a long tradition stretching from the Magna Carta to the Glorious Revolution, was 'an inheritable crown, an inheritable peerage, and a House of Commons and a people inheriting privileges, franchises, and liberties from a long line of ancestors' (ibid.: 33). Each of these, working together, 'preserves a unity in so great a diversity of its parts'. Any one part, unchecked, would come not only to dominate the others but thereafter to unravel the ties and values that held the nation together. In fostering a sense of patriotism and social cohesion among the people, Burke lays particular emphasis on two ingredients, religion and the nobility ('the spirit of a gentleman', ibid.: 79). Religion is important for Macaulay too, of course, though hers was a rational religion that served as the basis for the immutable truths that were the source of both government and personal virtue. Burke's emphasis, by contrast, was on revealed religion as not only the source and driver of moral behaviour but as the preserver of culture.

Within that culture, the nobility played a distinctive role, in cementing and stabilizing what was a naturally hierarchical society. They have acquired considerable swathes of property, and with it a great stake in society, through which they have learned the art of maintaining the system of which they are part. 'Long possession of Government; vast property; obligations of favours given and received; connexion of office; ties of blood, of alliance, of friendship', Burke argues, have taught the aristocracy the delicate and subtle skills required to maintain the complex balance and harmony of society (Burke, 1770: 21). This is exemplified in the way that the nobility serve as public benefactors, coming to understand this as an indispensable part of their role. 'Why', Burke asks,

> should the expenditure of a great landed property, which is a dispersion of the surplus product of the soil, appear intolerable to you or to me, when it takes its course through the accumulation of vast libraries . . . through great collections of ancient records, medals, and coins . . . through paintings and statues . . . through grand monuments of the dead, which continue the regards and connections of life beyond the grave . . . ?
>
> (Burke, 2009 [1790]: 162)

17.3 Edmund Burke: Key Points

- Burke argues that the principles and processes governing society are highly varied and complex and hence that political society should not be based on systems grounded in a few identifiable rational principles.
- Burke believed that over the course of generations societies develop the institutions and modes of organization that embody accumulated experience and wisdom about what is viable and stable.
- Burke recognized that societies must, and do, reform themselves over time, but argued that they should do so cautiously and incrementally.
- Burke viewed rights not as abstract, pre-political ideals to be discovered by speculation but social creations inherited from previous generations and passed on to the future.
- Society, according to Burke, is hierarchically arranged whereby the nobility learn the skills necessary to preserve the rights and prosperity of the whole.

17.4 Criticisms and relevance

How should we view the respective work of Macaulay and Burke in the light of contemporary moral and political perspectives? The considerable differences in social context between the eighteenth century and the present raises both interpretive questions and issues about how we can make use of their philosophy today.

17.4.1 Can Macaulay reconcile universal principles with social context?

Macaulay was an exemplary representative of the systematic, speculative approach to political philosophy and to which Burke vehemently objected (Burke, 2009 [1790]: 57). She grounded her system in immutable truths discoverable by reason. The most significant ideal politically was freedom, which was itself a product of a universal capacity for human reason through which human beings could discover the principles of both moral virtue and of good social organization. The principles of moral virtue are not only binding but should also be motivating as the people come to understand that their individual interests are inextricably bound together with the interests of others (Macaulay, 1790a: 169–170).

Expressed in these terms, Macaulay produced a cosmopolitan and inclusive political theory in which all human beings are in principle protected against arbitrary forms of intrusion and control in virtue of their status as rational agents. Although her work pre-dates modern ideas about democracy, it is democratic in nature, grounded in the belief that only collectively could people reliably come to converge on the optimal principles for government, in rather the same way that science is best done deliberatively by a community designed to identify efficient and true principles and discard weak or biased ones. Macaulay's is an emancipatory philosophy in which arbitrary, non-representative, non-democratic, inegalitarian rule is considered unjust and illegitimate, and where the oppressed are licensed and exhorted to rise up in revolution. England's seventeenth-century revolutions were, therefore, justified—though that of 1688, she argued, did not go far enough in constraining arbitrary power and securing freedoms—as were the eighteenth-century American and French Revolutions. Though Macaulay did not live to see the bloodshed, chaos, and devastation of the Reign of Terror in France, others writing in the same tradition would identify this as an inevitable, if deeply concerning, consequence of the corrupting nature of arbitrary power that depraves both dominator and oppressed in equal measure. This was the view taken by Wollstonecraft, who accepted that a gradual revolution conducted on rational principles would have been preferable but nevertheless reaffirmed the people's right to overthrow their tyrants (Wollstonecraft, 1794: vii, 68–72, 341–359).

Macaulay's approach nevertheless suffers from several potential weaknesses. Not least among these are whether her ideological principles are empirically sound, and whether their theological grounding hinders the acceptance of her ideals today. Karen Green raises both objections simultaneously. Green (2020b: 217–224) regards Macaulay's political philosophy as being intimately tied to a religious commitment to a form of human moral perfectibility—the belief that with rational application human beings can become ever more virtuous, not only individually but as a society under rational and virtuous laws—that is no longer widely held, even among religious believers today. Detached from these theological moorings, Green (ibid.: 218) believes that Macaulay gives us an empirical theory 'concerning how it is best, overall, for social, reasoning, self-conscious creatures to represent themselves to themselves'. This is an important consideration when evaluating Macaulay's continuing relevance. While her religious commitments are substantively part of Macaulay's political system, they are not necessary for a contemporary rendering of an ideal of a non-dominating, inclusive social and political organization that recognizes and treats all members as equals, and ensures that each has a voice in deliberating about the common good. On this score, then, her work continues to be both significant and relevant for our times, precisely because it promotes an equal and inclusive democratic system that could be characterized as republican (see Key Concept: Republicanism).

A potentially more troubling objection to Macaulay's approach is epistemological. While Macaulay is confident that she has identified immutable moral truths which she then applies using the power of reason, modern readers may find some of her substantive beliefs or assumptions more troubling. More generally, Macaulay faces a problem that confronts any philosopher arguing in abstract and universal terms, that their claims will embody tacit and implicit biases inherited from their culture that they cannot perceive. Feminists, for example, have noted that in Macaulay's long career in which she continually advocated for the singular importance for independence as an ideal, she nowhere makes an explicit argument for women's independence specifically, in the form of equal rights or citizenship. Indeed, it is not until her final work, the *Letters on Education*, that Macaulay even gives a sustained treatment of women's condition as dependent. On this feminist objection, she can plausibly be exonerated. Philip Hicks demonstrates that Macaulay accords women a much more prominent role as agents and political actors in her *Histories* than does Hume, foregrounding and analysing their interventions which others had 'unjustly ridiculed, omitted, praised for the wrong reasons, or not praised highly enough' (Hicks, 2002: 187–188). Wendy Gunther-Canada (forthcoming) shows how Macaulay develops a sustained critique of patriarchy throughout her *Histories*, drawing a parallel between the arbitrariness of the monarch and the husband. 'With each volume of the *History*', Gunther-Canada argues, 'her consideration of women's condition occupied a larger portion of the pages, underscoring how patriarchy was encoded in the social contract, and elements of monarchical rule reflected in the marriage contract' (ibid.: 35; see also Coffee, 2023).

Another blind spot for Macaulay is her apparent Orientalism, using terms that further stereotype and caricature Asian society, even where her target is to critique the treatment of women in Europe. She contrasts the relative subjection of European women with 'the abject slavery in which they have always been held in the east' (Macaulay, 1790a: 133), alleging that the unjustifiable suppression of the female understanding in Europe was more in keeping with 'regions of the east, because it accords with the state of slavery to which female nature in that part of the world has ever been subjected, and can only suit with the notion of a positive inferiority in the intellectual powers of the female mind' (ibid.: 31). She variously refers to 'the selfishness of Asiatic luxury' (ibid.: 135) and argues in response to Rousseau that his prescriptions for French women fit them rather more 'for the harem of an eastern Bashaw' than to be a wife as a man's companion (ibid.: 133). Against this, however, Macaulay fares better from a modern perspective in emphasizing that the 'natural equality of men' covers all races (ibid.: 160). She reminds her reader that

> persons even of deep reflection have pretended to discover an apparent difference in the mental qualities of the inhabitants of the east and the north, and have given to the effect of climate those virtues which alone depend on moral causes . . . [giving] to their own colour only, the quality of external beauty, and they persuade themselves, that the swarthy inhabitants of India and Africa, are a degree below them in the scale of intelligent Nature.
>
> (ibid.: 160–161)

There is a fundamental tension in Macaulay's writing. For all her commitment to the concept of immutable truths discoverable by reason, she is also highly, and perceptively, aware of the subtle but almost irresistible power of our social environment to shape what people actually believe. She understands how easily false ideas can become established as accepted social narratives and received wisdom. 'Every part of morals,' she observes, 'becomes fluctuation; and customs, manners, sentiments change according to the notions of those in power' (ibid.: 96). This sets up a difficult dilemma for her. It is the very elites who set the cultural and educational policies to educate the people on rational grounds whose own vested interests and implicit biases come to shape the public consciousness. This is a tremendous power to place unchecked in the hands of any social group. While she believes that her institutional design will prevent it from being abused, the danger remains that were the elite, consciously or unconsciously, to shape the social and cultural norms and beliefs to suit their own interests rather than those of the public interest, they would go a long way towards cementing their own dominance for a considerable period. While Macaulay is aware of this risk, she is optimistic that reason and principle will prevail over prejudice and error.

Whether Macaulay's optimism is warranted is a matter for debate. Her ideas, however, influenced Wollstonecraft, who developed them to outline a more robust republican position. Wollstonecraft's republicanism emphasized the need for participation by all sections of society—across gender, class, racial, and religious lines—to create a social background of beliefs, norms, practices, and values reflective of the perspectives of the entire community (Coffee, 2013). Others in the African American tradition of republican thought, such as Frederick Douglass, would develop similar arguments (Coffee, 2020) (read more about Douglass in Chapter 30).

17.4.2 Does Burke have sufficient safeguards against the abuse of power?

Macaulay's concern that social and political elites will be able to set the normative agenda in favour of their own partisan interests can be raised against Burke's philosophy. Burke vests considerable cultural and, thereby, political power in elite sections of society since their task is to safeguard the stability and prosperity that we have all inherited. Burke's emphasis on preserving norms and institutions puts groups that have traditionally been excluded from political influence, such as women and religious minorities, at a considerable disadvantage in raising their concerns and pressing for reform.

Burke was suspicious of, and hostile to, the idea of democracy which he regarded as either a misnomer or a fraud. Both monarchy and popular sovereignty, Burke acknowledged, brought risks—tyranny and anarchy respectively. Accordingly, he looked to the gentry and nobility to provide a moderating and mediating role that would mitigate these two opposing dangers. In so doing, Burke left himself open to the charge of being a dupe of the aristocracy, a fawning sycophant seeking to curry favour. Indeed, Macaulay opens her *Observations* on his *Thoughts* with this very jibe (Macaulay, 1770: 5–6; Bourke 2007: 430 gives a more charitable view). Cynicism aside, however, we can still ask whether Burke provides sufficient safeguards against the potential abuse of power.

One context in which questions concerning the justifiable exercise of power arise is that of empire and colonialism. In recent years, some commentators have come to regard Burke as an opponent rather than supporter of empire, or at least aspects of his philosophy have been interpreted as containing the seeds for such a rejection. The reasons can be found in Burke's rejection of the universal and rational principles used by Macaulay and which ultimately trace back to Locke. Uday Singh Mehta (1999) gives one such account. Although Mehta directs his arguments towards liberalism with its universal pretensions rather than to republicanism, their grounding in abstract rationalism is the same. On the surface, he argues, such universalist and rationalist approaches may appear to be cosmopolitan and egalitarian by appealing to a shared capacity for human reason. But, Mehta goes on, this capacity is not seen as having been developed to the same extent everywhere, thereby opening up the possibility that more developed societies could legitimately exercise colonial rule over other nations still in their infancy (like Britain over India in Mehta's analysis). On Mehta's account, then, Burke's rejection of reason and universal rights and principles, therefore, are not a weakness but represent his great strength. By viewing India as a distinct and particular society living under its own social institutions and practices that embody their own accumulated practical wisdom, rather than as inferior versions of ourselves, Burke is said to treat it as a self-governing society in its own right, thereby undercutting the normative basis for imperial rule. This is a powerful argument and, seen through the lens of twentieth-century postcolonial thinking, has much to commend it. Whether it accurately represents Burke's philosophy is another matter, which we do not have space to discuss here (for contrasting takes, see O'Neill, 2016 and Bourke, 2015).

Mehta's arguments must, however, be set alongside Burke's deeper logic of not only of empire but of power. A state can come legitimately to rule over the people of another territory through the 'right of conquest' (Burke both draws on and critiques Montesquieu on this principle. See Bourke, 2007 for an analysis in relation to Quebec, and see Chapter 11 to read more about Montesquieu). However, while Burke considers that victors in battle have the right to rule as they please, not all methods are expedient. The basic principles of enlightened rule apply to empires just as they do the state, even if the precise form that this takes may differ across an empire's territories (for example, Burke accepted and supported to some degree the American colonists' complaints that the British government had abandoned the principles and obligations of good government). In general, Burke believed that a vanquished people would come to accept their new rulers where this benefits them. So, where the pre-conquest style of government had enjoyed local support, this would count in favour of its being retained, though other factors such as the acceptability of this to the central government and the overall stability and prosperity of the empire as a whole may count against it. In the end, the solution will be pragmatic taking into account of both the rights of the conquerors as well as the prosperity of the whole. In his analysis of Burke's arguments concerning the rights of conquest and empire, Bourke (2007) emphasizes the role that Burke's understanding of human nature plays. At root, political subjection is a function of how humans behave rather than of abstract right or principle. Defeated peoples can be brought to acquiesce willingly, Burke believes, if they come to admire their new rulers.

The role of judgement, politics, and hierarchy in Burke's philosophy mean that there is an ever-present danger of supposedly enlightened rule lapsing into oppression. Unlike Macaulay, who saw arbitrary rule as the single cause of despotism, Burke accepts that each of the several competing factors that need to be balanced in society can come to exert a dominating influence. In the 1770s, for example, the monarch's overreach both at home and in America was said to represent the greatest danger, whereas in the build-up to the French Revolution the very spirit of freedom became the new threat. As we have seen, the American and French situations yielded different results concerning whether the population had a right to revolt. In general, Burke did not consider that subject populations had the right to rise up in revolution.

The social contract, according to Burke, is not made with our contemporaries but across time with our ancestors and with our descendants. The nature of our relations with our countryfolk is not merely transactional. 'The state', Burke argues, 'ought not to be considered as nothing better than a partnership agreement in a trade of pepper and coffee, calico or tobacco, or some other such low concern to be taken up for a little temporary interest, and to be dissolved by the fancy of the parties.' It should, instead, be viewed with 'reverence because it is not a partnership in things subservient only to the gross animal existence of a temporary and perishable nature: it is a partnership in all science; a partnership in all art; a partnership in every virtue, and in all perfection' (Burke, 2009 [1790]: 96). Since the ends of a such a partnership cannot be fully obtained even over many generations, he concludes that:

> each contract of each particular state is but a clause in the great primeval contract of eternal society, linking the lower with the higher natures, connecting the visible and invisible world, according to a fixed compact sanctioned by the inviolable oath which holds all physical and all moral natures, each in their appointed place.
>
> (ibid.: 97)

17.4 Criticisms and relevance: Key Points

- Macaulay has been criticized for relying on Orientalist stereotypes and for failing to argue for the independence of women.
- There is a tension in Macaulay's work between her commitment to immutable truths and her recognition that people's beliefs are shaped by their social environments and so open to manipulation by elites.
- Burke has been interpreted as both a defender and opponent of empire and can be challenged on whether he provides sufficient safeguards against the potential abuse of power.
- Burke believed that the social contract is made not with our contemporaries but with our ancestors and with our descendants.

17.5 Conclusion

Reading Macaulay and Burke in opposition to each other can be a fruitful exercise, with each shedding light on the weaknesses of the other. Burke provides a subtle and sophisticated appreciation of the complexity and range of social considerations and human motivations that contribute to a viable and productive state, while Macaulay develops a tightly worked-out framework around the fundamental political values of our society—freedom, equality, the common good, and public accountability. On the one hand, Burke's critique of systematic political philosophies that portray themselves as universal and based on a normative reason accessible to all identifies a potentially devastating blind spot in the republican and liberal traditions that Macaulay represents. On the other, Macaulay's insistence on a very high standard of equal protection and opportunity for all citizens—combined with an inclusiveness in reconstructing the background social context found in radical philosophers who built on her lead, such as Wollstonecraft and Douglass—provides a powerful rebuff to the dangers of elitism and hierarchy favoured by Burke.

Take your learning further by accessing the online resources for a library of web links to relevant videos, articles, blogs, and useful websites for this chapter: **www.oup.com/he/Ramgotra-Choat1e**.

Study questions

1. What concepts do Macaulay and Burke seem to share, and how are these understood respectively?
2. What is the relationship between independence, virtue, and equality for Macaulay (in each case, consider Burke's alternative conceptions)?
3. Is there a tension between Macaulay's reliance on public reason and her acknowledgement that people are deeply influenced by their social environment?
4. Why is Burke so suspicious of systematic philosophers?
5. Is freedom, as Macaulay maintains, the supreme value through which we should understand social and political relations?
6. How does Burke understand the relationship between conserving tradition and correcting it?
7. On what is the social contract based and what is the individual's place in society?
8. Can either Macaulay or Burke genuinely offer equality and freedom to women and members of minority social groups?

Further reading

Primary sources

Burke, E. (1999) *The Portable Edmund Burke*. Ed. I. Kramnik. Harmondsworth: Penguin.
   The fullest single-volume collection of Burke's important writings.

Burke, E. (2009 [1790]) *Reflections on the Revolution in France*. Oxford: Oxford University Press.
   The most popular of Burke's works.

Macaulay, C. (2020) *The Correspondence of Catharine Macaulay*. Ed. K. Green. Oxford: Oxford University Press.
   A valuable insight into Macaulay's intellectual life.

Secondary sources

Bourke, R. (2015) *Empire and Revolution: The Political Life of Edmund Burke*. Princeton, NJ: Princeton University Press.
A comprehensive, nuanced treatment of Burke's intellectual life and political career.

Green, K. (2020) *Catharine Macaulay's Republican Enlightenment*. London: Routledge.

Gunther-Canada, W. (forthcoming) *A Friend of Liberty: Catharine Macaulay and the Enlightened Republic*. Oxford: Oxford University Press.
These are two ground-breaking but accessible recent studies by the two leading Macaulay scholars writing today.

O'Neill, D. (2016) *Edmund Burke and the Conservative Logic of Empire*. Oakland, CA: University of California Press.
A systematic reconstruction of Burke's philosophy challenging the recent scholarly trend of viewing Burke in liberal terms.

References

Bergès, S. (2016) 'A Republican Housewife: Marie-Jeanne Phlipon Roland on Women's Political Role'. *Hypatia*, 31(1): 107–122.

Bourke, R. (2007) 'Edmund Burke and the Politics of Conquest'. *Modern Intellectual History*, 4(3): 403–432.

Bourke, R. (2009) 'Edmund Burke and International Conflict'. In I. Hall and L. Hill (eds), *British International Thinkers from Hobbes to Namier*. London: Palgrave Macmillan.

Bourke, R. (2015) *Empire and Revolution: The Political Life of Edmund Burke*. Princeton, NJ: Princeton University Press.

Bourke, R. (2018) 'What Is Conservatism? History, Ideology and Party'. *European Journal of Political Theory*, 17(4): 449–475.

Burke, E. (1757) *A Philosophical Enquiry into the Origin of Our Ideas of the Sublime and Beautiful*. London: R. and J. Dodsley.

Burke, E. (1770) *Thoughts on the Cause of the Present Discontents*. London J. Dodsley.

Burke, E. (1791) *An Appeal from the New to the Old Whigs, in Consequence of Some Late Discussions in Parliament Relative to the Reflections on the French Revolution*. London.

Burke, E. (2009 [1790]) *Reflections on the Revolution in France*. Oxford: Oxford University Press.

Coffee, A. (2013) 'Mary Wollstonecraft, Freedom and the Enduring Power of Social Domination'. *European Journal of Political Theory*, 12(2): 116–135.

Coffee, A. (2017) 'Catharine Macaulay's Republican Conception of Social and Political Liberty'. *Political Studies*, 65(4): 844–859.

Coffee, A. (2019) 'Catharine Macaulay'. In S. Bergès, E.H. Botting, and A. Coffee (eds), *The Wollstonecraftian Mind*. London: Routledge.

Coffee, A. (2020) 'A Radical Revolution in Thought: Frederick Douglass on the Slave's Perspective on Republican Freedom'. In B. Leipold, K. Nabulsi, and S. White (eds), *Radical Republicanism: Recovering the Tradition's Popular Heritage*. Oxford: Oxford University Press, pp. 47–64.

Coffee, A. (2023) 'Theories of the State'. In K. Detlefsen and L. Shapiro (eds), *The Routledge Handbook of Women and Early Modern European Philosophy*. London: Routledge.

Condorcet, N.C., Marquis de (1912) *The First Essay on the Political Rights of Women: A Translation of Condorcet's Essay 'Sur l'admission des femmes au droit de Cité' (On the Admission of Women to the Rights of Citizenship)*. Trans. A. Drysdale Vickery. Letchworth: Garden City Press.

Green, K. (2016) 'Reassessing the Impact of the "Republican Virago"'. *Redescriptions*, 19(1): 29–48.

Green, K. (2020) *Catharine Macaulay's Republican Enlightenment*. London: Routledge.

Gunther-Canada, W. (forthcoming) *A Friend of Liberty: Catharine Macaulay and the Enlightened Republic*. Oxford: Oxford University Press.

Harris, I. (2020) 'Edmund Burke'. In *The Stanford Encyclopedia of Philosophy*. Ed. E. Zalta. Stanford, CA: Stanford University Press.

Hicks, P. (2002) 'Catharine Macaulay's Civil War: Gender, History, and Republicanism in Georgian Britain'. *Journal of British Studies*, 41(2): 170–198.

James, C.L.R. (1963) *Beyond a Boundary*. London: Hutchinson.

Kramnik, I. (1983) 'The Left and Edmund Burke'. *Political Theory*, 11(2): 189–214.

Macaulay, C. (1763–1783) *The History of England from the Accession of James I. to that of the Brunswick Line*, 8 vols. London: J. Nourse, J. Dodsley and W. Johnston.

(Vols 5–8 are entitled The History of England from the Accession of James I. to the Revolution, London: C. Dilly.)

Macaulay, Catharine (1769). *Loose Remarks on certain positions to be found in Mr Hobbes' Philosophical Rudiments of Government and society with a short sketch of a democratical form of government in a letter to Signor Paoli by Catharine Macaulay. The Second edition with two letters one from an American Gentleman to the author which contains some comments on her sketch of the democratical form of government and the author's answer*. London: W. Johnson, T. Davies, E. and C. Dilly, J. Almon, Robinson and Roberts, T. Cadell.

Macaulay, C. (1770) *Observations on a Pamphlet entitled 'Thoughts on the Cause of the Present Discontents'*, 4th edn. London: Printed for Edward and Charles Dilly.

Macaulay, C. (1783) *A Treatise on the Immutability of Moral Truth*. London: A. Hamilton.

Macaulay, C. (1790a) *Letters on Education: With Observations on Religious and Metaphysical Subjects*. London: C. Dilly.

Macaulay, C. (1790b) *Observations on the Reflections of the Right Hon. Edmund Burke, on the Revolution in France, in a Letter for the Right Hon. The Earl of Stanhope*. London: C. Dilly.

Mehta, U.S. (1999) *Liberalism and Empire: A Study in Nineteenth-Century British Liberal Thought*. Chicago: University of Chicago Press.

Miller, D. (1981) *Philosophy and Ideology in Hume's Political Thought*. Oxford: Oxford University Press.

O'Gorman, F. (2004) *Edmund Burke*. London: Routledge.

O'Neill, D. (2016) *Edmund Burke and the Conservative Logic of Empire*. Oakland, CA: University of California Press.

Pettit, P. (1997) *Republicanism*. Oxford: Oxford University Press.

Priestley, J. (1791) *Letters to the Right Honourable Edmund Burke, Occasioned by His Reflections on the Revolution in France*. Birmingham: Thomas Pearson.

Skinner, Q. (1998) *Liberty before Liberalism*. Cambridge: Cambridge University Press.

Winch, D. (1985) 'The Burke-Smith Problem and Late Eighteenth Century Political and Economic Thought'. *The Historical Journal*, 28(1): 231–247.

Wollstonecraft, M. (1787) *Thoughts on the Education of Daughters with Reflections on Female Conduct, in the More Important Duties of Life*. London: Joseph Johnson.

Wollstonecraft, M. (1794) *An Historical and Moral View of the Origin and Progress of the French Revolution; and the Effect it Has Produced in Europe*, London: Joseph Johnson.

18 C.L.R. James
ROBBIE SHILLIAM

> **Chapter guide**
>
> This chapter examines a key tension in the political thought of C.L.R. James, the celebrated Trinidadian Marxist. James believed that the human condition was defined by a search for meaningful freedom through the pursuit of collective self-determination. Yet he was conflicted as to whether peoples of African descent had to depend for this meaning on the European civilization that had enslaved and colonized them. After an Introduction that sets out the stakes at play, this chapter details James's unique contribution to Marxist thought: a 'dialectic of freedom' that triangulates the struggle between the bourgeoisie, the masses, and the radical intelligentsia. Section 18.3 then considers the impact of colonial education on James's own development and the ways in which it made Black intellectual production, for him, intrinsically political and contentious. Section 18.4 explores the dualism with which James treated Blackness as a resource with which to struggle for meaningful freedom. The conclusion considers James's legacy as edifying precisely because of the intellectual forthrightness by which he lived his split ethical, theoretical, and political orientation towards Europe and Africa.

18.1 Introduction

We begin this chapter in 1982, in the apartment of C.L.R. James (1901–1989). A world-famous Trinidadian Marxist, an elderly James is spending his last years in Railton Road, South London. Linton Kwesi Johnson, Britain's most celebrated dub poet, has invited Mikey Smith, an up-and-coming Jamaican poet with Rastafari sympathies, to tour the UK. Here they are, discussing poetry with James.

James lays out to Johnson the evolution of his own special interest in English Romantic poetry—Wordsworth, Keats, and Shelley. Johnson then asks Smith what influence these poets had on him growing up. None, Smith replies, adding that he in fact 'detested them'. Smith feigns ignorance as a rhetorical parry to James's love of the English: he plays around with name pronunciation—Woodsrow for Wordsworth and Shak-e-spear for Shakespeare. James responds that 'no one in the Caribbean I have ever heard say "Shak-e-spear"; no-one ever told you about "Shak-e-spear"'. The three of them laugh at James's counter to Smith's provocation.

Smith continues with seriousness: 'to be honest, [the English poets] didn't have any impact on me'. 'I understand that', replies James immediately. Smith is surprised at James's understanding and explains further that he could never relate to the symbols, riddims (rhythms), and 'tongue twisting' of the English. James recalls that in his youth, English poetry was all there was, but that Smith is coming up in an era where Rastafari people have decided not to be dominated by the English and to instead retrieve the African retentions and Black innovations in Caribbean languages. James applauds Smith's generation: 'you tackled the most fundamental part of [domination]—the language.

And you created [a] dialect which is part of [that] language but [nonetheless enables] your own use of it, which I think was splendid.'

Smith was killed one year later at a political rally in Jamaica. Tragically cut short, his life could be fitted into James's exceedingly long biography four times over. Born in Trinidad at the turn of the twentieth century, by Smith's young age James had already written a novel as well as a treatise on Trinidadian self-determination. Becoming a Marxist after reading Leon Trotsky's *History of the Russian Revolution*, James then wrote the first anti-Stalinist history of the Communist International in 1937. Around the same time, James wrote *The Black Jacobins*, one of the first books in the English language to treat enslaved Africans as the principal authors of the Haitian Revolution (1791–1805) (African-American scholar Anna Julia Cooper had written a similar treatise before James in the French language). In the 1960s, James wrote another influential book, this time on the relationship between cricket, politics, and colonialism: *Beyond a Boundary*. At this point in time, when a new generation of students and scholars invested in Black Studies discovered his work written thirty years prior, he was already in his late sixties. He was still writing and lecturing through to his eighties.

Despite being generations apart in both birth and experience, the conversation between James and Smith reveals the core tenet of James's political thought and the abiding tension that resided in that tenet. The core tenet: that the human condition was moved ever onward towards meaningful freedom by the pursuit of collective self-determination; the core tension: that due to his colonial education, James believed the meaning of this freedom had to be drawn from European civilization, while those invested most in the struggling—Black peoples—often looked elsewhere for this meaning, and to that continent and peoples that Europe's colonial project had so often treated as less-than-human—Africa.

Read more about **James's** life and work by accessing the thinker biography on the online resources: www.oup.com/he/Ramgotra-Choat1e.

18.2 James's Marxism

18.2.1 The dialectic of freedom

James's singular contribution to Marxist theory emerged from a small intellectual group that he formed in the late 1940s with Raya Dunayevskaya and Grace Lee Boggs during his first US sojourn. The 'Johnson-Forest Tendency' set for itself the challenge of explaining why the Soviet Union—which should have ensured freedom to all its workers—had actually introduced new forms of unfreedom through the tight control that the Communist Party exerted over its population. To address this challenge, the group set for itself the early writings of Karl Marx, especially his 1844 *Economic and Philosophical Manuscripts*. Nowadays, these manuscripts are valued for the ways in which they bring to the fore Marx's concern for the meaning of freedom. But in the 1940s, they were still largely unknown in the English-speaking world. From these readings, James wrote *Notes on Dialectics*—a book that even towards the end of his life he considered his most crucial written work (Bogues, 1997: 119).

James and his comrades focused upon Marx's argument that bourgeois society was reprehensible principally because it robbed most individuals of exercising creativity in the act of labour, which was fundamental to the condition of being human. While labour should have been a self-directed activity that expanded freedom, in bourgeois society, labour was an act of unfreedom (James, 1980c: especially 175). James then applied this logic to evaluate Soviet society. Even if not bourgeois, the five-year economic 'Plans' in which the Communist Party compelled their workers to partake alienated their labour in ways similar to bourgeois society. In fact, James charged the Communist Party with exploiting the working classes as much as the bourgeoisie had done; the only difference was that the Party had perfected exploitation by commanding the state apparatus rather than by accumulating private property. Thus, James (1980c: 63, 67) claimed that the Soviet Union practised 'state capitalism'. By this reasoning, communism could in no way be said to have overturned bourgeois society. Hence James was compelled to rethink the Marxist narrative of class struggle.

Marxism told of the overcoming of feudalism by capitalism and then of capitalism by communism. Such a narrative was dialectical: every social system holds within it a tension or 'contradiction' that eventually tears it apart, leading to the creation of a new system; in this movement, some elements of the old system are discarded or overcome, and other elements take on new positions and meanings (see also Chapter 13 on Marx). In the Marxist understanding of dialectical change, every stage of human development comprises a specific struggle over the 'mode of production' between contending classes: the lords versus the peasants, the bourgeoisie versus the proletariat, etc. For James, the meaning of this struggle could be found in the degree of freedom that the masses enjoyed in self-directing their lives. But freedom had not advanced under the new stage of communism. Therefore, James devised a different story about the dialectic of freedom.

The innovative element of James's narrative lay in the interplay between three—not two—social forces: the masses, the bourgeoisie, and the petty bourgeoisie. The latter is usually glossed as small business owners, independent farmers, even teachers—anyone who has some small measure of autonomy when it comes to profession or property. But James was especially fascinated with that part of the petty bourgeoisie who were the radical intelligentsia—ideologues and organizers.

18.2.2 The radical intelligentsia and the masses

James presented the radical intelligentsia as a force that could pivot the struggle between the masses and the bourgeoisie towards a resolution it would otherwise not have had. If not the generators of historical movement, the intelligentsia could be, at critical moments, directors of it. Take, for instance, the French Revolution. For James (1980c: 187–189), the Jacobins—a small club of anti-royalist ideologues—were key to mobilizing the masses against the *ancien régime* in order to establish bourgeois society themselves. So, when it came to the French Revolution, if it weren't for the radical intelligentsia, the bourgeoisie would not have by themselves been able to win the struggle against the old classes to create bourgeois society.

Still, James pointed out, the intelligentsia often curtailed mass action. For instance, when it came to the Jacobins, in aspiring to run the state themselves, they forestalled a full revolution of the masses. In other words, the Jacobins directed the dialectic of freedom—they helped to get rid of an old unfreedom—but they also helped to create new unfreedoms in their attempts to command the state through, for instance, Robespierre's 'committee of public safety' and the 'terror' that it unleashed on the populace. James (ibid.: 200–209) explained the role of the intellectual apparatchiks (political or bureaucratic functionaries) of the Soviet Communist Party and their policy of 'state capitalism' along similar lines. The Bolsheviks, like the Jacobins, had been instrumental at directing the Russian Revolution to destroy the old Tsarist regime; and, at the same time, they had, under Stalin, raised the Communist Party to (an oppressive) leadership over the masses.

James never shook his distrust of small cabals of intelligentsia and ideologues seeking to pull the levers of history to the exclusion of the masses that they sought to direct. This distrust was a fundamental compass bearing for almost all the work that he undertook as he moved across a vast twentieth-century landscape. It is evident in his early considerations of what self-determination meant in the colonial Caribbean, and in the last decade of his life, when in 1981 James (1984b: 9–17) welcomed the formation of *Solidarność*, a trade union independent of the Polish state and thus Soviet influence.

Against this directorship of the petty bourgeoisie—especially the radical intelligentsia—James counter-posed a narrative of the masses. He was especially concerned to identify moments when the masses developed a self-awareness of their historical agency. James (1980c: 174) pointed to a set of revolutions, for instance, the risings across Europe in 1848, the French Commune in 1871, and the Russian Soviets (at least initially) in 1917, and later adding to this narrative the short-lived Hungarian People's Republic of 1956 (James et al., 2006). If James believed individual freedom to be the spirit of humanity, then that spirit moved with the masses, taking on the form of collective struggles for self-determination.

What was the source of the liberating tendencies of popular culture? Despite being a Marxist, James did not believe that the capitalist mode of production had created them; rather, he looked further back into the putative origins of Western civilization—ancient Greece. James (1993) took his cue from the Oxford-educated poet W.H. Auden, and presented ancient Greece as the moment wherein humanity was truly self-directed—when every individual could take part in every aspect of their society. James compared the 'universal man' of ancient Greece, who would plough in the morning and ruminate on metaphysics in the afternoon, with the dislocated life of modern humanity wherein individuals divided their energies into discrete and specialized activities often under the impress of a centralized bureaucracy or planning regime.

In a sense, James sought to detach ancient Greece from its late nineteenth-century anchoring within racist histories of European advance, which argued that only the Europeans had an ancient lineage that was ethically deserving of directing the present, and colonized peoples had no culture prior to their 'discovery' by Europeans. Still, James was clearly aware of the debilitating effect of this kind of teaching on the native intelligentsia. In his old age, he recalled seeing an exhibition of African art in London in 1933. It was only at that point that James (1984d: 207) 'began to realise that the African, the Black man, had a face of his own'. Up until that point, James had assumed that the proper face of humanity was a 'Graeco-Roman face'.

18.2.3 The dialectic of freedom in world history

With all these elements, James reframed the Marxist narrative of world history. Specifically, he proposed that humanity was living through a new stage in the dialectic of freedom: not simply the capitalists versus the proletariat but, more accurately, organized planning versus the self-activity of the masses (James, 1980a: 67; 1980c: 222). James painted a picture of this new stage quite soon after writing *Notes on Dialectics*, in a piece of writing he hoped would become a popular book (but which was never published in his lifetime)—*American Civilization*.

In this text, James claimed that the USA, as a settler colony, had skipped Europe's historical stage of feudalism. The ever-westward moving frontier provided the opportunity for settlers not just to practise their freedom but to associate freely with whomever they wanted (James, 1993: 30, 40). What's more, whereas culture in Europe was controlled by the old regime—the conservative and hierarchical aristocracy—in the USA, culture was far more authentically popular in essence (James, 1993: 36, 225). Take, for instance, the American creed—life, liberty, and the pursuit of happiness. The creed was evidence that the intelligentsia—that part of the petty bourgeoisie with which James was concerned—had to take the feelings and opinions of the masses far more seriously than their counterparts in Europe.

Opposed to this dialectical energy, however, lay an emergent twentieth-century phenomenon similar to Communist central planning. As a response to the Great Depression in 1930, President Roosevelt's 'New Deal' provided relief for poor people by enacting a series of federally-mandated rules and regulations, managed through large bureaucratic structures. Social life, heretofore remarkably free, became 'mechanized' through central planning (ibid.: 101, 104, 116). The intelligentsia were drawn into this national mechanization as they took their places in the new bureaucracy.

In sum, the American creed remained salient in the twentieth century but now only as an abstract promise of freedom, not as a substantive reality. The intelligentsia, who had heretofore tracked closely to the masses due to the prevalence of popular culture, had separated themselves by some degrees. Americans now pursued their freedom *vicariously*. Rather than fashion freedom from the self-direction of their own labour, Americans experienced it second-hand, via popular culture, and above all in the figure of the maverick individual—especially gangsters and private detectives—who lived freely until ultimately being bound by the law (ibid.: 121–127).

In the following years, James deployed his dialectic of freedom to explain political struggles the world over. For instance, he argued that most of the political organizations that came to power during the years of African independence, such as Kwame Nkrumah's Convention People's Party, were 'bastard imitations of the Russian one-party state' (James, 1982: 11, 14). Even with the rise of mass consciousness during the years of decolonization, the subsequent years of postcolonial rule had by and large led to the Indigenous intelligentsia distancing themselves from the masses in their governing regimes (ibid.: 15).

There is, though, a crucial dimension to *American Civilization* that requires further examination. James's book posed the question as to how the dialectic might be pushed forward in present conditions. In addressing this question, James retrieved a *racialized* dimension to the dialectic of freedom. He drew attention to a particular moment in US history: when, in the 1840s, President Andrew Jackson effectively gave over the South to the plantation owners. From that moment on, the pursuit of freedom would be regionally and racially divided between an industrial North and a slave-holding South and between whites versus Blacks.

Of course, in America it was the Black masses who had lived the contradiction between freedom and unfreedom most intensely. However, James (1977a: 250–251) insisted that, if not expressed publicly, white workers empathized deeply with the struggle of the Black masses for their freedom. In fact, he never failed to argue that the Black struggle for freedom was a universal struggle for the whole working class, regardless of whether white workers were racist or not (James, 1984b: 71). In James's estimation, slavery, more than any other phenomenon, sharpened the stakes at play for the general pursuit of freedom.

But what of the position of the *Black* intelligentsia—figures such as Booker T. Washington and W.E.B. Du Bois (see Chapter 31)? James was of the opinion that they had been drawn far more closely to these stakes—and the fates of the masses—than any other fraction of the petty bourgeoisie. Unlike the white intelligentsia, they exhibited an abidingly close association to the masses in their sharing of the Black Church and its pivotal role in the abolition movement, as well as their intimacy with musical genres such as jazz, blues, and spirituals (James, 1993: 202–209).

Key Concept: Black Studies

In 1968, pressure from students and freedom movements resulted in the inauguration of the first Black Studies programme in the US academy, at what was then called San Francisco State College. Black Studies sought systematically to analyse the lives of Black peoples. James did accept that Black intellectuals had been omitted from the 'canons' of social science and humanities. But he was also convinced that those who were best equipped to teach Black Studies were not necessarily Black professors, but professors who had been practically involved in the contemporary freedom struggle—white, Black, or whatever colour. Most importantly for James was his concern that a programme of study that ostensibly presented Black lives as separate and hermetically sealed might miss the fact that Black peoples were at the centre of a global and world-historical struggle over the fate of Western civilization. That fate was predicated, said James, on the struggle over slavery and the agency with which Black peoples fought that struggle.

Essentially, James (1993: 121–123) put forth a set of provocative propositions. Only in the USA was there a tradition of mass culture wherein the intelligentsia had to pay attention to and talk/walk with the masses. That mass culture had within it the potential to energize the struggle for freedom against capture by the state and its cadre of centralized planners. This struggle, James (ibid.: 161) intimated, should be seen as the exemplar of a global struggle, even against 'state capitalism' in the USSR. But, above all, the US struggle had, at its beating heart, a particularly intimate relationship between the Black masses and Black intelligentsia, such that the latter could not so easily 'sell out' the former and subvert and curtail the revolution.

In James's estimation, then, much rested on this relationship between the Black intelligentsia and the Black masses. To fully understand the stakes that James saw at play, we will now turn to his own biography, the development of his intellect in colonial Trinidad, and the ramifications of this development for his political thought.

18.2 James's Marxism: Key Points

- James provided a novel interpretation of Marxism with his idea of a 'dialectic of freedom' that drew the bourgeoisie, radical intelligentsia, and masses together in struggle.
- In so far as they robbed the masses of collective self-organizing, James considered Soviet communism and capitalism to be similarly oppressive systems.
- James considered the United States to be a peculiar society due to the way in which the cause of abolition created an especially close relationship between the Black intelligentsia and the Black masses.
- Due to this closeness, James believed that the Black intelligentsia had a special part to play in the dialectic of freedom in comparison to their white counterparts.

18.3 The native intelligentsia

18.3.1 Colonial education and European civilization

James's theorization of a dialectic of freedom was intimately informed by his own struggles to break from self-imposed isolation from the masses by embracing the struggle for freedom and self-determination from colonial rule. On more than one occasion James discussed the particular social standing of the native intelligentsia in colonies—that minority of non-white non-European (mostly) men who, like James, had received a European education and held some kind of administrative or educational position in the colony.

Colonial education was heavily ideological, presenting the imperial European 'homeland' as the source of all civilization and high culture. Indeed, despite his Marxist commitments, James's ethical orientation towards transformative change never rested solely upon the material analysis of various stages in the mode of production. Rather, James (ibid.: 171) identified the alienation of the individual from his self-directed activity—an alienation that was at the heart of his dialectic of freedom—as a problem deeper than class conflict, that is, as a problem of civilization itself. Notably, his comrades in the Independent Labour Party of Britain were always sceptical of the degree to which 'civilization' figured in James's logic instead of the category of 'class' (Dhondy, 2001: 41).

In the British colonies, education was designed, as James himself noted, to imbue the native intelligentsia with Victorian puritanical and bourgeois sensibilities while attributing base and primitive sensibilities to mass native culture (James, 1977b; Worcester, 1992). In fact, James's upwardly-aspiring mother often warned him that 'the road to the calypso tent was the road to hell'

(James, 2005: 21). The commandment to culturally distinguish oneself as a native intellectual from the native masses was internalized all the more by the fear that those few clerical or teaching positions in colonial administration could easily be taken away (see especially James, 1980e).

The impact of this schooling on James is clear. Just think, for instance, of the conversation between an elderly James and Mikey Smith in London, and of James's love for—and defence of—the English Romantic poets. The Romantics, who came to prominence around the time of the French Revolution and its aftermath, were very important to James. For him, they represented a 'tremendous expansion of the individual personality of the ordinary man'. Put another way, Romanticism was a movement that helped to break humanity from the staid order of the ancient regime with all its unfreedoms (James, 1984a: 195). Romanticism therefore captured the quintessence of the human spirit—a yearning for ever more freedom and self-directed activity.

Even in adult life, James considered himself to be a 'Black European' (Robinson, 2000: 285). Nonetheless, writing home during his first stay in London in the early 1930s, James (2003: 94) recounted that 'in the two things in which the English stand so high, the writing of poetry and political genius, it is unfortunate that I knew these things before I came'. Evident in this correspondence is an account not just of the importance of European civilization but also a recognition that its efficacy and extent were significantly fictionalized in colonial education.

The gap between education and reality was politicized by the fact that James from a young age feared the isolation that the native intelligentsia must necessarily endure from the masses (James, 2005: 4). James was always seeking to bridge this distance. His first published novel, *Minty Alley* (James, 1971), can be read as an attempt to report the 'common' life of his compatriots rather than the elite life of colonial masters and/or native intelligentsia. But more than anything else, cricket became the crucial medium by which James sought out a meaningful relationship with the masses.

For James, cricket embodied the fundamental conceit of colonialism that the English creed was one of 'fair play'. Moreover, it was only on the cricket field that colonized and colonizer could actually meet and engage in 'fair play'. Off the playing field, the entire structure of colonial Trinidad was hierarchical, iniquitous, and racialized when it came to wealth, land, labour, and representation. The groundsmen that James met through cricket were clearly far less infatuated with the English creed than he was (James, 2005: 148). Indeed, he was convinced that through the game the Trinidadian masses developed a sense of self-determination and postcolonial identity. For all these reasons, James conceived of the cricket field as a kind of public space wherein the dialectic of freedom worked out in colonial society: in cricket lived that contradiction that James gleaned in the US dialectic between formal and substantive freedom.

James retrospectively identified the fraught relationship that native intellectuals held with their masses also with respect to cricket. In his autobiography, James (ibid.: 65) laments the fact that as a youth he chose the 'wrong' team to play for: he could have joined the more 'proletariat' team but was impelled, instead, to join the one comprised of more elitist youth. This decision, he recounts, set back his intellectual and political development by years. But it was also a cricketer, Learie Constantine, who did much to break James's infatuation with the civilizational standing of the imperial centre. Constantine had invited James to England in 1932 to help write his autobiography. While staying with Constantine in Nelson, Lancashire, an old northern mill town with a radical labour history, James had complained of the comparatively 'low morals' that the Caribbean evinced vis-à-vis England. Constantine replied, simply, 'they are no better than we' (ibid.: 148).

18.3.2 The Haitian Revolution versus European civilization

It was while in Nelson that James started on a project that he had been toying with for a few years: a biography of the famous leader of the Haitian Revolution, Toussaint L'Ouverture (see Key Thinker: Toussaint L'Ouverture). The Haitian Revolution was a slave revolt led in particular by Toussaint L'Ouverture against the oppression of French colonial rule in Saint-Domingue (now Haiti). It began in 1791 and culminated in 1805 with the creation of the Haitian Republic under Jean-Jacques Dessalines. Eventually James's work would result in his most celebrated book, *The Black Jacobins*. However, he first arranged his thoughts in a play, 'Toussaint L'Ouverture: the story of the only successful slave revolt in history', which opened for the London theatre-going public in 1936.

James's play pivots around the tense relationship between Toussaint and his second-in-command, Dessalines. Toussaint, as James sketches him, is an almost one-dimensional Francophile. Toussaint wants freedom for the enslaved of the French colony of Saint-Domingue, yet not at any cost. The African enslaved, James's Toussaint bemoans, are practised warriors, but have no language and no education except what France has taught them (James, 2013: 94). Therefore, freedom will only be meaningful and efficacious if it preserves French culture and influence among the liberated Africans. Conversely, Dessalines, as James depicts him, is a Francophobe. He values nothing French, including language and education. He is convinced that freedom can only be achieved negatively—by irrevocably breaking with France in all respects.

Intriguingly, James suggests that Toussaint is the true leader of the people, despite the fact that Dessalines has their pulse more adroitly. Yet at the same time, when Toussaint has been tricked into captivity by Napoleon's forces and spirited away to die a lonely death in a prison in the French Alps, James (ibid.: 127) has him proclaim defiantly, at the end: 'You have got rid of one leader. But there are two thousand other leaders to be got rid of as well, and two thousand more when those are killed.' In his last words, James redeems Toussaint as a man of the people, even though the play suggests otherwise.

Soon after the play, James published *The Black Jacobins: Toussaint l'Ouverture and the San Domingo Revolution*. Note that the book, too, is about Toussaint, the leader of the revolution; it is not principally about the masses. Furthermore, James describes the revolutionaries in Francophile language: Jacobins—the radical intelligentsia so central to James's dialectic of freedom, albeit descriptively Black. By the time of the book's 1963 reprint, a whole new generation of activists and intellectuals had discovered James's history of Toussaint. On this occasion, James added an Appendix, seeking to connect the Haitian to the Cuban revolution that had occurred a handful of years previously. There, James argued that Black revolutionaries were always humanists and had always driven forward the dialectic of freedom 'without hatred or malice against the foreign, even the bitter imperialist past' (James, 2001b: 326).

Key Thinker: Toussaint L'Ouverture

Born into slavery, Toussaint L'Ouverture (c. 1743–1803) became a political and military leader of the Haitian Revolution. He eventually allied with France against the British and Spanish but was later arrested on the orders of Napoleon Bonaparte and died in prison in France, a year before Haitian independence. Recent research on the life of L'Ouverture suggests that the leader of the Haitian Revolution was not quite the Francophile portrayed by James. Although close to figures such as the French royalist Bayon de Libertat and a fellow Catholic, Toussaint also dabbled in Vodou practices and was a practitioner of African-based herbal medicine. In fact, his own father was a notable figure from the kingdom of Allada in West Africa who transmitted much of the Allada culture to his young son (Hazareesingh, 2020). As an adult revolutionary, Toussaint was conversant in various African languages and practices and for this reason was able to command a diverse army that included various African nations (Bell, 2005). It is very likely that Toussaint believed the best chance for freedom lay by tracking close to the French; but this does not necessarily imply that he was Francophile—or at least, Afro-phobic.

It's reasonably clear that there is some autobiography woven into James's characterization of Toussaint. In Toussaint, James compressed all of the tensions and hopes that he held for the Black intelligentsia as agents of the dialectic of freedom, including himself. His Toussaint was a lover of freedom and one who could direct the self-determination of the Black masses without compromising his commitment to European civilization. In addition, one can read into James's Toussaint a Black petty bourgeois who does not fully trust the Black masses to guide themselves towards a meaningful and progressive freedom.

Furthermore, in James's rendition of the Haitian Revolution lies an assumption that Blackness holds no meaning for freedom beyond its resistive power in the conscription of a mass of bodies against empire and capitalism. The meaning of freedom is derived from European civilization. It can be made Black as an adjective—as in Black Jacobin. But Blackness cannot function as a noun—as a reference point, an ethical directive, a horizon of possibility for humanity. European civilization, for James, never loses its humanist substance, even when it justifies the dehumanizing pursuits of empire and slavery.

> ### 18.3 The native intelligentsia: Key Points
>
> - James believed that European Romanticism was exemplary of the human yearning for ever more freedom.
> - Cricket was crucial to James insofar as it forced him to consider the ways in which colonial education might arrest the movement for anti-colonial self-determination.
> - James presented the political and ethical choice for the Black intelligentsia in paradoxical terms: the freedoms inherent in European civilization were to be embraced but not the colonialism and slavery that were part of the expansion of that civilization.
> - James scripted Toussaint L'Ouverture and the choices he made in the Haitian Revolution in a somewhat autobiographical fashion.

18.4 Black freedom/European civilization

18.4.1 Trinidad and the racial sources of self-determination

These tensions between Black freedom and European civilization were exposed early on in James's intellectual life. Prior to his arrival in Nelson, James had been finishing a biography of Captain Cipriani, founder of the Trinidad Labour Party, the colony's first political party to advocate for self-governance and equal representation. In this biography, published in 1933, James (1980d: 188) opined that it was Cipriani's heritage as a French creole that allowed him to draw on a long tradition of independent social and economic life, unlike the Black bourgeoisie of the islands. Note, here, the way in which James identified a French lineage with the cultural competencies that enabled the Romantic energies that he so admired—an individual personality fitting of self-directed activity and pushing for freedom in the form of collective self-determination.

James's critique might have been fair when it came to the Black bourgeoisie. But what kind of culture drove the Trinidadian masses? In his book on Cipriani, James addressed the case of Black Trinidadians. Unlike Cipriani's European lineage, claimed James (1933: 5–6), enslaved peoples in Trinidad had lost their African languages and cultures. As humans, though, they retained a capacity to learn language, and it was that capacity that allowed them to master English. This mastery meant that 'the negro who made the middle passage was now not African, he was a West Indian black' (James, 1980d: 174).

What is more, noted James in his biography of Cipriani, unlike Europeans, West Indian Blacks were forged as a people purely in the fires of 'modern industry'. Due to the specificities of the sugar production process, the plantation system required a tight fit between agricultural cultivation and product manufacturing, all of which took place in the same productive unit (ibid.: 176; see also Mintz, 1978). No cultural or practical remnants from the ancient regime mediated or buffered the brutal relationships of the plantation as they did in Europe. Rather, and unlike in Europe, the most modern industrial forces of production were driven forward by the most despotic relations of production in the form of the masters' whip. And that is why the desire of the Black masses for freedom and self-determination was so strong and so fundamental to the dialectic of freedom.

Effectively, then, James claimed that while the drive towards freedom came from the enslaved masses and their descendants, the meaning of freedom for the masses would be guided by the European culture of Cipriani, a white member of the petty bourgeoisie. But could the cultural tools that denied humanity to the Black masses really drive forward their collective freedom? What if the Caribbean masses were driven by a meaning of freedom that resonated with Europe's Romanticist movement, yet did so across a horizon of possibility that stretched beyond Europe? What if Blackness drove the human spirit forward in ways that were not indebted to European civilization, as James believed the Black intelligentsia—himself, Cipriani, and even Toussaint—were?

18.4.2 The challenge of Garveyism to James

In fact, the labour movement from which Cipriani emerged was just as influenced by Garveyism as it was European socialism or even Russian communism. In 1914, Marcus and Amy Ashwood Garvey set up the Universal Negro Improvement Association and African Communities League (UNIA) in Jamaica (see Key Thinker: Amy Ashwood Garvey). Initially a social reform society, by 1918, the UNIA was agitating for Pan-African self-determination under the motto: 'Africa for the Africans at home and abroad'. True, the UNIA practised a socialistic principle of collective self-reliance that James would have no problem with, but this practice occurred primarily within and between Black communities. The 'race first' motto associated with the UNIA was the quintessential logic of Garveyism.

Moreover, pomp and pageantry in the UNIA all focused on the redemption of an African identity. This identity was underpinned by Ethiopianism, an interpretive tradition of reading the Bible which claimed that enslaved Africans were God's chosen people who would save themselves in order to realize God's plan and make Heaven on Earth (see Shepperson, 1953). The UNIA even set up a Black Star shipping line to help Africans in the diaspora return home to the African continent from whence their ancestors had been kidnapped and enslaved.

So, while Garveyism—channelled through the UNIA—espoused the kind of self-determination that James celebrated, it did not do so through national lines, nor through strictly class lines nor even via a commitment to European civilization. Garveyism was avowedly Pan-African. The yearning of its spirit for an independent Black personality and for collective self-determination pointed towards a continent that James claimed Black peoples in the diaspora had been irrevocably separated from in all meaningful ways.

Consider this. At the time of the 1919 strike for higher wages, Garveyism had already begun to exert an influence on the Trinidad Workingmen's Association (TWA) (the forerunner of the Trinidad Labour Party). It is probably fair to say that among the TWA rank and file, the separation of Garveyism from trade unionism would have been nonsensical—the local UNIA branch and TWA regularly shared personnel and perhaps other resources (Thomas, 1987: 238; Singh, 1994: 21–22). Moreover, if Cipriani, as a French creole, could hardly become a Garveyite himself (nor would he have wanted to), other prominent positions in the TWA, such as the general secretary, were manned by Garveyites. James himself testifies to the synthesis by the Trinidadian masses of socialism with Garvey's

Pan-Africanism. Late in his life he still remembered talking, as an 18-year-old, to the waterfront strikers in 1919 and recalling that 'they were all Garveyites, even if they didn't say' (James, 1980b). Not to mention that, as a young man, James was a fellow reader of the UNIA's *The Negro World*.

It is no surprise that James accorded to Garveyism a historical role in mobilizing the Black masses. In a pamphlet published in 1938, entitled *A History of Negro Revolt*, James admitted that there had never before been a 'negro movement' like Garveyism. Garvey, in James's view, had 'created for the first time a feeling of international solidarity' among Black peoples by making the 'negro conscious of his African origin' (James, 1938: 68, 71). However, for James, this claim to origin was precisely the problem. Garvey's mass cultural and political movement did not reference the European civilizational strata that James had been taught to mine as a member of the native intelligentsia.

At the same time as acknowledging that Garveyism was integral to the movement of the Black masses towards freedom, James (ibid.: 69–71) described Garveyism as 'pitiable rubbish'. He argued that the Black masses didn't really believe any of the Garveyite ideology but that they were moved simply by the sentiment that it emoted. James also categorized Garvey not only as a petty bourgeoisie, but (unfairly) one with no thought about industrial organization, which would have made Garvey, in James's view, a conformist rather than radical member of the Black intelligentsia.

Yet it can be argued that James never managed to convince himself entirely of his own judgement on Garveyism. In 1935, James, along with Amy Ashwood Garvey, Chris Brathwaite, and others set up the International African Friends of Ethiopia to provide diasporic support to Ethiopia in its fight against Mussolini's fascist invasion (see Makalani, 2014). Notably, it is in this moment that James broke with the Independent Labour Party regarding their stance over support for Ethiopia. James was adamant that Europe could not and should not save Africa—Africa had to save itself (albeit with support from the European masses). James himself was not a million miles here from articulating the core beliefs of Garveyism.

Africa was on his mind. In 1935, James also turned his attention to the copper-belt strikes in southern Africa and the way in which the Watchtower movement in the region channelled the politics of self-determination. An African version of Jehovah's Witness, Watchtower—and its belief in the Second (Black) Coming of Christ—also articulated with existing forms of anti-colonial spirituality, such as Ethiopianism, and Pan-Africanism, especially Garveyism. Both Ethiopianism and Garveyism had been clearly influential in labour politics in southern Africa from the early 1920s onwards (see, in general, Hill and Piro, 1987).

Unlike his critique of the followers of Garvey in the Caribbean, James argued that the Watchtower movement in southern Africa was only 'absurd' on the surface, while its substance represented 'political realities' and expressed 'political apsirations far more closely than programmes and policies of parties with millions of members, numerous journals'. Far more than garnering just sentiment, Watchtower, for James (1938: 82–83), voiced 'what the thinking native thinks and what he is prepared to die for'. Here we can identify a meaningful freedom pursued by the Watchtower movement. Even if the movement partly drew upon Christian theology, it was not simply a product of European civilization.

Therefore, when it came to the prospect of Black freedom, it is possible to identify in James a relentless rethinking of the departure and end points of civilization beyond his initial disquiet of the Garvey movement. For instance, in the 1950s, James returned his attention to Haiti and the re-orientation by Haitian scholars and politicians of their history towards an embrace of the African influence. He accepted that the attempt to build a national culture post-independence upon emulation of the French had failed until Jean Price Mars decided to re-situate that culture in terms of 'Africa in the West Indies' (James, 1977b: 19). What Dessalines initially represented for James could no longer be simply defined as a brute reaction to unfreedom, but as a compass bearing towards an African-authored freedom.

18.4.3 The challenge of Rastafari to James

In 1967, James (1984c) reviewed a novel by soon-to-be-famous Jamaican sociologist Orlando Patterson entitled *The Children of Sisyphus*. Patterson—a fellow member of the Black (and Caribbean) intelligentsia—centred the story around the lives and travails of the most influential sons and daughters of Garveyism—the Rastafari. James found much to praise in the book. But he criticized Patterson's depiction of the Rastafari as tragic labourers towards a goal—repatriation to Africa—that would never happen. Instead, James (ibid.: 164–165) noted that despite Patterson's scripting of their 'colossal stupidities', the 'insanities' of the Rastafari were nonetheless 'consciously motivated by their acute consciousness' of their terrible social conditions and their 'conscious refusal to accept the fictions that pour in upon them from every side'.

It's important to grasp just how much James's estimation of the Rastafari was overflowing with the ascription of *conscious*—self-directed—action, a quality that was fundamental to his dialectic of freedom. Even if he thought their goal deluded, James nonetheless acknowledged that the Rastafari possessed a critical faculty with which to parse the lies of colonial and postcolonial elites. James even sought to humble Patterson by suggesting that his writing of the book for a British audience evinced the same desire to escape the Caribbean as his book's protagonists! Effectively, James was suggesting to Patterson that he and the Rastafari were not so far apart in position, but that Patterson's yearning for acceptance by the colonial culture might not be as progressive as the Rastafari yearning for an African-centred freedom.

A few years later and James (1984d: 214) reported that he had begun to read books on Africa's past 'high' civilizations. Advanced, in James's estimation, did not simply pertain to technological or productive capacity. Which criteria James used to evaluate 'high' rather than 'low' he did not say, but it is reasonably clear that he was invoking the values that animated European Romanticism—an expansion of the individual personality of the ordinary person, and a yearning for self-directed activity that drove a movement of collective self-determination. James then admitted that—contra claims he had made earlier in his life—he now appreciated that enslaved Africans had brought much of this civilization with them on the slave ships.

James connected this prospect to the work of Guyana historian, Marxist, and Black Power advocate Walter Rodney, whom he had mentored in the 1960s. Rodney undertook a PhD at SOAS, University of London, and, in the late 1960s, wrote a book entitled *Groundings with My Brothers* (Rodney, 1990). 'Grounding' is a Rastafari term for congregating, praising, and critical reasoning in a communal fashion and on a 'horizontal', non-hierarchical basis. The last chapter of Rodney's book reports on his experience in congregating with Rastafari outside of the University of West Indies, during his time in Jamaica. Recall how important to James's dialectic the pursuit of creative self-directed activity was. Now consider Rodney's (ibid.: 83) evaluation of the Rastafari:

> [Rastafari] are every day performing a miracle. It is a miracle how those fellows live. They live and they are physically fit, they have a vitality of mind, they have a tremendous sense of humour, they have depth. How do they do that in the midst of the existing conditions? And they create, they are always saying things. You know that some of the best painters and writers are coming out of the Rastafari environment. The black people in the West Indies have produced all the culture that we have, whether it be steelband or folk music. Black bourgeoisie and white people in the West Indies have produced nothing! Black people who have suffered all these years create. That is amazing.

In effect, Rodney was suggesting that the dialectic of freedom moved with the Rastafari—a group who in the 1960s were universally disparaged not just by the colonial administration but by Black bourgeoisie and the intelligentsia, many of whom would become the new governing class on independence. Ten years later, James held his own grounding with Mikey Smith in his South London flat.

18.4.4 Black women and the dialectic of freedom

We should not, though, return to that South London flat without coming to terms with the fact that the majority of historical figures that James engaged in his scoping out of a dialectic of freedom were men. James (1993: 200) was not blind to the fact that Black women played a role in anti-racist movements in the USA: 'I have known many revolutionary movements and I have known women in them, and those black girls in the movement . . . may not be strong on Marxist theory, but they are ready to take action . . . They are astonishing people' (James, 1984d: 212). Nonetheless, despite these acknowledgements, and despite his own personal relation to Amy Ashwood Garvey, the first wife of Marcus and putative co-founder of the UNIA, Black women are tellingly absent as part of the Black intelligentsia to whom James had given an outsized role in the struggle for meaningful freedom.

> **Key Thinker: Amy Ashwood Garvey**
>
> In the first part of his activist life, James enjoyed a working relationship with Amy Ashwood Garvey (1897–1969)—a co-instigator of the UNIA. Amy Ashwood was many things in her lifetime—a secretary, organizer, writer, orator, businesswoman—but always a Pan-Africanist. James held Ashwood Garvey in high regard, counting her among four of the most 'brilliant' conversationalists he had ever met, alongside the likes of Leon Trotsky (Martin, 2007: 144). James claimed that it was in Ashwood Garvey's Florence Mill's Social Club in London that the International African Friends of Abyssinian (IAFA) was gestated. The networks developed by the IAFA would eventually deliver the seminal 1945 Pan-African Congress in Manchester, to which Amy Ashwood herself made important contributions (Sherwood and Adi, 2003: 73). She was largely responsible for including five clauses in the Congress's resolution that pertained to gender equality in terms of pay, employment opportunities and conditions, and other considerations.

If James had set Ashwood Garvey rather than Marcus as his long-term intellectual and political provocateur, he might perhaps have spent more time considering alternative spaces wherein the dialectic of freedom worked its magic. One could say that Black women's work in cultivating the very spaces in which to collectively ruminate and organize might be seen as a fundamental element of his dialectic. But in much of James's narration, there is little time spent investigating this, perhaps the most fundamental work of community building and self-determination.

Erna Brodber, a Jamaican writer, can help us to think through the consequences of this gendered omission for James's dialectic of freedom. Broder, in fact, helps us to take the challenge of Rastafari to James in a new direction. She has in the past associated herself with a Rastafari organization—the Twelve Tribes of Israel. Perhaps more importantly, Brodber was one of a whole generation of Caribbean intellectuals whose development was marked by Walter Rodney's stay at the University of West Indies.

Rodney's practice of leaving the campus to reason with Rastafari communes in Kingston led students to demand that the University break with its colonial practices of teaching an ideal image of Western civilization and instead incorporate into its curricula the histories and experiences of the majority of the population—the economically impoverished African-Jamaican masses. For herself, Brodber realized that she could not pursue a degree in social policy if academia required her to take on a persona segregated from the communities that surrounded her and from which she hailed. She seems to have begun to question the native intelligentsia model in the course of undertaking a large oral history project documenting the lives and memories of elder Jamaicans. She was struck by their desire to talk of a past that was passionately associated with Africa, Atlantic slavery, and Garveyism (Brodber, 1985: 53).

So Brodber began to write novels. Many of them implicitly critique the assumptions and frameworks of academic disciplines—for example, history, sociology, anthropology, etc. Moreover, at least one of her novels explores the difficulties of male Black Caribbean Marxists such as James trying—and failing—to develop intimate and meaningful relationships through their politicking with ordinary folk (Brodber, 1980). Conversely, all of Brodber's novels unapologetically and immediately situate their protagonists in the geographies, languages, world-views, and traditions of her own peoples.

In these novels, global projects of domination and resistance are parsed through the lives of these 'little' people, living in 'little' spaces (small villages, backyards, etc.) practising 'little' traditions such as Ethiopianism. Often the key protagonists are women who operate not in the public sphere, chronicled by official archives, but in the spheres where oral accounts reside—within the politics of domesticity, familial relationships, folklore, healing arts, and spirit work (Roberts, 2006: 5–6, 33, 59). Yet these characters are by no means limited or provincial in their orientation. In fact, they tend to make audacious journeys between countryside and town, and between islands and continents. They are, in Brodber's estimation, as capable as understanding and directing the struggle for self-determination as the big male figures of history—Black or otherwise.

Due to the lack of memoirs and archives left by such peoples, Brodber argues that the retrieval of their histories of self-determination must be creative. Yet such creativity must be guided by a sense of the living and creative transmission of *all* heritages that make up a people—not just European. The writer must not be afraid to enter 'the minds and hearts of the ancestors through the children and grandchildren' (Brodber, 1983: 7). Brodber (1997: 80) is convinced that reasoning with the 'little traditions' of Black peoples might help to 'build the myths, the ideologies, the religious and political philosophy that will make us what this tradition thinks it can be— . . . self-directed souls'.

18.4 Black freedom/European civilization: Key Points

- To James, it seemed that the Black masses were animated by but misguided in taking up Garveyism.
- James struggled with but ultimately endorsed the proposition that 'Africans brought their cultures with them across the Atlantic'.
- In his later years, James found cultural value in the yearnings for African-centred self-determination by one of the most influential descendant groups of Garveyism—the Rastafari.
- James's understanding of Black self-determination was incomplete due to his gendered apprehension of the dialectic of freedom.

18.5 Conclusion

James is a controversial figure in the constellation of Black political thought. On the one hand, his writings have been extremely influential, and his intellectual activism is woven into the tapestry of twentieth-century Pan-Africanism through the Caribbean, North America, Europe, West and East Africa, and even as far as the Pacific. On the other hand, those expecting to find an Afrocentric thinker in James are almost bound to be disappointed, if not plain embarrassed by James's unrepentant love of European civilization.

This chapter has sought to make sense of this paradox. It presented the core tenet of James's thought: that the human condition is moved ever onward towards meaningful freedom by the pursuit of collective self-determination. It also interrogated the core tension in his thought: that the meaning of this freedom has to be drawn from European civilization, even by those Black masses whom European civilization determined to be less than human.

James is a scholar who is often fought over. We could claim that James's critique of Black Studies demonstrates that current attempts to 'decolonize' the white European 'canon' of political theory are misplaced, even dangerous. We could also claim James as a proponent of such attempts in so far as he was convinced that the relationship between the Black intelligentsia and the Black masses, and the particular resolution of the frictions in that relationship, would determine the struggle among humanity for ever-expansive freedom.

Regardless of where we might stand in that fight, pedagogically we must acknowledge that we do a disservice to the breadth, depth, and complexity of James's thought if we teach any one version of James. Recall that meeting between a young Mikey Smith and an elderly James. It is a meeting that is full of critique and generosity and, while laying out all the key issues for us to think through, ends with no clear resolution.

We can decide, for ourselves, whether Black freedom is served by European civilization, or whether European civilization is incomplete without Black freedom, or whether Black unfreedom makes of European civilization an impossibility, or whether Black freedom is all that we need, or that freedom will never make any sense until we engage in good faith with the intellectual and political work of Black women. But still, let us dwell in the space opened by James if only for a time, let us feel the weight of the dualisms and tensions, understand why they became weighty for James and how they leveraged his thought into a multitude of directions (but not into all available directions). We would do no less for Aristotle, Kant, Marx, or Foucault.

Take your learning further by accessing the online resources for a library of web links to relevant videos, articles, blogs, and useful websites for this chapter: www.oup.com/he/Ramgotra-Choat1e.

Study questions

1. What was original about James's version of Marxism?
2. Was James Eurocentric?
3. What is James's dialectic of freedom?
4. How, if at all, did James's colonial education create tension in his thought especially regarding Black people's struggle for freedom?
5. Does James consider the Haitian Revolution and its leader Toussaint L'Ouverture subversive of or products of European civilization?
6. What is Garveyism and why did James think the Black masses were misguided in following it?
7. What challenges did Garveyism and Rastafari present to James, as a member of the Black intelligentsia?
8. What theoretical consequences ensue from the absence of Black women in James's dialectic of freedom?

Further reading

Primary sources

James, C.L.R. (1982) *Nkrumah and the Ghana Revolution*. London: Allison & Busby.
 James applies his 'dialectic of freedom' to the fate of Kwame Nkrumah's rule of independent Ghana.

James, C.L.R. (1984b) *CLR James' 80th Birthday Lectures*. Ed. M. Busby and D. Howe. London: Race Today Publications.
 Towards the end of his life, James provides these lectures demonstrating his steadfast Marxist credentials; especially of note is the recording of his Q&As with the audience.

James, C.L.R. (1993) *American Civilization*. Malden, MA: Blackwell.
 Here James applies his 'dialectic of freedom' to make sense of US history via the conflict between the bourgeoisie, radical intelligentsia, and the masses.

James, C.L.R. (2001b) *The Black Jacobins: Toussaint L'Ouverture and the San Domingo Revolution*. London: Penguin Books.
 The famous book wherein James recounts the history of the Haitian Revolution and sketches out the character of Toussaint L'Ouverture.

James, C.L.R. (2005) *Beyond a Boundary*. London: Yellow Jersey Press.
 The famous autobiography wherein James demonstrates how the culture and gamesmanship of cricket provide a window into struggles for self-determination.

Secondary sources

Bogues, A. (1997) *Caliban's Freedom: The Early Political Thought of C.L.R. James*. London: Pluto.
 This book elucidates the original features of James's Marxism and also dwells on his engagement with the problem of race and racism.

Carby, H.V. (1998) *Race Men*. Cambridge, MA: Harvard.
 In Chapter 4, Carby uses James's writings on cricket and the Haitian Revolution to draw out the gendered dimension of his analyses and to demonstrate how important 'black manhood' was for him.

Høgsbjerg, C. (2014) *C.L.R. James in Imperial Britain*. Durham, NC: Duke University Press.
 This book provides a rich biography of James's early years in Britain and the transformations of his intellectual project that accompanied this sojourn.

Robinson, C. (2000) *Black Marxism: The Making of the Black Radical Tradition*. Chapel Hill, NC: University of North Carolina Press.
 Robinson famously situates James within a longer and wider 'Black radical tradition' of scholarship.

References

Bell, M.S. (2005) 'Toussaint Between Two Worlds'. *Journal of Haitian Studies*, 11(2): 30–44.

Bogues, A. (1997) *Caliban's Freedom: The Early Political Thought of C.L.R. James*. London: Pluto.

Brodber, E. (1980) *Jane and Louisa Will Soon Come Home*. London: New Beacon Books.

Brodber, E. (1983) 'Oral Sources and the Creation of a Social History of the Caribbean'. *Jamaica Journal*, 16(4): 2–11.

Brodber, E. (1985) 'Black Consciousness and Popular Music in Jamaica in the 1960s and 1970s'. *Caribbean Quarterly*, 31(2): 53–66.

Brodber, E. (1997) 'Re-Engineering Blackspace'. *Caribbean Quarterly*, 43(1/2): 70–81.

Dhondy, F. (2001) *C.L.R. James*. London: Weidenfeld & Nicolson.

Hazareesingh, S. (2020) *Black Spartacus: The Epic Life of Toussaint Louverture*. New York: Farrar, Straus and Giroux.

Hill, R.A. and Piro, G.A. (1987) '"Africa for the Africans": The Garvey Movement in South Africa, 1920-1940'. In S. Marks and S. Trapido (eds), *The Politics of Race, Class and Nationalism in Twentieth-Century South Africa*. London: Longman.

James, C.L.R. (1933) *The Case for West-Indian Self Government*. London: Hogarth Press.

James, C.L.R. (1938) *A History of Negro Revolt*. London: Fact.

James, C.L.R. (1956) 'Every Cook Can Govern: A Study of Democracy in Ancient Greece'. Marxists Internet Archive. Available at: https://www.marxists.org/archive/james-clr/works/1956/06/every-cook.htm.

James, C.L.R. (1971) *Minty Alley*. London: New Beacon Books.

James, C.L.R. (1977a) 'The Atlantic Slave Trade'. In C.L.R. James, *The Future in the Present*. London: Allison & Busby, pp. 235-264.

James, C.L.R. (1977b) 'The Mighty Sparrow'. In C.L.R. James, *The Future in the Present*. London: Allison & Busby, pp. 191-201.

James, C.L.R. (1980a) 'After Ten Years'. In C.L.R. James, *Spheres of Existence*. Westport, CT: Lawrence Hill and Co., pp. 59-69.

James, C.L.R. (1980b) 'Interview by Ken Ramchand'. Available at: www.marxists,org/archive/james-clr/works/1980/09/banyan.htm.

James, C.L.R. (1980c) *Notes on Dialectics: Hegel, Marx, Lenin*. London: Allison & Busby.

James, C.L.R. (1980d) 'The Making of the Caribbean People'. In C.L.R. James, *Spheres of Existence*. Westport, CT: Lawrence Hill and Co., pp. 173-190.

James, C.L.R. (1980e) 'The West Indian Middle Classes'. In C.L.R. James, *Spheres of Existence*. Westport, CT: Lawrence Hill and Co., pp. 131-140.

James, C.L.R. (1982) *Nkrumah and the Ghana Revolution*. London: Allison & Busby.

James, C.L.R. (1984a) 'Black Studies and the Contemporary Student'. In C.L.R. James, *At the Rendezvous of Victory*. London: Allison & Busby. pp. 186-201.

James, C.L.R. (1984b) *CLR James' 80th Birthday Lectures*. Ed. M. Busby and D. Howe. London: Race Today Publications.

James, C.L.R. (1984c) 'Rastafari at Home and Abroad'. In C.L.R. James, *At the Rendezvous of Victory*. London: Allison & Busby, pp. 163-165.

James, C.L.R. (1984d) 'The Old World and the New'. In C.L.R. James, *At the Rendezvous of Victory*. London: Allison & Busby, pp. 202-217.

James, C.L.R. (1993) *American Civilization*. Cambridge, MA: Blackwell.

James, C.L.R. (2001a) *Mariners, Renegades, & Castaways: The Story of Herman Melville and the World We Live In: The Complete Text*. Hanover, NH: Dartmouth College.

James, C.L.R. (2001b) *The Black Jacobins: Toussaint L'Ouverture and the San Domingo Revolution*. London: Penguin Books.

James, C.L.R. (2003) *Letters from London: Seven Essays by C.L.R. James*. Port of Spain: Prospect Press.

James, C.L.R. (2005) *Beyond a Boundary*. London: Yellow Jersey Press.

James, C.L.R. (2013) *Toussaint Louverture: The Story of the Only Successful Slave Revolt in History*. Ed. C. Hobsbjerg. London: Duke University Press.

James, C.L.R, Lee, G.C., Castoriadis, C., and Bracey, J.H. (2006) *Facing Reality: The New Society: Where to Look for It & How to Bring It Closer*. Chicago: Charles H. Kerr.

Makalani, M. (2014) *In the Cause of Freedom: Radical Black Internationalism from Harlem to London, 1917-1939*. Chapel Hill, NC: University of North Carolina Press.

Martin, T. (2007) *Amy Ashwood Garvey: Pan-Africanist, Feminist, and Mrs. Marcus Garvey No. 1 or a Tale of Two Amies*. Dover, MA: Majority Press.

Mintz, S.W. (1978) 'Was the Plantation Slave a Proletarian?' *Review (Fernand Braudel Center)*, 2(1): 81-98.

Roberts, J. (2006) *Reading Erna Brodber: Uniting the Black Diaspora Through Folk Culture and Religion*. Westport, CT: Praeger.

Robinson, C. (2000) *Black Marxism: The Making of the Black Radical Tradition*. Chapel Hill, NC: University of North Carolina Press.

Rodney, W. (1990) *The Groundings with My Brothers*. London: Bogle-L'Ouverture.

Shepperson, G. (1953) 'Ethiopianism and African Nationalism'. *Phylon*, 14(1): 9-18.

Sherwood, M, and Adi, H. (2003) 'Amy Ashwood Garvey'. In *Pan-African History: Political Figures from Africa and the Diaspora Since 1787*. London: Routledge, pp. 69-75.

Singh, K. (1994) *Race and Class Struggles in a Colonial State : Trinidad 1917-1945*. Kingston, Jamaica: University of the West Indies Press.

Thomas, R.D. (1987) *The Trinidad Labour Riots of 1937: Perspectives 50 Years Later*. St. Augustine, Trinidad: University of the West Indies Press.

Worcester, K. (1992) '"A Victorian with the Rebel Seed": C.L.R. James and the Politics of Intellectual Engagement'. In A. Hennessy (ed.), *Intellectuals in the Twentieth Century Caribbean*, vol. 1. Basingstoke: Macmillan, pp. 115-130.

19 Hannah Arendt

KEI HIRUTA

Chapter guide

This chapter considers the life and work of Hannah Arendt, one of the most original and influential political thinkers of the twentieth century. After a brief overview of her extraordinary life, it discusses her theory of totalitarianism and its central arguments and idiosyncratic methodology. It then turns to her attempt to form a new political theory attuned to the post-totalitarian present (Section 19.3), examining some of her key concepts, including action, speech, natality, plurality, freedom, and politics. This will be followed in Section 19.4 by a discussion of her theory of revolution, its shortcomings, and its enduring importance. Sections 19.5 and 19.6 consider her controversial stance on gender, race, and culture. It is argued that her legacy to feminist theory has been highly ambivalent, while some aspects of her political thought are undermined by her cultural biases and, to some extent, by her racial prejudices.

19.1 Introduction

No political thinker has made a more determined effort to understand the significance of twentieth-century totalitarianism than Hannah Arendt. Of course, totalitarianism—especially in its 'classical' Nazi and Stalinist forms—was seen as a foremost political challenge by many of her contemporaries, and the term 'totalitarianism' continues today to signify an especially oppressive form of government. However, Arendt differs from many others in insisting that totalitarianism is a phenomenon unknown prior to the twentieth century, and that a proper understanding of this 'novel form of government' requires a new form of political thinking (Arendt, 1979: 460–479). Although she is a versatile thinker, writing on numerous issues from *polis* life in ancient Greece to twentieth-century existential philosophy, much of her work may be seen as a continuing attempt to understand how totalitarianism came to emerge in the first place, and how the rise of a new totalitarianism might be averted in the post-war world. As Margaret Canovan writes, 'virtually the entire agenda of Arendt's political thought was set by her reflections on the political catastrophes of the mid-century' (Canovan, 1992: 7).

This chapter focuses on Arendt's major works in political theory, including *The Origins of Totalitarianism*, *The Human Condition*, and *On Revolution*. Although there are other writings by her that are important in their own right, such as *Eichmann in Jerusalem* and *The Life of the Mind*, they do not fall within the domain of political thought in a straightforward manner and consequently are not discussed in detail here.

The only child of a secular and assimilated German-Jewish family, Hannah Arendt was born in Hanover in 1906 and grew up in Königsberg. Having developed an interest in European philosophy and literature early on, she began her university education at a time when a new philosophical movement known as phenomenology was sweeping across Germany. She had the opportunity to attend seminars by the movement's founder, Edmund Husserl, but found greater inspiration in Husserl's former student Martin Heidegger. She not only attended Heidegger's courses in 1924-1925 but also had a romantic affair with him (an extramarital one, on his part). The difficult relationship between them, exacerbated by Heidegger's involvement with Nazism, continues to generate heated debate. Arendt completed her doctoral dissertation on 'The Concept of Love in Augustine', under the supervision of Karl Jaspers, in 1929.

> ### Key Thinker: Martin Heidegger
>
> Martin Heidegger (1889-1976) was one of the most brilliant and most controversial philosophers of twentieth-century Europe. He began his academic career as Husserl's research assistant. Instead of following his teacher's path, however, he developed his own brand of phenomenology, drawing on various sources such as Dilthey, Nietzsche, Kierkegaard, Kant, and Aristotle (read more about Nietzsche in Chapter 14, Kant in Chapter 29, and Aristotle in Chapter 3). He met Arendt while he was working on his masterpiece, *Being and Time*, published in 1927. While Heidegger's influence over Arendt's thought is undoubtedly significant, the precise nature of this influence has been a matter of scholarly dispute. While some accuse her of uncritically following Heidegger's work, others see her as creatively appropriating it for her own purposes. Added to this is a further controversy over Heidegger's Nazi sympathies. He joined the Nazi Party in 1933 and made various remarks that appear supportive of a purported rejuvenation of the German nation by Adolf Hitler.

Arendt's subsequent academic career was catastrophically disrupted by the rise of Nazism. As interwar democracy in Germany came to a violent end in the early 1930s, she realized that Jewish assimilation in the country had failed. This realization prompted her to undertake illegal work for the Zionist Federation of Germany, resulting in her arrest and an eight-day interrogation in Berlin. In 1933, she fled Germany and settled in Paris, where she met regularly with other German intellectuals in exile and continued her work for various Zionist organizations. The invasion of France by Nazi Germany in 1940 disrupted her life again, however, and she was sent to an internment camp in Gurs in south-western France. The absurdity of her situation was not lost upon her: she had been expelled from Germany because she was a Jew; when France was invaded, she was interned because she was a German; but once Germany had occupied France, she was not freed, again because she was a Jew (Arendt, 2007: 270).

Fortunately, Arendt escaped from Nazified Europe to the United States. Having arrived in New York in May 1941 as a refugee and a stateless person, she plunged into activity over the next decade. She learned English, while writing columns for a German-language newspaper; she began teaching at universities; and, once the war was over, she travelled to Europe on behalf of Jewish Cultural Reconstruction, Inc. to save Jewish cultural artefacts looted by the Nazis. She then published, in 1951, *The Origins of Totalitarianism*, establishing her reputation as one of her adopted country's most brilliant émigré intellectuals. This book, however, largely focused on the Nazi variant of totalitarianism and had relatively little to say regarding its communist counterpart. Arendt therefore began working on a new book, to be entitled 'Totalitarian Elements in Marxism'. Although she did not complete this project, the extensive research she conducted laid the foundation for her mature work in political theory.

> **Key Concept: Totalitarianism**
>
> Totalitarianism is a contested concept. Some use it broadly to mean oppressive government in general. Others use it more narrowly to designate twentieth-century fascist, Nazi, and communist regimes. Others use it even more narrowly, to refer to Hitler's Germany and Stalin's Russia specifically. Arendt's definition is at the narrowest end of this spectrum. She not only reserves the totalitarian label for Nazism and Stalinism, but sometimes goes so far as to argue that they became properly totalitarian only after the beginning of the Second World War. Arendt's decision to define totalitarianism narrowly stems from her wish to highlight its unprecedentedness. The downside of this, however, is that some regimes that should arguably be recognized as genuinely totalitarian, such as the Soviet Union after Stalin and today's North Korea, are excluded from the Arendtian definition.

While the theme of totalitarianism was not the direct focus of her work in the mid- and late 1950s, it re-emerged as a central issue when one of the key figures in the enactment of the Nazi extermination policy, Adolf Eichmann, was brought to trial in Jerusalem in 1961. Arendt wrote a series of essays on the trial for *The New Yorker* magazine, later published as *Eichmann in Jerusalem*. This sparked an intense controversy, for it not only raised extremely difficult moral questions surrounding the Holocaust but also discussed them in a provocative manner that was widely condemned as utterly inappropriate. Refusing to be intimidated, Arendt kept writing on pressing issues of her time, earning a reputation as a fearless public intellectual in post-war America. Meanwhile, she worked on what turned out to be an incomplete opus, *The Life of the Mind*, building on her earlier observation that Eichmann's evil might be accounted for by his sheer inability to think. Hannah Arendt died of a heart attack in 1975.

Read more about **Arendt's** life and work by accessing the thinker biography on the online resources: www.oup.com/he/Ramgotra-Choat1e.

19.2 The burden of our time

The unthinkable happened in the first half of the twentieth century. A totalitarian movement emerged at the heart of supposedly 'civilized' Europe, destroyed democracies, waged aggressive wars, and established a regime based on ideology and terror. It erected concentration camps across the continent and implemented extermination policies whereby millions of innocent men, women, and children were sent to their deaths. To comprehend this series of events, Arendt writes, is the 'burden which our century has placed upon us' (Arendt 1979: viii).

19.2.1 A new form of government

Arendt insisted that twentieth-century totalitarianism was a new form of government, without any historical precedent. Of course, it was neither the first nor the only type of regime to commit such evils and crimes as aggressive wars, massacres, foreign conquest, slavery, and state-sponsored racism. Even the signature institution of totalitarianism—concentration camps—had been used prior to the rise of Nazism and Stalinism. The notorious pioneers in this regard were the British, who sent tens of thousands of civilians to concentration camps, where some 45,000 died of disease and malnutrition during the Anglo-Boer War of 1898–1902 (Stone, 2017: 18). Nevertheless, it is a mistake, according to Arendt, to see totalitarianism as merely a more extreme version of 'traditional' forms of oppressive government. In fact, it flatly contradicts the classical definition of bad government as arbitrary power. This is the case because totalitarianism, far from being arbitrary, strictly adheres to what Arendt calls 'ideology': a comprehensive set of doctrines that explains literally everything in the past, present, and future. Moreover, it deploys violence and terror if reality as it is does not conform to reality as it ideologically ought to be. For example, if the racist ideology of Nazism stipulates that the law of nature condemns 'degenerate' races such as the Jews as unfit to live, the condemned are not only understood in such terms, but also become targets of extermination. Similarly, if the communist ideology of the Soviet Union stipulates that the law of history condemns aristocrats or wealthy landowning famers as a dying class, the condemned are not only understood in such terms, but also will be liquidated. Ideology and terror complement each other to form the twin pillars of totalitarianism.

Key Concept: Ideology

The term 'ideology' was coined in the late eighteenth century to mean the 'study of ideas', as sociology is the study of society. Under the influence of Marx and Marxists, however, it came to acquire pejorative connotations, highlighting the distorting influences of 'ideological' ideas (read more about Marx in Chapter 13). One may, for example, dismiss liberalism as a 'bourgeois ideology' if one thinks liberalism misrepresents reality, serves the interests of the bourgeoisie, and so on. In her 1950s work, Arendt went further and characterized ideology as not only distorting, but also totally fictitious, seeing Nazism and Stalinism as paradigmatically ideological movements. On this understanding, an ideology is a comprehensive set of ideas deduced from an axiomatically accepted premise such as the 'law' of nature or of history allegedly governing human conduct. Although this conception of ideology is somewhat antiquated today, it provided Arendt with an important tool to analyse key features of Nazism and Stalinism.

Nothing illustrates the infernal nature of totalitarianism better than concentration camps. On a general level, camps come in various forms and sizes, fulfilling functions ranging from confinement and forced labour to extermination. As such, they are not a uniquely totalitarian institution. Not only did imperial Britain use them during the Boer War; democracies today use them to confine refugees and asylum seekers (Parekh, 2016: 17–50; Kreichauf, 2018). However, according to Arendt, camps play a particularly important role under totalitarian regimes, in that they produce thoroughly dehumanized human beings, by means of total terror. Far from being confinement facilities, totalitarian camps are more than even death factories: their inmates are turned into 'living corpses' before finally being killed or left to die of disease, exhaustion, and malnutrition. In an especially chilling part of *The Origins of Totalitarianism*, Arendt characterizes the end of this dehumanization process as follows: 'Nothing . . . remains but ghastly marionettes with human faces, which all behave like the dog in Pavlov's experiments, which all react with perfect reliability even when going to their own death, and which do nothing but react' (Arendt, 1979: 455). Such comprehensive dehumanization, which Arendt calls 'total domination', is the ultimate aim of totalitarianism, because only when no human beings with the power to resist are left can totalitarianism declare its final victory. If unstopped, totalitarianism keeps killing and dehumanizing until the whole earth is filled with no one but 'ghastly marionettes'.

19.2.2 Crystallization

Arendt was by no means the only one trying to understand totalitarianism in the mid-twentieth century. She was aware of some of the competing explanations, but rejected them as exaggerating the continuity between totalitarianism and its alleged precursors. For example, she dismissed the anti-Germanic view, popular at the time, that purported to identify anticipations of totalitarian politics in the history of German thought and culture. She considered it absurd that German thinkers such as Nietzsche, Hegel, and Luther should be held accountable for 'what is happening in the concentration camps' (Arendt, 1994: 108). Similarly, she explicitly criticized the literature on 'political religion', represented by the work of Eric Voegelin, that saw totalitarianism as a kind of perverted religion in the age of secularism (Arendt, 1994: 401–408; Voegelin, 2000). On this view, totalitarianism commanded mass support because it fulfilled the spiritual craving that could no longer be fulfilled by traditional religions. It offered *Mein Kampf* or *Das Kapital* as a substitute for the Bible, the Party as a substitute for the Church, and so on. This body of work again struck Arendt as misguided, because it too 'failed to point out the distinct quality of what was actually happening' (Arendt, 1994: 405).

Arendt proposes the concept of 'crystallization' to characterize her own alternative approach. This elusive concept is open to multiple interpretations, but two aspects of it are worth highlighting. First, crystallization occurs when various elements coalesce under certain conditions. Second, what appears as a result of crystallization is different from any of the coalescing elements. Thus, although individual elements of totalitarianism, such as anti-Semitism, tribal nationalism, racism, and imperial expansion, had existed prior to the twentieth century, what those elements together crystallized into—totalitarianism—was entirely new. Furthermore, Arendt continues, most of the elements of totalitarianism originated from the 'subterranean stream of Western history', rather than its main currents (Arendt, 1979: ix). In other words, totalitarianism must be seen as a *usurper* of 'the dignity of our [i.e., Western] tradition', not a legitimate heir to it (ibid.: ix). This conviction led Arendt, on the one hand, to investigate various obscure sources of totalitarianism. Most notably, she made a pioneering effort to examine the connection between imperialism and totalitarianism, considering how atrocities committed by Europeans against colonial subjects boomeranged back to Europe, resulting in Europeans' atrocity towards each other. On the other hand, she firmly believed that such evils and wrongs as racism and imperialism belonged to 'the subterranean stream of Western history'. This raises the question as to whether she might have been 'whitewashing' the West: for is Western history without racism or imperialism even conceivable?

> ### 19.2 The burden of our time: Key Points
>
> - Arendt conceptualizes totalitarianism narrowly, to mean Nazism and Stalinism at their most violent.
> - According to Arendt, the goal of totalitarianism is 'total domination': the comprehensive dehumanization of each and every human being on Earth.
> - 'Crystallization' is the innovative concept Arendt employs to examine how totalitarianism emerged out of disparate elements belonging to the 'subterranean stream' of Western history.

19.3 The meaning of politics

Arendt has an acute sense of a fundamental historical rupture caused by the political disasters of the twentieth century. As we have seen, age-old concepts such as arbitrary power as the indicator of bad government are no longer adequate for understanding the worst form of government today. Similarly, other basic political concepts such as freedom, power, and indeed politics itself require fundamental reconsideration, because our traditional understandings no longer help us navigate through the new reality. On the basis of this conviction, Arendt undertakes two tasks in search of a new political theory. One is literally to 'think what we are doing' in light of 'our newest experiences and our most recent fears' (Arendt, 1998: 5). The other is to acknowledge the total breakdown of the tradition and to 'discover the past for ourselves—that is, read its authors as though nobody had ever read them before' (Arendt, 2006a: 201). Political thought must begin itself anew.

19.3.1 The specificity of the political

Arendt proposes to reconsider the meaning of politics itself. What is politics? How does it differ from other human activities? Part of her answer lies in the stark contrast she draws between the political and the economic. She conceptualizes the latter in the classical Greek sense of *oikos*, or household: as the sustenance of the biological life of the human animal. The things we do to keep ourselves alive and functioning as members of our biological species, such as procreation and the production and consumption of food, belong to the economic sphere. The political sphere, by contrast, concerns distinctly human life—the life of the citizen or of the member of a community. It is a sphere of freedom, where human life is no longer governed by thirst, hunger, and other biological needs and animal urges. Central to this sphere are action and speech: doing things on one's own initiative, on the one hand, and using words to persuade others and deliberate with others on matters of common concern, on the other. To be free in Arendt's sense is not to do whatever one wants to do, but to act and speak in the public realm. It requires the actualization of what Arendt calls 'natality' and 'plurality' (Arendt, 1998: 7–9, 178, 247). The former designates the innate ability of the human being to start something new and spontaneous; and the latter means the uniqueness of each and every single human being insofar as they are irreducible to mere specimens of *Homo sapiens*. The two human qualities remain dormant, however, unless one takes the opportunity to participate in politics, for it is only through political participation that one may cooperate with others to make a unique contribution to the world that one shares with them. The experience of political participation in turn gives one the sense of 'public happiness', that is, the joy of living in a distinctly human community that the Greeks used to call the *polis*.

Obviously, politics in this sense is very different from politics as we know it in our daily experience. This is the case even in liberal democracies, where citizens are in theory guaranteed the right to political participation. Indeed, individual democratic citizens today hardly ever 'act' or 'speak' in Arendt's sense. On the contrary, their principal form of political participation is voting, which one does alone and silently in a booth, to choose one's so-called representative (Arendt, 1972: 232). Similarly, some of the most extensively debated issues in today's Parliament or Congress—an institutionalized public realm where some action and speech do occur, at least among the representatives—are economic rather than political. They typically concern ways of sustaining biological life, such as the alleviation of poverty and the protection of public health. This makes contemporary politics look more like 'a gigantic, nation-wide administration of housekeeping' than politics in the classical sense (Arendt, 1998: 28).

Why is this the case? Why is politics today so different from what it used to be? Arendt answers this question in terms of the 'rise of the social' (ibid.: 38–49). This is a highly complicated process

(Pitkin, 1998), but her basic view is that the sphere of politics came to be eroded in modernity when economic activities accelerated exponentially to spill out of their original field and infiltrate the public realm, which used to be preserved for politics. 'The social' in Arendt's terminology designates this 'hybrid realm where private interests assume public significance' (Arendt, 1998: 35). One corollary of the expansion of this realm is that politics has come to be reconceptualized in economic terms. Our language of politics is indeed filled with economic metaphors such as 'career politicians' and 'political advertising'. What are we doing when we take part in politics today? Most of us, in Arendt's view, are behaving as though we were involved in an economic transaction.

19.3.2 Philosophy and politics

What is objectionable about the modern reconceptualization of politics as akin to economic activities? One answer Arendt gives is that such politics is powerless to contain the totalitarian threat. She does not think that totalitarianism naturally arises out of defective liberal democracy, wherein everyone sees politics as a kind of economic game for the pursuit of personal gain. This may well be bad politics, but in itself it does not give rise to totalitarianism. Empirically speaking, as we have seen, totalitarianism was an outcome of the crystallization of 'subterranean' elements of Western history. Nevertheless, opportunities to put a stop to a nascent totalitarian movement are likely to be wasted if politics is conducted on the economic model. Arendt takes this to be one of the key lessons of history from 1930s Germany, where most people did nothing to stop Nazism but kept worrying about their private security 'in the midst of the ruins of [their] world' (Arendt, 1979: 338). Unfortunately, the tradition of Western philosophy and political thought have been rather complacent about this sorry state of affairs. A significant part of this tradition has rationalized or even justified the anti-political mindset pervasive among the Germans of the interwar period. Arendt singles out the seventeenth-century English philosopher Thomas Hobbes (read more about Hobbes in Chapter 5) as an exemplar in this context, describing him as a prophet of the coming bourgeois age (ibid.: 139–147). He gave us an analysis of so-called 'human nature', but it was in fact a depiction of the egoistical modern individual terrified of fierce competition in the capitalist economy. Hobbes constructed a systematic political philosophy beginning with this view of 'human nature'. The result, however, was a thoroughly anti-political political philosophy, in which individuals never act or speak but are preoccupied with survival: with, that is, the sustenance of biological life. The Hobbesian modern individual knows no freedom (Hiruta, 2019: 28–29).

> **Key Concept: Tradition**
>
> Arendt accuses the mainstream tradition of Western philosophy and political thought of an anti-political bias. This began with Plato. Dismayed by the condemnation of his teacher Socrates by Athenian citizens, Plato defended a hierarchical division between the rational unity of philosophy and the confused multiplicity of politics (read more about Plato and Socrates in Chapter 2). This division has been inherited by generations of Western thinkers all the way down to Hegel and Marx, all of whom assumed the primacy of philosophy over politics. While Arendt's notion of 'the tradition' is somewhat simplistic, it made her realize the significance of unorthodox political thinkers such as Augustine and Machiavelli, who, on her reading, were partially exempt from the anti-political bias. It never occurred to Arendt, however, that she should study non-Western thought to see if this might provide some resources to counter some of the undesirable tendencies of the Western tradition. She never freed herself from the cage of Eurocentrism.

Hobbes's work, however, is but one variation of the deeper anti-political bias that animates the whole of the Western tradition. Arendt's indictment here is sweeping, stemming from her view that Western philosophy from Plato onwards has had built-in hostility to the contingency and unpredictability that action and speech bring to the human world (Arendt, 2005: 5–39). Philosophy has been monistic, while politics is by nature pluralistic. The former seeks *one* truth that silences all competing opinions, whereas the latter consists in debate, deliberation, negotiation, provisional decision-making, reconsideration, and further debate among a multiplicity of people. Consequently, Arendt continues, philosophers have viewed politics with suspicion, tempted to suppress the haphazardness of human affairs by appealing to the force of truth. She illustrates her point by way of discussing the eighteenth-century French thinker Mercier de la Rivière, who argued that the law of society that he had supposedly discovered should command the same 'despotic force' as does the law of geometry (Arendt, 2006a: 236). According to Arendt, however, Rivière merely articulated the same anti-political bias that tainted Hobbes's work.

In many of her essays devoted to the history of ideas, Arendt reiterates this same claim about the anti-political bias purportedly animating the Western tradition from a variety of angles (e.g. Arendt, 2005; 2006a: 17–169; 2018: 3–68). While her historiography simplifies a good deal, it should be noted that she is not concerned to interpret the Western tradition objectively and impartially. Rather, her intellectual project is to rescue from the past whatever is usable in order to navigate the post-totalitarian present, highlighting the originality of a handful of political thinkers, such as Augustine, Machiavelli, and Montesquieu, who had resisted this bias (see more on Machiavelli in Chapter 25, and Montesquieu in Chapter 11). Her source of inspiration here is her friend, the philosopher Walter Benjamin (1892–1940). Striking an autobiographical note, she writes that the task Benjamin set himself was 'to bend down, as it were, to select his precious fragments from the pile of debris' (Arendt, 1968: 200). As the Western tradition has been irreparably destroyed by the rise of totalitarianism, all those who think today are destined to be waste-pickers amid the ruins.

Key Thinker: Augustine

Augustine of Hippo (354–430), also known as Saint Augustine, is one of Arendt's surprising intellectual heroes. Born in what is now Algeria, he became a follower of Manicheanism as a young man, and his difficult spiritual journey to Christianity is vividly documented in his *Confessions*. Arendt's engagement with Augustine's work was lifelong, beginning with her doctoral dissertation on 'The Concept of Love in Augustine' and ending with her final book, *The Life of the Mind*. Arguably the most important idea that she derives from Augustine is that of natality. It may be doubted if Augustine was really the philosopher of natality she made him out to be; but this objection is perhaps beside the point, for Arendt was willing to inflict considerable interpretive violence on past thinkers if that was necessary to find 'precious fragments from the pile of debris' of the broken tradition.

19.3 The meaning of politics: Key Points

- Arendt conceptualizes the political as the sphere of freedom, in contrast to the economic as the sphere of biological necessity.
- Arendt attributes the transformation of the meaning of politics in modernity to the rise of the social.
- Arendt's sustained effort to reconsider central political concepts is based on her critical view of the tradition of Western philosophy and political thought as having had a persistent anti-political bias.

19.4 'The end of revolution is the foundation of freedom'

Arendt's historical analysis of modernity does not make for happy reading. It is a story of the rise of the social and the decline of the political, leading ultimately to the emergence of totalitarianism. But she is not completely pessimistic about modern history. On the contrary, she finds in it the development of an alternative tradition, in which politics is rediscovered and freedom experienced among ordinary people. This is the tradition of revolutionary politics.

19.4.1 France and America (and Haiti)

Arendt contrasts revolution with rebellion, writing that 'the end of rebellion is liberation, while the end of revolution is the foundation of freedom' (Arendt, 2006b: 133). A rebellion succeeds if the rebels overthrow an oppressive regime and release themselves from chains. A revolution succeeds, by contrast, if the revolutionaries create a new political order in which citizens can and at least occasionally do act and speak in the public realm. Although a revolution typically grows out of an act of rebellion, the successful overthrow of an oppressive regime does not automatically generate a new order of freedom. On the contrary, it sometimes leads to chaos, anarchy, and civil war, giving rise to the establishment of a new oppressive regime. Arendt deploys this conceptual scheme to examine the French and American Revolutions of the late eighteenth century. Her greater sympathy is with that of America, which she sees as a revolution in the proper sense of the term. Revolutionaries there not only overthrew the yoke of monarchical rule by the British but also established a new republic: the United States of America. The French Revolution, by contrast, fell short of being a fully-fledged revolution because it did not yield a stable political order but merely ended the *ancien régime*. To this contrast Arendt adds a further and highly controversial claim about the motives behind the two revolutions, based on her contention that colonial America, unlike pre-revolutionary France, knew no 'mass poverty' (ibid.: 148). According to her, what ultimately motivated the rebels in France was the desire to end material miseries, such as poverty and hunger, whereas what motivated the American revolutionaries was the hope of living in a free republic. In other words, the French were concerned with the social question, while the Americans were concerned with the political. It is little wonder that she held the latter in higher regard.

> **Key Concept: Liberty and freedom**
>
> In some of her writings, Arendt distinguishes explicitly between liberty and freedom. The former means liberty from arbitrary restraints; the latter designates the actual exercise of the distinctly human ability to act and speak in public. Although she does not always adhere to this terminological distinction, the conceptual distinction she draws is an important one, making her one of the most original theorists of freedom in the twentieth century. Her distinct contribution lies in her insistence on the inherent connection between freedom, politics, and action: 'The *raison d'être* of politics is freedom, and its field of experience is action' (Arendt, 2006a: 145). Of course, this idea has attracted criticism, especially from liberals who conceptualize freedom first and foremost as the freedom to choose between different options. To this, Arendtians have made various counter-arguments, and scholars continue to disagree over the 'true' meaning of freedom.

Arendt's discussion of the French and American Revolutions is more nuanced than might be surmised from the short overview of her *On Revolution* provided above. For example, she tells a complicated story as to how the revolutionary spirit that used to animate the early American republic came to be lost in subsequent years, turning the United States into a consumerist mass society (Arendt, 2006b: 207–273). Still, her contrast between the two revolutions has been criticized as simplistic, schematic, and hardly supported by empirical evidence. An especially harsh criticism came from the celebrated Marxist historian Eric Hobsbawm, who wrote that Arendt's discussion of the two revolutions 'at no point . . . touches the actual historical phenomena she purports to describe' (Hobsbawm, 1965: 258). Even some of Arendt's defenders concede her historical inaccuracies, although they regard them as insignificant, arguing that her highly stylized presentation of the two revolutions should be read as a 'fable', to which the normal standards of historical scholarship do not apply (Honig, 1991: 107–108; Young-Bruehl, 2004: 403–404). Arendt's theory of revolution has moreover been criticized for what it does *not* say as well as for what it does. Perhaps her most significant omission is any reference to the Haitian Revolution that unfolded in 1791–1804 in what was then the French colony of Saint-Domingue (read more about the Haitian Revolution in Chapter 18). This revolution would seem indeed to be an ideal case to illustrate Arendt's theory. Beginning as a revolt against slavery and colonial domination by the French, it ultimately led to 'the establishment of an independent Black state by former slaves and their free allies' (Gines, 2014: 74). Yet this extraordinary story of human freedom and new beginnings is completely ignored by Arendt, to many of her readers' disappointment.

Despite these limitations, it would be a mistake to dismiss *On Revolution* simply as bad history written by a theoretician compromised by 'white ignorance' (Mills, 2017: 49–71) (read more about Mills in Chapter 10). The book develops Arendt's highly original insight into the tragic nature of modern politics: politics *qua* action and speech has appeared almost exclusively in times of revolutionary upheavals in modern times, and has thus far lasted only briefly. Her study of revolutionary politics in *On Revolution* thus complements her analysis of the rise of the social in *The Human Condition*. The latter tells how politics came to decline in modernity; the former tells how it has occasionally resurfaced in extraordinary circumstances, unleashing men's and women's potential to act and speak in the public realm. There is a tension between these two sides of Arendt's analysis, however. An important question suggests itself, to which she does not give a satisfactory answer: can politics be institutionalized in modernity, when the conditions of its possibility are constantly undermined by social forces?

> **19.4 'The end of revolution is the foundation of freedom': Key Points**
>
> - Arendt draws a distinction between liberation as the overthrow of an old oppressive regime and revolution as the establishment of a new order of freedom.
> - Arendt's *On Revolution* has been criticized for its neglect of the Haitian Revolution as well as for its historical inaccuracies. It may, however, be read as an original attempt to delineate theoretically a modern revolutionary tradition.

19.5 Between feminism and anti-feminism

Arendt was a female thinker who lived in the male-dominated world of twentieth-century philosophy and political theory. But unlike some of her contemporaries, such as the pioneering French feminist Simone de Beauvoir (1908–1986), she showed little interest in feminist theory and had almost nothing to say on social and political issues concerning gender and sexuality. Moreover, the little she had to say about these issues seems inconsistent, and some of her remarks sound surprisingly conservative. She said, for example, 'I always thought that there are certain occupations that are improper for women, that do not become them, if I may put it that way. It just doesn't look good when a woman gives orders' (Arendt, 1994: 2–3). To take another example, Arendt gave the following advice to William Phillips, an editor, on how to deal with Beauvoir: 'The trouble with you, William, is that you don't realize that she's not very bright. Instead of arguing with her, . . . you should flirt with her' (Arendt and McCarthy, 1995: xiii). How should we assess Arendt's puzzling stance on gender and sexuality?

19.5.1 Arendt as an anti-feminist

Arendt presents her political thought in gender-neutral terms. She is concerned with general issues of high abstraction such as the *human* condition and the *human* capacity for action and speech, rather than with concrete issues specifically related to women's oppression, domination, exclusion, struggle, empowerment, and emancipation. This silence has raised the suspicion that her apparent gender neutrality in effect masks age-old gender biases, and *The Human Condition*, especially the second chapter entitled 'The Public and the Private Realm' (Arendt, 1998: 22–78), is often cited in support of this allegation. Drawing a seemingly inflexible distinction between politics and the public, on the one hand, and the household and the private, on the other, Arendt appears to associate the former pair with various 'masculine' virtues such as courage and responsibility, and the latter with various 'feminine' categories such as the family, the body, birth, nourishment, and species reproduction. Furthermore, her analysis of the 'rise of the social' sometimes strikes a gendered note, as if to say that the feminine sphere of human life—the household—came to contaminate the masculine sphere—the public—such as to undermine the latter's dignity. She writes,

> The distinction between the private and public realms, seen from the viewpoint of privacy rather than of the body politic, equals the distinction between things that should be shown and things that should be hidden . . . The fact that the modern age emancipated the working classes and the women at nearly the same historical moment must certainly be counted among the characteristics of an age which no longer believes that bodily functions and material concerns should be hidden.
>
> (ibid.: 72–73)

Although Arendt's discussion of the public and the private is more nuanced than is often supposed, passages like this have unsurprisingly maddened many a feminist. Adrienne Rich, for example, made the following remark about *The Human Condition*: 'To read such a book, by a woman of large spirit and great erudition, can be painful, because it embodies the tragedy of a female mind nourished on male ideologies' (Rich, 1979: 212).

It is, moreover, not only *The Human Condition* that has been seen as disappointing from a feminist perspective. Arendt's biographical study of the early nineteenth-century German-Jewish *salonnière* Rahel Varnhagen (Arendt, 1997) has attracted the charge that the author is far more interested in Varnhagen's predicament as a Jew than as a woman. A similar criticism has been levelled against Arendt's writings on Jewish issues more broadly. She has been taken to task for failing to extend her insight into the Jewish plight to that of women, at best missing an opportunity to contribute to feminist theory, and at worst ignoring or marginalizing sex and gender as *political* issues, notwithstanding their clear significance. Furthermore, her sporadic remarks on gender differences, as well as the apparently inflexible conceptual distinction she draws in *The Human Condition*, have been seen as suspiciously essentialist: that is, as taking such categories as 'men' and 'women' as givens, rather than as social constructs ideologically produced and reproduced within a specific historical context and power structure. In short, as Mary Dietz observes, some (especially early) feminist critics have taken Arendt to be 'a woman who thinks like a man' (Dietz, 1995: 23).

19.5.2 Arendt as a (proto-)feminist

Despite these criticisms, there is no shortage of feminist attempts to claim Arendt as an idiosyncratic feminist, or at least as someone whose work is not antithetical to feminism. Some partially accept the early reading of Arendt as an anti-feminist, while declining to dismiss her political thought as a whole as unequivocally anti-feminist. For example, Hanna Pitkin (1981; 1998) and Seyla Benhabib (1993; 2003) have both highlighted important ambiguities and inconsistencies discernible in Arendt's work, and proposed a reconstructed Arendtian theory incorporating certain key feminist demands. Others, by contrast, such as Bonnie Honig (1995), Amy Allen (1999), and Mary Dietz (2002), have vigorously repudiated earlier readings of Arendt as an anti-feminist, criticizing Rich and others for imposing *their* gendered and binary framework on Arendt's un-gendered and non-binary thought. By this account, Arendt is an anti-foundationalist *avant la lettre* and her primary contribution to feminism consists in her radically anti-identitarian conception of politics. Categories such as 'women' and the 'private', Honig and others argue, are for Arendt by no means fixed and given but are acquired, contested, and negotiated in a fluid manner, in an endless play of performative acts in politics.

This anti-essentialist reading, for its part, is in conflict with another reading by a different group of feminists, who see Arendt as a theorist of natality, birth-giving, pregnancy, and motherhood. They argue that her thought *is* indeed gendered, but it is so in a pro-feminist way, such as to give expression to women's experiences (Elshtain, 1986; Ruddick, 1989). This body of work has in turn been challenged by yet another group of feminists, according to whom Arendt's conception of natality is not naturalistically connected to the female body or to 'women's experiences' in the abstract. Rather, despite its abstract tendencies, it allows us to appreciate how actual births are experienced differently depending on social contexts and power structures, and how such inequality at birth may result in inequality in individuals' capacity to act, speak, and be free when they mature into adults and citizens (Cavarero, 2016; Söderbäck, 2018).

And so the interpretive debate continues. There is no end in sight to the dispute over 'the "woman question" in Arendt': whether there is a hidden feminist message in Arendt's work. Nor likewise to the dispute over 'the "Arendt question" in feminism': how to locate Arendt in the history of feminist thought (Maslin, 2013: 587–589). One thing that is beyond dispute, however, is that her work has inspired numerous feminist thinkers representing a range of theoretical strands, notwithstanding her own lack of interest in feminist theory. The credit here must go to Arendt's feminist readers as well as to Arendt. The bourgeoning literature on Arendt and (anti-)feminism is a testimony to the intellectual vigour of contemporary feminists, who have tirelessly engaged with and built on Arendt's thought in various ways.

> #### 19.5 Between feminism and anti-feminism: Key Points
>
> - While Arendt showed no interest in feminist theory, this does not necessarily mean that her work has nothing to contribute to it.
> - Although Arendt's work is sometimes seen as anti-feminist, it has inspired many feminist thinkers, who have reinterpreted it from a variety of innovative perspectives.

19.6 Arendt's 'Negro question'

As discussed in Section 19.2, 'The burden of our time', Arendt was one of the first scholars to underline the connection between imperialism and totalitarianism. In her view, it is the imperial experiences of racial domination, global conquest, bureaucratic rule, and administrative violence that made the emergence of totalitarianism 'experientially and conceptually possible if not inevitable' (Mantena, 2010: 91). Thanks to this insight Arendt has earned a reputation as a proto-postcolonial thinker and *The Origins of Totalitarianism* has been hailed as 'a constitutive book for postcolonial studies' (Grosse, 2006: 37; see also Lee, 2011). Nevertheless, both in this book and other writings, Arendt made a number of questionable remarks on race and culture, attracting the charges that she was not only Eurocentric but also a racist and even a 'white supremacist' (Frantzman, 2016). Are these allegations supported by the textual evidence?

19.6.1 Arendt's 'horrific racial stereotypes'

Arguably the most important text in what has come to be known as Arendt's 'Negro question' (Gines, 2014) is the section entitled 'The Phantom World of the Dark Continent' in the second part, on 'Imperialism', of *The Origins of Totalitarianism*. In this section she attempts to trace the beginnings of European racism by way of discussing the experience of Dutch settlers (the Boers) in southern Africa. While this may be a laudable goal, Arendt approaches the issue in a highly controversial manner, using a racially charged language indebted to Joseph Conrad's (2007) novel, *Heart of Darkness*. For example, she describes Africa before European colonization as a 'Dark Continent' inhabited by 'native savages' or 'black savages'. Although they were not literally inhuman or subhuman, the 'savages' were 'prehistoric men' who never transformed nature into a 'human landscape' but, on the contrary, 'treated [it] as their undisputed master' (Arendt, 1979: 190–192). Never having created a specifically human world, they lived 'without the future of a purpose and the past of an accomplishment' (ibid.: 192, 190). In short, Africa was 'a world of folly' (ibid: 191).

This was the world, Arendt continues, in which Dutch settlers arrived in the seventeenth century. Two things soon ensued. First, outnumbered by the native population, the settlers started to commit 'senseless massacre'. But this was, according to Arendt, an understandable reaction on the Boers' part, because such massacres were 'quite in keeping with the traditions of these tribes themselves' (ibid.: 192). Second, confronted by the additional problem of the infertility of the southern African soil, the settlers enslaved 'native savages'. Again, Arendt writes, this 'was a form of adjustment of a European people to a black race', because the Dutch settlers now had to live in fear and misery, surrounded by an entirely hostile nature (ibid.: 193). Besides, it was relatively easy for the Boers to institute a new slavery because, in Arendt's words, '[t]he natives . . . recognized them as a higher form of tribal leadership, a kind of natural deity to which one has to submit; so that the divine role of the Boers was as much imposed by their black slaves as assumed freely by themselves' (ibid.: 193). These are but samples of what Patricia Owens (2017: 405) calls the 'horrific racial stereotypes about Africans' in which Arendt appears to indulge in *The Origins of Totalitarianism*.

Arendt's discussion goes through an interesting turn as she shifts her attention from the Africans to the Boers. As they continued to live in Africa, she writes, this (formerly) European people came to be indistinguishable from 'native savages', notwithstanding the former's enslavement of the latter. They trekked, became nomadic, 'lost the European's feeling for a territory', and went wherever they needed to in order to reap the fruits of nature (Arendt, 1979: 196). Having developed an aversion to settling, cultivating, and creating a specifically human world, the Boers 'behaved exactly like the black tribes who had also roamed the Dark Continent for centuries' (ibid.: 196). Arendt calls this adjustment and change of lifestyle 'degeneration'—degeneration of 'Western man' into the savage (ibid.: 194). According to her, it was during this process of 'degeneration' that the Boers discovered racism. Now that the Boers had 'gone native' (Klausen, 2010: 404), the only thing that separated them from the original natives was the colour of their skin. Race became the only source of identity for the Boers. Thus, in Arendt's view, Boer racism was not something that the Dutch settlers brought from Europe to Africa. Rather, it 'was and remains a desperate reaction to desperate living conditions' (ibid.: 196). Arendt in this way distinguishes between the Boers' experientially-grounded racism and European writers' more theoretical race thinking, although her point is that these two distinct elements eventually merged into the racist ideology of Nazism. The validity of this larger claim need not concern us here, however. The relevant point is that Arendt sounds suspiciously like a racist in her discussion of southern Africa, identifying herself more with the slave-owning and murderous Boers than with the enslaved and massacred Africans.

19.6.2 The world and its other

How should we interpret Arendt's seemingly racist remarks about Africa and Africans? This question received little attention until recently, as the 'Imperialism' part of *The Origins of Totalitarianism* tended to be overlooked in the early Arendt scholarship (see King and Stone, 2007). Most scholars took it for granted that Arendt—a persecuted Jew—could not be a racist, assuming that she used racist language borrowed from Conrad selectively and tentatively, for the sole purpose of helping her readers to understand how the Boers discovered racism. On this reading, Arendt's use of such racist language is purely strategic; it by no means reflects her own views. This reading, however, has been vigorously challenged in recent years, as Arendt's stance on race and culture has come to be subjected to closer scrutiny (e.g., Presbey, 1997; Klausen, 2010; Gines, 2014; Owens, 2017). According to this new body of scholarship, Arendt not only failed to distance herself from the Boers, but also repeatedly made, in her own voice, racially biased comments on Africa and Africans. For example, when she contrasted Africans with Indians and the Chinese, and went on to say that treating the former 'as though they were not human beings' was 'humanly comprehensible' while treating the latter in the same way was not (Arendt, 1979: 206), she was not paraphrasing the Boers' opinions but was expressing her own misguided view of a civilizational hierarchy.

Unfortunately, moreover, *The Origins of Totalitarianism* is not the only work in which Arendt expressed her prejudices against Africans and, for that matter, against African-Americans. Of particular note here is her essay 'Reflections on Little Rock', occasioned by the controversy, beginning in 1957, over the desegregation of Little Rock Central High School in Arkansas (Arendt, 2003: 193–213). Although she never saw herself as a political conservative, Arendt ended up by taking a highly conservative position on this issue, mounting an attack on the school integration movement in the American South, about which she knew next to nothing (see ibid.: 193–213). Similarly, she was not at her best when she dismissed Swahili and African literature as 'nonexistent subjects' that should have no place in education, or when she misrepresented 'Negro students' as uniquely violent compared to their white counterparts during the student rebellion of the 1960s–1970s (Arendt, 1972: 192, 120–121). These errors of judgement, according to some critics, are due at least in part to Arendt's anti-Black racism. In a similar vein, it has been suggested that her anti-Black racism accounts for her aforementioned failure to include Black people's struggles for freedom, such as the Haitian Revolution, in her narrative of human freedom—as if to say that Black history is no part of human history.

The new critical scholarship on Arendt, race, and culture has not persuaded everyone, and some of her readers remain reluctant to accept the charges of racism alleged against her in recent years. By contrast, it is now widely accepted that Arendt is highly Eurocentric and that her work is infected by various *cultural* prejudices. For example, much of her political thought hinges on the distinction she draws between nature as the realm of necessity and the human world as the realm of freedom. Yet the image of the '*human*' world' that she tacitly assumes is the one she is most familiar with: Europe. It is for this reason that she offhandedly dismisses other modes of world-building that do not conform to this image as 'savage' and 'prehistoric', despite her evident lack of knowledge about those modes. As Gail Presbey (1997: 176) argues, it never occurred to Arendt that Africans might have their own 'ways of creating a cultural world that incorporates ritual, dress, ornamentation, and oral literature traditions', rather than exhibiting what Arendt took to be the markers of human civilization, such as building houses, temples, cathedrals, and city walls, on the one hand, and expressing ideas and feelings in the form of written literature, on the other. In short, Arendt's intellectual horizons were narrow when it came to culture. What this limitation implies is far from obvious, however. Does this mean that her political theory remains valid if and only if it is complemented by an additional, anthropologically informed theory of culture? Or do her cultural prejudices rot her theory to the core? Is it possible neatly to separate cultural prejudices from racial ones? Or do Arendt's cultural prejudices in fact slide into racism, as some of her critics have argued? Although Arendt scholarship in the last century largely sidestepped these and other difficult questions raised by her problematic stance on race and culture, an increasing number of researchers today bear the burden of tackling them squarely. We have every reason to hope that this development will continue.

> ### 19.6 Arendt's 'Negro question': Key Points
>
> - *The Origins of Totalitarianism* includes *both* questionable remarks on Africa and Africans *and* penetrating criticisms of imperialism and colonialism.
> - Arendt's racially biased comments are found not only in *The Origins of Totalitarianism* but also in her later work on American politics and society.
> - Arendt's political thought is compromised by her Eurocentrism and cultural prejudices. Whether these weaknesses amount to racism proper remains a matter of debate.

19.7 Conclusion

Hannah Arendt was a political theorist of many paradoxes. She was a Jewish woman and an idiosyncratic Zionist, who antagonized the Jewish community with the publication of *Eichmann in Jerusalem*. She was a female thinker who took little interest in feminist theory or social and political issues specifically related to gender and sexuality. She was a fierce critic of the Western tradition of philosophy and political thought, but she never attempted to expand her intellectual horizons beyond the West. She was in theory opposed to all forms of racism and yet made racially biased remarks in practice, especially with regard to Africa, Africans, and African-Americans. She also had a distinct style of writing, mixing long and densely composed sentences with short memorable ones, reminiscent of the great aphoristic writer Friedrich Nietzsche (more on Nietzsche in Chapter 14). For all these reasons, reading her work is often a disorientating experience, and her readers are presented with both prescient visions and surprising blindness, 'innovative insights alongside outrageous oversights' (Gines, 2014: 30).

It may be tempting to seek an easy way out from such disorientation, either by overlooking her blindness or by ignoring her prescience. Both of these paths are indeed well trodden, and Arendt has attracted blind admirers and bigoted detractors in equal measure. Neither group, however, has done much to help us understand her thought and its legacy. They are one-sided to the extent of becoming mirror-images of each other. A more helpful approach, such as I have attempted to take in this chapter, is to acknowledge the paradoxical nature of Arendt's work and ruminate upon it. I hope to have demonstrated, for example, that her highly complex conceptual apparatus has *both* the ability to expose some of the questionable practices that have been normalized in capitalist modernity *and* the downside of privileging a particular mode of world-building at the expense of others. Similarly, I have tried to show that Arendt's work has simultaneously been criticized for its alleged anti-feminism and praised for its purportedly hidden feminism. To read Arendt is often to navigate through such ambivalences and interpretive divides.

Nevertheless, serious readers of Arendt may agree on at least one thing: she could not be accused of intellectual cowardice. She unfailingly fulfilled what John Stuart Mill called the 'first duty' of a thinker, namely, 'to follow his [or her] intellect to whatever conclusions it may lead' (Mill, 2015: 34). Those who read her work today might be well advised to follow her own example in this respect and engage critically with her work, even if this leads to conclusions that would have surprised her, would disappoint her bigoted detractors, or would irritate her blind admirers.

Take your learning further by accessing the online resources for a library of web links to relevant videos, articles, blogs, and useful websites for this chapter: **www.oup.com/he/Ramgotra-Choat1e**.

Study questions

1. Evaluate Arendt's claim that totalitarianism is a 'novel form of government'.
2. How does Arendt conceptualize politics and what is distinct about her conceptualization?
3. What does Arendt mean by the 'rise of the social'?
4. Why does Arendt think that the tradition of Western philosophy and political thought is of little help to guide political life today?
5. Explain Arendt's distinction between liberation and revolution.
6. How should we assess Arendt's contributions to feminist theory?
7. Why do some scholars see Arendt as an important contributor to postcolonial studies?
8. Analyse the implications of Arendt's Eurocentric biases for her political theory.

Further reading

Primary sources

Arendt, H. (1972) *Crises of the Republic*. New York: Harcourt Brace.
  A collection of Arendt's essays on pressing social and political issues of the turbulent 1960s and 1970s.

Arendt, H. (1979) *The Origins of Totalitarianism*. 3rd edn. New York: Harcourt Brace.
  Arendt's *magnum opus* and a classic in the study of totalitarianism and twentieth-century political thought.

Arendt, H. (1998) *The Human Condition*. 2nd edn. Chicago: University of Chicago Press.
  Arendt's most important philosophical work, investigating the basic human activities of labour, work, and action.

Arendt, H. (2006a) *Between Past and Future: Eight Exercises in Political Thought*. London: Penguin Books.
  An accessible collection of Arendt's essays on political thought, displaying her brilliance as an essayist.

Arendt, H. (2006b) *On Revolution*. London: Penguin Books.
  Arendt's influential but controversial study of the American and French Revolutions.

Secondary sources

Baehr, P. (2010) *Hannah Arendt, Totalitarianism, and the Social Sciences.* Stanford, CA: Stanford University Press.
The best book-length study of Arendt's theory of totalitarianism.

Benhabib, S. (ed.) (2010) *Politics in Dark Times: Encounters with Hannah Arendt.* Cambridge: Cambridge University Press.
An outstanding collection of essays examining major aspects of Arendt's work.

Canovan, M. (1992) *Hannah Arendt: A Reinterpretation of Her Political Thought.* Cambridge: Cambridge University Press.
An exceptionally incisive study and a classic in Arendt scholarship.

Gines, K.T. (2014) *Hannah Arendt and the Negro Question.* Bloomington, IN: Indiana University Press.
A thought-provoking re-examination of Arendt's political theory, focusing on her problematic stance on race.

Hayden, P. (2014) *Hannah Arendt: Key Concepts.* New York: Routledge.
A reliable and accessible overview of Arendt's central ideas.

Hiruta, K. (ed.) (2019) *Arendt on Freedom, Liberation, and Revolution.* Cham: Palgrave Macmillan.
A collection of essays examining the continuing relevance of Arendt's political thought in light of events in the twenty-first century.

Honig, B. (ed.) (1995) *Feminist Interpretations of Hannah Arendt.* University Park, PA: Pennsylvania State University Press.
An excellent collection of essays by leading feminist thinkers, discussing Arendt's contested legacy to feminism from a variety of angles.

King, R.H. and Stone, D. (eds) (2007) *Hannah Arendt and the Uses of History: Imperialism, Nation, Race, and Genocide.* Oxford: Berghahn.
An important collection of essays critically examining the historical side of Arendt's work.

Villa, D. (2021) *Arendt.* New York: Routledge.
A comprehensive overview of Arendt's life and work by one of the leading authorities in the field.

Young-Bruehl, E. (2004) *Hannah Arendt: For the Love of the World*, 2nd edn. New Haven, CT: Yale University Press.
An indispensable biographical study of Arendt's life and work.

References

Allen, A. (1999) 'Solidarity after Identity Politics: Hannah Arendt and the Power of Feminist Theory'. *Philosophy and Social Criticism*, 25(2): 97–118.

Arendt, H. (1968) *Men in Dark Times.* New York: Harcourt Brace.

Arendt, H. (1972) *Crises of the Republic.* New York: Harcourt Brace.

Arendt, H. (1979) *The Origins of Totalitarianism.* 3rd edn. New York: Harcourt Brace.

Arendt, H. (1994) *Essays in Understanding, 1930–1954: Formation, Exile, and Totalitarianism.* Ed. J. Kohn. New York: Schocken Books.

Arendt, H. (1997) *Rahel Varnhagen: The Life of a Jewess.* Ed. L. Weissberg, trans. R. Winston and C. Winston. Baltimore, MD: Johns Hopkins University Press.

Arendt, H. (1998) *The Human Condition.* 2nd edn. Chicago: University of Chicago Press.

Arendt, H. (2003) *Responsibility and Judgment.* Ed. J. Kohn. New York: Schocken Books.

Arendt, H. (2005) *The Promise of Politics.* Ed. J. Kohn. New York: Schocken Books.

Arendt, H. (2006a) *Between Past and Future: Eight Exercises in Political Thought.* London: Penguin Books.

Arendt, H. (2006b) *On Revolution.* London: Penguin Books.

Arendt, H. (2007) *Jewish Writings.* Ed. J. Kohn and R.H. Feldman. New York: Schocken Books.

Arendt, H. (2018) *Thinking Without a Banister: Essays in Understanding, 1953–1975.* Edited by J. Kohn. New York: Schocken Books.

Arendt, H. and McCarthy, M. (1995) *Between Friends: The Correspondence of Hannah Arendt and Mary McCarthy, 1949–1975*. Ed. C. Brightman. New York: Harcourt Brace.

Benhabib, S. (1993) 'Feminist Theory and Hannah Arendt's Concept of Public Space'. *History of the Human Sciences*, 6(2): 97–114.

Benhabib, S. (2003) *The Reluctant Modernism of Hannah Arendt*. New edn. Lanham, MD: Rowman & Littlefield.

Canovan, M. (1992) *Hannah Arendt: A Reinterpretation of Her Political Thought*. Cambridge: Cambridge University Press.

Cavarero, A. (2016) *Inclinations: A Critique of Rectitude*. Trans. A. Minervini and A. Sitze. Stanford. CA: Stanford University Press.

Conrad, J. (2007) *Heart of Darkness*. Ed. O. Knowles and R. Hampson. London: Penguin Books.

Dietz, M.G. (1995) 'Feminist Receptions of Hannah Arendt'. In B. Honig (ed.), *Feminist Interpretations of Hannah Arendt*. University Park, PA: Pennsylvania State University Press, pp. 17–50.

Dietz, M.G. (2002) *Turning Operations: Feminism, Arendt, and Politics*. New York: Routledge.

Elshtain, J.B. (1986) *Meditations on Modern Political Thought: Masculine/Feminine Themes from Luther to Arendt*. New York: Praeger.

Frantzman, S.J. (2016) 'Hannah Arendt, White Supremacist'. *The Jerusalem Post*, 5 June. Available at: https://www.jpost.com/opinion/hannah-arendt-white-supremacist-456007 (accessed: 15 April 2020).

Gines, K.T. (2014) *Hannah Arendt and the Negro Question*. Bloomington, IN: Indiana University Press.

Grosse, P. (2006) 'From Colonialism to National Socialism to Postcolonialism: Hannah Arendt's *Origins of Totalitarianism*'. *Postcolonial Studies*, 9(1): 35–52.

Hiruta, K. (2019) 'Hannah Arendt, Liberalism, and Freedom from Politics'. In K. Hiruta (ed.), *Arendt on Freedom, Liberation, and Revolution*. Cham: Palgrave Macmillan, pp. 17–45.

Hobsbawm, E.J. (1965) 'Review [of Hannah Arendt, *On Revolution*]'. *History and Theory*, 4(2): 252–258.

Honig, B. (1991) 'Declarations of Independence: Arendt and Derrida on the Problem of Founding a Republic'. *American Political Science Review*, 85(1): 97–113.

Honig, B. (1995) 'Towards an Agonistic Feminism: Hannah Arendt and the Politics of Identity'. In B. Honig (ed.), *Feminist Interpretations of Hannah Arendt*. University Park, PA: Pennsylvania State University Press, pp. 135–166.

King, R.H. and Stone, D. (eds) (2007) *Hannah Arendt and the Uses of History: Imperialism, Nation, Race, and Genocide*. Oxford: Berghahn.

Klausen, J.C. (2010) 'Hannah Arendt's Antiprimitivism'. *Political Theory*, 38(3): 394–423.

Kreichauf, R. (2018) 'From Forced Migration to Forced Arrival: The Campization of Refugee Accommodation in European Cities'. *Comparative Migration Studies*, 6(7). doi: https://doi.org/10.1186/s40878-017-0069-8.

Lee, C.J. (2011) 'Hannah Arendt within Postcolonial Thought: A Prospectus'. *College Literature*, 38(1): 95–114.

Mantena, K. (2010) 'Genealogies of Catastrophe: Arendt on the Logic and Legacy of Imperialism'. In S. Benhabib (ed.), *Politics in Dark Times: Encounters with Hannah Arendt*. Cambridge: Cambridge University Press, pp. 83–112.

Maslin, K. (2013) 'The Gender-Neutral Feminism of Hannah Arendt'. *Hypatia*, 28(3): 585–601.

Mill, J.S. (2015) *On Liberty, Utilitarianism, and Other Essays*. Ed. M. Philip and F. Rosen. Oxford: Oxford University Press.

Mills, C.W. (2017) *Black Rights/White Wrongs: The Critique of Racial Liberalism*. Oxford: Oxford University Press.

Owens, P. (2017) 'Racism in the Theory Canon: Hannah Arendt and "the One Great Crime in Which America Was Never Involved"'. *Millennium: Journal of International Studies*, 45(3): 403–424.

Parekh, S. (2016) *Refugees and the Ethics of Forced Displacement*. New York: Routledge.

Pitkin, H.F. (1981) 'Justice: On Relating Private and Public'. *Political Theory*, 9(3): 327–352.

Pitkin, H.F. (1998) *The Attack of the Blob: Hannah Arendt's Concept of the Social*. Chicago: University of Chicago Press.

Presbey, G. (1997) 'Critics of Boers or Africans?: Arendt's Treatment of South Africa in *The Origins of Totalitarianism*'. In E.C. Eze (ed.), *Postcolonial African Philosophy: A Critical Reader*. Cambridge, MA: Blackwell, pp. 162–180.

Rich, A. (1979) *On Lies, Secrets, and Silence: Selected Prose, 1966–1978*. New York: Norton.

Ruddick, S. (1989) *Maternal Thinking: Toward a Politics of Peace*. New York: Ballantine Books.

Söderbäck, F. (2018) 'Natality or Birth?: Arendt and Cavarero on the Human Condition of Being Born'. *Hypatia*, 33(2): 273–288.

Stone, D. (2017) *Concentration Camps: A Short Introduction*. Oxford: Oxford University Press.

Voegelin, E. (2000) 'The Political Religions'. Trans. V.A. Schildhauer. In *Modernity Without Restraint: The Collected Works of Eric Voegelin*, vol. 5. Ed. M. Henningsen. Columbia, MO: University of Missouri Press, pp. 19–73.

Young-Bruehl, E. (2004) *Hannah Arendt: For the Love of the World*. 2nd edn. New Haven, CT: Yale University Press.

20 Zhang Taiyan

VIREN MURTHY

Chapter guide

Zhang Taiyan is perhaps most famous for promoting propaganda against the Manchu minority who ruled the Qing dynasty (Section 20.2). However, he was many things to different readers: a scholar, a revolutionary, a Buddhist, and a pan-Asianist (Sections 20.3 and 20.4). This chapter does not cover all of the different aspects of Zhang Taiyan's thought, but focuses on those elements that are relevant to political theory, namely, his ideas of revolution, nationalism, and especially his brief attempt to construct a new politics. Zhang has written an enormous amount and his complete works span eight volumes. He wrote numerous essays on history, philology, anti-Manchu propaganda and political theory, often influenced by Buddhism. It is recommended that students of political theory read both his writings against the Manchu government and also his Buddhist-inspired articles. In what follows, however, Zhang's anti-Manchu writings are outlined, before devoting space to his Buddhist writings. Section 20.5 finally shows how some of the ideas present in his Buddhist political theory are picked up by the post-war Japanese intellectual Takeuchi Yoshimi (1910–1977).

20.1 Introduction

Most studies on the works of Zhang Taiyan (1869–1936) are historical and therefore focus on the area where his impact is most clearly seen, namely his role as a propagandist during the 1911 Revolution. The 1911 Revolution overthrew the last Chinese Dynasty, the Qing dynasty, which was ruled by a Manchu minority from North-east China. (The majority ethnic group in China is the Han; today the Manchus are the largest minority ethnic group without an autonomous region.) This revolution signalled the end of over two thousand years of Chinese dynastic rule. From the standpoint of political theory, Zhang's anti-Manchu propaganda does not produce much that is new. But in the process of becoming a nationalist, he also transformed and came to anticipate Third World nationalism. As Zhang developed propaganda for the overthrow of the Qing government, he was incarcerated after a famous trial in 1903 and spent three years in jail. In jail, he avidly read Buddhist texts and these concepts fundamentally changed the nature of his political thought. In particular, after being released from jail, he mobilized concepts of 'Yocācāra', or 'consciousness-only Buddhism', to construct a new idea of universality that has great relevance to political theory. In short, this is a theory in which the universal does not eliminate or completely subsume the particular.

Read more about **Zhang's** life and work by accessing the thinker biography on the online resources: www.oup.com/he/Ramgotra-Choat1e.

20.2 Zhang Taiyan as anti-Manchu revolutionary

Zhang Binglin was born on 20 January 1869 in Yuhang prefecture of Zhejiang, a coastal province in South China. In recollections, Zhang noted that some of his earliest influences came from his maternal grandfather, Zhu Youqin, who taught Zhang to read the Chinese classics. In his *Autobiography*, Zhang explained that, at a young age, he learned about the distinction between the Manchus and the Han and described how he was moved when reading about scholars from the Ming dynasty (1368–1644). He was especially influenced by those scholars who were born during the Ming dynasty but whose lives traversed the Manchu-dominated Qing dynasty (1644–1911). These Ming loyalists were disappointed with the transition to the Qing dynasty and constantly dreamt of a return to the Ming. Zhang was extremely influenced by two loyalists in particular: Gu Yanwu (1613–1682) and Huang Zongxi (1610–1695), who are well known for advocating local autonomy against the imperial government (and whom, consequently, sinologists—those who study Chinese language, history, and culture—sometimes associate with Chinese early modernity). In fact, Zhang later took on the name Taiyan in order to honour Huang Zongxi (also known as *Tai*chong) and Gu *Yan*wu (Laitinen, 1990).

20.2.1 Zhang's classical learning amidst political events

Zhang first immersed himself in classical learning and although he had great success in his early studies of the classics with relatives, he never succeeded in passing the official examinations, which would have secured for him a job in the government. In 1883, when Zhang was 14 years old, his father told him to take the local district examinations, but he could not take the exams due to a fit of epilepsy a few minutes prior to the test. Zhang would never again take imperial examinations, and some suggest that Zhang's later criticism of the examination system and imperial government may be related to this early experience (Takada, 1974: 9). In the following years, Zhang continued to study the classics, but did not aim to take the examination and this allowed him the freedom to rethink the classics in creative ways, including mobilizing classical ideas against existing structures of power.

To understand the world that Zhang faced, we must briefly mention some of the setbacks that China faced beginning in the mid-nineteenth century. In 1842, China was famously defeated in the First Opium War. Chinese intellectuals and officials realized that they were technologically inferior to the West, but they did not want to fundamentally alter their culture. This led to the 'Self-Strengthening Movement'. The Chinese official Zhang Zhidong (1837–1909) pithily encapsulates the ideology behind this movement in his phrase 'Chinese learning as substance, Western learning as application.' By this, he meant that China could import technologies from the West, but should not alter its basic Confucian culture.

Key Thinker: Confucius

Confucianism is taken to be founded by the philosopher and political figure Confucius (551–479 BCE), whose teachings remain enormously important today in China and East Asia. His teachings were collected in the *Analects* long after his death. Confucius confronted a world in chaos and war; he believed that as the ancient rituals declined, people lost touch with practices such as humanity, righteousness, and filial piety. By rituals, Confucius meant specific rites, manners, and conventions, including sacrifices to ancestors. He believed that such practices had the power to transform human relations and make the polity harmonious. From the nineteenth century, many Chinese intellectuals had believed that because China needed to modernize, backward-looking philosophies such as Confucianism were obsolete. Others, however, argued that Confucius was actually a reformer who used the past to envision new political forms. They believed that the political philosophy of Confucius was meaningful beyond its specific historical context.

This movement was greatly challenged in 1895 when China lost the first Sino-Japanese War, between China's ruling Qing Dynasty and Japan, which was a watershed in Chinese intellectual history. In particular, the loss delegitimized much of the previous Self-Strengthening project, because much of its rhetoric was about making the country strong and yet it could not even defeat Japan, which Chinese historically considered a weaker and geographically smaller country.

Before the first Sino-Japanese War, not only did the Chinese think of themselves as superior to their neighbours because they were the central system in which neighbouring states would pay them tribute, but this view was also shared by the rest of the world (Elman, 2003: 84). After the first Sino-Japanese War, China began to see the need to catch up with various other nations, including the nations of Western Europe and Japan.

20.2.2 Zhang's nationalism in relation to reformers

At this time, many intellectuals were united in thinking that political reform required reforming political theory and this required rethinking both the West and China's own past. Intellectuals and officials, including Zhang Zhidong, Tan Sitong (1865–1898), Kang Youwei (1858–1927), and Zhang Taiyan would each combine religion with science to develop an ontology, which would be fundamentally political.

During the late Qing, politics was split between reformers and revolutionaries. Put simply, Kang Youwei and other reformers attempted to modernize politics within the Qing imperial system and transform China into a constitutional monarchy. Zhang Taiyan and his revolutionary cohorts, on the other hand, aimed to both overthrow the Manchu-led Qing dynasty and create a republic based on their image of Western countries, such as France. The ideal of a republic entailed overcoming the dynastic system and developing Western-style institutions including parliaments.

From this perspective, the political struggle between the reformers connected different narratives of the Chinese nation to the political form of China's future. Kang and the reformers proposed a relatively tolerant vision in which China is defined culturally and minority groups such as the Manchus could become Chinese by practising Chinese culture. Against this, Zhang and his cohort are famous for stressing that China must be ruled by the Han as opposed to the Manchus. They conceived of a racial opposition between the Han-Chinese and the Manchu invaders.

Much of the scholarship on Zhang has focused on this racialist dimension of his thought and, if one is not historically sensitive, one might even compare his emphasis on the Han race to white supremacism. However, during the late nineteenth and early twentieth centuries, when the Western biological concept of race entered China, the Manchus were a ruling minority. Therefore, Zhang mobilized the concept of race against the Manchu rulers and compared them to the British and the Moguls, who ruled India. Moreover, Zhang pushed this racialist logic to the extreme and contended that, after the revolution, the Manchus, Tibetans, and Mongols should be able to form their own nations. Note that when the 1911 Revolution actually occurred, most revolutionaries stopped being anti-Manchu, since it would have involved conceding a large amount of territory. Zhang also conceived of the Han race as more advanced than the other races in China and this could have formed the foundations for Han chauvinism as it has resurfaced in China during the past few decades. However, as we shall see, much of Zhang's Buddhist philosophy of equality goes against this idea of Han chauvinism. To understand this, we need to focus on the common temporal framework shared by both reformers and revolutionaries.

Nationalists are usually wedded to two conflicting narratives of time. On the one hand, nations claim to be more modern and advanced than previous forms of communities; on the other hand, they constantly struggle to show their ancient historical roots. In other words, they simultaneously attempt to be of the future and the past. In late developing countries, such as China, scholars reinterpreted the past in response to the West. The question was how they would do this.

With respect to the first gesture, namely, turning to the past, Kang and his cohort tended to return to the classical Chinese thinker Confucius and then see radical ideas there, while using Confucius to stress the cultural identity of China, which could constantly allow different ethnicities to become Chinese. However, they attempted to reconcile going back to Confucius with the project of legitimizing modern institutions. For example, Kang's younger colleague Tan Sitong contended that the many modern institutions, including a representative state, were already there in ancient China before the time of Confucius. From this perspective, although the West had overtaken China, they were only doing this because they unknowingly imitated the Chinese past. Kang Youwei thus famously claimed that Confucius was a reformer.

Zhang and other revolutionaries were critical of Confucius and some would argue this was precisely to attack the reformers. They would eventually become more interested in the margins of the Chinese philosophical traditions, including Buddhism and Daoism, and stress a different lineage going back to the Han Yellow Emperor. We could characterize this difference as a difference between cultural nationalism (reformers) and ethnic nationalism (revolutionaries). I will return to the problem of nationalism below, but first we should note that initially both revolutionaries and reformers underscored a concept of linear evolution, which entailed numerous changes in Chinese political theory.

Key Concept: Daoism

Daoism is a classical Chinese philosophy. Daoism was founded by Laozi (dates unknown, but usually thought to have lived around the sixth to the fourth century BCE). Daoism is usually thought of in opposition to Confucianism: Laozi and his followers believed that the rituals and concepts advocated by Confucius were themselves part of the problem and that one needed to return to nature or the way (the Dao). Laozi's most famous disciple is Zhuangzi and Zhang Taiyan wrote a famous commentary on his text.

As Chinese intellectuals and officials rethought notions of time, they began to use new political categories to characterize their pasts and futures around the world. Many of these categories came through the West, but were mediated by Japan. Once China saw Japan as a modern nation and Japan accepted its role as teacher, the two countries developed an exchange programme for Chinese students to study in Japan. During the first year of the programme in 1896, only six Chinese students went to Tokyo to study, but by the years 1905–1906, there were already between 8,000 and 9,000 (Harrell, 1992: 1–2). Zhang Taiyan would travel to Japan three times, and he constantly interacted with students and intellectuals in Tokyo, who were also engaged in spreading ideas of political reform and searching for new theories in Japanese translation. In many cases, Chinese scholars and students would use Japanese translations as a window into the world of Western political theory.

These translations helped to introduce Chinese intellectuals to a new temporality of politics and to put China in a frame of progressive history. As Satō (1996) explains, until the late nineteenth century, Chinese intellectuals translated a number of works on technology, but after the first Sino-Japanese War, there was a vast amount of political and social scientific works being translated into Chinese from both Western and Japanese sources. Various groups, including anarchists, republicans, and constitutional monarchists, proposed a number of different political visions of the future Chinese polity; however, despite profound differences in their views, Chinese intellectuals began to concur that the Chinese past should be called despotic (*zhuanzhi*) and that China should be called a 'monarchical despotism' (ibid.: 315). This was linked to a negative view of the past, and to evolutionary theories of politics and society, which asserted that various countries needed to advance through a stage of monarchical despotism before becoming either a constitutional monarchy or a republic.

> **Key Concept: Monarchical despotism**
>
> In the term 'monarchical despotism' (*junzhu zhuanzhi*), we should place the emphasis on 'despotism', which entails a clear negative value judgement. Before the early twentieth century, Chinese intellectuals used Indigenous terms to describe the political structures of their past. Now it would all be called despotic, suggesting a thorough negation of the past.

20.2.3 The revolutionary Zhang Taiyan

Kang Youwei reformulated a narrative of universal progress by drawing on Indigenous Confucian discourses of civilization. This narrative reimagined the Qing Empire as a modern nation state: a nation in which Chinese identity is culturally defined to include both Manchus and Han. In Kang's view, empire and nation exist in a mutually reinforcing relationship. He aimed to combine the strength of the nation with the respect for difference that he found in empires. Initially, Zhang followed the reformers and supported their civilizational narrative. Although he questioned the validity of Confucianism, he did not explicitly promote anti-Manchu revolution. After 1900, however, due to the failure of a series of reform attempts, Zhang advocated anti-Manchu revolution as part of an evolutionary narrative. During this period, Zhang shared with late Qing reformers and revolutionaries a broad framework informed by narratives of progressive civilization. We see this in the writings of Zhang's younger fellow revolutionary Zou Rong. Zou famously connected revolution to evolution in his famous text, *The Revolutionary Army*, for which Zhang wrote the preface. Zou writes:

> Revolution is the universal principle of evolution. Revolution is a universal principle of the world (*shijie zhi gongli*). Revolution is the essence of the struggle for survival or destruction in a time of transition. Revolution follows heaven and responds to human needs. Revolution rejects the corrupt and keeps the good. Revolution is the advance from barbarism to civilization. Revolution turns slaves into masters.
>
> (Tsou, 1968: 58, Zou, 2002: 8)

This passage lucidly connects revolution and evolutionary civilization. Zou weaves traditional ideas such as the belief that 'revolution follows heaven' (*shun tian*) into a vision of progressive history. From this perspective, heaven is not governed by cosmic principles, but by the scientific laws of the universal principle (*gongli*).

> **Key Concept: *Gongli***
>
> The term *gongli*, 'the universal principle', is a compound of two Chinese characters: 'gong 公', meaning public or universal, and 'li 理', meaning pattern or principle. The term 'principle' became important during the Song dynasty (960–1279), when Zhu Xi made it one of the central concepts of his interpretation of Confucianism. He combined it with the character for heaven (*tian*) and coined the term 'heavenly principle' or *tianli*. During the late Qing, as scholars became interested in Western science, they continued to use the term principle, but were sceptical of the Confucian idea of heaven. Consequently, they coined couplets, such as *wuli*, literally 'the principle of things', to translate physics. *Gongli* should be understood in the same light, but it applies more widely to society and history.

In this manner, Zou placed Chinese history on a linear passage moving away from despotism and he clearly took the West as a goal. Indeed, it is perhaps strange to find that one of the most famous revolutionary tracts of early Chinese nationalism begins with a sentence that advocates cleansing 'ourselves of 260 years of harsh and unremitting pain, so that . . . the descendants of the Yellow Emperor will all become Washingtons' (Tsou, 1968: 58, Zou, 2002: 7). By writing the preface for this book, Zhang endorsed the basic thrust of the book, but his vision of the world, history, and time would change in the next few years.

Zhang and Zou promoted evolution as part of their attack on the Manchu government and they made numerous statements against the emperor and the Qing dynasty. In 1903, after a famous trial, both Zhang and Zou were convicted of plotting to overthrow the Qing government and sentenced to jail. Zou Rong died in prison in 1905, but Zhang survived and, according to his own account, he was able to survive his experience in jail because he avidly read the texts of Yocācāra Buddhism. After his imprisonment from 1903 to 1906, Zhang rejected this narrative of evolution and reimagined anti-Manchu revolution in a way that emphasized the nation over universal evolution. Zhang links anti-Manchuism to a global movement against Western imperialism, and this shift coincides with his so-called turn to a Buddhist voice during the years 1906–1910.

Zhang moved away from the West during a period when many Chinese intellectuals vociferously resisted imperialism. This reached its high point in 1905, when Zhang was still in jail. At this point, people advocated boycotting American goods and protested against the ill treatment of Chinese workers in the United States. Moreover, during the early twentieth century, the Chinese identified with oppressed people around the world, which explains the popularity of the translation of *Uncle Tom's Cabin*, which was rendered as *Heinu yutian lu* ('Black Slaves Appeal to Heaven') (Meng, 2006: 126–127).

When Chinese intellectuals and officials linked the West with imperialism, they shifted their view of China in relation to weaker nations. Rather than warning the Chinese to avoid the fate of the colonized, they affirmed China's status as a poor nation, and moreover sought a narrative of resistance based on Asian unity. After Zhang left jail, he would also push his ideas in this anti-Euro-American direction. When Zhang was released from jail in 1906, he travelled to Japan and became the chief editor of *Minbao* (*The People's Journal*). In Japan, he met Japanese radicals, such as the anarchist Kōtoku Shūsui (1871–1911), and these meetings contributed to his increasingly critical stance towards the West and his promotion of Asian identity. During this period, Zhang participated in the Society for the Study of Socialism and the Asian Solidarity Society, to which I will turn next.

20.2 Zhang Taiyan as anti-Manchu revolutionary: Key Points

- Zhang Taiyan developed a theory of anti-Manchu revolution, which separated the Han and the Manchu races and advocated the overthrow of the Qing dynasty.
- He aimed to create a Republic with Western institutions such as a constitution, but eventually turned to become critical of Western imperialism.
- He was sent to jail in 1903 for plotting to overthrow the government and here he began to read Buddhism, which he used to construct a novel political theory, which would be part of his search for an alternative path for China and Asia.

20.3 Pan-Asianism and different types of transnationalism

In Tokyo, where he stayed until the 1911 Revolution, Zhang came into contact with numerous different leftist viewpoints, including Kōtoku Shusui's anarchism. In 1901, Kōtoku famously published a tract critically analysing imperialism (Kōtoku, 2004; Tierney, 2015), with which Zhang must have been familiar. In this text, Kōtoku not only criticized imperialism, but simultaneously attacked nationalism and the state, which allowed him to link his critique to an anarchist position. The second chapter of this book was about nationalist sentiment (*aikokushin*) and Kōtoku argued that national sentiment was produced by a mind of 'wild animal nature, superstition, craziness and belligerence' (Kōtoku, 2004: 48; Ishimoda, 1963: 400). Moreover, in other writings during the same period, he claimed that the Koreans must realize that the only way for them to be free from the humiliation of imperialism is to negate the concept of the state (ibid.: 391).

20.3.1 In defence of anti-colonial nationalism

Zhang follows the anarchist position to some extent. For example, drawing on Buddhist categories, he argues that the state was tantamount to a fiction. In this essay, 'On the State', published in 1907, he makes three points. First, the state is 'posited' and not real. Second, contrary to the claim of many late Qing thinkers that the state follows from principle, 'one establishes a state because the situational propensities (*shi*) leave one no other choice; it does not follow from principle' (Zhang, (1977 [1907]): 359). Finally, the state is extremely lowly rather than sacred. Of the three points, the first most directly draws on Buddhism and was one that his anarchist audience would have found appealing. The key Buddhist concept that Zhang uses is the 'atom' (*yuan zi*). He includes a note explaining that the early Buddhists had a theory of atoms, which he will use to analyse the state. Zhang is probably referring to the *paramāṇu* (*weichen*), which Yogācāra Buddhists used to designate the smallest unit.

Although anarchists would have liked the thrust of this essay, he ends up defending anti-colonialism nationalism in the present world. He contends that, in powerful countries, patriotism leads to imperialism, but weak countries need patriotism to resist being colonized (ibid.: 367). He repeatedly argued that just as India had fallen to Britain, China had already fallen to the imperialist Manchus and thus he conceived of his anti-Manchuism as part of a global struggle against imperialism.

In this manner, Zhang went against Kōtoku's arguments for anarchism and took the nation state as a vehicle through which greater transformation could be possible. Like Third World nationalists about a half a century later, he argued that the nationalism of oppressed nations could be the beginning of a transnational movement towards a new global order. As evidence of this, in Tokyo, he famously organized an Asia Solidarity Society, which brought together intellectuals from Japan, India, Burma, and other Asian, colonized nations, to resist imperialism. Zhang wrote the constitution for this Society, which gives us an insight into his logic:

> Among the various Asian countries, India has Buddhism and Hinduism; China has the theories of Confucius, Mencius, Laozi, Zhuangzi and Yangzi; then moving to Persia, they also have enlightened religions, such as Zoroastrianism ... About one hundred years ago, the Europeans moved east and Asia's power diminished day by day. Not only was their political and military power totally lacking, but people also felt inferior. Their scholarship deteriorated and people only strove after material self-interests. India fell first and then China was lost to the Manchus ... Only Siam and Persia remain independent; however, they are also in the process of declining.
>
> (Zhang, 1981: 428)

Zhang constructed a counter-discourse against a progressive vision of history with Europe at the centre by promoting the civilizational or cultural unity of Asia. He still aimed at realizing national independence, but considered nationalism as part of a transnational process involving regional unity. In this constitution, Zhang identifies Asia only in terms of culture, philosophies, and religions. He does not mention regional unity with respect to trade or political interplay. He only underscores that, in the eastern part, people treated each other with Confucian benevolence and almost never invaded one another. In Zhang's view, Asian states had separate boundaries, but they did not invade one another and were relatively peaceful until Western dominance. Zhang placed this original utopia in a larger temporal narrative of return. Zhang affirmed that nationalism was a type of return to a past before colonization; it was not a form of progression. Colonialism, therefore, is conceived as a rupture that makes pan-Asianism necessary.

Zhang explains that Europeans moved eastward about a hundred years ago and this transformed how Asians conceived of themselves. Once the Europeans invaded, Asian nations began to feel inferior: their view of themselves became mediated by the West. The term that Zhang used for feeling inferior—*zibei*—could also imply looking down on oneself. He explains why such a feeling emerges in the next sentence: 'scholarship declined and people strove after material interests'. Through the mediation of the West, Asian nations took material wealth as a standard and from this perspective did not measure up to the imperialist countries.

20.3.2 The roots of socialism in Chinese culture

In texts written during this period, Zhang attacks a culture that becomes dominant in capitalism. The interpretations of historians such as Hazama Naoki and Lin Shaoyang, who each claim that Zhang's critique of imperialism did not target capitalism (Hazama and Matsumoto, 1990: 249; Lin, 2014: 208), are to some extent correct: Zhang, unlike later Chinese and Japanese intellectuals, does not explicitly use the term for capitalism. Nonetheless, the concepts of imperialism and capitalism mutually entail one another, especially during this period: Zhang criticizes the effects of capitalism without always naming it. He narrates a transition from a world where scholarship dominates to one where people merely pursue their own interests. Early in Zhang's text, we see that by scholarship he includes Confucianism, Buddhism, and other religions that were connected to morality and self-respect. However, as Western imperialism encroaches on Asia, scholarship declines and is replaced by self-interest, where, as Marx and Engels (1978) would say, all holy shrines are washed in the cool waters of egoistic calculation. Zhang does not analytically separate capitalism from imperialism and analyse them or their connection, but he does identify a shift that takes place as capitalism becomes global through imperialism. His criticisms of capitalism are fewer than his attacks on imperialism. Nonetheless, he is conscious of this problem as he tries to revive tradition. We see this consciousness of capitalism in a speech given to Chinese exchange students in Tokyo, given shortly after he arrived in 1906. He makes the following point about the Imperial Examination System:

> Because of such a system, even poor people had hopes of becoming officials. Had this not been the case, study to gain official positions would have to have been left exclusively to the rich. The poor would have sunk to the bottom of the sea, and the day when they participated in political power would not come for a long time ... Our present reverence for our own tradition is nothing less than a reverence for our own socialism.
>
> (Shimada, 1990: 41)

By invoking the term 'socialism' (*shehuizhuyi*), Zhang implicitly criticises capitalism. Zhang translates the Chinese historical institution of the examination system into the socio-political project of socialism. Through this manoeuvre, the Chinese past (the tradition, the examination, and so on) becomes the future (socialism as a goal towards which to strive). This is a 'back to the future' effect in which the significance of temporal distinctions has changed. Capitalism is the unsaid present in Zhang's discourse. Zhang associates capitalism with the West and as something to be overcome or avoided through a socialist future. He expresses this same point by discussing China and the West earlier in the same speech when dealing with the equitable field system. He explains:

> What China has been particularly superb at, something the countries of the West can absolutely not approach, is the equitable field (*juntian*) system; this institution conforms to socialism, to say nothing of the well field (*jingtian*) system of the Three Dynasties of high antiquity. From the Wei and Jin eras through the Tang, the equitable field system was in effect.
>
> (ibid.: 40)

Zhang extols the Chinese past to legitimate the Chinese nation. However, the way in which he does this again gestures towards socialism, and by making the contrast with the West he implies an opposition to capitalism. The West will not be able to overcome their chronic inequalities because they have become capitalist. In Zhang's discourse, the opposition between China and the West resembles the opposition between socialism and capitalism. Through the mediation of the West, Zhang reinterprets the Chinese past as something that points beyond the present. However, imperialism and Eurocentrism block this movement to the future. Those who follow the ideology of Western superiority assert that a move back to an Asian past must imply being stuck in an anachronistic past, which cannot point to a different future.

20.3.3 India and China at the centre of Asian unity

Zhang counters the feeling of inferiority mentioned in the constitution by opening a space of Asian traditions to be used to imagine new political ideals. By re-evaluating Asian philosophies, he dislocates Asia from the spatio-temporal matrix that places it in the past and propels the Chinese classics into the future. Zhang aims to liberate Chinese and Indian pasts and by extension the Asian past. However, such a project is connected to actual anti-colonial struggles in Asia. After all, the Asian past became a problem primarily because of Western colonialism and, if there is insufficient resistance, various Asian nations would disappear. He explains how various nations in Asia have either come under the yoke of colonialism or have faced this threat in some way.

In his narration of successive colonialisms, the sequence is important. India is especially significant because it was colonized first and Zhang notes a similarity between India and China. The latter half of the constitution of the Asia Solidarity Society addresses the question 'what must be done to overcome the problem of imperialism?' The answer is now thought of in terms of international strategy and India and China become central to this.

> In the past, the thirty-six countries of Tianshan met with the invasions of the Tujue and Huihu barbarians; as the result the various races of Tianshan were destroyed. It appears that at a later time, China, India, Vietnam, Burma, the Philippines and other Asian countries will suffer a fate similar to the thirty-six countries of Tianshan. Learning from the experience of Tianshan, we establish the 'Asian Solidarity Society' in order to resist imperialism and protect our nation states. In the future, we hope to drive away the foreign races and stand mighty. The various groups of the South-east will mutually help each other and form a web of resistance. We must unite the various clans and resuscitate old, but broken friendships. We must revitalize our Hinduism, Buddhism, Confucianism and Daoism and develop our compassion in order to squeeze out the evil Western superficial morality. We will lead the sages to avoid being conquered by the whites. We will not follow separatism

and we shall not bow to form. All of our close friends of several different types have not completely united. First, India and China must unite to form a group. These two old countries of the East are huge and if they can be fortunate and obtain independence, they will form a shield for the rest of Asia. The remaining dozen neighbouring countries can therefore avoid being bullied. All nations of Asia who support independence, if you want to take this precious step and take an oath to unity, pray that such unity arrives.

(Zhang, 1981: 429)

In Zhang's view, the international situation of his time was similar to the situation of the Qin and Han dynasties and he implies that the Western invasion of Asia is similar to the barbarian invasion of the thirty-six countries of the Tianshan. Kang Youwei had already compared the Chinese past to the late Qing present. Zhang follows Kang in hoping to resist a full repetition of the past, since the first time the barbarians invaded, they transformed society. Yet while Kang aims for unity, Zhang underscores diversity. Zhang laments that after the barbarian invasion, the variety of races decreased and the place was unified. Zhang fears that this would happen again with contemporary Asian states, such as Burma, India and China: the West could annihilate the cultural plurality of Asia through force.

In Zhang's view, Asia became united because each of the individual states were invaded by Western powers; however, to resist this invasion, Asian nations must become self-conscious of this unity. In other words, he contends that by struggling for independence these nations would create a unity beyond their cultural diversity. He hopes to revive earlier teachings and religions to combat the morality of egoism. Asian people must fight imperialism both culturally and militarily. Moral ideology is of course imbricated in military battle, since moral teachings enable transcendence. The constitution of the Society asserts that Asian people should not bow to form, which implies that Asians should both resist the physical power of the imperialists and refuse their ideology of focusing on the outer form of material goods. Hinduism, Buddhism, Confucianism, and Daoism each emphasize the transcendence of material goods; by following such teachings pan-Asianists will not be seduced by the lure of the West, and they will also have the mental power to resist large military powers against the odds.

Just as in the case of nations that were colonized, we should note the sequence in which Zhang names these religions. Zhang notes that 'India has Buddhism and Hinduism', before referring to numerous Chinese teachings. Buddhism originated in India but developed throughout East Asia and it is important to note how Zhang mobilizes Buddhism against the West in works of this period as part of his overall plan of resistance. Zhang uses Buddhist terms throughout the constitution to discuss the difference between Asia and the West. He invokes, for example, the Buddhist term *zhantuoruo* (*cendala*) or evil to describe Western morality. He counters this evil morality by drawing on Buddhism to construct a new political theory.

20.3 Pan-Asianism and different types of transnationalism: Key Points

- Zhang's support for pan-Asianism implies that anti-imperialist nationalism and imperialist nationalism are fundamentally different.
- Zhang mobilizes a vision of Asian culture against what he sees as Western capitalist culture.
- Consequently, anti-imperialist nationalism is for Zhang connected to socialism.

20.4 Buddhism vs Hegel: towards a new universality

After he fled to Japan in 1906, Zhang began drawing on Yogācāra Buddhism intensely to formulate a critique of modernity and in particular linear time. During his time in Tokyo, he reread the Daoist classics and gave extremely influential lectures on the *Zhuangzi* (the writings of Laozi's disciple Zhuangzi and a foundational text of Daoism—see Key Concept: Daoism). Among the audience at these lectures were Lu Xun (1881–1936), the father of modern Chinese literature, and Chen Duxiu (1879–1942), who would go on to found the Communist Party of China. Zhang unfolds a type of synthesis of Buddhism and the *Zhuangzi*, to formulate an alternative theory of equality and difference. He undercuts the universality of the West, often presupposed by progressive visions of history, and he aims to realize a universality that is reconciled with particularity.

20.4.1 Zhang's confrontation with Hegel

G.W.F. Hegel (1770–1831) developed a philosophy with many dimensions, but for our purposes a bare outline of his position on history will suffice, since we are primarily interested in Zhang's critique. Unlike most modern philosophers, who presuppose that one can directly derive eternal truths, Hegel believed that knowledge and ideas were fundamentally conditioned by culture and history. In his philosophy of history, he shows how spirit or self-consciousness realizes freedom in history. According to Hegel, the story of freedom begins in Asian regions, such as China, but it remained extremely abstract. Freedom eventually evolved to become concrete in Greece and modern Europe. In Hegel's view, in China only the emperor was free and this freedom lacked the proper institutions to make this determinate. As European societies became modern, modern concrete freedom developed along with the emergence of market societies and the state. In such a configuration, people could realize individual freedom at the level of the market (civil society), but this would be reconciled with communal freedom at the level of the state. Zhang will use Buddhism and Daoism to attack both Hegel's evolutionary vision of history and what he took to be Hegel's privileging of community.

Zhang claims that Hegelian philosophy and evolutionary theory eclipse that which is different. Before we come to Zhang's critique, however, we should note that during the late Qing, a prevalent interpretation of Hegel involved seeing Hegel as eclipsing difference, even by proponents of his philosophy. Guan Yun, a student of Kang Youwei, stated in 1905:

> From Hegel's discussion of ethics and according to the principle that his philosophy establishes, the world is an expression of a great spirit and the individual is just a small part of this great spirit... Hence all things such as states, families, societies and countries do not have the goal of developing the individual, but only that of developing the great spirit of the world. According to Hegel's theory, the myriad things of the world are equal as one. It appears that there are differences, but in actuality there are none... Socialism and cosmopolitanism both take equality as their moral foundation and thus they both can be deduced from Hegel's theory.
>
> (Guan, 1977: 21)

From this perspective, the whole is greater than the parts and negates the parts in a one-sided manner. Note that in Guan Yun's interpretation of Hegel, there is no mention of the necessity of individual freedom; rather, one's individual freedom lies primarily in realizing the goal of spirit, which evolves through history. One of the first places where Zhang outlines a critique of Hegel is in his critique of evolutionary history, which he develops using Buddhist terminology. He does not doubt the validity of something like a process in which societies become technologically sophisticated, but he questions the moral overtones that Hegel, as he was read in China, bestows on such development. In Zhang's view, technological change and modern political apparatuses, such as the state, are inextricably connected to imperialism and an increase in general human suffering. In short, with evolutionary development, pleasure and suffering increase together. While we do not need to delve into the details of Zhang's critique here, the following passage from an essay published in 1907 outlines the main thrust of his argument:

> Some steal Hegel's theory of being, non-being, and becoming and believe that the universe emerged because of a goal and hence only things that accord with this goal are correct. If we take the universe not to have any knowledge/consciousness, then there is originally no goal. If we take the universe to have knowledge/consciousness, then it is as if this peaceful and happy self suddenly created the myriad things to bite into itself . . . If one speaks from the perspective of humans limited by their physical form, then both purity and contamination stem from one's will. What use is it to make loyalty and filial duty the goals of the universe? If one speaks from the perspective outside of form and matter, then the universe originally does not exist, so how can there be a goal?
>
> (Zhang, 1996: 264)

The above passage is a direct attack on Hegel's teleological vision of history. In short, rather than narrating a series of stages through which history progresses to enable greater freedom, Zhang counters with a scenario in which history or becoming leads to increasing disaster. Zhang thus anticipates later critics of what would be called modernization theory by uncovering the dark side of progress. He also underscores the manner in which tropes such as progress and civilization are used to justify imperialist aggression, which reinforces his sympathy for India and other colonized regions. When one makes this realization about the trajectory of history, one repents and attempts to find a way to end history as it now exists and create a new world. The transformation of the world required bringing together a philosophical reading of 'form and matter' with political revolutionary practice. For example, he advocated a refusal of existing form and matter, which Indians and Chinese exemplified by withdrawing from the British political economy and boycotting their goods. Zhang Taiyan's Japanese socialist cohort did not understand their Chinese friends' support of refusing Western goods, since the alternative was to buy commodities from Chinese capitalists. As we have seen above, Zhang believed that the nationalism of oppressed countries could resist both imperialism and capitalism and would go against the linear narrative in which all progress towards the same ideal.

20.4.2 Zhang's alternative to Hegel: a philosophy of difference

However, the above passage leaves an important question unanswered, namely what type of ideal did Zhang oppose to the Hegelian? One could say that Zhang applies Hegel's criticism to himself and contends that Hegel is unable to account for difference. Consequently, Zhang draws on the *Zhuangzi* and Buddhism to outline a world that affirms difference. He outlines this position with reference to Zhuangzi's concept of 'equalization' in an essay published in 1908, again attacking Hegel. He notes that, according to Zhuangzi's idea of the equalization of things:

> As Zhuangzi says, 'all things are so and all things are permissible (*wu wu bu ran, wu wu bu ke*)'. The literal meaning of this phrase is the same as Hegel's 'all events are in accord with principle and all things are virtuous and beautiful (*shi shi jie heli, wu wu jie shanmei*)'. [This is Zhang's rendition of Hegel's famous phrase 'what is rational is actual, what is actual is rational'.] However, the former takes people's hearts and minds to be different and difficult to even out, while the latter posits a final end, which is the process by which things are realized. This is a basic and huge difference.
>
> (ibid.: 304)

Zhang notes the similarity between the formulations of oriental philosophy, in this case, Zhuangzi and Hegel's own formulation. However, now it is Zhuangzi who is credited with actually grasping difference, while Hegel posits a telos (and end or a goal), which evens things out. Note that in Zhang's discussion of Hegel, the statement is stated in the affirmative, 'things are rational and beautiful'. From this perspective, the reasonable or the beautiful becomes the absolute standard against which various particulars can be measured. Here we return to the problem of using the world as method or standard, which in Zhang's view is one of the key tropes of imperialism. However, the citation from the *Zhuangzi* reads literally, 'there is no thing that is not so and no thing that is not possible'. In this formulation, there is no principle or ideal such as virtue and beauty to which things must conform. Rather, each thing is affirmed in its singularity and out of this would emerge a new universality. In Roy Bhaskar's (1994) terms, this would be a world in which the concrete singularity of each is the condition for the possibility of the flourishing of all.

Zhang explicates his theory of equality as difference most completely in his long essay, *An Interpretation of the Equalization of Things*, in which he uses Yogācāra Buddhism to read Zhuangzi. He was most proud of this work and famously claimed that each character was worth a thousand gold pieces. The opening passage explains the above point further by drawing on a Buddhist text, *The Awakening of Mahayana Faith*. He writes:

> 'Equalizing things' refers to absolute equality. If we look at its meaning carefully, it does not refer only to equality between sentient beings, such that there is no inferior and superior. It is only when [dharmas] 'are detached from the characteristics of speech; detached from the characteristics of naming cognition; and detached from of them as objects', that one understands absolute equality. This is compatible with the 'equalization of things'.
>
> (Zhang, 1982–1986, vol. 6: 4)

The *Awakening of Mahayana Faith* is a controversial text. It is supposed to be an Indian classic translated into Chinese, but scholars believe it to be a forgery created in China. It is significant to note Zhang does not quote the line immediately following the above passage, since it would have pushed the text in the direction of Guan Yun's reading of Hegel. The text reads: 'There is nothing but this One Mind and for this reason it is nominally called Suchness.' This suggests that there is one mind that exists even after one detaches from objects, cognition, and naming. Zhang does not cite this passage and constructs a radically negative position, which affirms radical difference and the new universality to which he gestures above. The play of difference and universality to which Zhang alludes has not yet come into being and consequently he can only gesture to it through paradoxical expressions connected to the trace. We find an excellent example of this in the following passage:

> One only uses traces to guide transformations. Without words nothing can appear and words have the nature of returning. Thus one uses words to signify things. This is what is said in the following passage [from *Zhuangzi*]: 'In speaking there are no words. One speaks one's whole life and has never spoken. One does not speak throughout one's life and has never stopped speaking (*wei chang bu yan*).'
>
> (ibid.: vol. 6: 6)

Zhang writes here of a trace that inscribes difference beyond our usual opposition between the particular and the universal. He posits a world in which there is no overarching dominant principle that determines a priori the nature of universality and that is then grafted onto particulars. The problem is that one cannot merely affirm the particular as it exists at present because such a particular is always already mediated by a false universal. Consequently, Zhang speaks of a future always to come because it must be constructed out of singularities; one can only use traces to guide transformations. Moreover, reified terms can never grasp what is always emerging: a totality constantly reconstituted by the emerging particulars. For this reason, Zhang develops a new language by bringing Yogācāra and Zhuangzi together. His language alternates between signification and silence and through this interplay, he gestures to a world that is not determined *a priori* by an ideal forced onto beings from the outside.

Drawing on a synthesis of Buddhism and Zhuangzi, Zhang attempts to discuss the problem of difference more fundamentally and opts for something like a metaphysics of democracy or a metaphysical democracy, which he believes would point the way to an ideal politics in the future. In other words, even in terms of what exists, one must begin from the singular, but this singular entity is only provisional and gets its meaning through a whole that does not yet exist. When applied to politics, such a view implies that the concrete singularity of each is the condition for the flourishing of all and flourishing of all is the condition for the singularity of each. Such a world requires institutions different from the modern nation state and for this reason, Zhang also wrote against the reality of the state. However, at the level of realpolitik, he also saw the necessity of anti-colonial nationalism as long as the world remained imperialist. His problematic, from this perspective, anticipates that of postcolonial thinkers who affirmed anti-colonialism, but were wary of with reproducing colonial structures unless one makes more fundamental transformations in one's consciousness and practice.

> **20.4 Buddhism vs Hegel: towards a new universality: Key Points**
>
> - Zhang draws on Buddhism to develop a critique of evolutionary history, which he believes Hegel embodied in his thinking.
> - He was partially attacking the influence of Hegel in Chinese thought during the late Qing dynasty.
> - Against Hegel, he reads Zhuangzi and Buddhism together to produce a philosophy of difference, which emphasizes a symbiotic relationship between concrete singularity and universality; this would be a universality that is constructed out of singularities.

20.5 Conclusion

We have seen how Zhang Taiyan began as an anti-Manchu revolutionary and eventually constructed a more radical theory drawing on Yogācāra Buddhism. After Zhang's imprisonment, he supported a version of nationalism similar to that which Third World nationalists would develop after the Second World War. Moreover, his political theory did not just stop at underscoring anti-imperialist nationalism; rather, drawing on Buddhism and Daoism, he outlined a theory of a new universality that does not extinguish particularity.

Scholars have usually believed that Zhang's political philosophy did not exert the influence that his political propaganda did. However, we can certainly speak of echoes of Zhang's thought, perhaps through his famous students such as Lu Xun. To conclude, I will briefly refer to a Japanese scholar of Lu Xun, the famous public intellectual, Takeuchi Yoshimi (1910–1977). I discuss Takeuchi because he, like Zhang in Tokyo, was a pan-Asianist and in the context of discussing pan-Asianism, returns to the problem of a new type of universality. In 'Asia as Method', published in 1960, he wrote:

> the Orient must re-embrace the West, it must change the West itself in order to realize the latter's outstanding cultural values on a greater scale . . . Such a rollback of culture or values would create universality. The Orient must change the West in order to further elevate those universal values that the West itself produced.
>
> (Takeuchi, 2005: 165; 1993: 469, translation amended)

Notice that the goal of Takeuchi's pan-Asianism is not merely to negate the West, but to take Western values to a higher level and produce a new type of universality that envelops and changes the West. With this gesture, Takeuchi continues Zhang's project of realizing a different type of world, where the abstract universal values are not mobilized to undermine the lives of those in the developing world. Zhang famously chastised the French for promoting freedom and equality in their own lands, but subjecting the Vietnamese to the greatest unfreedom. One would need a way beyond this fake universality and Zhang found this in rereading Zhuangzi and Yogācāra Buddhism. The point, however, as we have seen, is not merely to realize the existing universality, but to change the very nature of how universality is thought. Zhang's new universality is one that is constituted out of the particulars and, though he was no democrat, there is something fundamentally participatory about his universality. The particulars participate in creating the universality under which they will be subsumed.

For both Takeuchi and Zhang, the means to create this new universality is by confronting the West and this is through anti-imperialist nationalist struggle. This is the nationalist moment, which separates Zhang from some of his Japanese contemporaries, such as Kōtoku Shusui. The problem of how one moves from anti-imperialist struggle to a world beyond the opposition between the abstract universal and the concrete particular is a question that Zhang does not answer. Indeed, after 1911, Zhang did not spend as much effort articulating this political philosophy and devoted more time to philology and traditional forms of scholarship. However, his legacy lives in various twentieth-century theorists who resist the abstractions that govern our modern world.

Take your learning further by accessing the online resources for a library of web links to relevant videos, articles, blogs, and useful websites for this chapter: **www.oup.com/he/Ramgotra-Choat1e**.

Study questions

1. What was the conflict between the revolutionaries and the reformers and what was Zhang Taiyan's role in this political struggle?
2. How did Zhang envision Chinese nationalism in relation to pan-Asianism and what was his goal in such a movement?
3. How does Zhang's vision of the China and Asian nations differ from the situation in Asia today?
4. What was Zhang's critique of linear or evolutionary history?
5. How did his critique relate to his critique of imperialism?
6. How did Zhang use Daoism?
7. How does Zhang's socialism differ from how we understand the term today?
8. How do you think that Zhang understood politics?

Further reading

Primary sources

Unfortunately, little of Zhang Taiyan's work has been translated into English. There are some translations in Shimada's book, which was translated from Japanese. Part of the reason for this lack of translation is that his Chinese is notoriously difficult to read and he uses archaic characters and often alludes to events in Chinese history which contemporary scholars do not always know. I am currently working on a translation with a Chinese scholar, Yao Pei, of some of his key writings in political theory. This is scheduled to be published by Brill in 2024.

Zhang, T. 章太炎 (1977 [1907]) 'Guojia lun [On the State]'. Originally published in *Minbao*, 17 (1907): 359–369, in *Zhang Taiyan zhenglun xuanji*. Beijing: Zhonghuashuju, pp. 460–490.
In this essay, Zhang articulates his critique of the state from a Buddhist perspective.

Zhang, T. (1981) *Zhang Taiyan Xuanji-zhushiben* 章太炎選集—註釋本 [Zhang Taiyan: Selected Works, with Notes]. Ed. Zhu Weizheng 朱維錚 and Jiang Yihua 姜義華. Shanghai: Shanghai renmin chubanshe.
This is arguably the single most useful source to begin reading Zhang Taiyan's writings. Zhu Weizheng and Jiang Yihua have done a masterful job of providing detailed notes and also giving the meanings of obscure characters. Some of the essays cited in this chapter can be found in this text, including 'Yazhou heqinhui yuezhang' [The Constitution of the Asia Solidarity Society], pp. 427–432 of this volume.

Zhang, T. (1982–1986) *Zhang Taiyan quanji* 章太炎全集 [The Complete Works of Zhang Taiyan], vols. 4 and 6. Shanghai: Shanghai renmin chubanshe.
These are the complete works of Zhang Taiyan, an essential resource for studying his thought.

Zhang, T. (1996a) *Gegu dingxin de zheli Zhang Taiyan wenxuan* 革故鼎新的哲理: 章太炎文選 [The Philosophy of Reform and Improvement]. Shanghai: Shanghai yuandong.
This is another selection of Zhang's essays. It overlaps with the complete works, but gathers together many of his commonly cited essays. 'Wu wu lun' is an important political text since in it he uses Buddhism to propose a world without states and oppressive groups.

Zhang, T. (2019), *Qiwulunshi shishuzheng* 齊物論釋疏證 [An Annotated Edition of On the Equalization of Things], edited and annotated by M. Zhuo, Shanghai: Shanghairenmin chubanshe.
This is an extremely well-annotated version of Zhang Taiyan's interpretation of the equalization of things, highly recommended to anyone who would like to tackle this profound text. This is a key text, which will be helpful to students who have studied some Chinese.

Secondary sources

Laitinen, K. (1990) *Chinese Nationalism in the Late Qing Dynasty: Zhang Binglin as an Anti-Manchu Propagandist*. London: Curzon.
This is an early work on Zhang Taiyan in English and focuses on Zhang's nationalism and his anti-Manchu propaganda.

Murthy, V. (2011) *The Political Philosophy of Zhang Taiyan: The Resistance of Consciousness*. Leiden: Brill.
This book focuses primarily on Zhang's Buddhist writings and in particular attempts to bring Zhang's work in relation to Marx and German idealism.

Shimada, K. (1990) *Pioneers of the Chinese Revolution*. Trans. J. Fogel. Stanford, CA: Stanford University Press.
Shimada is a major Japanese sinologist and this collection contains an essay on Zhang Taiyan, which covers much basic information. Shimada also translates some essays by Zhang's Indian allies and his famous speech in front of exchange students in Tokyo in 1906.

References

Bhaskar, R. (1994) *Dialectics: The Pulse of Freedom*. London: Verso.

Elman, B. (2003) '"Universal Science" Versus "Chinese Science": The Changing Identity of Natural Science Studies in China, 1850–1930'. *Historiography East and West*, 1(1): 68–116.

Guan, Y. (1977) 'Pingdeng shuo yu zhongguo lunli zhi chongtu [The Theory of Equality and its Contradiction with Chinese Morality]'. In *Xinhai geming qian shinian qian shilun xuanji*. Beijing: Sanlian chubanshe, vol. 2, part 1, pp. 21–29.

Harrell, P. (1992) *Sowing the Seeds of Change: Chinese Students, Japanese Teachers, 1895–1905*. Stanford, CA: Stanford University Press.

Hazama, N. 狭間直樹 and Matsumoto, K. 松本健一 (1990) 'Shō heirin to meiji no ajiashugi' 章炳麟と明治のアジア主義 [Zhang Binglin and Meiji Pan-Asianism]'. *Chishiki* 知識, August.

Ishimoda, T. (1963) 'Kōtoku Shusui to chūgoku'. In T. Yoshimi (ed.), *Ajiashugi*. Tokyo: Chikumashobo, pp. 384–411.

Kōtoku, S. (2004) *Teikokushugi*. Annotated by Y. Susumu, Tokyo: Iwanami bunko.

Laitinen, K. (1990) *Chinese Nationalism in the Late Qing Dynasty: Zhang Binglin as an Anti-Manchu Propagandist*. London: Curzon.

Lin, S. 林少陽 (2014) 'Zhang Taiyan "zizhu" de lianya sixiang. 章太炎「自主」的連亞思想 [Zhang Taiyan's Ideas of Independence and Asian Unity]'. *Quyu*, 區域 1(3): 201–227.

Marx, K. and Engels, F. (1978) 'Manifesto of the Communist Party'. In *The Marx-Engels Reader*. Ed. R.C. Tucker, New York: W.W. Norton Company.

Meng, Y. (2006) *Shanghai and the Edges of Empires*. Minnesota, MN: University of Minnesota Press.

Satō, S. (1996) 'Taiyō na taisei kōzo'. In *Chūgoku kindai chishikijin to bunmei*. Tokyo: Tokyo daigaku chuppankai.

Shimada, K. (1990) *Pioneers of the Chinese Revolution*. Trans. J. Fogel. Stanford, CA: Stanford University Press.

Takada, A. (1974) *Sho Heirin, Sho Shiso, Ro Jin—Xingai no shi to sei to* [With the Life and Death of the 1911 Revolution: Zhang Binglin, Zhang Shizhao and Lu Xun]. Tokyo: Ryūkei shosha.

Takeuchi, Y. (1993) *Nihon to ajia*. Tokyo: chikuma gakugei bunko.

Takeuchi, Y. (2005) *What Is Modernity?*. Trans. R. Calichman. New York: Columbia University Press.

Tierney, R.T. (2015) *Monster of the Twentieth Century: Kōtoku Shusui and Japan's First Anti-Imperialist Movement*. Oakland, CA: University of California Press.

Tsou, J. (Zou Rong) (1968) *The Revolutionary Army: A Chinese Nationalist Tract of 1903*. Trans. J. Lust. Paris: Mouton & Co.

Zhang, T. 章太炎(1977 [1907]) 'Guojia lun [On the State]'. Originally published in *Minbao*, 17 (1907): 359–69, in *Zhang Taiyan zhenglun xuanji*. Beijing: Zhonghuashuju, pp. 460–490.

Zhang, T. (1981) *Zhang Taiyan Xuanji-zhushiben* 章太炎選集—註釋本 [Zhang Taiyan: Selected Works, with Notes]. Ed. Zhu Weizheng 朱維錚 and Jiang Yihua 姜義華. Shanghai: Shanghai renmin chubanshe.

Zhang, T. (1982–1986) *Zhang Taiyan quanji* 章太炎全集 [The Complete Works of Zhang Taiyan], vols. 4 and 6. Shanghai: Shanghai renmin chubanshe.

Zhang, T. (1996) 'Wu wu lun [On the Five Negations]'. In *Gegu dingxin de zheli Zhang Taiyan wenxuan* 革故鼎新的哲理: 章太炎文選 [The Philosophy of Reform and Improvement]. Shanghai: Shanghai yuandong, pp. 254–269.

Zou, R. 鄒容 (2002) *Geming jun* 革命軍 [The Revolutionary Army]. Beijing: Huaxia chubanshe.

Part V

Inclusion and Equality

21	Mary Wollstonecraft	Ashley Dodsworth	371
22	Iris Marion Young	Neus Torbisco-Casals	389
23	Bhikhu Parekh	Varun Uberoi	407
24	Gayatri Chakravorty Spivak	Nikita Dhawan	427

'Equality' is not the same as 'identity': people can be equal without being the same. Indeed, as many of the thinkers in this Part of the book argue, equality does not have to mean treating people in the same way.

Most people today would endorse some kind of equality. Precisely for this reason, however, equality is one of the most controversial and widely and intensely debated of all political concepts. Debate focuses, first, on the forms of equality and their relative desirability and feasibility. Almost everyone supports formal equality, which implies equal treatment—though there is disagreement about what this means. More substantive conceptions include equality of opportunity, which demands that all should start from equal conditions and have equal chances, and equality of outcome, which demands that all should be rewarded equally. Assessing whether and how these substantive forms of equality should be enacted requires understanding exactly what we mean by these terms. For example, does equality of opportunity mean that only a person's capabilities and skills—rather than the prejudices of others—should affect their life chances? Or does it mean that everyone should have an equal ability to achieve those capabilities? If equality of opportunity is desirable, then how should it be achieved? Does it require forms of unequal treatment such as positive discrimination (affirmative action)?

As well as analysing the relationships between different forms of equality—such as between equality of opportunity and equality of outcome—political thinkers also analyse the potential connections and conflicts between equality and other political concepts. For example, some argue that equality undermines freedom (because enforcing a more equal distribution of goods might necessitate restricting the liberty of some people), while others argue that equality is a necessary condition of freedom (because inequality limits people's freedom to act as they wish). We also need to consider what it is we want an equality *of*. Discussions of equality often refer to the distribution of wealth, but we might seek an equality of resources more generally, or of health, or happiness.

We also, of course, need to consider to whom equality applies: who is equal to whom? Since at least the American and French Revolutions in the late-eighteenth century, declarations of universal equality have been common. But in practice, and even explicitly in theory, this has meant equality for *men*—and very often only a minority of men, namely white property-owners. This is why *inclusion* is important: we must reflect on who is included in calls for greater equality (or freedom, justice, rights, etc.). Today, the language of 'EDI' (Equality, Diversity, Inclusion) is often used by institutions that are more interested in projecting supposedly progressive credentials than in initiating structural change, showing that calls for inclusion and equality can be co-opted and diluted. But as the chapters in this Part show, demands for equality and inclusion can also be radical and far-reaching.

A central—and arguably *the* central—inequality running through history is gender inequality. The eighteenth-century English philosopher Mary Wollstonecraft is often cited as one of the first feminist philosophers for her strident analyses of gender inequality. Wollstonecraft defended the rights of man announced by the 1789 French Revolution, but also insisted that such rights be extended to women—for the benefit of both women and society as whole. Identifying the causes of women's inequality in inadequate education and oppressive social structures, Wollstonecraft advocated radical political change. Yet, as Chapter 21 shows, her radicalism had its limits, and her arguments were not always as inclusive as we might expect or hope. While she argued for women to be recognized as equal citizens, she did so by pointing to the 'natural' role of women as mothers in raising the next generation of citizens. Although her later work considered the intersection of class and gender oppression, she could also be patronizing towards and dismissive of working-class women. She was an abolitionist who condemned the slave trade, yet she also relied on an Orientalist defence of enlightened civilization against a backward, barbarian 'Other'. The point in highlighting flaws and gaps in Wollstonecraft's arguments is not to draw up a kind of score sheet of her work—praising her for this, condemning her for that—but rather to facilitate a critical evaluation of her work, which reflects on who is included and who excluded by her theory.

This approach applies equally to contemporary thinkers. The remaining thinkers in this Part were all writing towards the end of the twentieth century and into the twenty-first century. The American philosopher Iris Marion Young, examined in Chapter 22, developed a novel theory of justice that was especially attentive to questions of inclusion and equality. She viewed inequality not primarily in terms of discrimination against individuals, but saw it rather as a consequence of oppressive social practices that are structurally reproduced. The remedy, Young therefore argues, is not to provide equal rights and opportunities within the existing (oppressive) system, but rather to call for structural change, transforming the conditions under which inequalities arise. Equality for Young essentially meant the participation and inclusion of all in political life. Against the liberal demand for 'neutral' and universal rules that apply equally to all, Young argued that equality may entail different treatment for marginalized and oppressed groups. This is because social structures separate individuals into groups, some of which are more privileged than others: women, Black people, and Indigenous groups, for example, have traditionally been marginalized, excluded, and oppressed.

The emphasis in Young's 'politics of difference' on the need to treat groups differently, combined with her recognition that groups are always internally diverse, has strong resonance with the politics of multiculturalism. Since the late-twentieth century, many discussions of inclusion and equality have taken place within debates around multiculturalism, which is a perspective that affirms cultural diversity within societies. Chapter 23 explores the work of one of the leading advocates of multiculturalism: the British political theorist Bhikhu Parekh, who served on the UK's Commission for Racial Equality and chaired the Commission on the Future of Multi-Ethnic Britain, known as the *Parekh Report*. Parekh defends cultural diversity as a prerequisite of intercultural dialogue, which he views as both inescapable and desirable. It has sometimes been claimed that multiculturalists wish to protect autonomous cultural communities, but Parekh is clear that all cultures are internally varied—as Young had also argued—and that intercultural learning allows cultural communities to develop and improve their beliefs and practices. Egalitarian critics of multiculturalism claim that states should treat all citizens equally, without special protections or exemptions for minority cultural groups, and that multiculturalism undermines equality. But Parekh enlists cultural diversity in a novel justification of equal treatment, which has traditionally been justified by reference to human uniformity: humans are fundamentally the same and so should be treated the same. But Parekh objects that one way in which we are all the same is that we all belong to different cultures, and therefore that equal treatment means citizens require both the same and different treatment.

The final chapter in this Part, Chapter 24, examines the work of the Indian theorist Gayatri Chakravorty Spivak and her contributions to feminism and postcolonial studies. In her analyses of political, social, and economic inequalities, Spivak adopts the term 'subaltern' from the Italian Marxist Antonio Gramsci to refer to those groups that are socially and politically excluded and subordinated. She gives special attention to subaltern women, who are doubly oppressed by economic and gender inequalities. In doing so, she complicates the notion of international feminist solidarity, questioning who is included in feminist demands and highlighting the ways in which Western feminists sometimes rely on imperialistic assumptions and stereotypes (about women in the Global South who need to be 'rescued', for example). This question of who can speak for disempowered groups is central to Spivak's work. The subaltern are those whose voices are silenced by oppressive social and political structures, yet claims by others to speak on their behalf are deeply problematic, not least because the subaltern is not a uniform group. Spivak coined the term 'strategic essentialism' to refer to the tactic of temporarily uniting an otherwise disparate group around a shared identity in order to pursue goals such as racial or gender equality. Like the other thinkers in this Part, therefore, Spivak sought equality and inclusion for oppressed groups while recognizing that such groups are never homogeneous.

21 Mary Wollstonecraft

ASHLEY DODSWORTH

> **Chapter guide**
>
> This chapter introduces the political thought of Mary Wollstonecraft, with a particular focus on her influential analysis of gender inequality. It first explores the different forms of writing Wollstonecraft employed, before focusing on her most famous work, *A Vindication of the Rights of Woman* and its radical arguments regarding gender, reason, and education (Section 21.2.2). Section 21.3 contextualizes her work within the republican tradition, which underpinned her opposition to slavery and her recognition of global inequalities. However, her arguments for emancipation are underpinned by problematic assumptions of universalism, which are further complicated by the tensions in her work surrounding class, motherhood, and Orientalism (Section 21.5). The chapter concludes by discussing her legacy and reception, both immediately after her death and in the twentieth and twenty-first centuries.

21.1 Introduction

One of the most infamous women of her time, the radical author and ground-breaking feminist philosopher Mary Wollstonecraft was born in 1759. Her father was abusive, wasting much of the family's money, and leaving Wollstonecraft to help raise her five younger siblings. Her education was infrequent and limited in scope, yet she was a passionate reader who sought out opportunities to learn wherever she could. She began work at 19, first as a lady's companion, before becoming a governess and school-teacher—as she would later note, for women in her position 'few are the modes of subsistence and those very humiliating' (Wollstonecraft, 1989b [1787]: 25). Wollstonecraft turned to writing, working as a translator, reviewer, and editorial assistant for the radical journal *Analytical Review*, and writing books for use in teaching (the textbooks *The Female Reader* and *Original Stories from Real Life*, and the teaching manual *Thoughts on the Education of Daughters*) alongside a semi-autobiographical novel called *Mary: A Fiction*. When the French Revolution began in 1789, Wollstonecraft was a passionate supporter. She wrote two influential political tracts in which she defended the principles of liberty, and the rights of all; *A Vindication of the Rights of Men*, published in 1790, and the revolutionary *A Vindication of the Rights of Woman* followed in 1792. She then moved to France in order to collect material for her book, *A Historical and Moral View of the French Revolution*, and was living in Paris during the beginning of the 'Reign of Terror', when the Revolution turned against itself, and thousands were sent to the guillotine. While in Paris, Wollstonecraft met and fell in love with an American author and businessman, Gilbert Imlay. Due to rising tensions between France and Britain, she had to register as Imlay's wife at the American embassy for her safety. However, the couple were never married, though they had a daughter, Fanny Imlay, born in May 1794 and seriously considered moving to America together. When their relationship ended, in part due to Imlay's infidelity, this stress and the increasing horror of the Revolution led Wollstonecraft to return to England, where she attempted suicide. Imlay then employed her to travel to Scandinavia

Read more about **Wollstonecraft's** life and work by accessing the thinker biography on the online resources: www.oup.com/he/Ramgotra-Choat1e.

on business for him, and she turned her letters from the trip into a travelogue. Published under the title *Letters Written During a Short Residence in Sweden, Norway and Denmark*, this was her most critically and commercially successful book. Recovering from a second suicide attempt, she and her daughter moved to the outskirts of London, where she began a relationship with the philosopher William Godwin and began writing a second novel, *The Wrongs of Women or Maria*. She did not live to complete the work, as she died in childbirth, in 1797, at the age of 38.

21.2 Women's emancipation

21.2.1 Form

One of the most notable things about Wollstonecraft is the range of work that she produced. In a ten-year writing career, she wrote two novels, two political tracts, three educational texts, a travelogue, and a history of the French Revolution. She also translated three books from French, German, and Dutch into English, in addition to writing hundreds of reviews and working as an editorial assistant. Such variety was in part due to the need to support herself, as for the majority of her life Wollstonecraft made a living from her writing, describing herself as 'the first of a new genus', a woman who was a professional radical author (quoted in Kelly, 2007: xiv). Her work for the *Analytical Review*, for example, brought in a steady income, enabling her to live alone and she openly stated that she wrote the *Letters* so that she could 'discharge all my obligations of a pecuniary kind' (Wollstonecraft, 1989e [1796]: 422). Engaging with a range of forms enabled Wollstonecraft to develop her own abilities as a writer, find her own voice and become self-sufficient and thus, she thought, truly free.

But there are intrinsic reasons for the variety of forms that she drew upon, in addition to the need to support herself. All of her works explore how to achieve emancipation and independence, particularly for women. Each type of writing acts as a lens through which she can view this problem and provide a different perspective on the difficulties involved in securing freedom for all. Her educational works, for example, are designed to promote changes in girls' education, or provide them with resources to supplement their inadequate lessons, thereby enabling young women to develop their knowledge of the world and critical thinking skills, while her travel writing includes a comparative analysis of civil liberties in Scandinavia. The range of writing also reflects her arguments regarding the need to break down the narrow boundaries of what is meant by the 'political', foreshadowing the third-wave feminist slogan 'the personal is political'. As Kelly highlights 'her achievement was to fashion a distinctively feminist discourse, in several kinds of writing' (Kelly, 2007: ix).

Looking at Wollstonecraft's novels demonstrates this point. It can seem surprising that Wollstonecraft wrote two novels, given her critique of both novels and the women who read them. Indeed, her first novel was called *Mary: A Fiction* specifically to distinguish it from a novel. She pours scorn on those 'who are amused by the reveries of the stupid novelists, who, knowing little of human nature, work up stale tales and describe meretricious scenes, all retailed in sentimental jargon, which equally tend to corrupt the taste and draw the heart aside from its daily duties' (Wollstonecraft, 1989d [1792]: 256). The link between the personal (the habit of reading 'stupid' novels) and the political consequences (the corruption of judgement, and failure to fulfil the duties that a successful society requires of its members) is clear. But this is a critique of a certain *type* of novel, not novels as a whole. If correctly written, Wollstonecraft believed that novels were the form that could most accurately convey the harm that is done to women by gendered oppression, because they can convey the inner life of female characters, thus showing how sexist prejudices damaged their perception of themselves and the world. Dolan highlights how Wollstonecraft uses the format of the novel to develop 'new narratives about women's desires and aspirations, [which] Wollstonecraft demonstrates, must emerge from women's own experiences' (Dolan, 2019: 133). These narratives are best constructed through the 'methodology' that is only possible in a novel, that of 'finding one's voice, exchanging stories with other women to achieve mutual recognition, and articulating this new understanding to a receptive audience in order to spur social change' (ibid.: 131).

Wollstonecraft identified the political possibilities inherent in the novel when discussing her second novel *The Wrongs of Women*, which is often seen as the second volume of *A Vindication of the Rights of Woman*, due to the title and the continuation of the arguments regarding the impact of gendered oppression. In this ground-breaking book, multiple women tell their stories, explaining how, despite their differences in class, they have all suffered from the denial of their civil and political rights, especially in their relationships with men. 'These appear to me', Wollstonecraft wrote to a friend, 'to be the peculiar Wrongs of Women, because they degrade the mind . . . it is the delineation of finer sensations which, in my opinion, constitutes the merit of our best novels' (Wollstonecraft, 1989f [1798]: 68). The approach of this book reflects the later feminist practice of consciousness-raising, as by telling their life stories, women realize the commonality of their experience and can therefore recognize structural oppression. In both the form of this book and in writing novels in general, the form of writing linked to female readers, Wollstonecraft seeks to build a shared recognition of women's oppression and turn one source of their subjection, the 'stale' and 'sentimental' tales that they are restricted to, into a tool to overcome their subjugation. Wollstonecraft always believed that the boundaries of the political should be expanded, and this argument was reinforced through the wide variety of works that she produced, each of which made political claims in new ways.

> **Key Concept: Gender**
>
> Sex refers to the labels that are given to different kinds of bodies, according to the classification of their physical features. Gender refers to the characteristics that are assigned to people by society on the basis of their sex, such as the assumption that those who are women are 'naturally' more caring. Gender is a social construct and is therefore not fixed, but can instead be altered as society's perceptions change. For Wollstonecraft, gender was a binary that referred to two categories, 'men' and 'women', however, this can be understood differently, as seen in the growing legal recognition for non-binary people or in cultures that recognize the existence of more than two genders, such as the Hijra people in South Asia.

21.2.2 *A Vindication of the Rights of Woman*

Wollstonecraft's most famous work is the political tract *A Vindication of the Rights of Woman*. This argument for gender equality earned her the reputation as one of the first feminist thinkers. But this text was a sequel to the earlier *A Vindication of the Rights of Men*, published two years before, and is best understood in light of this earlier work. The first *Vindication* was written in response to a scathing attack on the French Revolution by the influential statesman Edmund Burke in his *Reflections on the Revolution in France* (see Chapter 17).

As part of his criticism of the Revolution and its supporters, Burke singled out a sermon delivered to the Revolutionary Society by Dr Richard Price. Price was a friend and mentor of Wollstonecraft's, and she was furious at Burke's criticism, seeking to defend both the friend she admired and the ideals of the revolution. *A Vindication of the Rights of Men* was the first published response to Burke, appearing less than four weeks after his *Reflections* was published. It was the opening shot in a pamphlet war that came to be called the 'Revolution Controversy', which included contributions from Thomas Paine and Hannah More, and fundamentally shaped British politics to this day. In her response, Wollstonecraft furiously attacked Burke's character and principles, defending the rights of all against hereditary riches and property, and supporting reform and change instead of the corrupt status quo. Her book was an instant success, selling over three thousand copies and a second edition was soon produced. But while the first edition was published anonymously, the second edition was published with Wollstonecraft's name, creating a scandal and sexist backlash. As a critic in *The Gentlemen's Magazine* waspishly noted, 'we were always taught to suppose that the rights of women were the proper theme of the female sex'. Wollstonecraft fought back in response to these critics and to the release of the *Declaration of the Man and Citizen* in France, which did not keep the promises of gender equality made by the Revolution. (The *Declaration* was challenged by other feminist critics, including Olympes de Gouges.)

Key Thinker: Olympes de Gouges

Despite being forced into marriage at 16, Olympes de Gouges (1748–1793) became a writer and intellectual. In 1791, she published the *Declaration of the Rights of Woman and the Female Citizen* in protest at the denial of women's rights by the Revolutionary Assembly. She also wrote one of the first plays in French to feature a slave in a central, heroic role and condemned slavery. A supporter of the French Revolution, she was a member of the moderate faction and was arrested for her beliefs, particularly her call for a referendum to allow the French people to decide their new form of government. She was then executed, having once declared that if 'a woman has the right to mount the scaffold, she must equally have the right to mount the rostrum'.

While Wollstonecraft's first vindication argued for 'the rights of man—sacred rights!' (Wollstonecraft, 1989c [1790]: 34), in *A Vindication of the Rights of Woman* she demonstrates that 'the rights of humanity have been thus confined to the male line from Adam downwards' (Wollstonecraft, 1989d [1792]: 157). Wollstonecraft explains how this 'confinement' has been upheld and the damage it has done, both to women and to society as a whole, which cannot progress while one half of its inhabitants are denied their rights and confined to ignorance by custom and prejudiced social structures. Though all of Wollstonecraft's work examines questions of gender and women's equality, the causes of this inequality are most explicitly identified in this text. Wollstonecraft locates the main sources of gendered oppression in her society in inadequate education, prejudice, and structural inequalities—arguments that are unfortunately still applicable to contemporary politics. She thoroughly dismantles the prevailing prejudice of her day which said that women were naturally ignorant and frivolous, challenging the arguments of influential writers such as Jean-Jacques Rousseau (see Chapter 9). If women were ignorant, she argued, it was because they were trained to be through the preferences of society and poor education. By valuing women for their beauty and physical weakness, rather than their strength and intelligence, society stunted women's development, and then used their supposed inadequacies to justify denying them access to education and the public sphere.

Wollstonecraft demonstrated that gallantry and flattery harmed women, by promoting the view that they were at once above and below men, angels placed on pedestals but yet not worthy of respect, as opposed to rational creatures who were the equal of men. The prevailing view of women's education encouraged this belief, as it focused on ensuring that women were 'accomplished' in dancing, needlework, and music, rather than equipped with knowledge about the world and then taught to think critically for themselves. The inadequate education of women therefore harmed society as a whole, for women could not contribute to the running of society, nor educate their children. Any attempt to reform society and introduce fairer laws, or democratic government, was therefore doomed to fail unless it included full education for women: 'I therefore, will venture to assert, that till women are more rationally educated, the progress of human virtue and improvement in knowledge must receive continual checks' (ibid.: 109).

A Vindication does not just critique gendered oppression but develops solutions to fight gendered inequality. In Chapter 12, Wollstonecraft set out a radical alternative programme of education that would abolish distinctions of gender and class. She proposed that all children should go to the same nationally run school and study the same curriculum until they were aged 9. Then those 'intended for domestic employments or mechanical trades ought to be removed to other schools' to receive a technical education, while those 'of superior abilities or fortune' would be given a philosophical education (ibid.: 240). Despite this distinction, the call for all children to receive an education and to be taught together for several years was revolutionary for her time, and designed to foster a strong sense of community and benevolence among the next generation, in place of the divisions of her current society.

Key Thinker: Hannah More

Hannah More (1745-1833) was one of the most prominent women of her time, a passionate Evangelical Christian, writer and philanthropist, who set up several schools for poor children. As a writer, she initially wrote poems and plays, before turning to religious and social tracts, playing a key part in the development of a counter-revolutionary literature that sought to prevent the spread of radical politics in England. A social conservative, she so disagreed with Wollstonecraft's politics that she refused to read *A Vindication of the Rights of Woman*, believing the title to be a contradiction in terms. But she also sought to improve women's education and abhorred the slave trade, working closely with abolitionists such as William Wilberforce.

In addition to a new programme for education, Wollstonecraft also argued for radical structural change: 'I really think that women ought to have representatives, instead of being arbitrarily governed, without having any direct share allowed them in the deliberations of government' (ibid.: 217; and the following passage criticizes the lack of representation for the working class). She also attacks the laws and customs that denied women fair employment, for it was seen as shameful for upper- and middle-class women to work. Moreover, women who did work either could not access the same roles as men or were paid less—a problem which persists in contemporary working conditions. Furthermore, the type of work women could access, such as being servants, often made them vulnerable to harassment, a point highlighted in Wollstonecraft's novel, *The Wrongs of Women*, in which sexual harassment is a frequent feature of working women's stories. Thus, women were unable to support themselves, or develop their talents, leaving them in a position of vulnerability. However, the main structural problem that Wollstonecraft explores is marriage, which she likens to 'legal prostitution' (ibid.: 218). At that time, as Blackstone's (2016 [1765]) *Commentaries on the Laws of England* noted, 'the very being or legal existence of the women is suspended during the marriage, or at least is incorporated and consolidated into that of the husband'. Once married, a woman became part of her husband, losing control of all her property and her bodily autonomy, and with almost no way of escaping her marriage. Wollstonecraft's analysis therefore demonstrated how women were left dependent on men, as the majority of women had no way to support themselves outside of marriage, due to their inadequate education and lack of opportunities, but, once married, they had no legal or political identity, and they had no access to the political system that would enable them to change this.

> **21.2 Women's emancipation: Key Points**
>
> - Wollstonecraft wrote novels, political tracts, travel books, and educational textbooks, reflecting both the realities of being a working writer in the eighteenth century and her argument for expanding the scope of the political.
> - *A Vindication of the Rights of Woman* is grounded in the defence of rights that Wollstonecraft makes in her first *Vindication*, and focused specifically on women's rights.
> - Wollstonecraft challenges prevailing prejudice regarding women's ignorance and attacks the inadequate education women received, setting out an alternative plan for comprehensive education for all children.
> - She also explores the social structures that oppress women, particularly marriage.

21.3 Reason and republicanism

21.3.1 Reason

Central to the argument of both *A Vindication of the Rights of Woman* and all of Wollstonecraft's work is a belief in reason. She held that all human beings were created by God and equally endowed by him with both the ability to reason and a capacity for self-improvement. This belief underpinned her arguments for both equality and freedom. With regard to equality, Wollstonecraft believed that if all were created by God and given the same ability to reason, then all people, regardless of race or gender, were equal. 'Whatever effect circumstances have on the abilities, every being may become virtuous by the exercise of its own reason' (Wollstonecraft, 1989d [1792]: 90) and both society and its laws should reflect this. This belief in reason influenced her understanding of freedom as independence, as she thought that everyone had the ability to think and decide for themselves. Having the ability to reason could therefore free you from relying on custom and looking to authorities for guidance, thus enabling self-government for both people and society as a whole: 'tyrants would have cause to tremble if reason were to become the rule of duty in any of the relations of life' (ibid.: 221).

This understanding of reason is tied to virtue. Wollstonecraft argued that individuals were given passions, or strong emotions, in order to develop their character and gain experience through learning to control their emotions. This may seem to deny the importance of emotions, and can appear cold and unfeeling. But Wollstonecraft wanted men and women to exercise self-control so that they could direct their own lives, and be free from interference, whether from kings or their own impulses. To be virtuous therefore was to be guided by the head, not the heart, enabling people to better both themselves and society as a whole. This argument challenged the prevailing belief that women 'had only feelings' (ibid.: 164) and no ability to rise above their emotions. Hence, she claimed 'I do not wish [women] to have power over men; but over themselves' (ibid.: 131), to have the power to plan and direct their own lives and not rely on others for their happiness and self-respect. This reflects her argument that a woman's virtue should not be based on her sexual fidelity, but on the fulfilment of her duties towards society as a whole. So radical and seismic a change would this be, that it would involve 'a revolution in female manners' or actions, with positive consequence for all—for if women would 'labour by reforming themselves [they would] reform the world' (ibid.: 114). Reason is therefore both the basis of Wollstonecraft's argument for the equality of all, and the means by which that equality is realized, and all are able to live freely.

21.3.2 Liberalism or republicanism

Early responses to Wollstonecraft's work identified her with liberalism, seeing her work as part of a larger tradition that sought freedom for individuals through granting and recognizing their rights. But to position Wollstonecraft wholly within liberalism is to overlook several important aspects of her work. Recent scholarship has further contextualized her work within the intellectual debates of her time, and in doing so revealed the republican elements of Wollstonecraft's thought (see Coffee, 2013; Halldenius, 2015). This section examines how Wollstonecraft engaged with republicanism, and how this tradition influenced her understanding of what it is to be truly free.

> **Key Concept: Domination**
>
> Within liberalism, freedom is seen as either negative (there is nothing stopping you from doing what you want) or positive (you have the ability to do what you want). In contrast, the republican tradition offers a third understanding of freedom: freedom from domination. Domination is understood as the power of arbitrary interference, or whether someone else has the ability to intervene in your life without your consent. This is illustrated by the example of a slave with a kind master, for even if the master does not restrict the slave's actions and provides them with the resources they need to achieve their goals, the slave cannot be said to be free, as the master could change their mind at any time, and the slave would be powerless to stop them.

The republican tradition dates back to the classical period and played a key role in the justification of both the English Civil Wars and the American and French Revolutions, particularly with regard to the opposition to monarchy. Republicanism rejects the rule of kings and aristocrats in favour of self-government by virtuous citizens, who are all equal to one another, and work together to govern the republic. Central to this tradition is a rejection of arbitrary government, and Wollstonecraft passionately opposed all monarchies (Wollstonecraft, 1989c [1790]: 86, for one example). Yet she took this argument a step further, recognizing that the arbitrary despotism of kings the republicans opposed was identical to the power that men exercised over women. Wollstonecraft frequently compares marriage to slavery and despotism (Wollstonecraft, 1989d [1792]: 226, 215), as regardless of whether individual men were kind to their wives, all husbands dominated their wives because they had complete legal control over them, which they could exercise if they wished without their wives being able to prevent them. Thus, the heroine of her final novel speaks of 'her tyrant—her husband' (Wollstonecraft, 1989f [1798]: 86) for the terms are interchangeable with regard to the power they exert over their subjects. The experience of domination also explains why some women do not wish to be independent but instead seek to rely on men and be praised for their beauty: 'considering the length of time women have been dependent, is it surprising that some of them hug their chains and fawn like the spaniel' (Wollstonecraft, 1989d [1792]: 152)? Wollstonecraft could be highly critical of other women, but she did recognize that patterns of domination and habits of dependence were hard to break, and that it would take time and structural change for all women to be truly free (Coffee, 2013).

Wollstonecraft also opposed the system of aristocracy in general. She despised all distinctions of rank that were inherited rather than earned through virtue and hard work, believing them to corrupt both the entitled and those who paid them homage: 'from the respect paid to property flow, as from a poisoned fountain, all the evils and vices' (Wollstonecraft, 1989d [1792]: 211). As seen in her critique of French society before the Revolution, Wollstonecraft believed that valuing wealth and status over virtue and talent created an idle, stagnant society which discouraged progress and innovation.

Her work critiques not only the status of the aristocracy but their wealth, especially their landed estates. To be free from domination requires equality among the members of the republic, who prioritize the common good over their own benefit. Those who value money and wealth are held to be corrupt, putting their personal gain above doing what is best for the community as a whole: 'what has stopped . . . progress? Hereditary property—hereditary honours' (Wollstonecraft, 1989c [1790]: 10). These arguments were commonplace among the radicals of the eighteenth century, but Wollstonecraft developed these claims further by pointing out the gendered impacts. She highlights how the wealth and grand estates of the aristocracy were maintained through the subjection of the women of this class, first, through denying them the right to own or inherit property, and, second, through arranged marriages that increased the property their male relatives owned. Women were therefore not only treated as property, but exploited in the interests of property. Such injustice was the logical result of a societal structure that secured the riches of a minority over the equality of all.

Instead of a corrupt people who value only wealth and status, ruled by tyrants and kings, Wollstonecraft and her fellow republicans wished for virtuous independent citizens to be allowed to govern themselves in a condition of equality, a true republic. These citizens would balance the responsibilities of running the republic (such as holding office, participating in decision-making and raising children) with their rights, working together for the defence and continuation of the republic. Wollstonecraft used the republican emphasis on duty over rights to ground her claims that women should be treated as equal citizens. After all, women were carrying out the duties of the republic, especially with regard to raising the next generation of citizens (see the discussion of motherhood in Section 21.5.2). If they were not capable of critical thinking and exercising their reason, how could they teach their children to do so? Denying women the support they needed to fulfil these duties, such as an adequate education and the conditions needed for self-respect, was to doom the republic to failure, for if half the current citizens and all future citizens were unable to fulfil their duties, govern themselves or be independent, then the republic wound be undermined from within. Furthermore, to deny women the rights and privileges of a citizen, when they carried out the duties essential to the republic, was to break the pact of at the heart of republicanism and permit domination. Recognizing the republican elements of Wollstonecraft's thought therefore reveals the full extent of her opposition to the political structures of her time, especially those that ensured the domination of women, and the radical contribution that she made to the political arguments of her day.

> ### 21.3 Reason and republicanism: Key Points
>
> - Wollstonecraft believed all human beings were created by God and had the capacity to reason.
> - She therefore held that all were equal and should be allowed to govern themselves.
> - Though early commentary identified Wollstonecraft with liberalism, recent scholarship has demonstrated her engagement with the republican tradition.
> - Drawing upon the concepts of domination and citizenship, as well as the opposition to wealth and corruption, she then applied a gendered lens, expanding the scope of republican thought.

21.4 Slavery and the global context

Wollstonecraft frequently described women as being in a state of slavery, but she also explicitly condemned the practice of slavery, especially the Atlantic slave trade. She was a passionate supporter of abolition, believing that the slave trade was 'a traffic that outrages every suggestion of reason and religion' (ibid.: 14). The slave trade was described as 'a desperate disease' and one of her harshest criticisms of Burke's attack on the French Revolution is that his arguments could also be used to justify the 'infernal slave trade' (ibid.: 50). (While living in America, Wollstonecraft's lover Gilbert Imlay was part-owner of a slave ship, but he had lost the concession before he left for France and it is highly unlikely that Wollstonecraft knew of this connection).

Wollstonecraft's condemnation of slavery intersects with her analysis of the oppression of women. For example, in critiquing how her society valued women more for their ability to be pleasing to men than for the ability to be rational beings, she asks 'is one half of the human species, like the poor African slaves, to be subject to prejudices that brutalise them . . . only to sweeten the cup of man?' or 'is sugar always to be produced by vital blood?' (Wollstonecraft, 1989d [1792]: 215). This passage draws a link between the degradation of women's character and the horrific treatments of slaves through the comparison of sugar, one of the luxuries that literally and figuratively sweeten the life of others, at immense cost to those who produce them. Wollstonecraft therefore highlights the societal structures that prioritize the profit and comfort of rich, white men and maintain this through the exploitation of others. However, she also recognizes the role of white women in running slave plantations and maintaining racial hierarchies. Though the wives and daughters of plantation owners 'presumably hold no civil or political rights . . . [they were] infamous for their cruelty' (Howard, 2004: 68), and Wollstonecraft recognized that their exclusion from the public realm did not mean that these women would automatically empathize with those who were enslaved. For,

> where is the dignity, the infallibility of sensibility in the fair ladies whom, if the voice of rumour is to be credited, the captive negroes curse in all the agony of bodily pain, for the unheard-of tortures they invent? It is probable that some of them, after the sight of a flagellation, compose their ruffled spirits and exercise their tender feelings by the perusal of the latest imported novel.
>
> (Wollstonecraft, 1989c [1790]: 45)

Her work identifies not only the immense harm done to the enslaved, but also the corruption and damage done to the character of those who dominate them and are thereby cut off from the 'universal benevolence [that] is the first duty' of all (Wollstonecraft, 1989b [1787]: 30).

In addition to the Atlantic slave trade, she condemned both the use of slavery as punishment (Wollstonecraft, 1989e [1796]: 305–306) and the practice of press-ganging, in which men were forcibly enlisted into the navy (Wollstonecraft, 1989c [1790]: 15). Wollstonecraft argues that this practice stole the labour of the men forced to work on the ships and harmed the women and children left behind when the main breadwinner of the family was abducted to sea (Wollstonecraft, 1989f [1798]: 128). Though she did not liken press-ganging to slavery, her belief that property was only justified through labour, and that individuals should not be used for the benefit of others, underpinned her objection to both. It also formed part of her larger critique of exploitative economic practices, for she attacked the traders who 'like the owners of negro ships, never smell on their money the blood by which it is gained, but sleep quietly in their beds' (Wollstonecraft, 1989e [1796]: 344), even though they gain their wealth through exploiting others, a critique with echoes in today's arguments for fairer trading practices.

21.4.1 Global context

These arguments against slavery and exploitative trade are part of Wollstonecraft's engagement with global patterns of domination. Wollstonecraft was part of an international network of radical thinkers and writers, reading and reviewing works from across Europe and North America. She travelled extensively, visiting Portugal in 1785 and Sweden, Denmark, Norway, and Germany in 1795, in addition to living in Ireland while working as a governess, and in France. Her writings are therefore illustrated through examples of domination from across the world. She analyses the impact of Danish rule over Norway, for example, which she described as 'the cloven foot of despotism . . . the domineering state' (ibid.: 305) and compared to the British rule in Ireland, which she observed when working for Lord and Lady Kingsborough, who were the largest English landowners in Ireland. In the Preface to one of the works she translated, she 'pointedly inserted a passage of her own, enjoining the fair treatment of Native Americans' (Ferguson, 1992: 86), and she likens the injustice of slavery to the injustice of the caste system in India (Wollstonecraft, 1989c [1790]: 51). As Howard points out, Wollstonecraft demonstrates her points though 'a series of references to several sites of imperial irresponsibility . . . [to] include the Turkish Seraglio, China, ancient Sybaris, *ancien régime* France, the South Sea Islands, Circassia, Portugal, Italy, biblical Egypt and Russia' (Howard, 2004: 69). This is in part because, as noted in Section 21.3.1, Wollstonecraft believes reason to be a universal constant, a belief underpinned by her religious convictions, and leading her to argue that oppression and tyranny were wrong, wherever they occurred. This belief underpinned her arguments for racial and gender equality, for 'surely there can be but one rule of right, if morality has an eternal foundation' (Wollstonecraft, 1989d [1792]: 104). But there is a presumption of universality here, a claim that there is one 'correct' perspective that is superior to all others and that all history is the development towards a shared end state, a journey in which some nations have made more progress in than others. For though 'the civilisation which has taken place in Europe has been very partial' (Wollstonecraft, 1989c [1790]: 10), nevertheless 'Europe was emerging out of barbarism' (ibid.: 34), and 'civilisation is a blessing' (Wollstonecraft, 1989e [1796]: 250). Wollstonecraft is not arguing that European civilization is superior to other nations, but that there is one form of universal civilization, in the rule of God-given reason, and European nations are closer to this state, which other nations have yet to reach.

The problems of such universalization can be seen in one of Wollstonecraft's most frequent similes, that of the harem. Wollstonecraft imagined it to be a luxurious prison, in which women are trapped for the sexual gratification of the harem owner, a perfect example of gender domination. She likens the condition of women in England to that of the harem (Wollstonecraft, 1989d [1792]: 141 and 159 as but two examples), as they are educated for men's benefit and have no public existence. However, these references to the harem are an example of Orientalism (Howard, 2004; Brace, 2016), an othering discourse that constructs an image of 'the East' as a place of luxurious, corrupt, irrationality and despotism (the opposite of republican virtue) (see also Chapter 16 on Edward Said). The contrast with the harem is meant to highlight the inherent wrong in the way women are treated by British law and custom by linking it to the practices of 'barbaric' nations, a likeness that is meant to be shameful. This trope also occurs in Wollstonecraft's occasional references to Islam, which reflect the popular belief of her time that Islam denied the existence of a woman's soul—in criticizing Milton, she asks if 'in the true Mahometan strain, he meant to deprive us of souls' (Wollstonecraft, 1989d [1792]: 88; and see also 1989c [1790]: 45, where she makes the same critique of Burke) and says that English society 'in the true style of Mahometanism . . . treated [women] as a kind of subordinate beings' (Wollstonecraft, 1989d [1792]: 73). Zonana highlights this trend and its basis in a belief in universal reason when she describes Wollstonecraft's work as making 'what would in her time have been a relatively uncontroversial plea: that the West rid itself of its oriental ways, becoming as a consequence more Western—that is more rational, enlightened and reasonable' (quoted in Howard, 2004: 70). So though Ferguson has argued that 'Mary Wollstonecraft seems to have been the first writer to raise issues of colonial and gender relations so tellingly in tandem' (Ferguson, 1992: 87), this is complicated by her contrast between 'enlightened' freedom for women and a barbaric, backward 'Other', and the tensions in her belief in universal reason.

> **21.4 Slavery and the global context: Key Points**
>
> - Wollstonecraft opposed the slave trade and drew comparisons between the slave trade and gendered inequality.
> - Her belief in racial and gender equality, however, was grounded in an assumption of universal reason, which gave rise to a belief in 'civilization' that reflected Orientalist tropes.

21.5 Tensions

21.5.1 Class

A key critique of Wollstonecraft's work is that she, at best, overlooks the role of class and the position of working-class women and, at worst, believes them to be incapable of improvement—her radicalism appears to only go so far. *A Vindication of the Rights of Woman*, for example, specifically states: 'I pay particular attention to those in the middle class, because they appear to be in the most natural state' (Wollstonecraft, 1792: 75) and it is hard to reconcile her portrait of women who are indolent and idle with the hardships faced by working women. The references to servants are also problematic, suggesting the need for a continued servant class so that better educated women can thrive, as seen in Wollstonecraft's suggestion that an educated woman would be able to run her household 'with, perhaps, merely a servant maid to take off her hand the servile part of the household business' (ibid.: 213). Her first published work, *Thoughts on the Education of Daughters* was even more explicit, stating that 'servants are in general, ignorant and cunning' (Wollstonecraft, 1989b [1787]: 38). There is also an undercurrent of paternalism here, as she speaks of 'our superior judgement' (ibid.: 38) and suggests that 'we cannot make a servant wise or good, but we may teach them to be decent and orderly, and order leads to be some degree of morality' (ibid.: 39).

Wollstonecraft's later work did, however, shake off much of this paternalistic and slighting attitude, as seen in the defence of the poor women of France in response to Burke's critique in the first *Vindication* (Wollstonecraft, 1989c [1790]: 30) and her support for the rights of all. She highlights that the property of the poorest, whether in their goods or their labour, is not respected for 'it is only the property of the rich that is secure . . . when was the castle of the poor secure?' (ibid.: 15). In *Original Stories*, she sides with the poor and shopkeepers when she speaks of the injustice and harm that follows when the aristocracy do not pay their bills or treat tradesman fairly. But the main example of the development of her thought with regard to class, and her true radicalism, comes in her final work, *The Wrongs of Women*. This unfinished novel reflects the later feminist practice of consciousness-raising, as it features multiple female characters telling their stories in order to 'show the wrongs of different classes, of women, equally oppressive, though from the difference of education necessarily various' (Wollstonecraft, 1989f [1798]: 84).

In developing this approach, and seeking to tell these stories, Wollstonecraft begins to consider how poverty impacts the experience of gendered oppression, radically expanding on her explanation of how women are subjected. This is most clearly demonstrated in the character of Jemima, a guard at the asylum where the heroine, Maria, has been unjustly committed so that her husband can steal her property. In Chapter 5 of the book Jemima recounts her life story, beginning with her mother, a poor servant who died in childbirth. Jemima was treated badly by her stepmother, and then sent away to work as a maid when she turned 16. However, she is sexually assaulted by her employer and subsequently becomes pregnant. When the mistress of the house finds out, she blames Jemima, and throws her out, forcing her to turn to sex work. While the mistress of a wealthy man, she gains an education, but when she's made homeless again after his death, she cannot access better paid work and so must become a washerwoman. The physically demanding role means that Jemima is soon injured and, unable to work, she 'became a thief from principle' (ibid.: 118). She is caught and sent to jail, after which she enters the workhouse, where she meets the asylum owner, who offers her a job. Though she initially resists Maria's attempts at friendship, as she desperately needs to keep her job, she bonds with her after discovering that Maria has been separated from her new-born daughter, leaving the child as vulnerable and unprotected as Jemima once was. '[Jemima's] story is not just the story of one woman, but the story of several working-class women struggling to support themselves in an economy stratified by both class and gender' (Dolan, 2019: 140). Through Jemima's tale Wollstonecraft shows how poor women are made vulnerable and dominated, as through poverty and gendered oppression they are denied the conditions for security and independence.

The engagement with class in the novel also illustrates how interactions between different women maintain structures of privilege. Wollstonecraft notes that 'men who are inferior to their fellow men are always most anxious to establish their superiority over women' (Wollstonecraft, 1989f [1798]: 140) and this is also true of women, though in some cases it is driven by a need for self-preservation. Maria, for example, insults her father's mistress, a former servant in their home, whom she categorizes as 'the vulgar despot of the family; and assuming the character of a fine lady, she could never forgive the contempt which was sometimes visible on my countenance, when she uttered with pomposity her bad English or affected to be well bred' (ibid.: 133). Though Maria notes that this behaviour is in part because women are given 'but one way of rising in the world' (ibid.: 133), she fails to connect her condition, married to an abusive man with no legal remedy, with that of her father's mistress, who is even more vulnerable than she is. This parallel is repeated in Jemima's story, for when Jemima begins a relationship with a tradesman, she refuses to live with him unless he abandons the young servant whom he seduced and is now pregnant. The girl subsequently kills herself and Jemima is overcome with grief, ending the relationship, because she recognizes that she has perpetuated the cycle of harm, treating the pregnant servant the same way that Jemima herself had been treated: 'I thought of my own state and wondered how I could become such a monster!' (ibid.: 117).

There are also moments of cross-class connection between women. When Maria tries to flee her abusive husband, she meets several women when she is trying to find lodgings. Though these women frequently express sympathy with her plight, they are prevented from helping her by their husbands. Maria has the trappings of wealth and access to material comforts these women do not, but they are equally poor in the eyes of the law as, however meagre or extensive their property is, it belongs to their husbands. As one woman explains to Maria, when she tried to reclaim the clothes her husband stole from her, she was told 'it was all as one, my husband had a right to whatever I had' (ibid.: 164), reflecting Maria's inability to escape her husband and his sexual abuse of her. The novel therefore shows the harm done by gender, poverty, and the intersection of the two, in addition to Wollstonecraft's growth as a political theorist.

21.5.2 Motherhood

Wollstonecraft repeatedly stresses how important the duties of motherhood are and therefore she created a tension within her account of women's political existence. She emphasizes again and again that women should raise their children themselves (Wollstonecraft, 1989b [1787]: 22) and 'fulfil the peculiar duties which nature has assigned them' (Wollstonecraft, 1989d [1792]: 241), condemning those who leave their children to the care of others. She thought that breastfeeding was essential for a child's well-being, and attacks the practice of wet-nursing, whereby rich women pay another woman to breastfeed their child. Wollstonecraft believes this practice demonstrates how a desire to be seen as beautiful and attractive to men left women unable to connect with their children, harming the health of both mother and child (and thus society as a whole). Believing that 'maternal tenderness arises quite as much from habit as instinct' (Wollstonecraft, 1989b [1787]: 7), she argues that women will not love their children unless they carry out the actions of motherhood, such as breastfeeding or educating their children. But such actions are time-consuming and exhausting, tying women to the home and the family via the body and so preventing them from entering the public sphere via the exercise of their reason. As discussed above, she links her call for women's citizenship to the fact that they perform the essential duties of motherhood, strengthening the argument for women's citizenship at the expense of the argument for gender equality—after all, men's citizenship and education are not based on their role as fathers. She therefore 'does not succeed in proposing full gender equality: women's citizenship remains conditional on their performing certain biological duties' (Bergès, 2016: 217).

The tensions surrounding class also reoccur here:

> though I consider that women in the common walks of life are called to fulfil the duties of wives and mothers, by religion and reason, I cannot help lamenting that women of a superior cast have not a road open by which they can pursue more extensive plans of usefulness and independence.
>
> (Wollstonecraft, 1989d [1792]: 217)

Indeed, 'I do not mean to insinuate that they should be taken out of their families, speaking of the majority' (ibid.: 132). Troublingly, only exceptional women appear to move beyond the family and into the public sphere. But though Wollstonecraft keeps 'the majority' of women in the family sphere, she repeatedly argues that this sphere is political, and essential to the success of the political community as a whole. Wollstonecraft explicitly describes childcare as the means by which a woman will 'fulfil her part of the social compact' (Wollstonecraft, 1989c [1790]: 24), casting motherhood as a political act, which should be respected with mothers supported and rewarded for their efforts, viewed as part of the republic. Women are restricted to the private sphere, but that is not the same as excluding them from the political sphere, because Wollstonecraft breaks down the distinction between the two, a radical act even for contemporary politics. The exclusion of the majority of women from the public sphere, even implicitly, is highly problematic and runs counter to the aims of the feminist movement. Yet her argument for the recognition of the political work that is done within the private sphere, and the impact of the public sphere and its inequalities on the family, laid the groundwork for later feminist thought and activism.

Key Thinker: William Godwin

Mary Wollstonecraft's husband and the father of her second daughter, William Godwin (1756–1836) was a former minister who became a philosopher, author, and journalist, and played a key role in the radical circles of the 1790s. Like Wollstonecraft, he published across several genres, including plays, history books, children's books, and novels, including the best-selling *Caleb Williams*, a psychological thriller grounded in a critique of aristocratic privilege. His most influential work, *An Inquiry Concerning Political Justice*, argued against the existence of government, and so founded philosophical anarchism.

> ### 21.5 Tensions: Key Points
>
> - Wollstonecraft's arguments for freedom from domination and emancipation of women are undercut by tensions related to class and motherhood.
> - Her later work addresses some of the criticisms regarding class, exploring how class and gender intersect.
> - Though Wollstonecraft breaks down the distinction between the public and private sphere, she argued that women should focus their efforts on caring for their families.

21.6 Conclusion

Wollstonecraft died in September 1797, due to complications from the birth of her daughter, named Mary in her honour. Her husband, William Godwin, was heartbroken at her death and worked to compile her papers into an edition of *Posthumous Works*, which he published the following year along with an autobiography of Wollstonecraft, *Memoirs of the Author of the Vindication of the Rights of Woman*. Godwin's aim was to commemorate her life and her work, claiming that 'it has always appeared to me, that to give to the public some account of the life of a person of eminent merit deceased is a duty incumbent upon survivors' (Godwin, 1798: 1). But the memoir caused a scandal, as it revealed her dysfunctional childhood, her suicide attempts, the details of her relationship with Imlay, and that her first child, Fanny Imlay, was born out of wedlock. An outpouring of condemnation for her character followed, which either overshadowed her work or interpreted her writing in light of her life, with illegitimate children and unhappiness seen as the logical result of women's emancipation. The backlash against her personal life, combined with the increasing horror at the developments of the French Revolution that she championed, ensured that Wollstonecraft's work was reviled in England. Yet although there is a presumption that 'Wollstonecraft was not read for a century after her death' (Botting, 2013: 503), this is not the case. In England, her work was highly influential for the Romantic writers, such as Percy Bysshe Shelley and Robert Southey, and was particularly important in the work of her daughter, who became known as Mary Shelley, the author of *Frankenstein*. As Botting has shown, *A Vindication of the Rights of Woman* was widely read in Europe, the USA, and Brazil throughout the following century (ibid.).

Interest in Wollstonecraft's work rose and fell in line with the feminist movements of Europe and North America, as she was frequently labelled the 'mother' of feminism. There was an initial peak of interest during the first wave of feminism, for example, as seen in the new edition of *Vindication of the Rights of Woman* in 1891, with an introduction by prominent suffragist Millicent Fawcett in 1891. The development of the second wave of feminism meant that 'the 1970s was without question a crucial turning point in the reception of Wollstonecraft' (Murray, 2020: 61). Initially there was more interest in Wollstonecraft's life, with multiple biographies released in the 1970s, but gradually the focus shifted to her work, aided by the publication of a definitive edition of her complete works in 1989. Though the *Vindications* have received the most attention, more focus has recently been given to her two novels and the *Letters*, and there is a growing literature on her political thought, especially with regard to republicanism. There is also a flourishing discussion of her educational works, though her book on the French Revolution and her pieces for the *Analytical Review* remain comparatively underexplored.

Wollstonecraft's work is notable for its remarkable breadth and consistency—breadth in the range of forms that she uses, from travelogues, to novels, to political tracts, to educational works; and consistency in the focus throughout on political emancipation, particularly for woman. This chapter has set out her arguments for freedom, with a focus on her analysis of gendered oppression (Section 21.2), her engagement with republicanism (Section 21.3), and her arguments against slavery (Section 21.4). Her argument for freedom for all contains tensions, however, such as reconciling her claims for women's freedom with her strong belief in the importance of their duties as mothers (Section 21.5). While she radically expanded the question of political emancipation to include women, there are still questions over whether she saw this argument as applying to *all* women (though her work was far more nuanced in this regard that it is often perceived to be). More problematically, Wollstonecraft's arguments regarding reason, though underpinning her radical belief in the equality of all and her opposition to slavery, suggests a homogeneity that, when viewed in light of the Orientalist aspects of her work, is troubling. These are problems that the feminist movement still struggles with, and questions over class, motherhood, and globalization resonate today as, unfortunately, does Wollstonecraft's critique of the social and political structures that oppress women. Wollstonecraft was one of the first thinkers to argue that political questions *must* include gender, and her work demonstrates both the difficulty and the necessity of doing so.

Take your learning further by accessing the online resources for a library of web links to relevant videos, articles, blogs, and useful websites for this chapter: **www.oup.com/he/Ramgotra-Choat1e**.

Study questions

1. Which of Wollstonecraft's works are 'political'?
2. What factors does Wollstonecraft think account for women's subordinate status in society?
3. Why does Wollstonecraft oppose slavery?
4. What are the strengths and limitations within Wollstonecraft's account of universal reason?
5. How did republicanism influence Wollstonecraft's work and what does she add to this tradition?
6. Can Wollstonecraft's arguments for women's political emancipation and her belief in women's domestic duties be reconciled?
7. Does Wollstonecraft's later work answer the criticisms regarding class?
8. Should Wollstonecraft be considered the 'mother' of the feminist movement, and what would this imply for feminism in the twenty-first century?

Further reading

Primary sources

Wollstonecraft, M. (1989a) *The Works of Mary Wollstonecraft*, 7 vols. Ed. M. Butler and J. Todd. London: Pickering.
This is the standard edition of Wollstonecraft's work.

Wollstonecraft, M. (2004) *The Collected Letters of Mary Wollstonecraft*. Ed. J. Todd. New York: Columbia University Press.
This includes all her personal correspondence.

Secondary sources

Bergès, S., Botting, E.H., and Coffee, A. (eds) (2019) *The Wollstonecraftian Mind*. London: Routledge.
  A comprehensive collection of essays that covers her major works, their historical context, and her legacy. The section on 'Interlocutors' compares her work with that of other philosophers, such as Rousseau, Mill, Burke, and de Beauvoir.

Coffee, A. and Bergès, S. (eds) (2016) *The Social and Political Philosophy of Mary Wollstonecraft*. Oxford: Oxford University Press.
  An excellent edited collection, with a particular focus on Wollstonecraft's engagement with republicanism.

Gunther-Canada, W. (2001) *Rebel Writer: Mary Wollstonecraft and Enlightenment Politics*. Evanston, IL: Northern Illinois University Press.
  An engaging blend of biography and analysis of Wollstonecraft's political thought.

Howard, C. (2004) 'Wollstonecraft's Thoughts on Slavery and Corruption'. *The Eighteenth Century*, 45(1): 61–96.
  A thorough exploration of Wollstonecraft's comments on slavery that also introduces (and critiques) the previous works on this topic.

Johnson, C.L. (ed.) (2002) *The Cambridge Companion to Mary Wollstonecraft*. Cambridge: Cambridge University Press.
  The first collected edition to address Wollstonecraft's work as a whole and it remains an excellent starting point.

Johnson, N.E., and Keen, P. (eds) (2020) *Mary Wollstonecraft in Context*. Cambridge: Cambridge University Press.
  Explains the relevant historical and cultural contexts of Wollstonecraft's work, such as the contemporary debates over the rights of women and the literature of the period.

Sapiro, V. (1992) *A Vindication of Political Virtue: The Political Theory of Mary Wollstonecraft*. Chicago: University of Chicago Press.
  One of the first books to explore Wollstonecraft's political theory.

Taylor, B. (2003) *Mary Wollstonecraft and the Feminist Imagination*. Cambridge: Cambridge University Press.
  Highly influential study of Wollstonecraft's work which demonstrates the importance of her religious beliefs.

Todd, J.M. (1976) 'The Biographies of Mary Wollstonecraft'. *Signs*, 1(3): 721–734.
  An engaging account of the biographies of Wollstonecraft, beginning with Godwin's *Memoirs*, which highlights the relationship between reception of Wollstonecraft and the feminist movement.

References

Bergès, S. (2016) 'Wet-Nursing and Political Participation'. In A. Coffee and S. Bergès (eds), *The Social and Political Philosophy of Mary Wollstonecraft*. Oxford: Oxford University Press, pp. 201–217.

Blackstone, W. (2016 [1765]) *The Oxford Edition of Blackstone: Commentaries on the Laws of England*, vol. 1: *Of the Rights of Persons*. Ed. D. Lemmings. Oxford: Oxford University Press.

Botting, E.H. (2013) 'Wollstonecraft in Europe 1792–1904: A Revisionist History'. *History of European Ideas*, 39(4): 503–527.

Brace, L. (2016) 'Wollstonecraft and the Properties of (Anti)Slavery'. In A. Coffee and S. Bergès (eds), *The Social and Political Philosophy of Mary Wollstonecraft*. Oxford: Oxford University Press, pp. 117–134.

Coffee, A. (2013) 'Mary Wollstonecraft, Freedom and the Enduring Power of Social Domination'. *European Journal of Political Theory*, 12(2): 116–135.

Dolan, E.A. (2019) 'The Novels'. In S. Bergès, E.H. Botting, and A. Coffee (eds), *The Wollstonecraftian Mind*. London: Routledge, pp. 131–144.

Ferguson, M. (1992) 'Mary Wollstonecraft and the Problematic of Slavery'. *Feminist Review*, 42: 82–102.

Godwin, W. (1798) *Memoirs and Posthumous Works of Mary Wollstonecraft Godwin*. Dublin: Thomas Burnside for J. Rice.

Halldenius, L. (2015) *Mary Wollstonecraft and Feminist Republicanism*. London: Pickering and Chatto.

Howard, C. (2004) 'Wollstonecraft's Thoughts on Slavery and Corruption'. *The Eighteenth Century*, 45(1): 61–96.

Kelly, G. (2007) 'Introduction'. In *Mary and The Wrongs of Women or Maria*. New York: Oxford University Press, pp. ix–xxxi.

Murray, J. (2020) '1970's Critical Reception'. In N.E. Johnson and P. Keen (eds), *Mary Wollstonecraft in Context*. Cambridge: Cambridge University Press, pp. 57–63.

Wollstonecraft, M. (1989a) *The Works of Mary Wollstonecraft*, 7 vols. Ed. M. Butler and J. Todd. London: Pickering.

Wollstonecraft, M. (1989b [1787]) 'Thoughts on the Education of Daughters'. In M. Wollstonecraft, *The Works of Mary Wollstonecraft*, 7 vols. Ed. M. Butler and J. Todd. London: Pickering, vol. 4, pp. 1–52.

Wollstonecraft, M. (1989c [1790]) 'A Vindication of the Rights of Men'. In M. Wollstonecraft, *The Works of Mary Wollstonecraft*, 7 vols. Ed. M. Butler and J. Todd. London: Pickering, vol. 5, pp. 1–78.

Wollstonecraft, M. (1989d [1792]) 'A Vindication of the Rights of Woman'. In M. Wollstonecraft, *The Works of Mary Wollstonecraft*, 7 vols. Ed. M. Butler and J. Todd. London: Pickering, vol. 5, pp. 79–266.

Wollstonecraft, M. (1989e [1796]) 'Letters Written in Sweden, Norway and Denmark'. In M. Wollstonecraft, *The Works of Mary Wollstonecraft*, 7 vols. Ed. M. Butler and J. Todd. London: Pickering, vol. 6, pp. 237–348.

Wollstonecraft, M. (1989f [1798]) 'The Wrongs of Women: or Maria'. In M. Wollstonecraft, *The Works of Mary Wollstonecraft*, 7 vols. Ed. M. Butler and J. Todd. London: Pickering, vol. 1, pp. 75–184.

22 Iris Marion Young

NEUS TORBISCO-CASALS

Chapter guide

This chapter focuses on exploring the central contributions to contemporary political theory by American philosopher Iris Marion Young. Young remains well known as a leading socialist, feminist political theorist whose ground-breaking work on oppression, equality, and democratic theory has had an enduring impact despite her premature death. After introducing Young's multifaceted engagements with issues of justice and equality against the backdrop of her personal and political context, Section 22.2 examines her influential account of oppression. This analysis is essential to understanding Young's conception of equality as inclusion, as discussed in Section 22.3. Section 22.4 analyses her critique of the universal model of citizenship as delineated in her celebrated (1990) book *Justice and the Politics of Difference*.

22.1 Introduction

Iris Marion Young (1949–2006) was an accomplished thinker in many areas, including the social and philosophical analysis of the body; theories of justice, especially gender justice; ethics and international affairs; and responsibility, global justice, and public policy. Beyond her influential academic work, Young also built a reputation as a grassroots activist on social justice issues, such as workers' rights and women's rights, which led her to reflect critically on the meaning of democratic citizenship and political responsibility. Rather than engaging with Young's wide-ranging philosophical legacy, this chapter is dedicated to introducing her insights related to inclusion and equality. As will become apparent, the use of a gender lens permeates her analysis of these concepts.

The development of Young's feminist consciousness and her sensitivities towards difference and oppressive social structures are evoked in her narration of her difficult upbringing experience and family's 'different' home (Young, 2005a: 125–128). Young was born in 1949 in New York City, but her family soon moved to the suburbs of New Jersey, where her mother struggled with suburban isolation and expressed a 'passive resistance' to the gendered roles and divisions of labour prescribed for middle-class mothers in the 1950s. After the sudden death of her father, her 'too messy' home was deemed unsuitable and dangerous for the suburban eye, an expression of child neglect that eventually led Young and her siblings to be placed in foster care. Reflecting on the notion of 'negligence', which justified the bureaucratic welfare response, Young points to the relevance of formal and informal social rules and practices that her mother was expected to follow as a white, middle-class mother, which were impermeable to difference. She also points to the paternalistic understanding of what a suburban family should look like, one which failed to acknowledge a variety of experiences of care as well as the difficult position of her mother as a single parent (ibid.: 127).

This multifaceted account of equality, as distilled from her own personal account, is illustrative of Young's concern with oppression as a structural phenomenon (Young, 1990: 6). Young argues for a

Read more about **Young's** life and work by accessing the thinker biography on the online resources: www.oup.com/he/Ramgotra-Choat1e

conception of justice based on the affirmation, rather than the suppression, of group difference. In her account, difference is not simply relevant to *understanding* how individual lives and decisions are affected by social and institutional structures; it is also a value that enriches people's lives and needs to be considered as central in theories of justice. This insight leads to broader critiques of atomistic, depoliticized, and interest-based conceptions of liberal individualism as a basis for democratic politics, which she criticizes for sustaining a capitalist understanding of welfare, and ignoring the differing contexts and constraints affecting seemingly free individual choices.

Gendered social constraints become especially important in her theory, in that they allow understanding of how broader structures of oppression create specific meanings and harmful outcomes for women and vulnerable groups, even in the absence of direct forms of discrimination. Precisely for this reason, Young was also reluctant to embrace a communitarian political philosophy that, in her view, tends to privilege homogeneous values, which degrade difference *within* groups and punish non-conformity with established internal rules. Her writings on urban life and the politics of difference (Young, 1986: 19–23; 1990: 226–256) are particularly illuminating in this regard, as they reflect on the need to create spaces where a multiplicity of voices and perspectives can flourish and be positively appreciated.

Young's feminist engagement with a broad range of political and social issues—including the sexual division of labour, housing, urban life, and relationships of care—thus exposes how broader social structures create specific meanings and material outcomes, such as oppression, inequality, and inclusion. Section 22.2 begins by examining her influential account of oppression, a concept on which she wrote extensively, and which provided a distinctive foundation for her understanding of injustice as involving structural patterns of disadvantage between members in different social groups, and of gender as 'seriality'.

22.2 Oppression and structural inequality

Young's theory of oppression—originally delineated in her essay 'Five Faces of Oppression' (Young, 1988), and later included in her book *Justice and the Politics of Difference* (Young, 1990)—represents a major contribution, and reconceptualizes equality (and ultimately justice) beyond liberal ideals of redistribution. Her analysis provides a cohesive theme that connects her scholarship on feminist philosophy with her writings on political theory (especially her theory of equality and democracy). Gender provides a category that she uses to examine social structures of power, distinct from those of class or race (Young, 2005b: 12–26). In what stands today as one of the major contributions to contemporary political theory, Young argued that there are at least five distinct forms of oppression that cannot be reduced, or collapsed, into more fundamental dimensions of distributive justice related to individual desert: exploitation, marginalization, powerlessness, cultural imperialism, and violence.

Although each of them has certain significant traits, they are mutually entangled categories. *Exploitation* is associated with class division—a 'steady process of the transfer of the results of the labor of one social group to benefit another' (Young, 1990: 49). *Marginalization* is the system of exclusion of a group of people from participating in social and material life (ibid.: 53–55). *Powerlessness* is associated with the lack of authority to make decisions regarding policy, personal, or workplace autonomy, personal development and skills, and in relation to others (ibid.: 56–58). *Cultural imperialism* is described in terms of the prevalence of a certain group's experience over all other social groups (ibid.: 58–61). Finally, Young identifies *violence* in connection to group identities and relationships—for example, rape and domestic violence as being typically gendered (ibid.: 61–63).

While Young's analysis remains abstract, thus avoiding the historical or psychological dimensions of the origins and effects of oppression, her categorization emphasizes the positioning of individuals as members of differentiated groups, and so enables a better understanding of the nature of oppression and the roots of inequality beyond individual forms of discrimination. This allows her to stress the potential impact of social groups in hindering individual autonomy (self-development) and collective self-determination, both related to the domination of some groups over others (Young, 1979; 2000: 31). By 'self-development', Young refers to the conditions that enable people to acquire and exercise social skills and to make meaningful choices without experiencing coercion or other forms of constraint. Self-determination consists in 'being able to participate in determining one's action and the condition of one's action' (Young, 2000: 32). In her view, justice essentially consists in overcoming oppression in its different facets.

Young thus conceives of the individual as a socially grounded subject, and views their belonging to a social group as configuring 'social positions that people occupy which condition their opportunities and life chances' (ibid.: 94). This is because social groups produce structures in which individuals are arranged through a 'social organization of labor and production, the organization of desire and sexuality, the institutionalized rules of authority, and the constitution of prestige' (ibid.: 94). This relational conceptualization of individual agency and social difference allows for different degrees and forms of oppression within and across specific social identities, which are characterized as multifaceted and dynamic, rather than fixed and static.

Young's conception of social groups led critics to emphasize the risks of essentializing groups and group membership (Mouffe, 1995: 327–328; see also Cohen, 1997: 608–610). Young addresses such concerns first in her article 'Gender as Seriality' (Young 1994) and later in *Inclusion and Democracy* (Young 2000). In the former, Young builds on Jean-Paul Sartre's *Critique of Dialectical Reason* (Sartre, 2004 [1976]) to explore how material and social circumstances may mark a collective of persons without assuming a fixed, cohesive identity for the members of that collective (see Key Thinker: Jean-Paul Sartre). Young (2000: 99) contends that, despite the importance of group affiliations and affinities in the formation of a person's identity, '[t]he relation of individuals to groups, however, is not one of identity', as a person's identity is formed in active relation to their positioning within a constellation of different social groups. Hence, as she claims, the analysis of the forms of oppression that women suffer as a group cannot be disentangled from the analysis of oppression of other groups, including minority women (Green, 1995; Eisenberg and Spinner-Halev, 2005).

Key Thinker: Jean-Paul Sartre

Jean-Paul Sartre (1905–1980) was a philosopher, novelist, playwright, screenwriter, and literary critic. He is perhaps best known for his leading role in French existentialism, phenomenology, and Marxist theory and activism in the twentieth century. His theory of social seriality is of particular influence on Young's analysis of gender and the condition of women. In his *Critique of Dialectical Reason*, Sartre uses the metaphor of people waiting at a bus stop to coin his understanding of the concept. While these people 'do not care about or speak to each other and, in general, they do not look at one another', they do, however, 'exist side by side', and 'to the extent that the bus designates the present commuters, it constitutes them in their interchangeability: each of them is effectively produced by the social ensemble as united with his neighbors, in so far as he [*sic*] is strictly identical with them' (Sartre, 2004 [1976]: 256, 259).

For example, women as a group face exploitation of their labour and nurturing, as they still do a major proportion of unpaid work, consisting mainly of domestic and care-related tasks that are underappreciated and undervalued. They also have reasons to fear violence in the form of sexual assault, especially acute in the domestic sphere, and they remain significantly less visible and represented in the public realm. As sub-groups within this category, single mothers and migrant women, especially those belonging to racial or ethnic minorities, experience a higher level of powerlessness which increases the risk of exploitation and marginalization, and impacts negatively on health and other fundamental elements of well-being (see World Health Organization and Calouste Gulbenkian Foundation, 2014; American Psychiatric Association, 2017).

In sum, Young's understanding of social groups is attentive to the idea of difference within and between groups, producing multiple forms of oppression that have an impact beyond gender (including race, disability, sexual orientation, and class). Her emphasis on individual positionality and the social structures that produce specific group inequalities resonates with broader developments in feminist theory, especially postmodern, intersectional, and decolonial approaches to feminism (Crenshaw, 1989; Spelman, 1990; Ahmed, 2000; 2006; Lugones, 2010).

22.2.1 Social groups and structural inequalities

In exploring identity formation and group affiliation, Young thus contributes important insights on how social structures—and individual positioning in specific social groups—condition human agency:

> Persons are thrown into a world with a given history of sedimented meanings and material landscape, and interaction with others in the social field locates us in terms of the given meanings, expected activities, institutional rules, and their consequences. We find ourselves positioned in relations of class, gender, race, nationality, religion, and so on, which are sources of both possibilities of action and constraint.
>
> (Young, 2000: 100)

Here Young is not merely exploring the formation of someone's unique identity, but also how the social structures—such as gender, class, race, and so on, are—'determinate social positions that people occupy which condition their opportunities and life chances. These life chances are constituted by the ways the positions are related to one another to create systematic constraints or opportunities that reinforce one another' (ibid.: 94). Hence, individual agency neither develops nor is exercised in a vacuum, but is conditioned by social structures that we don't choose: 'we have no choice but to become ourselves under the conditions that position us in determinate relation to others. We act in situation, in relation to the meanings, practices, and structural conditions and their interaction into which we are thrown' (ibid.: 101).

In this scheme, the way social structures condition how people are positioned in society matters. It matters because these arrangements historically and systematically privilege members in some groups over others, thus producing social exclusion and injustice. For instance, women, Black people, Indigenous groups, and other identity groups suffer multiple forms of social marginalization in various domains, in a pattern that reveals the existence of what Young describes as *structural inequalities* (ibid.: 92–99, see Key Concept: Structural inequality).

Key Concept: Structural inequality

Structural inequalities involuntarily determine the status of people in society on the basis of their group belonging, consisting 'in the relative constraints some people encounter in their freedom and material well-being as the cumulative effect of the possibilities of their social positions, as compared with others who in their social positions have more options or easier access to benefits' (Young, 2001: 15). To a great extent, this is due to the historical configuration of social institutions, practices, and policies that reinforce one another, reproducing the relevance of an unfair delimitation between categories of people. This is because those structural inequalities stem from social structures, which are constantly reproduced via the interaction of individuals.

Building on the contributions of the British sociologist Anthony Giddens (1986), Young (1990: 131–132; 2000: 95) explains that while social structures are the product of previous coordinated and uncoordinated actions and interactions of individuals, they are constantly reinforced through these interactions. In her words, 'social structures exist only in the action and interaction of persons; they exist not as states, but as processes' (Young, 2000: 95).

Because of this reinforcing dynamic, those structures—and the inequalities they generate—are particularly difficult to change (ibid.: 95–98). A good example to illustrate this line of reasoning are the processes that produce and reproduce residential racial segregation in the USA. She explains that such segregation is the product of structural relations of race being imprinted in the physicality of cities:

> Racially discriminatory behaviour and policies limit the housing options of people of colour, confining many of them to neighbourhoods from which many of those whites who are able to leave do . . . Because of more concentrated poverty and lay-off policies that disadvantage Blacks or Latinos, the effects of an economic downturn in minority neighbourhoods are often felt more severely, and more businesses fail or leave. Politicians often are more responsive to the neighbourhoods where more affluent and white people live . . . As a result of the confluence of all these actions and processes, many Black and Latino children are poorly educated, live around a higher concentration of demoralized people in dilapidated and dangerous circumstances, and have few prospects for employment.
>
> (ibid.: 96–97)

Hence, the problem is not merely that Black people, and African-Americans in particular, were historically oppressed and mistreated, or remain discriminated against in violation of the Constitution or other legal rules (such as international human rights law); rather, the main problem is that the *effects* of historically entrenched patterns of social domination and prejudice persist, pervading current social practices and redistributive structures, even if legal norms formally recognize anti-discrimination principles. In other words, cultural hegemony and social arrangements, which are often a product of a history of group domination, continue to exert a strong influence on housing arrangements and residential segregation.

Young's concern with inequality as a social process that occurs as a consequence of different forms of oppression is therefore key to account for structural injustices, such as the one just described, as a distinctive kind of moral wrong that is irreducible to individual agency and responsibility (Young, 2006: 114). In her structuralist approach, histories of group domination matter not only for the purposes of recognizing past injustices (and asking redress in the form of compensation or reparation, for instance), but because they provide an account of the persistent dynamics and social interactions which create and reproduce exclusion and inequality. Indeed, '[s]tructural injustice occurs as a consequence of many individuals and institutions acting to pursue their particular goals and interests, for the most part within the limits of accepted rules and norms' (Young, 2011: 52).

In her posthumously published work, Young (ibid.) explores the application of her theory of justice to global injustices. She is especially interested in the question of how to conceive of responsibility for large-scale injustices that transcend borders and cannot be reduced to individual forms of harm or to single decision-making instances. She uses sweatshop labour as an example of an injustice that is structurally reproduced due to a range of actions and inactions by many agents, including consumers, transnational clothing companies, governments, and the workers who are forced to work in sweatshops in order to survive (ibid.: 125–134). Young argues that all individuals who are actually 'connected' to such injustice share *political*—as opposed to moral or legal—responsibility to struggle collectively against it. In this sense, consumers share responsibility for the working conditions of distant garment workers, even though they do nothing legally wrong when purchasing clothes.

> **22.2 Oppression and structural inequaly: Key Points**
>
> - Young argues that there are five distinct forms of oppression: exploitation, marginalization, powerlessness, cultural imperialism, and violence.
> - Social structures differentiate individuals and separate them into groups, thus *creating* structurally differentiated social groups in which individuals are arranged through an organization of labour and production, desire and sexuality, rules of authority, as well as the constitution of prestige.
> - Structural inequalities are *systematic* constraints that some individuals encounter in relation to others—barriers some people face in relation to their freedom and material well-being.

22.3 Equality, justice, and inclusion

Flowing from her account of oppression and her socially grounded conception of the self, Young's approach to equality contrasts significantly with that of contemporary liberal theories of justice which emphasize the distribution of resources (or welfare). Young distinguishes her approach from the distributive paradigm endorsed by prominent political and legal philosophers such as John Rawls (1999 [1971], see also Chapter 32) and Ronald Dworkin (1981). In her view, oppression, as the basis for inequality, cannot be understood through a logic of redistribution, exemplified by Rawls's (1999 [1971]) theory of justice, as this leads to overlooking the social and institutional context in which specific patterns of distribution emerge.

Rawls's idea of justice as fairness was primarily concerned with correcting an unjust distribution—in terms of resources, rights, or opportunities—and achieving a just society where even the most disadvantaged individuals could benefit from inequality: this is the essence of the second principle of justice, the difference principle (Rawls, 1993: 5–6, 1999 [1971]: 65–70). In contrast, Young's theory is primarily concerned with analysing the social processes and institutionalized patterns of oppression that uphold inequality. Her critique of distributive justice is related to the fact that it is insufficient as a remedy for social oppression, and therefore for tackling structural inequalities.

To give an example, the social stratification of employment, coupled with stereotypical gendered assumptions, significantly limit women's access to work, even more when they become mothers, and thus the possibility of exercising rights that are formally recognized. While acknowledging the relevance of redistribution in any plausible theory of justice, Young criticizes predominant liberal accounts for disregarding the pervasiveness of social institutional frameworks and the individual positioning and interactions that occur within such frameworks. Likewise, in her view, the logic of distribution implicitly assumes an individualized conception of the self which precedes social relationships, and is therefore not neutral, but more like that of a consumer merely focused on satisfying their interests or needs (Young, 1990: 36). According to Young, this atomistic and static depiction of individual choices and of social life is far too reductive. In fact, the dichotomy between choices and circumstances that is central to liberal egalitarian theories such as those of Rawls or Ronald Dworkin also fails to account adequately for the phenomenon of structural inequality.

Indeed, the form of distributive justice that Elizabeth Anderson (1999) has called 'luck egalitarianism' tends to obscure systemic patterns of discrimination under 'bad luck' scenarios; or, alternatively, it encourages members of marginalized groups to conclude that they are responsible for their circumstances (even though, in some accounts, this might be relevant to justify some form of redress or compensation) or that these are beyond transformation.

Yet, women, and members of marginalized social groups, are typically not victims of bad luck, or make individual bad choices for some reason relating to their capacity. On the contrary, their agency is restricted due to 'multiple forms of exclusion, unequal burdens or costs deriving from institutional organization, rules, or decisions, and the cumulative consequences of each' (Young, 2001: 8, 15); as compared with members in other groups better positioned to have easier access to education, benefits, and opportunities that have a direct impact on the definition of their choices and perceptions of self-worth.

Young thus regards predominant liberal egalitarian conceptions as reductionist, because they primarily focus on how individuals fare in relation to one another (Young, 1990: 15–38). Young contends that adopting a group-conscious standpoint that takes social positionality seriously provides a better grounding for justice. In her view, inequality is fundamentally related to oppression as a broader phenomenon involving a set of social processes and structures that create and reproduce what Nancy Fraser dubs 'status hierarchies' (Fraser, 2000) (see Key Thinker: Nancy Fraser). This form of group subordination produces harmful effects in the form of negative outcomes that disproportionately affect members in oppressed groups, such as constraints in freedom and autonomy or the risk of being subjected to various forms of violence, which are not the result of targeted acts of individual discrimination. Group-conscious assessments of discrimination are thus not merely metaphorical, but remain crucial to comprehending the subordinating character of those processes, as well as the kind of constraints affecting specific categories of peoples (Young, 2001).

Key Thinker: Nancy Fraser

Nancy Fraser (1947–) is an American philosopher, political theorist, and socialist feminist. She is renowned for her propositions of a post-socialist framework of Marxist emancipatory projects, one that goes beyond class-based analysis towards a more intersectional understanding of extra-economic forms of oppression and injustice. In Young's and Fraser's exchange in the *New Left Review*, they discussed issues of injustice and group differentiation. Fraser's framework runs on a more analytical level, differentiating between groups affected by socio-economic injustice—rooted in the political-economic structure of society—and cultural injustice, rooted in cultural domination. She explains that these two sorts of injustice invoke two different remedies: *redistribution* for socio-economic injustice, which often calls for the abolition of the group specificity that underpins the unequal distribution of resources; and *recognition* for cultural injustice, which highlights group specificity to promote their value in society. To solve this dilemma, she defends a model of socialist economics combined with deconstructive cultural politics.

Following from Young's perspective, it makes sense for social researchers to claim that women are discriminated *in relation to* men, Black people *in relation to* white people (or other predominant ethnicities in a given context), sexual minorities *in relation to* heterosexual persons, and so on. These categories help trace and unveil hierarchies of status and patterns of subordination embedded in social structures that *involuntarily* position individuals as members of particular identity groups. Therefore, rectifying or finding remedies for unjust (not chosen) structural inequalities *necessarily* requires disaggregating society into group categories (such as gender, race, ethnicity, etc.) in order to afford opportunities and resources to their members.

As we have seen, the idea of 'social structure' refers to a complex layering of elements (including legal institutions, the organization of family and sexuality, and the division of labour) in which individuals find themselves in a given *position*. This—largely unchosen—place significantly conditions their self-perceptions, their roles and ways of interacting with persons that occupy other positions within such social structures. Specific forms of subordination and inequality tend to be recreated through the performance of social agents acting in accordance with expectations and norms incorporated in those structures. Thereby, patterns of group subordination are created and reproduced which trigger inegalitarian effects that, as Owen M. Fiss (1976) argues, are unlikely to be legally actionable, as long as the ideal of equality is interpreted as merely embodying an individualistic interpretation of the anti-discrimination principle.

To summarize: Young's model of social justice focuses, overall, on challenging 'institutionalized domination and oppression' (Young, 1990: 10). Yet to achieve this goal in a context marked by structural inequalities, Young argues for a theory of justice based upon the affirmation, rather than the eradication, of social group differences. The argument is based upon the understanding that systemic oppression cannot be dismantled by standards of non-discrimination alone. In contrast with prevailing liberal theories that emphasize neutral (or 'difference-blind') rules applicable to all as a remedy for inequality, Young insists on the relevance of difference and context in order to identify, name, and accord responsibility to relationships of domination and oppression, which might otherwise be overlooked or dismissed. In her view, conceptions of formal impartiality, neutral rules, and equality as sameness can mask, thereby perpetuating, structural dimensions of domination and oppression (ibid.: 18, 21–22).

Moreover, the focus on distribution of material goods and resources, or on compensatory regimes—characteristic of distributive and remedial conceptions of justice—falls short of tackling the underlying social structures of domination that condition people's different opportunities or abilities to exercise their agency or develop their capacities (ibid.: 21–22). By contrast, Young's defence of a 'politics of difference' presupposes a broader scope of justice, which includes a conception of equality which she understands, first and foremost, as an ideal of political inclusion: '[E]quality as the participation and inclusion of all groups sometimes requires different treatment for oppressed or disadvantaged groups' (ibid: 158, see also Young, 1989: 270). This conception is seen as essential to transform (or dismantle) oppressive systems and alter the conditions under which members in certain groups often find themselves in a similar status of subordination. It also offers a framework for thinking critically about justice in concrete contexts, which contrasts with Rawlsian analytic approaches that aim at identifying a set of principles of justice for an ideal society engaging in an imaginary reasoning. This allows the incorporation of specific racial, gendered, or class perspectives on justice and inequality, and also of historical perspectives that are relevant to fully grasp pervasive forms of domination, such as the impact of regimes of slavery in today's racial subordination and inequality.

Young's theory offers an important basis for thinking of equality in a social world shaped by systemic patterns of oppression. Young's approach distinguishes between the provision of equal rights and opportunities within existing (and oppressive) systems—i.e., distributive justice—and altering the conditions under which oppression arises—i.e., what Young terms social justice. Such an approach can illuminate the work of contemporary global movements such as Black Lives Matter, which began in 2013 in response to the murders of numerous African Americans. Rather than relying simply on the individualistic legal language of racial discrimination, Black Lives Matter has emphasized *systemic racism*. At the core of the movement there is the idea, in line with Young's notion of structural injustice, that instances of violence against African Americans and other Black people are the product of centuries of racist policies and discrimination, which have systematically and disproportionally affected Black people as a distinctive social group.

> **22.3. Equality, justice, and inclusion: Key Points**
>
> - Young is critical of liberal egalitarian theories of justice, which focus on distributive paradigms rather than the social and institutional contexts from which specific patterns of distribution emerge.
> - She criticizes prevailing liberal theories that emphasize neutral ('difference-blind') rules applicable to all as a remedy for inequality on the basis that they can mask—and therefore perpetuate—structural dimensions of domination and oppression.
> - In contrast to the focus of liberal egalitarian theories on the distribution of material goods and resources, or else on compensatory regimes, Young defends a 'politics of difference' that presupposes a broader scope of justice, which includes a conception of equality as an ideal of political inclusion that sometimes requires different treatment for marginalized and oppressed groups.

22.4 Citizenship, democracy, and representation

22.4.1 Citizenship and the 'politics of difference'

Young's theory of equality as inclusion has a distinctive significance in her conception of democracy, essentially linked to a 'politics of difference', as she dubs it, grounded in a critique of the ideal of universal citizenship (Young, 1986; 1989; 1990; 2000). In her view, democracy and difference have a mutually reinforcing relationship and are closely intertwined with notions of inclusion and representation: without channels of representation and participation that acknowledge and promote the effective inclusion of diverse groups—especially marginalized ones—in political decision-making processes, a polity will hardly ever be fully democratic.

The defence of a group-differentiated conception of citizenship, linked to such 'politics of difference', is one of Young's most distinctive contributions. The commitment to difference is a form of attributing equal moral worth and value to the unique perspectives, experience, and histories of different social groups, which can never be adequately represented by outsiders. Young develops this model in opposition to the liberal universal conception of citizenship based upon a generalized, abstract, and homogeneous model to which she objects as potentially reinforcing oppression because it overlooks the claims of structurally marginalized social groups.

Indeed, discussing the ambiguous meaning of the term 'universality', she writes: 'universality in the sense of the participation and inclusion of everyone in moral and social life does not imply universality in the sense of the adoption of a general point of view that leaves behind particular affiliations, feelings, commitments and desires' (Young, 1990: 105). This nuanced distinction offers the basis for a critique of a liberal model of the 'normal' citizen typically based on the attributes of white, heterosexual, able-bodied, and patriotic males educated in the dominant language and culture (Young, 1989; 1990: 10–11, 54–55, 97, 110–120). As Young recalls, historically, citizenship has not been neutrally defined as a way of transcending all sorts of particularism. In depicting a model shaped by exclusive loyalties as well as by primordial identities or values—sex, language, or race—which are difficult or impossible to appropriate by everyone, most democratic states generated systematic exclusions. Minorities and Indigenous peoples, for instance, that deviated from a model of a unified demos based on a presumed common identity were coercively pressured to assimilate (multiculturalist theorists share this critique with Young—see Margalit and Raz, 1990; Kymlicka, 1991; 1995; Taylor, 1994). Women, Black, and gay identities were silenced, marginalized, and even criminalized in the public sphere.

Against this background, complex and multifaceted realities were obliterated for the sake of homogeneous, ethnocentric, racist, and gendered images of the polity that states typically promoted through standardized systems of public education, public symbols, and so on. As Benedict Anderson (1983: 6) famously put it, nations are thus 'imagined communities', not because they are completely invented, but because their existence depends upon acts of collective imagination which are arbitrated through cultural devices.

The historical processes of exclusion in the configuration of liberal democratic conceptions of citizenship remain embedded in the rules, policies, and dynamics that reproduce social systems of oppression, as described by Young. Aspects such as gender, language, or national identities have *already* been incorporated, remaining deeply embedded in roles and positions that have been structured in biased ways. This produces profoundly unequal results for a number of groups, which cannot be reversed through mere anti-discrimination statutes that take for granted that (1) neutrality is the norm; and (2) that every citizen is equally included in a conception of universal citizenship as generality (Young, 1989: 251).

In Young's view, a politics of difference is needed to tackle such indirect and unconscious forms of bias and discrimination—one that recognizes group-differentiated forms of citizenship and acknowledges that members of certain groups are included in the political community not only as individuals, but also through the group. Therefore, their rights would depend, in part, on their group membership (see also Kymlicka, 1995). Her proposal thus contrasts with the predominant liberal conception of citizenship as 'generality', linked to an individualist view of the self as a rational agent deprived of an identity—as modelled in Rawls's 'original position' (Rawls, 1999 [1971]: 15–19, 102–171; 2001: 14–18)—and of equality as requiring a commitment to difference-blindness.

22.4.2 Representation, deliberation, and inclusion

The appeal of Young's approach to citizenship lies in its better understanding of the relationship between claims of identity and structural inequalities. In many cases, legal and political institutions have been historically appropriated by dominant majorities that have enjoyed a privileged position to shape these institutions in accordance with their own culture, perspectives, and experiences; as a result, they often remain biased against traditionally marginalized groups, including women, the poor, national, or other minorities. Young's politics of difference provides a group-conscious framework to overcome the outcomes of such social structures and patterns of subordination, which typically lead to structural inequalities. 'Group-differentiated citizenship' is central to her conception of democratic politics, which seeks to ensure the effective inclusion of vulnerable and historically subordinated groups as equal members in the polity without making them assimilate or conform to the predominant mainstream culture.

Both inclusion and diversity thus play a key role in Young's conception of democracy, which she relates to guaranteeing equal and meaningful opportunities of participation in collective decision-making to all individuals concerned (Young, 1990: 173; 2000). In justifying the need for special representation of marginalized groups, she criticizes the idea of impartiality in moral and democratic theory as reductionist, as it expresses a misleading 'logic of identity that seeks to reduce differences to unity' (Young, 1990: 97). Accordingly, she rejects the assumption that there is a single perspective or standpoint available to rational beings, and that the true meaning of 'justice' is the 'impartial' application of rules to everyone, regardless of the particularities of the social context or positions. Young admits that standards of universality and impartiality characteristic of political liberalism have been used in favour of the emancipation of oppressed groups—for instance, liberal feminists invoke them as a main argument in favour of women's equality (Okin, 1989; Nussbaum, 2001); yet she claims this is insufficient to unsettle systemic inequalities, which tend to reproduce historical exclusions.

Hence, diversity and difference are indispensable elements of further political inclusion and democratic equality. In developing these connections, Young's defence of a deliberative model of democracy over an aggregative one is crucial. As she argues, aggregative models of democracy take the political process (and decision-making) as the sum of the most widely or strongly shared preferences of individual citizens, which are taken as formed outside political deliberation (Young, 2000: 19–20; see also Young, 1997). But there are three problems with such an approach. First, by taking political preferences as given, this model provides no basis from which to scrutinize their origins and motives, nor to evaluate their quality (Young, 2000: 20–21). Second, precisely because of the emphasis on aggregating preferences and votes, the democratic process becomes a competitive business: political parties and candidates will seek to offer solutions and platforms that cater to the wider demand (ibid.: 21–22). Third, the reasonability of decisions thus achieved is thin and individualistic to the extent that it requires no compromise to engaging in a broader dialogue, or to listening to others with a view to re-examining the correctness of one's own competing interests or preferences (ibid.: 20–21).

In contrast, deliberative models of democracy generally take participation and public discussions as essential elements of collective governance (see Bohman and Rehg, 1997; Koh and Slye, 1999; Bächtiger et al., 2018). As Young stresses, decision-making is reached through public debate on the fairness and reasonability of policies (Young, 2000: 22–23). Understanding democracy through the lens of deliberation not only holds a methodological value, providing a framework through which to understand how political preferences develop and change; it also harbours, as Young contends, a thicker normative dimension than the aggregative one, specifically for the attainment of four important ideals: inclusion; political equality; reasonableness; and publicity (see also Young, 1997: 362–364).

1. *Inclusion:* because deliberative models of democracy foreground discussion and exchange, it calls for the inclusion of all those affected by the issue under deliberation to participate in decision-making (Young, 1990: 198; 2000: 23).

2. *Political equality:* for deliberation to occur fruitfully, not only do those affected need to be included in the decision-making, but they also need to participate in it on an equal footing (Young, 1990: 173; 2000: 23–24). By 'equal footing', Young means the equal political opportunity to speak, question, respond, and criticize others—all of this while being free from a position where you may be coerced into accepting proposals or outcomes with which you do not agree (Young, 2000: 23–24). Political equality is crucial to guarantee the democratic legitimacy of decision-making, as citizens can see that decisions derive from their participation in reasonable discussions rather than from fear or false consensus (ibid.: 23).

3. *Reasonableness:* reasonableness refers to the disposition of participants to listen to others meaningfully, with a view to understanding different positions and reviewing one's own position whenever appropriate. This is particularly important for the trust of participants in democratic processes, as they will be able to enter deliberations with confidence that collective problems will be discussed through active listening and a disposition, among participants, to be persuaded of the wrongness or inappropriateness of their own opinions and preferences (ibid.: 24).

4. *Publicity:* in contrast to aggregative models—when participants are not required to engage with one another to discuss their preferences—deliberative democracy opens the door to a richer public discussion. Because participants need to discuss and therefore justify their claims and proposals for others, they often appeal to ideas of justice and the public good. This entails self- and collective reflection of what is publicly agreeable in terms of justice when resolving collective problems (ibid.: 25).

Young's defence of deliberative democracy does not ignore critiques of the premises embedded in some comprehensive accounts of this model, such as that of the German philosopher Jürgen

Habermas, which she perceives as based on a narrow conception of 'communicative action' that is limited to social interaction oriented to reach consensus (see Key Thinker: Jürgen Habermas in Section 29.4 of Chapter 29). More specifically, she is critical of a cognitive stance that relies on the validity of universal, rationally justified moral norms or contentions, which can be attained 'only by abstracting from the particularities of situation, feeling, affiliation, and point of view' (Young, 1990, 97). In Young's view, such understanding tends to devalue or exclude the speech patterns and interests of traditionally disadvantaged groups. In her essay, 'Communication and the Other: Beyond Deliberative Democracy', Young (1996) proposes a theory of communicative democracy that places the accent on difference and plurality by incorporating informal and situated modes of communication—such as greeting, rhetoric, and storytelling.

However, her proposal also attracted criticisms as to its practicality in the construction of a public space able to bring together different groups and individuals for democratic purposes. As Seyla Benhabib (1996: 83) writes:

> Greeting, storytelling, and rhetoric, although they may be aspects of informal communication in our everyday life, cannot become the public language of institutions and legislatures in a democracy for the following reason: to attain legitimacy, democratic institutions require the articulation of the bases of their actions and policies in discursive language that appeals to commonly shared and accepted public reasons . . . Young's attempt to transform the language of the rule of law into a more partial, affective, and situated mode of communication would have the consequence of inducing arbitrariness, for who can tell how far the power of a greeting can reach? . . . [W]hat about those who simply cannot understand my story?

Young revisits the question of communication modalities and democracy in *Inclusion and Democracy*. Building on her previous work on difference and social group positioning, her argument is much more detailed about the ways in which deliberants (especially members of marginalized groups) can use rhetoric or storytelling as modes of communication in order to contest hegemonic views (Young, 2000: 57–77, 115–120). The concept of difference thus plays a strong role in expanding the scope of deliberative democracy, as illustrated by her example of narrative in which feminist activism led to sexual harassment legislation (ibid.: 72–73). Young emphasizes that inclusive deliberations should engage with as wide a range of people's speeches and claims as acceptable 'unless and until they can be demonstrated as completely lacking in respect from all others, or incoherent' (ibid.: 70).

This interpretation thus aims at fully incorporating the perspective of marginalized groups in political deliberation, even if this might become detrimental to the 'rationalized' ideal of deliberation. As Young (ibid.: 39–40) notes, accounts of argumentative communication that privilege 'orderly', 'calm', and 'disembodied' norms of tone, grammar, and diction can be biased in favour of the speech culture of white, middle-class men. In contrast, the speech cultures of women and racialized minorities are often regarded as emotional, disorderly, and embodied. The problem with such hierarchization of speech forms for democratic deliberation is that it elects the first as 'neutral' and 'impartial', while the latter are depicted as their opposites.

Likewise, in *Inclusion and Democracy*, Young pays closer attention to the relevance of building shared values across differences through democratic deliberation (see Schwartz, 2015). Yet, in line with her broader justification of the virtues of deliberative democracy, her discussion of reasonableness as a basis for common understanding remains much more grounded in *listening* and cultivating dialogue across differences than on seeking an agreement as the most important outcome of deliberations. As she argues:

> Reasonable people enter discussion to solve collective problems with the aim of reaching agreement. Often they will not reach agreement, of course, and they need to have procedures for

> reaching decisions and registering dissent in the absence of agreement. Reasonable people understand that dissent often produces insight, and that decisions and agreements should in principle be open to new challenge. While actually reaching consensus is thus not a requirement of deliberative reason, participants in discussion must be aiming to reach agreement to enter the discussion at all. Only if the participants believe that some kind of agreement among them is possible in principle can they in good faith trust one another to listen and aim to persuade one another.
>
> (Young, 2000: 24)

The argument, however, remains unconvincing to some critics. As objected by Hekman (2005: 95-98), by assuming that differently situated individuals can come together and reach an agreement—especially on what it means to have 'justice', Young risks 'abandoning the "difference" aspect of the politics of difference', whereby difference, despite being the starting point of her model, is reduced to merely a 'stepping stone to uniformity'.

Young's theory of social positioning also has implications for her conception of deliberative democracy. Starting from the premise that individuals cannot bracket out their particular social positioning, she contests the prevailing understanding of objectivity in public deliberation and decision-making (Young, 2000: 112-114). Instead of suppressing difference and particularity in order to reach a supposedly impartial 'view from nowhere' (Nagel, 1986), democratic processes should aspire to reach a more nuanced and 'complete' public discussion, which might include multiple points of view (Young, 2000: 112-114).

To understand how Young operationalizes such a notion, it is important to recall the distinction between interests, opinions, and perspectives. While individuals can be represented in their interests—i.e., what they hold as important and influential to their life prospects and goals (ibid.: 134)—or even in their opinions—i.e., the principles, priorities, and values a person holds (ibid.: 135)—their social perspectives hold a specific value to democracy. This is because social perspectives constitute an individual's 'way of looking at social processes', shared with similarly positioned individuals (ibid.: 136-137). They thus refer to what is important or what affects the life prospects and goals of individuals (ibid.: 136); therefore, their inclusion helps to expand on the ways in which a social issue will be reflected on and decided upon via political decision-making. Because of this, even if a group may not hold a common interest or opinion, they can still be represented in their social perspective (ibid.: 136-137, 143-144).

For example, Black women of a certain age and class might be attuned to specific social issues that white men from another class might be less sensitive to. This does not mean that these Black women will converge entirely in their opinions, interests, or even on their interpretations of those issues. They will, however, bring a specific way of looking to specific issues, and it is by having multiple ways of looking represented in public deliberation that objective decision-making is reached.

Note that Young's concern with the inclusion of different social perspectives is also relevant in order to counteract structural inequalities affecting subordinated groups. In this regard, her defence of group representations implies adopting institutional mechanisms and devoting public resources to support the self-organization and empowerment of groups and also to foster the voicing of a group's perspective on how certain policies might affect them, and even granting veto power regarding policies that have a direct impact on their members—she uses, as examples, reproductive rights of women and use of reservation lands for Native Americans (Young, 1989: 261-262; 1990: 184). Young also discusses the idea of reserving a specific number of legislative seats for those groups (Young, 2000: 149-150) in line with the proposal on group representation also defended by Will Kymlicka (1995: 144-149). Although she recognizes that this tends to 'freeze both the identity of that group and its relations with other groups in the polity' and thus it should be a temporary option and a last resort.

22.4.3 Relations between representative and represented person

Another important reflection that Young's focus on social perspectives brings to representational politics is the recognition that individuals may hold similar—but not identical—social positions. This realization then exposes the inadequacy of expecting representatives to identically represent (and therefore 'substitute') their constituency (Young, 1997: 358, 361–362). The substitutive model is based on an identitarian 'descriptive' or 'mirror' logic that is impossible to realize (Young, 2000: 126–133). For instance, an Asian man who grew up in a predominantly African-American neighbourhood and social environment may be able to represent an African-American perspective—while most Asian-American men could not (ibid.: 147–148). Grounding representation on social positioning then moves past this identity framework. While individuals within a structurally differentiated social group may be better equipped to represent the perspectives of others similarly positioned, they will always do so to the extent that their own position allows them to share similar experiences and perspectives.

Moving beyond an identitarian logic, the problem of choosing *which* individual is better able to represent the perspectives of their group remains an issue. While the 'meritocratic' route is frequently argued as an option to solve this problem, Young rejects it. First, because current societies operate within a background of structural inequality, meritocratic systems will most likely present standards of merit evaluation that mimic norms and ideals of privileged groups and thus reproduce their dominant values (Young, 1990: 173, 200–204). Second, because similarity comes in degrees, applying those standards to pick representatives from systemically unprivileged groups can also result in the selection of members of unprivileged groups that have assimilated the cultural standards of merit set by privileged groups (ibid.: 212).

In contrast with merit-based ideas of representation, Young puts forward a *relationally constituted* model of representative politics that thinks of political representation 'as a process involving a mediated relation of constituents to one another and to a representative' (Young, 2000: 127). Drawing on Derrida's concept of *différance* (see Key Thinker: Jacques Derrida in Section 24.2.2 of Chapter 24), Young acknowledges that there is a difference and a separation between the representative and the constituents (Young, 1997: 355–359; 2000: 127–130). In this sense, no representative can speak for a plurality of other persons. In her view, however, the relationship between constituents and the representative, and among constituents themselves, is what makes such representation meaningful (Young, 2000: 127).

In simpler terms, what Young is elucidating here is a model of representational politics that takes into consideration the social positioning and perspective of citizens. When the representative holds a similar social standing in relation to their constituents, they will be able to represent the social perspective of the group without, however, pushing forward the idea that their views speak for the 'common identity' of the group. While the representative may decide differently than one of their constituents would—because of their different interests, opinions, experiences, and so on—their decisions would nonetheless have been informed by a sensitivity towards certain issues that is shared with their constituents.

In addition, this model of representation, which stresses social connections and positioning, allows a more active relationship between representatives and constituents. As posited by Young (ibid.: 128), '[r]epresentation systems sometimes fail to be sufficiently democratic not because the representatives fail to stand for the will of the constituents, but because they have lost connection with them'. Young's model requires a stronger sense of commitment to public debate both from representatives and constituents, whereby the representative is expected to act both as a delegate carrying the mandate of the constituents *and* as a trustee responsible for exercising independent judgement about the correct course of action within the political circumstances (ibid.: 128–129).

This dual delegate-trustee responsibility entails a representational dynamic that oscillates between moments of authorization and accountability (Young, 1997: 358–361; 2000: 129–130). In the first moment, representatives are authorized to act through a discussion process among constituents. In the second moment, representatives need to recollect the discussion process that led to their authorization, as well as anticipate the moment in which they will be held accountable, by their constituents, for acting on such authorization. This dynamic is therefore heavily dependent on public and reasonable debate for authorizing representational authority and public accounting of decision-making. More importantly, it allows a continued formation of public opinion through debate, as the constituents and representatives are engaging in discussions for both authorization and accountability (Young, 1997: 358–361; 2000: 131).

> **22.4 Citizenship, democracy, and representation: Key Points**
> - Although individuals within a group may share similarities, they will not necessarily share identities, opinions, or interests: there will invariably be intra-group differences in terms of positions, relationships, experiences, opinions, interests, and so on.
> - Objectivity in deliberative democratic processes is better achieved by seeking out a more nuanced and 'complete' overview of the problem as seen from multiple social points of view.
> - Although representation can never be identical, representatives can represent the perspectives of their structural social groups; for this to meaningfully happen, the representative needs to actively maintain a connection with their constituents.

22.5 Conclusion

Young's feminist theory of justice has a distinctive focus on equality and inclusion, which she also takes as central to democracy. Inequalities, in her view, are principally related to oppressive social practices and status hierarchies that are *structurally* reproduced, often unconsciously. In contrast with predominant liberal conceptions, the focus is placed on unsettling these group-based inequalities through social and political inclusion, rather than only through redistributive justice (whose fundamental aim is to neutralize 'brute bad luck' or compensate for individual disadvantages). Thus, tackling oppression, and the multiple forms in which it disproportionately affects marginalized groups, is a central concern that also informs her defence of a differentiated model of citizenship in her celebrated 1990 book *Justice and the Politics of Difference*. This critique is fully elucidated a decade later in *Inclusion and Democracy* (2000), which provides a broader critical democratic theory. Here, Young argues for a politics of democratic inclusion focused on affirming, rather than suppressing, group difference and group rights. Her relational understanding of gender and identity crucially informs her conception of representation and political communication, which draws strongly on Habermas' model of deliberative democracy, but remains critical of its predominant focus on coherent rationalization of public speech and consensual decision-making. Young's legacy remains highly relevant for current feminist and racial justice struggles as persistent social challenges. In her later writings on responsibility for global justice she articulates a response to injustice that acknowledges the need to account for asymmetrical relations of power and shared responsibilities (beyond intention and guilt) in a manner that allows confronting large-scale structural injustices that cannot easily be traced back to the intentions or the doings of individual persons. Overall, her rich account of the complexities inherent in overcoming oppression and inequality offers a distinctive contribution to theories of justice and democracy that remains highly relevant today.

Take your learning further by accessing the online resources for a library of web links to relevant videos, articles, blogs, and useful websites for this chapter: www.oup.com/he/Ramgotra-Choat1e.

Study questions

1. What are the five faces of oppression as theorized by Young?
2. What is the concept of social structures and how does it connect to the analysis of structural inequalities?
3. Why and how does Young criticize conventional liberal theories of distributive justice?
4. How, according to Young, does a representation of multiple social perspectives render political processes more objective?
5. How does a 'politics of difference' reconceptualize the notion of 'citizenship'?
6. In what ways do aggregative models of democracy differ from deliberative ones?
7. What are the main ideals of deliberative democracies?
8. What are the problems with 'descriptive representation'?

Further reading

Primary sources

Young, I.M. (1990) *Justice and the Politics of Difference*. Princeton, NJ: Princeton University Press.
   Young's best-known work, in which she explores in depth her conceptualizations of structural inequality and group difference and ways to rethink social justice.

Young, I.M. (2000) *Inclusion and Democracy*. Oxford: Oxford University Press.
   Young's main work on democratic theory from a perspective of difference and inclusion.

Young, I.M. (2011) *Responsibility for Justice*. Oxford: Oxford University Press.
   Young's posthumous monograph, more focused on the responsibility to address structural injustices.

Secondary sources

Ackelsberg, M. and Shanley, M.L. (2008) 'Reflections on Iris Marion Young's *Justice and the Politics of Difference*'. *Politics & Gender*, 4(2): 326–334.
   A short article that introduces many of Young's ideas on the politics of difference through a reading of three US Supreme Court decisions.

Allen, A. (2008) 'Power and the Politics of Difference: Oppression, Empowerment, and Transnational Justice'. *Hypatia*, 23(3): 156–172.
   A powerful critique of Young's conception of power and its shortcomings for addressing issues related to transnational justice.

Fraser, N. (1995) 'From Redistribution to Recognition? Dilemmas of Justice in a "Post-Socialist" Age'. *New Left Review*, (I/212): 68–93.
   Summarizes Fraser's understanding of injustices, group differentiation, and remedies, to which Young later responded.

Herr, R. (2008) 'Politics of Difference and Nationalism: On Iris Young's Global Vision'. *Hypatia*, 23(3): 39–59.
   An interesting piece that connects Young's vision of a politics of difference with nationalism in the global sphere.

Kymlicka, W. (2003) *Multicultural Citizenship: A Liberal Theory of Minority Rights*. Oxford: Oxford University Press.
Kymlicka's work shares with Young's several concerns with cultural pluralism and democracy.

Torbisco-Casals, N. and Boran, I. (2008) 'Interview with Iris Marion Young'. *Hypatia*, 23(3): 173–181.
An interview with Iris Marion Young that touches upon her personal story, as well as her views on contemporary issues of democracy and feminism.

References

Ahmed, S. (2000) *Strange Encounters: Embodied Others in Post-Coloniality*. London: Routledge.

Ahmed, S. (2006) *Queer Phenomenology: Orientations, Objects, Others*. Durham, NC: Duke University Press.

American Psychiatric Association (2017) *Mental Health Disparities: Diverse Populations*. Available at: https://www.psychiatry.org/psychiatrists/diversity/education/mental-health-facts (accessed 12 January 2023).

Anderson, B.R.O. (1983) *Imagined Communities: Reflections on the Origin and Spread of Nationalism*. London: Verso.

Anderson, E.S. (1999) 'What Is the Point of Equality?', *Ethics*, 109(2): 287–337.

Bächtiger, A. et al. (eds) (2018) *The Oxford Handbook of Deliberative Democracy*. Oxford: Oxford University Press.

Benhabib, S. (1996) 'Toward a Deliberative Model of Democratic Legitimacy'. In S. Benhabib (ed.), *Democracy and Difference: Contesting the Boundaries of the Political*. Princeton, NJ: Princeton University Press.

Bohman, J. and Rehg, W. (eds) (1997) *Deliberative Democracy: Essays on Reason and Politics*. Cambridge, MA: MIT Press.

Cohen, C.J. (1997) 'Straight Gay Politics: The Limits of an Ethnic Model of Inclusion'. *NOMOS: American Society for Political and Legal Philosophy*, 39: 572–616.

Crenshaw, K. (1989) 'Demarginalizing the Intersection of Race and Sex: A Black Feminist Critique of Antidiscrimination Doctrine, Feminist Theory and Antiracist Politics'. *University of Chicago Legal Forum*, 1989: 139–168.

Dworkin, R. (1981) 'What Is Equality? Part I'. *Philosophy and Public Affairs*, 10: 185–246.

Eisenberg, A.I. and Spinner-Halev, J. (eds) (2005) *Minorities within Minorities: Equality, Rights and Diversity*. Cambridge: Cambridge University Press.

Fiss, O.M. (1976) 'Groups and the Equal Protection Clause'. *Philosophy & Public Affairs*, 5(2): 107–177.

Fraser, N. (2000) 'Rethinking Recognition'. *New Left Review*, 3: 107–120.

Giddens, A. (1986) *The Constitution of Society: Outline of the Theory of Structuration*. Berkeley, CA: University of California Press.

Green, L. (1995) 'Internal Minorities and Their Rights.' In W. Kymlicka (ed.), *The Rights of Minority Cultures*. Oxford: Oxford University Press.

Hekman, S.J. (2005) *Private Selves, Public Identities: Reconsidering Identity Politics*. University Park, PA: Pennsylvania State University Press.

Koh, H.H. and Slye, R. (eds) (1999) *Deliberative Democracy and Human Rights*. New Haven, CT: Yale University Press.

Kymlicka, W. (1991) *Liberalism, Community, and Culture*. Oxford: Oxford: University Press.

Kymlicka, W. (1995) *Multicultural Citizenship: A Liberal Theory of Minority Rights*. Oxford: Clarendon Press.

Lugones, M. (2010) 'Toward a Decolonial Feminism'. *Hypatia*, 25(4): 742–759.

Margalit, A. and Raz, J. (1990) 'National Self-Determination'. *The Journal of Philosophy*, 87(9): 439–461.

Mouffe, C. (1995) 'Feminism, Citizenship, and Radical Democratic Politics'. In L. Nicholson and S. Seidman (eds), *Social Postmodernism: Beyond Identity Politics*. Cambridge: Cambridge University Press.

Nagel, T. (1986) *The View from Nowhere*. Oxford: Oxford University Press.

Nussbaum, M. (2001) *Women and Human Development: The Capabilities Approach*. Cambridge: Cambridge University Press.

Okin, S.M. (1989) *Justice, Gender, and the Family*. New York: Basic Books.

Rawls, J. (1993) *Political Liberalism*. New York: Columbia University Press.

Rawls, J. (1999 [1971]) *A Theory of Justice*. Cambridge, MA: Belknap Press of Harvard University Press.

Rawls, J. (2001) *Justice as Fairness: A Restatement*. Cambridge, MA: Harvard University Press.

Sartre, J-P. (2004 [1976]) *Critique of Dialectical Reason*. London: Verso.

Schwartz, J.M. (2015) 'Being Postmodern While Late Modernity Burned: On the Apolitical Nature of Contemporary Self-Defined "Radical" Political Theory'. In G.R. Smulewicz-Zucker and M.J. Thompson (eds), *Radical Intellectuals and the Subversion of Progressive Politics: The Betrayal of Politics*. New York: Springer.

Spelman, E.V. (1990) *Inessential Woman*. Boston: Beacon Press.

Taylor, C. (1994) 'The Politics of Recognition'. In A. Gutmann (ed.), *Multiculturalism: Examining the Politics of Recognition*. Princeton, NJ: Princeton University Press, pp. 25–74.

World Health Organization and Calouste Gulbenkian Foundation (2014) *Social Determinants of Mental Health*. www.who.int/publications-detail-redirect/.

Young, I.M. (1979) 'Self-Determination as Principle of Justice'. *The Philosophical Forum*, 11(1): 30–46.

Young, I.M. (1986) 'The Ideal of Community and the Politics of Difference'. *Social Theory and Practice*, 12(1): 1–26.

Young, I.M. (1988) 'Five Faces of Oppression'. *Philosophical Forum*, XIX(4): 270–290.

Young, I.M. (1989) 'Polity and Group Difference: A Critique of the Ideal of Universal Citizenship'. *Ethics*, 99(2): 250–274.

Young, I.M. (1990) *Justice and the Politics of Difference*. Princeton, NJ: Princeton University Press.

Young, I.M. (1994) 'Gender as Seriality: Thinking about Women as a Social Collective'. *Signs: Journal of Women in Culture and Society*, 19(3): 713–738.

Young, I.M. (1996) 'Communication and the Other: Beyond Deliberative Democracy'. In S. Benhabib (ed.), *Democracy and Difference: Contesting the Boundaries of the Political*. Princeton, NJ: Princeton University Press.

Young, I.M. (1997) 'Deferring Group Representation'. In I. Shapiro. and W. Kymlicka (eds), *Ethnicity and Group Rights*. New York: New York University Press, pp. 349–376.

Young, I.M. (2000) *Inclusion and Democracy*. Oxford: Oxford University Press.

Young, I.M. (2001) 'Equality of Whom? Social Groups and Judgments of Injustice'. *Journal of Political Philosophy*, 9(1): 1–18.

Young, I.M. (2005a) 'House and Home: Feminist Variations on a Theme'. In S. Hardy and C. Wiedmer (eds), *Motherhood and Space*. New York: Palgrave Macmillan US, pp. 115–147.

Young, I.M. (2005b) *On Female Body Experience*. Oxford: Oxford University Press.

Young, I.M. (2006) 'Responsibility and Global Justice: A Social Connection Model'. *Social Philosophy and Policy*, 23(1): 102–130.

Young, I.M. (2011) *Responsibility for Justice*. Oxford: Oxford University Press.

23 Bhikhu Parekh

VARUN UBEROI

Chapter guide

This chapter focuses on Bhikhu Parekh's texts on multiculturalism, as they are his best-known works and have had a significant impact on political philosophers, scholars in other disciplines, and policymakers. Section 23.1 introduces Parekh, and Section 23.2 examines his ideas about culture and cultural diversity. Section 23.3 considers why he values intercultural dialogue and Section 23.4 examines his approach to legitimizing cultural diversity in a polity. Section 23.5 examines Parekh's approach to fostering unity among the culturally diverse citizens of a polity and Section 23.6 considers how his practical political interventions relate to his ideas about what political philosophy is. Finally, Section 23.7 examines the reception of Parekh's work on multiculturalism and how best to interpret it and Parekh too.

23.1 Introduction

Parekh was born in 1935 in the Gujarat in colonial India. His father attended only primary school and his mother had even less schooling. But they were aspirational for their children and Parekh was an able student, so he completed undergraduate and master's degrees in India, and a PhD at the London School of Economics (LSE). He built a career at the University of Hull by writing books about thinkers as diverse as Jeremy Bentham, Hannah Arendt, Karl Marx, and Mahatma (Mohandas) Gandhi. He also initially wrote smaller pieces about cultural diversity in Britain that many inside and outside of academia valued, and he became not only a Professor of Political Theory, but also Deputy Chairman of the Commission for Racial Equality (1986–1990). In the 1990s, his work on cultural diversity became his main focus and he wrote his most important book, *Rethinking Multiculturalism* (hereafter *RM*). It was praised inside and outside of academia, and also inspired many scholars (Levey, 2019; Uberoi and Modood, 2019). Parekh was appointed to the House of Lords and elected a Fellow of the British Academy. Three aspects of his biography influenced his thought and work on multiculturalism.

First, Parekh's (1966) early life in India exposed him to differences of caste, money, and power. This sparked an interest in how to conceptualize equality so as to justify reducing these differences. But in India, and later in England, he also saw differences of culture and how these cannot be reduced without unacceptable levels of coercion, and perhaps not even then. Unlike other differences, he thought cultural differences should be valued, as those who do so are unlikely to discriminate against cultural minorities. Yet punishing discrimination and promoting equal treatment could just as easily help to reduce such discrimination. Parekh did not yet have a good reason to value cultural diversity. A second influence gave him one.

Parekh (1990: 39) found that Gandhi (see Chapter 27) valued cultural diversity as a source of intercultural learning; and Parekh's (2000a: 335) work on multiculturalism aims to show why cultural diversity is valuable for this reason. He thus does not aim to offer a 'liberal theory of minority rights' as many other political philosophers who write about multiculturalism do

Read more about Parekh's life and work by accessing the thinker biography on the online resources: www.oup.com/he/Ramgotra-Choat1e.

(Kymlicka, 1995: 71; Patten, 2014: 6). They aim to offer justifications for minority rights that are liberal, as such rights are shown to follow from individual autonomy and other values in the liberal tradition. Parekh's interests differed from such theorists, but he also wanted to avoid such a liberal theory for a reason that comes from a third influence.

The conservative and British Idealist thinker, Michael Oakeshott, mentored Parekh at the LSE, and Oakeshott's *Experience and its Modes* (hereafter *EM*) influenced Parekh. In *EM*, Oakeshott (1933: 348) showed that whereas history presupposes, for example, conceptions of time and change, and science presupposes conceptions of regularity and prediction, philosophy ideally presupposes nothing: it aims to be a presuppositionless inquiry. The German philosopher Georg Wilhelm Friedrich Hegel and many others had a similar view of philosophy; but Parekh (1979: 501; 1982a: 231) said that the version of this argument that he 'benefited from' came from *EM*. He thus noticed how those who aim to offer a 'liberal theory of minority rights' presuppose that a liberal theory will be closer to the truth than, for example, a socialist or conservative theory, as otherwise there is little need to offer a liberal theory; but they never defend this fundamental presupposition (Parekh, 2000a: 251). Parekh wanted to avoid such unexamined fundamental presuppositions, and proceeded differently.

Key Thinker: Michael Oakeshott

Michael Oakeshott (1933: 6) was influenced by the conception of philosophy of British Idealists such as F.H. Bradley and Bernard Bosanquet, as he noted in his book, *Experience and its Modes* (*EM*). But he is more commonly known as a conservative thinker because of pieces such as 'Rationalism in Politics', 'Political Education', and his final book, *On Human Conduct*. Parekh was influenced by *EM*, but he seldom mentions some of the other pieces above, and was critical of 'Political Education' and *On Human Conduct* (Parekh, 1979; 1991).

For Parekh, multiculturalism is not a multicultural society or policies of multiculturalism. Instead, it is a 'perspective', or a place from where we see how to think about culturally diverse polities, and it contains three ideas (Parekh, 2000a: 336). First, human beings are influenced by cultures; second, cultures are internally plural; and, third, cultural diversity is valuable as a source of intercultural learning. Parekh (ibid.: 12) presupposes a 'need' to defend these three ideas; thus, he spends the first third of *RM* showing why the greatest Western thinkers since antiquity deal inadequately with them. He thus shows how ancient Greek, Roman, and Christian thinkers ignored the significance of culture; how pluralist thinkers ignored its internal diversity; and that contemporary liberal thinkers show why culture is valuable but not why cultural diversity is (Uberoi, 2021). He then defends these three ideas and the political structures that can help to realize the value of cultural diversity as a source of intercultural learning. Many claimed that he does so in a way that is 'full of wisdom and insight' and I now will depict how he did so (Kymlicka, 2001: 128; Taylor, 2001: 4).

Key Thinker: Charles Taylor

Charles Taylor built his reputation through his book *Hegel* and went on to examine the nature of our ideas of identity in his path-breaking *Sources of the Self*. In 1994, he published an essay called 'The Politics of Recognition' (Taylor, 1994), which shows how dominant political beliefs and practices in a polity are an extension of the cultural majority's beliefs and practices. Hence, such majorities often feel at home and 'recognized' in their polity, while cultural minorities often do not. Parekh shared Taylor's interest in Hegel, but interpreted some of Hegel's ideas differently, and Parekh explicitly and repeatedly endorses the importance of Taylor's work.

23.2 Culture and cultural diversity

Different thinkers conceptualize culture in different ways (see Key Concept: Culture). But a well-known conception of it refers to a national or 'societal culture' that is 'territorially concentrated and based on shared language' and is used across 'the full range of human activities including social, educational, recreational and economic life encompassing both public and private spheres' (Kymlicka, 1995: 76). This conception of culture is important, but it refers to culture in only one sense. It does not describe the culture of a company or a university or a minority immigrant culture that is less 'territorially concentrated' as it travels with people from other countries.

> **Key Concept: Culture**
>
> Culture can and has been conceptualized in many different ways. But Parekh thought that any culture is composed of patterns of beliefs and practices that have emerged over time. These patterns of beliefs and practices also change over time and may be common, for example, among people in an organization or a national or a minority community, and thus we refer to 'organizational', 'national' or 'minority' cultures. Not every belief and practice is accepted by each member of a cultural group. Instead, these beliefs and practices are common among them; and are interpreted, related, and prioritized by them in a range of ways. Equally, as a culture emerges over time, it contains 'residual' beliefs and practices that once were popular among many of its members; and 'emergent' beliefs and practices that are becoming more widespread. A culture is thus always 'internally varied' (Parekh, 2000a: 144).

In comparison, Parekh's (2000a: 143) conception of culture emphasizes that cultures emerge over time among people and are composed of patterns of beliefs and practices that help them to 'regulate and structure their individual and collective lives'. He never assumes that cultures are internally uniform, as no culture is (Young, 2001: 118; Benhabib, 2002: 4; Mookherjee, 2015: 103).

Parekh (2000a: 144) showed how the common beliefs and practices of a culture have value as they generate common systems of meaning and morality that help people to understand 'what kind of life is worth living, what activities are worth pursuing and which human relationships are worth cultivating'. Such beliefs are also used to clarify what human beings have in common as members of the same species—what Parekh calls 'human nature'. Clearly, human beings share a common physiological and psychological structure and capacity to think and express themselves, as well as certain needs to eat and sleep. Yet different cultures help us to conceptualize, relate, and attach meaning and significance to these features of human life in different ways and thus we come to understand human nature in different ways too. Furthermore, as cultures help people to discern ways of thinking about their humanity and to create different moral systems, it is difficult to understand how any culture could have no worth.

> **Key Concept: Polity**
>
> A polity is a territorially concentrated group of people who govern their own collective affairs. The Greek *polis* was one type of polity and was a small city-state that differed from the medieval kingdoms with their allegedly divinely appointed rulers. The modern nation state is a contemporary form of polity and is often seen as implying that nations are territorially concentrated groups of people who share a history and culture and should regulate their own collective affairs. Yet many have argued that nation states are now undermined from within by cultural diversity and from without by globalization and new types of polities are needed.

Cultures differ as 'human creativity, geographical conditions' and 'different historical experiences' result in different beliefs and practices (Parekh, 2000a: 120). These help some to think that the good life is self-chosen, others to believe that it is about following God or living in harmony with nature. Different cultures thus favour different forms of life, and use certain ideas and judgements of worth, or values, to defend them. Moreover, as values often conflict, no culture realizes all of them. Each culture expresses and legitimizes a limited range of values and ways to live, and is silent about or delegitimizes others. But when cultures are exposed to one another, their members are alerted to the limits of their own ideas, and to the potential of those of others. Cultural diversity in a polity (see Key Concept: Polity) is thus valuable not for encouraging what John Stuart Mill (1991: 63) called 'experiments of living', as Mill had individual, not cultural, diversity in mind and was referring to individuals avoiding societal pressure (see also Chapter 12 on John Stuart Mill). Instead, following Gandhi, Parekh (2000a: 167) argued that cultural diversity is valuable as a source of intercultural learning.

> ### 23.2 Culture and cultural diversity: Key Points
>
> - Parekh argues, first, that cultures are vague but discernible patterns of beliefs and practices.
> - Second, cultures have value because their beliefs and practices generate moral systems and help people to understand their humanity.
> - Third, cultural diversity is valuable as it is a prerequisite for the knowledge that comes from intercultural learning.

23.3 Intercultural dialogue

Intercultural learning implies intercultural dialogue; and, unlike other political philosophers of multiculturalism, such as Will Kymlicka (1995) or Joseph Carens (2000), Parekh argued that intercultural dialogue is important for six reasons. First, a person can benefit from such dialogue, as those who are culturally different from us interpret our views and behaviour differently from us, and a dialogue with them can help us to see what we cannot see about ourselves. Parekh (2011: 128) thus noticed how such a dialogue offers what scholars, artists, and politicians, experience at times: through dialogue with others who have competing views, they see their own ideas more clearly, and why they might reform them.

> ### Key Thinker: Will Kymlicka
>
> Will Kymlicka's books, *Liberalism Community and Culture* and *Multicultural Citizenship*, began the turn towards multiculturalism in Anglophone political philosophy. In these books he shows why liberal political philosophers who value individual autonomy should value cultures, as individual autonomy implies individual choice and people mostly choose from among the options available in their culture; and, to make choices, people often use the beliefs in their culture. Such ideas inspired the 'liberal multiculturalism' of liberal political philosophers, such as Joseph Carens and Allen Patten, and Parekh is explicit about learning from Kymlicka.

Second, cultural communities benefit from intercultural dialogue. For example, through dialogues about gender equality, some minorities might come to see that their daughters are not solely wives and mothers in the making; and a cultural majority may see the culturally specific way in which they interpret gender equality. Muslim women demonstrate the point well when they explain why they *choose* to wear a *niqab* and *hijab*, and do not see doing so as a sign of domination any more than they see a 'mini-skirt as a sign of liberation' (al Hibri, 1999: 46). A culturally and historically specific way of interpreting gender equality has led many to ignore the choices of Muslim women (Mahmood, 2009: 860); and an intercultural dialogue can illuminate the need to reassess this sort of interpretation of gender equality. Thus, feminists use Parekh's idea of intercultural dialogue to show how it can help to develop understandings of gender equality that are less Western and more universal (Mookherjee, 2015).

> **Key Concept: Intercultural dialogue**
>
> Parekh's idea of intercultural dialogue is about people from different cultural backgrounds conversing, debating, and learning from one another. Through the dialogue, individuals learn about their unquestioned assumptions and new ways of thinking about common problems, as do the communities that they are part of. Such dialogue is also crucial to resolve disputes, reducing violence. Such a dialogue is also crucial to identify which values should be conceived as universal and which interpretations of them can be endorsed by all cultural groups.

Third, Parekh (2000a: 271) showed how intercultural dialogue should be used to resolve disputes in a polity about controversial minority practices. Parekh (1999: 74; 2000a: 284) noted that many of these disputes focus on minority practices relating to women, such as forced marriages and polygyny (a husband having more than one wife). Through a dialogue about forced marriage, courts have learned that duress is not just physical in nature. Some women fear being ostracized from their families and communities if they do not consent to a marriage, and this is a form of duress too. With regard to polygyny, a majority may learn through dialogue why some prefer it to secretive extra-marital affairs; and a minority may learn that making the practice consistent with gender equality would mean that women are permitted to take more than one husband. While Susan Moller Okin (1999) suggests that multiculturalism could be 'bad for women' if it permitted certain minority practices, Parekh argues that a feature of multiculturalism (intercultural dialogue) can help women (see also Key Thinker: Susan Moller Okin in Chapter 10). Although Parekh says little else about gender, one of the most important feminist thinkers of the late twentieth century, Iris Marion Young (2001: 122) notes how Parekh's approach to intercultural dialogue might 'mitigate some of the objections that some feminists', such as Okin, 'have to multiculturalism' (see also Chapter 22 on Young).

A fourth reason to value intercultural dialogue is that it can make parts of a political tradition created by a cultural majority more inclusive. For example, in 1989, Salman Rushdie published a book called *The Satanic Verses*. Many Muslims around the world found it offensive, and argued that the book should carry a notice saying that it is a work of fiction, or that it should be banned (Parekh, 1990; 2000a: 295–298). Yet many objected to such requests. Parekh and other UK minority intellectuals, such as Tariq Modood (see Key Thinker: Tariq Modood), began to argue that freedom of expression had never been unfettered in societies like the UK, for if it had been, blasphemy, incitement to hatred, and libel laws were inexplicable. If UK libel laws punish untruthful public comments about people, such laws should not be restricted to individuals. Instead, such libel laws should be extended to apply to the Muslim, Jewish, and other groups that people comprise. Regardless of whether this argument is plausible (Barry, 2001a: 32), these minority intellectuals used a dialogue to show how to extend *existing* practices that restrict expression (libel laws) within a political tradition.

This dialogue showed how minority needs can be consistent with the majority's political tradition, and how cultural minorities can influence parts of this tradition so as to make it their political tradition too.

> ### Key Thinker: Tariq Modood
>
> Tariq Modood and Bhikhu Parekh worked together at the Commission for Race Equality but got to know each other during debates over *The Satanic Verses*. Modood built his career at the University of Bristol where, unlike Kymlicka or Parekh, he placed the value of religion and religious identities at the centre of his work on multiculturalism. Like Parekh, Modood was influenced by Oakeshott's work. Thus, while he and Parekh differ, they are in certain ways like-minded too. Together they inspired a subsequent generation of scholars and Parekh, Modood, and others are sometimes called the Bristol School of Multiculturalism (Levey, 2019), whose ideas are shown to differ from those of liberal multiculturalists (Uberoi and Modood, 2019).

Fifth, while intercultural dialogue can fail and violence between groups in a polity can ensue, Parekh (1989a: 155; 2015: 289) claims that the prospect of such dialogue can still help restore peace. In such a situation, violence is physical and direct in nature and those who resort to it want only one view to prevail, and it is their own. Yet Parekh claims that moral and political views reflect cultural ones, and no matter how considered they might be, they are partial and benefit from other views. One view should thus seldom prevail. Likewise, violence often aims to separate people's beliefs from their actions so as to compel them to act against their beliefs. Their beliefs thus remain, as does a search for opportunities to act according to them; yet dialogue over time can alter such beliefs. Dialogue can thus seem preferable to violence if opponents keep channels of communication open and use them to ensure their opponents witness a sensitivity to each other's interests and a willingness to compromise. This can make a return to peace and dialogue to find a solution seem worthwhile (Parekh, 2008: 179).

A final reason to value intercultural dialogue is that it is a means to arrive at *universal* moral values. Such values are what we think *all* human beings everywhere should uphold—thus we need to give plausible reasons that will appeal to different cultural groups to do so. But this is not easy, as we cannot simply, as some claim, appeal to some notion of human worth. After all, we might claim humans have worth because they can think, reason, or forge visions of the good in ways that other species cannot, thus we should all value their right to life. But the issues of when life begins and ends and whether someone can waive this right to reduce their own suffering are seen differently by different cultural and national groups. Different cultural groups conceptualize life, reason, humanity, and so on in very different ways, thus there is a need to, in Immanuel Kant's words, 'woo the assent' of others on how universal values should be understood and why they should be cherished and upheld. This is especially true when such values often come to reflect some groups more than others. For example, the 1948 UN Declaration on Human Rights lists property rights as a human right, but Indigenous groups in Australia and Canada, as well as communists, may disagree (ibid.). Only some of this declaration's rights have a claim to universality, but Parekh sees it as the 'starting point' for dialogue among different cultural groups about which moral values are universal and should be upheld as such.

Some criticize Parekh by noting that cultural majorities may not be willing to engage in dialogue over controversial minority practices; and that, even if they do, they have the power to force their preferred decision (Kelly, 2003: 99). Yet this ignores how Parekh (2000a: 305) accepts that 'dialogue is not always available'. He defends minority protests to trigger self-doubt in those who avoid dialogue, collective rights, and affirmative action to increase the power of minorities.

> **Key Concept: Affirmative action**
>
> Affirmative action policies vary: some merely ensure that instead of using informal networks, positions are advertised among racial minorities and women; others can be more controversial. This is because these policies can increase the presence of minorities and women in professions, universities, or legislatures through quotas and other mechanisms. The motivation and rationale for affirmative action policies lie in the legacies of slavery, patriarchy, and colonialism that were legally and socially acceptable for long periods in our recent history and have helped create the unequal world in which we live (Mills, 1997). These legacies mean that even though, officially, citizens in a polity usually have the same legal and political status, unofficially their status is far from the same. Some are more likely to be accepted into prestigious universities and professions while other citizens are less likely to do so and more likely to suffer poor health and economic outcomes, more likely to be arrested, and so on. Many view affirmative action measures as temporary, to be removed once more equal societies have been achieved (see Devine, 2002; Mosely, 2002).

Some also note how Parekh's position is conservative as it favours the majority's interpretation of 'how we do things around here' (Barry, 2002: 232; Kelly, 2003: 99, 104). This is because Parekh (1998: 179) initially claimed that if there is an impasse in a dialogue with minorities over a controversial minority practice, the majority's view should prevail. But this changed in *RM*. Parekh (2000a: 271) argued that only if there is (1) an impasse in the dialogue and (2) 'the matter is urgent', as a minority practice is obviously 'morally unacceptable', the majority's view should prevail. For example, if there is an impasse in a dialogue over FGM (female genital mutilation), the majority's view should prevail, but not if there is an impasse about wearing a *niqab*, as it is not obviously morally unacceptable. Parekh altered his argument to avoid criticism; and showed why his approach need not always favour the majority's view (Uberoi, 2021).

> ### 23.3 Intercultural dialogue: Key Points
>
> - For Parekh, intercultural dialogue has value because, first, it allows us to identify other ways of thinking and behaving that can alter our individual lives.
> - Second, cultural communities can see how to improve their beliefs and practices.
> - Third, progress can be made towards settling disputes about controversial minority practices.
> - Fourth, the majority's political traditions can become the minority's.
> - Fifth, violence between communities can decline.
> - Sixth, and finally, we can arrive at values that are more universal as they do not reflect only one group.

23.4 Legitimizing cultural differences in a polity

Intercultural dialogue requires people to be secure enough to welcome what they can learn from other cultures. Cultural minorities in a polity are unlikely to exhibit such security if their cultural differences are widely perceived as troublesome, as this leads to defensive 'closed communities'. The cultural differences of minorities must thus be perceived as legitimate in the polity. To achieve this, Parekh justifies equal treatment in an original way.

In different ways, thinkers from Aristotle to Isaiah Berlin have noted how human beings are fundamentally the same, as they have a similar physiological and psychological structure and similar needs. Thus they must also be treated the same, as cases that are the same should be treated as such. As human beings are the same, they have the same legal and political requirements and should receive the same rights. Equal treatment is thus usually justified by an appeal to human uniformity. It entails treating people the same; yet, at times, doing so can be problematic. For example, if children in the UK must be treated the same and a school uniform mandates a cap, then children who wear a turban, yarmulke, or hijab must remove it to attend the school. They must sacrifice a religious belief to attend the school; yet children without a faith and children with other faiths do not. Treating people the same can, thus, at times, favour some over others.

Parekh (2000a: 239) thus altered the traditional justification for equal treatment, as he notices how it ignores one particular human uniformity: that humans are 'cultural beings'. As cultural beings, humans are the same in a way that makes them different, as they interpret their physiological and psychological structure as well as their needs through their cultures, such that in one culture, sex is a biological need akin to, as Bentham claimed, 'scratching an itch', and in another it is sacrosanct. To justify equal treatment through fundamental human uniformities, while ignoring the one uniformity that helps people to understand their other ones, is to be inconsistent. To include this uniformity entails accepting how human beings are the same *and different*, and thus they have the same *and different* legal and political requirements. They therefore require the same and different treatment; and ignoring this in the school uniform example resulted in some children sacrificing something to attend a school that others did not. To take account of how people, at times, have different legal and political requirements, children in this example can be given an exemption to wear their religious headdress, and be treated differently.

Of course, a child who wants to wear a baseball cap to school may complain that they are treated unequally compared to those wearing, for example, a turban. Yet the child who wants to wear a baseball cap must show that they are obligated to do so by patterns of belief and practices that generate moral systems and beliefs about humanity, just as those wearing a turban are. If true, the baseball cap and turban are equivalent and there is unequal treatment. Yet the baseball cap and turban are obviously not equivalent, and there is the following problem too.

Parekh (ibid.: 241) argues that 'opportunity is a subject-dependent concept' and for a turban-wearing child and their parents, there is no *real* opportunity to attend a school that mandates a cap. For them, attending the school is a logical option but not something they conceive as an opportunity as they have to sacrifice a religious belief to do so. To conceive the situation as an opportunity, they need a culture that is conducive to thinking of it as one. A turban-wearing child does not have an equal opportunity to attend the school that other children have; thus, once again, an exemption should be granted to allow the turban in the school.

In response, Brian Barry (2001a: 34) noted that all rules have a disproportionate effect on some. For example, speed limits have a disproportionate impact on fast drivers. Rules dictate people's 'choice sets', and the school uniform policy gives those who want to attend the school the same choice set (wear the uniform or go elsewhere), and thus all have an equal opportunity to attend the school. Yet Peter Jones (2015: 144) notes that we seldom ask conscientious objectors to fight in a war or priests to divulge what they learn in a confession, as we are hesitant to ask people to ignore sincerely held moral or religious beliefs. We realize that people are not free to ignore them as they feel obligated to live according to them, and this seems true of the turban-wearing child and their parents too. They will not see the school as an opportunity, but merely as a logical option. Jones, therefore, endorses Parekh's approach to granting such exemptions so that certain differences will become more legitimate in places like schools.

23.4 Legitimizing cultural differences in a polity: Key Points

- For Parekh, unlike others, cultural diversity is part of a justification for equal treatment.
- Parekh shows how equal treatment of all citizens can lead to cultural diversity being more legitimate in a polity.
- Parekh shows how equal opportunity can lead to cultural diversity being more legitimate in a polity.

23.5 Encouraging unity among culturally diverse citizens

But if cultural differences in a polity are divisive, they will not seem legitimate. The citizens of any polity must exhibit unity and be able to assume that they are a unit or a group so that they can from time to time conceive collective goals and challenges. In difficult times, such as war, citizens may need not only to assume they are a group, but to explicitly think of themselves as one and to be loyal to one another too. Like unity among family members or close friends, unity among citizens becomes more visible with need. Parekh shows how national identity can encourage such unity in a way that is distinct from liberal and conservative nationalists for four reasons.

First, liberal and conservative nationalists are silent about what identity is (Miller, 1995: 21; Scruton, 2006: 26). Yet, for Parekh (1995: 255), clarifying what national identity is requires us to clarify what identity is, as national identity is a type of identity. He thus notes that when we ask about the 'identity' of a person, or the racial and other groups that people comprise, we are asking who and what they are. Yet this is difficult to know, as the features of a group of people can be conceptualized, related, and prioritized in many ways; and explaining what a person is entails explaining why their identity remains the same over their life despite the ways in which they change during it. Despite these and other difficulties, we identify significant parts of a person that we refer to as their racial, religious, sexual, and other identities and salient features of a racial or a religious group's identity too (Uberoi, 2018).

Second, Parekh (2008: 54) shows how we think and talk about national identity in two related ways. First, as a person's national identity. This refers to part of what they are, just as their sexual or religious identity does. Hence, a person may, for example, say that they *are* British; or they may say that they feel part of Britain and influenced by its legal, political, and educational institutions by referring to their Britishness. Liberal and conservative nationalists also discuss a person's national identity. But Parekh noted how national identity also refers, for example, to Britain's identity, which is not the identity of a person but the identity of a territorially concentrated group. To describe this identity, we use the features that we think connect its individual members into a group, such as the territory they share or a history or tendencies in thought and behaviour that are common among them. Such features compose the vague but recognizable conceptions of, for example, Britain that we have in mind when we refer to Britain's identity. Intellectuals clarify such conceptions and schools promote them. Yet if conceptions of, for example, Britain as a white and Christian nation were widespread, many racial and religious minorities might well be reluctant to call themselves British. Hence, the two ways of thinking and talking about national identity are related.

Third, unlike nationalist thinkers (Scruton, 1990: 71; Miller, 1995: 25), Parekh (1994: 501) notes how national identity does not always entail being part of a nation whose members share a culture. A nation's culture is usually shared as people share a home. This is because when certain beliefs and practices are common among a territorially concentrated group, these beliefs and practices surround them and create a space in which they can feel safe and at ease, just as a home can. But the citizens of, for example, Canada do not share a culture in this way; nor do those of India. These are nations in the sense that all members of the United Nations are: they are states, or what Parekh calls 'polities'. Moreover, we still refer to people's Indian and Canadian identities, and to Canada or India's identity as forms of 'national identity'.

Fourth, liberal and conservative nationalist thinkers are called nation*alists* because, like Scottish or Welsh nationalists, they defend nation*alism*, and thus nations becoming states (Gellner, 1983: 1; Kedourie, 1998: 67). But Parekh does not. Instead, he shows why national identity can encourage unity among the citizens of a polity in the following way.

Those who 'feel American' often think of themselves as a group, just as those who share a religious identity, and are 'Muslim', or a sexual identity, and are 'gay' do. They often feel loyal to their 'fellow Americans', and they feel proud of one another's achievements, as they assume that they are a group. Equally, their vague yet discernible conceptions of America can help Americans to visualize themselves as a group. Yet Parekh notes that if a government demands that a person's national identity is more important than their ethnic or religious identity, then it is legitimizing uniformity, not difference. And if a government promotes or legitimizes conceptions of a polity that focus solely on a cultural majority, it is promoting or legitimizing conceptions of the polity that encourage minorities to seem like 'outsiders' even though they are citizens, and can help to legitimize the discrimination that minorities often suffer.

But a government can proceed differently. A government can use school curricula to teach children that they are part of a polity by discussing their rights and duties as citizens. Equally, when people go abroad, they encounter ideas of what is 'normal' and 'acceptable' that differ from their own ideas and those in their polity, and in doing so they often realize how 'British', for example, they are. To encourage this thought, children can go on foreign exchange schemes, and study beliefs and practices that are 'normal' in other polities. The type of education that can encourage a person's national identity has an international dimension. Likewise, no government can insist on a particular conception of the polity without it seeming artificial and imposed. Yet schools can teach children about the different cultural groups in their polity; and there can be school debates about the most plausible conceptions of the polity. Equally, a government can declare the polity to be multicultural so as to encourage conceptions of the polity in which it is a culturally diverse unit or group (Uberoi, 2008; 2018).

At times, Parekh (2000a: 231) also argued that citizens should have 'politico-institutional' conceptions of their polity that focus on 'institutions, values, modes of political discourse', as these are more inclusive than 'ethno-cultural conceptions' that focus on ethnicity and culture. Yet Tariq Modood (2001: 249) (see Key Thinker: Tariq Modood in Section 23.3) asked how conceptions of a polity that focus solely on institutions, values, and modes of political discourse can include ethno-cultural minorities in them. Realizing these sorts of problems, Parekh seldom repeated this claim. But he continued to note that citizens should have conceptions of their polity in which it is, among other things, a culturally diverse unit or group, as then they will see why they possess unity despite their cultural diversity. Like the Indian Constitution and the British Swann Report (1985), Parekh (2000a: 196) argues that a polity must legitimize the cultural diversity of its citizens and encourage unity among them. He uses national identity to show how this can be done and Parekh's most famous practical political intervention, *The Parekh Report* (Commission on the Future of Multi-Ethnic Britain and Parekh, 2000) does too.

23.5 Encouraging unity among culturally diverse citizens: Key Points

- Parekh defends national identity without advocating national cultures or nationalism.
- Unlike nationalist thinkers, Parekh notes how we think and talk about national identity in two ways: as, for example, a person's British or French identity and as Britain's or France's identity.
- Parekh shows how national identity in both senses can be used to encourage unity among the citizens of a polity while legitimizing their cultural diversity too.

23.6 *The Parekh Report*: political philosophy and practice

The Parekh Report was published in 2000, in the same year as *RM*. It was the report of the Commission on the Future of Multi-Ethnic Britain and has been studied by scholars in different countries (Joppke, 2004; Alidadi and Foblets, 2018). Parekh chaired this commission, which showed how Britain could be more at ease with its diversity. The report thus, inter alia, advocates policies that teach children about their polity's cultural diversity, and that declare a polity to be multicultural (Commission on the Future of Multi-Ethnic Britain and Parekh, 2000: 200). Both legitimize the cultural diversity of minorities in a polity while promoting a conception of it as a culturally diverse unit or group, just as in *RM*.

But this report also offers an ideal or a 'vision' of what a polity can become that citizens can try to live up to and realize. Such 'visions' reflect the place from where its author sees, and are thus like the 'perspective' that we saw Parekh offers in *RM*. Indeed, the 'vision' for Britain advocated in the first 100 pages of his report describes Britain as what Parekh had long called a 'community of citizens and a community of communities', or what the report also referred to in shorthand as 'a community of communities' (ibid.: ix, xiv, xviii, xx, 48, 56, 148, 224). This vision conveys four ideas about Britain (Uberoi, 2021).

First, Britain is comprised of individuals (Commission on the Future of Multi-Ethnic Britain and Parekh, 2000: ix). Second, these individuals form and are influenced by 'religious, ethnic, cultural and regional communities' (Parekh, 2001: 693; 2000b: ix). Third, despite individual and communal differences, people in Britain have developed over time a shared history and experiences that cultivate certain common ways of behaving, and thus we think of British people as forming a community too (Parekh, 2001b: 694). Hence, Britain is a 'community of *individuals* and a community of communities', which is the version of the phrase that Parekh (2000a: 23; 2001: 694, emphasis added) settled on when explaining what 'a community of *citizens* and a community of communities' means in the report (Commission on the Future of Multi-Ethnic Britain and Parekh, 2000: 105, emphasis added). Fourth, Parekh (2001: 694) recommends that British people 'picture' themselves as a community of individuals and a community of communities so as to help them to accept that their individual and communal differences are part of who they are collectively, and that these differences are not divisive, as, despite such differences, British citizens still form a community.

This vision was a 'conception' of Britain that Parekh thought British people should have as a culturally diverse unit or group; and he hoped to inspire a commitment to this idea of Britain. Yet Parekh (2010) states that his report 'was born an orphan', as those who were supposed to enthusiastically welcome it, did not do so. Many criticized it, especially the few paragraphs in a 352-page report that noted how Britishness had 'racial connotations' as 'the 'truly British' or 'naturally British' refers to white people. This was mischaracterized by some journalists as saying that being British was racist. Still, the UK government implemented 66 per cent of its recommendations within three years (Khan, 2015). Within ten years, politicians from different political parties were advocating a conception of Britain that includes minorities and a majority that seemed very similar to the ideas in the report (Uberoi and Modood, 2013: 7, 12). Twenty years later, amidst Black Lives Matter protests in Britain, articles were published that showed why fighting discrimination in Britain required its citizens to have conceptions of it that include minorities so that they do not seem like outsiders; and these articles encouraged policy-makers to re-examine *The Parekh Report* (Meer, 2020; Sealy, 2020; Uberoi, 2015; 2020).

Parekh agreed to chair this commission for at least two reasons. The first was that the conception of political philosophy implicit in *RM* inclined him to do so. Recall that Parekh follows Oakeshott in thinking that philosophy is ideally a presuppositionless inquiry. But Oakeshott (1993a: 131, 146) argued at times that *political* philosophy uses political life as a mere 'starting point'. This is because it moves away from political life by thinking 'out to the end' not only the concepts of political life, but all that they presuppose, such as social life, human life, existence, and so on. Parekh, however, thought that a political philosopher can minimize their presuppositions and gradually move towards political life by, for example, examining human life, why it is usually shared with others, why doing so requires a system of authority in which loyalty, obligation, liberty, and so on are conceived and related in ways that legitimize some institutions and laws and not others. This gradually shapes the 'framework' of our 'thought', 'choices', and recommendations for political life (Parekh, 2000a: 250; 2011: 40). Parekh (2000a: 11) thus begins *RM*, we saw in Section 23.1, by minimizing his presuppositions, and by its final chapters, he reaches the practical implications of his ideas, after which the next logical step that Parekh had to take were country-specific policy ideas. He took this step in his report in part to show where his arguments in *RM* lead.

Second, Parekh (2000b: ix) also took this step because he felt a 'political obligation' to do so. Parekh (1993: 241) argues that just as citizens have 'civil obligations' to obey laws, they have a 'political obligation' to 'take an interest' in how their polity is governed. Doing so helps to ensure politicians do not 'misuse . . . power and cut legal corners' and take defensible decisions. But all this requires citizens to have a 'capacity to grasp complex issues', balance values, and carefully reason so as to arrive at judgements. Those with such skills have a particular obligation to their polity (ibid.: 245; Parekh, 2019: 210). As a citizen, Parekh had a particular obligation to advocate ideas in his polity that he had developed for all culturally diverse polities in his capacity as a political philosopher. Parekh thus does so in his report.

Parekh's philosophical work led to practical political activity, but such practical activity also led him to 'rethink' what in political philosophy is regarded as politically relevant by others (Parekh, 2005: 14). After being appointed in 2000 to the House of Lords, he served on the Joint Human Rights Committee and he discussed what 'human rights' are. But his colleagues found doing so 'irrelevant', as they were not interested in what human rights are, but in how to uphold them. Political philosophers often think it useful to clarify political terms and the ideas they refer to so as to distinguish these ideas from others. But many ignore such clarification as it is less important in practical politics where political terms and the ideas they denote are used imprecisely because they often serve rhetorical purposes (ibid.: 14). In practical politics, there is also no time or need to read a detailed argument that is explained from minimal presuppositions. Such arguments are thus often ignored by those who are not philosophers, and thus the policies that follow from them are too. Showing such policy implications is philosophically important to demonstrate where an argument from minimal presuppositions leads; but it is unlikely to be perceived as politically relevant by others, so what will?

Such relevance is clear when, from time to time, political philosophers write works that are 'political' not because they discuss political thinkers or explain political life but because they have a clear potential to change political thought and behaviour. Such works focus not on fundamental presuppositions, but on political life or salient political issues. They clarify our questions and assess the coherence of our answers about them, show us how to reason about them, and offer 'a vision' of what sort of political life to 'strive for' (Parekh, 2011: 40). These and other practices show us how to think plausibly about political life and salient political issues, and 'where we change the way people think, we are well on our way to changing the way they behave' (ibid.: 40). Once a work's potential to alter political thought and behaviour is clear, so is its political relevance and so is a reason why not only political philosophers but also others should read it. Political philosophy does not, and need not, always take this form. But Parekh came to see that its political relevance is clear when it does.

> **23.6 *The Parekh Report*: political philosophy and practice: Key Points**
>
> - As in *RM*, Parekh justifies policies that legitimize cultural diversity and foster unity in *The Parekh Report*.
> - This report also offers a vision for Britain based on ideas in *RM*, and the report's vision was misinterpreted, yet its ideas continue to be discussed many years after its publication.
> - The conception of political philosophy implicit in *RM* led to practical political interventions, as did Parekh's ideas of political obligations.
> - Practical political interventions also shaped Parekh's views on when and why the political relevance of political philosophy is clear.

23.7 Reception and interpretations of Parekh's work

To understand how Parekh's work was received, consider the context in which he published his most important philosophical work, *RM*. It was published in 2000, before a time when multiculturalist ideas were widely criticized across Europe and North America (Uberoi and McGhee, 2012). Yet initial hostility to *The Parekh Report* suggests that, even in this context, criticism of such ideas was not far away. After the terrorist attacks in the USA on 11 September 2001 by extremist Islamist group Al-Qaeda, Islamophobia and a fear of immigration grew, causing many to fear multiculturalism, in the sense of what a multicultural society supposedly brings. Similarly, if multiculturalism is understood as government policies in which, for example, children learn about the multicultural nature of their society, then politicians in different countries have grown increasingly critical of these policies (for instance, David Cameron, Angela Merkel, and Nikolas Sarkozy criticized such policies in the UK, Germany, and France respectively). Likewise, the emerging consensus in the late 1990s about multiculturalist ideas in political philosophy was shattered by philosophical critiques of these ideas put forward by thinkers such as Brian Barry (2001b).

In a period when many were hostile to multiculturalism in these different senses, we might expect many to have rejected the ideas in *RM*. Yet politicians and journalists have endorsed many of its ideas (Goodhart, 2013: 208; Uberoi and Modood, 2013; Rietveld, 2014). Parekh's work on multiculturalism received widespread praise from philosophers such as Charles Taylor (2001), Will Kymlicka (2001), and Iris Marion Young (2001). Just as Kymlicka helped to found a school of thought that is often called 'liberal multiculturalism' that many are attracted to, Parekh did something similar. He mentored Modood, and younger scholars who came to work with Modood have sought to build on Parekh and Modood's work in their own different and wide-ranging ways (Levey, 2019; Uberoi and Modood, 2019). Parekh's work has thus been recognized as significant inside and outside of academia.

Like all prominent thinkers, however, there are debates about the most plausible way to interpret Parekh and his work on multiculturalism. Some argue that Parekh is really a liberal, despite (as we saw in Section 23.1) refusing to offer 'a liberal theory of minority rights'. This is because Parekh defends equal participation, democratic representation, accountability, and free speech, all of which are liberal beliefs (Kymlicka, 2001: 132). Yet as conservatives and socialists have such beliefs too, it is unclear why these are solely liberal beliefs; and no scholar shows that Parekh conceptualizes and relates these beliefs in ways that are common only among liberals. It is true that Parekh (2000a: 338) defends certain liberal ideas, but he explicitly rejects some of them too. For example, Parekh (2000c: 251) rejects the classical and contemporary liberal belief in which 'individuals are ultimate units of moral worth' (Kymlicka, 1989: 140), as this liberal belief is seldom defended. Hence, reasons are seldom given for when, why, and how to individuate people, as we cannot always do so as, at times, we wish to think of them as (for example) dependent children or parents and in doing so we unavoidably connect them to others. Those who claim that Parekh and his work on multiculturalism are liberal in nature do not offer any reasons to ignore the non-liberal aspects of his work so as to focus only on the liberal ones and thus define Parekh as a liberal. Yet both are necessary to plausibly deem Parekh and his work liberal.

Others, such as Paul Kelly, claim that Parekh and his work on multiculturalism are 'Oakeshottian'. This is because Parekh was influenced by Oakeshott at the LSE and he has similar interests to Oakeshott in political philosophy; and Parekh's work on multiculturalism contains some of Oakeshott's ideas too (Kelly, 2003: 99; 2009: 154). Yet Parekh also has other significant influences, such as Gandhi, whose ideas differ from Oakeshott's, thus the label 'Oakeshottian' is at best a partial description. At worst, it is an exaggeration, as Parekh, we saw in Section 23.6, also rejected Oakeshott's ideas about the nature of political philosophy. He also offered one of the most significant critiques of Oakeshott's *On Human Conduct* ever written (Parekh, 1979; 1982b; Uberoi, 2021). In short, Parekh was selective about which of Oakeshott's ideas he accepted; and referring to Parekh and his work as Oakeshottian implies only that Parekh is a disciple, and not also a critic who also rejected some of Oakeshott's ideas.

Parekh is also said to join Bernard Bosanquet, J.N. Figgis, Isaiah Berlin, Oakeshott, and others as part of a British tradition of political theory (Kelly, 2010: 27). Parekh contributes to this tradition, and he allegedly 'draws' from it by using Oakeshott's ideas and those of English Pluralists such as Figgis (1913: 80), who referred to a 'community of communities'. Yet there is no evidence that Parekh obtained the phrase 'community of communities' from Figgis and other English Pluralists. The Austrian and Israeli thinker Martin Buber (2002: 246) uses this phrase when discussing intercultural dialogue, as did the former Canadian prime minister Joseph Clark (1994: 25) when describing Canada's communal diversity; as did Gandhi when describing India (Parekh, 1990: 114; 1997: 100). The phrase may have come from outside the *British* tradition. While such a tradition may exist and Parekh may be part of it, if we say little else, we ignore how Parekh is also part of Indian traditions of political thought, to which he has contributed through his work on Gandhi. Moreover, the latter, we saw, influenced Parekh's work on multiculturalism (Parekh, 1989; 1990; 2015). We also minimize Parekh's contribution to this British tradition by omitting to mention how he introduced many of Gandhi's lesser-known ideas to Western thinkers. In doing so, he helps to reverse a trend in which Western thought influences non-Western thought but not vice versa. To acknowledge this fact, we might dwell not only on Parekh as part of a British tradition of political theory, but on how he connects this tradition to Indian traditions of thought through his work on multiculturalism.

We might also call Parekh an immigrant intellectual who, like Berlin, John Plamenatz, and Ernest Gellner, made significant contributions to philosophy in Britain. But unlike these figures, and more like Stuart Hall and Modood, Parekh, we saw, wanted to influence public life too. Equally, to claim that Parekh is an immigrant intellectual is to ignore the role that being a citizen with political obligations plays in motivating his public interventions relating to multiculturalism, as we saw earlier. It also ignores how he was influenced by certain English thinkers whom he spent many years studying, such as Oakeshott and Bentham.

Parekh's work on multiculturalism defies easy categorization. But if we focus on his magnum opus, *RM*, we can plausibly claim that it includes what Parekh learned while writing about other thinkers such as Oakeshott and Gandhi earlier in his career (Uberoi and Modood, 2019; Uberoi, 2021). The insights he gained while writing about these thinkers meant that he would not offer a liberal theory of minority rights, but would instead show why cultural diversity is a valuable source of intercultural learning that requires intercultural dialogue and certain types of political structures. The value of such intercultural learning is expressed not only explicitly, but also implicitly, as his argument reflects what he learned as an Indian in England, and from studying the beliefs and practices of Indian thinkers, such as Gandhi, and English ones, such as Oakeshott, in addition to what he learned from the differences in beliefs and practices of political philosophers and political practitioners in the House of Lords. Parekh's work on multiculturalism reflects his own intercultural learning; it defends such learning, and defends creating polities in which learning from cultural differences is more likely than fearing such differences. This work then set up the political interventions that he made.

> ### 23.7 Reception and interpretations of Parekh's work: Key Points
>
> - The significance of Parekh's work has been recognized both inside and outside of academia, but it has also been subject to criticisms and competing interpretations.
> - Parekh endorses certain liberal ideas, but to label Parekh's work on multiculturalism as 'liberal' is to ignore his defence of non-liberal ideas and the ways in which he has drawn on non-liberal thinkers.
> - Parekh's work on multiculturalism defies easy categorization and has been influenced by both British and Indian traditions of political thought.

23.8 Conclusion

By the time he wrote *RM*, Parekh had written extensively about thinkers as diverse as Oakeshott, Bentham, Marx, Arendt, and Gandhi. He thus had access to their repertoires of ideas, understood their mistakes, and had been thinking about his own experiences as an immigrant in England for more than thirty years. This enabled Parekh to see deeper and further than most about what culture is, why it and cultural diversity have value, why intercultural learning and intercultural dialogue are valuable, and how they require a polity to legitimize cultural diversity while also fostering unity among its citizens. These ideas structure his political thought about what political action is necessary and he defends such action in *The Parekh Report*, in debates in the House of Lords, and elsewhere. Few political philosophers combine what Hannah Arendt called the *vita contemplativa* (contemplative life) and the *vita activa* (active life) (see Chapter 19 on Arendt), and few of them also indicate how the two can be combined. Yet Parekh's (2006) work on multiculturalism does so: he once called these two types life his 'two great loves', neither of which he was willing to betray and both of which required his attention. His work indicates how a political philosopher not only can conceptualize and justify a more inclusive polity from minimal presuppositions, but also help to realize such a polity.

Take your learning further by accessing the online resources for a library of web links to relevant videos, articles, blogs, and useful websites for this chapter: **www.oup.com/he/Ramgotra-Choat1e**.

Study questions

1. How does Parekh's idea of culture compare to the way in which other thinkers, such as Kymlicka, conceptualize culture?
2. Explain why cultural diversity is important.
3. Analyse why Parekh thinks intercultural dialogue is important.
4. What is distinctive about the way in which Parekh justifies equal treatment?
5. How does Parekh's idea of national identity differ from those of nationalist thinkers?
6. What impact did Parekh have on other thinkers?
7. Explain why Parekh can be conceived as a liberal, and what might be wrong with this description too.
8. Is equal opportunity 'subject dependent'?

Further reading

Primary sources

Commission on the Future of Multi-Ethnic Britain and Parekh, B. (2000) *The Future of Multi-Ethnic Britain Report* (*The Parekh Report*). London: Profile Books.
This co-authored report was Parekh's most important intervention into public policy.

Parekh, B. (1974a) 'The Spectre of Self-Consciousness'. In B. Parekh (ed.), *Colour, Culture and Consciousness: Immigrant Intellectuals in Britain*. London: George Allen & Unwin.
This is perhaps Parekh's best text on what it is like to be immigrant.

Parekh, B. (2000a) *Rethinking Multiculturalism*. Cambridge, MA: Harvard University Press and Palgrave Macmillan.
This is perhaps Parekh's most important book relating to multiculturalism and reflects at least 25 years of thought on the subject and what Parekh learned from different thinkers.

Parekh, B. (2001) 'The Future of Multi-Ethnic Britain Report Reporting on a Report (The Parekh Report)'. *The Round Table*, 90(362): 691–700.
This is Parekh's reflections on this report.

Parekh, B. (2008) *A New Politics of Identity*. Basingstoke: Palgrave Macmillan.
This book was a follow-up to *Rethinking Multiculturalism* (*RM*). It is particularly good for understanding how Parekh conceptualizes identity and what the international implications of Parekh's ideas in *RM* are.

Parekh, B. (2011) *Talking Politics*. Oxford: Oxford University Press.
Ramin Jahanbegloo conducted a number of extended interviews with a number of prominent political philosophers such as Isaiah Berlin and Ashish Nandy. He conducted such interviews with Parekh and published them in this book. It summarizes Parekh's biography, intellectual influences, views on multiculturalism and India and is a useful to get an overview of Parekh's thought.

Secondary sources

Barry, B. (2001a) 'The Muddles of Multiculturalism'. *New Left Review*, 8, April.
Contains an important critique of *The Parekh Report*.

Jones, P. (2015) 'Liberty, Equality and Accommodation'. In V. Uberoi and T. Modood (eds), *Multiculturalism Rethought*. Edinburgh: Edinburgh University Press.
Offers an excellent reconstruction and recalibration of Parekh's approach to equal opportunity.

Kelly, P. (2001) '"Dangerous Liaisons": Parekh and "Oakeshottian" Multiculturalism'. *Political Quarterly*, 79(2): 428–436.
    Offers one of the best-known and perceptive critiques of Parekh.

Kelly, P. (2015) 'Situating Parekh's Multiculturalism: Bhikhu Parekh and Twentieth-Century Political Theory'. In V. Uberoi and T. Modood (eds), *Multiculturalism Rethought*. Edinburgh: Edinburgh University Press.
    Discusses the intellectual similarities between Parekh's ideas and those of other pluralist thinkers.

Levey, G. (2019) 'The Bristol School of Multiculturalism'. *Ethnicities*, 19(1): 200–226.
    This connects Parekh's ideas with those of scholars whom he and Modood have influenced.

Mookherjee, M. (2015) 'At the Borders of Otherness: Tracing Feminism Through Bhikhu Parekh's Multiculturalism'. In V. Uberoi and T. Modood (eds), *Multiculturalism Rethought*. Edinburgh: Edinburgh University Press.
    This text carefully shows how Parekh's multiculturalism should relate to feminist ideas.

Uberoi, V. (2018) 'National Identity: A Multiculturalist's Response'. *Critical Review of International Social and Political Philosophy*, 21(1): 46–64.
    Shows how Parekh's views on national identity differ from those of other scholars and are valuable as they contain insights that other scholars do not offer.

Uberoi, V. (2021) 'Oakeshott and Parekh: The Origins of British Multiculturalism in British Idealism'. *History of Political Thought*, 43(1): 730–754.
    Discusses the intellectual history of Parekh's ideas.

References

Al Hibri, A.Y. (1999) 'Is Western Patriarchal Feminism Good for Third World/Minority Women?' In S.M. Okin (1999) *Is Multiculturalism Bad for Women?* Ed. J. Cohen and M.C. Nussbaum. Princeton, NJ: Princeton University Press.

Alidadi, K. and Foblets, M. (eds) (2018) *Public Commissions on Cultural and Religious Diversity: National Narratives, Multiple Identities and Minorities*. London: Routledge.

Barry, B. (2001a) 'The Muddles of Multiculturalism'. *New Left Review*, 2001: 8.

Barry, B. (2001b) *Culture and Equality*. Cambridge: Polity.

Barry, B. (2002) 'Second Thoughts and Some First Thoughts Revived'. In P. Kelly (ed.) *Multiculturalism Reconsidered*. Cambridge: Polity.

Benhabib, S. (2002) *The Claims of Culture*. Princeton, NJ: Princeton University Press.

Buber, M. (2002) 'Comments on the Idea of Community'. In *The Martin Buber Reader*. Ed. A. Biemann. Basingstoke: Palgrave Macmillan.

Carens, J. (2000) *Culture, Citizenship and Community*. Oxford: Oxford University Press.

Clark, J. (1994) *A Nation Too Good to Lose*. London: Key Porter.

Commission on the Future of Multi-Ethnic Britain and Parekh, B. (2000) *The Future of Multi-Ethnic Britain Report*. London: Profile Books.

Devine, C.W. (2002) 'Preferential Policies Have Become Toxic'. In A. Cohen and C.H. Wellman (eds), *Contemporary Debates in Applied Ethics*. Oxford: Blackwell.

Figgis, J.N. (1913) *Churches in the Modern State*. London: Longmans, Green & Co.

Gellner, E. (1983) *Nations and Nationalism*. Oxford: Blackwell.

Goodhart, D. (2013) *The British Dream*. London: Atlantic Books.

Jones, P. (2015) 'Liberty, Equality and Accommodation'. In V. Uberoi and T. Modood (eds), *Multiculturalism Rethought*. Edinburgh: Edinburgh University Press.

Joppke, C. (2004) 'The Retreat of Multiculturalism in the Liberal State: Theory and Policy'. *British Journal of Sociology*, 55(2): 237–257.

Kedourie, E. (1998) *Nationalism*. Oxford: Blackwell.

Kelly, P. (2003) 'Identity, Equality and Power: Tensions in Parekh's Political Theory of Multiculturalism. In B. Haddock and P. Sutch (eds) *Parekh's Multiculturalism, Identity and Rights*. London: Routledge.

Kelly, P. (2009) 'The Oakeshottians'. In M. Flinders, A. Gamble, and C. Hay (eds), *The Oxford Handbook of British Politics*. Oxford: Oxford University Press.

Kelly, P. (2010) *British Political Theory in the Twentieth Century*. Oxford: Oxford University Press.

Khan, O. (2015) 'The Future of Multi-ethnic Britain: 15 Years On'. Available at: https://www.runnymedetrust.org/blog/the-future-of-multi-ethnic-britain-15-years-on (accessed 25 May 2018).

Kymlicka, W. (1989) *Liberalism, Community and Culture*. Oxford: Oxford University Press.

Kymlicka, W. (1995) *Multicultural Citizenship*. Oxford: Oxford University Press.

Kymlicka, W. (2001) 'Liberalism, Dialogue and Multiculturalism'. *Ethnicities* 1(1): 128–137.

Levey, G. (2019) 'The Bristol School of Multiculturalism'. *Ethnicities*, 19(1): 200–226.

Mahmood, S. (2009) 'Religious Reason and Secular Affect: An Incommensurable Divide?' *Critical Inquiry* 35(4): 836–862.

Meer, N. (2020) 'Britain Had a Chance to Talk About Race 20 Years Ago. Let's Get It Right This Time'. *The Guardian*. Available at: https://www.theguardian.com/commentisfree/2020/jul/12/britain-race-20-years-ago-stephen-lawrence-black-lives-matter (accessed 15 September 2021).

Mill, J.S. (1991) *On Liberty and Other Essays*. Oxford: Oxford University Press.

Miller, D. (1995) *On Nationality*. Oxford: Oxford University Press.

Mills, C. (1997) *The Racial Contract*. Ithaca, NY: Cornell University Press.

Modood, T. (2001) 'Their Liberalism, Our Multiculturalism'. *British Journal of Politics and International Relations*, 3(2): 245–257.

Mookherjee, M. (2015) 'At the Borders of Otherness: Tracing Feminism through Bhikhu Parekh's Multiculturalism'. In V. Uberoi and T. Modood (eds), *Multiculturalism Rethought*. Edinburgh: Edinburgh University Press.

Mosely, A. (2002) 'A Defense of Affirmative Action'. In A. Cohen and C.H. Wellman (eds), *Contemporary Debates in Applied Ethics*. Oxford: Blackwell.

Oakeshott, M. (1933) *Experience and Its Modes*. Cambridge: Cambridge University Press.

Oakeshott, M. (1993) *Religion, Politics and the Moral Life*. New Haven, CT: Yale University Press.

Okin, S.M. (1999) *Is Multiculturalism Bad for Women?* Ed. J. Cohen and M.C. Nussbaum. Princeton, NJ: Princeton University Press.

Parekh, B. (1966) 'The Idea of Equality in English Political Thought'. PhD thesis, London School of Economics.

Parekh, B. (1979) 'The Political Philosophy of Michael Oakeshott'. *British Journal of Political Science*, 9(4): 481–506.

Parekh, B. (1982a) *Marx's Theory of Ideology*. London: Croom Helm.

Parekh, B. (1982b) *Contemporary Political Thinkers*. Oxford: Martin Robertson.

Parekh, B. (1989) 'Britain and the Social Logic of Pluralism'. In Commission for Racial Equality (ed.), *Britain: A Plural Society*. Report of a seminar. London: Commission for Racial Equality, pp. 58–76.

Parekh, B. (1990) *Gandhi's Political Philosophy: A Critical Examination*. Basingstoke: Macmillan.

Parekh, B. (1991) 'Living as an Immortal'. *Cambridge Journal*, October, accessed at the LSE Oakeshott Archive.

Parekh, B. (1993) 'A Misconceived Discourse on Political Obligation'. *Political Studies*, 41(2).

Parekh, B. (1994) 'Discourses on National Identity'. *Political Studies*, 42(3): 492–504.

Parekh, B. (1995) 'The Concept of National Identity'. *New Community*, 21(2): 255–268.

Parekh, B. (1997) *Gandhi: A Very Short Introduction*. Oxford: Oxford University Press.

Parekh, B. (1998) 'Integrating Minorities'. In T. Blackstone, B. Parekh, and P. Sanders (eds), *Race Relations in Britain: A Developing Agenda*. London: Routledge.

Parekh, B. (1999) 'A Varied Moral World'. In S.M. Okin *Is Multiculturalism Bad for Women?* Ed. J. Cohen and M.C. Nussbaum. Princeton, NJ: Princeton University Press.

Parekh, B. (2000a) *Rethinking Multiculturalism*. Basingstoke: Palgrave Macmillan.

Parekh, B. (2000b) 'Preface'. In Commission on the Future of Multi-Ethnic Britain and Parekh, B., *The Future of Multi-Ethnic Britain: Report of the Commission on the Future of Multi-ethnic Britain (The Parekh Report)*. London: Profile Books.

Parekh B. (2000c) 'Theorizing Political Theory'. In N. O'Sullivan (ed.), *Political Theory in Transition*. London: Routledge.

Parekh, B. (2001) 'The Future of Multi-Ethnic Britain: Reporting on a Report (Parekh Report)'. *The Round Table*, 90(362): 691–700.

Parekh, B. (2005) 'CSD Interview'. *CSD Bulletin*, 12(2).

Parekh, B. (2006) 'The Man with Two Great Loves'. *Times Higher Education Supplement*, 8 September 2006.

Parekh, B. (2008) *A New Politics of Identity: Political Principles for an Interdependent World*. Basingstoke: Palgrave Macmillan.

Parekh, B. (2010) 'The Tenth Anniversary of the Parekh Report'. Political Studies Association Talk, Edinburgh.

Parekh, B. (2011) *Talking Politics*. Oxford: Oxford University Press.

Parekh, B. (2015) *Debating India*. Oxford, Oxford University Press.

Parekh, B. (2019) 'A Misconceived Discourse on Political Obligation'. In B. Parekh, *Ethnocentric Political Theory*. Basingstoke: Palgrave Macmillan.

Patten, A. (2014) *Equal Recognition*, Princeton, NJ: Princeton University Press.

Rietveld, E. (2014) 'Debating Multiculturalism in Britain: Competing Frames'. *Ethnicities*, 14(1): 50–71.

Scruton, R. (1990) *The Philosopher on Dover Beach: Essays*. Manchester, NH: Carcanet.

Scruton, R. (2006) *Arguments for Conservatism*. London: Continuum.

Sealy, T. (2020) 'What Can Multiculturalism Offer in the Fight Against Racism in Britain?' *Open Democracy*. Available at: https://www.opendemocracy.net/en/global-extremes/what-can-multiculturalism-offer-fight-against-racism-britain/ (accessed 15 September 2021).

Taylor, C. (1994) 'The Politics of Recognition'. In A. Gutman (ed.), *Multiculturalism*. Princeton, NJ: Princeton University Press.

Taylor, C. (2001) 'How to Be Diverse'. *Times Literary Supplement*, 20(1).

Uberoi, V. (2008) 'Do Policies of Multiculturalism Change National Identities?' *Political Quarterly* 79(3).

Uberoi, V. (2015) 'The Parekh Report—National Identity without Nations and Nationalism'. *Ethnicities*, 15(4): 509–526.

Uberoi, V. (2018) 'National Identity—A Multiculturalist's Response'. *Critical Review of International Social and Political Philosophy*, 21(1): 46–64.

Uberoi, V. (2020) 'Can Black Lives Really Matter in the UK Before Addressing Britishness?', Can Black lives really matter in the UK before addressing Britishness? | openDemocracy (accessed 15 September 2021).

Uberoi, V. (2021) 'Oakeshott and Parekh: The Origins of British Multiculturalism in British Idealism'. *History of Political Thought*, 43(1).

Uberoi, V. and McGhee, D. (2012) 'Social Integration in Britain'. In J. Fideres and J. Biles (eds), *International Perspectives Integration and Inclusion*. Montreal: McGill University Press.

Uberoi, V. and Modood, T. (2013) 'Inclusive Britishness and Multiculturalist Advance'. *Political Studies*, 61(1): 23–41.

Uberoi, V. and Modood, T. (2019) 'The Emergence of the Bristol School of Multiculturalism'. *Ethnicities*, 19(6): 955–970.

Young, I.M. (2001) 'Thoughts on Multicultural Dialogue'. *Ethnicities*, 1(1): 116–122.

24 Gayatri Chakravorty Spivak

NIKITA DHAWAN

> ### Chapter guide
>
> Described as a 'feminist Marxist deconstructivist' (MacCabe, 1988: ix), Gayatri Chakravorty Spivak, in addition to her formative contribution to Postcolonial Studies, has greatly influenced discussions on gender justice, human rights, and democracy. This chapter outlines Spivak's critique of the Eurocentric and male-centric nature of theories of the political and her contestation of exclusionary framings of political subjectivity. In offering a countermodel of individual and collective agency, Spivak expands and enhances our understanding of political normativity in the era of globalization. The chapter is divided into three sections: Section 24.2 focuses on Spivak's ground-breaking essay, 'Can the Subaltern Speak?' Section 24.3 engages with Spivak's counter-intuitive reflections on the relation between postcolonial states and international civil society. Section 24.4 examines the ambivalent relation between the European Enlightenment and the postcolonial condition and outlines Spivak's contribution to the process of decolonizing the Enlightenment.

24.1 Introduction

A key question for social and political theory is why subjects accept their own subordination. In the face of widespread political, social, and economic inequality, why do vulnerable groups not revolt against their disenfranchisement and dehumanization?

In addition to the conquest of geographical territories and exploitation of labour and resources, imperialism is also about colonization of the mind. Accordingly, decolonization is not the 'mere' transfer of power from European colonizers to the natives, but an intervention into the ideological constitution of imperial and subaltern (see Key Concept: Subaltern, in Section 24.2) subjects at both ends of the colonial divide. Given the persistence of social injustice in the postcolonial world, the question remains: How can the exploitative structures and 'epistemic violence' (Spivak, 1985) that result from Eurocentrism be overcome? Gayatri Chakravorty Spivak (1942–) explains that political and economic transformation must be supplemented by an 'epistemic change' (that is, changes to forms of knowledge and knowing) if we are to realize the project of decolonization: in addition to economic and political empowerment of subalterns, wherein the basic needs of subaltern groups are met, Spivak proposes undoing the discontinuity between the intellectual and labouring classes. Here, Spivak foregrounds the role of the postcolonial state as indispensable (see Key Concept: Postcolonialism). Spivak also proposes planetary ethics as an effort towards rethinking global solidarity and collective responsibility to reimagine a post-imperialist world.

> ### Key Concept: Postcolonialism
>
> Postcolonialism encompasses the study of the epistemic, economic, military, social, cultural, and political consequences of colonialism and the exploitation, dehumanization, and denigration of colonized people and societies. It is transdisciplinary and multidimensional, employing a variety of approaches and methods and exploring numerous world regions. Notable theorists include Frantz Fanon (see Chapter 28), Aimé Césaire, Edward Said (see Chapter 16), Gayatri Spivak, and Homi Bhabha. The 'post' in postcolonial does not signify the end of colonialism, but rather outlines the legacies of colonialism and its continuities. At the same time, postcolonial scholarship seeks to overcome Eurocentric knowledge production and systems of representation. The attempt is to identify and undermine the hierarchical oppositions between Occident/Orient, civilized/barbaric, developed/underdeveloped, and progressive/backward. This would result in decentring the clear demarcation line between 'the West and the rest' (Hall, 1992).

Although Spivak is one of the foremost intellectuals in the field of Postcolonial Studies, the scope and influence of her work are by no means limited to the analysis of the effects of colonialism. Her writings encompass a wide range of topics, from poststructuralist thought to literary criticism, feminism, psychoanalysis, and international political economy. Poststructuralism emerged in France during the 1960s as a movement deconstructing and decentring binary structures, such as male/female, reason/emotion, speech/writing, west/east, and challenged the Enlightenment assumptions about reason, representation, and universality. As a postcolonial feminist scholar, Spivak draws on both Marxism and poststructuralism. As such, Spivak's understanding of power and resistance is complex and eclectic; she is even accused of trying to 'ride two horses at once'. In defence of such efforts, it is argued that postcolonial scholars like Spivak are 'stunt riders' (Prakash, 1992: 184) who seek to address both material and epistemic aspects of power. Along similar lines, intersectional approaches, in focusing on the co-constitution of different categories such as race, class, and gender, offer a nuanced and dynamic understanding of power and domination. For instance, Spivak simultaneously addresses how Marxist approaches disregard gender when analysing questions of economic exploitation, while gender is weaponized by imperialist feminism. Thus, Spivak has greatly enriched feminist, Marxist, and poststructuralist scholarship by shifting focus to Third World gendered subjects, who have hitherto been excluded in the critical tradition (see Key Concept: The Third World). However, rather than reconciling the differences between feminism, Marxism, and poststructuralism or between the categories of race, class, gender, and caste, Spivak (1990: 15, 116) sees her task as preserving their discontinuities. In place of methodological purity, Spivak negotiates the fertile tensions between different theoretical approaches. Furthermore, her intellectual activity is informed and supplemented by her work as a trainer of elementary school teachers in rural West Bengal. In 1997, Spivak established the Pares Chandra and Sivani Chakravorty Memorial Foundation for Rural Education.

> ### Key Concept: The Third World
>
> In 1955, the Bandung Conference took place with participants from twenty-nine Asian and African countries, who adopted the term 'Third World' as a self-designation. The conference was an important expression of political independence of formerly colonized nation states and is considered the first postcolonial international conference. In the age of the Cold War, a perspective of a non-aligned 'Third World' was formulated, which positioned itself between the military blocs of the capitalist West (the 'First World') and the communist states (the 'Second World'). The common goals formulated included

ending colonial rule in all countries that were not yet independent, the right to self-determination and peaceful cooperation. Ironically this formerly positive term, the 'Third World' is often only associated with economic 'underdevelopment'. It is important to note that postcolonialism has not simply replaced the terms 'Third World' or 'Global South'; rather, one must be aware of the genealogies of each of the terms, even as one sometimes uses them interchangeably.

Read more about **Spivak's** life and work by accessing the thinker biography on the online resources: www.oup.com/he/Ramgotra-Choat1e.

24.2 Subalternity

The Italian thinker Antonio Gramsci employed the term 'subaltern' to describe the subordination of rural labourers and peasants (see Key Thinker: Antonio Gramsci in Section 9.3.1, in Chapter 9). Gramsci (2011) points out that 'subaltern' in military vocabulary is one who takes orders, one who obeys. He explains that subalternity is produced not just through economic oppression, but equally through social, political, and cultural subordination. He thereby departs from the orthodox Marxist focus on the class exploitation of industrial labourers to draw attention to the rural peasantry and their destitution. In his analysis of class conflict, Marx largely ignores the rural peasants, for, in his view, they lack revolutionary class consciousness, organization, and leadership, which disqualifies them from being agents of revolution (see Chapter 13 on Marx). In contrast, Gramsci provides a nuanced analysis of power and resistance to trace the multiple and complex dynamics of marginalization and disenfranchisement of subaltern classes that is not merely economic in nature.

Subalterns are nonhegemonic, and are not part of organized struggles, thus their dissident political practices are not perceived to systematically or coherently oppose power. Instead of victimizing or romanticizing the subalterns, Gramsci understands de-subalternization as the process of undoing conditions that place the subaltern in a submissive position with respect to hegemonic groups. It is a lesson that Spivak takes to heart and applies to the postcolonial-feminist predicament.

Key Concept: Subaltern

The term subaltern, according to Gramsci, designates nonhegemonic classes that are socially, politically, and geographically excluded and subordinated. Gramsci's writings greatly influenced the South Asian Subaltern Studies group of historiographers, who adapted the notion of subaltern to designate non-elite sectors of Indian society. In her writings, Spivak extends the term to describe ungeneralizable fringe groups of society such as 'subsistence farmers, unorganized peasant labour, the tribals and communities of zero workers on the street or in the countryside' (Spivak, 1988a: 288). Spivak draws on Gramsci and the South Asian Subaltern Studies thinkers, but also departs from them. She pays particular attention to the subject-position of the female subaltern in the Third World, who is 'doubly' vulnerable to economic exploitation as well as gender inequality. For Spivak, decolonization is incomplete without the process of desubalternization, or undoing subalternity, which entails activating subaltern agency by enabling access to the state and political participation in civil society.

24.2.1 Representation

In her thought-provoking essay 'Can the Subaltern Speak?' Spivak (1988a) addresses the issue of silenced subjects and hegemonic listeners. Spivak explores the processes by which subalterns were systematically silenced within colonial as well as anti-colonial discourses. The starting point of this canonical essay is the question of responsibility of representation, developed as a powerful critique of a dialogue between the poststructuralist thinkers Michel Foucault and Gilles Deleuze (see

Chapter 33 on Foucault, and Key Thinker: Gilles Deleuze in Section 33.3.2 in Chapter 33). Foucault (1977: 207) argues that the masses do not need intellectuals to enlighten them about their subjugation, but are capable of understanding and depicting their oppression. In distancing himself from questions of representation, Spivak contends that Foucault abdicates responsibility towards gendered subalterns in the Third World.

For Spivak, representation is indispensable in the process of decolonization. To explain the notion of representation, Spivak uses the example cited by Marx of nineteenth-century French agrarian society, in which small peasant proprietors, due to their social and economic conditions, were unable to have a class-consciousness. For Marx, these people do not collectively represent a coherent class, such that their absent collective consciousness is depicted symbolically by a political representative or a proxy from the middle class, who speaks on their behalf. Following Marx, Spivak distinguishes between two meanings of the word representation, namely, *Vertretung* (speaking for) and *Darstellung* (speaking about) (Spivak, 1988a: 276). According to Spivak, Foucault and Deleuze claim that only 'speaking about' is politically necessary and not 'speaking for'. However, in her view there is no *Darstellung* without *Vertretung*, whereby the two terms are linked even though they should not be conflated (ibid.: 277). In claiming that disempowered groups can speak for themselves, Foucault and Deleuze constitute them as coherent political subjects, who are able to express their political desires and interests in an unmediated manner. Spivak argues that this model of political representation, when applied to the Third World, distorts the relation between First World intellectuals and subaltern subjects. This is exemplified by Western feminism's tendency to speak on behalf of Third World women *as if* the former have unmediated access to the latter's perspectives and experiences. At the same time, the refusal to represent the silenced subaltern or the claim that the subaltern can speak for itself are equally problematic. By focusing on the relation but also discontinuity between speaking *for* and speaking *about*, Spivak demonstrates that subaltern political agency is not straightforwardly legible or intelligible for the representing intellectual (Morris, 2010: 2). This confronts the representing intellectual with an ethical dilemma, namely, how to speak in the name of those who cannot speak for themselves, without paternalizing or victimizing them.

What is original about Spivak's critique of Foucault and Deleuze is that, in a counter-intuitive move, she accuses them of romanticizing political action by constituting the masses as resistant speaking subjects (Moore-Gilbert, 1997: 81, 88). Spivak draws attention to the ideological constitution of subalterns, who consent to their subordination as inescapable and fateful. Subalterns do not have an understanding of themselves as subjects of political rights, such that they understand their marginalization as 'common sense' (what Gramsci calls *senso comune*). In Spivak's view, in order to undo subalternity, addressing the challenges of representation and ideology are unavoidable. Let us now turn to Spivak's critique of the South Asian Subaltern Studies collective's attempts to recover and reinstate subaltern agency.

24.2.2 Subaltern Studies

The South Asian Subaltern Studies collective, which was founded by the historian Ranajit Guha (see Key Thinker: Ranajit Guha in Section 37.1 in Chapter 37), was inspired by Gramsci's insights and detected parallels with the South Asian colonial and postcolonial situation. Guha and other 'subalternists', as they are called, are inspired by Gramsci's focus on rural peasants who had not been integrated into the industrial capitalist system. Drawing on Gramsci and Foucault, the subalternists contest the colonial and nationalist history of India and South Asia. The focus is on non-elite subaltern groups as agents of political and social change, who previously had been marginalized in both colonial and postcolonial historiography. They argued that in the hegemonic historical narratives of the British colonizers as well as the anti-colonial elites, the complex political agency of subaltern groups was erased. Subaltern insurgencies were dismissed as sporadic, violent, unorganized, and without leadership, and thereby pushed into the realm of criminality. Thus, postcolonial nation-building ended up being an elite project, where colonial interests were replaced by the interests of the privileged native, but did not automatically result in desubalternization. Combining Gramsci and Foucault, the subalternists propose a counter-history that addresses the role of subalterns as agents of resistance (Guha, 1999). The subalternists aim to contribute to the project of decolonization by recovering the voice, will, and consciousness—the *agency*—of subaltern groups.

As a postcolonial feminist, Spivak too is concerned with recuperating the silenced voices of the disempowered. Spivak particularly focuses on the gendered subaltern, who is doubly effaced through colonialism and patriarchy (Spivak, 1988a: 287). It is important to note here that Spivak is not merely substituting a gendered notion of the subaltern for a class-based notion; rather, she outlines how the exclusive focus on class overlooks the gendered processes of subalternization (Morton, 2003: 60).

Even as Spivak supports the efforts of the subalternists, she warns against the risks of valorizing subaltern agency as authentic and heroic. In the name of recovering subaltern voices, the historians project a subversive political will and consciousness onto the subaltern insurgent (Spivak 1988b: 203). Against the impulse to recover and represent the subaltern as a coherent political agent, Spivak counter-intuitively explains that subaltern agency becomes intelligible only through the mediation of the elite (Morton 2003: 54; 2007: 101–105).

In contrast to Foucault, who constructs an 'expressive' subject who knows and speaks about their exploitative conditions, and thus does not need to be represented, Spivak explains that the question 'Can the Subaltern Speak?' is rhetorical, because the impossibility of the subaltern being heard is implicit in the notion of subalternity. This insight has been one of the key contributions of Spivak's work, complicating the political programme of the subalternists' efforts to recover subaltern agency. Bringing in deconstructive (see Key Thinker: Jacques Derrida) and poststructuralist interventions into the Marxist political project, Spivak shows the limits of a straightforward revolutionary agenda.

Key Thinker: Jacques Derrida

Associated with poststructuralist and postmodern thought, the French philosopher Jacques Derrida (born in El Biar, French Algeria, in 1930) is best known for his ground-breaking approach called deconstruction. Deconstruction perceives language to be irreducibly complex, unstable, and open-ended, so that the meaning of words are impossible to define and determine. Accordingly, deconstruction is a criticism of the binary thinking that relies on oppositions such as being/nothingness, normal/abnormal, essence/appearance, mind/body, nature/culture, speech/writing, man/woman, white/Black. The ongoing task of deconstruction is to expose the violent hierarchy implicit in these dual concepts and undermine these oppositions. Derrida is the author of influential books including *Of Grammatology* (1967), which Spivak translated from French into English in 1976. Spivak wrote an immensely dense 79-page translator's introduction, which has been described as 'setting a new standard for self-reflexivity in prefaces' (Landry and MacLean, 1996: 1). Spivak's translation is considered responsible for introducing many in the English-speaking world to Derrida's work and to the concept of 'deconstruction' for the first time. He is considered one of the most influential thinkers of our times. He died, aged 74, in 2004.

In Spivak's view, there is no undivided subaltern consciousness that can easily be recuperated. She draws attention to the ways in which factors such as gender and caste create a heterogeneous (varied) field of subject-positions, and thus questions the claim that a counter-history merely involves making subalterns the subject of their own histories. Rather, Spivak urges us to undertake the more difficult project of attending to that which resists coherence and transparency, for example, the figure of woman. Against Foucault, Spivak argues that the postcolonial feminist cannot renounce the responsibility of representation, which is a more complex task than mere recovery of subalternized perspectives. Despite her misgivings, as a member of the Subaltern Studies Collective, Spivak endorses 'a *strategic use* of positivist *essentialism* in a scrupulously visible political interest' (Spivak, 1988b: 205).

> **Key Concept: Strategic essentialism**
>
> Strategic essentialism is a term coined by Spivak to refer to a political tactic of provisionally setting aside differences and heterogeneity within minority groups in the interests of unity to pursue chosen political ends. By strategically drawing on essentialist concepts, such as 'women' or 'Black', to invoke a shared identity, collective representation is made possible in order to achieve certain goals like gender or racial equality. Spivak (1993a: 3–4; 2008: 260) subsequently disavowed the term, indicating her dissatisfaction with how the term has been deployed to justify nationalist agendas.

Spivak draws attention to colonial debates on *Sati* (the practice of the self-immolation of widows on the funeral pyres of their husbands) in colonial India to illustrate the challenges of representing subalternity. As the act of taking one's life was strictly forbidden in ancient Hindu scriptures, the practice of widow self-immolation was an anomalous sacred ritual. The woman's 'choice' to die was considered an exceptional signifier of her free will and moral conduct (Spivak, 1988a: 300, 303). The exceptionality of the act of self-immolation is lost in translation and misconstrued by the British colonial administrators in the process of outlawing the practice in 1829. The Anglicized term *suttee* used to denote the ritual is a transliteration of the Sanskrit *sati*, which actually refers to the woman who performs the act. The Sanskrit term सती/satī simply means chaste wife and derives from सत्/sát (good). This was misrepresented by the British colonial administrators as *suttee* to denote the rite of widow sacrifice. Condemning the practice as an epitome of the barbaric and inhuman characteristics of Hindu society, they outlawed *suttee*. By rendering the native woman as an object of protection, imperialism as a civilizing mission was justified. Spivak describes this move in terms of 'White men are saving brown women from brown men' (ibid.: 297). While British colonial administrators claimed that they were rescuing Indian women from traditional Hindu patriarchal society, native men declared that 'the women wanted to die' (ibid.: 297). Rather than enabling native women's agency, both the British colonial administrators as well as elite Hindu men used the body of the widow as an ideological battleground for patriarchal and colonial power (Moore-Gilbert, 1997: 89–90). Subaltern women are caught between competing patriarchies, which mutually reinforce each other. In this context, Spivak (1988a: 308) argues that there is no space from which the subaltern as female can speak. She is allowed no subject-position, no site of enunciation since both white and brown men speak for her (ibid.: 297).

24.2.3 Imperialist feminism

The notion of 'double colonization', namely, that women in colonial contexts were subjected to both imperial ideologies and native patriarchies, is a crucial insight of postcolonial feminist discourse (Gandhi, 1998: 83). Postcolonial feminism shows how imperialism used gender violence as an alibi to legitimize itself.

As a simultaneous critique of white colonizers and Indigenous patriarchies, postcolonial feminism exposes anti-colonial nationalistic discourses' disregard of gender issues, such that in the struggle against the colonizers, the 'internal' hierarchies and injustices were erased. For example, the British colonial rulers in India declared that Indians were unfit for self-rule on account of their 'barbaric' attitudes towards women. Yet demands for gender equality set off fears among the anti-colonial nationalist elite of the 'Westernization' of Indian women and loss of authenticity. Between imperial and nationalist masculinities, the Third World woman was caught in the middle of competing patriarchal ideologies.

Equally significant is the critique of imperialist feminism offered by feminist postcolonial theory. The discourse about the 'emancipated' modern woman automatically evokes the image of the white, Western, bourgeois woman, with the 'other' woman automatically relegated to the role of the 'victim'. This goes hand in glove with the construction of the Third World as a site of gender oppression and 'oriental barbarism'. The 'emancipated' Western feminist is the one who has 'voice' in contrast to her 'mute(d)' Third World counterpart (Mohanty, 1988: 64).

Spivak unfolds the complicity of Western feminism in imperialistic discourses and problematizes the politics of 'global sisterhood'. Thus, in the name of solidarity with women in the Third World, Western feminism may unconsciously reproduce imperialist assumptions, such as the unquestioned liberal promotion of female autonomy as the greatest good. According to Spivak, the stereotyping of Third World women as 'helpless' justifies 'rescue narratives'. This reinforces paternalistic and condescending aid politics, which correspondingly constructs the Western feminist as benevolent and altruistic (for further elaboration, see Abu-Lughod, 2013).

Spivak advises elite women of the Global North but also in the Global South to unlearn the impulse to see themselves as role models for poor rural women (Ray, 2009: 56–59, 116). For an ethical relation between intellectuals and subalterns, the former need to 'earn trust' from the latter. Instead of gathering data about the other, the elite must take leave from the idea of themselves as knowledge producers.

In her book, *In Other Worlds* (Spivak, 1988b), Spivak argues that colonial epistemologies (that is, theories of knowledge) became authoritative by delegitimizing and disqualifying non-European systems of knowledge. For instance, Lord Thomas Macaulay (1965 [1835]), while introducing English education in colonial India, argued 'a single shelf of a good European Library was worth the whole native literature of India and Arabia'. This is a paradigmatic instance of canon formation, such that the process of naturalization of European discourse went hand in glove with the disqualification of other epistemic orders. However, instead of rejecting or censoring what Spivak calls the 'great male texts', namely the writings of Kant, Hegel, Freud, or Marx, she attempts to supplement them by drawing attention to hitherto excluded narratives and perspectives (Bilimoria, 2002: 160). Spivak suggests that the literary habits of transnational elites, in both Western and non-Western contexts, need to be 'rearranged'. This would function as a counter-measure to ethnocentrism by reconstituting the relation between the West as subject and the non-West as object. She furthermore focuses on texts from the Third World, such as the stories of the Bengali writer Mahasweta Devi (see Key Thinker: Mahasweta Devi).

Key Thinker: Mahasweta Devi

Born in Dhaka, British India, in 1926, Mahasweta Devi was an Indian writer in Bengali and an activist. She tirelessly worked for the rights and empowerment of the tribal people, with particular focus on *Adivasi* (Indigenous people), *Dalit*, and other marginalized female citizens of India. Mahasweta authored over 100 novels and over 20 collections of short stories primarily written in Bengali, which narrate experiences of caste, class, and gendered oppression. Many of her stories have been translated into English by Spivak and published in the three books *Imaginary Maps* (1995), *Old Woman* (1997), and *The Breast Stories* (1997). She died, aged 90, in 2016.

In *Death of a Discipline* (Spivak, 2003), Spivak suggests that critics interested in social justice should make efforts to protect the multiplicity of languages and literatures. Furthermore, Spivak understands reading itself to be an ethical negotiation with alterity. Entering into the idiom of 'the other' through translation and comparison can enable the decentring of the authoritative knowing Western self. Here the intellectual no longer sees themselves as agent of social change, but recognizes themselves as being part of the problem.

Since 'Can the Subaltern Speak?' appeared three decades ago, Spivak has been accused of neglecting subaltern perspectives and even of silencing them. Spivak responds that most people who claim to have heard the subaltern speak are unable even to imagine what she is referring to when she speaks of subalternity (Spivak, 1993a: 137). Instead of denying agency and voice to the gendered subaltern, Spivak attempts to show that when the oppressed are represented as speaking subjects, hegemonic structures that make it impossible for the subaltern to be heard are rendered invisible.

Critics like the Marxist thinker Terry Eagleton (1999) accuse Spivak of obscurantism, opaqueness, and eclecticism. In her defence, Spivak (1993b: 33) warns that 'plain prose cheats' and refuses to flatten the nuances and complexities of concepts and histories to make them more 'accessible'. Another point of criticism is that although Spivak argues that decolonization is impossible without desubalternization, she does not outline how to achieve this. While she accuses Foucault and Deleuze of abdicating the responsibility of representing the subaltern, she also understands subalternity as 'inaccessible blankness' (Spivak, 1988a: 294). Spivak explains that this thwarts hegemonic efforts to co-opt subaltern perspectives, thereby marking the limits of Eurocentric epistemic orders. Those who are in search of straightforward political programmes and agendas will be frustrated by Spivak's critical interventions.

24.2 Subalternity: Key Points

- Spivak links desubalternization with decolonization, arguing that representation is indispensable in the process of decolonization.
- Spivak focuses on the gendered subaltern subject, who is doubly effaced through colonialism and patriarchy.
- Gender is weaponized to justify colonialism as civilizing mission and Western feminists are often complicit in this process, notwithstanding claims of 'global sisterhood'.

24.3 Alter-globalization and subalternity

One of the cornerstones of democracy as a form of the collective exercise of political power is what the German philosopher Jürgen Habermas (1989) calls the public sphere (see Key Thinker: Jürgen Habermas in Section 29.4 in Chapter 29). This is the realm where citizens publicly deliberate over societal problems, thereby influencing political action.

The Habermasian public sphere has been assailed for disregarding categories of race, class, and gender and for ignoring the fact that socially vulnerable groups are not able to have their interests heard with the same ease as the more privileged actors. As an antidote to bourgeois public spheres, the political theorist Nancy Fraser (1992: 123) insists on the normative legitimacy and political efficacy of 'subaltern counterpublics', which extend democratic voice to previously marginalized groups. In recent decades, there has been a proliferation of protest movements and mass demonstrations that seek to draw attention to a range of issues such as police brutality, sexual assault, and climate change. Fraser identifies such spaces as 'transnational subaltern counterpublics', where marginalized social groups contest conditions of inequality and precarity and question their exclusion from political arrangements through counter-discourses.

The promise of transnational counterpublics as sites of de-subalternization goes against Spivak's understanding of subalternity. Spivak, from whom Fraser takes the term 'subaltern', contends that when a citizen is unable to claim the public sphere, itself a creation of colonial history, a certain kind of subalternity is produced (Spivak, 2008: 3, 154). According to Spivak, the concept of transnational subaltern counterpublics would be an oxymoron for, in her view, subalterns lack access to citizenship: they do not have entry into the structures of either the state or national and international civil society (Spivak, 2011). Subaltern groups, Spivak explains, are marginal to postcolonial nation-building even as they bear the impact of neo-colonial globalization. Through a 'complicity of colony and class', tools of democratic rights and equality are not always available to the gendered subaltern (Spivak, 2008: 154). Spivak (2009) presents a powerful critique of alter-globalization and the role of international civil society in the continued production of subalternity. Spivak thereby contests Eurocentric and male-centric framings of key ideas of political theory, such as the public sphere, deliberative democracy, and transnational justice.

24.3.1 Transnational solidarity

Spivak (2008) questions articulations of transnational solidarity and draws attention to the distance between those who 'dispense' justice, aid, and rights and those who are simply coded as 'victims of wrongs' and thus as passive 'receivers'. Any attempts at global ethics urgently needs to address the historical processes through which certain individuals are placed in a situation from which they can aspire to transnational solidarity. When progressive activists and intellectuals intervene 'benevolently' in the struggles of subaltern groups for greater recognition and rights, they ironically reinforce the very power relations that they seek to overcome. Only by being ideologically ignorant of the gendered international division of labour (see Key Concept: Gendered international division of labour) can one presume shared interests and aspirations between First World intellectuals and Third World gendered subaltern subjects. Spivak warns us not to disregard the complicities between liberal articulations of solidarity and the global structures of domination they claim to resist.

> **Key Concept: Gendered international division of labour**
>
> The concept of the international division of labour explains how current forces of globalization reinforce and consolidate the superexploitative processes of production established during colonialism. Whereas during colonialism raw materials were transported from the colonies to Europe, the current reorganization of production entails a spatial shift, with manufacturing industries moving from advanced capitalist countries to 'cheaper' locations in the Global South, where low-cost labour-intensive parts of the manufacturing processes are undertaken. This labour is increasingly feminized, flexible, and informal, involving reproductive and care work; it is grossly underpaid and precarious as it is considered unskilled. Spivak analyses how gendered divisions of labour on a global scale produce subalternity.

We commonly believe that an empowered civil society automatically strengthens democracy. However, as Gramsci has taught us, civil society is itself the site where hegemony is fashioned. Elite actors in civil society obtain remarkable amounts of political power and access to transnational public spheres, without being directly elected by the people whom they claim to represent. Spivak accuses the international civil society and its vanguardism of reproducing a 'Feudality without

Feudalism' (Davis and Spivak, 2019: 68), whereby the politics of representation in the name of 'we the people' is plagued by paternalism. Spivak argues that when it comes to disenfranchised groups, it is still within the territoriality of the state that the subaltern struggles have to be won, as there is no other agent capable of mediating between the subaltern groups and transnational power structures (Spivak, 2009). This is not a plea for statism; rather, Spivak warns of the dangers of replacing the state with non-state actors. One of the most effective strategies employed by extra-state collective action is to put pressure on the state, especially postcolonial states, by mobilizing international allies and extra-domestic forums, raising troubling questions of sovereignty, especially in recently decolonized countries.

24.3.2 Desubalternization

Aristotle claimed that not all persons were fit to become part of the governing class because not everyone had the necessary practical wisdom or ethical virtue (see also Chapter 3). Actual governmental practices in most postcolonial societies are still based on this premise that not everyone can govern. The challenge that Spivak poses is: How can the subaltern subject be transformed into a citizen?

In much of the postcolonial world 'class apartheid' (Spivak, 2008: 32) is produced by the system of education in place since formal decolonization. For Spivak, subalterns are not just 'the poor' or 'poor women' or even 'poor brown women'; rather, subalterns are those who are systematically deprived of any access to intellectual labour, with only their bodies being trained to serve elites. Accordingly, desubalternization is much more complex than enabling access to basic needs. Poverty alleviation, although clearly necessary, does not guarantee desubalternization (ibid.: 24–25). Deep asymmetries of power cannot be corrected simply by reorganizing income and wealth. Above all, subalterns must be enabled to unlearn the 'class-habit of obedience' (ibid.: 55) and inserted into the 'circuit of citizenship' (Davis and Spivak, 2019: 71) not through 'empowerment training' but by 'activating' habits of democracy (Spivak, 2008: 49).

Spivak warns that the processes of decolonization cannot be successful only through crisis-driven corporate philanthropy or impatient human rights intervention. NGOs building schools or Human Rights Watch shaming states into good behaviour is necessary but not sufficient, such that without the ethico-political education of the disenfranchised, the project of decolonization will repeatedly fail (ibid.: 35). Following Gramsci, Spivak emphasizes that democracy cannot mean merely that an unskilled worker becomes employable; rather, it entails every citizen being able to govern, with society placing them, even if only abstractly, in a general condition to achieve this (Spivak, 2009: 36).

Spivak criticizes the benevolence of human rights interventionists, even as she is wary of promises of 'justice under capitalism' offered by development politics and corporate social responsibility. She warns against regarding unmediated cyber-literacy as an unquestioned good, because, for her, broadening of digital access does not automatically translate into epistemic or political transformation (Spivak, 2008: 51). Economic empowerment is incomplete without the accompanying 'epistemic change' both in the Global North as well as the Global South (ibid.: 31), so that the vastly disenfranchised will not need to be patronized by aid. We urgently need to rethink and reimagine our understanding of politics by examining how, despite the best efforts of international civil society actors and institutions, subaltern groups remain objects of benevolence and not agents of transformation (Ray, 2009: 60–61).

A good example of this is the transnational feminist movement. Advocates of transnational feminism highlight the role of cross-border civil society networks as facilitating the participation of disenfranchised women in global politics. Critics like Benita Parry (2004: 23) accuse Spivak of being unwilling to hear the voice of subaltern women and of sacrificing the struggles against gender injustice and violence at the altar of high theory. But as Spivak (2009: 32) has repeatedly pointed out, subaltern women are located outside organized resistance and are neither part of any unified Third World women's movement nor any global alliance politics. The merging of women's local struggles with a global women's movement in past decades has consolidated the hegemony of elite feminist agendas, with the UN Cairo Conference (1994) and the Beijing Conference (1995) sparking intense debates on the complicities of the transnational feminist movement with imperialism.

The relationship of democratization and decolonization to the Indigenous subalterns is tenuous. Even as they bear the impact of neo-colonial globalization, subaltern groups remain marginal to both nation states as well as civil society. Despite the crisis of legitimacy of nation states, it is dangerous to disregard the immense political implications of anti-statist positions, which are hugely popular in radical discourses in the West, for subaltern populations in the South. Instead of a narrow understanding of the state as a repressive apparatus, which demands a *for* or *against* position vis-à-vis the nation state, a different state needs to be envisaged that is capable of articulating the will of the excluded subaltern populations.

Spivak focuses on how the interests and demands of disenfranchised groups can be articulated through institutionalization of the redistributive functions of the state. According to Spivak, subaltern groups should be enabled to make claims on the state within the formal grammar of rights and citizenship to activate a 'democracy from below'.

24.3 Alter-globalization and subalternity: Key Points

- Spivak focuses on the discontinuity between elite civil society actors, who 'dispense' solidarity, justice, aid, and rights, and subalterns, who are simply coded as 'victims of wrongs' and thus as passive 'receivers'.
- Subalterns have neither access to the structures of international civil society nor those of postcolonial states.
- International civil society puts pressure on the state, especially postcolonial states, raising troubling questions of sovereignty.
- Spivak suggests that subaltern groups should be enabled to make claims on the state within the formal grammar of rights and citizenship.

24.4 The European Enlightenment and empire

The project of decolonization poses some challenging questions: Is a move beyond the canon—a move which draws on non-white, non-European, non-heterosexist perspectives—the most efficient formula for 'decolonizing the mind'? Or does this end up essentializing and romanticizing 'the Other'? Is the poststructuralist 'decolonization from within' sufficient to purge the Eurocentrism of Enlightenment thought? Or do Marxism and poststructuralism need to be decolonized as well?

As has been pointed out by both Postcolonial and Holocaust Studies scholars, the Enlightenment's promise of attaining freedom through the exercise of reason has ironically resulted in domination by reason itself. Along with progress and emancipation, it has brought colonialism, slavery, genocide, and crimes against humanity. In light of these considerations, Latin American scholars like Walter Mignolo (2011) and Ramón Grosfoguel (2011) categorically reject European modernity, and criticize the ideological erasures and hollow claims of the emancipatory nature of the Enlightenment, advocating a 'return' to Indigenous cosmologies—the world-views of the peoples of the Americas prior to contact with European colonizers. Decolonial thinking, Mignolo (2011: 47) claims, functions as a counterpoint to modernity/coloniality through 'epistemic disobedience'. Rejecting Eurocentric Enlightenment and Western reason, the focus is on other memories, narratives, and cosmovisions (Indigenous world-views about the Earth, nature, and the universe). In delinking from European modernity, the effort is to recover non-European sources of knowledge and local histories in order to decolonize the imagination.

By contrast, normative political theorists accuse decolonial/postcolonial approaches of relativizing universal Enlightenment norms of secularism, human rights, democracy, justice, modernity, liberalism, and freedom (for further elaboration on the chasm between the Frankfurt School and Postcolonial Studies, see Allen, 2016). Normative theorists worry whether Postcolonial Studies can be truly critical if the universality of ideals is contested. An oft-repeated objection is that in questioning the validity of universal principles as inadequate for understanding the practices, experiences, and realities of the non-European world, Postcolonial Studies reinforces the difference between the West and the East. If, as claimed by proponents of universalism, human beings share common needs and interests independent of historical, cultural, and economic differences, then the postcolonial effort to 'provincialize' Europe (Chakrabarty, 2000) is rendered questionable in an increasingly interdependent world. Furthermore, the postcolonial critique of Enlightenment norms such as secularism and democracy, it is feared, may jeopardize emancipatory politics.

This characterization of Postcolonial Studies as anti-Enlightenment is misleading. Spivak (2008) explains that when she criticizes human rights politics or discourses of gender justice, it is not because norms like women's human rights originate in Europe and are thus not relevant in other cultural contexts; rather, she traces the violence exerted through the normative framing of both 'human' as well as 'rights'. This disenfranchises those individuals and communities that cannot fulfil these Eurocentric ideals. The notion of 'women's interests' shared by all women has led to advocating general solutions worldwide, like the United Nation's Millennium Development Goals. This has resulted in global programmes promoting gender justice, which often represent Third World women as 'in need of help', thereby legitimizing international intervention. Insofar as Western feminists have participated in these kinds of universalizing political discourses and denied the possibility of non-Eurocentric forms of gender justice, they have contributed to reinforcing Western bias in the pursuit of equality and emancipation, while holding onto a form of solidarity that reinforces established hierarchies. Spivak assails Western feminists like Martha Nussbaum for appropriating Third World women's narratives towards a 'philosophical justification for universalism' (Kapoor, 2008: 35). The problem of the universalization of human rights is particularly visible in discussions on sexual violence. The Convention on the Elimination of all Forms of Discrimination Against Women (CEDAW), for example, takes the Eurocentric notion of rights as emancipatory, while locating the source of Third World women's oppression mainly in the domain of traditional cultural practices, thereby perpetuating stereotypes of 'barbaric' and patriarchal African, Hindu, or Islamic traditions (ibid.: 35). This shifts focus from broader questions of global structural inequality. Although international development organizations promote gender rights, many Western governments have a history of supporting authoritarian regimes in the Global South. There is an inextricable link between gender-rights violations and structural adjustment policies—loans provided by the International Monetary Fund and the World Bank to countries that experience economic crises, often with onerous conditions attached—which are often promoted by the same donors who promote and protect human rights (ibid.; 36). Thus, according to Spivak, the liberal-universalist rights agenda serves to consolidate the institutional power of international organizations, while functioning as an alibi for military intervention, often under the pretence of 'responsibility to protect' (Spivak, 2008).

Although many decolonial critics of modernity explore modes of thinking untouched by Enlightenment rationality, Spivak does not believe in the recovery of 'pure' forms of thinking before and beyond the Enlightenment. The Enlightenment's disenchantment of the world, in her view, cannot be undone by overcoming the Enlightenment and its norms of human rights or democracy. Spivak argues that one cannot step outside of history to untouched pasts to retrieve pure knowledge, uncontaminated agency, and non-coercive political practices that will absolve us of complicity in structures of power and violence, an option that is claimed by the decolonial approach. As tempting and attractive as it seems, it disregards the risks and dangers of a categorical rejection of the Enlightenment and its legacies.

24.4.1 Decolonizing the Enlightenment

In defence of the European Enlightenment, Habermas questions the categorical condemnation of Western reason as destructive and dominant, and proclaims modernity to be an ongoing and incomplete project. Contrary to both Habermasian claims of the virtues of Western modernity as emancipatory and progressive and the decolonial rejection thereof, Spivak interprets the Enlightenment in terms of its ambivalence. Instead of understanding modernity as an ideal to be mimicked, the decolonial turn views it as a problem that can be solved by purging European modernity from the decolonized world. Spivak disputes the decolonial options' nostalgia for an idealized past as well as claims that recognition of non-European native perspectives functions as a recipe for decolonization. Instead of a categorical dismissal of the Enlightenment, Spivak's (2004) effort is to conceptually reposition its role in processes of decolonization, even as the Enlightenment itself must be decolonized. This is not a simple task of undoing the legacies of the Enlightenment and colonialism; rather it is a more challenging undertaking of reclaiming and reconfiguring the access to the 'fruits' of the Enlightenment to those who have been denied its benefits.

In *A Critique of Postcolonial Reason: Towards a History of the Vanishing Present* (Spivak, 1999), Spivak explores how the great minds of the European Enlightenment foreclosed the subaltern in their work (Morton, 2003: 115–116; 2007: 141–149). This 'sanctioned ignorance' (Spivak, 1999: 164) of European thinkers reinforced racist and imperialist tropes, while paradoxically claiming the superiority of Eurocentric ethical and political norms of freedom and equality as universally valid. However, even as Spivak condemns the colonialist attitude of the European Enlightenment, she also traces how the 'native informant', namely, Third World academics, activists, and other economic migrants from the Global South are complicit in dominant structures which are a legacy of the Enlightenment. Instead of viewing postcolonial scholars as victims of colonialism, Spivak emphasizes their agency-in-complicity (Sanders, 2006: 8).

As Spivak reminds us, the title of her book *Outside in the Teaching Machine* (Spivak, 1993a) is a grammatical dissonance, which outlines the complex relation between margin and centre. The title alludes to the conundrum of being outside *in* the teaching machine and not simply outside the teaching machine. She points to the paradoxical position occupied by postcolonial scholars. Rather than boycotting or censoring Western thinkers, the effort here is to pursue a more responsible role for the postcolonial critic. In an earlier article, Spivak (1989: 208) explains that when it comes to the Enlightenment and its legacies, postcolonial feminists speak from an ambivalent position that cannot be avoided (ibid.: 209). Spivak, referring to Kant, argues that 'even a brilliant imagination is no guarantee' (Spivak, 1999: 233) that Eurocentrism can be overcome. At the same time, she warns against censuring European thinkers like Kant despite their racism and sexism (see Chapter 29 on Kant).

In *An Aesthetic Education in the Age of Globalization* (Spivak, 2012), in place of the abandonment of European thought, Spivak suggests 'affirmative sabotage' (ibid.: 4) of the Enlightenment, which does not attempt to boycott it, but to deploy the tools of dominance to undermine its goals. This would serve the purpose of making these enabling tools available to subaltern classes, giving them the possibility of exercising intellectual labour and thereby inserting them into hegemony (ibid.: 436). From being 'subject of crisis' the subaltern is embedded into 'logic of agency' (ibid.: 436).

Spivak illustrates this with an incident that happened at one of her rural schools: after the local water well broke down, and since the aboriginal children could not access water in the main village due to the constitutionally illegal, but still prevalent, practices of untouchability, Spivak made repeated visits to government officials in Kolkata to request a new water well (Spivak, 2008: 47). When Spivak admonished one of the young Hindu teachers in the school who did not drink the water touched by her aboriginal students, one of the students spoke up in that teacher's defence, illustrating how caste rules are internalized by the children. Instead of initiating a fundraiser to acquire donations from national and international philanthropists, Spivak encouraged three of the schoolchildren to write a letter to the government officials, an effort that would ultimately be in vain. She explains her motivations as follows:

> We want the children to learn about the heartlessness of administrations, without short-term resistance talk. The bounty of some US benefactor would be the sharp end of the wedge that produces a general will for exploitation in the subaltern. All the same, I agree with W. E. B. DuBois rather than Booker T. Washington: it is more important to develop a critical intelligence than to assure immediate material comfort.
>
> (ibid.: 48–49)

Spivak could be accused of neglecting the pressing existential needs of the impoverished. After all, what could be more urgent than access to clean drinking water? However, Spivak argues that overcoming economic inequality is not simply a matter of attending to the 'basic needs' of the disenfranchised; rather, the effort should be to non-coercively 'rearrange desires' at both ends of postcoloniality. This would involve mapping the asymmetrical and non-reciprocal relation between the hegemonic and subaltern classes by undermining 'the necessity of "good" rich people solving the world's problems . . . Beggars receive material goods to some degree and remain beggars' (Spivak, 2012: 135). To this end, economic freedom and political emancipation for subaltern classes need to be recoded from an access to finance capital to a form of education that produces subalterns as 'problem solvers' rather than viewing them as a problem that needs to be solved (ibid.: 135).

Describing access to the European Enlightenment, particularly for subalterns, as an 'enabling violation', Spivak (2008: 156, 259, 263n2) proposes that one must strategically use the enablement even as the violation is renegotiated. The relation of postcoloniality to the Enlightenment—and its legacies of modernity, secularism, democracy, human rights, science, technology, hegemonic languages—is diagnosed as a 'double bind' (see Key Concept: Double bind).

Key Concept: Double bind

First described by the controversial anthropologist Gregory Bateson, who served in the Office of Strategic Services, a wartime intelligence agency of the United States during the Second World War and the predecessor of CIA, a double bind indicates a dilemma in which an individual or group receives contradictory demands, with one negating the other. Typically, the injunction is imposed upon the subject by someone whom the person respects or trusts. Even as the demand itself is inherently impossible to fulfil, it cannot be ignored. This creates a situation of confusion, anxiety, and distress as the subject can neither resolve nor escape the situation. Spivak describes the postcolonial relation to the European Enlightenment in terms of a double-bind experience.

Spivak advises that one should neither accuse European philosophers nor excuse them; rather, one ought to enter the protocols of the canonical texts of the Enlightenment to turn them around towards a more just and democratic postcoloniality (Spivak, 2012: 116–117). Spivak advocates *ab*-use of the Enlightenment (*ab* in Latin is 'from below'). This is not a position of inferiority or abasement, but one that embodies the double-bind of the postcolonial world with respect to the European Enlightenment. This is neither a misuse nor an abuse, but a critical relation to the structures that postcolonial societies so intimately inhabit. Spivak observes that when oppressed minorities ask for civil and political rights, they are making a demand within the Enlightenment discourse. Thus, rather than any wholesale rejection of the Enlightenment as dangerous and in bad faith, she recommends 'using it from below'.

In Spivak's view, we must confront the paradox that the Enlightenment, in spite of its white, bourgeois, masculinist bias, is eminently indispensable. As has been the experience in many postcolonial contexts, the critique of modernity has strengthened conservative nationalist political orders. Spivak advocates taking the Enlightenment beyond the confines of Europe and making it work for the Other, even as we are confronted with the challenge of trying to decolonize concepts like the public sphere, with its Westphalian frame. As colonial 'gifts', they are both present and poison, as Derrida reminds us. Such a project would entail saving the best of the Enlightenment and rethinking its relation to subalternized knowledges and their role in the project of decolonization. This would mark a departure from the orthodoxies of anticolonial critique; for, as Spivak reminds us, nationalism is a product of imperialism and is implicated in its violent structures. Thus, in her view, the banal opposition between the European Enlightenment and postcolonialism is an act of bad faith, which needs to be problematized by exploring how far our sense of critique is shaped by the Enlightenment, even as it is not limited to it. At the same time, the postcolonial experiences in the Global South offer important lessons for the future of critical political theories. Thus, instead of a politics of blame or a postcolonial anti-modernity, Spivak's writings urge us to revisit the Black feminist Audre Lorde's (1981) conundrum, namely, perhaps the master's tools can indeed be employed to dismantle the master's house.

> **24.4 The European Enlightenment and empire: Key Points**
>
> - In place of abandonment of European thought, Spivak suggests critical engagement of the Enlightenment through a renegotiation with the colonial episteme of modernity.
> - Spivak describes the postcolonial relation to the European Enlightenment in terms of a double-bind experience.
> - Instead of global ethics, Spivak proposes planetary ethics as a more responsible approach towards imagining non-imperialist futures.

24.5 Conclusion

If colonialism is not only about military domination and economic exploitation, but also about subject constitution, then decolonization cannot be achieved through a mere transfer of power from Europeans to native elites; rather, it involves a remapping of imperial and subaltern subject-formation through 'epistemic change'. Spivak warns that under conditions of neoliberal globalization 'monocultures of the mind' result through a uniform kind of education provided in a few hegemonic languages. To be literate under globalization requires more than mastery of reading and writing in the idiom of finance capital; rather, it is a form of critical practice linking literature and culture with economy. Transnational literacy (Spivak, 2008: 30) would work in different ways as a supplementary education for both the metropolitan elites and the rural subalterns, thereby undoing the discontinuity between these two groups. It is an effort to understand and transform geopolitical power and privilege through 'training in a literary habit of reading the world' (Spivak, 1999: xii).

In contrast to global ethics, Spivak proposes planetarity as a more sensitive and attuned way of understanding the materiality of the world and our collective place and responsibility within it. Rather than being 'global agents' we should instead imagine ourselves as 'planetary creatures' (Spivak, 2012: 339), inhabiting a planet that is merely 'on loan' to us (ibid.: 484). This calls us to rethink the notion of responsibility from the duty of the 'fitter self' *for* the other into responsibility *to* the other (Spivak, 2008: 26–28). We need to move from 'rights-based cultures' to 'responsibility-based cultures', wherein rights and responsibility are inextricably sutured together.

Planetary ethics thus entails forsaking formulas for solving global problems and critical self-vigilance on the part of transnational elites as important aspects of ethico-political practice (Ray, 2009: 82). This involves questioning the invincibility of one's convictions as well as another ethics of listening. Finally, it is political and ethical working 'with no guarantees' (Spivak, 2001: 15).

Take your learning further by accessing the online resources for a library of web links to relevant videos, articles, blogs, and useful websites for this chapter: **www.oup.com/he/Ramgotra-Choat1e**.

Study questions

1. Why does Spivak criticize Foucault and Deleuze in 'Can the Subaltern Speak?'
2. What is Spivak's understanding of gendered subalternity?
3. Why does Spivak argue that the subaltern woman is doubly silenced?
4. Is Western feminism imperialist?
5. Do protest movements and mass demonstrations contribute to sustained social, economic, and political transformation?
6. Do you agree with Spivak that the legacies of the European Enlightenment such as human rights and democracy can be mobilized for emancipatory struggles in postcolonial societies?
7. Why does Spivak describe the postcolonial relation to European Enlightenment in terms of a double-bind experience?
8. How can epistemic change lead to desubalternization?

Further reading

Primary sources

Spivak, G.C. (1988a) 'Can the Subaltern Speak?' In C. Nelson and L. Grossberg (eds), *Marxism and the Interpretation of Culture*. Chicago: University of Illinois Press, pp. 271–313.
Spivak's ground-breaking text outlining her understanding of subalternity.

Spivak, G.C. (1999) *A Critique of Postcolonial Reason: Toward a History of the Vanishing Present*. Cambridge, MA: Harvard University Press.
This text summarizes much of Spivak's contribution in recent decades to feminism, ethics, and political philosophy.

Spivak, G.C. (2008) 'Righting Wrongs'. In G.C. Spivak, *Other Asias*. New York: Routledge.
   Powerful critique of the idea of human rights and its enduring role in justifying neo-colonialism.

Secondary sources

Bilimoria, P. and Al-Kassim, D. (eds) (2014) *Postcolonial Reason and Its Critique: Deliberations on Gayatri Spivak's Thoughts*. Oxford: Oxford University Press.
   Collection of twelve critical essays that engage with Spivak's political thought. In an Afterword, Spivak responds to her critics.

Kapoor, I. (2004) 'Hyper-Self-Reflexive Development? Spivak on Representing the Third World "Other"'. *Third World Quarterly*, 25(4): 627–647.
   Excellent analysis of Spivak's critique of Western development politics.

Landry, D. and MacLean, G. (eds) (1996) *The Spivak Reader: Selected Works of Gayatri Chakravorty Spivak*. New York: Routledge.
   Offers a selection of Spivak's work with an insightful introduction to Spivak's thought and a useful interview on the question of the subaltern.

Moore-Gilbert, B. (1997) 'Gayatri Spivak: The Deconstructive Twist'. In B. Moore-Gilbert, *Postcolonial Theory: Contexts, Practices, Politics*. London: Verso.
   Engaging chapter that places Spivak's work in the context of Postcolonial Studies.

Morris, R. (ed.) (2010) *Can the Subaltern Speak?: Reflections on the History of an Idea*. New York: Columbia University Press.
   Collection of eight critical essays that situate Spivak's 'Can the Subaltern Speak?' within the development of subaltern and postcolonial studies and the quest for human rights. In an Afterword, Spivak reflects on the reception of her original essay and responds to her critics.

Morton, S. (2003) *Gayatri Chakravorty Spivak*. New York: Routledge.
   Accessible short introduction.

Morton, S. (2007) *Gayatri Spivak: Ethics, Subalternity and the Critique of Postcolonial Reason*. Cambridge: Polity Press.
   Useful introduction to Spivak's thought that situates her work in the wider context of political theory and ethics.

Ray, S, (2009) *Gayatri Chakravorty Spivak: In Other Words*. Hoboken, NJ: Wiley-Blackwell.
   In-depth introduction that explores the key concepts in Spivak's thought with particular focus on themes such as ethics, feminism, violence, and war.

Sanders, M. (2006) *Gayatri Chakravorty Spivak: Live Theory*. London: Continuum.
   Concise and accessible introduction.

References

Abu-Lughod, L. (2013) *Do Muslim Women Need Saving?* Cambridge, MA: Harvard University Press.

Allen, A. (2016) *The End of Progress: Decolonizing the Normative Foundations of Critical Theory*. New York: Columbia University Press.

Bilimoria, P. (2002) 'Postcolonial Critique of Reason: Spivak Between Kant and Matilal'. *Interventions*, 4(2): 160–167.

Chakrabarty, D. (2000) *Provincializing Europe: Postcolonial Thought and Historical Difference*. Princeton, NJ: Princeton University Press.

Davis, A. and Spivak, G.C. (2019) 'Planetary Utopias. Angela Davis and Gayatri Chakravorty Spivak in Conversation with Nikita Dhawan'. *Radical Philosophy*, 205 (Autumn 2019): 67–78.

Eagleton, T. (1999) 'In the Gaudy Supermarket'. *London Review of Books*, 21(10): 3–6.

Foucault, M. (1977) 'Intellectuals and Power: A Conversation between Michel Foucault and Gilles Deleuze'. In D.F. Bouchard (ed.), *Language, Counter-Memory, Practice: Selected Essays and Interviews by Michel Foucault*, Ithaca, NY: Cornell University Press, pp. 205–217.

Fraser, N. (1992) 'Rethinking the Public Sphere: A Contribution to the Critique of Actually Existing Democracy'. In C. Calhoun (ed.), *Habermas and the Public Sphere*. Cambridge, MA: MIT Press. pp. 109–142.

Gandhi, L. (1998) *Postcolonial Theory: A Critical Introduction*. Edinburgh: Edinburgh University Press.

Gramsci, A. (2011) *Prison Notebooks*, vols 1, 2, and 3. Ed. and trans. J.A. Buttigieg with A. Callari. New York: Columbia University Press.

Grosfoguel, R. (2011) 'Decolonizing Post-Colonial Studies and Paradigms of Political-Economy: Transmodernity, Decolonial Thinking, and Global Coloniality'. *Transmodernity: Journal of Peripheral Cultural Production of the Luso-Hispanic World* 1(1). Available at: http://dx.doi.org/10.5070/T411000004 (accessed 1 January 2023).

Guha, R. (1999) *The Elementary Aspects of Peasant Insurgency in Colonial India*. Durham, NC: Duke University Press.

Habermas, J. (1989) *The Structural Transformation of the Public Sphere: An Inquiry into a Category of Bourgeois Society*. Cambridge, MA: MIT Press.

Hall, S. (1992) 'The West and the Rest: Discourse and Power'. In S. Hall and B. Gieben (eds), *Formations of Modernity*. Cambridge: Polity Press, pp. 275–320.

Kapoor, I. (2008) *The Postcolonial Politics of Development*. New York. Routledge.

Landry, D. and MacLean, G. (eds) (1996) *The Spivak Reader: Selected Works of Gayatri Chakravorty Spivak*. New York: Routledge.

Lorde, A. (1981) 'The Master's Tools Will Never Dismantle the Master's House'. In C. Moraga and G. Anzaldúa (eds), *This Bridge Called My Back: Writings by Radical Women of Color*. Latham, NY: Kitchen Table Press, pp. 98–101.

Macaulay, T.B. (1965 [1835]) 'Minute on Education'. In H. Sharp (ed.), *Bureau of Education: Selections from Educational Records, Part I (1781-1839)*. Delhi: National Archives of India, pp. 107–117.

MacCabe, C. (1988) 'Foreword'. In G.C. Spivak, *In Other Worlds: Essays in Cultural Politics*, New York: Routledge, pp. ix–xix.

Mignolo, W. (2011) 'Epistemic Disobedience and the Decolonial Option: A Manifesto'. *Transmodernity: Journal of Peripheral Cultural Production of the Luso-Hispanic World*, 1(2): 44–66.

Mohanty, C.T. (1988) 'Under Western Eyes: Feminist Scholarship and Colonial Discourses'. *boundary 2*, 12(3): 333–358.

Moore-Gilbert, B. (1997) 'Gayatri Spivak: The Deconstructive Twist'. In B. Moore-Gilbert, *Postcolonial Theory: Contexts, Practices, Politics*. London: Verso.

Morris, R. (ed.) (2010) *Can the Subaltern Speak?: Reflections on the History of an Idea*. New York: Columbia University Press.

Morton, S. (2003) *Gayatri Chakravorty Spivak*. New York: Routledge.

Morton, S. (2007) *Gayatri Spivak: Ethics, Subalternity and the Critique of Postcolonial Reason*. Cambridge: Polity Press.

Parry, B. (2004) *Postcolonial Studies: A Materialist Critique*. New York: Routledge.

Prakash, G. (1992) 'Can the "Subaltern" Ride? A Reply to O'Hanlon and Washbrook'. *Comparative Studies in Society and History*, 34(1): 168–184.

Ray, S, (2009) *Gayatri Chakravorty Spivak: In Other Words*. Hoboken, NJ: Wiley-Blackwell.

Sanders, M. (2006) *Gayatri Chakravorty Spivak: Live Theory*. London: Continuum.

Spivak, G.C. (1985) 'Three Women's Texts and a Critique of Imperialism'. *Critical Inquiry*, 12(1): 243–261.

Spivak, G.C. (1988a) 'Can the Subaltern Speak?' In C. Nelson and L. Grossberg (eds), *Marxism and the Interpretation of Culture*. Chicago: University of Illinois Press, pp. 271–313.

Spivak, G.C. (1988b) *In Other Worlds: Essays in Cultural Politics*. New York: Routledge.

Spivak, G.C. (1989) 'A response to "The difference within: Feminism and critical theory"'. In E. Meese and A. Parker (eds), *The Difference Within: Feminism and Critical Theory*, Philadelphia, PA: John Benjamins Publishing Company, pp. 207–220.

Spivak, G.C. (1990) *The Post-Colonial Critic: Interviews, Strategies, Dialogues*. Ed. S. Harasym. London: Routledge.

Spivak, G.C. (1993a) *Outside in the Teaching Machine*. New York: Routledge.

Spivak, G.C. (1993b) 'An Interview with Gayatri Chakravorty Spivak'. *boundary 2*, 20(2): 24–50.

Spivak, G.C. (1999) *A Critique of Postcolonial Reason: Toward a History of the Vanishing Present*. Cambridge, MA: Harvard University Press.

Spivak, G.C. (2001) 'A Note on the New International'. *Parallax*, 7(3), 12–16.

Spivak, G.C. (2003) *Death of a Discipline*. New York: Columbia University Press.

Spivak, G.C. (2004) 'What Is Enlightenment? Interview with Jane Gallop'. In J. Gallop (ed.), *Polemic: Critical or Uncritical*. London: Routledge, pp. 179–200.

Spivak, G.C. (2008) *Other Asias*. New York: Routledge.

Spivak, G.C. (2009) 'They the People. Problems of Alter-Globalization'. *Radical Philosophy*, 157: 31–36.

Spivak, G.C. (2011) 'In Conversation with Bulan Lahiri'. Available at: https://www.thehindu.com/books/In-Conversation-Speaking-to-Spivak/article15130635.ece (accessed 11 January 2023).

Spivak, G.C. (2012) *An Aesthetic Education in the Era of Globalization*. Cambridge, MA: Harvard University Press.

Part VI
Violence, Power, and Resistance

25	Niccolò Machiavelli	Yves Winter	447
26	Emma Goldman	Ruth Kinna	465
27	Mohandas (Mahatma) Gandhi	Jimmy Casas Klausen	485
28	Frantz Fanon	Keally McBride	505

Power is at the centre of politics. Some thinkers explicitly define the activity and study of politics in terms of power. For these thinkers, politics arises from conflict over resources and concerns the distribution of those resources: politics is about who decides who gets what—or, in other words, who has the *power* to decide. Defined in this way, it can be claimed that politics is everywhere, because all relationships are in some way relationships of power. But even more conventional and narrower definitions of politics revolve around power. To say, for example, that politics refers to the activities of those in government or relations between governments is to raise the question of who holds or has access to power.

Yet the concept of power is subject to a huge variety of competing definitions. For some, power means the capacity to achieve a desired outcome—to do or get something. In this sense, a lone individual could have greater or lesser power to achieve some end. In politics, however, power usually refers to our relations to other people. The emphasis can be put on our need to work with others in order to achieve our goals—power as the capacity for people to act together—or on the ways in which other people can be obstacles to achieving our aims. Either way, when we refer to *political* power, we are usually referring not simply to our power to attain an object but our power over other people. Power in this sense refers to the ability to influence the behaviour of others, whether by persuading them to act collectively with us or by overcoming their opposition or resistance. As well as influencing behaviour—getting someone to do something that they would not otherwise have done—power in in this sense might mean restricting the choices of others, manipulating their desires, or even simply using force to compel them to act.

While political science has analysed how power *is* distributed, political theory and philosophy have tended instead to try to establish how power *should* be distributed. For many thinkers, this involves establishing the legitimacy of power, or who has authority. If power is often defined as the capacity to do something, then authority is the *right* to use power. Legitimate power is often defined as non-coercive: to act with authority is to do something that one has a recognized right to do, rather than using force. In this way, violence is often contrasted with politics, with the role of politics understood as the establishment of an order that overcomes or contains violence.

Yet the founding of any new political order is often—and arguably always—a violent act. Think of how many nation states have been founded by revolution, such as Haiti. Many thinkers explicitly defend a right to revolution, demonstrating that violence itself can be considered legitimate under certain circumstances. Nor does violence disappear once a political order has been established. Even legitimate peaceful and democratic regimes are ultimately guaranteed by the threat of violence, as a way of dealing with internal or external adversaries.

Violence, moreover, is a notoriously slippery concept. The word 'violence' calls to mind acts of physical force intended and executed by an identifiable agent. But to focus only on such acts would arguably be to ignore forms of systemic or structural violence. Poverty, racism, and sexism, for example, can be and have all been considered forms of structural violence—and many have argued that they can only be resisted or eradicated with further violence.

Like power, therefore, violence is arguably at the heart of politics. For this reason, it can be said that all of the thinkers in this book address these issues, even if they do so implicitly or indirectly. What distinguishes the four thinkers in this Part is that they address power and violence head on. The Part opens with Chapter 25 on the Florentine diplomat and thinker Niccolò Machiavelli, whose name has become a byword for those who seek to achieve and retain power by any means. Notwithstanding the validity of this posthumous reputation, Machiavelli's explicit discussions of power and violence mean that he is often cited as a central thinker in the realist tradition: he begins from the world as it is rather than how it should be, and his central concern is political stability—how power can be obtained and maintained. Unusually—though not uniquely—for a political thinker, his interest is in the realities of politics rather than philosophical ideals or grand questions about justice or the good life. His notoriety derives in part from his refusal to make violence an object of moral condemnation: he does not celebrate violence, but he defends its necessity under certain circumstances. As Chapter 25 demonstrates, however, Machiavelli is a rich and complex thinker who defends a republican conception of freedom and whose work has been used by radical thinkers.

The activist and thinker Emma Goldman likewise foregrounded the analysis of power, but in a very different way from that of Machiavelli. Chapter 26, on Goldman, is the only chapter in this book on an anarchist thinker. Like other anarchists, Goldman's critique of power emphasized the multiple and intersecting forms of domination that exist. Rejecting legal means of change, she advocated direct action as a form of resistance. She considered violence justifiable but sought to distinguish legitimate from illegitimate violence. While she insisted that women's liberation must be central to the transformation of society, she had less to say about racism and European colonialism.

In contrast, colonialism was the central concern of the final two thinkers considered in this Part. Probably the best-known and most influential anti-colonial activists of the twentieth century, Mahatma (Mohandas) Gandhi and Frantz Fanon had widely divergent views on resistance and violence. Drawing in part on Hindu traditions, Gandhi promoted and practised nonviolent resistance. Against the use of brute force, Gandhi advocated 'soul-force'. For Gandhi, this should not be equated with passive resistance: he insisted that it required active self-discipline and self-suffering, and its aim was the moral conversion of one's opponents rather than their destruction. As Chapter 27 suggests, Gandhi's status as an instantly recognizable global icon should not distract from his flaws: he at times expressed casteist and racist prejudices and his attitudes towards women were sometimes troubling.

Like Gandhi, Fanon believed decolonization must involve a total repudiation of the colonial order, including the forms of knowledge and culture by which it was sustained, and the development of new subjects capable of self-rule. But, in sharp contrast to Gandhi, Fanon believed that decolonization must be a violent event. As Chapter 28 argues, Fanon's attitude towards violence was similar to that of Goldman: violent resistance was a legitimate and necessary response to systemic violence—that of capital and government for Goldman and that of colonialism for Fanon. Like Goldman, Fanon did not simply celebrate violence: as explained in Chapter 28, he believed that some forms of violence could be counterproductive and psychologically damaging. Fanon nevertheless viewed violence as more than merely necessary, highlighting its potentially constructive role in developing individual and collective senses of self-respect.

The four thinkers in this Part all viewed violence in different ways, from Machiavelli's pragmatic assessments of its uses to Goldman's differentiation of legitimate and illegitimate violence, and from Gandhi's rejection of violent resistance to Fanon's embrace of the same. Yet what links them all is their willingness to acknowledge the central role that violence has played in political life. Rather than understanding politics merely as the application of normative values such as justice, they acknowledge the central place of power and struggles for power.

25 Niccolò Machiavelli

YVES WINTER

Chapter guide

This chapter focuses on the *Discourses on Livy* and on *The Prince*, Machiavelli's two major political works. Section 25.1 introduces Machiavelli's reception and biography, emphasizing the relation between his activities as Secretary of the Florentine chancery and his later theoretical work. It then turns to the centre of gravity of Machiavelli's thought: power and the state (Section 25.2). Section 25.3 introduces the two key concepts of his theory of history: *virtù* and *fortuna*. Section 25.4 develops Machiavelli's understanding of republican freedom along with the importance of conflict between the 'few' and the 'many'. Finally, Section 25.5 turns to questions of violence, conquest, and empire.

25.1 Introduction

Perhaps more than any other political theorist in the Western tradition, Machiavelli is read in diametrically opposed ways: some regard him as an advisor to tyrants, instructing them in the use of force and fraud; others argue that his works reveal the guarded secrets of tyranny, thereby empowering its subjects. Some view his subversion of Christian religion and conventional moral virtues as an attack on all values, whereas others see in him a passionate advocate of Roman republicanism. These controversies have various sources. They arise partly from Machiavelli's acerbic style; from his love of contradiction and paradox; and from the tensions between Machiavelli's works, for example, between the apparently autocratic politics of *The Prince* and the republican vision in the *Discourses on Livy*.

The polarization between readers has defined Machiavelli's reception from the sixteenth century onwards. His attacks on Christianity gave rise to his reputation as a heretic and landed his books on the *Index*, the list of books prohibited by the Catholic Church. Early on, some readers condemned him as an immoral teacher of evil. Champions of the counter-Reformation attacked him for imagining a secular space of politics, while others blamed him for the massacres perpetrated against French Protestants (Anglo, 2005; Kahn, 2010). In the seventeenth and eighteenth centuries, republican interpretations gained ground, with readers such as John Milton, Algernon Sydney, James Harrington, Baruch Spinoza (see Chapter 6), and Jean-Jacques Rousseau (see Chapter 9) interpreting Machiavelli as a clandestine republican who reveals the secrets of statecraft to his audience (Barthas, 2010).

This chapter argues that Machiavelli is a theorist of power and conflict with a political commitment to popular republicanism. Republicanism is a normative theory of self-government that has its origins in ancient Rome and which holds that politics should be based on legal and political equality and on freedom from arbitrary (such as monarchic or tyrannical) rule. Challenging many of the pieties of previous political theorists, Machiavelli insisted that to make sense of politics, we need to understand the forces at play in a concrete situation. Throughout his work, he was concerned with the problem of power—its nature, sources, social bases, modes of functioning, and the ways of managing and controlling it. The question of power is pivotal in modern political thought, and

Machiavelli was the author who pushed it to the forefront. Because of this primacy of power, historians of political thought sometimes portray Machiavelli as having broken apart the continuity of ethics and politics and to be exclusively concerned with force and fraud while lacking a moral conception of politics. This, I argue, is a mischaracterization of the Florentine thinker. While Machiavelli did indeed elevate power, the state, and violence to central topics for theoretical consideration, his is not a narrowly technical perspective on politics. On the contrary, Machiavelli had strong political commitments, most importantly a keen and lifelong allegiance to popular and anti-oligarchic republican government. At a time when republics were on the wane, and when broad-based, democratic republicanism had few defenders, Machiavelli stands out as a theorist committed to freedom, understood as collective self-government or sharing power.

25.2 Power and the state

25.2.1 Machiavelli's life and times

Niccolò Machiavelli (1469–1527) did not start out with a theoretical focus on politics. Above all, he was interested in politics as a sphere of action. His lucky break came in 1498 when the Florentine Republic appointed him to an executive position. From 1498 until 1512, Machiavelli served as second chancellor and secretary to the council that managed military affairs. It was a diplomatic position, which saw Machiavelli conduct multiple long missions to the French Royal court and to Italian rulers. The young Florentine upstart who came from a non-elite background relished his political role, and the experience he gained shaped his later writings. His political career spanned a short period during which Florence was a remarkably broad and participatory popular republic. Yet, in 1512, the republic abruptly fell when Spanish troops entered Florence and re-installed the Medici (a powerful Florentine banking family and political dynasty). Not only did Machiavelli lose his job, but because he was suspected of participating in a conspiracy against the Medici, he was imprisoned, tortured, and banished from the city (Tommasini, 1883; Vivanti, 2013).

The main body of Machiavelli's political and historical work was all written after these traumatic events. In the months following his expulsion from Florence, he wrote *The Prince* (1513), the book for which is most famous, followed a few years later by his main theoretical work, *The Discourses on Livy* (1517) and the *Florentine Histories* (1526). All these books were, however, published only posthumously, in 1531 and 1532.

Read more about **Machiavelli's** life and work by accessing the thinker biography on the online resources: www.oup.com/he/Ramgotra-Choat1e.

During Machiavelli's lifetime, the Florentine, Italian, and global political landscapes changed fundamentally. He lived through the tail end of the Florentine republic, and died a few years before the powerful Medici family officially transformed the city into a hereditary monarchy. He saw the Italian city-state system falling apart under the pressure of successive French and Spanish military invasions. And he was a contemporary to new forms of military and imperial conquest, from the Spanish *Reconquista* to the nascent European domination and plunder of the New World.

25.2.2 Principalities and republics

Machiavelli's theoretical work explores the problem of power and of the state. He opens *The Prince* with the assertion that 'all states, all dominions that have had and do have command over men, have been and are either republics or principalities' (Machiavelli, 2016: I, 39). On the surface, this assertion introduces a typology of states: principalities and republics. But on a deeper level, the opening line condenses Machiavelli's entire research programme. What does it mean for states to rule over people? (The Italian word is *imperio*, which can be translated as 'command', 'rule', or 'empire'.) What is the nature of this rule? What are its institutional forms? Who rules over whom, by what means, and to whose benefit? What forms of power operate between states? And how might a new power constitute itself on the Italian peninsula (Althusser, 1999)?

In *The Prince*, Machiavelli deals with these questions by theorizing the relation between a prince and his principality while in the *Discourses on Livy*, these issues arise in the context of a republican regime. *The Prince* begins with a typology of the different types of principalities, the manner in which they can be acquired and maintained and a discussion of the prince's position with respect to other political actors, especially the *grandi* and the *popolo* (see Key Concept: The *grandi* and the *popolo*) but also the church.

> **Key Concept: The *grandi* and the *popolo***
>
> The *grandi* or the 'few' are Machiavelli's term for the ruling elites, those who by birth, wealth, or reputation are considered the nobility; the *people* or the 'many,' by contrast, are those who lack any claim to social or political distinction. For Machiavelli, every society is internally divided between the privileged and the unprivileged, the wealthy and the poor, the nobles and the commoners. Machiavelli (2016: IX, 66) attributes to these groups distinct and opposed political desires and tendencies (what he calls 'humours'): the *grandi* desire 'to command to oppress the people' whereas the people 'desire to be neither commanded nor oppressed'. The resulting struggle between elite and popular factions is the most important political cleavage, both in republics and in principalities. In a principality, a prince therefore needs to decide whether to align himself with the elites or with the people. In a republic, how this conflict is managed will determine the prospects for stability and longevity. Machiavelli's abiding political sympathies, throughout his career as a political actor and theorist, are with the people.

25.2.3 Power

Power, for Machiavelli, designates a key category of his social ontology. Whereas Thomas Hobbes (see Chapter 5), writing a century and a half later, offers a crisp definition of power—the 'present means to obtain some future apparent good' (Hobbes, 1996: 62)—the reader searches in vain for a similar passage in Machiavelli's work. And whereas for Hobbes, power is a relation between agents and outcomes, for Machiavelli, power is a strategic constellation of asymmetric social relations. Power, for Machiavelli, corresponds to an agent's capacity not to effect outcomes but to influence the actions of others. The sources of power are multiple; among others, they include political office, violence (including military force), wealth, reputation, networks, appearances, as well as numbers. Power consists in a mobilization of these sources to govern, affect, and manipulate the actions of others. Yet for Machiavelli, power is not primarily coercive in character—it does not normally take the form of a compulsion whereby one agent forces another one to do something they would not otherwise do. This is no doubt an effect of Machiavelli's historical context. Renaissance states were not endowed with sophisticated mechanisms of surveillance, control, and coercion that a twenty-first-century reader might associate with the state. And even though Machiavelli thinks of power as not solely emanating from the state, he has a limited vocabulary to conceptualize types of coercion that occur outside the public domain, such as domestic violence, sexual assault, or workplace coercion.

Rather than coercive, Machiavelli thought of power as principally *strategic* (although he did not use that term). Power is strategic, insofar as it is always relational and relative; it is exercised from multiple points and generates asymmetric social relations. Indeed, Machiavelli would likely have concurred with Michel Foucault's famous line about power, penned nearly 500 years later that, 'where there is power, there is resistance' and this resistance is plural, irregular, and heterogeneous, some of it occurs in organized forms, others spontaneous; some instances of resistance are inevitable, others probable, and some unlikely; some forms of resistance can be co-opted, some are driven by specific interests, others take the form of martyrdom (Foucault, 1978: 95–96) (see also Chapter 33 on Foucault).

In *The Prince*, this relation between power and resistance is examined from the vantage point of a potential prince. Working through the mechanisms of obtaining and losing political support, loyalty, consent, and patronage, Machiavelli analyses power in terms of the cooperative, coercive, and communicative practices of leadership and contestation that are at the disposal of various agents. Yet even though the book is dedicated to a Medici prince, and ostensibly takes the form of a manual for how to acquire and maintain a principality, a strand of commentators beginning with the sixteenth-century jurist Alberico Gentili (1924: III.9) and including Jean-Jacques Rousseau (2007: 95; see also Chapter 9 on Rousseau) have interpreted the book as a critical analysis of autocratic regimes that discloses the secrets of statecraft. By revealing the hidden transcripts of rule to the people, *The Prince* is not only a handbook for aspiring monarchs but also an invitation for conspirators and rebels who are perhaps more in need of the knowledge it offers.

The candidness with which Machiavelli speaks about power (and as we shall see in Section 25.5, violence) makes him a unique figure in the history of Western political theory, certainly in his time. Later, other theorists, including Karl Marx (see Chapter 13), Friedrich Nietzsche (see Chapter 14), V.I. Lenin, Frantz Fanon (see Chapter 28), C.L.R. James (see Chapter 18), and Catharine MacKinnon openly discussed power and violence as constitutive elements of existing relations of domination, but in the early sixteenth century, Machiavelli was unusual in emphasizing power as the central feature of the state and violence as one of its pillars (Wolin, 2004: 197). The unvarnished approach to political life is not only a distinctive feature of his thought, but part of his programme to demystify politics. In *The Prince*, he famously complains that 'many have imagined republics and principalities that have never been seen or known to exist' and that in contrast to previous theorists, he will focus on 'the effectual truth' of politics (Machiavelli, 2016: XV, 85). 'Effectual truth' is a term coined by Machiavelli, and it has a double meaning: on the one hand, it refers to a truth that produces concrete results, a truth that is effective, that is successful in materializing itself in concrete ways. On the other hand, it refers to a truth that creates sensory effects, akin to the special effects that are used in cinema and in show business (Mansfield, 1996: 30; Del Lucchese, 2015: 26). Politics, Machiavelli argues, involves both of these effects, and if we want to investigate how these effects are produced, we have to inquire into the operations of power.

By focusing on the problem of power, Machiavelli introduces a new way of doing political theory, an approach that is no longer oriented towards abstract and ahistorical questions of the type 'What is justice?' but one that poses political inquiries at the scale of concrete societies that exist in a particular time and place (see Key Concept: Realism).

Key Concept: Realism

In political theory and political philosophy, realism describes a theoretical approach that begins with the political world as it is, rather than with how it might be. Whereas normative political theory/philosophy is concerned with how an ideal society can implement normative values, such as freedom, equality, and justice, realist political theory/philosophy is attentive to the constraints (including, for example, human psychology, interests, institutions, structural or systemic traits, existing power relations) that limit the scope for political change. Machiavelli is often described as a classical realist, because of his attention to moral psychology (the passions and emotions), to the role of power and conflict, and to the importance of judgement in politics. Yet whereas most realisms have a conservative tendency that arises from their efforts to accommodate reality rather than transform it, Machiavelli's realism has a 'popular' (Gramsci, 1957), 'radical' (Del Lucchese, 2009) and imaginative (Viroli, 2007) dimension.

Political power takes diverse forms. In all states, there are power relations between the people and the elites, but they are overlaid by different institutional vectors. In principalities, the salient power relations emanate from the prince, and Machiavelli analyses them in terms of three political passions: love, fear, and hatred, all three of which can and must be mobilized to sustain or undermine political authority. A prince has to navigate these passions, and while it would be best if he were both loved and feared, Machiavelli acknowledges that this is a difficult proposition. He notoriously concludes that if one must choose between the two, it is safer to be feared than to be loved. A prince who relies on being loved is at the mercy of his subjects: people are ungrateful and fickle, and they tend to withdraw their love for trifles. By contrast, a prince who relies on fear controls the relationship with his subjects, since it is in his hands whether and how to punish. Fear, however, is not a solution either. If love is fickle, the problem with fear is that it tends to morph into hatred, the stuff that revolts and uprisings are made of.

Fear and love are also inspired by laws and institutions, which Machiavelli understands as foundational to states (Machiavelli, 2016: XII, 74). Law institutionalizes the fear of punishment (Machiavelli, 2007: 1.29, 92), and since Machiavelli does not believe that people will 'do good' unless constrained by necessity (ibid.: 1.3, 33), law provides us with the requisite deterrent to ensure social order. Yet law is more than just the threat of punishment; it also embodies a set of customary norms and for this reason, it has a central role in organizing societies. While he does not advocate an absolute pre-eminence of law and acknowledges that there are occasions in which laws must be broken, he argues that when people become accustomed to flout the law, even when they have good reasons for doing so, eventually the legal order will break down (ibid.: 1.34, 101).

Along with law, the other vital political institution is religion, which Machiavelli regards as 'absolutely necessary for preserving society' (ibid.: 1.11, 56–57). Religion is the counterpart to force; if both violence and law inspire fear through the threat of force, religion installs a different kind of fear, namely the fear of God. But religion also incites political bonds (what Machiavelli calls 'love'). Just as law also inspires social cohesion, so religion is a major force of integration. Machiavelli insists that any well-ordered state, whether monarchy or republic, relies on religion as a mechanism of social integration and discipline. Yet not all religions fulfil this function equally well. While the pagan religious cults of ancient Rome were uniquely suited to strengthening civil bonds, to inculcating military valour, to generating solidarity, and to promoting republican freedom and self-government, early modern Christianity, with its deeply corrupt church and its demands of obedience, humility, and self-denial fared remarkably poor in all of these respects.

Conquest and political violence are therefore only half the story for how power can be established and maintained. In the words of the Marxist theorist Antonio Gramsci (1957), for Machiavelli, power consists of force + consent. A long-term strategy (whether for princes, republics, or indeed insurgent plebeians) to stabilize power demands a turn to institutions, especially law and religion, that can generate 'consent'.

25.2 Power and the state: Key Points

- Machiavelli's theoretical work is informed by his experience as an official of the Florentine republic between 1498 and 1512.
- Machiavelli attributes to the many and the few opposing political desires: whereas the few seek to dominate, the many endeavour to elude domination.
- Power in its various guises is at the heart of Machiavelli's political theory and of his realist analysis of force relations.

25.3 Virtue and fortune

25.3.1 Virtù

The most distinctive concept Machiavelli developed in his work is *virtù*, often translated as 'virtue'. Virtue was a major concept in ancient, medieval, and early modern philosophy (Hankins, 2019), yet Machiavelli uses it in an entirely unconventional manner. Etymologically, *virtù* derives from the Latin *virtus*, from *vir*, the Latin word for man, and it stands for moral excellence. For the Romans, it referred to desirable qualities associated with heroic masculinity: strength, courage, mercy, and dignity; the Christian tradition praises temperance, prudence, courage, and justice as its four cardinal virtues; and the Renaissance humanists who preceded Machiavelli insisted that fine character and practical wisdom make good rulers. Machiavelli's *virtù* has little in common with any of these, which is why there is great disagreement among scholars concerning its meaning (Price, 1973).

By *virtù*, Machiavelli means skill, expertise, and competence, as when we refer to a talented musician as a 'virtuoso'. *Virtù* refers to a faculty, a power, a capacity that is specific to its field. It includes such political skills as shrewdness, craftiness, as well as fraudulence and deceit, which neither Romans nor Christians would have recognized as virtuous. *Virtù* designates the capacity of political actors to shape the course of events, the adeptness to act and intervene effectively in the political field. A virtuous actor is one who can read the equilibrium of forces that make up a political situation and who sees and seizes opportunities for action.

The *virtù* that is called for in politics is of a different kind from that of other spheres of life; sometimes it coincides with moral virtue but often it does not and at times it even flagrantly challenges the expectations of morality. To highlight some of the most famous examples, in Chapter 7 of *The Prince*, Machiavelli lists as instances of political virtue: securing oneself against enemies, eliminating adversaries, using force or fraud as necessary, making oneself loved and feared by the people, and obeyed and respected by one's soldiers. The subsequent Chapter 8, which discusses princes who acquire their principality 'through crime' is deliberately ambiguous about whether criminal and evil political actions count as *virtù*. On the one hand, Machiavelli writes that 'one cannot call it virtue to kill one's fellow citizens, to betray one's friends, to be without faith, without compassion, without religion' but then goes on to do precisely that and invokes, not once but multiple times, the '*virtù*' of Agathocles the Sicilian, a prince who was unequivocally guilty of the very crimes Machiavelli said couldn't be called *virtù*.

Because *virtù* involves grasping the opportunities and limits of a particular historical situation, there is no such thing as generic political virtue that remains the same across time and space. What counts as *virtù* is going to be defined locally, in terms of a particular historical and political context. Sometimes, the conditions require political actors to do things for which they will be blamed, which is why it is important for them to learn how to be 'not good', in other words, to act against what public opinion regards as virtuous (Machiavelli, 2016: XV, 85). Indeed, often what seems virtuous is a recipe for disaster while what seems like vice turns out to be right in the long run. For example, a very generous prince who lavishly distributes gifts to his people will be loved temporarily; but if that magnanimity requires him to raise taxes, he will end up hated (ibid.: XVI, 86). Political action, in short, requires a different set of virtues than those that are upheld by writers, moralists, and priests. As Machiavelli puts it in Chapter 18 of *The Prince*, 'there are two kinds of combat: one with laws, the other with force' and a political actor needs to know how to engage in both. As models for how to combat with force, Machiavelli proposes the lion and the fox; from the former one can learn how to scare the wolves; from the latter, how to recognize traps (ibid.: XVIII, 91).

This contextual approach to virtue marks a key feature of Machiavelli's thought. His political philosophy does not seek to solve philosophy's eternal problems; indeed, he is entirely uninterested in them. Instead of solving philosophical problems, Machiavelli's thought addresses worldly concerns.

It is driven by a commitment to the concrete historical and political situation. This is why history and historical examples play such an important role in his work. They allow Machiavelli to reason inductively, from the concrete to the abstract, rather than the other way around.

25.3.2 Fortuna

The principal challenge to what Machiavelli calls *virtù*—the human capacity to actively shape politics and history—arises from the human condition itself. Humans make their own history, but we make it under conditions that are variable, volatile, and unpredictable. Machiavelli has a name for this undependable and mercurial condition: *fortuna*. *Fortuna* is Machiavelli's figure for contingency, chance, and danger; it marks the limits of the human ability to control and manage social life and a threat to political order. Politics, therefore, consists in an ongoing struggle between the virtuosity, skill, expertise, and mastery embodied by *virtù* and the hazards of *fortuna*, the unpredictable irruption of nature into the social field. Human action and ingenuity can achieve a great deal; but we act under conditions that are not of our choosing and that pose objective limits to the efficacy of even the most expertly devised plan. Machiavelli was not original in representing the human condition as struggle between *virtù* and *fortuna*—that trope can be traced back all the way to the Greeks. Yet what is distinctive about his interpretation is that he treats it as irreconcilable, insisting that facing the headwinds of history, one would be mistaken to follow what are conventionally regarded as virtues of moderation, caution, and compromise.

Machiavelli represents the contest between *virtù* and *fortuna* as a battle of the sexes, drawing on gendered tropes that juxtapose masculinized *virtù* and feminized *fortuna*. Fortune, Machiavelli writes, 'is a woman', associating the wild and intractable forces of nature, its whims and dangers with femininity. Although the gendered dimension of the clash between *virtù* and *fortuna* are not of Machiavelli's making, he dramatizes it as a scene of sexual conquest that vacillates between seduction and violence:

> it is better to be impetuous than cautious, for fortune is a woman, and it is necessary, if one wants to have it off with her, to strike her and to toss her down. And one sees that she lets herself be won more often by such men as these, than by those who proceed coldly.
>
> (ibid.: XXV, 117, trans. mod.)

Moving between the explicitly misogynist call to assault and physically subdue her, and the idea that she must be courted by displays of audacity, Machiavelli represents fortune/woman as both objectified and mysterious, as a pliable *object* of male action and as a mercurial *subject* who decides on her own accord whom she favours.

By investing the clash between *virtù* and *fortuna* with the sexist attitudes, desires, and fears that his presumptively male audience has towards women, Machiavelli turns the limits of human action into limits of masculinity and represents action as an exclusively masculine domain. In this respect, the image of fortune as a woman is indicative of the generic androcentrism, which feminist scholarship has highlighted across the Western tradition of political thought (see especially Okin, 1979; Pateman, 1988). In Machiavelli's texts, autonomy, citizenship, political action, and freedom are consistently associated with manliness while weakness, obsequiousness, and dependency are coupled with effeminacy and femininity. In line with both the venerable sexist tradition in the history of political thought as well as with the etymology of *virtù*, Machiavelli thus associates virtue with manliness while linking its absence with the unmanly, and mapping it on to the feminine. It therefore comes as no surprise that with very few exceptions, women do not make an appearance as actors in Machiavelli's political universe.

Yet as feminist readers have shown, in addition to this generic sexism there is also a Machiavellian twist, namely a profound ambivalence about the meaning of manhood and about the position of women that arises precisely because Machiavelli boldly affirms the role of desire in politics (Brown, 1988; Pitkin, 1999; Falco, 2004). Fortune, after all, does not passively await her conqueror but manifests a threat and danger. Thus, the feminine does not simply coincide with conventional attributes of unmanliness (weakness, timidity, obsequiousness) but also represents a menace. Indeed, Machiavelli figures women as not outside the political field but as nebulous threats from within, thematized most explicitly in the chapter of the *Discourses* that is notoriously titled 'How a State May Fall Through Women' (Machiavelli, 2007: 3.26, 335–336). There, Machiavelli argues (confusedly) that states have often been ruined because of women, but then he cites as examples cases that do not support this claim. Indeed, if one reads closely, it turns out that it is not women who ruin states, but men who lose popular support on account of adultery and sexual assault. In other words, the danger women pose to states arises not from their actions but from their objectification (Winter, 2019). This is a classic displacement, whereby sex and sexuality are projected onto women and represented as opaque threats to the socio-political order.

Although his representation is misogynistic, Machiavelli situates the philosophical problem of action and power squarely in the field of desire. It is a decisively gendered version of desire within a psychic space of male heterosexuality, but it remains a rare acknowledgement in the history of Western political thought, that politics is entirely shot through with desire. Insofar as Machiavelli understands politics as embodied and affirms the role of desire, women are not just relegated to a threatening natural force outside of the political domain. Rather than treating seduction as a problem outside of politics, Machiavelli explicitly figures political action as seduction and assault (Brown, 1988). The image of fortune as temptress and menace is indicative of his acknowledgement that 'politics is sexual . . . and sex is politics' (Brown, 1987: 7).

> ### 25.3 Virtue and fortune: Key Points
>
> - Political virtue is a type of practical knowledge that enables someone to act effectively in the political field, to interpret the relations of forces, and to seize opportunities.
> - Fortune is the name that Machiavelli gives to the limits of human action and control.
> - The encounter between the gendered figures of *virtù* and *fortuna* defines Machiavelli's theory of history.

25.4 Freedom and conflict

25.4.1 The Roman republic

Machiavelli's most important work of political theory is the *Discourses on the First Ten Books of Titus Livy*, a sprawling and intimidating text. For the modern reader, one of the difficulties the *Discourses* present is that it sets out Machiavelli's ideas as a commentary on Titus Livy's history of Rome (see Key Thinker: Titus Livius). Most of the first book focuses on the early history of Rome, but Machiavelli moves through Livy's text in a thematic rather than chronological sequence with a firm eye on the predicaments faced by Florence. Thus, the *Discourses* is a work that is *both* about republican Rome and about early sixteenth-century Florence, and the political quandaries of Florence motivate the work's trajectory.

The *Discourses* begins with the Roman constitution. Machiavelli argues that Rome was a 'perfect republic' because its mixed constitution blended the monarchic authority of two consuls, the aristocratic authority of a senate, and the popular authority of the tribunes of the plebs (i.e. the ordinary, lower classes) (Machiavelli, 2007: I.2, 30). But why Rome? For Renaissance humanists, Rome always had paradigmatic status (Burckhardt, 1960). Archaeologists excavated its monuments, statues, arches, and colonnades; travellers from all over Italy walked its streets; literary scholars edited the works of Latin poets, orators, and historians. Artists and architects looked to Rome for templates of aesthetic perfection and classical harmony. And Machiavelli saw in Rome an unparalleled blossoming of freedom and political virtue, which is why he looked to its constitution and history as keys to Florence's political dilemmas.

Key Thinker: Titus Livius

Titus Livius (59 BCE–AD 17), known as Livy in English, was one of the three great Roman historians (along with Sallust and Tacitus). He wrote a gigantic work on the history of Rome called *Ab urbe condita* [From the Founding of the City]. Written over 36 years, it chronicles the history of the Rome from the legendary moment when Aeneas arrived in Italy following the fall of Troy to the reign of Augustus, Rome's first emperor. It became an instant classic and exerted enormous influence on Latin style and historical writing. Of the originally 142 books (the length of which were constrained by the size of papyrus rolls), 35 survived, volumes 1–10 and 21–45. The first ten books, which are the object of Machiavelli's *Discourses* cover the period from the mythical founding of the city until about 292 BCE.

25.4.2 Freedom

At the heart of the *Discourses* is a theory of political freedom. Machiavelli shared the premise of political republicanism that freedom consists in the absence of dependency and domination and in the active participation in the collective self-government of one's community. To be free, for Machiavelli, means first of all, not to depend on the will of others and, second, to be able to collectively shape the conditions under which one lives (Viroli, 1998: 5–6). Dependency can have various sources; it can be military, political, economic, or social in nature. For example, someone who lives in a monarchy is dependent on the will of the king and is in this sense, unfree. Similarly, someone who lives in an oligarchic regime, where power is held by the few, is subject to domination and hence unfree. Political liberty is only possible in a broad-based republic, where laws are the product of collective decision-making. But citizenship in such a republic is no guarantee for freedom, either. A city such as Florence after the return of the Medici in 1512, where one family exercises tremendous informal power, through patron-client relationships and networks of dependency, is servile and unfree.

More generally, in republics that tolerate significant economic inequality and that lack mechanisms to safeguard political equality, wealthy elites tend to exercise far greater political power than the rest of the people. Indeed, the accumulation of wealth and the increase of economic inequality have all kinds of corrupting effects on republican government and citizenship, and one of Machiavelli's central concerns was to examine these repercussions for freedom. Corruption, Machiavelli argued, is not an individual moral vice nor an economic mechanism of enrichment for the unscrupulous but institutional degeneration and decay. Such degeneration occurs naturally; it is caused by the spread of bad customs that compromise virtue. While the deterioration of customs is a natural process, it is not uniform. Sound laws and institutions can mitigate the corrupting tendencies whereas growing inequality worsens them. Moreover, states that have political institutions and practices that are open and dynamic have a much better capacity to adapt and respond by reordering and reorganizing than states that are stuck in a political rigidity where institutions are unalterable (Raimondi, 2018). As the history of Rome demonstrates, such dynamism is much more likely under conditions of political and economic equality than under conditions of inequality.

There is disagreement among interpreters as to how robust Machiavelli's commitment to freedom was, and what level of political participation it implied. Some scholars believe that Machiavelli considered only elites to be competent political actors (de Grazia, 1989: 180–183; Mansfield, 1996: 307; Coby, 1999: 254–256). Others argue that Machiavelli thought people were primarily motivated by a desire for security, rather than an eagerness to share power (Pettit, 1997: 28; Skinner, 2002: 197). As a result, these scholars suggest that Machiavelli's notion of freedom was largely consonant with that of his fifteenth-century predecessors (Coluccio Salutati, Leonardo Bruni, and Poggio Bracciolini) who understood freedom as independence from foreign domination and self-government instead of being subject to a prince (Skinner, 1978: 157–158). My view is that Machiavelli's conception of freedom differs from that of his predecessors, insofar as he thought freedom requires a commitment to the commons and to public life. Unlike Aristotle, however, Machiavelli did not see participation in government as a moral virtue in itself; rather, he considered it essential to curb the deleterious effects of inequality and the relations of power and dependency that are promoted by wealth and patronage (see also Chapter 3 on Aristotle).

Machiavelli's focus on the adverse political consequences of inequality and his commitment to broad and inclusive political participation are features of his radically popular version of republicanism (McCormick, 2011; 2018). In contrast to most classical and early modern political theorists who regarded a just monarchy or a well-ordered aristocracy as the preferred regime, Machiavelli advocated for a Roman-style constitution that empowers the plebs. As readers from Gentili through Spinoza (see Chapter 6), Rousseau (see Chapter 9), and Gramsci have argued, Machiavelli's sympathies are with the people. Without romanticizing the people, he remarks that their purposes are more decent than those of the elites (Machiavelli, 2016 :IX, 67); the people are less ungrateful (Machiavelli, 2007: I.29, 90), wiser, more prudent, more stable, and have better judgement (ibid.: I.58, 146). The people do not always make the best decisions; nor are they incorruptible. But among the various threats to freedom in a republic, the most serious one emanates not from the masses but from ambitious political and economic elites. Refusing to distinguish between (good) aristocrats and (bad) oligarchs, Machiavelli insists that elites tend to be corrupted.

Yet elites are not simply going to disappear. In his *Florentine Histories*, Machiavelli shows that there are historical moments when the people have the upper hand and manage to disempower ruling elites, but these moments are invariably followed by the formation of new elites. Machiavelli anticipates early twentieth-century 'elite theories' which hold that there is an 'iron law of oligarchy', according to which all complex organizations, even if they start out democratically, ultimately develop into oligarchies (Michels, 1915; Mosca, 1980; Pareto, 2017). Yet whereas elite theorists acquiesce to oligarchic rule, Machiavelli describes the tendency to oligarchy as a form of corruption that can be challenged by the many in the interest of freedom.

If elites cannot be conclusively defeated once and for all, republics have to develop institutions and practices to deal with the threats they pose to freedom. For Machiavelli, elites cannot be trusted to safeguard freedom, because they have a strong motivation to usurp it (see Key Concept: The *grandi* and the *popolo*) and the only class that can be a reliable guard for freedom is the people (Machiavelli, 2007: 1.5, 36–37). His popular and democratic commitments distinguish Machiavelli's republicanism from his contemporaries, such as Guicciardini (1998; 2007), whose republican credos had a decisively oligarchic bent. While most Florentines were attached to the idea that their city was a free republic, many of the elites looked longingly to Venice, a city that was governed by an aristocratic senate. Venice lacked the broad political participation that made Florence—at least during Machiavelli's tenure as secretary—one of the most politically inclusive and democratic societies in early sixteenth-century Europe.

25.4.3 **Conflict**

With broad political participation comes turmoil, and Florence saw plenty of it. Among political and economic elites, there was a general consensus that political discord was detrimental to stability and freedom. Machiavelli, by contrast, insisted that conflicts, including the turbulences and commotions they generate, are a natural and healthy aspect of a free collective life. In Book 1 of the *Discourses*, he goes so far as to contend that the conflicts between plebeians and patricians (the Roman lower and upper classes) were the cause that made Rome free and powerful (Machiavelli, 2007: 1.4, 34–35). This is a remarkable and shocking claim that disputes both common sense, as well much of the learned judgements of ancient, medieval, and early modern political thought, which tended to promote the values of concord and consensus. In contrast to this received opinion, Machiavelli insists that civil conflicts are neither avoidable nor harmful for a state, as long as the institutions are set up to appropriately channel them.

This valorization of conflict is Machiavelli's most important intervention in the history of political thought (Lefort, 2012; Vatter, 2014; Del Lucchese, 2015; Gaille, 2018; Pedullà, 2018). It is also what distinguishes him from many contemporary neo-republicans, who understand the *demos* as primarily a passive force (Pettit, 1997; 2012). It is hard to overstate the profoundly radical nature of the idea that conflict is not a pathology of political life, but a source of freedom and even stability. Anticipating contemporary debates about populism, Machiavelli concedes that the problem of conflict is that it can quickly escalate into forms of violence that ultimately undermine security, order, and freedom. Hence one of his concerns was to distinguish forms of conflicts that could play the stabilizing role they performed in the Roman republic and forms that weaken freedom. In addition, Machiavelli proposes several institutions, modelled on templates from the Roman republic, to ensure that political struggle remains salutary and does not degenerate into civil war. Most important among these are class-based institutions, such as assemblies and offices that are only open to non-elite citizens, political trials for public officials accused of corruption, and arming the people (Machiavelli, 2007: 1.4–1.8, 34–49; McCormick, 2011).

Arming the people was one of Machiavelli's main political objectives, both during his time in office and in his writing. There is both a military and a political rationale for this. Governments in Machiavelli's time mostly relied on mercenaries for troops. But Machiavelli regarded mercenaries as unreliable: they are typically inadequately trained, undisciplined, and unmotivated. And if by chance they perform well on the battlefield, and are led by a skilful officer, then they are dangerous, because what stops them from turning against their employer? Thus militarily, arming the people means that states need not rely on mercenaries for troops and can instead draw on their own citizen militias.

In addition to the military argument for popular militias, there is also a political dimension to arming the people. Military discipline serves as a 'socializing process' through which people learn how to be citizens, oriented towards the common good (Pocock, 1975: 202). An armed population is much less likely to let itself be oppressed, either by corrupt elites or by a despotic monarch. Hence, for republics, a citizen militia is an obvious way to promote both citizenship and security. By contrast, Machiavelli's advice that principalities should do likewise is counterintuitive. By contending that princes should set up popular militias, Machiavelli rejects the prevailing view that the best way to secure a principality is to disarm the people. But how is a prince going to rule a people that is armed and militarily trained? His only option, at that point, is to enter into an alliance with the people against the oligarchs or risk being overthrown. Some readers have taken this point as evidence that even though *The Prince* appears to be a manual for princes, if princes actually followed his counsel, it would lead to their overthrow (Dietz, 1986).

> **25.4 Freedom and conflict: Key Points**
>
> - The *Discourses*, Machiavelli's chief work, advance a popular, anti-aristocratic political project.
> - Machiavelli defends a republican conception of freedom with a mixed constitution, modelled on Rome, where the people/plebs play the role of defending freedom against aristocratic conspiracies and tyrannical ambitions.
> - Whereas most political philosophers have emphasized the importance of concord, Machiavelli contends that conflict contributes to freedom and order.

25.5 Violence, conquest, and empire

25.5.1 Violence as spectacle

Perhaps even more than the discussion of power, it is his treatment of violence and cruelty that shocks many first-time readers of Machiavelli. His political works contain graphic depictions of instances of violence and cruelty, notably prominent historical examples of spectacular executions. They include the infamous fratricide by Romulus, the mythic founder of Rome; the massacre of the oligarchy and wealthiest citizens by Agathocles, the Greek tyrant of Syracuse; the cruelties of Hannibal, the famous Carthaginian general who invaded Italy and whom Roman sources, such as Livy and Cicero described as extremely cruel; the bloody 1378 revolt by the Florentine woolworkers, known as the Ciompi, which inspired Florentine elites with a fear of the masses that lasted for centuries; the executions and assassinations by Cesare Borgia, a contemporary of Machiavelli, and the illegitimate son of Pope Alexander VI, who was one of the most promising military and political figures of Machiavelli's lifetime.

Machiavelli's renditions of these events (and others) are notorious, because he refuses to simply condemn them on moral grounds and instead seeks to understand the political logics that animate them. Violence and cruelty, Machiavelli suggests, taint a prince's reputation, and he counsels readers to avoid them to the extent possible. But he insists on defending political actors who deploy violence under conditions when it appears necessary, whether in the case of war, punishment, or conspiracies and revolts. Instead of asking the moral question—when and under what conditions are certain types of violence morally justified?—Machiavelli seeks to render violence an object of political reflection (Kahn, 1994). Violence, Machiavelli contends, is a crucial instrument for establishing and maintaining political order, and those who deny this are either naïvely deluding themselves or intentionally deceiving their audience.

Most important among the mechanisms and logics of violence is the spectacle. Grisly scenes of spectacular executions are scattered across Machiavelli's work, and he insists repeatedly on the salutary political effects of publicly staged forms of punishment. It is tempting to read these passages simply as glorifications of violence, but a more context-sensitive interpretation suggests a different verdict. At issue, in these passages, is not the celebration of ferocious and bloody cruelty, as if to satisfy some ostensibly basic human instinct for violence. Rather, Machiavelli analyses the *modus operandi* of political violence. This is especially clear in his portrayal of Cesare Borgia's execution of his 'minister' Remirro de Orco, who, out of the blue, appears dead one morning in the town square of Cesena, bisected in two pieces 'with a piece of wood and a bloody knife' at his side. The 'ferocity of that spectacle' left the people 'at once satisfied and stupefied' (Machiavelli, 2016: VII, 59). Machiavelli interprets the execution as a clever machination whereby Cesare dissociates himself from the cruelty of his deputy. By emphasizing the *spectacle* and its satisfying and stupefying effects, Machiavelli shows that state-making is witnessed and staged and that theatricality is central to these effects. Violence, in other words, operates not primarily as a mechanism of coercion, whereby someone is forced to perform or forebear an action against their will, but by appealing to an audience. Political violence, for Machiavelli, is fundamentally communicative: it is designed to be seen and to leave behind traces. Violence in politics is a performance, and its sensory and dramatic aspects are part of its functioning (Winter, 2018: Chapter 1).

25.5.2 The paradox of conquest

Just as violence is an inescapable part of political life for Machiavelli, so is territorial conquest (Hulliung, 1983; Hörnqvist, 2004; Regent, 2011). While Machiavelli has curiously little to say about the conquest that turned out to be the most significant geopolitical event of his lifetime—the Spanish conquest of the Aztec Empire—the unsanctioned seizure of political office looms large in his political imagination, no doubt fuelled by the historical experience of Renaissance Italy, where coups, conspiracies, rebellions, and revolts were not infrequent.

Although he avoids the term 'conquest' and prefers instead the language of *acquistare*, to 'acquire', he considers the practice of taking possession of a territory in an unsanctioned manner an elementary component of political life. Scornful of hereditary rulers and the dynastic principle, Machiavelli identified two sources of conquest. On the one hand, it derives from an appetite for honour and glory that is fundamental to politics. In contrast to his analysis of the political humours, where the desire to dominate is specifically associated with elites, Machiavelli suggests that the desire for territorial expansion is universal: he calls it 'natural and ordinary' (Machiavelli, 2016: III, 47). On the other hand, conquest also results from the dynamics of political power, irrespective of the passions and appetites that motivate it (Machiavelli, 2007: 1.6, 41; 2.2, 165).

Machiavelli's theory of conquest is laid out in the first part of *The Prince* and the second book of the *Discourses*. It disaggregates conquest into two separate problems: how to *found* a state and how to *maintain* it. A successful conquest requires not only a military but also a political victory that constructs a solid foundation for political authority.

A prince can acquire power in two ways: either by heredity or by conquest. A ruler who accedes to office by inheritance is a natural prince or 'prince by birth'; he tends to inspire more loyalty, because he benefits from the authority that derives from ancestry (Machiavelli, 2016: II, 40). The conqueror, by contrast, lacks this natural resource, and in addition to the military problem of seizing territory, he must fashion an equivalent for the bond that the natural prince has with his subjects. Fortunately, for the conqueror, political loyalty is a social construct. While it helps to have the legitimacy conferred upon a ruler by an illustrious pedigree, allegiance can also be generated by addressing the political passions of one's subjects.

But there is a paradox at the heart of conquest: The conqueror who seizes power by means of violence thereby interrupts the prevailing relations of political legitimacy based on custom, lineage, or other sources. Yet insofar as the conqueror seeks to retain the power that was seized by violent means, conquest is also predicated on a return to the stability and chains of legitimacy that preceded it. The paradox of conquest is that even though conquerors acquire power by means of violence, they cannot publicly validate that violence, for that would invite others to depose them (Winter, 2011). To avoid acknowledging violence as a permissible mechanism of transferring power, successful conquerors must depict their conquest in such a way that dissimulates the principle of violent change. Machiavelli's (2016: XXIV, 113) solution is that conquerors should 'appear hereditary', that is, they should represent their conquest as a re-establishment of ancient order.

In emphasizing the political dimensions of conquest and in highlighting the paradox, whereby a successful conquest is predicated on its disavowal, Machiavelli unwittingly illustrates some of the problems that European conquerors of the New World faced. These conquerors faced the conundrum of how to transform their seizure of land into legal and political claims. In doing so, Machiavelli shifts the political predicament of conquest away from the narrowly technical realm of force to the sphere of representation. Conquest is not merely a successful employment of military technology but it consists in the manufacture of appearances. Force is futile if it is not accompanied by signs. This is one of the most important lessons of Machiavelli's political theory. While Machiavelli might have agreed with Mao Zedong's famous line that 'power grows out of the barrel of a gun', he would have insisted that this only captures half of the story. While the seeds of power may indeed be in the means of violence, power that is exclusively based on violence is unsustainable. To stay with Mao's metaphor, the problem is not only who wields the gun (a point that Mao highlighted and that is frequently omitted when his words are turned into a slogan) but also, as importantly, how the gun appears to others (Zedong, 1965: 224).

25.5.3 Republics and empire

One of Machiavelli's most controversial arguments about conquest is that it is not only a pursuit of self-absorbed princes, but that there is a political logic of conquest that not even popular republics can defy. As Machiavelli puts it in the *Discourses*, 'a city that lives free has two aims, one conquest, the other to remain free' (Machiavelli, 2007: 1.29, 91). While these two purposes—freedom and conquest—are analytically separate, Machiavelli takes them to be intimately linked. Lest we mistake Machiavelli, anachronistically, for a champion of modern imperialism, we must bear in mind that his conception of imperial power is decidedly ancient in character, and that especially the Roman Empire was a very different formation from modern empires.

On Machiavelli's interpretation of ancient history, there are two successful versions of republics: one that is aristocratic, small, territorially closed and non-expansionistic (modelled on Sparta and in Machiavelli's time embodied by Venice), and one is popular, large, expansionistic and seeks to build an empire (modelled on Rome) (ibid.: I.5, 36–38). Whereas most of Machiavelli's contemporaries would have looked to the Spartan-Venetian model, Machiavelli demurred and instead advocates for Rome (Gilbert, 1977). He acknowledges that the Spartan model has its advantages, most importantly longevity (Machiavelli, 2007: 1.2, 27; 1.6, 40). Whereas Rome was free for barely 400 years, Sparta endured more than 800 years as a republic (Machiavelli, 2003: 24). Yet even as he concedes the longevity, Machiavelli considers the advantages of the second model overwhelming. Most important among them, of course, is that Rome placed the 'guard of freedom' among the people rather than the nobility (Machiavelli, 2007: 1.5, 36–37). By contrast, Sparta had the nobility in control, thereby empowering those groups who pose the most danger to freedom. But there is a second advantage to the Roman model, which has to do with its openness and expansiveness. Unlike the closed republics of Sparta and Venice, Rome had an open citizenship policy, embracing foreigners and incorporating conquered subject populations. Because Rome was built on incessant territorial expansion and on unceasing incorporation of new populations, it had an enormous pool of military recruits to sustain its massive imperial armies. By contrast, the Spartan model must balance the military demands of having a sufficiently strong army to defend itself against potential aggressors with a non-expansionistic foreign policy. Even as he acknowledged the longevity of Sparta, Machiavelli was sceptical about this balancing act, arguing that if ever a Spartan-type republic is forced to conquer, it is doomed. Sooner or later states have to fight wars, and if they are strong enough to defeat their enemies, they face the predicament of conquest. Thus, against the conventional Aristotelian idea that a state should be balanced and neither too big nor too small (Aristotle, 1984, 1326a5–1326b25), Machiavelli argues that territorial and population growth are important factors for a republic's long-term success (see also Chapter 3 on Aristotle).

Scholars disagree about the implications of this claim. Did Machiavelli promote imperial expansion for the sake of glory (Hulliung, 1983; Regent, 2011)? As a strategy to redirect elites' domineering passions outwards, by offering them positions of military power (Hörnqvist, 2004: 74)? Because he regarded such expansion an inevitable consequence of building the military power a republic needs to defend itself (Pedullà, 2018: 174–176)? Or did he endorse territorial expansion only on the model of a voluntary alliance of free cities (Viroli, 1992: 162)? While these remain open questions, what is clear is that for Machiavelli, liberty and empire are not opposite political ideals but two sides of the same coin.

25.5 Violence, conquest, and empire: Key Points

- Political violence, for Machiavelli, functions as spectacle rather than as coercion.
- Machiavelli's theory of conquest highlights the paradoxes of conquest that materialized in early European colonial history.
- By adopting the Roman republic as a model for a free society, Machiavelli also embraces conquest and expansion.

25.6 Conclusion

Machiavelli's criticism of moral and metaphysical ideas led him to introduce a new approach to politics, one that seeks not abstract, timeless, and universal ideas but historically attuned political action. Such action must draw on a new form of practical knowledge, which Machiavelli dubs *virtù*, and it must confront the challenge posed by the changing and unpredictable conditions, which he calls *fortuna*. In contrast to the traditional concerns with ideals and principles, Machiavelli calls attention to the actual, the 'effectual truth' of politics. He demystifies politics by emphasizing the role of power and violence; and he proposes novel theories of how violence and conquest operate. Against the presumptive impartiality of political philosophy, he defends an unapologetically partisan political theory that champions the interests of the many. As the Florentine experience taught Machiavelli, inequality and the resulting concentrations of wealth and power are the greatest dangers to political freedom. In his view, freedom requires not only a republican regime but political and economic equality.

Take your learning further by accessing the online resources for a library of web links to relevant videos, articles, blogs, and useful websites for this chapter: **www.oup.com/he/Ramgotra-Choat1e**.

Study questions

1. What is freedom for Machiavelli and what are the conditions for its maintenance?
2. What kind of laws does Machiavelli's political science formulate, and how do they differ from moral injunctions?
3. In Machiavelli's theory of history, what is the role for human action?

4. If power, as Machiavelli suggests, is shaped by desire, what are the implications for politics?
5. What is the role of conflict for Machiavelli and why is it so important?
6. How does Machiavelli's realism differ from conventional understandings of realism?
7. What is the paradox of conquest and how does Machiavelli's work exemplify it?
8. Why does Machiavelli believe that republics have a tendency to become empires?

Further reading

Primary sources

Machiavelli, N. (1988) *Florentine Histories*. Ed. L. Banfield and H.C. Mansfield. Princeton, NJ: Princeton University Press.
A very good and accessible translation.

Machiavelli, N. (2003) *Art of War*. Trans. C. Lynch. Chicago: University of Chicago Press.
A recent translation of Machiavelli's work on military strategy and war.

Machiavelli, N. (2016) *The Prince: With Related Documents*. Ed. W.J. Connell. 2nd edn. Boston: Bedford/St. Martin.
The best contemporary English translation of *The Prince*.

Machiavelli, N. (2007) 'Discourses on the First Ten Books of Titus Livy'. In *The Sweetness of Power: Machiavelli's Discourses and Guicciardini's Considerations*. Ed. J.B. Atkinson and D. Sices, DeKalb, IL: Northern Illinois University Press.
The *Discourses on Livy* is notoriously difficult to translate. This careful edition brings together an elegant English text and a wealth of editorial notes.

Secondary sources

Althusser, L. (1999) *Machiavelli and Us*. Trans. G. Elliott. London: Verso.
An original Marxist interpretation of Machiavelli's *The Prince* that draws on Antonio Gramsci's discussions in the *Prison Notebooks*.

Del Lucchese, F. (2015) *The Political Philosophy of Niccolò Machiavelli*. Edinburgh: Edinburgh University Press.
A clear introduction to Machiavelli's political thought, legacy and reception from a Marxist perspective.

Gramsci, A. (1957) *The Modern Prince, and Other Writings*. Trans. L. Marks. New York: International Publishers.
This selection from the *Prison Notebooks* offers a revolutionary Marxist interpretation of *The Prince*.

Hankins, J. (2019) *Virtue Politics: Soulcraft and Statecraft in Renaissance Italy*. Cambridge, MA: Harvard University Press.
A remarkable and erudite re-interpretation of Renaissance political thought that foregrounds humanism and diminishes republicanism.

McCormick, J. (2011) *Machiavellian Democracy*. Cambridge: Cambridge University Press.
Proposes a provocative interpretation of Machiavelli as a democrat and offers a critique of the Cambridge School.

Pedullà, G. (2018) *Machiavelli in Tumult: The* Discourses on Livy *and the Origins of Political Conflictualism*. Trans. P. Gaborik and R. Nybakken. Cambridge: Cambridge University Press.
A key contribution to the anti-aristocratic interpretation of Machiavelli that focuses on his theory of conflict.

Pitkin, H.F. (1999) *Fortune Is a Woman: Gender and Politics in the Thought of Niccolò Machiavelli*. 2nd edn. Berkeley, CA: University of California Press.
A feminist interpretation of the gendered figures in Machiavelli's work, drawing on psychoanalytic theory.

Skinner, Q. (2019) *Machiavelli: A Very Short Introduction*. Oxford: Oxford University Press.
  The most accessible introduction to Skinner's influential interpretation, insisting on a contextual reading.

Strauss, L. (1958) *Thoughts on Machiavelli*. Chicago: Chicago University Press.
  Argues that Machiavelli was dealing with eternal philosophical questions, breaking fundamentally with ancient Greek and Christian conceptions of ethics and politics. Inspired an entire school of interpretations sometimes referred to as 'Straussian'.

Vatter, M.E. (2013) *Machiavelli's* The Prince*: A Reader's Guide*. London: Bloomsbury.
  A helpful and discerning introduction to *The Prince*.

Winter, Y. (2018) *Machiavelli and the Orders of Violence*. Cambridge: Cambridge University Press.
  Reconstructs Machiavelli's theory of violence with emphasis on the spectacle. Argues that violence, for Machiavelli, is not a generic political technology but a strategy that correlates with class conflict.

References

Althusser, L. (1999) *Machiavelli and Us*. Trans. G. Elliott. London: Verso.

Anglo, S. (2005) *Machiavelli—the First Century: Studies in Enthusiasm, Hostility, and Irrelevance*. Oxford: Oxford University Press.

Aristotle (1984) *Politics*. Trans. B. Jowett, The Revised Oxford Translation. Princeton, NJ: Princeton University Press.

Barthas, J. (2010) 'Machiavelli in Political Thought from the Age of Revolutions to the Present'. In J.M. Najemy (ed.), *The Cambridge Companion to Machiavelli*. Cambridge: Cambridge University Press.

Brown, W. (1987) 'Where Is the Sex in Political Theory?' *Women & Politics*, 7(1): 3–23.

Brown, W. (1988) *Manhood and Politics: A Feminist Reading in Political Theory*. Totowa, NJ: Rowman & Littlefield.

Burckhardt, J. (1960) *The Civilization of the Renaissance in Italy*. Trans. S.G.C. Middlemore. New York: New American Library.

Coby, J.P. (1999) *Machiavelli's Romans: Liberty and Greatness in the Discourses on Livy*. Lanham, MD: Lexington Books.

de Grazia, S. (1989) *Machiavelli in Hell*. New York: Vintage.

Del Lucchese, F. (2009) *Conflict, Power, and Multitude in Machiavelli and Spinoza*. London: Continuum.

Del Lucchese, F. (2015) *The Political Philosophy of Niccolò Machiavelli*. Edinburgh: Edinburgh University Press.

Dietz, M.G. (1986) 'Trapping the Prince: Machiavelli and the Politics of Deception.' *American Political Science Review*, 80(3): 777–799.

Falco, M.J. (ed.) (2004) *Feminist Interpretations of Niccolò Machiavelli*. University Park, PA: Pennsylvania State University Press.

Foucault, M. (1978) *The History of Sexuality*, vol. 1: *The Will to Knowledge*. Trans. R. Hurley. London: Penguin.

Gaille, M. (2018) *Machiavelli on Freedom and Civil Conflict*. Leiden: Brill.

Gentili, A. (1924) *De legationibus libri tres*. Trans. G.J. Laing. New York: Oxford University Press.

Gilbert, F. (1977) 'The Venetian Constitution in Florentine Political Thought'. In F. Gilbert, *History, Choice, and Commitment*. Cambridge, MA: Belknap Press.

Gramsci, A. (1957) *The Modern Prince, and Other Writings*. Trans. L. Marks. New York: International Publishers.

Guicciardini, F. (1998) *'Discorso di Logrogno': On Bringing Order to Popular Government*. Trans. A. Moulakis. Lanham, MD: Rowman & Littlefield.

Guicciardini, F. (2007) 'Considerations of the Discourses of Niccolò Machiavelli'. In *The Sweetness of Power: Machiavelli's Discourses and Guicciardini's Considerations*. Ed. J.B. Atkinson and D. Sices. DeKalb, IL: Northern Illinois University Library.

Hankins, J. (2019) *Virtue Politics: Soulcraft and Statecraft in Renaissance Italy*. Cambridge, MA: Harvard University Press.

Hobbes, T. (1996) *Leviathan*. Cambridge: Cambridge University Press.

Hörnqvist, M. (2004) *Machiavelli and Empire*. Cambridge: Cambridge University Press.

Hulliung, M. (1983) *Citizen Machiavelli*. Princeton, NJ: Princeton University Press.

Kahn, V. (1994) *Machiavellian Rhetoric from the Counter-Reformation to Milton*. Princeton, NJ: Princeton University Press.

Kahn, V. (2010) 'Machiavelli's Reputation to the Eighteenth Century'. In J.M. Najemy (ed.), *The*

Cambridge Companion to Machiavelli. Cambridge: Cambridge University Press.

Lefort, C. (2012) *Machiavelli in the Making*. Trans. M.B. Smith. Evanston, IL: Northwestern University Press.

Machiavelli, N. (2003) *Art of War*. Trans. C. Lynch. Chicago: University of Chicago Press.

Machiavelli, N. (2007) 'The Discourses on Livy'. In J.B. Atkinson and D. Sices (eds), *The Sweetness of Power: Machiavelli's Discourses and Guicciardini's Considerations*. DeKalb, IL: Northern Illinois University Press.

Machiavelli, N. (2016) *The Prince: With Related Documents*. Ed. W.J. Connell, second edition. Boston: Bedford/St. Martin.

Mansfield, H.C. (1996) *Machiavelli's Virtue*. Chicago: University of Chicago Press.

McCormick, J. (2011) *Machiavellian Democracy*. Cambridge: Cambridge University Press.

McCormick, J. (2018) *Reading Machiavelli: Scandalous Books, Suspect Engagements, and the Virtue of Populist Politics*. Princeton, NJ: Princeton University Press.

Michels, R. (1915) *Political Parties*. Trans. E. Paul and C. Paul. New York: Hearst's International Library Co.

Mosca, G. (1980) *The Ruling Class*. Trans. H.D. Kahn. Westport, CT: Greenwood Press.

Okin, S.M. (1979) *Women in Western Political Thought*. Princeton, NJ: Princeton University Press.

Pareto, V. (2017) *The Rise and Fall of Elites*. New York: Routledge.

Pateman, C. (1988) *The Sexual Contract*. Stanford, CA: Stanford University Press.

Pedullà, G. (2018) *Machiavelli in Tumult: The Discourses on Livy and the Origins of Political Conflictualism*. Trans. P. Gaborik and R. Nybakken. Cambridge: Cambridge University Press.

Pettit, P. (1997) *Republicanism: A Theory of Freedom and Government*. Oxford: Oxford University Press.

Pettit, P. (2012) *On the People's Terms: A Republican Theory and Model of Democracy*. Cambridge: Cambridge University Press.

Pitkin, H.F. (1999) *Fortune Is a Woman: Gender and Politics in the Thought of Niccolò Machiavelli*. 2nd edn. Berkeley, CA: University of California Press.

Pocock, J.G.A. (1975) *The Machiavellian Moment: Florentine Political Thought and the Atlantic Republican Tradition*. Princeton, NJ: Princeton University Press.

Price, R. (1973) 'The Senses of *Virtù* in Machiavelli'. *European Studies Review*, 3(4): 315–345.

Raimondi, F. (2018) *Constituting Freedom: Machiavelli and Florence*. Trans. M. Armistead. Oxford: Oxford University Press.

Regent, N. (2011) 'Machiavelli: Empire, Virtù, and the Final Downfall'. *History of Political Thought*, 32(5), 751–772.

Rousseau, J-J. (2007) *The Social Contract, and Other Later Political Writings*. Trans. V. Gourevitch, Cambridge: Cambridge University Press.

Skinner, Q. (1978) *The Foundations of Modern Political Thought*, 2 vols. Cambridge: Cambridge University Press.

Skinner, Q. (2002) *Visions of Politics: Renaissance Virtues*, 3 vols. Cambridge: Cambridge University Press.

Tommasini, O. (1883) *La vita e gli scritti di Niccolò Machiavelli nella loro relazione col machiavellismo*, 2 vols. Rome: Loescher.

Vatter, M.E. (2014) *Between Form and Event: Machiavelli's Theory of Political Freedom*. New York: Fordham University Press.

Viroli, M. (1992) *From Politics to Reason of State: The Acquisition and Transformation of the Language of Politics, 1250–1600*. Cambridge: Cambridge University Press.

Viroli, M. (1998), *Machiavelli*, Oxford: Oxford University Press.

Viroli, M. (2007) 'Machiavelli's Realism'. *Constellations*, 14(4): 466–482.

Vivanti, C. (2013) *Niccolò Machiavelli: An Intellectual Biography*. Trans. S. MacMichael. Princeton, NJ: Princeton University Press.

Winter, Y. (2011) 'Conquest'. *Political Concepts: A Critical Lexicon*. 1. http://www.politicalconcepts.org/conquest-winter/

Winter, Y. (2018) *Machiavelli and the Orders of Violence*. Cambridge: Cambridge University Press.

Winter, Y. (2019) 'Machiavelli and the Rape of Lucretia'. *History of Political Thought*, 40(3): 405–432.

Wolin, S. (2004) *Politics and Vision*. Princeton, NJ: Princeton University Press.

Zedong, M. (1965) 'Problems of War and Strategy'. In *Selected Works*, vol. II. Beijing: Foreign Languages Press.

26 Emma Goldman
RUTH KINNA

Chapter guide

This chapter discusses resistance in Emma Goldman's anarchism. The Introduction (Section 26.1) accounts for her reputation, indicates her detachment from conventional political theory and considers the criticism that she failed to investigate race as a category of oppression. Section 26.2 identifies two concepts, 'love with open eyes' and 'the spirit of revolt', to structure her concept of resistance and explain the gaps and silences in her thought. Section 26.3 examines Goldman's understanding of political theory as a practice informed by experience and uses it to explore her concepts of power and emancipation, specifically, her construction of the relationship between class power and women's oppression. Finally, Section 26.4 discusses 'slavery' and 'slavishness' to show how Goldman used rights to advocate resistance to domination. The argument is that her love of America reflected a New World ideal that the US Constitution had sullied and that her embrace of revolt highlighted the futility of struggles for inclusion.

26.1 Introduction

Emma Goldman (1869–1940) is one of the towering figures in the late-nineteenth- and early-twentieth-century anarchist movement. Habitually ignored by early commentators, she was rediscovered mid-century during Anglophone feminism's 'second wave', seen as a pioneering, pro-feminist anarchist who complicated 'first-wave' feminism and, by making issues related to women and sexuality central to anarchism, transformed it. Her reputation as a political thinker is less well established, as Kathy Ferguson (2013: 3–4) notes.

Goldman is detached from the major traditions of European political thought. As an anarchist, she rejected key foundational principles of mainstream political theory. For her, contract meant not consent to authority but 'surrender' (Goldman, 1979b [1911a]: 50). She identified political obligation with a pervasive political theology that taught that '*man is nothing, the powers are everything*'. This 'refrain' normalized power monopolies, inhibited individuals from becoming 'conscious' of themselves (ibid.: 51) and misled them into thinking that they were duty-bound to observe someone else's rules.

Goldman (1979o [1935]: 359) described herself as a 'free communist' and believed that 'the exploitation of man by man' was the source of 'all slavery and oppression'. Yet she rejected Marx (see Chapter 13 on Marx) and the parliamentary strategies that Marxist parties adopted, describing these as centralizing and dictatorial. Her critique hardened during the Russian Revolution of October 1917 when she witnessed the militarization of labour and the concentration of Communist Party power. She concluded that the libertarian revolution had been crushed by the 'Bolshevik idea': Marxism or 'fanatical governmentalism' (Goldman, n.d. [1923/1924]: 246). Stalin's efforts to forge an international anti-fascist alliance during the Spanish Civil War (1936–1939) provided her with the final proof. The cost of this policy was the destruction of the anarchist revolution that had erupted in 1936 when General Franco's Rebels had attempted to take control of the Spanish Republican government. Already convinced that there was a direct line of transmission leading from Marx and Engels to Lenin and Bolshevism, she argued in the late 1930s that Stalinism and Nazism were facets of the same phenomenon: totalitarianism.

Goldman adopted anarchism in America. Born in 1869 and brought up on the southern Baltic coast, she migrated from St. Petersburg in 1885, moving to New York's Lower East Side in 1889. In 1906, she founded the journal and publishing house *Mother Earth*, releasing her influential collection *Anarchism and Other Essays* four years later. This was followed by *The Social Significance of the Modern Drama* (1914), two books reporting her experiences of the Bolshevik Revolution (*My Disillusionment in Russia* (1923) and *My Further Disillusionment in Russia* (1924)) and her autobiography *Living My Life* (1931). Her last book, *Voltairine de Cleyre* (see Key Thinker: Voltairine de Cleyre) was published in 1932.

Key Thinker: Voltairine de Cleyre

Voltairine de Cleyre (1866–1912) was an educator and writer active in Philadelphia. Although critical of communist anarchism (de Cleyre, 1894 [1914]: 205–219), she protested against Goldman's arrest in 1893. First labelling herself 'individualist', she subsequently advocated 'anarchism without adjectives'. This indicated that social arrangements should be locally determined. Like Goldman, she wrote about women's emancipation, against marriage, 'sex slavery', and for free speech. She advocated direct action and refused to condemn the use of physical violence. In 1911, she supported the Mexican Revolution, comparing the brutal dispossession of Indigenous peoples to the Norman appropriation of English commons. De Cleyre and Goldman worked in the same networks, but de Cleyre was never part of the close-knit group that Goldman created around her journal *Mother Earth*. Goldman described de Cleyre as the 'most gifted and brilliant anarchist woman America has ever produced' (Goldman, 1932), also emphasizing her revisionism and admission of earlier 'error' (Goldman, 1970 [1931]: 505).

Goldman earned admiration and respect from both anarchists and liberals who joined her campaigns for free speech, birth control, and against conscription. Feared and loathed by the authorities, she was repeatedly arrested and demonized as a public menace. In 1901, when she defended US President William McKinley's assassin Leon Czolgosz, she became the focus of 'an unprecedented campaign of persecution' (Havel, 2018 [1910]: 125). Her involvement in the No-Conscription League in 1917 provided further proof to her enemies of her un-American pedigree and led to her trial and two-year imprisonment. On her release from prison, she was deported to Russia: J. Edgar Hoover, then on track to become the FBI's first Director, was instrumental in the process. He declared Goldman one of 'the most dangerous anarchists in America' (Ferguson, 2013: 22).

Goldman's approach to resistance was strategic, in that it demanded action against existing institutions, and also metaphysical, because it involved an idea of possibility that was fundamental to freedom (Caygill, 2013: 8–9). Both elements resulted in a commitment to direct action as a lawless movement against tyranny. Adapting the rallying cry that American revolutionaries had taken from the Reformation theologian John Knox, 'Resistance to tyranny is obedience to God', Goldman argued that resistance was disobedience to law. Progress, she argued, 'is ever renewing, ever becoming, ever changing – *never it is within the law*' (Goldman, 1979m [1917b]: 323; emphasis in original).

Goldman perhaps underestimated the biases of her politics. An important question asked about her anarchism is whether her conception of racism is adequate (Ferguson, 2013: 211–213). As Paul Burrows (2008) observes, Goldman's attitude to settlement betrayed a European bias. While she overlooked the brutal dispossession of Indigenous peoples in North America, she chided anarchist anti-Zionists for opposing Jewish immigration in Palestine. She used the Lockean proviso that the land 'should belong to those who till the soil' to defend the Jewish settlement programme (Goldman, 1938). To consider this neglect, Section 26.2 situates Goldman in the international anarchist movement and introduces two structuring concepts, 'love with open eyes' and 'the spirit of revolt'. This is followed by an examination of Goldman's approach to political theory as a practice informed by experience in Section 26.3. Her understanding of class power and women's oppression is explored here. Finally, Section 26.4 outlines her critique of 'slavishness' to examine how she used notions of right in resistance campaigns. It explains her 'unpleasantness' to those who struggled for inclusion (Hemmings, 2018: 12) and highlights her embrace of the avant-garde.

Read more about **Goldman's** life and work by accessing the thinker biography on the online resources: www.oup.com/he/Ramgotra-Choat1e.

26.2 Goldman's anarchism

Goldman's anarchism does not fit easily in the individualist or communist factions generally used to categorize anarchist thought (see Key Concept: Individualism and communism). In America, 'individualist anarchism' was associated with the politics of early European settlers who began to organize in the 1830s and 1840s. Abolitionism, transcendentalism, utopian socialism, and religious nonconformism were some of its major currents. It assumed definitive form in the early 1880s with the establishment of two influential journals—Benjamin Tucker's *Liberty* and Moses Harman's *Lucifer, the Lightbearer*. The advent of 'European' anarchism in communities arriving from Central, Eastern, and Southern Europe became the foil for individualism. A rough distinction between 'evolutionary' individualist and 'revolutionary' communist schools ensued.

Key Concept: Individualism and communism

The division between individualists and communists was the major line of facture in the Anglophone anarchist movement. Communism became the dominant current in the early 1880s. Philosophically, communist and individualist anarchism coalesced around the idea of individual sovereignty. For communists, individuals only ever exercised sovereignty in social contexts. Sovereignty therefore presumed interdependence. Individualists theorized a primary commitment to liberty and emphasized the need to protect individuals from coercion. This difference gave rise to contrasting attitudes to rights, particularly to property. Communists argued for common ownership and distribution according to need in order to inhibit future private accumulation. Individualists defended equal rights to property in order to prevent corporate monopoly. There were differences too, on questions of change and organization. Individualists typically called themselves evolutionists and rejected physical force. Yet the distinction between evolution and revolution was misleading. In reality, this issue cut across the main divide (Kinna, 2019: 116–133).

Goldman (1907b: 325) indicated her alignment with the European communist wing of the movement by dating the origins of American anarchism to the 1883 Pittsburgh Congress of the International Working People's Association, nullifying the longer history of individualism. Her critique of Tucker, who was known internationally as the leading exponent of anarchist individualism, also placed her in this camp. Although she acknowledged the positive impact of his journal *Liberty* and collaborated with Tucker on free speech, she criticized his detachment from the labour movement, and described his attitude to anarchist communists as sanctimonious, 'narrow' and rancorous (Goldman, 1970 [1931]: 232). Yet as a contributor to Moses Harman's journal *Lucifer* and an admirer of Harman's 'sex radicalism' (see Key Thinker: Moses Harman), she softened this position.

> ### Key Thinker: Moses Harman
>
> Moses Harman (1830–1910) was an egalitarian, anti-government free thinker who defended free speech as a 'sex-radical'. Goldman (1970 [1931]: 219) described him as 'the courageous champion of free motherhood and woman's economic and sexual emancipation'. His publication in 1886 of an account of forced sex in marriage, which he classified as rape, breached prohibitions on obscenity as defined in the Comstock Laws. It led to sustained legal harassment, prosecution, and imprisonment. Set up in 1883, *Lucifer* was renamed in 1907 as the *American Journal of Eugenics*. Goldman was supportive and set up a joint subscription for the new journal with *Mother Earth*. Harman advocated the 'right to be born well'. Comparing sexual passion to hunger, he advocated the exercise of reason to avoid excess and, describing mothers as 'race-builders', called for 'responsible motherhood' to safeguard the 'unwilling' and prevent the 'unfit' from having children (Harman, 1905: 19, 46).

Goldman launched *Mother Earth* as a non-sectarian paper. Its remit was to 'attract and appeal to all those who oppose encroachment on public and individual life' (Goldman and Baginski, 1906) and it provided 'a forum for anarchism of every school and variety', not just communism (Glassgold, 2000: xv). As a free communist, she advocated a social order based on voluntary co-operation and free federation (Goldman, 1979a [1908]: 36). She argued that communism was incompatible with 'rugged individualism', a doctrine she associated with free-market liberalism, (Goldman, 1979p [1940?]: 89) but declared it compatible with individuality, including the 'extreme individualism' of Max Stirner, the philosopher of egoism (Goldman, 1979i [1913b]: 192). Consequently, when she addressed the International Anarchist Congress (IAC) in 1907, she stressed her libertarianism. She was struggling for a society 'in which social, economic, or sexual subordination will be impossible'. Referring to a 'Communist principle of toleration' she rejected calls to regulate 'the personal habits of individuals, their manner of dressing or of wearing their hair, or smoking and so forth' (International Anarchist Congress, 1907). She later told her trusted comrade, the labour organizer Rudolf Rocker, that she was 'no doctrinaire' and 'never . . . a fanatic' (Porter, 1983: 94).

26.2.1 Radicalization: Haymarket

Choosing to avoid partisan principles to articulate her position, Goldman outlined the tenets of resistance in response to the Haymarket Affair (see Key Concept: The Haymarket Affair). Sometimes referred to as the first Red Scare, the Haymarket Affair was one of the defining events in anarchist history. It polarized American public opinion, radicalizing a generation of activists, on the one hand, and popularizing the stereotype of the anarchist as a 'foreign' bomb-throwing terrorist, on the other. Later describing it as 'the greatest event' of her life (Goldman, 1933), she remembered how the 'violence of the press, the bitter denunciation of the accused' and 'the attacks on all foreigners' (Goldman, 1970 [1931]: 7) affected her. Her biographer Richard Drinnon (1982: 25, 26) comments that 'the Haymarket tragedy shocked her beyond words'. Before Haymarket, 'anarchism' had been just a word. By the end of the trial, it had become a 'burning faith' (Goldman, 1970 [1931]: 10). Her epiphany had two triggers. The first was the flagrant disregard of legal process. As the 'worst frame-up in history' (ibid.: 8), Haymarket exposed the bankruptcy of the claim that America was 'the land of the free and the home of the brave' (ibid.: 10). The second was the example set by the accused: they had 'died for their ideal'. Now disillusioned with the US Constitution Goldman was inspired to follow their lead and revolt against the 'Old World'.

> **Key Concept: The Haymarket Affair**
>
> This refers to a meeting held in Chicago's Haymarket Square in 1886 and the subsequent trial of Georg Engel, Samuel Fielden, Adolf Fischer, Louis Lingg, Oscar Neebe, Albert Parsons, Michael Schwab, and August Spies, all prominent labour activists. The meeting, called to protest the shooting of workers involved in a bitter labour dispute, ended when a bomb exploded. Several police were killed. Forensics linked Lingg to the construction of the device, but there was no strong evidence against any of the accused. The judicial process was deeply flawed and conducted in an atmosphere of extraordinary prejudice. The criminalization of the defendants as anarchists was exacerbated by the immigrant status of Engel, Fischer, Lingg, Schwab, and Spies. A lengthy appeal process failed: Engel, Fischer, Parsons, and Spies were executed in 1887. Lingg committed suicide awaiting execution. Neebe, Fielden, and Schwab received prison sentences. All verdicts were quashed in 1893.

26.2.2 Love with open eyes

'Love with open eyes' described Goldman's feelings about America when she realized that the New World she had idealized was not so different from the old one she had left behind. She used the term in her commentary on the playwright August Strindberg (Goldman, 2005 [1914b]: 22) and again in her address to the jury at her trial for conspiracy in 1917 (Goldman, 1979m[1917b]: 324).

Goldman expressed her critical love for America in 1909 by re-writing the Declaration of Independence. In it, she contrasted the plight of the people—'[s]turdy sons of America' who 'tramped the country in a fruitless search for bread' and 'daughters driven into the street'—with the machinations of the 'wealth gatherers, unscrupulous lawmakers, and corrupt politicians'. These were the new kings who perpetuated 'poverty and disease' committed 'crime and corruption', fettered 'the spirit of liberty', throttled 'the voice of justice' and degraded and oppressed 'humanity' (Goldman, 1909). The betrayal of revolutionary ideals was also a key theme in the no-conscription campaign. In the December 1915 issue of *Mother Earth*, she compared the champions of 'cheap Americanism'— advocates of 'America first'—with the 'truly great' 'real Americanism' of founding father Thomas Jefferson and civil disobedience advocate Henry David Thoreau (Goldman, 1979l [1915]: 305). The June 1917 cover of the paper featured a dramatic image of a tomb inscribed 'In Memoriam: American Democracy'. Goldman (1970 [1931]: 603) commented: 'No words could express more eloquently the tragedy that turned America, the erstwhile torch-bearer of freedom, into a gravedigger of her former ideals.'

26.2.3 The spirit of revolt

The 'spirit of revolt' is the title of an essay by the anarchist Peter Kropotkin (1970 [1880]: 34–43) and it describes the feeling or commitment that spurs revolutionaries into action. Goldman used it frequently. For example, in her essay, 'Anarchism: What it Really Stands For' (Goldman, 1979a [1908]: 60), in her appreciation of the dramatist Gerhart Hauptmann (Goldman, 2005 [1914b]: 56) and in commentaries on labour conflict and direct action (Goldman, 1907b: 322).

Her explorations of the idea led to an extended debate with Alexander Berkman (see Key Thinker: Alexander Berkman) about political violence. Although she described herself as a Tolstoyan at heart (Goldman, 1979c [1911b]: 233), Goldman was in fact unable to accept Leo Tolstoy's (1908) doctrine of non-resistance. She considered violence both unavoidable and justifiable. Yet she also wrestled continually with the question of legitimacy. In 1892, she invoked just cause to defend revenge killing, 'collateral damage', and martyrdom. In 1907, she adjusted her position and advocated 'the right of rebellion on the part of the individual' alongside collective physical force (Goldman, 1907c: 316). In 1911, she wrote about the psychology of violence, emphasizing perpetrators' peculiar sensitivity to injustice (Goldman, 1979c [1911b]: 210–233). After her return to Russia, she considered the role of violence in revolutionary war. Her defence of armed struggle was directed against Bolshevik repression, and it relied on a distinction between the *exercise* of violence and its *monopoly*. On this view, the use of violence against 'domination' was permissible (Fellner, 1992 [1928]: 266). In Spain, witnessing Stalinist and fascist aggression against anarchist revolutionaries, Goldman restated her defence of armed struggle as the only practical response to counterrevolutionary violence. Her succinct view, '[a]narchism will win but not with kid gloves' (Porter, 1983: 321), distinguished legitimate from illegitimate violence by appealing to an anarchist commitment to non-domination (Goldman, 1970 [1931]: 88; n.d. [1923/1924]: 254; Porter, 1983: 220).

> ### Key Thinker: Alexander Berkman
>
> Alexander Berkman (1870–1936) was Goldman's soulmate and lifelong companion. They met in New York in 1889 and lived parallel lives. In 1892, prompted by the shooting of strikers at a Carnegie steel plant in Homestead, Pennsylvania, he attempted to assassinate Henry Frick, the plant manager. Goldman was complicit in the planning and subsequently defended the act. Frick survived and Berkman was jailed for 14 years. After his release, he edited *Mother Earth*, *The Social Significance of the Modern Drama*, and *Living My Life*. He also published *Prison Memoirs of an Anarchist* (1912), a frank reflection on his action and incarceration, and *The ABC of Communist Anarchism*, a classic introduction. In 1916, he established the journal, *The Blast*. Deported with Goldman following his involvement in the No-Conscription League, he also recorded his disillusionment with Bolshevism in *The Russian Tragedy* (1922) and *The Kronstadt Rebellion* (1923). When he committed suicide in 1936, Goldman considered following him.

In addition, Goldman invoked the spirit of revolt to extol the virtues of inspirational rebels: 'liberty-loving people' who struggled against oppression, 'pathfinders' who dynamited repressive social norms (Goldman, 2005 [1914b]: 5) and 'tender spirits' who stirred insurrection in 'the timid' (Goldman, 1907c: 316). While she considered Berkman's attempt on Frick (see Key Thinker: Alexander Berkman) a spirited act and said the same about Czolgocz's assassination of McKinley, the spirit of revolt was defined by 'idealism and sacrifice' and violence was only incidental to it. Mary Wollstonecraft (see Chapter 21) and Louise Michel were two of Goldman's role-models. Wollstonecraft had challenged 'every institution' of her age, grasping 'the new' as an 'annihilator of all stable habits and traditions' (Goldman, 2016b [1911c]: 76). Michel, who had joined the militia during the Paris Commune in 1871, was included for her courage, 'zeal' and daring (Goldman, 1970 [1931]: 166). Before her disillusionment in Russia, Goldman lauded the Bolsheviks in the same terms. They too possessed 'the zeal and courage of martyrs' (ibid.: 645). Shortly before they were executed for a robbery for which there were exonerated in 1977, she told the anarchists Nicola Sacco and Bartolomeo Vanzetti that their 'unflinching courage' in 'the struggle for our ideal' mirrored that of 'our martyred comrades in Chicago'. Here, as always, the spirit of revolt pointed to brighter future: 'every drop of blood and every beat of rebel's heart add so much force to the growing tide which will eventually purge the earth from the evils of despotism, greed and cruelty' (Goldman, 1927).

26.2.4 Goldman's anarchist imaginary

What are the problems with Goldman's concept of resistance? Neither of her two structuring concepts—'love with open eyes' and 'the spirit of revolt'—were overtly exclusionary, but both are problematic. Her concept of love idealizes the goal of resistance, while the spirit of revolt dramatizes the act by focusing attention on the avant-garde.

As Candice Falk (2008: 64) argues, Goldman's anarchism was instinctively inclusive. She was repelled by reports of anti-immigrant and racist violence. She spoke out against lynchings, vigilante violence, and the economic exploitation and social ostracism of former Black slaves, Mexicans, and Japanese minorities (Goldman, 1907b: 325). She repeatedly rejected 'Christian civilization' and the saviour culture associated with it. Acknowledging that America had been made by 'Christians, greedy of the new continent' who despoiled 'the American Indian' (Goldman, 1907a: 273), she constructed it as an international 'conglomeration of members of all European nations, with a considerable proportion of Asiatic and African races' (ibid.: 270). Nevertheless, the republic she imagined 'with open eyes' pointed to an ideal that was shaped by a narrow social imaginary.

Goldman's sustained critique of America was that its governing institutions tarnished the revolutionary principles on which the republic had been founded. America had been born in rebellion, but citizens were subject to tyrannical policing. The US Constitution guaranteed rights, but structured and concealed inequality. Justice was impartial, but law protected the interests of the propertied. As an immigrant who loved America critically and who found only 'superficiality', 'cant', and 'corruption' (Goldman, 1979m [1917b]: 324) in its corporations and consumer cultures, Goldman invariably evaluated the Constitution against a sanitized ideal of the republic. Neither the historic experience of slavery nor the distortions of settler narratives feature in her appreciation of Jeffersonian democracy, or in her construction of 'America as the promised land' (Goldman, 1917a). To use Kwame Anthony Appiah's (1990: 10–11) terms, she appeared more alert to expressions of 'intrinsic' racism buttressing 'racial solidarity' than to the pervasive 'extrinsic' systems that 'used race as the basis for oppression and hatred'. Criticizing a Black female prison guard for issuing extra rations to Black prisoners (Goldman, 1970 [1931]: 154–155), she complained that the officer's 'discrimination' against white inmates contravened needs-based equality. Yet when she argued that America's role was to offer 'a haven of refuge' to 'all the disinherited and oppressed people' who arrived 'on its shores', she described only the expectations of European immigrants (Goldman, 1979l [1915]: 305). Her narrative hardly captured the forcible transportation and enslavement of African people, let alone the experience of the Indigenous Americans displaced by European settlers.

The spirit of revolt was similarly double-edged. On the one hand, it was open to all manner of resistance activities: protesting, petitioning, fundraising, labour organizing, journalism, publishing, alternative lifestyles or, after Oscar Wilde, what Goldman called expressing 'personality', were all transformative activities. However, while resistance was open to all, manual workers and intellectual proletarians alike (Goldman, 1979k [1914a]: 176–185), the spirit of revolt spotlighted the actions of extraordinary beings. It was a kind of genius, reserved for special individuals equipped with the psychological wherewithal to stand apart from the downtrodden and possibly even their comrades. Goldman quoted Ibsen, '[t]he strongest man is he who stands most alone' and, for all her loathing of Puritanism, Martin Luther, 'Here I am and here I stand and I cannot do otherwise' (Goldman, 1979m [1917b]: 326). Configured in this way, revolt encouraged a distinction between the avant-garde and the 'mob'. As Goldman put it in *The Social Significance of the Modern Drama*, 'the possibility of greatness and fineness' existed in the 'soul of every man and every woman'. But not everyone possessed 'the strength to be true to the dominant spirit' (Goldman, 2005 [1914b]: 45).

Goldman's discussion of the barriers to revolt reinforced this distinction. Civilization was a powerful dampener of the 'idealists' flame (ibid.: 138). 'Mob spirit' was another (ibid.: 77, 143). 'Compromise and petty interest' also frustrated the spirit of revolt (ibid.: 114). Would 'the masses' ever rise above these obstacles? Goldman's answer was not without encouragement. Searching for idealists in America, Goldman obliquely contrasted the 'idealism' of European immigrants to the materialism of 'natives', betraying a racialized assessment of American passivity in the process. While she revised her 'superficial judgment' that 'Americans' had become too acquisitive to act heroically, she did not consider how far the contrast itself marginalized the experiences of non-European communities (Goldman, 1970 [1931]: 155). Likewise, when she told Sacco and Vanzetti that 'America cannot boast of many such rebels as you' (Goldman, 1927), she forgot about Geronimo, the Great

Sioux Wars, and Harriet Tubman. In short, her dedication to the 'enlightenment' of 'liberty-loving' American people cast whole sections of the oppressed 'mob' adrift (Goldman, 1970 [1931]: 155).

For all the silences and gaps in Goldman's thinking, the transformative energy of her concept of resistance was felt in her critique of patriarchal power. The next section shows how, by examining her approach to political theory as a practice informed by experience and underscored by her analysis of class and women's oppression.

> ### 26.2 Goldman's anarchism: Key Points
>
> - Goldman's advocacy of anarchist communism transcended divisions between individualists and communists.
> - Goldman's 'loving' critique of American republicanism narrowed her appreciation of racism in the New World.
> - Resistance entailed direct action and rejecting legal means of change.
> - The idea of the spirit of revolt introduced a distinction between the courageous and the 'mob'.
> - Goldman adopted a context-specific approach to questions of violence.

26.3 Theory and practice

This section looks at Goldman's approach to theory and practice in order to examine her conception of power and the place of class, sex and race within it. Section 26.3.1 describes her approach to political theory and, particularly, the role of experience. Section 26.3.2 discusses her critique of power. After outlining her structural account of state institutions—government, property, religion, and marriage—it describes how she explained compliance, focusing on women's oppression. Her critique of power shows why Goldman believed resistance necessary, and why she considered women's emancipation essential to it.

26.3.1 Theory and experience

Kathy Ferguson argues that Goldman performed her 'thinking in the streets', that is, in anarchist spaces and through her campaigns. Theory and practice were two aspects of a seamless process. For Goldman, '[t]hinking and acting were not separate political moments . . . her thinking was intertwined with acting, it was a kind of acting' (Ferguson, 2013: 6). This close interweaving of theory and practice explains why Goldman wrote principally as an essayist, and why so many of her most celebrated articles were delivered as lectures and speeches. Yet, as her response to political violence shows, Goldman also reviewed her positions as circumstances altered. If the relationship between theory and practice is imagined as a circuit, she built a delay into it, creating interruptions that enabled her to rewire her processes. Her involvement in the anarchist revolution during the Spanish Civil War (see Key Concept: The Spanish Revolution, 1936–1939), illuminated how the break operated. The dilemmas she confronted there were particularly testing. As a lifelong critic of parliamentary politics, she was close to Spanish anarchists who decided to join Republican institutions to protect revolutionary gains. Principle told her that their participation was wrongheaded. Her realization that Franco's Rebels possessed overwhelming military power told her that the principle was irrelevant to the revolution's plight. Writing from the Front, she told Rocker that while she had never been 'blind to the fact the reality often puts all theories on their head' (Porter, 1983: 94–95), Spain proved beyond doubt that 'life is more intricate, more contradictory and more compelling than any theory of philosophy about life' (ibid.: 125).

> **Key Concept: The Spanish Revolution, 1936–1939**
>
> In July 1936, a failed coup led by General Franco divided Spain into Nationalist and Republican zones, sparking a civil war. Anarchists, the most significant component of the Spanish left and crucial to the anti-Francoist resistance, organized militias and spearheaded a massive popular programme of collectivization of agriculture and industry (Leval, 1975). The international situation was messy: while refusing to support the Republic, France and Britain acquiesced to fascist interventions in support of Franco's campaign. Soviet involvement, conditional on the suppression of the revolution, presented anarchists with a dilemma: whether to work with the Republic against Franco or defend the revolution even if this meant fighting Soviet-backed Republican forces (Bolloten, 1979). Goldman made three trips to Spain during the period and campaigned throughout to rally international support. Critical of anarchists who participated in Republican institutions, she nevertheless defended them vigorously from anarchists who accused them of betrayal at some distance from the Front.

Jean Leca's distinction between political philosophy and political theory helps clarify Goldman's understanding. Leca describes political philosophy as a contemplative practice, focused on examining 'core concepts' and directed towards 'truth'. Political theory, on the other hand, is concerned with action and power, or its constraint (Leca, 2010: 525–526). By this measure, Goldman was a theorist, not a philosopher. Her determination to 'decide my own actions and reactions for myself' militated both against certainty and 'infallibility' (Porter, 1983: 292), as she put it. Driven to 'uphold what I consider right and attack what seems to me to be wrong' (ibid.: 292), she was in part concerned to rationalize her own intuitions. In the other part, she wanted to explain the divergence of American realities from professed ideals. As she told the jury in her 1917 trial: 'I am a social student. It is my mission in life to ascertain the cause of our social evils and of our social difficulties. As a student of social wrongs, it is my aim to diagnose a wrong' (Goldman, 1979m [1917b]: 317). Here, theory was a tool for the rectification of degraded institutions.

In thinking about this project, Goldman borrowed freely from 'canonical' anarchists notably Kropotkin, Pierre-Joseph Proudhon, and Michael Bakunin. She also incorporated concepts and insights gleaned from other 'dynamiters' of established norms. Friedrich Nietzsche (see Chapter 14) was a particular favourite. She relied on empathy, too. Theory involved 'something more than personal experience'. She continued: 'It is the quality of our response to the event and our capacity to enter into the lives of others that help us to make their lives and experiences our own' (Goldman, 1979n [1934]: 388). Towards the end of her life, Goldman returned to this theme. She had 'derived and developed' her convictions 'from events in the lives of others as well as from my own experience' (ibid.: 388).

If empathy intensified and broadened the scope of her anarchism, her approach was risky because it appeared to endorse 'speaking for others': becoming the authentic voice of 'the oppressed' without acknowledging fractures within it or the partiality of the speaker's perspective (Alcoff, 1991). To the extent that Goldman's interpretation of experience amounted to speaking 'for' rather than 'to' marginalized groups, it breached an established anarchist commitment to self-emancipation. Historically this was tied to critique of political representation and, as Goldman observed, to the oligarchic decision-making processes party organization involved. Playing with Bakunin's assessment of Marx's Bismarckian 'Prussian' orthodoxy, she once ridiculed American 'Bis-Marxian' socialists for subordinating themselves to German party leaders (Goldman, 1979a [1908]: 42). Goldman acknowledged that anarchists were not immune from the problem. In the non-conscription campaign, she decided that as an exempt woman she could 'not advise' men to refuse the draft and that, as an anarchist, she could not 'presume to decide the fate' of those who decided to enlist (Goldman, 1970 [1931]: 598). Nevertheless, her embrace of experience suggested that she was willing to give herself an authoritative voice. Section 26.3.2 will investigate how far she did this by looking at her analysis of power.

26.3.2 Power

Following Ferguson, Jane Gordon argues that Goldman spoke for the white working class. She 'could not suffuse her anarchism with an understanding of the uniqueness of racialization or forge substantive bridges between anarchist and specifically black American communities' (Gordon, 2015: 229). Like Ferguson, Gordon traces the fault to Goldman's conflation of race and class (ibid.: 239). Ferguson (2013: 217) explains: Goldman viewed race through a 'European class/state lens' which folded enslavement 'into a larger process of wage slavery' and explained racist violence as 'part and parcel of the violence of capitalism against workers'.

The argument of this section is that Goldman's analysis of power was flawed, but not for the reasons Gordon and Ferguson present. Goldman rejected conventional class theory and highlighted overlapping systems of domination. However, instead of matching this with an approach to resistance that recognized the multiplicity of actors within it, she placed a distinctive concept of women's liberation at its heart. Goldman did not entirely ignore racism as a relevant category of oppression, but she collapsed race into sex.

The Lockean claim opening Goldman's 'Declaration of Independence' is that 'people have the . . . right to rebel against, and overthrow' institutions that 'enslave, rob, and oppress'. She identified a mix of social structures, positions, and patterns of behaviour: property, law, Church and public opinion, 'national, racial, religious and sex superiority' and 'the narrow puritanical conception of human life' (Goldman, 1909). Her 1908 essay, 'What I Believe', included a slightly different list: property, government and marriage, militarism and 'churchism'. Goldman did not present a systematic account of the social structure, certainly nothing to rival Marx's crisp distinction between the economic structure ('base') and the political and ideological superstructure. However, looking at the relationships between institutions, she identified a four-part system of economic, political, legal, and moral domination and emphasized their interdependence. Her explanation of compliance was also multifaceted. Class featured in it, but Goldman did not define class narrowly as a relationship to the means of production. Nor did she consider class as the sole or even the major determinant of social transformation.

26.3.2.1 Social structure

Goldman's structural analysis was typically anarchist to the extent that she argued that the exercise of power in the state relied on the capacity of political elites to legitimize exploitation and the willingness of property owners to bankroll law enforcement. This interdependent relationship was illustrated by the organization of convict labour, cooperation between police and vigilante private militias against workers, and the award of government contracts to industrialists, particularly arms manufacturers. Following Proudhon (Goldman, 1979b [1911a]: 52), she defined property as the 'domination over things and the denial to others of the use of those things'

(Goldman, 1979a [1908]: 35). Government or state was 'organized authority ... to maintain or protect property and monopoly' (ibid.: 37). Borrowing from Bakunin, she described the state as the antithesis of liberty and the embodiment of law (Goldman, 1979b [1911a]: 55). Law meant 'the machinery of government, the club, the gun, the handcuff, or the prison'. It was entirely contrary to 'natural law', the principle of spontaneous and voluntary interaction arising from common needs for 'nutrition ... sex ... light, air and exercise' (ibid.: 56).

Extending the analysis, Goldman (1979d [1911d]: 139) described marriage as the 'sovereignty of the man over the woman'. It was 'an economic arrangement' that gave women a 'a life-long insurance policy' and men 'a perpetuator of his kind or a pretty toy' (Goldman, 1979a [1908]: 43). Militarism, 'part of the paraphernalia of government' was an incubator for capitalist greed (Goldman, 1979l [1915]: 303), breeding unquestioning obedience for the purposes of killing. It led to imperialism and despotism (Goldman, 1979a [1908]: 38–39). Churchism was religion transformed from naïve superstition into 'a nightmare that oppresses the human soul' (ibid.: 42). Goldman chose Christianity as her example. Dramatically parting company with Tolstoy (Goldman, 1979i [1913b]: 188), she used Nietzsche to express her contempt for religious resignation. The 'sick-room atmosphere' of Christian faith created 'all manner of social disorders ... to be cured with the preachment of love and sympathy' (ibid.: 192). This characterization resonated with Marx's metaphorical description of religion as 'opium of the people'. Yet Goldman's argument was that churchism did not conceal the nature of class antagonism and console workers, as Marx claimed, it enfeebled them. In the guise of 'Property Morality', it made even convinced socialists averse to property damage (Goldman, 1979g [1913a]: 128).

In sum, Goldman's account was comparable to Bakunin's. In the 1870s, he had credited Marx with developing a materialist analysis that revealed the material basis of political power, while arguing that the state existed independently of productive forces. For Bakunin, changes in the relations of production would only alter the character of state domination, not its reality. Similarly, Goldman outlined a pyramidal system in which power was monopolized by intersecting institutions to protect privilege and inequality. When Goldman talked about economic exploitation as the 'main evil' (Goldman, 1979b [1911a]: 50), she was making a moral and strategic judgement, not advancing a philosophical principle. Believing capitalists' and workers' interests to be irreconcilably opposed, she subscribed to an idea of class war (Goldman, 1979j [1913c]: 69) but she identified religion and militarism as separate axes of power.

26.3.2.2 Compliance

Goldman's account of compliance reinforced the intersectional quality of her approach but also altered the focus of the discussion. Paying special attention to women's oppression, she attempted to explain why women accepted subordination. She again referred to multiple types of power, notably, the domination of 'human mind', 'human needs' and 'human conduct' (Goldman, 1979b [1911a]: 52). But instead of using the typology to describe social structure, she explained how they affected women's choices. Marriage and prostitution were her two principal concerns.

Goldman regarded both as coercive institutions. Marriage was defiling and corrupting since it forced the woman to enter loveless heterosexual relationships, annihilating her 'social consciousness', paralyzing 'her imagination' and degrading and shaming her by buying 'her right to motherhood'. It was a snare that permitted children to be 'conceived in hatred, in compulsion' (Goldman, 1979f [1911f]: 165). Prostitution was less 'deplorable' because the contractual relationship did not involve a permanent or complete surrender of rights (Goldman, 1979e [1911e]: 151). Nevertheless, sex workers were treated as pariahs by the model citizens who created them: 'the financier, the priest, the moralist, the judge, the jailor' (Goldman, 1979g [1913a]: 131) and their 'virtuous' sisters, 'too pure' and too stupid to see the commonalities in their predicaments. Duly criminalized, sex workers were also subject to police extortion. Streetwalkers, '[d]esperate, needing protection and longing for affection' were 'absolutely at the mercy of graft-greedy police' (Goldman, 1979e [1911e]: 156).

Goldman's account of women's oppression anticipated Margaret Atwood's dystopian image of life in *The Handmaid's Tale*. The significant difference is that the wives in Atwood's fictionalized state of Gilead are complicit in the domination of handmaids; they are relieved of domestic labour and the children they appropriate are privileged and cherished. In the real world, Goldman saw no separation between the concubine and service classes. Wives were handmaids and domestics in one, maintained by husband-masters to do the housework and breed limitlessly (Goldman, 1979d [1911d]: 136). Family well-being was affected by class privilege. Raised to 'be ground into the dust by the wheel of capitalism' or 'torn into shreds in trenches and battlefields' (Goldman, 2016c [1916b]: 103), most children grew up in abject poverty. Yet sex monopoly affected all women, not just the poor.

Goldman found the linchpin for women's compliance in a double standard which recognized virility as a manly trait and valued chastity in women. This licensed promiscuity for men and stipulated ignorance for women. Men were encouraged to be sexually active. Women were prohibited from being so. As a result, most wives were 'shocked, repelled, outraged beyond measure' by the consummation of marriage and experienced sex as violation (Goldman, 1979f [1911f]: 161). Dictates of 'morality', notably the expectation that women would accede to their husbands' 'whims and commands', helped explain women's forbearance. In the other part, toleration was incentivized by marriage contracts which turned women into the property of their husbands, leaving them in 'absolute dependence on his name and support' (Goldman, 1979d [1911d]: 139). Goldman explained prostitution in the same way. Woman was 'easy prey' for as long as she 'was reared as a sex commodity' and kept in 'absolute ignorance of the meaning and importance of sex' (Goldman, 1979e [1911e]: 149). Starvation wages, safeguarded by women's starry-eyed dreams of finding 'Mr. Right' and reluctance to unionize, were the additional factors driving 'white . . . yellow . . . and black women' into the 'slave trade' (ibid.: 144).

26.3.3 Class, sex, 'race', and representation

Class struggle was no cure for women's compliance. As Goldman noted in Spain, 'most men . . . do not seem to understand the meaning of true emancipation'. They 'make themselves believe that women enjoy being kept in an inferior position'. Plantation owners had used the same argument against abolitionists, and Goldman felt it was as spurious in the Spanish context as it had been in pre-war America (Porter, 1983: 256). Women could help themselves by joining labour struggles and men could commit to women's liberation by forging new free and genuinely loving relationships. These were joint struggles, but women's liberation, not class struggle, was the common denominator.

Goldman had less to say about class and racism. As Ferguson notes, she tended to associate racism with violence, believing that the prejudices fuelling it were embedded in society, easily manipulated by but not fully explained by state domination. She also habitually linked racism to anti-Semitism (Falk, 2003: 300; 2008: 244), consequently downplaying what Frantz Fanon (see Chapter 28) referred to as the significance of 'Blackness' namely, white supremacist constructions of ethnicity (Fanon, 2009 [1952]: 259). How far she tied racism to economic competition is a moot point. The key point is that is that she was explicit about the transformative power of women's liberation.

Turning to Nietzsche to describe the kind of transformation she had in mind, Goldman talked about advancing 'untimely' ideas (Goldman, 1979k [1914a]: 178) and the 'transvaluation of values' (Goldman, n.d. [1923/1924]: 252–254). More concretely, she believed that revolution required the abandonment of 'sex monopoly' and the realization of 'free motherhood' and 'free love'. These concepts resonated with Harman's ideas (see Key Thinker: Moses Harman), but Goldman did not use responsibility to frame motherhood or share his worries about excess. In her view, free motherhood was an 'innate craving for motherhood' and woman's 'highest fulfillment' (Goldman, 1979d [1911d]: 138). Free love was the acceptance that love was 'the strongest and deepest element in all life', essential to 'beautiful personality' (ibid.: 139).

Mixing Romanticism with Harman's eugenics, Goldman argued that the achievement of women's liberation through free motherhood and free love would facilitate the foundation of a new, fully human race. Psychologically, love was the 'harbinger of hope, of joy, of ecstasy', the 'defier of all laws, of all conventions' (Goldman, 1979f [1911f]: 165). She explained: '[s]ex emotions and love are among the most intimate, the most intense and sensitive expressions of our being' (Goldman, 1979h [1912]: 169). The release of genuine passion would overwhelm Puritanical uniformity with colour and vitality and stifle petty jealousy. Her hope was that love's assertion over duty would prevent children being 'born in hatred and loathing' enabling 'race-conscious' women to nurture each child as a 'unit of society'. Goldman (2016c [1916b]: 103; 106) described this as the 'strongest factor in the building of a new world'. Enjoying a utopian moment in 1911, she imagined herself on a mountain peak, looking down on men and women, 'big and strong and free, ready . . . to bask in the golden rays of love'. Women's liberation would give rise to 'a new race, a new world'; a world of 'companionship and oneness' (Goldman, 1979f [1911f]: 167). A similar image sprang to mind in 1938 when she visited a children's colony in the Pyrenees: she had been 'filled to overflowing by the glowing day, the rich fount of love and generosity, the gaiety of the children and the ravishing mountain view' (Porter, 1983: 79).

In describing her vision, Goldman also betrayed its partiality. As a practitioner of free love, who regarded revolutionary idealism and motherhood as mutually exclusive alternatives (Goldman, 1970 [1931]: 153), she also claimed to speak 'for women' who had entirely different experiences and possibly alternative conceptions of motherhood, too. Even though she kept the full anguish of her romantic entanglements private (Falk, 1990), she frankly acknowledged that the domination symptomatic in marriage was also alive in free love. A Russian proverb captured the torment of one sexually fulfilling, psychologically dependent relationship: 'If you drink, you'll die, and if you don't drink you'll die' (Goldman, 1970 [1931]: 527). Choosing 'ecstasy' and humiliation over apathy and loneliness, she described the resolution of her dilemma, 'drink . . . drink!' as a bold move. Yet she never accepted that wives confronted the same dilemma, or credited them with similar determination when they opted to stay with their husbands. Moreover, while she considered herself free from 'antipathy' to gay and bi-sexual men and women (Goldman, 2016d [1923]: 118), her juxtaposition of marriage and 'free motherhood' resulted in a strongly heteronormative vision of anarchy. In short, by positioning herself as an authoritative voice on women's emancipation, she proposed free motherhood as a benchmark for universal emancipation. Having sketched the vision, her objective was to show how to realize it. The next section shows that her strategy hinged on overcoming slavishness.

26.3 Theory and practice: Key Points

- Goldman developed political theory as a critical practice incorporating experience into analysis.
- Goldman's critique of power illuminated multiple forms of domination.
- Goldman advocated class struggle as part of a broader resistance strategy.
- Women's liberation was essential to socialist transformation, not an 'add on'.
- Goldman's advocacy of 'free motherhood' assumed non-monogamous relationships.
- Free motherhood underpinned human well-being and social harmony.

26.4 Slavishness and rights

This section looks at Goldman's idea of 'slavishness' to show how she understood rights as levers for resistance. Goldman's view was that the eradication of 'slavery' would transform rights. This conception explained her embrace of the avant-garde and her 'unpleasantness' (Hemmings, 2018: 12) to those who struggled for inclusion. But it left open what role, if any, resistance would play in free communism.

26.4.1 Slavery and slavishness

Following the Haymarket anarchists, Goldman used a concept of enslavement to illustrate the tyrannical nature of American democracy. However, whereas they had invoked the 'transformation of slavery' (see Key Concept: Transformation of slavery) to explain the social mechanisms of corruption, Goldman used enslavement to uncover the power of American ideology and the pervasiveness of revolutionary myths. Declaring that a 'democracy conceived in the military servitude of the masses, in their economic enslavement . . . is not democracy at all' (Goldman, 1979m [1917b]: 324), she invited patriots to reflect on the disconnect between 'American values' and American institutions. To the extent that Americans could remain enchanted with the ideal but impervious to the reality, they were enslaved.

> **Key Concept: Transformation of slavery**
>
> Adopted by anarchists to critique the arbitrariness of private property rights (Kinna and Prichard, 2019: 225–228), the concept was given renewed impetus by the abolition of slavery. The Haymarket anarchists argued that abolition freed slaves without securing freedom from domination. Law guaranteed property rights, enabling owners to enforce exploitative contracts through dependence. All workers were now 'wage-slaves'. For Lucy Parsons, a Haymarket widow and the daughter of a slave, transformation illuminated the latitude for domination on the grounds of class, sex, and race under the constitution. However, it was sometimes used to depict the relative condition or moral status of free workers and chattel slaves, and highlight the peculiar harm of wage labour in ways that romanticized the Old South. *Mother Earth* published extracts from Paul Laurence Dunbar's poem 'To the South – On Its New Slavery', depicting the 'brutish' grind of wage work, without liberty 'nor a slave's delight' (Dunbar, 1907 [1904]: 51; Ramsey, 1999).

Goldman correlated slavishness to lying, identifying lies with ingratiation. Lying meant bowing to 'public opinion', respecting religious or family traditions or doing someone else's bidding for fear of rejection. Lies were hard to resist and habitually accepted as duties, strengthening repressive notions of respectability and enervating concepts of care. For as long as we remained 'bound by gratitude, tied and fettered by what we think we owe to others', we were 'weaklings and cowards' (Goldman, 2005 [1914b: 45).

Lying also bred resentment. Once duty became a burden, as Goldman believed was the case in marriage, victims expressed their frustration in bitterness and anger. Feminism showed how. Endorsing Nietzsche's maxim, '[w]hen you go to woman, take the whip along' (Goldman, 2016a [1910]: 45), Goldman argued that women were sponges for religious doctrines. Subordinating themselves to husbands, wives became 'petty quarrelsome, gossipy, unbearable' beings, 'reckless in appearance, clumsy in . . . movements, dependent in . . . decisions' and 'cowardly in . . . judgment', in short: 'a weight and a bore' (Goldman, 1979d [1911d]: 163–164). For Goldman, the feminist response was to attack the master by infiltrating the system of mastery. From the 'deepest red to the dullest grey' (Goldman, 1970 [1931]: 556) feminists misadvised women to fight for inclusion in existing political and economic institutions and organize independently of men. Goldman (1979d [1911d]: 142) conceded that the right to vote and civil rights were 'good demands'. And retrospectively, she argued that feminism had achieved some gains (Goldman, 2016e [1926]: 133–135). But in her view, feminism increased the prestige of the institutions responsible for 'slavery and dependence' (Goldman, 2005 [1914b]: 35). Feminists thus undermined socialist struggles and wrongly excluded men from 'their emotional life' (Goldman, 1979d [1911d]: 138).

Education was one means to combat slavishness. Like Wollstonecraft, Goldman expected mothers to cultivate transformative values in children, namely, 'freedom and opportunity to grow harmoniously'. However, she also implored mothers not to impose their 'own ideas and notions' on children, taking this 'vital' lesson from the playwright August Strindberg, a misogynist (Goldman, 2005 [1914b]: 25). While she adapted it as a supporter of women, it was difficult to see how feminists or wives could be up to the task or why free mothers should avoid socializing children as libertarians. Indeed, Goldman acknowledged the tension when she pinpointed the causes of women's enslavement in 'woman's inhumanity to man'. As carers, women had made men what they were (Goldman, 1970 [1931]: 557). Revolt, to secure new rights, was the only answer.

26.4.2 Rights and resistance

The impasse in libertarian education reflected a deeper tension between social stability and dynamic change or, in Goldman's terms, between resistance as disobedience to law and as continual renewal. While the first seemed to cast anarchy as the resolution of resistance, the second implied that, in lawless anarchy, resistance was also required. Goldman's consideration of rights suggested that there was scope for both positions.

Goldman's defence of rights attracted harsh criticism from within the anarchist movement. Ricardo Flores Magon, one of the inspirational figures of the 1911 Mexican Revolution, characterized her free speech campaigns as an attempt to court public favour. Playing to a bourgeois gallery, Goldman promoted rights in ways that concealed the reality of exploitation and drew attention to a mere effect of class antagonism (Magon, 1977: 85). To Voltairine de Cleyre, Goldman set too much store on petitioning government and on constitutional guarantees (de Cleyre, 1914 [1894]).

In some ways, both critiques were wide of the mark. Goldman (2005 [1914b]: 20) recognized that liberals wrongly reified 'constitutional rights and free speech'. By stubbornly testing the limits of constitutional rights in her campaigns, she highlighted the futility of this trust. Like the modern dramatists she most admired, her aim was to rouse intellectuals from their apathy and accelerate revolt in the 'mob' (ibid.: 3). Speaking freely—about sex monopoly, the evils of conscription or the exploitation of labour—was vital to this. Rather than appealing to the constitution to demand rights, Goldman incited the enslaved to assert their rights. She once remarked that libertarians believe 'with Stirner that man has as much liberty as he is willing to take' (Goldman, 1979b [1911a]: 61). Likewise, she described historical change as a 'ceaseless struggle for self-assertion' (Goldman, 2016a [1910]: 55).

The difference between Goldman and de Cleyre turned on the status of constitutionalism. De Cleyre's view was that constitutions were 'progressive expressions of progressive ideals . . . characterized by [eighteenth-century] metaphysical philosophy' (de Cleyre, 1914 [1894]: 209). Goldman, in contrast, attacked the existing constitution but not the principle. Asked at her trial in 1893 what she thought of the US Constitution and the Constitution of the State of New York, she replied that she would 'believe in' both if their articles were respected (Falk, 2008: 173). Her alternative

Declaration of Independence proclaimed that 'all human beings, irrespective of race, color, or sex, are born with the equal right to share at the table of life' and 'that to secure this right' there must be no government and 'economic, social, and political freedom'. It looked very different to the one agreed in 1776. Yet adopting the idea of a 'self-evident truth', Goldman (1909) added that 'lovers of liberty joyfully consecrate their uncompromising devotion . . . energy . . . intelligence . . . solidarity and their lives' to the Declaration. In this way, she presented it as the foundational statement for her social ideal. Her silences on racism and European settlement and her formula for women's emancipation suggested the possibility of further transvaluations of value. Yet Goldman left this question hanging.

> **26.4 Slavishness and rights: Key Points**
>
> - Goldman adapted the concept of the 'transformation of slavery' to develop an idea of slavishness as duty.
> - Slavishness reinforced the role of the avant-garde to inspire revolt.
> - Feminism bolstered obedience to slavish practices and militated against socialist transformation.
> - Rights were demands against constituted authority and instruments of social transformation.
> - Goldman's anarchy was an egalitarian social order rooted in a notion of constitutional right.

26.5 Conclusion

The starting point for this chapter was the idea that resistance can be understood as strategic action against exiting institutions and an idea of possibility fundamental to freedom. In combining these ideas, Goldman argued that strategic action was properly defined by the possibilities it contained and that it had a definite end.

The relationship between strategy and possibility turned on her understanding of slavishness. For her, resistance entailed the refusal to comply with institutional directives and norms. Struggles for inclusion, including civil rights campaigns and revolutionary regime change, contained no 'possibility' and, therefore, no strategic value. Goldman borrowed President Wilson's formulation to define her strategic goal. The 'ultimate base of our existence and liberty' was the expression of a 'new type of humanity' (Goldman, 1979m [1917b]: 319). It demanded free communism, free motherhood, and free love.

The implication of Goldman's argument is that anarchy marked not the start but the end of resistance. The shortcomings of her anarchism suggest that this would be an unsatisfactory utopia. Yet her view that the value of strategic goals is determined by the possibilities they contain also suggests that anarchy is imagined through revolt. For as long as the possibility of resistance is present, the strategic goal can be reimagined. In this respect, the outstanding feature of Goldman's resistance is the inspiration she has given to others.

Take your learning further by accessing the online resources for a library of web links to relevant videos, articles, blogs, and useful websites for this chapter: www.oup.com/he/Ramgotra-Choat1e.

Study questions

1. Explain and evaluate Goldman's 'free communism' as a critique of Marxism.
2. What role did class struggle play in Goldman's theory of change?
3. Feminist or anti-feminist: which best describes Goldman's anarchism?
4. Why did Goldman consider 'free motherhood' and 'free love' essential to liberation?
5. Is Goldman's silence about racism and European settlement indicative of a general flaw in anarchism?
6. How persuasive is Goldman's justification of political violence to resist domination?
7. Evaluate the strengths and weaknesses of Goldman's approach to political theory.
8. Was Goldman's appeal to the avant-garde elitist?

Further reading

Primary sources

Shulman, A.K. (1998) *Red Emma Speaks: An Emma Goldman Reader*. 3rd edn. Amhurst, NY: Humanity Books.
   Seminal collection of Goldman's writing on anarchism, women, labour, and violence.

Wilbur. S.P. (2016) *Anarchy and the Sex Question: Essays on Women and Emancipation, 1896–1926*. Oakland, CA: PM Press.
   An extensive collection of Goldman's writing on women and sex.

Secondary sources

Ferguson, K.E. (2013) *Emma Goldman: Political Thinking in the Streets*. Lanham, MD: Rowman & Littlefield.
   Uses poststructuralist theory to analyse Goldman's anarchist political theory.

Hemmings, C. (2018) *Considering Emma Goldman: Feminist Political Ambivalence and the Imaginative Archive*. Durham, NC: Duke University Press.
   Evaluates Goldman's significance to contemporary feminist thought, using 'ambivalence' as a lens to discuss race, gender, and sexuality.

Wexler, A. (1984) *Emma Goldman: An Intimate Life*. London: Virago.
   Critical yet sympathetic biography which examines the tensions in Goldman's public and private life.

References

Alcoff, L. (1991) 'The Problem of Speaking for Others'. *Cultural Critique*, 20: 5–32.

Appiah, K.A. (1990) 'Racisms'. In D. Goldberg (ed.), *Anatomy of Racism*. Minneapolis, MN: University of Minnesota Press, pp. 3–17.

Bolloten, B. (1979) *The Spanish Revolution: The Left and the Struggle for Power During the Civil War*. Chapel Hill, NC: University of North Carolina Press.

Burrows, P. (2008) ' "Apostle of Anarchy": Emma Goldman's First Visit to Winnipeg in 1907'. *Manitoba History*, 57: 2–15.

Caygill, H. (2013) *On Resistance: A Philosophy of Defiance*. London: Bloomsbury.

De Cleyre, V. (1914 [1894]) 'In Defence of Emma Goldman'. In A. Berkman (ed.), *Selected Works of Voltairine de Cleyre*. New York: Mother Earth.

Drinnon, R. (1982) *Rebel in Paradise: A Biography of Emma Goldman*. London: Phoenix Press.

Dunbar, P.L. (1907 [1904]) 'The New Slavery in the South'. *Mother Earth*, II(1): 51.

Falk, C. (1990) *Love, Anarchy and Emma Goldman*. New Brunswick, NJ: Rutgers University Press.

Falk, C. (2003) *Emma Goldman: A Documentary History of the American Years: Made for America, 1890–1901*. Urbana IL: University of Illinois Press.

Falk, C. (2008) *Emma Goldman: A Documentary History of the American Years: Made For America, 1890–1901*. Urbana, IL: University of Illinois Press.

Fanon, F. (2009 [1952]) 'The Fact of Blackness'. In L. Back, and J. Solomos (eds), *Theories of Race and Racism: A Reader*. London: Routledge, pp. 257–266.

Fellner, G. (1992) *Life of an Anarchist: The Alexander Berkman Reader*. New York: Four Walls Eight Windows.

Ferguson, K.E. (2013) *Emma Goldman: Political Thinking in the Streets*. Lanham, MD: Rowman & Littlefield.

Glassgold, P. (2000) *Anarchy!: An Anthology of Emma Goldman's Mother Earth*. New York: Counterpoint.

Goldman, E. (1907a) 'The Situation in America, Part I'. *Mother Earth*, II(7): 270–274.

Goldman, E. (1907b) 'The Situation in America, Part II'. *Mother Earth*, II(8): 320–329.

Goldman, E. (1907c) 'The International Anarchist Congress: Report by Emma Goldman'. *Mother Earth*, II(8): 307–319.

Goldman, E. (1909) 'A New Declaration of Independence'. [online] *Anarchist Library* . Available at: https://theanarchistlibrary.org/library/emma-goldman-a-new-declaration-of-independence (accessed 24 February 2020).

Goldman, E. (1917a) 'We Don't Believe in Conscription'. [online]. University of California Berkeley Library Emma Goldman Papers. Available at: http://awpc.cattcenter.iastate.edu/2017/03/21/an-anarchist-looks-at-life-march-1-1933/ (accessed 3 December 2022).

Goldman, E. (1927) 'Typed letter (copy) to Bartolomeo Vanzetti and Nicola Sacco, Toronto, Ontario, 18 July'. [online]. Boston Public Library. Available at: https://www.digitalcommonwealth.org/search/commonwealth:z603ss67w accessed 24 February 2020).

Goldman, E. (1932) 'Voltairine de Cleyre'. [online]. *Anarchy Archives*. Available at: http://dwardmac.pitzer.edu/Anarchist_Archives/goldman/egtribtovdc/index.html (accessed 24 February 2020).

Goldman, E. (1933) 'An Anarchist Looks at Life'. [online]. University of California Berkeley Library Emma Goldman Papers. Available at: https://awpc.cattcenter.iastate.edu/2017/03/21/an-anarchist-looks-at-life-march-1-1933/ (accessed 3 December 2022).

Goldman, E. (1938) 'Palestine and Socialist Policy: Emma Goldman's Views. Spain and the World'. [online]. *Freedom Press Archive*. Available at: https://freedomnews.org.uk/wp-content/uploads/2018/02/Spain-and-the-World-1938-08-26.pdf (accessed 24 February 2020).

Goldman, E. (1970 [1931]) *Living My Life*, 2 vols. New York: Dover.

Goldman, E. (1979a [1908]) 'What I Believe'. In A.K. Shulman (ed.), *Red Emma Speaks: The Selected Speeches and Writings of the Anarchist and Feminist*. London: Wildwood House.

Goldman, E. (1979b [1911a]) 'Anarchism: What it Really Stands For'. In A.K. Shulman (ed.), *Red Emma Speaks: The Selected Speeches and Writings of the Anarchist and Feminist*. London: Wildwood House.

Goldman, E. (1979c [1911b]) 'The Psychology of Political Violence'. In A.K. Shulman (ed.), *Red Emma Speaks: The Selected Speeches and Writings of the Anarchist and Feminist*. London: Wildwood House.

Goldman, E. (1979d [1911d]) 'The Tragedy of Woman's Emancipation'. In: A.K. Shulman (ed.), *Red Emma Speaks: The Selected Speeches and Writings of the Anarchist and Feminist*. London: Wildwood House.

Goldman, E. (1979e [1911e]) 'The Traffic in Women'. In A.K. Shulman (ed.), *Red Emma Speaks: The Selected Speeches and Writings of the Anarchist and Feminist*. London: Wildwood House.

Goldman, E. (1979f [1911f]) 'Marriage and Love'. In A.K. Shulman (ed.), *Red Emma Speaks: The Selected Speeches and Writings of the Anarchist and Feminist*. London: Wildwood House.

Goldman, E. (1979g [1913a]) 'Victims of Morality'. In A.K. Shulman (ed.), *Red Emma Speaks: The Selected Speeches and Writings of the Anarchist and Feminist*. London: Wildwood House.

Goldman, F. (1979h [1912]) 'Jealousy: Causes and a Possible Cure'. In A.K. Shulman (ed.), *Red Emma Speaks: The Selected Speeches and Writings of the Anarchist and Feminist*. London: Wildwood House.

Goldman, E. (1979i [1913b]) 'The Failure of Christianity'. In A.K. Shulman (ed.), *Red Emma Speaks: The Selected Speeches and Writings of the Anarchist and Feminist*. London: Wildwood House.

Goldman, E. (1979j [1913c]. 'Syndicalism: Its Theory and Practice'. In A.K. Shulman (ed.), *Red Emma Speaks:

The Selected Speeches and Writings of the Anarchist and Feminist. London: Wildwood House.

Goldman, E. (1979k [1914a]) 'Intellectual Proletarians'. In A.K. Shulman (ed.), *Red Emma Speaks: The Selected Speeches and Writings of the Anarchist and Feminist*. London: Wildwood House.

Goldman, E. (1979l [1915]) 'Preparedness: Road to Universal Slaughter'. In A.K. Shulman (ed.), *Red Emma Speaks: The Selected Speeches and Writings of the Anarchist and Feminist*. London: Wildwood House.

Goldman, E. (1979m [1917b]) 'Address to the Jury'. In A.K. Shulman (ed.) *Red Emma Speaks: The Selected Speeches and Writings of the Anarchist and Feminist*. London: Wildwood House.

Goldman, E. (1979n [1934]) 'Was My Life Worth Living?' In A.K. Shulman (ed.), *Red Emma Speaks: The Selected Speeches and Writings of the Anarchist and Feminist*. London: Wildwood House.

Goldman, E. (1979o [1935]) 'There Is No Communism in Russia'. In A.K. Shulman (ed.), *Red Emma Speaks: The Selected Speeches and Writings of the Anarchist and Feminist*. London: Wildwood House.

Goldman, E. (1979p [1940?]) 'The Individual, Society and the State'. In A.K. Shulman (ed.), *Red Emma Speaks: The Selected Speeches and Writings of the Anarchist and Feminist*. London: Wildwood House.

Goldman, E. (2005 [1914b]) *The Social Significance of Modern Drama*. New York: Cosimo.

Goldman, E. (2016a [1910]) 'Woman Suffrage'. In S.P. Wilber (ed.), *Anarchy and the Sex Question: Essays on Women and Emancipation, 1896–1926*. Oakland, CA: PM Press.

Goldman, E. (2016b [1911c]) 'Mary Wollstonecraft, Her Tragic Life and Her Passionate Struggle for Freedom'. In S.P. Wilber (ed.), *Anarchy and the Sex Question: Essays on Women and Emancipation, 1896–1926*. Oakland, CA: PM Press.

Goldman E. (2016c [1916b]) 'The Social Aspects of Birth Control'. In S.P. Wilber (ed.), *Anarchy and the Sex Question: Essays on Women and Emancipation, 1896–1926*. Oakland, CA: PM Press.

Goldman, E. (2016d [1923]) 'Louise Michel'. In S.P. Wilber (ed.), *Anarchy and the Sex Question: Essays on Women and Emancipation, 1896–1926*. Oakland, CA: PM Press.

Goldman, E. (2016e [1926]) 'Feminism's Fight Not in Vain'. In S.P. Wilber (ed.), *Anarchy and the Sex Question: Essays on Women and Emancipation, 1896–1926*. Oakland: PM Press.

Goldman, E. (n.d. [1923/1924]) *My Two Years in Russia: An American Anarchist's Disillusionment and the Betrayal of the Russian Revolution by Lenin's Soviet Union*. St. Petersburg, FL: Red and Black Publishers.

Goldman, E. and Baginski, M. (1906) 'Mother Earth'. *Mother Earth* [online]. 1(1). Available at: https://libcom.org/library/volume-1-issue-1 (accessed 24 February 2020).

Gordon, A.J. (2015) 'What Should Blacks Think When Jews Choose Whiteness?: An Ode to Baldwin'. *Critical Philosophy of Race*, 3(2): 227–258.

Harman, M. (1905) *The Right to Be Born Well*. Chicago: Harman.

Havel, H. (2018 [1910]) 'Introduction to Anarchism and Other Essays'. In N. Jun (ed.), *Proletarian Days: A Hippolyte Havel Reader*. Chico, CA: AK Press. pp. 88–135.

Hemmings, C. (2018) *Considering Emma Goldman: Feminist Political Ambivalence and the Imaginative Archive*. Durham, NC: Duke University Press.

International Anarchist Congress (1907) 'Proceedings' [online]. *Anarchist Library*. Available at: https://theanarchistlibrary.org/library/freedom-ed-the-international-anarchist-congress (accessed 24 February 2020).

Kinna, R. (2019) *The Government of No One*. London: Pelican.

Kinna, R. and Prichard, A. (2019) 'Anarchism and Non-Domination'. *Journal of Political Ideologies*, 24(3): 221–240.

Kropotkin, P. (1970 [1880]) 'The Spirit of Revolt'. In R.N. Baldwin (ed.), *Kropotkin's Revolutionary Pamphlets*. New York: Dover, pp. 34–43.

Leca, J. (2010) 'Political Philosophy in Political Science: Sixty Years On'. *International Political Science Review* 31(5): 525–538.

Leval, G. (1975) *Collectives in the Spanish Revolution*. London: Freedom Press.

Magon, R.F. (1977) *Land and Liberty: Anarchist Influences in the Mexican Revolution*. Orkney: Cienfuegos Press.

Porter, D. (1983) *Vision on Fire: Emma Goldman on the Spanish Revolution*. New Paltz, NY: Commonground Press.

Ramsey, W.M. (1999) 'Dunbar's Dixie'. *Southern Literary Journal*, 32(1): 30–45.

Tolstoy, L. (1908) 'Letter to a Hindu'. [online]. Anarchist Library. Available at: https://www.marxists.org/archive/tolstoy/1908/letter-to-a-hindu.html (accessed 1 June 2022).

27 Mohandas (Mahatma) Gandhi

JIMMY CASAS KLAUSEN

Chapter guide

Gandhi's political thought is thoroughly entangled with his life as an iconic activist. Accordingly, this chapter traces the development of Gandhi's theory *and* practice of nonviolent resistance in the context of British imperialism in Asia and Africa, thereby integrating what he wrote, how he projected himself, and how he conducted campaigns of resistance. The chapter first confronts Gandhi as icon (Section 27.2), before then sketching his argument for Indian self-rule (Section 27.3). Gandhi's book *Hind Swaraj* presents self-rule as personal/individual *and* political/collective and introduces the theory behind nonviolent resistance. In Section 27.4, a reading of Gandhi's *Autobiography* then reassesses his early activism, showing why anti-racist criticisms are not unfounded, and elaborates Gandhi's dilemmas in reconciling nonviolent theory and practice in nationwide political campaigns. Analysis of the *Salt Satyagraha* indicates how Gandhi had tried to resolve the tensions of nonviolent resistance on a mass scale. The chapter concludes with an overview of Gandhi's legacy and controversies.

27.1 Introduction

Better known by the honorific Mahatma, Sanskrit for 'great souled', Mohandas Karamchand Gandhi (1869–1948) seems more familiar as an activist than political theorist. A symbol of India's struggle for independence from British imperial rule, Gandhi is a 'founding father' of the postcolonial Indian nation, alongside Jawaharlal Nehru. Nonetheless, Gandhi left behind an immense corpus of writings. His two best-known books, *Hind Swaraj* and *An Autobiography*, present sometimes counterintuitive arguments on power, violence, and resistance, which Gandhi developed first in the context of *satyagraha* protests by the Indian community in southern Africa against European settlers' racial prejudice, and then in India's anti-colonial struggle against British overrule. Gandhian theory and practice have subsequently inspired dramatic and successful civil disobedience campaigns against dictatorships and white supremacy far beyond the South Asian subcontinent. Nonetheless, Gandhi himself has been accused of casteist and racist prejudices and authoritarian manipulations of his own. Despite being a complex, paradoxical, and in some ways quite a flawed figure, he nonetheless crucially influenced such important resistance strategists as Martin Luther King, Jr, and Nelson Mandela.

Read more about **Gandhi's** life and work by accessing the thinker biography on the online resources: www.oup.com/he/Ramgotra-Choat1e.

> **Key Concept: *satyagraha***
>
> Despite rendering *satyagraha* as 'passive resistance' in his own translation of *Hind Swaraj*, Gandhi distinguishes the two in *Autobiography* (Gandhi, 1993: 318–319). *Satyagraha* requires self-purification, discipline, and self-suffering, and calls for active strength of body and mind. By contrast, passive resistance could imply non-harm as a default for someone lacking robust strength to do harm (a weapon of the weak) or as the outcome of an ascetic (self-disciplining) renunciation of action. Passive resistance, too, could involve an outward willingness to suffer bodily while internally (mentally or emotionally) harbouring hatred towards the perpetrator. Motivated by altruistic love, *satyagraha*, means firm 'adherence to truth' and aims to convert wrong-doers to truth by the spectacle of the *satyagrahi*'s willingness to suffer for it. Although Gandhi remained optimistic that everyone had the capacity to practise *satyagraha*, he realized that most lacked spiritual discipline to practise true *satyagraha* in mass political campaigns.

27.2 Gandhi as global icon

With the possible exception of Karl Marx (see Chapter 13), no other political thinker is as visually iconic as Gandhi; certainly, he is the only one whose portrayal in film gained the actor an Academy Award, which Ben Kingsley won for his performance in *Gandhi* (dir. Attenborough, 1982). Gandhi appears on decals and t-shirts. Political parties and governments deploy his image strategically. He has been lionized with public statues and street names. 'Gandhi has become all things to all people . . . The poor love him and so do the rich', Arundhati Roy (2014: 40) notes. What explains the iconology of 'Gandhi'?

Gandhi himself understood the power of symbols and visual impressions and actively shaped his image, sometimes retrospectively. Born in Western India, and a timid and unimpressive student in arranged marriage to Kasturbai since the age of 13, Gandhi left Gujarat at age 18 to study law at University College London, defying family and caste members who worried he would succumb to Western ways. Indeed, although famously keeping his promise to his mother to abstain from alcohol, meat, and sexual temptation, Gandhi willingly cultivated an Anglicized persona in other ways. Keen to look the part of the Victorian gentleman, Gandhi adopted the sartorial self-presentation of a London barrister and maintained 'a besuited, starched collared style of dress for the next two decades' (Hyslop, 2011: 33). Though he adopted a more 'Indian' style of dress before returning to India in 1915, it was not until 1921 that he crafted his most well-known image of the sage or *sadhu* in the loin cloth, conveying simplicity and solidarity with the poor (Chakrabarty, 2002: 52).

When he arrived to work in the British colony of Natal, Gandhi suffered a shocking disconnect between his self-image, as Anglicized, modern, and civilized, and the settler-colonists' contempt for him as 'coloured'. The self-image that Gandhi had crafted in London and brought to southern Africa both launched and influenced his early political resistance, motivated more by respectability than race, and according to which educated Indians deserved a special place in Britain's Empire, different from Africans (Desai and Vahed, 2016).

In his early campaigns against anti-Indian discrimination in southern Africa, Gandhi intuited the importance of swaying public opinion by appeals to the mass media. Thus, in addition to crafting his own visual self-presentation in his personal relations, 'he became a master of reading the political moment and of the political use of the print media' (Hyslop, 2011: 30). He invited journalists to cover public protests for Indians' civil rights, started his own newspapers, and syndicated his own reports of events. Later in India, via print reportage and photojournalism, Gandhi won over international audiences with his determination and charming humility. Gandhi projected his ascetic image for camera and press, and chose potent symbols of arbitrary rule and economic domination. Journalists mass-mediated this iconology, which they co-constructed with him.

What 'Gandhi' signified varied considerably both before and after his assassination. As Judith Brown (2011: 54) astutely notes, 'many "Gandhis" developed in people's minds; many images of him took shape, as individuals and groups interpreted his work and teaching and appropriated him to further their own agendas'. In the eyes of critics in southern Africa and India, Gandhi appeared to be a sell-out who prioritized negotiations with imperial authority over community grievances. This view is reflected in the films *Dr Babasaheb Ambedkar* (dir. Patel, 2000) and *The Legend of Bhagat Singh* (dir. Santoshi, 2002), which portray Gandhi as foolish or cunning.

Key Thinker: B.R. Ambedkar

In 1927, B.R. Ambedkar (1891–1956) led a *satyagraha* for Dalits' right to access wells and water tanks forbidden to them by caste privilege. As a Dalit ('Untouchable'), Ambedkar clashed with Gandhi on caste politics, most famously in London in 1930, over whether Britain should award Dalits a separate electorate for provincial assemblies. Refusing to concede that Dalits might have interests separate from Hindus, Gandhi began a death fast in objection, forcing Ambedkar to change his position. Like Gandhi, Ambedkar studied law in London, yet, with a scholarship for caste-oppressed students, also earned master's and doctoral degrees from both Columbia University and the London School of Economics. Ambedkar published formidable, scholarly analyses of caste oppression, inequality, and democracy, and served as chair of the committee that drafted the Indian Constitution and first Law Minister post-independence. Angry at the lack of reform by privileged-caste Hindus, he converted to Buddhism before his death.

However, for peasants in northern India in the 1920s, 'Gandhi' embodied popular justice, inspiring sometimes armed agitation that the real Gandhi disowned (Pandey, 1988). As 'Mahatma', Gandhi represented for peasants a mythic figure endowed with miraculous powers, not a shrewd political leader of a mass anti-colonia nationalist movement who expected disciplined adherence to principles. Non-elite Indians thus circulated images of Gandhi that 'clashed with the basic tenets of Gandhism itself' (Amin, 1988: 342).

Despite crafting his own image, Gandhi represented diverse personae to distinct audiences: man of peace, scheming politician, saint of social justice, strategist, holy fool, ecologist. It is no wonder that controversies over statues of Gandhi are as heated as those over monuments to imperial, racist politicians. Projecting soft power across the Global South, the Indian government has deployed Gandhi's image for diverse purposes, including rejecting the argument that casteist treatment of Dalits amounts to racism (Krishna, 2014). Yet when the Indian embassy donated a statue of Gandhi to the University of Ghana in 2016, students and professors started a #GandhiMustFall petition, highlighting racist statements Gandhi made about Africans. The university removed the monument, prompting a counter-petition for the statue's return as a symbol of leadership and universalism (Barnargarwala, 2019). Nevertheless, some African leaders, most famously Nelson Mandela, honoured him as a model.

27.2 Gandhi as global icon: Key Points

- From his time in London onward, Gandhi shaped his own image.
- Gandhi masterfully utilized print media to publicize the causes of Indian civil rights in southern Africa and self-rule for India.
- Nonetheless, 'Gandhi' is a contested signifier, meaning different things to different audiences.

27.3 *Hind Swaraj*: anti-colonial resistance

Paradoxical and frustrating like Gandhi himself, *Hind Swaraj, or Indian Home Rule* presents a counterintuitive anti-colonial theory. Gandhi wrote *Hind Swaraj* in dialogue form, like Plato's *Apology* and the *Bhagavad Gita*, which served as inspirations (see Chapter 2 on Plato). In conversation with a Reader who hastily assesses injustice and offers solutions, the Editor counsels slow diagnosis of the root ills of India's political situation, and prescribes therapies for *swaraj*, self-rule. The Reader proposes killing for *swaraj*, so it is easy to cast the dialogue as a struggle between revolutionary violence and nonviolent soul-force (Hofmeyr, 2011). However, in the context of writing *Hind Swaraj*, Gandhi questions a range of political positions and models of resistance, from imperial liberalism (Skaria, 2016) to British suffragettes' rowdy direct action (Livingston, 2018).

> **Key Concept: *swaraj***
>
> Gandhi's argument for *swaraj* was ground-breaking (Sultan, 2020), despite its neo-traditionalist praise of Indian civilization. Whereas many anti-colonial nationalists argued that India must be free of alien rule for Indians to be free, *Hind Swaraj* argued that 'if we become free, India is free' (Gandhi, 1997: 73). *Swaraj* means achieving self-rule individually first, after which India collectively would become free. As such, *swaraj* cannot be granted by others, whether the British or other Indians, but must be 'experienced by each one for himself' through 'performance of duty' (ibid.: 73, 82). Political *swaraj*, national independence and sovereignty over national affairs and foreign policy, would not guarantee true freedom. True *swaraj* prioritizes moral before political authority, individuals, then the nation. Effectively, Gandhian *swaraj* inverted the order of freedom.

Two events, though, were notable enough to earn direct mention in the dialogue: the split between the Moderates and Extremists of the Indian National Congress in 1907, and Madan Lal Dhingra's assassination of Sir William Curzon-Wyllie in London in 1909 (Gandhi, 1997: 22–23, 77–78). The Extremists grew frustrated with the Moderates' strategy of petitioning imperial authorities for reform and backed more militant popular mobilization (Chandra et al., 1989: 135–142). Just before the split in 1907, Aurobindo Ghose argued in an influential Extremist pamphlet against treating passive resistance 'as an inelastic dogma'; under conditions of imperial 'hooliganism', active self-defence was a duty and even armed revolt possible (Ghose, 1952: 67, 62–63; Klausen, 2014). Indeed, secret terrorist cells had formed and made assassination attempts on British officials in India (Heehs, 1993), but it was revolutionary and pro-independence activist Madan Lal Dhingra's assassination of India Office official Sir Curzon-Wyllie in London that gained the most notoriety.

Gandhi wrote *Hind Swaraj* against this tumultuous background. He staged the conversation as a critique of available options for anti-colonial resistance. While it may not be justified to identify the Reader as unquestionably Extremist or terrorist, the dialogue clearly suggests he is persuaded by their ideas. Calling both Reader and Extremists 'impatient' (Gandhi, 1997: 14, 22), the Editor offers an alternative path forward.

In the first discussion of *swaraj*, the Reader parrots common positions among Indian nationalists: the British must leave because they enslave India and drain its wealth; nevertheless, home rule involves importing British institutions (ibid.: 27–29). The Editor rejects a definition of *swaraj* according to which Indians would 'want English rule without the Englishman' (ibid.: 28). True *swaraj* does not mean expelling the British while retaining Britain's modern developmental model (Sultan, 2020). The Editor argues conversely that Indians must discard the latter, though individual British could remain in India. According to Gandhi's unexpected diagnosis, British persons deserve not 'blame' for imperialism but rather 'sympathy'; they are sick without realizing it, diseased by modern civilization (Gandhi, 1997: 38). 'India', the Editor claims, 'is being ground down not under the English heel but under that of modern civilisation' (ibid.: 42).

The Editor criticizes the advent of modern civilization in India in terms of four main features: railways, sectarian enmity, doctors, and lawyers. These principal agents of modern civilization seduce Indians to 'violate our religious instinct' (ibid.: 64). Modern civilization weakens Indians' own self-reliance and forces them to rely on outsiders. Thus 'modern methods of violence to drive out the English' would not win India home rule (ibid.: 7). Indians cannot win independence by methods that render them dependent. Modernity is not morally neutral; it is the wrong means to the wrong end. What, then, constitutes the right means and end?

To answer this, the Editor defines 'true civilisation' as 'that mode of conduct which points out to man the path of duty. Performance of duty and observance of morality are convertible terms. To observe morality is to attain mastery over our mind and our passions. So doing, we know ourselves' (ibid.: 67). Duty or moral law encapsulates the central idea of 'true' civilization and instils self-knowledge and self-mastery, which results in self-limitation.

Gandhi contradicts the Eurocentric prejudice that India either lacked civilization or had long passed the age of decadence. Instead, he offers what Roy (2014: 83) calls 'a chauvinistic reverie of a mythical India' that excuses its poverty, romanticizes village life, and utterly ignores caste-based discrimination and violence. When the Reader objects to the Editor's reverie of blameless ancient wisdom, naming misogynistic customs, and animal sacrifice, the Editor admits that superficial 'defects' must be purged (Gandhi, 1997: 70–71). Whereas modern civilization is *essentially* vicious though 'not an incurable disease' (ibid.: 38), Indians' vices are *inessential* and do not detract from India's fundamentally virtuous civilization. Hence, Indians must 'revert to their own glorious civilisation' while British may remain in India if they 'become Indianised' (ibid.: 7). If the Editor accuses the Reader of wanting to make India British, *swaraj* for the Editor involves making India Indian again. Given this supremacist attitude, Roy (2014: 128–129) finds it unsurprising how easily today's Hindu right, including Narendra Modi, invoke Gandhi.

To the Editor, one achieves right ends—*swaraj*—not by any means whatsoever, but only by morally upright means, because means necessarily must comport with ends (Gandhi, 1997: 81). If the goal were simply to alter the face of rule from British to Indian, then force of arms would serve as appropriate, if regrettable, means. Indeed, the Reader blithely speculates: 'All [Indians] need not be armed. At first, we will assassinate a few Englishmen and strike terror; then, a few men who will have been armed will fight openly. We may have to lose a quarter of a million men, more or less, but we will regain our land.' Stunningly the Editor counters: 'What we need to do is to kill ourselves' (ibid.: 77). Indians' true freedom necessitates self-sacrifice, not the sacrifice of others. The British after all are sick and deserve Indians' pity. Moreover, the Reader's vision casually discards Indian lives too for *swaraj*.

Abstractly prioritizing collective political independence stokes selfishness, resulting in violence. In contrast, direct moral *swaraj* means consulting the interest of those with whom one holds immediate relations. Hence, true *swaraj* as the right end calls for morally upright means: what Gandhi names soul-force. Soul-force works by self-suffering and as such is the 'reverse' of brute force and armed resistance against others (ibid.: 90). Someone who perceives a wrong in the world and wants to correct it acts through pity, love, and truth if they do not violently impose their own perception of right on others but willingly suffer for it by themselves. Doing so, they provoke moral shock or agitation in the other person—whether that person is the perceived wrong-doer or a bystander—which can induce self-examination and moral transformation. If the *satyagrahi* turns out to have mistaken truth and wrong, then only they suffer, not the misperceived wrong-doer (Parekh, 1999: 172–174).

The anti-colonial nationalist armed resistance that the Reader advocates presumes that India's alien rulers cannot or will not change. Therefore, according to this position, only fear instilled by violence and terror will make them leave. Gandhi believes that the moral transformation of wrongdoers is possible. As the Editor says, to maintain otherwise is tantamount to claiming that they 'have no humanity in them' (Gandhi, 1997: 73–74). Soul-force appeals directly to this humanity in everyone. Therefore, anti-imperialist resistance by soul-force acts in the interest of possible wrongdoers, with the aim of saving them from their own propensity towards violent, harmful actions. For this reason, the Editor argues that the British may be Indianized.

Moral transformation through soul-force depends on a relatively optimistic understanding of humanity, both universally in history and individually within each person. Influenced by Russian writer Leo Tolstoy (see Key Thinker: Leo Tolstoy box), Gandhi believed that a divine or spiritual force dwells in and inspires humanity's moral progress. Progress on this view manifests itself not materially—as in the technological advancements that the Editor criticizes in modern civilization— but rather morally. When the Reader expresses doubt about the very possibility of soul-force, the Editor answers that its existence is proven by the very persistence of human beings, despite all the wars, enmities, and atrocities of history: 'The fact that there are so many men still alive in the world shows that it is based not on the force of arms but on the force of truth or love' (ibid.: 89); otherwise, humans would have destroyed each other long ago, and the world would not exist. Indigenous Australians, the Editor callously ventures in proof of his thesis, suffered nearly total genocide because they neglected to 'use soul-force in self-defence', and their settler-colonist perpetrators will face the same fate (ibid.: 89).

Key Thinker: Leo Tolstoy

Better known for his novels, Leo Tolstoy (1828–1910) also wrote extensively on anarchism and Christian spirituality. Indeed, Tolstoy's book *The Kingdom of God Is Within You* fuses the two. In it, Tolstoy argues that Christianity paradigmatically advocates nonviolence. Since governments claim to suppress evil by brute force, a properly Christian organization of social life calls for abolition of government. Tolstoy's book, Gandhi (1993: 137) claims, 'overwhelmed' him. Influenced also by Tolstoy's 'Letter to a Hindu', which insists on love as the basis for anti-colonial resistance, Gandhi subsequently sent the author *Hind Swaraj*. When Gandhi (1999: vol. 53, 4) entertained 'enlightened anarchy' as an ideal in which moral self-regulation would abolish the necessity of politics and the state, Tolstoy influenced his thinking. Nevertheless, Gandhi eventually judged the ideal unrealistic.

Humanity, then, is this balance of forces that has forever slightly favoured soul-force above brute force. The humanity that dwells in everyone makes them available to conversion or correction. Witnessing someone willing to suffer for truth or love can induce moral transformation in observers, so that their own internal balance of action is swayed away from untruth and harm and towards truth and nonviolence. *Satyagraha*, despite being called passive resistance, attempts actively to sway this balance of forces further in favour of soul-force, to convert each person individually and human beings collectively away from the egotism of the body and towards the soul's love of God and neighbour. In this sense, Gandhi's political theory does not succumb to utopian idealism (Mantena, 2012), because, although upholding a high ideal for humanity, Gandhi nevertheless views political outcomes as the result of strategic manoeuvring between forces of *himsa* and *ahimsa* (see Key Concept: *ahimsa* box), untruth and truth, egotism and love, body and soul, brute force and soul-force.

> **Key Concept: *ahimsa***
>
> *Ahimsa* means the absence or negation of *himsa*, violence or harm. Although seemingly straightforward, the line between violence/harm and nonviolence/non-harm was subject to interpretation. For many Hindu thinkers before and during Gandhi's lifetime, 'not all harm or destruction amounted to *himsā*' (Parekh, 1999: 124). Rather, *himsa* referred to *unjustified* harm, whereas *ahimsa* encompassed non-harm and justified harm. (This view informed Bhagat Singh's position discussed below, though he was not Hindu.) Gandhi rejected this permissive view of *ahimsa* and followed instead the stricter Jain and Buddhist positions. Jain and Buddhist thinkers defined *ahimsa* as the total absence of harm but allowed distinctions within the category *himsa* between justified and unjustified harm. Gandhi's views on self-purification show that *himsa*, moreover, encompassed harmful thoughts and words, not just physical violence. Soul-force and *satyagraha* call for such rigorous *ahimsa*.

Sections 27.4 and 27.5 suggest that Gandhi came to understand the struggle between these two sets of forces in more complex, subtle terms in the two decades after *Hind Swaraj*, and this more subtle understanding had consequences for his own practice of *satyagraha* and campaigns of political resistance.

> **27.3 *Hind Swaraj*: anti-colonial resistance: Key Points**
>
> - *Hind Swaraj* questions a range of political positions among Indian nationalists but argues directly against those advocating 'brute force'.
> - The tract develops an anti-colonial theory via a critique of 'modern civilisation', of which British imperialism is merely a symptom.
> - Therefore, *swaraj* involves not the substitution of Indian for British rulers but the rejection of modern civilization and a return to ancient Indian civilization's conception of duty.
> - The proper means to this end is not physical violence but rather 'soul-force'.
> - Resistance by soul-force disarms and converts colonial opponents morally rather than destroying them physically.

27.4 *An Autobiography*: struggle towards nonviolence

Published in 1927–1929, *An Autobiography* presents how Gandhi came to lead India's anti-colonial national resistance movement, though is not exactly a political biography (Parekh, 1999: Chapter 8). Ironically, although he titles it *The Story of My Experiments with Truth*, many historians distrust the accuracy of his account of his youth and career in South Africa. Jonathan Hyslop calls it 'both a wonderful resource and a source of danger' (Hyslop, 2011: 31). It is not that Gandhi lied outright, but, as Ashwin Desai and Goolam Vahed have claimed of Gandhi's retelling of his South African years, 'it was apparent that he indulged in some "tidying up"' (Desai and Vahed, 2016: 25).

27.4.1 Gandhi's hidden biases

Controversies around Gandhi's early attitudes and activism have exploded precisely because the *Autobiography* offers a partial, retrospectively self-vindicating account. In particular, it leaves the impression that Gandhi opposed racism generally and worked to advance the rights of all Indians indiscriminately because British and Afrikaner prejudice affected them equally. Indeed, no one less than Nelson Mandela perpetuated this image of Gandhi as an anti-apartheid warrior (ibid.: 23, 305). The reality, however, is more complex.

Certainly, in the *Autobiography*, Gandhi famously narrates in a very affecting manner his coming-to-consciousness of racism. Upon arriving in southern Africa, he secured a first-class train passage—which he presumed would befit the lifestyle of a London-trained barrister—but was thrown from the car with his luggage and slept the night on the platform. The next day he was humiliated when expecting superior accommodations on a stage coach and in a hotel. Soon after, he was kicked off a footpath, leading him to conclude that 'South Africa was no country for a self-respecting Indian' (Gandhi, 1993: 131). Years later, having gained renown—or, to white supremacists, infamy—for protesting discrimination, he was roughed up by a white mob upon disembarking from a visit to India. Composing this spectacle of himself as the target of discrimination (Lake and Reynolds, 2008: 114–118), Gandhi thus employs a seemingly straightforward fight against racial animus in general.

However, the *Autobiography*'s representation of events is ambiguous at best and effectively self-serving in multiple respects. First, while in some ways everyday discrimination and legislation in the British colonies, Afrikaner republics and, later, the Union of South Africa affected all Indians, there were significant differences between indentured labourers, including their descendants, who worked plantations and in menial service, and the 'passenger' Indians who came voluntarily to set up business ventures. All were slurred as 'coolies', prompting Gandhi to remark that, despite caste Indians' own vicious and invidious treatment of 'untouchables' and pariahs, all Indians 'have become the untouchables of South Africa' (Gandhi, 1993: 287), irrespective of privileged- or oppressed-caste position, economic class, or civil status as free or indentured. Nevertheless, Roy (2014) and Desai and Vahed (2016) show that Gandhi campaigned against discrimination as it affected principally the passenger Indians' interests and only belatedly came to widen his remit, deigning in 1913 to 'lead' indentured workers in protests and strikes they themselves had already initiated. Gandhi was and continued to be dismissive of indentured and working-class Indians, believing them unable to conduct themselves politically despite their own history of resistance. Gandhi himself, then, harboured prejudice against his fellow Indians. Despite saying he identifies with the poor (Gandhi, 1993: 153), he identifies also—or even more—with a racist respectability politics that condescends to less 'civilized' Indians and disdains their standards of cleanliness.

However, more ambiguous and self-serving still were Gandhi's representations of amaZulu and other native African peoples in the *Autobiography*. Though largely silent on British and Afrikaner settler-colonial expropriation and exploitation of Africans, Gandhi's *Autobiography* criticizes, though only in passing, the racial terror visited upon the amaZulu by the British during the Bambatha Rebellion in 1906. It 'was no war but a man-hunt', Gandhi concludes, contrasting British soldiers' flogging of prisoners with the Indians' corps' selfless succour to the Zulu wounded: 'but for us the Zulus would have been uncared for' (ibid.: 315–316).

Despite distancing himself from anti-Zulu views by referring to '*so-called* "uncivilized" Zulus' (ibid.: 316, emphasis added), Gandhi himself disparaged them as animalistic (Roy, 2014: 73). Although he bristled at the slur 'coolie', Gandhi himself persistently referred to native Africans by the derogatory term 'kaffirs' almost until his departure from South Africa (Desai and Vahed, 2016: 304). Although the *Autobiography* mentions that imprisoned Indians and Africans were subject to similar restrictions (Gandhi, 1993: 325), it does not disclose that Gandhi could scarcely tolerate sharing a jail cell with Africans: 'We could understand not being classed with the Whites, but to be placed on the same level with the Natives seemed to be too much to put up with' (Gandhi, 1999: vol. 8, 198). It is possible that Gandhi underwent a transformation in the two decades that passed between his objection to sharing prison accommodations with native Africans and the publication of

VIOLENCE, POWER, AND RESISTANCE

An Autobiography. Yet, if this were so, then it seems odd for him not to mention explicitly such an antiracist awakening in the course of what purports to be a report on self-realization and truth-seeking.

If Gandhi's political resistance in southern Africa was not directed against all forms of racial discrimination, then what principle drove his activism? The *Autobiography* in fact hints at it several times. Since 'I demanded rights as a British citizen', Gandhi reasons, 'it was also my duty, as such, to participate in the defence of the British Empire' (Gandhi, 1993: 214). Although he sympathized with Afrikaners and the amaZulu during their wars waged in resistance to British imperial consolidation in southern Africa, Gandhi nevertheless insisted that Indians should loyally support Britain's empire by active service in voluntary ambulance corps during the Anglo-Boer War and Bambatha Rebellion. Gandhi would later enjoin Indians likewise to serve the British military effort during the First World War but appealed for nonviolent resolution of the Second World War.

In short, Gandhi viewed racial politics through the eyes of Britain's better self: 'The colour prejudice that I saw in South Africa was, I thought, contrary to British traditions, and I believed that it was only temporary and local', and 'that British rule was on the whole beneficial to the ruled' (ibid.: 172). Like British liberal elites yet unlike most Afrikaners, Gandhi believed that the key dividing line was civilizational achievement rather than skin colour (Lake and Reynolds, 2008: Chapters 5, 9). Hence, according to this perspective, free, educated Indians came to British southern Africa as imperial citizens and merited—as fellow Aryans—more privileged treatment than either indentured and term-expired Indians or any native African. As Desai and Vahed (Desai and Vahed, 2016: 19) put it, Gandhi sought 'limited integration into white South African society' for respectable Indians like himself.

27.4.2 Self-purification and *satyagraha*

Although he criticizes Britain's civilization in *Hind Swaraj* as primarily materialistic progress driven by brute, bodily concerns, Gandhi upheld all the more fiercely a moralistic view of civilization, in which respectability, qua self-restraint and self-purification, served as the litmus test. One of the odder moments in Gandhi's *Autobiography* implicitly links imperial racism to moralistic restraint. The chapter 'Heart Searchings' begins with Gandhi's criticism of the Bambatha Rebellion 'man-hunt' (Gandhi, 1993: 315–316) but then devotes the remainder to his views on *brahmacharya* (see Key Concept: *brahmacharya* box).

> **Key Concept: *brahmacharya***
>
> Although often translated as 'celibacy', *brahmacharya* means not simply celibacy but more precisely sexual restraint or asceticism. Anti-colonial Indian thinkers prior to Gandhi 'contended that their countrymen had fallen prey to waves of foreign rule because they had become passive, effete and devoid of energy as a result of their sensuous and self-indulgent lifestyle' (Parekh, 1999: 204). Patriotic regeneration, on this view, demanded sexual discipline. Accordingly, Gandhi had masculinized chastity in *Hind Swaraj*, while vilifying women's sexuality (Gandhi, 1997: 97, 30). In arguing for *brahmacharya* in the *Autobiography*, Gandhi drew on more radically ascetic Jain and Hindu traditions which advocated not merely sexual continence but the rigid control of the senses. However, Gandhi's *brahmacharya* went even further—not just outward restraint of the sensual deeds and desires of the body, but mastery also of thoughts and words (Gandhi, 1993: 317).

For Gandhi, *brahmacharya* was not merely a spiritual quest but necessary for public service. To devote oneself to public service required not merely freedom from sexual temptation and familial duties (ibid.: 206) but also a careful disciplining and restraint of bodily desires. Civilization as human moral achievement required this bodily self-restraint that Gandhi saw neither in the brutish amaZulu nor in the British who hunted and flogged them.

By its juxtapositions, Gandhi's *Autobiography* identifies his ambulance corps service during the Bambatha Rebellion as a turning point, as 'The Birth of Satyagraha'. What links native rebellion and murderous British reprisals against 'so-called "uncivilized" Zulus' (ibid.: 316) to *brahmacharya* and *satyagraha*? Without contrasting them explicitly, *An Autobiography* seems to imply that Gandhi grew aware of a gulf between British and Zulu (and Afrikaner) motivations on one side and Indian motivations on the other. Although Gandhi personally sympathizes with the amaZulu against the British, he does not call for Afro-Asian political solidarity. Indeed, he urges Indians to perform public service in loyalty to the British Empire while giving basic medical aid to its Zulu victims. Nevertheless, he judges both the amaZulu and British to have fallen short of civilization. Unquestionably, each group expresses brutish selfishness differently: Zulu rebels pursue the right end, self-rule, for the wrong reason, egoism, and by the wrong means, brute force; whereas, as Gandhi understood in 1906, British imperialists pursue another right goal, 'the welfare of the world' (ibid.: 313), but with the same wrong reason and means as Zulu rebels.

Gandhi glimpsed in the Indians' public service an alternative that he elaborated in *Hind Swaraj*: resistance against brute force by soul-force. Since the soul is more real than the body (ibid.: 72), only it conveys real strength; thus, only soul-force can reconcile resistance, self-rule and the welfare of all, and its method is *satyagraha*.

In Gandhi's interpretation, *brahmacharya* demanded more than self-restraint; it demanded self-purification. It required not merely discipline of bodily desires but also of mental and verbal impulses as well—and moreover the endless project of extirpating, and not merely repressing, impure desires and impulses. Gandhi foresaw that a person might outwardly conduct *satyagraha* (see Key Concept: *satyagraha*) but inwardly hate or curse the target of conversion—a real possibility in settler-colonial and highly racist societies. Nonetheless, a violent thought or word could 'spoil' outward civil disobedience 'like a drop of arsenic in milk', he observed (ibid.: 437).

For this reason, Gandhi mentions that his encounter with the Sermon on the Mount 'delighted me beyond measure' (ibid.: 68). In the Sermon, Jesus of Nazareth enjoins followers not merely to turn the other cheek against aggression but also to love their enemy aggressors. Interpreters of the Sermon, such as Augustine of Hippo (1951), explicitly unified the two injunctions so that the victim of aggression willingly submits to further harm with genuine love in their heart for the welfare of the aggressor. To turn the other cheek but with hatred towards the aggressor would appear *superficially* Christian but would not accord *spiritually* with Christianity. Likewise, Gandhi argues that *brahmacharya* qua self-purification motivates a *satyagrahi* to do the right thing for the right reason. The outward comportment of *satyagraha* must be inwardly motivated. 'Experience has taught me that civility is the most difficult part of Satyagraha. Civility does not here mean the mere outward gentleness of speech cultivated for the occasion, but an inborn gentleness and desire to do the opponent good' (Gandhi, 1993: 437). Politics was necessarily spiritual or moral.

Nonetheless, Gandhi became fully aware how high an ideal a truly moral politics presented. After returning to India, Gandhi realized that *satyagraha* and *brahmacharya* would have to be reconciled to mass politics. *An Autobiography* concludes with Gandhi's 'Himalayan miscalculation' concerning the readiness of masses on a national scale to engage in nonviolent direct action, which we explore in Section 27.4.3.

27.4.3 Miscalculation: moral politics and the masses

After more narrowly focused campaigns against local exploitation of workers and peasants, Gandhi entered all-India politics in 1919, when the British government proposed bills that would severely restrict civil liberties. In response, Gandhi undertook his first *national* civil disobedience campaign.

In attempting to build an organization and sustain discipline, however, Gandhi realized with disappointment that 'partiality for exciting work, dislike for quiet constructive effort' characterized 'the popular attitude' (ibid.: 463). Ultimately, Gandhi had to call off the *satyagraha*. Some Indians had interpreted civil disobedience as destructive lawlessness. Meanwhile, British authorities had reacted violently and repressively to Indian 'disturbances': most shockingly, British-directed Indian troops massacred an unarmed gathering at the Jallianwala Bagh in Amritsar.

This was Gandhi's 'miscalculation' of 'Himalayan magnitude': he realized he had blundered gravely in inviting 'the people . . . to launch civil disobedience prematurely', before they were truly 'qualified' (ibid.: 470, 469). Civil disobedience demanded moral fitness and lawfulness. Only those who respected the law and knew how to obey it had 'qualified themselves' to judge whether specific laws were morally fit (ibid.: 470). In face of lawlessness, Gandhi corrected his course. Mass education in *satyagraha* would need to precede further campaigns. However, even in this, he found volunteers few and unresponsive to methodical training (ibid.: 471).

Despite the setback, in 1920, the Indian National Congress called upon Gandhi to design another nationwide resistance campaign. Gandhi proposed an all-India non-cooperation campaign, based on the idea that, in a situation in which only mere thousands of British persons on the ground ruled a country of more than three hundred million, imperial domination could not be maintained without Indians' cooperation; therefore, Indians should nonviolently withdraw their physical collaboration and moral complicity with British power. Inspired by Henry David Thoreau (see Key Thinker: Henry David Thoreau box) but different from civil disobedience per se, non-cooperation would subtract Indians' participation in their own subjugation and thus 'paralyse the mightiest government on earth' (Gandhi, 1987: vol. III, 137). Instead of negating a bad law as civil disobedience did, non-cooperation simply withheld force from bad authority. Non-cooperation involved therefore not a defiance of unjust laws but a mere refusal to continue buying British-made products, rejection of British services and institutions, even resignation from administrative posts (Shridharani, 1962: 34–42). The colonized would then substitute these with their own goods and services—Indian schools, locally produced cloth—and thus empower themselves, constructing *swaraj* while weakening imperial authority.

Key Thinker: Henry David Thoreau

Henry David Thoreau (1817–1862) weighs what a citizen owes to an unjust government in 'On the Duty of Civil Disobedience', which inspired Gandhi's thinking on resistance to unjust laws. Thoreau was jailed for refusing to pay his poll tax in protest at the US government's war on Mexico in 1846, which greatly extended the territorial scope of slavery. The essay justifies Thoreau's civil disobedience from participating in the distant injustice which his tax revenue would have supported. Although Thoreau's essay turns on the individual's conscientious objection to a democratic majority's complicity with or active contribution to state injustice, Gandhi found a way to make conscientious non-cooperation a *collective* endeavour for anti-colonial protest against non-democratic imperial authorities. The refusal not merely to pay the salt tax but, more defiantly, Gandhi's incitement of Indians to manufacture salt and raid government salt works bear Thoreau's influence but goes further.

Gandhi calls non-cooperation the 'only true resistance to the Government' and 'an inalienable right of the people' (Gandhi, 1993: 482). However, the *Autobiography* ends its narrative in 1920. Gandhi could have, but does not, recount the further trials of wedding moral principles to mass politics and the tragedies that ensued. Mass direct action continued to be fraught with the danger of descending into 'mobocracy' (Gandhi, 1987: vol. III, 146–151). Gandhi warned of mobocracy in 1920, little realizing that two years later it would arise in its most extreme form. In 1922, in Chauri

Chaura, a demonstrating crowd retaliated against the Indian police who fired at it by burning down the police station with officers inside, killing 25 persons altogether. Stunned, Gandhi called off once again an all-India campaign, yet omitted this fact from the narrative of his experiments in truth.

> **27.4 *Autobiography*: struggle towards nonviolence: Key Points**
>
> - Gandhi's *Autobiography* narrates his early activism in a misleading way, especially on racial questions.
> - Although Gandhi experienced racial discrimination in southern Africa, he was prejudiced against Indian indentured servants and African peoples.
> - Gandhi linked mental and bodily self-purification to altruistic service during the Bambatha Rebellion.
> - In India, Gandhi miscalculated the masses' moral fitness for civil disobedience and non-cooperation, leading him to call off nationwide campaigns.

27.5 Campaigns of nonviolent resistance: theory and practice

Gandhi's sudden command to demobilize the Non-Cooperation Movement stunned and disoriented Congress and the tens of thousands of Indians who came to participate in or follow anti-colonial national politics. Gandhi's decision to reverse the nationwide mobilization altogether because of sporadic local violence seemed opaque, monocratic, almost arbitrary. Congress leaders grew frustrated at Gandhi's utopian demand for moral purity from themselves and the newly mobilized masses. Nevertheless, years later, Congress's Working Committee decided to entrust to him yet again the conduct of a national campaign. By 1930–1931, the success of the Salt Satyagraha (or the Salt March, an act of nonviolent civil disobedience) allowed Gandhi to disprove his critics. The March to Dandi to produce salt and the national civil disobedience campaign it unleashed merit their fame (Dalton, 2012: Chapter 4). In executing this Salt Satyagraha, Gandhi proved himself a brilliant strategist and able leader of mass nonviolent direct action.

Gandhi had called the British authorities' tax on salt an 'injustice' already in *Hind Swaraj* (Gandhi, 1997: 19–20) and considered defying the salt tax in an earlier campaign. Though the choice amused his colleagues, Gandhi considered salt the perfect symbol of imperial domination. The tax affected all Indians, 'regardless of religion, caste, class or gender' (Brown, 2011: 53), but fell especially hard on the poorest households and functioned effectively as a regressive tax. Salt is necessary for human life, so none could avoid paying the tax. The law, moreover, prohibited Indians from making their own salt, thus proscribing a village industry in which the poor had been employed. In order to protect the imperial government's monopoly, officers would destroy salt that naturally accumulated on seashores, so that none could partake of nature's bounty (Gandhi, 1999: vol. 49: 1). The India Salt Act (1882) solidified imperial domination, but also intensified market domination by preventing both subsistence production and use of the commons. Finally, salt, though economically affecting entire households, unevenly burdened women in the gendered division of labour, forcing them to make difficult decisions about cooking expenses (Sarkar, 2011: 185).

Defiance of the tax also was less likely to generate violent reactions, whether by protesters, bystanders, or imperial authorities (Brown, 2011: 53), than had happened in 1922. Nevertheless, Gandhi had carefully programmed curbs on possible violence in his vision of the *satyagraha*. By the time of the Salt Satyagraha, he had more or less resolved three principal challenges represented by three groups: (1) the masses, who were ignorant of both the theory and the practice of nonviolence; (2) the Congress leaders, who could grasp the basic theory of nonviolence but practised it only instrumentally to advance their political goals; and (3) the 'revolutionary terrorists' (Chandra et al.,

1989: Chapter 20), whose theory of *swaraj* by violence Gandhi rejected but whose practical commitment to *swaraj* he admired.

The first challenge stemmed from Gandhi's 'Himalayan miscalculation' and concerns about 'mobocracy' (Chatterjee, 1986: 102–110; Guha, 1997: 135–150). Gandhi was forced again to reckon with how to reconcile the deep morality of *satyagraha* with mass politics on a national scale. Which persons were morally fit for how much direct action? In principle, Gandhi still maintained that it was possible to teach the masses the theory of nonviolence, but since doing so would involve much time and patience (Gandhi, 1999: vol. 48: 185–186), merely practising nonviolence by following the model provided by others would suffice in the meantime. Hence, the masses need not understand the theory of *ahimsa*, nor would they need to make decisions about its practice. They need only comply externally with the discipline imposed on them by trained leaders. Gandhi no longer expected the perfect alignment of theory and practice uniformly for all involved: 'Those who follow us may dispense with the rigid discipline we are going through, but for us there is no escape' (ibid.: vol. 48: 450). People could be followers of *satyagraha* and not *satyagrahis* per se.

Accordingly, Gandhi planned the *satyagraha* carefully from start to finish: 'my intention is to start the movement only through the inmates of the Ashram and those who have submitted to its discipline and assimilated the spirit of its methods' (ibid.: vol. 48: 348). He set out from near Ahmedabad with his walking stick and a hand-picked cadre of 78 trained *satyagrahis* for the 24-day march to Dandi. Tens of thousands, including newsreel filmographers and journalists, accompanied the march's progress, but the main action was confined to Gandhi and his cadre until he gave the signal on the morning of 6 April 1930. Gandhi would be the first to break the salt law by gathering natural sea salt. Others could then imitate him.

Riskier direct action likely to elicit physical repression from authorities required even more careful orchestration because *ahimsa* itself could be discredited by one undisciplined reaction. Jailed, Gandhi authorized only the most rigorously trained volunteers to participate in the Dharasana Salt Works protest in May 1930, because it would involve marching to the government-owned salt works to repossess it from the colonizers. When the police clubbed people in the first column without any response on their part, other protesters took away the injured, some with cracked skulls. Then the next columns would advance in perfect formation, each in turn meeting the same violence. Officers injured 320 protesters and killed two. Globally, media coverage of the brutal reaction to the Dharasana protest swayed public opinion against the British Raj. Within India, the flawless execution of committed suffering and bravery in the face of police repression set the example for subsequent raids by untrained masses (Chandra et al., 1989: 275).

Gandhi's second challenge leading up to the Salt Satyagraha involved confronting scepticism by already mobilized elites rather than masses of supposed novices at resistance. Many members of the Indian National Congress viewed *satyagraha* as a political weapon and not a religious creed. Their scepticism raised fundamental questions: Gandhi's declared 'ambition' was 'no less than to convert the British people through non-violence, and thus make them see the wrong they have done to India' (Gandhi, 1999: vol. 48: 366), but how could he expect to convert perpetrators while accompanied by apostate colleagues? Gandhi resolved this question by refusing any longer to demand moral purity. Ends and means need not coincide with motive. Both he and the sceptics in Congress wanted the same end, *swaraj*, by the same means, nonviolent civil disobedience; however, they accepted the means not for moral reasons—its rightness—but for political reasons: it produced results. This accommodation involved delicate calibrations between *Realpolitik* and idealism (Chatterjee, 1986: 108; Mantena, 2012). Accommodating *ahimsa* as 'mere policy', Gandhi consecrated the instrumentalization of nonviolent direct action.

Gandhi's biggest challenge around the time of the Salt Satyagraha, however, came from those who charismatically embraced physical force. He decried this 'cult of the bomb', 'cult of violence', and 'cult of political assassination' (Gandhi, 1999: vol. 48: 184; vol. 51: 385, 415). His most formidable rival in this regard was Bhagat Singh (see Key Thinker: Bhagat Singh box). Bhagat Singh and another young comrade from the Hindustan Socialist Republican Association threw a homemade bomb deliberately into an empty section of the Central Assembly in 1929. They allowed themselves to be arrested while shouting 'Down with imperialism!' Their goal had not been to harm anyone but rather to spotlight Indian politicians' collaboration with British imperialism and capitalism. Singh and colleagues had also assassinated a British officer the year before to avenge the death of the radical leader Lala Lajpat Rai. Singh's court statements redrew the line between *himsa* and *ahimsa*. The contemporaneous manifesto 'Philosophy of the Bomb' distinguished different uses of force: 'Force when aggressively applied is "violence" and is therefore morally unjustifiable, but when it is used in the furtherance of a legitimate cause, it has its moral justification' (Singh, 2007: 20). The point was not to employ force for its own sake. Singh disowned the label of terrorist (ibid.: 48). Whether force counted as violence depended on its ultimate aim.

Key Thinker: Bhagat Singh

By suddenly suspending the Non-Cooperation Movement in 1922, Gandhi had alienated many from mainstream anti-colonial politics altogether, including Bhagat Singh (1907–1931) (Lal, 2007). Singh went on to develop a more radical anti-capitalist critique of both British imperialism and Congress politics. He espoused socialist revolution, including the use of force, as the most just path to *swaraj*, and also avowed atheism in criticism of religious communalist tensions. With comrades, he formed the Hindustan Socialist Republican Association, which executed some spectacular actions, including an assassination of a British officer. Jailed after throwing a bomb in the Central Assembly, Singh staged well-publicized hunger strikes against prison conditions and influenced anti-colonial debates nationally with his eloquent statements in court. More than an assassin and supposed terrorist, Bhagat Singh was above all a subtle theorist of the uses of force and of class exploitation (Chandra et al., 1989: Chapter 20).

The revolutionaries' charisma, dramatic deeds, and seductive contention that the struggle for *swaraj* contemplated justifiable force compelled Gandhi to respond. He faced a storm of criticism for not interceding with the Viceroy forcefully enough to prevent Singh's death sentence. Gandhi thus walked a fine line in statements after Singh's hanging. He professed admiration but distinguished Singh's detestable 'deed'—'political murders'—from Singh's model 'spirit of bravery and sacrifice' (Gandhi, 1999: vol. 51: 385). To Gandhi, deliberate use of physical force only signalled 'despair' and 'helplessness' (ibid.: vol. 51: 320, 316). He considered it mindless and emotional. Gandhi could not envisage that one could argue rationally and reasonably for instrumental uses of physical force as Singh and his colleagues had done, even though, conversely, Gandhi conceded to Congress's sceptics an instrumental-rational argument for nonviolence.

27.5 Campaigns of nonviolent resistance: theory and practice: Key Points

- The Salt Satyagraha mobilized masses of Indians to produce salt in protest of a British tax and was a symbolic and strategic success.
- In the years leading up to the campaign, Gandhi had resolved three challenges to the theory and practice of nonviolent resistance.
- He no longer expected strict discipline from the masses and accepted that *satyagraha* could be a political instrument rather than a religious creed.
- Gandhi also honoured revolutionaries' political commitment while rejecting their methods.

27.6 Conclusion

Gandhi left an enormous legacy, stoked many controversies, and his ideas influenced many political resistance movements. One of Gandhi's most familiar legacies internationally was the adaptation of nonviolent direct action for the civil rights struggles of African-Americans in the United States during the 1950s and 1960s. Bayard Rustin (2015) carefully studied Gandhi's writings and visited India before becoming an important architect and theorist of the struggle for US racial equality and, later, gay rights. Rustin was one of several Gandhian influences on Martin Luther King, Jr, who incorporated nonviolent direct action in his most famous campaign in Alabama in 1963. Controversially, King mobilized children, even though protesters were threatened with police clubs and viciously trained dogs. In his account, including his famous 'Letter from Birmingham Jail', King invokes Gandhi as a model (King, 1964).

Yet before Gandhi could become a model for African-American Protestant Christian thinker-activists, Gandhi's ideas had to be cut loose from Hindu spiritualism. In some way, Gandhi had already performed this decontextualization in 1930, when he endorsed nonviolent resistance as a policy for sceptical Congress leaders rather than strictly a religious creed. Gandhi thus turned *satyagraha* into a political technique by sanctioning the possibility of a disjuncture between spirituality and politics.

Others, too, contributed to this secularization and instrumentalization. Krishnalal Shridharani insisted in *War without Violence* that 'this strategy of Satyagraha is no Oriental mystic doctrine baffling the Occidental mind but a hard-headed mass pressure technique . . . which can be utilised anywhere by any group or nation' (Shridharani, 1962: 1). Richard Gregg, a US citizen who travelled to India to investigate Gandhian theory and practice, published *The Power of Nonviolence* in 1934, in which he famously calls nonviolent direct action 'moral jiu-jitsu' (Gregg, 2018), and later sent the book to King (Immerwahr, 2007: 293). Continuing this trend, Gene Sharp's manual for nonviolent resistance *From Dictatorship to Democracy* (Sharp, 2010) mentions Gandhi not once but elaborates undeniably Gandhian techniques. Focus of the documentary *How to Start a Revolution* (dir. Arrow, 2011), Sharp was credited inaccurately as a principal influence on the anti-government activists of the Arab Spring in the 2010s. Sharp's mentors Arne Næss and Johan Galtung advanced Gandhian ideas in the areas of deep ecology and peace and conflict studies.

Scholars in the North Atlantic academy have studied Gandhi as political theorist since the 1970s but have tended to be hagiographic (Parekh, 1999; Iyer, 2000; Godrej, 2011; Dalton, 2012). However, figures in Subaltern Studies subjected Gandhi to incisive critique in the 1980s for his elitism (Chatterjee, 1986; Guha, 1997). A later generation reverted to more affirmative engagements by probing Gandhi's paradoxical ethics for politico-theological interpretations of sovereignty and unconditional giving (Mehta, 2010; Kumar, 2015; Skaria, 2016).

Antiracist and feminist critiques of Gandhi serve as counterweights to these more forgiving deconstructive analyses. Gender has played an important role in Gandhian scholarship. Gandhi may have subverted anti-colonial Indian masculinities, as Ashis Nandy argued (Nandy, 1983; 1987), but his words and deeds concerning women and sexuality are troubling, if nonetheless occasionally progressive enough to seem 'feminist' (Kishwar, 1985; Patel, 1988). Women in resistance campaigns pushed him out of his comfort zone, though. Gandhi originally forbade women to participate in the Salt March to Dandi, but commended militant women in subsequent salt-tax protests in a backhanded way: they 'acted with rare courage and calmness. But they would have done better to remain outside the venue of the men's fight' (Gandhi, 1999: vol. 49: 115). On one hand, he saw women as lacking the capacity for the rigours of political resistance. On the other, he used women to test his own capacity for *brahmacharya* by sleeping naked near young women towards the end of his life.

Gandhi's early racist ideas about Africans and the civilizational superiority of educated Indians have been scrutinized by Desai and Vahed (2016) and Roy (2014). His conceptions about *adivasis* (Indigenous peoples) were uninformed but suggested a similar civilizationist bias (Sarkar,

2011: 177–178). Thus, despite Mandela's honouring Gandhi as an early fighter against apartheid, anti-apartheid militants 'were breaking with Gandhi's politics, not carrying on his legacy' (Roy, 2014: 87) of prejudice against Africans, tribal societies, and descendants of indentured Asians.

Sankaran Krishna (2014) argues that Gandhi's anti-Black racism in South Africa parallels his casteism. Gandhi did pressure fellow privileged-caste Hindus to reform themselves and accept oppressed-caste persons and Dalits into quotidian and ritual activities and spaces. However, he conceived oppressed-caste 'uplift' as occurring from the top down and diminished and resisted Dalit-led initiatives (Sarkar, 2011: 178–184; Roy 2014). Likewise, in rejecting B.R. Ambedkar's representation of the grievances of fellow Dalits, Gandhi pompously insisted: 'I claim myself in my own person to represent the vast mass of the Untouchables' (Ambedkar, 2014b: 315). Ambedkar famously clashed with Gandhi over oppressed-caste politics and policy. In *Annihilation of Caste* (Ambedkar, 2014a), published in 1936, Ambedkar offered an unstinting critique of caste Hinduism. He ultimately advocated Dalits' right to exit Hinduism and caste-oppressive society altogether by religious conversion. Gandhi contended that 'untouchability' was ultimately a matter *internal* to Hinduism; therefore, Dalits must neither convert nor make autonomous political claims but rather await Hindus' repentant self-reform (Krishna, 2014). The Dalit Panthers, a Mumbai-based group inspired by the US Black nationalist group, The Black Panther Party, lambasted Gandhi for sacrificing Dalits at the altar of national unity (Dalit Panthers, 1986 [1973]).

Gandhi is more than an icon but was a paradoxical and controversial figure. He considered modern civilization the root cause of Indian subjugation, not British wrong per se, and found the path to Indian self-rule in moral duty. He launched his career against Africans and indentured Indians and struggled to translate his theory of *satyagraha* into mass practice. Nonetheless, he influenced the course of world politics through his innovative campaigns of nonviolent resistance. Globally, the Salt Satyagraha served as a model for nonviolent protest against white supremacy and dictatorship, despite Gandhi's own troubling views of race, caste, civilization, and gender. Although Gandhi aimed to rectify the political inequality between colonizer and colonized, and although his counterintuitive model for political resistance clearly inspired many, Gandhi's record on other kinds of inequalities was mixed and sometimes troubling.

Take your learning further by accessing the online resources for a library of web links to relevant videos, articles, blogs, and useful websites for this chapter: www.oup.com/he/Ramgotra-Choat1e.

Study questions

1. Why might nonviolent resistance demand, as Gandhi claimed, greater strength than would violence?
2. To what extent did Gandhi dilute the moral force of *satyagraha* by conceding to sceptics that it could be an instrumental technique instead of a spiritual creed?
3. Why was strategy so important to Gandhian nonviolent direct action?
4. How did the mass media contribute to Gandhi's success as an activist and to the success of his campaigns?

VIOLENCE, POWER, AND RESISTANCE

5. Regarding *satyagraha*, how does one distinguish the spectacle of suffering for truth as a morally legitimate appeal to another's conscience from moral or emotional manipulation?
6. Did Gandhi's hunger strikes constitute a morally coercive form of self-violence, as some have claimed?
7. What are the most persuasive arguments for and against removing public statues of Gandhi?
8. How does Gandhi's conception of 'civilization' aim to dismantle the colonizer-colonized relation yet simultaneously advance other inequalities?

Further reading

Primary sources

Brown, J. (ed.) (2008) *Mahatma Gandhi, The Essential Writings*, new edn. Oxford: Oxford World's Classics.
    This edition excerpts Gandhi's most important autobiographical and political writings.

Iyer, R. (ed.) (1987) *The Moral and Political Writings of Mahatma Gandhi*, 3 vols. Oxford: Clarendon Press.
    This comprehensive selection surveys Gandhi's copious oeuvre by theme and topic.

Secondary sources

Brown, J. and Parel, A. (eds) (2011) *Cambridge Companion to Gandhi*. Cambridge: Cambridge University Press.
    This volume presents aspects of Gandhi's thought, career, and reception in chapters written by experts across disciplines.

Chatterjee, P. (1986) *Nationalist Thought and the Colonial World: A Derivative Discourse?* London: Zed Books.
    Chatterjee situates Gandhi's political theory as a moment in the development of anti-colonial nationalist thought in India and compares anti-colonial nationalism to nationalist thought as it unfolded in Europe.

Coward, H. (ed.) (2003) *Indian Critiques of Gandhi*. Albany, NY: State University of New York Press.
    This multi-authored collection dedicates chapters to critiques of Gandhi by individuals and groups active in South Asian politics during his lifetime.

Dalton, D. (2012) *Mahatma Gandhi: Nonviolent Power in Action*, new edn. New York: Columbia University Press.
    This study interprets Gandhi's ideas in relation to key campaigns and by comparison to other thinkers, including Malcolm X.

Desai, A. and Vahed, G. (2016) *The South African Gandhi: Stretcher-Bearer of Empire*. Stanford, CA: Stanford University Press.
    This history of Gandhi's formative years as activist in South Africa critically reconstructs his anti-African views and distrust of indentured Indians' own traditions of resistance.

Parekh, B. (1999) *Colonialism, Tradition and Reform: An Analysis of Gandhi's Political Discourse*, rev. edn. New Delhi: Sage.
    Parekh's classic study contextualizes Gandhi's political theory as it emerges out of South Asian and Hindu traditions.

Roy, A. (2014) 'The Doctor and the Saint'. In B.R. Ambedkar, *Annihilation of Caste*, the Annotated Critical Edition. Delhi: Navayana Publishing.
    Roy's book-length essay analyses the clash between Gandhi and Ambedkar on caste privilege and racial inequality.

References

Ambedkar, B.R. (2014a) *Annihilation of Caste*. Annotated critical edn. Delhi: Navayana Publishing.

Ambedkar, B.R. (2014b) *Dr Babasaheb Ambedkar: Writings and Speeches*, vol. 5. New Delhi: Dr Ambedkar Foundation.

Amin, S. (1988) 'Gandhi as Mahatma'. In R. Guha and G. Spivak (eds), *Selected Subaltern Studies*. New York: Oxford University Press, pp. 288–348.

Augustine of Hippo. (1951) *Commentary on the Lord's Sermon on the Mount with Seventeen Related Sermons*. Trans. D. Kavanaugh. Washington, DC: Catholic University of America Press.

Barnargarwala, T. (2019) 'Debate Rages n About Gandhi's Legacy in Africa: Gandhi Statue in Africa to Be Relocated 3 Months After It Was Pulled Down'. *Indian Express*, 5 March: https://indianexpress.com/article/world/debate-rages-on-about-gandhis-legacy-in-africa-gandhi-statue-in-ghana-to-be-relocated-3-months-after-it-was-pulled-down-5611009/ (accessed 3 February 2021).

Brown, J. (2011) 'Gandhi as Nationalist Leader, 1915–1948'. In J. Brown and A. Parel (eds), *The Cambridge Companion to Gandhi*. New York: Cambridge University Press, pp. 51–68.

Chakrabarty, D. (2002) *Habitations of Modernity: Essays in the Wake of Subaltern Studies*. Chicago: University of Chicago Press.

Chandra, B., et al. (1989) *India's Struggle for Independence*. New Delhi: Penguin Books.

Chatterjee, P. (1986) *Nationalist Thought and the Colonial World: A Derivative Discourse?* London: Zed Books.

Dalit Panthers (1986 [1973]) 'Dalit Panthers Manifesto'. In B. Joshi (ed.), *Untouchable! Voices of the Dalit Liberation Movement*. London/New Delhi: Minority Rights Group/Zed Books, pp. 141–147.

Dalton, D. (2012) *Mahatma Gandhi: Nonviolent Power in Action*. New York: Columbia University Press.

Desai, A. and Vahed, G. (2016) *The South African Gandhi: Stretcher-Bearer of Empire*. Stanford, CA: Stanford University Press.

Gandhi, M. (1987) *The Moral and Political Writings of Mahatma Gandhi*, 3 vols. Ed. R. Iyer. Oxford: Clarendon Press.

Gandhi, M. (1993) *An Autobiography: The Story of My Experiments with Truth*. Trans. M. Desai. Boston: Beacon Press.

Gandhi, M. (1997) *Hind Swaraj and Other Writings*. Ed. A. Parel. Cambridge: Cambridge University Press.

Gandhi, M. (1999) *The Collected Works of Mahatma Gandhi (Electronic Book)*, 98 vols. New Delhi: Publications Division, Government of India.

Ghose, A. (1952) *The Doctrine of Passive Resistance*. Pondicherry: Sri Aurobindo Ashram.

Godrej, F. (2011) *Cosmopolitan Political Thought: Method, Practice, Discipline*. New York: Oxford University Press.

Gregg, R. (2018) *The Power of Nonviolence*. Cambridge: Cambridge University Press.

Guha, R. (1997) *Dominance without Hegemony: History and Power in Colonial India*. Cambridge, MA: Harvard University Press.

Heehs, P. (1993) *The Bomb in Bengal: The Rise of Revolutionary Terrorism in India, 1900–1910*. Delhi: Oxford University Press.

Hofmeyr, I. (2011) 'Violent Texts, Vulnerable Ideas: *Hind Swaraj* and Its South African Audiences'. *Public Culture*, 23(2): 285–297.

Hyslop, J. (2011) 'Gandhi, 1869–1915: The Transnational Emergence of a Public Figure'. In J. Brown and A. Parel (eds), *The Cambridge Companion to Gandhi*. New York: Cambridge University Press. pp. 30–50.

Immerwahr, D. (2007) 'Caste or Colony? Indianizing Race in the United States'. *Modern Intellectual History*, 4(2): 275–301.

Iyer, R. (2000) *The Moral and Political Thought of Mahatma Gandhi*, 2nd edn. Delhi: Oxford University Press.

King, Jr, M.L. (1964) *Why We Can't Wait*. New York: Harper & Row.

Kishwar, M. (1985) 'Gandhi on Women'. *Economic and Political Weekly*, 20(41): 1753–1758.

Klausen, J. (2014) 'Economies of Violence: The *Bhagavadītā* and the Fostering of Life in Gandhi's and Ghose's Anticolonial Theories'. *American Political Science Review*, 108(1): 182–195.

Krishna, S. (2014) 'A Postcolonial Racial/Spatial Order: Gandhi, Ambedkar, and the Construction of the International'. In A. Anievas et al. (eds), *Race and Racism in International Relations: Confronting the Global Colour Line*. London: Routledge, pp. 139–156.

Kumar, A. (2015) *Radical Equality: Ambedkar, Gandhi, and the Risk of Democracy*. Stanford, CA: Stanford University Press.

Lake, M., and Reynolds, H. (2008) *Drawing the Global Colour Line: White Men's Countries and the International Challenge of Racial Equality*. Cambridge: Cambridge University Press.

Lal, C. (2007) 'The Revolutionary Legacy of Bhagat Singh'. *Economic and Political Weekly*, 42(37): 3712–3718.

Livingston, A. (2018) 'Fidelity to Truth: Gandhi and the Genealogy of Civil Disobedience'. *Political Theory*, 46(4): 511–536.

Mantena, K. (2012) 'Another Realism: The Politics of Gandhian Nonviolence'. *American Political Science Review*, 106(2): 455–470.

Mehta, U. (2010) 'Gandhi on Democracy, Politics and the Ethics of Everyday Life'. *Modern Intellectual History*, 7(2): 355–371.

Nandy, A. (1983) *The Intimate Enemy: Loss and Recovery of Self under Colonialism*. New Delhi: Oxford University Press.

Nandy, A. (1987) *Traditions, Tyranny, and Utopias: Essays in the Politics of Awareness*. New Delhi: Oxford University Press.

Pandey, G. (1988) 'Peasant Revolt and Indian Nationalism'. In R. Guha and G. Spivak (eds), *Selected Subaltern Studies*. New York: Oxford University Press. pp. 233–287.

Parekh, B. (1999) *Colonialism, Tradition, and Reform: An Analysis of Gandhi's Political Discourse*, rev. edn. New Delhi: Sage.

Patel, S. (1988) 'Construction and Reconstruction of Woman in Gandhi'. *Economic and Political Weekly*, 23(8): 377–387.

Roy, A. (2014) 'The Doctor and the Saint'. In B.R. Ambedkar, *Annihilation of Caste*, Annotated critical edition. Delhi: Navayana Publishing.

Rustin, B. (2015) *Time on Two Crosses: The Collected Writings of Bayard Rustin*. Ed. D. Carbado and D. Weise. 2nd edn. New York: Cleis Press.

Sarkar, T. (2011) 'Gandhi and Social Relations'. In J. Brown and A. Parel (eds), *The Cambridge Companion to Gandhi*. New York: Cambridge University Press. pp. 173–195.

Sharp, G. (2010) *From Dictatorship to Democracy: A Conceptual Framework for Liberation*. 4th edn. East Boston: Albert Einstein Institution.

Shridharani, K. (1962) *War without Violence*. Bombay: Bharatiya Vidya Bhavan.

Singh, B. (2007) *Selected Speeches and Writings*. Ed. D. Gupta. Delhi: National Book Trust.

Skaria, A. (2016) *Unconditional Equality: Gandhi's Religion of Resistance*. Minneapolis, MN: University of Minnesota Press.

Sultan, N. (2020) 'Self-Rule and the Problem of Peoplehood in Colonial India'. *American Political Science Review*, 114(1): 81–94.

Films and documentaries

Arrow. R. (dir.) (2011) *How to Start a Revolution*. The Big Indy.

Attenborough. R. (dir.) (1982) *Gandhi*. Columbia Pictures.

Patel. J. (dir.) (2000) *Dr Babasaheb Ambedkar*. National Film Development Corporation of India.

Santoshi R. (dir.) (2002) *The Legend of Bhagat Singh*. Tips Films.

28 Frantz Fanon

KEALLY MCBRIDE

Chapter guide

This chapter will offer a brief account of Fanon's life and experiences, which provided the material for his analysis of the psychology of racialized colonialism. Section 28.3 will then investigate his account of the psychology of race and gender within a world where such categories operate to organize privileges. Section 28.4 will examine Fanon's discussions about the violence of colonization and decolonization, exploring the use of revolutionary violence. It will conclude with his warnings about the difficulties of transforming liberation movements into long-lasting regimes that provide freedom. Though less explored than his positions on the psychology of oppression and political violence, his predictions about the systemic dysfunctions of postcolonial regimes provide valuable tools for analysing contemporary global politics. Note that there are some terms in this chapter that are likely to trigger offence and other feelings. These terms are cited from Fanon's original work. He uses these terms to convey the racist and pejorative language of white supremacist ideology deployed to dominate Black people.

28.1 Introduction

Frantz Fanon (1925–1961) is best known as the author of *The Wretched of the Earth*, a volume that has been hailed as the handbook for revolutionaries around the globe since its publication in 1961. The book became famous for its declaration that revolutionary violence is an integral part of the process of decolonization: 'At the individual level, violence is a cleansing force. It rids the colonized of their inferiority complex, of their passive and despairing attitude' (Fanon, 2004: 51). As this chapter will explore, Fanon had more ambivalence about the use of violence in achieving liberation than this quotation suggests. While considering violence as a tool for liberation is a central argument that is linked to Fanon, it would be unfortunate to think that this was Fanon's biggest contribution to political thought. It was Fanon's apt combination of his knowledge of individual psychology, the dynamics of political movements, and the social, economic, and racial aspects of colonization that make him a touchstone for anyone interested in resistance and liberation in the twenty-first century. Fanon, as few others have, saw how the systemic and structural aspects of colonization created psychological responses in individuals. This means that achieving decolonization involves overcoming political and economic structures, social practices, cultural assumptions, and personal thoughts and feelings. Contemporary discussions about overcoming internalized racism, sexism, and heteronormativity all owe a great deal to the nuanced observations of Fanon.

28.2 Fanon's life

Frantz Fanon was born in Fort-de-France, the capital of Martinique in 1925; as the son of a customs inspector he was part of the Indigenous elite of the island. Fanon attended a prestigious state secondary school, Victor Schelcher, where one of his teachers was the poet Aimé Césaire, the founder of the *négritude* movement (see Key Thinker: Aimé Césaire). Fanon was taught in both public and private to see himself as absolutely French. 'When I am at home my mother sings me French love songs in which there is never a word about Negroes. When I disobey, when I make too much noise, I am told to "stop acting like a nigger"' (Fanon, 1967a: 191). During the Second World War, Fanon joined the army to defend what he considered his country. His subsequent experiences in the French Army led him to understand that he was not considered just another Frenchman; when the French looked at him, they saw above all 'a Negro'. His training camp in Morocco was governed by strict racial hierarchies. Fanon describes his shock with this system: 'I came into the world imbued with the will to find a meaning in things, my spirit filled with the desire to attain to the source of the world, and then found that I was an object in the midst of other objects' (ibid.: 109). He could not be seen for the person he was or define his own identity; he was 'an object' as opposed to a French citizen. He greatly struggled with the dissonance between the multidimensional person he knew himself to be, and the assumptions that were affixed to him by the French people. Nonetheless, his bitter disappointment in France did not prevent him from returning to the country in 1946 to start medical training.

Key Thinker: Aimé Césaire

Césaire (1913–2008) was a renowned poet, an elected leader, and Fanon's teacher and political mentor on Martinique. Césaire's words make many appearances in Fanon's texts, even though their conceptualizations of political struggle differed from one another. Husband and wife, Aimé and Suzanne Césaire were founders of the *négritude* movement, advocating for a revaluation of Black culture. They believed in a shared essence of Blackness that included cultural practices and ways of perceiving the world. In order to repudiate the systemic disparagement of Black culture inherent in colonialism, they articulated a new perspective on Blackness that valorized it as a common source of strength. A slogan that took its inspiration from the *négritude* movement was 'Black is Beautiful.' Césaire embraced communism and was elected and served as a member of the French National Assembly from Martinique under the communist banner. Later, he resigned from the *Parti Communist Français* (PCF) believing that a purely communist framework was not enough to overcome the damages of colonialism.

Initially, Fanon started a dentistry programme in Paris, but then left the city to pursue a medical degree in Lyon. He specialized in psychiatry. Fanon's exploration of Black identity within racialized colonialism was deeply influenced by his psychiatric training under François Tosquelles at the hospital Saint-Alban-sur-Limagnole. Tosquelles pioneered the idea of social therapy, arguing that mental illness was frequently accompanied by social alienation. Treating one would require addressing them both. Saint-Albans was set up to encourage social interaction and to give patients power within the hospital environment in order to give them a sense of agency. Fanon would continue similar innovations in treatment in his own medical practice during his career that were motivated by the insight that treating illness should also involve addressing injustice.

He started exploring themes of racial consciousness, personal identity, and colonial relationships by writing a volume that would eventually be published as *Black Skin, White Masks* (1952). The book was originally submitted as his medical thesis, but it was refused, in part because of its unusual way of making arguments. Adam Schatz has described its style as 'a dazzling work of bricolage, combining psychiatry, phenomenology, sociology, literary criticism and sudden eruptions of poetry (his debt to Césaire remained profound)' (Shatz, 2017). The volume offers two fundamental insights. First, oppressive social relations bring about twisted psychic results in individuals. Second, the experience of being a Black person cannot be separated from the cultural and political forces that define Blackness; what it means to be Black is defined by the projections of Blackness, not anything essential to Blackness itself. Fanon argued it was impossible to escape the projections of what Blackness means, and simply be oneself. Fanon took Georg Wilhelm Friedrich Hegel's basic idea about a master-slave dialectic, and provided many more details with the assistance of modern psychiatry. Even more explosively, he drew out the racial and sexual implications of these power relations, and the distorted experiences of self and sexuality that inevitably accompany them.

Next, Fanon spent three years in Algeria, working in the psychiatric hospital at Blida from 1953–1956 where he became involved in the violent struggle being waged in the colony to achieve independence from France. During his time in the hospital, Fanon treated the Algerian victims of French counterinsurgency, as well as the French soldiers tasked with suppressing the rebellion against French rule. During the bloody conflict, Fanon started to work closely with the National Liberation Front (FLN) in their organizing efforts, and this experience led to his commitment to anti-colonial struggles across the world. The FLN was outlawed, and its members were subject to arrest and torture, so Fanon took on great risks in allowing them to meet at the hospital in Blida, among his other supporting activities. Fanon would spend the rest of his very short life organizing and writing in support of Algerian independence from France and the global project of decolonization before dying of leukaemia in 1961.

The Wretched of the Earth is an analysis of the Algerian struggle and bears the stamp of Fanon's commitment to it, as he refers to Algerians as 'we' continuously throughout the text. Others have noted how odd it was that Fanon dropped his identity as Martinique and French and instead declared himself to be 'Algerian' after such a short time in the country. However, this shift of Fanon's provides a wealth of insight for his readers. His personal rebirth as an Algerian helps provide the key to understanding his assertion that 'Decolonization is truly the creation of new men' (Fanon, 2004: 2). Decolonization means a formerly colonized person is able to move beyond being defined from the outside, from their internalized sense of inferiority, and be reborn as a person who defines themselves and can act in the world (see also Key Concept: Decolonization). By reshaping one's self-conception, and changing one's position in the world, formerly colonized men are reborn with a new identity. Fanon also argued that the women who participated in the struggle for independence also created new possibilities for their identities in the world in an essay entitled, 'Algeria Unveiled'.

Key Concept: Decolonization

Decolonization involves a lot more than simply switching the reins of power from one set of hands to another. The process of colonization has created economies, cultural patterns, and systems of knowledge that support and serve to naturalize the rule of one culture over others. History must be rewritten, languages and religions recovered, educational systems must be reformulated, in order to start to address some of these issues. This was one reason that newly independent countries argued for the founding of UNESCO in order to highlight the historical contributions of cultures around the globe. Decolonization also means changing the patterns of self-understanding and behavioural patterns of those who have been colonized. This interior transformation was discussed by revolutionary leaders such as Ho Chi Minh, Gandhi (see Chapter 27), and Malcolm X.

Fanon's personal experience of several different colonies made it possible for him to write a more generalized narrative of decolonization as a historical process. In *The Wretched of the Earth*, he assumes the position of an outsider, illuminating the transnational struggle for decolonization.

Read more about **Fanon's** life and work by accessing the thinker biography on the online resources: www.oup.com/he/Ramgotra-Choat1e.

He describes the beliefs and ideologies of the revolution, with the insights one would expect from a participant in the struggle. But his training as a psychiatrist meant he was also an acute clinical observer. His descriptions detail the psychology of revolutionary struggle without being constrained by it. Fanon's personal history and training provided this exceptional perspective on what was unfolding as a furious political event in colony after colony at this particular historical juncture. For Fanon, the personal was political, and the political defined how we saw ourselves and others. His books describe this remarkable historical moment that ended formal colonization in the most personal and intimate terms. This is why his books were read in prison cells around the globe, and leaders from Oakland, California to Belfast, Northern Ireland thought that he spoke to their dilemmas, doubts, anger, and confusion. Even more importantly, he offered ideas about how the whole system of racialized colonization could be changed.

> ### 28.2 Fanon's life: Key Points
>
> - Fanon experienced French colonization in a number of different locales, and thereby gained insight into the colonial system more broadly.
> - Fanon combined his training as a psychiatrist with his political observations to develop a unique understanding of colonization as a process that becomes internalized by colonial subjects.
> - Fanon saw mental illness in relation to social injustice, and argued that changes in the world were necessary in order to overcome individual alienation and tendencies towards self-destruction.

28.3 Race, gender, and psychology

Without a doubt, one of Fanon's most important contributions to political thought was his analysis of the psychological impacts of colonialism and white supremacy more broadly. Although Fanon was focused on the legacies of colonialism, his work clearly has strong resonance in any society that has experienced systematic racial disparities. While fictional works such as Algerian-born author Albert Camus's *The Stranger* (1989 [1942]) had explored the alienation experienced in a colonial context, there had not been a systematic attempt to link together the political, economic, and social processes of colonization with the psychology of those subjected to them. As Fanon pointed out, 'The problem of colonialism includes not only the interrelations of objective historical conditions but also human attitudes towards these conditions' (Fanon, 1967a: 84). These human attitudes include our conceptions of others (which often remain unspoken) and our ambivalent feelings about ourselves.

Often feelings of insecurity, self-hatred and self-destructive tendencies are considered 'pathological'—a psychological disorder. *Black Skin, White Masks* explains how conditions in a colony would result in these behaviours; systemic social injustice creates psychological disorders. Fanon's descriptions of these psychological disorders are as intricate and complex as human emotions and thoughts tend to be. Fanon uses his own experiences as a basis for his analysis, so he generally speaks from the position of a Black man. It is helpful to conceive of his argument as a series of dialectics: a dynamic between two forces or terms put in relation to one another. For example, our understanding of strength impacts what we consider weakness, and those who wish to be viewed as strong will take care to position themselves apart from what they consider to be weakness. Identities are formed through a dialectical process; we start to understand who we are in relation to others and by observing differences and similarities. But these social relations and observations do not happen without being influenced by existing power relations between individuals and groups. Fanon argued that the colonial world impacts these processes of individual and group identification in particularly stark ways. Most distressing is the fact that we are frequently unaware that the most intimate thoughts and feelings that we have are not a result of some inner truth, but instilled from the outside. '[T]he collective unconscious, without our having to fall back on the genes, is purely and simply the sum of prejudices, myths, collective attitudes of a given group' (ibid.: 188).

First, Fanon identifies the dialectic between who is considered a subject and who is treated as an object in the colonial environment. The colonizer 'creates history' and is able to move through the environment and gain benefits from it. The colonized person is denied the same kind of agency, and instead is defined and treated as something to be controlled and changed. In the colony, the colonizer is a subject, meaning someone who creates the world and their path through it; the colonized is an object, someone who is at the mercy of their environment as opposed to being able to actualize themselves fully.

Fanon describes his struggle with being considered an incomplete person within this context: 'Nevertheless with all my strength I refuse to accept that amputation. I feel in myself a soul as immense as the world, truly a soul as deep as the deepest of rivers, my chest has the power to expand without limit. I am a master and I am advised to adopt the humility of the cripple' (ibid.: 140). How do you struggle to assert who you know yourself to be to a world that systematically denies that knowledge? The desire to seize control of one's life and self-definition within an environment that robs a person of the capacity to do so leads to confusion, frustration, and self-loathing. Fanon sees all of these responses being linked to colonization. 'What I want to do is help the black man to free himself of the arsenal of complexes that has been developed by the colonial environment' (ibid.: 30). However, in order to free the Black man from these complexes, they would need to be excavated and made public, so that what was diagnosed or experienced within an individual could be linked to larger historical systems of colonization.

The next dialectic that Fanon describes is the difficult relationship between one's mind and one's body. His body starts to seem like the enemy because it triggers negative responses from the colonial society. 'As I begin to recognize that the Negro is the symbol of sin, I catch myself hating the Negro. But then I recognize that I am a Negro' (ibid.: 197). This is perhaps one of the more difficult arguments that Fanon makes. His body itself makes it impossible to be in the world the way he would like to be in the world. But of course we have no way of being in the world other than through our bodies: 'Wherever he goes, the Negro remains a Negro' (ibid.: 173). Achieving harmony between body and mind means the Black person aspires to be white, or to lose their own body in order to find freedom. Since both of these possibilities are impossible, the colonized person feels trapped in their own body. Fanon asserts: '[T]he black man should no longer be confronted by the dilemma, turn white or disappear' (ibid.: 100).

Fanon's third dialectical relationship is that between two different groups—white and Black, colonizer and colonized, and male and female. The distorted sense of identity encapsulates every person involved in the process of colonization. 'The Negro enslaved by his inferiority, the white man enslaved by his superiority alike behave in accordance with a neurotic orientation' (ibid.: 60). Fanon saw the colonizer and the colonized as being locked into a dialectical relationship. While this formation of the master and slave dialectic originated with Hegel, Fanon takes the next step to argue how the complexities of race exacerbate the relationship of domination.

Culturally, Black and white are juxtaposed as the basic drama of our minds encapsulating instincts of goodness, light, sin and evil. As Fanon highlights, 'in Europe, whether concretely or symbolically, the black man stands for the bad side of the character' (ibid.: 189). You might object that we all have good and bad instincts. Yet this knowledge leads us to repress those elements within ourselves we do not like or value, and reinforce our desired self-conception by refusing contact with the bad elements we encounter in the world. We try and prove to ourselves and others that we as individuals are good and civilized by rejecting the 'dark'.

Fanon's analysis also includes complex considerations about the intersections of racial and gendered identities. *Black Skin, White Masks* addresses interracial sexual relationships which are invariably impacted by unequal racial identities. Fanon wrote, 'I know a great number of girls from Martinique, students in France, who admitted to me with complete candor . . . that they would find it impossible to marry black men' (ibid.: 47–48). Gaining status in the racial hierarchy through sexual liaisons becomes alluring for Black men and Black women alike. Fanon ruminates that being recognized as attractive by a white woman carries a special significance. 'By loving me she proves that I am worthy of white love. I am loved like a white man' (ibid.: 63).

Fanon points to Freud's argument about civilization being conceptualized as increasing power over and control of one's impulses, an increasing alienation from the body that in the end makes human beings unhappy. There is a fascinating convergence with narratives of colonization that state white Europeans are bringing civilization to the untamed Black population, as Fanon says: 'The Negro symbolizes the biological' (ibid.: 167). While this serves as a justification for colonialism, it also ends up feeding the insecurities of the white people. White men fear the sexual prowess of Black men, a dynamic that is exposed with lynching. Fanon mimics the thoughts and words of white people by stating: 'As for the Negroes, they have tremendous sexual powers. What do you expect, with all the freedom they have in the jungles! They copulate at all times and in all places' (ibid.: 157). This narrative serves many purposes, including justifying external control over the colonized population, and articulates a fundamental dividing line between white and Black populations. This logic also rationalizes violence against Black men by framing them as inherently uncontrolled and threatening. Yet it also haunts white male identity as they fear they are less powerful and less attractive than Black men. Fanon points out that the narratives of colonialism trap all participants into playing prescribed roles.

Key Concept: Psychopathology

Psychopathology is the scientific study of the source and effects of mental disorders. It is important to recognize the social origins of some illnesses, so we do not simply label victims of social discrimination as deviant or ill-adjusted. Fanon linked what was previously considered individual mental illness to social conditions, pointing to patterns of mental disturbances in his patients. To provide one example, our first instinct might be to label excessive hand washing as an individual psychological disorder (such as Obsessive-Compulsive Disorder). However, if the patient is trying to wash the Blackness off her skin, then Fanon points out this is a response to the social realities of white supremacy, not necessarily a mental illness that comes from individual pathology. In some ways, this desire to erase Blackness is a rational response to the devaluation of Black bodies in the world, and yet it causes great distress and social alienation for the individual engaging in this behaviour.

Fanon argued that healing the self and healing the world need to happen in conjunction with one another. Here he talks about the difficulties of reconciling mind and body, self-conception and social presence, and restoring a sense of agency to his patients:

> [I]f society makes difficulties for him because of his color, if in his dreams I establish the expression of an unconscious desire to change color, my objective will not be that of dissuading him from it by advising him from it by advising him to 'keep his place'; on the contrary, my objective, once his motivations have been brought into consciousness, will be to put him in a position to *choose* action (or passivity) with respect to the real source of the conflict—that is, toward the social structures.
>
> (ibid.: 100)

Ultimately, the only way to overcome these psychological pathologies completely is to change the world that played such a central role in creating them. And Fanon's career and life led him to participate in the political struggle that he saw as the only viable solution to the psychopathologies that he had identified.

> ### 28.3 Race, gender, and psychology: Key Points
>
> - Colonization was largely understood as a political and economic process, but Fanon points out how relationships of domination infuse processes of identity construction as well.
> - Individual identity construction happens in relationship with other people; if inequality pervades these relationships, an individual's sense of self can become distorted, and individuals might be unable to accept their identity if it is not as valued as other identities.
> - Overcoming colonization means seizing the opportunity to redefine oneself outside of colonial relationships.

28.4 The violence of colonization and decolonization

Fanon argued, 'Decolonization, which sets out to change the order of the world, is, obviously, a program of complete disorder' (Fanon, 2004:, 2). It might be helpful to draw some parallels between Fanon's and Gandhi's views on decolonization which were very similar, even though the methods they prescribed for achieving it were completely opposed (see also Chapter 27 on Gandhi). Fanon and Gandhi believed decolonization had two aspects. First, both thought that a total critique of the cultural aspects of colonization needed to ground anti-colonial movements. Both had a highly critical approach to the culture, systems of knowledge, and assumptions created by the colonizing power. Second, a refashioning of colonized subjects and their self-conceptions was necessary if countries were to achieve meaningful self-determination. Decolonization—or overcoming rule from outside forces—means interrupting the logic of that political order as well as developing the resources to rule from within.

The first step in overcoming colonial orders is the radical questioning of the logic, knowledge, and attitudes that accompanied colonizers. Gandhi pointed out the importance of standing outside of European civilization in order to repudiate European colonization: 'Those who are intoxicated by modern civilization are not likely to write against it' (Gandhi, 2009: 34). The proposal to stand outside of the current order and question its assumptions is a stance not unfamiliar in the genre of political theory. Friedrich Nietzsche (see Chapter 14) and Jean-Jacques Rousseau (see Chapter 9) were other radical critics who attempted to unearth the foundations of the thinkers who had preceded them. On one level, Fanon's work fits into the tradition of exposing the connections between one group's power and the knowledge that group produces. Edward Said's (1979) *Orientalism* is the most influential exposition of Fanon's basic insight that the structure of European knowledge is deeply complicit in the violence of colonialism (see Chapter 16 on Said). It would be hard to overstate the influence that Fanon's work has played in the development of postcolonial theories of epistemology, identity, and culture (see Jinadu, 1986; Fuss, 1994; McClintock, 1995; Bernasconi, 2001; Stoler, 2002; Gibson, 2003; Gooding-Williams, 2005; Gordon, 2007; Maldonado-Torres, 2007).

The Wretched of the Earth should be read as a guide for individuals, but also a lesson in how to read the motivations, delusions, behaviours, and dynamics of the political landscape at a given time. Fanon spends a great deal of time explaining the anger, insecurities, and desires of a person who has been colonized, as well as the logic of the colonizers. These common responses are not inescapable, but Fanon describes the calculations individuals are most prone to make in order to explain why the most immediate impulses to action might not be the most effective path to liberation.

The first common response to colonization that is described by Fanon is that the colonized person largely accepts the structural violence of colonialism, and tries to avert it by accepting the system of rule. Seeing the overwhelming political, military, and economic advantages of the colonizers, a response from the more privileged colonized people is to recognize the colonial systems in place, and accommodate themselves to them. Anyone who has ever argued that the only path to changing a system comes from working within it might be sympathetic to this response. Fanon knew this response intimately, because he assumed that he would be accepted as a Frenchman as long as he proved himself through the systems established by the French. Many of the relatively privileged colonial subjects might decide to benefit by working through the colonial system of administration. As Fanon explains: 'the colonized intellectual has invested his aggression in his barely veiled wish to be assimilated to the colonizer's world' (Fanon, 1967a: 22). The structure of colonial society rewards those who resemble the colonizers and openly adopt their values. However, Fanon prods his readers to understand that this disidentification from one's own culture and identity can be considered a form of violence against oneself.

Fanon points out that these assimilationist ambitions are ultimately thrown back upon this class of the colonized people. They will never achieve equality within a system that is fundamentally predicated upon their inequality. Furthermore, they will be drawn into participating in the suppression of their fellow colonized subjects. In a 'Letter to the Youth of Africa', Fanon tries to explain the reality of working within the colonial administration; 'every colonized person who today accepts a governmental post must know clearly that he will sooner or later be called upon to sponsor a policy of repression, of massacres, of collective murders in one of the regions of "the French Empire"' (Fanon, 1967b: 118). Working through the colonial system will not change the colonizers' views of the colonized, nor will it dismantle colonial power. Those who choose this route will end up participating in the violence of the colonizers against themselves and their communities, so other means must be adopted.

What happens if you decide to take anger about the injustices of colonialism and channel it outside of yourself? This is a second common response to colonization. Fanon observes that the initial externalization of this anger rarely aims at an appropriate target. After all, who is easily accessible and vulnerable to abuse? Other colonized people. 'The colonized subject will first train this aggressiveness sedimented in his muscles against his own people. This is the period when black turns on black, and police officers and magistrates don't know which way to turn when faced with the surprising surge of North African criminality' (Fanon, 2004: 15–16). This is an extremely important point: not all violence serves the goal of overcoming colonization. In fact, violence can be counterproductive because it confirms the narratives of the colonizers. Intracommunity violence leads the colonizers to point out the inherent instability and irrationality of the colonized, and to argue that it proves that they cannot be trusted with self-rule.

A third response to the distortions of a colonized world that Fanon points out is to dream of alternative worlds. Fanon recognizes the native's interest in magic as a way of reframing colonial existence into larger imaginary struggles, which one can control. 'The magical, supernatural powers prove to be surprisingly ego boosting. The colonist's powers are infinitely shrunk, stamped by foreignness. There is no real reason to fight them because what really matters is that mythical structures contain far more terrifying adversaries' (ibid.: 19). The colonized subject can fight these epic personal battles on their own terms. This insight is directly culled from Fanon's observations as a psychiatrist. While other doctors would have dismissed the phantasies of alternative worlds as simply delusional, Fanon saw it as an entirely rational response to being forced to exist in a world where personal control was taken away. Why not imagine other scenarios and powers that could interrupt the seemingly hopeless reality? Indeed, Fanon might have some insights into the popularity of superhero films today. Fanon also explores how the desire for physical freedom that is denied in the colonized world is realized through dreams. 'The first thing the colonial subject learns is to remain in his place and not overstep its limits. Hence the dreams of the colonial subject are muscular dreams, dreams of action, dreams of aggressive vitality' (ibid.: 15). The desire to achieve freedom is manifest in the imagination, because there is no clear way to achieve this freedom in the physical world.

Finally, the colonized person stops internalizing their aggression, trying to disappear through fantasy or subjecting their own community to violence. 'The colonized subject discovers reality and transforms it through his praxis, his deployment of violence and his agenda for liberation' (ibid.: 21). Fanon argues violence achieves a step towards decolonization in two ways: it transforms the individual, and creates the collective. 'At the individual level, violence is a cleansing force. It rids the colonized of their inferiority complex, of their passive and despairing attitude. It emboldens them, and restores their self-confidence' (ibid.: 51). Initially the colonized person was subject to the rule of others; suddenly the same individual can make their own destiny. The violence also transforms the colonizer from an active agent of history to an object, whose humanity is denied. Violence turns human beings into flesh, it denies recognition of their soul. In this way, violence creates a direct reversal of the dynamic of colonialism. The systemic violence of colonialism made the colonized into an object; revolutionary violence removes the humanity of the colonizers and turns them into objects. This is why Fanon argues that decolonization means simply, 'The first shall be last' (ibid.: 2).

Through violence, the colonized people also come to be joined together, and gain a sense of unity. 'This violent praxis is totalizing since each individual represents a violent link in the great chain, in the almighty body of violence rearing up in reaction to the primary violence of the colonizer' (ibid.: 50). Other theorists such as Ortega y Gasset (1994) and Elias Canetti (1984) have commented on the dynamic of crowds and mobs. When groups of people engage in simultaneous resistance, they see themselves as part of something greater than just simple revenge. From this moment of revolutionary violence, the first inklings of a new nationalist identification spring up.

There are similarities between Fanon's analysis of the violence of anti-colonial movements and Emma Goldman's considerations of revolutionary violence (see Chapter 26 on Goldman). Both thinkers see a connection between the injustices of the world, and how they are lodged in the psyches of observers. Goldman argues revolutionary violence is supposed to draw attention to the systemic violence that is frequently labelled as normal, pointing out, 'Compared with the wholesale violence of capital and government, political acts of violence are but a drop in the ocean' (Goldman, 1996). Fanon sees individual violence as a way of directly undoing the systemic violence of the colonial order.

> The violence which governed the ordering of the colonial world, which tirelessly punctuated the destruction of the indigenous social fabric, and demolished unchecked the systems of reference of the country's economy, lifestyles, and modes of dress, this same violence will be vindicated and appropriated when, taking history into their own hands, the colonized swarm into the forbidden cities.

(ibid.: 6)

> **Key Concept: Revolutionary leaders**
>
> *The Wretched of the Earth* was considered 'a bible' for leaders seeking to overturn formal colonization, racial oppression, or both. Bobby Sands (1954–1981), a leader of the Provisional IRA, read Fanon in his prison outside of Belfast, Northern Ireland, where he died from a hunger strike in 1981. Fanon was particularly influential in the Black Power movement. Stokely Carmichael (1941–1998) (who later changed his name to Kwame Ture after he moved to Ghana in 1968) referred to Fanon's work in the introduction to *Black Power*. Bobby Seale (1936) and Huey P. Newton (1942–1989) recounted reading *The Wretched of the Earth* as they started the Black Panther Party, and Eldridge Cleaver (1935–1998) once remarked, 'Every brother on a rooftop can quote Fanon.' Steve Biko (1946–1977) also circulated Fanon's work as he began actively organizing against the apartheid regime in South Africa, encouraging the adoption of 'black consciousness'.

Although *The Wretched of the Earth* focuses upon male revolutionaries and their attempt to seize the ability to define themselves, 'Algeria Unveiled' describes how revolutionary action allows Algerian women to overcome the predicament of experiencing their bodies as mere objects, and regain their subjectivity. The women affiliated with the FLN learned to use the stereotypes of Algerian women against their French adversaries in the struggle for self-determination, a strategy that is captured in *The Battle of Algiers*, a film that re-enacts the Algerian War. First, they alter their appearance to look like Europeanized Algerians, ones who accept colonial rule and their definitions of femininity. The French soldiers subconsciously assume that a light-skinned woman with European-style clothing would endorse the occupation of their country—they have adopted the logic of the colonizers. By playing the French soldiers' assumptions against them, these women were able to move bombs over the security checkpoints and achieve a disruption in the European neighbourhood. Later, they don veils in order to hide bombs underneath their dresses, resisting the soldiers searches by pretending to be a devout Muslim. The French soldiers subconsciously assume that such a woman cannot be a force for change or political action. The French soldier sees a traditional Algerian woman as helpless, and a Europeanized Algerian woman as a supporter. In manoeuvring between these two positions, the Algerian woman is able to act and overcome her identity as a passive entity that has been imposed by the colonizers. She puts on and discards the different roles society offers her, and from this dynamic, an authentic self is born. 'What we have here is not the bringing to light of a character known and frequented a thousand times in imagination or in stories. It is an authentic birth in a pure state, without preliminary instruction. There is no character to imitate' (Fanon, 1965: 50).

Despite Fanon's salutary descriptions of revolutionary violence and the rebirth of colonized men and women, *The Wretched of the Earth* concludes with many of his notes from the asylum at Blida in a chapter called 'Colonial War and Mental Disorders'. It is a decidedly unusual way to end his treatise, and it is hard not to believe that it sits there as a warning to his readers. Fanon would not want them to refuse the struggle, but wants them to be clear about the heavy price that it will incur. 'Perhaps the reader will find notes on psychiatry out of place or untimely in a book like this. There is absolutely nothing we can do about that. We had no control over the fact that the psychiatric phenomena, the mental and behavioral disorders emerging from this war, have loomed so large among the perpetrators of "pacification" and the "pacified" population' (Fanon, 1967a: 181). Fanon's notes recount how French soldiers and Algerian revolutionaries were similarly haunted by ghosts of those figures they had killed, and exhibited severe mental duress. The notes are deliberately organized by the disorder being detailed, with the French soldiers' and Algerian revolutionaries' testimonies mixed together. It seems clear that Fanon does acknowledge the irreparable harm of violence. Here, in presenting the truth of how the struggle impacts those who conduct it, Fanon provides recognition of common humanity, achieved at last.

VIOLENCE, POWER, AND RESISTANCE

> ### 28.4 The violence of colonization and decolonization: Key Points
>
> - Colonized individuals have a number of different responses to the fact of their colonization.
> - First, they might elect to work within the colonial system and try and gain personal advantages from doing so.
> - Second, anger at the systemic injustices of the colonial world may generate violence against oneself and one's community.
> - Third, colonized subjects can retreat from the world through an intensive fantasy life, refusing to acknowledge the world as it exists.
> - Finally, they can deploy violence more strategically in order to develop a sense of self-efficacy and control. Fanon believes this route may contain some disadvantages as well.

28.5 Achieving lasting decolonization

While Fanon's work hails the moment of rebirth by revolutionary people, it also contains warnings about what happens after this moment of struggle. Fanon saw many difficulties with overcoming the legacies of colonization and achieving a lasting decolonization.

Even as intellectuals and peasants alike become aware of the realities of their situation through the struggle, their mobilization into a collective unit can create a new barrier to self-rule. 'The militant who confronts the colonialist war machine with his rudimentary resources realizes that while he is demolishing colonial oppression he is indirectly building another system of exploitation' (ibid.: 94). The struggle was conducted on behalf of the nation in order to expel its alien governors. In 'The Pitfalls of National Consciousness', Fanon explains how anti-colonial nationalism can develop into a politics of oppression. Leaders do things on behalf of the people and nation, and consolidate their powers by controlling the population, instead of transforming or uplifting it. They also see that economic security is based upon a continuing alliance with the economic elites of the colonizing power, instead of taking a more difficult path to substantial economic development. Additionally, the colonial powers quickly come to recognize that there are advantages of giving up formal colonization, and embrace a system of neocolonialism. Fanon's predictions stand as a hauntingly accurate picture of the authoritarian political regimes and neocolonial economic structures that have frequently appeared in postcolonial countries.

> ### Key Thinker: Che Guevara
>
> Even though Fanon's work formed the bedrock of revolutionaries' reading lists, Guevara (1928–1967) eventually became the face that many associate with anti-colonial struggles. Like Fanon, he was a doctor and also defined decolonization as the rebirth of man. He believed humans were moral creatures, whose nature had been squashed by the imperative to work for material gain. Unlike Fanon, Guevara believed that revolutionary struggle had to be led by a small vanguard. He envisioned change being delivered by an exclusive group of people who would work for the party in order to achieve society's cultural and economic transformation. This is exactly the tendency that Fanon warned against in 'The Pitfalls of National Consciousness', in *The Wretched of the Earth*, arguing that having a small class of commanding officers and leaders could undermine progress towards freedom for all by becoming addicted to their own power.

First, there is the temptation to claim that decolonization happens through simple role reversal. But of course, having a different face at the top of the same exploitative structure does not create significantly different outcomes for the majority of citizens in the nation. Previously, the benefits from the country's production accrued to the colonizing power, now nationalization seizes these same means of production and claims them on behalf of the people. '[N]ationalization quite simply means the transfer into native hands of those unfair advantages which are a legacy of the colonial period' (Fanon, 1967a: 152). Even though property is seized and turned over to Indigenous elites, there is no significant shift in the way that agricultural production happens. 'The same old groundnut harvest, cocoa harvest, and olive harvest. Likewise the traffic of commodities goes unchanged. No industry is established in the country' (ibid.: 100).

Even more disturbingly, Fanon observes that frequently the oppression of the workers engaged in production increases under a new regime, all in the name of furthering the project of national pride and independence.

> In fact the landowners call on the authorities to increase a hundredfold the facilities and privileges now theirs but once reserved for the foreign colonists. The exploitation of farm workers is intensified and justified. Capitalizing on two or three slogans, these new colonists demand a colossal effort from these farm laborers—in the name of national interest of course.
>
> (ibid.: 102)

Therefore, what can happen after formal decolonization ends is that 'The people discover that the iniquitous phenomenon of exploitation can assume a black or Arab face' (ibid.: 94). Indeed, not the new world that revolutionary figures were hoping for. But remember, Fanon did point out that one of the temptations of the colonized person is simply to imagine themselves in the place of the colonizer as opposed to transforming the systems altogether.

Second, the leaders that the newly decolonized country turns to are frequently the educated elites. But these elites have been trained specifically to run the mechanics of the colonial state—they tend to be lawyers and bureaucrats, not visionary leaders who invent all new ways of doing things. They prove unable to fulfil the promise of economic development which requires great leaps of imagination, well beyond what the colonial economy offers as immediate options. Therefore, they tend to create alliances with the elites from other countries, and the former colonists. Extraction of raw materials continues, and production of goods that do not require investment in the workforce are prioritized. The economy 'develops' as the former colony achieves stability, and becomes an inviting location for vacations.

> The national bourgeoisie establishes holiday resorts and playgrounds for entertaining the Western bourgeoisie. This sector goes by the name of tourism and becomes a national industry for this very purpose. We have only to look at what has happened in Latin America if we want proof of the way the ex-colonized bourgeoisie can be transformed into 'party' organizer.
>
> (Fanon, 2004: 101)

And given their poor performance in actually transforming the economy, the new leaders decide to present their people with splashy projects that demonstrate the new nation's greatness. Military parades, new buildings, universities are built to display the competence and power of the regime, but without any of the sustained economic development that would be required to support them.

Third, nationalism itself can promote the same kind of magical thinking that characterized the individual native's response to colonialism. Now, the nation defines the citizens' enemies, and tells them *it* is the fetish that will protect them. 'Instead of inspiring confidence, assuaging the fears of its citizens and cradling them with its power and discretion, the State on the contrary, imposes itself in spectacular manner, flaunts its authority, harasses, making it clear to its citizens they are in constant danger' (ibid.: 111). The state labels dissent and organizing as a detriment to its future strengths, and tries to keep citizens from engaging in any public debate that might serve to weaken its image. Fanon was the first to predict the enlarged symbolic position of the state in postcolonial situations that emerges particularly when its capacities have not increased.

Just as it sets itself up as an irreplaceable protector of the interests of all citizens, the postcolonial state also wants to speak on their behalf. 'Since independence the party no longer helps the people to formulate their demands, to better realize their needs and better establish their power. Today the party's mission is to convey to the people the instructions handed down from the top' (ibid.: 115). In this way the national consciousness that was used to link the colonized together during the struggle for independence becomes deployed against the population, and the call for unity is now used to pacify and intimidate them. Because the state is not able to provide meaningful social and economic development, instead it resorts to threats and intensifies the role of the police. Even as infrastructure remains weak, the police force is strengthened. This means that life under the new regime comes to resemble life under the old colonial system more and more.

Key Thinker: Ali Shariati

Ali Shariati (1933–1977) was an Iranian intellectual who has been hailed as one of the inspirations behind the Iranian Revolution of 1977. In 1957, he went to Paris to study for a graduate degree in sociology, and became exposed to Marxist thought, and also the work of Frantz Fanon. He translated *The Wretched of the Earth* into Persian, and introduced the work to those who were organizing to overthrow the pro-Western regime of the Shah of Iran. Shariati also became involved in the struggle for Algerian Independence by assisting the FLN. His exposure to Marxism and Fanon's revolutionary work created a unique combination in Shariati's thought. He saw Islam as a tool to repudiate the Western and commercial forces that were governing Iran. He advocated for what has been labelled 'Red Shiism' which was a combination of Islamic principles and Marxist values, not dissimilar to the ideas of liberation theology that circulated in Latin America that combined Catholicism with social justice during the same period.

As the postcolonial state settles into these patterns of bombastically advertising its greatness and using its energies to control its own population, patterns of economic neocolonialism arise. 'To be more exact, the occupier can easily phase out the violent aspects of his presence. In fact, this dramatic phasing out not only spares the occupier much expense but also has the further benefit of allowing him to better concentrate his powers' (ibid.: 91). Now that the Indigenous government pays for the police and runs the government, former colonial elites can return to their original focus—exploiting the resources and labour of the country. While originally these companies would have taken great care to show deference to the new regime, eventually the need for pretence is dispensed. 'The former colonial power multiplies its demands and accumulates concessions and guarantees, taking fewer and fewer precautions to mask the hold it has over the national government' (ibid.: 112). Investors can demand concessions from the government, pay bribes in order to expedite their interests, or simply ignore the weak state's regulations altogether. The postcolonial regime will not draw its citizens' attention to its inability to control global investors since that would damage their image.

> **Key Concept: Neocolonialism**
>
> Neocolonialism refers to the continuing efforts of a colonizing power to exert influence and control over a former colony. There are two traps that newly independent nations can fall into. The first is enabling the Indigenous elite who were part of the colonial order to maintain power. These figures have not escaped the logic and values of the colonizers, and therefore their rule will not bring about significant change as they will continue to work for the interests of the colonizing powers even though formal colonial rule is suspended. Another tendency is for the new leaders of the nation to try and ensure material prosperity by continuing economic relations with the colonizing powers. The acceptance of new leaders by the former colonists makes it seem they have given up their power, but if economic exploitation continues, this is neocolonialism.

Fanon claims that none of these developments are inevitable, and that they could be countered by an insistence that the people claim the nation, and that the state serves them rather than the reverse. The only method of true decolonization is the development of the capacities and strength of the people. The task of decolonization 'means driving home to the masses that everything depends upon them, that if we stagnate the fault is theirs, and that if we progress, they too are responsible' (ibid.: 138). The postcolonial state's claim to be the new magical solution to all that ails them must be denied. The future of the country rests solely in the hands of the people, not in the decisions of a leader. Hence, Fanon warns his readers against the adoption of a 'nationalist consciousness' and instead urges them to take on a political consciousness rooted in analyses of the world as it currently exists. National consciousness can too easily become another method of warping people's perception of reality and incapacitating them.

The participants in the struggle need to see themselves as responding to the world historical context of colonization. The world they find themselves in was made by forces larger than the individual settlers before them. Personal vengeance will not bring this world to its end; only by seeing their experience in relationship to the historical framework of colonization can these individual fantasies of freedom be converted into a political restructuring of the world. Decolonization will require remaking the world that colonialism built; this remaking will require understanding the larger structures that are often obscured by individual, and then collective, experience. The task is momentous, since frameworks of knowledge, experiences of personal identity, global processes of extraction, and systems of law and politics were developed in conjunction with the colonial system. Colonialism is hegemonic (dominant), but like all hegemonies, incomplete. Fanon's historical perspective means being able to simultaneously see the greater forces at work, and the possibilities for human action within these perimeters.

Situatedness, or understanding one's potential actions through a realistic assessment of the conditions around oneself, will allow people to overcome the previous training of colonialism. Interestingly, it is also a direct opposition to the 'zone of nonbeing' that Fanon described in *Black Skin, White Masks* as a simultaneous presence and absence that colonized subjects experience. How they are perceived is not what they know themselves to be, but just as disconcertingly, how can one know oneself given only the distorted tools that society provides? Fanon argues that the process of understanding where the formerly colonized person exists in concrete time and space is the start of revolutionary consciousness. Revolutionary action can only occur when grounded by accurate perceptions of reality.

> **28.5 Achieving lasting decolonization: Key Points**
>
> - Fanon worried that systems of colonial oppression could remain in place, even though they were now headed up by Indigenous elites.
> - Fanon predicted that the capacities of postcolonial states might be weakened, and unable to control international economics.
> - Fanon also worried that the strong nationalism that was used to resist the colonizers and develop an independent state could be a double-edged sword: postcolonial leaders might ask their citizens to keep making sacrifices for the common good and stifle any dissent, hence returning to dynamics that are similar to the colonial order.

28.6 Conclusion

Though *The Wretched of the Earth* is seen as a handbook for revolutions of decolonization, it makes it clear that there is no set formula for success. In fact, the very core of Fanon's argument is that we should not let anyone tell us what the answer to our problems are. People need to be taught to apprehend reality accurately, and to act collectively in response to it. 'The living expression of the nation is the collective consciousness in motion of the entire people. It is the enlightened and coherent praxis of men and women. The collective forging of a destiny implies taking responsibility on a truly historical scale' (ibid.: 144). Therefore, while Fanon's name may be tossed about as shorthand for revolutionary violence, his ultimate message is that overcoming oppression means embracing collective responsibility for making and remaking the world that everyone lives in, regardless of the difficult conditions in which we find ourselves.

Take your learning further by accessing the online resources for a library of web links to relevant videos, articles, blogs, and useful websites for this chapter: www.oup.com/he/Ramgotra-Choat1e.

Study questions

1. Do you think personal experience is an accurate guide for political and social analysis?
2. How do colonial realities come to inhere in colonized subjects?
3. How do the positions of colonizer and colonized reinforce one another?
4. How do the psychologies of gender and race intersect?
5. How does violence lead to the birth of new men and women, according to Fanon?
6. Can you think of examples of oppressed persons engaging in violence within their own communities? Do you find Fanon's explication of this behaviour convincing?
7. Why did Fanon fear the nationalism of anti-colonial revolutions?
8. Do you think neocolonialism still operates today? How could that be changed?

Further reading

Primary sources

Fanon, F. (1965) *A Dying Colonialism*. Trans. H. Chevalier. New York: Grove Press.
   In this book, Fanon discusses the different strategies of anticolonial resistance and organizing. The most notable essay from this volume is 'Algeria Unveiled', which discusses the role of Algerian women in the revolutionary struggle, and the ways that the perceptions of colonists can be marshalled against them.

Fanon, F. (1967a) *Black Skin, White Masks: The Experiences of a Black Man in a White World*. Trans. C. Markmann. New York: Grove Press.
   This is the most complete exposition of Fanon's ideas about the psychology associated with racial subjugation and white supremacy. The book also addresses sexual insecurities and dynamics that are inflected by racial inequalities.

Fanon, F. (1967b) *Toward the African Revolution*. Trans. H. Chevalier. New York: Grove Press.
   A collection of Fanon's political writings that were published in the newspaper of the FLN, *El Moudjihad*. This book captures Fanon's direct appeals to members of the movement fighting for decolonization.

Fanon, F. (2004) *The Wretched of the Earth*. Trans. R. Philcox. New York: Grove Press.
   This book is considered the bible of revolutionary movements. It recounts common responses of those struggling against colonization, and makes predictions about different phases of the movements for independence.

Secondary sources

Gibson, N. (ed.) (2022) *Rethinking Fanon*. New York: Humanities Press.
   This volume contains many influential essays exploring the relevance and application of Fanon's theories of colonization, identity, and revolution.

Gordon, L. (2015) *What Fanon Said: A Philosophical Introduction to His Life and Thought*. New York: Fordham University Press.
   This volume explores Fanon's position in relation to philosophers throughout history, and traces Fanon's influence on critical race theory and contemporary social movements.

Jinadu, A.L. (1986) *Fanon: In Search of the African Revolution*. New York: Routledge.
   This book explores Fanon's theories in the context of African society. Jinadu provides a rich sociological account of the class, gender, and political dynamics in revolutionary Africa that influenced Fanon's understanding of the intricacies of decolonization.

Kohn, M. and McBride, K. (2011) *Political Theories of Decolonization: Postcolonialism and the Problem of Foundations*. Oxford: Oxford University Press.
   This book provides an overview of the different strategies used to achieve decolonization around the world, including a close investigation of Fanon's theories.

Macey, D. (2012) *Frantz Fanon: A Biography*. 2nd edn. New York: Verso.
   Considered the best biography of this complex man, giving a clear account of how his personal experiences and training as a psychologist informed the development of his theories of colonization, identity, resistance, and revolution.

References

Bernasconi, R. (2001) *Race*. New York: Wiley-Blackwell.

Camus, A. (1989 [1942]) *The Stranger*. Trans. M. Ward. New York: Vintage Books.

Cannetti, E., *Crowds and Power*. Trans. C. Stewart. New York: Farrar, Straus, and Giroux.

Fanon, F. (1965) *A Dying Colonialism*. Trans. H. Chevalier. New York: Grove Press.

Fanon, F. (1967a) *Black Skin, White Masks*. Trans. C. Farrington. New York: Grove Press.

Fanon, F. (1967b) *Towards the African Revolution*. Trans. H. Chevalier. New York: Grove Press.

Fanon, F. (2004) *The Wretched of the Earth*. Trans. R. Philcox. New York: Grove Press.

Fuss, D. (1994) 'Interior Colonies: Frantz Fanon and the Politics of Identification'. *Diacritics*, 24(2–3): 20–42.

Gasset, J.O.y. (1994) *Revolt of the Masses*. New York: W.W. Norton.

Gibson, N. (2003) *Fanon: The Postcolonial Imagination*. New York: Polity Press.

Goldman, E. (1996) 'The Psychology of Political Violence'. In A.K. Shulman (ed.), *Red Emma Speaks: An Emma Goldman Reader*. New York: Humanity Books.

Gooding-Williams, R. (2005) *Look, A Negro! Philosophical Essays on Race, Culture and Politics*. New York: Routledge.

Gordon, L. (2007) 'Through the Hellish Zone of Nonbeing: Thinking through Fanon, Disaster, and the Damned of the Earth'. *Human Architecture: A Journal of the Sociology of Self-Knowledge*, Summer: 5–12.

Jinadu, A.L. (1986) *Fanon: In Search of the African Revolution*. New York: Routledge.

Maldonado-Torres, N. (2007) 'On the Coloniality of Being: Contributions to the Development of a Concept'. *Cultural Studies*, 21(2): 240–270.

McClintock, A. (1995) *Imperial Leather: Race, Gender and Sexuality in the Colonial Context*. New York: Routledge.

Said, E. (1979) *Orientalism*. New York: Vintage Books.

Shatz, A. (2017) 'Where Life Is Seized'. *London Review of Books*, 39(2). January 19.

Stoler, A.L. (2002) *Carnal Knowledge and Imperial Power: Race and the Intimate in Colonial Rule*. Berkeley, CA: University of California Press.

Part VII

The Liberal Self and Black Consciousness

29	Immanuel Kant	Stella Sandford	527
30	Frederick Douglass	Kiara Gilbert and Karen Salt	545
31	W.E.B. Du Bois	Elvira Basevich	565
32	John Rawls	Maeve McKeown	581

This Part of the book brings together four chapters that explore liberalism in relation to race. It juxtaposes Immanuel Kant's Enlightenment and John Rawls's liberal conceptions of the self with Frederick Douglass' and W.E.B. Du Bois's understanding of Black consciousness and subjectivity, which developed through a long history of Black people's struggles to end slavery, domination, and racism. Both Kant and Rawls present idealistic conceptions of the self as rational that serve to construct a free and equal political state; whereas Douglass and Du Bois consider Black self-conceptions in relation to a state that constitutes and subjugates Black people. Although Rawls does not engage with these Black political thinkers, their ideas form a significant part of American history and self-understanding.

This Part situates John Rawls, who is widely considered to be the most influential liberal political philosopher of the last fifty years, in a context beyond that of analytical, historical, and ideological understandings of liberalism, socialism and communitarianism. Rawls composed his major political work *A Theory of Justice* (1971) in the midst of the Civil Rights movement that fought for Black people's suffrage and an end to segregation and racism. By placing Rawls alongside two influential Black American political thinkers and actors, we bring into academic debates about justice and the very foundations of being and knowing in the creation of a fair and equal society voices that have often been excluded, and yet are part of a broader political conversation within society, through both activist movements and political writings. Kant is included in this Part because Rawls explicitly builds on his conceptions of the self and reason. Moreover, Kant's Enlightenment philosophy has had an immense influence on political thinking since the eighteenth century. Yet, as we learn in Chapter 29, Kant developed a theory of race that he tried to define scientifically and philosophically as connected to geography and biology. By situating Kant in this Part, we challenge his conception of race as biological through the political theories of two Black thinkers who underline that racism is an ideology that operates to justify the domination of some people over others.

Chapter 29 examines Kant's understanding of the self as a free and rational being who has the capacity to act according to moral principles, notably to treat other human beings as ends in themselves, as persons, not as things. Kant understood human beings as imperfect empirical beings who had a physical existence influenced by bodily characteristics, desires, and needs; yet the human capacity for reason made human beings capable of moral judgement and action. This underpins his ethical conception of treating others as ends in themselves and not instrumentally. This chapter further examines his understanding of transcendental idealism, universal history, civilization, perpetual peace, and the view that human beings can live together ethically and peacefully. At the same time, it underscores the contradictions between the ideal and the real world and highlights Kant's problematic views of race and gender.

Rawls draws on elements of Kant's philosophy to develop his conception of the self and the construction of the original position. As Chapter 32 explains, the original position is an imaginary space in which individuals do not know their gender, class, race, sexuality, ability, or other characteristics that would associate one with a group or a particular identity. Rawls argues that, without this knowledge, individuals would choose liberal principles of justice as the foundations of political society. Therefore, Rawls conceives the liberal self as a rational being who would choose moral principles of freedom and equality for all. As such, he is said to develop an ideal conception of the human being and political society in which rational beings would opt to treat others according to principles of justice that would advance an equal distribution of economic and political goods and allow each person to pursue their own life plans. This conception of the liberal self is said to be colour-blind and to apply to all individuals without regard to race, gender, class, disability, or sexuality. And, arguably, it presupposes a sort of rationality that reflects the positionality of white heteronormative middle-class men who historically constituted the political sphere. Rawls's political theory is criticized for being ideal and lacking grounding in the non-ideal world in which the very real problems of racial, gender, and social inequalities are pervasive.

This understanding of the self operates from specific assumptions about human nature upon which it constructs political institutions. It does not consider how subjects are constituted by the political and social structures in which they are born and live. These structures shape people's conceptions of themselves, how they exist in the world and hence how they reason about the world and others. In other words, human beings are not blank slates; rather, there is a diversity of subjects and subjectivities whose awareness and consciousness are not reducible to a singular mode of reasoning, knowing, and being in the world. Chapters 30 and 31 on Douglass and Du Bois bring this into sharp relief.

Douglass was a fugitive who escaped slavery and later became not only a prominent activist for the abolition of slavery, but also politician and ambassador to Haiti. He speaks to the experience and consciousness of Black people who were dehumanized by a political system that exploited them for the privilege and profit of white supremacists. His reflections on how he reclaimed his humanity from brutal beatings that were meant to break his mind and body into servile subjection underline his strength and capacity to resist, and, hence, his consciousness. This consciousness and resistance against slavery and domination developed throughout his life and underpin his philosophical writings. Acts of resistance included learning to read and write, escaping slavery, and helping others to do the same. This chapter explores Douglass' conception of natural rights which he used to oppose slavery on the grounds that it violated enslaved people's natural right to freedom. Yet it also notes that after the US Civil War, Douglass' troubled relation with gender equality surfaced and he promoted suffrage for Black men, not Black women.

Du Bois was writing at the end of the nineteenth century and over the first half of the twentieth century. His work examined the periods of slavery and Reconstruction, and he protested against the racism that persisted in the USA and across the globe as a result of colonialism. He developed an innovative understanding of double consciousness, according to which Black people saw themselves both through the eyes of others, which constituted a false sense of self, and through their own sense of self. As this chapter observes, the first sense may be considered a constructed view imposed by the ruling part of society to denigrate Black humanity. Nevertheless, the strength of Black folk to resist domination and its attendant narratives characterized the second sense of self. As such, Black consciousness developed through the will to resist and a self-understanding that opposes or is indifferent to the views of others. This chapter further analyses Du Bois's understanding of the colour-line which divides Black and white, colonized and colonizer, and refers to white supremacy in the USA and globally. Both Douglass and Du Bois understand Black consciousness in the wider movements for Black liberation which overturned white supremacist myths of Black people and asserted their humanity, dignity, and integrity as equal, free, and rational human beings.

Overall, this Part of the book attempts to reframe how we read liberalism and conceptions of the subject in a broader context than simply that of the canon of political theory which neither contextualizes John Rawls in the contradictory history of the American republic's legacy of slavery and racism nor Kant in the context of colonialism. Simultaneously, it brings into relief Black political theories that demonstrate how ideologies of race construct subjects and political democracy but also how Black consciousness aims to resist racialization.

29 Immanuel Kant

STELLA SANDFORD

Chapter guide

This chapter focuses on what are commonly identified as Kant's primary political writings, and connects these to some of his relevant work in other areas. Section 29.1 introduces and explains Kant's important place in the history of Western philosophy and the reach of his influence. Section 29.2 gives a brief overview of some of the fundamental aspects of Kant's philosophy more generally, all of which are relevant for an understanding of his political philosophy. Section 29.3 sets out the main contours of Kant's political philosophy from the conventionally identified political writings, while Section 29.4 looks at Kant's influence on subsequent political philosophy and at the major problems in Kant's political thought, including its relation to a racial theory of development. The conclusion then considers the prospects for Kant's political theory today.

29.1 Introduction

Immanuel Kant (1724–1804) is one of the most influential European philosophers of the modern era. Indeed, so great is his contribution to the discipline of European philosophy that the period after the reception of his major works is referred to as 'post-Kantian'. His writings made him famous in his own lifetime and he was a popular teacher in his native Königsberg (now the city of Kaliningrad in Russia) where he spent all of his long life. He is mostly remembered now for his 'critical philosophy': the *Critique of Pure Reason* (Kant, 1997 [1781/1789]), the *Critique of Practical Reason* (Kant, 1996e [1788a]) and the *Critique of the Power of Judgment* (Kant, 2000 [1790])—the so-called First, Second, and Third Critiques.

In the subsequent history of Western philosophy, responses to and developments of Kant's critical philosophy and his doctrine of 'transcendental idealism' gave rise to the tradition of German Idealism associated with such thinkers as Fichte, Schelling, and Hegel. For some 50 years in the later 1800s and early 1900s a new interpretation of Kant's critical philosophy—'neo-Kantianism'—became the dominant philosophical movement in Germany. In the second half of the twentieth century, Western philosophy became increasingly polarized between two traditions—the Anglo-American 'analytic' tradition and the 'continental' or 'modern European' tradition. Both traditions, however, can be traced back to Kant's philosophy. Analytic philosophy is characterized by an emphasis on linguistic analysis and (usually) a rejection of metaphysical speculation. This rejection—the idea that we can only meaningfully talk about things that we can actually experience or things that can be expressed in logical form—is one interpretation of what Kant achieved in his first Critique, where he famously argues that we can have no knowledge, strictly speaking, of anything that is not a possible object of experience in space and time. 'Continental' philosophy has made the category of the 'subject' (the 'knower' or 'experiencer') central to its analyses in different ways. In all cases, however, Kant is either the inspiration or the antagonist. As Jacques Derrida (2002: 49) said, in Western philosophy it is as if the relation to Kant is 'tattooed on'.

> Read more about **Kant's** life and work by accessing the thinker biography on the online resources: **www.oup.com/he/Ramgotra-Choat1e.**

In one of his most famous essays—'An Answer to the Question: What Is Enlightenment?' (Kant, 1996b [1784a])—he describes the 'age of enlightenment' as the first to offer the possibility for humankind to free itself from its self-imposed immaturity. Maturity, for Kant, means the free exercise of one's reason, thinking for oneself, whereas immaturity is the state of being led by others—whether that be by the state, by religion, or by received philosophical ideas. In the Preface to the first edition of the *Critique of Pure Reason*, he writes: 'Our age is the genuine age of criticism, to which everything must submit' (Kant, 1997 [1781/1789]: Axi), indicating that there is nothing—including religion—which cannot legitimately be subject to rational investigation.

> **Key Concept: Transcendental idealism**
>
> 'Transcendental idealism' is a philosophical theory that aims to explain how it is possible for us to have objective knowledge of the external world. It argues that the knowing subject's mind contributes 'ideal' elements that structure that knowledge before all experience of the world. These elements are 'transcendental' because they make all meaningful experience of the world outside of us possible. This does not mean that we have no knowledge of 'reality', but that we contribute to what that 'reality' is *for us*. Although few today agree wholeheartedly with the doctrine of transcendental idealism, many have accepted the idea that humans (or 'the subject') necessarily contribute subjective elements to objective knowledge of the world.

29.2 Fundamentals of Kant's philosophy

Kant divided his work into 'theoretical' and 'practical' parts. The theoretical part (especially the First and Third Critiques and his work on the metaphysical foundations of science) deal with what can be said and known about the natural world (what *is*), whereas the practical part deals primarily with human action (what *ought to be*); it includes his moral and his political philosophy, and various works in physical and human geography and anthropology. The theoretical (we might also say 'logical') use of reason can make inferences about the physical world, and indeed its legitimate employment in knowledge is *limited to* claims about the physical world and to claims about what concepts and capacities of the mind make our knowledge of the physical world possible. His account of what makes objective and scientific knowledge of the world possible is the doctrine of 'transcendental idealism'. But reason is also driven to speculate beyond the limits of what we can legitimately claim to know, precisely because it is *free* from determination by the physical world. We cannot, strictly speaking, know anything about God, for example, but reason, according to Kant, inevitably posits the idea of God as a way to explain creation.

The term 'idea' has a specific, technical meaning in Kant's philosophy. An 'idea' is something that cannot in principle have any corresponding object in experience, or simply something that we cannot experience. But this does not mean that it is a mere fiction or an illusion. Ideas have an important theoretical role to play in orienting (or Kant would say 'regulating') our pursuit of knowledge and an important practical role to play in orientating our actions. The ideas of pure reason are part of the 'pure' elements of Kant's philosophy. By 'pure' he means 'purely rational' or 'purely rationally determined'—concepts or ideas of things and logical demonstrations that do not draw on experience and indeed are prior to all experience. These are the '*a priori*' elements of philosophy, or *a priori* forms of reasoning, contrasted with the '*a posteriori*' or 'empirical' elements.

> **Key Concept: *a priori—a posteriori***
>
> A quick way to remember the meaning of the distinction between '*a priori*' and '*a posteriori*' is to think of them as meaning 'before experience' (or 'not needing experience') and 'after experience' (or 'based on experience'). 'All bachelors are unmarried men' is true *a priori* because to assert the opposite would obviously be false (a married bachelor is a contradiction in terms). But *a posteriori* claims require something in addition to the claims themselves in order to be judged to be true or false. The claim that 'all professional basketball players are tall' needs to be verified (or falsified) empirically, that is, through appeal to experience. Only deductions *a priori* can be said to be universally true, because anything that relies on *a posteriori* verification can in principle be falsified by new experience. Kant thought that true, objective knowledge must be based on *a priori* elements; everything else would be merely provisional knowledge.

But *a priori* reasoning is also central to practical reason (or practical philosophy; including moral and political philosophy). Kant argues that we can always determine, in any situation, the right thing to do by applying a rational principle—or *the* rational principle of morality—which he calls the 'categorical imperative'. In every situation we have to ask ourselves whether we could rationally 'will' (that is, rationally want it to be the case) that the course of action that we are about to take could or should be 'universalized'. Say I am about to steal something. Can I rationally will that stealing should be a universal principle according to which everyone should act? Kant thinks that we could not *rationally* will such a thing, so stealing must be wrong and I must not do it. Morality means asking ourselves not 'what do I want to do?' but 'what *ought* I to do? What is it my duty to do?' (This kind of moral theory, based on duties and obligations rather than consequences, is called 'deontology'.) For Kant, when we act according to what we want to do (according to our desires and inclinations), we are not really free, because we are determined by those (ultimately sensual) desires. Only when we act out of duty, despite our desires to do something else, are we truly free and moral, and this is called 'virtue'.

> **Key Concept: The categorical imperative**
>
> The 'categorical imperative' is for Kant the supreme moral principle. It is contrasted with a 'hypothetical' imperative, which would take the form '*If* you want to achieve X, *then* you should do Y'. The categorical imperative commands instead something that is objectively necessary (something that you *must* or *must not* do) without any reference to an end to be achieved. It commands an action that is in-itself good, an action that any rational person would acknowledge to be so. Kant says that there is only one categorical imperative, but it can be expressed in different ways. In its most famous formulation it says: '*act only in accordance with that maxim through which you can at the same time will that it become a universal law*' (Kant, 1996d [1785b]: 73). It does not prescribe specific moral rules but a rational principle by which we can judge the morality of any proposed action *a priori*.

This distinction between desire/inclination and freedom/reason is fundamental to Kant's view of the essentially dual nature of human beings. That part of the human being that is rational, according to Kant, is in principle free from (not determined by) the physical world or the world of the senses.

This is a 'metaphysical' concept of freedom, not a political or social one. Freedom, for Kant, is effectively inseparable from reason. It is a power of the human soul, the existence of which cannot be proved by theoretical reason but which must be presupposed by practical reason if morality is to be possible. (So, 'freedom' is an idea of pure reason, Kant, 1996h [1797]: 376.) For Kant, all ideas about, and claims for, political freedom would be meaningless if we did not presuppose this kind of metaphysical freedom as a defining and therefore *universal* characteristic of human being. It is this part of the human being that raises it above its merely animal existence and gives human existence its 'absolute worth' (Kant, 1996d [1785b]: 78). A free will gives itself 'ends'—things that it wants to bring about—and in order to bring about these ends, it employs 'means'. But by virtue of its rationality every human being must be considered as an 'end in itself' and never merely as a means towards an end (ibid.: 79–80). As 'ends in themselves' human beings are 'persons' and not merely 'things'.

But human beings are also empirically determined, embodied creatures of passion and feeling. Reason allows human beings to transcend nature in certain respects, but humans are still part of nature. This is the animal (or 'empirical') aspect of human being—not just the accidents of birth (sex, natural talents, physical characteristics, and so on) but also sensual desires, passions, and inclinations. Indeed, it is *because* humans are also finite, imperfectly rational natural beings that we require morality. But morality is not subjection to an externally imposed law. Because we arrive at the 'categorical imperative' of morality through the free exercise of our own reason, we give the moral law to ourselves—we are *autonomous*. 'Heteronomy' of the will, on the other hand, is when it is determined by something other than itself, including our own desires or animal nature.

> **29.2 Fundamentals of Kant's philosophy: Key Points**
>
> - The idea of self-determination in thinking, religion, and politics presupposes, for Kant, the (metaphysical) idea of human freedom.
> - Morality is concerned with duty (what we ought to do) and what we ought to do is determined by the application of the pure rational principle of morality—the categorical imperative.
> - Humans are dual-natured beings, both free (rational) and empirically and sensually determined.

29.3 Kant's political philosophy

Although the distinction between theoretical and practical philosophy is often understood in terms of the distinction between what is and what ought to be, Kant's political philosophy deals with both. It is concerned with what social and political conditions—within and between states—necessarily arise because of what humans are, and what humans ought to do in order to facilitate the fullest expression of what humans ought to be.

Kant approaches these concerns from two different but interrelated perspectives. In a series of 'popular' essays, Kant addresses the political issues from the standpoint of 'universal history' (the history of humanity as a unitary whole) with its basis in a teleological conception of 'nature's plan' for humanity and ideas of the natural and moral 'ends' of the individual and the human species. In the first part of *The Metaphysics of Morals* (the 'Doctrine of Right', Kant, 1996h [1797]), on the other hand, the emphasis is firmly on the *a priori* deduction of the rightfulness of the state and of relations between states—that is, providing *a priori* foundations for political theory. Here the teleological standpoint is not rejected, but it only plays a supplementary role.

29.3.1 Universal history and teleology

First, in 'Idea for a Universal History with a Cosmopolitan Aim', Kant claims that in order to understand human history systematically we are justified in adopting a 'teleological' standpoint, where we see things in terms of purposes or 'ends'. We are justified, he says, in seeing history as proceeding according to an 'aim of nature', as if led by 'a guiding thread' (Kant, 1996c [1784b]: 108). Why? Because this is the only way that we can make sense of human history, as far as Kant is concerned (so it is a postulate of teleological reason) and because 'nature's plan' is another way of saying 'divine providence'. The fact that this could never be proved is acknowledged in the title of the essay—the 'Idea' for a Universal History is an idea of pure reason.

This teleological standpoint is valid when thinking about both individuals and about the human species as a whole. Kant claims that all of the 'natural predispositions' in any 'creature' 'are determined to develop themselves completely and purposively' (ibid.: 109), because it does not make sense (according to Kant) to think of creatures as being endowed with organs or capacities that have no purpose or use. The most important of the 'natural predispositions' in the human creature is the capacity for the development and full use of rationality itself (what he elsewhere calls 'Enlightenment'). However, reason does not operate instinctively but requires cultivation in the context of civilization, and the full development of rationality or 'the complete use of all of his natural predispositions' is too great a task for any one individual. The task of Enlightenment is passed from one generation to the next, each learning from its predecessor, so the full development of human predispositions occurs only in the species, not the individual (ibid.: 109). This allows us to see the species as slowly progressing towards the full development of its original dispositions (its potentialities, perhaps), even if this is not obvious at the level of the individual or of the nation. Given that humans can only progress towards 'perfection' in a civil state, Kant thinks that we can regard human history as a whole as the unfolding of a 'hidden plan of nature' to bring about a perfect state constitution (ibid.: 116).

Nature does this through what Kant (ibid.: 111) calls the 'unsociable sociability' of human beings. That is, humans have both an inclination towards society and a kind of natural antagonism or 'resistance' towards each other (each wants to get their own way). The contradiction between these two things is resolved by entering into a civil society. Kant (ibid.: 115) characterizes the situation of individuals before entering the civil state as 'the purposeless condition of savages'. Nature drives humans in a state of 'unbound freedom', through need, to enter the civil condition. But these states are then like 'savages' with a 'barbaric freedom' in relation to each other, in a condition of perpetually threatened or actual war. Nature then drives these states, again through need, to enter into a peaceable relation with each other, in what he here calls a 'federation of nations' (ibid.: 114).

As its title suggests, the essay 'Toward Perpetual Peace' is primarily concerned with this second aspect of human progress, the aim of a 'league of nations'. Again, he characterizes the various nations (of Europe, effectively) as if they were individuals 'in their natural condition (that is, in their independence from external laws)' (Kant, 1996g [1795]: 325). Just as individuals ought to want to relinquish their 'mad freedom' from external law in favour of a rational, civil freedom, so too should states in relation to each other. The immediate context of the essay was the French Revolutionary Wars (1792–1797), in which Kant's native Prussia had been involved until King Frederick William II withdrew and the Treaty of Basel (1795) was signed. This essay, probably the best known of Kant's political works, sets out various 'articles' that would be preliminary to or definitive for 'perpetual peace' among nations, so clearly spoke to the concerns of the moment. But it also seems to prefigure the aims of the international League of Nations, established in 1920, and its successor, the United Nations organization, established in 1945.

The articles in Kant's essay include what many might today see as basic conditions for the possibility of successful international relations, for example, the article that sets it down that 'No state shall forcibly interfere in the constitution and government of another state' (ibid.: 319). Others concern what is necessary for a peace treaty to really count as such and peacetime measures that even today seem radical, for example, that 'Standing armies . . . shall in time be abolished altogether' (ibid.: 318). Given that none of Kant's proposals have ever been instituted or respected in the subsequent history of international relations, they may seem utopian. But his point—as in the earlier 'Idea for a Universal History with a Cosmopolitan Aim'—is that these articles are 'ideal' in the technical sense that they represent aims that any rational state ought to work towards. Kant's political theory—like all of his practical philosophy—is premised on the claim that existing states of affairs cannot in themselves be any guide to how things ought to be. The 'guarantee' of perpetual peace in this essay, as before, is not to be found in any empirical survey of human history but in 'the great artist *nature*', the purposive course of the world or '*providence*' which we do not 'strictly speaking *cognize*' but posit ('*add it in thought*') for practical purposes (Kant, 1996g [1795]: 331–332). Although contemporary political theorizing would obviously not accept this idea of providence, the minimal interpretation of Kant's point here may be difficult to disagree with: if we do not theorize with the aim of something better in mind, does our theorizing make any sense?

29.3.2 *A priori* foundations for political theory

In 'Toward Perpetual Peace' Kant makes claims supported by means of *a priori* deduction. For some commentators (e.g., Flikschuh, 2000), this is the most important aspect of Kant's political philosophy. Although Kant was influenced by Rousseau's idea of the social contract (see Chapter 9), and people have often seen Kant (like Hobbes and Locke, see Chapters 5 and 7, respectively) as a contractarian thinker, what is really distinctive about Kant's political theory is his attempt to deduce the *obligation* for the civil contract that founds a rightful state (and the international 'contract' that would found a league of nations) from certain *a priori* premises—specifically from the idea of human freedom and the concept of right itself. Another way of saying this is that Kant (1996h [1797]: 371) aimed to provide metaphysical foundations for political theory, where 'metaphysics' means 'a system of *a priori* cognition from concepts alone'.

Kant maintains that every civil constitution (every state) should be 'republican'. By this he means not anti-monarchical, necessarily, but anti-despotic (or anti-tyrannical). A republican constitution is established 'first on principles of the *freedom* of the members of a society (as individuals [*Menschen*]), second on principles of the *dependence* of all upon a single common legislation (as subjects [*Untertanen*]), and third on the law of their *equality* (*as citizens* [*Staatsbürger*] *of a state*)' (Kant, 1996g [1795]: 322). The distinction between these three concepts—individuals (people; that is, particular human beings), subjects (or 'underlings'; the word Kant uses is now somewhat pejorative), and citizens—is crucial. Most important is this stress on the *freedom* of individuals, the *universality* of the principles of the constitution, and the *equality* of citizens.

The freedom of individuals is their original, positive freedom as human beings in the natural state. Although Kant does not use the terminology of the 'state of nature' or the 'social contract' in 'Toward Perpetual Peace' (or before), it is obvious that he is addressing the same kinds of issues that thinkers such as Hobbes, Locke, and Rousseau discussed with those phrases, and in *The Metaphysics of Morals* he uses the terminology explicitly. However, Kant positions himself against these thinkers by claiming that the 'state of nature' is already 'social' because it is comprised of family units, tribes, and so on. The state of nature is not opposed to a social condition but to civil society (Kant, 1797: 397), by which Kant means a state constituted by a particular form of 'right' or 'law'—specifically, the right of possession or what Kant (1996h [1797]: 451) calls 'distributive justice'.

'Right' in general, according to Kant, has to do with 'a practical relation of one person to another, insofar as their actions, as deeds, can have (direct or indirect) influence on each other'. The universal principle of right is: 'Any action is *right* if it can coexist with everyone's freedom in accordance with a universal law, or if on its maxim the freedom of choice of each can coexist with everyone's freedom in accordance with a universal law' (ibid.: 387). A 'maxim' is a rule or principle of action. In accordance with the categorical imperative, as in Kant's moral philosophy more generally, it must be able to be 'universalized'. If 'a certain use of freedom' (what Kant calls the 'mad' or 'wild' freedom of the state of nature) 'is itself a hindrance to freedom in accordance with universal laws', then that use of freedom is wrong (not in accordance with right) and right consists in opposing this use of freedom. The coercion that is opposed to this use of freedom is right: 'Right and the authorization to use coercion therefore mean one and the same thing' (ibid.: 388–389).

In Kant's sole explicit concession to the natural law tradition, he says that there is only one 'innate' or 'original' right that belongs to every human being by virtue of their humanity: freedom (ibid.: 393). Here 'freedom' means independence from being constrained by another person's freedom, and it is a right only to the extent that it coexists with the freedom of all or does not constrain the freedom of others. This 'internal' right is the social (but not yet civil) form of the metaphysical idea of freedom that distinguishes human beings from animals. As such, it is presupposed in political theory but there is nothing more to be said about it in itself. Kant's 'doctrine of right'—that is, his *a priori* justification of the political rights and duties in civil society—is concerned with 'external right', or rights enshrined in public law. But these political rights are the way of guaranteeing or allowing the rightful exercise of freedom, that is, of innate (internal) right.

Kant sees the civil contract as securing, first and foremost, rightful possession. In the state of nature there would be possession *in fact*, but not possession *in right*, strictly speaking, because others are as yet under no obligation to respect my claim to possession. Private right—the right of individuals in the state of nature—is therefore only provisional (ibid.: 409) and needs to be secured by public right, where 'public' can be understood to mean 'recognized by all'.

How, then, do we move to rightful possession? Kant's argument is very complex here, and the language in which it is expressed even more so. But the basic point is this. If I own an object, it is mine to use, or I am free to use it. When I lay claim to something as mine (a right to possession), this is the same as saying that it is not others' and that they have an *obligation* not to use it. Such a claim can only be made, however, if I also recognize that 'I in turn am under obligation to every other to refrain from using what is externally his' (ibid.: 409). Kant's point is not that, historically, at some point everyone agreed to this. His point is that when we analyse the concept of an obligation itself, corresponding to the concept of an external right, we see, through reason alone (so, *a priori*) that the very notions of obligation and right entail this universal rule. Still, no one person could will this unilaterally for every person (that would impinge upon others' freedom). Accordingly, 'it is only a will putting everyone under obligation, hence only a collective general (common) and powerful will, that can provide everyone this assurance' (ibid.: 409). The condition of being subject to a general, law-giving will *is* the civil condition. Kant says that it is therefore only in a civil condition that there is rightful possession, but he could also have said that only when there is rightful possession is there a civil condition. The one does not precede the other either empirically or logically.

Given that accepting the obligation not to use others' property is akin to giving up the right to the use of it, Kant (ibid.: 411) thinks that we must think of possession of things (including, importantly, land) on the basis of an original possession in common. The need to presuppose this makes it easier to see that any rightful limitation to this original possession in common could only be made 'through the united choice [effectively, freedom] of all who possess it in common' (ibid.: 413). This also helps us to see that rightful possession is 'nothing other than a relation of a person to persons' rather than, primarily, a relation between a person and a thing. So, Kant explicitly denies Locke's labour theory of property, which Kant sees as wrongly attached to the idea that right is established through the relation between a person and a thing (specifically, mixing one's labour with it). Kant's idea of original possession in common is also explicitly opposed to the idea of '*terra nullius*' (land that belongs to no one)—an idea that has been used to justify colonial appropriation of lands. The idea of original possession in common leads Kant (in ibid., at least) to deny that any nation has the right to found colonies by force (ibid.: 417–418). It also leads to the idea of 'cosmopolitan right'—'the right of citizens of the world *to try to* establish community with all and, to this end, to *visit* all regions of the earth' (ibid.: 489). Again, Kant denies, forcefully, that this extends to the right to make a settlement on the land of another nation, and writes in strong terms, in this late work, against the 'specious arguments' that try to justify the use of force in colonization, including Christianizing missions, where no amount of 'good intentions' can 'wash away the stain of injustice' (ibid.: 490).

In order to show that it is not just sensible to quit the state of nature, but more importantly that one *ought* to leave it for the civil condition (ibid.: 451), Kant presents it as commanded by the categorical imperative. If the well-being of a state lies in its constitution conforming to principles of right, 'it is that condition which reason, *by a categorical imperative*, makes it obligatory for us to strive after' (ibid.: 461). At its most basic, this is because only the civil condition, in which I accept my obligation to respects others' freedom, guarantees my freedom (of possession); thus, I am rationally obliged to accept it even if it is not in my immediate interest. Right, which is only possible in the civil condition, is the formal condition of outer freedom as universal law (ibid.: 513). Kant thinks that we arrive at this conclusion through the exercise of reason alone; that is, *a priori*.

This explains why Kant claims that there can be no justified resistance to or rebellion against a civil power. No resistance could be right, because right has as its condition submission to the general, legislative will which is represented by the head of state (whether a monarchy, an oligarchy, or in any other form) (ibid.: 463). 'Rightful rebellion' is for Kant a contradiction in terms. To act against the state contradicts the categorical imperative that impels one to act for it, and is thus contrary to reason. One may complain and petition for reform, in the executive authority, but never rebel or revolt (ibid.: 465). Indeed, the freedom to complain, or freedom of speech and publication, must be part of any rational state, because to outlaw this would be to constrain the public use of one's reason which is central to Kant's (1996b [1784a]) conception of Enlightenment.

The logic of the obligation of individuals to leave the state of nature and enter into a civil condition applies equally to nations in relation to each other. States, Kant (1996h [1797]: 482) says, are like 'moral persons', 'living in relation to another state in the condition of natural freedom and therefore in a condition of constant war'. Just as the private right of individuals in the state of nature was only provisional, needing to be guaranteed by the condition of right in civil society, so the rights of state are merely provisional in a global context: 'Only in a universal association of states (analogous to that by which a people become a state) can rights come to hold conclusively and a true condition of peace come about' (ibid.: 487). Once again Kant (ibid.: 487) recognizes that perpetual peace 'is indeed an unachievable idea' but striving towards this is a duty. A league of nations is thus a rational requirement and a practical duty: nations ought to leave the state of nature among themselves 'in order to enter a lawful condition'.

29.3 Kant's political philosophy: Key Points

- According to the teleological standpoint of universal history, the move from the state of nature to civil society and then to a league of nations is understood as nature's plan for the human species.
- According to the metaphysical standpoint, individuals are rationally obliged to enter the civil state to secure their freedom and right to possession.
- This rational obligation renders all revolution or rebellion against the state unjust.

29.4 'Ideal' and 'non-ideal' political theory

Aspects of Kant's political philosophy and the core of his moral philosophy have been and continue to be influential in political theory of various types. Some of the most important mainstream (and especially liberal) twentieth-century political theorists developed explicitly Kantian ideas. John Rawls (see Chapter 32) describes his conception of the 'original position' as an attempt to interpret Kant's claim that moral principles of legislation can only be 'agreed to under conditions that characterize men as free and equal rational beings'. He sees his 'principles of justice' as 'categorical imperatives in Kant's sense' (Rawls, 2005; 252–253). His 'liberal principle of legitimacy', which ties legitimate political power to a constitution that could in principle be agreed upon by all free, equal, and rational citizens (Rawls, 1993: 137), is clearly Kantian in inspiration. Aspects of his 'law of peoples' are easy to trace back to some of Kant's claims about a league of nations (Rawls, 1999: 36).

Jürgen Habermas's conception of 'discourse ethics' and his account of democratic legitimacy are also explicitly indebted to Kant (see Key Thinker: Jürgen Habermas). Robert Nozick's libertarian view of the minimal state appeals to Kantian principles (specifically, that version of the categorical imperative that forbids treating people as means). Without following him to the letter, many important theorists of international justice have found their starting point in Kant's discussions of cosmopolitanism; indeed, what can now be called the twentieth-century cosmopolitan tradition in general has its origin in Kant's work.

> ### Key Thinker: Jürgen Habermas
>
> Jürgen Habermas (1929–) is one of the most influential contemporary social philosophers in the West. He is the main figure of what many people consider the second generation of the Frankfurt School of Critical Theory (having been associated with the first-generation thinkers Theodor W. Adorno and Max Horkheimer). Habermas is known for his attempt to renew the Critical Theory tradition by outlining its normative foundations. Rethinking Kant's idea of 'public reason', he developed a theory of 'communicative rationality and action'. This is a theory that locates rationality in the process of reaching a consensus on the basis of a (transcendental) 'ideal speech situation'. Habermas is also known for defending the Enlightenment 'project of modernity' against its 'postmodern' critique.

The modern appeal of Kant's philosophy for political theorists lies in its postulation of the inherent and absolute dignity of *all* persons, irrespective of any empirical differences between them, the requirement to respect the freedom of others and to foster the conditions in which autonomous citizens might rightfully exercise this freedom, and the universality of the rights and duties ascribed to them on this basis. The initial postulate of respect for persons and the universality of the agreement required for any legitimate political constitution leads in Kant's political theory to the principle of the equality of all citizens before the law, and the extension of this to international relations is particularly attractive to some progressive strands in political theory, given the contemporary condition of increasing globalization. Some have developed a more extensive interpretation of Kant's idea of the right of hospitality to argue for the obligation of hospitality to refugees (e.g., Benhabib, 2008).

But some of the main criticisms of Kant and Kantian political theory (especially of Rawls and Habermas) touch directly on the 'ideal' nature of the supposed universality and equality at the basis of Kant's theory. Kant was explicit about the non-empirical nature of the concepts of duty, the social contract, right of state, perpetual peace, and so on. He argued that the principles drawn from the analysis of these concepts were rationally compelled, and hence principles with which every rational person would agree. In effect, this posits (in thought, not historical reality) an ideal situation at the origin of the social contract. In Rawls's (2005: 11) version, 'ideal theory' arrives at a conception of justice by following the guiding idea that the principles of justice are those that 'free and rational persons concerned to further their own interest would accept' in an 'initial position' of equality. Rawls argues that ideal theory must always come first, as it is only when certain basic principles have been established in this way that we can apply them to reforming our non-ideal (unequal) societies, acknowledging inequalities and taking into account the specific circumstances and needs of specific groups. But the basic criticism of ideal theory is that principles drawn from idealizing assumptions are likely to be inadequate as a basis for understanding how to promote justice in non-ideal—that is, actual—societies (see, for example, Moller Okin, 1989; Mills, 2005).

But there is another problem with Kant's 'ideal theory', which is that it fails to respect the very universality, equality, and safeguarding of freedom on which it is allegedly based. We can see this in two ways, which we will deal with here in turn: first, in relation to the *a priori* foundations for political philosophy; and, second, in relation to universal history and teleology, which we can connect to Kant's theory of 'race'.

29.4.1 Problems in the *a priori* foundations

In 'Toward Perpetual Peace' Kant (1996g [1795]: 322) makes an important conceptual and political distinction between the *individuals* (particular human members) of a society, the *subjects* of a common legislation, and the *citizens* of a state. It is the freedom of the individuals in a society (in the state of nature) that is the basis of the civil contract and which civil society guarantees. In civil society these individuals become subjects—that is, subject to the law that constitutes the civil condition, but a law that is the result of their common legislation, so one which does not compromise their autonomy. With regard to the various rights and duties then established in a civil society, they are treated as citizens of the state on a basis of equality.

However, Kant also maintains that there are certain requirements that have to be met for a subject to qualify as a citizen. As he puts it in 1793 (Kant, 1996f [1793]: 295): 'He who has the right to vote in this legislation is called a *citizen* . . . The quality requisite to this, apart from the *natural* one (of not being a child or a woman), is only that of *being one's own master (sui iuris)*, hence having some *property* . . . that supports him.' In *The Metaphysics of Morals*, this 'being one's own master' is characterized as an 'independence' that allows a member of the commonwealth to act from his 'own choice in community with others' (Kant, 1996h [1797]: 458). This gives Kant the distinction between 'passive' and 'active' citizenship, where only the latter are citizens proper (allowed to vote). 'Passive' citizens include:

> an apprentice in the service of a merchant or an artisan; a domestic servant; a minor . . .; all women and, in general, anyone whose preservation in existence (his being fed and protected) depends not on his management of his own business but on arrangements made by another (except the state). All these people lack civic personality . . . The woodcutter I hire to work in my yard; the blacksmith in India, who goes into people's houses to work . . . As opposed to the European Carpenter or blacksmith who can put the products of his work up as goods for sale. The private tutor . . . the tenant farmer . . . these are mere underlings of the commonwealth because they have to be under the direction or protection of other individuals, and so do not possess civil independence.
>
> (ibid.: 458)

This obviously seems to contradict the principles of equality and universality that are fundamental to Kant's political philosophy. In response, Kant claims:

> this thoroughgoing equality of individuals within a state, as its subjects, is quite consistent with the greatest inequality in terms of the quantity and degree of their possessions . . . and in rights generally . . . thus one must obey (as a child its elders or a wife her husband) and the other directs; thus one serves (a day labourer) and the other pays him, and so forth. But *in terms of right* . . . they are nevertheless all equal to one another as subjects.
>
> (Kant, 1996f [1793]: 292)

That is, equality at the level of the individual and the subject is quite compatible, according to Kant, with inequality (and indeed 'the greatest inequality') at the level of the citizen. He justifies this with the claim that the equality of subjects demands that any member of a civil society must be allowed to attain any rank within it that his talents allow (ibid.: 293) and that anyone may work their way up from passive to active citizenship (Kant, 1996h [1797]: 459). But as women are said to be *naturally* unfit for citizenship (Kant, 1996f [1793]: 295), this is a hollow claim for them. More generally, this claim reveals a problem with 'ideal theory'. As one commentator (Booth, 1993: 264) puts it: Kant 'presents us with an idealized picture of social relations in which coercion, understood as forcible assertions of one will over another, plays no role'. Kant writes as if the day labourer could choose *not* to sell their labour—but what choice do they *really* have? When social conditions of inequality are such as to effectively make it impossible for the day labourer to be anything other than a day labourer, the idea of equality of opportunity is rather empty.

Kant's justification for inequality is connected to the distinctions that he makes between various forms of possession. As we have seen, the civil condition secures rightful possession of, in the first instance, external objects or things for all people. But it also makes possible, second, rightful possession of 'another's *choice* to perform a specific deed' (Kant, 1996h [1797]: 402), the relevant example of which is 'a contract of *letting of work* on hire . . . that is, granting another the use of my powers for a specified price (*merces*). By this contract the worker is a hired help (*mercennarius*)' (ibid.: 433). For the duration of the contract, the 'hired help' is under the control of the hiring party, who is thus (in Kant's terminology) the owner of the help's 'choice'. The help is precisely not 'his own master', and thus does not qualify as an active citizen.

The civil condition also secures, third, rightful possession of another person or their status, or what Kant calls 'rights to persons akin to things'. This is, in a sense, possession of a person, and it has three forms: 'a *man* acquires a *wife* [marriage right]; a *couple* acquires *children* [parental right]; and a *family* acquires *servants* [right of the head of a household]' (ibid.: 426). There is some reciprocity in marriage right as far as 'sexual union' is concerned, as each makes use of the other's sexual organs for their own enjoyment, as if the other person were a thing (ibid.: 426–427). But, in addition, the man becomes the master of his wife: 'he is the party to direct, she to obey' (ibid.: 428). Parental right (which brings with it parental duties) is justified control of children (ibid.: 430). The right of a head of the household is formed by a contract which establishes a domestic society in which the servants belong to the head: he 'acquire[s] them as domestics' (ibid.: 431, 496).

In all cases possession of a person is a relation of inequality which seems, especially in the case of women and servants, to contradict the more general principle of equality. But, again, Kant (ibid.: 428) denies this, saying that the husband's control over his wife 'cannot be regarded as conflicting with the natural equality of a couple if this dominance is based only on the natural superiority of the husband to the wife in his capacity to promote the common interest of the household'. Kant offers no justification for this idea of the natural superiority of men in relation to women. Indeed, unjustified assertions about the incapacities of women are a common feature of Kant's anthropology, with significant consequences for the alleged universality of his moral philosophy, too. According to Kant (2012a: 631), women have no 'character'. Character is the capacity for control over one's desires and inclinations, manifest in the ability to follow objective (moral) rules and principles (ibid.: 438, 630). If women lack character, they thus lack the capacity to be full moral subjects, or they remain forever morally immature, which (for Kant) would justify their subjection to patriarchal control. As Inder Marwah (2013) has argued, this exclusion is not a contradiction in Kant's moral and political philosophy but is a requirement within it, because women are assigned particular roles in human history: the natural role of the reproduction of the species and the social role of using their feminine arts to civilize and 'moralize' men, to create the conditions in which men—but not women themselves—might develop a properly moral character.

29.4.2 Problems in relation to universal history and teleology: the theory of race and the colonial context

The idea of woman's role, or her 'purpose', returns us to the idea of natural teleology that we saw at work in Kant's political theory. The multi-generational task of rational development towards Enlightenment and perpetual peace that we saw there is also cast in terms of the development of 'seeds' or 'germs' (*Keime*). Kant (1996c [1784b]: 119) says, for example, that the presupposition of nature's plan for the human species allows us to imagine the species 'as finally working itself upward toward the condition in which all germs nature has placed in it can be fully developed and its vocation here on earth can be fulfilled'. This is not just an organic metaphor. One of the most consistent aspects of Kant's work, from the 'pre-critical period' of the 1770s to the mature period of the late-1790s, is his commitment to a theory developed as a contribution to the life sciences—what we would now call a 'biological' theory. It is developed, specifically, as a theory to explain the racial diversity of the human species—it is, therefore, a theory of 'race'.

> **Key Concept: 'Race'**
>
> Although other thinkers had used the *word* 'race' before, Kant is the first thinker to have tried to define the *concept* scientifically and philosophically (see Bernasconi, 2001). Kant was the first to give what we would now call a 'biological' explanation for the existence and persistence of different 'races', and many thus see him as having provided the basis for the essentialist, biological conceptions of race that ran through the nineteenth and twentieth centuries and which were used to justify slavery and racism in general. As many critical race theorists have argued, the consequences of this history still often structure the way people think about racial differences, even when the idea of a biological basis for race has been thoroughly discredited.

Kant adhered to the idea of 'monogenesis', which is to say that he believed that all human 'races' shared the same origin (and thus are members of the same species). But how, then, could the fact of human diversity be explained? Kant claimed that the popular idea that human differences were merely the effect of climate or other environmental factors could not be right, because this fails to account for the perpetuation of characteristics in species transplanted to other environments. Instead, he proposed a new theory. He claimed that the original 'stem' of the human species contained various germs and predispositions, which together equipped the species for survival in any part of the world. Not all of the germs and predispositions would develop in all of the members or groups within a species, only those that fitted them for the particular climate or circumstances to which it or they migrated. In his first essay on this topic, 'Of the Different Races of Human Beings', he writes:

> The human being was destined for all climates and for every soil; consequently, various germs and natural predispositions had to lie ready in him to be on occasion either unfolded or restrained, so that he would become suited to his place in the world and over the course of generations would appear to be as it were native to and made for that place.
>
> (Kant, 2007b [1775]: 90)

Human *physical* diversity is thus the effect of an 'enduring' development of some germs and predispositions as an adaption to the physical environment, especially to 'air' and 'sun', and in this way 'races' are established or become 'persistent': 'once a race has taken root and has suffocated the other germs, it resists all transformation just because the character of the race has then become prevailing in the generative power' (ibid.: 90–91, 96). Indeed, Kant actually suggests that there are 'germs which were originally placed in the stem of the human genus for the generation of the races' (Kant, 1996d [1785b]: 158, translation modified). For Kant (ibid.: 155; 2007c [1785a]: 148–149, 153–154; 2007d [1788b]: 210), the specific physical characteristic that distinguishes one 'race' from another is the only one that is unfailingly inherited, and this is skin colour.

Kant believed that there were four races. He characterized these geographically in different ways but most often in terms of skin colour: white, black, red, and olive (or yellow). In the essays on race, he contends that the identification of the races themselves belongs to 'physical geography' (Kant, 2007b [1775]: 97), but the essays are shot through with claims about the moral and behavioural characteristics of the different races, so also touch on what he calls 'moral anthropology' (Kant, 1996h [1797]: 372). Without exception, his remarks are ill-informed and trade in stereotypes. With regard to all 'races' except the white he is often profoundly racist. In the essays on race, in his lectures on anthropology, and in his lectures on physical geography, Kant assumes a hierarchy of the races, with white at the top and either black or red at the bottom. He claims, for example, that 'Humanity has reached its highest degree of perfection in the white race. The yellow Indians have a somewhat lesser talent. The Negroes are much lower, and lowest of all is part of the American races' (Kant, 2012b [1802]: 576). In the lectures on anthropology, he is reported as saying that 'the white race contains all incentives and talents in itself' (Kant, 2012a: 321). He frequently refers to some peoples outside of Europe as 'savages'.

Some scholars have tried to distinguish the racism of Kant the man from the thought of the philosopher, but these comments are part of his 'thought' and, according to his own procedure of justification, quite compatible with his political theory. In Kant's moral philosophy, individuals have a duty to cultivate their natural powers and to increase their 'moral perfection' (Kant, 1996h [1797]: 566), both of which can only be done in the civil condition. The collective work of moral self-perfection in the civil condition could be called culture in general. It is perfectly clear that Kant believes that not only have the white European nations achieved the greatest cultural development, but also that some people are incapable of culture, or at least incapable of an Indigenous culture. In his brief account of 'universal history', which charts a line of progress from ancient Greece and Rome, he says that we can discover 'a regular course of improvement of state constitutions in our part of the world (which will probably someday give laws to all the others)' (Kant, 1996c [1784b]: 119). Elsewhere he says that the 'Americans' are 'incapable of any culture' and that the 'Negro' ranks below even this (Kant, 2007d [1788b]: 211). Thus, Kant's political philosophy (encompassing aspects of his anthropology) is Eurocentric, according to Tsenay Serequeberhan's (1996: 142) definition: the belief 'that European existence is qualitatively superior to other forms of human life'. It is also Eurocentric in Emmanuel Eze's (1997: 117, 121) sense, as it takes European humanity as the 'ideal'. Dilek Huseyinzadegan (2019: 15) sums this all up well:

> Kant takes European history to be *the* universal or world history, the European mode of life and cultural activity to be *the* paradigm of human cultural production as such, and the European way of interacting with the world to be *the* primary model for all global relationships . . . his stated vision of a cosmopolitan world order has a distinctly European bent while masquerading as a universal ideal.

This contradiction between the universal idea of a human species involved in its common quest for moral and political perfection—one in which, in principle, all peoples participate equally—and the effective exclusion of so many people from active participation in this (mere followers of Europe) mirrors the contradiction between the universal equality of subjects and the inequalities of citizens described above. If Kant found no problem with the latter, we may safely conjecture that he would also find the former to be perfectly justifiable within his own terms; that is, *he* would have seen no contradiction between his Eurocentrism and the universalism of his political theory. Kant scholars have often seen 'an unresolved tension . . . between the core message of universality in [Kant's] ethics and frequent assertions that many different groups of people . . . are in a pre-moral state of development' (Louden, 2000: 15). But, in fact, Kant's philosophy encompasses that contradiction; it accepts and justifies it. This needs to be borne in mind in any discussion of Kant's relation to colonialism. In his late work he condemns colonial brutality and rejects the idea that capture of others' lands can ever be justified, not even in the name of a 'civilizing mission'. But the idea of a colony with its own constitution, legislation, and land over which another ('mother') state has 'supreme *executive* authority' (Kant, 1996h [1797]: 486) because of the supposed 'natural superiority' of the people of the mother state seems to him to be a decent outcome of war. Further, the injunction not to interfere in other states would not apply, for Kant, to a society that was in a 'state of nature'; indeed the 'civilized' state would have an obligation to bring 'peace' to relations between peoples, thus sanctioning, as Murad Idris (2019: 274) points out, imperial justifications for intervention. Kant sees the contradiction between the idea of a civilizing intervention and the barbaric violence that it most often entailed, but his political philosophy is nevertheless, as Idris (ibid.: 264) says, 'prone to retrospectively legitimating imperialism's historical consequences in the name of spreading peace, and to effacing empire and the asymmetries of power it re-entrenches'.

29.4 'Ideal' and 'non-ideal' political theory: Key Points

- The 'ideal' aspects of Kant's political theory (the freedom, dignity, and equality of all persons) continue to be influential and attractive.
- Kant sees these ideal aspects as compatible with certain 'natural' inequalities (specifically gender inequality) and with certain social or class inequalities (in relations of master and servant).
- The teleological unfolding of human predispositions is explained through a theory of 'germs' that aims primarily to account for the supposed existence of distinct human 'races'.
- Kant's 'universal history' is Eurocentric and racist; his teleological idea of human progress is compatible with a racial theory of development.

29.5 Conclusion

For a long time, Kant's racism and his Eurocentrism were overlooked in discussions of his work. That once might have been because of ignorance of these aspects of his work; to overlook them now is to choose to overlook prejudice and to remain ignorant of the influence that these aspects might have had in later political theorizing. But if we do acknowledge these aspects of his work, this does not mean that we have to reject everything else that Kant says. Some Kant scholars have argued that we can extract the universal egalitarian core of his political and moral philosophy while rejecting the sexist and racist content that fails to live up to this ideal. Indeed, some would say that any criticism of Kant on this score implicitly utilizes Kant's universal egalitarian ideal in that very criticism. Others would argue that we need to investigate the very notion of the 'universal' more critically. This is particularly the case with regard to the idea of 'universal history' (Spivak, 1999; Guha, 2003; Balibar, 2020).

One of the most sophisticated recent responses to Kant is Charles Mills's attempt to develop a 'black radical Kantianism' (see Chapter 10 on Mills). This works *with* the contradiction in Kant's works. Mills suggests that the Kantian idea of universal equality and respect for persons is crucial, to the extent that (contra European racism) 'blacks and other people of color *are* equal'. Mills (2018: 16) notes the extent to which the Black radical tradition has made its demands in Kantian terms: for 'equal recognition, equal dignity, equal respect, equal *personhood*'. This is particularly evident in the work of W.E.B. Du Bois (see Chapter 31). But at the same time Kant's Eurocentrism and racism unwittingly reveal another truth—that racial inequality has fundamentally shaped the modern world order (ibid.: 14). The modern state is (as Kant unwittingly revealed) a racial state; if we focus only on the 'ideal' aspects of Kant's theory, we fail to see this and thus fail to theorize adequately. Still, according to Mills, the 'key [egalitarian] principles and ideals of Kant's ethico-political thought' (ibid.: 3) are the tools we need to criticize the racial state and work out how to bring about a state of justice.

Take your learning further by accessing the online resources for a library of web links to relevant videos, articles, blogs, and useful websites for this chapter: www.oup.com/he/Ramgotra-Choat1e.

Study questions

1. Can we understand what it is to be a political actor without thinking about what we mean by 'freedom'?
2. What is a 'metaphysical', as opposed to a political or social, conception of human freedom?
3. What is 'Enlightenment', according to Kant?
4. What is a 'teleological standpoint'?
5. Should teleology have any place in modern political theory?
6. Is the European Union an example of a 'league of nations' as Kant envisaged it?
7. Is there a place for 'ideal theory' in politics?
8. How do we (or can we) justify continuing to study racist thinkers?

Further reading

Primary sources

Kant, I. (1996a) *Practical Philosophy*. Ed. M.J. Gregor. Cambridge: Cambridge University Press.
  This volume includes Kant's essays 'An Answer to the Question: What Is Enlightenment?' (1784a), 'Toward Perpetual Peace' (1795), and the longer, more difficult *The Metaphysics of Morals*. The first two essays are a good introduction to Kant's work.

Kant, I. (2007a) *Anthropology, History and Education*. Ed. G. Zöller and R.B. Louden. Cambridge: Cambridge University Press.

This volume includes Kant's essays on race (1775, 1785a and 1788b) and his 'Idea for a Universal History with a Cosmopolitan Aim' (1784b). This last essay is short, popular in style and a good place to start reading Kant.

Secondary sources

Huseyinzadegan, D. (2019) *Kant's Nonideal Theory of Politics*. Evanston, IL: Northwestern University Press.

Includes a short introduction to various debates over Kant's political philosophy from Rawls onwards, and explains why we should consider Kant's anthropology and geography as part of his political theory.

McCarthy, T. (2009) *Race, Empire, and the Idea of Human Development*. Cambridge: Cambridge University Press.

Treats the problem of 'ideal' political theory in general and in relation to Kant specifically.

References

Balibar, É. (2020) *On Universals: Constructing and Deconstructing Community*. Trans. J.D. Jordan. New York: Fordham University Press.

Benhabib, S. (2008) *Another Cosmopolitanism*. Oxford: Oxford University Press.

Bernasconi, R. (2001) 'Who Invented the Concept of Race? Kant's Role in the Enlightenment Construction of Race'. In R. Bernasconi (ed.), *Race*. Malden, MA: Blackwell.

Booth, W.J. (1993) 'The Limits of Autonomy: Karl Marx's Kant Critique'. In R. Beiner and W.J. Booth (eds), *Kant and Political Philosophy: The Contemporary Legacy*. New Haven, CT: Yale University Press, pp. 245–275.

Derrida, J. (2002) *Who's Afraid of Philosophy? Right to Philosophy I*. Trans. J. Plug. Stanford, CA: Stanford University Press.

Eze, E.C. (1997) 'The Color of Reason: The Idea of "Race" in Kant's Anthropology'. In E.C. Eze (ed.), *Postcolonial African Philosophy: A Critical Reader*. Oxford: Blackwell.

Flikschuh, K. (2000) *Kant and Modern Political Philosophy*. Cambridge: Cambridge University Press.

Guha, R. (2003) *History at the Limit of World-History*. New York: Columbia University Press.

Huseyinzadegan, D. (2019) *Kant's Nonideal Theory of Politics*. Evanston, IL: Northwestern University Press.

Idris, M. (2019) *War for Peace: Genealogies of a Violent Ideal in Western and Islamic Thought*. Oxford: Oxford University Press.

Kant, I. (1996a) *Practical Philosophy*. Ed. M.J. Gregor. Cambridge: Cambridge University Press.

Kant, I. (1996b [1784a]) 'An Answer to the Question: What Is Enlightenment?' In I. Kant, *Practical Philosophy*. Ed. M.J. Gregor. Cambridge: Cambridge University Press.

Kant, I. (1996c [1784b]) 'Idea for a Universal History with a Cosmopolitan Aim'. In I. Kant, *Practical Philosophy*. Ed. M.J. Gregor. Cambridge: Cambridge University Press.

Kant, I. (1996d [1785b]) 'Groundwork of the Metaphysics of Morals'. In I. Kant, *Practical Philosophy*. Ed. M.J. Gregor. Cambridge: Cambridge University Press.

Kant, I. (1996e [1788a]) 'Critique of Practical Reason'. In I. Kant, *Practical Philosophy*. Ed. M.J. Gregor. Cambridge: Cambridge University Press.

Kant, I. (1996f [1793]) 'On the Common Saying: That May be Correct in Theory, But it is of No Use in Practice'. In I. Kant, *Practical Philosophy*. Ed. M.J. Gregor. Cambridge: Cambridge University Press.

Kant, I. (1996g [1795]) 'Toward Perpetual Peace'. In I. Kant, *Practical Philosophy*. Ed. M.J. Gregor. Cambridge: Cambridge University Press.

Kant, I. (1996h [1797]) 'The Metaphysics of Morals'. In I. Kant, *Practical Philosophy*. Ed. M.J. Gregor. Cambridge: Cambridge University Press.

Kant, I. (1997 [1781/1789]) *Critique of Pure Reason*. Trans. P. Guyer and A.W. Wood. Cambridge: Cambridge University Press.

Kant, I. (2000 [1790]) *Critique of the Power of Judgment*. Trans. P. Guyer and E. Matthews. Cambridge: Cambridge University Press.

Kant, I. (2007a) *Anthropology, History and Education*. Ed. G. Zöller and R.B. Louden. Cambridge: Cambridge University Press.

Kant, I. (2007b [1775]) 'Of the Different Races of Human Beings'. In I. Kant, *Anthropology, History and*

Education. Ed. G. Zöller and R.B. Louden. Cambridge: Cambridge University Press.

Kant, I. (2007c [1785a]) 'Determination of the Concept of a Human Race'. In I. Kant, *Anthropology, History and Education*. Ed. G. Zöller and R.B. Louden. Cambridge: Cambridge University Press.

Kant, I. (2007d [1788b]) 'On the Use of Teleological Principles in Philosophy'. In I. Kant, *Anthropology, History and Education*. Ed. G. Zöller and R.B. Louden. Cambridge: Cambridge University Press.

Kant, I. (2012a) *Lectures on Anthropology*. Trans. R.R. Clewis, R.B. Louden, G.F. Munzel, and A.W. Wood. Cambridge: Cambridge University Press.

Kant, I. (2012b [1802]) *Physical Geography*. In I. Kant, *Natural Science*. Ed. E. Watkins. Cambridge: Cambridge University Press.

Louden, R. (2000) *Kant's Impure Ethics: From Rational Beings to Human Beings*. New York: Oxford University Press.

Marwah, I.S. (2013) 'What Nature Makes of Her: Kant's Gendered Metaphysics'. *Hypatia*, 28(3): 551–567.

Mills, C. (2005) '"Ideal Theory" as Ideology'. *Hypatia*, 20(3): 165–184.

Mills, C. (2018) ' Black Radical Kantianism'. *Res Philosophica*, 95(1): 1–33.

Moller Okin, S. (1989) *Justice, Gender and the Family*. New York: Basic Books.

Rawls, J. (1993) *Political Liberalism*. New York: Columbia University Press.

Rawls, J. (1999) *The Law of Peoples*. Cambridge MA: Harvard University Press.

Rawls, J. (2005) *A Theory of Justice*. Cambridge, MA: Harvard University Press.

Serequeberhan, T. (1996) 'Eurocentrism in Philosophy: The Case of Immanuel Kant'. *The Philosophical Forum*, XXVII(4): 333–356.

Spivak, G.C. (1999) *A Critique of Postcolonial Reason: Toward a History of the Vanishing Present*. Cambridge, MA: Harvard University Press.

30 Frederick Douglass

KIARA GILBERT AND KAREN SALT

Chapter guide

This chapter introduces the works of Black American abolitionist Frederick Douglass. It is organized roughly chronologically, as his political thinking was shaped by his respective experiences as enslaved, fugitive, and freed. Section 30.2 focuses on Douglass' conceptions of freedom as a natural right and his establishment of himself as a rational theorist. Section 30.3 focuses on the years between his emancipation and the start of the Civil War in 1861. It engages Douglass' understanding of the US Constitution as an anti-slavery text and his support for violence in insurrections against slavery. Section 30.4 analyses Douglass' political theory in post-Civil War America, particularly his thinking on American imperialism abroad.

30.1 Introduction

Frederick Douglass was born Frederick Bailey in 1818. Born into slavery, he escaped and fled to the Northern USA in 1838, and changed his name to avoid detection. After his escape, he perfected what Chicana feminist Gloria Anzaldúa later called a 'theory in the flesh', one in which 'the physical realities of our lives—our skin color, the land or concrete we grew up on—all fuse to create a politic born out of necessity' (Moraga and Anzaldúa, 2015: 23).

Throughout Douglass' life, he argued forcefully for the emancipation of all enslaved peoples in the USA. A few foundational beliefs guided his thinking. First, Douglass was a natural rights theorist. He believed all humans were endowed with a right to self-determination and freedom from enslavement. Douglass (2017 [1845]: 48) also believed that those robbed of the right to freedom were innately aware their natural rights were being violated. Slavery, he claimed, operated to dehumanize the enslaved and successfully convince them they were owed little as 'brutes'. Finally, Douglass viewed himself as an inheritor of the American tradition: he considered his vision of freedom to be aligned with that of his country's origins. Looking to the violence that erupted during the American Revolution, he argued that, in accordance with the forefathers of the United States, violence would be necessary to seize the freedom owed to disenfranchised parties.

Douglass' lifelong activism across a range of political groups, including among women's rights advocates, gave him a unique position to see the best and the worst of humanity. His early writings and speeches focused on slavery and abolitionism—the political movement to abolish slavery—but his full arc of work situates Douglass as an influential Black political actor, even though he never publicly ran for office. The so-called 'Sage of Cedar Hill' was more than a prominent abolitionist (Blight, 2020: 683). He changed the course of US history, and his theories on freedom and violence continue to influence struggles against racism.

Read more about **Douglass'** life and work by accessing the thinker biography on the online resources: www.oup.com/he/Ramgotra-Choat1e.

30.2 Slavery and freedom

When we first encounter Douglass as a political thinker, he is a fugitive. As he was still legally enslaved, to read early Douglass is to read the speeches, writing, and theories of a man who was legally ascribed the status of an object. Due to fugitive slave laws, whereby slave-catchers in the North had the right to capture enslaved persons, he was initially at constant risk of being kidnapped and forcibly returned to slavery. Douglass made a name for himself despite this risk, not having his freedom formally purchased until years after he emerged on the international stage. He eventually fled to Great Britain and Ireland in 1845, not returning until a sympathetic British abolitionist secured his legal liberation. This was done in 1846 for the sum of roughly $725 (*The Liberator*, 1847).

Despite his accomplishments as a theorist, Douglass was initially dismissed as a serious thinker. The white abolitionists Douglass worked alongside insisted that he only preach within the scope of their collective beliefs. He later complained that during this period of his life he was meant to focus 'on the facts, [while] white abolitionists [gave] the philosophy' (Douglass, 1892: 269). Douglass nevertheless managed to articulate the early foundations of his political and moral theories. He later credited his theoretical grounding to his experiences of slavery, from which he 'elaborated quite a lengthy chapter of political philosophy, applicable to the American people' (Douglass, 2018a [1867]: 232).

30.2.1 The fugitive's philosophy

Delivered in October 1841 at a local abolitionist gathering in Lynn, Massachusetts, this speech is perhaps Douglass' first to be recorded and circulated as abolitionist propaganda:

> My friends, I have come to tell you something about slavery—what I know of it, as I have felt it. When I came North, I was astonished to find that the abolitionists knew so much about it, that they were acquainted with its deadly effects as well as if they had lived in its midst. But though they can give you its history—though they can depict its horrors, they cannot speak as I can from experience; they cannot refer you to a back covered with scars, as I can; for I have felt these wounds; I have suffered under the lash without the power of resisting.
>
> (Douglass, 2018b [1841]: 5)

In this spontaneous address, Douglass gestured towards rival accounts of knowledge. First, there is the unsatisfactory knowledge of the white abolitionists—who 'knew so much', yet so little (ibid.: 5). This first type of knowledge is reflective of traditional understandings of reason and rationality—the 'disembodied' philosopher. Under these paradigms, theorizing from a 'racialized identity' does not grant a knower legitimate knowledge (Silva, 2018: 5). Learning about something at length—regardless of one's own relationship to the subject matter—is considered by most analytical theorists to be more important than citing experience. In fact, a claim to experiential knowledge can be regarded as nullifying one's claim to rational knowledge. With the second type of knowledge—imparted by a 'back full of scars'—Douglass (2018b [1841]: 5) offered a clear rebuke, underscoring that only from a personal perspective could he present his argument. In this way, Douglass underscored his subject-position as a Black enslaved man or, more broadly speaking, his Black subjectivity—the '*interior world*' from which he shaped and was shaped by racializing political constructs (Gibson, 2018: 6). This is reflected in his decisive opening line: he has 'come to tell' listeners about the brutality of slavery but can only 'tell [it]' as *he* knew it.

It is important to highlight that Douglass not only called attention to his own Black subjectivity, he also used it to wield epistemic authority: Douglass' enhanced knowledge was mediated by personal experience. His positionality informed both his testimony and political insights. Having 'felt the wounds' of slavery, Douglass (2018b [1841]: 5) pointed to himself as best positioned to speak on it, and—ultimately—to theorize upon its implications for both enslaved and enslaver. In pulling theory from his experiences as a slave, Douglass not only positioned himself as a rational thinker, he also demonstrated how lived experience grants special insight into sweeping ethical and political conundrums.

To underscore the importance of this moment in political theory, we need only examine the views of earlier thinkers. For Plato (see Chapter 2), to be a slave was to be 'deficient of reason' and thereby necessarily unable to articulate and engage with theoretical frameworks (Vlastos, 1941: 289). Philosopher David Hume once referred to Black intellectuals as 'parrots' limited by the deficiencies of their race: able to speak a few pretty words but lacking 'any symptom of ingenuity' (Hume, 1987 [1777]: 208). Douglass defied both philosophers by declaring his intelligence and his rationality. Still, Douglass' white abolitionist peers adopted a version of Hume's position regarding his work, as Douglass (1892: 269) was often pressured merely to repeat their ideas. Douglass' experiences of slavery were not viewed as a foundation from which he could philosophize. Ironically, his dealings with slavery were viewed as a foundation by which others could rationalize and theorize Douglass' experiences back to him.

Douglass not only rejected the narrow, racist parameters of *who* could rationalize, he also contested the parameters of classical rationality, which privileges a detached objectivity as the foundation of knowledge claims. He further challenged this model of epistemic authority by adding another dimension to his experiential claim to knowledge: emotion. Douglass (2018b [1841]: 5) spoke of slavery as he knew and had 'felt' it. Some of the most gripping moments in Douglass' early texts are those of unceasing despair—sorrow, pain, and anger that underscored the unnatural depravity of his enslaved condition. In invoking the emotion that coloured his experience, Douglass offered a comprehensive epistemological framework, one which established his authority on the topic of slavery. He experienced, he felt, he knew.

There is a third type of knowledge Douglass spoke to in this same address, one which anticipates his articulation of what it means to be human. This is the intrinsic knowledge of one's absolute rights, in this case, the positive right to freedom: 'A large portion of the slaves know that they have a right to their liberty—It is often talked about and read of, for some of us know how to read, although all our knowledge is gained in secret' (ibid.: 6).

This line is noteworthy in two ways. First, it demonstrates Douglass' view that those subjected to slavery maintained their humanity and agency out of the view of their oppressors. Second, Douglass (ibid.: 6) does not indicate this 'large portion of slaves' had been *taught* that freedom is an inherent right. As an aside, it could also be surmised that these enslaved people were largely illiterate, not having access—as Douglass did—to the abolitionist readings that partly inspired him to seek out freedom. Nevertheless, these enslaved Black Americans were presented as both innately aware that their social conditions were unjust and capable of rationalizing that slavery violated their rights.

This is important, as Douglass believed the ability to rationalize one's right to freedom legitimized one's right to freedom. In a later speech, 'Women's Suffrage Movement' (1870), Douglass asserted that one's 'natural powers'—namely the ability to reason—were 'the foundation of natural rights': 'Man can only exercise the powers he possesses, and he can only conceive of rights in the presence of powers' (Douglass, 2016: 493).

Key Concept: Natural rights

Douglass' abolitionism was grounded in natural rights theory. Put simply, natural rights theorists hold that 'individuals have certain rights—such as the rights to life, liberty, and property—in virtue of their human nature' (Paul et al., 2004: vii). Prominently featured in the US Constitution and Declaration of Independence, natural rights theory was frequently invoked during the American Revolution as a justification for self-determination. Douglass co-opted this language for his own purposes—championing these texts as containing the 'eternal laws of the moral universe' (Douglass, 1991 [1866]). He used natural rights to argue that enslaved persons—like all other rational beings—were intrinsically owed the right to liberty. Douglass centred his views on slavery around the proposition that the 'self-evident' desire for freedom was inherent in human nature (Douglass, 1857a: 273; Myers, 2008: 49–50).

In a letter that Douglass (1999 [1848]: 111) sent in 1848 to Thomas Auld, his former enslaver, he illustrated one such mode of this reasoning process—how he figured as a young child that slavery was inherently unjust and his escape inevitable:

> From that time, I resolved that I would someday run away. The morality of the [escape], I dispose as follows: I am myself; you are yourself; we are two distinct persons, equal persons. What you are, I am. You are a man, and so am I. God created both, and made us separate beings. I am not by nature bound to you, or you to me. Nature does not make your existence depend upon me, or mine to depend upon yours . . . We are distinct persons, and are each equally provided with faculties necessary to our individual existence. In leaving you, I took nothing but what belonged to me, and in no way lessened your means for obtaining an honest living.

In the above excerpt, Douglass advances three notable claims. First, he asserts that his escape from slavery was a *moral* escape. Second, he emphasizes that, by virtue of chaining the enslaved to the enslaver and vice versa, the arrangements of slavery are *unnatural* and violate the natural order by conjoining two men's needs into one. Third, he grounds his desire for self-emancipation in childhood, claiming he was no older than the age of 6 when he 'imbibed the determination to run away' (ibid.: 111). These points further underscore Douglass' claim that through experiences of slavery alone the slave is capable of recognizing their own humanity, and their innate right to freedom. Altogether, Douglass grounds his rights to and conception of freedom in the lived experiences, intuitions, and rationalizations of the slave.

30.2.2 Activating freedom

The ability to rationalize the ills of slavery was one basis of Douglass' claim to the 'natural rights' enslaved people possessed. Over the course of his career, Douglass would continue arguing that freedom was an inalienable feature of being a human being—not something you should have to buy or obtain from another person. It was a natural right, with every person having 'equal, but separate faculties' with which to navigate their 'individual experiences' (ibid.: 111).

Slavery was a totalizing system that attempted to stamp out all traces of humanity. Backed by brute force, it distorted familial relations, making parents either strangers to or owners of their offspring. It also placed Black women at special risk of sexual violence. Overall, slavery inscribed itself into the 'body, soul, and spirit' of enslaved persons, attempting to deprive the enslaved of either a past or a future (Douglass, 2017 [1845]: 48; Myers, 2008: 29). Perhaps most insidiously, those at the helm of slavery often attempted to convince the enslaved of the institution's legitimacy (Douglass, 1857a: 253–256). According to Douglass, the moment enslaved persons believed they did not have a natural right to freedom, they transformed into 'brutes', and ceased fighting for their own liberation (Douglass, 2017 [1845]: 48). When describing his lowest point as a captive, Douglass wrote: 'I was broken . . . My natural elasticity was crushed, intellect languished, the disposition to read departed, the cheerful spark that lingered about my eye died; the dark night of slavery closed in upon me; and behold a man transformed into a brute!' (ibid.: 48).

In order to maintain one's humanity in the throes of slavery, Douglass believed that everyone had a responsibility to *fight* for their own freedom. Despite Douglass considering freedom to be absolute, he nevertheless underscored the importance of taking concrete steps to seize it should it be stolen. Douglass (1876: 5) even reserved scorn for those who spent their time praying for liberation, declaring in numerous speeches that: 'When I was a slave, I tried praying for three years. I prayed that God would emancipate me, but it was not till I prayed with my legs that I was emancipated.' This is a tension we can reflect further on: How can we hold responsible those demoralized by a system *intended* to break them? In another speech, Douglass (1986 [1858]: 210) wrote that he '[detested] the slaveholder, and almost equally [detested] a contented slave. They are both enemies to freedom.'

> ### Key Concept: Dignity
>
> For Douglass, dignity is requisite to revolution. Political theorist Nicholas Buccola (2015: 230) argues that Douglass' account of dignity was a 'bridge . . . between [his] descriptive claim that human beings have certain natural powers and the normative claim that human beings have rights that ought to be respected'. Only a person who felt dignity for themselves believed that they too were worthy of respect and freedom, thus affirming their natural rights. In Douglass' (1857a: 236) own words: 'you may hurl a man so low . . . that he loses all ideas of his natural position, but elevate him a little and the clear conception of rights rises to life and power'. Here, Douglass (ibid.: 236) acknowledges that rational beings have a 'natural position,' but it's not until their '[elevation]'—until they claim their own dignity—that they're able to breathe 'life and power' into their newly 'clear conception of rights'.

Douglass (2017 [1845]: 44) often called attention to his personal experiences of resisting slavery, most notably the moment of his head-on battle with vicious 'slave breaker' Edward Covey who was known for using physical and psychological violence to break the human will. This was first detailed at length in the first of Douglass' three autobiographies, *Narrative of the Life of Frederick Douglass, an American Slave* (Douglass, 2017 [1845]). After one indignity too many, Douglass (ibid.:53) refused to further subject himself to abuse, and launched himself at Covey:

> This battle with Mr. Covey was the turning-point in my career as a slave. It rekindled the few expiring embers of freedom, and revived within me a sense of my own manhood . . . The gratification afforded by the triumph was a full compensation for whatever else might follow, even death itself . . . My long-crushed spirit rose, cowardice departed, bold defiance took its place; and I now resolved that, however long I might remain a slave in form, the day had passed forever when I could be a slave in fact. I did not hesitate to let it be known of me, that the white man who expected to succeed in whipping, must also succeed in killing me.

Two types of violence are mentioned here: Douglass' use of violence to resist and defend himself and Covey's oppressive violence to dominate and dehumanize. By refusing to submit to Covey's unjust violence, Douglass shattered the illusion of the invincible slaveholder and re-established his sense of self. If freedom is an inalienable right that is reserved for all and if one's humanity can never be completely stolen, then Douglass is only seizing back what he always had access to. Therefore his 'sense of manhood' is not established but 'revived' by his fight with Covey.

Alongside natural rights, Douglass also advanced a set of natural duties—responsibilities people owed one another. Nicholas Buccola (2015: 241) argues that Douglass conceived of natural duties as relating to institutionalized (in)justice. In this framework, everyone had a duty to uphold just political institutions and combat unjust ones. In his speech 'It Moves', Douglass (2018c [1883]: 382) stresses that everyone had a duty to create a political environment that made slavery untenable:

> Every well-formed man finds no rest to his soul while any portion of his species suffers from a recognized evil. The deepest wish of a true man's heart is that good may be augmented and evil, moral and physical, be diminished, and that each generation shall be an improvement on its predecessor . . .

In this conception of natural duties, the unfreedom of even a small sector of society should cause everyone alarm. Enslavers, naturally, failed to uphold these moral laws, and instead sought to benefit materially from injustice. In failing to protect the freedom of the enslaved, the enslavers put their own freedom—and humanity—at risk. Douglass (2018d [1883b]: 365) is one of the first formerly-enslaved theorists to explicate that the relative freedom of both the enslaved and the enslaver are entangled: 'No man can put a chain about the ankle of his fellow man without at last finding the other end fastened about his own neck.'

The unfreedom that enslavers imposed upon the slave was unnatural for both parties. The violence the enslaver used to maintain this unnatural relationship furthered an unnatural end. To follow this line of thinking, the violence an enslaved person would use to *end* such an unnatural relationship would re-establish a natural order. This will become relevant in Douglass' discussion of the US Constitution, the American Revolution, and his self-proclaimed inheritance of the US founders' principles. In the 1850s, Douglass (1892: 342) became increasingly convinced that slavery would not end by moral appeals, becoming 'less hopeful of [slavery's] peaceful abolition'. Moreover, he began to link the necessity of revolt against the British Crown to the necessity of revolt against Southern enslavers. Specifically, Douglass began to justify the use of violence to overthrow slavery on the same grounds that Americans used violence to overthrow British colonial domination.

30.2.3 Silences within slavery

While it is enlightening to read from Douglass' perspective, it is important to acknowledge the limitations of our engagement with his work. Douglass himself struggled to convey the brutality he witnessed. Despite compellingly articulating himself to a larger audience, there remained experiences and emotions that he could not relate to those who had never been enslaved.

In his first memoir, Douglass described a series of spontaneous songs he heard while young and on his first plantation. Performed by fellow slaves, these songs better expressed the 'horrible character of slavery' than 'whole volumes of philosophy on the subject could'. Though 'rude and incoherent' to the untrained ear, these were his 'first glimmering conception of the dehumanizing character of slavery'. Instead of describing them any further, Douglass (2017 [1845]: 20) asserted that readers would have to travel to the plantation, plant themselves in the woods, and listen intently for the 'soul-killing [sounds] of slavery' to understand just what he's describing.

To Douglass, those experiences are fundamentally unknowable to those who have never experienced them. What he does instead is act as a translator of sorts between what is unknowable and what is understandable to the contemporary reader, so as to motivate the reader to take concrete steps to overturn the institution of slavery.

🔑 30.2 Slavery and freedom: Key Points

- Douglass reclaimed his right to theorizing by centring Black subjectivity as the foundation of his political thought.
- He believed that freedom was a natural right to which everyone was entitled and that enslaved persons needed to take concrete action to 'activate' their natural right to freedom.
- He believed everyone had a natural duty to uphold just political institutions and dismantle unjust ones.

30.3 The freedman's philosophy

After Douglass escaped slavery, fled abroad, and returned to the USA as a freedman, tensions that had been brewing for years erupted among his Northern abolitionist allies. He felt intellectually stifled by his associates, who expected him to be little more than a mouthpiece for their own ideologies (Douglass, 1892: 269). At the head of this brigade was the then-highly influential William Lloyd Garrison—journalist, philosopher, and staunch abolitionist. It was Garrison who first introduced Douglass to the abolitionist circuit and set him up as a public speaker. Douglass identified as a Garrisonian for the first decade or so after his initial escape, and Garrison regarded Douglass as his protégé.

Key Thinker: William Lloyd Garrison

William Lloyd Garrison (1805-1879) was born in Massachusetts, where he founded renowned abolitionist newspaper *The Liberator* in 1830. In 1833, Garrison established the American Anti-Slavery Society, the largest and most influential abolitionist organization in the United States. The group served as a springboard for formerly enslaved public intellectuals, most notably Frederick Douglass and William Wells Brown. Garrison had a few principles that guided his political work: First, that the US Constitution was an explicitly racist, pro-slavery text—'a Covenant with Death'—and made the US government unredeemable (Garrison and Garrison, 1889: 100). Second, committing any kind of violence for political aims was unconscionable (Garrison would amend this position at the outbreak of the Civil War). Third, there would be no 'Union with Slaveholders'—the North should secede from the slaveholding South (ibid.: 100).

This façade began to crack in 1846. The question of purchasing Douglass' freedom threw into clear relief the two men's differences. Garrison believed that purchasing a fugitive slave's freedom was a capitulation to the institution of slavery and a negation of the enslaved person's humanity. Douglass (2017 [1845]: 53) firmly disagreed, reaching back to his distinction of being a 'slave in form' versus a 'slave in fact'. Like Garrison, Douglass disavowed he was a slave by nature, but recognized that he remained a legal one. This disagreement cemented the break between the two men and their respective abolitionist philosophies.

Douglass' personal strife was a microcosm of the discord engulfing the country. The Civil War of 1861-1865 rocked the political stability of the United States (see Key Concept: Civil war or slave rebellion?). Though only lasting four years, the Civil War destroyed families, wreaked violence on communities and encouraged Douglass, a now older agitator and abolitionist, out on the speakers' circuit. Douglass' speeches in the lead-up to the war brought together his praxis and theory. Free to intellectualize as he pleased, Douglass spoke on the relevance of the US Constitution and the necessity of violence in burgeoning slave insurrections. He further bolstered the political careers of sympathizers—most notably that of Abraham Lincoln, who became president in 1861.

Key Concept: Civil war or slave rebellion?

Southern US states feared that, under Abraham Lincoln's presidency, slavery would be abolished. They subsequently banded together and seceded, declaring themselves the Confederate States of America in 1861. A bloody war followed. Initially, the Union promised to leave slavery intact if the Confederates cooperated. The Union eventually made abolition its core rallying cry as 400,000 enslaved persons fled from the South and crossed over into the Union (Hahn, 2009: 61). Of those enslaved persons, 150,000 joined the Union Army (ibid.: 57). These men and women changed the course of the Civil War and, ultimately, the course of the country. As Steven Hahn argues, the US Civil War should be read as 'the greatest slave rebellion in modern history' (ibid.).

30.3.1 Heroic violence

Before the eruption of the Civil War, Douglass also revised his stance on pacifism. He openly and derisively acknowledged his break from the Garrisonian sect of abolitionists:

> Your humble speaker has been branded as an ingrate, because he has ventured to stand up on his own and to plead our common cause as a colored man, rather than as a Garrisonian. I hold it to be no part of gratitude to allow our white friends to do all the work, while we merely hold their coats.
>
> (Douglass, 1857b: 21)

Douglass consistently argued that an enlightened slave should take concrete steps to secure their own freedom, lest they fall into the trap of believing—like 'brutes'—they did not deserve it (Douglass 2017 [1845]). He now began to expand the boundaries of what constituted action. Specifically, Douglass advocated for outright violence against deterrents of freedom.

Four years before the start of the Civil War, we can observe a clear articulation of his views on violence in his speech 'West Indian Emancipation' (Douglass, 1857b), delivered on the 23rd anniversary of the British Caribbean abolition of slavery. Douglass launched two core arguments: first, that anyone who chose not to fight for their freedom negated their right to freedom; second, using violent insurrection as a tool against enslavement was an effective political strategy.

Slavery was officially abolished in British Caribbean colonies in 1834, thirty years before it was abolished in the USA. Douglass used the emancipation of the Caribbean as a framing device for Black American struggles towards freedom. To Douglass, Black Americans ought to follow the example of their Afro-Caribbean peers and revolt en masse to hasten their liberation. Although Douglass used the Caribbean as a comparative example, it is important to note key contextual differences between plantation populations in the USA and other parts of the Americas. As one example, apart from Spanish colonies, Caribbean 'populations were generally about 70 to 90 per cent Black' and mostly enslaved (Engerman and Higman, 2003: 45). In contrast, according to the 1860 census, only about 13 per cent of the US population comprised of enslaved Black Americans (US Bureau of the Census, 1976: 14). In the South, enslaved populations made up roughly one-third of the total population size. Consequently, enslaved populations in the British Caribbean were more highly concentrated and could more effectively organize widespread revolts.

In the opening lines of his West Indian Emancipation speech, Douglass (1857b: 20) declared it 'just' that a 'man who does not fight for [his own freedom] is not worth being fought for by others'. He argued that without putting up resistance to oppressive conditions, the enslaved would be showing their oppressors they would 'quietly submit' to the 'injustice . . . imposed upon them' (ibid.: 22):

> Negroes will be hunted at the North and held and flogged at the South so long as they submit to those devilish outrages and make no resistance, either moral or physical . . . If we ever get free from the oppressions and wrongs heaped upon us, we must pay for their removal. We must do this by labor, by suffering, by sacrifice, and if needs be, by our lives and the lives of others.

Note to whom Douglass speaks to in the speech: 'If *we* ever get free from the oppressions . . .' (emphasis added). Though information on attendees of the speech has been lost to posterity, it is clear Douglass was not directing this speech to white Northern abolitionists. Douglass is uninterested in paternalistic arguments that paint such abolitionists as the ultimate saviours of Black enslaved populations. To Douglass, there were blatant political disadvantages to enslaved communities being passively guided to freedom by white outsiders. If you did not fight for your own freedom, then you did not have control over your post-emancipation future.

After establishing that the enslaved needed to fight for their own freedom before turning to others to assist them, Douglass (ibid.: 23) raised the argument that violent struggle was politically advantageous: slaves needed to show the United States that slavery was 'dangerous'. After all, 'outbreaks and violence' helped to secure the freedom of those enslaved in British Caribbean colonies. Douglass also used the example of Stateside rebellions to prove his point. On Nat Turner, the leader of a slave revolt that killed sixty white persons in 1831, he wrote 'Virginia was never nearer emancipation than when General Turner kindled the fires of insurrection at Southampton' (ibid.: 24).

Douglass was clearly no longer a pacifist. He lamented those who 'professed to favor freedom [while deprecating] agitation', likening such abolitionists to those 'who wanted crops without plowing up the ground' (ibid.: 22). In the most famous passage of the speech, he underlined that power did not concede without 'struggle':

> The whole history of the progress of human liberty shows that all concessions . . . have been born of earnest struggle. The conflict has [to be] exciting, agitating, all-absorbing, and for the time being, putting all other tumults to silence. It must do this, or it does nothing. If there is no struggle, there is no progress . . . Power concedes nothing without a demand.
>
> (ibid.: 21–22)

Douglass would return to these words during the Civil War a few years later, compelling Black American men to assist the Union against the Confederates at all costs.

Douglass' views on violence should be read in tandem with his views on the Constitution. He associated the violence of the American revolutionaries—used to throw off the yoke of imperialism—with the violence he considered necessary for the abolition of slavery. In both instances, violence considered justifiable is used to overturn unjust institutions. This can be seen most clearly in 'The Heroic Slave' (Douglass, 2015 [1852a]), his only foray into fiction. The short story centred on the tale of Madison Washington, a Creole enslaved man who killed the captain of a slave ship before redirecting the ship's course to Barbados. In the closing dialogue of the short story, Douglass wrote what he imagined to be Washington's response to being labelled a 'Black murderer':

> I am not a murderer. God is my witness that LIBERTY, not *malice*, is the motive for this night's work. I have done no more to those dead men yonder, than they would have done to me in like circumstances. We have struck for our freedom, and if a true man's heart be in you, you will honor us for the deed. We have done that which you applaud your fathers for doing, and if we are murderers, *so were they* (emphasis in original).
>
> (ibid.: 48)

This dialogue served as an eerily relevant precursor to the eruption of the Civil War, in which—once again—two opposing forces battled violently to remake the United States in their own image.

30.3.2 The promise of the US Constitution

Before the onset of Douglass' split with Garrison, he espoused all the major Garrisonian positions. One of these key positions was that the US Constitution was an irredeemably racist text. As Douglass became increasingly involved in politics, however, he began to preach that the soul of the nation could be saved. Douglass' and Garrison's philosophies further diverged: Garrison believed that systemic inequalities *reflected* the founding principles of the United States, and the USA was a lost cause. Douglass believed that systemic inequalities *distorted* the founding principles of the United States. This shift in Douglass' thinking is articulated clearly in 'What to the Slave is the Fourth of July?' (Douglass, 2018e [1852b]), arguably his most famous address.

In 1852, the Rochester Ladies' Anti-Slavery Society invited Douglass to give the annual Fourth of July lecture. He accepted but moved his speech to the 5th of July, the commemorative date of New York's abolition of slavery in 1827. From the start of the address, Douglass (ibid.: 61) reminded listeners of the bravery of the men who fought against British colonial oppression. In retelling this story, Douglass moved beyond a tale of anti-colonialism, protests against taxation, and questions of American self-determination. He emphasized instead that the purpose of the revolution was one of transformation and sacrifice for a greater cause: freedom.

Although he acknowledged that these noble origins were a past to celebrate, he further challenged readers to recognize the founders' work was incomplete. He condemned the nation's desire to claim the revolutionary power of the Fourth of July while slavery persisted (ibid.: 76). The forces that shaped the colonies into a democratic republic conflicted with the active 'enslavement [of] three million of its countrymen'. He recalled 'the doleful wail of fettered humanity', and likened enslaved Black Americans to 'horses, sheep and swine knocked off to the highest bidder'. After reflecting on the brutalities of slavery, which 'disturbed and endangered the [state of the] Union', he presented the US Constitution as the roadmap to salvation (ibid.: 87).

Douglass' goal was to establish himself as a rightful heir to both the Constitution and the US founders' legacy of championing freedom. To do this, he needed to argue that the founders had no intention of encoding slavery into the fabric of the country's laws and nascent identity. Naturally, this would affirm Douglass' point that slavery was an illegal and immoral institution, and that the perpetuation of slavery went against the spirit of the nation.

Douglass aimed to accomplish this by presenting the Constitution as being in accord with his own visions for the country, declaring anyone who charged the Constitution with racism to be '[slandering] the memory' of its framers (ibid.: 87). In opposition to those Northerners, surely with the Garrisonians in mind, he argued that the Constitution was in fact an anti-slavery document '[containing] principles and purposes entirely hostile to the existence of slavery' (ibid.: 90). Douglass further stated that his 'spirit was cheered' by the 'Declaration of Independence, the great principles it contained, and the genius of American Institutions'.

As modern-day readers of Douglass, we can question the premises of his argument. In an essay entitled 'Douglass and "Original Intent"', philosopher Charles Mills (1998: 167) described Douglass' views as 'simultaneously inspiring and naïve'. As seen here, debates over the Constitution's pro- or anti-slavery nature stretch even into recent history. This is due in part to the document's authors. Torn between their complicity in the institution of slavery and the promotion of Enlightenment ideals of freedom and equality, most of the founders of the United States settled into a guilty complacency. Despite (or perhaps because of) this, some of the Constitution's authors—including enslavers—were especially determined to reflect egalitarian principles in the document. This namely involved refusing to reference, let alone condone, slavery in the original text.

Nevertheless, historians who disagree with Douglass (Waldstreicher, 2010; Rutherglen, 2013; Gilhooley, 2020), point to clauses like the three-fifths clause as proof the Constitution was 'operationally pro-slavery' without ever mentioning the institution by name (Waldstreicher 2015). The three-fifths clause allowed slave-permitting US states to count three-fifths of the total number of enslaved peoples as part of the represented population. Even though enslaved persons could not vote, this augmented both the number of seats these states were allocated in the US Congress and the total electoral count these states received towards the presidency. Consequently, slave-permitting states wielded disproportionate political power—power they would use to protect slavery. In addition, the slave trade clause, without mentioning slavery, banned Congress from prohibiting the 'migration or importation' of people until twenty years after the Constitution's signing (The Constitution of the United States, 1789: art. I, sec. 9). Though debated, constitutional scholar Carl Bogus (1998: 371) also claims the Second Amendment—which protects the 'right to bear arms' and gather a militia—was written with slave revolts in mind (The Constitution of the United States, 1789: amend. II).

In a later address, 'The American Constitution and the Slave', Douglass (2018f [1860]) favourably highlighted the absence of pro-slavery rhetoric in the Constitution and offered more structured support for his anti-slavery interpretation. Regarding the three-fifths clause, for example, he reasoned that since a 'black man in a free State is worth just two-fifths more than a black man in a slave State', the Constitution 'encourages freedom by giving an increase of "two-fifths" of political power to free over slave States' (ibid. 168). He even dismissed the Fugitive Slave clause—which enforced the return of enslaved persons who escaped out-of-state—claiming that the clause applied in theory not to enslaved people, but to indentured labourers. Douglass also championed the words of James Madison (1920 [1787])—one of the Constitution's signers, eventual US President (1809–1817), and owner of at least one hundred slaves—who insisted it would be 'wrong to admit in the Constitution the idea that there could be property in men'.

Douglass was aware of the tension in his defence of the framers, choosing to celebrate the most inclusive iteration of their ideals. In his 5th of July 1852 address, for example, he stated that though his personal views on the framers were not necessarily 'the most . . . favorable,' he recognized that 'the [American] principles they contended for' demonstrated a 'love of country' over personal interests (Douglass, 2018e [1852]: 63–64). Despite these tensions, Douglass had few political alternatives; the most popular abolitionists, the Garrisonians, advocated for the nullification of the Constitution and secession of the North from the South. Other abolitionists sought to return enslaved populations back to the African continent, uprooting millions to a homeland they had never seen. Douglass firmly disagreed with either approach. He felt these so-called solutions would leave Northerners unaccountable to an injustice they both profited from and helped to establish: 'The American people in the Northern States have helped to enslave the black people. Their duty will not have been done till they give them back their plundered rights' (Douglass, 2018f [1860]: 182).

Douglass' stance on the Constitution directly challenged such approaches. Though viewed as 'naïve' by some, Douglass' position on the Constitution allowed him to explicitly link the country's struggle for freedom with the slaves' struggle for freedom, reinforcing, as well, that the enslaved were included in the founders' vision for the country. This would further allow Douglass to portray the issue of slavery as antithetical to the founding of the United States—to own slaves was not only immoral under this framework, but also deeply un-American. Additionally, Douglass could use the Constitution to argue that white Americans were not only failing his personal moral and political standards, but also their *own* standards on the dilemma of the peculiar institution.

It bears noting that, after the Civil War, Douglass' stance on the Constitution and the nation's founding became more nuanced. In contrast to his 1852 and 1860 speeches, Douglass (2018a [1867]: 223) later instructed an audience to '[discard] all Fourth of July extravagances about the Constitution, and about its framers' and instead emphasized the importance of treating the Constitution as a living text. According to Douglass, the Constitution needed to have its 'defects' corrected and be removed from the 'shadows of . . . slavery' (ibid.: 229). On this basis, he began to champion the 13th Amendment, which barred slavery except as a 'punishment for a crime', and advocated for the 14th and 15th Amendments, which respectively protected citizenship and granted Black men the right to vote (U.S. Const. amend. XIII). This shift in perspectives on founding US texts suggests Douglass indeed partially sought to champion them insofar as they advanced his political goals. Once Douglass began viewing the texts as obstructive to progress, he prioritized amending, rather than defending, them to fit the changing times.

30.3.3 Suffragists, Natives, and the Constitution

Douglass' interpretation of the Constitution as protective of natural rights extended not only to the enslaved. He famously advocated on behalf of women's rights. He was the only Black American to speak at the Seneca Fall's Convention in 1848, often billed as the first women's rights gathering in the United States, and the only man to sign the Seneca Fall's Declaration (McMillen, 2009: 95). He was also one of relatively few men to speak out in favour of women's right to vote (ibid.). To this end, he co-founded the American Equal Rights Association, a political organization dedicated to the universal suffrage movement. In short, Douglass' position on gender equality was quite radical for the period.

The expansion of Douglass' politics to encompass women's rights resulted from close friendships with leading suffragists, particularly Elizabeth Cady Stanton (see Key Thinker: Elizabeth Cady Stanton in Chapter 2). At their urging, Douglass (1892: 575) publicly denounced the US government for its failure to include women as political actors, writing: 'In this denial of the right to participate in government, not merely the degradation of woman and the perpetuation of a great injustice happens, but the maiming and repudiation of one-half of the moral and intellectual power of the government of the world.'

Initially, abolitionists and suffragists worked to bring about universal suffrage across gender and racial lines. Once universal suffrage was considered politically unviable, Douglass began leading a political faction that prioritized suffrage for Black men. Concurrently, another sect of leading suffragists prioritized securing suffrage for largely middle-class white women. A rift grew between Douglass and key white suffragists. This coincided with national political campaigns for the 15th Amendment, which constitutionally guaranteed the right to vote to all men.

Though he would support women's rights over the course of his life, Douglass began voicing frustration with the suffragists' cause. He stated in one letter that since 'white men have been enfranchised always . . . white women, whose husbands, fathers, and brothers are voters, [were not being] generous' enough if refusing to support Black men's suffrage (Borome and Douglass, 1948 [1868]: 470). In other words, Douglass argued that white women's proximity to political power diminished their claim to urgency on matters of voting rights. This completely disregarded the suffragist point that women deserved complete political independence from the men in their lives.

Among the white suffragists, the arguments over whether Black men should receive the right to vote before white women were similarly bitter. Such disagreements ultimately led to an organizational schism. The racist attitudes of some suffragist leaders became apparent: Elizabeth Cady Stanton (1997 [1869]: 237), for example, declared that 'Sambo and Hans and Yung Tung' and other 'lower order' citizens didn't deserve the right to vote before 'American women of wealth, education, virtue and refinement'. Stanton and Susan B. Anthony thereafter founded the National Woman Suffrage Association, which disallowed the enrolment of any Black members (including women). A faction of the largely white suffragists sided with Douglass on the practicality of supporting the 15th Amendment, including prominent abolitionist-suffragists like the Grimké sisters, who championed both gender- and race-based inclusion. Those women, Douglass, and a slate of progressive men joined the staunchly pro-15th Amendment American Woman Suffrage Association (AWSA).

Prominent Black suffragists like Sojourner Truth (see Chapter 2) and Frances Ellen Watkins Harper also joined the new AWSA coalition. Grossly underrepresented, Black women were often in the troubling position of having to side with either white feminists or Black men who would 'vote against [Black women] as soon as [they] got [their] vote' (Harper, 2019 [1896]: 98). A national organization for the benefit of Black women specifically—the National Association for Colored Women—would not be founded until the late 1890s by Harper, Harriet Tubman, and Frederick's daughter Rosetta Douglass, among others (White, 1999; Cooper, 2017).

The exclusion of Black women from suffragist spaces is also apparent in Douglass' recorded correspondences. One of Douglass' primary arguments was that Black men needed access to the ballot to combat the violent racism they experienced in their daily lives. During a heated argument against universal suffrage, Douglass once contended that:

> When women, because they are women, are hunted down through the cities of New York and New Orleans, when they are dragged from their houses and hung upon lamp posts; when their children are torn from their arms . . . then they will have an urgency to obtain the ballot equal to our own.

(Stanton et al., 1881: 382)

When asked to clarify how Black women—also obvious victims of racist violence—related to this claim, Douglass is quoted as indignantly responding that '[this] is true for the Black woman but not because she is a woman but because she is Black!' (ibid.: 382). As evidenced, Douglass failed to see how Black women had unique political concerns that both overlapped and differed from either his own or those of white women.

It should be noted that Black women were not often considered political actors in Douglass' body of work. Even his first wife, Anna Douglass, who helped organize his escape and paid for his passage to freedom, faded into the background of his narrative, despite her central role in it. There are clear exceptions: Douglass (1892: 342–343) referred to Sojourner Truth as an 'old friend' and 'advocate of the sword' during the Civil War. He was also an admirer and avid supporter of anti-lynching crusader Ida B. Wells (2014 [1892]: 6), whom he lauded for doing 'a service' so critical it 'could neither be weighed or measured'.

Although Douglass did not fundamentally disagree with women's active inclusion in citizenship and politics, this sentiment did not extend to Native Americans, whom Douglass occasionally held up as derogatory counterparts to Black Americans. In the immediate aftermath of the Civil War, while on the campaign trail, Douglass observed bitterly that despite the 'romantic reverence . . . of the Indian, they rejected [US] civilization' (Douglass, 1991 [1866]: 130). By contrast, he asserted: 'The negro is despised . . . [though] the negro accepts [US civilization]. He is with you, of you, been here for the last two hundred and fifty years . . . living, flourishing with you, accepting all that is valuable in your civilization and serving you at every turn' (ibid.: 130).

Douglass could be said to have political aims for suggesting white Americans and Black Americans were kindred spirits who 'flourished' together during the years of slavery. At the same time, he continued to double down on the dual passivity and defiance of Indigenous peoples in comparison to Black Americans, writing a few years later that: 'The Indian [is] . . . refusing to imitate, refusing to follow the fashion . . . and the consequence is, that he dies or retreats before the onward march of your civilization – [whereas the Black man] becomes just what other people become, and herein is the security for his continued life' (Douglass, 2018g [1869]: 259–260).

Douglass paints a portrait of Indigenous communities as intrinsically unable to participate in larger US civilization. As Indigenous scholars observe (Hall, 2008; Tuck and Yang, 2012), this 'imitation' that Douglass demands of Natives necessarily involves both their erasure and concession of their land to the colonial settler state that the Constitution establishes. The USA depended on the gradual disappearance of Native Americans to further its expansionist project, and Douglass—while reiterating Black Americans were fully committed to the USA—affirmed this.

30.3 The freedman's philosophy: Key Points

- Douglass viewed himself as an inheritor of the American Revolution's foundational principles.
- Douglass argued that the US Constitution was an inherently anti-slavery document, and that its true purpose had been distorted by racist enslavers.
- Though a supporter of women's rights in words and deeds, Douglass prioritized the enfranchisement of Black men.
- Douglass' conception of citizenship did not extend to Native Americans resisting US imperialism.
- Douglass eventually turned away from pacifism, arguing that violence was both effective and necessary as a political tool.

30.4 The statesman's philosophy

After the Union prevailed in the Civil War, Douglass felt that America was reborn, finally able to claim its rightful place as a nation steeped in democracy and equality. As discussed above, constitutional amendments were passed that abolished slavery, granted citizenship to formerly enslaved persons, and accorded voting rights to Black men. Douglass' optimistic sentiment, however, would not last.

The Reconstruction Era encompassed the roughly twelve-year period after the Civil War ended. In the War's aftermath, Republican politicians fought to preserve Black American rights, reconstruct the South after brutal warfare, and seamlessly reunite the country. Such policy efforts were overall limited in their impact. Voting rights for Black American men—seemingly won with the passage of the 15th Amendment—were eventually withdrawn by means of force, and not regained until the 1964 Voting Rights Act. After the Compromise of 1877—which settled the disputed 1876 presidential election and saw the end of the Reconstruction Era, with federal troops withdrawn from the South—discrimination was encoded in Jim Crow Laws, thus legalizing racial segregation.

As state governments responded to the emancipation of Black Americans with fear, suspicion, and segregation, racial violence erupted. The number of lynchings across the South rose exponentially and became a rallying cry for Douglass in the final years of his life. The hope he espoused at the immediate conclusion of the Civil War turned to despair:

> I have sometimes thought that the American people are too great to be small, too just and magnanimous to oppress the weak, too brave to yield up the right to the strong . . . I have fondly hoped that this estimate of American character would soon cease to be contradicted or put in doubt . . . but the immediate future looks dark and troubled. I cannot shut my eyes to the ugly facts before me.
>
> (Douglass, 2018h [1894], 454–498)

While grappling with the post-Civil War failures of US politics, Douglass nonetheless became increasingly enmeshed with them. Over two decades, Douglass the fiery abolitionist and orator would become Douglass the political ambassador and insider, taking up the role of President of the US Freedmen's Bank (1874), US Marshall (1877–1881), Recorder of Deeds (1881–1886), and US Minister Resident to Haiti (1889–1891). Now a key political actor, Douglass was divided between representing the USA on the global stage and continuing to protest the country's anti-Black racism. To engage this tension, we will turn to one of Douglass' final theoretic shifts near the close of his life and analyse his support of US imperialism.

30.4.1 (Re)colonizing the Caribbean

In 1871, the westward expansion of the United States and its colonization of Indigenous territories coincided with an increased focus on the Caribbean. Of particular interest was Santo Domingo, the other half of the island of Hispaniola and what is now the Dominican Republic. The US eyed Santo Domingo for annexation, despite Haitian interests that sought to bring the full island under Haitian jurisdiction. When debated by the US Congress, what was often discussed was whether a self-avowed Black nation like Haiti should territorially acquire Santo Domingo. Permeating these discussions were dangerous presumptions about national rights, powers, sovereignty, and a kind of white supremacist benevolence that sought to save Santo Domingo from being subsumed by Haiti.

Nearly two decades later, Douglass was sent to Haiti as the US Minister Resident by US President Benjamin Harrison, who sought to secure a strategic naval port off the coast of the island-nation, among other activities in the region. Haitian politicians were rightfully suspicious, presuming the USA would use such a port to wield political influence. One of those politicians, Anténor Firmin, ultimately refused to acquiesce the port to US control, despite assurances from Douglass that the naval port was no 'menace to the autonomy of [his nation]' (Dubois, 2016: 105).

In 1891, Douglass resigned his post as Minister Resident, and in his final memoir stated: 'Haiti is no stranger to Americans or to American prejudice. [A white diplomat would] play the hypocrite [were he to] pretend to love negroes in Haiti when he is known to hate negroes in the United States' (Douglass, 1892: 730).

In the same memoir, however, he included a long passage about his views on colonization, illuminating the prevailing views on transnational rights and freedoms after the US eradication of slavery (ibid.: 731):

> It was a shame to American statesmanship that, while almost every other great nation in the world had secured a foothold and had power in the Caribbean Sea, where it could anchor in its own bays and moor in it its own harbors, we, who stood at the very gate of that sea, had there no anchoring-ground anywhere.

This would have been a curious passage from Douglass the abolitionist, who promoted natural rights and freedom. Douglass the statesman, however, did not believe his defence of abolition was in contradiction with imperialist aims: 'While slavery existed, I was opposed to all schemes for the extension of American power and influence. But since its abolition I have gone with him who goes farthest for such extension' (ibid.: 732). With these short lines, Douglass the firebrand appears to become Douglass the imperialist, or at least an imitator of more expansionist-minded American politicians. He would take up his pen and hit the circuit for annexation of Santo Domingo, but not stop there. He would suggest that Haiti and even Cuba should become a part of the USA. As David Blight (2020: 543) remarks, 'Douglass saw Reconstruction's egalitarian promises – the end of slavery, equality before the law, birthright citizenship, and the right to vote – as catalysts and justifications for American expansion.' This expansionist model would bring the new USA—the post-Civil War America that had renewed its commitment to racial equality—to the world as 'the model for "human rights" above all conceptions of racial or ethnic identities' (ibid.: 544). For Douglass, freedom had become the USA's duty to others—even if it meant denying other nations' sovereignty. Eventually, however, the failures of Reconstruction would complicate Douglass' argument for imperialism.

30.4 The statesman's philosophy: Key Points

- Douglass initially believed that the USA had fulfilled its liberatory promise as the 'Land of the Free' upon the conclusion of the Civil War, but ultimately became despondent over the state of the country.
- Douglass argued for the 'farthest' expansion of the USA over Caribbean nations and colonies, arguing the goal was to spread the 'egalitarian promise' of his country.

30.5 Conclusion

Frederick Douglass' life would end markedly different than it began, having died a freedman on 20 February 1895. His life was marked by profound transitions: from slave to freedman, from freedman to national hero. Along the way, he developed a significant and influential political theory that promoted a rigorous conception of liberty, which challenged the institution of slavery and led to its abolition. Douglass considered freedom to be a natural right, and the defence of freedom-granting institutions to be a social duty. Where freedom wasn't granted, Douglass defended the just use of violence to achieve liberation from violent structural oppression. He spent over half of his life clamouring against slavery, which he understood to be a deep violation of a person's humanity. Douglass' theory mirrored his life in that it always strove towards freedom, even if it did not always hit the mark.

Douglass was a complex figure whose views were sometimes contradictory. His relationship to the early women's rights movement was both complicated and occasionally exclusionary. He struggled to acknowledge the claims of Indigenous peoples outside of US imperial efforts, not extending to them his philosophy of freedom or violence. Despite these glaring faults, it still remains that Douglass was a significant activist, theorist, and statesman whose philosophical and political warfare against the institution of slavery changed the United States, and the world, for the better.

Take your learning further by accessing the online resources for a library of web links to relevant videos, articles, blogs, and useful websites for this chapter: www.oup.com/he/Ramgotra-Choat1e.

Study questions

1. Describe Douglass' three ways of knowing conveyed in his speech 'I Have Come to Tell You.'
2. What did Douglass believe was necessary to 'activate' a claim to freedom?
3. Why did Douglass' claim that a 'slaveholder' was 'almost equally' detestable as 'a contented slave'?
4. Why did Douglass consider the US Constitution an anti-slavery text in contrast to other abolitionists who saw it as pro-slavery?
5. Are Black women accounted for in Douglass' theory?
6. How did Douglass describe Native Americans in the aftermath of the Civil War?
7. Why did Douglass defend the necessity of violence as a political tool? Do you agree with his conclusions?
8. Did Douglass' later position on US imperialism contradict his earlier claims?

Further reading

Primary sources

Douglass, F. (1892) *Life and Times of Frederick Douglass*. London: Park Publishing Company.
This is the third of Douglass' three autobiographies. The longest and most detailed of Douglass' memoirs on his life's trajectory to a few years before his death.

Douglass, F. (2014 [1857]) *My Bondage and My Freedom*. New Haven, CT: Yale University Press.
The second of Douglass' three autobiographies that it adds more nuance and detail to iconic scenes like Douglass' battle with Edward Covey.

Douglass, F. (2017 [1845]) *Narrative of the Life of Frederick Douglass, An American Slave, Written by Himself: Authoritative Text Contexts Criticism*, 2nd edn. Ed. W.L. Andrews and W.S. McFeely. New York: W.W. Norton & Company.
The first and most famous of Douglass' three autobiographies.

Douglass, F. et al. (2018) *The Speeches of Frederick Douglass: A Critical Edition*. New Haven, CT: Yale University Press.
This text offers historical context for some of Douglass' most important political speeches and includes excerpts from texts that influenced Douglass.

Sprague, R.D. (1923) 'Anna Murray-Douglass: My Mother as I Recall Her'. *The Journal of Negro History*, 8(1): 93-101.
This recollection written by Rosetta Douglass Sprague, Douglass' daughter, offers a vital account of Anna Douglass' contribution to Frederick Douglass' legacy.

Secondary sources

Blight, D.W. (2020) *Frederick Douglass: Prophet of Freedom*. New York: Simon & Schuster.
The most comprehensive and incisive biography of Douglass.

Bromell, N.K. (2021) *The Powers of Dignity: The Black Political Philosophy of Frederick Douglass*. Durham, NC: Duke University Press.
A detailed overview of Douglass' political philosophy, particularly in relation to his conception of democracy and citizenship.

Buccola, N. (2015) '"The Essential Dignity of Man as Man": Frederick Douglass on Human Dignity'. *American Political Thought*, 4(2): 228-258.
A detailed overview of Douglass' conception of dignity, dignity as a virtue, and natural rights and duties.

Fought, L. (2017) *Women in the World of Frederick Douglass*. New York: Oxford University Press.
An examination of the role and influence that various women, including family members, political adversaries, and close confidantes, had on Douglass.

References

Blight, D.W. (2020) *Frederick Douglass: Prophet of Freedom*. New York: Simon & Schuster.

Bogus, C. (1998) 'The Hidden History of the Second Amendment'. *U.C. Davis Law Review* 31(2): 311-408.

Borome, J. and Douglass, F. (1948[1868]) 'Two Letters of Frederick Douglass'. *The Journal of Negro History*, 33(4): 469-471.

Buccola, N. (2015) '"The Essential Dignity of Man as Man": Frederick Douglass on Human Dignity'. *American Political Thought*, 4(2): 228-258.

Cooper, B.C. (2017) *Beyond Respectability: The Intellectual Thought of Race Women*. Champaign, IL: University of Illinois Press.

Douglass, F. (1852) 'The Colonization Scheme'. vol. 5 no. 5, 22 January. Available at: https://exhibits.library.pdx.edu/exhibit/show/gates/item/16.html (accessed 11 January 2023).

Douglass, F. (1857a) *My Bondage and My Freedom*. New York: Orton & Mulligan.

Douglass, F. (1857b) 'West India Emancipation'. In C.P. Dewey (ed.), *Two Speeches, by Frederick Douglass: One on West India Emancipation, Delivered at Canandaigua, Aug. 4th, and the Other on the Dred Scott Decision, Delivered in New York, on the Occasion of the Anniversary of the American Abolition Society, May, 1857*. C.P. Dewey, American Office.

Douglass, F. (1876) 'Self-Made Men'. *The New York Herald*, 16 November. Available at: https://www.loc.gov/resource/sn83030313/1876-11-16/ed-1/?sp=5&r=-0.225,-0.153,1.461,0.93,0 (accessed 11 January 2023).

Douglass, F. (1892) *Life and Times of Frederick Douglass*. New York: Park Publishing Company.

Douglass, F. (1986 [1858]) '"Citizenship and the Spirit of Caste"'. In J.W. Blassingame (ed.), *The Frederick Douglass Papers*. New Haven, CT: Yale University Press.

Douglass, F. (1991 [1866]) '"We Are Here and Want the Ballot Box"' (1866). In J.W. Blassingame (ed.), *The Frederick Douglass Papers Volume 4, Series One: Speeches, Debates, and Interviews, 1864-1880*. New Haven, CT: Yale University Press).

Douglass, F. (1999 [1848]) 'Letter to Thomas Auld (September 3, 1848)'. In P.S. Foner (ed.), *Frederick Douglass: Selected Speeches and Writings*. Chicago: Lawrence Hill Books, p. 111.

Douglass, F. (2015 [1852a]) *The Heroic Slave: A Cultural and Critical Edition*. Ed. R.S. Levine, J. Stauffer, and J.R. McKivigan. New Haven, CT: Yale University Press.

Douglass, F. (2016) 'Woman Suffrage Movement'. In *The Portable Frederick Douglass*. Ed. J. Stauffer and H.L. Gates, Jr. New York: Penguin.

Douglass, F. (2017 [1845]) *Narrative of the Life of Frederick Douglass, an American Slave, Written By Himself: Authoritative Text Contexts Criticism*. 2nd edn. Ed. W.L. Andrews and W.S. McFeely. New York: W.W. Norton.

Douglass, F. (2018a [1867]) '"Sources of Danger to the Republic": An Address Delivered in St. Louis, Missouri, 7 February 1867'. In J. Husband, H. Kaufman, and J. McKivigan (eds), *The Speeches of Frederick Douglass*. New Haven, CT: Yale University Press, pp. 217–246.

Douglass, F. (2018b [1841])' "I Have Come to Tell You Something about Slavery": An Address Delivered in Lynn, Massachusetts, October 1841'. In J. Husband, H. Kaufman, and J. McKivigan (eds), *The Speeches of Frederick Douglass*. New Haven, CT: Yale University Press, pp. 3–8.

Douglass, F. (2018c [1883a]) '"It Moves," or the "Philosophy of Reform": An Address Delivered in Washington, D.C., 20 November 1883'. In J. Husband, H. Kaufman, and J. McKivigan (eds), *The Speeches of Frederick Douglass*. New Haven, CT: Yale University Press, pp. 374–400.

Douglass, F. (2018d [1883b]) '"This Decision Has Humbled the Nation": An Address Delivered in Washington, D.C., 22 October 1883'. In J. Husband, H. Kaufman, and J. McKivigan (eds), *The Speeches of Frederick Douglass*. New Haven, CT: Yale University Press, pp. 356–373.

Douglass, F. (2018e [1852b]) '"What to the Slave Is the Fourth of July?": An Address Delivered in Rochester, New York, 5 July 1852'. In J. Husband, H. Kaufman, and J. McKivigan (eds), *The Speeches of Frederick Douglass*. New Haven, CT: Yale University Press, pp. 55–92.

Douglass, F. (2018f [1860]) '"The American Constitution and the Slave": An Address Delivered in Glasgow, Scotland, 26 March 1860'. In J. Husband, H. Kaufman, and J. McKivigan (eds), *The Speeches of Frederick Douglass*. New Haven, CT: Yale University Press, pp. 151–185.

Douglass, F. (2018g [1869]) '"Let the Negro Alone": An Address Delivered in New York, New York, 11 May 1869'. In J. Husband, H. Kaufman, and J. McKivigan (eds), *The Speeches of Frederick Douglass*. New Haven, CT: Yale University Press, pp. 247–266.

Douglass, F. (2018h [1894]) '"Lessons of the Hour": An Address Delivered in Washington, D.C., 9 January 1894'. In J. Husband, H. Kaufman, and J. McKivigan (eds), *The Speeches of Frederick Douglass*. New Haven, CT: Yale University Press, pp. 454–498.

Dubois, L. (2016) 'Frederick Douglass, Anténor Firmin, and the Making of U.S.- Haitian Relations'. In E.M. Dillon and M. Drexler (eds), *The Haitian Revolution and the Early United States*. University Park: PA: University of Pennsylvania Press, pp. 95–110.

Engerman, S.L. and Higman, B.W. (2003) 'The Demographic Structure of the Caribbean Slave Societies in the Eighteenth and Nineteenth Centuries'. In F.W. Knight (ed.), *General History of the Caribbean*, vol. III: *The Slave Societies of the Caribbean*. New York: Palgrave Macmillan US, pp. 45–104.

Garrison, W.P. and Garrison, F.J. (1889) *William Lloyd Garrison, 1805-1879: The Story of His Life Told by His Children*. New York: Century Company.

Gibson, D.G. (2018) *Frederick Douglass, a Psychobiography: Rethinking Subjectivity in the Western Experiment of Democracy*. Cham: Palgrave Macmillan.

Gilhooley, S.J. (2020) *The Antebellum Origins of the Modern Constitution: Slavery and the Spirit of the American Founding*. Cambridge: Cambridge University Press.

Hahn, S. (2009) *The Political Worlds of Slavery and Freedom*. (Nathan I. Huggins lectures). Cambridge, MA: Harvard University Press.

Hall, L.K. (2008) 'Strategies of Erasure: U.S. Colonialism and Native Hawaiian Feminism'. *American Quarterly*, 60(2): 273–280.

Harper, F.E.W. (2019 [1896]) *Minnie's Sacrifice*. New York: Blackberry Publishing.

Hume, D. (1987) *Essays, Moral, Political, and Literary*, Ed. E.F. Miller, Indianapolis, IN: Liberty Fund.

Madison, J. (1920) 'Madison Debates (1787)'. In J.B. Scott, and G. Hund (eds), *The Debates in the Federal Convention of 1787*. Oxford: Oxford University Press. Available at: https://avalon.law.yale.edu/18th_century/debates_825.asp (accessed 11 January 2023).

McMillen, S.G. (2009) *Seneca Falls and the Origins of the Women's Rights Movement*. Oxford: Oxford University Press.

Mills, C.W. (1998) 'Whose Fourth of July?: Frederick Douglass and "Original Intent"'. In *Blackness Visible: Essays on Philosophy and Race*. Ithaca, NY: Cornell University Press, pp. 167–200.

Moraga, C. and Anzaldúa, G. (eds) (2015) *This Bridge Called My Back: Writings by Radical Women of Color*.

4th edn. Albany. NY: State University of New York (SUNY) Press.

Myers, P.C. (2008) *Frederick Douglass: Race and the Rebirth of American Liberalism*. Lawrence, KS: University Press of Kansas.

Paul, E.F., Miller, F.D., and Paul, J. (eds) (2004) 'Introduction'. In E.F. Paul, F.D. Miller, and J. Paul (eds), *Natural Rights Liberalism from Locke to Nozick, Social Philosophy and Policy*. Cambridge, Cambridge University Press, pp. vii–xv.

Rutherglen, G. (2013) *Civil Rights in the Shadow of Slavery: The Constitution, Common Law, and the Civil Rights Act of 1866*. New York: Oxford University Press.

Silva, G.J. (2018) 'On the Difficulties of Writing Philosophy from a Racialized Subjectivity'. *APA Newsletter on Hispanic/Latino Issues in Philosophy* 18(1) 2–6.

Stanton, E.C. (1997) 'The Sixteenth Amendment (1869)'. In S.K. Sewell, S.B. Anthony, and T.G. Miller (eds), *The Selected Papers of Elizabeth Cady Stanton and Susan B. Anthony: Against an Aristocracy of Sex, 1866 to 1873*. Ed. A. D. Gordon. New Brunswick, NJ: Rutgers University Press.

Stanton, E.C., Anthony, S.B., Gage, M.J., and Harper, I.H. (eds) (1881) *History of Woman Suffrage*. Rochester, NY: Charles Mann.

The Constitution of the United States (1789) in National Archives. Available at: https://www.archives.gov/founding-docs/constitution-transcript (accessed 11 January 2023).

The Liberator (1847) 'The Ransom of Douglass', 15 January. Available at: https://www.theliberatorfiles.com/the-ransom-of-douglass/ (accessed 11 January 2023).

Tuck, E. and Yang, K.W. (2012) 'Decolonization Is Not a Metaphor'. *Decolonization: Indigeneity, Education & Society*, 1(1): 1–40.

US Bureau of the Census (1976) *Historical Statistics of the United States: Colonial Times to 1970*. Washington, DC: US Government Printer.

Vlastos, G. (1941) 'Slavery in Plato's Thought'. *The Philosophical Review*, 50(3): 289.

Waldstreicher, D. (2010) *Slavery's Constitution: From Revolution to Ratification*. New York: Hill and Wang.

Waldstreicher, D. (2015) 'How the Constitution Was Indeed Pro-Slavery'. *The Atlantic*, 19 September. https://www.theatlantic.com/politics/archive/2015/09/how-the-constitution-was-indeed-pro-slavery/406288/ (accessed 11 January 2023).

Wells, I.B. (2014 [1892]) *Southern Horrors: Lynch Law in All Its Phases*. New York: Floating Press.

White, D.G. (1999) *Too Heavy a Load: Black Women in Defense of Themselves, 1894–1994*. New York: W.W. Norton.

31 W.E.B. Du Bois

ELVIRA BASEVICH

Chapter guide

This chapter introduces W.E.B. Du Bois's original political thought and his strategies for political advocacy. Du Bois's political thought concentrates on the politics of race, colonialism, gender, and labour, among other themes, in order to redefine how political thinkers and activists should build a democratic polity that is truly free and equal for all. His work presents a *serious*, *systematic*, and wholly *unmet* challenge to any liberal theory of justice and democracy that pays attention to non-ideal racial realities. Additionally, this chapter defines some key concepts that Du Bois developed to scrutinize a white-controlled world that does not welcome members of vulnerable groups as equals. These trailblazing concepts include: the doctrine of racialism, double consciousness, and Pan-Africanism. Finally, Sections 31.3 and 31.4 defend Du Bois's contributions to Black feminist thought and American labour politics, which inspired major social justice movements in the twentieth century.

31.1 Introduction

W.E.B. Du Bois's scholarship and activism span over six decades. It is difficult to present an overview of his major writings and legacy in and outside of academia, given his wide-ranging and developing views. Du Bois is recognized as an influential civil rights leader who fought against lynching and racial segregation in the USA. He was born in Great Barrington in rural western Massachusetts in 1868 and died in 1963, the night before Martin Luther King Jr's March on Washington for Jobs and Freedom, during which King gave his now famous 'I have a dream speech'. Along with Ida B. Wells-Barnett (see Key Thinker: Ida B. Wells-Barnett) and others, he co-founded the political and civil rights organization, The National Association for the Advancement of Colored People (NAACP) in 1910, and was the founding editor of its main magazine *The Crisis* from 1910 to 1934. Trained as a historian, he was the first African American to receive a doctoral degree from Harvard University in 1895. Aldon Morris (2015: 15–54) notes that Du Bois pioneered the discipline of modern sociology by developing empirical methods to study segregated Black neighbourhoods in Philadelphia and Atlanta. At the time, public policy-makers and white academics paid scant attention to the living conditions in segregated Black communities. Du Bois's important book *The Souls of Black Folk* (Du Bois, 2007b [1903]) is not only a vital text in African-American arts and letters, but a classic of modern American literature and philosophy. It begins his lifelong inquiry into the legacy of slavery and Jim Crow segregation on modern American society. What is more, he was a philosopher and a poet. One can say without exaggeration that he pursued every path available in his lifetime to theorize and fight for Black dignity and equality.

Key Thinker: Ida B. Wells-Barnett

Ida B. Wells-Barnett (1862–1931) was born into slavery in Holly Springs, Mississippi. Wells-Barnett became a prominent civil rights leader, Black suffragist, and journalist. After her close friends were lynched by a white mob, she dedicated herself to investigative journalism, covering lynchings across the

> USA and campaigning for the US Congress to pass an anti-lynching bill, which it finally did in 2005. As a Black suffragist, she established the National Association of Colored Women's Club, highlighting the vulnerability of Black women to political disenfranchisement, sexual violence, and economic exploitation at the hands of white men (Feimster, 2009: 39–61). Though she often worked together with Du Bois, they also clashed. Du Bois failed to acknowledge her role in the co-founding of the NAACP and, as an editor of *The Crisis*, seldom recognized her substantial contributions to investigative journalism covering racist violence against the segregated Black community.

Du Bois's political thought considers the question of what it means for a person or a group to be a part of a political community—and why victimized groups are often cruelly excluded. Du Bois's writings primarily focused on the African-American community as a marginalized social group; and the relevant larger political community that he often had in mind was the United States, though his criticism of the USA was embedded in an account of global racial injustice. For he theorized a Black diaspora in the context of global Pan-African and decolonial movements in the early twentieth century. Yet it is striking that in his early career, namely, with the publication of the now classic books, *The Souls of Black Folk* (Du Bois, 2007b [1903]), *John Brown* (2007c [1909]), and *Darkwater* (Du Bois, 1999 [1920]), he argued that African Americans must publicly assert their status as free and equal persons, a principle that is foundational to the modern political philosophy of political liberalism. He employs this elemental principle to novel effect by casting the USA—and the world—in a light in which the powerful refuse to see the non-ideal reality, preferring to view major political institutions as if they were basically decent, fair, and democratic. The noted philosopher Charles W. Mills thus argues that Du Bois was a 'black radical liberal ... centrally focused on ... the world of sociopolitical oppression and the challenge, in the United States in particular, of how to overcome illiberal white supremacy in what was supposedly a liberal democratic state' (Mills, 2018: 34–35. See also Chapter 10 on Mills). If Du Bois asks the question of what it means to be part of a political community, his proposed answers analyse why and how a political community functions like an exclusionary, often violent, white supremacist mob. He presses political theorists, philosophers, and activists alike to define fair and inclusive terms of political membership that can truly represent all persons in a modern constitutional democracy.

Consider that Du Bois participated in the NAACP to safeguard the dignity of Black Americans as rights-bearers who should, ideally, command political power in government. His critique of American democracy often draws on the first successful slave uprising, the St. Domingue Revolution in Haiti, which ousted the French colonial slavocracy in 1804. (A 'slavocracy' is a political regime in which slaveowners control political and economic power.) For many Black public intellectuals, as for Du Bois, the St. Domingue Revolution was an inspirational embodiment of Black self-determination in modern government. For the first time in the Americas, a constitutional republic explicitly rid itself of the scourge of slavery—and it was led by Black revolutionaries (Roberts, 2015: 5–8). Du Bois contended that if the American people wish to avoid a violent uprising, the polity must welcome Black self-determination and learn to forge a just interracial political community inclusive of all the people, Black and nonBlack. By way of constructing an interracial political community—or an 'abolition democracy', the preferred term Du Bois uses in his magnum opus, *Black Reconstruction in America*—he centred the input and moral imagination of voices excluded from the democratic process (Du Bois, 1992: 215–258).

Du Bois's unique take on political liberalism underscores 'new revolutionary ideals' that would challenge the status quo and the moral blind spots of the American people (Du Bois, 1999 [1920]: 107). He envisioned that those who are denied formal political standing are the key historical agents of change: enslaved Africans, instigators of slave uprisings, ex-slaves, and African-American women and girls. For him, inclusive democratic practices are the by-products of grassroots social justice movements, often spearheaded by the most vulnerable and disrespected groups in society. In sum, ideally, an inclusive democracy expands the rights and privileges of all, as formally excluded groups refashion the norms and values of the public sphere and lay out a new political agenda for reconstructing the polity. The promise of Du Bois's inclusive democratic vision underscores the profound structural inequalities underpinning American democracy.

Read more about **Du Bois's** life and work by accessing the thinker biography on the online resources: www.oup.com/he/Ramgotra-Choat1e.

31.2 The problem of exclusion

Du Bois reinterprets American history and contemporary racial realities through the lens of the idea of white supremacy. Du Bois is often considered a political theorist of the segregated US South, but he viewed the problem of white supremacy as a national and, ultimately, a global problem (ibid.: 17–46). Du Bois used the term 'the color line' to refer to the sociohistorical phenomenon of white supremacy. He famously writes in *Souls* that 'the problem of the Twentieth Century is the problem of the color line' (Du Bois, 2007b [1903]: 3). White supremacy is the inheritance of the country and the world. It was historically moulded by the institutions of the trans-Atlantic slave trade and colonialism, and was upheld by state-enforced racial segregation that continued in Du Bois's day, widely known as Jim Crow laws and upheld by the US Supreme Court ruling in the case of *Plessy v Ferguson* (1896). Some twenty years after the abolition of Black chattel slavery, the court formally legalized using state power to separate racial groups in public and civil spaces, including housing, public schools, and businesses. The ruling appealed to the doctrine of 'Separate but Equal', reasoning that the enforced separation of racial groups is consistent with their legal equality under the Constitution.

In Du Bois's view, Jim Crow segregation created a deeply unequal world that denied People of Colour in general, and African Americans specifically, basic rights and opportunities. Jim Crow segregation not only fuelled economic and political disenfranchisement in vulnerable racial communities, but bolstered white mob violence that resulted in thousands of lynchings and the destruction of entire Black neighbourhoods and business districts. Du Bois reasoned that racial whiteness reflects an objective social location that disproportionately grants political and economic power to white Americans, whereas non-white racial groups *as a group* tend to lack political and economic power, though some non-white individuals might have more or less privilege, money, or power. The idea of white supremacy represents the overall impact of racialized social location on a person's life prospects, tracking the sociohistorical racial hierarchy persons occupy due to their racial identity. Du Bois thus highlights structural inequalities, including the lack of equitable access to basic resources, rights, and power. However, he also links white supremacy to a social system of values that encourages racially denigrating attitudes and cultural values. White supremacy is therefore not just about structural inequalities in the distribution of resources and opportunity, but is a social system that devalues the beauty, social worth, and the culture of those groups subjugated by the colour line, namely Black and brown people.

The colour line consists of two central dimensions that illustrate the sociohistorical phenomenon of white supremacy: an objective dimension and a subjective dimension. Both dimensions are a key feature of an unjust racial reality. The objective dimension represents the external structure of the world. For example, a white supremacist polity denies political and economic power to Black and brown communities, resulting in staggering racial inequalities in healthcare, housing, education, wealth, and personal safety. Labour markets create profits that tend to enrich white neighbourhoods and white wealth. This is not to say that poor whites do not exist or matter in Du Bois's picture of the colour line. Rather, for Du Bois, though poor whites have relatively fewer resources than their rich counterparts, they still share an objective social location with other white people that grants them better standing than *an average Black and Latinx household in the USA*. What poor whites lack in resources, Du Bois adds, they are compensated for by 'the wages of whiteness'. The latter imparts a psychological feeling of superiority. Even if they don't have much, Du Bois reasons that they 'buy' into a status quo that diminishes their economic prospects because, at least, they can feel good about their racial whiteness.

As staggering and disturbing as this picture is, the external structure of an unequal world does not fully capture the colour line. In addition to striving to represent the external world accurately, Du Bois also strove to represent accurately and compassionately what it *feels* like *not* to be welcomed into a political community on account of one's racial identity. He illustrated the Black experience of the colour line, inviting his reader to contemplate with him, what does it 'feel' like to be a 'problem' in a political community that does not want you there? He stressed the devastating emotional and psychological impact that racial exclusion has on the well-being and self-perception of members of vulnerable racial groups. In addition to the objective dimension of the colour line, he also highlights the *subjective* dimension of the Black experience of the colour line, and is perhaps best known for his original account of the psychological turmoil captured by the concept of 'double consciousness' (Du Bois, 2007b [1903]: 8).

An unjust racial reality produces in Black Americans the 'peculiar sensation' of 'double consciousness' (see Key Concept: Double consciousness):

> After the Egyptian and Indian, the Greek and Roman, the Teuton and Mongolian, the Negro is a sort of seventh son, born with a veil, and gifted with second-sight in this American world,—a world which yields him no true self-consciousness, but only lets him see himself through the revelation of the other world. It is a peculiar sensation, this double-consciousness, this sense of always looking at one's self through the eyes of others, of measuring one's soul by the tape of a world that looks on in amused contempt and pity. One ever feels his two-ness,—an American, a Negro; two souls, two thoughts, two unreconciled strivings; two warring ideals in one dark body, whose dogged strength alone keeps it from being torn asunder.
>
> (ibid.: 8)

Double consciousness conveys the way a Person of Colour might perceive their Self in self-consciousness, when they take their own Self as an 'object' for self-reflection. Self-consciousness elicits our sense of self-value, that is, how we discern our worth: when you contemplate your Self, do you think you're beautiful, smart, or possess inalienable moral entitlements that are worth fighting for? Self-perception is informed by the way that other people see us. We often weigh up how we might come across to others. We figure out who we are, and would like to become, by gauging how we stand in other people's eyes. The development of self-consciousness through social interaction should be a healthy, normal part of human development. However, in a hostile environment, a person is often judged unfairly, and this negative feedback impacts their subjective sense of self-worth. For example, a Jim Crow society treats Black Americans as lacking beauty and social worth, and expects them to *accept* that they do *not* deserve the basic rights and opportunities that are denied to them by the hostile, white-controlled political community. The influential Du Bois scholar Robert Gooding-Williams (2009: 78) notes that double consciousness is premised on 'a racially prejudiced disclosure of Negro life that misrepresents and obscures Negro life as it is'. Because the 'eyes of others' are hostile, the 'revelations' of a white-controlled world are hurtful. The dominant social system of values denigrates Black humanity and undermines the formation of a 'true self-consciousness'. Black Americans never receive the social recognition that they deserve. Ultimately, Du Bois cautioned that prolonged mistreatment can severely damage a person's sense of self-value, so much so that it makes it difficult for them to 'see' their true moral and social value as a complete human being.

> **Key Concept: Double consciousness**
>
> Imagine walking into a room and everyone stares at you. They make hurtful comments about you and the people with whom you share a physical feature. Du Bois believed that this is what it is like when skin colour assumes denigrating social significance. As a member of a vulnerable racial group, you are forced to look at yourself from the point of view of hostile white spectators. As a consequence, your sense of self begins to destabilize: your consciousness 'doubles'. On the one hand, there's the 'you' as you want to see yourself and, on the other hand, there's the 'you' as the white world sees you. Think about how awkward it is to have judgemental eyes follow you around for no reason. Now imagine that those judgemental eyes *constantly* follow you around. What is more, they threaten public humiliation and violence against you. Du Bois feared that under these circumstances the self-esteem of the most psychologically healthy person would soon be crushed and that they would experience 'inevitable self-questioning, self-disparagement, and lowering of ideals' (Du Bois, 2007b [1903]: 12).

31.2.1 Du Bois's philosophy of resistance and race

31.2.1.1 Resistance

Du Bois's challenge to political liberalism places the problem of white supremacy and racial exclusion as central to the project of forming a fair and inclusive political community, in which persons stand as free and equal in dominant institutional arrangements. As we have seen, Du Bois aimed to represent the non-ideal racial realities in the objective structure of the external world, as well as the subjective impact of the colour line on the way vulnerable racial groups feel and experience the world. His challenge to liberalism champions a group-based model of political advocacy and struggle. Though he too emphasized the importance of individual rights, he argued that group-based forms of political action that hone the shared experience of oppression best realize individual rights and make dominant institutions more welcoming of historically excluded groups. In underscoring our responsibilities towards the oppressed, Du Bois set himself apart from most liberal political philosophers, however much else he had in common with them. For he rejected the notion that individuals alone can protect their rights and self-interest without a larger social whole working on their behalf.

African-American political philosophy and Africana philosophy have numerous, often clashing, models of group-based political advocacy that draw on the shared Black experience of oppression. Du Bois rose to national prominence in the early twentieth century in a public debate with the influential Black political leader Booker T. Washington (see Key Thinker: Booker T. Washington). Washington advocated for Black capital in Black hands. Rather than fight Jim Crow directly, he defended Black self-improvement through the exercise of the social virtues of thrift, personal responsibility, and hard work. These virtues, Washington posited, could help build wealth in impoverished and segregated Black communities. Du Bois responded that Washington's approach, in effect, blamed Black Americans for the social ills affecting their communities by suggesting that the poor need to work harder in order to overcome their difficult circumstances. Du Bois protested that Washington's advocacy of Black 'self-reliance' amounted to a 'self-help' philosophy that put too great of a burden on the oppressed to achieve economic gains; and it allowed the country at large to remain complicit in structural inequalities upheld by the Jim Crow laws. Against Washington, Du Bois argued that whatever material gains the Black community might secure through hard work would be precarious in a white-controlled world, in which Black labourers had no political representation or legal protection from the government or in the workplace.

Key Thinker: Booker T. Washington

Born into slavery in 1856, Booker T. Washington gained political influence among white segregationists and the Black community. He founded the Tuskegee Institute in Alabama for Black vocational training as skilled labourers and farmers, but did not stress the value of Black liberal arts colleges. He is today perhaps best known for delivering the 1895 'Atlanta Compromise' speech, in which he declared that: 'In all things purely social we can be as separate as the five fingers, and yet one as the hand in all things essential to mutual progress' (Du Bois, 2007b [1903]: 34). His speech galvanized popular support for state-enforced racial segregation. However, Washington's legacy is more complicated than it first appears (Jagmohan, 2020). He privately donated to desegregation legal case funds. Moreover, unlike Du Bois who grew up in western Massachusetts and attended an integrated high school, Washington's brutal, first-hand experience of slavery may have led him to advocate for more practical solutions that did not rely on the aid or goodwill of a white-controlled world to employ or support Black Americans. Though Du Bois had initially criticized Washington's call for Black economic self-reliance, later in his life he would also come to advocate for Black economic cooperation in a historical context in which white employers exploited Black and brown labourers.

31.2.1.2 Philosophy of race

Du Bois defended Black individual rights before the state, as well as that of Black cultural difference (Marable, 2004; Jeffers, 2013). He did not believe that it was racist to acknowledge the existence of—or to cultivate—racial differences. He was a 'realist' about race. As many critical race theorists agree today, race is 'real' because it is a sociohistorical phenomenon that reflects structural inequalities that impact group-based opportunities and experience. In a white supremacist polity, persons objectively stand in a racial hierarchy that denotes their racial identity. Du Bois's philosophy of race is controversial because it supports the idea that objective social location 'racializes' a group, but he adds that the doctrine of 'racialism' is also important for theorizing the cultural and political meaning of race (Du Bois, 1986: 817–819). The racialist doctrine claims that a 'race ideal' conveys the 'inner thought' of a racial group and should represent their distinct cultural or spiritual life. To be sure, Du Bois did not think physical differences explained the 'spiritual' differences to create a unique Black culture. He argued, instead, that spiritual differences should mould a distinct and unified principle to guide group-based political action and cultural production (ibid.: 818–820). Unsurprisingly, his philosophy of race still inspires Du Bois scholars to debate whether or not he was an essentialist about race. 'Essentialism' in this context refers to the widely rejected view that individuals have the same personality traits, feelings, or thoughts because they happen to look alike or be subject to racial oppression. While contemporary scholars agree that objective social location 'groups' individuals together on account of race, many disagree that individuals who share an objective social location or racial phenotypic features also share a unified subjective viewpoint as a group. Yet Du Bois's racialist theory of race posits an underlying 'spiritual' ideal that can 'unify' what it means to be Black (Outlaw, 1992; Gooding-Williams, 1996; Taylor, 2000; Jeffers, 2013).

Key Concept: Racialism

The doctrine of racialism asserts a racial ideal, through which members of a racial group interpret the world, but racialist doctrines provide different explanations of the nature of the underlining 'spiritual' unity of racial groups. For example, we can distinguish classical racialism from cultural racialism. Classical racialism supported the popular white supremacist ideologies of Social Darwinism, fascism, and eugenics.

> Classical racialism assumed that racial biology 'fixes' the human species' moral and psychological traits. It defended a racial hierarchy in human biology that viewed nonwhite racial groups as natural inferiors in intelligence and moral sensibility. Du Bois's racialism, by contrast, is cultural and egalitarian. It does not appeal to racial biology to explain cultural differences nor does it use racial biology to defend racial hierarchy or chauvinism. Rather, his cultural racialism seeks to articulate the possible cultural and political commitments that members of a vulnerable racial group might share as free, equal, and creative group agents (Jeffers, 2013).

Du Bois's racialist philosophy of race defends two contentious points. First, a race ideal should inform how members of a racial group interpret the world. His racialist philosophy of race also contends, second, that not only should the existence of racial differences be acknowledged, but they should be actively cultivated and celebrated as unique cultural artefacts. He offered excellent reasons to support these two points, which suggests that his racialism is not 'essentialist' after all. In his view, racial groups must cultivate racial differences in order to pursue political goals. His racialism is part of a philosophy of history that uses robust social bonds to engender Black political solidarity as an instrument of progress: a racial ideal should thus form 'a distinct sphere of action and an opportunity for race development' (Du Bois, 1986: 818–820). Black racial identity must be 'conserved' because it has a role to play in democratic politics: it can pragmatically foster Black intragroup political solidarity against white supremacy (Shelby, 2005; Jeffers, 2013). Moreover, Du Bois rejected Black cultural assimilation into the white-controlled world. As he put it, Black liberation that secures a scheme of rights, resources, and opportunities for Black individuals should not entail Black 'self-obliteration' as a distinct cultural group (Du Bois, 1986: 821). He maintained that the innate value of Black cultural difference has yet to be fully appreciated by the world-at-large.

31.2 The problem of exclusion: Key Points

- Du Bois affirms inclusion as a democratic ideal, but his primary focus is on how and why a nominally liberal democracy excludes vulnerable racial groups.
- White supremacist ideology—or the idea of the 'colour line'—determines the objective standing of racial groups and access to political and economic power as well as informing a shared subjective and group-based experience of racial exclusion.
- The concept of 'double consciousness' captures the destructive impact of racist social values on the psychological well-being of members of vulnerable racial groups.
- Du Bois opposed Booker T. Washington's social philosophy of self-help, arguing that it burdened the segregated Black community to redress the destructive impact of Jim Crow laws.
- A racialist philosophy of race encourages vulnerable racial groups to strengthen their 'spiritual' differences in order to cultivate intragroup political solidarity and resist cultural assimilation into a white-controlled world.

31.3 Du Bois on gender and the Black family

31.3.1 Slavery and the Black family

Du Bois has an uneven record as a feminist. Hazel Carby (1998: 10) criticizes the 'masculine' elitism of his political thought, pointing to his 'complete failure to imagine black women as intellectuals and race leaders'. His biographers D.L. Lewis (1993; 2000) and Manning Marable (2004) reveal the often-strained relationships that he had with the women in his household. Yet his prodigious writings also offer incisive feminist analyses. Notwithstanding his personal failings as a feminist ally to Black women, he both aligned himself with the women's right movements, and criticized the exclusion of women of colour from it. For example, he defended the role of Black suffragists in the passage of the 19th Amendment, which gave American women the right to vote in 1920. He lobbied the labour movement for gender parity; and, in his work as an editor, he elevated the careers of young Black women artists and writers.

Du Bois's emphasis on the historical experiences of women showcases his constructive critique of liberalism in action, in that he notes the importance of group-based advocacy to define political goals and realize justice. His notable contribution to Black feminist thought is his contention that the treatment of Black and brown women is a crucial measure of whether or not American democracy realizes the values of freedom and equality for all. In asserting inclusion as a democratic ideal, he underscores the social values and violent practices through which Black women were denied—and continue to be denied—full standing as American citizens and as dignified human beings:

> I shall forgive the white South much in its final judgment day: I shall forgive its slavery, ... I shall forgive its fighting for a well-lost cause and for remembering that struggle with tender tears; I shall forgive its so-called 'pride of race'... but one thing I shall never forgive, neither in this world nor the world to come: its wanton and continued and persistent insulting of the black womanhood which it sought and seeks to prostitute to its lust. I cannot forget that it is such Southern gentlemen ... who insist upon withholding from my mother and wife and daughter those signs and appellations of courtesy and respect which elsewhere he withholds only from bawds and courtesans.
>
> (Du Bois, 1999 [1920]: 100)

The white supremacist patriarchy that 'honours' white women simultaneously withholds 'signs and appellations of courtesy and respect' from women of colour. In other words, in its so-called 'defence' of white women, the polity not only locked white women into dependence on white men, it also fostered the extreme economic and political insecurity of Black women, and treated them as 'undeserving' of gender-based expressions of courtesy, respect, and patriarchal 'protection'.

Du Bois foregrounds the 'history of insult and degradation' against Black women and girls on slave plantations, noting that 'The crushing weight of slavery fell on black women' (ibid.: 98). In particular, he stressed that systematic sexual violence was institutionalized on slave plantations in the South. The rape and sexual brutalization of Black women and girls were routine practices on slave plantations and integral to the growth of the slave economy. Du Bois illustrated that Black women were reduced to instruments of productive labour and endured sexual assault by slave-masters and their families and associates.

In the American slavocracy, enslaved Black families were extremely vulnerable and routinely degraded and destroyed. For enslaved persons there was 'no legal marriage, no legal family, no legal control over children' (ibid.: 98). Enslaved persons were often forced to stand by as witnesses to the physical and sexual brutalization of their loved ones—their partners and children. And they were routinely separated from them by slave markets. In *Black Reconstruction in America*, Du Bois recounted that slaves 'could be sold—actually sold as we sell cattle with no reference to calves or bulls, or recognition of family. It was a nasty business [b]ut it was a stark and bitter fact' (Du Bois, 1992: 11). In documenting the practice of family separation, he gathered original newspaper notices from the antebellum period (that is, the period before the US Civil War) that offered cash rewards for the return of runaway slaves, noting in a melancholy reverie that often the runaways were children looking for their mothers or fathers trying to catch a glimpse of their wife and children on a distant plantation (ibid.: 12). The newspaper notices used disgusting racist depictions to characterize the desire of an enslaved Black person to reunite with their families. They considered slaves' rudimentary desire to re-establish their family units the machinations of mere 'animals'.

31.3.2 Motherhood and the freedom to love

The attack on enslaved families on plantations prompted Du Bois to defend what he calls the 'freedom to love', which requires protecting Black familial bonds against external encroachment and public disrespect (Du Bois, 2007b [1903]: 11). In articulating the idea of the 'freedom to love', he centred the historical experiences of Black women and girls, positioning them as central agents in American democracy after the end of the Civil War and within the legal abolition of slavery in the USA. In the postbellum republic, he argued that Black women were vital in redefining the ideals and values of democratic life and in charting their own destinies as free ex-slaves.

One might wonder why Du Bois regarded the idea of the 'freedom to love' as essential to the historical struggle of emancipated Black women. In order to understand why this idea is so central for him, we must appreciate that the freedom to love has two dimensions: a formal legal dimension and a moral dimension, both of which connect to the right to 'motherhood' (Du Bois, 1999 [1920]: 95–108). The formal legal protection of the right to motherhood included the newfound legal rights of Black women as parents with custodial rights. Custodial rights established Black mothers as the principal authorities in the lives of their children, rather than that of the state or whites, as had been the case in the South during the antebellum era. Relatedly, the extension of formal legal protection also included the legal recognition of romantic partnerships in which a marriage contract became legally binding. A legal marriage contract, for Du Bois, indicated a germ of public acknowledgement that Black people should be free to choose who to love and to stay in partnered relationships with their beloved without the white-controlled world intervening in their personal affairs. Custodial rights and the marriage contract were thus long overdue basic legal protections for the Black family. Black women were historically denied these basic legal protections, whereas white women took such protections for granted and overlooked their cruel suppression in the lives of their sisters of colour. In the historical context of a republic emerging from the shadow of slavery, Black women asserting the legal right to raise their own children and to forge their own familial bonds against external encroachment was unprecedented. In other words, he viewed rights associated with defended families to be central to the enrichment of democratic ideals and politics.

Du Bois's contribution to Black feminist thought intimates a crucial, but often overlooked, difference in the fragility of familial bounds with respect to the intersection of race and gender. This difference of historical experience would later impact the US women's rights movement in the twentieth century. White women fought to *exit* their family units and to *enter* the labour force. They sought to leave the pedestal that cemented their patriarchal dependence on white men as sole earners. In contrast, women of colour and Black women in particular were often forced to labour outside their homes, with little compensation for their productive labour and few opportunities to connect with their own children and families. In contrast to white women's political agenda, women of colour have fought and continue to fight for the chance to *enter* their own families and to reconstitute their family unit on their own terms. Not only were Black women often forced to work outside of their own homes, but they were often forced into domestic and care-oriented labour, looking after white children. To have the chance to be with their own families and to administer to the needs of their own children remains difficult.

Additionally, Du Bois defended the moral—in addition to the formal legal—dimension of the right to motherhood. For him, informal social practices often devalued Black persons as loving parents and partners. He argued that Black women should have the freedom to make their own decisions about bearing children and pursuing intimate relationships—and that freedom should be publicly respected as a moral right. He thus asserted Black women's 'freedom to love' during the Jim Crow era. Lawrie Balfour (2011: 104) observes that 'he defended the importance of sexual freedom for any meaningful conception of women as free citizens'. In a historical context that systematically targeted Black and brown women's bodies for abuse and exploitation in American domestic life and in violent colonial encounters, Du Bois argued that it was absolutely essential to protect their bodily security and to cultivate public respect for their sexual agency. Du Bois asserted their freedom and dignity as sexual agents, and as such rejected the colonial and white supremacist objectification of Black and brown women. While defending 'the freedom to love' and Black women's custodial rights, however, he was careful not to invoke traditional gender conventions that praise the cult of domesticity for Black women. 'We cannot imprison women again in a home or require them on pain of death to be nurses and housekeepers' (Du Bois, 1999 [1920]: 103). The exercise of sexual agency, for him, must be linked to equal opportunity for securing fairly compensated employment, education, and political power. He defended Black women as free agents whose desire to pursue sexual relations and to bear children—including outside of wedlock—is a legal and a moral right (ibid.: 107). He refused to confine Black women to the nuclear family and patriarchal gendered mores.

> **31.3 Du Bois on gender and the Black family: Key Points**
>
> - Du Bois often failed to make his personal relationships with women conform to his vision of gender equality.
> - Du Bois emphasized that Black women and girls endured sexual violence and abuse on slave plantations.
> - After the abolition of slavery and with the rise of Jim Crow, Black women fought to assert their dignity as free sexual agents, political equals with the right to love, and as parents with custodial rights.
> - The legal recognition of Black custodial rights and the marriage contract was an important political gain.
> - The informal social recognition that respects Black women—and their moral right to have children outside of wedlock—is an important counterpart to the advance of Black civil and political rights.

31.4 Du Bois's socialist politics

31.4.1 Du Bois among liberals and labour organizers

Du Bois's Marxist politics is a contentious topic in Du Bois scholarship. Although he officially joined the Communist Party USA in 1961, at the age of 93, he considered himself a socialist throughout his long life and there are good reasons to resist thinking that his Marxist sympathies only began in the 1960s. In his application to join the party, he wrote: 'Capitalism cannot reform itself . . . No universal selfishness can bring universal good to all.' But Du Bois was a radical democratic socialist who did not believe that the basic values of liberalism, such as freedom and equality for all persons before representational domestic and global governing bodies, are incompatible with Marxist calls for economic and labour rights. Du Bois's labour politics have recently received renewed attention (Douglas, 2019; Myers, 2019), and it has several unique features. Here we explore his defence of, first, interracial labour alliances and, second, democratic control of the economy and the workplace. In presenting each feature, we provide an overview of his rebukes to the American labour movement and the National Association for the Advancement of Colored People (NAACP), of which he was a co-founder and long-time member until 1934.

31.4.1.1 Critique of the American labour movement

By way of presenting Du Bois's defence of interracial labour alliances, we must engage his incisive critique of the American labour movement. He criticized its racially exclusionary character in the late nineteenth and early twentieth centuries. It had neglected the abolition movement against slavery and failed to advocate on behalf of slaves as a hyper-exploited labour force. In fact, the white-controlled labour movement often referred to *themselves* as the 'white slaves' of capitalism, ignoring the existence of actual slaves (Du Bois, 1992: 356). After the abolition of slavery, the American labour movement enabled the emergence of what Du Bois described as a 'second slavery' for the African-American community. It barred workers of colour from joining its ranks and failed to represent their economic interests in the workplace.

> Contrary to all labor philosophy, they [the white-controlled labour movement] would divide labor by racial and social lines and yet continue to talk of one labor movement. Through this separate union, Negro labor would be restrained from competition and yet kept out of the white race unions where power and discussion lay.
>
> (Du Bois, 1992: 356)

In effect, the white-controlled labour movement fought for protections for white labourers: its moral imagination was just as segregated as the social world. For it viewed the Black and brown labour force as another competitor, rather than as a potential and indispensable ally for an interracial labour alliance. Du Bois highlights that just as the American women's suffrage movement would exclude women of colour, the American labour movement had excluded persons of colour from its ranks, and in his view these exclusionary tendencies led to the weakening of these movements.

Du Bois upheld the ideal of interracial labour solidarity as pivotal for economic justice for all labourers. He viewed the ideal of interracial labour solidarity to be essential in sustaining a viable labour movement that could exert pressure on white capitalists who exploited the colour line for profits, driving down Black wages and placing a ceiling on white wages. The philosopher Chike Jeffers thus aptly observes that 'Du Bois wishes to treat marginality as opportunity'—an indispensable reference point for reimagining political advocacy (Jeffers, 2017: 247). According to Du Bois, the ultimate 'test' of American socialism was to overcome the colour line, which necessitated an ongoing political engagement with segregated Black communities (Du Bois, 1913: 140). Indeed, he argued for an interracial economic democracy, with democratic control of the state *and* the workplace.

31.4.1.2 Critique of the NAACP

Du Bois co-founded the NAACP but left the organization in 1934 for its failure to redress the economic needs of the segregated Black community, reeling from the effects of the Great Depression. After publishing *Black Reconstruction in America* in 1935, he began to reframe his thinking about political and economic equality. He argued that in a real democracy the people should control the parts of their lives where they are the most vulnerable: their subordinate relation to the free market and the workplace. He merged this sensibility to care for the urgent economic needs of the segregated Black community, suffering serious economic insecurity.

Du Bois was particularly sensitive to Black labourers' subordination to white capitalists. Former slaves and their descendants still had little control over the institutional conditions of their labour. White employers often resented having to pay Black people a wage at all. Du Bois defended granting workers' democratic control over the means of production. He surmised that democratic rights were empty without the chance to exercise democratic control over the conditions of labour and means of production. In other words, his expanded political vision included protecting civil and politics rights, as well as what 'touches the matters of daily life [and] are nearest to the interests of *the people*' (Du Bois, 1999 [1920]: 90–91). Democratic politics should concentrate on 'the vital, everyday interests of all', which he describes as that of 'work and wages' (ibid.: 90–91).

Du Bois became an unpopular figure later in his life. Neither the American labour movement nor major civil rights associations such as the NAACP stressed Black economic needs. So, he began to favour a version of Black nationalism that was reminiscent of Washington's original call for Black economic self-reliance, though with some modifications. Du Bois still favoured challenging Jim Crow directly, demanding that the state should extend equal legal protections to Black Americans. But he also conceded the importance of members of segregated Black communities working together to achieve economic security. He hoped that Black consumer cooperatives could build up material wealth and thereby lessen Black dependence on white employers. Unsurprisingly, his new proposals were controversial. Many former allies in the civil rights movement distanced themselves from him. He became increasingly isolated with the rise of the Cold War and McCarthyism (the practice of making accusations of subversion and treason, especially when related to communism and socialism).

During this dark period in American history, prominent progressive intellectuals and activists chose to abandon progressive causes but, in his advanced age, Du Bois instead aligned himself more closely with progressive causes. Narrowly escaping imprisonment for his peace activism, in 1961, he accepted an invitation from the socialist revolutionary and pan-African leader Kwame Nkrumah to resettle in Ghana. Nkrumah was the first President of Ghana after its emancipation from Britain and was a formidable intellectual in his own right, trained in Britain and the USA. He was also a public intellectual who supported the Pan-African philosophy of which Du Bois was by this point a strong exponent. At the end of his life, Du Bois went into exile, gave up his American citizenship, and died in Ghana. The next day Nkrumah organized a state funeral attended by thousands.

Key Concept: Pan-Africanism

Pan-Africanism was a political philosophy and global political strategy for forging regional and global political alliances in the Black diaspora. As a political strategy, it encompassed an international federation of states, with newly independent Ghana playing a major role in creating an international Pan-African alliance that still exists today. But it also sought to cultivate international relations with former European colonies in South America and Asia. As a political philosophy, Pan-Africanism aimed to secure the substantive economic independence of former European colonies from Europe and achieve lasting global peace in the aftermath of brutal colonial wars. It sought to redefine the intellectual and historical identity of African and Afro-descendent peoples on their own terms, inviting a global conversation about race and national identity among formerly colonized African peoples. Du Bois was deeply involved in the Pan-African movement, organizing several Pan-African Congresses before relocating to Ghana. He believed that a Pan-African global justice movement must help advance racial justice in his former homeland, the USA.

31.4 Du Bois's socialist politics: Key Points

- Du Bois advocated interracial political solidarity in the American labour movement, which had failed to represent the economic interests of the Black and brown labour force.
- The scope of democratic ideals should be extended to include workers' democratic control of the production process and the institutional conditions of their labour.
- Persecuted during the Cold War and McCarthyism in the USA, Du Bois went into exile in Ghana, where he died in 1963.

31.5 Conclusion

W.E.B. Du Bois is a unique, creative, and hitherto neglected political theorist. He accomplished much in his lifetime, as a theorist, activist, creative writer, and journalist. His political thought puts pressure on the liberal principle of freedom and equality for all: in order to better understand how to deliver this principle to the American people, his writings foreground the politics of race, gender, and labour in its analysis of the promise—and limits—of American and global democracy.

As laid out in Section 31.2, Du Bois's political critique scrutinizes how white supremacist ideology has shaped modern societies to create the colour line. The colour line consists of an objective dimension and a subjective dimension. The objective dimension tracks race-based inequalities in the external world, whereas the subjective dimension relates victims' feelings of psychological distress that stem from being subject to systematic racial exclusion. Though the colour line inflicts a serious moral injury that can cause double consciousness, Du Bois adds that the shared experience of oppression can also be the basis for collective resistance. For this reason, as explained in Section 31.2.1, he develops a racialist theory of race. The adoption of certain 'racial ideals' can help members of vulnerable racial groups achieve political goals to redress their hardships. Additionally, he posits that conserving cultural differences among racial groups has innate moral value because it fills out an important feature of human plurality. Racial groups, especially those subjected to a long history of racial injustice, need not seek their cultural self-obliteration in order to liberate themselves from white supremacist ideology.

Du Bois's political critique is context-sensitive and responds to historical injustices. Section 31.3 related Du Bois's compassionate account of the impact of the institution of slavery on the families of enslaved persons, citing his extensive historical documentation of routine sexual violence against Black women and girls, as well as the separation of family members by slave markets. Yet Du Bois's discussion of the family does not uncritically defend the nuclear family unit. Instead he defends the self-determination of Black women to exercise their sexual autonomy apart from traditional gender expectations, affirming their moral right to have children outside of wedlock. Finally, Section 31.4 showed that although Du Bois was a lifelong socialist, he only officially joined the Communist Party USA in 1961 at the age of 93. His reluctance to join a party platform reflected his misgivings about the prevailing organizational tactics of the labour movement. For example, he criticized the white-controlled labour movement for failing to develop interracial labour coalitions against the owners of capital and the means of production. He also came to criticize the NAACP, a civil rights organization that he helped co-found, for to its failure to assail the crushing economic distress of Black American communities in the aftermath of the Great Depression.

Tke your learning further by accessing the online resources for a library of web links to relevant videos, articles, blogs, and useful websites for this chapter: **www.oup.com/he/Ramgotra-Choat1e**.

Study questions

1. How should non-ideal racial realities factor into how political philosophers theorize and defend the ideal of political inclusion in modern democratic states?
2. Can you think of some examples that capture how a 'colour line' works in your country, neighbourhood, or classroom?

3. What effect do you think the experience of double consciousness might have on someone's motivation to join a social justice movement?
4. Is there any way to avoid some of the more devasting psychological consequences of double consciousness? Offer some concrete examples for how one might lessen the negative effects of double consciousness.
5. Why did Du Bois believe that Washington's social philosophy of self-help was dangerous for the segregated Black community to adopt?
6. Why was it vital for Du Bois to centre the history of sexual violence on slave plantations against Black women and girls in his critique of American democracy?
7. Du Bois's message to 'conserve' Black racial difference aimed to build a strong Black domestic and global community. Do you think that white people should also cultivate or conserve their 'racial' difference?
8. Du Bois theorized many original concepts for thinking about racial injustice: how might they capture—or not—the shared experience of oppression based on gender, sexuality, or religion?

Further reading

Primary sources

Du Bois, W.E.B. (1982) *Writings by Du Bois in Non-Periodical Literature Edited by Others*. Ed. H. Aptheker, Millwood: Kraus-Thomson Organization Limited.
Collects in one volume Du Bois's essential essays published in pamphlets, volumes, and magazines edited by others.

Du Bois, W.E.B. (1995) *W.E.B. Du Bois: A Reader*. Ed. D.L. Lewis. New York: Henry Holt and Company.
Useful collection of some of Du Bois's works.

Du Bois, W.E.B. (2007a) *The Oxford W.E.B. Du Bois*, 19 vols. Ed. H.L. Gates, Jr. Oxford: Oxford University Press.
The 2007 Oxford Series of Du Bois's complete works is the best and most comprehensive representation of Du Bois's monographs; each work is introduced by a key contemporary figure in Africana/African-American/Black studies.

Du Bois, W.E.B. (2015) *W.E.B. Du Bois and the Problem of the Color Line at the Turn of the Twentieth Century*. Ed. N.D. Chandler. New York: Fordham University Press.
Collects in one volume Du Bois's essential early essays from 1894–1906.

Secondary sources

Appiah, K.A. (2014) *Lines of Descent*. Cambridge, MA: Harvard University Press.
A unique book that combines intellectual biography and philosophy to connect Du Bois's writings to modern German philosophy.

Balfour, L. (2011) *Democracy's Reconstruction: Thinking Politically with W.E.B. Du Bois*. New York: Oxford University Press.
Original monograph that interrogates how Du Bois reimagines the nature of the US political community, particularly with respect to the history of anti-Black racial injustice.

Bromell, N. (ed.) (2018) *A Political Companion to W.E.B. Du Bois*. Lexington, KT: University of Kentucky Press.
Interdisciplinary collection of essays on Du Bois's democratic theory.

Gillman, S. and Weinbaum, A.E. (eds) (2007) *Next to the Color Line: Gender, Sexuality, and W. E. B. Du Bois*. Minneapolis, MN: University of Minnesota Press.
Singular and comprehensive collection of essays on Du Bois, gender, and sexuality.

Gooding-Williams, R. (2009) *In the Shadow of Du Bois: Afro Modern Political Thought in America*. Cambridge, MA: Harvard University Press.
An influential *tour de force* monograph about Du Bois's political philosophy and philosophy of race, covering his intellectual background and political milieu.

Hooker, J. (2017) *Theorizing Race in the Americas: Douglass, Sarmiento, Du Bois, and Vasconcelos*. Oxford: Oxford University Press.
Establishes Du Bois's intellectual and political legacy in relation to Latinx political thought in continental South America.

Jeffers, C. (2013) 'The Cultural Theory of Race: Yet Another Look at Du Bois's "The Conservation of Races"'. *Ethics*, 123: 403–426.
An important recent article defending Du Bois's philosophy of race as part of a 'cultural theory of race'. It includes a brief survey of critical philosophy of race today and an overview of an important debate in Du Bois scholarship about whether or not Du Bois is an 'essentialist' about race.

Lewis, D.L. (1993) *W.E.B. Du Bois: Biography of a Race, 1868–1919*. New York: Henry Holt.
Part I of Pulitzer-winning essential biography of Du Bois.

Lewis, D.L. (2000) *W.E.B. Du Bois: The Fight for Equality and the American Century, 1919–1963*. New York: Henry Holt.
Part II of Pulitzer-winning essential biography of Du Bois.

Marable, M. (2004) *W.E.B. Du Bois: Black Radical Democrat*. New York: Routledge.
Indispensable intellectual biography of Du Bois as a radical democratic socialist.

Rabaka, R. (2021) *Du Bois: A Critical Introduction*. Cambridge: Polity.
Presents Du Bois's influence in critical race theory, emphasizing postcolonialism, Black Marxism, and Black feminist philosophy.

Taylor, P.C. (2004) 'What's the Use of Calling Du Bois a Pragmatist?' *Metaphilosophy*, 32(1–2): 99–114.
Develops a line of thought that begins with the work of Cornell West situating Du Bois in the American pragmatist philosophical tradition.

Valdez, I. (2019) *Transnational Cosmopolitanism: Kant, Du Bois, and Justice as a Political Craft*. Cambridge: Cambridge University Press.
Presents Du Bois's cosmopolitan theories of global justice in relation to his involvement in decolonial and the Pan-African movements in the twentieth century, as well as challenging contemporary debates in Kant scholarship about race and colonialism.

West, C. (1989) *The American Evasion of Philosophy: A Genealogy of Pragmatism*. New York: Palgrave.
A classic, covering Black thought in the development of American pragmatism.

References

Balfour, L. (2011) *Democracy's Reconstruction: Thinking Politically with W.E.B. Du Bois*. New York: Oxford University Press.

Carby, H. (1998) *Race Men*. Cambridge, MA: Harvard University Press.

Douglas, A.J. (2019) *W.E.B. Du Bois and the Critique of the Competitive Society*. Athens, GA: University of Georgia Press.

Du Bois, W.E.B. (1913) 'Socialism and the Negro Problem'. *New Review*, 1(5): 138–141.

Du Bois, W. E. B. (1986) 'On the Conservation of Races'. In *W.E.B. Du Bois: Writings*. New York: The Library of America, pp. 817–819.

Du Bois, W.E.B. (1992) *Black Reconstruction in America*. New York: Free Press.

Du Bois, W.E.B. (1999 [1920]) *Darkwater: Voices from within the Veil*. Mineola, NY: Dover.

Du Bois, W.E.B. (2007b [1903]) *The Souls of Black Folk*. Oxford: Oxford University Press.

Du Bois, W.E.B. (2007c [1909]) *John Brown*. Oxford: Oxford University Press.

Feimster, C. (2009) *Southern Horrors: Women and the Politics of Rape and Lynching* Cambridge, MA: Harvard University Press.

Gooding-Williams, R. (1996) 'Outlaw, Appiah, and Du Bois's "The Conservation of Races"'. In B.W. Bell, E.R. Grosholz, and J.B. Stewart (eds), *W.E.B. Du Bois on Race and Culture: Philosophy, Politics, and Poetics*. New York: Routledge, pp. 39–56.

Gooding-Williams, R. (2009) *In the Shadow of Du Bois: Afro Modern Political Thought in America*. Cambridge, MA: Harvard University Press.

Jagmohan, D. (2020) 'Booker T. Washington and the Politics of Deception'. In M.L. Rogers and J. Turner (eds), *African American Political Thought: A Collected History*. Chicago: University of Chicago Press.

Jeffers, C. (2013) 'The Cultural Theory of Race: Yet Another Look at Du Bois's "The Conservation of Races"'. *Ethics*, 123: 403–426.

Jeffers, C. (2017) 'W.E.B. Du Bois's "Whither Now and Why"'. In E. Schliesser (ed.), *Ten Neglected Classics of Philosophy*.Oxford: Oxford University Press, pp. 222–255.

Kirkland, F.M. (1993) 'Modernity and Intellectual Life in Black'. *The Philosophical Forum*, 24(1–3): 136–165.

Lewis, D.L. (1993) *W.E.B. Du Bois: Biography of a Race, 1868-1919*. New York: Henry Holt.

Lewis, D.L. (2000) *W.E.B. Du Bois: The Fight for Equality and the American Century, 1919-1963*. New York: Henry Holt.

Marable, M. (2004) *W.E.B. Du Bois: Black Radical Democrat*. New York: Routledge.

Mills, C.W. (2018) 'W. E. B. Du Bois: Black Radical Liberal'. In N. Bromell (ed.), *A Political Companion to W.E.B. Du Bois*. Lexington, KT: University Press of Kentucky, pp. 19-56.

Morris, A. (2015) *The Scholar Denied: W.E.B. Du Bois and the Birth of Modern Sociology*. Oakland, CA: University of California Press.

Myers, E. (2019) 'Beyond the Psychological Wage: Du Bois on White Domination'. *Political Theory*, 47(1): 1–18.

Outlaw, L. (1992) 'Against the Grain of Modernity: The Politics of Difference and the Conservation of "Race"'. *Man and World*, 25: 443–468.

Roberts, N. (2015) *Freedom as Marronage*. Chicago: University of Chicago Press.

Rogers, M.L. (2012) 'The People, Rhetoric, and Affect: On the Political Force of Du Bois's *The Souls of Black Folk*. *American Political Science Review*, 106(1): 188–203.

Shelby, T. (2005) *We Who Are Dark: The Philosophical Foundations of Black Solidarity*. Cambridge, MA: Harvard University Press.

Taylor, P.C. (2000) 'Appiah's Uncompleted Argument: W.E.B. Du Bois and the Reality of Race'. *Social Theory and Practice*, 26: 103–128.

32 John Rawls

MAEVE MCKEOWN

> ### Chapter guide
>
> This chapter focuses on what is arguably the most influential text in contemporary Anglo-American political philosophy: John Rawls's *A Theory of Justice* (1971). Section 32.2 explores the basics of Rawls's difficult text, while Section 32.3 addresses the Rawlsian self in what he calls 'the original position'. Feminists and critical race theorists disagree over the potential of this self for generating a non-sexist, anti-racist society, and philosophers of disability highlight its ableist assumptions. Section 32.4 addresses the Rawlsian society governed by a just 'basic structure'. It highlights three issues: (1) the ambiguity of the concept of a basic structure separate from individual behaviour and other institutions; (2) the concern that focusing on the basic structure fails to address power relations between groups; and (3) that it limits the scope of justice to the nation state. While acknowledging the profound contributions of Rawls, the chapter concludes that Rawlsian ideal theory is not the best approach from the perspective of feminist, anti-racist, and anti-ableist philosophy.

32.1 Introduction

John Rawls (1921–2002) is without doubt one of the most influential political philosophers of the twentieth century. While few may have heard of Rawls outside of academia, within the academy his influence is unparalleled. Since the publication of *A Theory of Justice* in 1971, political philosophy in the English-speaking world has been dominated by Rawls, his followers, and his critics.

Rawls's work spanned four decades and over 2000 pages of text, but it is *A Theory of Justice* (Rawls, 1971; hereafter *TJ*) that dominated debates among political philosophers in the late twentieth and early twenty-first centuries, and is our focus. The secondary literature on Rawls is vast; we will focus on his heterodox critics (philosophers working outside the mainstream), who have highlighted that Rawls was writing at the height of the Civil Rights and Women's Liberation movements in the USA, yet his theory of justice neglects race and women. Rawls's commitments to universalism, liberal neutrality, and ideal theory meant that the crucial forms of *in*justice of his time were overlooked, or at least subsumed under more general themes. Some think that Rawlsian liberalism can be rescued for feminism and critical philosophy of race, but others think that these gaps render his work irrelevant. This chapter begins by looking at the background to Rawls's theory and the basics of his approach, before addressing the heterodox critiques of his interpretation of the self and the just society.

Rawls began his work within two established traditions in political philosophy: liberalism and social contract theory. As a liberal, Rawls wanted to balance freedom and equality. Liberals are primarily concerned with individual liberty, but they also recognize the equal moral worth of individuals. They believe that a fully egalitarian society that distributed resources equally to every individual would violate the individual's liberty to do whatever one wants with one's time and resources. However, people start out from different social positions and have different capabilities and talents, so letting individuals do whatever they want will lead to social and economic inequalities.

Rawls came up with an ingenious solution: the two principles of justice—the liberty principle and the egalitarian principle—that are explained in Section 32.2.4. Rawls hoped to show that liberals could keep their fundamental commitment to freedom, while also ensuring a degree of equality. It is this commitment to redistribution and equality that makes Rawls a left-liberal, rather than a right-liberal.

Rawls revived the social contract tradition when it seemed obsolete and the dominant mode of moral and political philosophy was utilitarianism. Utilitarians argue that society should be organized to maximize utility for the greatest number of people (see also Chapter 12 on Mill). Rawls, like many others, rejects this on the grounds that individuals' liberty can be overridden in the interests of maximizing utility: 'Justice denies that the loss of freedom for some is made right by a greater good shared by others' (ibid.: 25). In making calculations about overall utility, utilitarianism denies 'the distinction between persons' (ibid.: 24). For Rawls (1988: 251), the just society must prioritize the 'right' over the 'good', meaning that the principles of justice 'set limits to permissible ways of life'.

In addition, Rawls rejected 'intuitionism' in philosophy, whereby a philosopher draws on their intuitions to determine which principles of social justice seem correct (Rawls, 1971: 34). Instead, Rawls argues that there should be constructive criteria against which to judge competing principles. This is established through a process of 'reflective equilibrium', in which a person weighs competing conceptions of justice and revises their judgements to accord with them (ibid.: 42–43). Rawls thinks that in the abstract, without the complications of real life and real politics, free, equal, and rational individuals would choose his principles of justice over utilitarianism or intuitionism.

Moreover, the just society must be determined by people together. Thus, he thinks about what rational, free and equal persons would agree to if they were in a fair dialogue with one another deciding upon an 'original agreement' for the principles to regulate a just society; this is Rawls's theory of 'justice as fairness' (ibid.: 10). He doesn't think that the social contract is something that actually happened in history; rather, he thinks that if we abstract away from the world as it is, we can think more clearly about the kind of contract individuals would choose to govern a just society. Rawls is credited with creating a new, rigorous methodology, reviving social contract theory for the twentieth century, and indeed for reviving the entire field of normative political philosophy.

Read more about **Rawls's** life and work by accessing the thinker biography on the online resources: www.oup.com/he/Ramgotra-Choat1e.

32.2 *A Theory of Justice*: The basics

Rawls's *TJ* is dense and difficult to understand for first-time readers with no background knowledge. Here we will establish the basics.

32.2.1 The basic structure

Rawls opens *TJ* thus: 'Justice is the first virtue of social institutions' (Rawls, 1971: 3). He means that justice refers to the ways in which institutions organize society. People are born into social positions that are determined by the political system and by economic and social circumstances. These social positions, some of which are more advantaged than others, affect people's chances in life and yet they have nothing to do with merit or desert. These are the inequalities that a theory of justice should address—the inequalities that are rooted in what Rawls calls the 'basic structure' of society.

Within society, individuals produce and use resources and services, and participate in the economy, social interactions, and political processes. This 'social cooperation' generates benefits and burdens. The role of the basic structure is to distribute these benefits and burdens fairly, as well as determining individuals' rights and duties. The basic structure refers to the 'major social institutions': these are the political constitution and the principal economic and social arrangements, which include legal protection of freedom of thought and liberty of conscience, competitive markets, private property in the means of production, and the monogamous family (ibid.: 6).

The main idea is this: because the effects of these institutions on our lives are so profound, and are present from birth, these are the institutions that a theory of justice should be concerned with. Some other institutions, like religion, are not basic, because they are not fundamental in determining our life chances. Rawls (ibid.: 6–7) writes:

> Taken together as one scheme, the major institutions define men's [sic] rights and duties and influence their life prospects, what they can expect to be and how well they can hope to do. The basic structure is the primary subject of justice because its effects are so profound and present from the start.

Note that Rawls's is a theory of *social* justice: it is not a theory about all advantages and disadvantages that we might consider unjust, for instance, injustice within a private association like a corporation, or injustice in social norms. It only refers to those advantages and disadvantages that arise from the basic structure. Also, it is a theory of justice within one nation state, not between states or globally. This is because it refers to justice between individuals who are engaged in social cooperation under the same public institutions (ibid.: 7).

32.2.2 Ideal theory

Rawls thinks that we should figure out what a society would look like in the ideal. He describes his theory as a 'realistic utopia': it is utopian because it is more just than any existing society, but it is realistic because 'it depicts an achievable world' that coheres with 'the actual laws of nature' (Rawls, 1999: 6, 12–13; Swift and Stemplowska, 2014: 115). To provide a blueprint of the ideal society, Rawls assumes a situation of 'strict compliance': everyone in the society accepts the principles of justice, which they agree to in the original position, and people abide by the laws and uphold the political institutions. He calls this a 'well-ordered society' (Rawls, 1971: 8).

Rawls makes this assumption because he thinks that ideal theory is necessary to determine what a just society would look like, giving us a standard against which to judge existing problems. Once an ideal theory is in place, then we can start looking at questions of non-ideal theory, including topics like a theory of punishment, just war theory, opposing unjust regimes, civil disobedience, conscientious objection, revolution, compensatory justice, and institutional injustice (ibid.: 8). Ideal theory will help us to determine how best to respond to these problems, and in what order, because we know what we are working towards.

32.2.3 The original position

Perhaps Rawls's greatest and most unique innovation is 'the original position': a thought experiment, or a 'device of representation', wherein citizens agree to the principles of justice for the ideal society. Rawls aimed to find an impartial perspective on what a just society should look like. One of the philosophical antecedents is Hume's 'judicious spectator' (Freeman, 2019). Hume wanted to explain how people make moral judgements and he argued that they do this by abstracting away from their own particular interests and taking the view of an impartial spectator in their imagination. Other philosophers used the idea of an impartial perspective not only to explain how individuals make moral judgements, but to create a basis against which to justify moral rules and principles; examples include Kant's 'categorical imperative', Adam Smith's 'impartial spectator', and Henry Sidgwick's 'point of view of the universe' (ibid.).

Rawls's original position is an account of the moral point of view with regards to justice. But it is different because it is socially conceived (it's a general agreement between 'parties' in the original position, not one person's view). This ties into the social contract tradition. Rawls's original position is an alternative to the state of nature. In state of nature theories, like Locke's, humans have rights and claims prior to membership in a political community. In contrast, Rawls thinks we are fundamentally social beings and we must determine these rights and claims together.

Importantly, the original position is not a historical event; it is a hypothetical situation or a thought experiment, similar to those proposed by classical social contract theorists, such as Hobbes, Locke, and Rousseau (see Part II in this volume). But, unlike other contract theorists, for Rawls, the foundation of society is not only about the legitimacy of the political constitution and law, but also private property, social and economic arrangements, educational and work opportunities, and social positions—i.e., the entire 'basic structure' of society. The parties agree to principles that regulate the basic structure and ensure it is just.

In Rawls's original position, participants are under a 'veil of ignorance': the parties in the original position do not know anything about themselves. More specifically, they do not know their social status or class, their natural talents or abilities, such as level of intelligence or strength, or their 'conception of the good' (their own interpretation of the good life) (Rawls, 1971: 11). In addition, they don't know what kind of society they live in; specifically, they do not know historical facts about their society, the size of the population, its level of wealth and resources, what religious institutions there are, etc. (ibid.: 118). This is to ensure that no one is advantaged or disadvantaged by the choice of principles of justice in the original position (because, for example, if a person knows that they are a rich, white man, then he may choose principles of justice that favour rich, white men).

The parties in the original position *do* know general facts about the natural and social sciences, such as economics (supply and demand), psychology, political science, biology, human behaviour, and psychological development (ibid.: 119). They also know that they are living in the 'circumstances of justice': 'the normal conditions under which human cooperation is both possible and necessary' (ibid.: 109). There is moderate scarcity: there is enough to go round, so the citizens are not under threat of a famine or war, but they are not living in a state of abundance; decisions have to be made collectively about how to distribute resources. There are also conflicting interests. The parties have different conceptions of the good (even if they don't know their specific content), limited knowledge, and different philosophical and religious beliefs (ibid.: 110).

The parties know that they are heads of families (ibid.: 111). Rawls includes this to ensure intergenerational justice: the participants will endorse a 'just savings principle' to ensure justice for their children and hence future generations more generally. The parties are 'mutually disinterested' (ibid.: 12, 112): they are not willing to sacrifice their interests for others. This does not mean they are selfish: they care about their own interests, the interests of their loved ones, and the causes they care about; they are like trustees (Freeman, 2019). They are not motivated by envy or resentment (Rawls, 1971: 124); instead, they are simply trying to do the best for themselves and those in their trust.

Parties know about the desirability of the primary social goods—'things that every rational man is presumed to want' (ibid.: 54). The natural primary goods are health and vigour, intelligence, and imagination; these are not things that can be controlled by the basic structure. The social primary goods are the fundamental liberties, access to social positions, income and wealth, and the social bases of self-respect, and these are under the control of the basic structure.

In the original position, the participants are given a list of conceptions of justice from Western political philosophy: utilitarianism, perfectionism, intuitionism, rational egoism, Rawlsian justice as fairness, and some mixed conceptions (ibid.: 107). They compare the different conceptions and ultimately agree that Rawlsian justice as fairness is the most rational. This is a selection process, not a deliberation (Freeman, 2019). They are motivated by their own rational interests (getting an adequate share of the primary goods). In order to achieve an adequate share of the primary goods, participants will specifically choose Rawls's two principles of justice, to which we now turn.

32.2.4 The principles of justice

Rawls thinks that the participants in the original position would choose two principles of justice. 'First: each person is to have an equal right to the most extensive scheme of equal basic liberties compatible with a similar scheme of liberties for others' (Rawls, 1971: 53). The basic liberties are: the right to vote and hold public office; freedom of speech and assembly; liberty of conscience and thought; freedom from psychological oppression and physical assault; the right to own personal property; freedom from arbitrary arrest. The fact that Rawls prioritizes a liberty principle as the first principle of justice puts him squarely in the liberal tradition: he wants to ensure the protection of basic freedoms and rights.

The second principle of justice is composed of two parts: 'social and economic inequalities are to be arranged so that they are both (a) reasonably expected to be to everyone's advantage, and (b) attached to positions and offices open to all' (ibid.: 53). Rawls gives priority to clause (b)—the principle of fair equality of opportunity—over clause (a)—the difference principle. So, the order is basic liberties, fair equality of opportunity, the difference principle.

The principle of fair equality of opportunity rules out explicit discrimination in the distribution of jobs; an individual's opportunity to access jobs should not depend on their socio-economic background. To use an example, say, the talent to be a philosopher is evenly distributed across the population: a third of philosophers would come from the lowest economic group, a third from the middle group, and a third from the wealthiest group. A person's class background should not preclude them from access to educational or work opportunities (see also Wenar, 2021).

The difference principle is a more distinct and original proposition. This is not a principle of full egalitarianism: it allows for social and economic inequalities—but only if they can make the least advantaged as well-off as possible. Thus, Rawls rules out a society where everyone has an equal income. Instead, there can be inequality in income, but only if it improves the situation of the worst-off. The rationale for Rawls is that inequality creates an incentive mechanism and an enabling mechanism (Van Parijs, 2006: 203–204). The incentive mechanism is that entrepreneurs will work harder and take risks. The enabling mechanism is that capitalist competition keeps removing wealth, and hence economic power, from poor innovators or unwise investors, concentrating it in the hands of those who find the cheapest way to produce goods and satisfy consumer demand. This mechanism would be destroyed if profits were redistributed in an egalitarian way. Thus, Rawls thinks this is more efficient than pure egalitarianism.

A basic structure governed by these two principles of justice would, Rawls believed, ensure a distribution of the primary social goods that would benefit the worst-off members of society. Rawls thought his theory was eminently rational and sensible, as do many other political philosophers, who have been spellbound by it over the last half-century. Undoubtedly, *TJ* is a remarkable intellectual achievement, rivalled by few. Its vision of social democracy is far more egalitarian than the liberal democracies in which most people in the Global North currently live, yet it still feels viable. But the criticisms of Rawls are powerful.

32.2 *A Theory of Justice*: The basics: Key Points

- Rawls designed a theory of justice in the liberal and social contract traditions that revived normative political philosophy.
- He argues that justice applies to the basic structure of society and understands his theory as a 'realistic utopia'.
- The principles of justice are discovered in a hypothetical thought experiment called the original position where participants are behind a veil of ignorance.
- He proposed a liberty principle and an equality principle.

32.3 The original position and the Rawlsian self

Rawls stripped parties in the original position of self-knowledge and knowledge about their society for reasons based on equality and liberty. From the perspective of equality, if parties do not know their social position or level of wealth, they will agree that the position of the worst-off person in society should be maximized; thus, they choose the difference principle and the principle of fair equality of opportunity. From the perspective of freedom, if parties do not know their conception of the good, they will choose principles that allow everyone to pursue their own conception of the good; thus, they choose the liberty principle. This seems plausible, but *who* exactly are these parties in the original position?

The Rawlsian self in the original position is a disembodied, unattached, free-floating reasoner seemingly separate from its community, social group, or any markers of identity or difference. Communitarians were the first major Rawlsian critics, questioning who 'is the shadowy "person" that exists independently of, and able freely to choose, the ends that give her life meaning and value?' (Mulhall and Swift, 2002: 10). Communitarians were especially critical of this Rawlsian self, because it placed the individual prior to its community, when many people see their identity as fundamentally bound up with their community (Sandel, 1984: 179). They argued that the self cannot exist in this independent way because it is formed in the context of a cultural and linguistic community (Taylor, 1985); Rawls misunderstands what the self is and how it is formed. Michael Sandel (1984) pejoratively described it as an 'unencumbered self'.

> **Key Concept: Communitarianism**
>
> Communitarianism is not a systematic theory, but rather refers to a certain kind of response to liberalism. While most communitarian theorists were responding to Rawls's *TJ*, some were responding to liberalism more broadly and also to what they perceived to be the problems in actually existing liberal societies in the late twentieth century, including social atomism and the disintegration of community. Thinkers include Alasdair MacIntyre, Michael Sandel, Charles Taylor, and Michael Walzer. Unlike liberal thinkers who draw on Locke (see Chapter 7), Kant (see Chapter 29), and Mill (see Chapter 12), communitarians draw on thinkers like Aristotle (see Chapter 3) and Hegel, who emphasize virtue and the cohesive social whole. Each communitarian thinker has a different theory, but they generally share at least one of two ideas in common: ontological holism—that the community is prior to the individual *in reality*; or ethical holism—we *should* give priority to the community.

While communitarians prioritized the community over the individual, feminists and critical race theorists highlighted another issue. The worst-off for Rawls is defined by class. Thus, sex or race (or their intersections with class) are not reasons by virtue of which someone would count as the worst-off in society. Why? Rawls thought that the question of race was settled, but the question of class was not: 'we are confident that religious intolerance and racial discrimination are unjust ... But we have much less assurance as to what is the correct distribution of wealth and authority' (Rawls, 1971: 17–18). When it comes to sex, Rawls included 'heads of households' as the parties to the original position, which implicitly means men. Following criticism, Rawls later included sex and race as things that parties in the original position did not know, but they remain heads of families. Some people think these amendments can rescue Rawlsian justice theory from the criticisms of feminism and critical race theory, but others highlight the way these inclusions have reverberations for the rest of the theory that remain under-theorized or potentially fatal.

32.3.1 **The feminist critique**

Unlike previous social contract theorists, such as Locke, Rousseau, and Kant, who explicitly subordinated women in a 'sexual contract' (see Chapter 10), Rawls seems to include women by populating the original position with disembodied, reasoning 'parties' (Pateman, 1988: 43). Yet this is not entirely true: Rawls smuggled in the gender of the parties by stealth. As Jane English (1977) and Susan Moller Okin (1989: 91) pointed out, in the original version of *TJ*, Rawls did not specify gender as something the parties in the original position would not know about themselves and assumed they would be 'heads of households'. Rawls's reasoning for this, as we saw, is to ensure justice between generations: the 'ties of sentiment' that heads of households would have for their children would ensure that they adopt the 'just savings principle' that guarantees the state saves money to ensure the maintenance of a just basic structure into the future. But including 'heads of households' in the original position is obviously not neutral. Rawls talked about intergenerational justice in terms of 'fathers' and 'sons', and, when Rawls was writing, heads of household were assumed to be men (ibid.: 90). Even though family forms have become more plural in the fifty years since *TJ*'s publication, this is still the default assumption. Rawls's sexism here was inadvertent, but has important implications that he did not address.

If the parties in the original position did not know their gender, Okin (ibid.: 95–105) thinks this would change the conclusions they would reach, which could have critical feminist potential. A proper application of the liberty principle would rule out the assumption that women should take primary responsibility for domestic labour and childcare, because this renders them less free than men, and it would ensure equal representation of women in politics. If Rawls is serious about the social bases of self-respect as a fundamental primary good (a claim he never really investigates), then all genders would grow up with an equal sense of self-respect and expectations of themselves, which would require things like the regulation of pornography. Okin optimistically thinks that the original position encourages parties not to take the view from nowhere, as communitarians complain, but rather 'to think from the perspective of *everybody*', which requires developing a sense of empathy and the capacity to listen to others (ibid.: 101).

Other feminists are not convinced. Iris Marion Young (1990) (see also Chapter 22) rejects Okin's claim that the parties in the original position will reason from the perspective of everybody, arguing instead that they will take the perspective of a Rawlsian impartial spectator. A number of theorists have pointed out that while Rawls claims to care about pluralism, he in fact imposes a certain perspective on justice. The parties in the original position are all the same: they all have the same moral powers and come to the same conclusions about the principles of justice. What they experience in the original position is not an act of agreement, but 'an act of cognition' (Honig, 1993: 134) where they realize the truth about justice.

Young argues that reasoning from the perspective of an impartial viewpoint 'denies or represses difference' (Young, 1990: 100). When put into practice in the real world, a unified perspective derived in a hypothetical thought experiment as supposedly impartial and neutral will have the effect of marginalizing and denigrating anyone who doesn't conform or dissents. Historically, these groups have included women, People of Colour, the disabled, LGBTQI+ people, and immigrants. Indeed, Rawls thinks that whenever a person is unsure about a political problem, they can return to the original position and reflect on it through the process of reflective equilibrium, answering their questions in relation to the agreed-upon principles of justice. Bonnie Honig (1993: 136) suggests that the reason for this is 'the regime's perpetual need to reinscribe unruly subjects into the order'.

Young (1990: 116) argues further that we don't need this notion of impartiality to engage in moral reasoning: 'Instead of a fictional contract, we require real participatory structures in which actual people, with their geographical, ethnic, gender, and occupational differences, assert their perspectives on social issues within institutions that encourage the representation of their distinct voices.' What we need is radical democracy for real people. Furthermore, the Rawlsian ambition to create a rational, impartial method for generating right answers to political questions expels feelings (historically associated with women), which 'lurk as inarticulate shadows' (ibid.: 103). These shadows will come back to haunt us, because, in the real world, politics is bound up with emotions.

32.3.2 The critical race critique

In the original edition of *TJ*, just like gender, race was not specified as one of the things the parties in the original position did not know, but this was later amended (Mills, 2009: 164). Rawls's remarks on race are brief and few and far between (ibid.). Given that the United States was founded on the expropriation and genocide of Indigenous peoples, the enslavement of Africans, and the subsequent repression of African-Americans, such an omission in the foremost book of the twentieth century about *justice* seems startling. The USA, and the modern world more generally, were founded on a 'racial contract', which subordinated racialized populations to the benefit of 'free and equal' white men (Mills, 1997) (see also Chapter 10).

But supporters of Rawls point out that he made it clear that racism was fundamentally opposed by *TJ*. Discrimination on the basis of race is a violation of the liberty principle. Rawls states that we know racial discrimination is unjust and this counts as a 'provisional fixed point' which any theory of justice must fit (Rawls, 1971: 17–18; Shelby, 2004: 1698–1699). Moreover, Rawls discusses how no one in the original position would 'put forward the principle that basic rights should depend on the color of one's skin or the texture of one's hair. No one can tell whether such principles would be to his advantage' (Rawls, 1971: 129; Shelby, 2004: 1700).

Tommie Shelby (ibid.) argues that Rawls's formulation of the original position, where parties do not know about themselves or about their society, can produce anti-racist principles of justice. Rawls assumes that all parties have the two 'moral powers': reasonableness (the capacity for justice) and rationality (the ability to form and revise a conception of the good), and he specifies that this applies, regardless of race. The original position will produce a basic structure that mitigates against institutional racism, and the fair equality of opportunity principle will ensure that everyone has the opportunity to pursue their conception of the good. Thus, Shelby argues that Rawls's abstraction away from race ensures 'that racial bias is not codified in or further entrenched by our shared conception of justice' (ibid.: 1700). But, again, not everyone agrees.

In *TJ*, the above remarks are some of the only references to race in the 600-page book (Mills, 2009). Charles Mills argues that Rawls doesn't discuss race because of his focus on ideal theory. In the ideally just society, there is no racial injustice and no history of racial injustice, so Rawls doesn't address it. Mills, therefore, argues that we should abandon ideal theory and focus instead on non-ideal theory (see Key Concept: Ideal theory as ideology). But this does not mean getting rid of the original position as a device for thinking about the just society. Instead, Mills argues that the veil of ignorance should be thinner than the one suggested by Rawls. Mills wants to retain the element of self-ignorance, but he argues that ignorance about society should be reduced (Pateman and Mills, 1997: 119).

Instead of starting at ground zero and coming up with an ideally just society, Mills suggests starting from the point of view of there having been many different kinds of unjust society, and parties choose between these societies (ibid.: 119). Because of this, they would be motivated to choose principles of *corrective* justice that would ensure that those who have suffered from a history of discrimination and marginalization would receive compensation to enable them to be fully equal members of society.

Mills claims that the social contract tradition is white and male not only because it has historically been written by these people for themselves, but more fundamentally because they take the perspective of free and equal contracting parties, failing to recognize that most people have been rendered unfree and unequal throughout human history. Mills thinks that only a white audience would accept the view that society is 'a cooperative venture for mutual advantage' (Rawls, 1971: 4); from the perspective of People of Colour and colonized people, the social contract is a 'domination contract' founded on white supremacy. This perspective requires the acknowledgement and full integration of corrective justice. Parties in this later, non-ideal original position would know about the history of slavery, colonialism, expropriation of land from Indigenous peoples, genocide, settler-colonialism, and racist ideologies, and would want to correct it. Rawls's failure to recognize any of this (and the failure of his many commentators and followers) is 'an abdication of both moral and theoretical responsibility, producing a grotesquely sanitized and Eurocentric picture of the history of the last few hundred years, one from which race, racial conquest, and racial authority have been whitewashed out' (Mills, 2009: 172).

Key Concept: Ideal theory as ideology

The Rawlsian topic that has received most attention in recent years is his commitment to 'ideal theory'. Ideal theory plays two roles for Rawls: a 'target role'—explaining where we want to go; and a 'urgency role'—giving us an order for what needs to be reformed, depending on how far it deviates from perfect justice (Swift and Stemplowska, 2014: 117). Supporters claim that these are valid goals, especially for disadvantaged social groups (Shelby, 2013). But Charles Mills (2005) argues that since it is implausible to think that we can end oppression by *not* theorizing about it, that ideal theory is serving some sort of purpose. It is serving the interests of the privileged—white, upper-class men, who for a very long time have dominated academic philosophy—by not challenging the status quo. Mills thinks these people do not experience cognitive dissonance when doing this kind of theory because their experiences come closest to the ideal. What we actually need are concepts that capture the essential features of oppression, rather than ignoring them—concepts like patriarchy, white supremacy, and class. While these terms are abstractions, they are not idealizations; instead, they reflect group experiences, and therefore illuminate rather than obscure subordination. To fully address oppression, subordination, inequality, etc., we must do non-ideal theory.

32.3.3 The disability critique

Some feminists and critical race theorists believe that the sexless and raceless reasonableness and rationality of the parties in the original position means that Rawlsian justice theory is valuable, but philosophers of disability have highlighted that this appeal can have unintended ableist consequences. Rawls specifies that the parties know that they have psychological capacities and physical needs 'within the normal range' (Rawls, quoted in Simplican, 2016: 82). Rawls thinks of people with disabilities as a 'hard case' for a theory of justice, which distracts us by thinking about 'people distant from us whose fate arouses pity and anxiety' (Rawls, quoted in ibid.: 82). Thus, in the original position, not only does Rawls want to exclude emotions (anxiety, pity), and he assumes that disabled people arouse these emotions in the able-bodied, he also excludes reasoning about the needs of disabled people, so their needs go unaddressed. It is 'we normal people' who are parties to the contract; thus 'economic redistributions to disabled people are depoliticized and made the purview of charity or virtue. Disability is thus out of sight, out of mind, and out of politics' (ibid.: 86).

Women and People of Colour might be able to participate in a revised original position because they are 'normal', but cognitively disabled people cannot and physically disabled people are ignored. The social contract is a 'capacity contract', excluding those lacking, or perceived to be lacking, the requisite capacities (ibid.). As Shelley Tremain (2018: 38) argues, mainstream liberal philosophers since Rawls 'cast disability as a natural, negative, and inert state of affairs... they have largely removed disability from the realm of philosophical inquiry'. One effect of this is to fail to recognize, as disability rights movements have done, that disability is socially constructed, and thus justice for people with disabilities involves uncovering the power relations that construct certain bodies as disabled or that create barriers to their inclusion in society. It will also result in failure to create policies that address these social disadvantages (ibid.: 37).

Rawls was aware of some of these criticisms. The communitarian critique is arguably the one that troubled him the most. In his second major work, *Political Liberalism* (Rawls, 1993), he acknowledged that a theory of justice should be 'political not metaphysical'. He argued that there are different communities in society with their own 'comprehensive doctrines' (their own world-views, such as a religious world-view). What mattered was that these communities could reach an 'overlapping consensus' based on shared 'public reasons'. Not only does this accommodate some communitarian concerns about the importance of community, it also makes for a more stable political system over time, because different groups in society have their own reasons for committing to it.

This rethink both won and lost Rawls fans. Some were pleased that Rawls recognized the historical and cultural specificity of *TJ* and was trying to accommodate political and religious diversity. But it was still too liberal for communitarians who thought that the idea of liberal political neutrality was implausible. Some feminists objected that justice as fairness (with revisions) offered women the opportunity of genuine equality but that *Political Liberalism*, in allowing communities to have comprehensive religious doctrines, threatened to perpetuate the repression of women (Okin, 2005). And, as Mills notes, *Political Liberalism* still had very little to say about race (Mills, 2009: 165). Disability remained excluded as a 'hard case' (Kittay, 1999; Simplican, 2016).

Key Concept: Political liberalism

In his second major work, *Political Liberalism* (1993), Rawls admits that *TJ* presented a 'comprehensive' form of liberalism that will not be acceptable to all groups in a multicultural society. Thus, in *Political Liberalism* he starts from 'the fact of reasonable pluralism': Rawls accepts that people will hold different comprehensive conceptions of the good and that this fact needs to be accommodated by a theory of justice. He also addresses the problem of stability: if a liberal conception of justice relied on a comprehensive conception of the good, it would be inherently unstable because of the fact of reasonable pluralism. So, a well-ordered society has to accommodate reasonable pluralism. To achieve this, Rawls argues for a conception of justice that is 'political, not metaphysical'. The political conception of justice is determined by the use of 'public reason': political values shared by free and equal citizens that do not conflict with their comprehensive doctrines. In fact, citizens will reach an 'overlapping consensus': they will find reasons internal to their comprehensive doctrines to support liberal political institutions, thus ensuring stability.

32.3 The original position and the Rawlsian self: Key Points

- The parties in Rawls's original position have no self-knowledge or knowledge about their society.
- Communitarians reject this 'unencumbered self' as failing to take community and formation of the self in a community seriously.
- Feminists disagree about the value of the Rawlsian self for delivering a feminist theory of justice.
- Critical race theorists disagree about the value of the Rawlsian self for delivering an anti-racist theory of justice.
- Critical philosophers of disability have argued that the Rawlsian conception of the self is ableist.

32.4 The basic structure and the Rawlsian society

Rawls's principles of justice apply to the 'basic structure': the political constitution and the principal economic and social arrangements (legal protection of freedom of thought and liberty of conscience, competitive markets, private property in the means of production, and the monogamous family). Rawls thinks that if the basic structure is just, then individuals are free to pursue their own life plans against a just background structure. Individuals cannot and should not be burdened with ensuring that distributions of primary goods across society is fair, nor with protecting due legal process. Instead, they should be free to live their lives.

Rawls, as a left liberal, has a relatively expansive understanding of the basic structure and the redistributive state. Right liberals were deeply wary of his proposal. Famously, the libertarian theorist Robert Nozick described tax as theft: the state is stealing the fruits of individuals' labour (Nozick, 1974: 169). Rawls thought that individuals' labour is mixed up with inherited social positions and natural talents, both of which are undeserved, and thus the fruits of which can be rightly distributed. Theorists on the left welcome this recognition that natural talent is arbitrary and that social position often has more to do with inheritance of wealth or status than with individual hard work. But they pose a range of other challenges to Rawls's conception of the basic structure.

Key Thinker: Robert Nozick

Robert Nozick (1938–2002) was a contemporary of Rawls at Harvard, and though they shared some philosophical predecessors, like John Locke, and some premises, such as a rejection of utilitarianism, Nozick promoted a very different type of liberalism, known as libertarianism. In his famous treatise *Anarchy, State and Utopia* (1974), Nozick argues for a 'nightwatchman state': an absolutely minimal state that exists purely to protect individuals' private property. Starting from the Lockean premise that individuals have natural rights to life, liberty, and property, Nozick believes that if property is justly acquired and justly transferred, then individuals are entitled to the fruits of it without any state intervention; this is an 'entitlement theory' of justice. Taxation is theft because it steals the fruits of people's talents, labour, and property. Nozick claimed there is no such thing as society; only an aggregation of individuals who cannot be expected to make any sacrifices for anyone else or some notion of a common good. It is a radical defence of capitalism.

32.4.1 What is the basic structure?

The exact content of the basic structure is unclear. It seems to be 'the *broad coercive outline* of society' (Cohen, 1997: 19), but the family is included. G.A. Cohen argues that if the family is included, the line is crossed from coercive to non-coercive institutions and, crucially, that individuals' behaviour can be constitutive of non-coercive structure. For example, women doing the majority of the domestic labour in heterosexual couples does not have to be enforced by law; it is enforced by patterns of behaviour across society. But behaviour can change. Therefore, what is needed to create a just society is an 'egalitarian ethos', as well as just institutions (ibid.: 23). Iris Marion Young goes further, demonstrating how 'structural injustice' is embedded in social, political, and economic structures, that go far beyond the basic structure institutions, to encompass the daily habits, choices, and behaviours of everyday life (Young, 2011: 43–72). Overcoming structural injustice involves collective action (ibid.: 111–113).

The problem of the family not only highlights the role of individuals' behaviour in perpetuating injustice, but raises problems for the idea of separate basic structure institutions. Rawls equivocates about the role of the family. On the one hand, he clearly includes it in the basic structure, but, on the other, he claims in *Political Liberalism* that the family is like other 'voluntary institutions' and so the principles of justice should not 'regulate [the family] internally' (Chambers, 2013: 82).

Okin thinks that Rawls should 'make good' the claim that the family is a basic structure institution, following through on the application of the principles of justice to the family's internal life. But Clare Chambers (ibid.: 76) argues that 'the family illustrates deep-seated difficulties with Rawlsian justice as a whole'. Rawls claims that the principles of justice 'apply directly' to basic structure institutions and not to non-basic structure institutions. When it comes to the family, for instance, a husband cannot stop his wife from voting as this would violate the liberty principle; however, no institutions can violate a citizen's right to vote, including non-basic structure institutions like churches or employers (ibid.: 84–85). Thus, there is no clear way in which Rawls can distinguish between the principles of justice applying to the basic structure and to other institutions. This debate about the family, therefore, has thrown into question the entire premise that the basic structure can be separated out from society and other institutions.

Rawls's commitment to justice exclusively applying to the basic structure is brought out in his discussion of 'civil disobedience'. This was a fundamental political issue when Rawls was writing, in the midst of the nonviolent Civil Rights movement of the 1960s. Influenced by political events and the liberal tradition, Rawls defines civil disobedience as the nonviolent breaking of laws to highlight injustice within a frame of reference accepted by the majority population. Civil disobedience, for Rawls, is only acceptable as a 'last resort' and is only justified if the liberty principle or principle of equality of opportunity are being violated. Systemic injustice, for Rawls, is therefore limited to situations where there is a gap between how the basic structure should be in theory, and has been agreed to in the original position, and how it is operating in practice (Pineda, 2021: 36).

However, such an approach, Erin Pineda (ibid.: 41) argues, is to 'see like a state': to take the state as a starting point, assuming the state is legitimate, assuming a standardization of the citizens and their claims, abstracting away from political realities, and denying local forms of knowledge. This assumes that racial injustice, such as segregation, is an aberration; a gap between the principles of a 'mostly just' white state and how they are being implemented. By contrast, Black social movements stressed that segregation and the denial of voting rights were a symptom of a fundamentally unjust system.

32.4.2 Critique of the 'distributive paradigm'

Social movements, rather than the state or abstract principles derived from philosophers' thought experiments, often have unique insights into injustice. Iris Marion Young thinks that instead of thinking about the ideally just society, we should focus on injustice and the claims made by social movements about injustice. Based on the new left social movements of the 1960s–1980s, she highlights three types of injustice that are missing from Rawls's theory: (1) decision-making power (who gets to make the decisions?); (2) the division of labour (why are some jobs populated by and/or associated with certain social groups?); and (3) culture (stereotypes, symbols, and narratives that affect people's social standing) (Young, 1990: 22–24).

Young argues that social justice should be less concerned with creating a just basic structure—'a small sub-set of institutions' (Young, 2011: 70)—and instead with ending domination and oppression (see Chapter 22, for further discussion of Young's work). She argues further that the 'distributive paradigm' of justice is ideological (Young, 1990: 18–30). First, the focus on the distribution of primary goods takes for granted the fact that there is a welfare state that collects taxes and redistributes resources; it doesn't question whether these institutions are the right ones. Second, it over-extends the concept of distribution. For instance, Rawls considers one of the primary goods to be the 'social bases of self-respect', but how can that be distributed? It is not a thing that can be measured and parcelled out. Overcoming domination and oppression involves more than creating a just basic structure and reassessing distribution. It includes an assessment of power relations between social groups (not just individuals). It requires celebrating and affirming group difference to overcome negative stereotypes and exclusion. And it involves radical democracy—including people in genuinely inclusive democratic debate, where different voices and perspectives on politics can be heard and people explain what injustice looks like from their particular point of view.

In recent debates, and drawing on Young, relational egalitarian theorists have insisted that we care about distributions across society not for their own sake, but because of the ways in which they create and maintain hierarchies between different social groups. Social movements have focused on relations of inferiority and superiority, such as gender, race, class, and the ways in which the superior are entitled to inflict violence on inferiors, to segregate and exclude them, to treat them with contempt, to force them to obey or work in ways that suit the superior (Anderson, 1999: 312). Egalitarians have two goals: a negative goal to eliminate oppression and a positive goal to create a social order where people live in relations of equality (ibid.: 313). Elizabeth Anderson calls this 'democratic equality'. Distribution is not irrelevant to achieving democratic equality, but it should be differently conceived along the lines of the capabilities approach advocated by Amartya Sen and Martha Nussbaum (see Key Thinker: Amartya Sen and Martha Nussbaum). The distribution of resources for the purpose of achieving capabilities is not an end in itself; rather, the end goal is equal social relations (ibid.: 320). Chris Lebron (2014) adds that those positioned as superior in society need to cultivate the appropriate civic virtues to develop a 'human point of view': to be able to see the world from the perspective of those marked as inferior.

Key Thinker: Amartya Sen and Martha Nussbaum

The economist and philosopher Amartya Sen (1933–) famously critiqued Rawls's dismissal of disability as a 'hard case' for a theory of justice. Sen argued that the currency of Rawlsian justice (primary goods) is an inadequate way to think about just distributions. Instead, the focus should be on ensuring people can achieve certain 'capabilities' (Sen, 1979). Every individual should be able to be and do certain things, and this means they will need different kinds of resources. For instance, a wheelchair-user will require a wheelchair and accessible buildings in order to be able to move around freely. Sen refused to commit to a list of basic capabilities as he thought they would be culturally specific. Martha Nussbaum (1947–), however, built on this initial approach to produce a list of ten capabilities from a feminist perspective: life; bodily health; bodily integrity; senses, imagination, and thought; emotions; practical reason; affiliation; interaction with other species; play; and control over one's environment (Nussbaum, 2006). The capabilities approach has been influential on the United Nations' Human Development Index, Millennium Development Goals, and Sustainable Development Goals.

32.4.3 The scope of justice

Why does the basic structure only apply within one society? Rawls thought that domestic justice and international justice were different, so his theory applied only to a 'closed system': 'The significance of this special case is obvious and needs no explanation' (Rawls, 1971: 7). But, in fact, it does. Cosmopolitan theorist Charles Beitz (1999: 125–136) pointed out that if we care about sharing the benefits and burdens of social cooperation, then the fact of globalization means that there is sufficient social cooperation at the global level to trigger Rawls's theory of justice. He argues further that nationality is arbitrary from the moral point of view, just like the other morally arbitrary features excluded by Rawls in the original position; thus, in the original position, the parties would not know their nationality and would apply the difference principle to the worst-off person globally, which would entail significant global redistribution of wealth (Beitz, 1999: 136–143).

Rawls later responded in his third major book *The Law of Peoples* (Rawls, 1999) that his theory of justice only applies to 'liberal peoples', not to other kinds of peoples around the globe. Instead, there should be a two-tiered theory of justice: one for the domestic sphere and another for the international sphere. The latter applies not between individuals, but 'peoples' who are groups ruled by a common government, are bound by common sympathies, and share a common conception of justice. In the international original position, parties are representatives of 'liberal' or 'decent hierarchical peoples' ('burdened' and 'outlaw' societies are excluded). Under the veil of ignorance, they do not know the size of their territory, population, or military strength. They agree to eight principles of justice, including the principle of non-intervention, observing treaties, respecting minimum human rights and the rules of war, and duties of assistance to burdened societies. Rawls aims to tolerate difference between peoples and to affirm the difference between the basic structures at the domestic and international levels. Decolonial critics think Rawls is right to respect state sovereignty, but that he neglected the ways in which domestic politics are shaped by international pressures, an unjust international order, and neo-colonialism (Rao, 2010; Forrester, 2019; Getachew, 2019; Murad, 2021).

Key Concept: Cosmopolitanism

Cosmopolitanism has been around in various forms in philosophy since ancient times. For instance, Diogenes the cynic described himself as 'a citizen of the world' and Kant argued in the eighteenth century for a principle of cosmopolitan 'hospitality'. But cosmopolitanism became a fully-fledged school of thought from the 1970s onwards, partly in response to Rawls's *TJ*. Cosmopolitan critics of Rawls, such as Charles Beitz and Thomas Pogge, argued that, for the sake of consistently removing all morally arbitrary factors from the original position, nationality ought to be included. This would generate a global difference principle and therefore global distributive justice. But cosmopolitanism does not have to be Rawlsian in form. The core tenets of cosmopolitanism are individualism (individuals come first, not groups); universality (all humans are equal and are the ultimate unit of moral concern); and generality (this applies to everyone everywhere). There are utilitarian, Kantian, Aristotelian, rights-based, and autonomy-based cosmopolitanisms, and there are at least three branches of cosmopolitan theory: moral, institutional, and cultural (Brock, 2013).

32.4 The basic structure and the Rawlsian society: Key Points

- Rawls applies his principles of justice to the basic structure of society, but feminists have shown that the idea of a separate basic structure is ambiguous.
- Iris Marion Young critiqued Rawls's 'distributive paradigm' of justice and argued instead for a focus on actually existing domination and oppression highlighted by social movements.
- Relational egalitarians argue that we should care about distributions for the sake of creating just relations between social groups.
- Cosmopolitans have critiqued the restriction of Rawlsian justice to a closed society.

32.5 Conclusion

The inputs in Rawls's original position generated the outputs that Rawls wanted: a social democracy governed by individual liberty with quite an extensive scheme of redistribution. But once other inputs are included in the original position, it generates different outputs. Consider the Rawlsian self. If sex is excluded from the original position and the family is genuinely considered a basic structure institution, then the family would be governed according to the basic liberties and prioritizing the least-advantaged, which would radically challenge the gendered division of labour in the household and gender stereotypes. If race was taken more seriously, then, arguably, corrective justice would be included in the principles of justice and reparations would be included in designing the basic structure of society. If disability was taken seriously, then care work and differing needs would be considered, potentially generating a whole new principle of justice (Kittay, 1999: 113). The more we try to amend Rawls's framework to be inclusive, the further away it moves from his original vision.

We then also have to consider whether the outputs Rawls achieved are the desired ones. The Rawlsian society involves a sharp separation between citizens and the state. The state takes responsibility for justice, while citizens are left to their own devices. But what does this mean for forms of injustice that are perpetuated in everyday life rather than through institutions and what does this mean for relations between citizens? Does this mean that power relations of domination and oppression go unchecked? Can the state really be neutral and thus fair to all citizens despite their different communities, identities, and needs?

Perhaps, then, the problem is the underlying methodology. Can ideal theory generate the correct answers as to what justice should be like when we live in circumstances of pervasive and structural injustice? My own view is that ideal theory will not generate the right answers. Rawlsian ideal theory is infused with assumptions about gender, race, and ability that are insurmountable. An ideal theory that tries to incorporate these concerns about deep real-world injustice becomes a kind of Frankenstein's monster with bits added here and there, some of which conflict. Moreover, as Mills (2005: 179) points out, once these real-world forms of injustice are included, it ceases to be ideal theory, because it incorporates real facts about society. But an ideal theory that doesn't address facts about injustice is potentially useless and, worse, can function as ideology by obscuring what really matters. Many others disagree and believe that a Rawlsian sex- and race-blind methodology has generated a 'realistic utopia' worth fighting for (at least in theory).

Take your learning further by accessing the online resources for a library of web links to relevant videos, articles, blogs, and useful websites for this chapter: www.oup.com/he/Ramgotra-Choat1e.

Study questions

1. Why does Rawls think that the device of the original position will produce the best theory of justice?
2. Can the original position produce principles of justice that address sexism, racism, and ableism?
3. Can Rawls be defended against the feminist, critical race, and disability critiques of the Rawlsian self?
4. To what extent does Rawls privilege the individual over the community?

5. Should the concept of justice only apply to the basic structure?
6. Should a theory of justice focus on real-world power relations of oppression and domination?
7. In the context of globalization, should we think of the basic structure as global?
8. Is an ideal theory of justice required in order to discuss injustice?

Further reading

Primary sources

Rawls, J. (1971) *A Theory of Justice*, rev. edn. (1999). Cambridge, MA: The Belknap Press of Harvard University Press.
  Rawls's magnum opus and the most influential text in Anglo-American contemporary political philosophy.

Rawls, J. (1993) *Political Liberalism*. New York: Columbia University Press.
  Rawls's attempt to create a political rather than a comprehensive theory of liberalism.

Rawls, J. (1999) *The Law of Peoples*. Cambridge, MA: Harvard University Press.
  Rawls's theory of international justice.

Rawls, J. (2001) *Justice as Fairness: A Restatement*. Ed. E. Kelly. Cambridge, MA: The Belknap Press of Harvard University Press.
  A shorter, summary version of *A Theory of Justice*, including amendments in response to his critics.

Rawls, J. (2007) *Lectures on the History of Political Philosophy*. Ed. S. Freeman. Cambridge, MA: Harvard University Press.
  Rawls's lectures on the liberal tradition in the Western canon and how he fits in.

Secondary reading

Abbey, R. (2013) 'Biography of a Bibliography: Three Decades of a Feminist Response to Rawls'. In R. Abbey (ed.), *Feminist Interpretations of John Rawls*. University Park PA: The Pennsylvania State University Press, pp. 1–23.
  Abbey provides a chronological survey of the feminist debates on Rawls from the 1970s to the 2010s; the book as a whole offers differing feminist perspectives on Rawls.

Forrester, K. (2019) *In the Shadow of Justice: Postwar Liberalism and the Remaking of Political Philosophy*. Princeton, NJ: Princeton University Press.
  Forrester's is the first book to 'historicize' Rawls, placing him in his contexts.

Freeman, S. (2006) *The Cambridge Companion to Rawls*. Cambridge: Cambridge University Press.
  A collection of essays by leading Rawlsians and other key mainstream philosophers addressing the core topics in Rawls.

Mills, C.W. (2009) 'Rawls on Race/Race in Rawls'. *The Southern Journal of Philosophy*, XLVII: 161–184.
  Mills surveys the discussions of race in Rawls and advances his view that a theory of justice must incorporate corrective justice.

Mulhall, S. and Swift, A. (2002) *Liberals and Communitarians*, second edition. Oxford: Blackwell.
  Introduction to the liberal/communitarian debate, covering Rawls's views, Sandel, MacIntyre, Taylor, and Walzer's critiques, Rawls's response, and a discussion of liberal neutrality.

Young, I.M. (1990) *Justice and the Politics of Difference*. Princeton, NJ: Princeton University Press.
  The classic, blistering critique of Rawls's 'distributive paradigm' of justice from a critical feminist perspective.

References

Anderson, E.S. (1999) 'What Is the Point of Equality?' *Ethics*, 109(2): 287–337.

Beitz, C.R. (1999) *Political Theory and International Relations*. 2nd edn. Princeton, NJ: Princeton University Press.

Brock, G. (2013) 'Contemporary Cosmopolitanism: Some Current Issues'. *Philosophy Compass*, 8(8): 689–698.

Chambers, C. (2013) '"The Family as a Basic Institution": A Feminist Analysis of the Basic Structure as Subject'. In R. Abbey (ed.), *Feminist Interpretations of John Rawls*. University Park PA: The Pennsylvania State University Press, pp. 75–94.

Cohen, G.A. (1997) 'Where the Action Is: On the Site of Distributive Justice'. *Philosophy and Public Affairs*, 26(1): 3–30.

English, J. (1977) 'Justice Between Generations'. *Philosophical Studies*, 31: 91–104.

Forrester, K. (2019) *In the Shadow of Justice: Postwar Liberalism and the Remaking of Political Philosophy*. Princeton, NJ: Princeton University Press.

Freeman, S. (2019) 'Original Position'. In *The Stanford Encyclopedia of Philosophy*. Summer 2019. Stanford, CA: Stanford University Press. https://plato.stanford.edu/cgi-bin/encyclopedia/archinfo.cgi?entry=original-position.

Getachew, A. (2019) *Worldmaking After Empire*. Princeton, NJ: Princeton University Press.

Honig, B. (1993) *Political Theory and the Displacement of Politics*. Ithaca, NY: Cornell University Press.

Kittay, E.F. (1999) *Love's Labor: Essays on Women, Equality, and Dependency*. London: Routledge.

Lebron, C. (2014) 'Equality from a Human Point of View'. *Critical Philosophy of Race*, 2(2): 125–159.

Mills, C.W. (1997) *The Racial Contract*. Ithaca, NY: Cornell University Press.

Mills, C.W. (2005) '"Ideal Theory" as Ideology'. *Hypatia*, 20(3): 165–184.

Mills, C.W. (2009) 'Rawls on Race/Race in Rawls'. *The Southern Journal of Philosophy*, XLVII: 161–184.

Mulhall, S. and Swift, A. (2002) *Liberals and Communitarians*, 2nd edn. Oxford: Blackwell.

Murad, I. (2021) 'The Kazanistan Papers: Reading the Muslim Question in the John Rawls Archives'. *Perspectives on Politics*, 19(1): 110–130.

Nozick, R. (1974) *Anarchy, State and Utopia*. Oxford: Blackwell.

Nussbaum, M.C. (2006) *Frontiers of Justice: Disability, Nationality, Species Membership*. Cambridge, MA: Belknap Press.

Okin, S.M. (1989) *Justice, Gender and the Family*. New York: Basic Books.

Okin, S.M. (2005) '"Forty Acres and a Mule" for Women: Rawls and Feminism'. *Politics, Philosophy & Economics*, 4(2): 233–248.

Pateman, C. (1988) *The Sexual Contract*. Oxford: Polity Press.

Pateman, C. and Mills, C.W. (1997) *Contract & Domination*. Cambridge: Polity Press.

Pineda, E.R. (2021) *Seeing like an Activist: Civil Disobedience and the Civil Rights Movement*. Oxford: Oxford University Press.

Rao, R. (2010) *Third World Protest: Between Home and the World*. Oxford: Oxford University Press.

Rawls, J. (1971) *A Theory of Justice*. Rev. edn, 1999. Cambridge, MA: The Belknap Press of Harvard University Press.

Rawls, J. (1988) 'The Priority of Right and Ideas of the Good'. *Philosophy & Public Affairs*, 17(4): 251–276.

Rawls, J. (1993) *Political Liberalism*. New York: Columbia University Press.

Rawls, J. (1999) *The Law of Peoples*. Cambridge, MA: Harvard University Press.

Sandel, M. (1984) *Liberalism and the Limits of Justice*. Online edition. Cambridge: Cambridge University Press.

Sen, A. (1979) 'Equality of What?' In *The Tanner Lectures on Human Values, 1979*. Available at: www.tannerlectures.utah.edu

Shelby, T. (2004) 'Race and Social Justice: Rawlsian Considerations'. *Fordham Law Review*, 72: 1697–1714.

Shelby, T. (2013) 'Racial Realities and Corrective Justice: A Reply to Charles Mills'. *Critical Philosophy of Race*, 1(2): 145–162.

Simplican, S.C. (2016) 'Disavowals of Disability in Rawls' *Theory of Justice* and His Critics'. In B. Arneil and N.J. Hirschmann (eds), *Disability and Political Theory*. Cambridge: Cambridge University Press, pp. 79–99.

Swift, A. and Stemplowska, Z. (2014) 'Rawls on Ideal and Nonideal Theory'. In J. Mandle and D.A. Reidy (eds), *A Companion to Rawls*. London: John Wiley & Sons, Inc.

Taylor, C. (1985) 'Atomism.' In C. Taylor, *Philosophy and the Human Sciences*, vol. 2. Cambridge: Cambridge University Press.

Tremain, S.L. (2018) 'Philosophy of Disability as Critical Diversity Studies'. *International Journal of Critical Disability Studies*, 1(1): 30–44.

Van Parijs, P. (2006) 'Difference Principles'. In S. Freeman (ed.), *The Cambridge Companion to Rawls*. Cambridge: Cambridge University Press, pp. 200–240.

Wenar, L. (2021) 'John Rawls'. In *Stanford Encyclopedia of Philosophy*. Summer 2021. Stanford, CA: Stanford University Press. Available at: https://plato.stanford.edu

Young, I.M. (1990) *Justice and the Politics of Difference*. Princeton, NJ: Princeton University Press.

Young, I.M. (2011) *Responsibility for Justice*. Oxford: Oxford University Press.

Part VIII

Sex and Sexuality

33 Michel Foucault	Paul Patton	603
34 Shulamith Firestone	Victoria Margree	621
35 Angela Y. Davis	Manjeet Ramgotra	639
36 Judith Butler	Clare Woodford	657

Sex is a fundamental and universal human activity ('universal' in the sense that it has necessarily been practised by all cultures at all times, if not by all individuals). Yet it has often been marginalized within the study of politics, treated as a purely private matter. This is not necessarily because mainstream political thinkers have ignored sex or sexuality. To the contrary, canonical thinkers from Plato to Kant and beyond have discussed sex—albeit often in dismissive or condemnatory terms—while others have analysed related topics such as marriage and other family relations. Even the views of canonical thinkers, however, have traditionally tended to be neglected when it comes to sex. In this Part, we examine a range of thinkers for whom sex and sexuality are primary objects of study—though, as we shall see, their theories also go far beyond sex.

'Sex' can refer either to the act or activity of sex or to an identity. 'Sexuality' can likewise be used to refer to sexual activity in general or to an identity: a person's sexual preferences or orientation (queer, straight, bisexual, etc.). There are at least two ways in which sex and sexuality can be understood as political. First, because the state intervenes in our sex lives. Second, because sex and sexuality always involve relations of power and conflict.

The first of these understandings points towards the formal political and legal status of sex. The state prohibits certain acts and regulates others: with whom we can have sex, where, and under what circumstances are all determined by the laws of each state. At the time of writing, for example, more than seventy countries in the world criminalize consensual gay sex. The role of the state in regulating sexuality raises a number of normative questions. On what basis should the state be able to interfere in our sex lives? Is it only certain acts that the state can prohibit, or also certain preferences? What are the limits of state interference?

These kinds of questions have long been debated by political thinkers, even if these debates have not always been accorded a central place within the study of politics. To use an example: the English utilitarian philosopher Jeremy Bentham (see Key Thinker: Jeremy Bentham in Section 12.1 in Chapter 12) concluded in his 1785 essay 'Offences Against Oneself' that consensual same-sex relations between men should be decriminalized because they increase pleasure rather than pain. These conclusions were controversial enough that the essay was not published until almost two hundred years after it was written. In contrast, Bentham's contemporary Immanuel Kant (see Chapter 29) concluded that sexual relations were legitimate only within the institution of marriage (which for Kant could only occur between a man and a woman). The questions of consent, harm, right, and dignity that are raised by Bentham and Kant can be and still are used today to analyse the role of the state in governing sexuality.

While the role of state in regulating sexual activity has long been of interest to political thinkers, it was arguably the second wave of feminism, inaugurated in the 1960s, that did most to foreground sex and sexuality as topics of political analysis. Through their discussions of and activism around issues including abortion, pornography, contraception, rape, and domestic violence, second-wave feminists drew attention to the ways in which the state involves itself in our sexual lives (for good or for ill), demonstrating that supposedly 'private' or domestic issues are subject to laws made by governments. The second-wave slogan 'the personal is political' also points to the second way in which sex and sexuality can be understood as political: regardless of the actions of the state, sex and sexuality are in themselves political because they always involve questions of power and conflict—over meanings, identities, and resources. This understanding of sex and sexuality as necessarily and inherently political challenges the traditional understanding of politics as the study of government: politics is no longer seen as something that happens only in the public realm; if politics is about power, then even our most intimate personal relations are political.

Second-wave feminists typically insisted on distinguishing sex, which they argued is biologically given, from gender, which they defined as socially or culturally constructed. Much of their work then involved arguing that phenomena that had traditionally been ascribed to the former, such as roles in childrearing or participation in public life, in fact belonged to the latter. The category of gender was in this way used to denaturalize forms of oppression: if something which has been assumed or claimed to have been given to us by nature—and is therefore difficult or even impossible to change—can be shown to be socially and culturally constructed, it can then be challenged and reconstructed in different ways. Many gay liberation activists and, later, queer theorists pursued a similar strategy, showing that the 'natural' or 'biological' are social and historical. In the case of queer theory, this has often involved exploring the boundaries between forms of sexuality that were permitted as 'natural' or 'normal' and those condemned as 'unnatural' or 'abnormal' and demonstrating the historically contingent character of the boundaries between the two.

This understanding of sex and sexuality as political because they involve power and conflict—rather than simply because they are regulated by the state—thus raises a different set of questions. Are sexual power relations equal? What forms has sexual oppression taken and how has it intersected with other forms of oppression such as racism? Are our sexual identities determined by nature, imposed by society, or individually chosen?

For many in the women's and gay liberation movements, and for many activists since, the goal has been to liberate forms of sexuality from repression. This understanding of sexuality—as in need of liberation from repression—draws in part on the hugely influential work of Sigmund Freud, who perhaps more than any other single thinker made sex a legitimate and significant topic of intellectual inquiry (see Key Thinker: Sigmund Freud in Section 34.4.1 in Chapter 34). Yet Freud believed that repression was necessary, both for the individual, who must repress certain infantile desires before entering adulthood, and for society, whose cultural and civilizational development depends on the repression of sexual and aggressive impulses.

The idea that sexuality has been repressed—whether this is viewed as necessary, as for Freud, or as something from which we must be liberated—was rejected (or, at least, complicated) by the twentieth-century French historian and philosopher, Michel Foucault. He did so for both historical and conceptual reasons, arguing that in fact sex has been widely discussed and subject to political intervention and that it is *produced* rather than simply repressed by power. Foucault conceptualized power not in the conventional sense as a thing possessed by an individual or group who use it to oppress others, but rather as a relation that is everywhere and which is primarily productive rather than repressive—producing knowledge and subjects. As Chapter 33 shows, Foucault analysed power within a wide range of contexts and institutions, and his work has been enormously influential across the social sciences and humanities. His work has been particularly useful for feminists and queer theorists because of the way it has historicized sexuality: rather than viewing sex simply as a natural instinct that is then either permitted or restricted, Foucault has sought to show that sexual experiences, representations, and practices vary historically and are inseparable from power relations.

A historical approach was also taken by the US second-wave feminist Shulamith Firestone, but in a very different way from that of Foucault. Firestone drew on Marx and Engels to explore the origins and persistence of women's oppression. Whereas most second-wave feminists sought to denaturalize—showing that gender roles are not natural or biological but cultural and social and hence mutable—Firestone in sharp contrast argued that women's oppression was rooted in biology: in particular, women's role in childbirth and childrearing made them dependent on men. Crucially, however, Firestone believed that technology could change nature and liberate women. Firestone's arguments were thus quite different from those of other second-wave feminists. Yet, as Chapter 34 argues, like many other white second-wave feminists, she advanced an understanding of race and racism that was at best inadequate, and at worst relied on racist stereotypes.

For this reason, Firestone and other white feminists were criticized by Black feminists, such as Angela Davis, who is the subject of Chapter 35. Davis has shown how Black women have been doubly marginalized and excluded—by white women within the feminist movement and by Black men within the Black liberation movement. In doing so, she has interrogated the category of 'woman', seeking to expand and transform this category so that it can also include Black women and other women of colour, as well as working-class and trans women. As well as analysing the oppression of women, and the role that sexual violence has played in such oppression, Davis's work has ranged over a number of issues, including arguing for the abolition of prisons. All of her work has explored the interconnections of gender, race, class, sexuality, and other axes of oppression in a way that might today be called 'intersectional'.

While Davis and Firestone are, in their different ways, keys figures of second-wave feminism, the US theorist Judith Butler is sometimes cited as a key figure in feminism's third wave. Both Firestone and Butler unsettled the second-wave distinction between the biological or natural (sex) and the social or cultural (sex), but in very different ways. Firestone foregrounded nature, trying to show that both the causes of women's oppression and the possibility of transformation lie in biology. Butler pursued a contrary strategy, drawing on Foucault to foreground culture and discourse and in effect arguing that both sex and gender are social. For Butler, there is no purely 'natural' body that exists before culture: the ways that we distinguish between the sexes (whether by anatomy, chromosomes, hormones, etc.), and even how many sexes there are, are socially determined. This does not mean that biological differences are nonexistent or irrelevant, but rather that which biological characteristics become salient can vary. As Chapter 36 demonstrates, these arguments have made Butler a highly influential but also controversial figure for feminists, queer theorists, and trans theorists.

While probably best known for her work on gender, Butler has written on a huge variety of topics. Indeed, this is true of all four thinkers in this Part: while all of them have changed the ways we think about sex and sexuality, demonstrating clearly that these are political issues, they have all also illuminated many other political issues.

33 Michel Foucault

PAUL PATTON

Chapter guide

This chapter focuses on Michel Foucault's work during the 1970s, including but not limited to his work on sexuality. Section 33.2 outlines the approach and key outcomes of *The History of Sexuality*, volume 1: *An Introduction* (1978) [henceforth *The History of Sexuality*]. Section 33.3 discusses Foucault's analyses of discourses and truth before turning to the concept of power that informed his approach to sexuality and prisons. Critical questions about this concept raised in his 1975–1976 lectures '*Society Must Be Defended*' led to its eventual abandonment in favour of a concept of power as government. Section 33.4 discusses the ideas of biopower and race raised in the final chapter of *The History of Sexuality* before taking up his approach to liberal and neoliberal government in *Security, Territory, Population* (2007) and *Birth of Biopolitics* (2008) and the concept of power outlined in the light of this approach. The conclusion summarizes Foucault's impact on thought and politics around sexuality and the wider impact of his work on power, biopower, and government.

33.1 Introduction

Foucault (1926–1984) was an idiosyncratic political thinker. He published histories of the emergence of institutions such as asylums, hospitals, and prisons that were also histories of the associated forms of knowledge: psychiatry, clinical medicine, criminal anthropology and criminology (Foucault, 1973 [1963]; 1977a [1975]; 2006 [1961]). He wrote several volumes of a projected history of European sexuality, the structure of which changed dramatically after it was first announced (Foucault, 1978 [1976]; 1985 [1984]; 1986 [1984]; 2021[2018]). His lectures at the *Collège de France* sketched histories of modern ideas about the nature and function of government, as well as ancient forms of self-care. He became a very public political figure with a distinctive conception of the role of intellectuals in assisting progressive social transformations. He never sought to provide normative foundations for his own political activism, preferring to align himself with Weber and Nietzsche in accepting that all his work depended on certain values, while refusing the demand to justify those values or the choices that informed his political activity. The historian and his colleague at the Collège de France, Paul Veyne, suggested that 'Foucault's originality among the great thinkers of our century lay in his refusal to convert our finitude into the basis for new certainties' (Veyne, 1993: 5).

In a lecture at the beginning of his 1982–1983 course, Foucault located his work in the critical tradition that extends from Hegel through Nietzsche (see more on Nietzsche in Chapter 14), Weber, and the Frankfurt School, describing it as a critical ontology of the present (Foucault, 2010: 21). Unlike others in that tradition, he did not develop a comprehensive account of history, modernity, or modern society. Rather, he proposed conceptions of discourse, power, and ethics while making it clear that these were not global theories but conceptual scaffolding designed to support particular genealogical studies. He used the term 'genealogy' in the sense that Nietzsche (1994 [1887]) proposed a genealogy of morality, namely to refer to a certain kind of historical understanding of how things came to be as they are.

Foucault offered multiple accounts of the purpose of such genealogies. At times, he suggested that the aim was to assist movements for social change by exposing the historical and contingent character of contemporary ways of thinking and acting. Genealogical histories show that it was not inevitable that madness be considered a mental illness and become caught up in the institutional and scientific apparatus of psychiatry, just as it was not inevitable that judicial punishment, incarceration, and techniques of disciplinary power come together in the modern penal system. In 'What Is Enlightenment?', Foucault summed up this conception of the aim of genealogical critique in the question: 'in what is given to us as universal, necessary, obligatory, what place is occupied by whatever is singular, contingent and the product of arbitrary constraints?' (Foucault, 2000: 315). Some commentators suggest that Foucault's diagnostic and descriptive genealogies do more than expose the contingency of our ways of thinking and acting: they can also help us to think more effectively about possible changes (Koopman, 2013: 44). At times, however, Foucault insists on a more open-ended aim of his genealogical approach to the present, pointing to the political effectivity of historical analyses that simply 'seek to detect types of practice, institutional forms etc. which exist and function for a time in certain places ... The problem is to let knowledge of the past work on the experience of the present' (Foucault, 2008: 130).

33.2 Sexuality

First published in 1976, *The History of Sexuality* introduced a projected six-volume history of modern sexuality in Western Europe. It was a product of the historical moment during the 1960s and 1970s that saw the emergence of movements such as women's liberation, gay liberation, and children's liberation. These movements aimed at overcoming forms of oppression and injustice perpetrated on particular social groups. They often shared a concern with the liberation of sexualities that were supposed to be repressed or confined in the interests of biological reproduction and the productivity of labour. The promised combination of new social relations and new forms of freedom and pleasure, Foucault suggested, took the form of 'a great sexual sermon' that echoed across Western industrial societies, assuming the 'lyricism and religiosity that long accompanied the revolutionary project' (Foucault, 1978 [1976]: 8).

Foucault's attitude towards these movements was complicated. On the one hand, as he later explained in 'The Subject and Power' (Foucault, 1982), his genealogical histories of aspects of the present always took as their starting point the 'forms of resistance against different forms of power': 'the power of men over women, of parents over children, of psychiatry over the mentally ill, of medicine over the population', and so on (Foucault, 2000: 329). These histories were intended to support struggles against particular forms of power in their efforts to bring about 'a new economy of power relations' (ibid.: 329).

On the other hand, he rejected key elements of the liberation sermon. He questioned the historical accuracy of the claim that sex had been repressed since the beginnings of the capitalist era. This 'repressive hypothesis', as he called it, was built in part on Freud's argument in *Civilization and Its Discontents* (Freud, 2002 [1930]) that the repression of the sexual drive was necessary for the development of civilization. Freud's argument, first published in 1930, was taken up in various forms of 'Freudo-Marxism' that were popular during the 1960s and 1970s. Along with a conception of power as essentially negative, these provided the intellectual context of Foucault's project. They drew on the work of the Austrian psychoanalyst Wilhelm Reich, who had argued in the 1930s that sexual repression was linked to class oppression. Herbert Marcuse further developed the link between psychic repression and alienated labour in *Eros and Civilization: A Philosophical Inquiry into Freud* (Marcuse, 1955).

The History of Sexuality did not deny particular forms of sexual repression, but pointed out that sex was also one of the things most spoken about in modern European societies. Christianity had long been concerned not only with sexual behaviour but also with the sexual thoughts and desires that became a particular focus of confession. The twentieth century saw the emergence of psychoanalysis and other therapeutic practices in which sex remained a primary concern. Foucault argued that European modernity from the seventeenth century onwards had been accompanied by a proliferation of discourses on sex and an intensification of relations of power and pleasure associated with the sexual conduct of individuals. He challenged a key tenet of Freudo-Marxism by pointing out that this sexualization and control of bodies developed among the emerging bourgeoisie, rather than in the attempt to repress working-class sexual expenditure in order to maximize the productivity of labour. As such, he suggested it should be seen as 'the self-affirmation of one class rather than the enslavement of another' (Foucault, 1978 [1976]: 123).

In light of these historical corrections, Foucault doubted whether repression is really the most important mechanism of power in the modern period. He wondered whether the discourse of sexual liberation really signalled a rupture with a supposed era of repression rather than belonging to 'the same historical network as the thing it denounces' (ibid.: 10).

He argued that the repressive hypothesis was misleading as a historical claim, as a conception of the nature of power, and as a conception of sexuality: 'Sexuality must not be thought of as a kind of natural given which power tries to hold in check, or as an obscure domain which knowledge tries gradually to uncover. It is the name that can be given to a historical construct . . .' (ibid.: 105).

The proliferation of discourse around sexuality from the seventeenth century onwards included a discourse on female hysteria that understood the female body as entirely 'saturated with sexuality'; a discourse on childhood masturbation and the moral and physiological dangers this entailed for individuals and for the population; a political and medical discourse on reproduction, birth control practices, and the relationship between these and the conditions of population growth; and, finally, towards the end of the nineteenth century, a psychiatric taxonomy of anomalous or perverse forms of sexual behaviour. These discourses were accompanied by a more or less co-ordinated series of strategies and tactics of power that included 'hysterization' or subjecting women's bodies to medical treatment for the 'hysteria' they supposedly acquired by virtue of their sex; 'pedagogization' of the sexual behaviour of children evident above all in the campaign against masturbation in the course of the eighteenth and nineteenth centuries; 'socialization' of procreative behaviour that included state control of practices of birth control; and a 'psychiatrization' of sexual behaviour that nineteenth-century taxonomies deemed abnormal, along with the development of technologies for the correction of such abnormalities (ibid.: 104–105).

Key Concept: Discourse

Discourse refers to how we speak or think about things and what we take to be a 'normal' belief or point of view. Foucault analysed the way that our ability to speak or think about a concept is shaped by power relations that structure what it is possible to think or say either in general or in a specific area of knowledge (a particular discourse). For example, in economics, human beings are understood as rational utility maximizers, while in religious discourse, they are understood to have souls. See also the analysis in Section 33.3.1.

Together these strategies and associated discourses produced the objects of knowledge and intervention that defined what Foucault called the '*dispositif*' of modern European sexuality. This term is controversially translated either as 'deployment' or 'apparatus' of sexuality (Kelly, 2013: 132–134). Either way, the object to which it refers comprises all of the figures representing the successive discourses and fields of intervention listed above: the hysterical woman, the masturbating child, the Malthusian couple, and the perverse individual. On Foucault's account, these were socially constructed identities rather than natural kinds. He did not deny the biological and physiological realities that underpin human sexual reproduction and the differences between male and female bodies, although his commentary on the text by the hermaphrodite Hercule Barbin showed that these are more complex than a simple dichotomy between male and female would suggest (Foucault, 1980b [1978]). He acknowledged the physiological and psychological realities of 'bodies and pleasures' that underpin sexual behaviour, but also argued that sexuality should be understood as 'the set of effects produced in bodies, behaviours, and social relations by a certain deployment deriving from a complex political technology' (Foucault, 1978 [1976]: 127).

Foucault's denaturalization of sexuality and his insistence that the ways in which bodies and pleasures are experienced are a historical phenomenon that cannot be separated from the forms of exercise of power within society made his work attractive to feminist scholars. At the same time, his work was widely criticized from feminist points of view for its lack of attention to the ways in which modern sexuality was bound up with the subordination of women in European societies (Diamond and Quinby, 1988; Sawicki, 1991; McNay, 1992; Hekman, 1996; McWhorter, 1999; McLaren, 2002; *Foucault Studies*, 2013; Taylor, 2013). A focus of much criticism was his discussion of what would now be considered the sexual assault of a young girl by an itinerant male labourer from her village in nineteenth-century France. The perpetrator, Charles Jouy, was reported to the authorities and subsequently spent the rest of his life in a psychiatric asylum where his case became the subject of investigation and an eventually published report. Foucault discussed the case in the context of illustrating the novel kinds of discourse about sex produced in eighteenth- and nineteenth-century Europe (Foucault, 1978 [1976]: 31–32; 2003b: 292–303). His remarks were accused of trivializing the incident and showing no interest in or sympathy for the experience of the young victim Sophie Adam (Woodhull, 1988; Hengehold, 1994; Alcoff, 1996; Cahill, 2000, Taylor, 2009; 2017: 70–78, 276–277, 304–315; Kelly, 2013: 36–38). Tremain (2013) offers a different perspective on the incident from the perspective of critical disability studies.

The History of Sexuality has been an especially important text for the development of Gay and Queer theory (Halperin, 1995; Spargo, 1999). Judith Butler (1990) built on Foucault's description of sexuality as an effect of discourse and power to elaborate an account of gender as the effect of repeated performance of behaviours codified as masculine or feminine (see more on Butler in Chapter 36). This approach denied any stable connection between gender norms and biological sex, thereby allowing for the critical or parodic performance of behaviours in ways that transgress the heterosexual norms of modern European societies. More recently, Lynne Huffer (2010; 2018) has argued that Foucault's *History of Madness* provides an important resource for queer theory in part because of its focus on the dual emergence of the modern rational and ethical subject through practices of exclusion.

Foucault's plan to write a further five volumes on the history of sexuality was never fulfilled, although a draft version of one of the books proposed in the initial series was published in 2018 as *The History of Sexuality 4: Confessions of the Flesh* (Foucault, 2021 [2018]). After a diversion into the study of governmentality in 1977–1978 and 1978–1979, the focus of his research shifted to ways in which (male) individuals became engaged in making themselves subjects of certain kinds through the practice of 'techniques of the self'. The two volumes published shortly before his death in 1984 examined ancient Greek and Roman accounts of such techniques: *The Use of Pleasure*: *The History of Sexuality*, vol. 2 (Foucault, 1985 [1984]) and *The Care of the Self: The History of Sexuality*, vol. 3 (Foucault, 1986 [1984]).

> ### 🔑 33.2 Sexuality: Key Points
>
> - Foucault's *The History of Sexuality* challenged the 'repressive hypothesis' about sex in European modernity on both historical and conceptual grounds: sex was widely discussed and an object of political intervention; it was produced rather than repressed by power.
>
> - He proposed a six-volume series outlining the major discursive components and forms of intervention that make up the modern 'deployment' of sexuality.
>
> - Because of its historicization of sexuality and its insistence on power relations, *The History of Sexuality* has been a controversial but influential text in feminist, gay, and queer scholarship.

33.3 Discourse, truth, and power

33.3.1 Discourse and truth

Foucault's proposed history of sexuality sought to identify the important ways in which sex became an object of discourse: who spoke about it, from what positions and points of view; within what institutions sex was spoken about and how these institutions 'store and distribute the things that are said' (Foucault, 1978 [1976]: 11). In addition, as suggested by the French title, *La volonté de savoir*, literally 'The will to know', this book proposed an analysis of the will to truth or knowledge that developed in concert with the exercise of power over sex. In these ways, Foucault's history of discourse in relation to sexuality drew upon the original approach to the history of pre-scientific forms of knowledge that he had pursued in earlier work. His major thesis for the state doctorate, *History of Madness* (Foucault, 2006 [1961]), sought to examine the historical development of what counted as truth in the domains of psychopathology and psychiatry. *The Order of Things* (Foucault, 1970 [1966]) analysed the presuppositions of seventeenth- and eighteenth-century theories of language, living things, and the production of wealth. *The Birth of the Clinic* (Foucault, 1973 [1963]) described the discursive and institutional sources of modern clinical medicine.

Foucault described these historical studies as an 'archaeology' of knowledge, by analogy with the manner in which archaeology uncovers the buried remnants of past physical structures and ways of life. The archaeology of what once passed for knowledge similarly uncovers forgotten structures or forms of thought in particular empirical domains. In 1969, he published *The Archaeology of Knowledge*, a retrospective methodology of these attempts to identify the underlying conditions of empirical knowledge (Foucault, 1972 [1969]). In contrast to other ways of doing the history of ideas, sciences, or proto-sciences, he defined his aim as the identification of singular formations of discourse, where 'discourse' was a technical term that he defined with reference to *énoncés*, translated as 'statements'. By 'statements', Foucault meant linguistic events of a very particular kind, distinct from propositions (timeless and independent of their form of expression), utterances (tied to a particular time and place), and speech-acts (tied to particular social institutions). Foucault's 'statements' are at once tied to a historical context of utterance and yet capable of repetition. Certain kinds of regularity between statements, and between statements and non-discursive procedures that enabled their production, allowed him to define distinct discursive formations. These regularities included the type of subject-position or 'enunciative modality' presupposed by a given statement (who is entitled to say what, under what conditions, and in relation to which institutional sites?); the type of theoretical object to which it may refer (bodily humours? sexual desires? features of a population?); and the empirical or institutional domains in relation to which these objects function (such as churches, hospitals, prisons, or national populations).

Foucault's (1981) inaugural lecture delivered at the *Collège de France* in December 1970 referred to the history of such formations of discourse as a history of the will to know or, more simply, a history of truth. He suggested that the distinction between truth and falsehood could be regarded as one of the systems of exclusion that defined the order of discourse in modern Western societies, alongside others such as the distinction between reason and madness, or the different prohibitions that govern who can speak about what and under what conditions, especially in the highly charged fields of politics and sexuality. The first lecture of his 1970–1971 course entitled 'The Will to Know' began with the suggestion that this phrase could equally well describe the object of the historical analyses of discourse that he had undertaken up to this point, as well as many he would like to undertake: 'I think all these analyses—past or still to come—could be seen as something like so many "fragments for a morphology of the will to know"' (Foucault, 2013: 1).

In a 1977 interview with Bernard-Henri Levy, 'Power and Sex', Foucault (1988: 112) suggested that the aim of his projected history of sexuality was 'not to write the social history of a prohibition but the political history of a production of truth'. Drawing on the methodological precepts of his earlier archaeology of knowledge, he outlined an analysis of the form taken by modern knowledge of sex in the course of the nineteenth century. He argued that, because it evolved out of religious discourse on sexual behaviour, knowledge of sex assigned a privileged role to confession. As a result, a number of theoretical postulates and transformations in the form of such confessional discourse were necessary before it could be adjusted to the norms of nineteenth-century science (Foucault, 1978 [1976]: 65–67). Foucault clearly intended that the history of the modern discourse about sexuality should serve as an archaeology of psychoanalysis (ibid.: 130). That is why he describes the project as answering a further question, namely how has it come about that 'Sex has always been the forum where both the future of our species and our "truth" as human subjects are decided' (Foucault, 1988: 111).

33.3.2 Disciplinary power

Foucault claimed in an interview that the whole point of his proposed six-volume history of sexuality lay in the re-elaboration of the theory of power (Foucault, 1980a: 187). Whereas in *History of Madness* he had relied upon a traditional conception of power as an essentially juridical mechanism that prohibits certain kinds of conduct, a persistent theme of his analyses during the 1970s involved criticism of this conception. In *The History of Sexuality*, he challenged the predominant juridical image of power in suggesting that 'In political thought and analysis, we still have not cut off the head of the king' (Foucault, 1978 [1976]: 88–89). In lectures delivered earlier in 1976 he sketched an account of the historical reasons why this juridical conception had become dominant, noting that the constitution of a body of law that regulated the exercise of monarchical power and maintained civil peace had played a crucial role in the establishment of absolute secular authority in Europe. The rule of law remained central to criticism of monarchical authority throughout the sixteenth and seventeenth centuries: 'From the sixteenth and especially the seventeenth century onward, or at the time of Wars of Religion, the theory of sovereignty then became a weapon that was used both to restrict and to strengthen royal power' (Foucault, 2003a: 34–35).

The enduring grip of this juridical concept of power was partly explained by the fact that the legal apparatus of sovereignty has continued to provide the institutional framework of modern, democratic political power. However, Foucault argued that this juridical concept was inadequate to account for other ways in which power was exercised in modern European societies. From the seventeenth century onwards there emerged a disciplinary form of power that applied directly to bodies and activities rather than land and its products. It extracted time and labour from bodies rather than commodities and wealth from the fruits of their labour as had occurred under the feudal system. It was exercised through constant surveillance of their activity rather than through systems of taxation and obligation. It relied upon a closely meshed grid of material coercions that ordered bodily movements, activities, and the disposition of individuals in space and time. It sought to increase both the subjugated forces of bodies and the efficacy of their subjugation. This new form of power was 'absolutely incompatible with relations of sovereignty' as well as being 'one of bourgeois society's great inventions. It was one of the basic tools for the establishment of industrial capitalism and the corresponding type of society' (ibid.: 36).

> **Key Concept: Disciplinary power**
>
> *Discipline and Punish* provides a detailed analysis of discipline as a new way of exercising power over bodies, distinguished by its continuous supervision of bodily movements and gestures. The aim was the efficient integration of bodily movements into functional activities undertaken for military, educational, productive, or penal aims. Foucault used primary sources from the seventeenth, eighteenth, and nineteenth centuries to demonstrate the spatial and temporal techniques of discipline: the enclosure and partitioning of camps, factories, classrooms, and prisons along with the minute control of the temporal succession of actions or activities through timetables, the integration of bodily actions with functional processes, and the articulation of bodies and gestures with the tools or instruments of those processes. 'These methods, which made possible the meticulous control of the operations of the body, which assured the constant subjection of its forces and imposed upon them a relation of docility-utility, might be called "disciplines"' (Foucault, 1977a [1975]: 137).

Foucault's focus on disciplinary power and its enduring impact on modern European societies owed much to his involvement with prisons and penal reform during the early 1970s. In 1971, he was one of the founders of the *Prisons Information Group* (Zurn and Dilts, 2016; Thompson and Zurn, 2021). *Discipline and Punish* (Foucault 1977a [1975]) traced the emergence of disciplinary power in the seventeenth century and its progressive adoption in the key institutions of modern society: armies, factories, schools, hospitals, and eventually prisons. Where Marxism tended to regard institutional forms of power as superstructural phenomena necessary for the perpetuation of relations of production and class domination (read more about Marx in Chapter 13), Foucault drew attention to the ubiquity and autonomy of power relations. He argued that power was diffused throughout society and that disciplinary power was an indispensable element of capitalist forces and relations of production. As a consequence, power should be studied not at the sovereign centre of the social order but at the periphery, from the ground up, in its effects on individual bodies (Foucault, 1978 [1976]: 94–97; 2003a: 29–34). So, for example, rather than trying to understand the nature or the justification of punishment from the point of view of the sovereign power that punishes, whether monarchical or democratic, Foucault looked at the institutions, practices and 'actual apparatuses' of punishment (Foucault, 2003a: 28). From this 'peripheral' perspective, it is the local forms of power throughout society that are primary. The power exercised over servants, workers, criminals or the mentally ill should be understood as supports on which political power rested, rather than as effects of state or class domination:

> Between every point of a social body, between a man and a woman, between the members of a family, between a master and his pupil . . . there exist relations of power which are not purely and simply a projection of the sovereign's great power over the individual; they are rather the concrete, changing soil in which the sovereign's power is grounded, the conditions which make it possible for it to function.
>
> (Foucault, 1980a: 187)

In opposition to the juridical concept of power, *Discipline and Punish* relied upon a concept of power comprised of two key ideas: first, that power was essentially productive of certain comportments and behaviours; and second, that 'one should take' as the model for power relations 'a perpetual battle rather than a contract regulating a transaction or the conquest of a territory' (Foucault, 1977a [1975]: 26). Foucault's concept of power as a form of war explains the militaristic language of 'tactics', 'manoeuvres', and 'strategies' throughout *Discipline and Punish*. Similarly, *The History of Sexuality* proposed as the basis for understanding power 'the moving substrate of force relations which, by virtue of their inequality, constantly engender states of power' that are always local and unstable (Foucault, 1978 [1976]: 92). Alluding to Clausewitz's dictum that war is politics by other means, Foucault suggested that the underlying multiplicity of force relations 'can be coded – in part but never totally – either in the form of "war", or in the form of "politics"' (ibid.: 93). Foucault took the idea that power relations are formed on the basis of underlying relations of force from Gilles Deleuze.

Key Thinker: Gilles Deleuze

Foucault and French philosopher Gilles Deleuze (1925-1995) became friends in the early 1960s, reviewing each other's books and collaborating as editors of Nietzsche's works. Deleuze's reconstruction of Nietzsche's concept of will to power in terms of force relations in *Nietzsche and Philosophy* (Deleuze, 1983 [1962]) formed the basis of Foucault's concept of power in *The History of Sexuality*. Among other shared political and intellectual activities, Deleuze participated in the *Prisons Information Group* and in Foucault's seminar in 1971-1972. A high point of their mutual engagement was the 'Intellectuals and Power' interview published in 1972 (Foucault, 1977b: 205-217). However, their political positions and their views on theoretical issues such as the relationship between desire and power diverged after 1976 and they drifted apart (Patton, 2019). Deleuze (1988 [1986]) published *Foucault* in 1986. His 1990 'Postscript on Control Societies' outlined a conception of what came after Foucault's disciplinary society (Deleuze 1995 [1990]: 177-182).

Foucault's conviction that 'the question of power needed to be formulated not so much in terms of justice as in those of technology, of tactics and strategy' (Foucault, 1980a: 184) led to the 'military-technological' concept of power that is perhaps his most widely known contribution to political philosophy. Helpfully summarized and discussed in Kelly (2013: 62-71) and Taylor (2017: 115-138), it has been the subject of exhaustive debate and fierce criticism, especially in relation to the lack of any overt normative dimension to the resulting analysis of power (Fraser, 1981; Philp, 1983; Walzer, 1986; Taylor, 1984; Habermas, 1985). Political philosophers tended to see his work as fatally flawed, confused, or nihilistic on the grounds that it endorsed no values that might enable moral or political evaluation. For example, Michael Walzer took Foucault's methodological injunctions about the study of power to imply that: 'Citizenship and government alike have been superseded. And yet the whole point of modern political theory, since the absolutist state provided the ground on which it was constructed, has been to account for these two things' (Walzer, 1986: 53).

For Walzer (ibid.: 66-67), the task of modern political theory was to provide a kind of 'philosophical jurisprudence' that explained and justified the institutions of the liberal state, and the absence of any such principles amounted to a 'catastrophic weakness' in Foucault's political philosophy. As noted above, Foucault repeatedly contrasted his own approach to power with the 'juridico-political' model of sovereign power. However, contra Walzer, he never argued that the juridico-political apparatus of sovereign power disappeared altogether. Rather, he argued that the political structure of modern societies since the nineteenth century involved a system of public right articulated around a principle of democratic sovereignty, the exercise of which was delegated to the state, in concert with 'a tight grid of disciplinary coercions that actually guarantees the cohesion of that social body ... A right of sovereignty and a mechanics of discipline. It is, I think, between these two limits that power is exercised' (Foucault, 2003a: 37).

Foucault's reluctance to pursue the standard questions and approach of modern political philosophy must be understood in the light of his approach to power as well as his rejection of the traditional conception of the philosopher as judge. He sought to describe the non-sovereign mechanisms of disciplinary power in a manner that was not concerned, with *why* but rather with *how* power is exercised, by what mechanisms and to what ends (ibid.: 24; see Foucault, 2000: 336–337). At the same time, as we will see, his understanding of power changed significantly between 1975 and 1980.

> ### 33.3 Discourse, truth, and power: Key Points
>
> - Foucault's *The History of Sexuality* proposed a history of the 'will to knowledge' or 'will to truth' in relation to sexuality.
> - Building on the theory of discourse and discursive formations developed in *The Archaeology of Knowledge*, he identified specific features of modern forms of 'knowledge' of sexuality, such as the confessional origins of psychoanalysis.
> - Foucault criticized the predominance in political thought of the juridical model of power, focused on the justification, legitimacy, and limits of the power of the sovereign.
> - His analyses of discipline and sexuality were framed by a 'military-technological' model of power as based on struggle between contending forces.
> - Foucault's analyses of power should be understood in the context of his genealogical approach as opposed to the jurisprudential conception of the task of political philosophy.

33.4 Race, government, and power

33.4.1 Biopower and state racism

The final chapter of *The History of Sexuality*, 'Right of Death and Power Over Life', introduced several novel themes in Foucault's work: the idea that state power in modern societies is a power over life rather than a power to inflict death, and the suggestion that this 'biopolitical' character of modern power explains the emergence of state racism in the nineteenth century. It also introduced a shift of focus from the forms of micro-social power to the forms of government by the state that continued in his 1977–1978 (*Security, Territory, Population*) and 1978–1979 (*Birth of Biopolitics*) lectures. Foucault developed a historical and descriptive approach to the exercise of state power focused on what he called 'governmentality': the nature, purpose, and mechanism of the exercise of sovereign power. None of these themes was foreshadowed in the preceding chapters of *The History of Sexuality*. Nevertheless, he commented in an interview that this concluding chapter is 'the fundamental part of the book' (Foucault, 1980a: 222).

This chapter and the final lecture of Foucault's 1975–1976 course 'Society Must be Defended' develop the argument that the European eighteenth and nineteenth centuries saw 'the acquisition of power over man insofar as man is a living being' (Foucault, 2003a: 239). The sovereign had always been endowed with a power of life and death but for a long time this was exercised in a negative fashion: the sovereign could take life or allow to live. It was only from the seventeenth century onwards that sovereign power developed the capacity to actively manage both individual lives and the life of the larger unities of community, race, and species. In the eighteenth century the power of government began to be exercised over rates of birth and death, endemic diseases, and the relation of people to the urban and natural environment in which they lived and worked. Unlike disciplinary power exercised over bodies and small groups, this new power operated at the level of the whole population. Rather than the detailed control of bodily forces and movements, it involved mechanisms that rely on forecasts, statistical models, and measures designed to maintain and to regulate states of relative security and equilibrium within populations. It sought to regulate not 'by training individuals, but by achieving an overall equilibrium that protects the security of the whole from internal dangers' (ibid.: 249). Foucault sometimes used the term 'biopower' in a limited sense to describe this form of power, but he also used the term in a broad sense that encompassed both discipline and these regulatory mechanisms directed at the security of the population. It is in this broad sense that power took possession of life in the nineteenth century: 'thanks to the play of technologies of discipline on the one hand and technologies of regulation on the other, [it] succeeded in covering the whole surface that lies between the organic and the biological, between body and population' (ibid.: 253).

The Covid-19 pandemic drew renewed attention to Foucault's remarks about biopower, prompting more than one commentator during that period to suggest that 'We live in Foucauldian times' (Schubert, 2021: 1). The widespread recourse to pre-modern techniques of controlling the spread of disease by the closing of borders and quarantining those infected led some to question the claim that biopolitics was born in the eighteenth century, and to propose a more long-term and diverse history of biopolitical practices (Meloni, 2022). Others were led to explore previously neglected aspects of Foucault's analysis of European biopower, such as the relations between biopolitical and Marxist analyses of modernity and the degree to which biopolitics always involved a politics of differential vulnerability on the part of different social groups (Lorenzini, 2021). Calls for a more democratic biopolitics were indicative of the need to move beyond a simplistic moral and political evaluation of biopower as something to be resisted always and everywhere.

In his own analysis, Foucault suggested that the development of modern biopower explained not only why sexuality became such a focus of attention during the nineteenth century, involving as it did both the behaviour of individual bodies and the reproduction of the population as whole, but also the nature and function of racism. Once state power had become primarily a matter of supporting and sustaining life, how was it possible for that power to cause death? Racism enabled biopower to exercise the traditional right of the sovereign to kill. It provided an apparently biological way to fragment or divide the life that is under the control of the state so that only some life had to be protected. Other kinds of life that were different, weaker, or that posed a threat to the valued life could be allowed to die. The enemy was no longer a protagonist so much as a biological threat.

Foucault's hypothesis was not about the origins of racism 'as such' or 'the ordinary racism that takes the traditional form of mutual contempt or hatred between races' (Foucault, 2003a: 258). It was rather a specific claim about a kind of racism that emerged during the latter half of the nineteenth century and that was bound up with the exercise of biopower:

> We are dealing with a mechanism that allows biopower to work. So racism is bound up with the workings of a State that is obliged to use race, the elimination of races and the purification of the race, to exercise its sovereign power. The juxtaposition of—or the way biopower functions through—the old sovereign power of life and death implies the workings, the introduction and activation, of racism.
>
> (ibid.: 258)

Blood relations and the symbolism of spilling blood played an important role in the mechanisms, manifestations, and rituals of the pre-modern form of sovereign power. By contrast, in modern European societies the mechanisms of power function less in terms of a 'symbolics of blood' than in terms of 'an analytics of sexuality': they were addressed to bodies, to life, and to whatever reinforced the species (Foucault, 1978 [1976]: 148). In his 1974–1975 lectures, Foucault suggested that the disqualification of the criminal, the poor, the sexually or psychologically deviant was bound up with a 'racism against the abnormal' (Foucault. 2003b: 316). At the same time, in a variety of colonial and domestic contexts, 'the mythical concern with protecting the purity of the blood and ensuring the triumph of the race' continued to play a role in the conceptualization and administration of state power' (Foucault, 1978 [1976]: 149). Nazism was the most elaborate and disastrous combination of biopower and the atavistic symbolics of a superior blood. However, state racism was manifest in a range of other phenomena during this period, such as the colonization of Africa and the fantasy of a global citizenship embracing all of the British colonies settled by the 'White race' (Bell, 2016).

Foucault wrote very little about colonialism but his work has nevertheless become an important resource for postcolonial studies (see, for example, Stoler, 1995; Young, 1995; Nichols, 2010; Chow, 2018). Biopower and its relation to racism also serve as a point of departure for Achille Mbembe's (2003) influential elaboration of the concept of necropolitics in order to describe the multiple forms of subordination of life to the power of death, such as slavery, colonial occupation, and apartheid regimes. The influence of Foucault on queer theory has been further developed by the emergence of studies in queer necropolitics (Puar, 2007; Haritaworn, Kuntsman and Prosocco, 2014).

33.4.2 Liberal and neoliberal government

Foucault's *Security, Territory, Population* outlined an account of liberalism as a novel form of government that sought to reconcile the practice of sovereign government with the operation of a market economy. He illustrates the emergence of liberal government by reference to proposals put forward in France in the middle of the eighteenth century to deal with the problem of grain shortage. This was a threat to governments since it could lead to revolt on the part of urban populations. Previously, it had been dealt with by regulations including controls on the price of grain, the prohibition of hoarding, limits on the export of grain, and limits to the extent of land under cultivation (Foucault, 2007: 32). French government edicts in 1763 and 1764 introduced a new policy that aimed at ensuring food security for the population by allowing the free circulation of goods and relying on market mechanisms to stabilize the supply and the price of grain. They recommended the removal of restrictions on hoarding, on the export and import of grain, and on the extent of land devoted to its production. Foucault commented that this manner of exercising power was 'profoundly linked to the general principle of what is called liberalism . . . not interfering, allowing free movement, letting things follow their course; *laisser faire, passer et aller*' (Foucault, 2007: 48).

This new policy worked through the decisions of individual producers, merchants, and consumers. It exercised power indirectly by acting on the actions of others considered as free agents endowed with certain irreducible interests and the capacity to calculate optimal ways of satisfying those interests. It was a government of *homo oeconomicus* exercised neither over bodily forces, as the analysis of disciplinary power supposed, nor over juridical subjects of right, but over subjects of interest. In this manner, he argued, by virtue of its reliance on the individual governed as a subject of interest and by virtue of its mode of acting indirectly on the actions of the governed, the form of government advocated by the eighteenth-century political economists introduced 'some of the fundamental lines of modern and contemporary governmentality' (ibid.: 348).

> **Key Concept: Governmentality**
>
> Foucault embarked on the study of 'governmentality' from the fourth lecture of his 1977–1978 course, *Security, Territory, Population*. He outlined a history of some of the most important understandings of the exercise of state power in the European tradition. These included pastoral government modelled on the ancient idea of the ruler as shepherd, the early modern 'reason of state' doctrine and its associated theory of the policing of the social and economic life of the polity, and the emergence of liberal government during the eighteenth century (Lemke, 2019). The first lecture of the 1978–1979 course *Birth of Biopolitics* gave a concise explanation of 'governmentality': not the actual practice of government but 'the reasoned way of governing best and, at the same time, reflection on the best possible way of governing' (Foucault, 2008: 2). In short, the study of governmentality involved 'the study of the rationalization of governmental practice in the exercise of political sovereignty' (ibid.: 2).

Apart from a few remarks about Bentham, Foucault's analysis of liberal government in *Birth of Biopolitics* (2008) skips over the nineteenth century in order to focus on the twentieth-century neoliberal reinvention of liberal governmentality, first, in the work of German 'Ordoliberals' and, second, in the work of American thinkers associated with the Chicago School (Harvey, 2005; Gane, 2018). Despite the considerable differences between these two approaches, they shared a concern for the role of the state in sustaining the free market as the core institution of government and society. Whereas the problem of classical liberalism was how to limit the activities of an existing state to make room for the market, the issue for neoliberalism was how to take the free market as the 'organizing and regulating principle of the state' (ibid.: 116). Foucault points to the tension at the heart of liberal political thought between a governmentality exercised over predominantly juridical subjects and a governmentality exercised over predominantly economic subjects. The overarching concern of his 1978–1979 lectures is to identify this heterogeneity between the market and the contract, between *homo oeconomicus* and *homo juridicus*, and to point to some of its consequences for political theory (Patton, 2016).

These lectures provoked extensive debate over whether he was critical of or sympathetic towards neoliberal approaches to government (Zamora and Behrent, 2016; Sawyer and Steinmetz-Jenkins, 2019). They should rather be read as delineating a field of investigation adjacent and complementary to the 'philosophical jurisprudence' that, for Walzer and many others, defines the task of political theory.

33.4.3 Power and the government of conduct

In his lectures at the beginning of 1976, Foucault raised a series of critical questions about the 'war-repression' schema in terms of which he had thought about power up to this point: 'Are we really talking about war when we analyse the workings of power? Are the notions of "tactics," "strategy," and "relations of force" valid? To what extent are they valid? Is power quite simply a continuation of war by means other than weapons and battles?' (Foucault, 2003a: 18).

Interviews make it clear that Foucault was actively questioning the war-repression schema: see, for example, 'The Eye of Power' (Foucault, 1980a: 164), 'The Confession of the Flesh' (ibid.: 208), and 'Truth and Power', in which he comments that 'it's astonishing to see how easily and self-evidently people talk of warlike relations of power or of class struggle without ever making it clear whether some form of war is meant, and if so what form' (Foucault, 2000: 124). The fact that *The History of Sexuality* continued to make use of this schema shows that, at this point, he had not developed an alternative. This only came later, after his discussion of the exercise of sovereign power in the government of populations in his 1977–1978 and 1978–1979 lectures.

In 'The Subject and Power' (Foucault, 1982), Foucault proposed a definition of power that responded to the conceptual questions posed in 1976. In contrast to the concept of power as a struggle between opposing forces, the parties to power relations were conceived as subjects capable of action and in fact free to act in a number of ways. Power, he suggested, was a way of directing or governing the actions of others that did not essentially involve struggle between contending forces. Rather, it was a way of acting on the 'field of possibilities' that circumscribed the actions of others:

> ... less a confrontation between two adversaries or their mutual engagement than a question of 'government' ... The relationship proper to power would therefore be sought not on the side of violence or of struggle, nor on that of voluntary contracts (all of which can, at best, only be the instruments of power) but, rather, in the area of that singular mode of action, neither warlike nor juridical, which is government.
>
> (Foucault, 2000: 341)

The predominant approach to the analysis of power in political theory involves definition of conditions under which an agent A may be said to exercise power over another agent B. Definitions have been proposed that emphasize the capacity to get someone to do something they would not otherwise do (Dahl, 1969), the capacity to affect someone in a manner contrary to their interests (Lukes, 2005), or the capacity to 'strategically constrain' the environment within which somebody acts (Wartenberg, 1990: 85). Forst (2015: 112) has further developed the idea that power involves action on the actions of others by arguing that it needs to be understood as belonging to the 'space of reasons, or the normative space of freedom and action' and that power is exercised 'when someone acts for certain reasons for which others are responsible'. Whereas the definitions by Dahl and Lukes present a negative conception of power, Wartenberg's 'field' concept and Forst's 'noumenal' concept allow that the exercise of power is not necessarily contrary to the will or the interests of those over whom it is exercised.

For Foucault too, power understood as governing the conduct of others can be exercised in all kinds of social relations and not only by political authorities. However, commentators tend to overlook his repeated insistence that he was not interested in a theory of power as such but rather in an 'analytics' that would provide the concepts needed for the description of historically specific mechanisms of power (Foucault, 1978 [1976]: 82). The definition of power as 'action on the actions of others' proposes a concept of power adequate for the description of the kinds of liberal and neoliberal government of conduct that have developed in modern industrial societies.

33.4 Race, government, and power: Key Points

- The final chapter of *The History of Sexuality* argued that a new form of power over life, or biopower, emerged in Europe in the eighteenth century.
- Foucault suggested that the development of biopower explained why sexuality became a focus of attention, given its role in the propagation of the population; it also provided a new rationale for the state's power to take life, in the form of the state racism that emerged in the latter part of the nineteenth century.
- Foucault's 1977–1978 lectures *Security, Territory, Population* introduced 'governmentality', or conceptions of the nature, purpose, and mechanisms of government, as a primary object of study, providing an account of the emergence of liberal governmentality as a form of government that sought to reconcile the actions of the sovereign with the laws of a market economy.

- His 1978–1979 lectures dealt with German and American forms of neoliberal governmentality and have given rise to a debate over whether or not Foucault was critical of neoliberalism.
- The study of liberal and neoliberal government enabled Foucault to respond to his earlier critical questions about the 'war-repression' model of power that informed his analysis of discipline and sexuality: he proposed a different conception of power as action on the actions of others.

33.5 Conclusion

The History of Sexuality had a significant impact on thought and politics surrounding sexuality. It undermined the belief in human sexuality as a natural object repressed for social and economic reasons in favour of a conception of sexuality as a complex historical phenomenon that was the effect of diverse political strategies and forms of knowledge. Despite a lack of focus on the differential position of men and women, his work played an important role in the development of feminist, gay, and queer theory. Building on his earlier work on the history of discourses, Foucault developed novel conceptions of knowledge and its relation to power. These informed his claims about the emergence of complex apparatuses of power and knowledge such as sexuality or penal incarceration. They also informed his influential comments about biopolitics and biopower in Europe and the development of state racism in the nineteenth century.

While Foucault's analyses of power, knowledge, and their role in the constitution of new forms of subjectivity have contributed to a broader understanding of what counts as political, he is best known in political thought at a theorist of power. His discussions of disciplinary power and sexuality relied on a 'military-technological' model of power as arising through struggle between contending forces. His shift of focus after 1976 to the forms of exercise of sovereign power and his outline of a genealogy of modern state government led him to a different conception of power as action on the action of others that is more suited to the analysis of liberal and neoliberal government.

Take your learning further by accessing the online resources for a library of web links to relevant videos, articles, blogs, and useful websites for this chapter: www.oup.com/he/Ramgotra-Choat1e.

Study questions

1. What did Foucault mean by 'the repressive hypothesis' in relation to sexuality and what did he think was wrong with it?
2. What is 'sexuality', according to Foucault?
3. What does Foucault mean by the history of truth and how does his history of sexuality contribute to this?
4. Why is disciplinary power important and how does it relate to the sovereign power of government?
5. What is 'biopower', according to Foucault, and why is it important?
6. What does Foucault contribute to studies of race and racism?

7. What does Foucault mean by 'governmentality' and what is the interest of this concept for political philosophy?
8. What is Foucault's final concept of power and how does it relate to analytical definitions of power?

Further reading

Primary sources

Foucault, M. (1977a [1975]) *Discipline and Punish*. Trans. A. Sheridan. London: Allen Lane/Penguin.
An exemplary genealogy of the prison and modern penal science that developed novel conceptions of power and the relationship between power and knowledge.

Foucault, M. (1978 [1976]) *The History of Sexuality*, vol. 1: *An Introduction*. Trans. R. Hurley. London: Allen Lane/Penguin.
Key text in the evolution of Foucault's thought regarding power, sexuality, and truth.

Foucault, M. (1982) 'The Subject and Power'. In M. Foucault, *Essential Works of Foucault 1954-1984*, vol. 3: *Power*, Ed. J.D. Faubion, trans. R. Hurley et al. New York: New Press, pp. 326-348.
The final concept of power in Foucault's work.

Foucault, M. (2003a) *'Society Must Be Defended': Lectures at the Collège de France 1975-76*. Ed. M. Bertani and A. Fontana, trans. D. Macey. London: Allen Lane.
Raises a series of conceptual and historical questions about the understanding of power in terms of war and struggle between contending forces. The final lecture introduces important ideas about racism and the emergence of biopower.

Foucault, M. (2007) *Security, Territory, Population: Lectures at the Collège de France 1977-78*. Ed. M. Senellart, trans. G. Burchell. Basingstoke: Palgrave Macmillan.
Introduces the concept of governmentality and explores the eighteenth-century emergence of liberal governmentality.

Foucault, M. (2008) *The Birth of Biopolitics: Lectures at the Collège de France 1978-79*. Ed. M. Senellart, trans. G. Burchell. Basingstoke: Palgrave Macmillan.
Pursues the discussion of liberal and neoliberal government, framed by the contrast between subjects of right and subjects of interest.

Secondary sources

Kelly, M.G.E. (2013) *Foucault's History of Sexuality, vol. 1: The Will to Knowledge*. Edinburgh: Edinburgh University Press.
Helpful analysis of this key text and Foucault's initial approach to the history of sexuality.

Lemke, T. (2019) *Foucault's Analysis of Modern Governmentality: A Critique of Political Reason*. Trans. E. Butler. London: Verso.
Thorough examination of the concept of governmentality and its place in Foucault's work.

Sawicki, J. (2005) 'Queering Foucault and the Subject of Feminism'. In G. Gutting (ed.), *The Cambridge Companion to Foucault*, 2nd edn. Cambridge: Cambridge University Press, pp. 379-400.
Helpful discussion of responses to Foucault by feminist theorists and Judith Butler's queer poststructuralism.

Taylor, C. (2017) *The Routledge Guidebook to Foucault's The History of Sexuality*. London: Routledge.
Wide-ranging exploration of the central ideas of Foucault's text and its reception among feminist theorists.

References

Alcoff, L. (1996) 'Dangerous Pleasures: Foucault and the Politics of Pedophilia'. In S.J. Hekman (ed.), *Re-Reading the Canon: Feminist Interpretations of Michel Foucault*. University Park, PA: Pennsylvania State University Press, pp. 99–135.

Bell, D. (2016) *Reordering the World: Essays on Liberalism and Empire*. Princeton, NJ: Princeton University Press.

Butler, J. (1990) *Gender Trouble: Feminism and the Subversion of Identity*. New York: Routledge.

Cahill, A.J. (2000) 'Foucault, Rape, and the Construction of the Feminine Body'. *Hypatia*, 15(1): 43–63.

Chow, R. (2018) 'Foucault, Race, and Racism'. In L. Downing (ed.), *After Foucault: Culture, Theory and Criticism in the 21st Century*. Cambridge: Cambridge University Press, pp. 102–121.

Dahl, R.A. (1969) 'The Concept of Power'. In R. Bell, D.V. Edwards, and R.H. Wagner (eds), *Political Power: A Reader in Theory and Research*. New York: Free Press, pp. 79–93.

Deleuze, G. (1983 [1962]). *Nietzsche and Philosophy*. Trans. H. Tomlinson. Minneapolis, MN: University of Minnesota Press.

Deleuze, G. (1988 [1986]) *Foucault*. Trans. S. Hand, Minneapolis, MN: University of Minnesota Press.

Deleuze, G. (1995 [1990]) *Negotiations 1972–1990*. Trans. M. Joughin. New York: Columbia University Press.

Diamond, I. and Quinby. L. (eds) (1988) *Feminism and Foucault: Reflections on Resistance*. Boston: Northeastern University Press.

Downing, L. (ed.) (2018) *After Foucault: Culture, Theory and Criticism in the 21st Century*. Cambridge: Cambridge University Press.

Forst, R. (2015) 'Noumenal Power'. *Journal of Political Philosophy*, 23(2), 111–127.

Foucault, M. (1970 [1966]) *The Order of Things: An Archaeology of the Human Sciences/*, Trans. A. Sheridan. London: Tavistock.

Foucault, M. (1972 [1969]) *The Archaeology of Knowledge*. Trans. A. Sheridan. London: Tavistock.

Foucault, M. (1973 [1963]) *The Birth of the Clinic*. Trans. A. Sheridan. London, Tavistock.

Foucault, M. (1977a [1975]) *Discipline and Punish*. Trans. A. Sheridan. London: Allen Lane/Penguin.

Foucault, M. (1977b) *Language, Counter-Memory, Practice: Selected Essays and Interviews*. Ed. D.F. Bouchard, trans. D.F. Bouchard and S. Simon. Ithaca, NY: Cornell University Press.

Foucault, M. (1978 [1976]) *The History of Sexuality*, vol. 1: *An Introduction*. Trans. R. Hurley. London: Allen Lane/Penguin.

Foucault, M. (1980a) *Power/Knowledge: Selected Interviews and Other Writings 1972–1977 Michel Foucault*. Ed. C. Gordon. New York: Pantheon Books.

Foucault, M. (1980b [1978]) *Herculine Barbin: Being the Recently Discovered Memoirs of a Nineteenth-Century Hermaphrodite*. Trans. R. McDougall. New York: Vintage.

Foucault, M. (1981) 'The Order of Discourse'. Trans. I. McLeod. In R. Young (ed.), *Untying the Text: A Poststructuralist Reader*. Boston: Routledge & Kegan Paul, pp. 48–78.

Foucault, M. (1982) 'The Subject and Power'. In *Essential Works of Foucault 1954–1984*, Vol. 3: *Power*. Ed. J.D. Faubion, trans. R. Hurley et al. New York: New Press, pp. 326–348.

Foucault, M. (1985 [1984]) *The Use of Pleasure: The History of Sexuality*, vol. 2. Trans. R. Hurley. New York: Pantheon.

Foucault, M. (1986 [1984]) *The Care of the Self: The History of Sexuality*, vol. 3. Trans. R. Hurley. New York: Pantheon.

Foucault, M. (1988) *Michel Foucault. Politics, Philosophy, Culture: Interviews and Other Writings 1977–1984*. Ed. L.D. Kritzman. New York: Routledge.

Foucault, M. (2000) *Essential Works of Foucault 1954–1984*, vol. 3: *Power*. Ed. J.D. Faubion, trans. R. Hurley et al. New York: New Press.

Foucault, M. (2003a) *'Society Must Be Defended': Lectures at the Collège de France 1975–76*. Ed. M. Bertani and A. Fontana, trans. D. Macey. London: Allen Lane.

Foucault, M. (2003b) *Abnormal: Lectures at the Collège de France 1974–1975*. Ed. V. Marchetti and A. Salomoni, trans. G. Burchell. London: Verso.

Foucault, M. (2006 [1961]) *History of Madness*. Ed. J. Khalfa, trans. J. Murphy and J. Khalfa. New York: Routledge.

Foucault, M. (2007) *Security, Territory, Population: Lectures at the Collège de France 1977–78*. Ed. M. Senellart, trans. G. Burchell. Basingstoke: Palgrave Macmillan.

Foucault, M. (2008) *The Birth of Biopolitics: Lectures at the Collège de France 1978–79*. Ed. M. Senellart, trans. G. Burchell. Basingstoke: Palgrave Macmillan.

Foucault, M. (2010) *The Government of Self and Others: Lectures at the Collège de France 1982–83*. Ed. F. Gros, trans. G. Burchell. Basingstoke: Palgrave Macmillan.

Foucault, M. (2013) *Lectures on the Will to Know: Lectures at the Collège de France 1970–71*. Ed. D. Defert, trans. G. Burchell. Basingstoke: Palgrave Macmillan.

Foucault, M. (2021 [2018]) *The History of Sexuality*, vol. 4: *Confessions of the Flesh*. Ed. F. Gros, trans. R. Hurley. London: Penguin.

Foucault Studies (2013) Issue 16, Special Issue: 'Foucault and Feminism'.

Fraser, N. (1981) 'Foucault on Modern Power: Empirical Insights and Normative Confusions'. *Praxis International*, 3: 272–287.

Freud, S. (2002 [1930]) *Civilization and Its Discontents*. London: Penguin.

Gane, N. (2018) 'Foucault's History of Neoliberalism'. In L. Downing (ed.), *After Foucault: Culture, Theory and Criticism in the 21st Century*. Cambridge: Cambridge University Press, pp. 44–60.

Habermas, J. (1985) *The Philosophical Discourse of Modernity*. Trans. F.G. Lawrence. Cambridge, MA: MIT Press.

Halperin, D.M. (1995) *Saint Foucault: Towards a Gay Hagiography*. New York: Oxford University Press.

Haritaworn, J., Kuntsman, A. and Posocco, S. (eds) (2014) *Queer Necropolitics*. Abingdon: Routledge.

Harvey, D. (2005) *A Brief History of Neoliberalism*. Oxford: Oxford University Press.

Hekman, S.J. (ed.) (1996) *Re-Reading the Canon: Feminist Interpretations of Michel Foucault*. University Park, PA: Pennsylvania State University Press.

Hengehold, L. (1994) 'An Immodest Proposal: Foucault, Hysterization, and the "Second Rape"'. *Hypatia*, 9(3): 88–107.

Huffer, L. (2010) *Mad for Foucault: Rethinking the Foundations of Queer Theory*. New York: Columbia University Press.

Huffer, L. (2018) 'Foucault and Queer Theory'. In L. Downing (ed.), *After Foucault: Culture, Theory and Criticism in the 21st Century*. Cambridge: Cambridge University Press, pp. 93–106.

Kelly, M.G.E. (2013) *Foucault's History of Sexuality*, vol. 1: *The Will to Knowledge*. Edinburgh: Edinburgh University Press.

Koopman, C. (2013) *Genealogy as Critique: Foucault and the Problems of Modernity*. Bloomington, IN: Indiana University Press.

Lemke, T. (2019) *Foucault's Analysis of Modern Governmentality: A Critique of Political Reason*. Trans. E. Butler. London: Verso.

Lorenzini, D. (2021) 'Biopolitics in the Time of Coronavirus'. *Critical Inquiry*, 47(4): S40–S45.

Lukes, S. (2005) *Power: A Radical View*, 2nd edn. Basingstoke: Palgrave Macmillan.

Marcuse, H. (1955) *Eros and Civilization: A Philosophical Inquiry into Freud*. Boston: Beacon Press.

Mbembe, A. (2003) 'Necropolitics'. *Public Culture*, 15(1): 11–40.

McLaren, M.A. (2002) *Feminism, Foucault, and Embodied Subjectivity*. Albany, NY: SUNY Press.

McNay, L. (1992) *Foucault and Feminism: Power, Gender and the Self*. Cambridge: Polity Press.

McWhorter, L. (1999) *Bodies and Pleasures: Foucault and the Politics of Sexual Normalization*. Bloomington, IN: Indiana University Press.

Meloni, M. (2022) 'An Unproblematized Truth: Foucault, Biopolitics, and the Making of a Sociological Canon'. *Social Theory & Health*, published online 7 March: https://doi.org/10.1057/s41285-022-00177-5.

Nichols, R. (2010) 'Postcolonial Studies and the Discourse of Foucault: Survey of a Field of Problematization'. *Foucault Studies*, 9: 111–144.

Nietzsche, F. (1994 [1887]) *On the Genealogy of Morality*. Ed. K. Ansell-Pearson, trans. C. Diethe. Cambridge: Cambridge University Press.

Patton, P. (2016) 'Government, Rights and Legitimacy: Foucault and Liberal Political Normativity'. *European Journal of Political Theory*, 15(2): 223–239.

Patton, P. (2019) 'Michel Foucault'. In G. Jones and J. Roffe (eds), *Deleuze's Philosophical Lineage II*. Edinburgh: Edinburgh University Press, pp. 293–313.

Philp, M. (1983) 'Foucault on Power: A Problem in Radical Translation?' *Political Theory*, 11(1): 29–52.

Puar, J.K. (2007) *Terrorist Assemblages: Homonationalism in Queer Times*. Durham, NC: Duke University Press.

Sawicki, J. (1991) *Disciplining Foucault: Feminism, Power and the Body*. New York: Routledge.

Sawyer, S.W. and Steinmetz-Jenkins, D. (eds) (2019) *Foucault, Neoliberalism and Beyond*. New York: Rowman & Littlefield International.

Schubert, K. (2021) 'Biopolitics of Covid-19: Capitalist Continuities and Democratic Openings'. *Interalia: A Journal of Queer Studies*, 16. https://doi.org/10.51897/interalia/OAGM9733

Spargo, T. (1999) *Foucault and Queer Theory*. New York: Totem Books.

Stoler, A.L. (1995) *Race and the Education of Desire: Foucault's History of Sexuality and the Colonial Order of Things*. Durham, NC: Duke University Press.

Taylor, C. (1984) 'Foucault on Freedom and Truth'. *Political Theory*, 12(2): 152–183.

Taylor, C. (2009) 'Foucault, Feminism, and Sex Crimes'. *Hypatia*, 24(4): 1–25.

Taylor, C. (2013) 'Infamous Men, Dangerous Individuals, and Violence Against Women: Feminist Re-readings of Foucault'. In C. Falzon, T. O'Leary, and J. Sawicki (eds), *A Companion to Foucault*. Oxford: Blackwell, pp. 419–435.

Taylor, C. (2017) *The Routledge Guidebook to Foucault's The History of Sexuality*. London: Routledge.

Thompson, K. and Zurn, P. (eds) (2021) *Intolerable: Writings from Michel Foucault and the Prisons Information Group (1970–1980)*. Minneapolis, MN: University of Minnesota Press.

Tremain, S. (2013) 'Educating Jouy'. *Hypatia*, 28(4): 801–817.

Veyne, P. (1993) 'The Final Foucault and His Ethics'. *Critical Inquiry*, 20, 1–9.

Walzer, M. (1986) 'The Politics of Michel Foucault'. In D. Couzens Hoy (ed.), *Foucault: A Critical Reader*. Oxford: Blackwell, pp. 51–68.

Wartenberg, T.E. (1990) *The Forms of Power: From Domination to Transformation*. Philadelphia, PA: Temple University Press.

Woodhull, W. (1988) 'Sexuality, Power, and the Question of Rape'. In I. Diamond and L. Quinby (eds), *Feminism and Foucault: Reflections on Resistance*. Boston: Northeastern University Press, pp. 167–176.

Young, R.J.C. (1995) 'Foucault on Race and Colonialism'. *New Formations*, 25: 57–65).

Zamora, D. and Behrent, M.C. (eds) (2016) *Foucault and Neoliberalism*. Cambridge, Polity Press.

Zurn, P. and Dilts, A. (eds) (2016) *Active Intolerance: Michel Foucault, the Prisons Information Group, and the Future of Abolition*. Basingstoke: Palgrave Macmillan.

34 Shulamith Firestone

VICTORIA MARGREE

Chapter guide

This chapter explores Firestone's analysis of women's oppression in her 1970 feminist manifesto, *The Dialectic of Sex*. Section 34.2 introduces the Women's Liberation Movement and its strands of liberal, socialist, and radical feminisms. Firestone's thesis that the origins of women's oppression lie in their procreative capacities is the focus of Section 34.3. Section 34.4 explores her vision of the utopian society that might be created through a feminist revolution in which women seize control of reproductive technologies. Finally, Section 34.5 deepens the argument of the chapter as a whole: that despite the serious flaws of Firestone's book—in particular its treatment of 'race'—it possesses renewed relevance today in relation to 'queer' politics and movements for reproductive justice.

34.1 Introduction

Shulamith Firestone (1945–2012) has helped to extend our conceptualization of the political. Along with other feminists of the 'second-wave' feminist movement, she argued that areas of life previously considered 'private' as opposed to 'public', and as such, as being without political significance, were in fact calling out for political analysis. Such 'private sphere' activities included marriage, housework, and childcare, with feminists arguing that the liberation of women required a radical transformation of these areas of life. But Firestone went even further, contending that the origins of women's oppression lay deeper still, in the very physical differences between the sexes that gave men and women different roles in reproducing the species. As such, Firestone brought concepts such as 'sex' and 'biology' into the field of political thought in a way that was unprecedented for feminist thinkers and political theorists.

This chapter will focus on Firestone's *The Dialectic of Sex: The Case for Feminist Revolution* (Firestone, 2015 [1970]). This is the only book she wrote on feminism and while it was a bestseller upon its release, Firestone withdrew from feminist campaigning shortly thereafter. As such, the *Dialectic* has an unusual status. Though credited with being an inspiration for the emerging second-wave movement and a canonical text of 'radical' feminism, the book's author never returned to its arguments in order to defend them from criticism or to revise them. The result is that her ideas have suffered neglect by subsequent feminists for whom the *Dialectic*'s flaws are exemplary of wider problems with second-wave feminism. More recently, however, Firestone's book has begun to be reclaimed for feminist theory.

This context for the *Dialectic*'s appearance is crucial. Firestone was writing in 1969, on the cusp of a decade that would witness the reawakening of a feminist consciousness not seen since the 'first-wave' feminist movement had culminated in the early twentieth century in the achievement of the vote for women. Inspired by the wider radicalism of 1960s counterculture, feminist radicals such as Firestone believed that an incomplete revolution in gender relations could be reinvigorated, and society transformed root and branch. Firestone's writing is characterized by anger at the oppression of women and other groups but also by optimism about the kind of alternative society that might be created. As such, it is also characterized by a deep utopianism.

The *Dialectic* is a *manifesto*, in the sense of being 'a piece of ephemeral writing drafted in and for a specific historical moment' (Weeks, 2015: 735). It attempts to communicate to mainstream society the urgency of a renewed feminist movement at a time when, as Firestone noted in one of her articles, 'To be called a feminist has become an insult' and young women are 'ashamed to identify in any way with the early women's movement' (Firestone, 1968). It is frequently anecdotal, acerbic and witty. But it is also a work of serious political theory, that draws upon thinkers including Karl Marx (read more about Marx in Chapter 13), Friedrich Engels, Simone de Beauvoir, and Sigmund Freud to build a new framework for feminist analysis. Indeed, I share Kathi Weeks' view that Firestone's significance lies partly in her being one of the first feminists to attempt a 'systematizing theory', capable of analysing not just individual symptoms of women's oppression but the underlying structures that link them (Weeks, 2015: 742). Lastly, though, it is important to remember that the *Dialectic* was conceived not as an abstract exercise in theory but as a contribution to activism. Firestone would have agreed with Marx that the task of the philosopher is not merely to understand the world but to intervene into it.

Read more about **Firestone's** life and work by accessing the thinker biography on the online resources: **www.oup.com/he/Ramgotra-Choat1e**.

34.2 The Women's Liberation Movement

The Women's Liberation Movement (WLM) is the name given to the organized feminist campaigns that took place in the 1960s and 1970s, primarily in the capitalist countries of the Western world. It is often used interchangeably with 'second-wave feminism' and I will adopt that practice here. The WLM emerged in the wake of a post-war period in which middle-class women had been persuaded to re-enter the home after having entered the workforce in unprecedented numbers to support the war effort. By the early 1960s, dissatisfaction with their roles as wives and homemakers was already leading many women to question this state of affairs. Many became part of the hippie, youth, and civil rights movements that opposed traditional values and practices (respect for church and family, sexual monogamy, racial segregation, imperialism, and consumerism). Yet women increasingly discovered that one mainstream value that countercultural movements were less prepared to challenge was sexism, and they left these organizations to form women-only groups. Where first-wave feminism had concentrated upon obtaining legal rights for women (to own property, sign a contract, vote), second-wave feminism extended its reach to the social and cultural ways in which women were attributed inferior status, campaigning against women's sexualization in advertising and beauty contests, for example. While second-wave feminism can be credited with having made possible many advances for women since the 1970s, it is also generally accepted by feminists today that its predominantly middle-class and white membership produced serious limitations in thinking through issues of race and class. We will see evidence of this problem in Firestone's own work.

34.2.1 The personal is political

One of the key insights of the WLM is that 'the personal is political'. This formulation insists that politics is not restricted to activities within government or political parties but is also a character of everyday life. Our daily interactions are also political in that they are conditioned and regulated by wider structural relationships of power. For example, when a husband suffering from a cold receives more care from his wife than he provides when she is sick, this is an *inequality* and it reflects a division of labour (she is considered more responsible for supplying emotional care than he is). That division of labour is not an arrangement that the couple have arrived at independently, however. Instead it reflects a wider gendered division that many feminists argue the capitalist economy depends on: men do paid work to generate profit for an employer; women do unpaid domestic work to look after men's physical and emotional needs, in order that their husbands can labour productively. Feminists of the WLM as such insisted that even the most intimate aspects of our lives could be illuminated by political analysis. Who performed the housework and looked after the kids; how and when a couple had sex; whether or not a woman continued with a pregnancy—all these things called for explanation in terms of concepts such as exploitation, power, and oppression. Firestone (2015 [1970]: 36) herself argued that the contemporary feminist movement was 'the first to combine effectively the "personal" with the "political"'.

The distinctive form that political organization took in the WLM reflected this attention to the personal. While feminists did organize larger-scale events such as public protests and conferences, the key organizational unit was the small, woman-only group (such as those founded by Firestone herself). The small group was thought most conducive to 'consciousness-raising': the activity by which women could confide in each other their dissatisfactions with marriage, motherhood, or work, and through sharing these experiences come to understand their political (rather than simply personal) character. One of the aims of consciousness-raising was to enable women to develop analytical frameworks appropriate to their situations, rather than rely upon ill-fitting theories taken from male-dominated political traditions.

34.2.2 Liberal, socialist, and radical feminisms

That is not to say that these political traditions were ignored. Second-wave feminism can be distinguished into three main strands, two of which explicitly situate themselves within a particular lineage of political theory.

Liberal feminism addressed the situation of women from the perspective of political liberalism, arguing that women had the same right as men to exercise personal freedom without being impeded by unjust laws or authority. John Stuart Mill (see more on Mill in Chapter 12) was a major nineteenth-century liberal feminist, arguing for the removal of the 'legal disabilities' that prevented women from developing their individual faculties and putting these to use in public life (Mill, 1869). In the 1960s, the key representative of liberal feminism was Betty Friedan (see Key Thinker: Betty Friedan box), who helped kick-start the women's movement with her bestselling book, *The Feminine Mystique* (Friedan, 2010 [1963]), and who founded the National Organization for Women (NOW) in 1966. Friedan and other liberal feminists called for women to have equality of opportunity with men, campaigning for laws against unequal pay and discrimination in the workplace. The influence of liberal feminism would diminish in the 1970s, as more radical forms of feminism gained traction. Firestone (2015 [1970]: 25) herself wrote in complimentary terms about Friedan's book, which had 'documented so well' women's 'caged hell'. But she was dismissive of NOW for focusing on 'the more superficial symptoms of sexism', and labelled liberal feminists the 'conservative' feminists (ibid.: 30–31).

Key Thinker: Betty Friedan

Betty Friedan's (1921–2006) *The Feminine Mystique* (2010 [1963]) argued that women across America were suffering from the 'Problem that Has No Name'—a condition of unhappiness that apparently lacked explanation, since according to popular ideology the middle-class American mother and housewife had fulfilled her destiny as a woman. Friedan argued that an explanation in fact lay in the 'feminine mystique'— the myth peddled to women that fulfilment lay in domestic duties and a life restricted to the home. Her answer was for women to find an arena for their untapped talents and ambitions by entering into public life and paid employment (a solution that ignored that many working-class women were already in paid employment—often in the homes of the middle-class women with whom Friedan commiserated). In her campaigning work, Friedan advocated for the Equal Rights Amendment and for abortion law reform, but she was often critical of what she saw as the more extreme wings of second-wave feminism.

Socialist or Marxist feminists argued that while classical Marxism had failed adequately to account for forms of oppression beyond class oppression such as sexism and racism, this was a redeemable failing rather than a fatal flaw in the theoretical apparatus (see, for example, Mitchell, 1966). Socialist feminists thus aimed to bring to Marx and Engels' historical materialist framework an explicitly feminist analysis of women's role in the capitalist system, focusing on women as a reserve labour force in times of shortage (such as wars) and on women's role in *reproducing* the workforce (see Section 34.2.1, 'The personal is political'). Socialist feminism is a revolutionary form of feminism since, unlike liberal feminism, it called for a radical transformation of society's base (economics) and superstructure (laws and institutions), contending that only with capitalism's overthrow would women be free. But Firestone (2015 [1970]: 32) rather provocatively categorized the socialist/leftist feminists of her day with the liberals as 'reformist' as opposed to 'revolutionary' feminists. Her objection was partly that they were too keen to force women's issues into an 'existing leftist analysis and framework' where women's issues would always be marginalized (ibid.: 33). But she also considered that tracing women's oppression even to the economic substratum of society failed to penetrate deeply enough—as we shall shortly see.

Radical feminists typically rejected existing political traditions and sought to build up new theoretical frameworks from the consciousness-raising activity of women's groups (see, for example, Millett, 1970). They were suspicious of liberal feminist calls for legal *equality*, deeming this a project that sought only to argue that women could be like men and that therefore endorsed male-defined standards of behaviour. Instead, many radical feminists were interested in the ways in which women were *different*—physically and psychologically—from men and sought to affirm these supposed distinctively female traits. The very concept of 'patriarchy' is attributable to radical feminists, for whom this described a society governed by men in the interests of men. They helped popularize the term 'oppression' (as opposed to the liberal term 'discrimination') to capture the idea that within patriarchal cultures women were being denied the opportunity to develop their full potentials as human beings. While Firestone is usually identified as a radical feminist, her belonging to this strand is more complicated than might at first appear. As we shall see, in several respects she went against the grain of radical feminist thinking. But she was also unusually open to Marxism (signalled in her book's adoption of the term 'dialectic'), believing that Marx's analysis of economic oppression in relation to production was needed alongside an analysis of women's oppression in relation to reproduction. She is better understood as seeking to subsume socialist feminism within her own highly particular version of radical feminism.

34.2.3 Reproductive rights

A cause around which liberal, socialist, and radical feminists came to unite was that of reproductive autonomy. In 1969, the female oral contraceptive pill was widely available to married women in the USA but it was not legally available to *un*married women, apart from in a handful of states. Abortion was also widely illegal, with just some states having decriminalized it in only the specific cases of incest or endangerment to a woman's life. The consequence was widespread illegal 'backstreet' abortion, from which an estimated 5,000 US women died each year (NARAL: Pro-Choice America, 2015). The legal right to abortion was established only in 1973 through the *Roe v Wade* Supreme Court judgment. Before that, when Firestone was writing, a sexually active woman had few options to protect herself against unwanted pregnancy, and the very real prospect of becoming a 'mother' against her will.

34.2 The Women's Liberation Movement: Key Points

- Firestone was a proponent of the second-wave feminist idea that 'the personal is political'.
- Both liberal feminism and socialist feminism were considered by Firestone to be inadequate responses to the depth of women's oppression.
- Firestone's belonging to radical feminism is complicated by factors including her endorsement of much Marxist theory.

34.3 Reproductive biology and women's oppression

The thesis for which Firestone is famous is that women constitute a class exploited for their reproductive labour. They are *exploited* because, denied the ability to control their reproductive capacities (through contraception or abortion) they are made to take on the physical and social burdens of childbearing, while their inferior social position also means that they are denied many of the economic and cultural benefits produced on the back of their work. Firestone thus sees gender inequality as being rooted in the physical differences between the sexes: the fact that it is women and not men who become pregnant and give birth. She claims that liberating women from oppression therefore requires 'changing a fundamental biological condition' (Firestone, 2015 [1970]: 3)—the facts of human procreation.

34.3.1 A historical materialism rooted in sex

Part of Firestone's argument is thus an historical one about how male domination first arose and took hold in human societies. In early human history, she believes, 'before the advent of birth control', women 'were at the continual mercy of their biology' (ibid.: 9). Females from the age of menarche to menopause were subject to an endless cycle of pregnancy, 'painful childbirth, wetnursing and care of infants' (ibid.: 9). This led inevitably to women's diminished participation in other areas of social life, including the important realm of productive labour. As such, they were dependent upon men for the provision of the necessities of life: food, shelter, clothing, etc. According to Firestone, this natural division of labour between the sexes led directly to a system of domination. Men enjoyed their power, Firestone postulates, and went on to reinforce it through social customs and laws that further disempowered women. Firestone termed this the 'sex class' system (see Key Concept: Sex class box). It was the original oppression within human history, and from it sprang further oppressions in the form of the creation of economic classes, castes, and 'race'.

Key Concept: Sex class

Firestone (2015 [1970]: 3) opens the *Dialectic* with the claim that 'Sex class is so deep as to be invisible.' She is adapting Marx's idea that outside of communist societies people are distributed into economic classes in which a ruling class that owns the means of production (e.g. bourgeois factory owners in the nineteenth century) exploits an oppressed class (e.g. the proletariat) by siphoning off the value produced by their labour. Marx saw the struggle that arises between classes as being the driving force of history. Firestone's innovation is to argue that before there were economic classes, women were already a class that was being exploited for its—reproductive—labour. But, for Firestone, because *this* class antagonism is in a sense natural and as such, is to be found *everywhere*, it has usually escaped recognition within political theory.

Firestone, as such, departs from Friedrich Engels' account of women's oppression in his *Origins of the Family, Private Property and the State* (Engels, 1884). Engels had argued that the earliest human groupings had been characterized by a primitive form of communism in which there was collective ownership of goods and equality between the sexes. Engels thought it was only when private property emerged that the patriarchal family appeared: to be sure of passing down their property to their biological heirs, men needed to control women's sexuality and enforce on them a rigid monogamy. This Engels called the 'world historical defeat of the female sex'. Many socialist feminists had taken succour from this account because it posited an historical *origin* to women's oppression and indicated that male domination would be overcome once private property was abolished. But Firestone rejects this. In common with other radical feminists, she believed that the oppression of women was a phenomenon that had existed in all societies for all time.

Firestone did, however, locate her aetiology (causal explanation) of women's oppression within Marx and Engels' historical materialist method. A Marxist account of history is materialist in the sense that it begins with the physical conditions within which human beings produce the means of sustaining life: how they generate food and shelter, for example. But Firestone argues that the Marxist focus upon production obscures the equally important role of reproduction: the conditions in which the human species replenishes itself through pregnancy, childbirth, and the care of infants. Firestone is arguing that in order to be fully materialist, analysis must enquire into the making of human beings themselves. She argues that had Engels pursued his analysis more deeply, he would have seen that this biological division of labour (women undergo pregnancy, men do not) already established an unequal power relationship even before private property emerged.

One frequent objection to Firestone is that her analysis is *dehistoricizing*: that in insisting that all human societies have been patriarchal, she misses the varied ways in which different societies have organized gender relations. Firestone herself would insist that hers is the only properly *historicizing* account, since it is the only one that identifies changes in reproduction (increasing human control over fertility) as being as central to historical change as Marx and Engels recognized changes in productive forces to be. It is certainly the case that while Firestone holds that all societies have been patriarchal, she does not hold that they have all been patriarchal *in the same way* (she recognizes the existence of matriarchies, for example, but considers these as giving symbolic prestige to the 'Female Principle' [Firestone, 2015 [1970]: 159] while largely maintaining male control over women). She also holds that the form that the family (the unit of reproduction) takes is something that changes historically. Whether this is sufficient to refute the criticism is something for readers to consider.

34.3.2 Natural oppression

In locating the origins of women's oppression in the facts of biology, Firestone was venturing into territory where most feminists feared to tread. It might seem to be conceding an anti-feminist argument—think how frequently gender inequalities are justified even today by claims that women are the natural homemakers or men are biologically more suited to succeed in certain jobs (typically the better paid ones). Indeed, for Firestone, the oppression of females really is in one sense natural. For her, that we have no examples of genuinely sexually egalitarian societies means that we are forced to conclude that the problem originates in something deeper than phenomena such as laws (cf. liberal feminism) or economics (cf. socialist feminism). Evidence lies even with the animal kingdom, she thinks: 'Anyone observing animals mating, reproducing, and caring for their young will have a hard time accepting the "cultural relativity" line' (ibid.: 9). Noting that 'feminists have to question . . . even the very organization of nature' she acknowledges that 'Many women give up in despair' (ibid.: 4).

But, for Firestone, despair is not warranted, because while natural conditions help *explain* women's oppression, they do not *justify* it or establish it as needing to continue (see also Sandford, 2010).

'To grant that the sexual imbalance of power is biologically based is not to lose our case', she writes, since 'We are no longer just animals. And the kingdom of nature does not reign absolute' (Firestone, 2015 [1970]: 10). Firestone is adopting from Marx and Simone de Beauvoir an anti-naturalist position (see Key Concept: Anti-naturalism box), according to which nature is neither intrinsically good nor unchangeable. Human beings have the distinctive capacity to use science to change natural facts to suit their own ends, she believes, so if women's oppression is rooted in natural conditions, we can use technology to transform those conditions.

> **Key Concept: Anti-naturalism**
>
> There is an anti-naturalist strain in Marxist thought, with Marx stressing that human beings transform the natural environment and their own natures through their labour. Firestone herself quotes affirmatively from Beauvoir, who claims that 'Human society is an antiphysis—in a sense it is against nature; it does not passively submit to the presence of nature but rather takes over the control of nature on its own behalf' (Beauvoir, quoted in Firestone, 2015 [1970]: 10). Xenofeminism (XF) is a twenty-first-century feminist movement that is also committed to anti-naturalism and to 'hacking' technologies in order to overcome any inequalities rooted in nature. One of its proponents, Helen Hester, explicitly acknowledges Firestone's influence. She writes: 'XF is an anti-naturalist endeavour in the sense that it frames nature and the natural as a space for contestation—that is, as within the purview of politics' (Hester, 2018: 19).

Nonetheless, Firestone's identification of the origins of women's oppression in nature or biology has been highly controversial. Indeed, she has been accused of biological determinism—of crudely reducing complex human social arrangements to biological conditions and without recognizing the role played by human agency (see, for example, Barrett, 1988; Haraway, 1991). I would argue, however, that she is better understood as offering a deterministic account only in her discussion of the earliest stages of human history, before human beings had an understanding of the causes of pregnancy or the means to do much to prevent it. What is often missed by Firestone's critics is her repeated insistence that 'the oppressive power structures set up by nature' are 'reinforced by man' (Firestone, 2015 [1970]: 15). Human agency re-enters the picture then with the cultural, legal, and economic fortifications by which men entrench women's dependence upon them (for example, nineteenth-century laws which prohibited married women from owning property). Indeed, I think Firestone can be interpreted as holding that as human technological control of fertility increases, the balance of contribution to upholding male supremacy shifts from biological to social factors. Women's oppression is not *simply* natural then; it is also culturally reinforced.

34.3.3 Pregnancy and childbirth

'*Pregnancy is barbaric*' writes Firestone (ibid.: 180, 181), and childbirth like 'shitting a pumpkin'. It becomes clear that her objection to female reproductive processes is not only to the limitations she sees these as imposing on women's ability to do other things, but also to the physical processes themselves. Clearly discernible here is the influence of Beauvoir (see Key Thinker: Simone de Beauvoir), who had depicted pregnancy as an alienating experience in which a woman is drained of strength and vitality by an invading parasitical being. Beauvoir saw women's reproductive biologies as making them 'the victim of the species' (Beauvoir, 1997: 52) in that the painful burdens of pregnancy and childbirth, while necessary for the continuation of the species, came at the cost of women achieving their individual ambitions. When Firestone (2015 [1970]: 180) writes that 'pregnancy is the temporary deformation of the body of the individual for the sake of the species', she is undoubtedly echoing Beauvoir.

> ### Key Thinker: Simone de Beauvoir
>
> Simone de Beauvoir (1908–1986) was born in Paris, France. She studied at the prestigious École Normale Supérieure where she met Jean-Paul Sartre, the existentialist philosopher who would become her lifelong friend and intellectual collaborator. A prolific writer, Beauvoir is nonetheless most famous for *The Second Sex* (1945; translated 1953), which is credited with being a major inspiration for second-wave feminism. The book explored the situation of women through the framework of existentialism, with Beauvoir arguing that in order to flee the existential anguish of recognizing their true freedom, women accepted their cultural conditioning as significant only in their relationships to men (wives, girlfriends, mothers, etc). But she argued that women could refuse their secondary status and assert themselves as agents. Firestone (2015 [1970]: 7) applauds Beauvoir for being 'the one who came close to . . . the definitive analysis' of women's condition. But where Beauvoir denied that women's physical embodiment played a causal role in their oppression, Firestone, as we have seen, contended that it did.

Firestone's negative view of gestation put her at odds with other radical feminists, many of whom were celebrating female procreative capacities as the '*basis of women's powers*' (Alpert, 1974: 7). It has also opened Firestone up to charges of internalized misogyny. According to this criticism, she is viewing female bodies through a patriarchal lens, and as such can see their differences from male bodies only in terms of deviancy. Indeed, Elizabeth Spelman sees Firestone's book as evincing 'somatophobia', or fear of and disdain for the body. Spelman (1988: 130) argues that both Firestone and Beauvoir have been so anxious to sever a misogynistic philosophical association of women with the body and nature (viewed as inferior to 'male' mind and culture) that they 'think and write . . . as if we would be better off if we were not embodied'.

So is Firestone guilty of somatophobia? Or is there some justice in characterizing the processes of reproduction as she does? These questions lack easy answers. But what might be said for Firestone is that she is drawing attention to the persistent reality that reproductive labour really does involve significant costs. These include the potential physical harms of pregnancy and childbirth, as well as psychological harms such as birth trauma and post-natal depression. The mechanics of gestation in the human species have evolved in such a way as to be unusually destructive. Even today, tens of thousands of women die in childbirth each year. Firestone's treatment of gestation is certainly one-sided and negative. Yet perhaps there is also value in her foregrounding of what Sophie Lewis (2019: 1) has called 'pregnancy's morbidity, the little-discussed ways that, biologically speaking, gestating is an unconscionably destructive business'. Firestone brings biological reproduction into the purview of political theory, and in so doing also makes it visible as what Lewis (ibid.: 9) calls 'work under capitalism'.

34.3 Reproductive biology and women's oppression: Key Points

- Firestone called for a materialist account of history that would start with procreation, to analyse how a sex class system with its origins in biological conditions became reinforced socially.
- The natural origins of women's oppression were not considered by Firestone a reason for despair, since human beings can change nature through technology.
- Firestone's account of women's oppression has been criticized for being dehistoricizing, for biological determinism, and for somatophobia.

34.4 Reproductive technology and feminist revolution

Firestone's solution to women's oppression is a revolution in which both capitalism and patriarchy are overthrown. Returning to Marx, she argues that 'just as to assure elimination of economic classes requires the revolt of the underclass (the proletariat) and . . . their seizure of the means of *production*, so to assure the elimination of sexual classes requires the revolt of the underclass (women) and the seizure of control of *reproduction*' (Firestone, 2015 [1970]: 11). This would clear the way for a post-revolutionary society characterized by a 'cybernetic communism' (ibid.: 213) in which people's material needs would be met regardless of their ability to participate in work. Indeed, alienated labour—Marx's term for toil under capitalist conditions—would have been abolished. Firestone believed that developments in computing would soon make it possible for boring, dangerous, or physically arduous work to be taken over by machines, freeing human beings to perform only 'work' that had personal value (e.g. artistic creation). Similarly, women's alienated reproductive labour would disappear through the humane deployment of technologies of human fertility.

Firestone believed that revolution was possible at this moment in human history because technology (see Key Concept: Technology) had developed sufficiently to free human beings from natural constraints. She held that reproductive technologies had nearly reached the point where women could have full control over their reproductive capacities and the problem of female dependence on men could thus be eliminated. These included the existing technologies of contraception, abortion, sterilization and artificial insemination, and technologies 'just around the corner' such as sex-selection and 'test-tube fertilization' (ibid.: 179). But the problem was that these were currently being controlled by men (doctors and politicians) who would not willingly give up this control. Firestone has sometimes been accused of technological determinism—of assuming that technological development will inevitably unfold in such a way as to solve the problem of gender oppression (see, for example, O'Brien, 1981). In my view and that of several others, however, this is a misreading (see also Bassett, 2010; Franklin, 2010; Paasonen, 2010). It is clear that Firestone thinks feminist agency is required: women themselves must wrest control of reproductive technology from the patriarchal establishment in order to liberate its progressive potential.

> **Key Concept: Technology**
>
> Firestone's attitude towards technology is unusual for feminists of the second wave. Many radical feminists saw technology as a masculine endeavour to gain mastery over a natural world that feminists ought to be celebrating. We have already seen that Firestone rejects such a view of nature. By 'technology', she means the 'accumulation of skills for controlling the environment' (Firestone, 2015 [1970]: 155). Intrinsically, technology is 'liberating' (ibid.: 179) because it allows us to intervene into any natural conditions that constrain human freedom or equality. She recognizes that technology is frequently put to oppressive use (her key example is the atomic bomb) but claims this is a consequence of how technology becomes *mis*used within patriarchal cultures. Firestone's pro-technology position can be seen as anticipating cyberfeminism (see Halbert, 2004), and it is another influence on Xenofeminism.

The prospect eventually of entirely 'artificial reproduction'—gestation in artificial wombs—was welcomed by Firestone (2015 [1970]: 181) as offering not merely the amelioration of women's role as gestators but its elimination. It should be noted that she proposed this only as an *option* for individuals. But it is a proposal that has nonetheless led to frequent derision. In the 1970s it appeared to many readers to be fantastical speculation that tipped the *Dialectic* into the genre of science fiction rather than serious political analysis. Today, however, with the increasing likelihood of *ectogenesis* (extra-uterine development of embryos) becoming scientific reality, Firestone's speculations start to look both prescient and pertinent. If extra-uterine reproduction were to become possible, would this be to women's benefit? One obvious objection is that people may not want pregnancy and childbirth abolished. Many women describe these as positive experiences (fulfilment in pregnancy, ecstatic births) or at least as neutral ones. The question about somatophobia resurfaces here. Is Firestone's proposal for artificial reproduction a good solution to the 'problem of pregnancy' (Lewis, 2019: 1)—the aforementioned destructiveness of gestation to gestators? Or is it the most extreme expression of her desire to flee from (female) embodiment?

Firestone can also be criticized for a myopic focus on white women's experiences of reproduction and reproductive technologies. As Shatema Threadcraft (2016: 2) has pointed out, 1970s feminists who protested the forced exploitation of women's reproductive capacities often failed to recognize how this 'diverged sharply along racial lines', with reproduction being encouraged for (wealthy) white women but repressed in women of colour. Firestone makes only passing reference to the state-sponsored targeting of African-American women for involuntary sterilization that was ongoing when she wrote. Involuntary or non-consensual sterilization to control reproduction by the state is referred to as eugenics. Over the latter part of the nineteenth century and well into the twentieth, many Black, Latino, Native American, and disabled women were forcibly sterilized to control the reproduction of these populations. This was often and falsely justified on the grounds that these women were mentally unfit, feeble-minded, sexually promiscuous, or their gene pool was weak. While Firestone would undoubtedly consider this an instance of technology being abused, her inattention to this practice and its eugenicist history associates her with the white birth control campaigners whom Angela Davis (2019 [1981]: 194) criticized for failing to enquire into the reasons for 'their Black sister's . . . suspicion toward their cause' (read more about Davis in Chapter 35).

34.4.1 Abolishing the family

Firestone saw the technological mediation of reproduction as making possible the abolition of the *biological* family. Many feminists of the period wanted to disband the *nuclear* family (see Key Concept: The nuclear family), seeing this as one of the chief sites of women's oppression. But Firestone wanted to go further, and render obsolete the very biological unit of male sperm-giver, female egg and womb-provider and genetic offspring. For Firestone, where the biological family had necessarily (until now) been a constant in human history, the particular social form that the family had taken had varied, with the patriarchal nuclear family being only a relatively recent form. She held that the socialist revolutions of the twentieth century had failed to deliver gender equality because they had transformed economic relationships alone and had not reached down into the fabric of the family, to destroy the 'tapeworm of exploitation' itself (Firestone, 2015 [1970]: 12).

> **Key Concept: The nuclear family**
>
> The 'nuclear family' refers to the unit of husband, wife, and dependent children. In the 1960s, the husband was likely to be sole or primary breadwinner and considered authoritative head of the family. Where the nuclear family is typically a central value of conservative political discourse, it has long been an object of critique for the left. Marx and Engels considered it a central mechanism for the perpetuation of class society since it ensured the inheritance of private wealth. They understood the bourgeois family of their own time to be an economic unit shrouded in sentimentalizing ideology, in which women were forced to sell their sexual and reproductive services in return for a living. Marxist and radical feminists saw the nuclear family as institutionalizing women's oppression and looked forward to its overthrow.

In her critique of the family, Firestone draws upon Sigmund Freud (see Key Thinker: Sigmund Freud), transforming his account of the Oedipus complex. Freud had claimed that a young boy forms an affectionate and erotic attachment to his mother which leads him to perceive his father as a rival. The boy eventually breaks this attachment in order to avoid paternal punishment, which he typically understands would take the form of removal of his penis—his 'castration complex'. Firestone (2015 [1970]: 44) rewrites this scenario in a way that reads it as a response to the 'hierarchy of power' within the family. The boy represses his love for his mother and hostility towards his father because he recognizes that while currently he shares his mother's powerlessness, his father is offering him an eventual place in the privileged world of the male—'the exciting world of "travel and adventure"' (ibid.: 47). The girl also desires access to this world, but knowing that it is denied to her, envies her brother's privilege (Firestone's rewriting of Freud's 'penis envy') and adopts 'servility and wiles' (ibid.: 49) in her attitude towards her father.

Key Thinker: Sigmund Freud

The founder of psychoanalysis, Sigmund Freud (1856–1939) believed that erotic life began in early infancy ('infantile sexuality') before becoming subject to various repressions. As adults, many of our sexual wishes exist in our 'unconscious' minds, becoming expressed only in disguised forms in dreams and neurotic symptoms. Freud's work includes many notorious pronouncements about women: for example, that women unconsciously wish they had a penis, and that they form a weaker 'superego' (ethical faculty) than do men. Freud was thus for a long time rejected as an enemy of feminism. Firestone is one of the earliest feminists to take his work seriously, arguing that Freudianism and feminism agree in recognizing the fundamental importance to human life of sex (although Firestone's reading of Freud is reductive—see Margree, 2018). Subsequent thinkers have also tried to rid Freudianism of its elements of sexism (and racism and heteronormativity) in order to harness its radical potential.

Firestone (2015 [1970]: 98) thus reads Freud as offering an invaluable *metaphorical* account of how the 'power hierarchy' of the family shapes children's minds, 'creat[ing] the psychology of sexism'. It forms boys and men who are psychologically deformed by having to sacrifice loving identifications with women in order to ascend to their position of supremacy, and girls and women whose potential is repressed by coerced submissiveness. She even argues that the power dynamics of the nuclear family provide a way of understanding the 'psychology of racism' (ibid.: 98) and its equivalent deformations.

34.4.2 The 'racial family'

Firestone's account of racism has been widely denounced. Using her rewriting of Freud's Oedipal drama she attempts to show that Black men in America are in the position of the male child, torn between identification with the powerless white Mother and an urge to degrade her in their rivalry for patriarchal status with the white Father; while Black women are relegated to the position of either 'traditional passive female' or 'Whore' (ibid.: 110, 104). As critics have observed, Firestone thereby repeats racist stereotypes of African-American men as constituting a sexual threat to white women (Davis, 2019 [1991]: 163), while denying African-American women political agency (Spillers, 2003). This is all the more egregious, Spillers (ibid.: 159) observes, given that 'Firestone addresses black women's issues in a single chapter', meaning that 'everywhere else in the book, "woman" . . . does not mean *them*'.

The failures of Firestone's attempt to address racism proceed in part from her insistence that sexism is *causative* of racism. '*Racism is sexism extended*' (Firestone, 2015 [1970]: 97)—an extension of exploitation by groups of men who have come to love dominating others. Racism in white women is 'an inauthentic form of racism' since 'it arises from a false class consciousness' in which white women misguidedly identify 'their own interests with those of their men' (ibid.: 99)—a claim that looks suspiciously like an attempt to exculpate white women of responsibility for their own racism. In making the pathologies of the family her model for understanding US race relations, Firestone entirely neglects to situate racism as an ongoing legacy of the plantation slavery upon which the American economic and political system was built (in contrast, see the much more nuanced accounts of racism and the family offered by bell hooks (2015)—see more on bell hooks in Chapter 3). Arguably, insisting on 'sex class' as the glue of a systematizing theory leads Firestone to gravely distort the character of other oppressions. But Firestone's inadequate treatment of racism is also symptomatic of a wider problem evident across second-wave feminisms (liberal, Marxist, and radical). The white and middle-class feminists who often dominated the movement frequently failed to recognize sufficiently the overlapping oppressions faced by women of colour, and in effect excluded them from the category 'woman' even as this was being mobilized as a supposedly *unifying* political identity.

34.4.3 The household

Firestone's alternative for how children might be raised is a form of collective parenting called the 'household'. A group of adults who wished to be involved in child-rearing would contract to live together for a limited period of time. The children may or may not be genetically related to any of the adults. Firestone imagines that with the technological transformation of reproduction (potentially including artificial wombs), the biological connectedness of children to adults would cease to have the significance we accord it today. The work of caring for the young would be shared by men and women alike, and parenting would be opened up as a possibility to older people and those who cannot biologically have children. Key to Firestone's vision is that the cultural imperative to have children would have disappeared. She envisages households as existing alongside other arrangements for adults who don't wish to be involved in child-rearing (single professional life and 'living together') and these would be equally valued by society. Within the household, she believes, reproduction would be transformed: for women, by eliminating its physical burden and associated dependencies; for men, by allowing the development of previously repressed emotional qualities such as the capacity to nurture; and for children, by enabling freedom and independence.

34.4.4 Children's oppression

Indeed, a significant contribution of Firestone to political theory is her contention that in patriarchal societies children, as well as women, are oppressed. She believes that the power hierarchy of the traditional family also involves the domination of children, which takes the form of an artificial extension of their dependency upon adults. Citing historical research that shows that the concept of 'childhood' is relatively recent—children in the medieval period had been considered apprentice adults—Firestone proposes that children are actually capable of much more than our current ideas about them allow. Presently, she thinks, 'parental satisfaction is obtainable only through crippling the child' (Firestone, 2015 [1970]: 205). This is a result of 'ego investments' (ibid.: 206) that parents make in 'their' children as the biological extensions of themselves. For men, she thinks, a child is an opportunity for 'the "immortalizing" of name, property, class, and ethnic identification'. For women, motherhood provides 'the justification of [their] existence' in a society that otherwise devalues them (ibid.: 205). Both men and women are thus supplied with a powerful motivation to maintain children in a condition of dependence.

Within the household, in contrast, children would be accorded unprecedented rights—including the right to opt out of a household if they were unhappy. Firestone (ibid.: 213) proposes that non-compulsory education guided by a child's own interests would replace the current system of schooling, which actually represses children's spontaneous curiosity in its focus upon producing 'the average bland adult' needed by capitalism. Children would form relationships with the various adult members of the household according to their preferences. Firestone also proposes that what she considers the sexual feelings of children, repressed within the nuclear family, could be expressed to whatever degree the child was ready. Disturbingly, this leads her to propose that sexual relationships between adults and children might become possible. While it is clear that Firestone envisages these as loving and non-abusive, her blindness to the dangers of adult sexual predation is concerning.

> ### 34.4 Reproductive technology and feminist revolution: Key Points
>
> - For Firestone, feminist revolution requires that both patriarchy and capitalism are overthrown.
> - Key to achieving this are modern reproductive technologies, which enable the biological family to be transcended.
> - Firestone's deeply flawed discussion of racism indicates a wider problem of racialized exclusion within second-wave feminist theory.
> - Within the 'household', women would be liberated from the burdens of child-bearing; child-rearing shared equally with men; and children emancipated from their own oppression.

34.5 Sexual and reproductive politics in the twenty-first century

After the 1970s, *The Dialectic of Sex* entered into a period of 'active repudiation' (Weeks, 2015: 741). From the perspective of a third-wave feminism that became increasingly poststructuralist and/or intersectional, Firestone's deployment of the singular, unproblematized term 'woman' was unacceptable. The very attempt to produce 'systematizing theory' (ibid.: 742) was seen as theoretical overreach that contributed to over-generalizations and distortions in Firestone's analyses. The *Dialectic* became considered exemplary of the worst excesses of second-wave feminism, including biological determinism, somatophobia, technological determinism, and a blindness to the experiences of women of colour. Readers will have seen that I believe some of these criticisms hit their target, while others are less justified. More importantly, I hope you will interrogate Firestone and reach your own conclusions.

Since about the 2010s, however, there has been a resurgence of interest in Firestone. In Section 34.5.1, I will focus on two ways in which her significance as a political theorist is increasingly becoming clear.

34.5.1 Queering sex and gender

Firestone's ideas about transforming sexuality and gender are becoming acknowledged for their radicalism. Lisa Downing (2018), for example, has proposed that Firestone be considered a 'proto-queer theorist'. 'Queer theory' refers to a body of work inaugurated in the 1990s that saw sexuality as a fundamentally destabilizing force that productively unsettled identities such as 'man', 'woman', 'gay', or 'straight'. The basis for such a view is to be found in Firestone's belief that with the elimination of the sex class system, 'genital differences between human beings would no longer matter culturally'. There would be a 'reversion to an unobstructed *pansexuality*— Freud's "polymorphous perversity"' (Firestone, 2015 [1970] : 11) (see Key Concept: Polymorphous perversity).

> **Key Concept: Polymorphous perversity**
>
> Contrary to the dominant view that sexuality appeared only at puberty, Freud believed that even very small babies were capable of a physical, sensuous pleasure that should be recognized as the first manifestation of the human sexual instinct. 'Infantile sexuality' was 'polymorphous' (taking many forms) because it focused not initially upon the genitals but upon the parts of a child's body that would be stimulated through breastfeeding and toileting: the mouth and the anus particularly. It was 'perverse' only from the perspective of so-called 'normal' adult sexuality, in which the capacity for experiencing pleasure beyond the organs involved in heterosexual, reproductive sex had been repressed. Importantly for Firestone's affirmation of pansexuality, the polymorphously perverse child forms erotic attachments to males and females indiscriminately (Freud's 'original bisexuality' idea).

Firestone holds that among patriarchy's distortions of our emotional and psychological lives is the deformation of sexuality. We are conditioned to rigidly separate out sexual from affectionate feeling—which in men results in a need to degrade a woman in order to experience sexual desire for her. But with the abolition of the patriarchal family and its associated sexual repressions, the conditions would be in place for a 'free sexuality' in which all affectionate relationships would include physical intimacy to some degree (Firestone, 2015 [1970]: 215). Monogamy would fall by the wayside, but so too 'would probably . . . hetero/homo/bi-sexuality' because we would fall in love with persons and not body parts and feel no need to categorize our desires. Indeed, Firestone (ibid.: 11) holds that 'the end goal of feminist revolution must be . . . not just the elimination of male *privilege* but of the sex distinction itself'. There would still be anatomical differences between people, but these would cease to predict anything about what individuals might be like.

Firestone's pronouncements on sexuality and gender combine radical with more regressive aspects. She understands heterosexuality as a regime maintained only by societal enforcements. But elements of homophobia appear in her thoughtlessly disparaging comments about male homosexuals, and female same-sex relations are rendered invisible. More positively, her vision of a post-gender world seems to anticipate the challenges to binary gender that we are witnessing today, where a 'gender fluid generation' is increasingly at ease with identifications such as agender, multigender, queer trans, transfeminine and transmasculine (although we should note that Firestone emphasizes androgyny—possibly about homogenization rather than proliferation of genders). A case may even be made for Firestone as a trans-positive radical feminist, in a context where many second-wave radical feminists have become trans-exclusionary. There is no acknowledgement of trans people in the *Dialectic*, and Firestone never questions her equivalence of 'women' with persons with a womb. But her insistence on the irrelevance of the genitalia you are born with to the person that you (could) become anticipates some (though not all) strands of transfeminist thought (see Hester, 2018).

34.5.2 Reproductive politics

Arguably, what Firestone had insisted was the class exploitation of women for their reproductive capacities continues today, and even those limited increases in reproductive autonomy won by 1970s feminism are under assault, from defunding of women's healthcare provision and a push-back against abortion rights (in the USA, Poland, and Nicaragua, for example). At the same time, however, radical movements are increasingly putting reproduction at the forefront of politics.

One example is Social Reproduction Theory (SRT), a recent re-articulation of Marxist feminism. SRT holds that labour towards the 'making of people'—childbearing and other caring duties within the family—is increasing under neoliberalism, which requires 'more hours of waged work per household' while 'withdrawing state support for social welfare' (Fraser et al, 2018: 121, 122). Firestone is not, to my knowledge, cited as an influence by Social Reproduction Theorists, but there are clear connections with her own insistence that childbearing is work exploited under capitalism, and that the spheres of reproduction and production cannot be separated.

The Reproductive Justice framework is an initiative originated in 1994 by a group of African-American women which campaigns for reproductive autonomy. Its emphasis on 'justice' foregrounds a situation of unequal access to maternal healthcare, in which women of colour and women from poorer backgrounds have often been materially prevented from making use of their legal rights to contraception and abortion (many states have so few abortion clinics, for example, that the cost of travelling to one is prohibitive). However, while organizations such as SisterSong lobby for the right to end an unwanted pregnancy, they also insist that reproductive justice means having access to the material provisions needed to continue a wanted pregnancy and to 'parent the children we have in safe and sustainable communities' (SisterSong, n.d.). The Reproductive Justice framework is a legacy of the activism of Black feminists in the 1970s, who organized around the specific issues that 'patriarchal control of reproduction' presented to African Americans, and who 'are the reason we refer to a "reproductive-rights" and not simply an "abortion-rights" movement' (Threadcraft, 2016: 2, 5). Many African-American women in the 1970s were actually fighting for the right to a family life in the face of attempts to limit Black fertility. The failure of Firestone among other white feminists to recognize this constitutes another instance of the race-blindness of much second-wave feminism.

Yet at the same time there is a way in which Firestone's work dovetails with the Reproductive Justice framework and its demands. As we have seen, what she was agitating for was precisely that childbearing and child-raising be transformed so that their oppressive elements would be removed, and she was insistent that this could only be achieved through meeting the material needs of children and care-givers—regardless of the latter's capacity to participate in paid employment. If Firestone's work is marred by race-blindness and even unwitting racism, is there nonetheless a way in which certain of its coordinates might be repurposed for a feminism that centres reproduction while being explicitly intersectional and anti-racist?

> ### 34.5 Sexual and reproductive politics in the twenty-first century: Key Points
>
> - The *Dialectic* can be read as providing support for queer politics, gender abolitionism, and transfeminism.
> - Social Reproduction Theory and the Reproductive Justice framework both politicize reproduction (biological and social) in ways that connect with Firestone's ideas.

34.6 Conclusion

Firestone's significance is to have extended the purview of 'politics' to include the family, childhood, and the organization of human reproductive biology ('sex'). She helped shift the framework of feminist analysis away from liberal feminism towards a structural analysis capable of showing that patriarchy and capitalism were interlocking systems that deformed the lives of women, children, and men. The utopianism of her thought led for a long time to its dismissal as impractical or absurd. Yet it is perhaps precisely this that gives it its greatest interest today (see also Weeks, 2015). Firestone was offering her proposals for a post-revolutionary society tentatively, in the spirit of thought experiments designed to challenge us to think beyond existing social, political, and economic arrangements—to dare to imagine that a better society might be possible.

The automation of work and the transformation of biological reproduction through technology are around us today. That these may have brought with them undesirable consequences (making supermarket workers redundant; exploitative IVF and surrogacy industries) is not necessarily a point against Firestone—she had always insisted this would be the case for as long as such technologies operated under conditions of patriarchal capitalism. Her work prompts us to imagine what could be the case if technology were mobilized instead to extend human freedom and equality. What if capitalist technologies that strip the planet of its resources were to be supplanted with green technologies directed towards sustainable living? (Firestone [2015 [1970]: 176] claimed that 'a revolutionary ecological movement would have the same aim as the feminist movement: control of the new technology for humane purposes'.) If the automation of jobs is going to increase unemployment, should the material needs of everyone be met through a universal basic income? Should we start planning for a post-work world? If biomedical technologies are making the apparent sex of the body you are born with less significant, how might we reconceive identities? Might we be able to reimagine love and care beyond the genetic family? These are questions that Firestone asked in 1970. Arguably they are more relevant, not less, in the twenty-first century.

Take your learning further by accessing the online resources for a library of web links to relevant videos, articles, blogs, and useful websites for this chapter: www.oup.com/he/Ramgotra-Choat1e.

Study questions

1. What is Firestone's argument about the biological origins of women's oppression and is it plausible?
2. Analyse how Firestone adopts and adapts Marxist theory.
3. In what respects is Firestone's thought both typical and atypical of radical feminism?
4. Would a society in which children are born through artificial wombs be utopian or dystopian?
5. Evaluate Firestone's claim that the family is an oppressive institution.
6. Evaluate Firestone's claim that children are oppressed.
7. What, if any, are the problems with Firestone's treatment of racism?
8. Analyse how Firestone's ideas might contribute to LGBTQ politics.

Further reading

Primary sources

Firestone, S. (1998) *Airless Spaces*. South Pasadena, CA: Semiotext(e).
Firestone's second and final book is little known. A series of sketches of lost souls in New York, it becomes increasingly apparent that at least some of the stories are autobiographical.

Firestone, S. (2015 [1970]) *The Dialectic of Sex: The Case for Feminist Revolution*. London: Verso.
Firestone's famous 1970 manifesto and her only book-length publication on feminist theory.

Secondary sources

Downing, L. (2018) 'Antisocial Feminism? Shulamith Firestone, Monique Wittig and Proto-Queer Theory'. *Paragraph*, 41(3): 364–379.
Argues for Firestone as a 'significant precursor' of queer theory.

Grogan, K. (2015) 'Love Unimpeded: *The Dialectic of Sex* Revisited'. *Oxonian Review*, 28(4). Available at: http://www.oxonianreview.org/wp/love-unimpeded-the-dialectic-of-sex-revisited/
Thoughtful reconsideration of Firestone that focuses on her often neglected discussion of human love.

Halbert, D. (2004) 'Shulamith Firestone: Radical Feminism and Visions of the Information Society'. *Information, Communication and Society*, 7(1): 115–135.
An astute discussion of Firestone's significance in the Internet age: locates Firestone as an inspiration for cyberfeminism and compares her thought with Donna Haraway's cyborg theory.

Hester, H. (2018) *Xenofeminism*. Cambridge: Polity.
Hester's articulation of Xenofeminism explicitly situates Firestone's influence on her own brands of technomaterialism, anti-naturalism, and gender-abolitionism.

Lane-McKinley, M. (2019) '*The Dialectic of Sex*, After the Post-1960s'. *Cultural Politics*, 15(3): 331–342.
Explores the resources in the *Dialectic* for a trans-positive feminism, and argues for it as resonating with the critical utopianism of 1970s' queer feminist science fiction.

Margree, V. (2018) *Neglected or Misunderstood: The Radical Feminism of Shulamith Firestone*. Washington, DC: Zero Books.
Accessible introduction to Firestone that calls for critical re-engagement. Final two chapters explore twenty-first-century reproductive issues, including IVF, egg-freezing, surrogacy, and feticide laws.

Merck, M., and Sandford, S. (eds) (2010) *Further Adventures of the Dialectic of Sex: Critical Essays on Shulamith Firestone*. New York: Palgrave Macmillan.
A landmark publication in the rediscovery of Firestone; contains specially commissioned critical reflections on Firestone's ideas.

Threadcraft, S. (2016) *Intimate Justice: The Black Female Body and the Body Politic*. Oxford: Oxford University Press.
Doesn't reference Firestone, but an important study of the history of racialized control of reproduction that Firestone marginalizes, and its consequences for political theory.

Weeks, K. (2015) 'The Vanishing Dialectic: Shulamith Firestone and the Future of the Feminist 1970s'. *The South Atlantic Quarterly*, 114(4): 735–754.
Impressive discussion of the *Dialectic* as participating in the genre of utopian manifesto.

References

Alpert, J. (1974) *Mother Right: A New Feminist Theory*. Pittsburgh, PA: Know, Inc. Available at: https://cdm15957.contentdm.oclc.org/digital/collection/p15957coll6/id/669

Barrett, M. (1988) *Women's Oppression Today: The Marxist/Feminist Encounter*. London: Verso.

Bassett, C. (2010) 'Impossible, Admirable, Androgyne: Firestone, Technology and Utopia'. In M. Merck and S. Sandford (eds), *Further Adventures of the Dialectic of Sex: Critical Essays on Shulamith Firestone*. New York: Palgrave Macmillan.

Beauvoir, S. de (1997) *The Second Sex*. Trans. H. M. Parshley. London: Vintage.

Davis, A.Y. (2019 [1981]) *Women, Race and Class*. London: Penguin.

Downing, L. (2018) 'Antisocial Feminism? Shulamith Firestone, Monique Wittig and Proto-Queer Theory'. *Paragraph*, 41(3): 364–379.

Engels, F. (1884) *Origins of the Family, Private Property and the State*. Available at: https://www.marxists.org/archive/marx/works/1884/origin-family/ch02c.htm

Firestone, S. (1968) 'The Women's Rights Movement in the USA: New View'. In *Notes from the First Year*. New York: The New York Radical Women. Available at: https://www.marxists.org/subject/women/authors/firestone-shulamith/womens-rights-movement.htm

Firestone, S. (2015 [1970]) *The Dialectic of Sex: The Case for Feminist Revolution*. London: Verso.

Franklin, S. (2010) 'Revising Reprotech: Firestone and the Question of Technology'. In M. Merck and S. Sandford (eds), *Further Adventures of the Dialectic of Sex: Critical Essays on Shulamith Firestone*. New York: Palgrave Macmillan.

Fraser, N., Bhattacharya, T., and Arruzza, C. (2018) 'Notes For a Feminist Manifesto'. *New Left Review*, 114: 113–134.

Friedan, B. (2010 [1963]) *The Feminine Mystique*. London: Penguin.

Halbert, D. (2004) 'Shulamith Firestone: Radical Feminism and Visions of the Information Society'. *Information, Communication and Society*, 7(1): 115–135.

Haraway, D. (1991) *Simians, Cyborgs and Women: The Reinvention of Nature*. New York: Routledge.

Hester, H. (2018) *Xenofeminism*. Cambridge: Polity.

hooks, b. (2015) *Yearning: Race, Gender, and Cultural Politics*. New York: Routledge.

Lewis, S. (2019) *Full Surrogacy Now: Feminism Against Family*. London: Verso.

Margree, V. (2018) *Neglected or Misunderstood: The Radical Feminism of Shulamith Firestone*. Washington, DC: Zero Books.

Merck, M. and Sandford, S. (eds) (2010) *Further Adventures of the Dialectic of Sex: Critical Essays on Shulamith Firestone*. New York: Palgrave Macmillan.

Mill, J.S. (1869) *The Subjection of Women*. London: Longmans, Green, Reader and Dyer. Public Domain Kindle edition.

Millett, K. (1970) *Sexual Politics*. New York: Doubleday.

Mitchell, J. (1966) 'Women: The Longest Revolution'. *New Left Review*, I(40): 11–37.

NARAL: Pro-Choice America (2015) 'The Safety of Legal Abortion and the Hazards of Illegal Abortion', p. 5. Available at: https://www.prochoiceamerica.org/wp-content/uploads/2016/12/2.-The-Safety-of-Legal-Abortion-and-the-Hazards-of-Illegal-Abortion.pdf

O'Brien, M. (1981) *The Politics of Reproduction*. London: Routledge & Kegan Paul.

Paasonen, S. (2010) 'From Cybernation to Feminization: Firestone and Cyberfeminism'. In M. Merck and S. Sandford (eds), *Further Adventures of the Dialectic of Sex: Critical Essays on Shulamith Firestone*. New York: Palgrave Macmillan.

Sandford, S. (2010) 'The Dialectic of *The Dialectic of Sex*'. In M. Merck and S. Sandford (eds), *Further Adventures of the Dialectic of Sex: Critical Essays on Shulamith Firestone*. New York: Palgrave Macmillan.

SisterSong (Women of Colour Reproductive Justice Collective) (n.d.) 'Reproductive Justice'. Available at: https://www.sistersong.net/reproductive-justice

Spelman, E.V. (1988) *Inessential Woman: Problems of Exclusion in Feminist Thought*. Boston: Beacon Press.

Spillers, H. (2003) *Black, White and in Colour: Essays on American Literature and Culture*. Chicago: University of Chicago Press.

Threadcraft, S. (2016) *Intimate Justice: The Black Female Body and the Body Politic*. Oxford: Oxford University Press.

Weeks, K. (2015) 'The Vanishing Dialectic: Shulamith Firestone and the Future of the Feminist 1970s'. *The South Atlantic Quarterly*, 114(4): 735–754.

35 Angela Y. Davis
MANJEET RAMGOTRA

Chapter guide

This chapter presents some of the core ideas of the radical Marxist, abolitionist political theory of Angela Davis. Section 35.1 gives a brief overview of how her life experiences of racism, sexism, and imprisonment underpin her activism to create a better world without the oppressions of the capitalist, white supremacist, heteropatriarchal state. Section 35.2 examines her Marxist-communist philosophy and understanding of the state structures that maintain the domination of one group of people over many others. Section 35.3 reviews her arguments for the abolition of prisons and Section 35.4 looks at her feminism and her understanding of how Black women in particular confront multiple and intersecting oppressions of gender, race, class, and sexuality.

35.1 Introduction

Angela Y. Davis's (1944–) political theory has been shaped by her lived experience and forms the moral foundations for her activism and lifelong struggle for freedom and justice. Davis (2021 [1974]: xxi) is a radical feminist, Marxist, communist, and Professor of Philosophy who calls for the abolition of the neo-liberal, capitalist, heteropatriarchal, racist, and imperialist institutions and structures of power embodied by the state, notably the American state. She has fought for the complete eradication of structural racism, sexism, homophobia, classism, and ableism as well as the abolition of prisons and the penal system that criminalizes and exploits Black, Indigenous, and Latinx people. Significantly, she has struggled for the elimination of the epistemic and physical violence that maintains these ideologies and system in place. The importance of this struggle and her commitment to it are encapsulated in her claim that for many activists there has been 'no alternative but to offer our lives—our bodies, our knowledge, our will—to the causes of our oppressed people' (ibid.: xxx).

The persistent violence against Black people, including police violence, lynchings, and the disproportionate imprisonment of Black people for minor misdemeanours or on false pretences, along with her own incarceration, shape Davis's outlook. Her lifelong activism in numerous groups is inseparable from her political thinking and has influenced the vocabularies with which she articulates her ideas to oppose complex oppressions that intersect across race, class, gender, and sexuality (ibid.: xvi–xviii). Her education, from a segregated school in Birmingham, Alabama, via the Frankfurt School of Critical Theory, to completing a PhD at the University of California San Diego reinforced her leftist Marxist views.

Davis was falsely implicated in the Marin County Courthouse (California) revolt and was imprisoned for almost two years (1970–1972). This experience deeply informed her activism and conviction that prisons be abolished. In August 1970, at a hearing in the California Courthouse, 17-year-old Jonathan Jackson used a gun registered in Davis's name to take the judge and four others hostage in an effort to bargain for the freedom of three Black men known as the Soledad

Brothers—one of whom, George Jackson, was his brother. These men had been imprisoned on different charges but were later charged with killing a prison guard. A shoot-out ensued in which Jonathan Jackson, the judge, and two prisoners died, and others were wounded. Davis was placed on the FBI's ten most wanted list. Her reaction was to 'go underground' (ibid.: xix). After being on the run for a few months, she was found, incarcerated, charged with 'murder, kidnapping, and conspiracy', denied bail and put on death row (ibid.: 6–14, 242–249; Associated Press, 1970; Hattenstone, 2022). Her incarceration sparked a worldwide campaign to free Angela Davis and all political prisoners. On 4 June 1972, she was acquitted of all charges.

During her time in prison, Davis got to know the women with whom she was imprisoned and learned of their plight. Many were in prison on minor charges but could not afford bail. With these women, Davis discussed issues regarding oppression and inequality and she read George Jackson's book, *Soledad Brother*. These small acts of resistance maintained their humanity. In the third preface to her autobiography, written in 2021, Davis reflects on how her time 'behind bars' shaped her 'activist trajectories', 'political journey', 'intellectual vocation' and notably her 'interests in the intersection of race and feminism' developed the way they did because of her experience in the 'jail cell' (ibid.: xxii–xxiii).

Davis's (ibid.: x) view that racism is systemic underpins her politics and call for revolutionary changes such that 'the masses of Indigenous, Black, Latinx, Middle Eastern, Asian, and working-class white people' can 'begin to enjoy the material and intellectual benefits of life in an advanced industrial society—or even life on this planet, regardless of the level of development in a particular region'. She advances a moral conception of social justice in which all people would have the means to live full, healthy, and worthy lives free from violence, exploitation, imprisonment, and bondage. These are conceptualized as collective ideals or a collective freedom and democracy in which people would participate freely and equally as there would not be classes of oppressors and oppressed. This view differs radically from the liberal conception of individual freedom as the right to property ownership and the right to do and be what one wants without interference from the state (Kelley, 2012: 7).

In their activist work, Davis (2021 [1974]: x) and her comrades recognize that the murders and incarceration of countless Black people cannot be treated as 'isolated instances of racist state violence'. In the 1960s and 1970s, Davis and her fellow activists were 'emboldened by revolutionary struggle' across the world, believing in 'the end of capitalism' and 'the possibilities of socialism'. Yet they failed to 'attend to the contradictions in our assumption that we could call on the existing judicial system to prosecute official agents of the state for committing acts that were actually extensions of the logic of the systems they represented' (ibid.: xi). In Davis's view, it is impossible to change structures from within or with the tools of those structures, rather, for real change to take place, these structures must be dismantled and abolished to lay the ground for new possibilities.

In the 1960s, Davis worked for Black Liberation through the Student Nonviolent Co-ordinating Committee. They tried to merge with the US revolutionary organization the Black Panthers, but this dissolved due to ideological differences. She was disenchanted with the Black Panther Party leadership that considered 'Marx irrelevant to Black Liberation' and socialism as 'the white man's thing' (ibid.: 140–145). In addition, she noted the sexism of some Black male activists who confused 'their political activity with an assertion of their maleness' and who saw 'Black women as a threat to their attainment of manhood' (ibid.: 139–140, 157). Inspired by Lenin and Du Bois (see Chapter 31), Davis joined the American Communist Party (CPUSA) in 1968. She ran as their vice-presidential candidate in the US presidential elections in 1980 and 1984 and left the Party in 1991 because it failed to democratize. She was active in the Black cell of the CPUSA–Che-Lumumba Club—which sought to infuse Marxist-Leninist ideas into the Black Liberation struggle in LA (ibid.; 164).

Read more about **Davis's** life and work by accessing the thinker biography on the online resources: www.oup.com/he/Ramgotra-Choat1e.

35.2 Davis's radical political theory

35.2.1 Marxism and Communism

Davis's philosophy was greatly influenced by Marx and Engels (see Chapter 13). In particular, she drew on Marx's understanding of social relations in terms of the conflictual relationship between the capitalist owners of the means of production—the ruling class under the capitalist mode of production—and the working classes, who are obliged to sell their labour in order to live. Even though their relationship is conflictual and contradictory, the existence of one class depends on the other. Marx and Engels believed that this social conflict would eventually erupt in clashes and lead to the creation of a new order.

To Davis, these relations of exploitation and domination are reproduced in race and gender relations, notably through the intersection between white supremacist and patriarchal forms of power. Although she considered the Black working classes—many of whom were sharecroppers, tenant farmers, factory workers, and domestic workers—and working-class women as part of the wider working-class movement (Davis, 2019 [1981]: 135; 2021 [1974]: 95), she moves beyond Marxist conceptions of working-class oppression to include racial and sexist exploitations as part of the struggles against the capitalist state. Solidarity across these oppressed groups would bring about revolution and structural change. Although this unity was lacking at the beginning of the twentieth century, since the US Socialist Party excluded Black people, the Industrial Workers of the World and eventually the Communist Party included Black workers in their struggles against capitalism and 'recognised the centrality of racism in US society' (Davis, 2019 [1981]: 136). This informs her conception of Marxism and Communism that the exploitation of Black people, women, and the working classes furthered the ends of capitalism and the privileges of the white supremacist middle classes. Today she articulates this in terms of the struggles of Black, Indigenous, Latinx people, LGBTQ+, and women against the racism and sexism of the white supremacist, heteropatriachal, capitalist state.

Of course, she was not the first to argue that capitalist exploitation was not limited to class but included race. Cedric Robinson and C.L.R. James (see Chapter 18) had developed conceptions of Black Marxism and racial capitalism (Davis, 2021 [1974]: 205). However, Davis and other Black women activists and thinkers, such as Claudia Jones, expanded these conceptions to include Black women and the dual oppression of sexism and racism they suffer. 'Because the structures of female oppression are inextricably tethered to capitalism, female emancipation must be simultaneously and explicitly the pursuit of black liberation and of the freedom of other nationally oppressed peoples' (Davis, 2000: 173).

Key Thinker: Claudia Jones

Born in Trinidad, raised in the USA, Jones (1915–1964) was a noted communist, activist, and journalist. She joined the Communist Party USA in 1936 and became Negro Affairs editor for the *Daily Worker*. As a communist, Jones considered Black people's liberation allied to working-class struggles. Her article 'An End to the Neglect of the Problems of the Negro Woman!' (1949) is widely considered a precursor to intersectionality; for Jones highlighted Black women's leadership in struggles for Black liberation and in industrial action for better working conditions and challenged patriarchal understandings of the role of Black women, especially chauvinistic attitudes that silenced them and slotted them in domestic service roles. In the late 1940s and early 1950s, Jones was imprisoned for her communist views and eventually deported to the United Kingdom in 1955 where she founded the *West Indian Gazette* and in response to the Notting Hill race riots of 1958 organized the annual Caribbean (Notting Hill) Carnival (Atkinson, 2020).

To Davis, racial capitalism operates to exploit and dominate both People of Colour and women in order to maximize the interests of the ruling classes. She draws on Marx and Herbert Marcuse (see Key Thinker: Herbert Marcuse) to explain how capitalism requires human beings to exploit each other, and uses the Marxist concept of alienation to demonstrate that the white supremacist, patriarchal ruling classes' domination and exploitation of others is a function of a capitalist apparatus. Davis argues that when human beings as producers are severed from both nature and other producers, they become fragmented and lose touch with the context in which they live to the extent that production of material goods is no longer based on material needs for a decent life, for the reproduction of the family and community. Rather, the end-goal of the production of commodities becomes 'the reproduction of capital', that is, profit (Davis, 2000: 158–159). The separation of the producer from nature and from other human beings further produces a fracture within the self as the individual then functions to maximize self-interest, to reproduce capital with disregard for others. This process also creates a fracture of the self from its humanity and humaneness. It is this distancing that allows the exploitation of workers, the confinement and subjugation of women to the domestic sphere, and the enslavement of Black people. The oppression of and violence against women and Black, Indigenous, and Latinx people persist since capitalist structures continue to exploit people for their labour power. Davis substantiates such exploitation in terms of the appalling conditions in which the majority of Black Americans live; this includes 'substandard schools', poor medical care, expensive and rundown housing, and the lack of a decent welfare system. These conditions under capitalism contribute to their oppression.

Key Thinker: Herbert Marcuse

Marcuse (1898–1979) was a neo-Marxist political and social thinker from Germany. With Max Horkheimer and Theodor Adorno, he is considered one of the leading thinkers of the Frankfurt School of Critical Theory. His work examined art and society and grappled with how individual action was not entirely shaped by social and political structures, but could contribute to changing these through political activism and practice. In addition, he worked on technological reason and domination, which informs his best-known work *One-Dimensional Man*. As a German Jew, he sought refuge in the USA in the 1930s. He taught at Brandeis University—where he encountered Davis—and at UC San Diego. He supported Davis in her plight and advocated publicly on behalf of Black women who suffered sexist and racist oppressions. His book, *Eros and Civilisation: A Philosophical Enquiry into Freud* imagines a non-repressive society.

35.2.2 Consciousness

Davis's thinking goes beyond Marxist and communist modes to include conceptions of the nonhuman and to traverse the boundary that separates human beings from animals as beings that share the planet. This awareness underpins our social consciousness of being part of a collective body. To Davis, consciousness is becoming aware that structures, ideas, and ideologies shape and produce subjects in their particular social and political contexts. When people come to terms with these and realize that they are constructed and contingent, then they can be overthrown. At its core, consciousness amounts to understanding that racism and sexism are systemic and structural and not the result of individual misbehaviour. Once people begin to understand this, then they can think independently and develop a political awareness that aims to dismantle structures of domination that oppress and perpetuate inequality. Davis (2000: 16–17) describes revolutionary, anti-capitalist, and socialist consciousness as awakenings and calls to action. Consciousness is cultivated through activism in movements that seek to defend the cause of the oppressed and disadvantaged members of society against the privileged whose very privilege reproduces exploitative hierarchies and inequalities.

With regard to race, Black consciousness is about coming to terms with the fact that racism does not simply reflect individual attitudes or ignorance, but rather it is systemic and institutional, for it is built in the coercive structures—policing, judicial, and prison systems—of the state. Racism is an ideology that supports systems of slavery, racial capitalism, colonial imperialism, and oppression and that depicts Black, Indigenous and People of Colour as intellectually and spiritually inferior to white people in order to dominate them.

Black consciousness is about reclaiming one's humanity and not allowing the discursive myths that criminalize and degrade Black people to shape their being; radical Black feminist consciousness operates in the same way but includes resisting sexist tropes regarding Black women as matriarchs, domestic help, and sexual objects (Davis, 2019 [1981]: 155–181). Radical Black feminism is distinct from the feminist movement of the 1960s–1980s, which Davis criticizes, notably in the work of Shulamith Firestone (see Chapter 34), for reproducing the myth that Black men harbour uncontrollable sexual desire for white women. In turn, this 'reinforces racism's open invitation to white men to avail themselves sexually of Black women's bodies' (Davis, 2019 [1981]: 163; Srinivasan, 2021: 11).

The repudiation of exploitative and oppressive ideologies also allows people to contest laws and punishment, especially since the laws operated to protect property-owning white people and criminalized black people. Davis (2016b [1971]: 27) argues for an 'inherent right of resistance' against 'unjust, immoral laws and the oppressive social order from which they emanate'. She highlights the glaring contradictions between democracy and the capitalist economy and stresses that 'the people are not the ultimate matrix of the laws and the system which govern them – certainly not Black people and other nationally oppressed people, but not even the mass of whites. The people do not exercise decisive control over the determining factors of their lives' (ibid.: 27–28).

From her prison cell in 1971, Davis called for the overthrow of capitalism and imperialism and believed that Blacks and people from the Global South, the working classes, and victims of capitalism would spearhead the revolution. She argued that the ideology of racism is not only political but economic as well, since capitalists have extracted massive profits from the underpaid labour of People of Colour 'with the aid of a superstructure of terror'. 'This terror', she claims, along with 'more subtle forms of racism have further served to thwart the flowering of a resistance, even a revolution which would spread to the working class as a whole' (ibid.: 40–42). Moreover, the capitalist class has cultivated the white population's fear of the other and hence their consent to racism and terror to quell the resistance.

35.2 Davis's radical political theory: Key Points

- To Davis, racism is structural and not the result of individual attitudes or behaviours.
- When people become aware that the structures and ideologies that produce subjects are contingent, then they can develop a revolutionary consciousness.
- Davis extends Marxist insights on class domination to include race and gender and she considers how capitalist, white supremacist, heteropatriarchal state structures intersect to produce multiple oppressions.
- To Davis, as producers become alienated from nature and other human beings, they will exploit these for their own profit.

35.3 Abolition of prisons

35.3.1 Prisons, racism, and slavery

Davis is one of the foremost advocates for the abolition of prisons and the legal system that maintains these. Her book, *Are Prisons Obsolete?* develops historical and theoretical justifications for abolition. The call to abolish prisons is an extension of the call to abolish the slavery and racism on which the capitalist economic system is built (Davis, 2016a: 23). Although the Thirteenth Amendment of the American Constitution (1865) abolished slavery and involuntary servitude, it was nevertheless reinstated 'as punishment for crime whereof the party shall have been duly convicted' (cited in Davis, 2003: 28). As such, slavery persisted as punishment through the prison system in which racism became institutionalized (Allen, 2007: 313). By breaking down the relationship between wrong conduct and punishment, she creates the space not only to imagine prison abolition but to rethink anew how society judges and determines right and wrong conduct not only among individuals but among groups and how certain groups are criminalized according to race, gender, class, and sexuality.

It is hard to imagine a world without prisons, Davis observes, especially since people consider these as permanent parts of society. Although they are a pervasive part of everyone's lives, they are hidden from everyday life. Prisons operate in society's imagination and ideology as sites to which so-called 'evil-doers' are removed from society to make people feel more safe and secure (Davis, 2003: 9–14). It seems overly idealistic and impracticable to abolish them. Nevertheless, Davis echoes Michel Foucault (see Chapter 33) in highlighting that the prison is a relatively recent institution, prior to which people were subject to other forms of punishment, including brutal torture and public executions. The prison or penitentiary system arose in the eighteenth century, with the social role of managing and controlling the population, disciplining and correcting deviant behaviour. However, in the USA, these institutions were abused, and the rehabilitative capacity of labour was exploited.

After the abolition of slavery, Black people were punished and (re)enslaved for the tiniest misdemeanours. In the American South, new laws known as 'Black codes' severely restricted and regulated Black people's freedom and behaviour. These 'legalized convict labor, prohibited social intercourse between Blacks and whites, gave white employers an excessive degree of control over the private lives of Black workers, and generally codified racism and terror' (Davis, 2016b [1971]: 29). These codes and laws established crimes 'for which only black people could be "duly convicted"' (ibid.: 28). Black people were imprisoned, sentenced to hard labour back on the plantations, often in worse conditions than before, and were literally worked to death. They became targets of the Convict Lease System, whereby prisons leased convicts, often in groups or chain gangs, to private companies for their labour. As such, crime became racialized. Davis concurs with Frederick Douglass (see Chapter 30) who criticized this tendency to 'impute crime to colour' (ibid.: 30). By contrast, whiteness operated and was possessed as a property. Through such ownership, white people affirmed their entitlements to rights, liberty, and self-identity. Moreover, mob rule of groups like the Ku Klux Klan and the Jim Crow laws violated and denied Black people's political and civil rights. The legal and penitentiary systems were skewed and manipulated to criminalize, convict, and redeploy Black people as slaves and to profit from their forced labour. This 'transformation of petty thievery into a felony' condemned many Black people to involuntary servitude, which in fact built many city centres, streets, and railroads. Today prisoners' labour produces furniture for American universities (Davis, 2003: 32–35). Davis further draws a parallel between the measure of labour-value in terms of time spent working and the length in time of prison sentences not only to quantify the expected amount of labour-value that can be extracted from prisoners, but also to compute 'the value of capitalist commodities' (ibid.: 44).

35.3.2 Prisons and policing

Davis contests the use of imprisonment as a form of punishment and questions the Prison Industrial Complex or the increased construction of new prisons in which a disproportionate number of Black, Indigenous, and Latinx people have been incarcerated. Moreover, she protests the political justifications and media spin for building new prisons on the basis that crime was on the rise, since crime rates had been falling (ibid.: 9–21, 92). She criticizes harsher sentencing for minor crimes leading to imprisonment as a way to deal with 'human surplus' as the US economy deindustrialized and unemployment rose (ibid.: 91; Allen, 2007: 317). The proliferation of prisons over the last three decades has become a global phenomenon tied to global capitalism (Davis, 2003: 85–86, 97–102).

> **Key Concept: Prison industrial complex**
>
> The US Marxist Mike Davis (1995) coined the term 'prison industrial complex' to describe the 60 per cent rise in the number of prisons built in California in the 1980s and 1990s. Activists and scholars use this term to protest the notion that increased levels of crime have driven the need for more prisons. Rather, they argue that the increase in prisons fuels the drive to fill these with human bodies and that this is supported by 'ideologies of racism and the pursuit of profit' (Davis, 2003: 84–85; 84–103). Financial incentives underlying the prison industrial complex include business for developers and other industries to provide for prisoners' basic needs, a pool of cheap labour, and it removes People of Colour and the poor from society. The US War on Drugs and Bill Clinton's Violent Crime Control and Law Enforcement Act (1994) increased funding for prisons and policing. Consequently, the US prison population quadrupled from 474,000 to 2,000,000 between the 1980s and 2010s (Zamalin, 2017: 119).

Like Foucault, Davis rehearses the history of the judicial and penitentiary systems, though she criticizes Foucault for disregarding race. She formulates an incisive critique of this system and argues that punishment and the penal system were established to maintain social control (Davis, 2003; 2016b [1971], Allen, 2007: 313; Zamalin, 2017: 124–126). Davis depicts prisons as 'instruments of class domination'. The protection of private property is central to this conception: in societies where wealth is unevenly distributed, 'crime is inevitable' and the law and prisons aim to protect the 'haves' from the encroachment of the 'have-nots'. Davis (2016b [1971]: 34–35) underlines the injustice of this inequality where 'society's resources' move 'in the wrong direction' and property crimes and anti-social acts are the expressions of 'profound but suppressed social needs' and reflect the problematic nature of capitalism. Nonetheless, these crimes and acts simultaneously represent protests against capitalism as well the desire to take part in its 'exploitative content' (ibid.: 35).

Furthermore, Davis (ibid.: 36) underlines that many Black and brown people are railroaded into prison without having committed a crime. Rates of unemployment are twice as high in the ghettos and 'even higher among Black women and youth' (ibid.: 38). In both good and bad times, Black people confront poverty and are often the first victims of economic duress. She considers that the incarceration of Black people is political, first, since their activism threatens the capitalist state and, second, because the political order perpetuates racial inequality subjecting Black people to dire conditions of poverty, exclusion, and undue police surveillance (ibid.: 33).

Davis argues that to reduce criminality to individual acts ignores the systemic nature of oppression. She defines political prisoners as those who violate a law to further the 'interests of a class or a people whose oppression is expressed either directly or indirectly through that particular law'. These people are 'reformists' or 'revolutionaries' and are 'interested in universal social change'. Although those who break the law to further their own interests 'might be called criminal', she emphasizes that in many cases, these people are victims of the system (ibid.: 29–30). Black prisoners are political prisoners because the system had either already criminalized them or had 'reduced their possibilities of subsistence and survival' that they had no other alternative but to violate the rules of society (ibid.: 36). However, even political acts that challenged the status quo were criminalized in an effort to 'discredit radical and revolutionary movements' (ibid.: 33). Her distinction between law breaking and being criminalized is important, for once people are criminalized, they are already considered law breakers, even if they have not broken the law (Allen, 2007: 314; Zamalin, 2017:124).

In discussing institutionalized racism and violence in policing, Davis evokes Frantz Fanon's critique of colonial police in settler colonies to show that policing in American ghettos is equally oppressive and dehumanizing (see Chapter 28 on Fanon). Police presence maintains social disparity, poverty, and violence in Black ghettos. They maintain the boundaries between the haves and have-nots, white and non-white, and are the 'domestic caretakers of violence'. They are 'the oppressor's emissaries, charged with the task of containing us within the boundaries of our oppression'. Ultimately, she argues that the police protect and preserve the interests of 'our oppressors' and serve Black people 'nothing but injustice'. Moreover, 'Arrests are frequently based on whims.' Bullets from their guns murder human beings on little or no pretext, aside from the universal intimidation they are charged with carrying out. Far from being there 'to protect and serve the people', the massive deployment of police patrols in Black communities are 'there to intimidate Blacks, to persuade us with their violence that we are powerless to alter the conditions of our lives' (Davis, 2016b [1971]: 39).

35.3.3 Delinking crime from punishment

In making the case to abolish prisons, Davis distinguishes between crime and punishment, for there is no logical link between crime and punishment: many people violate laws, but they do not suffer the same punishment, depending on their race, class, and gender. For instance, historically, white people who lynched and murdered Black people were almost never tried and convicted, whereas Black and Indigenous people are subject to racial profiling, incarcerated for minor felonies, or indeed shot by police on mere suspicion. The focus on individual criminal acts and trying to reduce crime in general misses the structural aspects of punishment, which include economic, political, and ideological elements.

Davis contends that we usually think 'about punishment as an inevitable consequence of crime', but by recognizing that '"punishment" does not follow from "crime" in the neat and logical sequence offered by discourses that insist on the justice of imprisonment', then we can begin to imagine alternatives to the prison system. She advances this argument since the ends of imprisonment are 'linked to the agendas of politicians, the profit drive of corporations, and media representations of crime' (Davis, 2003: 112) rather than the rehabilitation of the offender to correct their behaviour.

In her view, justice should not be retributive, where a wrong begets a corresponding punishment, but should rather be reparative and seek to heal the social ills that criminalize people. To Davis, in order to abolish the prison, we need to disarticulate relationships of 'crime and punishment, race and punishment, class and punishment, and gender and punishment' not only within the prison system but also in 'all the social relations that support the permanence of the prison' (ibid.: 112). By pulling apart crime from punishment, Davis argues that we can discern the hidden racist, classist, and sexist structure of the penal system and demonstrate that the social role of the prison system has not been a more humane way of treating people who violate society's laws, but rather the prison system has benefited government through population control and management, and profited private companies through the exploitation of labour and creation of services to maintain prisons and their inmates.

35.3.4 Reparative justice

Davis (ibid.: 113) conceptualizes alternatives to prison that aim at decriminalizing not only specific acts that have been criminalized, 'but also criminalized populations and communities'. She draws on the work of others who promote 'radical transformations within the existing justice system' such as the Dutch criminologist Herman Bianchi, who contends that we ought to change how we think of crime and criminal law. Were society to consider those who violate the law as debtors—as people who are liable and who have a duty 'to take responsibility for their actions and assume a duty to repair'—rather than as evil-minded, then we can reimagine the criminal justice system (ibid.: 113–114). By thinking of violations of the law in terms of reparative justice rather than retributive justice, we can change the overall penal system and abolish prisons. To Davis, this would 'create an entirely different – and perhaps more egalitarian – system of justice' (ibid.: 105). She proposes gradual decarceration and several alternatives to prisons. These require radical transformations of society that include: addressing 'racism, male dominance, homophobia, class bias and other structures of domination'; transforming schools from militarized spaces of discipline to spaces of learning; providing free physical and mental healthcare; and creating 'a justice system based on reparation and reconciliation rather than retribution and vengeance' (ibid.: 107–108; Allen, 2007: 316–321; Srinivasan, 2021, 172).

Davis rejects alternatives such as house arrest and electronic surveillance bracelets, which echo the retribution of prisons. Rather, she promotes a more humane approach that comprises the decriminalization of sex work and drug use; the creation of centres to help people overcome addiction; defending immigrant rights, decriminalizing undocumented immigrants, and supporting women who flee their countries to 'escape sexual violence' rather than criminalizing, incarcerating, and subjecting them to a continued cycle of violence; and tackling domestic violence and violence against women, especially since women are frequently imprisoned for fighting 'back against their abusers'. In addition, Davis includes 'job and living wage programs, alternatives to the disestablished welfare system, [and] community-based recreation' (Davis, 2003: 109–113). These are all alternative ways to 'reverse the impact of the prison industrial complex on our world' (ibid.: 111). With regard to the question of murderers and rapists, Davis proposes a system of reconciliation between the perpetrator and the victim or the victim's family along the lines of the South African Truth and Reconciliation Commission. Yet it is hard to see how this in practice might work and also it does not deal with serial offenders. Davis's proposals for an alternative system of justice that does not rely on the prison industrial complex nonetheless aims at the eradication of racist, sexist, and classist domination in society overall. There is a growing movement against criminalization of oppressed communities and for the adoption of reparative justice among Indigenous, Black, and marginalized groups in North America, not only to recognize and correct historical wrongs but to implement in the current operations of the penal system.

35.3 Abolition of prisons: Key Points

- To Davis, the abolition of prisons is part of a history to abolish slavery, since the US Constitution allows for the enslavement and involuntary servitude of prisoners.
- Davis argues that punishment ought to be delinked from crime, because it is not an inevitable consequence of wrongdoing and it lays bare the racist, classist, and sexist dimensions of the carceral system.
- Black people in the USA are disproportionately incarcerated and are criminalized as a group; the Prison Industrial Complex compounds this situation.
- Abolition of prisons creates a new space to rethink justice in terms of reparation and decriminalization of sex work and drug use and the creation of better education, healthcare, welfare, and living conditions.

35.4 Women, race, and class

35.4.1 Black women's struggles and resistance

Davis's (2019 [1981]) highly influential book *Women, Race and Class* explores gender oppression within an imperialist, racial capitalist system built on slavery. She dispels the myth that enslaved women were mainly used for domestic labour in the home; rather, they had to work in the fields even when they were pregnant. Like men, they were not exempt from punishment and flogging if they did not produce what slave-owners required. Enslaved women were subject to rape and sexual abuse, which was an 'expression of the slaveholder's economic mastery and the overseer's control over Black women as workers' (ibid.: 5). Black women were valued for their fertility. When the slave trade was abolished, they were used to replenish the slave population. They were coveted if they could produce ten or more children but, Davis notes, they did not enjoy the status of motherhood in the way that white women did. For enslaved women were considered 'breeders – animals whose monetary value could be precisely calculated in terms of their ability to multiply their numbers', with their children taken away and sold 'like calves from cows' (ibid.: 4–5; Barnett, 2003: 20). At the same time, so as not to break the 'chain of command' of white male supremacy, Black men were emasculated.

Davis (ibid.: 19–20) observes that rape was a weapon of domination and repression; it was used to break 'slave women's will to resist, and … to demoralize their men'. While *Women, Race and Class* focuses on the use of rape as a weapon against women, her later work also highlights the rape of boys and men, as well as gender violence against trans people (Davis, 2016a, 2021 [1974]: Preface). She also emphasizes that sexual and gender violence is prevalent in prisons. Gender structures prisons and reflects the deep levels of prison violence and control. Not only is the routine internal search of women's bodies a sexual violation, but also prison guards' sexual abuse of prisoners is tolerated, as they are rarely brought to account (Davis, 2003: 60–83).

Against the extreme violence of slavery, Davis (2019 [1981]: 12) highlights that enslaved people resisted and maintained their humanity and dignity: 'As they tried desperately and daily to maintain their family lives, enjoying as much autonomy as they could seize, slave men and women manifested irrepressible talent in humanizing an environment designed to convert them into a herd of subhuman labor units.' Enslaved women 'resisted sexual assault', 'defended their families, … participated in work stoppages and revolts', 'poisoned their masters … joined maroon communities and fled northward to freedom'. She underlines that those who accepted enslavement passively were 'the exception rather than the rule' (ibid.: 16). An important act of resistance was learning to read and write, which allowed them to develop their consciousness and to reclaim their humanity (ibid.: 18).

In the composition of *Women, Race and Class*, Davis draws on works of philosophy, Black political thought, history, fiction, poetry, and testimony to construct her reading and analysis of the role of Black women in the history of emancipatory struggles in the USA. She chronicles the founding of anti-slavery societies in the 1830s (the American Anti-Slavery, the Philadelphia and Boston Female Anti-Slavery societies), which attracted both middle- and working-class white women, who learned about oppression through these societies and began to campaign for women's rights (ibid.: 28–34). Initially, anti-slavery and women's movements were aligned but, with the approach of civil war, rifts began to appear. White women feared that they would be neglected as enslaved people acquired freedom (ibid.: 59). Solidarity between the movements waned.

Davis traces the evolution of what started as a movement against racist and sexist oppression but ended up supporting white women's suffrage only to advance white supremacy. Towards the end of the nineteenth century, white suffragists gradually withdrew their support for Black people's political rights to vote, even though they had previously worked with prominent Black activists such as Ida B. Wells and Frederick Douglass and promoted the abolition of slavery (ibid.: 98). Elizabeth

Cady Stanton (see Key Thinker: Elizabeth Cady Stanton in Section 2.2.3 in Chapter 2) and Susan B. Anthony, for instance, did not want to alienate white women from the South and therefore excluded Black people from the National American Woman Suffrage Association (NAWSA) convention in 1893 (ibid.; 99). These women were motivated by expediency and wanted to acquire voting rights at the cost of excluding Black and working-class women. Soon after, the association passed a motion to support the suffrage only of women who could read and write, effectively excluding most Black, immigrant and working-class women (ibid.: 102). The NAWSA did not take a stand against the rising racism in the USA that legalized segregation, tolerated lynchings, and overturned the 1875 Civil Rights Act (Wells, 2014). Rather, Davis observes, racism operated insidiously in the NAWSA, under the guise of promoting human rights and political equality that ultimately were only for some but not all (Davis, 2019 [1981]: 99–103).

Davis (ibid.: 107) explains how a potent ideological mixture of racism and sexism resulted in a union of 'White supremacy and male supremacy' which portrayed People of Colour across the world as 'incompetent barbarians' and women as inferior, as 'mother-figures' whose duty was to nurture their men. This racist and sexist propaganda promoted white women as the 'mothers of the race' whose role was to safeguard white supremacy. To Davis, along with racism, the 'cult of motherhood' crept into the white women's suffrage movement and became more and more pervasive to the point that white women's suffrage became 'the most expedient means to achieve racial supremacy'. This mutually reinforcing combination of racism and sexism underscored white and male supremacy and eugenics (ibid.; 107–110) (see Key Concept: Eugenics). Davis concludes that the NAWSA—the bourgeois white women's movement for suffrage—no longer promoted sisterly solidarity or the defeat of male supremacy: 'It was not women's rights or women's political equality but, rather, the reigning racial superiority of white people which had to be preserved at all costs' (ibid.: 111).

To be sure, these middle-class white supremacist movements were countered by more radical Black feminist movements that sought to defend their own against violent racist attacks. In 1892, Josephine St. Pierre Ruffin, the partner of the first Black judge in Massachusetts, founded The Women's Era Club in Boston, and, in 1895, Black women held their first national convention. Black women organized and founded clubs across the USA, including the Women's Loyal Union in New York and the Chicago Women's Club, that included both middle- and working-class Black women. In 1892 and 1896, Black women including Wells, Mary Church Terrell, Anna Julia Cooper, and Harriet Tubman founded the Colored Women's League and then the National Association of Colored Women's Clubs, which advocated suffrage for Black women and men, and women in general. Davis draws attention to the Chicago Women's Club that 'raised funds to prosecute a policeman who had killed a Black man' (Davis, 2019 [1981]: 117). All of these clubs and associations struggled for Black Liberation. They constitute a long legacy for contemporary movements such as Black Lives Matter that continue to fight for the same goals: freedom, the eradication of structural racism that underpins the often murderous and violent oppression Black people, and, especially for Davis, the abolition of prisons.

Key Concept: Eugenics

Eugenics refers to the racially biased study and practice that aim to improve the genes of the human population by promoting the reproduction of those deemed to have desirable characteristics and preventing the reproduction of those who do not. This genetic control of population reproduction underpins white supremacist ideologies such as Nazism, apartheid in South Africa, and White Supremacy in the USA. It has justified genocide, the murder of many People of Colour with impunity, and the forced sterilization of many women of colour.

The control of women's reproductive rights presents another form of institutionalized sexism and racism. Davis is critical of the abortion rights movement for disregarding the elements of eugenics in the history of the US birth control movement. Abortion rights became legal in the United States in 1973 with the Supreme Court *Roe v Wade* ruling, which was overturned in 2022. However, Davis remarks that the women who fought for this were silent on the issue of forced sterilization, notably of Black, Indigenous, Latinx, immigrant, working-class, and so-called 'unfit' women. At the beginning of the twentieth-century, the birth rate of white Americans fell, which led to campaigns to encourage more births among the white middle classes to avoid 'race suicide' and to control the birth rate among Black people, immigrants, and the poor through forced sterilization (ibid.: 182–189). While forced sterilization was justified on the grounds that it prevented the birth of 'mentally deficient persons' (ibid.; 195), it was also used to control the reproduction of non-white people. As a result, in 1932, twenty-six states had legislated for compulsory sterilization. The practice was prevalent until the late 1970s and continues today. In North Carolina, of over 7500 forced sterilizations, 5000 Black women were sterilized between the 1930s and the 1970s. In 1976, 24 per cent of Indigenous women had been sterilized. Moreover, in 1977, the US government withdrew federal funds for abortions save 'those involving rape and risk of death or severe illness', yet federal funds were available for sterilizations, which were free for poor women (ibid.: 199). Black women had been performing abortions since the days of slavery so as not to bring children into 'a world of interminable forced labour, where chains and floggings and sexual abuse for women were the everyday conditions of life' (ibid.: 184). So it is not that they were against campaigns for abortion rights, it was more that these campaigns focused on white women's concerns and rights and did not consider those of Black, Latinx, poor, and immigrant women.

Although the NAWSA and the suffragists of the Equal Rights Association held anti-Black positions, Davis highlights the radical movements that pushed against these conservative voices. She traces a brief history of working-class women's movements of the mid-nineteenth century and of Communist Women of the early twentieth century (ibid.: 123–154). Her portrayal of the history of these opposing political movements is dialectical and underscores the many tensions and contradictions between the ruling conservative middle-class groups of society and the radical, exploited, and oppressed groups that include Black and Indigenous people, People of Colour, and the working classes, especially the immigrant women who replaced white working-class women when they began to move out of factory work. As women left the home to work, they were not treated as 'full-fledged wage workers' (ibid.: 206). Hence, working-class women were active in organizing for better working conditions and, in the USA, working-class Black women demonstrated against the dual racist and sexist exploitation of Black women and People of Colour (ibid.: 138).

Davis traces the history of women's subordination to men through production and reproduction. She agrees with Marx and Engels that sexual inequality arose with the ownership of property. In pre-capitalist and pre-industrial times, women's contribution to the economy through the production of basic material necessities, social reproduction, and caring for children put them on a par with men, but as technology progressed and much of the basic necessities were produced in factories, and as the division between the domestic home economy and the profit-driven capitalist economy grew, women's roles were diminished. Domestic labour was seen to be an inferior form of labour and service, even if a 'precondition' of capitalist production (ibid.: 202–206, 211). Women became increasingly subordinated to men and were 'ideologically redefined as the guardians of a devalued domestic life' (Davis, 2016a: 206).

Middle-class women, in particular, were relegated to the category of 'housewife'. Simultaneously, however, many immigrant women worked in factories. By contrast, slave women and men were equals in labour and there was greater sexual equality in the home. Moreover, after emancipation, Black women worked and hence housework was never a 'central focus of their lives'. Although they did not fall into the middle-class white American trope of housewife, Black women have borne 'the double burden of wage labor and housework' (Davis, 2019 [1981]: 206–209). In her concluding chapter to *Women, Race and Class*, Davis criticizes the international campaign that advocated that caring notably in the home should be paid, wages for housework, as a reformist measure and calls for structural change whereby women would not be defined by their domestic functions (ibid.: 211; Bhandar and Ziadeh, 2020b: 13–15). She calls for 'the abolition of housework as the private responsibility of women', a move that would entail 'the socialization of housework – including meal preparation and childcare'. In her view, this has 'explosive revolutionary potential' as effectively it would dismantle the sexist hierarchies and domestic structures on which capitalism depends (Davis, 2019 [1981]: 219).

35.4.2 The category of woman

Even in the latter half of the twentieth century, many Black women and women of colour did not identify with white feminisms which were racist and perpetuated social hierarchies (Combahee River Collective, 1977; Srinivasan, 2021:11). As a result of these exclusions, the very definition of the category woman was debated. Davis discerns that 'the struggle for women's rights was ideologically defined as a struggle for white middle-class women's rights, pushing out working-class and poor women, pushing out Black women, Latinas, and other women of color from the discursive field covered by the category "woman"' (Davis, 2016a: 95). From these debates the 'radical women-of-color feminist theories and practices arose'. But it was at the World Conference on Women in 1985 that

> the slogan 'Women's Rights Are Human Rights' arose and many women of colour thought that if the category was expanded to include Black, Latinx, Indigenous, Asian women and so on, the category would overcome its exclusive nature. At the time, however, they did not consider rewriting the category to include transwomen and in particular transwomen of color.
>
> (ibid.: 96–98)

To Davis, transwomen's struggles for inclusion in the 'category "woman"' echo the struggles of Black women and women of colour. These women bring a deeply feminist approach 'because it is performed at the intersection of race, class, sexuality, and gender' and because these women are 'the *most* harassed by law enforcement, *most* arrested and incarcerated' (ibid.: 98–99). Davis contends that the struggles of transwomen prisoners are very telling about the reach and nature of the prison industrial complex. Many transwomen are incarcerated in men's prisons where they are subject to the most violent treatment by guards and other male prisoners who target them; in addition to which transwomen are 'often denied their hormonal treatments'. Again, Davis highlights the institutionalized nature of this violence and stresses the extent to which it reaches beyond violations of the body to violations of one's mental health and identity. Furthermore, the experiences of transwomen ought to make us 'learn how to think and act and struggle against that which is ideologically constituted as "normal"'. For instance, prisons are considered normal, yet the abolitionist movement calls on people to question the role of prisons in society. To Davis, if we change our thinking of what is normal, we can change society (ibid.: 99–100).

She questions the notion of being assimilated into a category and argues that this will not necessarily produce revolutionary change. For assimilation means becoming part of an existing category or group, which entails adapting to and reproducing the norms of this category or group that has broadened its membership but has not changed its fundamental principle. Therefore, the category of 'woman' must change so as not to 'simply reflect normative ideas of who counts as women and who doesn't' (ibid.: 101). Gender does not simply refer to a binary structure of male and female at opposite poles. It is a contested concept constructed through 'social, political, cultural, and ideological' norms. However, Davis discerns that 'bringing trans women, trans men, intersex, many other forms of gender nonconformity into the concept of gender . . . radically undermines the normative assumptions of the very concept' (ibid.: 101).

Davis's reflections on the use of language to define gender and sexuality are critical to her promotion of the abolition of the structures and norms that hold racism, sexism, and classism in place by defining and controlling populations. She draws attention to the methodologies of feminist, queer, and trans activists because they do not consider that bodies and body parts—such as uteruses and penises—are linked to notions of gender identity, characteristics, intelligence and roles, including parenting. In turn, this produces a reconceptualization of cultural, social, and legal norms, practices, and ideologies. In other words, feminist and queer methodologies deconstruct the premise that because one has a penis, one is a man and therefore must adapt to the identity, role, and characteristics that the category man entails. Queer theorists argue that by rethinking gender binary norms that are based on the association of body parts and roles, we would no longer pathologize those who do not fit these norms. For, as Davis emphasizes, body parts do not make anyone who they are and are certainly not measures for determining superiority or inferiority (ibid.: 102).

Davis claims that these feminist methodologies examine how categories can be challenged and disrupted by marginal aspects or anomalies, which, in turn, allows 'researchers, academics, . . . activists and organizers' to rethink them anew. Challenging a category and pushing it to its boundaries can actually 'bust up' the category (ibid.: 103). The questioning of the very categories used to define people and to determine who belongs and who does not can shatter the very foundations of social and political power. Davis brings this to the fore in her recent work, yet in *Women, Race and Class* she already intimated the implications of how categories operate to exclude and control populations who do not conform (Barnett, 2003). She highlights both the epistemic violence done to those who do not fit categories and the real physical violence.

Davis is concerned about these forms of sexual violence as well as gender-based violence especially as it impacts Black, trans, Black trans women, and women of colour in society, the home, and prisons. She argues that 'the institutional violence of the prison complements and extends the intimate violence of the family, the individual violence of battery and sexual assault' (Davis, 2016a: 105). That is to say that these forms of violence are structural and are means of punishment and control of usually men over women and trans women. Again, this violence asserts masculinist power, but disturbingly it is often tolerated violence that is institutionalized in the prisons and among the police (Srinivasan, 2021: 177).

35.4 Women, race, and class: Key Points

- Davis traces how gradually the anti-racist anti-sexist women's suffragist movement excluded Black women and mutated to support white supremacy and the political dominance of white men.
- Davis shows that Black women organized to defend their rights in opposition to middle-class white women's movements and underlines that even in the 1970s these movements reproduced racist myths regarding Black men and women.
- To Davis, movements to defend reproductive rights ought to include the abolition of forced sterilization and recognize that the early movements for birth control in the USA included eugenics.
- Sexual and gender violence structure and pervade the prison system, according to Davis.
- Davis celebrates that Black women, women of colour, and trans women have expanded and radically transformed the category of 'woman' that previously essentialized white women.

35.5 Conclusion

Davis reiterates the 'old adage' that 'the personal is political'. She discerns 'a deep relationality that links struggles against institutions and struggles to reinvent our personal lives, and recraft ourselves'. Moreover, she reflects, the 'political reproduces itself through the personal' (Davis, 2016a: 106). We are structured by the system, yet when we push back against it, we find the space to reinvent and recraft ourselves and our futures. She gives an example of how deeply inscribed retributive justice is within us, since our emotional response to an attack usually is to fight back. Her point is that we must unlearn these structures in order to think anew. In particular, both white people and People of Colour must 'unlearn racism' and apprehend that it is not individual but structural. She does not see this process as a psychological one but one that requires dismantling 'the structures of racism' that begin with the institutions—the prisons, the police, and the legal system—that uphold it. This also means dismantling the ideology and reconceptualizing the categories through which we understand social relations. To do this she draws on both abolitionist and feminist ideas and methodologies in her abolition feminism. Davis observes that there is more to feminism than 'gender equality'. Her Marxism shines through in this call for revolution and the dismantling of the imperialist, heteropatriarchal, and capitalist state along with all of its institutions of racial, sexual, and social control. Her call for abolition democracy promotes a more humane and inclusive society based on radical conceptions of community, caring, and solidarity (Kelley, 2012: 15; Lester, 2021).

*Take your learning further by accessing the online resources for a library of web links to relevant videos, articles, blogs, and useful websites for this chapter: **www.oup.com/he/Ramgotra-Choat1e**.*

Study questions

1. How does Angela Davis transform Marxist conceptions of exploitation and oppression?
2. What is consciousness to Davis?
3. How do myths and narratives about race operate to maintain the power of the ruling classes?
4. Why does Davis argue that prisons should be abolished?
5. How do gender, race, and class intersect to oppress groups of people?
6. According to Davis, why should racism be understood as structural and not individual?
7. Why does Davis delink punishment from crime?
8. Does Davis's conception of revolution seek to overthrow or reform the imperialist, capitalist, heteropatriarchal state?

Further reading

Primary sources

Aptheker, B. and Davis, A.Y. (2016 [1971]) (eds) *If They Come in the Morning . . . Voices of Resistance*. London: Verso.
   Davis' first edited book, written in prison, in which she articulates early arguments for prison abolition.

Davis, A.Y. (2003) *Are Prisons Obsolete?* New York: Seven Stories Press.
Theoretical argument as to why prisons should be abolished along with an excellent historical overview of the prison system.

Davis, A.Y. (2005) *Abolition Democracy: Beyond Prisons, Torture, Empire*. New York: Seven Stories Press.
Interviews with Davis where she develops her views on abolition and considers in greater depth torture and sexual violence notably in light of the US war on terror.

Davis, A.Y. (2012) *The Meaning of Freedom and Other Difficult Dialogues*. San Francisco: City Lights.
An excellent collection of Davis's recent speeches and public lectures on the theme of freedom.

Davis, A.Y. (2019 [1981]) *Women, Race and Class*. London: Penguin Random House.
The classic work that traces the history of Black radical feminism.

Davis, A.Y. (2021 [1974]) *Angela Davis: An Autobiography*. London: Hamish Hamilton Penguin Random House.
A re-edition with a 2021 preface of Davis's early autobiography, in which she explains her politics and activism through her experience in prison.

Davis, A.Y., Dent, G., Meiners, E. and Richie, B. (2022) *Abolition. Feminism. Now*. London: Haymarket Books.
A recent work on abolition politics and radical feminism.

Joy, J. (ed.) (1998) *The Angela Y. Davis Reader*. Oxford: Blackwell.
A comprehensive collection of Davis' main writings.

Secondary sources

Allen, A. (2007) 'Justice and Reconciliation: The Death of the Prison? Scholar's Symposium: The Work of Angela Y. Davis'. *Human Studies*, 30(4): 311–321.
A short article that examines Davis' argument for the abolition of prisons.

Kelley, R.D.G. (2012) 'Foreword'. In A.Y. Davis, *The Meaning of Freedom and Other Difficult Dialogues*. San Francisco: City Lights, pp. 7–16.
A short and concise explanation of Davis' theory of freedom and radical conception of emancipatory community and politics.

Zamalin, A. (2017) 'Angela Davis, Prison Abolition, and the End of the American Carceral State'. In A. Zamalin, *Struggle on Their Minds: The Political Thought of African American Resistance*. New York: Columbia University Press, pp. 119–149.
A good chapter that critically examines Davis' views on prison abolition.

References

Allen, A. (2007) 'Justice and Reconciliation: The Death of the Prison?' Scholar's Symposium: The Work of Angela Y. Davis'. *Human Studies*, 30(4): 311–321.

Associated Press. (1970) 'Angela Davis Is Sought in Shooting That Killed Judge on Coast'. *New York Times*. August 16.

Atkinson, C. (2020) 'Claudia Jones, Brief Life of an Intersectional Activist: 1915–1964'. *Harvard Magazine*. September–October. Available at: https://www.harvardmagazine.com/2020/09/features-vita-claudia-jones [accessed 4 September 2022].

Barnett, B.M. (2003) 'Angela Davis and *Women, Race, & Class*: A Pioneer in Integrative RGC Studies'. *Race, Gender & Class*, 10(3): 9–22.

Bhandar, B. and Ziadeh, R. (2020b) 'Introduction'. In B. Bhandar and R. Ziadeh (eds), *Revolutionary Feminisms: Conversations on Collective Action and Radical Thought*. London: Verso, pp. 1–30.

Combahee River Collective (1977) 'Statement'. Available at: https://combaheerivercollective.weebly.com/the-combahee-river-collective-statement.html# (accessed 4 September 2022).

Davis, A.Y. (2000) 'Women and Capitalism: Dialectics of Oppression and Liberation'. In J. James and T.D. Sharpley-Whiting (eds), *The Angela Y. Davis Reader*. Oxford: Blackwell Publishers, pp. 146–182.

Davis, A.Y. (2003) *Are Prisons Obsolete?* New York: Seven Stories Press.

Davis, A.Y. (2016a) *Freedom Is a Constant Struggle: Ferguson, Palestine, and Foundations of a Movement*. London: Haymarket Books.

Davis, A.Y. (2016b [1971]) 'Political Prisoners, Prisons and Black Liberation'. In A.Y. Davis (ed.), *If They Come in the Morning . . . Voices of Resistance*. London: Verso, pp. 27–43.

Davis, A.Y. (2019 [1981]) *Women, Race and Class*. London: Penguin Random House.

Davis, A.Y. (2021 [1974]) *Angela Davis: An Autobiography*. London: Hamish Hamilton Penguin Random House.

Davis, M. (1995) 'Hell Factories in the Field: A Prison Industrial Complex'. *The Nation*. 20 February.

Hattenstone, S. (2022) 'Angela Davis on the Power of Protest: 'We Can't Do Anything Without Optimism''. *The Guardian*, 5 March.

Jones, C. (1949) 'An End to the Neglect of the Problems of the Negro Woman!' In National Women's Commission, *Political Affairs*. New York: CPUSA.

Kelley, R.D.G. (2012) 'Foreword'. In A.Y. Davis, *The Meaning of Freedom and Other Difficult Dialogues*. San Francisco: City Lights, pp. 7–16.

Lester, Q. (2021) 'Whose Democracy in Which State? Abolition Democracy from Angela Davis to W.E. B. Du Bois'. *Social Science Quarterly*, 102: 3081–3086.

Srinivasan, A. (2021) *The Right to Sex*. London: Bloomsbury Publishing.

Wells, I.B. (2014) 'The Lynch Law in All its Phases (1893)'. In M. Bay and H.L. Gates Jr (eds), *The Light of the Truth: Writings of an Anti-Lynching Crusader*. New York: Penguin Books, pp. 96–114.

Zamalin, A. (2017) 'Angela Davis, Prison Abolition, and the End of the American Carceral State'. In A. Zamalin, *Struggle on Their Minds: The Political Thought of African American Resistance*. New York: Columbia University Press, pp. 119–149.

36 Judith Butler

CLARE WOODFORD

> **Chapter guide**
>
> This chapter provides an overview of Judith Butler's intellectual trajectory. Section 36.2 situates Butler's work in relation to feminism and gay and lesbian studies. Section 36.3 summarizes Butler's argument on performativity and parody; and explores the theoretical underpinnings of this in their theory of subjectivity. It concludes by considering her later work (often referred to as the 'turn to ethics'). Section 36.6 reflects on Butler's continuing relevance for political thought today. (Note: This chapter uses they/them pronouns to refer to Butler.).

36.1 Introduction

Unlike most political theorists, Judith Butler (1956–) has crossed the divide from academia to popular culture, achieving iconic celebrity status. Although part of a much wider movement, often referred to as queer theory, it is Butler, more than any of her other contemporary theorists, who has captured the public imagination as the superstar academic of gender performativity. Yet publicity comes at a price. Butler has acquired the dubious accolade of uniting in condemnation those who are at other times vociferously opposed across the political spectrum. Criticized by left-wing feminist scholars and activists for undermining feminism with an 'evil' critique of sex and gender (Nussbaum, 1999), religious leaders and right-wing activists have protested that Butler's 'queer theory' undermines the natural order of gender, sexuality, and the family.

What is often missed is that Butler's theorization of gender stems from a broader concern about which lives matter, whose lives get to count as human, and whose are constrained, curtailed, and subjected to unbearable violence. This leads Butler to question the way that any identity functions to define not just who we are but how, and if, we can live. Far less media space is devoted to their wider politics, which calls for a radical egalitarian society that resists neoliberalism, decries war, criticizes US and Israeli foreign policy, defends public services and insists that left politics must be nonviolent. Indeed, Butler has used the notoriety achieved by their theory of gender to speak up for those whose lives are made unbearable by all forms of inequality. Yet, gender is never far from their concerns. Their understanding of what it is to live does not assume a bare minimum of survival, but incorporates a certain meaningful sense of existence, including not just our ability to eat or breathe, but our capacity 'to desire, to love and to live' (Butler, 2004a: 8). This assigns our need to love and be loved a much higher importance than it is usually accorded in political thought.

Yet in seeking such a world, Butler's aims could be described as modest. They do not foresee that we could live without norms (a sense of what is 'normal' and should be the case), including gender norms. They simply call for a world in which the impact of norms and conventions is minimized, such that the need to conform does not provoke violence against those who do not fit—where behaviours such as gay-bashing and sexual abuse are no longer ordinary occurrences for those who live differently.

Read more about **Butler's** life and work by accessing the thinker biography on the online resources: www.oup.com/he/Ramgotra-Choat1e.

36.2 Gender, feminism, and identity

Whether or not Butler is a feminist thinker is a contested topic. Although claiming to work 'in the interstices of the relation between queer theory and feminism' (Butler, 1997c: 1), she has posed challenges to traditional feminist theory through their problematization of the term 'woman' and her questioning of the category of sex. Their intention was not to undermine feminism, but to expand it, asking why it is that feminism often only speaks for certain women: why it has to establish in advance who/what woman is and why too often it assumes a narrow, white, stereotypically heterosexual, and middle-class understanding of woman. Arguing that this assumption inadvertently delegitimizes those of minority genders and sexualities as well as non-whites and the working class, Butler sought to explore how the category 'woman' is produced in the first place.

In answer, Butler theorized the way that all social norms and identities are maintained through performativity and repetition. Beginning with gender, they argued that there is no 'true' underlying gender that one's male or female behaviour expresses. Instead we 'perform' our gender through repeating its dominant norms. We learn to dress, talk, walk, and shape our desires in accordance with the dominant idea of what it is to be male or female, and this regulates our expectations and judgements of which appearances and behaviours are masculine and feminine. We come to expect men and women to look and act a certain way because the ongoing repetition of this performance retroactively creates the illusion that there is an inner core of gender 'essence': gender is constructed.

More controversially, Butler then questions the division between sex and gender, arguing that if the latter is culturally constructed, there is no necessary connection between sex and gender: there is no reason why male bodies have to be gendered as masculine or female bodies gendered as feminine. Further, there is no reason why we should recognize only two types of gender. This begins to challenge our notion of sex: if there is no reason to presuppose only two genders, then we might also wonder if there are only two sexes. If a 'male' body can be gendered as feminine, what does it mean to talk of a 'male' body in the first place? Butler thus proposed that gender creates sex. This is a bold and perhaps puzzling claim, yet it becomes clearer if we realize that Butler wants us to think about what we mean by 'sex' and how and why we identify every human being as either one or the other sex from the moment of birth.

Butler argues that there are many exceptions to the 'rule' of binary biological sex identification, and cites one medical paper's claim that a 'good ten percent of the population has chromosomal variations that do not fit neatly into the XX-female and XY-male set of categories'. If it is not sufficient to rely on chromosomes or the presence of male or female genitalia to denote sex identity, then on what are we basing our judgement? Butler's answer is that sex is not the concrete biological fact that we assume it to be and is actually discursive: it is an effect of discourse.

If there is no naturally sexed body that exists before culture, this is not to say that our fleshly bodies do not exist with their differences and similarities. It is just to say that they only *come to be understood as sexed* through and for the purposes of our social order to the benefit of some and cost to others. Butler therefore asks: if it is rather difficult to assign sex to a body, why is it so important that we continue to do so, and why does that initial assignment make such an impact on the life opportunities and chances that will be open to that body?

Butler's question had wide-reaching implications for social and medical theory as well as legislation. Widely acclaimed on the one hand as addressing the difficulties faced by gender and sexual minorities, Butler's theory was reviled by those who were horrified by the idea that the sexual distinction between male and female may not be as stable as they had assumed. It was also rejected by many who felt that the category of woman was necessary in order to mobilize a feminist politics. Many of these thinkers were instead committed to a form of politics known as 'identity politics' (see Key Concept: Identity politics), which emerged prominently in the 1970s in the civil rights, women's, gay, and lesbian movements.

By the 1980s, many identity-based movements were facing challenges by those who felt excluded from their particular definitions of woman, gay, or lesbian. For example, as feminism departed further from liberal and Marxist forms which were said to still be constituted in male terms (constructed by and for men), it sought to restart theory from the position of the woman, to theorize women's oppression from a specifically female perspective (e.g., see the work of Mary Daly, Robin Morgan). The importance of this was that it enabled recognition of the way that our ideas of things such as the body, housework, heterosexual sex, and sexuality were political. It helped develop practices by which women-centred knowledge could be produced, free of the interests of men and patriarchal power.

> **Key Concept: Identity politics**
>
> A political strategy moving away from broad party-based politics towards alliances based on shared features of identity, such as sex, race, or gender. This includes, for example, movements such as the civil rights movement, Black resistance, feminism, postcolonial, and gay and lesbian politics.

However, this meant that emergent 'radical feminists' such as Catharine MacKinnon and Andrea Dworkin had to rely even more strongly on a concept of woman that could fit all women. Others responded by asserting that woman—understood as one singular experience—does not exist. Instead there is a plurality of positions that are not men, and that feminism could embrace this difference in a way that still enables it to form a united movement (see variations of this in the work of Carole Gilligan in the USA, Luce Irigaray in France, and Adriana Cavarero in Italy). Many of these 'difference feminists' sought to consider how the various aspects of a woman's identity such as class, race, and gender, interrelated and whether they could be separated out or had to be dealt with together. This latter 'intersectional' approach (see Kimberlé Crenshaw, bell hooks, Angela Davis, and Gayatri Spivak) still, however, retained a particular importance for identity within political and cultural struggle, even though these identities were understood to overlap and interlock with others (read more about hooks in Chapter 3, Spivak in Chapter 24, and Davis in Chapter 35).

The gay liberation movement also struggled with identity politics. Emerging in the wake of the Stonewall protests of 1969, it had initially sought the abolition of all sexual identity (homosexuality and heterosexuality) to be replaced by an understanding of humans as 'essentially polymorphous and bisexual' (Altman, 1972: 74). However, it soon started to assume a particular definition of homosexuality. This provoked arguments concerning who was included in this definition (with objections that it was male-dominated, patriarchal, white, and middle-class); whether homosexuality was an identity category at all; that homosexual identities often imitated heterosexual ones; that gay politics was being dominated by masculinity, excluding lesbians from the movement; and between lesbians over the extent to which butch-femme culture recreates heterosexual, patriarchal standards.

It is important to remember that Butler's *Gender Trouble* was intended primarily as an intervention in these debates—one that sought to loosen our attachments to identities altogether. This loosening was necessary for Butler, since, although identity politics can further the particular struggles of specific groups, it cannot offer us a broader conception of how we are to live together, within our diverse identities. This critique of identity politics has become known as queer theory (see Key Concept: Queer theory).

> **Key Concept: Queer theory**
>
> The term 'queer theory' was coined by Teresa de Lauretis (1991) to distinguish her work from gay and lesbian studies. Queer theory uses the term 'queer' to denote resistance to essentialism, and to definitions in general, meaning that it is impossible to define 'queer' in itself. The term 'queer' was reclaimed by gay and lesbian activists in an affirmative way to resist the use of the label 'queer' as an insult. This inspired the development of a practice of 'queering' that takes categories of identity (such as insulting names) and reuses them in ways that demonstrate the contingency at play. Although adopted by many theorists who operate in the 'queer' field of questioning norms and identities, many acclaim Butler as the leading theorist of queer theory due to their significant contribution to its theoretical framework.

Over time, the assumed distance between Butler's theory of gender and other feminist positions has lessened. Where Butler's *Gender Trouble* was initially misunderstood as championing merely individualistic actions of resistance (Nussbaum, 1999) and implying that gender was volitional—something we could choose to enact or not, at will—their subsequent work, sought to clarify that this was not the case. Against claims that the theory of performativity overlooked women's concrete lived experience (MacKinnon, 2000: 701) and dismissed the importance of legal challenge, collective action, and material transformation (Nussbaum, 1999), Butler insists that political, legal, and economic resistance themselves operate performatively.

> **36.2 Gender, feminism, and identity: Key Points**
>
> - Butler's work has challenged and reshaped feminism and gay and lesbian studies.
> - Butler problematizes the concept of 'woman' and claims that gender constructs sex.
> - Butler's work seeks to deconstruct identity.
> - Butler is famed for their contribution to 'queer theory'.

36.3 Parody and performativity

Performativity is not the same as performance. Although Butler argues that gender is in some way performed, it is not the case that we can simply choose to act like 'a woman' one day or a man the next, depending for example, on how we choose to dress. Instead, performativity acknowledges that social existence is a realm of performance into which we are born, and that exceeds and shapes our own roles. An individual subject does not get to choose freely (of their own volition) their gender, since we each already exist in a context where certain preordained performances are presented to us as the full range of what is possible. Other ways of living may be unknown or less easily available, and some may bear heavier penalties or prohibitions depending on context. The concept of performativity thus asserts that social existence is performative, not that social existence is performed. Just because our ability to live and communicate with one another requires us to engage in identity performance, this does not mean we have the autonomy to choose which roles we are born into nor the performance(s) that we may find ourselves compelled to play.

Butler theorizes gender performativity by drawing on the work of Jacques Derrida. Responding to J.L. Austin's work on the way speech can perform certain acts (such as pronouncing a couple married or the making of a promise—see Key Concept: Speech acts), Derrida (1988) argues that this is only possible because of the accrued history of the performative element which repeats what has gone before. This repetition builds a precedent of historical force. A felicitous (successful) performative 'draws on and covers over the constitutive conventions by which it is mobilized' (Butler, 1993: 172).

> **Key Concept: Speech acts**
>
> According to J.L. Austin (1911–1960), speech is able to act because certain 'performative' utterances 'do things', such as make a promise, make a request, issue an invitation, or apologize. Austin (1962) divided performative utterances into three types. A locutionary act refers to a speaker making a statement that says something that can be understood by the listener. An illocutionary act refers to a speaker saying something with a purpose, such as to inform, and a perlocutionary act refers to saying something that causes someone else to act. Examples of illocutionary acts given by Austin include: 'I now pronounce you man and wife' at a wedding; and 'I christen this ship' at a ship's naming ceremony. Austin notes that these only have the force to succeed (to be 'felicitious') if they enact an already established convention and are pronounced in the right context at the right time by the right people, e.g. children playing may pronounce that a couple are married but would not actually be marrying anyone.

Butler argues that gender is comprised of a collection of actions that iterate 'normal' male and female behaviour, thereby excluding homosexuality just by dint of its absence from the dominant iterations. The requirement for repetition makes the maintenance of norms vulnerable, since to subvert conventions all that needs to be done is to carry out this iteration imperfectly. If difference is inserted into each iteration, Butler argues, the conventions underlying it are drawn upon but at the same time *revealed* rather than covered over. For Butler, subversion of norms is a type of imitation with a twist: an iteration in which something is not quite right, where the copy is not exact. In their obvious and purposeful failure to imitate completely, parody and mimicry can subvert by revealing the contingency of the original.

The weakness of the heterosexual norm is highlighted by revealing its failure to apply in all cases, indicating that it is clearly not as necessary or natural as may have been thought. Since our behaviours are performed and constructed, they *could be otherwise*. By asserting the contingency of norms, Butler argues that it is possible to construct new ways of living and to overturn the normative order that oppresses, excludes, and subordinates those whose gender and sexual identity do not fit heterosexual expectations.

Famously, this subversion is demonstrated through the example of drag. In *Undoing Gender*, Butler (2004a: 213) narrates how while watching male drag artists perform femininity 'better than I ever could'. It became evident that gender is something we perform rather than 'are'. Drag can reveal to us the contingency of our heteronormative practices and thereby demonstrate the possibility that such practices could be less violent: after realizing their contingency, we may no longer enforce them violently. Although drag will not *always* have this effect, Butler notes that it may at times be one way of subverting heterosexual norms by demonstrating their contingency.

Why might such subversion be necessary? Butler's work draws attention to something called 'normative violence'. This refers to the way that norms cause violence just by enforcing certain behaviours and prohibiting others. Denoting everyday conventions as violent in this way may sound melodramatic unless we consider what is at stake. Such violence is the invisible or primary violence that makes certain ways of living possible while prohibiting other ways of life. If a person attempted to live a life not approved by norms, that person would become unintelligible socially, with no place, no sense of being, that could be recognized by others. In addition to the dislocation this could create, it also marks someone out as in need of correction or elimination. This may sound exaggerated until we ask what it is that, for example, makes people rape and murder women, homosexuals, and transgender people. Butler's argument is that this is made possible by normative violence, the violence of having to conform with norms, to ensure that they remain effective. Normative violence in this sense then is a primary form of violence that makes subsequent 'physical violence' possible by creating the context in which it will be generated (see Chambers and Carver, 2008: 76).

> ### Key Thinker: Susan O'Neal Stryker
>
> Professor of Transgender Studies at the University of Arizona, Susan Stryker (1961–) is one of the first openly trans* academics. Her career was famously launched via her dramatic speech in June 1993 at a conference at the University of California, later published as 'My words to Victor Frankenstein above the village of Chamounix'. Along with Paisley Currah, she established *Transgender Quarterly* (TGQ) magazine and authored *Transgender History* detailing trans* history in the USA. Stryker has won numerous awards for filmmaking, literature, and LGBTQ+ advocacy work.

Butler's work on performativity and normative violence is seen by many to have contributed to trans* studies: the problematization of binary sex and gender, the critique of essentialized female identity, and concerns about (hetero)normative violence, together comprise a theoretical framework in which it is possible to think trans* lives. Nonetheless, as we will see, the precise relationship between Butler's work and trans* studies is controversial.

The term trans* refers to all people who do not accord with prevailing expectations of male and female, and those who in various ways live a different sex or gender to that assigned at birth. Trans* can refer to both transgender and transsexual. Examples might include drag kings and queens, heterosexual male cross-dressers, butch lesbians, who are all often referred to as transgender; as well as people who have received surgery or medication to alter their biological sex, often referred to as transsexual. Rather than producing a single definition for 'trans', transgender or transsexual, trans* studies provides space in which trans lives can be spoken and thought, often in order to resist the pressure for definitions. In particular, trans* allows thinkers to engage with the problem of volition which ensnares Butler's early work on performativity. Are sex and gender unalterable parts of our subjectivity, even if they do not match up with the sex or gender assigned at birth, and does that mean they are somehow essential (Stone, 2005; Stryker and Whittle, 2006)? Or are our lived practices of sex and gender somehow operating in a space between the materiality of our bodies and the representative performativity of the ways we live? To what extent can the subject reflexively interact with sex and gender? In this way, although trans* is often treated as an identity, it is also a space of fluidity that further develops the problematization of sex, gender, and their inter-relation as theorized by Butler.

Central to the idea of trans* is recognition that individuals may not identify with the identities assigned to them by others, and instead should be able to self-identify. Although this can seem to be supported by much of Butler's work, criticism of Butler has emerged, in particular from those who see themselves as having a 'real' gender or sex identity that is different from that assigned at birth. Butler's critique of identity could be seen to undermine such a claim for a 'real' identity. Butler's work could also be seen to counter the need to construct a space for a trans* identity that is different from either heterosexual or homosexual identity (see Prosser, 1998;

Namaste, 2000) in order to provide a basis for trans* politics. Hence Butler's critique of normativity as *hetero*normativity has been interpreted as overemphasizing the violence of binary male/female identities without also noting these identities as possible spaces of resistance to normative violence.

> ### 36.3 Parody and performativity: Key Points
>
> - Butler argues that sex/gender are performative; they function through iteration.
> - Performativity has a parodic element—by repeating norms 'wrong' we can subvert the normal operation of gender and sex categories, opening up the potential to live differently.
> - Butler's work has contributed to trans* studies, but the critique of identity politics that it develops has clashed with some trans* theory.

36.4 Subjectivity, resistance, and the psyche

Butler's unique approach to sex and gender emerges from an interest in the philosophical conceptualization of the subject, a topic which has occupied them ever since their doctoral thesis, later published under the title *Subjects of Desire*.

> ### Key Thinker: Georg Wilhelm Friedrich Hegel
>
> G.W.F. Hegel was born in Stuttgart, Germany, in 1770. After rejecting a career in the Church, Hegel worked as a tutor while struggling to establish an academic career. He eventually achieved acclaim for his works of Idealist philosophy, among the most famous of which are the *Phenomenology of Spirit* and *Elements of the Philosophy of Right*. Hegel developed one of the most systematic and detailed post-Kantian philosophies, incorporating many theories that have been enormously influential, including a teleological and dialectical theory of history. He died, aged 61, in 1831.

Subjects of Desire traces the development of the self-conscious subject in the work of Hegel (see Key Thinker: Georg Wilhelm Friedrich Hegel) and its critique by twentieth-century French thinkers, first by Kojève, Hyppolite, and the existentialist thinkers Sartre, de Beauvoir, and Jean Wahl and, second, by French poststructuralists Derrida, Lacan, Foucault, Kristeva, and Deleuze. In it, Butler argues that each critical reading remained captured by Hegel's desiring subject.

Like many other interpreters, Butler (1987: 21) does not read Hegel's description of the emergence of consciousness (see Key Concept: Hegel's theory of recognition) as a factual account but instead as a series of 'instructive fictions'. Butler's reading is distinctive, however, in its interpretation of desire as a 'vehicle' that, in a much-quoted passage 'careens' like the car of the visually challenged 1950s US cartoon character Mr Magoo (Butler, 1987: xv). This reading of Hegel's theory of consciousness as a bumbling, accidental, and non-directed story is a comical counter-narrative to the prevailing interpretation of this theory, usually read as progressing in a neat and ordered teleological process. Where traditional philosophy reads each stage as the successful attainment of the next level in our journey to absolute understanding, Butler sees a series of failures that compulsively prompt the little car to set out again.

> **Key Concept: Hegel's theory of recognition**
>
> Hegel's *Phenomenology of Spirit* (2018 [1807]) contains a famous account of how consciousness emerges from the realm of nature and becomes self-consciousness. At first, the self encounters the other as something to be appropriated—e.g. eaten or used. It cannot at first understand this other apart from itself and its own needs. Experience teaches the self that others have an independent existence since they do not always give in to the self's own need and desires. To preserve itself, consciousness learns to subordinate the other to itself. This initially occurs through violent struggle. Yet if the self kills the other, it would destroy the only means each had of being recognized as a person. It is preferable for the victor to enslave the loser. However, this Lord-bondsman relationship is unsatisfactory since the recognition that the bondsman can give the Lord will only ever be the recognition of a slave rather than a free man and the bondsman is only recognized as an enslaved being. Through his labour, the bondsman is able to unite ideas with raw materials and in the process realize his own consciousness in his ability to master the world around him. This superiority compels the master to free the slave. This leads to a state of equal consciousnesses where each receives recognition. The self knows that it is rational because another rational being recognizes its autonomy.

For Hegel, the subject is desiring: the desire to encounter others moves the subject out of a rather self-obsessed relationship with itself. Borrowing from Heidegger's concept of human existence as outside of itself or 'ek-static', Butler's (2004a) subject is characterized by its operation in a plane of relations with others, through which, in living our various lives, we navigate our ability to be recognized or to fail to be recognized as socially viable beings. As Butler's work progresses, it focuses more on the processes that create us as sexed and gendered desiring subjects, reading desire as principally sexual and erotic. To theorize the desiring subject, Butler draws increasingly on psychoanalysis and, in the process, the comic, bumbling Mr Magoo in his little car of desire is transformed back into a more tragic subject. Its tragic form is more specifically a melancholy one, still stumbling blindly, but now in search of its lost object: that which it lacks but can never recover.

The transformation from comedy to melancholy happened gradually. *Gender Trouble*, with its focus on the parodic nature of subject formation, could be said to have remained in the comic realm. Later works responded to concerns that the theory of performativity implied a volitional subject (Butler, 1990: xxvi)—a subject who could recognize the operation of norms and choose when and where to subvert them. In *Bodies that Matter* and *The Psychic Life of Power*, Butler seemed to turn away from the use of parody to clarify that subjects are not merely self-constituting but are themselves constituted by norms. They operate within a field of power relations that limits their ability to see the constraints of norms and to act to subvert them. Here Butler emphasized that the reading of the formation of the subject in Hegel is of a subject formed through the tragic motif of loss. The self can only find itself again through its reflection in another. But this is not a return to a prior state. That prior state is forever lost, and forever mourned. Thus the relationship to the other is ambivalent. The emergence of the other is what marked the loss of the self but also what makes possible a (re)turn to the self. In undergoing this loss, the self can never again be free of the other. As such, its 'relationality' to the other 'becomes constitutive of who the self is' (Butler, 2004a: 147–148). This understanding of ourselves as irreducibly interconnected with others will go on to form the linchpin of Butler's ethics (see Section 36.5).

In *Bodies that Matter*, the centrality of loss for Butler's subject emerges in the discussion of heterosexual melancholia. This follows Freud's theory of melancholia as a process of ego formation through which we incorporate aspects of loved others into our own psyche because we cannot bear to give them up as a loved object even if they disappoint or abandon us. Provocatively Butler argues that the straight man or straight woman has to give up the possibility of same-sex love.

Heterosexuals therefore incorporate into themselves the same-sex love object or ideal that they had to give up when they assumed a straight identity. This leaves them with an inadmissible melancholic grief for their lost same-sex love objects. Thus Butler argues that homosexuality is the 'constitutive outside' of heterosexuality. It is that upon which heterosexuality is dependent, but which it simultaneously disavows.

In *The Psychic Life of Power*, Butler seems to want to return to the question of what it is that makes performativity able to challenge norms. Although some have argued that Butler (1997a: 3) never offers a direct answer to this question (Disch, 1999; Lloyd, 2007; Woodford, 2017: 165-166), perhaps it is more that Butler reframes the focus to 'how a subject is produced' in order to understand how a subject might resist being produced one way or another, how it might turn against its constituting conditions in order to effect change. Butler observes that although the moment of the inauguration of the subject is theorized in the work of Hegel, Nietzsche (see more on Nietzsche in Chapter 14), Althusser and Foucault (see more on Foucault in Chapter 33), none of these thinkers alone explain how the turn back on the self is possible—the moment in which the subject can resist the way it is being produced. Butler suggests that there is a blind spot in these theories concerning the psychic workings of power that overlooks the passionate attachments by which a subject comes into being (ibid.: 7). Butler proposes that any investigation into the emergence of the subject needs to appreciate both the social and the psychic workings of power. However, because psychoanalysis too easily assumes that there is some sort of unconscious essence that is resistant to normalization (ibid.: 88), they read psychoanalysis alongside Foucault's productive theory of power.

In turning to this task, Butler reviews the work of Hegel, Nietzsche, Freud, Foucault, and Althusser, identifying the psychic features of melancholia in each theorization of the emergence of the subject. Although melancholia is a theory developed by Freud, Butler uses it slightly differently. Rather than asserting that melancholia is an experience that we all undergo, Butler (1997b: 108) instead wants to use the Freudian account as a useful 'allegory' for thinking about how subjectivity is produced. Reflecting on Freud's argument that melancholia involves disavowal of loss while the healthier process of mourning involves acknowledgement of loss, Butler indicates that politicizing mourning might enable us to find a healthier way to live together. This does not just mean feeling that it is acceptable to share one's feelings in public, but identifying hitherto disavowed losses and recognizing them publicly, in order to make society more inclusive while simultaneously weakening the strong identities that depend on disavowal. This may mean loosening our attachments to identities such as gay or straight, woman or man, not in order to advocate the possibility of a neutral position, but to acknowledge that it is through strong identifications that we are compelled to disavow other lives lived. Ambivalence enables us to break from the passionate attachments associated with melancholia. Although we can never re-claim the 'lost object' of the self, we might come to terms with our melancholia so that it is less damaging.

Butler concludes by emphasizing that we come into being as subjects through our social communicability. It is therefore through playing in this field of meaning, which Butler (1997a: 196-198) renders as a field of speakability, of voice and of speech acts (see Key Concept: Speech acts), that we are formed but also can form our existence as subjects. This prefigures Butler's next book *Excitable Speech*, published in the same year, where, in a critique of the legislation against hate speech. Butler argues that language is a weapon we can use to resist subordination. In response to arguments by thinkers including Richard Delgado and MacKinnon concerning the banning of hate speech and of pornography, interpreted as a type of hate speech, Butler argues instead for a performative doubling of language, whereby offensive labels, such as racist or sexist insults, or the aforementioned term 'queer', could be used affirmatively to resist their performative force. This is speech that 'talks back' to those who call names, appropriating that name as something positive and thereby resisting and rendering futile its intended negative connotations.

> **36.4 Subjectivity, resistance, and the psyche: Key Points**
>
> - Butler follows Hegel in assuming that subjects are motivated by desire; Hegel's subject is moved out of itself through an encounter with another: it is ek-static.
> - The subject is formed by a process through which it realizes it can never be fully self-sufficient; once lost, this almost pathological belief in its self-sufficiency is something that can never be retrieved but is experienced as a loss.
> - This leads to Butler's understanding of the subject as 'melancholic': in order to avoid melancholia from harming us, we need to recognize what we have had to lose in order to become the people we are expected to be in today's world; this could enable us to acknowledge and, where necessary, 'mourn' these losses in a healthy manner, thereby avoiding resentment and vengeance, and highlighting the damage done when we normalize judgements that certain ways of life are evil or unacceptable.
> - One way to resist such judgements is to use speech in an 'insurrectionary' manner, taking insults and using them affirmatively; this can weaken their capacity to hurt or undermine us.

36.5 Morality and ethics

Although *Giving an Account of Oneself* is described on its cover as Butler's turn to moral theory, the interest in morality and its imbrication in the formation of the subject is evident in earlier work. In *The Psychic Life of Power*, Butler (1997a: 4) suggests that as soon as we seek to give an account of the formation of the subject, we are 'confronted with the tropological presumption made by any such explanation, one that facilitates the explanation but also marks its limit'. Tropology is a practice of reading scripture to draw out its meaning for our current way of life, specifically with regards to morality. Why, though, would any account of the formation of the subject imply for us specifically a concern for our moral way of life as opposed to any other facet of our life together? In their reading of Hegel, Butler (ibid.: 32) explains that the Lord's freeing of the bondsman launches him into an 'ethical world subjected to various norms and ideal'. Our so-called freedom from domination by others is what moves us into a relationality with others regulated not just by norms, but by norms that always have an ethical dimension (of right and wrong). These norms are not formed after we emerge as a subject into this world nor are they 'merely' self-imposed (ibid.: 33). Instead they are 'the precondition of the subject's very formation' since the subject could not exist without these norms to structure it (ibid.: 33). Thus we can see from *The Psychic Life of Power* that, for Butler, life together with others is already a moral life and all norms are in some sense ethical in the sense of being value-laden.

Butler's focus on morality and ethics, however, becomes more explicit in *Giving an Account of Oneself*, which opens by asking 'how it might be possible to pose the question of moral philosophy' (Butler, 2005: 3). Here the moral is identified as any 'conduct . . . in the contemporary social frame' (ibid.: 3) and Chapter 1 clarifies the implicit moral argument of *Psychic Lives*. Butler further adds that our task is 'to find a way of appropriating [norms], taking them on, establishing a living relation to them' (ibid.: 9). But because we recognize that the 'I' is not just reduced to the norms that shape it, the 'I' has to reflect on those norms in order to distinguish itself from them and operate within them. This involves deliberation that is both ethical and critical (ibid.: 8). It creates a space for creativity in the form of navigating norms by reflecting on them critically for oneself, rather than simply going along with the popular viewpoint.

Butler argues that the scene of the formation of the self requires us to give an account of oneself. According to Nietzsche (1969), we emerge as subjects in a moment of accusation, of having caused suffering and being liable for punishment—an accusation to which we have to respond with an account (Butler, 2005: 10). However, inspired by Adriana Cavarero (2000: 20-29), Butler questions whether the subject only emerges from a scene of punishment and whether it could emerge instead from a will to know about the other who might emerge in response to the question 'who are you?' In tracing the difficulties of answering this question, Butler notes how this self is opaque not only to others but also to itself. There is a limit to what can be known or recounted according to the norms that shape us. It is in the space of wrestling between the 'I' that seeks to be more than the norms and the norms themselves that the 'I' emerges. As Butler has already argued, this is an 'I' that has already lost something—it is 'dispossessed'—through the scene of recognition as a subject. This subject only exists through recognition by the other and in its being shaped by norms. The self is only knowable in its relation to others (how it treats and interacts with others) (Butler, 2005: 81), and since it is in this space of the relation between subjects that we become ethical and responsible, we see that ethics shapes our very existence as subjects.

As beings, Butler argues we are limited and ignorant of ourselves and others. An awareness of our own limits should create a humble attitude and an attitude of forgiveness towards others for their own limitations (ibid.: 42). Following the work of Emmanuel Levinas and Cavarero, Butler suggests that this limitedness manifests itself in our vulnerability to both physical and psychic injury as well as our ability to injure. Butler asserts that an ethics should start from an acceptance of this vulnerability rather than trying to deny or hide our vulnerability, since this can make us more considerate of the vulnerability of others (ibid.: 100). This ethics of vulnerability involves a particular understanding of responsibility that concerns how we respond to injury: do we retaliate or forgive (ibid.: 102)? For Butler (2000: 81), this is a type of humanism that does not seek to limit who or what counts as human but to make us consider which lives we constantly overlook and ignore, despite their vulnerability. Such a response 'risks ourselves', or at least our secure sense of self. It opens us up to others, to the risk of this secure sense of self being 'undone'—but being willing to be undone is, according to Butler (2005: 136), what it takes to become human. In addition, Butler emphasizes that we suffer unequally from something called precarity. It is this that 'designates that politically induced condition in which certain populations suffer from failing social and economic networks of support more than others, and become differentially exposed to injury, violence and death' (Butler, 2015: 33). Precarity indicates our unequal conditions of existence.

In *Precarious Life*, Butler turns to consider what this form of taking responsibility might look like in the USA post-9/11. This work seeks to think about a 'nonviolent, cooperative, egalitarian international relations' that might change social and political conditions and avoid terrorist events happening in future (Butler, 2004b: 17). Butler again asks about the values accorded to different lives that make some more grieved than others, in particular in the context of US foreign policy that excuses its own 'accidental' killing of innocent civilians whilst seeking revenge for the killing of each and every US citizen.

Butler continued to emphasize 'grievability' in subsequent work, and asks if the way in which the subject comes to be 'dispossessed' as it comes into being could help reorientate future politics towards peace in a way that need not depend on violent Western-centric thought (ibid.: 28). Since so much damage comes from attempts to protect ourselves from this vulnerability, by lashing out at others, for example, Butler hopes that if instead we can come to somehow accept the vulnerability of our existence, we might be able to live more peacefully together. Butler posits this ontology of the human as inherently vulnerable, precarious, and grievable as an alternative to the dominant liberal ontology of independent, powerful individuals and their belligerent states.

As we saw above, ethics for Butler is intimately connected with critical, reflexive thought. They appears to hold out faith that critical thinking can make us more open to others. Butler draws on Foucault's argument that ethics is a type of critique that offers a 'perspective on established and ordering ways of knowing which is not immediately assimilated into that ordering function' (Butler, 2002: 215). This is not ethics as a form of prescription. It cannot be reduced to an external moral code that simply tells us how to behave. Indeed, such a code could contribute to further normative violence if we seek to punish those who do not conform. Instead, Butler's ethics is a certain reflexive practice which maintains a critical relation to order.

> ### 36.5 Morality and ethics: Key Points
> - Butler contends that ethics and morality are implied in any relation: as soon as we live with others, we are in the realm of ethics.
> - For Butler, human beings are dispossessed, vulnerable, and precarious.
> - Butler argues that critical reflexiveness can help make us more disposed towards the other.

36.6 Politics

Butler's more recent writing on US military campaigns, torture, and violence directed towards Muslims in the age of the 'War on Terror', the critique of the Israeli occupation of Palestine, and her wider concerns about xenophobia and racism all indicate a particular politics of solidarity with the oppressed. Butler calls for 'an ethos of solidarity that would affirm mutual dependency, dependency on workable infrastructures and social networks, and open the way to forms of improvisation in the course of devising collective and institutional ways of addressing induced precarity' (Butler, 2015: 21–22). This repeated emphasis on public services such as healthcare, education, and housing support all hint at some form of radical democratic left politics, although its precise contours are yet to be clarified.

Butler (2013) follows the work of Hannah Arendt (see Chapter 19), who recognizes that we must cohabit the world not from our own choice but because that is the situation in which we find ourselves. If we are to avoid the violence of seeking to eliminate all those with whom we disagree, our only option is to find a way to coexist together peacefully (Butler, 2013, 166). Butler's aim is to consider how we might be able to find ways to live in this world without rendering the lives of some unliveable.

Butler has accordingly taken an increasing anti-war stance, denouncing state belligerence. Outside the academy Butler supports groups fighting oppression or occupation and those working for peace. *Precarious Life* criticizes the rise of US nationalism following 9/11 and the treatment of prisoners in Guantanamo Bay. Motivated by a 2002 speech by the President of Harvard University, in which he seemed to equate anti-Semitism with any criticism of Israel, Butler developed an argument in *Precarious Life* and *Parting Ways* that defends the possibility of a specifically Jewish critique of the Israeli state that is not anti-Semitic. Developing an understanding of Jewishness that stems from relationality and dispossession, Butler argues that their Jewish identity bestows an ethical responsibility to criticize Israeli treatment of Palestinians. Continuing the anti-war theme, *Frames of War* argues that even if our lives are not destroyed when the state we live in goes to war, something of our lives is destroyed since war destroys others to whom we are connected just by dint of being alive. This theme returns in

Notes Towards a Performative Theory of Assembly where Butler emphasizes that the politics we need must be nonviolent (Butler, 2015: 187–192). This argument was developed in *The Force of Nonviolence*, which theorizes nonviolence as a way of channelling our political anger to show that alternatives are possible through our everyday practices. Rather than countering war and state violence with more of the same, Butler argues that we would do better to demonstrate that other ways of living and organizing ourselves are possible.

Butler's emphasis on living differently leads to a call for us to engage in a politics of refusal, refusing to go along with something Butler refers to as 'neoliberal rationality'. Dominated by an aggressive commitment to free-market policies combined with hostility to the state and public ownership, Butler (2015: 14) identifies neoliberalism with a particular individualist ontology and as the cause of the precarity that they are keen to challenge. Here again we see that, for Butler, ethics cannot be separated from politics, for in this argument neoliberal rationality is seen to have within it a morality that shapes its politics.

How might we resist neoliberal politics then? In the wake of the Arab Spring in 2010 and the wave of protests between 2011–2012 that formed the Occupy! movement, Butler celebrates the power of mass protest to assert popular sovereignty against repressive state power. Butler notes that demonstrations are not simply good things, and could represent various forms of politics (ibid.: 124). It is also recognized that many people may not be able to be present at such demonstrations such as those who are incarcerated or disabled (ibid.: 151). Yet Butler suggests that there is a power associated with appearing in public that asserts the right of those appearing to be able to do so. Butler hopes demonstrations might 'produce a rift within the sphere of appearance' (ibid.: 50). We reveal our precarity and interdependence in such demonstrations, directly disproving neoliberal expectations of individual responsibility. Yet, rather than seeking to unite us in a unified and homogeneous anti-neoliberal movement, Butler argues that we need to build alliances and coalitions. This is particularly important for understanding the turn to ethics. Butler has not abandoned gender politics. Instead, this later work just calls for a wider coalition of the precarious and those who recognize the vulnerability of the human condition.

Butler has increasingly emphasized the infrastructures we need to make our lives liveable: from healthcare to public amenities such as pavements, street lights, sanitation, running water, and housing. Butler insists that we need to begin again to think about how these can be provided, and at times recommends that we start to provide them for one another, celebrating political occupations where medicine and social support are provided by protesters for one another. Butler notes that, for many, neoliberal rationality seems shocking because we are used to the social-democratic consensus that asserted that people do and should care for one another. Butler's work persistently asks 'what does it mean to act together when the conditions for acting together are devastated or falling away?' Butler answers that in gathering together we can signify our 'persistence and resistance' to neoliberalism (ibid.: 23). Furthermore, political resistance to neoliberalism has to be radically egalitarian if we are to recognize the value of life without asserting vitalism (the celebration of all that is living just because it is living). Instead, Butler simply asserts that all life is valuable, incalculably so, and life here means not merely survival but livability and grievability too.

Butler's celebration of life is distinctive. It acknowledges that the emphasis on the value of life could undermine claims to 'bodily integrity and self-determination' so important to many political movements for the rights to be free of violence and rape; the right to abortion; and sexual freedom (Butler, 2004b: 25). In response, Butler has distinguished this argument from the 'pro-life' position on the grounds of equality. Butler argues that many 'pro-life' positions are 'committed to inequality' because they 'privilege some forms of life, or living tissue (e.g., the fetus), over others (e.g., teenage or adult women)' (Butler, 2020: 109). But alongside this argument Butler is critical of the mainstream liberal approach which bases arguments for rights on liberal understandings of sovereign selfhood.

Instead, Butler's approach indicates that much more work is needed if we are to adequately consider in such debates 'whether we are referring only to human life, to cell tissue, and embryonic life, or to all species and living processes, and thus to the ecological conditions of life' (ibid.: 141). Somewhat surreally, given the extent of religious critiques of Butler's work, this leaves Butler searching for terminology concerning how we might value life in a way that complements theological arguments much more closely than many of their contemporaries, albeit while strongly eschewing the pro-life position.

Indeed, given the aforementioned observations that Butler has often been caricatured as the figurehead of either a postmodern attack on religion and tradition, on the one side, or a liberal watering down of radical theory on the other (Chambers, 2014), it is worth noting the importance of Butler's argument that, contrary to popular opinion, progressive politics need not be associated with secularism. This is key to Butler's critique of the Western-centrism of political theory, which suggests that secularity is itself structured by religion, in particular a certain Western-centric interpretation of Christianity. Secularists will often accuse religions of absolutism and dogmatism while overlooking their own absolutist and dogmatic tendencies (Butler, 2009). In contrast, (2013: 116) argues that religious education can contribute towards the formation of a politically critical subject. Butler's openness towards religion is specifically motivated by the desire to avoid the anti-Islam narrative popularized by the War on Terror. Yet in a more general sense it also comprises part of Butler's decolonization of political thought by providing greater legitimization to non-Western beliefs. Perhaps the puzzled reception of Butler's critique of secularity indicates just how strongly we continue to rely upon Western-centric political cleavages in political theory. This challenge to the usual alignment of religion with the conservative right is just one example of the trouble Butler's work has provoked in mainstream political thought. Unlike many political theorists, Butler does not patronize those with opposing views, but takes seriously the possibility of alliances of plurality and diversity beyond the Global North.

36.6 Politics: Key Points

- Butler calls for a nonviolent and radically egalitarian politics.
- Critical of US nationalism and Zionism, Butler has also spoken out against a certain dogmatic Western secularism which can be just as harmful as religious fundamentalism.
- Butler challenges the traditional Western understanding of the relationship between politics and religion and has developed a unique perspective in contemporary ethical theory.
- Since we must cohabit in the world, Butler seeks to find a way that we can do so without resorting to violence, arguing that this requires resistance to neoliberalism and theorization of how we can develop non-oppressive structures of support.

36.7 Conclusion

Through critiques of US foreign policy, Israeli politics, xenophobia, and neoliberal precarity, Butler has become a vocal critic of Western-centrism and developed a nonviolent, anti-war politics that emphasizes the need for all of us to live differently, to oppose neoliberal rationality and individualism by seeking to make life liveable, even in small ways, in the face of the forces that exploit, dominate, and destroy. In conclusion, we can see that Butler's work has dramatically unsettled the terrain in which political theory operates today. It uses the fame associated with the theory of gender to refocus attention on the vulnerable and the precarious; to prompt us to make theory more inclusive; to put inequality and injustice back on the agenda; and to encourage us to reject calls for violence with a firm commitment to peace. Although, as befits such a rich body of work, the details of Butler's thinking will likely always attract criticism and provoke debate, it is difficult to dispute that Butler has made a remarkable contribution to redirecting political theory towards a more compassionate agenda.

Take your learning further by accessing the online resources for a library of web links to relevant videos, articles, blogs, and useful websites for this chapter: www.oup.com/he/Ramgotra-Choat1e.

Study questions

1. Is Judith Butler a feminist?
2. How does Butler's work challenge identity politics?
3. How are sex and gender related?
4. What is the difference between performance and performativity?
5. Do you think that performativity can change our normal ways of behaving? How?
6. What is 'insurrectionary speech' and how does it work?
7. Why does Butler argue that we are all vulnerable?
8. Should egalitarian politics be nonviolent?

Further reading

Primary sources

Butler, J. (1990) *Gender Trouble*. London: Penguin.
  Butler's most famous text, outlining the theory of performativity.

Butler, J. (2020) *The Force of Nonviolence*. London: Verso.
  A good summary and outline of Butler's political theory and intellectual contribution.

Butler, J. and Athanasiou, A. (2013) *Dispossession: The Performative in the Political*. Cambridge: Polity Press.
  A conversation with Athena Athanasiou about the concept of 'dispossession' in the context of riots and uprisings of the early twenty-first century.

Butler, J. and Gambetti, Z. (2016) *Vulnerability in Resistance*. Ed. L. Sabsay. Durham, NC: Duke University Press.
  A collection of essays on the theme of vulnerability introduced by Judith Butler, developing a new conception of embodiment.

Secondary sources

Brady, A. and Schirato, T. (2011) *Understanding Judith Butler*. London: Sage.
  Useful introduction to Butler's thought that situates it in the wider context of cultural theory.

Carver, T. and Chambers, S. (eds) (2008) *Judith Butler's Precarious Politics: Critical Encounters*. London: Routledge.
  A collection of critical essays. Of note are Lloyd's contribution on the limitations of Butler's ethics and Dean's critique of Butler's politics.

Chambers, S. and Carver, T. (2008) *Judith Butler and Political Theory: Troubling Politics*. London: Routledge.
  An engaging introduction that summarizes Butler's thought and interprets it from the perspective of political theory.

Devenney, M. (2019) 'The Performative Politics of a Brick'. In *Towards an Improper Politics*. Edinburgh: Edinburgh University Press.
  A defence of Butler's ontology and an application of Butler's work on resistance.

Disch, L. (1999) 'Judith Butler and the Politics of the Performative'. *Political Theory*, 27(4): 545–559.
  A critical review.

Hennessey, R. (2000) *Profit and Pleasure*. New York: Routledge.
  A critique from queer Marxism.

Honig, B. (2010) 'Antigone's Two Laws: Greek Tragedy and the Politics of Humanism'. *New Literary History*, 41(1): 1–33.
  A critical essay concerning Butler's ontology of vulnerability.

Lloyd, M. (2007) *Judith Butler*. Cambridge: Polity Press.
  An in-depth introduction that places Butler's work in context.

Lloyd, M. (ed.) (2017) *Butler and Ethics*, Edinburgh: Edinburgh University Press.
  A collection of critical essays.

Salih, S. (2002) *Judith Butler*. London: Routledge.
  An accessible short introduction.

Shulman, G. (2011) 'On Vulnerability as Judith Butler's Language of Politics: From Excitable Speech to Precarious Life'. *Women's Studies Quarterly*, 39(1&2): 227-235.
  A critique of Butler's ethics of vulnerability.

References

Altman, D. (1972) *Homosexuals: Oppression and Liberation*. Sydney: Angus and Robertson.

Austin, J.L. (1962) *How to Do Things with Words: The William James Lectures delivered at Harvard University in 1955*. Oxford: Oxford University Press.

Butler, J. (1987) *Subjects of Desire*. New York: Columbia University Press.

Butler, J. (1990) *Gender Trouble*. London: Penguin.

Butler, J. (1993) *Bodies that Matter*. London: Routledge.

Butler, J. (1997a) *The Psychic Life of Power*. Stanford, CA: Stanford University Press.

Butler, J. (1997b) *Excitable Speech*. New York: Routledge.

Butler, J. (1997c) 'Against Proper Objects'. In E. Weed and N. Schor (eds), *Feminism Meets Queer Theory*. Bloomington, IN: Indiana Press.

Butler, J. (2000) *Antigone's Claim: Kinship between Life and Death*. New York: Columbia University Press.

Butler, J. (2002) 'What Is Critique? An Essay on Foucault's Virtue'. In D. Ingram (ed.), *The Political: Readings in Continental Philosophy*. London: Basil Blackwell.

Butler, J. (2004a) *Undoing Gender*. New York: Routledge.

Butler, J. (2004b) *Precarious Life*. London: Verso.

Butler, J. (2005) *Giving an Account of Oneself*. New York: Fordham University Press.

Butler, J. (2009) *Frames of War*. London: Verso.

Butler, J. (2013) *Parting Ways*. New York: Columbia University Press.

Butler, J. (2015) *Notes Towards a Performative Theory of Assembly*. Cambridge, MA: Harvard University Press.

Butler, J. (2020) *The Force of Nonviolence*. London: Verso.

Cavarero, A. (2000) *Relating Narratives: Storytelling and Selfhood*. Trans. P.A. Kottman. London: Routledge.

Chambers, S. (2014) 'Subjectivation: The Social and a (Missing) Account of the Social Formation'. In *Bearing Society in Mind*. London: Rowman & Littlefield.

Chambers, S. and Carver, T. (2008) *Judith Butler and Political Theory: Troubling Politics*. London: Routledge.

De Lauretis, T. (1991) '"Queer Theory": Lesbian and Gay Sexualities'. *Differences: A Journal of Feminist Cultural Studies*, 3(2): iii-xviii.

Derrida, J. (1988) 'Signature, Event, Context'. In S. Webber and J. Mehlman (eds), *Limited Inc*. Evanston, IL: Northwestern University Press.

Disch, L. (1999) 'Judith Butler and the Politics of the Performative.' *Political Theory*, 27: 545–560.

Hegel, G.W.F. (2018 [1807]) *The Phenomenology of Spirit*. Trans. and ed. T. Pinkard. Cambridge: Cambridge University Press.

Lloyd, M. (2007) 'Radical Democratic Activism and the Politics of Resignification'. *Constellations*, 1(4): 129–146.

MacKinnon, C. (2000) 'Points against Postmodernism'. *Chicago-Kent Law Review*, 75(3): 687–712.

Namaste, V. (2000) *Invisible Lives: The Erasure of Transsexual and Transgender People*. Chicago: University of Chicago Press.

Nussbaum, M. (1999) 'The Professor of Parody: The Hip Defeatism of Judith Butler'. *The* New Republic, 22 February.

Nietzsche, F. (1969) *On the Genealogy of Morals*. Trans. W. Kaufman. New York: Random House.

Prosser, J. (1998) *Second Skins: The Body Narratives of Transsexuality*. New York: Columbia University Press.

Stone, A. (2005) 'Towards a Genealogical Feminism: A Reading of Judith Butler's Political Thought'. *Contemporary Political Theory*, 4: 4–24.

Stryker, S. and Whittle, S. (eds) (2016) *The Transgender Studies Reader*. New York: Routledge.

Woodford, C. (2017) *Disorienting Democracy: Politics of Emancipation*. London: Routledge.

Part IX

The Environment, Human, and Non-Human

37	Dipesh Chakrabarty	Eva-Maria Nag	679
38	Donna Haraway	Claire Colebrook	697
39	Indigenous Ecologies	Esme G. Murdock	713

We opened this book by reflecting on the boundaries of the political (Part I: Chapters 2–4). Indeed, these are questions that, in some sense, run through all of the chapters in this book: what is politics, where does it take place, and who or what does it involve? One boundary that has traditionally been highly significant is that between the human world and the 'natural' world, typically with only the former judged to be political. This does not mean, however, that the natural world has played no role in political thought. Non-human animals in particular have been used to delineate the boundaries of the political: many (though by no means all) political theories base themselves, explicitly or implicitly, on a theory of human nature, and what is 'human' is very often defined in contrast to what is 'animal'. Thinkers across the centuries have excluded animals from politics on the basis that they lack some characteristic claimed to be specifically human, variously identified as speech, reason, creativity, free will, or any one of numerous other candidates.

Yet this traditional identification of animal life as non-political is highly questionable. First, even if animals are different to humans in some essential way, our lives are intimately entwined with theirs: we make use of animals for food, clothing, medicine, and entertainment; they enter and live in our towns and cities, and we build in and travel through their territories. As such, it is legitimate and even necessary to examine human-animal relations using political concepts, such as obligation, justice, exploitation, and rights. Second, it can reasonably be argued that the lives of animals are themselves political—depending, of course, on how we define 'politics'. Animals come into conflict with each other, and they develop, defend, and contest social hierarchies between themselves, competing for resources and establishing relations of power. Third, it can be said that the differences between human and non-human animals have been exaggerated. We may be closer to animals than we like to think: animals, after all, also use technology, communicate with each other, and organize themselves into (often hierarchical) groups. The boundary between human and non-human animals is more complex or porous than has often been claimed.

The tendency in European thought has been to separate the human world not only from the animal worlds but from the natural world more generally. 'Nature' has very often been portrayed as something given to man (and traditionally it has been *men*) for him to control and master. This attitude has deep roots, going back at least as far as the claim in the Old Testament that God gave man 'dominion over ... all the earth, and over every creeping thing that creepeth upon the earth' (Genesis 1:26). This belief has simultaneously been gendered and racialized, with women and non-white populations frequently characterized as closer to or part of the natural rather than the human world—and hence open to exploitation by white men.

Yet, global heating and other looming ecological disasters expose the hubris of the claim that humans are masters of the natural world: humans have unleashed forces and processes that they may not be able to control or predict. The urgent need to understand and address the existential threat of climate change, and environmental degradation more generally, highlights the importance of political thought while simultaneously posing challenges to conventional approaches to politics. Environmental problems are never purely natural, biological, or scientific: they are simultaneously social, economic, and political. The destruction of the non-human environment has political consequences for humans, giving rise to food shortages, conflict, increased migration, pandemics—and potentially even the end of human life itself. These problems in turn demand political solutions, which may vary from free-market fixes, through calls for greater state intervention, to forms of eco-anarchism. The persistent failure actually to implement any solutions that might slow or reverse ecological destruction also calls for political analysis: are solutions impeded by our political or economics systems, or by some flaw in our human nature?

The impact of human activities upon the Earth has been so great that the term 'the Anthropocene' has been coined to refer to the current period of the Earth's history as one in which, for the first time, humans are having a decisive influence on the Earth's geology, climate, and ecosystems. There is disagreement about when the Anthropocene started, with suggestions including the dawn of settled agriculture 12,000 years ago, the start of the Industrial Revolution in the eighteenth century, or the detonation of the first nuclear bomb at the end of the Second World War. The concept has been criticized, however, for the way in which it glosses over the highly differentiated causes and impact of environmental problems. Not all humans, for instance, are equally affected by or culpable for climate change: it has mainly been caused by rich people in the Global North and its worst effects have been on poor, mostly non-white people in the Global South. The term 'the Capitalocene' has been proposed to highlight the role of capitalism as the cause of our current predicament and obstacle to necessary change.

The concept of the Anthropocene is central to the recent work of Indian historian Dipesh Chakrabarty (Chapter 37). While he is critical of capitalism, Chakrabarty contends that the climate crisis cannot be reduced wholly to capitalism. He argues that political thinking must be planetary and go beyond human-centred critiques of capitalism, colonialism, and globalization. Chakrabarty is an interesting example of a political thinker for whom the ecological crisis demands new directions of research: as Chapter 37 explores, Chakrabarty's recent writings build on but also challenge his earlier contributions to postcolonialism.

The US thinker Donna Haraway—whose work crosses numerous disciplines—is one of those who prefers the term 'Capitalocene' to 'Anthropocene'. Indeed, as Chapter 38 explains, she has also used the term 'the Plantationocene', to emphasize the role of colonialism and slavery in transforming the Earth, and has coined her own term 'the Chthulucene'. This latter term is intended both to allude to the multiple histories that make up the present and to lessen human exceptionalism (without denying the impact of human activities on the planet). All of Haraway's work has sought to highlight human beings' entanglement with and reliance upon both non-human life—from the animals that live and work with us to the microbes that live inside us—and technology, as captured by Haraway's influential concept of the 'cyborg'.

Haraway's unsettling of the traditional boundaries and oppositions between animals and humans and animals, nature and culture, is relatively novel within 'Western' political thought, but similar manoeuvres have long been common in other traditions. Chapter 39 examines Indigenous political and ecological thought, looking at the forms of knowledge of people whose sovereignty was violently suppressed by settler colonialism, with a special focus on Indigenous peoples from what is currently called North America. There are sharp contrasts between Indigenous thought, which emphasizes reciprocity, balance, and interdependence, and what the chapter calls 'Western industrial thinking', which is centred on human domination over nature.

Chapter 39 is the only chapter in this book which does not name at least one specific thinker in its title. This is categorically not because we think that Indigenous thinkers deserve less respect and recognition than non-Indigenous thinkers: numerous Indigenous scholars are discussed and cited throughout the chapter. Nor is it because we think that all forms of Indigenous thought are homogeneous or indistinguishable. As the chapter eloquently shows, even where there are shared features and principles, Indigenous thought remains enormously diverse. But naming the chapter 'Indigenous ecologies' highlights that the production and dissemination of knowledge can take varied forms. Not all traditions venerate individual authors or rely on textual—rather than oral—transmission. While we think that there are pedagogical advantages to categorizing ideas according to individual thinkers—as we explained in Chapter 1—this is certainly not the only way of organizing and studying political thought, as Chapter 39 shows.

Nor should we imagine that Indigenous forms of knowledge production are somehow anachronistic. Chapter 39 not only discusses numerous present-day Indigenous scholars, it also demonstrates the salience of continuing Indigenous resistance to pipelines, mining, and other corporate extractive practices. Far from being outmoded, Indigenous thought offers insights into the interdependence of human and non-human life that are remarkably pertinent to our current malaise and with which Western thinkers are only now beginning to catch up.

37 Dipesh Chakrabarty

EVA-MARIA NAG

Chapter guide

This chapter offers an overview of Dipesh Chakrabarty's contribution to political thinking that is concerned with the human condition in the age of climate change. Chakrabarty contends that human-centred ways of thinking about the world and about humanity itself are no longer appropriate. In his widely cited article 'The Climate of History: Four Theses', he makes a case for bringing together natural and human history; for humans having become a non-human, geological force upon the planet; for capitalism having only a limited role in climate change; and for a new focus on planetary history, not merely human history. After introducing Chakrabarty as a postcolonial historian and political thinker, the chapter will examine his conceptualization of the Anthropocene as a new historical and planetary era. Section 37.3 will explore the complex connections between freedom, capitalism, and climate change. Section 37.4 will introduce Chakrabarty's image of humanity as a geological force. This has considerable implications for how he rethinks familiar ideas of justice, the topic of Section 37.5.

37.1 Introduction

Dipesh Chakrabarty (1948–), born in Kolkata, India, is, in his own words, a 'practising historian with a strong interest in the nature of history as a form of knowledge' (Chakrabarty, 2009: 198). At the time of writing, he holds the post of Lawrence A. Kimpton Distinguished Service Professor of History, South Asian Languages and Civilizations at the University of Chicago. His work is shaped by the confluence of personal and intellectual trajectories that span the anti- and postcolonial era of the second half of the twentieth century and the era of globalization and its discontents in the early twenty-first century. With a background in physics, Chakrabarty came to study history as a postgraduate student under the tutelage of the Marxist historian Barun De (Dimova-Cookson, 2012: 60). His writings self-consciously reflect his diverse identities as a Bengali Brahmin, a former Maoist revolutionary during his youth, and an academic straddling an 'insider/outsider relationship' with the United States, India, and Australia (Chakrabarty, 2018b: xxxii). Chakrabarty does not describe himself as a political theorist who builds systems of political ideas, but as a political thinker who 'cuts his or her own way through a jungle' (Dimova-Cookson, 2012: 70). A multidisciplinary social scientist, his writings are located in various fields and geographies: South Asian history and literature, Marxist political economy, twentieth-century globalization, and large-scale planetary history.

As part of India's Subaltern Studies group (see Key Thinker: Ranajit Guha, and also Section 24.2.2 of Chapter 24 on Subaltern Studies), Chakrabarty's early contributions to the study of Indian history and postcolonialism stemmed from his critique of epistemological and ethical deficiencies of universalism and rationalism found in both classical Marxist and liberal thought. He argued that the abstract thought and universal concepts which characterize classical Marxism and European liberalism could not relate to the lived experiences of human rootedness, belonging, and difference.

Read more about **Chakrabarty's** life and work by accessing the thinker biography on the online resources: www.oup.com/he/Ramgotra-Choat1e.

Further, the repressive and violent Eurocentric processes of modernization had been the opposite of the ethical claims of modern Western political thought to justice and equality (Dimova-Cookson, 2012: 66).

> ### Key Thinker: Ranajit Guha
>
> The Indian historian Ranajit Guha (born in 1923 in Siddhakati, Backergunje, British India) was a founding member and intellectual driver of the Subaltern Studies movement that emerged in India in the early 1980s, and was also the editor of the group's first set of anthologies. Initially conceived as a project rooted in 'anti, and not postcolonial, thought' (Chakrabarty, 2012: 3), today the term has influential reach outside of India and within numerous disciplines, including postcolonialism. Scholars associated with the Subaltern Studies movement include Partha Chatterjee, Shahid Amin, David Arnold, Gyan Pandey, David Hardiman, and Gayatri Chakravorty Spivak (see also Chapter 24). The original aim was to counter both colonialist elitism and bourgeois-nationalist elitism that dominated the historiography of Indian nationalism (Guha, 1982: 1). Neither approach took seriously 'the contribution made by the people *on their own*, that is, *independently of the elite* to the making and development' of Indian nationalism (ibid.: 3). Instead, Guha shows colonial and national power to be the exercise of 'dominance without hegemony' (Guha, 1997), coexisting but separate from the autonomous domain of non-elite politics and culture. This shift in focus was also a significant departure from Eurocentric Marxism's 'history from below' with its emphasis on the universality of historical progress and the unity of political classes (see also Chapter 13 on Marx).

The later project of decentring and 'provincializing Europe' was a further critique of the homogenizing forces of Western-centric globalization and capitalism (Chakrabarty, 2008). In rejecting the idea of history as a uniform and linear trajectory of development, Chakrabarty argues that there are several and distinct histories of political modernity, of which the mythical construct of 'Europe' represents only one, albeit vested with the colonizing power that came from being seen as 'the original home of the modern' (ibid.: xiv). Yet the postcolonial concepts of difference, power, oppression, and justice are the backdrop rather than the foreground to his more recent thinking on politics in the era of climate change, triggered by his traumatic experience of the 2001–2009 'Millennium Drought' in Australia. In his writings on the Anthropocene, Chakrabarty aims to explore what is new about this era by pointing to the limitations of old ways of thinking about human societies (Chakrabarty, 2021). Crucially, the new ways of thinking are not to supplant or transcend older ideas. Instead, political thinking has to constantly move between the old and the new, requiring that political subjects inhabit multiple perspectives about the world and about themselves at the same time.

The term Anthropocene stands for a new stage of both human and planetary history in which 'humans collectively have become a geophysical force capable of changing the planet's climate to the detriment of humanity' (Chakrabarty, 2018b: xxxii, see also Key Concept: Anthropocene in Section 37.2). Thus, postcolonial thinking cannot stop at critiques of globalization, but 'may need to be stretched to adjust itself to the reality of global warming' (Chakrabarty, 2012: 1). Section 37.2 will set out Chakrabarty's analysis of our changing social and material worlds, and why the social sciences must connect with the natural sciences in unprecedented ways, especially with earth sciences and environmental sciences.

37.2 What is the Anthropocene?

Most social science disciplines have generally concerned themselves with human societies on their own terms, disconnected from their physical environments. The realities of climate change mean that the social sciences can no longer be indifferent to the rapidly changing external conditions in which societies find themselves. The intensive exploitation of the Earth's natural resources, especially of fossil fuels since the late 1800s, have led to changing levels of certain chemical compounds found within the Earth's atmosphere. The rise of heat-trapping gases such as carbon dioxide, methane, and various fluorinated greenhouse gases in particular have led to rising temperatures and shifts in weather patterns. The consequences of climate change include droughts, flooding, extreme weather events, rising sea levels, acidification of the oceans, melting of polar ice caps, damage to food chains, and the rapid loss of biodiversity. These environmental changes now pose catastrophic threats to the functioning of human societies, namely threats to livelihoods, to access to food and water, to health and well-being, and to the ability of humans to survive and thrive on a planet that will be unable to sustain the necessary conditions for biological life.

Natural scientists had already noted changes to the Earth's atmosphere as early as the mid-nineteenth century. Although 'scientific studies of global warming are often said to have originated with the discoveries of the Swedish scientist Svante Arrhenius in the 1890s' (Chakrabarty, 2009: 198), it would be more accurate to credit the beginnings of climate science to the American amateur scientist and natural philosopher, Eunice Foote (Mariotti, 2019) (see Key Thinker: Eunice Foote). Foote's experiments were a precursor to later experiments by John Tyndall in 1860 that described the greenhouse effect. Yet it was only in 1938 that the steam engineer and amateur climatologist Guy Callendar demonstrated the quantitative connection between global warming and emission of greenhouse gases through human activity (Hawkins, 2013). Even so, discussions of human-induced global warming remained separate from critiques of globalization in the social sciences. These discussions only connected in the 2000s (Chakrabarty, 2009: 198–199).

Key Thinker: Eunice Foote

Eunice Foote (1819–1888) was a scientist, inventor, and women's rights campaigner who only very recently has been credited with being the first scientist to discover the absorption of thermal radiation by carbon dioxide and water vapour. These discoveries have been foundational to our understanding of the greenhouse effect and of climate change (Jackson, 2019: 105). Her discoveries were published in 1856 in the *American Journal of Science and Arts*. Although her findings were noticed by a small number of physicists in the USA, her ground-breaking work was ignored by scientists in Britain and Europe. Today, more efforts are being made by contemporary historians of science to highlight Foote's status as a climate science pioneer.

In the twenty-first century, the main propositions of climate science have finally entered the public domain, with profound implications for how the social sciences think about human history and the modern, industrialized world (Chakrabarty, 2009: 198). Key to this have been the 2006 Stern Review on the Economics of Climate Change, the 2007 Fourth Assessment Report of the Intergovernmental Panel on Climate Change (IPCC) of the United Nations, and the many books that have been published by scientists and scholars seeking to explain the science of global warming. Assuming that the main propositions of climate science are accurate, Chakrabarty uses the commonplace but highly contested term 'Anthropocene' to describe this particular period of planetary and human history (see Key Concept: Anthropocene). Coined in the 1970s by the American marine biologist, Eugene F. Stoermer, it gained popular acceptance in the 2000s when the Dutch Nobel Prize-winning chemist Paul Crutzen reinvented it.

> **Key Concept: Anthropocene**
>
> The word Anthropocene is derived from the Greek words *anthropos*—man—and *cene*—new. Earth scientists work with chunks of time known as geologic timescales. These are descending lengths of time called eons, eras, periods, epochs, and ages. Officially we are in the Meghalayan Age of the Holocene Epoch, which began 11,700 years ago after the last major ice age. For earth scientists, the Anthropocene Epoch is an *unofficial* unit of geologic time as it can only be declared a new epoch if the changes to the earth system made by humans can be reflected in the rock strata and can be identified as human-made. So far, the term has not been formally adopted by the International Union of Geological Sciences (IUGS), the international organization that names and defines epochs. However, many scientists agree that the informal term 'Anthropocene' is highly useful in describing 'a period of Earth's history during which humans have a decisive influence on the state, dynamics and future of the Earth System'. (http://quaternary.stratigraphy.org/working-groups/anthropocene/)

For Chakrabarty, the impact of humans on the planet itself means that the time has come for social scientists to connect their fields of study with the climate sciences. This is not easily done, as natural scientists and social scientists work with different conceptual and methodological tools. With reference to his own work, he notes that

> as the crisis gathered momentum in the last few years, I realized that all my readings in theories of globalization, Marxist analysis of capital, subaltern studies, and postcolonial criticism over the last twenty-five years, while enormously useful in studying globalization, had not really prepared me for making sense of this planetary conjuncture within which humanity finds itself today.
>
> (Chakrabarty, 2009: 199)

So far, the task of historians and social scientists has been to discern and judge humans' purposeful actions in constructing their social, cultural, and economic worlds. Natural events were relegated to the background (ibid.: 203). This differentiation between natural history and human history has a long tradition in European thought, going back to 'the old Viconian-Hobbesian idea that we, humans, could have proper knowledge of only civil and political institutions because we made them, while nature remains God's work and ultimately inscrutable to man' (ibid.: 201). This idea remained powerful, even in twentieth-century secular, materialist, and sociological thinking (ibid.: 204). This partly had to do with the relatively slow pace of change of humankind's external environment compared with fast-moving changes within human societies. Moreover, human history did not appear to have any impact on 'eternal' nature, nor did the seemingly slow changes in environmental conditions impose binding constraints on how human societies functioned (ibid.: 204).

Today, the changes to our natural environment are radical and rapid, and many societies and economies are greatly affected by these changes. It seems intuitive that knowledge of the Earth's systems matters if human societies are to rise to the practical challenges posed by climate change. Yet, as Chakrabarty argues, knowledge in itself does not provide a compelling reason for action to combat climate change. Humans act on judgements, motivations, and choices. These in turn are driven by moral and political considerations such as justice, fairness, and obligation. He identifies two obstacles to acting on the knowledge of climate science. First, deep-rooted socio-economic and political divisions stand in the way of collective and solidaristic action on climate change. The second obstacle is the difficulty of grasping the vastly different spatial-temporal scales of the non-human environment. This is to say that 'motivating human action on global warming necessarily entails the difficult, if not impossible, task of making available to human experience a cascade of events that unfold on a non-human scale' (Chakrabarty, 2018b: 222). The social sciences in the age of the Anthropocene are thus tasked with rethinking human agency in historical *and* geological time to provide answers to the questions of 'how did we get here?' and 'what can we do to preserve our future'?

37.2.1 Historical time and geological time

The concept of the Anthropocene as 'a measure of not geological time but of the *extent* of human impact on the planet' (Chakrabarty, 2018a: 7) requires that we think of time simultaneously as human-centred and planet-centred. Importantly, climate change and the Anthropocene are not quite the same. The former is part of the planet's natural climatic conditions that have changed over the c. 4.5 billion years of its existence. Such changes have also enabled the emergence of basic life on Earth, not long after the planet was formed. To be able to imagine such vast scales of time, natural scientists use planet-centred geological timescales, to also answer 'general questions of habitability of a planet, questions to which humans are not central' (Chakrabarty, 2018a: 25). Geological time is a measurement of changes to the planet such as the emergence as well as the extinction of certain life forms. These are known as boundary events. Ever greater consensus is forming around the idea that the Anthropocene is a specific, human-triggered boundary event. It is recognizably a period of mass extinctions of many forms of animal, insect, and plant life. It is also a period of significant changes to the Earth's atmosphere and changes to the Earth's upper layers that now bear traces of our material lives, for instance, in the form of microplastics and toxins.

Historical time is human-centred and not planet-centred. It is based on recording, tracking, and tracing events that have communicable meaning for humans. Although part of geological time, historical time is recent and is recorded on much more comprehensible scales. Historical time can be divided into deep and recorded history, that is to say from the time human societies began to the time societies began to record and transmit information through written signs.

> **Key Concept: Recorded and deep history**
>
> Recorded history goes back c. 5000 years, starting with the first written texts. Deep history cannot rely on texts but due to advances in archaeological analysis, gene mapping, and evolutionary ecology, is traced back as far as 2.6 million years. It aims to understand trends and processes in the evolution and spread of human societies on this planet. For Chakrabarty (cited in Cohen, 2011), deep history has a role 'in retelling the human story' and bringing to the table 'a sense of contingency in human affairs'. Deep history is a useful tool that counters teleological readings of human history which foreground European dominance within recorded history, in particular within the period of early modernity and modernity of the last four hundred years.

One of the key differences between geological and historical time is that only the latter transmits a sense of agency and affect, involving the language of 'hope and despair' (Chakrabarty, 2018a: 13). Therefore, it is not the scientific and neutral language of climate change but the emotive language of the Anthropocene that calls for a new kind of political thinking. Central to this language is the idea of freedom. Section 37.3 will explore Chakrabarty's thesis that links humans' historical quest for freedom with a reliance on fossil fuels. Paradoxically, these freedoms are threatened by the natural effects of cumulative and high-intensity fossil fuel usage.

> **37.2 What is the Anthropocene?: Key Points**
>
> - Chakrabarty reads the Anthropocene as a new era in the Earth's history that connects planet-centred geological time and human-centred historical time.
> - It signifies a challenging period of climate change brought about by human activities, in particular by the burning of fossil fuel for energy, with profoundly negative implications for all life on this planet.
> - Human-triggered climate change means the natural world cannot be seen as a mere backdrop to human activities.
> - Knowledge of how societies function has to be compounded by knowledge of the planetary conditions of human existence; yet human existence and activities are undermining these very conditions and, conversely, these changing climatic conditions are shifting how societies function.
> - The Anthropocene thus poses the dual challenge of finding practical as well as political solutions to global warming and energy-intensive globalization.

37.3 A story of globalization and capitalism: freedom and fossil fuels

Chakrabarty contends that most human freedoms—ranging from freedom from natural hazards to living autonomous and acquisitive lives—were made possible by the extraction of the Earth's non-renewable but plentiful carbon resources and the utilization of these resources as fuel. For almost 300 years, the use of coal has underpinned energy-intensive technological developments in industry, agriculture, and lifestyles that are at the heart of modern economic systems of growth and consumption. Despite rising inequalities within and among states, for a long time these developments led to an overall flourishing of human beings.

37.3.1 Freedom

According to Chakrabarty, freedom is 'a blanket category for diverse imaginations of human autonomy and sovereignty' and is 'the most important motif of written accounts of human history of these two hundred and fifty years'. He refers to a diverse range of ideas and movements, found, for example, in the works of Kant, Hegel, or Marx; in ideas of progress and development; in class struggle; in the struggle against slavery; in various resistance movements and revolutions; in decolonization movements; and in civil rights discourses. Although different in their concrete aims, these movements shared a concern for freedom from dominance, or 'the injustice, oppression, inequality, or even uniformity foisted on them by other humans or human-made systems' (Chakrabarty, 2009: 208).

Other freedoms go back even longer to the beginnings of agriculture more than 10,000 years ago. These are material freedoms that are key to physical survival, such as the freedom from starvation, disease, early mortality, and burdensome manual labour. From the mid-twentieth century onwards, the exponential rise in the use of cheap and plentiful fossil fuels that are used globally in transportation, food production, medicine, and consumer goods enabled more people, including the poor, to live longer lives (Chakrabarty, 2017: 28). Alongside are the freedoms to acquire tradeable goods and to reproduce in big numbers. A carbon- and industry-based economic system is therefore at the heart of commonplace aspirations to economic growth, improvement in living standards, creation of jobs and the reduction of poverty. These are societal goals subscribed to by most modern states and societies. While some recent socio-economic thinking is shifting to ideas such as 'de-growth' (Hickel, 2020), 'post-GDP worlds' (Fioramonti, 2017), or a Great Deceleration to counter the Great Acceleration of the second half of the twentieth century, none of these models considers curtailing fundamental freedoms as enshrined for instance in the Universal Declaration of Human Rights (adopted in 1948) or the International Covenant on Economic, Social and Cultural Rights (adopted in 1966). These bundles of rights recognize universally held claims to sovereignty and autonomy of individuals and states through material and non-material development with the free use of natural resources and wealth (United Nations, 1967: ICESCR, Article 1, para 2).

This line of thinking that legitimizes the extraction and exploitation of natural resources has a long lineage with no specific geographic, religious, or cultural source. It can be traced to societies across the world. Clearly, not all societies had or have the political and economic power to exploit natural and human resources in the same way. Moreover, there are alternative views about non-exploitative relations between human societies and their environments, as reflected in many strands of Indigenous political thinking (McGregor, Whitaker and Sritharan, 2020). Ultimately, Western-led globalization with its deep socio-political and cultural roots in colonialism, industrialization, and industrial agriculture proved to be a dominant model for human activities that are now linked to climate change. Today, many social scientists concerned with human well-being, autonomy, and justice, analyse not whether, but *how* the processes and structures of globalization and global capitalism pose fundamental threats to universal aspirations to freedom and to the capacity for the Earth's system to sustain the rate of growth of human numbers and material consumption.

37.3.2 Global capitalism

Though a critic of elite-centred globalization and capitalism, Chakrabarty departs from analyses that connect climate change primarily with the socio-economic systems of global capitalism. Seemingly going against the grain of his intellectual commitments to the political left, he offers two reasons for claiming that 'the whole crisis cannot be reduced to a story of capitalism' (Chakrabarty, 2009: 221). The first is that capitalism was historically preceded by other systems of growth and accumulation. The second is that critics of capitalism generally do not differentiate between global and planetary history. The global stands for ideas such as justice, equality, power, and resistance. It is about the fine-grained history of domination and subjugation within human-centred socio-economic and political systems. Planetary history happens on a much larger scale and is about the central role of earth systems in the evolution of the bio-chemical conditions for the emergence of life. Knowledge of the planet's history means having knowledge about the conditions of the habitability of the planet by various life forms, including humans. We now know that human activity has changed the course of planetary history by changing its background conditions, bringing it to the brink of inhabitability caused by rising temperatures (Chakrabarty, 2014). Over the next 20 years, temperatures are set to rise by 1.5 to 2 degrees above pre-industrial levels, considered critical thresholds for irreversible perils (Masson-Delmotte et al., 2021).

37.3.3 The global and the planetary

With the habitability of the planet at stake, Chakrabarty states that the impact of climate change will be felt by all of humanity, arguing that runaway global warming would in the end affect the rich as well as the poor. This would not happen at once but would certainly happen in the case of credible boundary events like the extinction of human life, or the extinction of the lives of the poor upon which the modern capitalist system of cheap labour relies. In the case of a likely planetary crisis, 'unlike in the crises of capitalism, there are no lifeboats here for the rich and the privileged' (Chakrabarty, 2009: 221). Moreover, while globalization is about individuals and human societies, planetary conditions are dependent on much larger scales of forces. The human species itself falls into this category, acting with collective agency and as a non-purposeful geological force. Critical analyses of globalization and capitalism reject such collectivism and the notion of human agency without purpose. Social and political history has not been about sameness and homogeneity, as Chakrabarty himself has shown in his work on postcolonialism and Eurocentrism. In writing about the Anthropocene, he now shifts his position to consider both human and planetary scales of space and time. Social scientists need to understand how human societies were able to develop within planetary history, and conversely how humans' global history of extraction and consumption is affecting these very conditions of life on the planet. This requires the conceptual ability 'to move back and forth between thinking on these different scales all at once' (Chakrabarty, 2018b: 203).

To illustrate, Chakrabarty posits that 'anthropogenic climate change is not inherently—or logically—a problem of past or accumulated intrahuman injustice' (Chakrabarty, 2014: 11). Rather, the problem lies in the total output of greenhouse gases, resulting from the *mass* consumption of fossil fuels. Without these energy sources, humans would not be able to pursue many of freedoms valued by most people and societies, including the rights to freely reproduce, produce, and consume (Chakrabarty, 2012: 14). He hypothesizes that even a non-capitalist and egalitarian distribution of wealth would have led to the climate crisis, perhaps in worse ways. The reasoning is that

> [the] collective carbon footprint would only be larger—for the world's poor do not consume much and contribute little to the production of greenhouse gases—and the climate change crisis would have been on us much sooner and in a much more drastic way. It is, ironically, thanks to the poor—that is, to the fact that development is uneven and unfair—that we do not put even larger quantities of greenhouse gases into the biosphere than we actually do. Thus, logically speaking, the climate crisis is not inherently a result of economic inequalities—it is really a matter of the quantity of greenhouses gases we put out and into the atmosphere.
>
> (Chakrabarty, 2014: 11)

37.3.4 Critical debates and defence

To his critics, this unjustifiably shifts the responsibility for the climate crisis from rich and powerful states and corporations to an abstract humanity. Slavoj Žižek (2010: 330–336) was one of the first to respond to Chakrabarty's Four Theses, and highlighted the primary role of capitalism as causing the current ecological crisis. Since then, several others have stressed the links between global warming and the specific geopolitical history of capitalism, rejecting Chakrabarty's interpretation of the Anthropocene as a species-wide history (see Malm and Hornborg, 2014). These thinkers are generally part of Marxist traditions and are those with whom Chakrabarty directly engages. They criticize the very notion of the Anthropocene, arguing that terms like the Capitalocene would be more accurate descriptors (see Moore, 2017, see also Chapter 38 on Haraway). Their counter-arguments are compelling, citing that there are indeed 'lifeboats for the rich', that consumer power resides primarily in the West and not everywhere, that the accumulation of goods is specific to capitalism, and that tackling global warming will not and cannot come from species solidarity but from the solidarity of the subalterns to counter the economic and ecological power of global and national elites (Emmett and Lekan, 2016).

Criticism has also been levelled at the tension between Chakrabarty's own work on postcolonialism, with its concerns about difference, power, and positionality, and his writings on the Anthropocene that bring in a 'quietist, highly abstract liberal universalism and a Malthusian population politics' (Boscov-Ellen, 2020: 73). There is a worry that the dual focus on an unexplained commonality of the human species and their inescapable socio-political differences leads Chakrabarty to a position of theoretical and practical paralysis (ibid.: 75). These are examples for ongoing debates between Chakrabarty and others within political theory and across other disciplines, including geology, earth sciences, paleoclimatology, geography, biodiversity, sustainability, ecology, and history. In his rebuttals, Chakrabarty claims that both pro-capitalists and anti-capitalists are unable to leave behind human-centred approaches to climate change, hoping to either buy or innovate themselves out of the crisis, thereby underestimating the implications of a Great Extinction event for all of humanity (Chakrabarty, 2019b: 25). The era of the Anthropocene does not signal an end to critiques of capitalism or to ongoing struggles for justice and freedom from oppression. The politics of race, gender, caste, and class is far from over. However, critiques of capitalism have to continue *alongside* the incorporation of new analytical perspectives, such as planetary and species thinking.

To better understand his arguments, Section 37.4 will explore Chakrabarty's views of the human as characterized by agency and diversity while constituting an impersonal and undifferentiated geological force at the same time. These are described as old and new images of the human, although the old and new are not sequential or temporal categories but exist simultaneously.

37.3 A story of globalization and capitalism: freedom and fossil fuels: Key Points

- Chakrabarty posits that human-centred political thinking on globalization and capitalism has reached its limits in understanding and dealing with the implications of climate change for life on Earth and for the future of humanity.
- Political thinking in the Anthropocene calls for a recognition of large-scale shifts across time and space to differentiate between the planetary and the global.
- The global is defined as the sphere of human-centred socio-economic and political systems, dealing with questions of justice, distribution, locality, and power.
- The planetary refers to the central role of earth systems, even though these are independent of human agency and will.
- Unless critical thinking about humans' social systems can find ways of accommodating knowledge of the planet and the conditions of habitability of the planet, human societies will be existentially threatened.

37.4 Old and new images of the human: free agent and geological force

The idea of the human is central to political thinking. A society's assumptions about what human beings are and what they ideally should be are 'manifested in its social codes, formal laws, informal behaviour systems, its high art, its self-conscious theory' (Kaviraj, 1979: 16–17). One such assumption has been the distinction between humans as natural, biological beings and humans as makers of constructed, socio-cultural histories. It served an important purpose of distinguishing the realms of freedom and agency from deterministic views of human beings as driven by their biology. However, this dualism was never recognized by environmental historians and thinkers (Chakrabarty, 2009: 205). Today, eco-centric and hybridist theories are moving beyond traditional 'green' thinking on balanced relations between humans and nature. Thinkers like Bruno Latour (2004; 2018) or Jairus Grove (2019) point to social and political worlds that are not static or merely interlinked with the natural world. Rather, humans, non-humans, technologies, and natural events interconnect through complex associations with each other, often in unpredictable ways. This thinking also challenges Eurocentric and elitist models of development that have been violent and extractive towards those with less power or agency.

Chakrabarty's work intersects with these recent developments in political ecology but takes a different turn. He scales up the view to focus on the impersonal dimension of humanity as a species with power over planetary history. As such, human beings are not only differentiated, autonomous agents consciously acting out their own histories, but also constitute an undifferentiated species that is unwittingly acting as a *non*-human geological force (Chakrabarty, 2009: 206). The sheer numbers of humans, their technologies, and their collective activities of consumption and reproduction have had an impact on the planet that is only possible through having enough of 'a force on the same scale as that released at other times when there has been a mass extinction of species' (ibid.: 209-207). No other species has exercised this level of collective force or changed the planetary conditions of habitability. Thinking about humans as a species is not an original idea, but it takes two distinct forms in Chakrabarty's work. The first connects with his roots in postcolonial thought. The second is found in his approach to political thinking as border crossings.

37.4.1 Different, equal, and conjoined

Anticolonial views perceived humans as equal sovereign subjects and creators of their own destinies (Chakrabarty, 2012: 4). Postcolonial theories challenged this uncritical acceptance of the essentialist idea of the human and instead emphasized differences in people's manifold identities and respective positions vis-à-vis power (Balibar, 2020: 8). Humans are not simply abstract bearers of universal rights but are 'endowed everywhere with what some scholars call "anthropological difference"—differences of class, sexuality, gender, history, and so on' (Chakrabarty, 2012: 2). This was an attempt at a deeper engagement with human nature, taking into account that individual lives are complex, contradictory, and shaped by relations of power. To these two images Chakrabarty adds a third view of humanity as an impersonal force. The three images of the human are the rights-bearing, abstract human who emerged out of the seventeenth- and eighteenth-century European Enlightenment, the twentieth-century postcolonial human embodying difference, and the twenty-first-century human as part of the human species wielding impersonal, geological force. Human beings thus are different in their respective positions and situations, but equal in their aspirations and rights, and conjoined in their collective impact on the planet.

Drawing on the work of the postcolonial thinker Homi Bhabha, Chakrabarty contends that human beings thus occupy not one but multiple positions simultaneously. This simultaneity is explained through the imagery of border-crossings and contradictions (Bhabha, 1994). Borders are both conceptual and actual. Bhabha claims that globalization epitomizes continuous border crossings. Although twentieth-century globalization celebrated interdependence, openness, and mobility, borders have not been eradicated. Bhabha elucidates how humans, in particular subaltern groups of people, in crossing geographical and political borders constantly mediate and create multiple identities, e.g., of insiders and outsiders, survivors and civic participants at the same time. Chakrabarty borrows from this idea to assert that the era of the Anthropocene is a new frontier to be crossed. Like the borders constructed by humans (such as political boundaries and social identities), the Anthropocene is not only a new temporal era but is also a space that exists alongside the spaces of states, economies, and cultures, and within which a specific form of humanity as a geological force has emerged.

> **Key Concept: Humanity and human species**
>
> Chakrabarty connects species thinking 'to the enterprise of deep history' (Chakrabarty, 2009: 213). This view departs from Marxian thought about the 'species being' of humanity realizing itself through freely chosen conscious activity. Instead, taking his cue from climate scientists, Chakrabarty differentiates between the Greek word for human, 'anthropos', and the Latin word, 'homo'. 'Anthropos' in anthropogenic climate change is a neutral term signifying a long-term causal relationship between human beings, their existence on this planet and their collective impact on the planet without assigning moral culpability. It is about the non-human force of the human species as an undivided collective. The 'homo' is the divided, and moral figure of humanity (Chakrabarty, 2015: 157–159), and is the subject of the politics of climate change, in particular of climate justice.

37.4.2 Species thinking

Species thinking is contested and problematic (see Dibley, 2012b). Chakrabarty concedes that the idea of humans constituting an undifferentiated collective is of serious concern for historians and social scientists who criticize the determinism and essentialism inherent in this idea (Chakrabarty, 2009: 214). For this reason, the term 'species' to denote human beings is rarely, if ever, used by historians and critical thinkers analysing globalization. In using this term, he points to an overlap between the biological sciences and cultural studies. Neither discipline considers species as homogeneous entities embodying a particular essence, for example of human-ness or fish-ness (ibid.: 214). Moreover, species thinking is not a call to seek out the true nature of human beings but is a conceptual tool that works at three different levels. First, it brings to the fore the role of the planet as the site of flourishing of all species, including humans. Second, it stands for the human species as constituting an impersonal, a-political force that has reversed the planetary conditions of flourishing. Third, it is a placeholder term for a simultaneously divided *and* conjoined collective of humans that share the same existential threats despite their differences. Section 37.5 will examine the implications of Chakrabarty's species thinking for a new kind of political thought that criss-crosses between justice-sensitivity and what Chakrabarty denotes as 'justice-blindness'.

> ### 37.4 Old and new images of the human: free agent and geological force: Key Points
>
> - Political thinking is intrinsically linked to questions of who human beings are, what they can be, and what they ought to be; such thinking can focus on commonalities and on differences.
> - In modern Western political thought, a major point of contestation has revolved around the question of whether humans are abstract beings bearing universal rights such as freedom, development, and security, or whether they are differentiated beings with unique localized histories, aspirations, and relations to sites of social and political power.
> - According to Chakrabarty, these views of the human do not supersede or compete with each other, as these different and often contradictory modes co-exist in the same space and at the same time.
> - This is possible as politics always takes place on a multiplicity of scales such as communities, cities, states, and international organizations; in the Anthropocene, the planet is a new site of politics, leading to a new view of human beings as a geological force.
> - Species thinking stands for the collective power of human beings over planetary conditions; Chakrabarty emphasizes that other views of human beings are not cancelled out but retain their importance in the context of climate change as an ethical and political issue.

37.5 Justice-sensitivity and justice-blindness

The idea of justice has been a perennial feature of political thinking across centuries and across the world. Regardless of how human nature is viewed, humans mostly live in social groups. Politics is about the structure and legitimacy of these groups, with debates on the role and place of the individual, on what is due to individuals and to groups, on the right and lawful means of distribution of a range of material goods (income, wealth, assets) and non-material goods (status, opportunities, freedoms, power). Crucially, these are intra-human arguments about the scope and aims of justice. Climate change is now changing the context and scope of justice. Chakrabarty delineates three kinds of thinking about justice in this new era. First, intra-human justice retains a central role, especially in the context of climate justice. Second, sharing the limited space of the planet with other species who are facing anthropogenic extinction means that inter-species justice matters for political thinking. Third, the impersonal force of humanity implies a certain kind of justice-blindness that is new to political thought.

37.5.1 Intra-human justice

The shared existential threats posed by climate change have not subsumed humans' divisions. Humanity's diverse political and technological responses to climate change are inevitably grounded in anthropological differences. Intra-human justice thus remains a central feature of politics, especially in the realm of climate justice that considers the unequal burdens of climate change on the rich and poor, developed and developing countries, as well as on present and future generations (Chakrabarty, 2019b: 22). Species thinking does not negate the historical role of mainly Western nations in generating the currently dangerous levels of greenhouse gases. The politics of common but differentiated responsibilities in trying to curb emissions is critical to this pushback (Chakrabarty, 2009: 218). However, Chakrabarty offers two additional perspectives. First, the pursuit of justice also takes place in the context of the pursuit of energy-intensive freedoms, for instance, economic development. The trade-offs between development and redistribution mean that ideals of intra-human justice are inevitably pursued on longer timescales than climatic tipping points allow for. As the pursuit of justice in a particular period of time might in fact lead to existential risks further down the line, this calls for resituating humanocentric notions of justice that have to date taken the planetary basis for existence for granted (Chakrabarty, 2021: 178). Second, the Anthropocene is more than climate change caused by greenhouse gas emissions. It is also the era of the sixth Great Extinction of non-human species, caused by an ecological overshoot of humans in terms of appropriating the limited resources and room on the planet (Chakrabarty, 2018b: 201–212; 2019b: 23).

37.5.2 Inter-species justice

This brings up a second idea of justice, namely of inter-species justice. In his various writings on the Anthropocene, Chakrabarty only briefly but critically questions the legitimacy and legacy of humans colonizing the Earth in the way Europeans colonized and appropriated others' lands and goods for their exclusive use (Chakrabarty, 2014: 16). This kind of dominance raises the issue of obligations to the dispossessed who are not necessarily other humans but other species. Chakrabarty does not have clear or systematic answers to this question. He contends that

> we could act as a responsible species – by which I do not mean as do-gooders—but only if we had a multispecies government. But we have a human government, we only have domination by this species on this planet . . . It is not enough—hough I welcome the gesture—to extend (human) rights to non-humans.

(Chakrabarty, 2018b: 266)

Extending fundamental rights to animals or other life forms remains problematic given that conceptions of justice are human-focused (Chakrabarty, 2019b: 27). At the same time, exponential population growth and rapid spread are a practical form of domination. While the idea of 'population' or over-population is highly contested (Connelly, 2010), in Chakrabarty's work it takes on the distinct meaning of viewing human populations as a human biomass that is crowding out non-human biomass. This is a question of justice as the fair distribution of life chances. In the most general way, Chakrabarty's critique is a call for new kinds of political systems that take seriously the rights and interests of the dominated, whether humans or non-humans.

37.5.3 Justice-blindness

Going beyond conceptions of justice that require awareness of ourselves and others, Chakrabarty claims that 'we also have a collective mode of existence that is justice-blind. Call that mode of being a "species" or something else, but it has no ontology, it is beyond biology, and it acts as a limit to what we also are in the ontological mode' (Chakrabarty, 2012: 14). Justice-blindness is a consequence of viewing human beings as part of a non-political collective. Chakrabarty relates this back to the thinking of the German philosopher, Karl Jaspers (1883–1969), in particular, Jaspers' notion of epochal consciousness which he 'tied to the question of humans' perceived capacity to project themselves into the world as collective, sovereign agents' (Chakrabarty, 2015: 144). It is described as a 'shared perspectival and ethical space' that arises at momentous times in human history. Further, it is a pre-political perspective in that humanity's divisions matter less than its commonalities at these moments. Momentous times can be achievements like the moon landing or dangers such as the detonation of the first nuclear weapon. Epochal consciousness does not lend itself to finding practical solutions to shared problems in the first instance, but rather constitutes a collective ethical position towards the world, formalized by legal treaties in international law, for instance. Globalization engendered a similar consciousness about the dangers of global capital, technologies, and environmental destruction.

Climate change calls for yet another kind of epochal consciousness that raises collective awareness of the planet as a new political category. It is a moment of recognition that 'the institutions of human civilization, including technology, have interfered with some critical planetary processes.' These are processes that have no moral or ethical dimensions as they take place on non-human scales of time and space. Human action changed the planet's atmospheric and environmental conditions. Yet there are no rational, single, or justice-based solutions that can reverse these changes within the timescale needed to prevent the current crisis from tipping into the irreversible event of mass extinction of life. Moreover, 'with regard to the planet, ... we are no more special than other forms of life. The planet puts us in the same position as any other creature' (Chakrabarty, 2019a: 28–29). Ultimately, human-centric ideas and ideals of justice cannot in the short term change the boundaries of habitability that are now closing in on all species.

37.5 Justice-sensitivity and justice-blindness: Key Points

- Anthropogenic climate change necessitates new ways of political thinking about justice.
- Justice was always conceptualized in many different ways, but these debates took place within and among human societies only.
- Political thinking in the Anthropocene sharpens the role of justice as the burdens of climate change fall on societies in unequal ways.

- It further connects the concept of human justice with the rights of and obligations towards non-human species that are suffering from changing environmental conditions and from human domination over their lives and habitats.
- At the same time, natural, though human-induced, planetary processes are leading to existential risks faced by all species; given the non-human scale of these processes, these threats cannot be met by the human-centred politics of justice that operate on human scales of time and space.

37.6 Conclusion

Chakrabarty's contribution to political thinking of the twenty-first century is to ask probing questions about the politics *in* the Anthropocene, not merely the politics *of* climate change. In line with thinkers who defend the idea of the Anthropocene as human-induced and as a shared challenge for all of humanity, he argues that the era of climate change requires new perspectives on politics that go beyond traditional critiques of capitalism, colonialism, and globalization. He calls for a rethinking of methods in the social sciences and for extending the scope of the subjects of politics. On the former, he believes that the social sciences must connect with the natural sciences to grasp the implications of rapid changes to the earth systems for the functioning of human societies. Relatedly, his views on human history as contingent, indeterminate, and dependent on planetary processes serve to rethink conceptualizations of historical time as linear, progressive, and fully controlled by humans. Regarding the scope of political thinking, he contends that political thinking must scale up to include the planet as a new site of politics that affects all human societies. Humanity too is recast as a non-political geological force, implying that politics can no longer be solely human-centred. Moreover, the scope of the politics of justice also has to encompass the non-human realm. Chakrabarty's insistence on the simultaneity of perspectives and scales leads him to being both an optimist and a pessimist about solutions to the climate crisis. As a liberal, he is optimistic about the role that the enlightened self-interest of the rich could play in combating climate change, and about the possibility of a solidaristic politics between the rich and poor (Chakrabarty, 2019b: 26). As a theorist of postcolonial difference, he is pessimistic about the coming together of unequal social groups in the near future. As a critic of global capitalism, he highlights that governments across the world debate solutions to climate change from dominant, Western, developmentalist positions. These are undemocratic and elitist debates, ignoring the publics who are often intentionally kept uninformed about the politics of the climate change (ibid.: 31). Chakrabarty's core theses are complex and are subject to much critical debate. In breaking with anthropocentric methods of political thinking, he has laid himself open to the charges of having crossed the boundaries of what is considered to be properly part of politics and political thinking. He is also regarded as having diminished the roles of colonialism and capitalism in climate change. These are important discussions still to be had. Ultimately, Chakrabarty's theses end in the politics of contradiction, trade-offs, and imperfection. His conceptualization of the Anthropocene is useful in identifying new questions and rethinking old analytical frameworks. Without providing just, rational, or simple solutions, it is a soberingly realistic assessment of the political conundrums of the day.

Take your learning further by accessing the online resources for a library of web links to relevant videos, articles, blogs, and useful websites for this chapter: www.oup.com/he/Ramgotra-Choat1e.

Study questions

1. Is Dipesh Chakrabarty right in saying that the capitalism alone cannot explain the crisis of climate change?
2. What is the link between the consumption of fossil fuels and the exercise of freedom?
3. Why does Chakrabarty believe that historians need an understanding of geological time?
4. How compelling are Chakrabarty's arguments that the planet is a new agent of change in the Anthropocene?
5. What are the three images of the human in the era of climate change and how do they relate to each other?
6. How does Chakrabarty differentiate between humans as 'species beings' and humans as 'rights-bearing individuals'?
7. Why does intra-human justice still matter in the age of climate change?
8. Why is the dominance of the human species a problem for humanity?

Further reading

Primary sources

Chakrabarty, D. (2009) 'The Climate of History: Four Theses'. *Critical Inquiry*, 35(2): 197–222.
  A seminal article which argues that climate change poses limits to human-centred political thinking.

Chakrabarty, D. (2012) 'Postcolonial Studies and the Challenge of Climate Change'. *New Literary History*, 43(1): 1–18.
  Explores the challenge of rethinking human agency over multiple and incommensurable scales.

Chakrabarty, D. (2014) 'Climate and Capital: On Conjoined Histories'. *Critical Inquiry*, 41(1): 1–23.
  Connects the history of the earth system with the history of human evolution and industrial civilization.

Chakrabarty, D. (2017) 'The Politics of Climate Change Is More Than the Politics of Capitalism'. *Theory, Culture & Society*, 34(2–3): 25–37.
  Takes issue with the complexity of climate change as being only one manifestation of humanity's impact on the planet.

Chakrabarty, D. (2018a) *The Crises of Civilization: Exploring Global and Planetary Histories*. New Delhi: Oxford University Press.
  Essays on the contested, crisis-ridden nature of the global and thoughts on the implications of climate change for human history.

Chakrabarty, D. (2018b) 'Anthropocene Time'. *History and Theory*, 57(1): 5–32.
  Discusses the difference between historical time and geological time.

Chakrabarty, D. (2019a) 'The Planet: An Emergent Humanist Category'. *Critical Inquiry*, 46(1): 1–31.
  Foregrounds ESS (Earth System Science) as a tool for differentiating between the planetary and the global.

Chakrabarty, D. (2021) *The Climate of History in a Planetary Age*. Chicago: University of Chicago Press.
  Systematically sets out ideas of the planet as a new category of political theorizing, and connects this category with the globe.

Secondary sources

Boscov-Ellen, D. (2020) 'Whose Universalism? Dipesh Chakrabarty and the Anthropocene'. *Capitalism, Nature, Socialism*, 31(1): 70–83.
   Critically examines Chakrabarty's turn from anti-universalism to a universalist humanism with regard to shared human responsibility for climate change.

Dalby, S. (2016) 'Framing the Anthropocene: The Good, the Bad and the Ugly'. *The Anthropocene Review*, 3(1): 33–51.
   A review of various interpretations of the Anthropocene and prospects for interdisciplinary thought.

Dibley, B. (2012a) '"The Shape of Things to Come": Seven Theses on the Anthropocene and Attachment'. *Australian Humanities Review*, 52: 139–153.
   An exploration of various implications of the Anthropocene as a new epoch and as a political discourse.

Dibley, B. (2012b) '"Nature Is Us:" The Anthropocene and Species-Being'. *Transformations: Journal of Media and Culture*, 21: 1–15.
   Develops the idea of humans as species beings, in tension with humans as having geological agency.

Emmett, R. and Lekan, T. (2016) 'Whose Anthropocene? Revisiting Dipesh Chakrabarty's "Four Theses"'. *RCC Perspectives Transformations in Environment and Society*, No. 2.
   Short, multidisciplinary, and critical essays engaging with Chakrabarty's 2009 article.

Žižek, S. (2010) *Living in the End Times*. London: Verso.
   An overview of current-day debacles, including a critique of Chakrabarty's arguments about the limits of capitalism as a useful analytical tool for understanding the implications of climate change.

References

Balibar, É. (2020) 'Ontological Difference, Anthropological Difference, and Equal Liberty'. *European Journal of Philosophy*, 28(1): 3–14. doi: 10.1111/ejop.12512.

Bhabha, H. (1994) *The Location of Culture*. London: Routledge.

Boscov-Ellen, D. (2020) 'Whose Universalism? Dipesh Chakrabarty and the Anthropocene'. *Capitalism, Nature, Socialism*, 31(1): 70–83. doi: 10.1080/10455752.2018.1514060.

Chakrabarty, D. (2008) *Provincializing Europe*, 2nd edn. Princeton, NJ: Princeton University Press.

Chakrabarty, D. (2009) 'The Climate of History: Four Theses'. *Critical Inquiry*, 35(2): 197–222.

Chakrabarty, D. (2012) 'Postcolonial Studies and the Challenge of Climate Change'. *New Literary History*, 43(1): 1–18.

Chakrabarty, D. (2014) 'Climate and Capital: On Conjoined Histories'. *Critical Inquiry*, 41(1): 1–23. doi: 10.1086/678154.

Chakrabarty, D. (2015) 'The Human Condition in the Anthropocene'. *The Tanner Lectures in Human Values*, pp. 139–188.

Chakrabarty, D. (2017) 'The Politics of Climate Change Is More Than the Politics of Capitalism'. *Theory, Culture & Society*, 34(2–3): 25–37. doi: 10.1177/0263276417690236.

Chakrabarty, D. (2018a) 'Anthropocene Time'. *History and Theory*, 57(1): 5–32.

Chakrabarty, D. (2018b) *The Crises of Civilization: Exploring Global and Planetary Histories*. New Delhi: Oxford University Press.

Chakrabarty, D. (2019a) 'The Planet: An Emergent Humanist Category'. *Critical Inquiry*, 46(1): 1–31. doi: 10.1086/705298.

Chakrabarty, D. (2019b) 'The Politics of Climate Change Is More Than the Politics of Capitalism'. In K-K. Bhanvnani et al. (eds), *Climate Futures: Reimagining Global Climate Justice*. London: Zed Books, pp. 21–31.

Chakrabarty, D. (2021) *The Climate of History in a Planetary Age*. Chicago: University of Chicago Press.

Cohen, P. (2011) 'History That's Written in Beads as Well as in Words'. *The New York Times*, https://www.nytimes.com/2011/09/27/arts/deep-history-takes-humanity-back-to-its-origins.html (accessed 13 June 2022).

Connelly, M. (2010) *Fatal Misconception: The Struggle to Control World Population*. Cambridge, MA: Harvard University Press.

Dibley, B. (2012b) '"Nature Is Us:" The Anthropocene and Species-Being'. *Transformations: Journal of Media and Culture*, 21: 1–15.

Dimova-Cookson, M. (2012) 'Subaltern Studies, Post-Colonial Marxism, and "Finding Your Place to Begin from": An Interview with Dipesh Chakrabarty'. In G. Browning (ed.), *Dialogues with Contemporary Political Theorists*. Basingstoke: Palgrave Macmillan, pp. 58–73. doi: 10.1057/9781137271297_4.

Emmett, R. and Lekan, T. (eds) (2016) 'Whose Anthropocene? Revisiting Dipesh Chakrabarty's "Four Theses"'. *RCC Perspectives Transformations in Environment and Society*, 2: 15–20.

Fioramonti, L. (2017) *The World After GDP: Economics, Politics and International Relations in the Post-Growth Era*. Cambridge: Polity Press.

Grove, J.V. (2019) *Savage Ecology*. Durham, NC: Duke University Press.

Guha, R. (ed.) (1982) *Subaltern Studies I: Writings on South Asian History and Society*. New York: Oxford University Press.

Guha, R. (1997) *Dominance without Hegemony: History and Power in Colonial India*. Cambridge, MA: Harvard University Press.

Hawkins, E. (2013) 'On Increasing Global Temperatures: 75 Years after Callendar'. *Quarterly Journal of the Royal Meteorological Society*, 139(677).

Hickel, J. (2020) *Less Is More: How Degrowth Will Save the World*. London: William Heinemann.

Jackson, R. (2019) 'Eunice Foote, John Tyndall and a Question of Priority'. *Notes and Records: The Royal Society Journal of the History of Science*, 74: 105–118. doi: https://doi.org/10.1098/rsnr.2018.0066.

Kaviraj, S. (1979) 'Concept of Man in Political Theory: Part One'. *Social Scientist*, 8(3): 15–30.

Latour, B. (2004) *Politics of Nature*. Cambridge, MA: Harvard University Press.

Latour, B. (2018) *Down to Earth: Politics in the New Climatic Regime*. Cambridge: Polity Press.

Malm, A. and Hornborg, A. (2014) 'The Geology of Mankind? A Critique of the Anthropocene Narrative'. *Anthropocene Review*, 1(1): 62–69. doi: 10.1177/2053019613516291.

Mariotti, A. (2019) 'Female Climate Science Pioneer Steps Out of Obscurity'. *Nature*. https://www.nature.com/articles/d41586-019-02117-2 (accessed 23 June 2020).

Masson-Delmotte, V. et al. (2021) *IPCC: Climate Change 2021: The Physical Science Basis*. Cambridge: IPCC.

McGregor, D., Whitaker, S. and Sritharan, M. (2020) 'Indigenous Environmental Justice and Sustainability'. *Current Opinion in Environmental Sustainability*. 43: 35–40. doi: 10.1016/j.cosust.2020.01.007.

Moore, J.W. (2017) 'The Capitalocene, Part I: On the Nature and Origins of Our Ecological Crisis'. *Journal of Peasant Studies*. 44(3): 594–630. doi: 10.1080/03066150.2016.1235036.

Žižek, S. (2010) *Living in the End Times*. London: Verso.

38 Donna Haraway

CLAIRE COLEBROOK

Chapter guide

Donna Haraway began her career as a historian of science in the late twentieth century. She forged connections between the emergent fields of science and technology studies, feminist theory, and what would come to be known as 'history of consciousness' studies (a mode of inquiry that assumes that 'mind' and 'humanity' have complex histories and are neither timeless nor foundational). This chapter explores the various disciplinary and political dimensions of Haraway's work and explores her journey from her first book on metaphors to her twenty-first-century negotiation of the inter-disciplinary problem of the Anthropocene. After a brief introduction to Haraway's contributions to standpoint theory and posthumanism, Section 38.2 turns to an examination of Haraway's concept of the cyborg. Section 38.3, on organisms, mechanisms, and vitalism, looks at her critique of science and leads into Section 38.4 on her alternative way of considering the world in which the boundaries between the human and non-human disappear. Section 38.5 outlines various ways to think about planetary change and presents Haraway's conception of the Chthulucene that captures the complexity of the present, including the transformation of nature through human histories.

38.1 Introduction

Donna Haraway (1944–) is a feminist, postmodernist, standpoint theorist, animal rights activist, posthumanist, socialist, historian of science, scientist, and new materialist, but she is also *not quite* any of these things. The best way to capture her work is to detail all the ways in which she marks herself as different from all these broad categories. Her best-known figure is that of the cyborg: the human body is inextricably intertwined with technology, and this includes the various technologies (including metaphors) that enable humans to know the world.

One of Haraway's most cited essays, 'Situated Knowledges', takes up feminist standpoint theory (see Key Concept: Standpoint theory). Rather than think of science (or any field of knowledge) as an objective and value-free exercise, standpoint feminists argue that all forms of knowledge are made possible by the specific situation of the scientist. What looks like neutrality or objectivity is really a shared standpoint: most scientists up until the twentieth century were white European males. It made sense that from such a point of view the world would appear as passive matter available for experimentation and manipulation. Women, to think of just one other possible standpoint, are often caregivers, nurturers, and carriers of other living beings; it makes sense that feminist science would have less clear subject/object boundaries. Haraway accepts that knowledge is situated, and that there is no pure objective world that might somehow be grasped without any inflection of the scientist's experience. This does not amount to a simple relativism. The supposed 'objectivity' of science has been achieved by one specific standpoint (white European male) not recognizing its partiality, but partiality does *not* mean that there is no objectivity, truth, or reality. Haraway insists

Read more about **Haraway's** life and work by accessing the thinker biography on the online resources: www.oup.com/he/Ramgotra-Choat1e.

that the situated and partial nature of knowledge generates a strong form of objectivity, where the world can be known in quite specific and multiple ways. Rather than a binary between some mythic pure objectivity and an 'anything goes' relativism, Haraway argues that there are multiple, situated, and partial knowledges that make up the rich and complex worlds that all sorts of humans and non-humans inhabit. Second, while Haraway accepts that those who have traditionally been disempowered may have more of a sense of the partial nature of knowledge, there is no privileged position of innocence that would give a more accurate or unmediated representation of the world, (Haraway, 1988: 583).

> **Key Concept: Standpoint theory**
>
> Rather than assume that knowledge can be grasped objectively, and that the position of the scientist or thinker should be irrelevant, standpoint theory argues that all forms of knowledge emerge from located subject positions that are culturally and historically inflected. This is not to say that knowledge is biased or subjective, but rather that knowledge is only possible if there are initial interests and assumptions. Feminist standpoint theory argued that gender was crucial to different modes of knowledge production.

Science is made, but it is not *made up*. The multiple, situated, and partial perspectives that allow a scientific grasp of the world amount to a more complex objectivity: 'You will have strong objectivity when you are seriously enlarging the kinds of things that you take account of, including enlarging the "you" who's doing the knowledge-making, "included" and "excluded" or "otherwise." It's not just a matter of increasing the numbers of women in science' (Haraway, 2016a: xiii). Haraway's rejection of postmodern relativism (where knowledge is simply constructed) stems from her recognition of non-human worlds and forces. Humans are not the only knowers and world-makers, but they do have distinct histories and ways of knowing that compose the politics of the present. Rather than a posthumanism that would not attend to the specific world formations that have marked human culture, Haraway attends to the relationships between humans and non-humans, recognizing the contributions and responsibilities of non-humans (see Key Concept: Posthumanism). Nearly every aspect of her work accords with the concept of cyborg: there is no natural, essential human subject, but there are many different compositions of humans and world-generating technologies.

> **Key Concept: Posthumanism**
>
> The tradition of humanism grants human beings an exceptional nature, either by privileging human rationality, morality, language, or complexity, or by arguing that only humans can transform their world. Posthumanism not only refuses to grant human beings a distinct and separate essence in relation to non-human animals, it also questions the simple unity of 'the human' by suggesting that the human species varies historically and culturally. Posthumanism also focuses on the significance of forces that are outside the realm of conscious and intentional action. Science and culture rely on animals, objects, and broader planetary forces. Not only do humans have no essential nature, bound up as they are with technology; *no* living being possesses the mythic wholeness or integrity that Western thought has attributed to the organism.

Haraway is a feminist and socialist, even though she criticizes feminism for assuming a single category of women, rather than thinking about the complex differences among women of colour, transgender people, and women whose contributions to the global labour market do not grant them the privileges of domesticity and privacy that have defined liberal feminism (see Section 34.2.2 in Chapter 34 on Firestone). Just as 'the human' is a technological composite, so is 'woman'. Haraway's socialist and Marxist commitments prompt her to consider the conditions of labour, colonization, and technology that differentiate women; but Haraway also takes issue with Marxism and socialism for their emphases on 'man' as a world-making and history-forging being, and instead insists that human existence is made possible by the work and companionship of non-humans, ranging from carrier pigeons and domestic dogs, to the microbes that make up the human biome. As long as feminism assumes the natural unity of women as a group, and as long as socialism relies on the figure of man as the maker and master of history, such movements will be unable to create the alliances for a future that no longer rely on privileged perspectives. There is no 'humanity' or 'woman' in general, only distinctly composed, overlapping, and dynamic groupings.

38.2 Cyborg

38.2.1 'A Cyborg Manifesto'

'A Cyborg Manifesto' was published in 1985 in *Socialist Review* (Haraway, 2016a). In this article, Haraway offers a feminist response to broadly Marxist accounts of the relationship between technology and history, while also reconfiguring and responding to feminist forms of socialism. Marxism and the forms of socialist theory indebted to Marxism usually offer a progressive yet critical understanding of technology. Technology begins as a way of harnessing the powers of nature, but technological forces become increasingly alienated from human needs to the point that ever-increasing production of goods requires further and further reduction of life and the globe to capitalist markets. Once human actions are reduced to wage labour, and once nature is nothing more than raw material for the creation of goods, humans become fully subjected to relations of production. Because nature and human existence are caught up in mass production, and because all goods are valued *not* for how they might be used but rather in terms of their monetary or exchange value, capitalism can be understood as the increasing development of technology that coincides with increasing alienation. It is against this notion of technology as alienation that Haraway wrote 'A Cyborg Manifesto'. In this short polemical text, Haraway outlines a series of claims that, from the point of view of the twenty-first century, might appear to be prescient or less polemical than they were in the mid-1980s. Most of the claims made in the manifesto are developed and intensified in Haraway's later work on companion species, primatology, the Anthropocene, and science studies.

'A Cyborg Manifesto' is not only one of Haraway's most cited and anthologized works, it also captures the *troubling* nature of her work. The genre of the manifesto, to which she would return nearly twenty years later in *The Companion Species Manifesto* of 2003, is a polemical form, making manifest and declaring an interest that demands to be heard, but that also aims to create a grouping in its call to action. Throughout her work Haraway has resisted the notion that political identities precede or ground political expression and representation, and instead focuses on the work of creating alliances. The cyborg is an avowedly manufactured figure that Haraway creates in a spirit of irony and blasphemy:

> This experience is a fiction and fact of the most crucial, political kind. Liberation rests on the construction of the consciousness, the imaginative apprehension, of oppression, and so of possibility. The cyborg is a matter of fiction and lived experience that changes what counts as women's experience in the late twentieth century. This is a struggle over life and death, but the boundary between science fiction and social reality is an optical illusion.
>
> (Haraway, 2016a: 5)

The cyborg's explicitly manufactured and hybrid composition refuses *both* the humanist attachment to one's own species and bloodlines *and* the heteronormative valorization of families and biological reproduction: 'The cyborg skips the step of original unity, of identification with nature in the Western sense' (ibid.: 7). The figure of the 'cyborg' is *not* the outcome of familial and heterosexual reproductive lineage, and pushes back against one strand of radical feminism that valorized women as maternal and fertile beings. Already the 'cyborg'—despite its passionate attachment to fabrication and technology—is an ambivalent figure that does not signal a techno-utopia where humans are liberated from the demands of the body or the earth; the utopia Haraway imagines is one of complication: 'The cyborg is resolutely committed to partiality, irony, intimacy, and perversity. It is oppositional, utopian, and completely without innocence' (ibid.: 9).

38.2.2 Cyborgs, humans, and non-humans

In 'A Cyborg Manifesto', Haraway looks at the ways in which the messy and monstrous nature of her fictional being will produce breaks and ruptures with the world:

> Cyborgs are not reverent; they do not re-member the cosmos. They are wary of holism, but needy for connection—they seem to have a natural feel for united-front politics, but without the vanguard party. The main trouble with cyborgs, of course, is that they are the illegitimate offspring of militarism and patriarchal capitalism, not to mention state socialism.
>
> (ibid.: 9)

She makes a similar claim in her later manifesto on companion species, where she begins with the particular and singular, and not a comprehensive theory: 'Dogs, in their historical complexity, matter here. Dogs are not an alibi for other themes; dogs are fleshly material-semiotic presences in the body of technoscience' (Haraway, 2016a: 97–98). Haraway begins from the singular and the displaced, rather than the unified and coherent.

In addition to beginning from the particular, and the other-than-human, Haraway continues to think about the complicated and messy species-being of humans. She does not assume a natural human unity, nor a human nature, but she does insist that her work begins from a specific position—both the long history of Western thought in general, and her socialist feminist position in particular. This is why she declares her work to be ironic: the Western tradition imagines science and technology as a journey of progress freeing itself from the body in order to dominate nature. The figure of the cyborg is created as the blasphemous endpoint of the history of technology. Rather than find some place of innocence outside patriarchal capitalism, the cyborg takes the humanist ideal of technological progress and explores all the ways in which it disrupts dreams of human integrity:

> The cyborg is a creature in a post-gender world; it has no truck with bisexuality, pre-oedipal symbiosis, unalienated labour, or other seductions to organic wholeness through a final appropriation of all the powers of the parts into a higher unity. In a sense, the cyborg has no origin story in the Western sense—a 'final' irony since the cyborg is also the awful apocalyptic telos of the 'West's' escalating dominations of abstract individuation, an ultimate self untied at last from all dependency, a man in space.
>
> (Haraway, 2016a: 8)

Haraway's work is populated by the contributions of non-human companions, such as dogs and apes, whose own ways of making their way in the world allow humans to recognize that there are worlds that are different from the world that has been brought into being by various human knowledge practices. Beings emerge from complex relations, and this includes human beings who are the outcome of a long history of various contradictory, overlapping, and distinct practices and institutions.

Human beings are creations as much as they are creators. They are cyborgs insofar as they are pieced together by multiple components, rather than emerging seamlessly from nature. Although Marxism had long insisted that history is the outcome of making and fabrication, it nevertheless relied upon human beings as the sole makers of history. For Haraway, human history is the outcome of human *and* non-human agents. Such non-human agents include the animals with whom we share our domestic space, the microscopes that allow us to write stories about the world, the microbes that inhabit our bodies, and all the technical devices that we add to our own bodies. The first important implication of Haraway's figure of the cyborg is that there is no human nature, no essence to which politics and ethics might return, no foundation or normative subject who is the privileged author or agent of history.

The second implication is the end to human exceptionalism. To refer to all human beings as cyborgs is to see them as effects of a long history of making, where history and what we have come to know as nature are already intertwined with technology. Whereas Marxism understands history to follow from the relations of production among humans, with capitalism giving workers the greatest insight into the path to revolution, Haraway sees history as composed by humans and non-humans in complex relations of transformation across species and their environments. To think of humans as cyborgs is both to acknowledge that there is no foundational or proper human nature *and* that all other beings are also multiple and as transformative of the world as 'we' humans believe ourselves to be.

The third implication of recognizing humans as cyborgs is the transformation of the political concept of production. Marxism and socialism explain the polity, and the sense of human existence made possible by the polity, through the foundational concept of production. It is economic production and the subjection of workers to wage labour that allow Marxism to argue that the proletariat will be the agents of the revolution, and that it is wage labour that is the primary relation of alienation. Because wage labour is essentially exploitative (with workers producing a surplus that is then enjoyed by those who own the means of production), there needs to be some representation of the world that makes sense of this uneven distribution. Ideology is a way of depicting this unnatural state of affairs as natural, either by depicting wage labour as something far more joyous than it is, or by depicting class relations as natural and unchangeable, as simply the way things are. The task of the Marxist critic is to expose or demystify what appears to be inevitable, and the Marxist critic can do this—have this privileged insight—because they understand the economic determination of social relations. The Marxist could explain to the worker that their sense of pride in having a factory job for 20 years, or their sense of loyalty to a political party that serves the interests of corporations and does so in the name of 'the market', is illusory and a way of masking economic exploitation. If the worker were to consider their social existence as an effect of economic history, their desires and interests would be revolutionary. Against this notion that economic or wage production is the driver of social relations, Haraway (like other feminists) draws attention to unpaid, non-wage, domestic, and more complex forms of production—including the work women do in the home to reproduce social relations. If Marxism focuses on the economy as foundational, and feminists focus on reproduction within the family as foundational, Haraway insists on multiple and complex forms of production, including the non-humans upon whom we rely and who transform us. Rather than an ideology critique (or exposing illusions), Haraway's thought is itself productive: showing all the ways in which humans are in relation to other productive forces, such as the technologies that make our lives possible.

38.2.3 Production and reproduction

Before looking at Haraway's account of the transformed relations of labour and production in the late-twentieth century, it is essential to understand one of her key interventions in the feminist conception of the sexual division of labour. Focusing on the work of liberal and anti-pornography feminists such as Catharine MacKinnon, who argued that pornography produces and reinforces the sexual objectification of women, Haraway objects to feminism's criticism that women have become objects (Haraway, 2016a: 25). In even broader terms—and this is in keeping with Haraway's affirmation of the figure of the cyborg—not even objects are objects. Haraway criticizes liberal feminists for accepting the humanist conception of the self as an autonomous subject. Rather than subjects and objects, humans and animals, culture and nature, and rather than humans leading and causing a history in which the rest of the world is passive, the concept of the cyborg defines human beings as composed *with* all the other complexities of the world.

At the time of writing the manifesto, Haraway was arguing that new technologies demanded a reformulation of the ways in which Marxists and feminists think about the human body's relationship to technology. Writing in 1985, well before the development of smartphones, widely used personal computers, the internet, and digital media, Haraway possessed a Marxist sense of humans co-evolving with the machines that enable and form their lives. Humans are increasingly hybrid beings, constantly being supplemented and transformed by the things around them. Even though Haraway sees the cyborg as a late-capitalist concept, she is not claiming that prior to the twentieth century human beings were distinct and autonomous organisms. Her broader approach to the philosophy of life and the history of science is to think of all figures, including the concept of the cyborg, as fabulations that are bound to the time and place of their emergence.

There are, then, two senses in which Haraway's work is historical. She recognizes that there is no timeless human nature, and that humans are composed from different relations among bodies, including non-human animals and machines. She also makes it clear that her own composition of the cyborg proceeds from her political investments as a feminist and a socialist, concerned with achieving new forms of political relation that do not assume capitalist or patriarchal modes of value. The cyborg is a way of reading a specific moment in human history: the point at which new technologies create new forms of relation. It is also a way of imagining a different historical trajectory; rather than assuming that history unfolds from who 'we' are, the figure of the cyborg insists on the creation of the political terrain and future, even if—as cyborgs—humans are never fully in control of their environment.

The cyborg is a political and historical figure that expresses and advocates for an alteration of human existence, both in terms of sexual politics, class politics, and race. In addition to drawing upon work in socialist feminism that insists on *reproduction* and sexual-domestic labour, Haraway argues that the conditions of work and social relations have altered dramatically in the late-twentieth century to include the widespread feminization of labour. Socialist feminists had already argued that the division of labour in the domestic sphere requires a complex account of sexual reproduction, but for Haraway considering labour in its broadest sense requires going beyond the family and beyond the liberal polity to consider the global forms of political domination and labour relations that make any individual existence possible. No matter how private and privileged a subject considers themselves to be, their existence is made possible by complex webs of human and non-human living beings, and multitudes of things. As Haraway examines late capitalism, she observes the new forms of labour that can no longer be understood through the older public-private distinctions that would divide wage labour from domestic labour.

The cyborg is typical of how Haraway understands human existence in late capitalism—as humans become increasingly bound up with machines—but her general approach is to see human existence in general as made possible by way of connections with the non-human.

> **38.2 Cyborg: Key Points**
>
> - Haraway invents the figure of the cyborg to argue that all human life is made possible through technology.
> - The cyborg contests the association of women with nature, and argues for a form of feminism that embraces the potentials of technology.
> - The cyborg is an explicitly fictional device that makes manifest the ways in which knowledge is always in part an event of the imagination.

38.3 Organisms, mechanisms, vitalism

Published in 1976, *Crystals, Fabrics, and Fields* traces the transition in twentieth-century science from two competing paradigms (vitalism and mechanism) to organicism. In the background of this history of science undertaken by Haraway is her methodological commitment to the concept of scientific paradigms: scientists do not look at the world from a position of neutrality, but develop their questions about and perceptions of the world through a range of already given forms, which include the types of questions posed, what counts as an observation, and how observations are validated. The notion of a scientific paradigm that creates a background assumption for scientific projects goes back to Thomas Kuhn's work, *The Structure of Scientific Revolutions* (Kuhn, 1962), which argues that scientific questions and answers should not be understood in simple terms of truth and error, but rather rely upon background methods and assumptions that establish criteria for what counts as normal science and/or falsifiable claims (see Key Thinker: Thomas Kuhn).

> **Key Thinker: Thomas Kuhn**
>
> Thomas Kuhn (1922–1996) is a central and influential figure in the philosophy of science. Prior to Kuhn's intervention, science studies were dominated by positivism, or the commitment to a direct transition from observation and experiment to objective truth. Positivism in the twentieth century was a reaction against metaphysics and speculation, where scientific theories were not fully distinct from spiritual and grand philosophical systems. In his 1962 book, *The Structure of Scientific Revolutions*, Kuhn challenged the positivist ideal of straightforward and objective observation by arguing that all scientific procedures are made possible by background assumptions and ways of posing problems. Scientific revolutions occur when presuppositions come under so much pressure that new ways of thinking come into being to generate new paradigms. Kuhn argued that paradigms were incommensurable. Rather than think of Newton as wrong and Einstein as right, it is better to think of their claims being true and falsifiable within their distinct paradigms.

Rather than looking at the history of science as a straightforward march of progress to a more accurate capture of the real world, and rather than looking at earlier eras of science as simply erroneous, Kuhn argued that scientists operated in communities that had structuring metaphors that enabled truth and falsity. This is not to say that science bears no relation to truth, or is *merely* constructed, but that questions, perceptions, and methods are social and political events, and that scientific revolutions occur when a question and event ruptures the received ways of making sense of the world.

Haraway's earliest work on the history of scientific problems, in *Crystals, Fabrics, and Fields*, has three-fold significance. First, she argues for a richer conception of the formation of scientific knowledge than the abstract notion of paradigm, referring to 'sensuously lived metaphors' (Haraway, 2004: xviii). A science emerges not simply from a way of thinking, but from bodily and creative engagements, so that the scientists she studies are celebrated for their 'vivid artistic sensibilities'. Scientists are creators, but creators who feel the world they study with a transformative intensity. Throughout her work Haraway will develop this nuanced version of scientific paradigms, where the grounds that make science possible are not simply ideas or norms but fleshy, creative, and felt experiences of connection with objects of study. Rather than think of things as discrete entities that enter into relations, or that can be encountered through some neutral relation of 'knowledge', it matters very much *how* relations take place. Haraway frequently quotes the anthropologist Marilyn Strathern on partial connections and the relations that are used to think others' relations:

> It matters what matters we use to think other matters with; it matters what stories we tell to tell other stories with; it matters what knots knot knots, what thoughts think thoughts, what descriptions describe descriptions, what ties tie ties. It matters what stories make worlds, what worlds make stories.
>
> (Haraway, 2016b: 10)

Where Kuhn had thought of scientific paradigms as something like conceptual schemes, Haraway will increasingly stress non-conceptual forces in relations, including affects. How we feel and the forms of bodily life we inhabit and encounter, have as much formative power on knowledge as ideas, concepts, and theory. The concept of paradigm that Haraway takes from Kuhn still harbours a subject-object distinction, where metaphors shape ways of knowing and determine what can be seen. For Haraway, the collective, embodied, and affective ways in which the world is known are complex and dynamic affairs of mutual interaction and transformation.

In addition to a radical sense of the situated nature of knowledge—not just the scientist's standpoint, but their desiring relation to their field of study—the second strand of significance that runs through *Crystals, Fabrics, and Fields* is the attention paid to embryology. The specific scientific revolution charted by Haraway concerns the boundaries of living beings, and charts the resurgence of a theory of epigenesis.

Epigenesis—or the theory that characteristics acquired by an individual could be passed on to subsequent generations—had been consigned to the scientific past once Charles Darwin, and later geneticists, put forward a theory of evolution. Darwinian evolution did away with notions of intelligent design: complex life forms could emerge from chance and mutation, with survival being the result of a random changes fitting better with an environment. Evolutionary theory could explain the way living beings appeared to be made for their world by arguing that contingent variation would produce some forms that would be more successful than others. No intelligence need be invoked. Haraway's study begins with the opposition between mechanism and vitalism, where mechanism is the blind and random mutation of matter that generates complex forms, while vitalism posits some non-material force that organizes life.

Materialism has a long history dating back at least to ancient Greece, but modern scientific materialism is specifically focused on providing explanations for the world that do not rely on any spiritual or intentional force. Materialism as an anti-theological and specifically scientific method begins most explicitly in René Descartes's (1596–1650) dualism, where there is *either* mind *or* matte, either thinking stuff (*res cogitans*) or extended stuff (*res extensa*) (see Key Thinker: René Descartes in Section 6.2.1 in Chapter 6). This Cartesian mind/body distinction was crucial to the early formation of the natural sciences as distinct from theology and philosophy. Bodies could be studied as mechanisms. Late-nineteenth-century theories of evolution further tilted the battle between vitalism and mechanism in the latter's favour by arguing that forms that appeared to be the outcome of design emerged *only* because other variants did not survive. As with many of her projects, Haraway refuses to accept the opposition between mechanism and vitalism; life operates neither by some basic matter that yields complexity by way of an algorithm *nor* through some organizing principle.

Haraway describes the emergence of a new paradigm by situating organicism as *neither* vitalism *nor* mechanism. The organicism she charts is quite distinct from pre-modern forms. Prior to modern mechanism and science, Aristotelian understandings of living beings saw matter as the means through which forms come into existence, and forms were immaterial and timeless design patterns instantiated in matter.

Haraway's organicism, as described in *Crystals, Fabrics, and Fields*, is not a return to the privilege of form over matter; rather, it explores what happens when there is no strict binary between matter and a forming power. According to theories of epigenesis, a body's relationship with the world and the changes a body undergoes can transform genetics; matters can take on formative powers. One might think of this as overcoming 'nature versus nurture' debates and 'social construction versus essence' debates. Rather than think of a body as a blank slate that is imprinted by its environment, the body's nature/genetics is transformed by relations to the world. 'Nature' is not fixed but dynamic and relational.

The third strand of significance that runs through *Crystals, Fabrics and Fields* (and that looks forward to 'A Cyborg Manifesto') is Haraway's posing of the question of the political and social force of science paradigms. If science is fabricated, then it is important to look not only at how science is made but *also* the forms of thinking and existing that make any science and its field of study possible. This, for Haraway, requires a shift in thinking that goes beyond a single science, and beyond science in general. All forms of knowledge are in a dynamic relation to a world which, in turn, has a complexity and that requires far more responsive forms of inquiry (Haraway 2004: 17).

38.3 Organisms, mechanism, vitalism: Key Points

- Rather than think of science as a literal truth that is communicated through metaphors, Haraway argues that science is made possible by metaphors.
- Figures of speech do not stand in the way of objective truth, but make the understanding of the world possible.
- Until the twentieth century, science had tended to be either organicist or mechanistic in its metaphors; life was understood either to be a complex, organized, intentional, and inter-related whole (organicism) *or* nothing more than a single matter that can be studied quantitatively (mechanism).
- The concept of epigenesis argues that matter itself can develop tendencies through time, combining the organizational tendencies of organicism with the possibilities of chance and contingency of mechanism.

38.4 The reinvention of nature

The title of Haraway's 1991 collection of essays, *Simians, Cyborgs, and Women: The Reinvention of Nature*, captures the rich relations of her thought. Simians (apes or monkeys) allow Haraway to think about a non-human species in a way that challenges what we thought the human might be. Just as *Crystals, Fabrics, and Fields* (see Section 38.3) had charted the history of the life sciences to show the emergence of a dynamic and relational understanding of organisms, so Haraway's long engagement with primatology exposed the ways in which studies of primates were both determined by patriarchal ways of seeing, while also opening the way to understand life collectively.

In *Primate Visions* (Haraway, 1989), Haraway studies a range of practices (photography, science, taxidermy, and museum exhibits) that create stories about supposedly 'natural' sexual and social hierarchies. Crucial to Haraway's argument is that science is a narrative and creative affair, and so is her own account of scientists' lives and journeys. The narratives of primatology she examines are ways of maintaining the dominance of some humans over others: men over women, capitalists over workers, Westerners over the colonized, whites over People of Colour. Her own task will be to rewrite stories that include the labour and lives of those who were often the objects and not the subjects of science writing. In *Primate Visions*, Haraway offers a sharp sense of the invention of nature:

> Nature is such a potent symbol of innocence partly because 'she' is imagined to be without technology. Man is not in nature partly because he is not seen, is not the spectacle. A constitutive meaning of masculine gender for us is to be the unseen, the eye (I), the author, to be Linnaeus who fathers the primate order. That is part of the structure of experience in the Museum, one of the reasons one has, willy nilly, the moral status of a young boy undergoing initiation through visual experience. The Museum is a visual technology. It works through desire for communion, not separation, and one of its products is gender . . . Social relations of domination are built into the hardware and logics of technology, producing the illusion of technological determinism. Nature is, in 'fact,' constructed as a technology through social praxis.
>
> (ibid.: 54)

In both *Primate Visions* (implicitly) and *Simians, Cyborgs, and Women* (explicitly), Haraway creates a new form of science that is positively fabricated. Rather than think of the construction of science as something that is imposed on an otherwise meaningless world, Haraway will see the realm of the non-human as playing its part in creating science and in challenging the subject-object hierarchies that science has assumed and enforced. While primates provide a clear example of the ways in which scientists repeated and reinforced hierarchies, assuming a dominance in nature that inflected their practices and theories, it was the exploration of other 'companion species' that allowed Haraway to create a new vision of science and humanity.

Haraway's later work will intensify and multiply various senses of what she refers to as 'SF': 'science fiction, speculative fabulation, string figures, speculative feminism, science fact, so far' (Haraway, 2016b: 2). *When Species Meet* (Haraway, 2008) refers to the non-human (rather than posthuman) force of 'sf worlding'. Haraway argues for working *with* other species, asking questions and speculating about others, in an ongoing ethical labour. Humans exist and are distinct even if their world is composed of processes that are non-human. This yields a non-humanism of working with others, rather than a posthumanism that assumes a single and unified whole of interconnected life: 'Maybe that's all *nonhumanism* means. But in that little "all" lies permanent refusal of innocence and self-satisfaction with one's reasons and the invitation to speculate, imagine, feel, build something better. This is the sf worlding that has always lured me. It is a real worlding' (ibid.: 92).

'SF' begins as a way of thinking about the fictions that hold us together, and extends to include the importance of speculation, where humans strive to imagine what those others who humans are becoming-with might think and imagine in their worlds. It also includes string figures, a practice of taking a simple matter—string—and exploring all its possible capacities for varying creation. The string in its simplicity enables the creation of figures and stories. Without these simple matters humans would not be able to tell stories (Haraway, 2016b: 3).

'SF' is tied to a refusal of any single abstraction that might explain the whole; there is no unified theory of life, and no privileged system of relations that enables an account or view of the whole. 'SF' is bound up with *sympoesis* and not autopoesis, becoming-with and not the autopoetic myth of self-formation that has exempted humans from the multiple and complex forces of the Earth. In this respect, Haraway's binding of humans to companion species is part of what has come to be known as 'new materialism' (see Key Concept: New materialism).

> **Key Concept: New materialism**
>
> Materialism's long and complex philosophical history can be captured by contrasting materialism with its opposite: idealism, or the notion that it is mind, thinking, or ideas that form the world and are the basis for knowledge and all that is given as the real world. Materialism insists that everything begins with matter. One might refer to the brain, atoms, or light being registered by the eye. *New* materialism—which is associated with Haraway and others including Bruno Latour, Jane Bennett, and Rosi Braidotti—argues for a far more complex and plural sense of matter, so that the feelings and affects of the human body, along with multiple non-human agents (such as microscopes, telescopes, lab rats, institutions, and working spaces) play a role in the composition of knowledge. Matter is no longer a simple object that can be known directly, but is dynamic and produces many complex perspectives.

The worlds we create are made possible by the complexity of matters. Matter is not some blank substance available for making; instead, matter is complicated and captured best in the many senses of 'SF'—capable of fictions, figures, and speculation. To think about 'sf worlding' is to consider the ways in which non-human species compose our world. Those beings whom we call, so generically, 'animals' are also composed through our fictions, not just through processes of domestication, farming, experimentation, breeding, and transportation, but through co-evolving technologies and the passions we develop for consuming, co-habiting, and culling. Carrier pigeons, rodents, feral cats, fungi, spiders, and primates compose Haraway's world of companion species (Haraway, 2008: 165).

> **38.4 Reinvention of nature: Key Points**
>
> - Nature is not opposed to culture, but is transformed through the ways in which it is known, just as knowledge practices adapt and come into being through interactions with a dynamic nature.
> - 'SF' is a manifestly creative label for thinking about the multiple relations between science and fiction: the 'S' can stand for science, speculation, and the string of string figures that create patterns; the 'F' for fiction and figures is not opposed to an objective nature but marks the ways in which the formation of patterns and stories are natural events.
> - 'SF' can also be thought of as socialist feminism, which no longer ties women to a supposedly ahistorical and passive nature, and no longer defines socialism in terms of nature-dominating labour.

38.5 Anthropocene, Capitalocene, Plantationocene, Chthulucene

The concept of the Anthropocene, though coined in the 1980s by Eugene Stoermer, came to prominence when atmospheric chemist Paul Crutzen proposed the term in 2000 as a way to think about the human-caused transformation of the Earth as a living system (see also Section 37.2 of Chapter 37). Haraway recognizes the force and power of the various terms used to think about planetary change. She has some sympathy for those who have sought to think of the 'Capitalocene' rather than the Anthropocene. Not all human ways of life have the hyper-consuming, nature-dominating, and fossil-fuel dependent ways of the capitalist West, and not all cultures assume the grand story of Man as privileged agent of history:

> Still, if we could only have one word for these sf times, surely it must be the Capitalocene. Species Man did not shape the conditions for the Third Carbon Age or the Nuclear Age. The story of

> Species Man as the agent of the Anthropocene is an almost laughable rerun of the great phallic humanizing and modernizing Adventure, where man, made in the image of a vanished god, takes on superpowers in his secular-sacred ascent, only to end in tragic detumescence, once again.
>
> (Haraway, 2016b: 47)

In addition to expressing some sympathy for Jason Moore's (2015) theorization of the Capitalocene, Haraway also considers the concept of the Plantationocene; it was not just industrial production that transformed the Earth, for this relied upon a long history of colonization, displacement of Native Peoples, industrialized agriculture, and slavery. Ultimately, though, Haraway coins her own term, the Chthulucene, which does not deny or erase human-caused planetary change (Anthropocene), or the importance of thinking capitalism and colonization, but holds onto the problem of these terms while adding the important dimension of dynamic time and matter. The Anthropocene aims to capture a new geological age, discernible in the reading of the Earth's strata. It imagines that just as geologists today can read layers of time in the past, the events of a species will be discernible in the Earth's sedimented layers. In keeping with her early work on this history of science, Haraway thinks of the writing of this new Earth science as proceeding from specific types of beings—those who are of the Earth, humans as earthbound—and from a specific time—this present moment of mass extinction which demands new ways of thinking about how to live with others.

In *Staying with the Trouble*, Haraway (2016b) repeats and intensifies her understanding of science as an affair of desire, fiction, risk, and responsibility. In addition to combining the sense of 'chthonic' as earthbound, so that humans are no longer beings who master or own the Earth, Haraway adds the sense of time, and specifically refers to *kainos* (or newness). The present is one in which a number of histories and competing futures demand recognition; rather than the single line of history with a central agent—either humanity or capitalism—Haraway imagines an entangled present:

> Nothing in *kainos* must mean conventional pasts, presents, or futures. There is nothing in times of beginnings that insists on wiping out what has come before, or, indeed, wiping out what comes after. Kainos can be full of inheritances, of remembering, and full of comings, of nurturing what might still be.
>
> (ibid.: 2)

When Haraway declared that her cyborg figure of 1985 was blasphemous and ironic, she captured a feature that would be even more present in *Staying with the Trouble*. Her work is ironic in that it does not seek to find some innocent outside or future; by 'staying with the trouble' she inhabits the texts, terrain, and alliances of the present, but then aims to create new relations and formations from matters at hand. Working against the revolutionary and apocalyptic notion that the world as we know it might be swept away to generate a utopia, Haraway instead remains within the story-building capacities already in place, and tries to imagine what monstrous possibilities they might yield. The irony of adopting a voice and exploring its mutations is also akin to a form of blasphemy—not being faithful to the voices and doctrines one has inherited.

Perhaps Haraway's most controversial blasphemy is her argument for making 'kin' and not babies. Rather than reproduction of one's own kind, one might think of forging new relations with companion species. In some ways, 'A Cyborg Manifesto' had already taken a strong stance against feminist valorizations of biological reproduction, and had declared the era of the cyborg to be one of replication as opposed to reproduction (Haraway, 2016a: 29). In 'A Cyborg Manifesto', Haraway questioned whether women's role in the polity could be captured with the notion of reproduction, and instead argued for an expanded notion of labour beyond socialism's figure of the worker and feminism's figure of woman as mother (ibid.: 30). In *Staying with the Trouble*, Haraway goes beyond description and affirmation of the ways in which reproductive labour neither captures women as a group nor generates feminism's political focus. Here she suggests that the political goal of reproductive freedom needs to confront the problem of human numbers (Haraway, 2016b: 6–7).

Population control has always been a politically difficult concept; it tends to demonize the poor who are perceived as surplus humans, when really the problem is over-consumption rather than over-population. Population control also harbours racial implications, given that the affluent West tends to use more of the world's resources than the world's poor, who also do not have the luxury or desire for the small and bounded nuclear family. Haraway explored this problem in an edited volume, *Making Kin Not Populations* (Clarke and Haraway, 2018), which takes two projects that are normally in conflict—population control and racial justice—and combines the challenge of thinking how the planet's number of humans might be reduced without bringing in the spectre of the population *control* that would take the form of a top-down management of the world's peoples by some privileged Western elite. The project of *Staying with the Trouble* is a broader version of this ambivalence towards the human species. On the one hand, Haraway's work is driven by the attempt to forge a new mode of human existence that is just to *all* humans; in this respect, her feminism goes beyond women (in the narrow or restrictive sense) to include trans and non-binary subjects, and her socialism goes beyond the figure of the worker to include those precarious and vulnerable lives not in the workforce in any traditional sense. On the other hand, from the figure of the cyborg to the carrier pigeons, spiders, and primates that are Haraway's companions, her work strives to demote humans from the overwhelming right to life that has silenced all possibility for thinking that the planet might be better off with fewer human beings.

> **38.5 Anthropocene, Capitalocene, Plantationocene, Chthulucene: Key Points**
>
> - The Chthulucene is a term created by Haraway to capture the complexity of the present, including the ways in which nature has been transformed by human histories, and the multiple and competing histories that comprise any account of the present.
> - Chthulucene also aims to forge links with the non-human world, downplaying the traditional privilege attached to human life.
> - Haraway's slogan of 'making kin not babies' is both an extension of her career-long sense that human life is hybrid and intertwined with the non-human, but also a controversial argument for population control.

38.6 Conclusion

As this chapter has explored, Haraway is a feminist, posthumanist theorist of technology and ecology. Her work ranges from feminist interventions in science studies, where she challenged conceptions of objective truth by looking at the institutional shifts in scientific method, to animal studies and environmental criticism. Her entire body of work can be defined as posthumanist, both because she refuses any conception of a simple and unchanging humanity, and because she stresses the importance of non-human animals in the creation of various human worlds, including the world of science. Haraway's feminist and socialist study of science focuses on the multiple ways in which the world is known. For Haraway, all forms of knowledge are made possible by specific standpoints. There is no single 'human' world, but various ways of knowing and being human, each bearing a distinct relation to non-humans (both animals and things).

Take your learning further by accessing the online resources for a library of web links to relevant videos, articles, blogs, and useful websites for this chapter: www.oup.com/he/Ramgotra-Choat1e.

Study questions

1. Why, according to Haraway, are partial points of view necessary to form scientific objectivity?
2. How does Haraway define the cyborg?
3. Why, according to Haraway, does nature need to be reinvented?
4. What is the Chthulucene?
5. How does Haraway transform the concept of the paradigm?
6. What are Haraway's objections to liberal feminism?
7. Why is the question of population important, and controversial, for Haraway?
8. How does thinking about 'companion species' challenge conventional humanism?

Further reading

Primary sources

Clarke, A. and Haraway, D. (eds) (2018) *Making Kin Not Populations: Reconceiving Generations*. Chicago: Prickly Paradigm Press.
A collection of essays exploring the problem of population control.

Haraway, D. (1988) 'Situated Knowledges: The Science Question in Feminism and the Privilege of Partial Perspective'. *Feminist Studies*, 14(3): 575–599.
Article arguing that all science proceeds from a specific standpoint; partiality enhances objectivity.

Haraway, D. (1989) *Primate Visions: Gender, Race, and Nature*. London: Routledge.
In this important text, Haraway argues that the stories told by primatologists are bound up with the imagination of how humans ought to be.

Haraway, D. (2004) *Crystals, Fabrics, and Fields: Metaphors That Shape Embryos*. Berkeley, CA: North Atlantic Books.
Originally published in 1976, this book emerged from Haraway's doctoral research on the paradigm shift from disputes between mechanism and vitalism to organicism and epigenetics.

Haraway, D. (2008) *When Species Meet*. Minneapolis, MN: University of Minnesota Press.
Haraway's broad conception of companion species is founded on her insistence that all living beings are composed through dynamic relations to others.

Haraway, D. (2016a) *Manifestly Haraway*. Minneapolis, MN: University of Minnesota Press.
This collection includes the very influential 'A Cyborg Manifesto,' the later *Companion Species Manifesto* of 2003, and an interview with Cary Wolfe.

Haraway D. (2016b) *Staying with the Trouble: Making Kin in the Chthulucene*. Durham, NC: Duke University Press.
Rather than accepting the concept of the Anthropocene—or the idea that humans as a species have transformed the Earth as a living system—Haraway argues for an earthbound and entangled understanding of planetary change and ecological fragility.

Haraway, D. (2018) *Modest_Witness@Second_Millennium.FemaleMan©_Meets_OncoMouseTM*, 2nd edn. London: Routledge.
The concept of modest witnessing ties all scientific knowledge to an observer whose point of view is both partial and essential.

Secondary sources

Bell, D. (2007) *Cyberculture Theorists: Manuel Castells and Donna Haraway*. London: Routledge.
An introductory guide that situates Haraway within the broader problem of digital culture.

Cox, L. (2018) 'Decolonial Queer Feminism in Donna Haraway's "A Cyborg Manifesto" (1985)'. *Paragraph*, 41(3): 317–332.
Haraway's early manifesto explored from the point of view of queer theory and decolonization.

Kroker, A. (2012) *Body Drift: Butler, Hayles, Haraway*. Minneapolis, MN: University of Minnesota Press.
Examines Haraway as a complex and apocalyptic figure who pushes the imaginative potential of hybrid technologies.

Lewis, S. (2017) 'Cthulhu Plays No Role for Me'. *Viewpoint Magazine*, May. Available at: https://viewpointmag.com/2017/05/08/cthulhu-plays-no-role-for-me/.
A feminist criticism of Haraway's argument for population control.

Schneider, J. (2005) *Donna Haraway: Live Theory*. London: Continuum.
An introduction and overview.

Wark, M. (2017) 'Donna Haraway: The Inhuman Comedy'. In M. Wark, *General Intellects: Twenty-One Thinkers for the Twenty-First Century*. London: Verso.
A short and original assessment of Haraway.

References

Clarke, A. and Haraway, D. (eds) (2018) *Making Kin Not Populations: Reconceiving Generations*. Chicago: Prickly Paradigm Press.

Haraway, D. (1988) 'Situated Knowledges: The Science Question in Feminism and the Privilege of Partial Perspective'. *Feminist Studies*, 14(3): 575–599.

Haraway, D. (1989) *Primate Visions: Gender, Race, and Nature*. London: Routledge.

Haraway, D. (2004) *Crystals, Fabrics, and Fields: Metaphors That Shape Embryos*. Berkeley, CA: North Atlantic Books.

Haraway, D. (2008) *When Species Meet*. Minneapolis, MN: University of Minnesota Press.

Haraway, D. (2016a) *Manifestly Haraway*. Minneapolis, MN: University of Minnesota Press.

Haraway D. (2016b) *Staying with the Trouble: Making Kin in the Chthulucene*. Durham, NC: Duke University Press.

Haraway, D. (2018) *Modest_Witness@Second_Millennium.FemaleMan©_Meets_OncoMouseTM*, 2nd edn. London: Routledge.

Kuhn, T. (1962) *The Structure of Scientific Revolutions*. Chicago: University of Chicago Press.

Moore, J.W. (2015) *Capitalism in the Web of Life: Ecology and the Accumulation of Capital*. London: Verso.

Schneider, J. (2005) *Donna Haraway: Live Theory*. London: Continuum.

39 Indigenous Ecologies

ESME G. MURDOCK

> **Chapter guide**
>
> This chapter will focus on Indigenous philosophies that uniquely wed ecological and political relations. It will provide an overview of key tenets of Indigenous thinking and contrast them to prominent features of Western industrial thinking in Section 39.2. The following Sections will explore how these Indigenous philosophies give rise to unique understandings of Indigenous peoples and the more-than-human world as interdependent, creating what is called Indigenous ecologies. These Indigenous ecologies are deeply related to how Indigenous peoples construct and craft their governance systems that aim to be balanced and reciprocal with their ecologies. Section 39.6 further explores interruptions and disruptions to Indigenous ecologies and governance systems through examining colonization and the racialized and gendered violence that accompanies that process, especially through resource extraction.

39.1 Introduction

The term 'Indigenous' is a broad, complex, and sometimes contested term. This chapter, however, understands Indigenous peoples to refer to the approximately 400 million people worldwide who practised, and still practise, sovereignty and political governance before the arrival of other human groups who interrupted their lifeways and governance structures through processes of territorial aggression, dominance, and oppression such as colonialism, settler colonialism, and imperialism. These colonial governments and powers are largely recognized internationally as the dominant or primary political sovereigns in these territories, even while Indigenous nations continue to exist and practise their sovereignty. As such, the category and term Indigenous capture multiple experiences, histories, and heritages globally. The chapter will only be able to touch on specific examples that are not representative of the diversity and uniqueness of all Indigenous peoples.

This chapter will focus on examples of Indigenous governance and ecological philosophies emanating from and situated upon Turtle Island—the name given by many Indigenous peoples to what is currently referred to as North America, particularly the colonial settler states of the United States and Canada. This will be the chapter's focus because it is the geographical region of the world that I am most familiar with as a scholar of non-dominant environmental philosophies and ethics, particularly Indigenous ones. While the USA and Canada often loom large and are overrepresented in the scholarly academic literature, they are not and should not be understood as the sole or primary political sovereigns of this geographical territory. In fact, to do this would be to reaffirm the Eurocentric logics and erase the colonial legacies of violence that account for the USA's and Canada's existence and coming into being. The USA and Canada are instead relatively young settler states that surround and encompass hundreds of Indigenous nations who are very rarely engaged in the same literature that dominates transnational and global academic scholarship. In this sense, both the Haudenosaunee and Anishinaabe (Indigenous peoples of the Great Lakes area in the USA and Canada) traditions explored in this chapter are neither American nor Canadian but, rather and importantly, they are grounded in the thinking of sovereign Indigenous nations and as such represent an international analysis.

While Indigenous political philosophies are non-identical and globally diverse, they can be analysed and explained as having shared features and general principles. This chapter examines some of those shared principles and features towards understanding and arguing that Indigenous governance systems are distinct from Western ones in many ways. A main focus of this chapter will be how Indigenous ecologies or holistic understandings of land and ecological relationships inform Indigenous political philosophies and governance structures.

> **Key Concept: Ecologies**
>
> As a branch of biology, ecology treats the relations of living beings to each other and to their environment. Here it is taken to mean the reciprocal balance attended to by peoples and lands as well as their more-than-human relatives, including plants and animals, through relationships attuned to the needs and agency of the world around us. The term is also taken to refer to interdependent systems of life that overall would not survive without each other.

39.2 Indigenous thinking vs. industrial thinking

To begin, we will examine the ways that Indigenous thinkers conceptualize their orientations to the world. While it is difficult to outline or define an Indigenous world-view, Indigenous philosophies do share similar principles of organization that are meaningful in expressing a world-view. Anishinaabe scholar and activist Winona LaDuke has contributed to this important work by outlining prominent features of what she calls 'Indigenous thinking'. She does this largely by examining the principles of an Indigenous world-view that inform the ways Indigenous peoples think and behave and contrasting them to the ways people think in an industrial world-view. Thus, Indigenous thinking is presented as a fundamentally different world-view from what LaDuke calls 'industrial thinking'. In what follows, I will examine the principles of LaDuke's Indigenous thinking and underline how it differs from industrial thinking.

> **Key Thinker: Winona LaDuke**
>
> Winona LaDuke (1959–) is an Anishinaabe economist, scholar, and activist from the Ojibwe White Earth Reservation in Minnesota. She was formally trained in Economics at Harvard and used her Western education paired with her Indigenous knowledge to work for Indigenous justice. Her activism began in her work in the mid-1980s when she helped co-found the Indigenous Women's Network and also helped address issues of forced sterilization of Indigenous Women in the Americas through her work with Women of All Red Nations. She has also been involved in fighting for the recovery of Anishinaabe lands through her advocacy and organizing to buy back her reservation's own lands through the White Earth Recovery Project. She has published and written about crucial principles of Indigenous thinking and philosophy as well as different case studies of Indigenous peoples fighting for land and environmental justice.

The first principle of Indigenous thinking is the pre-eminence of natural law. It is important to note that this natural law is different from the understanding of natural law within the European Enlightenment tradition which sees nature or states of nature largely as inferior to 'civilization'. Natural law, according to LaDuke, is the highest law to which all of us as beings of Earth are accountable. Similarly natural law is 'superior to the laws made by nations, states, and municipalities' (LaDuke, 1993). In this way, Indigenous societies, governments, and political structures are all created and built in accordance with and respect for natural law. In contrast to the pre-eminence of natural law in Indigenous thinking, industrial thinking believes in the human species' dominion over nature. In this conception that favours human dominion and control, natural law is not something that needs to be respected or taken seriously, rather natural law is a limitation to be both overcome and overruled by humans' interest. In this way, nature becomes a subject of particular human rule and is used for human purposes with little regard for the consequences of that kind of uneven relationship.

The second principle of Indigenous thinking is the understanding of time as cyclical (ibid.). This is related to the first principle discussed above, namely the respect for natural law as the highest law. Nature continually produces and reproduces itself by balancing its various aspects and cycles. Indigenous thinking is grounded in careful and continuous observation and relationship with nature as a guide for how to live correctly (Cajete, 2016). This involves paying close attention to and in some ways mirroring the practices and cycles of nature. Time, then, is broadly understood as a series of cycles that repeat and balance continuously. Interrupting or interfering with these processes and cycles has consequences that affect all other parts of the natural world, including human activities. In contrast to the cyclical notions of time common to Indigenous thinking, industrial thinking is modelled on conceptions of linear time. Under this model, time is akin to a straight line that marches on in a predictable fashion. This forward motion of time is in industrial societies often associated with the notion of progress. LaDuke underlines that the notion of progress in industrial society is associated with things like technological innovation and economic growth (LaDuke, 1993). The prioritization of this kind of understanding of time and progress reflects an indifference, if not open hostility, to the limits and needs of the natural world, subordinating natural law for the purposes of particular human desires and projects.

The third principle of Indigenous thinking is reciprocity with nature (ibid.). This is a principle guided by an understanding of human beings as a part of a larger interdependent whole. In this way, humans are one part or aspect of nature and need to balance their actions with the limits of natural law and coordinate their actions with the cyclical time of the land. LaDuke gives the example of harvesting and only taking as much as you need as well as giving back whenever you take (ibid.). This is done to ensure the continuance of what is taken and to be in a balanced and equal relationship that allows the flourishing of all beings. In industrial thinking, however, reciprocity is foregone for the imposition of particular humans' will in the processes of taming or civilizing what is wild. This relies on an understanding of humans as distinct from and superior to nature instead of an equal part or reflection of nature. This type of thinking has not only led to degradation and destruction of nature, but also to oppressive systems imposed on some humans by other humans, such as colonialism and imperialism. In her discussion of this feature of industrial thinking, LaDuke states:

> My experience is that people who are viewed as 'primitive' are generally people of color, and people who are viewed as 'civilized' are those of European descent. This prejudice still permeates industrial society and in fact even permeates 'progressive' thinking. It holds that somehow people of European descent are smarter and they have some better knowledge of the world than the rest of us. I suggest that this is perhaps a racist worldview, that it has racist implications. That is, in fact, our experience.
>
> (ibid.)

This othering of nature that we find in the industrial world-view is deeply related to other dangerous structures that still permeate our societies, such as racism and colonialism. This is also another way in which linear time and linear thinking can be hitched to particularly harmful projects that disrespect natural law and also devalue other beings, including other human beings.

The fourth principle of Indigenous thinking is linguistic, and acknowledges the creation of languages that respect and reflect the animacy of the natural world (ibid.). The Indigenous scholar and botanist, Robin Wall Kimmerer describes this as a 'grammar of animacy' (Kimmerer, 2017). LaDuke and Kimmerer discuss this grammar of animacy using examples from their native languages, which both belong to the language family of Anishinaabe peoples: *anishinaabemowin*. Anishinaabemowin is 60–70 per cent verb-based, which results in a language that reflects the animacy and aliveness of the natural world (ibid.). In Anishinaabemowin, common words referred to as nouns in English are animate and perform respect for the inherent value and agency of natural beings. For example, '*wiikwegama*', in Potawami, is translated in English as 'bay', but a truer translation is actually 'to be a bay', which reflects a world-view in which water is alive and has agency. Water could have any number of manifestations: a lake, a river, etc., but *wiikwegama* expresses water as being a bay (ibid.). LaDuke states, 'Looking at the world and seeing most things are alive, we have come to believe, based on this perception, that they have spirit' (LaDuke, 1993). Conversely, LaDuke characterizes industrial thinking as bound in a language of inanimacy that reduces the sacredness of the natural world and commodifies it. Languages of industrial societies and colonizing societies such as English, Spanish, French, Portuguese, etc., are primarily noun-based and are overpopulated with inanimate nouns. This overdetermination of nouns and objects, LaDuke argues, creates and performs a fundamentally different relationship to the rest of world in a penchant (when wedded to other features such as linear thinking and economic growth) for objectifying and commodifying beings (ibid.). To stay with the example of water, think about the ongoing controversies over private multinational corporations such as Nestlé asserting private ownership of water. In European philosophies, this process has also been observed and described as an inclination for 'thingification', transforming beings into things or commodities. This kind of commodification or objectification of natural beings (including some humans) can and has been used as a kind of perverse justification for mistreatment or extraction.

The final principle of Indigenous thinking for LaDuke is an economic organization of Indigenous societies based on what she calls 'conspicuous distribution' (ibid.). Conspicuous distribution prioritizes and values the amount that is given away or gifted rather than valuing the amount that is consumed or accumulated. In a society that practises conspicuous distribution, everyone shares resources based on their need rather than resource hoarding by some, which leads to resource-lack for the many. Under industrial thinking, LaDuke argues that capitalism and its primary focus on massive accumulation and consumption disregard natural law, which leads to negative consequences that we experience globally, such as the global ravages of climate change. This kind of capitalist accumulation thinking promotes greed and unsustainable consumption that is entirely out of sync with the needs and functions of the natural world. This leads to highly unbalanced ecologies, which produce adverse consequences for all, such as the extreme weather conditions and natural disasters of climate change. LaDuke argues that industrial societies have much to learn from the conspicuous distribution models of economic organizations found within Indigenous societies and Indigenous thinking.

39.2 Indigenous thinking vs. industrial thinking: Key Points

- LaDuke proposes that there are five key principles of Indigenous thinking in contrast to industrial thinking.
- First, natural law vs. human dominion over nature.

- Second, cyclical/non-linear time vs. linear time.
- Third, reciprocity (give and take) with nature vs. taming or civilizing wilderness.
- Fourth, languages of animacy (aliveness) vs. languages of inanimacy (object-oriented).
- Fifth, economic organization of conspicuous distribution vs. economic organization of conspicuous accumulation and consumption (capitalism).

39.3 Indigenous governance

Now that we have an idea of the key characteristics of Indigenous thinking, we will explore how those tenets of thinking are employed in societal organization and structure, particularly how self-rule or sovereignty is actualized in and through Indigenous governance. We can say that all forms of governance and rule are bound by particular physical and ecological realities. Thus, conceptions of ecology and place are fundamental to both the shapes and forms that societies and governance take. Care for and relation with the environment and ecology are a key tenet centred in Indigenous forms of governance and rely once more on how Indigenous peoples view and understand the world. Take, for example, the centrality of interdependence, balance, and responsibility for harmony with the natural world prioritized in Anishinaabe traditions.

> Interdependence highlights reciprocity or mutuality between humans and the environment as a central feature of existence. In Anishinaabe traditions, reciprocity is also systematized. That is, environmental identities and responsibilities are coordinated with one another through complex social, cultural, economic, and political institutions. Interdependence suggests a much larger system of 'reciprocities' that characterize many hundreds of relationships of interlocking/intersecting relationships across entire societies.
>
> (Whyte, 2018: 128)

Importantly, in Anishinaabe traditions, interdependence forms a central pillar of Anishinaabe identity and existence that is therefore embedded in and reflected through the organization of Anishinaabe societies. Reciprocity, or the symbiotic relationship of balance between beings, the eternal give and take, is systematized in Anishinaabe societies. In this way, reciprocity and interdependence are not just abstract ideals divorced from the physical or ecological realm but guide important related forms of value and valuing. For example, Whyte states further:

> Interdependence is a source of identity for how humans understand whom and what they are in the world . . . [I]nterdependence is also a means to motivate humans to exercise their caretaking responsibilities to their relatives, human and nonhuman, which helps motivate these relatives to exercise their reciprocal responsibilities to nourish and support one another in diverse ways.
>
> (ibid.: 127–128)

Here, interdependence is both intrinsically and instrumentally valuable because it ensures specific norms of interaction with the natural world such that the value of interdependence is preserved through reciprocity. In this way, interdependence within Anishinaabe traditions both facilitates and preserves reciprocity or good, balanced relationships among relatives/relations, which importantly here also encompass non-humans. This facilitation and preservation of good relations through reciprocity translate and realize other goods that outsiders might call different things, such as sustainability or biodiversity. Institutions are often important expressions of cultural values. So, if we look at societal structuring through the institutions that exist and are supported and prioritized, we can trace or track the values of any particular community. For example, our current reliance upon and commitment to expanding extractive industries, such as oil drilling and pipeline construction in our industrial, capitalist society, can track our particular commitment and valuing of fossil fuels as well as fossil fuel infrastructure, which is extremely out of balance with notions of ecological interdependence and reciprocity. Indeed, we could say that a society that prioritizes extracting and taking without giving back, or in other words with no care for reciprocity, is a highly unbalanced and unsustainable society/political organizational structure.

39.3.1 Indigenous governance in action: the Haudenosaunee Confederacy

> We are a part of everything that is beneath us, above us, and around us. Our past is our present, our present is our future, and our future is seven generations past and present.
>
> — Haudenosaunee teaching (quoted in LaDuke, 2016: xi)

An interesting example of Indigenous sovereignty and governance is the Haudenosaunee Confederacy. Haudenosaunee (also called Iroquois) peoples are Indigenous to Turtle Island and their ancestral lands encompass the north-eastern territories currently referred to as upstate New York and parts of both English and French Ontario. As such, Haudenosaunee territories pre-exist and transcend the colonial borders of both the USA and Canada. The Haudenosaunee Confederacy is an important example of Indigenous governance not only for its long history and political power, but also because of its sophistication as a confederacy of six Indigenous Haudenosaunee nations that 'is among the most ancient continuously operating governments in the world' (as quoted from the 'Haudenosaunee Statement to the World' in LaDuke, 2016: 12). The Haudenosaunee Confederacy is a type of representative democracy, in fact it is the first federal constitution on the North American continent and a spiritual, political, social, and ecological governance agreement between six nations (Wilkins, 2006b: 129). Those nations include the Mohawk, Oneida, Onondaga, Cayuga, Seneca, and Tuscarora. These nations form a political, territorial, and social alliance unified under a primary law *Kaienarakowa*, which has been translated as the Great Law of Peace and a Good Mind.

This Law is embodied by the Haudenosaunee Confederacy and the relations of the six nations. This is similar to the way in which the principle of interdependence and reciprocity was systematized in Anishinaabe traditions politically, socially, economically, and culturally through institutions, as described by Whyte. The Great Law of Peace and a Good Mind ensures that all voices embodied in the confederate structure of the six nations were consulted and also consented to decisions. This arose out of histories of conflict and discord that spurred the shared governance structure of the confederacy. Indeed, the Haudenosaunee Thanksgiving Address centres the fostering of consent through diversity by beginning each part with the notion: 'We bring our minds together . . .' (Kimmerer, 2015). As David E. Wilkins elaborates:

> The strength of this democratic process was that the Onondaga, after having heard the subject analyzed from multiple perspectives, were able to discern the general sense of discussion and give their final consent to a decision that by the end of deliberation reflected the collective voice of the assembled leaders. This sophisticated yet clearly demarcated process reflects the strong emphasis the Iroquois placed on checks and balances, public debate, and consensus, the idea being to foster unity.
>
> (Wilkins, 2006b: 130)

This process was subject to several levels of consent and approval, first, internally through an individual nation in the confederacy and then by each subsequent nation in the confederacy until an agreement or consensus was reached. Importantly, dissent was also encouraged and accommodated. Dissent was not viewed as negative or disruptive. This idea of working to foster unity within difference, and indeed to respect difference within a unified whole or confederate structure, directly reflects principles of the Great Law of Peace and a Good Mind. This Law requires respect of difference and processes of deliberation to reach consent that necessitate fostering discourse, discussion, and allowing the voices of others to be heard and listened to seriously. If this sounds familiar to some of the readers in the Western context, then it should, as this representative form of democracy was not something foreign or introduced through European arrival, intervention, influence, settlement, or colonization on Turtle Island. Rather, this sophisticated and elaborate form of political governance and social organization grew out of the distinct and strong relationships the Haudenosaunee had nurtured and maintained with their lands over millennia.

This respect for difference and deliberation follows directly from an Indigenous world-view that does not define equality as similarity or sameness. That each nation is equal within the confederacy and can be heard does not rely on an assimilation or erasure of their differences or distinctness. This practice and principle of political organization follow from an intimate relationship and collaboration with the natural environment or ecology. Robert Venables (2010: 26–27) elaborates:

> 'Balance' is a key word in Haudenosaunee society, and in fact the whole Haudenosaunee worldview is based on balance—not 'either/or.' When things go wrong, as indeed they do in any and all human societies, answers posed by the Haudenosaunee are based on the idea of finding ways to *rebalance* the situation. Progress—the adaptation to new ideas—was important, but not as important as balance. In turn, balance does not work without equality, and thus equality pervades the entire Haudenosaunee worldview. The Haudenosaunee believe that all life forms, including human beings, are equal and that all life forms have equal spiritual consciousness—'souls'.

This principle of equality is in many ways recognized in and taught to the Haudenosaunee, and in fact all humans if we pay close enough attention, by the natural world. This principle of political governance is structured in a way that mirrors the reality of the cooperation of different entities and beings and their factual interdependence on each other, on every part. Therefore, that someone does a different kind of work or develops a different kind of skill based on their gifts or familial tradition does not degrade or place them in an unequal hierarchy, but rather contributes necessarily and meaningfully to the functioning and purpose of the whole. This is key to constructing a flexible system of political governance informed by the versatility and resilience of ecologies. In times of struggle or massive disruption, such as natural disasters or, say, global climate crisis, it makes more sense to have a fluid and adaptable structure to accommodate and adapt to change. This fluidity and non-rigidity equally apply to many traditional Indigenous systems of gender. The Haudenosaunee peoples organized work and landscapes in gendered fashions, but this gendering cannot and must not be read through the exclusive and binary logics of the dominant sex/gender/sexuality system, as explored in Section 39.3.2.

39.3.2 Gender systems and land

As introduced in Section 39.3.1, it is a well-supported sociological and anthropological thesis that institutions are a crucial way of tracking both cultural differences as well as cultural priorities or values between different societies or traditions. Structures of governance are one such institution; gender systems are another foundational institution through which we can track cultural priorities and values. For example, the Haudenosaunee have a clear way in which they organized their landscapes, sometimes referred to in archaeological research as the creation of cultured landscapes. The existence of cultured landscapes refers to the ways in which human communities have always affected and shaped their physical places and ecological conditions. In the case of the Haudenosaunee, a fundamental cultured landscape took the form of the organization of their societies and settlements around woods and clearings, which were organized to reflect different 'spheres of responsibility' (Venables, 2010: 27). Traditionally, people socialized as women were responsible for the clearings and for cultivation and agriculture, while people socialized as men were responsible for the woods for hunting and gathering as well as strategic defence of the settlements, such as the Haudenosaunee longhouses, and farms of the clearings. While these activities were and are gendered, they are not hierarchical or exclusive in the way we know commonly understand gender systems through our own familiarity and experience in a divisive, hierarchical, unequal, and oppressive binary sex/gender/sexuality system. The different spheres of responsibility, gendered landscapes, and gendered activities were interdependent and reciprocal and relied on each other. As such, they were both equally important to the proper functioning and healthy balance of the whole, not only within each nation, but across the whole of the confederacy. In this way, Venables reminds us not to read Haudenosaunee gender systems or relations through the perspective of our colonial inheritance of a hierarchical binary gender system. 'The Haudenosaunee [gender] system was/is not rigid because it is based on maintaining balance in the real world, not a world based on abstract principles. A balanced reality calls for pragmatic solutions. The principle of balance carried over into Haudenosaunee politics' (ibid.: 34). This reinforces once again how the Haudenosaunee system of political governance and social organization was not living in just the abstract sense, but also in the literal sense—in the ways that ecologies are alive and depend on the gifts and responsibilities as well as spheres of duty of the whole, each interdependent part. Again, a strict and hierarchical gender system that has only rigidity and presumes the gendered activity to emanate and reside in the being who performs it alone is not an adaptive or flexible system that can cope with and overcome hardship or change. As we are currently seeing, ecological conditions are changing drastically and rapidly in ways inhospitable to the current rigid systems, which are struggling to adapt precisely because they have not been constructed with a deep awareness or prioritizing of balance and interdependence. It is to the clash between world-views and governance structures that this chapter now turns, in order to understand the changes to Indigenous ecologies wrought by external disruptions and the attempted imposition of foreign systems of dominance.

39.3 Indigenous governance: Key Points

- Key features of Indigenous governance for the Anishinaabe and Haudenosaunee include reciprocity, balance, interdependence, and flexibility, all of which are importantly learned from and modelled on ecologies.
- Reciprocity is a governance principle that recognizes the wisdom of respecting give and take.
- Balance is closely related to reciprocity in attending to the need to keep natural systems, including human ones, in a state of equilibrium or balance.
- Interdependence is a governance principle that understands that we as individuals are all part of the greater whole, nations are a part of greater political systems (such as confederacies), and that all beings are part of a larger ecosystem.
- Flexibility refers to the ways governance structures should be created to ensure all of the principles above, but also should be understood as a living and changing being to be able to adapt to ecological and political changes.

39.4 Interruptions and disruptions of Indigenous ecologies and sovereignties

There have been and remain many challenges, disruptions, and interruptions of Indigenous sovereignty globally, but perhaps the most prominent of these historical and continuous challenges is colonization (the action or process of settling among and establishing control over the Indigenous people of an area). Particularly in the context of the Americas, including Turtle Island (what is currently called North America), colonization takes the form of settler colonialism. Settler colonialism is a specific form of colonialism in which lands are stolen and used for economic extraction, and where the colonizers arrive, displace the original inhabitants, and never leave (see Key Concept: Settler societies in Section 10.2.4 in Chapter 10). This is clearly a highly disruptive and oppressive form of colonialism and domination that significantly affects Indigenous sovereignty and nationhood, as well as the flourishing of Indigenous ecologies that are both a foundational and integral part of Indigenous governance systems, as explored in Section 39.3.

In fact, the territoriality—the dispossession of lands and territories from Native peoples for the use and benefit of the colonizers—and ecological violence of settler colonialism are in many ways its primary features. Settler colonialism is a mode of domination achieved through various complex and ongoing practices that aims to *displace* Indigenous peoples, ecologies, and their subsequent governance structures, such as sovereignty, for the purpose of establishing different ecological relations that support settler nation states. In the case of North America, settler colonialism has manifested in the attempted transformation of hundreds of Indigenous nations into the three settler colonial nation-states of the USA, Canada, and Mexico. However, Indigenous nations and tribes still hold unique political status in both the USA and Canada that recognize the sovereignty and political uniqueness of both First Nations in Canada and American Indian governments in the USA that complicate not only political understandings of Indigenous peoples, but also comparisons to other racialized and minoritized groups on Turtle Island.

This is an essential component to understanding how settler colonialism both recognizes and denies Indigenous sovereignty for the purposes of ecological and territorial domination through the creation of settler nation states. For example, the USA is a much younger and relatively new political formation as a nation state, especially in comparison to the hundreds of Indigenous nations in the same geographical area that pre-date its sovereignty and existence by thousands of years. Yet, the USA globally is recognized as the primary sovereign of that same territory. Similarly, Indigenous nations and Indigenous peoples are often constructed within both the USA and Canada as racial and cultural minorities, which is often used as a way to further degrade Indigenous sovereignty, and the unique political status of Indigenous nations. Indigenous peoples are not only the first inhabitants of Turtle Island, however; they also formed sovereign nations that constituted the majority in pre-colonial contexts. Indigenous nations and peoples in North America were only later minoritized and racialized through the violent and continuous realities of settler colonialism. This point is not well understood generally in mainstream scholarship or political discourse. As David E. Wilkins explains within the US context: 'The fact of *treaty making*, which no other resident American group (states are also precluded from negotiating treaties) participated in, and the products of that process—the actual treaties, agreements, and negotiated settlements—confirmed nation-to-nation relationship between the negotiating tribal and nontribal parties' (Wilkins, 2006a: 46).

The nascent and emergent settler colonial state of the USA negotiated and made treaties with hundreds of Indigenous nations and acknowledged the treaty-making power of these Indigenous nations within the US Constitution itself. In this sense, Indigenous nations have a unique political status, and treaties between Indigenous nations and other nations, such as the settler State of the

US, form international nation-to-nation agreements. This stands regardless of the prevalent and almost universal practice of the US refusal to honour treaties with American Indian nations.

> **Key Concept: Racialization and minoritization**
>
> Racialization and minoritization refer to the processes through which race becomes a primary feature of our social world, and the processes through which peoples who are not minorities within their own cultural contexts become seen as cultural minorities. In this way, racialization and minoritization are features that affect how Indigenous peoples, Black peoples, and People of Colour more broadly are represented and viewed in a dominant Euro-centric society. In the case of Indigenous peoples in the Americas, however, prior to colonization they were the majority population and did not conceive of themselves in these racialized and minoritized ways. The same could be said of Africans who were targeted and trafficked in the transatlantic slave trade. Indigenous peoples have always maintained their political status and orientation as sovereign autonomous nations even after being forcibly made citizens through US law. However, this political status did not exist for African Americans (even though many were Indigenous to Africa) and post-emancipation they became citizens of the state in a different political sense than Indigenous peoples. This means that the pathways to justice for American Indians and African Americans are different, even though they experience similar racialization and minoritization processes.

The racialization and minoritization of Indigenous peoples on Turtle Island were and remain a prominent feature of Euro-Western colonization, imperialism, and globalization. The incorrect construction of Indigenous peoples as racial and cultural minorities is a pernicious attempt to dissolve further Indigenous nations' unique political status and sovereignty. As Wilkins (2006a: 45) explains, '[t]he situation of the 562 indigenous polities in North America is and has always been distinctive in comparison to the status and place of African Americans, Asian Americans, Latino Americans, women, and other racial or ethnic groups in the country'. This is not to say that Indigenous peoples have not been subject to the negative consequences of racialization and minoritization that other racial and cultural minorities face in North America. But their racialization and minoritization have different political consequences for Indigenous nations considering the ability and distinct possibility, in the USA, Canada, and Mexico, of the termination of Indigenous nations legally and politically by the settler state. This unique political status has often been misunderstood by both settlers and also other racialized and minoritized groups in the USA. But understanding the particular unique and distinct struggles Indigenous nations face is a key component to the deep and necessary forms of solidarity necessary for Indigenous justice, and justice for all other prominently oppressed groups in North America and worldwide, specifically Afrodiasporic peoples enslaved to build the New World order of settler states.

39.4 Interruptions and disruptions of Indigenous ecologies and sovereignties: Key Points

- Prominent and ongoing interruption and disruption of Indigenous ecologies and governance are due to colonialism and settler colonialism.
- The dominant form of governance on Turtle Island is settler colonialism, which continuously works to transform many hundreds of Indigenous nations and governance systems to three settler colonial states: Canada, the USA, and Mexico.

- Settler colonialism is a form of colonialism in which a foreign or external power comes to lands already occupied by inhabitants and through ecological, physical, and political violence asserts their own dominance and form of society.
- In some ways, settler colonialism can be understood as the attempted and ongoing uprooting of Indigenous ecologies for the insertion and functioning of settler ecologies in their place.
- An important feature of settler colonialism is that settlers come to a new territory to stay.

39.5 Difference, incommensurability, and solidarity

To say that oppression or the collective experience of oppressive social structures fosters shared identity is true but insufficient. Even within oppressed groups that are externally identified as similar or the same, there are important distinctions and incommensurabilities to how that oppression is experienced and resisted. Naturally this makes solidarity and coalitional work difficult not only across groups, but also within groups themselves. Here, I will focus specifically on the solidarity struggles and successes between American Indians and African Americans, with a special focus both on the ways in which solidarity requires respect for difference and on sites of incommensurability between Black and Indigenous struggles in North America. Colonization in North America relied fundamentally on Indigenous dispossession and attempted genocide as well as on the forced labour of enslaved Africans brought to the Americas. It should also be noted that de facto enslavement of Indigenous peoples was critical to the production of the wealth and landscapes that the USA as a settler state boasts today (see Miranda, 2010; 2013). In this sense, African Americans or descendants of enslaved Africans on Turtle Island have a different status and history than both European colonizers/settlers and voluntary immigrants to North America from other places. This distinction is increasingly emphasized in both Black Studies and Native Studies.

One site of difference or obstacle to solidarity is the incommensurability of Indigenous forms of resistance that do not work within the shared framework of securing rights from the settler nation state through campaigns for equal citizenship in practice. Historically, citizenship of and within the settler nation state has been a fraught concept for both Indigenous peoples and African Americans on Turtle Island. There are important histories of forced citizenship (or citizenship conferred non-consensually) to the USA for both Indigenous peoples and African Americans. For example, under the General Allotment Act (1887), some Indigenous peoples were conferred citizenship by the USA if they received land from the government in the form of allotments—a transaction that both forcibly removed them from the political and legal status of citizens of their own tribe and registered them as citizens of the settler nation (Wilkins, 2006a: 55, see also here https://iltf.org/land-issues/history/). Additionally, in 1924, the General Citizenship Act declared that all non-citizen American Indians were now federal citizens. This was in many ways a method of forced assimilation directed at the process of dissolving and eliminating Indigenous nations as political sovereigns within the geopolitical space of the USA (ibid.: 59). If citizens of Indigenous nations through 'acquiring' land under Western private property regimes become US citizens, they lose or are often required to forfeit their unique political status as members of sovereign nations and come into and under nation-state rule, which strengthens and solidifies the US claims to primary political sovereignty of the geographical space of Turtle Island and fortifies the US political dominance in the region. This was importantly related to requiring assimilation of Indigenous peoples in the form of private property regimes, which disrupted the communal property relations of Indigenous nations, and broke up the geographical contiguity of Indigenous lands through land parcelling and sale to white settlers (LaDuke, 1993).

Similarly, post-emancipation, the USA faced the 'Negro question' of what to do both politically and legally with the new massive populations of formerly enslaved African Americans (Du Bois, 1998). There was a period of time when formerly enslaved African Americans belonged to no nation in the sense that they were neither citizens of the USA nor citizens of any other nation (except perhaps for the Freedmen who were citizens of Indigenous nations and Black Indians on Turtle Island). With the passing of the 14th Amendment in 1866, African Americans were legally decreed citizens of the USA. In both instances detailed above, becoming citizens was a result of the practices of the USA and solidified the settler state's sovereignty and political dominance. Importantly, however, Indigenous justice has been and remains rooted in the USA respecting its treaty obligations that assert and recognize Indigenous nations as political sovereigns and international nations, while African Americans—largely because they were unilaterally made citizens of the USA in 1866—have historically and continuously struggled for recognition by the USA of their constitutionally-mandated status as equal citizens of the state. So, while both Indigenous peoples and African Americans in the USA share in racialization, minoritization, violence, and oppression at the hands of the state, their positions and experiences are in many ways incommensurable. This is why attempts to erase difference for the purposes of solidarity between various marginalized and vulnerable groups often fail or result in conflict. It is important both to realize shared oppressive circumstances in the fight for justice but also to avoid erasing or conflating the very real distinctions that matter for solidarity work and progress.

African Americans and American Indians are often the communities most overburdened with environmental injustice in the USA (LaDuke, 2016). In writing on the differences in conceptions of environmental justice, a movement to achieve healthy, safe, and liveable environments for all, Dina Gilio-Whitaker (2019) provides an important analysis of the preconditions for the emergence of the capitalist nation state through violence to both Indigenous peoples and enslaved Africans on Turtle Island. The central precondition is settler colonialism. Environmental justice in the USA has focused on the structure of environmental racism (Bullard, 1990): the overburdening and targeting of racialized, minoritized groups as the communities for toxic dumping and ecological externalities of capitalist industry. Yet Gilio-Whitaker urges us to view state violence against racialized, minoritized groups as emerging within a settler colonial national framework which only achieves normative power in and through colonialism. Racism, then, can be understood as a denial or diminishment of rights based on an understanding of their distribution in a national citizenship framework (Gilio-Whitaker, 2019: 22–23). In the case of racialized and minoritized communities, this looks like a denial of their fair share of rights as promised or conferred through their membership in the nation-state as citizens or being overburdened with harms not placed on other communities, mainly white affluent communities.

As such, this grounding of environmental justice as a movement and theoretical framework is State-centric and already works within the confines and dictates of the settler colonial nation-state. This makes mainstream environmental justice ill-suited for articulating Indigenous justice, which is necessarily a state-to-state relationship and not a vying for more equal rights among or within the settler nation-state. Gilio-Whitaker (ibid.: 24) importantly notes that capitalism is not a consequence of colonialism, but rather that colonialism is a precondition for capitalism because the wealth generated and accumulated as capital for Europe and within the 'New World' 'could only accumulate from centuries of violent Indigenous displacement, genocide, and land theft'. Additionally, she states that '[c]olonialism is inextricably bound up with slavery, having paved the way for the transatlantic slave trade initiated by Columbus in his first voyage to the "New World"'(ibid.: 24).

So, capitalism grows out of and becomes normative or normalized through the violent processes of colonization and slavery that both shape and inform current society and fights for justice on Turtle Island and the planet more broadly. Under capitalism, justice becomes understood as a matter of distribution and redistribution. But this framework says hardly anything about the preconditions of colonization by which the wealth to be distributed or redistributed is accumulated in the first place. This colonization, as Gilio-Whitaker states, is predicated on the genocide, dispossession, and displacement of Indigenous peoples and the displacement and enslavement of African peoples. So, for Gilio-Whitaker and other scholars, environmental injustice is not something reducible to environmental racism alone (which is not to minimize the deadly effects it has for both Indigenous peoples and racialized, minoritized communities): we must understand the whole historical and ongoing process of colonization and colonialism as the supreme environmental injustice (Whyte, 2016; Gilio-Whitaker, 2019). Part of the ongoing injustice of settler colonialism is that it obscures other ways of being or other ways even of understanding ourselves outside of settler colonial capitalist frameworks or realities. Indigenous peoples pose a threat, still, to settler colonial state-making and statecraft because their very existence disproves the generally considered fact of settler colonial sovereignty as accomplished and irreversible. This threat posed by Indigenous nations explains, in part, why Indigenous nations are so viciously attacked through settler colonial capitalist violence, which includes ecological violence such as physical invasion, land theft, genocide, and corporate extractivism.

39.5 Difference, incommensurability, and solidarity: Key Points

- While both Indigenous peoples and African Americans face similar harms from racialization and minoritization, their experiences are not the same.
- One difference has to do with Indigenous nations' unique political status in relationship to settler colonial states.
- Whereas African Americans are constructed as a racial minority within the state, who attempt to achieve justice through intra-state mechanisms, such as having their rights as citizens respected and enforced, Indigenous peoples fight for their unique political status and sovereignty to be respected.
- An important historical point that positions Indigenous peoples and descendants of enslaved Africans in the Americas in solidarity is the fact that colonization and slavery generated the wealth that made what we understand as capitalism today possible.
- When we consider what justice entails as a matter of redistribution of wealth, we must answer for and think critically about where that wealth comes from and how it was generated—through colonization and slavery.

39.6 Extractivism, fossil fuels, and Indigenous lands

Much Western media attention has recently been given to the massive organizations against corporate fossil fuel extractive practices by Indigenous peoples globally. While this attention is important, the problem of corporate extractivism—the removal of resources, including fossil fuels, from the Earth by corporations for profit—on Indigenous lands is not a new reality. In fact, the ecological violence that these forms of extractivism pose is indicative of ongoing practices of colonization and resource colonization for at least the past 500 years in the context of the Americas. Non-Indigenous scholar Naomi Klein has developed a comprehensive definition of extractivism that is useful in thinking about a philosophy that encourages unsustainable and environmentally degrading resource extraction globally. Importantly, for Klein, extractivism is both a (neo-)colonial philosophy and a set of practices that relies on understandings of the world filtered through the ideology of capitalism. Klein (2015: 169) describes extractivism as a 'nonreciprocal, dominance-based relationship with the earth, one purely of taking . . . It is the reduction of life into objects for the use of others, giving them no integrity or value of their own – turning living complex ecosystems into "natural resources".' Compare, then, the non-reciprocal extractive orientation of capitalism to the reciprocal relations called for and required by a centralizing of natural law examined earlier in this chapter.

Capitalism paired with the practice and philosophy of extractivism is for Klein a mentality of endless taking and extraction, that necessarily relies on creating places as sites of extraction that do not matter, or what Klein (ibid.: 169–170) terms sacrifice zones: 'places that, to their extractors, somehow don't count and therefore can be poisoned, drained, or otherwise destroyed, for the supposed greater good of economic progress'. A philosophy and way of being that ignore natural law for unprecedented and conspicuous accumulation would have to blind itself to the unsustainability of such practices. A non-ethic of endless domination and exploitation, which is what both capitalism and colonialism suggest as world-views, always needs to believe there is another place to exploit, to exhaust, to dominate. This has been and remains the experience of Indigenous peoples and nations globally for centuries, especially in the Americas. Significantly for Indigenous nations in the Americas, their lands have historically and continuously been targeted for resource-extractive industries, which constitute further violations to both Indigenous nations' lands and sovereignties.

Take, for example, the No Dakota Access Pipeline (#NODAPL) movement currently ongoing in South Dakota in the USA, which saw the gathering of over 15,000 people camped at Standing Rock Sioux reservation to oppose the construction of an oil pipeline that would imperil Indigenous lands and lives. Now, some detractors and even proponents of the movement against the pipeline mistakenly understand these practices of resource extraction and the forms of resistance to which they have given rise as new. As many Indigenous scholars argue, however, this is just another episode in a centuries-long and multigenerational assault on Indigenous peoples (Whyte, 2018; Estes, 2019; Gilio-Whitaker, 2019). Importantly for Indigenous nations' resistance to extractivism is understood not as just protest against pipelines or mining, but as the defence of lands, waters, and non-human relations that are importantly alive and related to collective survival. As Oceti Sakowin historian and scholar Nick Estes (2019: 47) writes:

> #NoDAPL was also a struggle over the meaning of land. For Oceti Sakowin, history is the land itself: the earth cradles the bones of the ancestors. Because Native people remain barriers to capitalist development, their bodies needed to be removed—both from *beneath* and *atop* the soil—therefore eliminating their rightful relationship *with* the land.

Thus, the rampant extractivism of capitalist colonialism is not just an assault on both human lives and land, but also targets and attacks whole networks of relationships and life that exist to nourish other sovereignties and other realities than those carved into the land through extractivist practices.

Importantly, extractivism and capitalism fundamentally change or reorient the very meaning of relationships—human relationship to land, non-human relationships to each other, and human-to-human relationships. Diné historian Melanie Yazzie describes this loyalty to extractivist world-views as a 'death drive' and positions multi-generational Indigenous resistance against the world-destroying power of resource extraction as a 'relational politics of life' (Yazzie, 2018: 29). This death drive and world-destroying power reflect a fundamental perversion of extractivism via capitalism that takes whole living interconnected systems of being and life and objectifies them or singles them out for profit. Importantly, extractivism and capitalism via colonialism also understand power as dominance and order as hierarchy, which is both empirically absurd and wreaks havoc on the living systems it attempts to relate to in this way.

One example of this is the way that resource extraction sites are historically and continuously also sites of extreme gender and sexual violence, largely against Indigenous women and women of colour. The domination of the land embodied in extractivist capitalism is mirrored and encouraged in human-to-human relationships that naturalize the unnatural practices of gender oppression and sexual violence. These realities exist in the presence of 'man camps' that are all-men work encampments for the resource-extractive projects in the areas that are related to high rates of gender and sexual violence and human trafficking largely of Indigenous women and girls in the surrounding areas (Deer, 2015). As Estes (2019: 79–80) explains, this is not a novel reality, but one that dates back centuries to colonization and the development of another extractive industry, the European fur trade in North America: 'In some ways, trading forts were the first man camps—the vanguards of capital that extracted wealth not only from the land, but also through the conquest of Indigenous women's bodies. Later, these trade forts also became border towns, the white-dominated settlements that today ring Indigenous reservations.' The system of taking without consent which is embodied in resource extraction easily bleeds into human-to-human relations.

The destruction and potential destruction of more Indigenous lands through the ever-expanding need to feed the beast of capitalism and settler colonial expansion mean that the foundational principles of Indigenous lifeways and governance structures are constantly under direct attack. One cannot live, survive, and thrive if the very basis of life is being attacked from all sides. This is why the Oceti Sakowin philosophy of 'Mni Wiconi' or 'Water is Life' is not a slogan or metaphor, but a direct expression of the natural law of relation and interconnection (ibid.). Pipelines, mines, and other extractive practices threaten the possibility of the continuance of all life, not just Indigenous life and not just human life. The ability of Indigenous nations to continue and flourish is predicated exactly on this understanding of natural law, or as Yazzie (2018) put it a 'relational politics of life'. We can also see how threats such as climate change, global pandemics like Covid-19, and extractive practices to support fossil fuel industries endanger Indigenous communities already made vulnerable through centuries of colonization, land theft, and segregation into reservations/reserves. Colonization and settler colonial rule have at every turn attempted to undermine Indigenous nations' ability to continue, and yet, they continue all the same.

39.6 Extractivism, fossil fuels, and Indigenous lands: Key Points

- Extractivism is a philosophy that normalizes or naturalizes non-reciprocal, non-consensual taking for the purposes of massive capital accumulation.
- Extractivism is one way of understanding how living, diverse ecosystems can be perceived as mere objects or commodities that are only considered valuable in their ability to generate profit.
- Extractivism helps to explain the steadfast commitment we, especially in the West, have to unsustainable resource extraction and societies built on and around the continuous unearthing of fossil fuels.
- Extractivism also helps explain the overburdening of communities of colour in general, but Indigenous communities specifically, with harms related to environmental degradation from resource extraction.
- Indigenous peoples all over the world continue to resist colonization, including resource colonization, by rejecting the capitalist death drive encapsulated in philosophies of extractivism and by defending lands and waters through a 'relational politics of life' (Yazzie, 2018).

39.7 Conclusion

Indigenous ecologies are, thus, a critical and crucial philosophy, a way of life, and reality that continue to be actively targeted for the elimination of Indigenous nations and Indigenous peoples. Indigenous philosophies have some of the most beautiful, resilient, and complex political philosophies and ecologies. This chapter has provided only a very brief overview of some of the essential features of Indigenous thinking and governance in a particular geographical space. An exploration of these political systems and insights points to the fact that we must work in solidarity, and follow the lead of Indigenous nations and peoples globally to both imagine and create a world that fosters the principles of Indigenous thinking not as our property or our right, but as our duty to both the human and more-than-human world to which our current dominant industrial thinking has laid siege again and again. Indigenous governance and ecologies have never ended. We must work together to foster Indigenous futures through realizing that, while we are not the same, the future of life on Earth depends on imagining otherwise through the traditions and knowledges of Indigenous peoples.

Take your learning further by accessing the online resources for a library of web links to relevant videos, articles, blogs, and useful websites for each chapter: **www.oup.com/he/Ramgotra-Choat1e**.

Study questions

1. What are the five features of 'Indigenous thinking' and 'industrial thinking'?
2. How is closely observing nature related to Indigenous governance systems?
3. What distinguishes settler colonialism from colonialism?
4. How is the acceptance of difference important for building solidarity and coalitions?
5. What makes Indigenous nations unique politically in contrast to other racialized and minoritized groups in the USA?
6. In what ways is colonization a precondition of capitalism?
7. How does extractivism exhibit a capitalist death drive?
8. How is a lack of consent in extractivism related to sexual violence?

Further reading

Primary sources

Anderson, K., Campbell, M., and Belcourt, C. (eds) (2018) *Keetsahnak: Our Murdered and Missing Indigenous Sisters*. Edmonton: The University of Alberta Press.
Examines the crisis of murdered and missing Indigenous women in North America, especially in connection with colonization and resource extraction.

Burkhart, B. (2019) *Indigenizing Philosophy through the Land: A Trickster Methodology for Decolonizing Environmental Ethics and Indigenous Futures*. East Lansing, MI: Michigan State University Press.
Presents Indigenous philosophies and the centrality of land to them, combatting Eurocentric presentations of environmental ethics and promoting Indigenous justice.

Cajete, G. (2016) *Native Science: Natural Laws of Interdependence*. Santa Fe, NM: Clear Light Publishers.
Presents central and foundational tenets of Indigenous science and its practices while also contrasting them with Western science.

Coulthard, G.S. (2014) *Red Skin, White Masks: Rejecting the Colonial Politics of Recognition*. Minneapolis, MN: University of Minnesota Press.
Addresses Indigenous rejections of politics of colonial recognition, specifically the ways in which colonial governments fail to recognize Indigenous nations as sovereign states.

Gilio-Whitaker, D. (2019) *As Long as Grass Grows: The Indigenous Fight for Environmental Justice, from Colonization to Standing Rock*. Boston: Beacon Press.
Reorients environmental justice as a much older concept by posing that environmental injustice is enacted in the North American context primarily through colonization and slavery.

Kimmerer, R.W. (2015) *Braiding Sweetgrass: Indigenous Wisdom, Scientific Knowledge and the Teachings of Plants*. New York: Milkweed Editions.
Presents stories and lessons of plants as a way of understanding Indigenous philosophies and relations to place.

LaDuke, W. (2016) *All Our Relations: Native Struggles for Land and Life*. Chicago: Haymarket Books.
Examines different Indigenous peoples' experiences of environmental injustice and their fights to combat them.

Penashue, T.E. (2019) *Nitinikiau Innusi: I Keep the Land Alive*. Ed. E. Yeoman. Winnipeg: University of Manitoba Press.
Memorializes the experiences and life of an Innu land and water defender, especially in resistance to Canadian/European military pollution and environmental degradation.

Simpson, A. (2014) *Mohawk Interruptus: Political Life Across the Borders of Settler States*. Durham, NC: Duke University Press Books.
Presents Mohawk (Haudenosaunee) political philosophies, especially in relation to asserting sovereignty against the state of Canada, and offers a politics of refusal as a strategy Indigenous peoples use globally to survive and dismantle colonization.

Simpson, L.B. (2017) *As We Have Always Done: Indigenous Freedom through Radical Resistance*. Minneapolis, MN: University of Minnesota Press.
Addresses Nishnaabeg philosophy and Ninshaabeg cultural resurgence in fights for Indigenous freedom.

References

Bullard, R.D. (1990) *Dumping in Dixie: Race, Class, and Environmental Quality*. Boulder, CO: Westview Press.

Cajete, G. (2016) *Native Science: Natural Laws of Interdependence*. Santa Fe, NM : Clear Light Publishers.

Deer, S. (2015) *The Beginning and End of Rape: Confronting Sexual Violence in Native America*. Minneapolis, MN: University of Minnesota Press.

Du Bois, W.E.B. (1998) *Black Reconstruction in America, 1860–1880*. Ed. D.L. Lewis. New York: Free Press.

Estes, N. (2019) *Our History Is the Future: Standing Rock Versus the Dakota Access Pipeline, and the Long Tradition of Indigenous Resistance*. London: Verso.

Gilio-Whitaker, D. (2019) *As Long as Grass Grows: The Indigenous Fight for Environmental Justice, from Colonization to Standing Rock*. Boston: Beacon Press.

Kimmerer, R.W. (2015) *Braiding Sweetgrass: Indigenous Wisdom, Scientific Knowledge and the Teachings of Plants*. New York: Milkweed Editions.

Kimmerer, R.W. (2017) 'Learning the Grammar of Animacy'. *Anthropology of Consciousness*, 28(2): 128–134.

Klein, N. (2015) 'Beyond Extractivism: Confronting the Climate Denier Within'. In. Klein, *This Changes Everything: Capitalism vs. The Climate*. New York: Simon & Schuster, pp. 161–187.

LaDuke, W. (1993) 'Voices from White Earth: Gaa-waabaabiganikaag'. In Thirteenth Annual E.F. Schumacher Lectures, New Haven, October. Available at: https://centerforneweconomics.org/publications/voices-from-white-earth-gaa-waabaabigaanikaag.

LaDuke, W. (2016) *All Our Relations: Native Struggles for Land and Life*. Chicago: Haymarket Books.

Miranda, D.A. (2010) 'Extermination of the Joyas: Gendercide in Spanish California'. *GLQ: A Journal of Lesbian and Gay Studies*, 16(1): 253–284.

Miranda, D.A. (2013) *Bad Indians: A Tribal Memoir*. Berkeley, CA: Heyday.

Venables, R.W. (2010) 'The Clearings and the Woods: The Haudenosaunee (Iroquois) Landscape—Gendered and Balanced'. In S. Baugher and S.M. Spencer-Wood (eds), *Archaeology and Preservation of Gendered Landscapes*. New York: Springer-Verlag, pp. 21–55.

Whyte, K.P. (2016) 'Indigenous Experience, Environmental Justice and Settler Colonialism'. In B. Bannon (ed.), *Nature and Experience: Phenomenology and the Environment*. Lanham, MD: Rowman and Littlefield.

Whyte, K.P. (2018) 'Settler Colonialism, Ecology, and Environmental Injustice'. *Environment and Society*, 9(1): 125–144.

Wilkins, D.E. (2006a) *American Indian Politics and the American Political System*, 2nd edn. Lanham, MD: Rowman & Littlefield Publishers.

Wilkins, D.E. (2006b) 'Indigenous Governments: Past, Present, and Future'. In D.E. Wilkins, *American Indian Politics and the American Political System*, 2nd edn. Lanham, MD: Rowman & Littlefield Publishers, pp. 125–162.

Yazzie, M.K. (2018) 'Decolonizing Development in Diné Bikeyah: Resource Extraction, Anti-Capitalism, and Relational Futures'. *Environment and Society*, 9(1): 25–39.

Index

Notes

vs. indicates a comparison.

Entries in **bold** indicate a Key Thinker or Key Concept box.

A

a priori foundations, Kant 530, 532, 536-8
a priori, *a posteriori* vs. **529**
The ABC of Community Anarchism (Goldman) 470
Abduh, Muhammad 258, **259**
abortions 650
absolute rights, Douglass 547
absolute sovereignty,
    Hobbes 89-90
    Locke 127
    Montesquieu 194
abuse of power, Burke 307-9
    Montesquieu 192
accountable government,
    Macaulay 298-9
Achebe, Chinua 280
activating freedom, Douglass 548-50
Adorno, Theodor W. 535, 642
Aeschylus 275, 276
An Aesthetic Education in the Age of Globalization (Spivak) 439-40
affirmative action 413
African philosophy 569
African-Americans 173, 723-4
    political philosophy 569
agon 239, **244**, 245-6, 249
agriculture 684-5
    Indigenous agriculture 124-5
    Montesquieu 188
ahimsa 490, **491**, 497-8
Ahmad, Aijaz 277
Ain't I a Woman: Black Women and Feminism (hooks) 53
'Ain't I a woman' speech (Sojourner Truth) 32, 33-4
al-'Azm, Sadiq Jalal 277
Al-Qaeda 257, 419
Althusser, Louis 223, 232, 665
alter-globalization, Spivak 434-7
amaZulu 492-504
Ambedkar, B. R. **487**
American Civilization (James) 316, 317
American Revolution (1776-1783) 164, 292, 303, 550
    Arendt 339-40
Amin, Shahid 680

Amo, Anton Wilhelm 141
amour de soi (self-love), Rousseau 151
anarchism 355, 383, 490
    Goldman 467-72
    Marx 232-3
Anarchism and Other Essays (Goldman) 466
anarchy, international, Hobbes 86-7
Anarchy, State and Utopia (Nozick) 591
Anderson, Elizabeth 394-5, 593
Anglo-Boer War (1898-1902) 333-4
Anishinaabe 714, 716-18
Anishinaabemowin 716
'An Answer to the Question: What is Enlightenment' (Kant) 528
Anthony, Susan B. 556, 649
Anthropocene 676, 680-4, **682**, 707-9
anti-colonial resistance, Gandhi 488-91
anti-colonial nationalism, Zhang Taiyan 355-6
anti-feminism, Arendt 341
anti-Manchu revolution, Zhang Taiyan 350-4
anti-naturalism **627**
Antiphon 22
anti-semitism 250-1, 282, 335, 668
Anvikshaki (philosophy of science) **59**, 70
Are Prisons Obsolete (Davis) 644
Arendt, Hannah 292-3, 331-48, 668
    American Revolution (1776-1783) 339-40
    anti-feminism 341
    crystallization 335
    feminism 340-2
    French Revolution 339-40
    government forms 333-4
    Haitian Revolution 339-40
    meaning of politics 336-8
    'Negro question' 342-5
    philosophy and politics 337-8
    proto-feminism 342
    racial stereotypes 343-4

    specificity of the political 336-7
    world and the other 344-5
aristocracy, Wollstonecraft 377-8
Aristotle 18, 39-56, **40**, 436
    household 49-52
    human nature 46-7
    knowing and being 43-4
    private sphere 122
    slavery 50-1
    women 51-2
Armitage, David 126
Arnold, David 680
Arthaśāstra (Kautilya) 57-74
artificial reproduction 629-30
Asian unity, Zhang Taiyan 357-8
Astell, Mary 9-10, 76-7, 131-46
    consent 138-40
    freedom 140-2
    human nature 135-6
    interpretative puzzle 132-3
    marriage 142-4
    slavery 140-2
    social contract theory 133-42
    sovereignty 136-8
Atwood, Margaret 476
Augustine of Hippo **338**, 494
Austen, Jane 279, 280
Austin, J. L. 660-1
authorization, Hobbes 87-9
Awakening of Mahayana Faith (Zhang) 361

B

The Bacchae (Euripides) 275
Bailey, Frederick *see* Douglass, Frederick
Bakunin, Michael 232-3, 473-5
balance of power, Montesquieu 189-94
Balibar, Étienne 100, 107
Bambatha Rebellion 493-4
Bandung Conference (1955) 428
Barbauld, Anna Laetitia 298
Barry, Brian 414
base, superstructure and, Marx 224-6
basic structure, Rawls 591-4
de Beauvoir, Simone 157, 340-1, **628**, 663
Beijing Conference (1995) 436-7

INDEX

Being and Time (Heidegger) 332
Beitz, Charles 593-4
Benhabib, Seyla 342, 400
Bennett, Jane 707
Bentham, Jeremy **203**, 407, 414, 420, 421, 599-600, 614
Berkman, Alexander 469, **470**
Berlin, Isaiah 89, 413, 420
Beyond Good and Evil (Nietzsche) 240, 242, 246, 250
Bhabha, Homi **277**, 428, 688
Bianchi, Herman 647
biopower, Foucault 611-13
Birth of Biopolitics (Foucault) 611, 614
The Birth of the Clinic (Foucault) 607
Black consciousness 523-98, 643
    see also Douglass, Frederick; Du Bois, W. E. B.; Kant, Immanuel; Rawls, John
Black family 53, 571-2, 574
Black freedom, James 321-6
The Black Jacobins: Toussaint l'Ouverture and the San Domingo Revolution (James) 280, 314, 320
Black Lives Matter 396
Black men, right to vote 53-54, 556
Black Panther Party 252, 640
Black Reconstruction in America (Du Bois) 572
Black Skin, White Masks (Fanon) 251, 508, 510, 518
Black Studies **317**
Black women
    alienation, hooks 53-4
    Davis 648-51
    Douglass 548, 556-7, 560
    Du Bois 566, 571-8
    James 325-6
    representation, Sojourner Truth 31-3
    right to vote 556-7
bodies, minds and, Spinoza 100-2
Bodies that Matter (Butler) 664
Bodin, Jean 89, **190**, 194
Boers 343-4
Boggs, Grace Lee 314
Boone, Joseph 278
Bosanquet, Bernard 420
boundaries of the political 17-74
    see also Aristotle; hooks, bell; Kautilya; Plato; Socrates; Sojourner Truth
Bourke, Richard 297
brahmacharya **493**, 494, 499
Bradley, F. H. 408

Braidotti, Rory 708
Brathwaite, Chris 323
The Breast Stories (Devi) 433
Broad, Jacqueline 140-1
Brodber, Erna 325-6
Buccola, Nicholas 549
Buddhism, Zhang Taiyan 359-62
Burke, Edmund 295, 301-5, 373
    abuse of power 307-9
    conservation 302-3
    correction 302-3
    criticism of 305-9
    rights as convention 303-4
    spirit of a revolution 304-5
    spirit of religion 304-5
    see also Macaulay, Catherine
Burrows, Paul 466
Burton, Richard 276
Butler, Judith 99, 601, 606, 657-73
    gender, feminism, identity 658-60
    gender parody & performativity 660-3
    morality & ethics 666-8
    politics 668-70
    subjectivity, resistance, psyche 663-6

C

Cabral, Amical 235
Callendar, Guy 681
Cambridge School 9
Camus, Albert 508
Canada, colonialism 713
Canovan, Margaret 331
Capital (Marx) 225, 227-8, 234
capitalism
    end of 234
    global, Chakrabarty 685
    Marx 227-31
    Qutb 264-5
Capitalocene 676, 686, 707-9
Carby, Hazel 571-2
The Care of Self: The History of Sexuality vol. 3 (Foucault) 606
Carens, Joseph 410
Caribbean
    recolonisation, Douglass 558-9
    slavery abolition 552
Carlyle, Thomas 214
Categorical imperative 247, **529**, 530, 533-5, 583
category of women, Davis 651-2
Cavarero, Adriana 659
CEDAW (Convention of the Elimination of all Forms of Discrimination Against Women) 438

Césaire, Aimé 285, 428, **506**
Chakrabarty, Dipesh 676, 679-95
    critical debates 686-7
    different, equal, cojoined 688
    freedom 684-5
    geological time 683, 687-9
    global capitalism 685
    global habitability 685-6
    historical time 683
    human free agent 687-9
    intra-human justice 690
    intra-species justice 690-1
    justice blindness 691
    justice sensitivity 690-2
    planetary 685-6
    species thinking 689
Chatterjee, Partha 680
childbirth, Firestone 627-8
The Children of Sisyphus (James) 324
children's oppression, Firestone 632-3
China
    Asian unity 357-8
    Revolution (1911) 349, 351
Chthulucene 707-9
Churchism 475
citizenship 536-7
    Young 397-8
civil contracts, Kant 533
civil rights 3, 30, 53, 156, 189, 195, 293, 479, 480, 486, 487, 489, 499, 523
Civilization and Its Discontents (Freud) 604
claim rights and liberty rights, Hobbes **82**
class 222-35, 639, 641, 643, 644, 646, 648-52
    Goldman 476-7
    Locke 119-21
    Wollstonecraft 381-2
    see also sex class
classical learning, Zhang Taiyan 350-1
de Cleyre, Voltairine **466**, 479
climate change 2, 70, 228, 434, 676, 679-92, 716, 727
climatology, Montesquieu 188
Collingwood, R. G. 5-6
colonial domination 181-290
    see also Marx, Karl; Mill, John Stuart; Montesquieu, Charles-Louis de Scondat Baron de la Brede et de; Nietzsche, Friedrich; Qutb, Sayyid; Said, Edward W.
colonial education, James 318-19

colonialism 713, 721
  Fanon 511-19
  Hobbes 86
  Kant 538-40
  Locke 123-6
  Montesquieu 197
  Nietzsche 249-51
  Pateman 175-6
  Qutb 259-63
  see also decolonization; postcolonialism
Coloured Women's League 649
Combahee River Collective 2, 22, 235
commerce, Montesquieu 185-7, 189, 193-4, 197-8
commercialism **165**
commodification, Marx 227-8
communism 224, 226, 232-5
  Davis 641-2
  individualism and **467**, 468
Communist Manifesto (Marx & Engels) 224, 227-8, 232, 235
communitarianism 207, 292, 390, **586**, 590
The Companion Species Manifesto (Haraway) 699-700
compliance, Goldman 475-6
Components of the Islamic Conception [Muqaw-wimat al-Tasawwur al-Islmai] (Qutb) 261
concentration camps 334
The Condition of the Working Class in England (Engels) 222
The Confessions of the Flesh: The History of Sexuality vol. 4 (Foucault) 614
Confucius 293, **350**, 352, 355
conquest 7, 62, 89, 118, 127, 168, 173, 176, 186, 196, 199, 230, 279, 451, 458-61
  Montesquieu 196
  paradox of, Machiavelli 459-60
consciousness, Davis 53, 601, 630, 639, 642-3
consent 68, 75, 76, 79, 80, 93, 105, 115, 117, 134, 148, 166, 178, 191, 205, 231, 279, 303, 450, 718, 719, 727
  Astell 138-40
  contracts and 170
  political obligation 139
conservation, Burke 302-3
conspicuous distribution, LaDuke 716
constitutional theory, Montesquieu 190
contract **164**

contracts, consent and 68, 75, 79, 80, 89, 92, 105, 115, 133, 170
contractualism 164-6
  see also Mills, Charles; Pateman, Carole
contrapuntal reading **280**
A Contribution to the Critique of Political Economy (Marx) 224-5
Convention of the Elimination of all Forms of Discrimination Against Women (CEDAW) 438
Cooper, Anna Julia 314, 649
Cooper, Anthony Ashley 123-4
cosmopolitanism 534-5, **594**
Covid-19 pandemic 612, 727
Crenshaw, Kimberlé 22, 659
critical race critique, Rawls 588-9
Critique of Dialectical Reason (Sartre) 391
A Critique of Postcolonial Reason: Towards a History of the Vanishing Present (Spivak) 439
Critique of Practical Reason (Kant) 527
Critique of Pure Reason (Kant) 527, 528
Critique of the Gotha Programme (Marx) 233
Critique of the Power of Judgment (Kant) 527
Crutzen, Paul 681, 707
crystallization, Arendt 335
Crystals, Fabrics and Fields (Haraway) 703-5
cult of womanhood 32
cultural diversity
  legitimization, Parekh 413-14
  Parekh 409-10
  unity in, Parekh 415-16
cultural imperialism, Young 390
culture 240-3, **409**
  physician of, Nietzsche 240-3
Culture and Imperialism (Said) 278-9, 280
Curzon-Wyllie, William 488
'A Cyborg Manifesto' essay (Haraway) 699-700, 705, 708
cyborgs, Haraway 697, 698, 699-703, 708, 709
cyclical time, Montesquieu 194
Czolgosz, Leon 466

D

Daoism **352**, 358, 359, 362
Darkwater (Du Bois) 566
Davis, Angela Y. 601, 639-55
  Black women 648-51
  category of women 651-2

communism 641-2
consciousness 642-3
crime-punishment delinking 646
Marxism 641-2
policing 645-6
prison abolition 644-7
radical political theory 641-3
reparative justice 647
Davis, Mike 645
Daybreak (Nietzsche) 240
De Cive (Hobbes) 86
Death of a Discipline (Spivak) 434
debates, Chakrabarty 686-7
Declaration of the Rights of Women and the Female Citizen (De Goges) 169, 374
decolonization 10-11, **507**
  the Enlightenment, Spivak 439-41
  Fanon 511-19
  see also colonialism
deep history **683**
Deleuze, Gilles 429-30, 434, **610**, 663
deliberation
  will and, Hobbes **80**
  Young 398-401
Democritus 100
democracy 18, 22, 40, 76, 89, 103, 106-9, 189, 211-13, 248-51, 397-403
  Mill 204-5, 211-13
  Nietzsche 248-52
  Spinoza 106-10
Democracy in America (de Tocqueville) 211
democratic equality 593
Derrida, Jacques 8, 12, 402, **431**, 441, 527, 660-1, 663
Desai, Ashwin 491
Descartes, René 99, 153, 704
despotism, Montesquieu 193-4
Dessalines, Jean-Jacques 319
desubalternization, Spivak 436-7
Devi, Mahasweta **433**
The Dialectic of Sex: The Case for Feminist Revolution (Firestone) 621
dialectics 224
dialectics of freedom, James 314-15, 316-18, 325-6
Dietz, Mary 341
difference principle, Rawls 394, 585-6, 594
dignity **549**
direct action, Gandhi 496-8
disability critique, Rawls 589-90

INDEX

disciplinary power, Foucault 608–11, **609**
Discipline and Punish (Foucault) 609
discourse **605**, 658
  Foucault 607–8
Discourse on Political Economy (Rousseau) 148
Discourse on the First Ten Books of Titus Livy (Machiavelli) 454, 459
Discourse on the Origins of Inequality (Rousseau) 148, 151
Discourses on Livy (Machiavelli) 447, 448, 454
distributive justice 394–6, 532, 581–95
distributive paradigm, Rawls 592–3
divided sovereignty, Montesquieu 189–91
division of labour, gendered international **435**
domestic analogy 85
domestic slavery, Montesquieu 199
domination **377**, 666, 676, 685, 690, 691
double bind **440**
double consciousness, Du Bois 568, **569**
Douglass, Frederick 24, 52, 523, 524, 545–63, 644, 648–9
  activating freedom 548–50
  Caribbean recolonisation 558–9
  freedman's philosophy 550–7
  fugitive philosophy 546–8
  heroic violence 552–3
  silences within slavery 550
  slavery 545–50
  statesman's philosophy 558–9
  suffragists & natives 555–7
  US Constitution 553–7
Downing, Lisa 633–4
drag 661–2
Drake, Judith **141**
Du Bois, W. E. B. 317, 523, 524–5, 565–80
  American labour movement 574–5
  Black family 571–2
  exclusion problem 567–71
  freedom to love 573–4
  labour organizations 574
  liberals 574
  motherhood 573–4
  NAACP criticism 575–6
  race 570–1
  resistance 569
  socialist politics 574–6
Dunayevskaya, Raya 314
Dunbar, Paul Laurence 478

Dunn, John 6
Dutch East India Company 97
Dutch West India Company 97
Dworkin, Andrea 659
Dworkin, Ronald 394

E

Eagleton, Terry 434
East India Company 216–17
ecologies **714**
  Indigenous *see* Indigenous ecologies
Economic and Philosophical Manuscripts (Marx) 222, 314
economic determinism, Marx 225
education 25–6, 29, 31
  Aristotle 42
  hooks 44–5
  Macaulay 301
Eichmann, Adolf 333
Eichmann in Jerusalem (Arendt) 331, 333
The Eighteenth Brumaire of Louis Bonaparte (Marx) 225, 232
emancipation 23, 52, 183, 223, 224, 225, 230, 251, 371–5, 376, 384, 385, 398, 435, 437, 438, 440, 465, 472, 476, 477, 480, 545, 641, 650
  Douglass 545
  Socrates 29–30
Emile (Rousseau) 148
empire 185–7, 213, 218
  Machiavelli 460–1
  Mill 216–17
  resistance to, Said 280–1
  Said 278–89
Engels, Friedrich 221–35, **222**, 356, 466, 601, 622, 624, 626, 630
English Civil War (1642-1649) 164
English, Jane 587
Enlightenment 98, 101, 108, 110, 148, 174, 182, 183, 185, 187, 189, 199, 242, 257, 261, 270, 427, 437–41, 472, 531, 535, 538
  decolonization of, Spivak 439–41
  individualism 101
environment 675–730
  see also Chakrabarty, Dipesh; Haraway, Donna; Indigenous ecologies
Epicurus 100
epigenesis 704
Equal Rights Association 650
equality 367–444
  Macaulay 299–300
  Nietzsche 248–52
  opportunities of, Rawls 585

Pateman & Mills 167–8
Young 394–7
  see also Parekh, Bhikhu; Spivak, Gayatri Chakravorty; Wollstonecraft, Mary; Young, Iris Marion
Equiano, Olaudah 141
Eros and Civilization: A Philosophical Inquiry into Freud (Marcuse) 604
ethics, Butler 666–8
Ethics (Spinoza) 98-103
An Ethics of Sexual Difference (Irigaray) 243
Euben, Roxanne 4, 258, 266, 270
eudaimonia (happiness) 47
eugenics **649**
Euripides 275
Eurocentrism
  Chakrabarty 686
  Gandhi 489
  Mill 217
  Nietzsche 251
European civilisation, James 318–19
European Enlightenment, Spivak 437–41
European fundamental laws, Montesquieu 197
'The Eye of Power' essay (Foucault) 614
Excitable Speech (Butler) 665
exclusion problem, Du Bois 567–71
executive power, Montesquieu 189
exile, figure of (Said) 286
experience, theory and, Goldman 472–4
Experience and it's Modes (Oakeshott) 408
exploitation **229**
  Marx 228–30
  Young 390
extractivism 725–7

F

Falk, Candice 471
families
  Black families, Du Bois 571–2
  Firestone 630–1
  nuclear family **630**
  racial family, Firestone 631–2
Fanon, Frantz 251, 285, 428, 446, 505–21
  biography 505–8
  colonization 511–19
  decolonization 511–19
  race, gender, psychology 508–11

The Female Reader
  (Wollstonecraft) 371
The Feminine Mystique (Friedan) 623
feminism 10-11, 21, 40, 53, 54, 99,
  342, 345, 369, 384, 392, 428,
  582, 586
  anti-feminism, Arendt 341
  Arendt 340-2
  Butler 658-60
  critique, Rawls 587-8
  imperialist feminism,
    Spivak 432-4
  liberal feminism, Firestone 623-4
  Machiavelli 453-4
  Marxism 624
  Mill 214
  postcolonialist feminism 431
  proto-feminism, Arendt 342
  radical feminism, Firestone
    623-4
  second-wave feminism 600
  socialist feminism *see* socialist
    feminism
feminist revolution, reproductive
  technology 629-33
Figgis, J. N. 420
Filmer, Robert 122, 138
Firestone, Shulamith 10, 601,
  621-38
  children's oppression 632-3
  families, abolishing of 630-1
  household 632
  liberal feminism 623-4
  natural oppression 626-7
  personal is politics 622-3
  pregnancy & childbirth 627-8
  queering sex 633-4
  racial family 631-2
  radical feminism 623-4
  reproductive biology 625-8
  reproductive politics 635
  reproductive rights 624
  reproductive technology &
    feminist revolution 629-33
  socialist feminism 623-4
  technology **629**
  women's oppression 625-8
Florentine Histories
  (Machiavelli) 448
Foote, Eunice **681**
The Force of Nonviolence
  (Butler) 669
Forster-Nietzsche, Elisabeth 245
fortuna
  Machiavelli 453-4
  virtù vs. 453
fossil fuels 725-7
Foucault, Michel 7, 250, 449-50,
  600, 603-20

biopower 611-13
disciplinary power 608-11, **609**
discourse & truth 607-8
government of conduct 614-16
liberal government 613-14
neoliberal government 613-14
race, government & power
  611-16
sexuality 604-7
state racism 611-13
Fraser, Nancy **395**, 434
free speech, Mill 206
free will, Rousseau 100, 101,
  153-4, 530
freedman's philosophy,
  Douglass 550-7
freedom 291-365
  Astell 140-2
  Chakrabarty 684-5
  characterization of 291
  constraints on 291-2
  free will of, Rousseau 151
  individual *see* individual
    freedom
  liberty and, Arendt **339**
  to love, Du Bois 573-4
  Qutb 266
  see also Arendt, Hannah; Burke,
    Edmund; James, C. L. R.;
    liberty; Macaulay, Catherine;
    Zhang Taiyan
French Revolution (1792-1797)
  292, 315, 531
  Arendt 339-40
  Burke 303
Freud, Sigmund 241, 433, 510, 600,
  604, **631**, 664-5
Friedan, Betty **623**
fugitive philosophy, Douglass
  546-8
Fukuyama, Francis 278-9
Fuller, Margaret 298
*Fundamental Constitution of
  Carolina* (Locke) 127
*The Future Belongs to this Religion
  [Al-Mustaqbal li-hādhā al-Din]*
  (Qutb) 261

G

Garrison, William Lloyd 24, **551**
Garvey, Amy Ashwood 323, **325**
Garvey, Marcus 322-3, 325
gay liberation movement 600, 659
The Gay Science (Nietzsche) 240,
  250
gender binary norms 652
gender inequality 51, 54, 198, 243,
  368, 371, 429, 625

gender **373**
  Astell 135
  Butler 658-60
  Fanon 508-11
  Goldman 475
  Hobbes 84-5
  Indigenous governance 719-20
  Kautilya 67-70
  Locke 121-3
  Mill 214-16
  Nietzsche 242-3
  Plato 26-7, 28
  Qutb 261-2
  Rawls 586
  Said 278
  sex division 658
  social constraints, Young 390
gender parody, Butler 660-3
gender performativity, Butler
  660-3
gender politics
  Aristotle 47, 49-50
  hooks 48
Gender Trouble (Butler) 659-60, 664
gendered international division of
  labour **435**
genealogy 246, **250**, 603
Genealogy of Morality (Nietzsche)
  244, 246, 251
general will 147, **149**, 150, 154-9
Gentili, Alberico 450
geological time, Chakrabarty 683,
  687-9
The German Ideology (Marx and
  Engels) 223, 225
Gandhi, Mohandas (Mahatma) 407,
  446, 485-515
  anticolonial resistance 488-91
  biography 486-7
  global icon as 486-7
  hidden biases 491-3
  moral politics 494-6
  nonviolent resistance 496-8
  satyagraha 485, **486**, 490,
    493-4, 497
  self-purification 493-4
Gilbert, Olive 23
Gilio-Whitaker, Dina 723-4
Gilligan, Carole 659
Giving an Account of Oneself
  (Butler) 666
global capitalism,
  Chakrabarty 685
global habitability,
  Chakrabarty 685-6
global injustices, Young 393
The Glorious Revolution (1688-1689)
  164, **296**, 303, 304
Godwin, William **383**

INDEX

Goldman, Emma 10, 446, 465–83
  anarchism 467–72
  anarchist imaginary 470–2
  class 476–7
  compliance 475–6
  love with open eyes 469
  power 474
  race 476–7
  radicalization 468
  representation 476–7
  resistance 479–80
  rights 479–80
  sex 476–7
  slavery 478–9
  slavishness 478–9
  social structure 474–5
  spiritual revolt 469–70
  theory and experience 472–4
  theory and practice 472–7
gongli 353
Gooding-Williams, Robert 568
Gorgias 22
de Gouges, Olympes 169, 298, **374**
governmentality 611–6, **614**
Gramsci, Antonio **158**, 369, 429–31, 435, 436, 451, 456
grandi, popolo vs. **449**, 456
Greek city-states 18
Green, Karen 306
Grosfoguel, Ramon 437
Grotius, Hugo **86**, 150, 153
de Grouchy, Sophie 298
Grove, Jairus 688
Grundrisse (Marx) 223, 225, 228, 234
Guevara, Che **515**
Guha, Ranajit 281, 430–1, **680**
Gunther-Canada, Wendy 306–7

H

Habermas, Jürgen 400, 402, 434, **535**
Haitian Revolution 280, 292–3, 566
  Arendt 340, 344
  James 314, 319–21
hakimiyyah (divine sovereignty), Qutb 263–7, **265**
Hall, Stuart 7, 287, 420
The Handmaid's Tale (Atwood) 476
Haraway, Donna 676, 697–711
  cyborgs 700–1
  non-humans 700–1
  organisms, mechanisms, vitalism 703–5
  production & reproduction 702
  reinvention of nature 705–7
Hardiman, David 680
Hare, Thomas 212

harem 380
harm principle (liberty principle) 205
Harman, Moses 467, **468**, 476–7
Harrison, Benjamin 558
Haudenosaunee 714, 718–20
The Haymarket Affair 468, **469**
Hays, Mary 298
Hazama Naoki 356
Heart of Darkness (Conrad) 280
Hegel, G. W. F. 100, 222, 224, 251, 293, 335, 337, 359–61, 408, 433, 507, 527, 586, **663**
  theory of recognition 664
  Zhang Taiyan, confrontation with 359–60
Heidegger, Martin 8, 11–12, **332**, 664
'The Heroic Slave' essay (Douglass) 553
heroic violence, Douglass 552–3
Hicks, Philip 306
Hind Swaraj (Gandhi) 488–91
Hindustan Socialist Republican Association 498
Hippias 22
Hirschmann, Nancy 85
A Historical and Moral View of the French Revolution (Wollstonecraft) 371
historical materialism, *see* history, materialist conception of, Marx
historical time, Chakrabarty 683
history, materialist conception of, Marx 223–7
History of England (Macaulay) 295, 298
History of Madness (Foucault) 606, 608
A History of Negro Revolt (James) 323
history of political thought 2–5
  field of study 8–12
  history of 5–8
The History of Sexuality (Foucault) 604, 605, 606, 610
History of the Russian Revolution (Trotsky) 314
Hobbes, Thomas 76, 79–95, 133, 167, 175, 302
  absolute sovereignty 89–90
  authorization 87–9
  covenanting 89–90
  gender 84–5
  laws of nature 82–4
  legacy of 92
  liberty 89
  protection 91

  protection and obligation 91
  rebellion 91–2
  representation 87–9
  right to rebel 91
  social contract 87–91
  state breakdown 91–2
  state of nature 81–2, 85–7
Hohfeld, Wesley 82
holy war (*jihad*), Qutb 267–9
homeplace, hooks 52–4
Honig, Bonnie 342, 587
hooks, bell 40, 632
  Black women alienation 53–4
  homeplace 52–4
  households 41–2
  knowing and being 44–5
  subjectivity 48–9
Hoover, J. Edgar 466
Horkheimer, Max 535, 642
household
  Aristotle 49–52
  Firestone 632
  hooks 41–2
Human, All Too Human (Nietzsche) 240, 249
The Human Condition (Arendt) 331, 340, 341
human exceptionalism 676, 701
human nature 25, 39, 49, 81, 82, 126, 134, 150, 151, 153, 207, 223, 239, 244, 247, 248, 249, 252, 303, 337, 372, 409, 524, 675, 688, 690, 700, 702
  Aristotle 46–7
  Astell 135–6
human species 530, 538, **689**
humanity 490, 530, **689**
Hume, David **185–6**, 297, 306, 547, 583
Huntington, Samuel 257, 278–9
Huseyinzadegan, Dilek 539
Husserl, Edmund 332
hybridity, Said 278–89

I

IAC (International Anarchist Congress) 468
ideal theory
  as ideology **589**
  Kant 535–40
  Rawls 583, 588–9, 595
idealism
  materialism *vs.* 226, 707
  transcendental idealism 527, **528**
identity, Butler 658–60
identity politics **659**
ideology **334**

INDEX

Arendt 334
  ideal theory as **589**
  liberalism as 182-3
  Marx 100, 102, 226, 701
  racism as 40, 643
ignorance, states of, Qutb 261-3
Imaginary Maps (Devi) 433
IMF (International Monetary Fund) 438
imperialism 1, 11, 173, 183, 205, 208, 209, 210, 216, 218, 264, 279, 280, 343, 344, 432, 553
  totalitarianism and 342
  see also empire
imperialist feminism, Spivak 432-4
In Other Worlds (Spivak) 433
In the Shade of the Qur'an (Qutb) 260
inclusion 367-444
  Young 394-7, 398-401
  see also Parekh, Bhikhu; Spivak, Gayatri Chakravorty; Wollstonecraft, Mary; Young, Iris Marion
Inclusion and Democracy (Young) 391, 400, 402
Indigenous Americans 126, 471
Indigenous ecologies 713-30
Indigenous governance 717-20
  Haudenosaunee 718-19
Indigenous lands, exploitation of 725-7
Indigenous thinking, industrial thinking *vs.* 714-17
individual freedom 98, 104, 117, 118, 127, 171, 185, 196, 199, 200, 204, 209, 261, 266, 316, 359, 640
  Kant 532
  Montesquieu 189-94
individualism **101**, 120, 167, 182, 226, 390, 594
  communism and **467**, 468
individuality, Mill 207-8
industrial thinking, Indigenous thinking *vs.* 714-17
inequality **152**
  see also gender inequality; structural inequality
intersectionality 9, 21, **22**, 641
institutionalism, Rawls 582
intellectual vocation, Said 285-6
intercultural dialogue **411**
  Parekh 410-13
interdependence, Anishinaabe 717-18
interior world, Douglass 546
International Anarchist Congress (IAC) 468

international anarchy, Hobbes 86-7
International Monetary Fund (IMF) 438
International Workingmen's Association 233
An Interpretation of the Equalization of things (Zhang) 361
intra-species justice, Chakrabarty 690-1
Irigaray, Luce **242-3**, 659
Iroquois *see* Haudenosaunee
Islamic Law *(shari'ah)* 263-4
Islamophobia 419

J

Jacobins 315
Jahilliyyah, Qutb 259-63
James, C. L. R. 7, 280, 292, 313-29, 641
  Black freedom 321-6
  Black women 325-6
  colonial education 318-19
  dialectic freedom 316-18
  dialectic of freedom 314-15, 325-6
  European civilisation 318-19
  Garveyism 322-3
  Haitian Revolution 319-21
  Marxism 314-18
  native intelligensia 318-21
  racial sources of self-determination 321-2
  radical intelligensia 315-16
  Rastafari 324
Jameson, Fredric 227
Jaspers, Karl 332
jihad (holy war), Qutb 267-9
Jim Crow laws 567, 568, 569, 644
John Brown (Du Bois) 566
Johnson, Linton Kwesi 313
Jones, Claudia 235, **641**
Jouy, Charles 606
Julie, ou La Nouvelle Héloïse (Rousseau) 148
justice
  blindness, Chakrabarty 691
  intra-human justice, Chakrabarty 690
  intra-species, Chakrabarty 690-1
  power of 608-9
  principles of, Rawls 585
  reparative justice, Davis 647
  scope of, Rawls 593-4
  sensitivity, Chakrabarty 690-2
  theory of, Young 393
  Young 394-7

Justice and the Politics of Difference (Young) 390
Justice, Gender and the Family (Okin) 171

K

kainos 708
Kang Youwei 351
Kangle, R. P. **58**, 61, 62, 65, 69
Kant, Immanuel 523, 524, 527-43
  colonialism 538-40
  ideal political theory 535-40
  non-ideal political theory 535-40
  philosophical fundamentals 528-30
  political philosophy 530-4
  political theory 532-4
  a priori foundations 536-8
  race 538-40
  teleology 531-2
  universal history 531-2
Kautilya 19, 57-74
  end of political rule 62-4
  foreign policy 60-7
  gender 67-70
  morality 64-6
  philosophy 58-60
  political reality 64-6
  social order 68-70
  states 60-7
Kelly, Paul 420
Kimmerer, Robin Wall 716
King, Jr., Martin Luther 485, 499, 565
The Kingdom of God is Within You (Tolstoy) 490
knowledge 18
  being and, hooks 44-5
  being and, Aristotle 43-4
  power relationship, *Orientalism* (Said) 275
  Socrates 30
  Spinoza **102**
Knox, John 466
Kōtoku Shūsui 353
The Kronstadt Rebellion (Goldman) 470
Kuhn, Thomas **703**
Kymlicka, Will 401, **410**, 412, 419

L

labour organizations, Du Bois 574
LaDuke, Winona **714**, 715, 716
land, Indigenous governance 719-20
Lane, Edward 276
Latour, Bruno 688, 707

INDEX

The Law of Peoples (Rawls) 594
laws of nature, Hobbes 82–4
Leca, Jean 473
legislative power, Montesquieu 189
Leibniz, Gottfried Wilhelm 132
Lenin, V. I. 233, 450, 466, 640
'Letter Concerning Toleration' (Locke) 117
'Letter to the Youth of Africa' essay (Fanon) 512
Letters Written During a Short Residence in Sweden, Norway and Denmark (Wollstonecraft) 372
Leviathan (Hobbes) 79–92, 167
 religious imagery **88**
Levy, Bernard-Henri 608
Lewis, D. L. 571–2
liberal feminism 623–4, 698–9
liberal government, Foucault 613–14
liberal modernity 181–290
 see also Marx, Karl; Mill, John Stuart; Montesquieu, Charles-Louis de Scondat Baron de la Brede et de; Nietzsche, Friedrich; Qutb, Sayyid; Said, Edward W.
liberal self 523–98
 see also Douglass, Frederick; Du Bois, W. E. B.; Kant, Immanuel; Rawls, John
liberalism 76, 182–3, 334, 523–5, 591
 Astell 134
 communitarianism *vs.* 291–2, 586
 Du Bois 566, 569, 574
 Firestone 623
 Foucault 613–4
 Locke 118, 119, 122, 126
 Marx 226
 Mill 203–18
 Montesquieu 185
 political liberalism **590**
 Qutb 259, 264, 270
 Rawls 581, 590
 Spinoza 98, 110
 Wollstonecraft 377–8
 Young 398
Liberalism, Community and Culture (Kymlicka) 410
liberty 191
 freedom and, Arendt **339**
 action of, Mill 206–7
 Hobbes **89**
 Mill 204–5
 thought of, Mill 206
 see also freedom
liberty principle (harm principle) 205

liberty rights 81–2
 claim rights and, Hobbes 82
The Life of the Mind (Arendt) 331, 333
Lin Shaoyang 356
linear time, Montesquieu 194
Living My Life (Goldman) 466
Livy (Titus Livius) **455**
Locke, John 76, 115–30, 132, 140–2, 167, 175, 302
 class 119–21
 colonisation 123–6
 gender 121–3
 global considerations 123–8
 hierarchies 119–23
 property 125–6
 race 126–7
 sexual identities 119–23
 slavery 126–7
 social contract theory 133–4
 social identities 119–23
 sovereignty 116–19
 state of nature 116–19
lokasamgraha (collective benefit and happiness) 60, 62–3, 70
Lorde, Audre 441
love with open eyes, Goldman 469, 470
L'Ouverture, Toussaint 319, **320**
Lucretius 100
Luther, Martin 335, 471
lying 478–9

M

Macaulay, Catherine 10, 295, 297–301
 accountable government 298–9
 education 301
 equality 299–300
 government 301
 independence 299–300
 universal principles and social context 305–7
 virtue 299–300
 see also Burke, Edmund
Macaulay, Thomas 433
Machiavelli, Niccolò 105, 106, 447–64
 biography 448
 conflict 457–8
 empire 460–1
 fortuna 453–4
 paradox of conquest 459–60
 political freedom 455–6
 power 449–51
 principalities 448–9
 republics 448–9, 460–1
 Roman Empire 454–5

 violence as spectacle 458–9
 virtù 452–3
MacIntyre, Alasdair 586
MacKinnon, Catharine 659
Macpherson, C. B. 92, **120–1**
Madison, James 555
Magon, Ricardo Flores 479
Making Kin Not Populations (Clarke and Haraway) 709
Malcolm, Noel 85–6
Maldonado-Torres, Nelson 266
mandala (circles of states) 60–2
Mandela, Nelson 487
Mansfield Park (Austen) 279, 280
Manuscripts, Economic and Philosophic (Marx) 222–3
Mao Zedong 460
Marable, Manning 571–2
Marcuse, Herbert 604, **642**
Marin County Courthouse (California) revolt 639–40
Marine Lover of Friedrich Nietzsche (Irigaray) 243
marriage
 Astell 142–4
 Goldman 475
 Pateman 170–2
Marwah, Inder 538
Marx, Karl 183, 221–37, 314
 anarchism 232–3
 base and superstructure 224–6
 capitalism 227–31
 commodification 227–8
 end of capitalism 234
 exploitation 228–30, **229**
 ideology 226
 materialist conception of history 223–7
 modes of production 223–4
 primitive accumulation 230–1
 state and ruling class 231–2
 value **228–9**
Marxism 7–8
 Davis 641–2
 feminism 624
 James 314–18
Mary: A Fiction (Wollstonecraft) 371, 372
Masham, Damaris Cudworth **132**
mass sovereignty, Rousseau 149–50
materialism
 idealism *vs.* 226, 707
 new **707**
materialist conception of history, Marx 223–7
Maududi, Abu A'la **261**
Mazarin case **139**
McKinley, William 466
Mehta, Uday Singh 124, 308

INDEX

Meir, Golda 282
The Metaphysics of Morals (Kant) 530
Mignolo, Walter 10, 266, 437-8
Mill, Harriet Taylor **214-15**
Mill, John Stuart 203-20
   democracy 211-13
   empire 216-17
   gender 214-16
   government 210-11
   individuality 207-8
   liberalism 204-10
   liberty 204-5
   liberty of action 206-7
   liberty of thought 206
   race 213-14
   utilitarianism 204-10
Millennium Development Goals (MDGs) 438
Millett, Kate 3
Mills, Charles 21, 76, 77, 99, 116, 163-80, 226, 566, 588
   equality 167-8
   hypocrisy 173-4
   peaceful agreements 164-8
   people and state 166-7
   prostitution 171-2
   racial contract 172-5
   settler contract 175-6
   sexual contract 169-72
   social contract 162-8
   universalism 173-4
   violence 168
   whiteness and ignorance 174
   women & marriage 170
   see also Pateman, Carole
minds, bodies
   Aristotle 46-7, 49
   Spinoza 100-2
minoritization, racialization **722**
modernity 172-3, 181-290, 359, 437-40, 489, 535, 605
   Arendt 339-40
   Chakrabarty 680, 683
modes of production, Marx 223-4
Modood, Tariq 411, **412**
monarchical despotism **353**
monarchy, Montesquieu 192
Montesquieu, Charles-Louis de Secondat, Baron de la Brede et de 185-202
   balance of power 189-94
   climatology 188
   commerce 197-8
   conquest 196
   divided sovereignty 189-91
   economic change 187
   government types 192-4
   individual freedom 189-94
   political change 187

   separation of power 191-2
   slavery 198-9
   time and progress 194-6
   transatlantic commerce 187
moral politics
   Gandhi 494-6
   realpolitik *vs.* 66
morality 4
   Butler 666-8
   Douglass 548
   Gandhi 489
   Hobbes 80, 83, 92
   Kant 529-30
   Kautilya 64-6
   Nietzsche 246-8
   Parekh 409
   Qutb 264, 265
   Socrates 29
   Spinoza 108
   Zhang 358
More, Hannah 374, **375**
motherhood
   Du Bois 573-4
   Wollstonecraft 382-3
Mouffe, Chantel 3
Multicultural Citizenship (Kymlica) 410
Multiculturalism 368, 397, 407-21
multitude, unity of, Spinoza 108-10
Muslim Brotherhood *(al-Ikhwan al-Muslimeen)* 259, **260**
My Disillusionment in Russia (Goldman) 466
My Further Disillusionment in Russia (Goldman) 466

N

NAACP *see* National Association for the Advancement of Colored People (NAACP)
Naipaul, V. S. 277
Narrative of Sojourner Truth: A Northern Slave (Garrison) 24
Narrative of the Life of Frederick Douglass, an American Slave (Douglass) 549
National American Woman Suffrage Association (NAWSA) 649
National Association for the Advancement of Colored People (NAACP) 565, 566, 574, 575-6
National Association of Colored Women's Clubs 649
National Organization for Women (NOW) 623
nationalism 415
   Black nationalism 156, 576
   Butler 668

   Fanon 515-6
   Nietzsche 250-1
   Parekh 415
   Qutb 259
   Said 284-5
   Spivak 441
   Zhang Taiyan 349, 351-2, 355-6, 360, 362
Native Americans 173, 380, 401, 557, 630
native intelligentsia, James 318-21
natural law
   Hobbes 82-4
   Kant 533
   pre-eminence of 715
natural rights **547**
   Douglass 545, 549, 555
natural sociability, Rousseau 150
nature 675-730
   state of *see* state of nature
NAWSA (National American Woman Suffrage Association) 649
Nazism 11-12, 466, 613, 649
   Arendt 332-4, 337, 344
'The Negro Question' essay (Mill) 214
neocolonialism 517, **518**, 594
neoliberal government, Foucault 613-14
New Deal (Roosevelt) 316
new materialism **707**
Newton, Huey P. **252**, 514
Nietzsche, Friedrich 8, 183, 239-55, 511
   Agon 245-6
   colonisation 249-51
   contrasting truth of opposite values 243
   democracy 248-52
   equality 248-52
   foundation of morality 247
   gender issues 242-3
   perpestivism 241-2
   physician of culture 240-3
   racism 249-51
   sexism 249-51
   slavery 246
   truth 242-3
   will to power 244-8
nihilism 183, 240, **241**, 244
No Dakota Access Pipeline (NODAPL) 726
non-cooperation, Gandhi 495-6
non-ideal political theory, Kant 535-40
nonviolent resistance, Gandhi 496-8
Norris, John 132

INDEX

Notes Towards a Performative Theory of Assembly (Butler) 668–9
Nozick, Robert 535, **591**
nuclear family **630**
Nussbaum, Martha 438, **593**

O

Oakeshott, Michael **408**, 417–8, 420–1
obligation, Hobbes 91
Observations on a Pamphlet entitled 'Thoughts on the Cause of the Present Discontent' (Macaulay) 292, 308
Of Grammatology (Derrida) 431
'Of the Different Races of Human Beings' essay (Kant) 538
Okin, Susan Moller 11, **171**, 411, 587, 592
Old Woman (Devi) 433
On Human Conduct (Oakeshott) 408, 420
On Liberty (Mill) 204, 205, 209, 210, 214
On Revolution (Arendt) 331, 339–40
On the Genealogy of Morality (Nietzsche) 240
'On the Jewish Question' essay (Marx) 225–6
On the Subjection of Women (Mill) 215
opportunity, equality of 368, 537, 585–6, 588, 592, 623
oppression, Young 390–4
The Order of Things (Foucault) 607
oriental despotism, Montesquieu 199
Orientalism (Said) 273, 274–8, 280, 511
  criticisms of 276–8
The Origin of the Family, Private Property and the State (Engels) 222, 626
original position, Rawls 583–4, 586–90
Original Stories (Wollstonecraft) 371, 381
The Origins of Totalitarianism (Arendt) 331, 332, 334, 343, 344
Outside the Teaching Machine (Spivak) 439

P

Paine, Thomas 296, 297, **299**, 374
Palestine 281–5
pan-Africanism 323, 326, **576**
pan-Asianism 355–8
Pandey, Gyan 680

Parekh, Bhikhu 368, 407–25
  cultural difference legitimization 413–14
  cultural diversity 409–40
  intercultural dialogue 410–13
  reception and interpretations 419–21
  unity in cultural diversity 415–16
Parekh Report 417–18
Paris Commune 233, 470
Parry, Benita 436–7
Parsons, Lucy 478
Parting Ways (Butler) 668
Pateman, Carole 10, 77, 84–5, 116, 121, 163–80
  equality 167–8
  peaceful agreements 164–6
  people and state 166–7
  prostitution 171–2
  settler contract 175–6
  sexual contract 169–72
  social contract 162–8
  violence 168
  women & marriage 170
  see also Mills, Charles
Peloponnesian War 23
people, the **166**
People of Colour 9
perfectibility, Rousseau 151
The Persian Letters (Montesquieu) 186
The Persians (Aeschylus) 275
perspectivism, Nietzsche 241–2
Phenomenology of Spirit (Hegel) 664
Phillips, Wendell 24
Philosophical Enquiry into the Origin of Our Ideas of the Sublime and Beautiful (Burke) 302
Pineda, Erin 592
Pitkin, Hannah 342
Pitt, William 297
Plantationocene 707–9
Plato 19, 23, 25–9, 30
  ideal state 26–7
  race 546–7
  women guardians 28
Plessy v. Ferguson (1896) 567
Pocock, J. G. A. 6
policing, Davis 645–6
polis 18–9, **41**, 46–7, 50, 144, 409
  Arendt 336
political liberalism **590**
Political Liberalism (Rawls) 590, 592
Political Treatise (Spinoza) 105
politics
  boundaries of the 17–74
  see also Aristotle; hooks, bell; Kautilya; Plato; Socrates; Sojourner Truth

definition 3
difference of, Young 397–8
equality, Young 399
freedom, Machiavelli 455–6
meaning of, Arendt 336–8
personal as, Firestone 622–3
philosophy and, Arendt 337–8
realism 3–4
reality, Kautilya 64–6
servitude, Montesquieu 199
specificity of, Arendt 336–7
virtue 192
The Politics (Aristotle) 40–1, 51–2
polity 409
polymorphous perversity **634**
popular government, Rousseau 152
popular militias 457
popolo, *grandi* vs. **449**, 456
positionality 9, 45, 118, 392, 395, 524, 686
  and standpoint **48**
postcolonialism 277, 343, **428**, 429, 613, 680
  Chakrabarty 679, 686
  Said 273, 274, 276, 278
  Spivak 427–8, 438, 441
  see also colonialism
posthumanism **698**, 706
poststructuralism 8, 278, 287, 428, 437, 633, 663
potentia, Spinoza 108
potestas, Spinoza 108
power **108**, 440–521
  abuse of, Burke 307–9
  balance of, Montesquieu 189–94
  concept as 107
  disciplinary **609**
  Goldman 474
  judicial concept of 608–9
  Kautilya **62**
  knowledge relationship, *Orientalism* (Said) 275
  Machiavelli 449–51
  separation of, Montesquieu 191–2
  Spinoza 103–5
  strategic power 449–50
  see also Fanon, Frantz; Gandhi, Mohandas (Mahatma); Goldman, Emma; Machiavelli, Niccolò
The Poverty of Philosophy (Marx) 227, 232
Precarious Life (Butler) 667, 668
pregnancy, Firestone 627–8
Presbey, Gail 344
Price, Richard 297, 373
Price Mars, Jean 323
Priestley, Joseph 296, 297, 299, 303
Primate Videos (Haraway) 706

INDEX

primitive accumulation, Marx 230–1
The Prince (Machiavelli) 447, 448, 449, 450, 459
principalities, Machiavelli 448–9
principles of justice, Rawls 585, 587, 588, 591, 592, 594
prison industrial complex **645**
Prison Information Group 609
Prison Memoirs of an Anarchist (Goldman) 470
Prison Notebooks (Gramsci) 158
prisons
    abolition, Davis 644–7
    racism & slavery 644
private sphere **122**
production
    Haraway 702
    modes of, Marx 223–4
progress, time and, Montesquieu 194–6
property
    Indigenous ecologies 723
    Locke 125–6
    Mill 216
prostitution
    Goldman 475–6
    Pateman 171–2
proto-feminism, Arendt 342
Proudhon, Pierre-Joseph **232**, 473, 474–5
psyche, Butler 663–6
The Psychic Life of Power (Butler) 664, 665, 666
psychology, Fanon 508–11
psychopathology **510**
public spaces, Aristotle 42
Pythagoras 22

Q

queer theory 600, 606, 613, 616, 633–4, 657–9, **660**
querelle des femmes 135
The Question of Palestine (Said) 282, 283
Quijano, Anibal 10, 266
Qutb, Sayyid 257–72
    colonialism 259–63
    gender issues 261–2
    hakimiyyah 263–7
    intellectual context 259–61
    jahilliyyah 259–63
    jihad (holy war) 267–9
    sovereignty 263–7

R

race **538**
    in antiquity **40**
    Arendt 343–4
    Davis 648–52
    Du Bois 570–1
    Fanon 508–11
    Foucault 611–15
    Goldman 476–7
    Kant 538–40
    Locke 126–7
    Mill 213–14
    Rawls 588–9
racial capitalism, Davis 642
The Racial Contract (Mills) 77, 172–5
racial sources of self-determination, James 321–2
racialism **570–1**
racialization, minoritization **722**
racism 570–1
    Marx 225–6
    Nietzsche 249–51
    origins of, Foucault 612–13
    prisons & slavery 644
    state racism, Foucault 611–13
    systemic racism 396
radical equality, Astell 135
radical feminism 3, 639, 659, 700
    Firestone 622, 623–4, 626, 628, 629, 630, 634
radical intelligentsia, James 315–16
rape, domination as 648
Rastafari, James 324
rationality **126**
Rawls, John 3, 143, 394, 523, 581–98
    basic structure 591–4
    critical race critique 588–9
    disability critique 589–90
    distributive paradigm 592–3
    feminist critique 587–8
    original position 583–4, 586–90
    principles of justice 585
    scope of justice 593–4
    see also A Theory of Justice (Rawls)
realism 4, 86, 92, 98, 104, **450**
    Kautilya 58, 61, 66
reason, Wollstonecraft 376
reasonableness, Young 399
rebellion
    Hobbes 91–2
    Locke 117, 122, 127
reciprocity with nature 715
recognition, theory of, Hegel **664**
Reconstruction Era 558
recorded and deep history **683**
Reflections on the Revolution in France (Burke) 297, 299, 302, 373
religion
    critiques of, Spinoza 99–100
    imagery in *Leviathan* (Hobbes) 88
    Machiavelli 451
    spirit of, Burke 304–5
reparative justice, Davis 647
representation
    Goldman 476–7
    Hobbes 87–9
    Spivak 429–30
    Young 398–401, 402–3
repressive hypothesis, Foucault 605
reproduction, Haraway 702
reproductive biology, Firestone 625–8
Reproductive Justice framework 635
reproductive politics, Firestone 635
reproductive rights
    control of 650
    Firestone 624
reproductive technology 629–33
The Republic (Plato) 19, 28
republicanism 142, **300**
    Machiavelli 455, 456
    Wollstonecraft 307, 377–8, 384–5
republics
    Machiavelli 448–9, 460–1
    Montesquieu 192–3
resistance 440–521
    Butler 663–6
    Du Bois 569
    Goldman 479–80
    Indigenous ecologies 723
    see also Fanon, Frantz; Gandhi, Mohandas (Mahatma); Goldman, Emma; Machiavelli, Niccolò
resistance to empire, Said 280–1
ressentiment **247**
Rethinking Multiculturalism (Parekh) 407–21
revolution 291–365
    Marx 222, 225, 233, 234, 235
    Rousseau 148–54
    spirit of, Burke 304–5
    Zhang Taiyan 353–4
    see also Arendt, Hannah; Burke, Edmund; James, C. L. R.; Macaulay, Catherine; Zhang Taiyan
revolutionary leaders **514**
Ricardo, David 222, 228
Ricoeur, Paul 241
rights 303–4, 373–5, 478–80, 624–5
    convention as, Burke 303–4
    Goldman 479–80
    natural **547**
    see also claim rights and liberty rights, Hobbes
The Rights of Man (Paine) 299
de la Rivière, Mercier 337
Robespierre, Maximillian **149**
Robinson, Cedric 231, 641

INDEX

Rochester Ladies Anti-Slavery Society 553-4
Rodney, Walter 324
Roman Empire, Machiavelli 454-5
Roosevelt, Theodor 316
Rousseau, Jean-Jacques 77, 108, 147-62, 169, 302
  commanders-in-chief 159
  free will 153-4
  mass sovereignty 149-50
  revolution 148-54
  solitariness 150-2
  sovereignty by choice 154-9
  sustained by virtue 155-8
  will 155-8
Rushdie, Salman 411
The Russian Tragedy (Goldman) 470

S

Said, Edward W. 183, 273-90, 428, 511
  empire 278-89
  hybridity 278-89
  intellectual vocation 285-6
  nationalism 284-5
  Orientalism 274-8
  Palestine 281-5
  resistance to empire 280-1
Salih, Tayeb 280
Salt Satyagraha 496-7
Sandel, Michael 586
Sappho **52**
Sartre, Jean-Paul 156-7, **391**, 628, 663
The Satanic Verses (Rushdie) 411
Sati 432
satyagraha, Gandhi 485, 486, 490, 493-4, 497
Schmitt, Carl 3, 11-12, 17-18
scope of justice, Rawls 593-4
Scott, David 7
The Second Sex (de Beauvoir) 628
Second Treatise of Government (Locke) 115-28, 142-3, 167
second-wave feminism 3, 9, 600-1, 621-3, 628, 629, 632, 633, 634, 635
Security, Territory, Population (Foucault) 611, 613, 614
self-determination, racial sources of, James 321-2
self-knowledge, Socrates 30
self-love *(amour de soi)*, Rousseau 151
self-ownership, Locke 118
self-purification, Gandhi 493-4
Sen, Amartya **593**
separation of power, Montesquieu 191-2

A Serious Proposal to the Ladies (Astell) 132, 136, 138, 142, 143
settler colonialism 282-3, 713, 721-3, 724-5
settler contract, Pateman & Mills 175-6
settler societies **168**
sex 599-601
  gender division 658
  Goldman 476-7
  historical materialism 625-6
  see also Butler, Judith; Davis, Angela Y.; Firestone, Shulamith; Foucault, Michel
sex class **625**
This Sex Which is Not One (Irigaray) 243
sexual contract, Pateman & Mills 169-72
The Sexual Contract (Pateman) 169, 172
sexuality 599-673
  Butler 657-70
  Davis 639-52
  Firestone 621-35
  Foucault 603-15
shari'ah (Islamic Law) **263-4**, 265, 266
Shariati, Ali **517**
Shelby, Tommie 588
Shelley, Mary 298
Shilliam, Robbie 11
Sidgwick, Henry 583
Signposts along the Road [Ma'alim fil al-Tariq] (Qutb) 2, 262
Simians, Cyborgs, and Women: The Reinvention of Nature (Haraway) 705-7
Singh, Bhagat **498**
Skinner, Quentin 6-7, 83, 300
slavery 97
  Aristotle 50-1
  Astell 140-2
  Douglass 545-60
  global context of, Wollstonecraft 379-80
  Goldman 478-9
  Locke 126-7
  Mill 214
  Montesquieu 187, 196, 198-200
  Nietzsche 246
  prisons & racism 644
  transformation of **478**
  Truth 23-5, 30-4
  Wollstonecraft 378-81
slavishness, Goldman 478-9
Smith, Adam 222, 228, 231, 583

Social Contract (Rousseau) 169
social contract theory 75-180
  Astell 133-42
  authorization 87-9
  Hobbes 87-91
  Locke 133-4
  Pateman & Mills 162-8
  Rawls 582
  see also Astell, Mary; Hobbes, Thomas; Locke, John; Mills, Charles; Pateman, Carole; Rousseau, Jean-Jacques; Spinoza, Baruch
social identities, Locke 119-23
Social Justice in Islam (Qutb) 259, 265
Social Reproduction Theory (SRT) 635
The Social Significance of the Modern Drama (Goldman) 466, 470, 471
socialism, Zhang Taiyan 356-7
socialist feminism
  Firestone 623-4
  Haraway 702
socialist politics, Du Bois 574-6
Society Must be Defended (Foucault) 250
Socrates 22, 26, 29-31
  knowledge and politics 27-8
Soledad Brothers (Jackson) 640
Solidarność 315
solitariness, Rousseau 150-2
Some Reflections Upon Marriage (Astell) 131, 132-3, 136, 137, 138, 139, 143, 144
Sophists **22**, 30
soul-force, Gandhi 489-90
The Souls of Black Folk (Du Bois) 565, 566, 567
sovereignty **166**
  Astell 136-8
  choice by, Rousseau 154-9
  divided, Montesquieu 189-91
  duties of 90
  Hobbes 89-90, 133
  Locke 116-19
  mass sovereignty, Rousseau 149-50
  Qutb 263-7
Spanish Civil War/Revolution (1936-1939) 465, 472, **473**
Speculum of the Other Woman (Irigany) 242-3
speech acts 660, **661**, 665
Springborg, Patricia 134, 140-1
Spinoza, Baruch 97-113
  bodies and minds 100-2
  democracy 106-10

knowledge 102
politics 98–103, 105–6
politics and power 103–6
religious critiques 99–100
unity of multitude 108–10
The Spirit of the Laws (Montesquieu) 185–7, 198–9
spiritual revolt, Goldman 469–70
Spivak, Gayatri Chakravorty 368, 427–44, 680
  alter-globalization 434–7
  decolonizing the Enlightenment 439–41
  desubalternization 436–7
  European Enlightenment 437–41
  imperialist feminism 432–4
  representation 429–30
  subaltern studies 430–2
  subalternity 429–34
  transnational solidarity 435–6
Sreedhar, Susanne 84, 91
standpoint 19, 44, 45, 174, 395, 398, 697–8, 704, 709
  and positionality 48
standpoint theory 697, **698**
Stanton, Elizabeth Cady **24**, 556, 648–9
state 26–28, 80–86, 91–92, 106–10, 116–18, 166–7, 231–4, 245–6, 448–51, 611–13
  breakdown, Hobbes 91–2
  Kautilya 60–7
  people and, Pateman & Mills 166–7
  ruling class and, Marx 231–2
state of nature 75–180, 195, 532, 534, 540
  Hobbes 81–2, 85–7
  Locke 116–19
state racism, Foucault 611–13
Staying with the Trouble (Haraway) 708–9
Stoermer, Eugene F. 681, 707
Stonewall protests (1969) 659
The Story of My Experiments with Truth (Gandhi) 491
Stowe, Harriet Beecher 24
The Stranger (Camus) 508
strategic essentialism 369, **432**
structural inequality **392**
  Young 390–4
The Structure of Scientific Revolutions (Kuhn) 703
Stryker, Susan O'Neal **662**
subaltern 369, **429**, 427–42
subaltern studies 430–2, 499, 679–80, 682

subalternity, Spivak 429–34
'The Subject and Power' essay (Foucault) 604, 615
subjectivity
  Butler 663–6
  hooks 48–9
Subjects of Desire (Butler) 663
suffragettes 488
suffragists 555–7, 572, 648, 650
superstructure, base and, Marx 224–6
surplus value 230
survival (*yogakshema*), Kautilya 60, 62, 70
swaraj 485, 486, **488**, 490, 491, 494, 495–8
systemic racism 396

T

Tan Sitong 351, 352
Taylor, Charles **408**, 419, 586
Teaching to Transgress (hooks) 45
technology, Firestone **629**
teleology 43–4, 360, 663
  Kant 530–2, 536, 538–40
telos **43**, 46, 47, 50, 361
Terrell, Mary Church 45, 649
territoriality 721
Theaetetus (Plato) 30
theory of justice, Young 393
A Theory of Justice (Rawls) 3, 523, 581–95
  ideal theory 583
  structure 582–3
Thiong'o, Ngũgĩ wa 280
The Third World 273, 350, 355, 362, **428**
Thoreau, Henry David 469, **495**
Thoughts Concerning Education (Locke) 117
Thoughts on the Education of Daughters (Wollstonecraft) 371, 381
Thrasymachus 22
Thus Spake Zarathrustra (Nietzsche) 240
Timaeus (Plato) 28
time
  cyclicity of 715
  progress and, Montesquieu 194–6
de Tocqueville, Alexis **211**
toleration 117–18, 182, 468
Tolstoy, Leo 469, 475, **490**
totalitarianism 292–3, **333**, 466
  Arendt 331–46
'Toward Perpetual Peace' essay (Kant) 531–2, 536

Tractatus Theologico Politicus (Spinoza) 98, 100, 103, 105, 106, 107
tradition 4, 10, 13, 79, 80, 173, 203, 270, 276, 277, 303, 310, 326, **337**, 344, 352, 357, 420, 421, 438, 446, 465, 478, 493, 527, 581, 623, 624
trans* studies 662–3
transatlantic commerce, Montesquieu 187
transcendental idealism 524, 527, **528**
transformation of slavery **478**
Transgender History (Stryker) 662
transnational solidarity, Spivak 435–6
transnationalism, Zhang Taiyan 355–8
Treaty of Basel (1795) 531
Trinidad 321–2
Trinidad Workingmen's Association (TWA) 322–3
Trotsky, Leon 153, 314
Trouillot, Michel-Rolph 6
'true womanhood, cult of' **32**
truth 18, 19, 46, 133, 135, 173, 183, 206, 242–3, 250, 287, 295, 299, 301, 338, 359, 408, 473, 541
  Foucault 607–8
  Nietzsche 242–3
'Truth and Power' essay (Foucault) 614
Truth, Sojourner 23–5, 29–34
  Black women representation 31–3
  narrative and humour 33–4
Tubman, Harriet 472, 556, 649
Tully, James 6
Twilight of the Idols (Nietzsche) 249
Two Treaties of Government (Locke) see *Second Treatise of Government* (Locke)

U

Undoing Gender (Butler) 661–2
United States of America (USA)
  American Indians 723–4
  colonialism 713
  Constitution, Douglass 553–7
  Indigenous Americans 126
  labour movement, Du Bois 574–5
universal history, Kant 530, 531–2
universal suffrage, Mill 212
US Civil War (1861–1865) 214, 545–60, **551**, 573

INDEX

The Use of Pleasure: The History of Sexuality vol. 2 (Foucault) 606
Utilitarianism 203, **208**
    Mill and 204, 208–9
    Rawls and 582, 584
'Utilitarianism, Utility or the Greatest Happiness Principle' essay (Mill) 208–9

V

Vahed, Goolam 491
value **228–9**
variable-sum power, zero-sum power *vs.* **64**
Varnhagen, Rahel 341
Venables, Robert 719–20
A Vindication of the Rights of Men (Wollstonecraft) 371, 373
A Vindication of the Rights of Woman (Wollstonecraft) 169, 371, 373–6, 381, 384
violence 440–521
    Pateman & Mills 168
    spectacle as, Machiavelli 458–9
    see also Fanon, Frantz; Gandhi, Mohandas (Mahatma); Goldman, Emma; Machiavelli, Niccolò
virtù
    fortuna *vs.* 453
    Machiavelli 452–3
virtue 23, 25, 26, 29, 30, 33, 35, 48, 62, 75, 102, 104, 106, 108, 135, 139, 165, 173, 208, 227, 241, 257, 261, 266, 267, 292, 296, 298, 301, 304, 307, 309, 452–4
    Aristotle 41
    Macaulay 299–300
    Montesquieu 188, 194
    political virtue, Montesquieu **193**
    Rousseau 156–8
vitalism, Haraway 703–5
Voltairine de Cleyre (Goldman) 466
von Humboldt, Wilhelm 206–7

W

Wahl, Jean 663
Walzer, Michael 586, 610, 614
Warren, Mercy Otis 297
Washington, Booker T. 317, 440, 569, **570**
Watkins, Gloria *see* hooks, bell
Wells, Ida B. 557, **565–6**, 648–9
West, Cornel 250
When Species Meet (Haraway) 706
Whigs 132, 133, 141, 143, **298**, 302, 304
white ignorance 340
Wilkins, David E. 718, 721–2
will
    deliberation and, Hobbes **80**
    to power, Nietzsche 244–8
    Rousseau 155–8
Williams, Eric 231
The Will to Power (Nietzsche) 244–5
Wollstonecraft, Mary 169, 298, 371–87
    class 381–2
    global context of slavery 379–80
    liberalism 377–8
    motherhood 382–3
    reason 376
    republicanism 377–8
    slavery 378–81
    women's emancipation 372–6
womanhood, cult of true **32**
Woman's Liberation Movement (WLM) 622–5
women 28–29, 170–2, 372–5, 622–4, 648–52
    Aristotle 51–2
    category of, Davis 651–2
    emancipation, Wollstonecraft 372–6
    historical experiences 572
    oppression, Firestone 625–8
    Pateman & Mills 170
Women, Race and Class (Davis) 648–52
World Bank 438

The Wretched of the Earth (Fanon) 507, 511–12, 514
Wright, Frances 298
The Wrongs of Women (Wollstonecraft) 372, 373, 374, 381

Y

Yazzie, Melanie 726–7
yogakshema (survival), Kautilya 60, 62, 70
Young, Iris Marion 368, 389–406, 587–8
    citizenship 397–8
    deliberation 398–401
    equality 394–7
    inclusion 394–7, 398–401
    justice 394–7
    oppression 390–4
    politics of difference 397–8
    representations 398–401, 402–3
    represented persons 402–3
    social groups 392–3
    structural inequality 390–4

Z

zero-sum power, variable-sum power *vs.* **64**
Zhang Taiyan 293, 349–65
    anti-cultural nationalism 355–6
    anti-Manchu revolution 350–4
    Asian unity 357–8
    Buddhism 359–62
    classical learning 350–1
    Hegel confrontation 359–60
    nationalism *vs.* reform 351–2
    pan-Asianism 355–8
    philosophy of difference 360–2
    revolution 353–4
    socialism 356–7
    transnationalism 355–8
Zhang Zhidong 350, 351
Zionism 282, 332, 466–7
Žižek, Slavoj 686